THE ROUTLEDGE HANDBOOK OF THE COMMUNICATIVE CONSTITUTION OF ORGANIZATION

This Handbook offers state of the art scholarship on the perspective known as the Communicative Constitution of Organization (CCO). Offering a unique outlook on how communication accounts for the emergence, change, and continuity of organizations and organizing practices, this Handbook systematically exposes the theoretical and methodological underpinnings of CCO, displays its empirical diversity, and articulates its future trajectory.

Placing communication firmly at the centre of the organizational equation, an international team of expert authors covers:

- The key theoretical inspirations and the main themes of the field
- The debates that animate the CCO community
- CCO's methodological approaches
- How CCO handles classic management themes
- Practical applications

Offering a central statement of CCO's contributions to the fields of organization studies, communication, and management, this Handbook will be of interest to organization studies and communication scholars, faculty, and graduate and advanced undergraduate students, as well as anyone associated with CCO theorizing seeking a comprehensive overview of the theoretical, methodological, and practical tenets of this growing area.

Joëlle Basque is Assistant Professor in the Department of Human Sciences, Arts and Communication at Université TÉLUQ in Montréal, Canada.

Nicolas Bencherki is Associate Professor in the Department of Human Sciences, Arts and Communication at Université TÉLUQ in Montréal, Canada.

Timothy Kuhn is Professor in the College of Media, Communication and Information at the University of Colorado Boulder, USA.

ROUTLEDGE STUDIES IN COMMUNICATION, ORGANIZATION, AND ORGANIZING

Series Editor: François Cooren

The goal of this series is to publish original research in the field of organizational communication, with a particular—but not exclusive—focus on the constitutive or performative aspects of communication. In doing so, this series aims to be an outlet for cutting-edge research monographs, edited books, and handbooks that will redefine, refresh and redirect scholarship in this field.

The volumes published in this series address topics as varied as branding, spiritual organizing, collaboration, employee communication, corporate authority, organizational timing and spacing, organizational change, organizational sense making, organization membership, and disorganization. What unifies this diversity of themes is the authors' focus on communication, especially in its constitutive and performative dimensions. In other words, authors are encouraged to highlight the key role communication plays in all these processes.

For a full list of titles in this series, please visit www.routledge.com.

Methodological and Ontological Principles of Observation and Analysis
Following and Analyzing Things and Beings in Our Everyday World
Edited by François Cooren and Fabienne Malbois

Dis/Organization as Communication
Exploring the Disordering, Disruptive and Chaotic Properties of Communication
Edited by Consuelo Vásquez and Tim Kuhn

Authority and Power in Social Interaction
Methods and Analysis
Edited by Nicolas Bencherki, Frédérik Matte and François Cooren

Organizing Inclusion: Moving Diversity from Demographics to Communication Processes
Edited by Marya L. Doerfel and Jennifer L. Gibbs

Whistleblowing, Communication and Consequences
Lessons from The Norwegian National Lottery
Edited by Peer Jacob Svenkerud, Jan-Oddvar Sørnes and Larry Browning

Speaking with One Voice
Multivocality and Univocality in Organizing
Edited by Chantal Benoit-Barné and Thomas Martine

Communicating Authority in Interorganizational Collaboration
Rebecca M. Rice

The Routledge Handbook of the Communicative Constitution of Organization
Edited by Joëlle Basque, Nicolas Bencherki, and Timothy Kuhn

THE ROUTLEDGE HANDBOOK OF THE COMMUNICATIVE CONSTITUTION OF ORGANIZATION

Edited by
Joëlle Basque, Nicolas Bencherki, and Timothy Kuhn

Routledge
Taylor & Francis Group
NEW YORK AND LONDON

Cover image: © Nature Picture Library/Alamy Stock Photo

First published 2022
by Routledge
605 Third Avenue, New York, NY 10158

and by Routledge
4 Park Square, Milton Park, Abingdon, Oxon, OX14 4RN

Routledge is an imprint of the Taylor & Francis Group, an informa business

© 2022 Taylor & Francis

Library of Congress Cataloging-in-Publication Data
Names: Basque, Joëlle, editor. | Bencherki, Nicolas, editor. |
Kuhn, Timothy, editor.
Title: The Routledge handbook of the communicative constitution of organization /
edited by Joëlle Basque, Nicolas Bencherki and Timothy Kuhn.
Description: New York, NY: Routledge, 2022. |
Series: Routledge studies in communication, organization, and organizing |
Includes bibliographical references and index.
Identifiers: LCCN 2021058641 (print) | LCCN 2021058642 (ebook) |
ISBN 9780367480707 (hbk) | ISBN 9780367480721 (pbk) |
ISBN 9781003224914 (ebk)
Subjects: LCSH: Communication in organizations. | Organizational behavior.
Classification: LCC HD30.3 .R69 2022 (print) |
LCC HD30.3 (ebook) | DDC 658.4/5–dc23/eng/20220120
LC record available at https://lccn.loc.gov/2021058641
LC ebook record available at https://lccn.loc.gov/2021058642

ISBN: 978-0-367-48070-7 (hbk)
ISBN: 978-0-367-48072-1 (pbk)
ISBN: 978-1-003-22491-4 (ebk)

DOI: 10.4324/9781003224914

Typeset in Bembo
by Newgen Publishing UK

To Jim, Elizabeth, Bob, Linda, and the entire CCO community.

CONTENTS

Contents

Contents

FIGURES

TABLES

CONTRIBUTORS

Helle Kryger Aggerholm holds a position as Head of Research at the Danish School of Media and Journalism, Denmark. Her research examines the role of communicative practices in strategic processes in public and private organizations, communication within a strategy-as-practice context, organizational communication (CCO), and language as social interaction. Her most recent work in these areas has been published in *Journal of Management Inquiry*, *The International Journal of Strategic Communication*, *Journal of Management Communication*, *Public Relations Review*, *Business Ethics: A European Review*, and *Corporate Communication: An International Journal*.

Oana Brindusa Albu is Associate Professor in the Department of Management and Marketing at University of Southern Denmark, Odense. Her research involves ethnographic studies of transnational institutions and non-profit organizations working in the Middle East and North Africa contexts, with a focus on governance and new information and communication technologies use. Her research has been published in journals such as *Management Communication Quarterly*, *Business and Society* and *The International Encyclopedia of Organizational Communication*. She received and successfully managed large grants awarded by the Danish Ministry of Science, Innovation and Higher Education, and the Danish Ministry of Foreign Affairs.

Birte Asmuß is Associate Professor at the Department of Management at Aarhus University, Denmark. In her research, she investigates communicative practices in various workplace settings focusing specifically on communicative actions like complaints, requests, and emotional displays. Based on video data of authentic workplace interaction, she applies an ethnomethodological, multimodal conversation analytic approach to identify the sequentially ordered and intersubjective nature of workplace interaction.

Joëlle Basque is Professor in the Département Sciences humaines, Lettres et Communications at Université TELUQ, Canada. She obtained her PhD in organizational communication at Université de Montréal in 2013 and was Research Fellow at HEC Montréal from 2013 to 2017. Her research focuses on discursive approaches to organizational communication, individual and organizational identity, and practice theories of strategy and organizational change. Her work has appeared in *Organization Studies*, *M@an@agement*, as well as *The SAGE Handbook* *of Qualitative Business and Management Research Methods*, 2017, and *The Cambridge Handbook of Open Strategy*, 2019.

Nicolas Bencherki is an associate professor of organizational communication at Université TÉLUQ, Montréal, Canada, and an affiliate professor at Université du Québec à Montréal. He studies the role of communication and materiality in constituting organizational reality, thus revisiting classic notions of management such as strategy, membership, and authority, as well as property. Empirically, his work mostly focuses on non-profit organizations and inter-organizational collaboration. He has published in outlets such as *Academy of Management Journal, Organization Studies, Human Relations, Journal of Communication*, and *Communication Theory*. He co-edited *Authority and Power in Social Interaction: Methods and Analysis*, published in 2019 by Routledge.

Chantal Benoit-Barné is Associate Professor in the Department of Communication at the Université de Montréal in Canada. She received her PhD from the University of Colorado at Boulder. Her research draws on rhetorical theories and Communication as Constitutive of Organization (CCO) perspectives to explore the constitutive dimensions of communication in work interactions, public deliberations, and sociotechnical controversies. Her work appears in academic journals such as *Quarterly Journal of Speech, Communication Monographs*, and *Management Communication Quarterly*.

Ryan S. Bisel is Professor of Organizational Communication at the University of Oklahoma, USA. His research interests focus primarily on issues surrounding leadership communication, organizational culture, and behavioral ethics. His 2018 book titled *Organizational Moral Learning: A Communication Approach* was honored with Book of The Year Awards from two divisions of the National Communication Association. Additionally, Bisel's work is published in communication and management journals, such as *Communication Monographs, Journal of Applied Communication Research, Small Group Research, Human Relations, Management Communication Quarterly*, and *Leadership Quarterly*.

Blagoy Blagoev is Professor of Organization at Technische Universität Dresden, Germany. Blagoy holds a doctoral degree from Freie Universität Berlin and his work focuses on the interplay of time and temporality with processes and practices of organizing. Among other things, he has studied the persistence of organizational time regimes, the temporal coordination of organizational routines, and the entanglement of organizational remembering with materiality.

Geneviève Boivin is Assistant Professor in the Communication Department at the Université de Sherbrooke in Québec, Canada. Her research interests include the communicative constitution of organization, institutional theory, intercultural communication, and expatriation. Her work on the establishment of CCO scholarship in organizational communication has been published in journals such as *Management Communication Quarterly*.

Boris H. J. M. Brummans is Professor in the Département de Communication at the Université de Montréal in Canada. His research interests include agency, conflict management, mindful organizing, organizational communication, organizational ethnography, and process philosophy. He has contributed chapters to several edited books and his articles appear in international peer-reviewed journals such as *Communication Monographs, Human Relations, Information, Communication & Society, Journal of Communication, Management Communication*

Quarterly, *Organization Studies*, and *Qualitative Inquiry*. His edited volume, *The Agency of Organizing: Perspectives and Case Studies*, received the 2018 Outstanding Edited Book Award from the Organizational Communication Division of the National Communication Association, and he served as Associate Editor of *Management Communication Quarterly* from 2015 to 2019.

Letizia Caronia is Professor at the Department of Education, University of Bologna, Italy. She studies language, interaction, and culture in institutional as well as ordinary contexts with an emphasis on the management of knowledge in interaction and the local construction of (epistemic and deontic) authority. Her recent publications include "Following and Analyzing an artifact: Culture-through-things", in F. Cooren, F. Malbois (Eds.), *Methodological and Ontological Principles of Observation and Analysis*, 2019; "Morality in Scientific Practice" (with André H. Caron), *Human Studies*; "Challenging the Interprofessional Epistemic Boundaries: The Practices of Informing in Nurse-Physician Interaction" (with M. Saglietti, A. Chieregato), *Social Science & Medicine*.

Theresa Castor is Professor in the Department of Communication at the University of Wisconsin-Parkside, USA. Her area of research includes the analysis of decision-making discourse in human-nonhuman system interactions. Her recent work includes the examination of decision-making interactions during crises such as natural disasters and freshwater controversies. Her work has been published in *Management Communication Quarterly*, *Journal of Business Communication*, *Discourse Studies*, *Journal of Pragmatics*, *Electronic Journal of Communication*, and *Annals of the International Communication Association* (formerly, *Communication Yearbook*). She is the author of *Climate Risks as Organizational Problems: Constructing Agency and Action*, 2018.

Mathieu Chaput is Professor in the Département Sciences humaines, Lettres et Communications at Université TELUQ, Canada. He obtained his PhD in organizational communication at Université de Montréal in 2012. He worked as a postdoctoral researcher at the University of Lund from 2012 to 2013 before coming home to his alma mater to lecture extensively in organizational communication, rhetoric, and written communication from 2013 to 2017. His research focuses on the communicational constitution of political organizations. His work has appeared in *Management Communication Quarterly*, *The Handbook of Business Discourse*, and *The Cambridge Handbook of Strategy as Practice* (2nd edition).

Lars Thøger Christensen is Professor in Communication and Organization at the Copenhagen Business School, Denmark. His research interests include talk-action dynamics, hypocrisy, identity, voice, corporate social responsibility, and transparency. He approaches these topics through a communication lens focused on how organizations talk themselves into new realities. In addition to six books and contributions to several edited volumes, his research appears in *Communication Theory*, *Organization Studies*, *Organization*, *Journal of Business Research*, *Human Relations*, *Management Communication Quarterly*, and elsewhere.

Boukje Cnossen is a Post-Doctoral Researcher affiliated with the Institute for Sociology and Cultural Organization at Leuphana University of Lüneburg, Germany. She holds a PhD from the Tilburg School of Economics and Management (Tilburg University), the Netherlands, and has published in *Human Relations*, *Journal of Organizational Ethnography*, and other outlets. Her research interests include the communicative constitution of organization in the context of the arts, with a focus on space and materiality, and the role of creativity discourses in new organizational contexts such as co-working spaces.

François Cooren is Full Professor and former Chair of the Department of Communication at the Université de Montréal, Canada. His research interests include organizational communication, language and social interaction, and communication theory. He authored and co-authored five books, edited seven volumes, and published more than 40 book chapters and 60 articles in international peer-reviewed journals such as *The Academy of Management Annals, Organization Studies, Human Relations, Long Range Planning, Organization, Management Communication Quarterly, Communication Monographs, Journal of Communication,* and *Communication Theory.* He is a Fellow and Past President of the International Communication Association (ICA), a distinguished scholar of the National Communication Association (NCA), and the recipient of several awards, including the Frederic M. Jablin Memorial Award for Contributions to the Organizational Communication division of the ICA.

Veronica R. Dawson is Assistant Professor of Communication Studies at the California State University, Stanislaus, USA. She is interested in how social media interactions between organizations and their stakeholders become organizational text, where text is seen performatively as the routine practices defining organizational identity and branding. She has presented her research at national and international conferences and publishes in communication, management, and media journals.

Leonhard Dobusch is Professor of Business Administration with focus on Organization at the University of Innsbruck, Austria. He holds degrees in Law and in Business Studies and his main research interests include the management of digital communities, regulation via standards, and various forms of open organizing.

Sophie Del Fa is a PhD student at the University of Quebec in Montreal, Canada. She wrote a thesis on alternative universities for which she conducted an ethnographic fieldwork in two of these institutions. Her interests lie in alternative organizations and social movements. She adopts a constitutive approach of communication and critical perspectives. Her work has been published in *Tamara: Journal for Critical Organization Inquiry, Alternates Routes: Journal of Critical Social Research, Recherches en communication, Questions de communication, Communication et organisation,* and *Communication, lettres et sciences du langage.*

Gail T. Fairhurst is Distinguished University Research Professor of Organizational Communication at the University of Cincinnati, USA. She specializes in organizational and leadership communication processes, including those involving paradox, problem-centered leadership, and framing. She is a Fellow of the International Communication Association, Distinguished Scholar of the National Communication Association, and a Fulbright Scholar.

Stephanie Fox is Professor in the Département de Communication at the Université de Montréal in Canada. Her research interests include interprofessional collaboration, health communication, narrative, and interaction analysis.

Shiv Ganesh is Professor in the Department of the Communication Studies in Moody College of Communication, at the University of Texas at Austin, USA. He studies communication and collective organizing in the context of globalization and digital technologies. His work spans critical-institutional and post structural approaches to communication and is currently composed of two strands: studies of transformations in collective action and studies of dialogue, conflict, and social change. His research is largely qualitative but has incorporated quantitative elements, and he has done fieldwork in a number of countries, including India, Aoteaora New Zealand, the United States, and Sweden.

Michael Grothe-Hammer is Associate Professor of Sociology (Organization and Technology) in the Department of Sociology and Political Science at the Norwegian University of Science and Technology in Trondheim, Norway. Before, he was a researcher at the Institute of Social Sciences at Helmut Schmidt University Hamburg, and at the Department of Management at Freie Universität Berlin, Germany. His field is organizational sociology with a focus on socio-logical systems theory, communication- and decision-centered approaches, and relational soci-ology. He is currently particularly interested in new forms of organization, the effects of new digital technologies on organizations and society, and the relationship between organizations and macro-societal differentiation.

Heidi Hirsto works as Associate Professor in University of Vaasa, Finland. Her work focuses on discourse and communication across a range of disciplines and topics, spanning from media studies and cultural consumer studies to organizational communication. Her current work revolves around current and historical discourses of saving and investment, as well as emotion discourse in the context of organizational and leadership communication. Her work has appeared in academic journals including *Organization Studies, Consumption, Markets and Culture,* and *Equality, Diversity and Inclusion: An International Journal,* as well as in research books.

Joel O. Iverson is currently Professor at the University of Montana, USA, and researches organizations as enacted through communication (communicative constitution of organiza-tion) and communities of practice theory. He applies this work in several contexts including organizational knowledge, communities of practice, risk and crisis communication, nonprofit organizing, and communities.

Jody Jahn is Associate Professor in the Department of Communication at the University of Colorado at Boulder, USA. Her main research interests include constitutive explanations of organizing, and safety documentation.

Sam James is a PhD student at the University of Texas at Austin, USA. Her research interests center on affective organizing and the influence technology has on our communication in a globalized world. Much of Sam's work emphasizes the transition from online to in-person organizing at the global and local level and takes a critical perspective. Sam completed an accelerated Bachelor of Arts degree and earned her MA in Communication Studies at the University of Alabama, where she focused on organizational and intercultural communication research while gaining industry experience at a small communication consultancy.

Henrik Ladegaard Johannesen received his PhD from Aarhus University, Denmark, in 2018. His work explores temporal aspects of organizing from an ethnomethodological and conversation analytical perspective. One of his main research interests is the moral ordering of working time and its impact on people's working lives. He is an External Lecturer at Roskilde University, Denmark.

Dan Kärreman is Professor in Management and Organization Studies at Copenhagen Business School, Denmark, and Professor in Management at Royal Holloway, University of London, UK. He is also affiliated to the LUMOS group at Lund University, Sweden. His research interests include critical management studies, knowledge work, organization communication, identity in organizations, leadership, organizational control, and research methodology.

Peter Knoers is a hybrid professional combining a decades-long career as Manager and Senior Consultant in the field of communication and organizational development with a position as lecturer on twenty-first-century strategy and leadership at the University of Twente, Netherlands. In both positions he focuses on the new challenge organizations encounter in this so-called "network society". He explores new ways of organizing, co-operating, and communicating needed to be successful in this day and age. Helping organizations to see "the broader picture", the multiplicity of stakeholders, and the fluidity of societal demands, he became convinced that "listening" is the most important communicative skill.

Matthew Koschmann is Associate Professor in the Department of Communication at the University of Colorado Boulder, USA. His research focuses on organizational communication and collaboration, with an emphasis on the civil society sector and nonprofit organizations. His work has been published in outlets such as *Academy of Management Review*, *Management Communication Quarterly*, *Journal of Communication*, and *Communication Monographs*. He also was a Fulbright Scholar and Visiting Research Professor at Ateneo de Manila University, where he studied civil society collaboration in the Philippines, focusing on housing relocation of urban informal settlement communities and shelter reconstruction after natural disasters.

Timothy Kuhn is Professor in the Department of Communication at the University of Colorado Boulder, USA. His research addresses how authority, agency, knowledge, and identity are constituted in sociomaterial, power-laden, and dis/orderly communication practices. He is a former Associate Editor at the interdisciplinary journal *Human Relations* and chair of the organizational communication division of the International Communication Association. His research has been published in *Academy of Management Review*, *The Academy of Management Annals*, *Organization*, *Organization Studies*, *Management Communication Quarterly*, *Communication Monographs*, and *Communication Theory*, among other outlets.

Salla-Maaria Laaksonen (@jahapaula) is Senior Researcher and Adjunct Professor at the University of Helsinki, Finland. Her research focuses on technology, organizations, and new media, including organizational reputation in the hybrid media system, the organization of online social movements, and the use of data and algorithms in organizations. She is also an expert of digital and computational methods.

François Lambotte is Professor of Organisational Communication at École de Communication of Université Catholique de Louvain, Belgium. He is the founder of UCLouvain Social Media Lab, a research program exploring fabrics of data intelligibility in a professional context (www. socialmedialab.be). His work focuses on collaborative processes in organizational context (i.e. organizational change projects or audits, dashboarding practices, strategic decision-making).

Elizabeth Wilhoit Larson is Assistant Professor of Communication in the School of Communication and Journalism at Auburn University, Alabama, USA. Her research focuses on non-human agency in the communicative constitution of organization, particularly how non-humans communicate and the role of space in the constitution of organizations. Her research has been published in outlets including *Organization Studies*, *Communication Theory*, *Management Communication Quarterly*, *Organization*, and *Gender, Work & Organization*.

Jeanne Mengis is Professor of Organizational Communication at the Faculty of Communication Sciences at the Universita della Svizzera italiana (USI), Switzerland, where she is director of the Institute of Marketing and Communication Management. She is also Associate Honorary Professor at Warwick Business School, UK. In her research, she works with a practice theoretical perspective and has a particular interest in how communication and materiality (i.e. artefacts, space) come together in organizational phenomena, such as cross-disciplinary collaboration, knowledge work, organizational learning, or innovation. She published her work in journals such as *Organization Science, Organization Studies, Organizational Research Methods, Organization, Management Learning*, and *Social Science & Medicine*.

Colleen E. Mills is Professor of Management at the University of Canterbury, Christchurch, New Zealand, and an International Affiliate Faculty (IAF) at Audencia Business School, Nantes, France. She is a longstanding Executive Member and a Past President of the Australian and New Zealand Communication Association and has served as the International Communication Association's Board Member-At-Large for Africa and Oceania. Her award-winning research examines organizations during periods of ambiguity and change, usually using communication and sensemaking lenses. She is currently the Editor-In-Chief of *Communication Research and Practice* and on the Advisory Boards of *Group and Organization Management, International Journal of Entrepreneurial Behaviour and Research*, and *Journal of International Education in Business*.

Jamie McDonald is Associate Professor in the Department of Communication at the University of Texas at San Antonio, USA. His research interests include identity and difference in organizational settings and feminist and queer approaches to organizing. His work has appeared in peer-reviewed journals such as *Communication Theory, Management Communication Quarterly, Management Learning, The Journal of Applied Communication Research*, and *Gender, Work & Organization*.

Robert D. McPhee is Emeritus Professor in the Hugh Downs School of Human Communication at Arizona State University, USA. Specializing in communication theory and methods and in organizational communication, he served as Chair of the Organizational Communication Division of the National Communication Association, as Associate Editor of *Human Communication Research*, and as Book Review Editor of *Communication Theory*. His work has received honors such as the Golden Anniversary Monograph Award from the (national) Speech Communication Association, and he was awarded the International Communication Association's Fredric M. Jablin Outstanding Member Award in Organizational Communication.

Karen K. Myers is Professor in the Department of Communication at the University of California, Santa Barbara, USA. Her current research includes membership negotiation (socialization, assimilation), vocational anticipatory socialization, workplace flexibility and work-life balance issues, organizational identification, and interaction between generational cohorts in the workplace. Her work has appeared in *Management Communication Quarterly, Human Communication Research, Journal of Applied Communication Research, Communication Monographs, Communication Yearbook, Human Relations*, and elsewhere.

Nicola Nasi is a PhD candidate in Education Sciences at the University of Bologna, Italy. He graduated in Linguistics at the University of Turin, Italy, and Dresden, Germany. His research interests include language teaching, language socialization in heterogeneous settings, child discourse, and children's peer cultures. In his PhD project, he combines ethnography and Conversation Analysis to analyze children's peer socializing practices in primary schools characterized by language and culture contact. In this regard, he also focuses on children's social organization and local enactment of authority in the peer group.

Ellen Nathues is a PhD student in Faculty of Behavioural, Management and Social Sciences at the University of Twente, Netherlands. Her research interests focus on organizational communication, social interaction, and team learning. For her dissertation, she draws on a communicative constitutive (specifically ventriloquial) lens to study how interorganizational teams work across and around their various differences and boundaries. Prior to starting her PhD, Ellen completed an MSc in Communication Studies (Cum Laude) at University of Twente and gained industry experience in an international corporation as marketing manager (EMEA).

Visa Penttilä is a Postdoctoral Researcher at Hanken School of Economics in Helsinki, Finland. His research revolves around corporate social responsibility and communication in organizational and societal settings. Currently, he studies how civil society organizations and corporations interact in the context of regulatory initiatives for corporate responsibility.

Mie Plotnikof is Associate Professor of Public Governance and Organization at Danish School of Education, Aarhus University, Denmark. Her work questions the constitutive processes and politics of organizing by studying matters of discourse, meaning, subjectivity, dis/order, and power/resistance. She has published in various journals such as *Gender, Work & Organization*, *Scandinavian Journal of Management*, and *ephemera*, as well as in Danish journals and edited volumes. Mie is also a member of the editorial collective of *ephemera*, as well as associate editor at *Gender, Work & Organization*.

Linda L. Putnam is Distinguished Research Professor Emerita in the Department of Communication at the University of California, Santa Barbara, USA. Her current research interests include organizational tensions, materiality and space, and organizational conflict. She is the co-editor of *Building Theory of Organization: The Constitutive Role of Communication* (2009) and a constitutive approach to the study of contradictions and paradoxes in *The Academy of Management Annals* (2016).

Rebecca M. Rice is Assistant Professor in the Department of Communication Studies at University of Nevada, Las Vegas, USA. Her research focuses on interorganizational collaboration around security threats and emergency response work.

Jean A. Saludadez is Professor and Faculty Administrator at the University of the Philippines Open University, Philippines, where she teaches communication theory, organizational communication, and research at the graduate level. Her research interest is in understanding organizations through the lens of the Communication as Constitutive of Organization (CCO) perspective.

Dennis Schoeneborn is Professor of Organization, Communication and CSR at Copenhagen Business School, Denmark, as well as Visiting Professor of Organization and Management at Leuphana University Lüneburg, Germany. His current research is focused primarily on the communicative constitution of new forms of organizing.

David Seidl is Full Professor of Organization and Management at the University of Zurich, Switzerland, and Research Associate at the Centre for Business Studies at Cambridge University, UK. He is Associate Editor of *Organizational Theory* and a member of several editorial boards, including *Organization Studies*, *Strategic Organization*, *Organization*, and *Scandinavian Journal of Management*. He was a member of the executive board of the European Group for Organizational Studies (EGOS), Past Chair of the SAP Interest Group at the Academy of Management, and co-organizer of the EGOS Standing Working Group on "Strategizing: Activity and Practice". He has widely published on organization, strategy, and the philosophy of science. His papers have appeared in leading international journals, including *Academy of Management Journal*, *Academy of Management Review*, *Academy of Management Annals*, *Organization Science*, and *Strategic Management Journal*. He has (co-)produced several special issues and books, including, most recently, *The Cambridge Handbook of Routine Dynamics* (2021).

Viviane Sergi is Associate Professor in Management in the Department of Management and Technology at ESG UQAM in Montréal, Canada. Her research interests include process thinking, performativity, new work practices, leadership, and materiality. She also has a keen interest in methodological issues related to qualitative research and in the practice of academic writing. Her work has been published in journals such as *Academy of Management Annals*, *Human Relations*, *Scandinavian Journal of Management*, *Long Range Planning*, *International Journal of Project Management*, and in *Qualitative Research in Organizations and Management*, among others.

Mathew L. Sheep is Professor of Management and Associate Dean at Florida Gulf Coast University, Florida. His research focuses on discursive perspectives of paradoxical tensions (that often intertwine in knots) in organizational and identity work, leadership and followership, innovation, spiritual belief systems, and work-home boundaries. His work is published in *Academy of Management Journal*, *Organization Studies*, *Human Relations*, *International Journal of Management Reviews*, *Journal of Business Ethics*, *Research in the Sociology of Organizations*, *Journal of Management Inquiry*, as well as numerous book chapters. Sheep served as Associate Editor for *Human Relations* from 2012 to 2019 and is on its editorial board.

Leo Feddersen Smith is External Lecturer at Aarhus University, Denmark, and Head of Research in Talents Unlimited. He did his PhD on the communicative constitution of employer brands in face-to-face encounters. His research is driven by reconceptualising various organisational processes as grounded in communication, for instance employer branding and supply chain management.

A. Paul Spee is Associate Professor in Strategy at the University of Queensland Business School, Australia. Paul's research on strategy is at the nexus of communication theory, in particular Communication as Constitutive of Organization and social practice theory. His research is particularly known for advocating strategy-as-practice as an alternative perspective to traditional strategy theory. Some of his work appeared in the *Academy of Management Journal*, *Accounting, Organization & Society*, *British Journal of Management*, *Organization Science*, *Organization Studies*, and in influential handbooks. Paul currently serves as Senior Editor for *Organization Studies*, and as Outgoing Chair for the Strategizing, Activities & Practices Interest Group within the Academy of Management.

Cynthia Stohl is Distinguished Professor in the Department of Communication at the University of California, Santa Barbara, USA. She is past director of UCSB's Center for

Information Technology and Society. Her recent work explores global dynamics related to corporate social responsibility, collective action, emerging communication technologies, and the management of visibility in the digital age.

Neva Štumberger is External Lecturer in the Department of Management, Society and Communication at the Copenhagen Business School, Denmark. Her research focuses on sensemaking of and organizing around various communication and organization phenomena—primarily, in the area of corporate social responsibility (CSR)—to better understand complexities and dynamics behind actions that lead to organizational and social change.

Hannah Trittin-Ulbrich is Assistant Professor for business ethics at Leuphana University Lüneburg, Germany. She holds a PhD from the University of Zurich, Switzerland. Her research interests include corporate social responsibility (CSR), CSR communication, diversity management, and digital communication technologies. Her research is published in journals like *Journal of Management Studies*, *Journal of Business Ethics*, *Journal of Management Inquiry*, and *Organization*.

Consuelo Vásquez is Associate Professor in the Département de Communication Sociale et Publique at the Université du Québec à Montréal, Canada. Her research interests include ethnography, the communicative constitution of dis/organization and the epistemologies of the South. Her work appears in such venues as *Communication Theory*, *Human Relations*, and *Qualitative Research in Organizations and Management*. She is the principal investigator of Volunteering on the move, funded by the Social Sciences and Humanities Research Council of Canada. She is the co-founder of the Research Group Organizing and Communication (RECOR) and the Red Latinoamericana de Investigacion en Comunicacion Organizacional (RedLAco).

Camille Vézy is a doctoral candidate in the Département de Communication at the Université de Montréal in Canada. Her research interests include care ethics and consent, the ethics of artificial intelligence (AI), mindful organizing, organizational ethnography, and sociomateriality. Her doctoral research, funded by the Fonds de Recherche du Québec - Société et Culture (FRQSC), the Université de Montréal's Faculté des Arts et Sciences, and a MITACS Acceleration grant, explores how ethics get materialized with care in the practices of designing an AI system.

Florence Villesèche is Associate Professor and Academic Director of the Diversity and Difference Platform at Copenhagen Business School, Denmark. She holds a PhD from the University of Geneva, Switzerland. She is a Carlsberg Foundation fellow and a Marie Curie Alumni. Her research focuses on the topics of gender, diversity, identity, networks, and the corporate elite. Publications on these topics include a book on identity and diversity in the workplace and a diversity methods companion, as well as contributions to journals such as *Work, Employment and Society*, *Human Relations*, and *European Management Review*.

Mark van Vuuren is Associate Professor of Organizational Communication at the University of Twente, Netherlands, in the Faculty of Behavioural, Management and Social Sciences. His main research interest is the process of communication, specifically in the context of organizations. He studies identity work, work meanings, and the ways professionals make sense of the content and significance of their work, and how this comes about in their interacting and organizing.

Régine Wagnac is a PhD candidate at the Department of Communication of the Université de Montréal, Canada. She has worked in a variety of settings, including medical and military ones, where she developed an interest in research and organizational communication. Various interdisciplinary academic experiences have led her to use qualitative and quantitative research methods. Mobilizing conversation analysis principles, her doctoral thesis aims to contribute to the literature on identity work, by studying it from conversations between military members, especially senior leaders coming from different environments and occupations.

ACKNOWLEDGEMENTS

The idea for this handbook emerged in 2018 in Tallin, Estonia, during the EGOS conference, when Joëlle Basque pointed out the absence of a reference work reflecting the diversity and richness of the CCO community. From that initial suggestion, the project gradually gained more materiality over the three next years, as authors enthusiastically accepted our invitation to contribute to the handbook and turned in drafts of their papers, until we excitedly held in our hands a complete set of final chapters.

Getting to fruition a handbook project with 61 authors across over 30 chapters would not have been possible without the invaluable help of Simon Mallette-Brochu, who acted as the project's coordinator. Simon dealt with the overwhelming number of emails such a project inevitably generates and found a way to keep track of the multiple versions of each document we worked with. Saying we are grateful to him does not begin to express our appreciation of his important role in making this handbook a reality.

We also want to thank the authors who wrote multiple drafts of their chapters and patiently applied our comments and suggestions. We demanded a lot from them, and we are all the more thankful that much of their work took place in the midst of a global pandemic. While the handbook is very comprehensive, many more people conduct CCO research than we could possibly include in a book. All of them make our community a vibrant and exciting one, that encourages daring ideas and intellectual exploration.

FOREWORD

The Emerging Paradigm of Communication Constitutes Organization (CCO)

Linda L. Putnam

Scholars in organizational communication and organizational studies have ushered in a major paradigm shift in theory and research. Dedicated to understanding "organization" not as a container or a pre-existing entity, this approach focuses on how communication constitutes organization (CCO). In this work, the terms *organization* and *communication* are not taken for granted or held as abstractions (Putnam, Nicotera, & McPhee, 2009), rather the two become interwoven and mutually constituted. Thus, scholars focus on how an organization is composed, enacted, and sustained through communication. Moreover, in this approach, communication is not a vehicle for transmitting information "inside" an organizational container, rather it consists of language, discourses, texts, conversations, interactions, and meaning that actively constitute organizing and organization. As Brummans, Cooren, Robichad, and Taylor (2014, p. 173) highlight, "what sets [CCO] apart from other areas of inquiry is its novel way of theorizing and analyzing how organization as a discursive-material configuration is produced and reproduced from ongoing interactions".

CCO work, however, is not simply one school of thought, rather it has become a proliferation of perspectives that share a common goal and embrace similar tenets. This *Handbook* showcases these perspectives, including the three original schools (Brummans et al., 2014; Schoeneborn, Blaschke, Cooren, McPhee, Seidl, & Taylor 2014), that serve a catalyst for a large body of theoretical and empirical work on communication and organization. This volume explores these multiple perspectives through emphasizing their similarities and differences as well as their links to practice theory, discourse studies, sociomateriality, and ethnomethodology as cognate areas (see Aggerholm, Asmuß, Ladegaard Johannesen & Feddersen Smith; Albu & Stumberger; Castor; Jahn & Rice; Larson & Mengis; this volume). In this way, it focuses on the core issues that form the very foundation of CCO. Thus, it provides a "State of the Art" picture of CCO work and its expansion, including theories, research topics, methodologies, and practice. In doing so, it shows how this approach has become "institutionalized" through publications in mainstream journals, the development of field-configuring events, and extensions to interdisciplinary and international domains (Boivin, Brummans, & Barker, 2017).

In this Foreword, I revisit the history of CCO and unpack central constructs that I believe emerged from the earliest stages of its development. Then, I provide an overview of each of the three major schools of CCO, their similarities and differences regarding communication and the organization-communication relationship, and the central constructs that surfaced from this extensive work. Finally, I ascertain how CCO has emerged a paradigm in the field and the contributions that it is making to organizational communication and organizational studies.

Revisiting the History and Development of CCO

Multiple narratives tell the story of CCO and its evolution in organizational communication studies. These histories aim to capture CCO's conceptual foundations and dominant themes (Cooren, Taylor, & Van Every, 2006), its theoretical and philosophical roots (Scherer & Rasche, 2017; Taylor & Van Every, 2000), its position in organizational discourse studies (Fairhurst & Putnam, 1999, 2004, 2015; Putnam, Phillips, & Chapman, 1996), its role in the field of communication writ large (Ashcraft, Kuhn, & Cooren, 2009; Taylor, 2011) and its emergence in organizational communication studies, in particular (Ashcraft et al., 2009; Bisel, 2010; Boivin et al., 2017; Brummans et al., 2014; Putnam et al., 2009; Taylor & Van Every, 2011). Several of these scenarios are brief historical summaries (Bisel, 2010) while others aim to explicate the implicit and explicit origins of CCO (Ashcraft et al., 2009; Boivin et al., 2017).

To introduce this *Handbook*, I revisit and recast the history of CCO by tracking its development in organizational communication and organizational studies. Hence, my story departs from other CCO narratives through examining three stages of CCO emergence: (1) the early work on communicative processes of organizing and the key constructs that emanate from this period; (2) the three main CCO schools of thought and the key constructs that surface across these schools; and (3) the emergence of a generic paradigm of CCO with alternative perspectives, applications in organizational studies, and central premises. These three stages lay the groundwork for this *Handbook*, especially for the chapters on discourse, materiality, agency, order and disorder, and decision-making as well as the application of CCO to classic management themes.

Stage 1: Communication Constitutes Organizing

As many histories of CCO note (Ashcraft et al., 2009; Putnam et al., 2009), the earliest work in organizational communication focused on messages sent through vertical or horizontal channels or transmission networks (Putnam & Cheney, 1983; Tompkins, 1984). Grounded in positivism and functionalism, these early studies treated communication and organization as distinct phenomena, as tangible social facts, or as reified objects that existed apart from the processes that created them (Putnam, 1983). The interpretive turn in the field challenged these assumptions and ushered in two threads of work that, in my mind, served as precursors to CCO: (1) communication as co-constructing organizing (that is, constituting organizing) and (2) language/discourse as the performative enactment of organization.

Interaction Patterns as Organizing. In the early 1980s, scholars focused on interaction patterns that co-created activities and jointly constituted organizing as a communication process. This approach challenged the view of an organization as a container or a reified entity through examining how patterns and sequences of communication co-constructed organizational phenomena (Putnam & Cheney, 1985). As Putnam (1983, p. 53) notes, "Communication [was] not simply another organizational activity; it created and recreated the social structures that formed the crux of organizing". Inspired by systems-interactions views of communication (Fisher, 1978) and Karl Weick's (1979) theory of organizing, scholars coded the order and development of utterances and their links to organizational constructs. For example, researchers investigated interaction patterns that jointly constructed leadership in organizing (Fairhurst, Rogers, & Sarr, 1987), verbal messages that coordinated tasks and accomplished rules and resources (Poole & DeSanctis, 1992), and interactions that constituted negotiation and bargaining as organizing (Putnam, 1985). In the early 1990s, the use of adaptive structuration to study organizational teams moved interaction analysis beyond micro levels to ways of co-constructing institutional texts (Putnam et al., 1996, p. 393).

Hence, through focusing on patterns of coordinated interactions, scholars began to center on communication as "the capacity to create, maintain, and dissolve organizations" (Hawes, 1974; Krone, Jablin, & Putnam, 1987, p. 393). This work drew on meta-models of communication as constitutive, that is, composing, constructing, or forming phenomena (Ashcraft et al., 2009; Craig, 1999). It gave rise to a definition of organizational communication as "the study of messages, information, meaning, and symbolic activity that constitutes organizations" (Putnam & Cheney, 1985, p. 131). Embedded streams of CCO were also evident in the way that communication constructed organizational cultures, produced power and politics, and formed interorganizational networks (Ashcraft et al., 2009). Thus, the work on communication as constituting organizing began in the early 1980s and laid the foundation for studying CCO. However, scholars in this period clearly focused too strongly on examining organizing as a verb, which obscured the role of organization as a noun or an agent (Taylor, 2013). With the exception of Hawes's (1974) linguistic work on social collectives, scholars held weak conceptions of a collective rationality and were unable to show how the organization emerged from jointly produced interaction processes.

Language/Discourse as Enacting Organizing/Organization. In the 1990s and early 2000s, organizational communication scholars began to focus on discourse, conversations, and language patterns as performances that enacted both organizing and organizations (Putnam & Fairhurst, 2001). Even though this early work centered on talk "inside of" organizations and institutions, studies of ethnography of speaking, conversational performances, and language as texts treated communication as a way to accomplish organizing (Banks, 1994; Trujillo, 1985). In addition, researchers began to view texts and intertextuality as metaphors of the organization, ones grounded in self-reflexive discursive practices, local experiences, and global social meanings (Cheney & Tompkins, 1988; Thatchenkery, 1992; Thatchenkery & Upadhyaya, 1996).

At the same time, scholars in management and organizational studies began to focus on discourse and organization and to examine how agencies as actors constituted client identities in discursive struggles (Phillips & Hardy, 1997), how storytelling performances constructed Disneyland as a postmodern organization (Boje, 1995), how talk accomplished work (Gronn, 1983) and how conversations produced organizational change (Ford & Ford, 1995). (For full reviews, see Keenoy, Oswick, & Grant, 1997; Grant, Hardy, Oswick, & Putnam, 2004.)

Scholars also referenced the work of Boden (1994), a sociologist who developed a theory on the reflexive relationship between talk and organization. Drawn from patterns of conversational turn-taking, she showed how the sequencing of texts became laminated or layered to form structures that moved from individuals to groups to form an organization. Even though Boden's work examined talk and organization, Cooren and Taylor (1997) criticized it for failing to capture the constancy or transitional nature of the organization. However, Boden's (1994) work helped pave the way for communication "to be seen as a constitutive force of organizations" and the organization to be viewed as a "discursive construction'" (Boivin et al., 2017:, p. 334; Fairhurst & Putnam, 2004; see Castor, this volume).

Taylor's books, *Une organization n'est q'un tissue de communication: Essais theoriques* (1988) and *Rethinking the Theory of Organizational Communication* (1993), were the first publications to theorize the communication-organization relationship. His thinking drew from speech acts, conversational analysis, narratology, and pragmatics to shift the ground away from organizing as a verb to organization as a noun (see Cooren & Seidl, this volume). Inspired by the notion of autopoiesis as a self-productive system, Taylor (1993) set forth *conversation* as the process of the organization and *text* as structured events that transcended immediate conversations. In this view, communication did not just produce the organization; rather "the organization [could] be found in the maneuverings and interpretations of its many conversations" (Fairhurst & Putnam, 1999, p. 9; see Dawson, this volume).

Taylor's (1993) work was also inspired by Ruth Smith's (1993) paper on root metaphors in organizational communication. In this essay, she reviewed ways that scholars had conceptualized the communication-organization relationship based on three categories: containment (i.e., communication contained in organizations), production (i.e., one produced the other or both were mutually constitutive), and equivalence (i.e., the two were one and the same). Her essay showed that most researchers treated communication either as a phenomenon that occurred "inside" the organization or a process that produced organizing (Taylor, 2013). Differing from this approach, Fairhurst and Putnam (2004) shifted these three orientations to alternatives: object (i.e., an entity that contains discourse), becoming (i.e., discourse as existing prior to and producing organization), and grounded-in-action (i.e., the organization as anchored in the continuous flow of discursive conduct in which action and structure are mutually and recursively constituted). Unlike Smith, Fairhurst and Putnam (2004) treated communication and organization as distinct phenomena (not equivalent) and set forth three ingredients of constitution—communicative action, discursive structures, and interpretive processes. They contended that the interplay of the three orientations held the key to anchoring organization in action. In effect, the "discursive constitution of organization" served as a precursor to the formal development of CCO theories (Boivin et al., 2017; see Castor, this volume).

Emergent CCO Constructs. Three key constructs that emerged from this stage of development became central to CCO thinking; namely, constitutive, performativity, and recursive relationships. The term *constitutive* means to form, frame, or make something what it is (Brummans et al., 2014; Putnam et al., 2009). It surfaces in the work on interaction patterns as constituting organizing as well as theoretical thinking about the discursive construction of organization. Used interchangeably with co-creation or co-constructed, constitutive entails more than simply arranging or combining parts, it refers to how multiple actors and actions come together and jointly enact organizing/organization. Although aligned with the system terms *production* and *reproduction*, constitutive entails a central focus on the "doing" or the ongoing developing that is not always salient in the work on production or enactment of the organization.

The second key construct that emerges from this period is *performativity,* which refers to the "how questions ... the concrete activities through which particular realities are generated, sustained, and changed" (Kuhn, Ashcraft, & Cooren, 2017, p. 41). Drawing from studies of speech acts and discursive patterns, scholars focus on the ways that utterances bring activities into being (Austin, 1962; see Cooren & Seidl, this volume). Hence, discourse and language engage in doing; they are "productive, generative, and active processes", not just ways of reflecting already formed things (Kuhn et al., 2017, p. 41). As such, storytelling and conversational practices enact organizational performances, such as leading, negotiating, and changing.

Although clearly rooted in organizing, research on interaction analysis, language, and discourse processes embraces performativity as a key construct of constitution.

A recursive relationship between communication and organizing is a third major CCO construct that surfaced during this period. A recursive relationship is a repeated pattern or routine in which the output at each stage is typically applied to the input of succeeding stages. In the studies of interaction patterns, repeated processes of communication become the input for recurrent organizational activities. Recursive relationships, also evident in Giddens's (1984) structuration, emerge in successive grammatical structures, repeated discursive routines, and the idea of "defining a thing in terms of itself". A recursive relationship lies at the core of treating an organization as a self-productive system—an important issue for the three main CCO schools.

Stage 2: The Emergence of Three Major Schools of CCO

In 2000, scholars from two of the three major schools of CCO thinking produced landmark publications—*The Emergent Organization: Communication at its Site and Surface* (Taylor & Van Every, 2000) and "The Communicative Constitution of Organizations: A Framework for Explanation" (McPhee & Zaug, 2000). These publications mark the beginning of the Montreal School and the Four Flows approach, respectively. A third school originated from translations and applications of Luhmann's *Social Systems* (1995) theory to CCO thinking (Seidl & Becker, 2005, 2006; Schoeneborn, 2011). These three schools while unified in their commitment to CCO (Ashcraft et al., 2009; Boivin et al., 2017; Brummans et al., 2014; Cooren, Kuhn, Cornelissen, & Clark, 2011) differ in their metatheoretical underpinnings, the properties of CCO, and explanations for what constitutes an organization (Bisel, 2010; Schoeneborn et al., 2014). In effect, while CCO emerged as a field of inquiry in organizational communication, it was not a unified enterprise.

The next sections provide brief overviews of the three schools through recapping how CCO occurs in each of them and then contrasting them in terms of their notions of communication and descriptions of the communication-organization relationship (Schoeneborn et. el., 2014). It culminates by extrapolating three additional constructs that are now pivotal to CCO work.

The Montreal School of CCO. As noted above, the Montreal School draws from the recursive nature of language to show how the organization emerges from its many conversations and texts (Taylor & Van Every, 2000). Conversations co-orient around something to be done and how to do it. They consist of the sayings and doings in situated practices and are fleeting while texts, as what's done, have the capacity to be stored to transcend local interactions. Importantly, the two function recursively, that is, texts enable and constrain conversations while conversations continually update and alter texts (see Dawson, this volume).

As both linguistic and material (non-human) in form, texts have the capacity to act or to display agency since they can "make a difference" in both constituting and representing an organization (Cooren, 2004). Thus, anything that "participates in the mode of communicating of an organization" (for example, a building, logo, directive, memo, or document) embodies it and materializes it as an organization (Schoeneborn et al., 2014). Texts then express missions, legitimate official positions, and enact policies as they constitute the organization.

This recursive relationship between conversations and texts leads to metaconversations and metatexts through successively embedding many different conversations and texts in each other. Metaconversations form communities or networks of practice that become loosely coupled self-organizing systems. A person or macro actor emerges from these communities to speak for or represent the organization; thus, the organization takes on authority through authoring and enlisting texts that cross time and space, link together different worldviews, and transform texts into symbols and standardized practices (e.g., strategic plans, codes of conduct, rules and regulations). Through communication then the organization functions as a collective actor capable of making itself known to its members and representing itself to others (Brummans et al., 2014).

The many communities of practice then often speak and act as one voice through multiple actors, such as texts, artifacts, emotions, buildings, and material objects (see Basque, Hirsto, & Wagnac, this volume). Cooren and his colleagues (Cooren et al., 2014) have developed several constructs to illustrate this speaking and acting as one entity, for instance, ventriloquism (Cooren, 2010; see Nathues & Van Vuuren, this volume), presentification and re-presentification (Cooren, Brummans, & Charrieras, 2008), and incarnation (Brummans & Cooren, 2011). The organization as one then is translated back to the many through aligning it with a *third person*; that is, using references such as *they, it, he,* or *she,* to invoke its name and to legitimate and authorize a representative. Thus, "the organization is constituted as an entity. Such entities, however, have no existence other than in discourse, where their realities are created and sustained" (Taylor & Cooren, 1997, p. 429).

The Four-Flows School. In the Four-Flows School, four distinct types of communication processes or "flows" constitute the organization (McPhee & Zaug, 2000; see Iverson, Myers, & McPhee, this volume). Grounded in Giddens's (1984) structuration theory (see Cooren & Seidl, this volume), an organization is a coordinated system of dynamic interaction episodes and social practices that emerge as flows. The flows and intersections between them contribute to CCO in different ways, but each one is necessary for an organization to function. These flows set forth the conditions for organizational existence, ones that are both orderly and disorderly, cooperative and competitive, and enabling as well as constraining.

The four flows consist of membership negotiation, reflexive self-structuring, activity coordination, and institutional positioning (McPhee & Zaug, 2000). Membership negotiation centers on the communicative practices and strategies that constitute identities, positions, and boundaries. Communication integrates members through storytelling, instruction, dismissive rules, and boundary framing (inclusion/exclusion) that reference the organization and designate who speaks on behalf of it. Reflexive self-structuring refers to interactions that produce rules and resources that steer the organization in a particular direction. These interactions generate policies, formal charts, and informal norms and practices, ones that become retained, regularized, or reflexively altered.

Activity coordination, the third flow, focuses on communication that enacts task roles and work processes through connecting and assembling joint actions. In this process, organizational members negotiate activities, engage in trial-and-error interactions, and coordinate how to work. Activity coordination then parallels co-orientation in the Montreal School. The fourth flow, institutional positioning, refers to interactions aimed at situating the organization within a system of suppliers, regulators, customers, competitors, and partners. It occurs through legitimating and distinguishing the organization from other agencies, developing and maintaining a place for it in a larger social system, and establishing a niche for it in inter-organizational relations.

The four flows together account for coordinated episodes and transactions between them, interweaving the local with the global (and vice versa), transferring patterns across space and time, and forming sub-systems linked to each other (McPhee, Poole, & Iverson, 2014). In this way, the organization is constituted communicatively as "a level of effective integration" among sets of people engaged in social practices and positioned in a larger social system (McPhee & Iverson, 2009, p. 62).

The Luhmannian School. Like the other schools, scholars who apply Luhmann's theories to CCO treat the organization as a closed system that maintains its own operations and creates its own boundaries (see Grothe-Hammer, this volume). For Luhmannian scholars (Seidl, 2005; Seidl & Becker, 2006; Schoeneborn, 2011), however, the organization is nothing but a communication system or a system of information (content), utterances (form and purpose), and understanding (meanings). In this thinking, communication happens when the form and purpose of interaction is understood (Luhmann, 2006, p. 47), but it is the system itself that develops understanding, which becomes detached from humans who are considered part of the environment. Communication selects from the environment what is information and what is understanding as it invites responses, redundancy, negotiation, and differentiation. Thus, communication constitutes the organization through self-referencing or self-production (see Cooren & Seidl, this volume); that is, it develops a logic of operations that differentiates the organization from its environment (Luhmann, 1995, p. 13).

More specifically, organizations are constituted by decision communication. As noted by March and Simon (1958), communication selects courses of action or decisions that produce more decisions as the medium and outcome of choice. Decision communication, though, functions paradoxically in that the selection of one alternative excludes other options and thus reveals the undecidability of choice. To counter this factor, the organization aims to conceal this paradox by producing and storing decision premises that make choice seem predictable and reasonable for a particular time or a set of powerful actors (Brummans et al., 2014).

Importantly, only communication events participate in constituting the organization. Communication authors other communicative events and form networks of interconnected decisions. In this school, unlike the Montreal and Four Flows approaches, the organization is authorless or agentless; communication events constitute it, but the organization does not act as a separate agent. It exists as a social system that is sustained and changed through decision communication (Schoeneborn, 2011).

Comparison/Contrast of the Three Schools. As these descriptions suggest, the three schools of thought are similar yet are different in several ways (see Schoeneborn et al., 2014, for a full discussion). Two areas though seem pivotal to developing CCO thinking, that is, assumptions about communication as well as the communication-organization relationship.

All three approaches cast communication as a dynamic, ongoing process that is precarious and indeterminate; however, they differ regarding the salient features that enact CCO. Drawing from the dialectic of conversation and text, scholars in the Montreal School treat communication as a transactional process that entails human and non-human agents who are co-orienting around a task. As agents produce metaconversations and metatexts, representatives come forth to speak on behalf of the organization. In this way, communication enacts relationships among human and non-human agents as both engage in organizing and in authoring the organization as a collective.

In the Four Flows School, communication refers to different interactional functions that are deemed necessary for organizations to exit. Even though this school recognizes symbolic meaning, only humans can act. Thus, unlike the Montreal School, non-humans cannot have agency. In the Luhmannian School, communication is not a type of action/transaction; rather it centers on selecting out information, choosing utterances, and developing understanding through distinguishing the organization from the larger environment. Importantly, in this school, understanding operates retrospectively, that is, subsequent communication interprets preceding ones; hence, meaning does not reside in humans per se, but in a network of decision communications (Blaschke, Schoeneborn, & Seidl, 2012).

Although the three differ in this regard, they share a common bond that communication constitutes the organization—as speech acts/conversations/texts that form and maintain a collective whole and speak on behalf of the collective (Montreal School, Taylor & Cooren, 1997); as four interrelated flows that interface to give rise to the organization (Four Flows, McPhee & Zaug, 2000), and as interconnected decisions that produce networks of communication (Seidl, 2005). In effect, an organization emerges as a processual entity through communication as transactional exchanges (Montreal), flows or interlocking communication events (Four Flows), or decision premises, networks, and understandings that shape continued decision communication (Luhmann).

Emergent CCO Constructs. These three schools serve as metatheories for guiding research and explanatory thinking about CCO. As such, a metatheory functions as an umbrella of central constructs and principles that generate explanations and modes of inquiry. Each of the three has produced complex and detailed nomenclature to guide research questions, methodologies, and extended theory development. In addition, as metatheories, they give rise to constructs that govern what CCO is and is not. The three constructs previously reviewed—constitutive, performativity, and recursive relationships—form the foundation that underlies all CCO thinking. However, the schools bring to the table three additional CCO constructs; namely, *entity/collective*, *materiality* (non-humans), and *distanciation* (i.e., crossing time and space). Even though the schools differ in their views of them, the three surface as additional constructs that have become pivotal to CCO thinking.

The first construct, the *entity* or *collective*, is the focal point of the communication-organization relationship. CCO work, however, differs from typical studies of the firm, institutions, or agencies that presume an a priori existence prior to communication. In this way, it challenges the age-old problem of entitativity that casts a collective as "real" or as an abstraction that exists apart from its construction. Even though the three schools agree that communication constitutes the organization, they differ regarding what the entity or collective is.

The Montreal School treats the entity as a macro-actor formed through meta-conversations/texts produced in communities of practice; thus, it surfaces as a communicative collective developed through self-organizing networks of interactions. The organization then is incarnated by anything that presents or represents it, including a logo, a text, a building, or a spokesperson. For the Four Flows School, the entity is a collective or a functional system that is (re)produced in day-to-day interactions. These interactions (i.e., assemblages of communicative processes) create membership boundaries, engage in self-structuring, perform task activities, and communicate with other organizations (e.g., competitors, regulators). Like the Four Flows, Luhmannian scholars cast the collective as a system, but a meso-level one distinguished from society and dyadic interactions by its reliance on decision communication; thus, the organization is "a network of interrelated processes of decisions connecting to other decisions" (Schoeneborn et al., 2014, p. 293). In summary, all three schools concur that the entity/collection is produced by and exists only in and through communication.

A second important construct that emanates from CCO schools is *materiality* or *non-human* actors (see Larson & Mengis, this volume). All three schools decenter or de-emphasize the role of human agents through focusing centrally on communication as the impetus for organizing.

The Montreal School moves a step further in endowing material objects and non-human actors with agency or the capacity "to make a difference" in organizations. The other two schools recognize materiality but give it less credence in constituting the organization. The Four Flows treats materiality as potentially enabling or constraining actions, but not as having its own agency; only humans have the capability to act. Similarly, the Luhmannian school recognizes material forms (e.g., objects, bodies, sites), but treats them as part of an organization's environment and not as communication per se. In effect, while the three schools differ regarding the role that non-humans play in constituting the organization, they believe materiality is important and critical to CCO.

The third construct that surfaces from the three schools is *distanciation* or the critical role of *distance, time,* and *space* in theorizing how communication constitutes the organization. *Distanciation* focuses on the way that agents bind communication and organizing across time and space or in local-global interactions (McPhee et al., 2014). All three schools embrace the notion that an organization crosses time and space, now and then, here and there, not simply as a social fact or a permanent building, but as ongoing processes of being constituted and reconstituted. Based on Giddens's (1984) work, the Four Flows school embraces distanciation to examine how interactional encounters move from one social system to another, how time-space trajectories cross locales, and how virtuality becomes rooted in structures (McPhee & Canary, 2013; McPhee et al., 2014).

Drawn from Ricoeur's (1981) notion of distanciation, scholars in the Montreal School explore distance through the ways that conversations become detached from texts (Taylor & Van Every, 2000, 2011), texts surface as objects that can be stored and archived (Spee & Jarzabkowski, 2011), objects come to represent the organization (Koschmann, Kuhn, & Pfarrer, 2012; Kuhn, 2008), and the organization becomes incarnated in artifacts, protocols, and routines (Cooren, Matte, Taylor, & Vásquez, 2007). Mobilizing agents to speak on behalf of the organization intertwines the past, present, and future through time trajectories that draw from previous conversations and direct future actions (Koschmann et al., 2012). In this way, the Montreal School investigates two key processes that take place in distanciation—decontextualizing and depersonalizing. Decontextualizing occurs when actors detach a text from its local situation and cast it as an abstraction while depersonalizing separates the text from the individuals who produced it and cast it as 'a what' (Lohuis & van Vuuren, 2017).

In the Luhmannian School, the construct of distanciation functions implicitly, especially in decision communication that produces premises for future decisions. As networks of decisions, communication travels across time and space. Moreover, the Luhmannian School also contends that the organization assures its presence across time and space through boundary communication that continually separates it from its environment. The organization then moves across time and space as a self-referential system, mediated by a network of communication decisions that produce decisions (Seidl, 2005).

In effect, the emergence and continued development of three schools paves the way for institutionalizing CCO thinking and for spreading its reach to international and interdisciplinary domains (Boivin et al., 2017). The three schools function as meta-theories or umbrellas in which other approaches draw on explanatory insights and key constructs to investigate how communication constitutes organization (Cooren et al., 2011). Even though they differ in terms of the communication features salient in CCO, they share common assumptions and central constructs that differentiate CCO work from other perspectives. In particular, the three schools embrace the fundamental belief that organizations "do not predate communication but come into being ... [through] communicative processes that attribute actorhood to the organizational endeavor" (Schoeneborn et al., 2014, p. 309). In this way, CCO has become "a paradigmatic perspective" or "a common enterprise" in which new and alternative approaches are surfacing to address "what is an organization?".

Stage 3: The Spread of CCO and the Emergence of a Generic Paradigm

The latest stage in CCO development is more difficult to date but it surfaces in the last decade through field-configuring events, the interdisciplinary and international spread of CCO, and the emergence of alternative CCO thinking. These developments have contributed to "the institutionalization of CCO scholarship" (Boivin et al., 2017) and culminated in a generic paradigm—one that embraces central constructs and tenets of CCO work.

Several field-configuring events have contributed to the advancement of CCO perspectives. A field-configuring event (Lampel & Meyer, 2008) is a "temporary social organization" or a professional gathering of scholars from different disciplines who join together, share concerns, exchange information, and advance a field of study (Boivin et al., 2017). These events are linked to pre-conferences, panels, symposia, and forums on CCO at professional meetings. Books, publications, forums, and special issues of journals stem from ideas sparked during these field-configuring events (see, for example, Blaschke & Schoeneborn, 2017; Cooren et al., 2006; Cooren, Vaara, Langley, & Tsoukas, 2014; Robichaud & Cooren, 2013; Putnam & Nicotera, 2009, as well as *Management Communication Quarterly*, 2010, 2013, 2014; *Organization Studies*, 2011). The growth of these events aids in establishing CCO as a field of inquiry and in developing alternative perspectives (Boivin et al., 2017).

These field-configuring events also foster the interdisciplinary and international spread of CCO. While the early work was primarily based in North America among organizational communication scholars, Boivin et al., (2017) note the rapid growth of CCO thinking in multi-disciplinary circles, as evident in mainstream management journals and applications to traditional organizational concepts. The interdisciplinary/international spread of CCO ties to the existence of a Standing Work Group on "Organization as Communication" in the European Group for Organization Studies (EGOS) from 2013 to 2021 (and now renewed for 2022–2025). Since the inception of this group, scholars from business schools, sociology, corporate communication, public relations, and other disciplines have presented and responded to CCO papers, deliberated about theory and research, and explored alternative methods for studying CCO. Relatedly, the number of publications authored by interdisciplinary scholars has increased in the past decade and CCO articles have gained traction in management journals, such as *Organization Studies* (12), *Human Relations* (5), *Academy of Management Review* (3), *Journal of Management Studies* (3), and *Academy of Management Annals* (2) (see Boivin et al., 2017).

Another indicator of the interdisciplinary spread is the growth in research that applies CCO thinking to traditional organizational topics, such as leadership (Fairhurst, 2007; Fairhurst & Cooren, 2009; Holm & Fairhurst, 2018; Koch, 2017; see Bisel, Fairhurst, & Sheep, this volume), organizational identification (Cornelissen, Christensen, & Kimuthia, 2012; Piette, 2013; Seidl, 2005, 2007; see Chaput & Basque, this volume), organizational change and learning (Browning, Sitkin, Sutcliffe, Obstfeld, & Greene, 2009; Matte & Cooren, 2015), interorganizational collaboration (Arnaudi & Mills, 2012; Koschmann, 2013; Koschmann et al., 2012; see Koschmann, this volume), and networks (Blaschke, Schoeneborn, & Seidl, 2012; Blaschke, 2017).

Importantly, applying CCO to particular research concepts often leads to reframing these arenas in innovative ways. In leadership studies, CCO work on textual "authoring" led to distinguishing leadership from authority, two concepts that have been habitually conflated (Holm & Fairhurst, 2018; see Benoit-Barné & Fox, this volume). In organizational strategy, for instance, Fenton and Langley (2011) recast strategic planning as textual narratives that infuse infrastructures, metaconversations, and coherence. Similarly, Spee and Jarzabkowski (2011) examine how a strategic text becomes de-contextualized and detached from its production and how it disciplines members, shapes subsequent managerial conversations, and enacts legitimacy and authority for future actions (see Spee, this volume). Other studies apply Luhmann's CCO thinking to investigate the routines that shape decision communication in strategy (Faure & Rouleau, 2011; Hendry & Seidl, 2003). CCO thinking has also added a communicative approach to institutional theory through reconceptualizing stakeholder theory and knowledge-based theories of the firm (Kuhn, 2008, 2012) and through tracking how communicative practices scale up from local, situated events to metaconversations as opposed to drilling down from organizational logics (Cornelissen, Durand, Fiss, Lammars, & Vaara, 2015; Sandhu, 2017).

Applying CCO to a variety of topics has led to alternative approaches that veer from the three major schools. This work draws on different European theorists (e.g., Foucault, 1979; Habermas, 1987; Honneth, 1996; Gunther, 1979) to explore power conditions (Leclercq-Vandelannoitte, 2011), ethics and moral communication (Jensen, 2017; Scherer & Rasche, 2017), and struggles for recognition (Fassauer, 2017) in the communicative constitution of organization (see Cooren & Seidl, this volume).

One alternative that has gained considerable traction is the role of communication in constituting disorder and disorganization (see Vásquez, Kuhn, & Plotnikof, this volume). In contrast to CCO studies that privilege ordering moves (Cooren, 2000), this perspective focuses on conflict, struggles, and irrationality, not as ineffective or dysfunctional, but as an unavoidable and necessary feature of organizational life (Cooren et al., 2011; Cooper, 1986). CCO models are particularly well-suited to studying dis/organization through focusing on the dialectical relationship between order and disorder in negotiating meanings, examining power (Mease, 2021), and in struggles among texts (Putnam, 2019; Vásquez & Kuhn, 2019). This alternative also shifts research agendas to concepts such as paradox, contradictions, and tensions (Putnam, Fairhurst, & Banghart, 2016) and to dis/organizing processes (Cooren & Caidor, 2019), such as producing visibility through invisibility (Albu, 2019; Stohl & Stohl, 2011), oscillating between stability and flexibility (Grothe-Hammer, 2019), and examining the interplay between equilibrium/disequilibrium in the "knotting" of multiple tensions (Sheep, Fairhurst, & Khazanchi, 2017).

In effect, CCO has emerged as a generic paradigm of theory and research in organizational communication as well as organizational studies writ large. The growth of field configuring events, the spread of CCO to interdisciplinary and international scholars, the applications of CCO to traditional organizational scholarship, and the emergence of alternative perspectives—all attest to a new framework or a paradigm for conceiving of what constitutes an organization. This paradigm, rooted in communicative processes and practices, includes a set of common elements and basic premises that emanate from these three stages of development and that guide CCO theory and research.

Common Elements and Premises of the CCO Paradigm

In a scientific community, a paradigm implies a general agreement on a way of thinking, common elements, basic premises, and key constructs. Although scholars differ in their perspectives, they share an overall goal; that is, to examine how communication constitutes organization. To this end, theorists concur on common elements and premises. For CCO, communication as constituting organization is the focal point of an investigation. Common elements subsumed under this umbrella include language, conversations, texts, flows, utterances, nonverbal communication, bodies, information, metaphors, non-human agents, artifacts, and meaning/understanding. Importantly, CCO scholars focus on the interactive configurations or sets of arrangements that emerge from the multiplicity of these elements; for example, among conversations, texts, and nonhuman actors in the Montreal School, flows and meaning in the Four Flows School, and information, utterances, understandings, and decisions in the Luhmannian School. Alternative perspectives privilege struggles among these elements, for example, tensions and contradictory discourses, meanings, and texts as constituting dis/organization.

These sets of arrangements exist in reciprocal relationships; that is, they begin and end with interconnections that reflect back on and build on each other. In some CCO approaches, these dynamic and evolving relationships exist as a dance among agencies (Montreal) or a complex interwoven social system (Luhmann). Thus, "who and what is acting is always an open question" (Cooren et al., 2011, p. 1152) and texts such as strategies and mission statements act in the name of the organization (Montreal). Relationality among agents, flows, or decisions, then, underlies how the three major CCO schools decipher patterns among these elements.

Adding to these elements, three key premises characterize CCO work (Cooren et al., 2011; Schere & Rasch, 2017). First, scholarship focuses on processes or "segments of ongoing, situated streams of socio-discursive practices", not isolated episodes or singular occurrences (Cooren et al., 2011, p. 1151). It examines the interactive processes and communicative practices as they evolve over time. Thus, scholars center on "what happens *in* and *through* communication to constitute (re-)produce, or alter organizational forms and practices" (Cooren et al., 2011, p. 1151, emphasis in original).

A second and related premise is that CCO targets joint production, or the co-orientating and co-constructing of performances and meanings. Meanings then are negotiated as "provisional and temporary-situated accomplishments" (Cooren et al., 2011). Because they are co-produced or co-constructed among multiple actors, they typically differ from the sender's intended meaning. A third premise closely tied to the first two is that CCO scholarship focuses on *both* the processes of organizing and the constitution of the organization. Focusing only on the process of organizing privileges an individualistic view and downplays the role of communication in constituting the collective. Thus, CCO scholars center on "how people get organized" and "how organizations come to be re-enacted and reproduced through these activities" (Cooren et al., 2011, p. 1153).

These premises form the assumptive ground for the six constructs that surface from tracing CCO history. Focusing on ongoing, situated streams of socio-material practices captures the *performative* nature of communication and the role of *materiality or non-humans* (socio-material practices) in *constituting* organizational forms. The *entity* or *collective* as a self-organizing system arises from the *recursive relationships* between organizing and organization as the third premise mentioned above. These relationships then become *distanciated* or detached from their situated construction to cross time and space in constituting the collective. Hence, as a common framework, CCO scholars focus on communicative elements and their recursive relationships in constituting organizing and organization. Five of the constructs—constitutive, performative, recursive relationships, entity/collective, and distanciation—surface as essential ingredients in all CCO studies while materiality is primarily a theme characterizing the Montreal School. Overall, though, these paradigmatic features distinguish CCO thinking from other types of organizational theory and scholarship.

Another characteristic of a paradigm is a common methodology or a shared epistemology. CCO research embraces a wide array of qualitative and quantitative research approaches, including narrative analysis, network studies, ethnography, conversational analysis, semiotics, and use of artifacts and architectural elements (Cooren et al., 2011). As this list suggests, the majority of studies are qualitative in nature. Even so, CCO research is methodologically diverse which can lead to a lack of transparency in describing data collection and analytical techniques

(Boivin et al., 2017, p. 346). One common methodological concern, however, is that CCO investigators focus on communication per se; thus, they share an epistemology centered on communicative events and practices grounded in the realm of action rather than on phenomena removed from observable interactions (Cooren et al., 2011).

As a paradigm, then, CCO represents a type of *unified diversity* (Eisenberg, 1984; see Boivin & Brummans, this volume) that shares common elements, premises, and constructs, but differs in perspectives, metatheoretical underpinnings, methodologies, and links to mainstream organizational literature (Boivin et al., 2017; Cooren et al., 2011). As this volume suggests, CCO scholarship has expanded its purview and paradigmatic reach to include an array of new approaches.

CCO Contributions to the Field

As a major theoretical lens, CCO has made several contributions to both organizational communication and organizational studies. A first key contribution is that CCO as a paradigm originates in organizational communication as opposed to in social theories writ large (Boivin, 2017; Putnam & Mumby, 2014). In this way, it challenges the social constructionist and critical approaches that minimize communication and materiality. CCO concepts and dynamic interrelationships surface from language, interactions, texts, utterances, nonverbal cues, and materialities rather than from structural, psychological, or mental models. For example, CCO work on sensemaking has moved away from its roots in cognition to focusing on language and dynamic interactions that constitute collective sensemaking (Cornelissen & Clarke, 2010). Thus, as demonstrated in previous discussions of organizational strategy and institutional theory, a second (and key) contribution of CCO is its capacity to reframe and alter the nature of organizational concepts through treating them as situated performances rather than preordained structures, individual cognitions, or cultural meanings.

Three additional contributions merit attention. First, CCO studies focus on ways that communication transcends the here and now. Rather than privileging norms and rules as structural or cultural phenomena, scholars focus on how transcendence occurs, ways that networks of practices and chains of interactions cross distances, how interactions intertwine past, present, and future (Browning et al., 2009; Vásquez & Cooren, 2013). Another important contribution of CCO work is its recent focus on disorder and disorganization. Criticized for a bias for order (Bisel, 2009, 2010), CCO work has responded to its critics and branched out to examine the disruptive, disordering, and chaotic properties of communication (Vásquez & Kuhn, 2019). This contribution advances an important and largely ignored agenda in organizational studies.

A third contribution that surfaces from CCO work is the research on *organizationality*: that is, what makes communication practices more or less "organizational" (Dobusch & Schoeneborn, 2015; see Schoeneborn, Blagoev, & Dobusch, this volume). Organizationality moves beyond the conceptions of organization as a noun or a verb to examine it as an adjective or a loose and fluid social phenomenon, such as movements, communities, and terrorist networks that have degrees of organizationality (Schoeneborn, Kuhn, & Kärreman, 2019). For example, Wilhoit and Kisselburgh (2015) show how a community of commuter bicyclists stabilize communicative practices of spatial resistance that form a social collective.

A fourth contribution, as noted previously, is the way CCO addresses the classic micro-macro divide in organizational studies (Kuhn, 2012). Rather than reducing one level to another or treating them as discrete arenas, CCO work centers on navigating boundaries, scaling up and down through chains of interactional episodes, and ways that communication flows transcend levels in self-structuring and coordination activities. A CCO lens, as Kuhn (2012) aptly demonstrates, alters our understanding of traditional macro topics by situating them in micro routines of socio-material accomplishments, dialogues that nurture multiple stakeholder relationships, and discursive resources in decision-oriented episodes. Focusing on communicative performances then counters the dualisms in debates between micro-macro levels.

The Exigencies for a CCO Handbook

As this essay suggests, CCO has not only reached maturity and developed clear conceptual foundations, it is now an alternative paradigm for studying communication and organization. This paradigm encompasses meta-theories as overarching schools of thought, alternative perspectives that spin off these theories, and general agreement on the goals, elements, central premises, and key constructs of CCO.

As scholars develop alternative perspectives and engage in dialogue across fields, a *Handbook* of CCO work is needed to take stock of theory and research, track developments in methodologies, and explore CCO pedagogy and practice. The wide interdisciplinary and international appeal of CCO suggest that empirical and theoretical work in this area will continue to grow and to focus on consequential problems that affect organizations and society today (Albu, 2019; Porter, Kuhn, & Nerlich, 2017; Schoeneborn, Vásquez, & Cornelissen, in press). Yet, in some circles, CCO has become a "catch all" phrase for any work on the communication-organization relationship (Boivin et al., 2017). A *Handbook* can aid in avoiding this conceptual drift by articulating commonalities among perspectives.

Although it may be premature to draw boundary lines, CCO scholars need to center on the configurations and interactive relationships among features of communication in constituting organization. They need to target how these elements jointly produce streams of ongoing, situated interactions and socio-material practices in both organizing and organization. Finally, based on historical development, they need to attend to six foundational constructs, namely, *constitutive, performativity, recursive relationships, entity/collective, materiality,* and *distanciation,* that serve as focal points for CCO work.

The CCO paradigm has become one of the most refreshing and generative frameworks in the field. It will continue for decades to be fertile ground for reframing traditional organizational concepts, for bridging the micro-macro divide, and for generating provocative insights as to what an organization is and how communication constitutes it.

References

Albu, O. B. (2019). Dis/ordering: The use of information and communication technologies by human rights civil society organizations. In C. Vásquez & T. Kuhn (Eds.), *Dis/organization as communication: Studying tensions, ambiguities and disordering* (pp. 151–171). New York: Routledge.

Arnaud, N., & Mills, C. E. (2012). Understanding interorganizational agency: A communication perspective. *Group & Organization Management, 37,* 452–485.

Ashcraft, K. L., Kuhn, T. R., & Cooren, F. (2009). Constitutional amendments: "Materializing" organizational communication. *The Academy of Management Annals, 3*(1), 1–64.

Austin, J. L. (1962). *How to do things with words.* Cambridge, MA: Harvard University Press.

Banks, S. P. (1994). Performing public announcements: The case of flight attendants' work discourse. *Text and Performance Quarterly, 14,* 253–267.

Bisel, R. S. (2009). On a growing dualism in organizational discourse research. *Management Communication Quarterly, 22*(4), 614–638.

Bisel, R. S. (2010). A communicative ontology of organization? A description, history, and critique of CCO theories for organization science. *Management Communication Quarterly, 24*(1), 124–131.

Blaschke, S. (2017). Organizing and organization: The micro and the macro of networks of communication episodes. In S. Blaschke & D. Schoeneborn (Eds.), *Organization as communication: Perspectives in dialogue* (pp. 177–190). New York: Routledge.

Blaschke, S., & Schoeneborn, D. (Eds.). (2017). *Organization as communication: Perspectives in dialogue.* New York: Routledge.

Blaschke, S., Schoeneborn, D., & Seidl, D. (2012). Organizations as networks of communication episodes: Turning the network perspective inside out. *Organization Studies, 33*(8), 879–906.

Boden, D. (1994). *The business of talk: Organizations in action.* Cambridge, UK: Polity Press.

Boivin, G., Brummans, B. H. J. M., & Barker, J. R. (2017). The institutionalization of CCO scholarship: Trends from 2000 to 2015. *Management Communication Quarterly, 31*(3), 331–335.

Boje, D. M. (1995). Stories of the storytelling organization: A postmodern analysis of Disney as "Tamaraland". *Academy of Management Journal, 38*, 997–1035.

Browning, L. D., Greene, R. W., Sitkin, S. B., Sutcliffe, K. M., & Obstfeld, D. (2009). Constitutive complexity: Military entrepreneurs and the synthetic character of communication flows. In L. L. Putnam & A. M. Nicotera (Eds.), *Building theories of organizations: The constitutive role of communication* (pp. 89–116). New York: Routledge.

Brummans, B. H. J. M., & Cooren, F. (2011). Communication as incarnation. *Communication and Critical/Cultural Studies, 8*(2), 186–187.

Brummans, B. H. J. M., Cooren, F., Robichaud, D., & Taylor, J. R. (2014). Approaches to the communicative constitution of organization. In L. L. Putnam & D. K. Mumby (Eds.), *The SAGE handbook of organizational communication* (3rd edn., pp. 173–194). Los Angeles, CA: Sage.

Cheney, G., & Tompkins, P. K. (1988). On the facts of the text as the basis of human communication research. In J. A. Anderson (Ed.), *Communication yearbook 11* (pp. 455–481). Newbury Park, CA: Sage.

Cooper, R. (1986). Organization/disorganization. *Social Science Information, 25*, 199–335.

Cooren, F. (2000). *The organizing property of communication.* Amsterdam: J. Benjamins.

Cooren, F. (2004). Textual agency: How texts do things in organizational settings. *Organization, 11*, 373–393.

Cooren, F. (2010). *Action and agency in dialogue: Passion, incarnation and ventriloquism.* Amsterdam: John Benjamins.

Cooren, F., Brummans, B. H. J. M., & Charrieras, D. (2008). The coproduction of organizational presence: A study of Medecins sans Frontieres in action. *Human Relations, 61*(10), 1339–1370.

Cooren, F., & Caïdor, P. (2019). Communication as dis/organization: How to analyze tensions from a relational perspective. In C. Vásquez & T. Kuhn (Eds.). *Dis/organization as communication: Studying tensions, ambiguities and disordering* (pp. 36–59). New York: Routledge.

Cooren, F., Kuhn, T. R., Cornelissen, J. P., & Clark, T. (2011). Communication, organizing and organization: An overview and introduction to the special issue. *Organization Studies, 32*(9), 1149–1170.

Cooren, F., Matte, F., Taylor, J. R., & Vásquez, C. (2007). A humanitarian organization in action: Organizational discourse as a stable mobile. *Discourse and Communication, 1*(2), 153–190.

Cooren, F., & Taylor, J. R. (1997). Organization as an effect of mediation: Redefining the link between organization and communication. *Communication Theory, 7*(3), 219–260.

Cooren, F., Taylor, J.R., & Van Every, E. J. (Eds.). (2006). *Communication as organizing: Empirical and theoretical explorations in the dynamic of text and conversation.* Mahwah, NJ: Lawrence Erlbaum.

Cooren, F., Vaara, E., Langley, A., & Tsoukas, H. (2014*). Language and communication at work: Discourse, narrativity, and organizing.* Oxford, UK: Oxford University Press.

Cornelissen, J., Christensen, L. T., & Kinuthia, K. (2012). Corporate brands and identity: Developing stronger theory and a call for shifting the debate. *European Journal of Marketing, 46*, 1093–1102.

Cornelissen, J., & Clarke, J. S. (2010). Imagining and rationalizing opportunities: Inductive reasoning, and the creation and justification of new ventures. *Academy of Management Review, 35*, 539–557.

Cornelissen, J. P., Durand, R., Fiss, P. C., Lammers, J. C., & Vaara, E. (2015). Putting communication front and center in institutional theory and analysis. *Academy of Management Review, 40*(1), 10–27.

Craig, R.T. (1999). Communication theory as a field. *Communication Theory, 9*(2), 119–161.

Dobusch, L., & Schoeneborn, D. (2015). Fluidity, identity, and organizationality: The communicative constitution of Anonymous. *Journal of Management Studies, 52*, 1005–1035.

Eisenberg, E. M. (1984). Ambiguity as strategy in organizational communication. *Communication Monographs, 51*(3), 227–242.

Fairhurst, G.T. (2007). *Discursive leadership: In conversation with leadership psychology.* Thousand Oaks: Sage.

Fairhurst, G. T., & Cooren, F. (2009). Leadership as the hybrid production of presence(s). *Leadership, 5*(4), 469–490.

Fairhurst, G. T., & Putnam, L. L. (1999). Reflections on the communication-organization equivalence question: The contributions of James Taylor and his colleagues. *The Communication Review, 3*(1/2), 1–19.

Fairhurst, G. T., & Putnam, L. L. (2004). Organizations as discursive constructions. *Communication Theory*, *14*, 5–26.

Fairhurst, G. T., Rogers, E., & Saar, R. (1987). Manager-subordinate control patterns and judgments about the relationship. In M. McLaughlin (Ed.), *Communication Yearbook 10* (pp. 395–415). Beverly Hills, CA: Sage.

Fassauer, B. (2017). Organization as communication and Honneth's notion of struggles for recognition. In S. Blaschke & D. Schoeneborn (Eds.), *Organization as communication: Perspectives in dialogue* (pp. 27–44). New York: Routledge.

Fauré, B., & Rouleau, L. (2011). The strategic competence of accountants and middle managers in budget making. *Accounting, Organizations and Society*, *36*, 167–182.

Fenton, C., & Langley, A. (2011). Strategy as practice and the narrative turn. *Organization Studies*, *32*(9), 1171–1196.

Fisher, B. A. (1978). *Perspectives on human communication*. New York: Macmillan.

Ford, J. D., & Ford, L. W. (1995). The role of conversations in producing intentional change in organizations. *Academy of Management Review*, *20*(3), 541–570.

Foucault, M. (1979). *Discipline and punish: The birth of the prison*. Harmondsworth: Penguin.

Giddens, A. (1984). *The constitution of society: Outline of the theory of structuration*. University of California Press.

Grant, D., Hardy, C., Oswick, C., & Putnam, L. L. (Eds.). (2004). *The SAGE handbook of organizational discourse*. Thousand Oaks, CA; Sage.

Gronn, P. C. (1983). Talk as the work: The accomplishment of school administration. *Administrative Science Quarterly*, *28*, 1–21.

Grothe-Hammer, M., & Schoeneborn, D. (2019). The queen bee out lives her own children: A Luhmannian perspective on project-based organizations (PBOs). In C. Vásquez & T. Kuhn (Eds.). *Dis/organization as communication: Studying tensions, ambiguities and disordering* (pp. 60–79). New York: Routledge.

Günther, G. (1979). Life as poly-contexturality. In *Beiträge zur grundlegung einer operationsfähigen dialektik* (Vol. 2, pp. 283–307). Hamburg: Meiner.

Habermas, J. (1987). *The theory of communicative action* (Vol. 2). Boston, MA: Beacon Press.

Hawes, L. C. (1974). Social collectives as communication: Perspectives on organizational behavior. *Quarterly Journal of Speech*, *60*, 497–502.

Hendry, J., & Seidl, D. (2003). The structure and significance of strategic episodes: Social systems theory and the routine practices of strategic change. *Journal of Management Studies*, *40*, 175–196.

Holm, F. & Fairhurst, G.T. (2018). Configuring shared and hierarchical leadership through authoring. *Human Relations*, *71*(5), 692–721.

Honneth, A. (1996). *The struggle for recognition*. Cambridge: Polity Press.

Jensen, T. (2017). Organization as communication and Gunther's notion of polycontexturality. In S. Blaschke & D. Schoeneborn (Eds.), *Organization as communication: Perspectives in dialogue* (pp. 45–68). New York: Routledge.

Keenoy, T., Oswick, C., & Grant, D. (1997). Organizational discourses: Text and context. *Organization*, *4*, 147–157.

Koch, J. (2017). Organization as communication and the emergence of leadership: A Luhmannian perspective. In S. Blaschke & D. Schoeneborn (Eds.), *Organization as communication: Perspectives in dialogue* (pp. 121–140). New York: Routledge.

Koschmann, M. A. (2013). The communicative constitution of collective identity in interorganizational collaboration. *Management Communication Quarterly*, *27*(1), 61–89.

Koschmann, M. A., Kuhn, T., & Pharrer, M. (2012). A communicative framework of value in cross-sector partnerships. *Academy of Management Review*, *37*(3), 332–354.

Krone, K. J., Jablin, F. M., & Putnam, L. L. (1987). Communication theory and organizational communication: Multiple perspectives. In F. M. Jablin, L. L. Putnam, K. H. Roberts & L. W. Porter (Eds.), *Handbook of organizational communication: An interdisciplinary perspective* (pp. 18–40). Newbury Park, CA: Sage.

Kuhn, T. (2008). A communicative theory of the firm: Developing an alternative perspective on intra-organizational power and stakeholder relationships. *Organization Studies*, *29*(8/9), 1227–1254.

Kuhn, T. (2012). Negotiating the micro-macro divide: Thought leadership from organizational communication for theorizing organization. *Management Communication Quarterly*, *26*(4), 543–584.

Kuhn, T., Ashcraft, K. L., & Cooren, F. (2017). *The work of communication: Relational perspectives on working and organizing in contemporary capitalism*. New York: Taylor & Francis.

Lampel, J., & Meyer, A. D. (2008). Field-configuring events as structuring mechanisms: How conferences, ceremonies, and trade shows constitute new technologies, industries, and markets. *Journal of Management Studies*, *45*, 1025–1035.

Leclercq-Vandelannoitte, A. (2011). Organizations as discursive constructions: A Foucauldian approach. *Organization Studies, 32*(9), 1247–1271.

Lohuis, A. M., & van Vuuren, M. (2017). Organization as communication and strategic change: The dynamics of distanciation. In S. Blaschke & D. Schoeneborn (Eds.), *Organization as communication: Perspectives in dialogue* (pp. 191–212). New York: Routledge.

Luhmann, N. (1995). *Social systems*. Stanford, CA: Stanford University Press.

Luhmann, N. (2006). System as difference. *Organization, 13*(1), 37–57.

March, J. G., & Simon, H. A. (1958). *Organizations*. New York: John Wiley.

Matte, F., & Cooren, F. (2015). Learning as dialogue: An "on-the-go" approach to dealing with organizational tensions. In L. Filliettaz & S. Billett (Eds.), *Francophone perspectives of learning through work* (pp. 169–187). Cham, Switzerland: Springer.

McPhee, R. D., & Canary, H. E. (2013, July). *Distanciation and organizational constitution*. Paper presented at the European Group for Organizational Studies Conference, Montreal, Canada.

McPhee, R. D., & Iverson, J. (2009). Agents of constitution in Communidad: Constitutive processes of communication in organizations. In L. L. Putnam & A. M. Nicotera (Eds.), *Building theories of organization: The constitutive role of communication*. New York: Routledge, 49–88.

McPhee, R. D., Poole, M. S. & Iverson, J. (2014). Structuration theory. In L. L. Putnam & D. K. Mumby (Eds.), *The Sage Handbook of Organizational Communication* (3rd edn., pp. 75–100). Los Angeles, CA: Sage.

McPhee, R. D. & Zaug, P. (2000). The communicative constitution of organizations: A framework for explanation. *The Electronic Journal of Communication, 10*, 1–16.

Mease, J. J. (2021). Techniques and forces and the communicative constitution of organization: A Deleuzian approach to organizational (in)stability and power. *Management Communication Quarterly, 35*, 226–255.

Phillips, N., & Hardy, C. (1997). Managing multiple identities: Discourse, legitimacy and resources in the UK refugee system. *Organization, 4*, 159–185.

Piette, I. (2013). Restructuring identity through sectorial narratives. In D. Robichaud & F. Cooren (Eds.), *Organization and organizing: Materiality, agency, and discourse* (pp. 150–170). New York: Routledge.

Poole, M. S., & DeSanctis, G. (1992). Microlevel structuration in computer-supported group decision-making. *Human Communication Research, 19*, 5–49.

Porter, A. J., Kuhn, T. R., & Nerlich, B. (2017). Organizing authority in the climate change debate: IPCC controversies and the management of dialectical tensions. *Organization Studies, 39*(7), 873–898.

Putnam, L. L. (1983). Organizational communication: Toward a research agenda. In L. L. Putnam & M. E. Pacanowsky (Eds.), *Communication and organizations: An interpretive approach* (pp. 31–54). Beverly Hills, CA: Sage.

Putnam, L. L. (1985). Bargaining as organizational communication. In R. D. McPhee & P. K. Tompkins (Eds.), *Organizational communication: Traditional themes and new directions* (pp. 129–148). Beverly Hills, CA: Sage.

Putnam, L. L. (2019). Constituting order and disorder: Embracing tensions and contradictions. In C. Vásquez & T. Kuhn (Eds.), *Dis/organization as communication: Studying tensions, ambiguities and disordering* (pp. 17–35). New York: Routledge.

Putnam, L. L. & Cheney, G. (1983). A critical review of research traditions in organizational communication. In M. S. Mander (Eds.). *Communications in transition: Issues and debates in current research* (pp. 206–224). New York: Praeger.

Putnam, L. L., & Cheney, G. (1985). Organizational communication: Historical development and future directions. In T. W. Benson (Ed.), *Speech communication in the 20th Century* (pp. 130–156). Carbondale, IL: Southern University Press.

Putnam, L. L., & Fairhurst, G. T. (2001). Discourse analysis in organizations: Issues and concerns. In F. M. Jablin & L. L. Putnam (Eds.), *The new handbook of organizational communication: Advances in theory, research, and methods* (pp. 78–136). Newbury Park, CA: Sage.

Putnam, L. L., & Fairhurst, G. T. (2015). Revisiting "organizations as discursive constructions": 10 years later. *Communication Theory, 25*(4), 375–392.

Putnam, L. L., Fairhurst, G. T., & Banghart, S. (2016). Contradictions, dialectics, and paradoxes in organizations: A constitutive approach. *The Academy of Management Annals, 10*, 65–171.

Putnam, L. L., & Mumby, D. K. (2014). Introduction: Advancing theory and research in organizational communication. In L. L. Putnam & D. K. Mumby (Eds.), *The SAGE handbook of organizational communication* (3rd edn., pp. 1–18). Los Angeles, CA: Sage.

Putnam, L. L. & Nicotera, A. (Eds.). (2009). *Building theories of organization: The constitutive role of communication*. New York: Routledge.

Putnam, L. L., Nicotera, A. M. & McPhee, R. D. (2009). Introduction: Communication constitutes organization. In L. L. Putnam & A. M. Nicotera (Eds.). *Building theories of organizations: The constitutive role of communication*. New York: Routledge, 1–19.

Putnam, L. L., Phillips, N., and Chapman, P. (1996). Metaphors of communication and organization. In S. R. Clegg, C. Hardy, and W. Nord (Eds.), *Handbook of organizational studies* (pp. 375–408). London: Sage.

Ricoeur, P. (1981). *Hermeneutics and the human sciences* (J. B. Thompson, Ed. and Trans.). Cambridge, UK: Cambridge University Press.

Robichaud, D., & Cooren, F. (Eds.). (2013). *Organization and organizing: Materiality, agency, and discourse*. New York: Routledge.

Sandhu, S. (2017). Organization as communication and institutional theory: Opportunities for communicative convergence? In S. Blaschke & D. Schoeneborn (Eds.), *Organization as communication: Perspectives in dialogue* (pp. 79–102). New York: Routledge.

Scherer, A. G., & Rasche, A. (2017). Organization as communication and Habermasian philosophy. In S. Blaschke & D. Schoeneborn (Eds.), *Organization as communication: Perspectives in dialogue* (pp. 3–25). New York: Routledge.

Schoeneborn, D. (2011). Organization as communication: A Luhmannian perspective. *Management Communication Quarterly, 25*, 663–689.

Schoeneborn, D., Blaschke, S., Cooren, F., McPhee, R. D., Seidl, D., & Taylor, J. R. (2014). The three schools of CCO thinking: Interactive dialogue and systematic comparison. *Management Communication Quarterly, 28*(2), 285–316.

Schoeneborn, D., Kuhn, T. R., & Kärreman, D. (2019). The communicative constitution of organization, organizing, and organizationality. *Organization Studies, 40*(4), 475–496.

Schoeneborn, D., Vásquez, C., & Cornelissen, J. P. (in press). Theorizing the role of metaphors in co-orienting collective action towards grand societal challenges: The example of the Covid-19 pandemic. *Research in the Sociology of Organizations*.

Seidl, D. (2005). Organization and interaction. In D. Seidl & K. H. Becker (Eds.), *Niklas Luhmann and organizational studies* (pp. 145–170). Oslo, Norway: Copenhagen Business School Press.

Seidl, D. (2007). General strategy concepts and the ecology of strategy discourses: A systemic-discursive perspective. *Organization, 28*, 197–218.

Seidl, D., & Becker, K. H. (2006). Organizations as distinction generating and processing systems: Niklas Luhmann's contribution to organization studies. *Organization, 13*, 9–35.

Smith, R. C. (1993, May). *Images of organizational communication: Root-metaphors of the organization-communication relationship*. Paper presented at the annual meeting of the International Communication Association, Washington DC.

Sheep, M.L., Fairhurst, G.T., & Khazanchi, S. (2017). Knots in the discourse of innovation: Investigating multiple tensions in a reacquired spin-off. *Organization Studies, 38*(3–4), 463–488.

Spee, A. P., & Jarzabkowski, P. (2011). Strategic planning as communicative process. *Organization Studies, 32*(9), 1217–1245.

Stohl, C., & Stohl, M. (2011). Secret agencies: The communicative constitution of a clandestine organization. *Organization Studies, 32*(9), 1197–1215.

Taylor, J. R. (1988). *Une organization n'est q'un tissu de communication: Essais théoriques* [The organization is but a web of communication]. Montréal, QC: Université de Montréal.

Taylor, J. R. (1993). *Rethinking the theory of organizational communication: How to read an organization*. Norwood, NJ: Ablex.

Taylor, J. R. (2011). Organization as an (imbricated) configuring of transactions. *Organization Studies, 32*(9), 1273–1294.

Taylor, J. R. (2013). Organizational communication at the crossroads. In D. Robichaud & F. Cooren (Eds.), *Organization and organizing: Materiality, agency, and discourse* (pp. 207–221). New York: Routledge.

Taylor, J. R., & Cooren, F. (1997). What makes communication "organizational"? How the many voices of a collectivity become the one voice of an organization. *Journal of Pragmatics, 27*, 409–438.

Taylor, J. R., & Van Every, E. J. (2000). *The emergent organization: Communication as its site and surface*. Lawrence Erlbaum.

Taylor, J. R., & VanEvery, E. J. (2011). *The situated organization: Case studies in the pragmatics of communication research*. New York: Routledge.

Thatchenkery, T. (1992). Organizations as "texts": Hermeneutics as a model for understanding organizational change. In W. A. Pasmore & R. W. Woodman (Eds.), *Research in organizational development and change* (Vol. 6, pp. 197–233). Greenwich, CT: JAI Press.

Thatchenkery, T. J., & Upadhyaya, P. (1996). Organizations as a play of multiple and dynamic discourses: An example from a global social change organization. In D. M. Boje, R. P. Gephart, & T. J. Thatchenkery (Eds.), *Postmodern management and organization theory* (pp. 308–330). London: Sage.

Tompkins, P. K. (1984). The functions of human communication in organizations. In C. Arnold & J. W. Bowers (Eds.), *Handbook of rhetorical and communication theory* (pp. 659–713). Boston, MA: Allyn & Bacon.

Trujillo, N. (1985). Organizational communication as cultural performance: Some managerial considerations. *Southern Speech Communication Journal, 50,* 201–224.

Vásquez, C., & Cooren, F. (2013). Spacing practices: The communicative configuration of organizing through space-times. *Communication Theory, 23,* 25–47.

Vásquez, C., & Kuhn, T. (Eds.). (2019). *Dis/organization as communication: Studying tensions, ambiguities and disordering.* New York: Routledge.

Weick, K. E. (1979). *The social psychology of organizing.* Reading, MA: Addison-Wesley.

Wilhoit, E. D., & Kisselburgh, L. G. (2015). Collective action without organization: The material constitution of bike commuters as collective. *Organization Studies, 36,* 573–592.

INTRODUCTION

Nicolas Bencherki, Joëlle Basque and Timothy Kuhn

Because CCO is far from being a homogeneous theory or a clearly defined object of interest, editing a handbook on the Communicative Constitution of Organization (CCO) presents quite a challenge. Linda Putnam and Anne Nicotera (2010) suggest that CCO is not a single stance, but a "collection of perspectives" that are united by a single central question: *what is the role of communication in the ontology of an organization?* For Taylor and Van Every (2000), the question that became the quest of CCO research is even broader: it is *What is an organization?* Whichever way the question is posed, though, "the closer one looks at the literature, the less evident the answer to the question becomes" (p. ix). This frustration with traditional theorizing unites CCO scholars, though their own answers to it also diverge greatly.

Such apparent disagreement may have to do with the fact that the two key terms – communication and organization – are very differently understood. "Organization" can be taken as a noun: an organization is a thing out there that we may study. It may, however, also be taken as a verb: organiz*ing* is something that we do together, a process through which we coordinate and control activity to "get organized". Or, it may also be an adjective: "organization*ality*" is a feature that different collectives, from a crowd to a social movement, might exhibit to varying degrees (Schoeneborn et al., 2019).

The way we understand communication also varies greatly. Communication looks rather different across the "schools" that are usually distinguished in CCO scholarship – the Montréal School, the Luhmannian perspective, and the Four Flows – but important distinctions also occur within each of them (Schoeneborn et al., 2014). Communication has been variously understood as an action (for instance, following speech act theory à la Austin, 1962; or American pragmatism, see Lorino, 2018; Misak, 2013), as the synthesis of information, utterance and understanding (according to Luhmann, 1992), a linking (Cooren & Caïdor, 2019), or as a symbolic interaction (McPhee, 1998), to name a few. It may take the empirical form of narratives (Robichaud, 2003), conversations (Cooren, 2007), sensemaking activities (Taylor & Robichaud, 2004), social media posts (Dobusch & Schoeneborn, 2015; Etter & Albu, 2021), internal magazines (Basque & Langley, 2018) or any other kind of "communication episode" (Blaschke et al., 2012).

Such variability in how it understands its own core concepts has led some to question whether CCO actually knows what it is studying (Sillince, 2009). In response, we could say

DOI: 10.4324/9781003224914-1

that CCO is not defined by an object, as is the case for some fields of study. In the same way as William James (1904/1977) said of pragmatism that it is the "attitude" of looking at consequences and effects rather than at categories, in the same way CCO is perhaps better understood as a sensibility: an attention attuned to asking, for each facet of our collective life, how it came to exist in the first place, and how it continues to sustain itself and to change. In that sense, although CCO scholars have been accused of lacking a critical agenda (an issue we'll return to in a moment; see also Del Fa and Kärreman's chapter in this volume), it shares with critical studies the reflex of not taking things for granted, of looking beneath the surface at how beliefs and realities that might appear "normal" are in fact constituted and maintained through what we say and do (Deetz, 1982).

The diversity of issues CCO scholarship has taken on – as is reflected by the chapters in Part 3 of this Handbook – should not, then, be understood as a lack of focus, but rather as a desire to unscrew the idols of management and organization theory. CCO shows that an organization is not made up of discrete features that can be dealt with independently, such as authority (Benoit-Barné & Fox, 2017), collaboration (Koschmann, 2016), diversity (Trittin & Schoeneborn, 2017), identity (Chaput et al., 2011), social responsibility (Christensen et al., 2013) or strategy (Aggerholm et al., 2012; Spee & Jarzabkowski, 2011). Instead, CCO highlights the fluidity between these issues, as they all materialize through communication and implicate each other. For instance, strategizing involves the performance of authority (Bencherki, Sergi, et al., 2019; Vásquez et al., 2018), and collaboration supposes the creation of a collective identity (Koschmann, 2013). Corporate social responsibility, for its part, supposes listening to (and thus the competition among) a diversity of voices (Cooren, 2020; Schoeneborn & Trittin, 2013) and collaborating with outside stakeholders (Christensen et al., 2011). Adopting a CCO sensibility thus avoids dealing with issues in silos – which often follow the hermetic distinction between disciplines and university departments – and encourages a more integrative view of organizational reality.

Such holistic thinking, though, still has some difficulty finding its way in some journals and conferences. Organization and management journal editors and reviewers at times fall short of understanding that communication is a mode of explanation that can illuminate organizational phenomena, rather than an object in itself. In other words, CCO papers are rarely *about* communication: instead, they adopt a communication *perspective* on a variety of questions. Alternatively, organization and management scholars may have difficulty recognizing their own concepts when they are described as communicative performances. This is exactly what CCO is about: shaking up traditional ways of describing things and showing, for instance, that Max Weber did not say all there is to know about authority (Bourgoin et al., 2020), that project management is far more than what the standard "body of knowledge" claims it to be (Sergi et al., 2020), or that strategizing is far more pervasive than it is usually believed to be (Bencherki, Sergi, et al., 2019; Cooren et al., 2015). That being said, more and more CCO papers are published in journals beyond the discipline of communication, and CCO-minded scholars sit on those journals' editorial boards, suggesting a growing embrace of a CCO sensibility.

Towards Intellectual Institutionalization

The idea that communication constitutes organizations is still presented as "new" at academic conferences and in articles, even though it is nearly 35 years old. It can be traced back to 1988, when James R. Taylor published, in French, a collection of essays collectively titled *An Organization is but a Fabric of Communication* (Taylor, 1988, our translation). However, it took nearly another decade for this idea to reach a wider, English-speaking audience, with a

Communication Theory paper by Taylor and then-PhD students François Cooren, Nicole Giroux and Daniel Robichaud, where they suggest looking for organization "between the conversation and the text" (Taylor et al., 1996). The second half of the 1990s saw a multiplication of similarly minded publications, such as Jeffrey Ford and Laurie Ford's famous piece on the way organizational change is produced through conversation (Ford & Ford, 1995). The year 2000, though, is often described as a turning point, with the publication of Taylor and Van Every's (2000) *The Emergent Organization* and Cooren's (2000) *The Organizing Property of Communication*, which both offered a systematic overview of communication's constitutive power, but also of Robert D. McPhee and Pamela Zaug's (2000) article "The communicative constitution of organizations", which was the first to make use of the term that became the perspective's name and a rallying cry for a rich and diverse community.

Whichever birthdate we assign to the CCO perspective, at anywhere between 22 and 35 years of age, it is mature enough today to fully participate in academic deliberations over communicating and organizing, and the pressing social issues that surround the intersection of the two. CCO has witnessed increasing "institutionalization" (Boivin et al., 2017), with volumes and special issues systematically laying out its foundations and materializing it (e.g., Cooren et al., 2011; Robichaud & Cooren, 2013), as well as events bringing together its representatives throughout the world. For instance, Schoeneborn and Vásquez (2017) identify the 2002 preconference organized by Linda Putnam and Ann Nicotera at the National Communication Association convention, and the 2008 preconference of the International Communication Association conference, organized by Cooren, Robichaud and Giroux, in honor of Taylor, as two key structuring events. In addition, the funding that Steffen Blaschke and Dennis Schoeneborn received between 2010 and 2013 from the German National Science Foundation was also instrumental in establishing CCO as a research community (see also Blaschke & Schoeneborn, 2016). In particular, it led to the creation of the "Organization as Communication" network, which later engendered a standing working group of the same name at the European Group for Organization Studies (EGOS) – and its successor, the "Communication, Performativity and Organization" standing working group – and stimulated conversations between Luhmann-inspired researchers and their peers from around the world.

Despite these important milestones, CCO had been lagging in at least one important respect. While even more recent perspectives or phenomena have had handbooks published to inventory their respective state of the art, such an effort had yet to be made for CCO. The important edited book by Putnam and Nicotera (2009) has played a pivotal role for legitimating the subfield, but its chapters mostly consist in elaborations by North American authors regarding McPhee and Zaug's (2000) pioneering article (which is reprinted as the book's second chapter), thus centering its scope around the Four Flows perspective. Since then, the constitutive perspective has diversified in an important manner, a diversity this Handbook attempts to better capture. In addition to its founding geographical poles – Montréal, Québec; Tempe, Arizona; Boulder, Colorado – it now includes researchers from across the globe, although, regretfully, CCO (and social science research more broadly) still has to pay better attention to research conducted, for instance, in Latin America, Africa or some parts of Asia. Authors within this Handbook live and work in the US and in Canada, but also in Austria, Australia, Belgium, Denmark, Finland, Germany, Italy, the Netherlands, New Zealand, Norway, the Philippines and Switzerland. They are in departments and schools of communication, education, management, organization, sociology, or work outside of academia. The typical distinction between "schools" within CCO – The Montréal School, the Luhmannian approach, and the Four Flows – only partly accounts for the diversity of ways in which research is conducted and how it leads to a myriad of theoretical proposals with equally diverse axiological agendas (Schoeneborn et al., 2014; Winkler & Bencherki, 2020). Yet, despite this diversity, this handbook of course only includes a portion of the research being conducted within and around the CCO umbrella today. Our hope, however, is that this Handbook serves to spark conversations and help isolated researchers realize they are, in fact, part of a rich community.

Key Questions Animating CCO Scholarship

What unites this diverse community? To answer this question, we must start by pointing out some of the key differences that adopting the CCO sensitivity makes. To begin, we can distinguish CCO from its older cousin, the interpretive tradition that began much earlier in organizational communication research and with which it is regularly confused (Putnam & Pacanowsky, 1983). Indeed, CCO scholarship is sometimes accused of not bringing anything new to the table, given that interest in the way people talk has been around for a while. A key distinction between interpretive and constitutive research is that the latter locates the organization in individual or social cognition: it is what people *understand* that interests the researcher. These understandings may be shared or even imposed upon others (this is, for instance, how Gioia & Chittipeddi, 1991, understand the notion of sensemaking). In contrast, CCO researchers hold that communication *does* things, with or without the mediation of human interpreters. Stories connect different events together and present the organization as their author, signs continue to warn against danger, tables participate in calculations, conversations weave time and space together, etc. (Cooren & Bencherki, 2010; Cooren & Matte, 2010; Vásquez, 2016).

The matter is made more complex by the fact that some research adopts a constitutive lens, without necessarily drawing from CCO literature or labeling itself as such. This is the case, for instance, of organizational researchers adopting an ethnomethodological approach (e.g., Clark & Pinch, 2010; Kwon et al., 2014; Samra-Fredericks, 2010), of studies that look at how discourse intertextually weaves the organization into new configurations, or which use Boden's (1994) notion of lamination to look at the way talk recursively refers to yet other talk (Grant et al., 2005; Oswick & Richards, 2004). Boje's (1991, 2003) and Gabriel's (1991, 1995) views of narratives have also had a deep influence on CCO. Similarly, the critical stance of Mumby (2000, 2018) and Deetz (1992) feeds CCO's aspirations to this day. We can consider these studies as "CCO-friendly", as they also pay attention to what communication concretely does to constitute organizational reality, beyond the sum of individual interpretations (see Ashcraft et al., 2009).

Besides this commitment to the tangible effects of communication, it is not entirely clear that CCO has a core credo or single method on which all would agree, although different attempts to delineate shared theoretical and methodological commitments have been formulated. François Cooren, Timothy Kuhn, Joep Cornelissen and Tim Clark (2011) suggested that CCO scholarship is based on "six premises:"

1. It studies communicational events;
2. It should be as inclusive as possible about what we mean by (organizational) communication;
3. It acknowledges the co-constructed or co-oriented nature of (organizational) communication;
4. It holds that who or what is acting is always an open question;
5. It never leaves the realm of communicational events;
6. It favors neither organizing nor organization.

Kuhn (2012) offers a more succinct characterization of CCO research, and more broadly of what it means to "take communication seriously", consisting of four "tenets": portraying communication as constitutive of social realities, seeing organizations not as containers for communication, but intrinsically *as* communication, staying in the realm of communicational events both conceptually and methodologically, and, finally, not reducing communication to "meaning convergence". In 2013, during a pre-colloquium development work of the European Group for Organizational Studies conference, Cooren also suggested that CCO has a common "origin" and named a few "precursors", including Chester Barnard (1938/1968), Mary Parker Follett (1940), Gabriel Tarde (1893/2012) and Karl Weick (1979), who each contributed defining some of its defining features (see also Cooren & Robichaud, 2019).

Yet CCO scholars are well aware that creeds, origin stories and other rituals, if they are important in constituting an organization – or a research subfield – are communicatively constituted themselves and are resources for action rather than entrenched paths (see Basque & Langley, 2018, as well as Basque, Hirsto & Wagnac, this volume). Being aware of their role in our community can help us build upon them, but also move ahead without fearing to appear ungrateful to our predecessors.

Moving past such conventional ways of describing and dividing CCO scholarship, though, some common theoretical, methodological and empirical issues are raised from the moment we suppose that organizing takes place through communicating. For instance, Schoeneborn and Vásquez (2017) identify three issues that animate CCO studies: the ontological question (what is an organization?), the composition problem (how can singular events assemble into an organization?), and the question of agency (how does an organization act when people act on its behalf?). Other scholars have also identified the issue of authority as a key concern for CCO research (see in particular Taylor & Van Every, 2014, and the interview with Taylor in this volume). While all of these issues are intimately interconnected, based on the chapters included in this handbook, we can reorganize the themes that have been identified before, and distinguish at least four questions that cut across current CCO investigations.

An Expanded Ontological Question

The question pursued by Taylor and Van Every (2000) over two decades ago – "What is an organization? – has since been stretched to include a broader concern for the way organizing processes and features of organizationality can be detected even beyond conventional organizations. In this sense, CCO – in particular through the contribution of its the Luhmannian branch – has incorporated the work of Arhne and Brunsson (2011) on partial organizations to develop new analytical insights (Dobusch & Schoeneborn, 2015; Schoeneborn et al., 2019). This new intellectual equipment has allowed CCO to answer some of its most stringent critics, including Sillince (2009), who argued that CCO was unable to distinguish between organizations and other forms of collective entities.

Rather than attempting an impossible definition, CCO scholarship has justified its interest in the diversity of ways in which collective endeavors unfold, by pointing out that being an organization is a matter of degree rather than a clear distinction. To be able to produce such an answer, CCO did not only draw from McPhee and Zaug's (2000) four flows– membership negotiation, reflexive self-structuring, activity coordination, and institutional positioning – but also incorporated "membership, hierarchy, rules, monitoring and sanction", as well as decisions, as key features of the constitution of organizations to look for in its empirical investigations (Ahrne & Brunsson, 2011, p. 86).

CCO has also expanded its reach by never hesitating to graft onto its intellectual tree new theories and perspectives, thus freeing itself from its origin story. In addition to regular engagement with management and organization theory, among other such expansion projects, it has dipped its toes in the fields of ethics and law (Brummans et al., 2021; Cooren, 2015, 2016; Denault & Cooren, 2016; Laasch, 2021; Matte & Bencherki, 2019), shown its relevance for public relations (Buhmann & Schoeneborn, 2021), forayed into linguistics (Asmuß, 2012), caught the attention of sociologists (Donges & Nitschke, 2018), and has entered a dialogue with philosophers such as Étienne Souriau, Gilbert Simondon and Gilles Deleuze to highlight the organization's ontological plurality and the continuous nature of its individuation (Bencherki & Elmholdt, 2018; Bencherki & Iliadis, 2019; Mease, 2021) .

By drawing from outside its traditional theorizing, CCO was thus able to explore new organizational forms, such as clandestine and anonymous organizations (Dobusch & Schoeneborn, 2015; Schoeneborn & Scherer, 2012), social media communities (Dawson, 2018; Dawson & Bencherki, in press; Etter & Albu, 2021), art collectives (Cnossen & Bencherki, 2018), entrepreneurial projects (Kuhn, 2017; Kuhn & Marshall, 2019) or even scientific and social controversies (Porter et al., 2018). CCO has shown it is able to answer its ontological question in each of those settings, but these expansions have also helped it clarify some of its other key concepts: agency, authority and the notion of situation.

A Richer View of Agency

A key issue animating CCO research across all of its perspectives is the notion of agency (Brummans, 2018). While authors working in each of its schools might disagree on crucial facets of what agency means – an issue we will return to shortly – it is undeniable that CCO supposes questioning taken-for-granted assumptions about agency. Communication has long been associated with people's ability to act (Bencherki, 2016), but this relationship takes on a particular shade with CCO theorizing. Indeed, it is concerned with how an *organization* might act, which relates to notions of organizational action and actorhood (Bencherki & Cooren, 2011; Grothe-Hammer, 2019). These notions have traditionally been addressed in management and organization theory through an emphasis on decision-making, rule following, and ecological adaptation, with issues of ambiguity and interpretation throwing some confusion in the mix (see March, 1996). Agency is all the more important, since it connects with the very existence and status of the organization: in other words, depending on how we suppose it acts, we also question whether it *exists* – and if so, how – or whether it is "mere" fiction (Savage et al., 2018). Conventional views have often limited the role organizations play in their own action, making organizational theory "a theory without a protagonist" (King et al., 2010, p. 290).

Such pronouncements ignore the contribution CCO scholars had already been making. Indeed, for CCO scholars, the organization is a *metaconversation* (Robichaud et al., 2004). This means that it consists in a mesh of conversations that recursively incorporate prior conversations, and in doing so reify them as texts available for collective scrutiny (Taylor et al., 1996; Taylor & Van Every, 2000). The Luhmannian perspective puts the emphasis on a particular set of texts: decisions, which are iteratively based on prior decisions, at once confirming them and opening up the possibility of alternatives (Schoeneborn, 2011). For the Four Flows perspective, reflexive monitoring is a key aspect of (human) agents' ability to reproduce the structures that, in turn, constrain them, as they account for their own actions and ask for other to explain theirs, thus embedding them into a structure (Iverson et al., 2018).

In a CCO view, organizational action consists, then, in the communicative embedding of prior conversations, decisions and descriptions into other descriptions that position the organization as the author of action. In this sense, through communicative practices, some aspects of the organization – a rule, a way of doing things, a budget, etc. – may be positioned as co-authoring what people (and other beings) do and say, making them "authoritative" texts (Kuhn, 2008, 2012;

Vásquez et al., 2018). Such sharing of agency between people and the organization may take place through nested narratives (Robichaud, 2003) or through attributive practices (Bencherki & Snack, 2016), but also through communication's inherent *ventriloquial* property (Cooren, 2010; Cooren et al., 2013). Ventriloquism refers to the fact that any actor may also be described as a *passer*, as what they do or say can be positioned as a being motivated by someone or something else that speaks or acts through them, thus blurring authorship and allowing one to consider these words and deeds as the organization's (Cooren & Sandler, 2014; Nathues et al., 2020; Wilhoit, 2016).

Authority. CCO's view of agency is intimately related to its treatment of authority (see Benoit-Barné & Fox, as well as Caronia & Nasi, this volume). A key question of authority – who speaks and acts for the organization? – may indeed be rephrased as an issue of shared agency between the organization and its spokesperson. Rather than formal positions and organizational charts, such a construal of authority invites us to look at the many ways in which the organization is *presentified* and made to express its wishes (Benoit-Barné & Cooren, 2009; Benoit-Barné & Fox, 2017). Authority, then, is not the property of some individuals, but rather a feature of each situation that may require people to act in a certain way all the while they are contributing to shaping it (Bourgoin et al., 2020; see also Follett, 1940). This also means that authority is not the prerogative of human beings alone, as contracts, tools, principles and other "non-humans" may also contribute to guiding collective action, a reality captured through both the notion of "textual agency" and that of "authoritative text", illustrating the proximity between agency and authority (Brummans, 2007a; Cooren, 2004a; Cooren & Matte, 2010; Hollis, 2018; Koschmann & Burk, 2016).

Situation. The notions of agency and authority help CCO scholars understand organizations, organizing and organizationality because they help it analyze how *situations* are assembled through what people and things do and say, and in return direct these actions and words. In that sense, the notion of situation is CCO's response to the "composition problem" that Schoeneborn and Vásquez (2017) and Kuhn (2012) identified. Each communication event includes attempts at shaping the ongoing situation. As that situation gradually stabilizes, it also increasingly constrains further communication events. To the extent that people "obey" what the situation requires from them, it gains *authority* over their actions (Benoit-Barné & Cooren, 2009; Bourgoin et al., 2020; Cooren, 2010).

"Composing" the organization from diverse communicative events, thus, is not something done outside of the concrete interactions that take place in each of these events. As people and things communicate, they also attribute those same actions to the situation in which they find themselves, i.e., to an organizational "third", thus presenting it as defining and guiding what they do and say (Bencherki & Cooren, 2011; Bencherki & Snack, 2016; Kuhn, 2012). They may also appropriate communicative events that took place elsewhere and at another time, to *presentify* them into their situation (Cooren, 2004b; Cooren et al., 2008; Vásquez, 2013). As particular ways of defining the situation gain autonomy, for instance through (authoritative) texts, the organization emerges as a constraining actor of its own.

Though it emerged in interactional literature, and in particular in Goffman's (1959) work, Taylor and Van Every (2011) extend the notion of situation to make it key in understanding the organization's role as "thirdness", as that to which people and things both contribute and co-orient as they define their ongoing relationship. They thus recognize the "fundamental role of framing a situation" (p. 14), as it is the situation that defines roles and identities, dictates what can and cannot be done, and how people should behave relative to one another. The organization, thus, is always "situated".

(Dis)organization

A last issue that animates CCO research is that of the relationship between organization and dis-organization, or between order and disorder. Researchers' inclination to look for coherence has led them to attend to organization and order, and to consider disorder as a mere backdrop (Kuhn, 2012). In doing so, they have tended to ignore the messiness that cohabitates with organization. However, adopting a constitutive view of communication stresses the fact that order is "a local, emergent, and transitory phenomenon" (Bauman, 1992, p. 189; cited in Kuhn, 2012, p. 550).

For Four Flows researchers, while some communicative practices can lead to organizing, others may lead to disorder (Bisel, 2009), and other conditions besides communication may also affect whether it can engender order (Bisel, 2010). For their part, the Montréal School and Luhmannian perspective agree that the same communicative event can be at once organizing and disorganizing, as (dis)organization is a property of communication itself, and both order and disorder are present at once in any situation. (Dis)organization results from language's ability to escape its author's control and the possibility of other meanings to "haunt" what is said or written, thus making communication always susceptible to surprise (Vásquez et al., 2016). A similar argument is made by Grothe-Hammer and Schoeneborn (2019) using a Luhmannian lens. They note that communicating a decision always paradoxically also communicates the existence of alternatives to that decision, thus at once reproducing the organization the decision supposes, but also raising the possibility of disorganization (see also Schoeneborn, 2008).

The simultaneous existence of organization and disorganization, finally, may be seen as a matter of perspective. The same situation may promote the existence and interests of some people or things, while hindering those of others: Cooren and Caïdor (2019) give the example of a lumberjack following instructions to cut down trees in a particular area – thus displaying orderliness – causing havoc for animals and ecosystems, or possibly even leading competitors to experience disorganization if they counted on that contract.

Current Conversations in the Community

While CCO scholars broadly share a common sensitivity, adhere broadly to similar principles and are animated by the above issues, different ways of understanding and addressing these issues co-exist within the research community. Without reflecting the rich conversations and debates that take place during conferences and in the pages of journals, we can summarily identify two fundamental areas around which research perspectives branch out. Indeed, CCO scholars do not entirely agree on what counts as a meaningful communicative event, and – as we have hinted above – they theorize agency in diverging ways. While below we caricature the positions of each of the CCO "schools", these conversations do not always neatly follow these demarcation lines.

What Counts as a Meaningful Communication Event?

The first of the "premises" suggested by Cooren, Kuhn, Cornelissen and Clark (2011) is that CCO studies communication events, and already researchers are debating what unit of analysis should be object of study. The various understandings of what a communication event is lead to equally various methodological choices. For Montréal School researchers, the tendency has been to prioritize naturally occurring communication events, which are usually recorded, such as meetings and other formal or casual conversations (Bencherki et al., 2016; Cooren, 2007; Cooren et al., 2008; Robichaud, 2003).

This definition of communication events rests, to some extent, on the Montréal School's roots in ethnomethodology and conversation analysis, which similarly favor naturally occurring events. Yet, it is also justified by the school's view of communication as action, and its extension of agency to non-human actants (as we will see in the next section), which, when combined, require paying attention to what language concretely *does* and how it relates to other situated actions. In that sense, traditional qualitative investigation tools such as interviews, rather than collecting "facts" or individual interpretations, would be viewed as interactional episodes between the interviewer and the interviewee, during which organizational realities are co-constructed (but interviews are also much more; see Alvesson, 2003).

That being said, the Montréal School has also been criticized for over-privileging interactions and, in particular, talk, at the expense of other forms of communication (Wilhoit, 2016). Perhaps as a testament to a generational shift and an extrication from its ethnomethodological roots, a growing number of researchers do not hesitate to explore Montréal School concepts using interviews (Jahn, 2016), visual elicitation (Wilhoit, 2017), archival methods (Basque & Langley, 2018) and other approaches, thus also broadening its definition of what counts as a communication event.

The Luhmannian perspective, which had initially introduced the notion of communication event (Schoeneborn, 2011), shares with the Montréal School its tendency to explore naturally occurring events. While Luhmannian theory would target communication events surrounding *decisions*, which it views as the ones specific to organizing (see Grothe-Hammer, this volume), the fact is that empirical studies have observed a range of communicative phenomena. Research in the Luhmannian perspective has also been inclusive when it comes to the tangible form communication episodes might take and how to study them. That is why, for instance, the Luhmannian perspective comprises quantitative and network analysis of collaboration between people (Blaschke et al., 2012), interviews about how decisions are "programmed" (Grothe-Hammer & Berthod, 2017), as well as the study of documents such as presentation slides (Schoeneborn, 2013). Contrary to the Montréal School's conceptualization of communication as action, for Luhmann communication includes *understanding*, which lies in subsequent communication's uptake of preceding ones, meaning that communication can only be understood as a string of events rather than as isolated moments (as Seidl explains in Schoeneborn et al., 2014; see also Luhmann, 1995).

Finally, the Four Flows perspective is not as explicit as the others on what it identifies as a relevant communication event, which may result from its being based on structuration theory, though "Giddens was notoriously brief in his discussion of communication" (McPhee & Iverson, 2009, p. 52). For Four Flows researchers, not all communication leads to organizational constitution (Bisel, 2009). Indeed, "speech does not in itself, or even mainly, constitute an organization, and can be delusional or involve unusual registers" (McPhee in Schoeneborn et al., 2014, p. 301). The perspective focuses on communication that relates to (a) membership negotiation, (b) activity coordination, (c) reflexive self-structuring and (d) institutional positioning. Each of these flows, in turn, is an assemblage of communicative processes, such as, in the case of membership negotiation, "role learning, power accumulation, identification and disidentification" (McPhee in Schoeneborn et al., 2014, p. 294). In the case of activity coordination, McPhee gives the example of mutual adjustment as an example of underlying communicative process. Reflexive self-structuring would rely on creating membership boundaries, while institutional positioning concerns relations between the organization and others surrounding it.

In that sense, the Four Flows perspective can be described as "meta-theoretical" to the extent that it directs the attention of scholars interested in organizational constitution to relevant communication processes, without these processes being themselves germane to the Four Flows approach. For instance, identification, which McPhee suggests is crucial to membership negotiation, has been studied by Montréal School researchers (Chaput et al., 2011). The same goes for the creation of membership boundaries, which has been shown to be a communicative achievement using both the Montréal School and the Luhmannian perspective (Bencherki & Snack, 2016; Dobusch & Schoeneborn, 2015). Much work has also been devoted to the way organizations present themselves online or to inter-organizational collaboration, thus addressing institutional positioning (e.g., Dawson, 2015; Koschmann, 2013). As for activity coordination, it arguably represents the bulk of CCO research, for instance through work about the coordination of resistance online or about (strategic) planning (Albu, 2019; Bencherki, Sergi, et al., 2019; Etter & Albu, 2021; Grothe-Hammer & Berthod, 2017). Thus, it appears that the Four Flows' segmentation of communication events is the most widely accepted in CCO theorizing, although it is rarely explicitly referred to as such.

An important distinction between the Four Flows approach and the two others, though, is its restriction to communication to human beings, in line with its view of agency, as we will see below. Indeed, for McPhee, communication depends on human beings' interpretive resources, and it is important to recognize – if we seek to explain organizational constitution – "that human agents' interpretive systems include resources that lead an individual to think of himself or herself as able to (fallaciously) speak for, or even to be, an organization" (Schoeneborn et al., 2014, p. 301). This contrasts with the Montréal School's desire to "open up the scene" of communication to other-than-humans (Cooren, 2008), as well as with Luhmann's provocative suggestion that "[h]umans cannot communicate [… o]nly communications can communicate" (2002, p. 169; cited in Seidl & Becker, 2006, p. 20).

Who (or What) "Has" Agency and What Place to Give to Materiality?

As already partly covered earlier (also see Putnam's Foreword, this volume), a key concern for CCO scholars is the question of agency, and each school's different take on the notion is crucial for understanding its theorizing, as well as its conception of relevant communication events and the methods it adopts in studying them. The Four Flows perspective's restriction of communication to humans, due to their interpretive capacity, is paralleled by an equal restriction of agency to humans. This restriction is justified by Giddens's definition of agency as "to be able to 'act otherwise'" (Giddens, 1984, p. 14), which is understood to mean that agents should also possess the "ability to account for and reflect on actions in meaningful ways" (Iverson et al., 2018, p. 44). Indeed, the ability of non-humans to act is mediated by the interpretation humans make of their role, and is conceptualized in terms of resources and constraints on human agency (McPhee & Iverson, 2011). Most importantly, even if it might grant some role to technology and other non-human actors, the Four Flows perspective rejects the "minimization of the difference between human agents (who alone can understand communications) and other elements and systems" (McPhee in Schoeneborn et al., 2014, p. 299).

Although some of its authors have similarly questioned the Montréal School's apparent conflation of human and non-human agency (Jansen, 2016), the Luhmannian perspective has a radically different perspective on agency. To begin with, Luhmannians consider human agency to be at the intersection of different systems: a human being is "made up", for instance, of organic and psychic systems, which constitute it and its ability to act (Seidl & Becker, 2006), a point echoed by some Montréal School theorizing that sits somewhat outside its canon (e.g., Bencherki & Iliadis, 2019; Brummans, 2007b). However, it also agrees with the Montréal School in "de-centering" agency from human beings to the extent that it focuses on communication itself as productive of systems and of further communication events, which "gain agency in their own right" (Schoeneborn et al., 2014, p. 306).

The Four Flows and the Luhmannian perspectives have often formulated their views of agency in reaction to the Montréal School's liberal extension of the notion to non-human entities, which is largely a result of its borrowing from actor-network theory, and in particular from Bruno Latour (Bencherki, 2017; Cooren, 2010; Latour, 2013). This extension of agency is instrumental in the Montréal School's proposal that conversations gain endurance through their inscription in texts, such that what people say and do can move through time and space, "scaling up" to constitute an organization (Cooren & Fairhurst, 2009; Robichaud et al., 2004; Taylor & Van Every, 2000). This key idea has led Montréal School researchers to develop the notion of textual agency (Brummans, 2007a; Cooren, 2004a), and to recognize that an organization is a "plenum of agencies" (Cooren, 2006).

More recently, though, and perhaps under the influence of Luhmannian thinking (see Cooren & Seidl, 2020), Montréal School researchers have begun considering communication itself as material (rather than resting on non-human agents), and to position communication's materiality as participating in a relational ontology view of organizing (Ashcraft et al., 2009; Cooren, 2018; Kuhn et al., 2017). In other words, relationality is substantiated in communication (Cooren et al., 2012). This seemingly slight shift in the way the Montréal School views agency and materiality is consequential, in the sense that it allows viewing communication not only as constitutive of organizations within which human beings live and work, but also as constitutive of humans themselves, with a growing number of researchers interested in notions such as affect and performativity, and connecting the Montréal School with different philosophical approaches (e.g., Ashcraft, 2020; Del Fa, 2017).

Future Trajectories: Ensuring the Practical and Academic Relevance of CCO

These conversations have kept CCO scholarship on its toes, always looking to renew and refine their theorizing of the communication–organization relationship. In exploring new avenues, CCO is opening up exciting future trajectories, but is also faced with potential challenges.

As discussed in Del Fa and Kärreman's chapter in this volume, a first important area of development for CCO concerns its ability to articulate a critical posture. Indeed, CCO has been at times accused of limiting itself to describing organizational phenomena as they take place, without positioning itself regarding what constitutes good and/or ethical organizing (Reed, 2010). This lack of critical engagement is all the more surprising given that CCO, in revealing the communicative underpinnings of organizing, parallels the efforts of many critical authors (e.g., Clegg, 1987; Deetz, 1992). In developing its own critical voice, CCO can build on the efforts of "friendly" research that has pointed out, for instance, how communication enables resistance and submission (Mumby, 2005), how "ideal" professional identities are constituted (Ashcraft, 2016, 2017), how gender and class intersect in "dirty work" (Tracy & Scott, 2006), how particular forms of organizing are rendered invisible (Cruz, 2015, 2017), or how brands gain agency to reproduce capitalism (Mumby, 1998, 2018). It can also count on CCO research that has already touched upon some of the central themes of critical theory, albeit not from a critical stance as such, in particular power and authority (Bencherki, Matte, et al., 2019; Benoit-Barné & Cooren, 2009; Benoit-Barné & Fox, 2017), diversity (Trittin & Schoeneborn, 2017), and ethics (Cooren, 2016; Matte & Bencherki, 2019). Genuine CCO critical research is still in its nascent stage, with studies on the way alternative organizations are constituted (Del Fa, 2017; Del Fa & Vásquez, 2019), calls to decolonize the epistemologies that underpin constitutive approaches (Vásquez et al., 2021), and the proposal that communicative relationality might allow escaping capitalism's position as the overarching and deterministic framework within which organizing unfolds (Kuhn et al., 2017). More efforts are still needed, though, to unpack CCO's critical potential.

A second area of development for CCO is for it to find its full relevance for practitioners, as van Vuuren and Knoers explain in their chapter in this volume. Indeed, while CCO can pride itself on conducting quality empirical work, few research projects truly employ its rich theorizing to reach out to practitioners and respond to their concerns (exceptions include rare action-research work; see Vásquez et al., 2018). While CCO's relevance for practice has been the topic of at least two workshops held prior to the 2014 and 2017 colloquiums of the European Group for Organizational Studies, engaging with practitioners and working with them on making theory actionable for them remains an underexplored area (not unlike CCO pedagogy, incidentally; see Kuhn & Schoeneborn, 2015).

As CCO researchers explore these avenues, however, they also face the challenge of losing their specificity. Indeed, the strength of CCO has been, so far, its ability to pinpoint the communicative processes in practices through which organizing takes place; its descriptivist stance was its distinctive trait. By developing its critical reach or its relevance to practitioners, it will need in both cases – albeit differently – to adopt instead a normative or prescriptive vocabulary, and in doing so risk diluting its distinctiveness. CCO scholars will therefore be careful to make sure to reflect on how they can formulate critique or guidance that builds on their unique analytical ability and remains a distinctive voice in the concert of organizational (communication) studies.

That being said, CCO probably has more to gain than to lose in reaching out to neighboring research communities. As, until recently, CCO scholars have been busy building and legitimating their original approach, they have also somewhat neglected their engagement with broader debates and conversations, leading some to perceive them as somewhat of a clique. In that sense, we have perhaps missed some opportunities to better explain our perspective(s) to other researchers and to demonstrate our relevance to them. Toning down the impression that CCO is an exclusive club would therefore allow us to show what we can do, but also to enrich ourselves, as we help address the challenges that preoccupy organization studies and management, other fields of communication studies, as well as other disciplines.

Outline of the Handbook

Since the beginning of this handbook project, a constant preoccupation for us as co-editors has been to include authors reflecting the diversity of our community, as witnessed during the academic conferences and events that bring us together. In particular, we wanted to reflect diversity in terms of *generations* of CCO scholars. Indeed, given the maturity of our research tradition, we see emerging young scholars representing what is now the fourth generation of CCO scholars, who bring along new concerns and new theoretical vistas, and are unburdened with some older intellectual traditions and cleavages. From early on, CCO scholars have been inspired by their students (as illustrated in Chaput and Basque's interview with James R. Taylor, in this volume) and have never hesitated to collaborate with young researchers from around the world (e.g., Nathues et al., 2020; Taylor & Virgili, 2008). In our desire to capture this vivacity, we chose to give a voice not only to the established scholars who defined the field, but also to mid-career and early-career scholars who are active contributors to our research community, as well as PhD students who enrich CCO thinking.

Roughly speaking, the different sections of this book can be understood as corresponding to the concerns of these different "generations". While early on CCO was preoccupied with establishing theoretical basis – as is the case in our first section, with many first- or second-generation researchers – it has since moved on to seeking to diversify its methods (second section) and to engage with the concerns of its sister fields of study, in particular management and organization studies (third section), and now seeks to find resonance with practitioners in new territories and applications (fourth section). At each step, and in each section, a greater number of younger scholars join their voice to the conversation. In that sense, 7 of the handbook's 33 chapters (21%) include a student or postdoc author, and the number would be greater if we counted recent graduates with either faculty or out-of-academia positions.

Another preoccupation for us, the co-editors, was to make a conscious effort to achieve gender parity among the books' authors. In 2022, gender parity may seem like something one may take for granted, but recent research has shown that gender equality is still a challenge in the academic world (Blithe & Elliott, 2020; Munar et al., 2017). A constant effort is thus needed to make sure women's voices are heard and given the same importance. For these reasons, authors were asked to do their best, in their teams, to accomplish both generational and gender parity. They have responded well to our call: of this handbook's 33 chapters, 26 include at least one woman among their authors (79% of all chapters), 23 include at least 50% of women among their authors (70% of chapters), and 13 are written entirely by women (40% of chapters).

Geographical parity was also a challenge in the co-editors' mind from the initiation of the project. The handbook reflects that CCO remains concentrated in North America, with Americans representing 28% of authors and Canadians 23%, for a total of 51%. Denmark follows at 18%, and all other Europeans combined reach 26%. Non-Europeans – all three of them – only represent 5% of authors. While this lack of geographical diversity could be blamed on a variety of reasons, the fact is that it does represent our community, and points to the need to continue recent efforts to "de-Westernize" CCO thinking and draw inspiration from other parts of the world, as suggested by Vásquez, Guillén & Marroquín (2021), in the case of Latin America.

The first section of the handbook offers an overview of the key theoretical debates that animate our research community. As indicated above, CCO scholarship has developed in conversation with a wide array of thinking in social theory, philosophy, and allied academic disciplines. Although the story of this engagement is often told as revolving around the three schools of CCO thought (as we've done in this Introduction), the vectors of intellectual lineage are more complicated. The field's theoretical influences are the central concern of François Cooren and David Seidl's chapter on the roots of CCO, which explores the multiple sources of inspiration undergirding the three schools of CCO thought, displaying areas of convergence as well as differentiation. Following this is Geneviève Boivin and Boris Brummans's chapter on the value that the notion of ambiguity has played in the development of CCO scholarship by turning the spotlight on the very scholars mentioned in the pages of this Handbook: the social collective of CCO researchers themselves. Far from navel-gazing, this chapter examines discourse at relevant conferences to consider how ambiguity participates in the creation of this vibrant and growing scholarly community. The third chapter in this section, by Veronica Dawson, considers how the conversation-text dialectic has served as a key conceptualization of the communicative event for CCO scholarship, particularly the line of work associated with the Montréal School. Next is Joel Iverson, Karen Myers and Robert McPhee's explication of the Four Flows framework, which employs the compelling example of Trump University to illustrate the communicative flows and their intersections. The ensuing chapter introduces the

Luhmannian school of thought, as Michael Grothe-Hammer cogently presents Luhmann's theorizing and describes how decisions can take center stage as the foundational communicative events in CCO thinking.

After considering the grounding of the field and its main conceptual traditions, the remaining chapters in the first section take up core theoretical concerns that cross the schools of thought. In Elizabeth Wilhoit Larson and Jeanne Mengis's chapter, the authors outline four approaches to the study of materiality in studies of organizing, with particular attention to CCO engagements with this complex notion. Next, Consuelo Vásquez, Timothy Kuhn and Mie Plotnikof pursue the insights to be gleaned from rejecting any opposition between order and disorder and, instead, framing dis/organization as a heuristic vision of the social practice CCO scholars study. A further exploration into the complexity of organizing is offered by Dennis Schoeneborn, Blagoy Blagoev and Leonhard Dobusch's chapter on organizationality. The notion of organizationality was introduced above, but this chapter deepens understandings of this novel concept through two case studies, which also display organizing to be more fluid than conventionally understood. Then, because authority is at issue for all the authors in this section, Letizia Caronia and Nicola Nasi unpack the notion by distinguishing between epistemic and deontic authority, illustrating these types (and their junctures) with a detailed analysis of episodes of interaction associated with antibiotic use in a hospital ward. The next chapter, by Sophie Del Fa and Dan Kärreman, is a provocation, challenging CCO scholarship to more fully embrace a critical orientation, one that entails a thoroughgoing critique of the neoliberal capitalism that serves as the foundation upon which organizing and communicating unfolds. And, finally, Jamie McDonald's chapter continues the critique of CCO's theoretical foundations, providing a model for how scholars might interrogate heteronormative conceptions of organizing by building on queer theorizing to center difference; in so doing, argues McDonald, new vistas for organization studies will emerge. Taken together, then, the 11 chapters in this first section not only display CCO scholarship's central theoretical tenets, but also demonstrate the field's willingness to challenge its fundaments in the pursuit of continuing growth.

In the second section, chapters address the burgeoning methodological diversity and the many ways in which CCO research is conducted. While CCO research regularly expresses its commitment to studying communication episodes, it has only rarely reflexively examined its own methodological choices (Nathues et al., 2020; Wilhoit, 2016). To remedy this, Theresa Castor first offers a thorough review of the many ways in which discourse has been conceptualized, and how CCO has engaged with the variety of discourse analysis. Ellen Nathues and Mark Van Vuuren then offer a hands-on approach to analyzing discourse data in a CCO perspective, and more specifically using François Cooren's ventriloquial perspective (Cooren, 2010; Cooren et al., 2013). In the third chapter in this section, Helly Kryger Aggerholm, Birte Asmuß, Leo Feddersen Smith and Henrik Ladegaard retrace CCO's roots in ethnomethodology and conversation analysis, and present readers with fruitful avenues to conduct EM/CA analysis in search for organizing. Joëlle Basque, Heidi Hirsto and Régine Wagnac then move past a focus on language as such, to invite CCO scholars to engage with organizing's temporality through the use of archival methods. Finally, Boris H.J.M. Brummans and Camille Vézy offer a poignant plea for a more "adventurous" engagement with ethnography, to capture the processuality and eventfulness of communication. Through these many chapters, this handbook's second section thus constitutes a rare opportunity to review the different strategies available to observe communication's constitutive power.

As the third section reveals, CCO theorizing, combined with appropriate methods, sheds a different light on crucial managerial and organizational notions. Chantal Benoit-Barné and Stephanie Fox address one of CCO's key concerns, authority, which finds resonance in Ryan

Bisel, Gail Fairhurst and Matthew Sheep's treatment of leadership among each of the three schools of CCO. Mathieu Chaput and Joëlle Basque, for their part, engage with another crucial theme, identity, by introducing the notion of "identity matters" as CCO's unique contribution to scholarship on the topic. Then, Viviane Sergi and Paul See each bring to our attention key evolutions in the way organizations are managed: Sergi shows how CCO can fruitfully converse with literature on project-based organizing, and Spee offers an overview of literature intersecting CCO and strategic management. The next two chapters hint at CCO's potential for more responsible organizing: Lars T. Christensen, Visa Penttilä and Neva Štumberger review the important work that has been conducted so far in connecting a constitutive view of communication with corporate social responsibility, revealing how talk may produce responsible organizational action; Shiv Ganesh, Cynthia Stohl and Samantha James, for their part, suggest the term "lenticulation" to address the role of visibility in the way we have been studying globalization. Continuing on the project of making organizations better places, Matthew Koschmann then reviews the ways in which a constitutive approach to communication can help understand collaboration between civil society organizations, and Hannah Trittin-Ulbrich and Florence Villesèche show how CCO can contribute to, but also learn from, literature on organizational diversity. Finally, the section's two last chapters engage with areas of research that CCO has overlooked for the moment: the first is that of digital media, which has only recently started to catch the attention of a new generation of scholars, even though, as Jean Saludadez argues, CCO is well equipped to shed a new light on technology; the second is organizational memory, for which Salla-Maaria Laaksonen and François Lambotte offer a rich theorizing that goes beyond simple information storage and retrieval.

Lastly, in the fourth section, chapters reveal how CCO can illuminate concrete, day-to-day practice in a variety of organizational settings. This last section is all the more important given that – as we have already mentioned – CCO scholarship has regularly been accused of falling short on formulating useful advice for managers and for the other people who, every day, make their organizations thrive. First, Mark van Vuuren and Peter Knoers, in a very original and provocative chapter, explain how the CCO view can help practitioners understand the problems they face in their work. Relying on their experience as both academics and consultants and on the many occasions they had to build bridges between theory and practice, they challenge the CCO community to engage more closely with professionals to equip them with CCO's particular lens to overcome naiveté about communication and start questioning the "taken-for-grantedness" of organizations. Next, Boukje Cnossen offers a thorough examination of organizational research in the arts, and reveals how a theorizing of both the art organization and of the impact of the artwork on it is mostly absent from this literature. She explains how a relational view, informed by a CCO perspective, can bring a unique contribution to address this omission, and provide a better comprehension of the role of artistic practices in organizing for researchers and artists alike. Using CCO to study difficult and unusual settings, Oana Albu and Neva Štumberger examine spatial assemblages in refugee camps through the work of humanitarian organizations. They describe the volatility of agencies in these contexts, and explain how a communicative understanding of space can help volunteers consider political and ethical aspects of humanitarian organizing. Also demonstrating the variety of research contexts that inspire CCO authors, Colleen Mills brings us to a very different setting where spatiality is also prominent: a food-processing factory. Through this chapter, she shows the relevance of one feature of CCO – namely the rejection of the language/materiality dualism – for practitioners. In a similar vein, Jody Jahn and Rebecca Rice engage with the high reliability organizing (HRO) literature to identify its shortcomings in theorizing the role of materiality in organizing and sensemaking in these risky contexts. They show how a CCO approach can reveal how material objects orient the construction of the tactical possibilities HRO members see as available to them when they consider various courses of action. Last but not least, Stephanie Fox and Jody Jahn propose a CCO perspective to address a very concrete problem faced by practitioners in multidisciplinary work teams, especially in the healthcare system: how to navigate status asymmetry while deciding on action.

In addition to the agenda each chapter set for itself, this Handbook also aims at a purpose beyond its value as a pedagogical tool to introduce students to CCO: we hope it helps both delineate and galvanize the community of researchers interested in the communicative power of communication. That is why, among other reasons, we include, in lieu of a postface, an interview with James R. Taylor, whom many consider to be the father of CCO. His interview, in addition to telling the tale of CCO's early days, also reveals some of the values central to our community, such as intellectual curiosity, eclecticism, collaboration across generations and individual projects, and, most importantly, kindness to each other. In shaping this publication project the way we did, we recognize that handbooks have often played a *performative* role, in the sense that they have not so much reflected the prior existence of a community around a research topic, but rather rallied scattered research efforts and made individuals aware of their shared trajectory. By considering this performative role, the CCO community can reflexively apply its own theorizing to its efforts to structure itself as a legitimate academic field (Boivin et al., 2017).

Of course, the limited number of chapters in this handbook means that it cannot include, as authors, all the diverse people who make up our community. However, many more people will be present as their work is ventriloquized and as each chapter incorporates multiple voices in an effort to offer a broad overview of the debates taking place around its specific topic (Cooren et al., 2013; Cooren & Sandler, 2014).

References

Aggerholm, H. K., Asmuß, B., & Thomsen, C. (2012). The role of recontextualization in the multivocal, ambiguous process of strategizing. *Journal of Management Inquiry, 21*(4), 413–428. https://doi.org/10.1177/1056492611430852.

Ahrne, G., & Brunsson, N. (2011). Organization outside organizations: The significance of partial organization. *Organization, 18*(1), 83–104. https://doi.org/10.1177/1350508410376256.

Albu, O. B. (2019). Dis/ordering: The use of information and communication technologies by human rights civil society organizations. In C. Vásquez & T. Kuhn (Eds.), *Dis/organization as communication: Exploring the disordering, disruptive and chaotic properties of communication* (pp. 151–171). Routledge.

Alvesson, M. (2003). Beyond neopositivists, romantics, and localists: A reflexive approach to interviews in organizational research. *Academy of Management Review, 28*(1), 13–33. https://doi.org/10.5465/amr.2003.8925191.

Ashcraft, K. L. (2016). Resistance through consent?: Occupational identity, organizational form, and the maintenance of masculinity among commercial airline pilots. *Management Communication Quarterly, 19*(1), 67–90. https://doi.org/10.1177/0893318905276560.

Ashcraft, K. L. (2017). 'Submission' to the rule of excellence: Ordinary affect and precarious resistance in the labor of organization and management studies. *Organization, 24*(1), 36–58. https://doi.org/10.1177/1350508416668188.

Ashcraft, K. L. (2020). Communication as constitutive transmission? An encounter with affect. *Communication Theory,* 1–22. https://doi.org/10.1093/ct/qtz027.

Ashcraft, K. L., Kuhn, T., & Cooren, F. (2009). Constitutional amendments: "Materializing" organizational communication. *The Academy of Management Annals, 3*(1), 1–64. https://doi.org/10.1080/19416520903047186.

Asmuß, B. (2012). Conversation analysis and meetings. In *The Encyclopedia of Applied Linguistics*. Wiley. https://doi.org/10.1002/9781405198431.wbeal0210.

Austin, J. L. (1962). *How to do things with words*. Harvard University Press.

Barnard, C. (1968 [1938]). *The functions of the executive*. Harvard University Press.

Basque, J., & Langley, A. (2018). Invoking Alphonse: The founder figure as a historical resource for organizational identity work. *Organization Studies, 39*(12), 1685–1708. https://doi.org/10.1177/017084061 8789211.

Bauman, Z. (1992). *Intimations of postmodernity*. Routledge.

Bencherki, N. (2016). Action and agency. In K. B. Jensen & R. T. Craig (Eds.), *The international encyclopedia of communication theory and philosophy*. John Wiley & Sons. https://doi.org/10.1002/9781118766 804.wbiect030.

Bencherki, N. (2017). Actor–network theory. In C. R. Scott & L. Lewis (Eds.), *The international encyclopedia of organizational communication*. John Wiley & Sons. https://doi.org/10.1002/9781118955567. wbieoc002.

Bencherki, N., & Cooren, F. (2011). Having to be: The possessive constitution of organization. *Human Relations, 64*(12), 1579–1607. https://doi.org/10.1177/0018726711424227.

Bencherki, N., & Elmholdt, K. T. (2018). *The organization's synaptic mode of existence*. Tallinn, Estonia: European Group for Organizational Studies.

Bencherki, N., & Iliadis, A. (2019). The constitution of organization as informational individuation. *Communication Theory*, 1–21. https://doi.org/10.1093/ct/qtz018.

Bencherki, N., Matte, F., & Cooren, F. (Eds.). (2019). *Authority and power in social interaction*. Routledge.

Bencherki, N., Matte, F., & Pelletier, É. (2016). Rebuilding Babel: A constitutive approach to tongues-in-use. *Journal of Communication, 66*(5), 766–788. https://doi.org/10.1111/jcom.12250.

Bencherki, N., Sergi, V., Cooren, F., & Vásquez, C. (2019). How strategy comes to matter: Strategizing as the communicative materialization of matters of concern. *Strategic Organization*. https://doi.org/ 10.1177/1476127019890380.

Bencherki, N., & Snack, J. P. (2016). Contributorship and partial inclusion: A communicative perspective. *Management Communication Quarterly, 30*(3), 279–304. https://doi.org/10.1177/0893318915624163.

Benoit-Barné, C., & Cooren, F. (2009). The accomplishment of authority through presentification: How authority Is distributed among and negotiated by organizational members. *Management Communication Quarterly, 23*(1), 5–31. https://doi.org/10.1177/0893318909335414.

Benoit-Barné, C., & Fox, S. (2017). Authority. In C. R. Scott & L. Lewis (Eds.), *The international encyclopedia of organizational communication* (pp. 1–13). Wiley. https://doi.org/10.1002/9781118955567. wbieoc011.

Bisel, R. S. (2009). On a growing dualism in organizational discourse research. *Management Communication Quarterly, 22*(4), 614–638. https://doi.org/10.1177/0893318908331100.

Bisel, R. S. (2010). A communicative ontology of organization? A description, history, and critique of CCO theories for organization science. *Management Communication Quarterly, 24*(1), 124–131. https:// doi.org/10.1177/0893318909351582.

Blaschke, S., & Schoeneborn, D. (Eds.). (2016). *Organization as communication: Perspectives in dialogue*. Routledge.

Blaschke, S., Schoeneborn, D., & Seidl, D. (2012). Organizations as networks of communication episodes: Turning the network perspective inside out. *Organization Studies, 33*(7), 879–906. https:// doi.org/10.1177/0170840612443459.

Blithe, S. J., & Elliott, M. (2020). Gender inequality in the academy: Microaggressions, work-life conflict, and academic rank. *Journal of Gender Studies, 29*(7), 751–764. https://doi.org/10.1080/09589 236.2019.1657004.

Boden, D. (1994). *The business of talk: Organizations in action*. Polity Press.

Boivin, G., Brummans, B. H. J. M., & Barker, J. R. (2017). The institutionalization of CCO scholarship: Trends from 2000 to 2015. *Management Communication Quarterly, 31*(3), 331–355. https://doi. org/10.1177/0893318916687396.

Boje, D. M. (1991). The storytelling organization—a study of story performance in an office-supply firm. *Administrative Science Quarterly, 36*(1), 106–126.

Boje, D. M. (2003). Using narrative and telling stories. In D. Holman & R. Thorpe (Eds.), *Management and language: The manager as practical author* (pp. 41–53). Sage.

Bourgoin, A., Bencherki, N., & Faraj, S. (2020). "And who are you?": A performative perspective on authority in organizations. *Academy of Management Journal, 63*(4), 1134–1165. https://doi.org/ 10.5465/amj.2017.1335.

Brummans, B. H. J. M. (2007a). Death by document: Tracing the agency of a text. *Qualitative Inquiry, 13*(5), 711–727.

Brummans, B. H. J. M. (2007b). Travels of a Buddhist Mind. *Qualitative Inquiry, 13*(8), 1221–1226. https://doi.org/10.1177/1077800407308225.

Brummans, B. H. J. M. (Ed.). (2018). *The agency of organizing: Perspectives and case studies.* Routledge. https://doi.org/10.4324/9781315622514.

Brummans, B. H. J. M., Higham, L., & Cooren, F. (2021). The work of conflict mediation: Actors, vectors, and communicative relationality. *Human Relations,* 0018726721994180. https://doi.org/10.1177/0018726721994180.

Buhmann, A., & Schoeneborn, D. (2021). Envisioning PR research without taking organizations as collective actors for granted: A rejoinder and extension to Hou. *Public Relations Inquiry, 10*(1), 119–127. https://doi.org/10.1177/2046147X20987337.

Chaput, M., Brummans, B. H. J. M., & Cooren, F. (2011). The role of organizational identification in the communicative constitution of an organization: A study of consubstantialization in a young political party. *Management Communication Quarterly, 25*(2), 252–282. https://doi.org/10.1177/0893318910386719.

Christensen, L. T., Morsing, M., & Thyssen, O. (2011). The polyphony of coporate social responsibility: Deconstructing accountability and trasparency in the context of identity and hypocrisy. In G. Cheney, S. May, & D. Munish (Eds.), *Handbook of communication ethics* (pp. 457–474). Routledge.

Christensen, L. T., Morsing, M., & Thyssen, O. (2013). CSR as aspirational talk. *Organization, 20*(3), 372–393. https://doi.org/10.1177/1350508413478310.

Clark, C., & Pinch, T. (2010). Some major organisational consequences of some 'minor', organised conduct: Evidence from a video analysis of pre-verbal service encounters in a showroom retail store. In N. Llewellyn & J. Hindmarsh (Eds.), *Organisation, interaction and practice Studies of ethnomethodology and conversation analysis* (pp. 140–171). Cambridge University Press.

Clegg, S. R. (1987). The language of power and the power of language. *Organization Studies, 8*(1), 61–70. https://doi.org/10.1177/017084068700800105.

Cnossen, B., & Bencherki, N. (2018). The role of space in the emergence and endurance of organizing: How independent workers and material assemblages constitute organizations: *Human Relations, 72*(6), 1057–1080. https://doi.org/10.1177/0018726718794265.

Cooren, F. (2000). *The organizing property of communication.* J. Benjamins.

Cooren, F. (2004a). Textual agency: How texts do things in organizational settings. *Organization, 11*(3), 373–393. https://doi.org/10.1177/1350508404041998.

Cooren, F. (2004b). The communicative achievement of collective minding: Analysis of board meeting excerpts. *Management Communication Quarterly, 17*(4), 517–551. https://doi.org/10.1177/0893318903262242.

Cooren, F. (2006). The organizational world as a plenum of agencies. In F. Cooren, J. R. Taylor, & E. J. Van Every (Eds.), *Communication as organizing: Practical approaches to research into the dynamic of text and conversation* (pp. 81–100). Lawrence Erlbaum.

Cooren, F. (Ed.). (2007). *Interacting and organizing: Analyses of a management meeting.* Lawrence Erlbaum Associates.

Cooren, F. (2008). The selection of agency as a rhetorical device: Opening up the scene of dialogue through ventriloquism. In E. Weigand (Ed.), *Dialogue and rhetoric* (pp. 23–37). John Benjamins.

Cooren, F. (2010). *Action and agency in dialogue: Passion, ventriloquism and incarnation.* John Benjamins.

Cooren, F. (2015). In the name of law: Ventriloquism and juridical matters. In K. McGee (Ed.), *Latour and the passage of law* (pp. 235–272). Edinburgh University Press.

Cooren, F. (2016). Ethics for dummies: Ventriloquism and responsibility. *Atlantic Journal of Communication, 24*(1), 17–30. https://doi.org/10.1080/15456870.2016.1113963.

Cooren, F. (2018). Materializing communication: Making the case for a relational ontology. *Journal of Communication, 68*(2), 278–288. https://doi.org/10.1093/joc/jqx014.

Cooren, F. (2020). A communicative constitutive perspective on corporate social responsibility: Ventriloquism, undecidability, and surprisability. *Business & Society, 59*(1), 175–197. https://doi.org/10.1177/0007650318791780.

Cooren, F., & Bencherki, N. (2010). How things do things with words: Ventriloquism, passion and technology. *Encyclopaideia, Journal of Phenomenology and Education, 28,* 35–61.

Cooren, F., Bencherki, N., Chaput, M., & Vásquez, C. (2015). The communicative constitution of strategy-making: Exploring fleeting moments of strategy. In D. Golsorkhi, L. Rouleau, D. Seidl, & E. Vaara (Eds.), *The Cambridge handbook of strategy as practice* (pp. 370–393). Cambridge University Press.

Cooren, F., Brummans, B. H. J. M., & Charrieras, D. (2008). The coproduction of organizational presence: A study of Médecins Sans Frontières in action. *Human Relations*, *61*(10), 1339–1370. https://doi.org/10.1177/0018726708095707.

Cooren, F., & Caïdor, P. (2019). Communication as dis/organization: How to analyze tensions from a relational perspective. In C. Vásquez & T. Kuhn (Eds.), *Dis/organization as communication: Exploring the disordering, disruptive and chaotic properties of communication* (pp. 36–59). Routledge.

Cooren, F., & Fairhurst, G. T. (2009). Dislocation and stabilization: How to scale up from interactions to organization. In L. L. Putnam & A. M. Nicotera (Eds.), *The communicative constitution of organization: Centering organizational communication* (pp. 117–152). Lawrence Erlbaum Associates.

Cooren, F., Fairhurst, G. T., & Huët, R. (2012). Why matter always matters in (organizational) communication. In P. M. Leonardi, B. A. Nardi, & J. Kallinikos (Eds.), *Materiality and organizing: Social interaction in a technological world* (pp. 296–314). Oxford University Press.

Cooren, F., Kuhn, T., Cornelissen, J. P., & Clark, T. (2011). Communication, organizing and organization: An overview and introduction to the special issue. *Organization Studies*, *32*(9), 1149–1170. https://doi.org/10.1177/0170840611410836.

Cooren, F., & Matte, F. (2010). For a constitutive pragmatics: Obama, Médecins Sans Frontières and the measuring stick. *Pragmatics and Society*, *1*(1), 9–31. https://doi.org/10.1075/ps.1.1.02coo.

Cooren, F., Matte, F., Benoit-Barné, C., & Brummans, B. H. J. M. (2013). Communication as ventriloquism: A grounded-in-action approach to the study of organizational tensions. *Communication Monographs*, *80*(3), 255–277. https://doi.org/10.1080/03637751.2013.788255.

Cooren, F., & Robichaud, D. (2019). Les approches constitutives. In S. Grosjean & L. Bonneville (Eds.), *La communication organisationnelle: Approches, processus et enjeux* (pp. 140–175). Chenelière.

Cooren, F., & Sandler, S. (2014). Polyphony, ventriloquism, and constitution: In dialogue with Bakhtin. *Communication Theory*, *24*(3), 225–244. https://doi.org/10.1111/comt.12041.

Cooren, F., & Seidl, D. (2020). Niklas Luhmann's radical communication approach and its implications for research on organizational communication. *Academy of Management Review*, *45*(2), 479–497. https://doi.org/10.5465/amr.2018.0176.

Cruz, J. (2015). Dirty work at the intersections of gender, class, and nation: Liberian market women in post-conflict times. *Women's Studies in Communication*, *38*(4), 421–439. https://doi.org/10.1080/07491409.2015.1087439.

Cruz, J. (2017). Invisibility and visibility in alternative organizing: A communicative and cultural model. *Management Communication Quarterly*, *31*(4), 614–639. https://doi.org/10.1177/089331891 7725202.

Dawson, V. R. (2015). "Who are we online?" Approaches to organizational identity in social media contexts. *The Journal of Social Media in Society*, *4*(2), Article 2. www.thejsms.org/tsmri/index.php/TSMRI/article/view/102.

Dawson, V. R. (2018). Fans, friends, advocates, ambassadors, and haters: Social media communities and the communicative constitution of organizational identity. *Social Media + Society*, *4*(1), 205630511774635. https://doi.org/10.1177/2056305117746356.

Dawson, V. R., & Bencherki, N. (in press). Federal employees or rogue rangers: Sharing and resisting organizational authority through Twitter communication practices. *Human Relations*.

Deetz, S. (1982). Critical interpretive research in organizational communication. *Western Journal of Communication*, *46*(2), 131–149.

Deetz, S. (1992). *Democracy in an age of corporate colonization: Developments in communication and the politics of everyday life*. State University of New York.

Del Fa, S. (2017). The embodiment of the alternative: A communicational and constitutive approach of an "alternative university". *Tamara: Journal for Critical Organization Inquiry*, *15*(3–4), 219–236.

Del Fa, S., & Vásquez, C. (2019). Existing through differantiation: A Derridean approach to alternative organizations. *M@n@gement*, *Vol. 22*(4), 559–583.

Denault, V., & Cooren, F. (2016). La personnalisation des témoins lors de procès: Rhétorique et ventriloquie lors des questions introductives. *International Journal for the Semiotics of Law - Revue Internationale de Sémiotique Juridique*, *2*(30), 321–349. https://doi.org/10.1007/s11196-016-9496-3.

Dobusch, L., & Schoeneborn, D. (2015). Fluidity, identity, and organizationality: The communicative constitution of anonymous. *Journal of Management Studies*, *52*(8), 1005–1035. https://doi.org/10.1111/joms.12139.

Donges, P., & Nitschke, P. (2018). Political organizations and their online communication. *Sociology Compass*, *12*(2), e12554. https://doi.org/10.1111/soc4.12554.

Etter, M., & Albu, O. B. (2021). Activists in the dark: Social media algorithms and collective action in two social movement organizations. *Organization, 28*(1), 68–91. https://doi.org/10.1177/135050842 0961532.

Follett, M. P. (1940). *The Dynamic Administration: The Collected Papers of Mary Parker Follett.* Routledge.

Ford, J. D., & Ford, L. W. (1995). The role of conversations in producing intentional change in organizations. *Academy of Management Review, 20*(3), 541–570. https://doi.org/10.5465/AMR.1995.9508080330.

Gabriel, Y. (1991). Turning facts into stories and stories into facts: A hermeneutic exploration of organizational folklore. *Human Relations, 44*(8), 857–875.

Gabriel, Y. (1995). The Unmanaged organization: Stories, fantasies and subjectivity. *Organization Studies, 16*(3), 477–501. https://doi.org/10.1177/017084069501600305.

Giddens, A. (1984). *The constitution of society: Outline of the theory of structuration.* Polity Press.

Gioia, D. A., & Chittipeddi, K. (1991). Sensemaking and sensegiving in strategic change initiation. *Strategic Management Journal, 12*(6), 433–448. https://doi.org/10.1002/smj.4250120604.

Goffman, Erving. (1959). *The presentation of self in everyday life.* Doubleday.

Grant, D., Michelson, G., Oswick, C., & Wailes, N. (2005). Guest editorial: Discourse and organizational change. *Journal of Organizational Change Management, 18*(1), 6–15. https://doi.org/10.1108/095348 10510579814.

Grothe-Hammer, M. (2019). Organization without actorhood: Exploring a neglected phenomenon. *European Management Journal, 37*(3), 325–338. https://doi.org/10.1016/j.emj.2018.07.009.

Grothe-Hammer, M., & Berthod, O. (2017). The programming of decisions for disaster and emergency response: A Luhmannian approach. *Current Sociology, 65*(5), 735–755. https://doi.org/10.1177/00113 92116640592.

Grothe-Hammer, M., & Schoeneborn, D. (2019). The queen bee outlives her own children: A Luhmannian perspective on project-based organizations (PBOs). In C. Vásquez & T. Kuhn (Eds.), *Dis/organization as communication: Exploring the disordering, disruptive and chaotic properties of communication* (pp. 60–79). Routledge.

Hollis, D. J. D. (2018). *"It's the secret to the Universe": The communicative constitution and routinization of a dominant authoritative text within a UK cosmetics company* [Phd, The Open University]. http://oro.open. ac.uk/56164/.

Iverson, J., McPhee, R. D., & Spaulding, J. A. (2018). Being able to act otherwise: The role of agency in the four flows at 2-1-1 and beyond. In B. H. J. M. Brummans (Ed.), *The agency of organizing: Perspectives and case studies* (pp. 43–65). Routledge. https://doi.org/10.4324/9781315622514.

Jahn, J. L. S. (2016). Adapting safety rules in a high reliability context: How wildland firefighting workgroups ventriloquize safety rules to understand hazards. *Management Communication Quarterly, 30*(3), 362–389. https://doi.org/10.1177/0893318915623638.

James, W. (1977). What pragmatism means. In J. J. McDermott (Ed.), *The writings of William James. A comprehensive edition* (pp. 376–390). Chicago University Press. (Original work published 1904)

Jansen, T. (2016). Who is talking? Some remarks on nonhuman agency in communication. *Communication Theory, 26*(3), 255–272. https://doi.org/10.1111/comt.12095.

King, B. G., Felin, T., & Whetten, D. A. (2010). Perspective—Finding the organization in organizational theory: A meta-theory of the organization as a social actor. *Organization Science, 21*(1), 290–305. https://doi.org/10.1287/orsc.1090.0443.

Koschmann, M. A. (2013). The communicative constitution of collective identity in interorganizational collaboration. *Management Communication Quarterly, 27*(1), 61–89. https://doi.org/10.1177/08933 18912449314.

Koschmann, M. A. (2016). The communicative accomplishment of collaboration failure. *Journal of Communication, 66*(3), 409–432. https://doi.org/10.1111/jcom.12233.

Koschmann, M. A., & Burk, N. R. (2016). Accomplishing authority in collaborative work. *Western Journal of Communication, 80*(4), 393–413. https://doi.org/10.1080/10570314.2016.1159728.

Kuhn, T. (2008). A communicative theory of the firm: Developing an alternative perspective on intra-organizational power and stakeholder relationships. *Organization Studies, 29*(8–9), 1227–1254. https://doi.org/10.1177/0170840608094778.

Kuhn, T. (2012). Negotiating the micro-macro divide: Thought leadership from organizational communication for theorizing organization. *Management Communication Quarterly, 26*(4), 543–584. https://doi.org/10.1177/0893318912462004.

Kuhn, T. (2017). Communicatively constituting organizational unfolding through counter-narrative. In S. Frandsen, T. Kuhn, & M. Lundholt (Eds.), *Counter-narratives and organization* (pp. 17–42). Routledge.

Kuhn, T., Ashcraft, K. L., & Cooren, F. (2017). *The work of communication: Relational perspectives on working and organizing in contemporary capitalism*. Routledge.

Kuhn, T., & Marshall, D. (2019). The communicative constitution of entrepreneurship. In J. J. Reuer, S. F. Matusik, & J. Jones (Eds.), *The Oxford handbook of entrepreneurship and collaboration* (pp. 81–113). Oxford University Press. https://doi.org/10.1093/oxfordhb/9780190633899.013.15.

Kuhn, T., & Schoeneborn, D. (2015). The pedagogy of CCO. *Management Communication Quarterly*, *29*(2), 295–301. https://doi.org/10.1177/0893318915571348.

Kwon, W., Clarke, I., & Wodak, R. (2014). Micro-level discursive strategies for constructing shared views around strategic issues in team meetings. *Journal of Management Studies*, *51*(2), 265–290. https://doi.org/10.1111/joms.12036.

Laasch, O. (2021). *Principles of management: Practicing, ethics, sustainability, responsibility* (2nd edn.). Sage.

Latour, B. (2013). "What's the Story?" Organizing as a mode of existence. In D. Robichaud & F. Cooren (Eds.), *Organization and organizing: Materiality, agency and discourse* (pp. 37–51). Routledge.

Lorino, P. (2018). *Pragmatism and organization studies*. Oxford University Press.

Luhmann, N. (1992). What is communication? *Communication Theory*, *2*(3), 251–259. https://doi.org/10.1111/j.1468-2885.1992.tb00042.x.

Luhmann, N. (1995). *Social systems*. Stanford University Press.

Luhmann, N. (2002). How can the mind participate in communication? In *Theories of distinction: Redescribing the descriptions of modernity* (pp. 169–184). Stanford University Press.

March, J. G. (1996). Continuity and change in theories of organizational action. *Administrative Science Quarterly*, *41*(2), 278–287.

Matte, F., & Bencherki, N. (2019). Materializing ethical matters of concern: Practicing ethics in a refugee camp. *International Journal of Communication*, *13*, 5870–5889.

McPhee, R. D. (1998). Giddens' conception of personal relationhips and its relevance to communication theory. In R. Conville & E. Rogers (Eds.), *The meaning of "relationship" in interpersonal communication* (pp. 83–106). Praeger.

McPhee, R. D., & Iverson, J. (2009). Agents of constitution in Communidad: Constitutive processes of communication in organization. In L. L. Putnam & A. M. Nicotera (Eds.), *Building theories of organization: The constitutive role of communication* (pp. 49–87). Routledge.

McPhee, R. D., & Iverson, J. (2011). Materiality, structuration, and communication. In T. Kuhn (Ed.), *Matters of communication: Political, cultural, and technological challenges to communication theorizing* (pp. 101–122). Hampton Press.

McPhee, R. D., & Zaug, P. (2000). The communicative constitution of organizations: A framework for explanation. *Electronic Journal of Communication*, *10*(1–2).

Mease, J. J. (2021). Techniques and forces and the Communicative Constitution of Organization: A Deleuzian approach to organizational (in) stability and power. *Management Communication Quarterly*, *35*(2), 226–255.

Misak, C. J. (2013). *The American pragmatists*. Oxford University Press.

Mumby, D. K. (1998). Organizing men: Power, discourse, and the social construction of masculinity(s) in the workplace. *Communication Theory*, *8*(2), 164–183.

Mumby, D. K. (2000). Power and politics. In F. M. Jablin & L. L. Putnam (Eds.), *The new handbook of organizational communication: Advances in theory, research, and methods* (pp. 585–623). Sage.

Mumby, D. K. (2005). Theorizing resistance in organization studies: A dialectical approach. *Management Communication Quarterly*, *19*(1), 19–44. https://doi.org/10.1177/0893318905276558.

Mumby, D. K. (2018). Targeting Alex: Brand as agent in communicative capitalism. In B. H. J. M. Brummans (Ed.), *The agency of organizing: Perspectives and case studies* (pp. 98–122). Routledge.

Munar, A. M., Khoo-Lattimore, C., Chambers, D., & Biran, A. (2017). The academia we have and the one we want: On the centrality of gender equality. *Anatolia*, *28*(4), 582–591. https://doi.org/10.1080/13032917.2017.1370786.

Nathues, E., van Vuuren, M., & Cooren, F. (2020). Speaking about vision, talking in the name of so much more: A methodological framework for ventriloquial analyses in organization studies: Organization Studies. https://doi.org/10.1177/0170840620934063.

Oswick, C., & Richards, D. (2004). Talk in organizations: Local conversations, wider perspectives. *Culture and Organization*, *10*(2), 107–123. https://doi.org/10.1080/14759550420002533404.

Porter, A. J., Kuhn, T. R., & Nerlich, B. (2018). Organizing authority in the climate change debate: IPCC controversies and the management of dialectical tensions. *Organization Studies*, *39*(7), 873–898. https://doi.org/10.1177/0170840617707999.

Putnam, L. L., & Nicotera, A. M. (2009). *Building theories of organization: The constitutive role of communication*. Lawrence Erlbaum.

Putnam, L. L., & Nicotera, A. M. (2010). Communicative constitution of organization is a question: Critical issues for addressing it. *Management Communication Quarterly, 24*(1), 158–165. https://doi.org/10.1177/0893318909351581.

Putnam, L. L., & Pacanowsky, M. E. (1983). *Communication and organizations, an interpretive approach*. Sage.

Reed, M. (2010). Is communication constitutive of organization? *Management Communication Quarterly, 24*(1), 151–157. https://doi.org/10.1177/0893318909351583.

Robichaud, D. (2003). Narrative institutions we organize by: The case of a municipal administration. In B. Czarniawska & P. Gagliardi (Eds.), *Narratives we organize by: Advances in organization studies* (pp. 37–54). John Benjamins.

Robichaud, D., & Cooren, F. (Eds.). (2013). *Organization and organizing: Materiality, agency and discourse*. Routledge.

Robichaud, D., Giroux, H., & Taylor, J. R. (2004). The metaconversation: The recursive property of language as a key to organizing. *Academy of Management Review, 29*(4), 617–634. https://doi.org/10.5465/amr.2004.14497614.

Samra-Fredericks, D. (2010). The interactional accomplishment of a strategic plan. In N. Llewellyn & J. Hindmarsh (Eds.), *Organisation, interaction and practice: Studies of ethnomethodology and conversation analysis* (pp. 198–217). Cambride University Press.

Savage, P., Cornelissen, J. P., & Franck, H. (2018). Fiction and organization studies. *Organization Studies, 39*(7), 975–994. https://doi.org/10.1177/0170840617709309.

Schoeneborn, D. (2008). *Alternatives considered but not disclosed: The ambiguous role of PowerPoint in cross-project learning*. Deutscher Universitätsverlag. https://doi.org/10.1007/978-3-8350-5528-5.

Schoeneborn, D. (2011). Organization as communication: A Luhmannian perspective. *Management Communication Quarterly, 25*(4), 663–689. https://doi.org/10.1177/0893318911405622.

Schoeneborn, D. (2013). The pervasive power of PowerPoint: How a genre of professional communication permeates organizational communication. *Organization Studies, 34*(12), 1777–1801. https://doi.org/10.1177/0170840613485843.

Schoeneborn, D., Blaschke, S., Cooren, F., McPhee, R. D., Seidl, D., & Taylor, J. R. (2014). The three schools of CCO thinking: Interactive dialogue and systematic comparison. *Management Communication Quarterly, 28*(2), 285–316. https://doi.org/10.1177/0893318914527000.

Schoeneborn, D., Kuhn, T. R., & Kärreman, D. (2019). The communicative constitution of organization, organizing, and organizationality. *Organization Studies, 40*(4), 475–496. https://doi.org/10.1177/0170840618782284.

Schoeneborn, D., & Scherer, A. G. (2012). Clandestine organizations, al Qaeda, and the paradox of (in)visibility: A response to Stohl and Stohl. *Organization Studies, 33*(7), 963–971. https://doi.org/10.1177/0170840612448031.

Schoeneborn, D., & Trittin, H. (2013). Transcending transmission: Towards a constitutive perspective on CSR communication. *Corporate Communications: An International Journal, 18*(2), 193–211. https://doi.org/10.1108/13563281311319481.

Schoeneborn, D., & Vásquez, C. (2017). Communicative constitution of organizations. In C. R. Scott, J. R. Barker, T. Kuhn, J. Keyton, P. K. Turner, & L. K. Lewis (Eds.), *The international encyclopedia of organizational communication* (pp. 1–21). Wiley. https://doi.org/10.1002/9781118955567.wbieoc030.

Seidl, D., & Becker, K. H. (2006). Organizations as distinction generating and processing systems: Niklas Luhmann's contribution to organization studies. *Organization, 13*(1), 9–35. https://doi.org/10.1177/1350508406059635.

Sergi, V., Crevani, L., & Aubry, M. (2020). Process studies of project organizing. *Project Management Journal, 51*(1), 3–10. https://doi.org/10.1177/8756972819896482.

Sillince, J. A. A. (2009). Can CCO theory tell us how organizing is distinct from markets, networking, belonging to a community, or supporting a social movement? *Management Communication Quarterly, 24*(1), 132–138. https://doi.org/10.1177/0893318909352022.

Spee, A. P., & Jarzabkowski, P. (2011). Strategic planning as communicative process. *Organization Studies, 32*(9), 1217–1245. https://doi.org/10.1177/0170840611411387.

Tarde, G. (2012). *Monadology and Sociology* (T. Lorenc, Trans.). re.press. http://re-press.org/book-files/9780980819724-Monadology_and_Sociology.pdf. (Original work published 1893)

Taylor, J. R. (1988). *Une organisation n'est qu'un tissu de communication: Essais théoriques*. Université de Montréal.

Taylor, J. R., Cooren, F., Giroux, N., & Robichaud, D. (1996). The communicational basis of organ-ization: Between the conversation and the text. *Communication Theory, 6*(1), 1–39. https://doi.org/10.1111/j.1468-2885.1996.tb00118.x.

Taylor, J. R., & Robichaud, D. (2004). Finding the organization in the communication: Discourse as action and sensemaking. *Organization, 11*(3), 395–413. https://doi.org/10.1177/1350508404041999.

Taylor, J. R., & Van Every, E. J. (2000). *The emergent organization: Communication as its site and surface.* Lawrence Erlbaum Associates.

Taylor, J. R., & Van Every, E. J. (2011). *The situated organization: Studies in the pragmatics of communication research.* Routledge.

Taylor, J. R., & Van Every, E. J. (2014). *When organization fails: Why authority matters.* Routledge.

Taylor, J. R., & Virgili, S. (2008). Why ERPs disappoint: The importance of getting the organisational text right. In B. Grabot, A. Mayère, & I. Bazet (Eds.), *ERP systems and organisational change* (pp. 59–84). Springer. https://doi.org/10.1007/978-1-84800-183-1_5.

Tracy, S. J., & Scott, C. (2006). Sexuality, masculinity, and taint management among firefighters and cor-rectional officers: Getting down and dirty with "America's heroes" and the "scum of law enforcement". *Management Communication Quarterly, 20*(1), 6–38. https://doi.org/10.1177/0893318906287898.

Trittin, H., & Schoeneborn, D. (2017). Diversity as polyphony: Reconceptualizing diversity management from a communication-centered perspective. *Journal of Business Ethics, 144*(2), 305–322. https://doi.org/10.1007/s10551-015-2825-8.

vásquez, c. (2013). spacing organization: or how to be here and there at the same time. In D. Robichaud & F. Cooren (Eds.), *Organization and organizing: Materiality, agency and discourse* (pp. 127–149). Routledge.

Vásquez, C. (2016). A spatial grammar of organising: Studying the communicative constitution of organ-isational spaces. *Communication Research and Practice, 2*(3), 351–377. https://doi.org/10.1080/22041451.2016.1221686.

Vásquez, C., Bencherki, N., Cooren, F., & Sergi, V. (2018). From 'matters of concern' to 'matters of authority': Reflecting on the performativity of strategy in writing a strategic plan. *Long-Range Planning, 51*(3), 417–435. https://doi.org/10.1016/j.lrp.2017.01.001.

Vásquez, C., Marroquín Velásquez, L., & Guillén Ojeda, G. (2021). Décoloniser les perspectives CCO: écouter les voix des traditions critiques latino-américaines en communication. *Communication & Organisation, 59.*

Vásquez, C., Schoeneborn, D., & Sergi, V. (2016). Summoning the spirits: Organizational texts and the (dis)ordering properties of communication. *Human Relations, 69*(3), 629–659. https://doi.org/10.1177/0018726715589422.

Weick, K. E. (1979). *The social psychology of organizing* (2d edn.). Addison-Wesley.

Wilhoit, E. D. (2016). Ventriloquism's methodological scope. *Language Under Discussion, 2*(1), 45–49.

Wilhoit, E. D. (2017). Photo and video methods in organizational and managerial communication research. *Management Communication Quarterly, 31*(3), 447–466. https://doi.org/10.1177/0893318917704511.

Winkler, P., & Bencherki, N. (2020, July 2). *Axiological tensions of CCO: What is the value of giving a voice?* 67th colloquium of the European Group of Organizational Studies, Hamburg.

PART I

Theoretical Discussions

1

THE THEORETICAL ROOTS OF CCO

François Cooren and David Seidl

In this chapter, we will present the various theories that have influenced or even defined the three schools of CCO thinking for the past 30 years (Boivin, Brummans and Barker, 2017; Brummans, Cooren, Robichaud and Taylor, 2014; Schoeneborn, Blaschke, Cooren, McPhee, Seidl and Taylor, 2014). Regarding the four-flows model, proposed by Robert McPhee and Pamela Zaug (2000), we will describe the key role Anthony Giddens's (1979, 1984) Structuration Theory has played since its inception. Regarding the roots of the system of self-referential communication systems proposed by Niklas Luhmann (1992, 1995, 2018), we will highlight the role of Edmund Husserl's (1979; 1982) phenomenology, Maturana and Varela's (1980; 1992) theory of self-referential systems and George Spencer-Brown's (1969) observation theory. Finally, the theoretical roots of the Montreal school, initiated by James R. Taylor's (1993; Taylor, Cooren, Giroux and Robichaud, 1996; Taylor and Van Every, 2000, 2011, 2014) text/conversation model, will be introduced through the presentation of some key authors' works, namely pragmatists such as John Dewey (1916) and Charles Sanders Peirce (1991), but also John Langshaw Austin (1962), Harold Garfinkel (1967, 2002), Algirdas Julien Greimas (1987), and Bruno Latour (1986, 2005, 2013a). Beyond their differences, we will also insist on what unifies the theoretical foundations of these three respective schools of thought.

Anthony Giddens's Structuration Theory as Theoretical Root of the Four-Flows Model

Although the CCO perspective can arguably be traced back to James R. Taylor's (1988) book, titled "Une organisation n'est qu'un tissu de communications: Essais théoriques" (*An Organization is but a Web of Communications: Theoretical Essays*), we historically owe the label "Communicative Constitution of Organization" to Robert D. McPhee and his then PhD student, Pamela Zaug, who coined this phrase in their landmark essay, "The communicative constitution of organizations: A framework for explanation", published in 2000 in the *Electronic Journal of Communication*. This article, which was later republished in a volume edited by Linda Putnam and Anne Nicotera (2009), proposes that the constitution of any complex organization requires four types of message flows or interaction processes, which they identify as membership negotiation, self-structuring, activity coordination, and institutional positioning.

DOI: 10.4324/9781003224914-3

Although McPhee and Zaug (2009) identify several theoretical foundations for their four-flows model (namely, Karl Weick's (1979) sensemaking model of organizing, Ruth Smith's (1993) root metaphors of organizational communication, Deirdre Boden's (1994) conversational approach to organizations, James R. Taylor's (1993) text-conversation model, as well as Stan Deetz and Dennis Mumby's (1990) critical perspective on organizational constitution), they explicitly borrow the idea of constitution from Anthony Giddens's (1984) landmark book, *The Constitution of Society*. As they point out, Giddens never explicitly defines what he means by "constitution", but McPhee and Zaug explicitly associate this idea with his key notion of *duality of structure*.

Agent and Agency

To understand the notion of duality of structure, we first need to present the way Giddens (1984) conceptualizes the notions of *agent* and *agency*. To define what characterizes agents, Giddens highlights, following Garfinkel (1967) and Schutz (1973), people's capacity to reflexively monitor activities, not only their own, but also others'. This monitoring is associated with their *practical consciousness*, which can be distinguished from what he calls their *discursive consciousness*, that is, their capacity to verbally *account for* their own actions, others' actions and, more generally, the context in which they evolve. Agents, for the British sociologist, are therefore *competent actors*, not only because of the knowledge they practically mobilize to act in their daily life, but also because of their capacity to rationalize what they do and what others do.

Regarding the question of agency, Giddens (1984) defines it as people's *capacity of doing things*, noting that it is especially characterized by the possibility that they could "have acted differently" (p. 9). Although many philosophers tend to associate agency with intentionality (e.g. Davidson, 1980), Giddens takes care to point out that "agency refers not to the intentions people have in doing things but to their capability of doing those things in the first place" (p. 9). This allows him to insist on the key role *unintended consequences of intentional conduct* play in sociological phenomena, but also to make an important connection between power and agency. As he points out, "action depends upon the capability of the individual to 'make a difference' to a pre-existing state of affairs or course of events. An agent ceases to be such if he or she loses the capability to 'make a difference', that is, to exercise some sort of power" (p. 14).

This conception of agency thus calls into question any sociological theory, which Giddens (1984) associates with what he calls "objectivist social science" (p. 16), that would reduce human agents to docile bodies acting like automata. On the contrary, he insists on agents' capacity to resist forms of domination and norms of action, a resistance that he associates with what he calls "the dialectic of control in social systems" (p. 16). Giddens then points out that in order to act, agents draw upon rules and resources – which he captures with the umbrella term "structure" – that are presented as "the means of system reproduction" (p. 19). Rules and resources, which Garfinkel (1967) would associate with ethnomethods, tend to be *tacitly* known by agents, which is why the latter can be identified as competent actors. When these rules and resources are called into question (like in Garfinkel's famous breach experiments), the agents' *ontological security* appears threatened, that is, the sense of orderliness and continuousness that they usually rely on with regard to their experiences and activities seems to be called into question (Giddens, 1991).

The Duality of Structure

Structure is preserved, according to Giddens, as memory traces and is considered "out of time and space" (p. 25) and "marked by an 'absence of the subject'" (p. 25). People thus draw upon these memory traces to conduct themselves in their daily life, as structures (under the form of signification, domination, and legitimation) both constrain and enable their social actions. In contrast, *social systems* (organizations, for instance) are considered reproduced social practices. They reproduce themselves across time and space through human agents' situated activities, activities that recursively draw upon the rules and resources that define structure. There is therefore *structuration* to the extent that these social systems are (re-)produced through the multiple interactions by which human agents knowledgeably mobilize these rules and resources. To account for this phenomenon, Giddens speaks about the *duality of structure*, according to which structures are both the medium and outcome of human action. He contrasts this notion of duality with that of a dualism. In his definition, a dualism would imply the existence of agents and structures as completely independent, while a duality entails that structures, through the form of the rules and resources, are *internal* to agents and their actions. They indeed exist as memory traces and are constantly mobilized in social practices by constraining and enabling them.

McPhee and Zaug (2009) draw upon this notion of duality of structure to put forward their four-flows model. As they point out, they use Giddens's sense of "constitution" according to which "a pattern or array of types of interaction constitute organizations insofar as they make organizations what they are, and insofar as basic features of the organization are implicated in the system of interaction" (p. 27). Communication thus has constitutive force, but they specify that not all communication can be called organizational as that this constitutive force can only express itself if "a complex relation among organizational communication processes" (p. 29) exists. Echoing Mintzberg (1979) and Lash and Urry (1994), they propose to call these processes "flows" to emphasize that communication is about "circulating systems or fields of messages" (29).

According to their model, any organization is constituted through four flows of communication that make it what it is: (1) agents negotiate their membership of an organization through recruitment, socialization, and the (re-)definition of what it means to be a member of this organization (Membership Negotiation); (2) some members are in charge of structuring activities through various media such as procedures, protocols, organizational charts, directives, which all materialize the formal structure of the organization by dividing labor and allocating resources (Organizational Self-structuring); (3) within this division of labor, members still have, however, to coordinate their activities in order to get things done by adapting to specific situations (Activity Coordination); and (4) some members are in charge of communicating on behalf of the organization to deal with other entities such as suppliers, consumers, competitors, governmental bodies, a form of communication that position the organization vis-à-vis its environment (Institutional Positioning).

The Theoretical Roots of Niklas Luhmann's Theory of Self-Referential Communication Systems

In developing his particular communication approach to the social world in general and to organizations in particular, Luhmann drew inspiration from a wide range of different disciplines, including sociology, philosophy, linguistics, law, cybernetics, biology and even mathematics. Amongst these many influences, however, there are arguably three bodies of theory that had a particularly important impact on Luhmann's approach, which we will focus on in the following: Husserl's phenomenology, the theory of self-referential systems and Spencer-Brown's observation theory.

Husserl's phenomenology

Edmund Husserl's phenomenological work had a profound influence on Luhmann's communication approach – according to Nassehi (2012) even more profound than any of the other influences – although Husserl himself was more concerned with human consciousness than communication. As founding father of phenomenology, Husserl was interested in the phenomena in our mind and, thus, how we subjectively experience the world around us. He thereby distinguished clearly between the way that things appear in our mind (i.e. the phenomena) and how things might be in themselves. That is, the *perceived* star, the *perceived* cow or the *perceived* weather in contrast to the star, the cow or the weather as such. Thus, he was concerned with the realm of meaning: how meaning is constituted and processed. In trying to identify the structures and processes of meaning construction, he stressed, we need to focus on the internal workings of the mind and should bracket out any transcendental questions about the natural world as such (phenomenological reduction).

For Husserl (1982), a central element of conscious experience was intentionality; that is, consciousness is always actively directed at something. As Luhmann (2013, p. 57) explained: "the operations of consciousness can take place only if they are concerned with phenomena – that is, if they *intend* a phenomenon, no matter what the environment may be." A thought is always a thought about something; a thought about a new employee, a thought about a building or even a thought about thoughts. By highlighting the intentionality of experience, Husserl makes clear that consciousness is not passively shaped by external influences but that experiences are active operations of consciousness. As Baecker in the foreword to Luhmann's *Social Systems* explains: "For Husserl, the external world of material objects presents itself to consciousness in the form of a spatio-temporal field of unactualized perceptions that surround it like a 'halo of background intuitions' (Husserl 1982: 35). The flux of actual experience is constituted in a series of 'intentional acts' that seize upon particular objects within this field" (Luhmann 1990, p. XXVI). Thus, the content of the consciousness is actively created by the acts of consciousness that seize upon something around it; in other words, the consciousness only experiences what it makes itself attend to.

While each experience is differentiated from others by the particular object it intends, it only comes about as part of a stream of experiences. Thereby, each experience is embedded into a particular "horizon of experiences" (Husserl, 1973, p. 42), which provide a background to the focal experience. This horizon of experience is made up, on the one hand, of earlier experiences, which provide the backdrop from which the focal experience is made sense of. In other words, the backdrop of earlier experience contributes to the particular focal experience. On the other hand, the horizon of experience also contains potential future experiences. That is, the focal experience is always defined in reference to other potential experiences in the future. For example, when we perceive a hammer we relate this perception to earlier experiences with hammers and we might also relate it to potential future experiences of using this hammer for particular tasks at hand. Apart from references to potential experiences of the same object, the horizon of experiences also contains potential experiences of other objects. For example, the experience of a hammer might be followed by experiences of nails, paintings or walls. Taken together, a focal experience is not an isolated event but is an event that is embedded into a horizon of other potential experiences that define the focal event. One could also say, the horizon of potential experiences is a constitutive part of the focal experience.

This reference of a given focal experience to other potential future experiences adds a dynamic element to the operations of the consciousness. Whenever we have a focal experience the horizon of potential experiences suggests other experiences that could follow. Thus, the mind is constantly stimulated to move from one experience to another. And as the horizon of potential experiences is re-created with each new experience, we can never exhaust and thus never transgress this horizon. Thus the stream of experience is moved on indefinitely.

Having studied his work intensely during his early career, Luhmann recognized that a lot of what Husserl had written about the workings of the human consciousness could be applied, with some slight adaptations, to the realm of communication as well. Like the operations of our mind, communication can be understood as the processing of meaning. Every communicative event is *about* a particular phenomenon. We always communicate *about* something; about the customer, about the product, about the market or about the communication itself. The focal communicative event thereby can be understood as an *active selection*. From the horizon of *possible* communication contents, it selects a particular content that it *actually* communicates about. As a selection, a focal communicative event is as much defined by the un-actualized possibilities of communication as by the actualized ones. The meaning of a focal communicative event is defined in relation to the horizon of what could have been communicated instead.

In the same way as all our intentions take place within the horizon of our consciousness, communication can be said to take place within the horizon of potential communications. Every communicative event takes place within the horizon of potential communications, which is reproduced with every new communicative event and which co-determines its meaning. For example, when we communicate about the hiring of a new employee, the meaning of this communicative event is determined in part by the reference to earlier communications about replacing some employees or extending the workforce and the prospect of future communications about related hires or about onboarding the employee. Like the operations of consciousness, communications, thereby, can only stay within this horizon of potential communications, which is re-created with every new communicative event and which the communications themselves can never transgress.

Analogously to the realm of consciousness, the reference of a focal communicative event to potential future communicative events adds a dynamic element to communication. Each actualization of a potential communicative event stimulates the actualization of a follow-on communicative event that stimulates further actualizations to follow. The asking of a question calls forth the communication of an answer; the communication of an opinion calls forth the communication of an agreement or disagreement; the communication of a decision calls forth the communication about the implementation of the decision. In this way, a stream of communicative events is created that will continue indefinitely.

Husserl's phenomenological studies also highlighted the central importance of the temporality of meaning, which becomes an important part of Luhmann's communication theory. As Husserl stressed, experiences can only take place in the present moment, which he illustrates with the example of listening to a melody. At each present moment in time, our consciousness perceives only the individual tone; "the first tone sounds, then comes the second tone, then the third, and so on [...] when the second tone sounds, I hear *it*, but I no longer hear the first tone, etc. In truth, then, I do not hear the melody but only the single present tone. That the elapsed part of the melody is something objective to me, I owe [...] to memory; and that I do not presuppose, with the appearance of the currently intended tone, that this is *all*, I owe to anticipatory expectation". (Husserl, 2012, p. 25). Analogously to the experience of musical tones, communicative events happen in the present moment; they are "events that disappear as soon as they come into being" (Luhmann 2018, p. 205). Each communicative event follows the other. While the different communicative events are only meaningful in relation to each other, they do not co-exist. The answer to a communicated question comes after the communication of the question, which has already disappeared when the answer is given. Yet, like listening to a melody, the focal present communicative event carries along the preceding communicative events in the form of a reference to those communicative events and it also anticipates some future communicative events in the form of references to future potential communicative events. Or to put it differently, the past only "exists" to the extent that it is referred to in the focal present communication and, similarly, the future only exists in the form of anticipatory references in the present focal communicative event (Langenmayr, 2016). As Luhmann (2018, p. 207) writes, "the memory accompanies every operation [i.e. communication], regulating what is to be recalled and what can be forgotten."

Theory of Self-Referential Systems

Next to Husserl's phenomenology, another important inspiration for Luhmann's communication approach to organizations was the development of self-referential systems theory, based on the one hand on the concept of autopoiesis by the Chilean cognition biologists Humberto Maturana and Francisco Varela and on the other hand on second-order cybernetics by the Austrian American thinker Heinz von Foerster. While Luhmann's interest in systems thinking goes back to his study of Parsons's works, it is this new development in systems theory from the 1970s and 1980s that became central to his communication approach. In contrast to the traditional open systems paradigm that also characterized Parsons's theory (1968), the new paradigm highlighted the recursivity of the system's operations. As Varela (1984, p. 25) explained, in the open systems paradigm a system was characterized "by the specific ways in which it interacts with its environment, through a well-defined set of inputs followed by a transfer function." In the self-referential systems paradigm, in contrast, a system is characterized by the particular ways in which the system's operations interact with themselves; that is, how the operations of the system shape what other operations of the system come about. One could also say, with the transition from one systems paradigm to the other there is a shift in emphasis on the different forces operating on the system. While open systems theorizing highlights the environmental forces on the system, bracketing the internal forces within the system, self-referential systems thinking highlights the internal forces within the system, bracketing the forces from outside (Seidl & Schoeneborn, 2016). Thereby, external forces are conceptualized as unspecific "noise" or "perturbations," whose recognition, interpretation and processing are determined entirely by the internal forces; thus, environmental forces become secondary to the internal forces.

This shift in emphasis between different forces operating on a system had important implications for the understanding of a system. As Von Foerster (2002) pointed out, with the recognition of the self-referential forces operating in the system, systems are no longer treated as "trivial machines," that is, as machines whose behaviour is predictable and can be described by an input–output function. Instead, systems become "non-trivial machines," whose operations depend on the particular state they are in, rendering their behaviour history-dependent and unpredictable.

Maturana and Varela coined the term "autopoiesis" (from Greek "auto" meaning self and "poiesis" meaning production) to describe the self-referential mode of operation of a system. Focussing particularly on biological systems, they described how such systems produce their own components through their own components. As Varela (1979, p. 13) defined: "An autopoietic system is organised (defined as a unity) as a network of processes of production (transformation and destruction) of components that produces the components that: 1. through their interactions and transformations continuously regenerate and realize the network of processes (relations) that produces them; and 2. constitute it (the machine) as a concrete unity in the space in which they exist by specifying the topological domain of its realization as such a network." Taking the example of a plant, they explained that the cells that make up a plant are produced by the very cells of the plant. Cells cannot be imported from outside but only be produced internally. In this sense, autopoietic systems can be said to be *operatively closed*. This operative closure, however, does not mean that the system is closed off from the environment – as was the case in the initial closed systems paradigm. As Luhmann clarified, operative closure just means that "the system itself has at its disposal all of the causes that are necessary for selfproduction" (Luhmann, 2005, p. 57). For example, the plant uses energy and matter from the environment to produce its cells – but it is the plant itself and not the environment that produces the cells. In addition to that, autopoietic systems can react to their environment on the basis of their own operations. For example, plants react to sunlight by growing in its direction. Yet again, the way the plant reacts to the sunlight is determined by the internal operations. Luhmann in this sense also speaks of operational closure as a precondition for interactional openness (Luhmann, 1995, p. 9). Only *because* the autopoietic system is operatively closed, i.e. controls all its own operations, can we speak of the *system* reacting to the environment – rather than the environment controlling the system.

Luhmann (1995) argued that the very concept of autopoiesis can be abstracted from its biological roots and turned into a general systems concept applicable also to social systems. He argued that analogously to biological systems, social systems can be understood as self-reproducing systems of communication. "Social systems", he explained, "use communications as their particular mode of autopoietic reproduction. Their elements are communications which are recursively produced and reproduced by a network of communications and which cannot exist outside of such a network" (Luhmann, 1986, p. 174). To the extent that individual communicative events are defined in their meaning only by the network of other communications in which they are embedded, we can say that it is the network of communicative events – in other words: the communicative system – that "produces" that particular communicative event. He explains: "A communication system is therefore [an operatively] closed system that creates the components out of which it arises through communication itself. In this sense a communication system is an autopoietic system that (re)produces everything that functions as a unity for the system through the system itself. [...] Formulated more concretely, this means that the communication system itself specifies not only its elements whatever the ultimate units of communication are – but also its structures. What is not communicated cannot contribute anything to it. Only communication can influence communication. Only communication can break down the units of communication [...]. And only communication can control and repair communication" (Luhmann, 1992, p. 254).

Associated with the operative closure of the social system is a clear differentiation between thoughts as the operations of the psychic system, i.e. the mind, and communications as the operations of the social system. As Luhmann (1995) stresses, neither can the operations of the mind contribute to the reproduction of the social system nor can the operations of the social system contribute to the operations of the mind. Psychic and social systems "are self-referentially closed systems that are limited to their own mode of autopoietic reproduction. A social system cannot think and a psychical system cannot communicate" (Luhmann, 1992, p. 257). Instead, social and psychic systems are part of each other's environment. Yet, this does not mean that social and psychic systems are irrelevant for each other. On the contrary, as Luhmann points out, treating the psychic system as environment of the social system "does not mean that the human being is estimated as less important than traditionally. Anyone who thinks so [...] has not understood the paradigm change in systems theory. Systems theory begins with the unity of the difference between system and environment. The environment is a constitutive feature of this difference, thus it is no less important for the system than the system itself"

(Luhmann, 1995, p. 212). Social systems depend on the psychic system not least for the formulation of words that the social system can treat as utterance and use for constructing a communicative event from it. However, the meaning processed in the social system is determined by the self-referential dynamics of communication, while the meaning processed in the psychic systems of the participating human beings is determined by the self-referential dynamics of their thoughts. The two systems create perturbations in the respectively other system, but how those perturbations are processed is determined entirely by the receiving system (Luhmann, 2002a).

In line with the general characterization of social systems as autopoietic communication systems, Luhmann (2018) characterizes organizations as systems reproducing themselves on the basis of particular types of communication: communicated decisions. In this sense, he defines organizations as systems "made up of decisions, and capable of completing the decisions that make them up, through the decisions that make them up" (Luhmann, 2003, p. 32).

Spencer-Brown's Observation Theory

A further important influence on Luhmann's communication approach to organizations was the theory of observation by the British mathematician and thinker George Spencer-Brown, which he developed in his magnum opus *Laws of Form* (Spencer-Brown, 1969). To underline the significance of Spencer-Brown's work, Luhmann (2007, p. 45) even indicated that this theory of observation would allow transcending the systems-theoretical foundations of his own communication approach – even though Luhmann himself held on to systems thinking. He wrote, "I suspect that we could develop a very general theory that would transcend even systems theory on the basis of this very general concept of form that we can detach from its specifically mathematical use in Spencer-Brown."

At the heart of Spencer-Brown's theory is the concept of observation, defined as the operation of drawing a distinction and focusing, or as he says: indicating one of the two sides – creating a "marked," i.e. observed, and an "unmarked," i.e. unobserved, side of the distinction. In this sense, the *Laws of Form* start with the instruction: "Draw a distinction" (Spencer-Brown, 1969, p. 3). For example, observing a company logo on the front of a factory means distinguishing the logo from the factory front and indicating the logo rather than the factory front. Depending on what I distinguish and what side of the distinction I indicate, I observe something different. If I distinguish the window in the factory front from the rest of the factory front, I will observe a window instead and will not observe the logo. Thus, if we want to understand observation we need to study the use of distinctions. Generalizing from visual observations, Spencer-Brown claims that all operations that happen in the world, whether the operations of machines or the communications of human beings, can be conceptualized as observations, i.e. as the drawing of a distinction and the selection of one side to focus on. Every communication communicates a particular content, the marked side of the distinction, which it distinguishes from other contents that it *could* have communicated about, the unmarked side. In Husserl's terms, every communication draws a distinction between the particular content it actualizes and the horizon of other, non-actualized possibilities of communicating.

The crucial point in this concept of observation is that after you have drawn a distinction and indicated one side, you cannot see anything but the marked side. In particular, the observer cannot see the very distinction that brought about the observation. In this regard, Von Foerster (1981) also speaks of the "blind spot" of observation. Any observation at the same time creates a blindness for other things (Seidl, 2007) or as Weick and Westley (1996, p. 446) wrote, " 'To see', we must 'not see'." When we communicate about something we draw a distinction between that which we communicate and that which we do not communicate; yet, the very distinction we use in this communication is itself not communicated. The communication, so to speak, remains "blind" to the distinction it is constituted by.

Only a second-order observer can observe the distinction used by the original observer. For this, the second-order observer has to use another distinction that distinguishes and indicates the distinction used by the original observer. While this second-order observer is herself blind for her own observational distinction, she can see the distinction of the first-order observer. "Second-order observation," Luhmann explains, "is indeed not only first-order observation. It is both more and less. It is less because it observes only observers and nothing else. It is more because it not only sees (= distinguishes) its object but also sees what the object sees and sees how it sees what it sees, and perhaps even sees what it does not see and sees that it does not see that it does not see what it does not see" (Luhmann, 2002b, pp. 114–115).

Applied to the field of organization studies, this means that we as organization researchers can be understood as second-order observers observing how organizations observe; or to the extent that organizations also observe themselves, we are even third-order observers, observing organizations observing themselves how they observe (Luhmann, 2018). As a social rather than psychic or living system, organizational observations materialize as communicative events and particularly as decision communication. Every decision communication draws a distinction between that which it actually decides and all possible decisions. While the focal decision communication only actualizes a particular decision content, the horizons of other potential decision communications, though only latent, are on the one hand constitutive for the meaning of the particular decision communication and on the other hand constitute the possibilities for ensuing decision communications. In this regard, organizational processes can be conceptualized as the successive drawing of distinctions: a first communication draws a distinction indicating a particular communication content in contrast to all possible communications on its unmarked side; after that, the next communication "crosses" to the unmarked side of the first communication, rendering the originally marked side unmarked and actualizing one of the *potential* communications within the originally unmarked side; the next communication, in turn, crosses the new distinction again actualizing yet another of the communicative possibilities within the previously unmarked side. The organizational process, in this sense, can be described as successive actualizations of particular communication contents, which at the same time reproduce a horizon of potential future communications. As organization researchers we can observe this processing of observational distinctions and can see how it allows the organization to see particular things while making them blind to others.

As observers of organizations we are ourselves just observers whose observations depend on the distinction used for observing the organization. While there are many distinctions that organization scholars could use, Luhmann suggests that we use the system/environment distinction. This distinction has the advantage that it corresponds to the distinction the organization itself uses in observing itself – after all, the organization has to distinguish itself from the environment. In using the system/environment distinction, "[t]he theoretician must use the pointer or indication in such a way that it indicates the system and not the environment. The environment remains outside. The system is on one side, the environment on the other" (Luhmann, 2013, p. 50).

Organizations distinguish between themselves and the environment by distinguishing between their own decision communications and all other communications happening around them (as well as anything else). Every decision communication needs to distinguish, at least implicitly, between decision communications belonging to the same organization (and thus as something that it can connect to) and those that belong to its environment. In this way, every decision communication redraws the distinction between the organization (as a network of all decision communications that are attributed to the organization) and the environment (as everything that is not attributed to the organization). Based on this insight, Luhmann reformulated the concept of autopoiesis as self-production of the system/environment distinction: "If we describe organizations as autopoietic systems, we are therefore always concerned with the generation and reproduction of a difference (systems-theoretically: between system and environment), and the concept of autopoiesis means that an observer who uses it presupposes that this difference is generated by the system itself and reproduced by systemic operations" (Luhmann, 2018, p. 62). In this sense, organizations are conceptualized as systems of decision communications that reproduce the distinction between organization (as network of decision communication) and its environment with every decision communication that it produces.

The Theoretical Roots of the Montreal School

In comparison with the four-flows model, which positions itself in continuity with a renowned sociologist, Anthony Giddens, the Montreal School of organizational communication shares with the Luhmannian approach a reliance on multiple origins, even if this third school appears, at first sight, much more scattered. It is, however, key to understand that the initiator of this third school, James R. Taylor, has the ambition of offering a truly communicational theory of organization, an ambition that can be traced back to his 1988 book but that is also explicitly mentioned in his 1993 monograph, *Rethinking the Theory of Organizational Communication: How to Read an Organization*, as well as his magnum opus, *The Emergent Organization: Communication as Site and Surface*, published in 2000 with Elizabeth Van Every.

Pragmatism

What does it mean to offer a communicational theory of organization? For James Taylor (1988), it especially means being inspired by a quote from John Dewey's (1916) *Democracy and Education*. According to Dewey, "[s]ociety not only continues to exist *by* transmission, *by* communication, but it may fairly be said to exist *in* transmission, *in* communication" (p. 10). This quote is not fortuitous as it positions the Montreal school in direct filiation with pragmatism, the nineteenth-century American philosophical movement initiated by Charles Sanders Peirce (1877) and popularized by William James and others. Incidentally, Robert T. Craig (1999), who defends a constitutive model of communication, does not hesitate to also position the communication field as being mainly inspired by this American philosophical movement (Craig, 2007; see also Russill, 2004, 2005, 2008).

Although the definition of pragmatism is far from being consensual (even Peirce and James disagreed about what it meant, which led Peirce to propose another name, *pragmaticism*, to refer to his own philosophy), we would argue that it mainly consists of *acknowledging the multiple agencies that compose our world and bring it into being*. For instance, Peirce (1877), in his famous anti-Cartesian article, *The fixation of belief*, underscored the possibility that our beliefs be *contradicted* by our experiences, which is at the basis of any scientific enterprise (what Popper (1959), for instance, would much later call the falsifiability of scientific investigations). For Peirce, we, as human beings, are certainly characterized by our capacity to act, i.e., to make a difference in the world, but this capacity is also shared, and this is a key point for pragmatists, by other entities that also compose our world.

It is therefore not by chance that communication tends to be a focal point for pragmatists, a focus that led, for instance, to the foundation of a whole field of study in linguistics, called "pragmatics" (Levinson, 1983; Mey, 1998; Morris, 1946). After all, taking into account the pragmatic dimension of an utterance consists of acknowledging not only its performative dimension, i.e., the effects it produces, as an act, on its recipients, but also the key role elements of the context play in this performativity (Cooren, 2008). Whether we are dealing with *pragmatism* as a philosophical movement or *pragmatics* as a linguistic subfield, the idea thus consists of taking into account the multiple sources of agency that bring into being a specific situation.

Speech Act Theory

Although John Langshaw Austin (1962) was not a pragmatist per se (he tends to be identified as an ordinary language philosopher), the influence of his posthumous book, *How to do Things with Words*, was truly exceptional in pragmatics (Levinson, 1983) and in communication studies in general.[1] To account for the organizing property of communication (Cooren, 2000), Taylor (1993) thus took up Austin's ideas concerning the general performativity of language, i.e., speech act theory. If organization and organizing had indeed to be found *in* communication and *in* transmission, Austin provided an ideal theoretical apparatus to show why starting from communication made sense to understand the constitution of social and organizational forms.

What does speech act theory tell us? That when people speak, and more generally, communicate, they *always* do things with words, that is, they act. This actional dimension means that by communicating, people *alter* the situation in which they find themselves. For instance, when a vice-president is saying, "This pandemic situation is really catastrophic for our sales" during a top management meeting, she is making an *assertion*, that is, she is claiming something about the pandemic situation and the state of the organization's sales. What difference does she make? It depends, of course, on the way other persons present in the room react to what she has just said, but if they heard and understood her, her contribution will make at least some difference: she will have indeed made a claim, a claim that might have consequences regarding how the meeting evolves (for instance, by leading other participants to start thinking about what should be done based on this statement).

While philosophers at that time were obsessed with questions of truth-conditionality, that is, questions related to the truth or falsehood of assertions, Austin (1962) thus demonstrated that studying language could also consist in examining its *performativity*, that is, what producing an utterance is *doing* in specific situations. Finding organization in communication, for James R. Taylor (1993; Taylor and Van Every, 2000), thus consists in examining the multiple ways by which people not only get organized, but also sustain an organization through various acts of communication. People not only claim things ("You look tired" – assertives), but they also commit themselves ("I will do it!" – commissives), give orders or make suggestions ("Bring me these files, please" – directives), authorize others to do things ("Okay, you can do it" – accreditives), sanction what has been done ("That was a nice job, congrats!" – expressives), and transform the world in declaring it to be something ("I declare this session opened" – declarations) (Cooren, 2000, 2015; see also Searle, 1979).

All these speech acts, according to the Montreal School approach, contribute to creating the building blocks by which organizing takes place and organizations emerge, get reproduced and change. While Austin (1962) mainly focused on verbal performances, Jacques Derrida (1988) pointed out, however, that the performativity of all forms of communication had to be acknowledged, especially writing. Writing, as we know, is especially important in organizations and this is no coincidence, as it contributes to their stabilization. How? Because writings (or any form of recording for that matter) have this capacity to say the same thing over and over (Cooren, 2000, 2010).

What is a procedure or protocol, for instance? It is a way of doing things that has been officially established and that is usually put in writing. When organizational members refer to it, they can repeatedly *be told* what to do in specific situations. The same logic applies for organizational charts, task descriptions, policies, etc. As we see, what we tend to call the *formal structure of an organization* is actually made of writings, tables or schemas that prescribe who is in charge of what and how things have to be done. While traditional sociology tends to contrast action and structure, which implies that structural elements do not act, the Montreal School of organizational communication shows, through their Derridean reinterpretation of speech act theory, that *we never leave the realm of action*. In other words, even texts (and therefore the structures they represent) have a form of agency (Brummans, 2007; Cooren, 2004, 2008, 2009; Jahn, 2018; Vaara, Sorsa and Pälli, 2010).

This does not mean, of course, that people lose their agency. For instance, when people follow a protocol, they also make a difference as they make sense of what this protocol tells them to do in the situation they find themselves in. Ascribing agency to texts does not mean that people are reduced to automata that blindly follow what texts tell them to do. In keeping with Giddens (1984) and Garfinkel (1967), the Montreal School acknowledges people's capacity to make a difference, that is, to disregard, for instance, what a protocol tells them to do if they feel that this should be done. What this school, however, points out is that disregarding a protocol is a decision that is then made *in the name of* a principle or value that appears to *contradict* what the protocol tells them to do. In other words, when people act, they act for specific reasons that can retrospectively be identified as *having made a difference* in their decisions (Cooren, 2010).

In keeping with the tenets of pragmatism, multiple forms of agency can thus be identified in any situation, including the agency of principles, values, emotions, rules, attitudes, etc. (Van Vuuren and Cooren, 2010). Finding organization in communication thus consists of acknowledging that when people communicate, other forms of agency express themselves and possibly make a difference in what is happening. For instance, invoking a rule is not only a way to make it say something in the context of a conversation, it is also a way to *lend weight* to what is being said by adding a *co-author* of one's position. It is not only someone who says that this should be done, it is also a rule that prescribes us to do so, hence the effect of *authority* this invocation can have (Taylor and Van Every, 2014).

Greimas's Narratology

It is therefore no coincidence that another important scholar, the semiotician and linguist Algirdas Julien Greimas (1987), keeps having a profound influence on the representatives of the Montreal School (Bencherki and Cooren, 2011; Taylor and Cooren, 2006). Echoing pragmatists, Greimas also shows that our world is filled with agencies, what we could call, echoing Garfinkel (1988), a *plenum* of agencies (Cooren, 2006). By studying narratives, Greimas indeed demonstrates how making sense of a situation consists of ascribing agency to a multitude of beings that appear to play various roles in a story development. For Greimas, it thus makes sense to say that, for instance, a medication, an object or a document is an agent to the extent that it is portrayed as doing something in the context of a story. In other words, Greimas sides with pragmatists who pointed out that people *act* on the world as much as they *react* to it (Mead, 1932/1980).

But what Greimas's (1987) narrative analysis also shows us – and this is a key point for the Montreal School – is that these multiple agents' contributions either *articulate* with each other or, on the contrary, *disarticulate* one another. Greimas calls this the *polemical* dimension of narratives, which the Montreal School extends to the polemical dimension of action in general. Some agents indeed position themselves or are positioned as *obstacles* or *opponents* while others position themselves or are positioned as *helpers* or *partners* (Cooren, 2000). Furthermore, Greimas also shows that articulation implies a form of *embedment* of specific actions within others, an embedment that explains how *organizing* can take place.

Taylor and Van Every (2000) use the term *imbrication* to speak about this form of articulation, while Cooren (2000) prefers to use the term *submission*. When we study organizational processes from a CCO perspective, one indeed cannot help but notice that some programs of action appear to be imbricated, embedded or submitted to others. For instance, when a supervisor (X) entrusts her supervisee (Y) with the task of taking care of an important client (C), this speech act (entrusting), which is both a directive and an accreditive, consists of embedding Y's program of action (taking care of C) *within* X's program of action (taking care of multiple clients, a task that she is in charge of distributing to her multiple supervisees). Embedding takes place to the extent that what Y is doing is done under X's authority, an authority that is also confirmed when sanction takes place, that is, when Y is evaluated by X for his performance (what, in speech act theory, is called expressives).

As we see through this illustration, analyzing organization and organizing from this perspective thus consists of acknowledging the *hierarchization effects* that are communicatively created, not only through the distribution of roles, tasks and responsibilities (as performed, for instance, through the design of an organizational chart), but also through the embedding of various programs of action within others, which sometimes creates *invisibilization effects*. By having one's program embedded within another program of action, one's action indeed runs the risk of becoming invisible to others to the extent that it is subjected to a form of *appropriation* by the supervisor. What one does becomes what my supervisor is doing (Bencherki and Snack, 2016), as authorship is directly related to authority.

In contrast to these embedding effects that render some actions invisible, one can note the *visibilization effects* that obstacles and opponents produce. If, for instance, Y does not perform as X expected (for instance, because X does not have the requisite competence or because he encountered unexpected obstacles, e.g., a pandemic or a competitor who took clients from him), this will result in disarticulation to the extent that Y's program of action (or lack thereof) now appears to run against X's capacity to fulfill hers. As we see in this illustration, obstacles and opponents are rendered visible to X because they prevent the fulfillment of her own programs of action.

As illustrated in this case, hierarchization effects take place on the *terra firma of interaction* (Cooren, 2006a), that is, when we act, we always act *in the name of* something or someone that is then positioned as *animating* us (Cooren, 2006b). Greimas thus helps us think about action and activity as implying a form of *passion* and passivity. We are not only actors, but also passers, that is, when we act, others always proceed into action. Studying organization in communication thus consists of unveiling these various forms of agency that explicitly or implicitly express themselves when people talk, write, or more generally communicate to each other. It is thanks to them that people get organized and (re-)produce an organization.

Harold Garfinkel's Ethnomethodology

Although Garfinkel's (1967, 2002) work does not affiliate with pragmatism (his intellectual influences have rather to be found in Alfred Schütz's (1973) phenomenology and Talcott Parsons's (1968) theory of social action), his research program can be reinterpreted according to a pragmatist perspective, even if some decentering then needs to take place.[2] Why is Garfinkel so important to the Montreal School? Because his work enjoins us to find *in interaction*, that is, *in communication*, the very root of social order (and therefore of organizational order). What is also crucial is his *empirical program* to the extent that ethnomethodology and especially its sister's discipline, conversation analysis (initiated by Harvey Sacks (1992)), are always relying on observations and recordings to develop their insights about social life.

This focus on naturally occurring interaction (Peräkylä, 2016) leads Garfinkel (1967) to show that people are not, as he famously pointed out, *judgmental dopes*, that is, that they are usually capable of evaluating, reflecting and acting on what can or should be done in a given situation. Studying human communication thus consists of analyzing what methods, procedures or recipes people mobilize to go about their daily life, whether in organizational contexts or not. In this regard, Garfinkel notes that human (inter-)action is characterized by its *reflexivity*. By this, he means that people's action *constitutes* the situations they find themselves in. For instance, when an employee speaks *as* an office clerk when serving a client, she actively constitutes the situation of service that both the client and her find themselves in. This also means that she can decide to switch from one register to another if she deems it relevant (for example, she could, at some point, start speaking *as* a parent or *as* a citizen, making the conversation topics respectively evolve toward questions of parenthood or politics). It also goes without saying that this reflexivity has to be *negotiated* by the participants, that is, in this case, the clients and her.

Another important feature of actions and situations identified by Garfinkel (1967) is their *accountable* character. This accountability is essential as it is what allows people to *make sense* of the situation they not only find themselves in, but which they also constitute (Pomerantz and Fehr, 2011). As he points out, people are indeed capable of accounting for what they do and what others do, that is, they can rationalize, justify, explain or, on the contrary, condemn, denounce or criticize what is being done. In his famous breach experiments, Garfinkel was, for instance, able to show that when someone appears to break a rule (for instance, the rule that consists of waiting for one's turn when queuing), others often do not hesitate to react by calling out this person, which means that people are able to account for what they consider to be an unacceptable behaviour. Here also, ethnomethodology insists on the negotiable character of these situations to the extent that the violator could also attempt to justify what led him to break the rules ("I'm sorry, I did not see there was a line").

A third important feature of interaction that Garfinkel (1967) identifies is their *indexicality*, which, incidentally, directly connects his position with pragmatism. By highlighting the indexical character of interactions, Garfinkel points out that the meaning of what is communicated depends on the circumstances in which interactions take place. In other words, what is said or done indexes or points to some elements of a situation in which this communication is taking place. For instance, if at some point the office clerk tells the client, "I need you to fill this in," the meaning of this request depends on what the clerk is referring to when using the demonstrative "this." If we are observing this interaction, we can then note that while using this demonstrative, the clerk is also handing a form to the client, which shows that by "this," she means the form she is now handing to the client. In other words, Garfinkel implicitly acknowledges the pragmatic dimension of utterances by acknowledging not only its performative dimension, i.e., the effects it produces, as an act, on its recipients, but also the key role elements of the context play in this performativity.

Although Garfinkel remains a phenomenologist, which means that he is essentially interested in how people interactively make sense of the situations they both constitute and find themselves in, it is noteworthy that there is a way to decenter his analytical position, which is precisely what the Montreal School proposes to do. The representatives of this school indeed take seriously the pragmatist idea that *the world acts on us as much as we act on it*. For instance, when the clerk says, "I need you to fill this in," the verb "need" expresses the fact that she is following an organizational procedure that enjoins her to have clients fill in this form when they make a specific request. In other words, when the office clerk asks her client to fill in this form, it is also the procedure she previously learned that expresses itself through this action. If we go back one more step, we could also point out that she is acting on behalf of the organization she represents (i.e., makes present again), an institution that, through its procedures, enjoins her to have this form filled in.

Actor Network Theory

This brings us to the last root of the Montreal School (but not the least), namely Actor Network Theory (ANT) (Callon, 1986; Latour, 2005, 2013a, 2013b). This influence should not be surprising to the extent that ANT itself not only echoes many of the tenets of pragmatism (especially through John Dewey and William James), but was also directly influenced by Austin's speech act theory (for its notion of performativity), Greimas's narratology (for its acknowledgment of nonhuman agency), and Garfinkel's ethnomethodology (for its empirical focus on interaction and how people make sense of situations). Although Actor Network Theory can be considered one of the roots of the Montreal School, the fact that both approaches share several influences also means that a family resemblance exists between the two, a resemblance that has been acknowledged on many occasions (Latour, 2010; Vásquez, Bencherki, Cooren and Sergi, 2018).

What especially characterizes ANT is its *analytical decentering*, that is, the fact that human beings are certainly important elements to understand what is happening in our world (we just have to think about the emergence of the Anthropocene and its consequences on our planet), but that the performativity of their actions should not render other contributions invisible. For instance, Callon (1986) famously showed how it was difficult to understand a specific controversy surrounding the cultivation of scallops in the St Brieuc Bay, France, without acknowledging what the scallops themselves and the technologies involved were literally doing in this situation. Similarly, Latour (1996) brilliantly demonstrated that a world without objects, that is, a world where the active contribution of artifacts and technologies are unrecognized, cannot be intelligible.

What would indeed be an organization without the buildings that host its activities, the technologies that actively participate in its operations or the procedures that define how and what things have to be done? In order to get organized, ANT reminds us, we need to mobilize texts, machines, procedures, etc. that actively participate in the structuration of our world. While Giddens (1984) still speaks about the *duality* of structure, ANT scholars invite us to acknowledge the multiple sources of agency that compose our (organizational) world. Echoing ethnomethodology, it insists on people's capacity to disregard certain rules or enforce others, but in contrast with this phenomenological perspective, it takes a pragmatist stance according to which humans are not alone on the construction site: they react to what the world does, as much as they act on it.

While ANT scholars tend not to be that interested in the detailed study of interaction, the Montreal School representatives are keen to study what precisely happens *in* communication, not only in its eventfulness, but also in its iterability. They especially highlight the multiple voices that can be recognized when people speak, not only absent persons' voices (for instance, when a member speaks about the dead founder of an organization in order to make a point), but also the voices of rules, protocols or procedures (as when a clerk invokes a rule to turn down a client's request), or the voices of emotions, such as anger, which can be heard and felt when someone feels betrayed or unfairly treated.

Conclusion

Although the three CCO schools definitely share a common stance, which is that communication constitutes organization, this chapter highlighted various intellectual roots that allow us to distinguish them from each other. One could, however, point out that James R. Taylor (1995) never hesitates to acknowledge the key role Maturana and Varela's (1980, 1992) ideas play in the elaboration of his theory, which shows that both Luhmannians and Montreal School representatives share at least an interest in the self-organizing properties of communication. Similarly, Taylor and Van Every (2000) definitely side with Giddens's (1984, 1991) structuration theory when time comes to critique both functionalist/structuralist and hermeneutic/interpretive perspectives. Quoting the British sociologist, they point out that "[f]unctionalism proposes 'an imperialism of the social object' [while] interpretivism is founded, by contrast, on an 'imperialism of the subject'" (Taylor and Van Every, 2000, p. 150).

Both Giddens (1984) and Taylor (1999) thus try, each in their own way, to fight against these two imperialisms, even if they disagree about the means to win this fight, especially regarding the role communication plays in their respective models. While Taylor and Van Every (2000) conceive communication as a central modality for the constitution of organization, communication just remains, for Giddens (1984), the way by which the modality of *signification* is realized in interaction. In other words, Giddens conceives of communication as not playing any role in the two other modalities he identifies, that is, *domination* and *legitimation*. This position is highly problematic for the Canadian scholars, especially regarding the questions of authority and collective agency, which have, for them, to always be established communicatively.

Additionally, if Luhmannians and Montrealers tend to agree on the central role communication plays in the constitution of organization, Luhmann (1988) does not hesitate to write that "humans cannot communicate; not even their brains can communicate; not even their conscious minds can communicate. Only communication can communicate" (p. 371), which seems entirely consistent with his social systems theory, but appears at odds with Taylor and his followers' position. Indeed, for Luhmann, it is irrelevant to know what is in people's minds to infer that communication occurs or even succeeds, as mutual comprehension has always to be displayed *in* communication. Communication is therefore conceived by the German sociologist as an *autonomous* realm of reality (Cooren and Seidl, 2020).

Although the Montreal School representatives agree with this position, they would not go as far as denying human actors the capacity to communicate. On the contrary, they even side with Actor Network Theory regarding the capacity of other-than-humans (collectives, texts, technologies, architectural elements) to communicate too, which appears unconceivable for both Luhmann and Giddens. While Luhmann (2018) implicitly acknowledges the relative character of autopoiesis and self-organization, he never really leaves the organization's perspective, which means that humans or their technologies remain mere *irritations* for this communication system (Cooren and Seidl, 2020; Schoeneborn, 2011). In contrast, Taylor and his followers do not hesitate to highlight the heteronomous dimension of autonomy, which allows them to ascribe the capacity to communicate to multiple actors, whether humans or other-than-humans.

We hope that this chapter will have contributed to clarifying the various positionings of these three schools through the examination of their respective roots. Many more influences could have, of course, been acknowledged (e.g. Karl Weick's [1979] theory of organizing or Fritz Heider's [1959] media theory) but a lack of space unfortunately prevents us from addressing them here (for more details, see Boivin, Brummans and Barker, 2017, or Jahraus et al., 2012). At least, we wish that readers can now better acknowledge some of the giants' shoulders that the CCO movement stands on.

Notes

1 It is also noteworthy that this posthumous book was published from the William James lectures he gave in Harvard in 1955, which means that the connection with pragmatism was at least present in this regard.
2 It is noteworthy that ethnomethodology and conversation analysis played a key role in the development of pragmatics as a subfield of linguistics. For more on this influence, see Levinson (1983).

References

Austin, J. L. (1962). *How to do things with words*. Cambridge, MA: Harvard University Press.

Bencherki, N., & Cooren, F. (2011). Having to be: The possessive constitution of organization. *Human Relations, 64*(12), 1579–1607.

Bencherki, N., & Snack, J. P. (2016). Contributorship and partial inclusion: A communicative perspective. *Management Communication Quarterly, 30*(3), 279–304.

Boden, D. (1994). *The business of talk: Organizations in action*. Cambridge, UK: Polity Press.

Boivin, G., Brummans, B. H. J. M., & Barker, J. R. (2017). The institutionalization of CCO scholarship: Trends from 2000 to 2015. *Management Communication Quarterly, 31*(3), 331–355.

Brummans, B. H. J. M. (2007). Death by document: Tracing the agency of a text. *Qualitative Inquiry, 13*(5), 711–727.

Brummans, B. H. J. M., Cooren, F., Robichaud, D., & Taylor, J. R. (2014). Approaches in research on the communicative constitution of organizations. In L. L. Putnam & D. K. Mumby (Eds.), *Sage handbook of organizational communication* (pp. 173–194). Thousand Oaks, CA: Sage.

Callon, M. (1986). Some elements of a sociology of translation: The domestication of the scallops and the fishermen of St Brieuc Bay. In J. Law (Ed.), *Power, action and belief* (pp. 196–233). London: Routledge & Kegan Paul.

Cooren, F. (2000). *The organizing property of communication*. Amsterdam: J. Benjamins.

Cooren, F. (2004). Textual agency: How texts do things in organizational settings. *Organization, 11*(3), 373–393.

Cooren, F. (2006a). The organizational world as a plenum of agencies. In F. Cooren, J. R. Taylor, & E. J. Van Every (Eds.), *Communication as organizing: Empirical and theoretical explorations in the dynamic of text and conversation* (pp. 81–100). Mahwah, NJ: Lawrence Erlbaum.

Cooren, F. (2006b). Arguments for the in-depth study of organizational interactions: A rejoinder to McPhee, Myers, and Trethewey. *Management Communication Quarterly, 19*(3), 327–340. https://doi.org/10.1177/0893318905280325.

Cooren, F. (2008). Between semiotics and pragmatics: Opening language studies to textual agency. *Journal of Pragmatics, 40*, 1–16.

Cooren, F. (2009). The haunting question of textual agency: Derrida and Garfinkel on iterability and eventfulness. *Research on Language and Social Interaction, 42*(1), 42–67.

Cooren, F. (2010). *Action and agency in dialogue: Passion, ventriloquism and incarnation*. Amsterdam: J. Benjamins.

Cooren, F. (2015). Speech act theory. In K. Tracy, C. Eli, and T. Sandel (Eds). *International encyclopedia of language and social interaction*. Oxford, UK: John Wiley & Sons.

Cooren, F., & Seidl, D. (2020). Niklas Luhmann's radical communication approach and its implications for research on organizational communication. *Academy of Management Review, 45*(2), 479–497. https://doi.org/10.5465/amr.2018.0176.

Craig, R. T. (1999). Communication theory as a field. *Communication Theory, 9*(2), 119–161. doi: 10.1111/j.1468-2885.1999.tb00355.x.

Craig, R. T. (2007). Pragmatism in the field of communication theory. *Communication Theory, 17*(2), 125–145. doi: 10.1111/j.1468-2885.2007.00292.x.

Davidson, D. (1980). *Essays on actions and events*. London: Oxford University Press.

Deetz, S., & Mumby, D. K. (1990). Power, discourse, and the workplace: Reclaiming the critical tradition. *Annals of the International Communication Association, 13*(1), 18–47. doi:10.1080/23.

Derrida, J. (1988). *Limited inc*. Evanston, IL: Northwestern University Press.

Dewey, J. (1916). *Democracy and education*. New York: The Macmillan Company.

Garfinkel, H. (1967). *Studies in ethnomethodology*. Englewood Cliffs, NJ: Prentice Hall.

Garfinkel, H. (1988). Evidence for locally produced, naturally accountable phenomena of order, logic, reason, meaning, method, etc. in and as of the essential quiddity of immortal ordinary society, (I of IV): An announcement of studies. *Sociological Theory, 6*(1), 103–109. https://doi.org/10.2307/201918.

Garfinkel, H. (2002). *Ethnomethodology's program: Working out Durkheim's aphorism*. Lanham, MD: Rowman & Littlefield Publishers.

Giddens, A. (1979). *Central Problems in social theory: Action, structure and contradiction in social analysis.* London: McMillan.

Giddens, A. (1984). *The constitution of society*. Cambridge, UK: Polity Press.

Giddens, A. (1991). *Modernity and self-identity: Self and society in the late modern age*. Cambridge, UK: Polity Press.

Greimas, A. J. (1987). *On meaning: Selected writings in semiotic theory* (P. J. Perron & F. H. Collins, Trans.). London: Frances Pinter.

Heider, F., 1959. Thing and medium. *Psychological Issues, 1*, 1–34.

Husserl, E. (1973) *Experience and judgment: Investigations in a genealogy of logic* (J. S. Churchill & K. Ameriks, Trans.). Evanston: Northwestern University.

Husserl, E. (1982) *Ideas pertaining to a pure phenomenology and to a phenomenological philosophy – First Book: General introduction to a pure phenomenology* (F. Kersten, Trans.). The Hague: Nijhoff.

Husserl, E. (2012). On the phenomenology of the consciousness of internal time (1893–1917). Dordrecht: Springer.

Jahn, J. L. S. (2018). Genre as textual agency: Using communicative relationality to theorize the agential-performative relationship between human and generic text. *Communication Monographs, 85*(4), 515–538.

Jahraus, O., Nassehi, A., Grizelj, M., Saake, I., Kirchmeier, C., & Müller, J. (2012). *Luhmann-Handbuch: Leben–Werk–Wirkung*. Berlin. Springer.

Langenmayr, F. (2016). *Organisational memory as a function: The construction of past, present and future in organisations*. Springer.

Lash, S., & Urry, J. (1994). *Economies of signs and space*. London: Sage.

Latour, B. (1986). The powers of association. In J. Law (Ed.), *Power, action and belief. A new sociology of knowledge?* (pp. 264–280). London: Routledge & Kegan Paul.

Latour, B. (1996). On interobjectivity. *Mind, Culture, and Activity, 3*(4), 228–245.

Latour, B. (2005). *Reassembling the social: An introduction to Actor-Network Theory*. London: Oxford University Press.

Latour, B. (2010). Foreword — Who is making the dummy speak? In F. Cooren (Ed.), *Action and agency in dialogue: Passion, incarnation and ventriloquism* (pp. xiii–xvi). Amsterdam/Philadelphia: John Benjamins.

Latour, B. (2013a). *An inquiry into modes of existence: An anthropology of the moderns*. Cambridge, MA: Harvard University Press.

Latour, B. (2013b). "What's the story?" Organizing as a mode of existence. In D. Robichaud & F. Cooren (Eds.), *Organization and organizing: Materiality, agency, and discourse* (pp. 37–51). New York: Routledge.

Levinson, S. C. (1983). *Pragmatics*. Cambridge: Cambridge University Press.

Luhmann, N. (1986). The autopoiesis of social systems. In F. Geyer and J. Van d. Zeuwen (Eds.), *Sociocybernetic paradoxes: Observation, control and evolution of self-steering systems* (pp. 172–192). London: Sage.

Luhmann, N. (1988). How can the mind participate in communication? In H. U. Gumbrecht & K. L. Pfeiffer (Eds.), *Materialities of communication* (pp. 371–388). Stanford, CA: Stanford University Press.

Luhmann, N. (1990). *Essays on self-reference*. New York: Columbia University Press.

Luhmann, N. (1992). What is communication?. *Communication Theory, 2*(3), 251–259.

Luhmann, N. (1995). *Social systems*. Stanford: Stanford University Press.

Luhmann, N. (2002a). How can the mind participate in communication? In W. Rasch (Ed.), *Theories of distinction: Redescribing the descriptions of modernity* (pp. 169–86). Stanford, CA: Stanford University Press.

Luhmann, N. (2002b). Identity: What or how. In W. Rasch (Ed.), *Theories of distinction: Redescribing the descriptions of modernity*. Stanford, CA: Stanford University Press.

Luhmann, N. (2003). Organization. In T. Hernes & T. Bakken (Eds.), *Autopoietic organization theory: Drawing on Niklas Luhmann's social systems perspective* (pp. 31–52). Copenhagen: Copenhagen Business School Press.

Luhmann, N. (2005). The concept of autopoiesis. In D. Seidl & K. H. Becker (Eds.), *Niklas Luhmann and organization studies* (pp. 54–63). Copenhagen: Liber & Copenhagen Business School Press.

Luhmann, N. (2007). What is communication? In R. T. Craig & H. L. Muller (Eds.), *Theorizing communication: Readings across traditions* (pp. 301–307). Los Angeles, CA: Sage.

Luhmann, N. (2013). *Introduction to systems theory*. Cambridge, UK: Polity.

Luhmann, N. (2018). *Organization and decision.* Cambridge University Press.

Maturana, H., & Varela, F. (1980). *Autopoiesis and cognition: The realization of the living.* Dordrecht: Reidel.

Maturana, H., & Varela, F. (1992). *The tree of knowledge: The biological roots of understanding.* Boston: Shambhala.

Mey, J. L. (1998). Pragmatics. In J. L. Mey (Ed.), *Concise encyclopedia of pragmatics* (pp. 716–737). Oxford: Elsevier/Pergamon.

Mintzberg, H. (1979). *The structuring of organizations: A synthesis of the research.* Englewood Cliffs, NJ: Prentice-Hall.

Nassehi, A. (2012). Luhmann und Husserl. In O. Jahraus & A. Nassehi (Eds.), *Luhmann-Handbuch. Leben – Werk – Wirkung* (pp. 13–18). Stuttgart: JB Metzler.

McPhee, R. D., & Zaug, P. (2000). The communicative constitution of organizations: A framework for explanation. *The Electronic Journal of Communication / La revue électronique de communication, 10*(1/2), 1–16.

McPhee, R. D., & Zaug, P. (2009). The communicative constitution of organizations: A framework for explanation. In L. L. Putnam & A. Nicotera (Eds.), *Building theories of organization: The constitutive role of communication* (pp. 21–47). New York: Routledge.

Mead, G. H. (1932–1980). The physical thing. In A. E. Murphy (Ed.), *The philosophy of the present* (pp. 119–139). Chicago: The University of Chicago Press.

Morris, C. W. (1946). *Signs, language and behavior.* New York: Prentice-Hall.

Parsons, T. (1968). *The structure of social action.* New York: Free Press.

Peirce, C. S. (1877). The fixation of belief. *Popular Science Monthly, 12*(November), 1–15.

Peirce, C. S. (1991). *Peirce on signs: Writings on semiotic.* Chapel Hill, NC: University of North Carolina Press.

Peräkylä, A. (2016). Conversation analysis. In G. Ritzer (Ed.), *The Blackwell encyclopedia of sociology.* New York: Blackwell.

Pomerantz, A., & Fehr, B. J. (2011). Conversation analysis: An approach to the analysis of social interaction. In T. A. Van Dijk (Ed.), *Discourse studies: A multidisciplinary introduction* (pp. 165–190). London: Sage.

Popper, K. R. (1959). *The logic of scientific discovery.* London: Hutchinson & Co.

Putnam, L. L., & Nicotera, A. M. (Eds.). (2009). *Building theories of organization: The constitutive role of communication.* New York: Routledge.

Russill, C. (2004). *Toward a pragmatist theory of communication.* The Pennsylvania State University.

Russill, C. (2005). The road not taken: William James's radical empiricism and communication theory. *The Communication Review, 8,* 277–305.

Russill, C. (2008). Through a public darkly: Reconstructing pragmatist perspectives in Communication Theory. *Communication Theory, 18,* 478–504.

Sacks, H. (1992). *Lectures on conversation.* Oxford: Blackwell.

Schoeneborn, D. (2011). Organization as communication: A Luhmannian perspective. *Management Communication Quarterly, 25*(4), 663–689.

Schoeneborn, D., Blaschke, S., Cooren, F., McPhee, R. D., Seidl, D., & Taylor, J. R. (2014). The three schools of CCO thinking: Interactive dialogue and systematic comparison. *Management Communication Quarterly, 28*(2), 285–316.

Schutz, A. (1973). *Collected Papers I: The Problem of Social Reality.* The Hague: Martinus Nijhoff.

Searle, J. R. (1979). *Expression and meaning: Studies in the theory of speech acts.* Cambridge, UK: Cambridge University Press.

Seidl, D. (2007) The dark side of knowledge. *Emergence: Complexity & Organization, 9,* 13–26.

Seidl, D., & Schoeneborn, D. (2016) Systems theory. In R. Craig (Ed.), *International encyclopedia of communication theory and philosophy* (pp. 1–11). Chichester: Wiley Blackwell.

Smith, R. C. (1993). Images of organizational communication: Root-metaphors of the organization-communication relation. Paper presented at the annual conference of the International Communication Association, Washington DC.

Spencer-Brown, G. (1969). *Laws of form.* London: Allen & Unwin.

Taylor, J. R. (1988). *Une organisation n'est qu'un tissu de communications: Essais théoriques.* Montréal, QC: Université de Montréal.

Taylor, J. R. (1993). *Rethinking the theory of organizational communication: How to read an organization.* Norwood, NJ: Ablex.

Taylor, J. R. (1995). Shifting from a heteronomous to an autonomous worldview of organizational communication: Communication theory on the cusp. *Communication Theory, 5*(1), 1–35.

Taylor, J. R. (1999). What is "organizational communication"? Communication as a dialogic of text and conversation. *The Communication Review, 3*(1–2), 21–63.

Taylor, J. R., & Cooren, F. (2006). Making worldview sense: And paying homage, retrospectively, to Algirdas Greimas. In F. Cooren, J. R. Taylor, & E. J. Van Every (Eds.), *Communication as organizing: Empirical and theoretical explorations in the dynamic of text and conversation* (pp. 115–138). Mahwah, NJ: Lawrence Erlbaum.

Taylor, J. R., Cooren, F., Giroux, N., & Robichaud, D. (1996). The communicational basis of organization: Between the conversation and the text. *Communication Theory, 6*(1), 1–39.

Taylor, J. R., & Van Every, E. J. (2000). *The emergent organization. Communication as site and surface.* Mahwah, NJ: Lawrence Erlbaum Associates.

Taylor, J. R., & Van Every, E. J. (2011). *The situated organization: Case studies in the pragmatics of communication.* New York: Routledge.

Taylor, J. R., & Van Every, E. J. (2014). *When organization fails: Why authority matters.* New York: Routledge.

Vaara, E., Sorsa, V., & Pälli, P. (2010). On the force potential of strategy texts: A critical discourse analysis of a strategic plan and its power effects in a city organization. *Organization, 17*(6), 685–702.

Van Vuuren, M., & Cooren, F. (2010). 'My attitude made me do it': Considering the agency of attitudes. *Human Studies, 33*, 85–101.

Varela, F. (1984). Two principles of self-organization. In H. Ulrich and G. J. B. Probst (Eds.), *Self-organization and management of social systems: Insides, promises, doubts and questions* (pp. 25–32). Bern: Haupt.

Vásquez, C., Bencherki, N., Cooren, F., & Sergi, V. (2018). From 'matters of concern' to 'matters of authority': Studying the performativity of strategy from a communicative constitution of organization (CCO) approach. *Long Range Planning, 51*, 417–435.

Varela, F. (1979). *Principles of biological autonomy.* New York: Elsevier.

Von Foerster, H. (1981). *Observing systems.* Seaside, CA: Intersystems.

Von Foerster, H. (2002). On natural magic. In *Understanding understanding: Essays on cybernetics and cognition.* New York: Springer.

Weick, K. E. (1979). *The social psychology of organizing.* New York: Random House.

Weick, K. E., & Westley, F. (1996). Organizational learning: Affirming an oxymoron. In S. R. Clegg, C. Hardy, and W. R. Nord (Eds.), *Handbook of organization studies* (pp. 440–58). Thousand Oaks, CA: Sage.

2

WHAT'S PRAGMATIC ABOUT AMBIGUITY IN THE COMMUNICATIVE CONSTITUTION OF ORGANIZATIONS?

The Case of CCO Scholarship's Establishment

Geneviève Boivin and Boris H. J. M. Brummans

Since Karl Weick's (1979) *The Social Psychology of Organizing*, organizational scholars have come to believe that the multiplicity of meanings is at the heart of organizing processes. In Weick's view, "individuals enact environments that vary in their degree of *equivocality*, which in turn leads everything that 'happens' in and around organizations to be subject to multiple (and often competing) interpretations" (Eisenberg, 2006, p. 1696, emphasis added). Inspired by Weick, among others, James Taylor and Elizabeth Van Every (2000) began suggesting in the 1990s that people organize *by* communicating, leading to what's now known as research on the communicative constitution of organizations (CCO).

While the correspondences between Weick's work and that of Taylor and Van Every's are indisputable (e.g., see Taylor & Van Every, 2000, pp. 274–275; Weick, Sutcliffe, & Obstfeld, 2005, p. 413; see also Eisenberg, 2006), it's surprising that the role of Weick's notion of equivocality has not received more explicit attention in CCO research so far. Organizational communication scholars seem to agree that people "communicate in an effort to reduce the number of possible interpretations, and *in so doing* make coordinated action possible" (Eisenberg, 2006, p. 1696, emphasis added). Yet few have conceptualized, let alone empirically investigated, how equivocality, or rather the now more popular concept of *ambiguity* (see Castor, 2017; Eisenberg, 2007), drives the communication through which organizations are constituted.

To begin addressing this question, this chapter examines how ambiguity plays into the constitution of a very particular social collective: the community of CCO researchers itself. This scholarly community is becoming increasingly organized as a distinct area of inquiry, for example in the form of the European Group for Organizational Studies (EGOS) Standing Working Group: Organization as Communication (see also Schoeneborn, Kuhn, & Kärreman, 2019). CCO research, in other words, is showing increasing degrees of *organizationality* (Dobusch & Schoeneborn, 2015; Schoeneborn et al., 2019). As a collective, it (1) engages in the ongoing

DOI: 10.4324/9781003224914-4

demarcation and negotiation of its own identity in relation to other areas of research and larger fields or disciplines; (2) has increasing ability to act as an actor and be attributed actorhood by other actors; and (3) displays the interconnection of instances of decision-making taking place on its behalf. In addition to these organizationality criteria, CCO scholarship is also becoming more "organizational" (and organized) because it's showing signs of *institutionalization*; it's becoming established in such fields as organization studies and organizational communication (see Boivin, 2018; Boivin, Brummans, & Barker, 2017).

To theorize how ambiguity plays into CCO scholarship's communicative constitution, we build on Hélène Giroux's (2006) writings on the pragmatic usefulness of ambiguity for collective action. More specifically, we explain how CCO researchers' use of ambiguities in their academic discourse contributes to CCO scholarship's communicative institutionalization or establishment. Investigating CCO scholarship as if it were an "exotic tribe" is helpful, we believe, not so much as a navel-gazing exercise, but to encourage reflexivity as Pierre Bourdieu imagined it (see Bourdieu & Wacquant, 1992; see also Brummans, 2015). Practicing reflexivity reveals how individual human actors and fields, whether academic or non-academic (e.g., politics, arts, law, or medicine), are mutually constitutive and exist in a relationship of *ontological complicity* (Bourdieu & Wacquant, 1992). Cultivating collective "self"-awareness as an area of inquiry through Bourdieu's reflexivity could therefore help prevent CCO scholarship's institutionalization "from becoming dysfunctional" (Kuhn, 2005, p. 623). Put differently, this practice is important since actors tend to "construct around themselves an environment that constrains their ability to change further in later years" (DiMaggio & Powell, 1983, p. 149, cited in Kuhn, 2005, p. 623).

In what follows, we situate our chapter in the extant literature on ambiguity, organizing, and communication. We subsequently demonstrate the value of studying the role of pragmatic ambiguity in the communicative constitution of organizations by examining how this ambiguity plays into the communicative establishment of an area of research like CCO scholarship through an empirical analysis of conference discourse at the 2015 EGOS conference. To conclude, we discuss the implications of our work for CCO research.

Ambiguity, Organizing, and Communication

Ambiguity may have lost some of its currency in organizational communication studies and beyond (see Castor, 2017), but opposing or contradictory meanings are still of great interest to those who investigate how tensions, contradictions, and paradoxes emerge and intermingle with organizational practices (see Putnam, Fairhurst, & Banghart, 2016). This research parallels studies that examine organizational cultures from a "fragmentation" perspective, which highlights ambiguity as "the essence of a culture" (Martin, 2002, p. 191) and focuses attention on "irony and paradox—irreconcilable tensions that coexist in an uneasy balance" (p. 106; see also Brummans & Putnam, 2003). Thus, ambiguity is "a normal, salient, and inescapable part of organizational functioning" (Martin, 2002, p. 105).

Weick's idea of equivocality clearly influenced ambiguity research. In particular, Eric Eisenberg (1984) drew from Weick's work to develop his concept of *strategic ambiguity*. Ambiguity becomes strategic, Eisenberg suggests, when it's used intentionally (by management) to achieve specific aims. It can therefore "[foster] the existence of multiple viewpoints in organizations" (p. 233), facilitate organizational change, and preserve privileged organizational positions. However, Eisenberg subsequently moved away from viewing ambiguity as a mere instrument of managerial control to conceive of it instead as an "aesthetic of communication" that aims to reject fundamentalism and cultivate a life-affirming, contingent view of the world, grounded in openness and relationality (see Eisenberg, 2007).

Within the context of CCO scholarship, Taylor and Van Every's pioneering research both benefited from Weick's work and influenced it in return (see Taylor and Van Every, 2000, pp. 147–149; Weick, Sutcliffe, & Obstfeld, 2005, p. 409, p. 413). Taylor and Van Every (2000) suggested that Weick's theory of organizing could have been "more influential in empirical communication studies" if it had shown more clearly how "to operationalize the concept of ambiguity reduction in discourse" (p. 148). For his part, Weick has increasingly come to embrace Taylor and Van Every's conception of communication (see Taylor & Van Every, 2000, p. 58, cited in Weick et al., 2005, p. 413; see also Eisenberg, 2006, p. 1699). Similarly, Taylor and Van Every (2000) were partly influenced by Eisenberg's work when they wrote that "[i]t is not crucial that there be unanimity in the diverse cause maps, but it is crucial that everyone subscribe to an agreed-upon text, whatever reservations they may privately continue to entertain" (p. 149).

Despite the importance of ambiguity in Taylor and Van Every's early work, CCO scholars have yet to explicate and operationalize its role in the communicative constitution of organizations. One promising avenue for addressing this question is the conceptual lens Giroux developed while working with Taylor on her doctoral research at the Université de Montréal in the 1990s (see Giroux, 2006; Giroux & Taylor, 1999, 2002). According to Giroux (2006), the strategic intent behind Eisenberg's concept should be questioned because in actual communication situations, the source of a message never quite controls its degree of ambiguity. Hence, strategic ambiguity is never fully "strategic", and messages are, in fact, often unintentionally ambiguous (see also Brummans & Miller, 2004). Giroux consequently proposes the concept of *pragmatic ambiguity*, which puts less emphasis on strategic intent, and highlights how ambiguity is a matter of "choice—strategic or inadvertent—of polysemic words and equivocal grammatical structures … [as well as] the use of certain tropes" (p. 1228). Pragmatic ambiguity can contribute to our understanding of the dissemination of concepts such as Total Quality Management (TQM), for "the equivocality of concepts allows for *different courses of action* while maintaining a semblance of unity" (p. 1232, emphasis in original). Drawing on research on the *interpretive viability* of management fashions (see Benders & van Veen, 2001), Giroux notes that if concepts are pragmatically ambiguous, they can be interpreted—or *translated* (Callon, 1986; Latour, 1987)—differently according to different parties' interests, thus securing their broad, discursive dissemination and "admitting more than one course of action" (p. 1229). Equivocality or ambiguity is therefore *practiced*, strategically or inadvertently, in everyday communication through the interplay between conversation, text, and intertextuality, which drives organizing processes (see also Taylor & Van Every, 2000).

Researchers have used Giroux's concept to investigate the interpretive viability of such concepts as *corporate social responsibility* (Fassin & Van Rosem, 2009) and the *Balanced Scorecard* (BSC) as a strategic management system (Braam, 2012). On the whole, these studies show that "conceptual ambiguity is not a coincidence but could be considered a precondition for ideas to 'flow' (Røvik, 2002) and become popular among managers" (Braam, 2012, p. 100). Surprisingly, however, Giroux's work has not been mobilized to investigate how organizations are communicatively constituted. If ambiguity is pragmatically useful for establishing entire management movements based on single concepts, such as TQM or corporate social responsibility, what constitutive force might it have in communicatively establishing areas of research like CCO scholarship? The framework we develop next is helpful for gaining insight into this question.

The Role of Pragmatic Ambiguity in Communicatively Establishing an Area of Research

In this chapter, we examine how the use of pragmatic ambiguity in CCO scholars' discourse contributes to establishing CCO research as a legitimate area of inquiry within the organizational communication discipline and other fields. Our starting point is therefore that institutions such as organizations or academic fields "are constituted *in* discourse" (Phillips, Lawrence, & Hardy 2004, p. 646, emphasis added); that is, we aim to gain insight into CCO scholarship's communicative establishment by analyzing the discursive dynamics underlying this institutionalization process.

Since our previous research looked at the role of *published discourse* (books, book chapters, and journal articles) in the institutionalization of CCO research (see Boivin et al., 2017), this chapter focuses on how using ambiguity in *academic conference discourse* (formal presentations of research papers, respondent/discussant comments, Q&A, discussion, etc.) plays into CCO scholarship's establishment (see also Hardy & Maguire, 2010). Using *ambiguity* (admitting more than one meaning), *generality* (encompassing several elements or being applicable across situations), and *vagueness* (lacking precision and leaving room for doubt) (Giroux's modalities of pragmatic ambiguity) in conference discourse when talking about CCO theories, concepts, and methods contributes to establishing CCO research, we postulate, for it increases their interpretive viability and thus their dissemination. Through scholars' pragmatic use of ambiguity, that is, CCO theories, concepts, and methods

> stand a chance of broad dissemination [, because they] lend [themselves] to various interpretations [and appropriations/translations] ... . [Their] interpretative viability allows that different parties can each "recognize" their own version of the [theory, concept, or method].
>
> *Benders & van Veen, 2001, p. 38, cited in Giroux, 2006, p. 1228*

Studying CCO researchers' pragmatic use of ambiguity in their conference talk is useful, we argue, in turn, because it can reveal how the interpretive viability of CCO theories, concepts, and methods enables conferees to "become aware of their common concerns, join together, share information, coordinate their actions, shape or subvert agendas, and mutually influence [the] structuration [of their emerging area of inquiry]" (Anand & Jones, 2008, p. 1037, cited in Hardy & Maguire, 2010, p. 1366). Hence, their talk "is not 'mere talk' dissociated from action" (Giroux, 2006, p. 1237), but central to the communicative constitution of the CCO scholarly collective's organizationality (Dobusch & Schoeneborn, 2015). In pragmatically ambiguous talk, "patterned approaches to problem solving" (Kuhn, 2005, p. 620) are therefore not only generated and formalized in the form of new CCO theories, concepts, and methods—what institutional theorists Pamela Tolbert and Lynn Zucker (1996) would call a process of *habitualization*; they're also increasingly accepted and championed by leading CCO scholars (*objectification*), and eventually become broadly disseminated, making them persistent over time (*sedimentation*) (see also Kuhn, 2005).

To demonstrate the value of our theoretical framework, we'll now present the results of an empirical study on the pragmatic use of ambiguity during the 2015 EGOS conference. To conduct this study, the first author collected data during this conference in Athens, Greece. While CCO research originally emerged in North America, this international conference marked the beginning of the first official Standing Working Group (SWG 05) dedicated to "Organization as Communication". It was thus an important *field-configuring event* (Hardy & Maguire, 2010) that brought together organizational communication scholars who associate themselves with one (or more) of the three main CCO schools (the Four Flows Model, the Montréal School, and the Luhmannian School), as well as scholars from other disciplines. The three-day meeting provided a unique opportunity to investigate how the pragmatic use of ambiguity in conference discourse plays into CCO scholarship's communicative establishment. In fact, in the subsequent years, this annual meeting became a key institutional "force" for CCO research (for a detailed description of our data collection and analysis methods, see Boivin, 2018).

The Role of Pragmatic Ambiguity in Communicatively Establishing CCO Scholarship During the 2015 EGOS Conference

In this section, we show how the pragmatic use of ambiguity in conferees' talk played into CCO scholarship's communicative establishment during the 2015 EGOS conference by examining the use of (1) conceptual ambiguities, (2) ambiguities in positioning SWG 05's subtheme, and (3) ambiguities in positioning within CCO schools.

The Pragmatic Use of Conceptual Ambiguities

This first subsection focuses on how the pragmatic use of ambiguous language in the development of concepts plays into CCO scholarship's establishment. It also reveals how conferees' questioning of this kind of ambiguity figures into this process.

To start, we focus on Robert (to protect participants' identities, we use pseudonyms), a professor and well-known CCO scholar who is presenting his research on the role of organizational tensions in an NGO's organizing. Following Robert's presentation, Sophie, a professor who is very familiar with his research, asks:

> My question is more of a broader question. I'm not sure when you talk about tensions in organization, if your interest is to understand how tension, organizational tensions, are communicatively constituted, or if tensions constitute organization. It seems that you shift. And not in this paper, but in another study you did, you shifted from one to the other.

As can be seen, Sophie points out the ambiguity in Robert's conception of (organizational) tensions by stating that he alternates between two possible meanings of the constitutive nature of tensions.

Their discussion continues as follows:

ROBERT: Could it be both?

SOPHIE: Yes, but then analytically how do you distinguish them? How do go from one to the other?

ROBERT: Yeah, that is a really interesting point. So, I don't know, maybe you can tell me ((general laughter in the audience)). But maybe I don't want to ... , Ha-ha! Maybe we, I don't have to choose, but for me it would be to explain it to kind of justify it. Here's that side of it, the tension that constitutes and then here's the other side the constitutive kind of tension. So, but, but ... .

SOPHIE: Maybe it's not choosing one or the other but being clear on what is one or the other.

In his response, Robert agrees that he hasn't questioned the possible double meaning of the constitutive nature of tensions. By asking Sophie to help him figure this out, Robert admits that he doesn't have an answer yet. Moreover, the second part of the discussion suggests that although both meanings associated with the tension-constitution relationship might be pertinent for his research, Robert still needs to reflect on how to analyze this distinction (how tensions constitute organization vs. how tensions are communicatively constituted). Because Robert's work has a strong empirical focus, he needs to tease out this distinction, as Sophie suggests.

While this is just a micro-moment in the larger conversation of CCO scholarship, the discussion between Sophie and Robert reflects CCO scholarship's struggles to formalize certain concepts. By going back and forth between two possible meanings, Robert appears to feel pushed by Sophie to "stabilize" his conceptual definition. Moreover, we see how Sophie uses this ambiguity to point out a lack of formalization in the way Robert (and possibly other CCO scholars) have operationalized this concept, thus echoing the general lack of formalization of CCO methodology/methods we discovered in our analysis of CCO researchers' published discourse (see Boivin et al., 2017). Coming to grips with the double constitutive meaning of organizational tensions, both theoretically/conceptually and analytically/operationally, is important for moving CCO research on this topic forward, Sophie and Robert seem to acknowledge through their respective interventions.

This scholarly exchange illustrates how ambiguity is pragmatically useful in establishing CCO scholarship. Figuring out how to conceptualize and operationalize the constitutive nature of organizational tensions is productive, because it contributes to the formalization of CCO research. In addition, because the concept of organizational tensions has such a high degree of interpretive viability (Benders & van Veen, 2001), scholars may devote future conference papers, journal articles, and book chapters to this ambiguity, thus contributing to CCO scholarship's objectification (see Tolbert & Zucker, 1996). Furthermore, this example also shows that CCO research on a particular topic may be published in reputable journals *before* CCO scholars have formalized research on this topic—Robert has already published an article on organizational tensions that didn't grapple with the mentioned ambiguity in *Communication Monographs*, a flagship journal of the communication discipline.

Another example of the role of conceptual ambiguity in the establishment of CCO scholarship can be observed during Kim's presentation on the concept of *work*—another concept with high interpretive viability. Kim and her co-author aim to explore the role of work in organizing processes through an empirical study, because the concept of work has not received much attention in CCO scholarship. They propose to investigate this concept from a CCO perspective by analyzing interactions on Twitter. As Kim says during her presentation,

> We are not locating ... this practice inside an organization. And this is an intriguing element, because in CCO, given the ontological question that CCO scholarship explores, of course, the question of what is an organization and organizing are central, but here we are outside of that. What we're saying also is that work, of course, is very much present in CCO scholarship, but as a concept, as a theoretical concept, it's a bit less explored. And what we're suggesting ... with this exploration of work, starting from work practices done by workers, that maybe we can use work as a way to deepen CCO reflections.

What Kim suggests here is that the meaning of work in CCO scholarship is vague (one of Giroux's modalities of pragmatic ambiguity), because it has not been conceptually defined or empirically investigated. CCO researchers' conceptualization of work, Kim seems to suggest, could benefit from greater precision, and their paper aims to begin to provide such precision. This example illustrates how identifying the imprecise aspects of a concept in CCO scholarship can contribute to this area of inquiry's legitimacy. By highlighting the vagueness of specific concepts from a CCO perspective, researchers are able to introduce new concepts to CCO scholarship, thus proliferating its conceptual apparatus.

As the next excerpt shows, Kim proposes to manage the pragmatically ambiguous nature of work as a CCO concept by appropriating Taylor and Van Every's (2000) well-known conversation-text dialectic (perhaps *the* most established CCO concept), thereby giving their work more weight and authority:

> So, when we talk about talk-text form, we highlight the fact that in those tweets, we see the textual, that is, making the talk visual in the text, but there is also this possibility of conversation. It is not a conversation that will happen around the tweets, but through the tweets. So the conversation becomes textual. So the text can morph into conversation, can become conversation. And what's also interesting in the tweets is that they embody characteristics that are usually associated with either talk or text, and also that they tend to be mutually exclusive. […] So they can be more or less one or the other. So it's not a question of talk or text, of being one or the other, but it's the possibility of moving from one to the other. So we have here a textual form that can move out of the text and become talk.

Although this is again a mere micro-moment in the larger CCO conversation, this excerpt shows how Kim's talk contributes to CCO scholarship's legitimization by using the ambiguous concept of work and by demonstrating the value and relevance of CCO scholarship's arguably most-used concepts for research (the dialectic between conversation and text). Through her talk, then, she also reinforces the persistence of Taylor and Van Every's concept over time.

Similar to Robert's example, we see here how Kim and her co-author's research identifies a pragmatically ambiguous concept in CCO research, which allows them to explore the concept of work in a new empirical context. As mentioned, by contributing to the proliferation of CCO concepts, their work contributes to CCO scholarship's objectification. To gain more legitimacy as an area of inquiry, though, more concerted, systematic, empirical CCO research is needed (see also Boivin et al., 2017).

Next, we'll explore how the pragmatic use of ambiguities in language that positions Standing Working Group 05's CCO conference subtheme and that positions individual participants within a CCO school figures into CCO scholarship's communicative establishment. Although we distinguish these "positional" ambiguities from the conceptual ambiguities we've previously discussed, the two are closely related and both contribute to the institutionalization of this area of inquiry.

The Pragmatic Use of Ambiguities in Positioning the CCO Subtheme

This subsection shows that EGOS conferees were also pragmatically ambiguous in the language they used to position the SWG 05 Communication as Organization subtheme itself in the broader context of the EGOS conference—as well as their own positioning within this subtheme. To start, we zoom in on how Simon, a professor who is one of the conveners, is pragmatically ambiguous in positioning the subtheme. During his opening speech of the first session on day one of the conference, Simon introduces the subtheme as follows:

> We made a proposal, I think, two years ago, to start the Standing Working Group, to find a home for those people who are interested in studying the relations of organization and communication—some would say the constitutive relations, those who like the label CCO, communication as constitutive of organization. But we … the label "communication as organization", we understand it more broadly. So, it's not only about CCO papers. We've got all kinds of papers that come from people that are interested in studying organization from a communication, narrative, discursive lens.

By defining the subtheme as "not being only about CCO papers", Simon—who is speaking on behalf of the other conveners ("we")—distances himself, at least somewhat, from CCO scholarship because, according to him, the subtheme is not solely about CCO research or for CCO scholars. However, his definition is rather general, for a vast number of studies investigate "organization[s] from a communication, narrative, discursive lens". So, Simon uses Giroux's generality modality of pragmatic ambiguity to include as many people as possible.

Simon then continues to introduce the subtheme without further explaining what he means by "studying organization from a communication, narrative, discursive lens". A few minutes later, though, he elaborates his view when he introduces the subtheme's keynote speaker, Tom—who played an important role in the conference, not only as keynote speaker, but also as a discussant in one of the other sessions:

> We invited Tom, who's a very active member of another working group, a friendly working group, friends of ours, […] because we think there's utility to bring the conversation with this community as well, because we think it's right spot on for things that we're discussing over the next few days. We are interested in the relation also of talk and action and the performativity of language, but also of ((inaudible)) of language, which is a focus area that Tom will talk about.

In this excerpt, Simon positions Tom's research as not being an official part of SWG 05's subtheme. By saying that Tom is "a very active member of another working group, a friendly working group, friends of ours", Simon positions him both outside and inside the community. He then continues to say that Tom's work focuses on subjects that are also of great interest to SWG 05 members. However, to a certain extent, Simon also excludes Tom from the subtheme, even if Tom clearly adopts "a communication, narrative, discursive lens" in his work. The latter could also be due to the EGOS Conference's structural constraints, which groups people into streams. Hence, Simon needs to make a formal connection to allow Tom to participate in the "Organization as Communication" stream. Interestingly, throughout the introduction (of which we only analyze a snippet here), Simon uses general terms that allow him to position the Organization as Communication subtheme as not focusing exclusively on CCO research. In so doing, Simon oscillates between a general definition of the subtheme and a more specific, exclusive definition.

Other participants, however, seem to favor a more exclusive definition. For instance, during the discussion after the keynote speech, one conferee starts her intervention by stating: "We are in a session which is about communication as being constitutive of organization." Furthermore, during some presentations, presenters say things like "in our CCO tradition". By using this specific, non-ambiguous language, participants position the SWG 05 subtheme more squarely within CCO scholarship and appear to want to make its meaning less general. Jennifer's (a well-known senior professor who was invited as a discussant) comments on a set of papers are especially interesting, in this regard. Jennifer concludes her remarks by stating:

> Well, let me summarize by saying, "My gosh, what a long way we've come". I've responded to a lot of panels in communication and a lot of CCO panels, and I really believe that these are really pushing important kinds of ways that we're thinking about what is it that we're doing and where we are going.

By saying that she has "responded to a lot of panels in communication and a lot of CCO panels", Jennifer marks the specificity of CCO scholarship in relation to more general communication research. By using the word "we", Jennifer then switches to a language that suggests that she's speaking on behalf of an already established CCO community ("that we're thinking about what is it that we're doing and where we are going"). What remains somewhat ambiguous (vague) in her statement, though, is if this community is mainly defined by (organizational) communication scholars (because in the previous sentence, she refers to "panels in communication"), or if it also includes scholars from other fields.

Thus, the excerpts in this subsection show how conferees give different and often general or vague meanings to SWG 05's subtheme throughout the conference, thereby positioning CCO research in ambiguous ways in relation to other areas of inquiry and larger fields. By creating the sense that the subtheme is inclusive of other communication perspectives and other kinds of research, conveners like Simon avoid *discursive closure* (Christensen, Morsing, & Thyssen, 2015) that would exclude certain scholars. In this regard, we see how pragmatic ambiguity is used to create a sense of "unified diversity" (Eisenberg, 1984, p. 8). Other participants nevertheless define the subtheme more precisely and exclusively as focusing on CCO scholarship.

Conferees' language was similarly ambiguous when it came to positioning their own research within one of the three main CCO schools of thought, as we'll show next.

The Pragmatic Use of Ambiguities in Positioning within CCO Schools

There seems to be a social consensus among CCO researchers that CCO scholarship has three main "pillars", even though other pillars are and have been emerging. Most CCO review articles and book chapters indeed divide CCO scholarship into the Four Flows Model, the Montréal School, and the Luhmannian School (see Brummans, Cooren, Robichaud, & Taylor, 2014; Cooren, Kuhn, Cornelissen, & Clark, 2011; Koschmann & Campbell, 2019; Schoeneborn et al., 2014; Schoeneborn & Vásquez, 2017). Returning to Giroux's notion of generality, the term "CCO research" is general, because it's a category that includes these schools of thought. Thus, scholars who refer to their work as "CCO research" use more general language than those who specify the school within which they position their work in their published and conference discourse.

Our analysis of published CCO discourse revealed that most researchers tend to refrain from positioning their research within one of these schools and refer to the more general term of "CCO research" (see Boivin et al., 2017). The same can be observed in the language used during the 2015 EGOS conference: few presenters positioned their work within a single school, even though they were sometimes more precise and explicit in the papers they submitted for the subtheme. Specifically, from the 19 presentations the first author recorded, only three presenters clearly positioned their work within a particular school (two in the Montréal School and one in the Luhmanian School). What we observed more frequently is that presenters situated their research by referring to a well-known individual CCO researcher without explicitly mentioning the CCO school with which this scholar is typically associated. Some would, for example, mention that they used concepts like Taylor and Van Every's conversation-text dialectic or Cooren's ventriloquism, but they would not explicitly situate their research within these scholars' school of thought (the Montréal School).

This lack of public positioning within CCO schools may also contribute to creating a sense of "united diversity" within the CCO community. That is, by not verbally taking positions within one of the schools, conferees mainly emphasized the similarities between CCO researchers and created an *esprit de corps*. In so doing, they evaded key debates between the schools. Elucidating the unique contributions of each school may be important, though, because clarifying the strengths of each of the CCO pillars may help advance CCO scholarship's objectification as a unique area of inquiry that is composed of distinct approaches to studying the constitutive force of communication in processes of organizing. Hence, our analysis suggests that it will be beneficial for CCO scholarship's communicative establishment to organize more public fora (preconferences, panels, roundtables, etc.), similar to some of the already published fora (see Cooren et al., 2011; Schoeneborn et al., 2014), that tease out the differences between its existing and emerging pillars.

Conclusion

This chapter has highlighted the key role of pragmatic ambiguity in the communicative constitution of organization through the analysis of academic conference discourse. In this final section, we'll discuss the implications of our work for CCO research and suggest avenues for future inquiry.

First, this chapter shows how integral ambiguity is to understanding the communication practices through which organizations are produced and sustained. As mentioned, the concept of equivocality is key in Weick's (1979) model of organizing, which was not only an important source of inspiration for Taylor and Van Every (2000), but also for Robert McPhee and Pamela Zaug in their seminal 2000 article on the Four Flows Model, as well as for many other scholars who were trained or inspired by these CCO pioneers. It could be argued, then, that Weick's idea that "people communicate [or interact] in an effort to reduce the number of possible interpretations, and in so doing make coordinated action possible" (Eisenberg, 2006, p. 1696) sparked for an important part the foundational work that led to CCO scholarship as an area of research, which increasingly has "a legitimate identity of its own" (Kuhn, 2005, pp. 621–622).

As we've shown, equivocality or ambiguity is indeed what makes people communicate and, in so doing, organize. More precisely, however, it's a *discursive resource* that enables *and* constrains people in the communication through which social collectives are organized. Hence, ambiguity is pragmatically useful in the communicative constitution of organizations. And because "meaning is always indeterminate" (Vásquez & Kuhn, 2019), it's worth studying how ambiguity figures into the communication that generates both processes of organizing and *dis*organizing (see also Brummans, 2007; Vásquez, Schoeneborn, & Sergi, 2016).

Second, in line with the observation that studying pragmatic ambiguity is useful for gaining insight into dis/organizing processes, our exploratory research suggests that pragmatic ambiguity may advance and impede processes of organizational institutionalization. Scholars are increasingly agreeing that communication is vital to institutionalization processes (see Cornelissen et al., 2015; Kuhn, 2005), yet few studies have examined the communicative constitution of organizations from a (neo-)institutional perspective (see also Schoeneborn et al., 2019). Giroux's (2006) concept of pragmatic ambiguity could provide a useful linchpin for connecting CCO and institutional scholarship. Our research reveals, for example, that investigating how the pragmatic use of ambiguity in conference talk (as well as published texts; see Boivin et al., 2017) contributes to the dis/establishment (or dis/institutionalization) of fluid social collectives like the CCO research community (see Dobusch & Schoeneborn, 2015). As Leonhard Dobusch and Dennis Schoeneborn (2015) note, social collectives with fluid boundaries and latent, contested, unclear—and, we might add, ambiguous—membership still achieve a certain degree of organizationality. Their empirical analysis of Anonymous shows that "if social collectives are fluid in the sense of having unclear membership, they can activate organizational actorhood at least temporarily through carefully prepared and staged performances of identity claims" (p. 1007). This chapter advances this research on organizationality by revealing that making numerous *ambiguous* identity and positioning claims may both benefit and hinder the establishment of a more or less fluid collective like the CCO scholarly community.

Third, this chapter illustrates the importance of practicing reflexivity as a scholarly community or field of practice in the making. Through this reflexivity, scholars can become more aware of their blindfolds, investments in contests for various forms of social, cultural, and symbolic capital, and attachments to positions (see Bourdieu & Wacquant, 1992; Brummans, 2015). However, practicing this reflexivity as a scholarly community requires that the community "rewards" scholars for questioning the consequences of their actions in the world, so this kind of criticality becomes part of the mutual constitution between scholars and field of practice. It's imperative, then, for a field to reflect systematically on its modes of operating in order to prevent itself from getting caught up in its own dynamics. For instance, this could be achieved by opening a stream to conferees from other streams during an academic conference, as could be seen during the 2015 EGOS conference when Tom was invited to give a keynote presentation. Researchers could also work more actively with colleagues from other fields or disciplines. This reflexivity may destabilize a field's communicative constitution, yet it does not trivialize, deny, or delegitimize its operations. To the contrary, it's key for understanding how certain modes of operating inhibit or derail the field's production of knowledge (in his 2005 essay, Timothy Kuhn makes a similar argument from a neo-institutional perspective, citing DiMaggio & Powell, 1983).

In line with these ideas, this chapter shows how useful it is for the CCO scholarly community to reflect on the ways its members' own communication practices play into its dis/organization (or dis/organzing), and how useful Giroux's pragmatic ambiguity lens is for cultivating this reflexivity in their conference (and also published) discourse. It illustrates that conferences offer rare opportunities to discuss, debate, and address questions that are central to the communicative dis/establishment of a budding scholarly field of practice. These meetings are events during which "disparate constituents [can] become aware of their common concerns, join together, share information, coordinate their actions, shape or subvert agendas, and mutually influence [the] structuration [of their field]" (Anand & Jones, 2008, p. 1037, cited in Hardy & Maguire, 2010, p. 1366) by publicizing and discussing their work. Because such events provide an opportunity to open multiple discursive spaces that can influence the configuration of a field of practice (Hardy & Maguire, 2010), they can become important public fora for reflecting on a field's modes of operating and, thereby, affecting its communicative constitution.

A conference's field-configuring force was exemplified during the 2014 "CCO in Practice" EGOS preconference in Rotterdam, the Netherlands. This event brought together CCO scholars and organizational practitioners to discuss how CCO research can inform organizational practice. As the second author (who participated in the event) recalls, CCO scholars seemed to become more and more aware through their preconference talk that theoretical/conceptual ambiguities were becoming the norm within CCO research, and that such ambiguities could adversely affect the sedimentation (Tolbert & Zucker, 1996) of their scholarship within different academic *and* professional fields. In turn, this collective practice of reflexivity created concerns about the "academic-professional gap" (see Van Vuuren & Knoers, this volume) within the CCO research community that prevail to this day (see also Koschmann & Campbell, 2019), even though the development of theoretical concepts continues to be CCO scholars' central matter of concern.

References

Anand, N., & Jones, B. C. (2008). Tournament rituals, category dynamics, and field configuration: The case of the Booker Prize. *Journal of Management Studies, 45*(6), 1036–1060.

Benders, J., & van Veen, K. (2001). What's in a fashion? Interpretative viability and management fashions. *Organization, 8*(1), 33–53.

Boivin, G. (2018). *The institutionalization of an area of research through published and public discourse: The case of CCO scholarship* [Unpublished doctoral thesis]. Université de Montréal.

Boivin, G., Brummans, B. H. J. M., & Barker, J. R. (2017). The institutionalization of CCO scholarship: Trends from 2000 to 2015. *Management Communication Quarterly, 31*(3) 331–355.

Bourdieu, P., & Wacquant, L. J. D. (1992). *An invitation to reflexive sociology.* The University of Chicago Press.

Braam, G. (2012). Balanced scorecard's interpretative variability and organizational change. In C.-H. Quah & O. L. Dar (Eds.), *Business dynamics in the 21ˢᵗ century* (pp. 99–112). InTech.

Brummans, B. H. J. M. (2007). Death by document: Tracing the agency of a text. *Qualitative Inquiry, 13*(5), 711–727.

Brummans, B. H. J. M. (2015). "Turning the lens on ourselves": Bourdieu's reflexivity in practice. In A. Tatli, M. Özbilgin, & M. Karatas-Özkan (Eds.), *Bourdieu, organization and management* (pp. 70–94). Routledge.

Brummans, B. H. J. M., Cooren, F., Robichaud, D., & Taylor, J. R. (2014). Approaches to the communicative constitution of organizations. In L. L. Putnam & D. K. Mumby (Eds.), *The SAGE handbook of organizational communication: Advances in theory, research, and methods* (3rd edn., pp. 173–194). SAGE.

Brummans, B. H. J. M., & Miller, K. I. (2004). The effect of ambiguity on the implementation of a social change initiative. *Communication Research Reports, 21*(1), 1–10.

Brummans, B. H. J. M., & Putnam, L. L. (2003). New directions in organizational culture research: A review of Martin's "Organizational culture: Mapping the terrain" and Alvesson's "Understanding organizational culture". *Organization, 10*(3), 640–644.

Callon, M. (1986). Some elements of a sociology of translation: Domestication of the scallops and the fishermen of St Brieuc Bay. In J. Law (Ed.), *Power, action, and belief: A new sociology of knowledge* (pp. 196–233). Routledge.

Castor, T. R. (2017). Ambiguity. In C. R. Scott & L. K. Lewis (Eds.), *The international encyclopedia of organizational communication* (pp. 1–11). Wiley Blackwell.

Christensen, L. T., Morsing, M., & Thyssen, O. (2015). Discursive closure and discursive openings in sustainability. *Management Communication Quarterly, 29*(1), 135–144.

Cooren, F., Kuhn, T., Cornelissen, J. P., & Clark, T. (2011). Communication, organizing and organization: An overview and introduction to the special issue. *Organization Studies, 32*(9), 1149–1170.

Cornelissen, J. P., Durand, R., Fiss, P. C., Lammers, J. C., & Vaara, E. (2015). Putting communication front and center in institutional theory and analysis. *Academy of Management Review, 40*(1), 10–27.

DiMaggio, P. J., & Powell, W. W. (1983). The iron cage revisited: Institutional isomorphism and collective rationality in organizational fields. *American Sociological Review, 48*(2), 147–160.

Dobusch, L., & Schoeneborn, D. (2015). Fluidity, identity, and organizationality: The communicative constitution of Anonymous. *Journal of Management Studies, 52*(8), 1005–1035.

Eisenberg, E. M. (1984). Ambiguity as strategy in organizational communication. *Communication Monographs, 51*(3), 227–242.

Eisenberg, E. M. (2006). Karl Weick and the aesthetics of contingency. *Organization Studies, 27*(11), 1693–1707.

Eisenberg, E. M. (2007). *Strategic ambiguities: Essays on communication, organization, and identity.* SAGE.

Fassin, Y., & Van Rossem, A. (2009). Corporate governance in the debate on CSR and ethics: Sensemaking of social issues in management by authorities and CEOs. *Corporate Governance, 17*(5), 573–593.

Giroux, H., & Taylor, J. R. (1999). L'évolution du discours sur la qualité: D'une traduction à l'autre. *Communication & Organisation, 15*, 36–68.

Giroux, H., & Taylor, J. R. (2002). The justification of knowledge: Tracking the translations of quality. *Management Learning, 33*(4), 497–517.

Giroux, H. (2006). "It was such a handy term": Management fashions and pragmatic ambiguity. *Journal of Management Studies, 43*(6), 1227–1260.

Hardy, C., & Maguire, S. (2010). Discourse, field-configuring events, and change in organizations and institutional fields: Narratives of DDT and the Stockholm Convention. *Academy of Management Journal, 53*(6), 1365–1392.

Koschmann, M. A., & Campbell, T. G. (2019). A critical review of how communication scholarship is represented in textbooks: The case of organizational communication and CCO theory. *Annals of the International Communication Association, 43*(2), 173–191.

Kuhn, T. (2005). The institutionalization of Alta in organizational communication studies. *Management Communication Quarterly, 18*(4), 595–603.

Latour, B. (1987). *Science in action: How to follows scientists and engineers through society.* Harvard University Press.

Martin, J. (2002). *Organizational culture: Mapping the terrain.* SAGE.

Phillips, N., Lawrence, T. B., & Hardy, C. (2004). Discourse and institutions. *Academy of Management Review, 29*(4), 635–652.

Putnam, L. L., Fairhurst, G. T., & Banghart, S. (2016). Contradictions, dialectics, and paradoxes in organizations: A constitutive approach. *Academy of Management Annals, 10*(1), 65–171.

Røvik, K. A. (2002). The secrets of the winners: Management ideas that flow. In K. Sahlin-Andersson & L. Engwall (Eds.), *The expansion of management knowledge: Carriers, flows, and sources* (pp. 113–144). Stanford University Press.

Schoeneborn, D., Blaschke, S., Cooren, F., McPhee, R. D., Seidl, D., & Taylor, J. R. (2014). The three schools of CCO thinking: Interactive dialogue and systematic comparison. *Management Communication Quarterly, 28*(2), 285–316.

Schoeneborn, D., Kuhn, T. R., & Kärreman, D. (2019). The communicative constitution of organization, organizing, and organizationality. *Organization Studies, 40*(4), 475–496.

Schoeneborn, D., & Vásquez, C. (2017). Communication as constitutive of organization. In C. R. Scott & L. K. Lewis (Eds.), *The international encyclopedia of organizational communication* (pp. 1–21). Wiley Blackwell.

Taylor, J. R., & Van Every, E. J. (2000). *The emergent organization: Communication as its site and surface.* Lawrence Erlbaum.

Tolbert, P. S., & Zucker, L. G. (1996). The institutionalization of institutional theory. In S. R. Clegg, C. Hardy, & W. R. Nord (Eds.), *Handbook of organization studies* (pp. 175–190). SAGE.

Vásquez, C., & Kuhn, T. (Eds.). (2019). *Dis/organization as communication: Exploring the disordering, disruptive and chaotic properties of communication.* Routledge.

Vásquez, C., Schoeneborn, D., & Sergi, V. (2016). Summoning the spirits: Organizational texts and the (dis)ordering properties of communication. *Human Relations, 69*(3), 629–659.

Weick, K. E. (1979). *The social psychology of organizing* (2nd edn.). McGraw-Hill.

Weick, K. E., Sutcliffe, K. M., & Obstfeld, D. (2005). Organizing and the process of sensemaking. *Organization Science, 16*(4), 409–421.

3

ORGANIZATION AS CONVERSATION AND TEXT

Veronica R. Dawson

Imagine that you work for a marketing and advertising agency and your team is charged with managing the social media presence for an all-natural candy manufacturer. You've just gathered with your team and client representatives in a swanky meeting room to discuss the brand's social media plan for the next three months. In front of you is the meeting agenda, last month's minutes, the company's social media policy, a list of the products that the client wants to promote next, another list with ideas the client has brought for an upcoming Facebook contest and a few pages of clippings representing the most outstanding social media interactions on Facebook, Instagram, and Pinterest for the past month. Going down the agenda, you discuss the items in order, the Facebook product contest, the number of recipe shares on Pinterest, the "Eat in Color" Instagram posts, and engagement with each of these items. The conversation weaves in and out of topic; you all agree that you are creating "a friendly, colorful brand", which should guide the company's social media marketing strategy moving forward. The agenda, meeting minutes, and the next month's strategy (down to each post to be scheduled for posting on individual platforms) are printed in a document to be reviewed, followed, adjusted, and discussed, with actionable feedback throughout the month and at the next meeting. The formatting of the documents is always the same, the different content is determined by the ongoing communication on various company social media platforms.

This short example comes from a meeting[1] I attended a couple of years ago as part of a research project interested in the impact of social media interactions on organizational identity ("the friendly, colorful brand" description feeds into employees' notion of who they are as an organization). I sat through many such social media marketing meetings with the same company, and they inevitably followed a similar structure, driven by organizational goals and strategies, resulting in specific practices to meet these goals, all further encased in guiding policies. The structure had to be rigid enough to provide guidance about social media marketing strategy, yet flexible enough to be modified quickly in response to the fast pace of social media platform interactions.

In CCO terms, what this example demonstrates is communication as the site (studied as the conversation in the meetings and the interactions taking place on social media platforms) and the surface (studied as the text of social media policy, agendas, minutes and so on) of an organization (Taylor, 1999). Conversation and text, as the site and surface of an organization, are a

DOI: 10.4324/9781003224914-5

dynamic dialectic (Putnam, 2013): conversations scale up to text (i.e. policy) and text continuously guides conversations (i.e. enacting said policy in interaction). The relationship between conversation and text is a recursive tension and is the basis of the communicative definition of organization. In the rest of this chapter, I explore this foundational relationship by explaining the basic theorizing behind it, its connection to notions of materiality in organizations and communication, current methodological approaches and empirical applications of the dynamic, and conclude with suggested future directions in theorizing and research utilizing conversation-text. The argument I make is that interpreting organizations as conversation-text is historically significant to CCO, continually generative of theory and research, and an important intellectual tool in understanding the complexities of organizations as communication.

The Duality of Conversation and Text Explained

Organization emerges "in the intersection of a) an ongoing object-oriented conversation specific to a community of practice, and b) the text that names, represents, or pictures it" (Taylor, 2006, p. 156). Stated like this, the communicative constitution of organization materializes (more on materialization later) in the conversation and text dynamic, two of the building blocks of the Montreal School approach to CCO. Everyday object- and goal-oriented conversation specific to a given community of practice is the "doing" of organization and the recorded forms of these conversations might accumulate to become the "authoritative" text of the organization, to be referred to again and again (i.e. minutes, agenda, and strategy in the meeting example above). Authoritative texts are abstractions of conversations that nevertheless induce a common reading (Koschmann, 2013) and whenever they are invoked in conversation by organizational members, they have the power to coordinate and control activity (Kuhn, 2008). Any time we refer to what the policy says at work or the strategy we agreed upon in a meeting, we are referring to an authoritative text, which informs our present conversations with colleagues or clients and, in a sense, represents the organization. Put another way, the goal of conversation is to sustain interaction to the effect of co-orientation (more on co-orientation shortly) toward shared tasks; the goal of text is to produce a collectively negotiated interpretation of the (organizational) world across time and space, which in turn repeatedly guides co-oriented actions toward task completion (Taylor & Van Every, 2000).

Conversation and text exist in a recursive relationship defined by circumstances such as time, space, identity, occasion, history, and purpose (Robichaud, Giroux, & Taylor, 2004; Taylor, 1999). Conversation is somewhat temporary, situated, fleeting interaction. Even when we have the same conversations again and again, until the matter of the conversation is recorded in some form, it remains situation specific. Imagine a professor covering class policy in the beginning of the semester. As a professor she may instruct the students to perform certain actions, but unless the demands are specified in the syllabus (the class contract), the professor's right to hold students accountable for whether they perform these actions or not, just because the professor said so at one time, can be questioned by the students and by the university. Text, on the other hand, is somewhat more permanent, or *transcendent* (Cooren, 2006; Taylor, 1999; Taylor, Cooren, Giroux, & Robichaud, 1996). The notion of transcendence has a rich theoretical history (for more, see the works of Derrida, Austin, and Garfinkel), but my aim doesn't require us to go into this history. The transcendence of text simply allows for its relative permanence or iterability (capacity to be repeated in different contexts), allowing for us as communicators to refer to it, as a sign of recorded communication beyond local interactions.

Because the notion of text is somewhat more abstract than that of conversation (interaction), it is worth thinking of texts as either *concrete* or *figurative* (Kuhn, 2008). Concrete texts are the symbolic representations of communication, such as lists, emails, policies and so on. Concrete texts are what most people would identify as a text and are characterized by more or less permanence. Figurative texts are abstract representations of repeated organizational activity, such as practices, rituals, and communities of practice, and, as such, they are rarely "written". Thus, if the professor's demands are part of class policy or assignment outlined in the syllabus, they also become a somewhat permanent part of a *concrete* organizational text representing not just the particular class, but also the university. Professor and students can refer to the syllabus when checking and conversing over the rules of the class and during their efforts to achieve its learning outcomes (goals). This professor-student interaction of going over the syllabus also begins to create the *figurative* organizational text of a particular class, (what one hopes develops into) a community of practice with its own unique dynamics, practices, rules and rituals, that may or may not be typical of what college classes are like in general.

To summarize, in order to understand the constitution of organization through communication, we must analyze both the conversations and documents that make up the routines of organizational life (Cooren, 2015). This relationship, in which conversation and text recursively shape one another, allows for communication to become *distanciated*: to extend through space and time. Distanciation (Ricoeur, 1981) is achieved through text, which in its relative permanence can transcend space, time, and context and thus inform future conversation that occurs in different contexts. Texts that achieve this kind of iterability are called authoritative texts and materialize conversation.

The Materialization of Communication

How did conversation and text come to explain and represent the process of organizing in the CCO literature? Can employee conversations and the texts they produce really be called an organization in the brick and mortar sense of the word? By answering these questions, we would be able to better understand the theoretical foundations and empirical usefulness of the conversation-text dynamic, which I address in the next section. To start, we ought to backtrack a bit and look at the relationship between discourse and materiality or, put otherwise, between human and non-human action.

From its inception, CCO has wanted to better understand how the process of communication produces, reproduces and stabilizes the material aspects of organizations and organizing practices. Understanding this is predicated on defining (and re-defining) the relationship between discourse and materiality which has resulted in the "material turn" (explained in detail by Cooren, 2020); the term keeps with previous "turns" in organizational communication, such as the "linguistic turn" of the 1980s. While not entirely new, the move to recognize, and ameliorate, the anthropocentric focus of the social sciences (organizational communication being among those) has been ongoing for about 20 years, and the material turn is now identified as the "new materialism" (for examples see Cooren, 2020; Kuhn, Ashcraft, & Cooren, 2019, and the journal issue their article introduces). The conversation-text dynamic is both reflective of and resulting from the material turn, as it represents the central relationship entertained therein, that of discourse and materiality. Hence, I loosely base the following explication on Cooren's (2020) perspectives on the relationship between discourse and materiality.

The relationship between conversation and text in CCO has been described and interpreted in various ways. One such way is as a dialectic, a tension among opposites held together and managed through "both-and" strategies (most notably, by Putnam, 2013, 2015). A dialectical relationship is at once unresolvable, productive, and recursive. When viewed as a dialectic, conversation and text are seen as separate, but intertwined, dependent on one another—akin to a company policy (the text) and how it is continuously enacted by organizational members in practice (the conversation). Like the more encompassing relationship between discourse and materiality, the relationship between conversation and text has also been interpreted through the lens of "sociomateriality" (notably by Novak, 2016; Orlikowski, 2007, 2010; Orlikowski & Scott, 2008; Scott & Orlikowski, 2014; Szabo, 2016). When Orlikowski came up with the concept of sociomateriality, she meant that "the social and the material are considered to be inextricably related—there is no social that is not also material, and no material that is not also social" (Orlikowski, 2007, p. 1437). In organizations, the social are the employees and the various interactions (conversations) they have among one another and importantly, with the material, which most frequently is technology (text) or the "things" of organization (computers, software, and even online search engines and social media platforms). Technology as text possesses (non-human) agency in organizing, which means that it facilitates human action and can itself act to direct and coordinate conversation. This toggling between conversation and text, and their sociomaterial agencies, in organizations produces an emerging structure called imbrication, an essential CCO process and term covered in its own right in the next section of this chapter. In reference to the conversation-text relationship, imbrication indicates the agencies' mutual constitution through interaction. From an imbrication perspective (perhaps best known through Leonardi, 2011, 2012, 2013), agency—who or what can act to constitute organization—becomes a central problematic. The resolution of this problematic is that agency is a "both/and" issue for CCO: it is, thus, always multiple (see Larson & Mengis, this volume).

Understanding how theorizing the discursive-material relationship over the years has influenced the conversation-text dynamic is of theoretical and empirical importance because it explains the constitutive properties of conversation-text and underscores its future theory and research-generative potential. The discursive and material relationship defines communication (and communication defines that relationship) in a way similar to how the conversation and text relationship defines organization (and organization represents that relationship). Interpreting organizations as the relationship between conversation and text (which was theorized by Taylor in the late 1990 and early 2000) predates, and makes possible, our discussions of the new materialism in communication studies and, as I will show in my discussion of empirical research, is impacted by what Cooren (2020) calls the materialization of communication.

The Conversation-Text Dynamic and Its Mediating Processes

Thus far, I've described the conversation-text relationship as essential in CCO, because it concisely represents the revolutionary idea put forth by Taylor and Van Every (2000) that communication doesn't only happen in organizations, but that organization also happens in communication. But how, might we ask, does conversation-become-text-become-organization? The answer, for CCO, is through a number of mediating processes that build on each other to achieve self-structuring: lamination, imbrication, coordination and translation. Below I review these processes in pairs.

Lamination and Imbrication

Lamination, a term first associated with Goffman (1974) and notably with Boden (1994), who writes of "the laminated effect of meeting upon meeting" (p. 91), is the process of interlacing conversations and interactions into a recognizable pattern of communication. If texts are the representations of the collective organizational voice, then the multiple texts that come to represent any single organization are all "laminated" onto one another to create "a global interactive and representational tissue [of the organization] held together by information flows" (Taylor & Van Every, 2000). Boden's lamination paves the road of a CCO specific concept, that of imbrication, the scaling up of everyday conversation to organizational text.

Imbrication, also thought of as tiling because it reminds one of overlapping roof tiles (Taylor & Van Every, 2000), is the connected, overlapping structure that emerges from goal-oriented organizational conversation over time and space. Imbrication is the process of transition from fleeting conversation to more stable organizational text and back to conversation. It "constitutes the map of the organization, its essential structure, which is found in the conversational dynamics of its members" (Taylor & Van Every, 2000, p. 323). Above, I described the relationship between conversation and text as recursive; imbrication is what mediates this recursive relationship. I will briefly illustrate imbrication with an example using the concept of organizational identity constructed in the marketing meeting presented earlier in this chapter.

An organization's identity is a text that has emerged from the tiling of numerous conversations attempting to answer the question "Who are we as an organization?" Organizational identity has been defined differently based on the background of the authors defining the concept—ranging from a rather enduring and unchangeable characteristic of an organization, to a continuously negotiated flexible process, to a dialectic that is *both* enduring *and* flexible. Early on, organizational identity was defined as what is central, distinct, and enduring about an organization (Albert & Whetten, 1985). Ten years later, the definition had evolved to the "unfolding and stylized narratives about the soul and essence of the organization" (Ashforth & Mael, 1996, p. 21). The turbulent organizational and communicative environments in which people operate today have challenged any completely stable notion of identity, thus conceptualizing organizational identity as "adaptive instability" (Gioia, Schultz, & Corley, 2000). However, and also in response to the turbulent age we live in, both "individuals and organizations are in hot pursuit of solid, favorable, identities even as such identities become harder to capture and sustain" (Cheney & Christensen, 2001, p. 241). So, even though organizational identity is a dialectical concept (Larson & Gill, 2017), we can agree, for the purposes of this writing, that this dialectic is *both* multiple and contested *and* stable and consistent (Alvesson, 2010; Sveningsson & Alvesson, 2003).

The example opening this chapter describes a monthly marketing meeting, which deals with social media strategy designed to represent an organization and its product. We can assume that the organization's social media strategy is informed by relatively stable artifacts such as company values, a mission statement, and what those who work in social media strategy call "organizational voice". Here is how a marketing manager described her organization's voice on social media during a one-on-one interview with me:

> It is just a playful, authentic being, um, that, you know playful is the perfect word: playful, realistic, it is concerned with the causes that revolve around the processes of making our products. We really talk about the bees. I think authentic, playful, colorful, sincere, are all great words that I would use to describe the brand and then the voice of how we communicate online.

When I attended the meetings at the marketing office, I heard this description, using almost the exact same words, repeated multiple times by various employees of the company or the agency they worked with. This description was illustrated in the company's printed marketing materials, where colorful, playful imagery dominated. More importantly, the colorful, playful imagery continued in all internal paperwork, including the printed paper agenda for every meeting. Given the social media strategy and imagery, not surprisingly, others I interviewed described the company as "colorful", "authentic", "playful", and deeply concerned with the pollinator environmental crisis. If one is to visit this organization's website today and click on their origins story, the first image is that of a bee. Imbrication is anchored in the practices that led to the strategy, the posts, the meetings, the printed materials, and the website, where "the object becomes clear, and roles are not for the moment up for negotiation" (Taylor, 2009, p. 161), and decisions made during numerous meetings solidify. And while the social media strategy, posts, and materials might be agreed upon for the moment, they will again be questioned, amended, or reiterated at the next meeting, based on interactional developments online. Despite their relative fluidity, the elements described here make up how organizational employees answer the ever-important question "Who are we as an organization?"

Coorientation and Translation

Conversation is the interactive, situated events in which organizing occurs (Taylor et al., 1996; Taylor & Robichaud, 2004). Coorientation is the relationship that makes certain conversations organizational. It is the process by which organizational members orient toward something to be done and around the ways in which to do it (Taylor & Van Every, 2000, 2011). Communication is in the center of coorientation, as both the thing to do and how to do it are negotiated. Text, then is the recording of past cooriented conversations that now marks the result of collective action and upon which future conversations unfold. For example, in organizational texts emerges the identity of an organization or what Taylor and Cooren (1997) call the "us-ness" and Taylor and Van Every (2011) call the "we-ness" of organization that is conversationally referred to over and over again in the process of work.

The act of organizing, then, is mostly a matter of coorientation by which people orient to a common objective, creating imbrication between various actions (Cooren, 2015). How coorientation and imbrication create organization becomes clearer if we follow Cooren's thinking and break down cooriented collective action into sub-orientations, which correspond to various "tiled" sub-actions. Consider the marketing meeting in the beginning of this chapter. The big act of the meeting is creating the next social media strategy. The candy company has its own marketing team and they have recruited the help of an agency team. Throughout the meeting, the strategy is broken down into parts, such as the Facebook product contest, the number of recipe shares on Pinterest, the "Eat in Color" Instagram posts, and engagement with each of these items. Throughout the meeting, a different actor reports on each subject in detail and proposes new actions to become part of the strategy next. All of these sub-actions are cooriented toward one big objective: the next social media strategy. These coorientation systems (i.e. team members' orientation toward an object of importance, the strategy) "tile up" and eventually translate into structured organizational strategy text (there, quite literally, is a template).

Communication, understood as the ongoing effort to make sense of circumstances in which people collectively find themselves, involves both conversation and sensemaking (for more on sensemaking, see Weick's work). In terms of conversation, people interact to make sense of a situation. Sensemaking, however, involves translating experience into language, spoken or written, and the production of symbols or text (Cooren, 2010; Taylor & Van Every, 2000). Recursively, conversation has to be translated into text and text into conversation for organizing—and communication more generally—to happen. Studying organization as emergent from the conversation-text relationship necessitates that we discuss this translation. Translation is the process by which conversation and text enter into the structuring of the dynamic processes of communication and organization. Text is the (re)presentation of laminated conversation. An authoritative text, in particular, is what makes the organization meaningfully present to its members—in logos, mission statements, value statements, rules, and so on. The authoritative text is also the script that coordinates and controls the actions of organizational members, and which they reflexively follow to (re)produce the organization in conversation (Kuhn, 2008; Koschmann, 2013).

Recall the earlier discussion of sociomateriality and the assertion within CCO that humans share their actions (and thus their agency) with, for example, technology to the extent that technology allows organizational employees to get work done. Now consider the professor's syllabus presented earlier, imagine an operations manual, or remember your most recent employee handbook. Such organizational texts are, on the one hand, the product of human and technological (e.g. word-processing program) agency and, on the other hand, represent the organization (re)interpreted symbolically as authoritative text that guides action (thus has agency) in various contexts. But while context influences how we interpret such texts, it doesn't determine that interpretation-texts have certain autonomy, which they have achieved through the lamination of cooriented action (Cooren, 2010). Importantly, (authoritative) texts do not determine employee actions, but rather help actors perform the organization into being through deliberate action. Consider this dynamic during your next customer service call when a representative quotes you the policy as explanation of why an action can/not be taken.

So, how does conversation-become-text-become-organization? Simply put, through the processes that mediate the conversation-text dynamic: the cooriented tiling (lamination and imbrication) of fleeting conversations translated into permanent texts (structures). Some of these texts become authoritative and come to coordinate and control organizing actions (acquire agency). Such texts become representative of the organization itself.

Current Methodologies and Research

It has been more than 20 years since Taylor (1999) "opened up a field of inquiry" and wrote in an introduction to a special issue in *Communication Review*, "It is our hope that the presentation of our preliminary reflections in this issue will stimulate others to take up the gauntlet and develop the theory further" (p. 23). Since then, many have taken up the gauntlet of theory development, and CCO and the Montreal School, which James Taylor represents, have become a considerable force of inquiry within organizational communication. Below I provide a glimpse into the current developments in methodology and research concerning and utilizing the conversation-text dynamic.

Methodologies Utilizing the Conversation-Text Dynamic

Although I have conceptually delineated cooriented systems of conversations and the resulting organizational authoritative texts, it is important to acknowledge that organizational actors and researchers alike come to take the *organizationality* (an adjective denoting "organization-like", or what makes communicative practice more or less organizational) of organizations for granted. Thus, to glance into the process of organizational emergence from the conversation-text dynamic, CCO scholars have utilized utterance-based methods such as conversation analysis (CA) (notably, Cooren's extensive work), critical discourse analysis (CDA) (see Szabo, 2016, where she demonstrates the unique ways in which discourse, agency, and materiality culminate in organizing the economy), and speech act analysis (see Dobusch & Schoeneborn, 2015, a work that is also of note because the speech acts studied occurred in online communication to constitute organizationality rather than organization; more on this below). Methodologies focusing on communication events most readily allow for researchers to look *at* communication, rather than *through* it to understand organizational processes (Schoeneborn, Kuhn, & Kärreman, 2019). The focus on singular communication events, though, has been critiqued (see Blaschke, Schoeneborn, & Seidl, 2012) for missing the forest for the trees and thus losing sight of the organization as an entity in favor of the constitutive events comprising it. In their critique the authors offer a communication-centered social network analysis methodology aiming to illuminate *the* organization.

Although not explicitly in an effort to step outside of the utterance-based research methodology paradigm, CCO scholars utilizing, at least partially, the conversation-text dynamic also approach organizing ethnographically. Often, to gather the kind of data that allows the observation and recording of conversation and performances, along with its (concrete or figurative) textual representation, researchers seek out first-hand attendance (see Novak, 2016, and his critical-interpretive analysis of the work of "homelessness"; see Laapotti & Mikkola's 2019 study of the constitutive effects of "problem talk" in hospital management meetings) or recordings of organizational meetings and/ or cases to be analyzed (see Kuhn's work on a theory of the firm). Along with primary data sources such as meetings, other instances of conversation/text are frequently engaged, such as technology (see Leonardi's work) and social media (see Dawson, 2018; Kavada, 2015; Orlikowski & Scott, 2012). Finally, and indicative of the tension ever-present in the conversation-text dynamic, ethnographic tension-centered forms of analysis have been utilized to understand how conversation-text constitute organization (see Putnam's work), authority (i.e. Porter, Kuhn, & Nerlich, 2018), and even disorganization (see edited volume by Vásquez & Kuhn, 2019).

Emergent Organization in Meetings and Observation

If communication is the site and surface of the emergent organization, then the careful analysis of organizational meeting communication has been the prevalent method and context of revealing the dynamics of its emergence. Research framed by CCO's foundational dynamic builds on direct and indirect observations of organizational meetings and resulting decision-making. Taylor and Robichaud (2004) provide one of the foundational studies exemplifying the constitutive power of the conversation-text dynamic through the observation, recording, and conversation analysis of a senior management meeting. It is precisely in this earlier work where the authors explain conversation as the site of organizing, coorientation as organizational members' relation to a common object of concern, and text as "recollections and understandings" (p. 397) formed over time (through sensemaking) and referred to in future conversations. An important value of this early study is the delineation of terminology and the empirical application of the conversation-text dynamic. Importantly, coorientation, this article demonstrates, is easily observed during organizational meetings, a valuable methodological takeaway.

Indeed, organizational meeting observations have since become a preferred method to empirically study the conversation-text dynamic. Pälli and Lehtinen (2013) study managerial meetings to uncover the communicative "(re)construction" of organizational strategy; specifically, they demonstrate how texts are attributed agency and then used in persuasive ways to legitimize action. Szabo (2016), creatively using Kuhn's (2008) theorizing of authoritative texts to interpret organizational rituals differently, suggests that rituals observed in meetings act as authoritative texts: produced, authorized, and reproduced by a collective to guide organizational action. Sometimes, meetings are followed up by ethnographic interviews, which provide context and perspective to the observations. Koschmann (2013) showed the formation of collective identity during an interorganizational collaboration (one organization with many subcommittees) utilizing both public meeting observation and follow-up interviews. In this study, he shows that an organization's identity is an authoritative text, frequently called upon by organizational actors for their own intents and purposes.

Conversation-Text, a Generative Force

The conversation-text dynamic is generative of new theories, concepts, and ideas. For example, Kuhn (2008) builds his *communicative theory of the firm* on the concept of authoritative text as he reviewed a second-hand account of General Motors' governance struggles. It is primarily the concept of the authoritative text that makes the theory of the firm (a pre-existing set of theories, actually) *communicative*, as that text is what (1) when bound up with practice creates value and ensures the longevity of the organization, (2) marshals consent, and (3) attracts social, cultural, and economic capital, thus greatly enriching the conceptualization of the firm. Cooren (2010, 2012) based his concept of *ventriloquism* on authoritative texts. When a speaker (or a collective of speakers, such as organizational members or students in a class) invokes a text, they give it a voice, a body, a form (the class syllabus "says"); the speaker or collective is similarly invoked by the text in its authoring and reading (we as a class have agreed that the text of the syllabus is our class creation and contract). The concept of ventriloquism illustrates a more complex aspect of the conversation-text dynamic where human actors make contracts, policies, and other non-human organizational actors "speak" by representing their motivations and obligations in conversations. Alternatively, texts provide actors with motivations and obligations in organizational decision-making.

More recently, some CCO researchers have shifted their attention from the emerging organization to the idea of *(dis)organization*, to explore disorder, disruption and chaos in organizing (for an in-depth look, see the edited volume by Vásquez and Kuhn, 2019; see also Vásquez, Kuhn, & Plotnikof, this volume). Due to its organizing properties, the conversation-text dynamic is also foundational in the examination of the disorder, sometimes chaos, and renegotiation that accompanies organizing and its accomplishment in management meetings (see Vásquez, Schoeneborn, & Sergi, 2016). (Dis)ordering and (dis)organization are communication-based processes founded by the same conversation-text dynamic as ordering and organizing and, thus, can be studied by utilizing it. Texts, for instance, have the property of simultaneously establishing meaning in a more or less permanent form, yet also allowing for meaning to escape the control of a single author (as we see when texts are interpreted), thus incorporating the order/organization-disorder/disorganization duality. Concepts such as authoritative text and ventriloquism, theories such as the communicative theory of the firm, and ideas such as (dis) ordering and (dis)organizing as communicative practices animate, complicate, and evolve the conversation-text dynamic. They are also necessary in the development of the relationship as we continue to study organizations as a life form.

Technology-as-Conversation-Text

Somewhat more recently, CCO researchers have become interested in technology as both site for conversation and as text. As noted earlier, acknowledging technology as an organizational actor (and a context where interactions occurs) reflects a renewal of interest in non-human actors in organizations and, more broadly, a renewed interest in materiality in communication (see Larson & Mengis, this volume).

Of particular interest in this chapter is the development of technology with respect to the conversation-text dynamic. Focusing on conversation, Martine, Cooren, Bénel, and Zackland (2016) analyze interactions during the introduction of novel organizational wiki. They refocus a popular argument that (social) technologies facilitate and improve knowledge management on the process of communication and, specifically, how knowledge sharing translates in everyday interaction and in turn how the expressed "matters of concern" become constitutive of organization. Alternatively, Güney and Cresswell (2012) write about *technology-as-text*, a concept which describes how technology becomes the text that "writes organization into being" (Taylor & Van Every, 2000), and study its role in the negotiation and (re)constitution of organizational authority. Reading technology-as-text can extend understandings of the mobilization of agency, embedded in and enacted through technology, in the structuring of organization and how this is achieved (in this particular case, through IT governance documents).

Related to the constitutive role of technology-as-conversation-text, CCO research has also applied the conversation-text dynamic to online communication and social media interaction in particular. Online communication has been shown to be more than just a means to convey information, as exchanges over new technology and the internet also contribute to constituting organizational reality (Albu & Etter, 2016; Dawson, 2018; Kavada, 2015; Leonardi & Vaast, 2017; Treem & Leonardi, 2013). As much communication by organizations takes place online, and on social media specifically, the context cannot be ignored. Research has engaged both with social media use within organizations (see Leonardi, 2011; Treem & Leonardi, 2013) and with various (external) stakeholders (see Dawson, 2018, Kavada, 2015). Kavada, for example, demonstrates how social media interactions co-create the Occupy Movement as a collective actor with its own identity. Dawson (2018) demonstrates how organizations cultivate social media communities of users, which in turn co-construct the organization's identity through interaction. Albu and Etter (2016) take to Twitter specifically to show how hashtags are used by organizations to create a hypertext *both* constitutive *and* contesting of organizational identity, thus shining light on the dialectical tensions embedded in the conversation-text dynamic. CCO work that uses interactional and textual data available on social media grapples with the discursive co-constitution of the organization by internal and external stakeholders and larger questions stemming from these interactions about organizationality.

Indeed, mobilizing technology-as-conversation-text has allowed for the exploration of flexible forms of organization. The concept of organizationality is used in reference to loose and fluid social collectives, such as online hacktivist networks or bike commuter communities (Dobusch & Schoeneborn, 2015; Wilhoit & Kisselburgh, 2015) and thus suggests a similarly fluid conceptualization of organization, often aided by technology. Possessing a certain level of organizationality might be the best way to describe various organizing talk and organizational forms on the internet (for an overview of the communicative constitution of organization, organizing, and organizationality, see Schoeneborn et al., 2019).

Conclusion and Future Directions

In the early days of the communicative constitution of organization, when the theory was in relative nascency and much of the foundational characteristics of the conversation-text dynamic were still to be empirically demonstrated, Taylor and Van Every (2000, pp. 324–325) argued that organizations are a form of life and should be studied in a way that respects their aliveness.

In the basis of this life form are two opposites, they wrote, that of conversation and text, and they sum up their relationship beautifully:

> there are opposite poles in the spectrum of communication as well, and the space between them is where we must look for the emergence of organization. Those poles are text and conversation: text because, in its own way, it fixes a state of the world (sometimes, as in religious or great creative literature, for centuries and even millennia) and lends itself to faithful reproduction; conversation because its outcomes are never quite predictable and, unless rendered by recording into a texted equivalent, are as evanescent as smoke.

Looking to the future, current research indicates the development of potential new directions within the scope of organizationality, which might benefit from considering the conversation-text relationship. Questions about where organizations are located, what identifies a space as work space, and who or what can contribute to organizing, besides organizational members and the non-human materialities of organizations (Bencherki & Snack, 2016; Dawson & Bencherki, 2021; Grothe-Hammer, 2019; Larson, 2020a, Larson, 2020b; Wilhoit & Kisselburgh, 2019), have become more pertinent as work has become more flexible. These authors argue that activities (like bike commuting) not traditionally labeled "organizational" occur "at the edges of organizations" instead (Wilhoit & Kisselburgh, 2019), that when any space gets appropriated as a work space, it becomes organizational (Larson, 2020a), and that contributorship is a form of communicative organizational action that can be performed when, say, an employee is on vacation (Bencherki & Snack, 2016) or on Twitter (Dawson & Bencherki, 2021). Such claims direct our attention to the materiality (and materialization) of work and organizations, and also present fertile ground for further development of the emergent organization paradigm.

Building on the direction of organizational locale and contributorship, another area where the conversation-text dynamic can challenge and expand our knowledge is the study of organizational membership. Indeed, authors who write about contributorship have already suggested that one need not be *at* work to contribute communicatively *to* work and, thus, organizing. In the past several years, with the advent of social media in areas such as corporate communication, corporate social responsibility, and marketing, advertising and public relations, a different type of organizational membership has emerged—that of the influencer. Part fans, part customers, and part contractors, influencers are not organizational members, yet one could argue that they contribute both communicatively and financially to organizational goals, usually and primarily through their conversations over social media platforms (e.g. YouTube and Instagram) and the texts they produce there. Accounting for their place at the edge of organization and contributorship, the question we ought to answer about influencers then might be: how do the texts these actors produce through social media interaction influence those we conventionally consider to be "organizational" (and in some sense authoritative)?

The concept of organizationality encompasses the future directions mentioned above and provides a more general direction for future research where the conversation-text dynamic can be applied and developed further. As work becomes more diffuse and as a result permeates our everyday non-work existence, including the very spaces we considered private, it is important for CCO research to reach out to spaces that may have been not entirely organizational until recently. Focusing on the work of communication and the changing role of communication in the new economy (see Kuhn, Ashcraft, & Cooren, 2017) opens up research possibilities for the study of new types of work that may lack traditional organizationality, such as certain types of entrepreneurship (e.g. creative work), personal branding, and the aforementioned social media influencing.

In conclusion, the conversation-text dynamic represents an essential CCO relationship that accounts for the emergent organization. Indeed, organization becomes and is found within the conversation-text pillars. The dynamic is important within communication in general in that it holds evident the materialization of communication in its very nature (fleeting conversation translated into stable text informing future communicative action). Much research has been carried out through the application of the conversation and text relationship interpreted on a spectrum from opposites to different sides of the same process. There is more research to come as we explore new forms of work and organizing and grapple with different ways of constituting authority (and authoritative texts).

Note

1 Company and personal identifying information has been masked.

References

Albert, S., & Whetten, D. A. (1985). Organizational identity. In *Organizational Identity: A Reader* (pp. 89–118). Oxford: Oxford University Press.

Albu, O. B., & Etter, M. (2016). Hypertextuality and social media: A study of the constitutive and paradoxical implications of organizational Twitter use. *Management Communication Quarterly, 30*(1), 5–31.

Alvesson, M. (2010). Self-doubters, strugglers, storytellers, surfers and others: Images of self-identities in organization studies. *Human Relations, 63*(2), 193–217.

Ashforth, B. E., & Mael, F. A. (1996). Organizational identity and strategy as a context for the individual. *Advances in Strategic Management, 13*, 19–64.

Bencherki, N., & Snack, J. P. (2016). Contributorship and partial inclusion: A communicative perspective. *Management Communication Quarterly, 30*(3), 279–304.

Boden, D. (1994). *The business of talk: Organizations in action*. Cambridge, UK: Polity Press.

Blaschke, S., Schoeneborn, D., & Seidl, D. (2012). Organizations as networks of communication episodes: Turning the network perspective inside out. *Organization Studies, 33*, 879–906.

Cheney, G., & Christensen, L. T. (2001). Organizational identity: Linkages between internal and external communication. In F. M. Jablin & L. L. Putnam (Eds.), *New handbook of organizational communication: Advances in theory, research, and methods* (pp. 231–269). Thousand Oaks, CA: Sage.

Cooren, F. (2006). The organizational world as a plenum of agencies. In F. Cooren, J. R. Taylor, & E. J. Van Every (Eds.), *Communication as organizing: Empirical and theoretical explorations in the dynamic of text and conversation* (pp. 81–100). Mahwah, NJ: Lawrence Erlbaum Associates.

Cooren, F. (2010) Figures of communication and dialogue: Passion, ventriloquism and incarnation. *Intercultural Pragmatics, 7*(1): 131–145.

Cooren, F. (2012). Communication theory at the center: Ventriloquism and the communicative constitution of reality. *Journal of Communication, 62*(1), 1–20.

Cooren, F. (2015). *Organizational discourse*. Cambridge, UK: Polity Press.

Cooren, F. (2020). Beyond entanglement: (Socio-)materiality and organization studies. *Organization Theory, 1*(3), 1–24.

Dawson, V. R. (2018). Fans, friends, advocates, ambassadors, and haters: Social media communities and the communicative constitution of organizational identity. *Social Media + Society, 4*(1), 1–11.

Dawson, V. R., & Bencherki, N. (2021). Federal employees or rogue rangers: Sharing and resisting organizational authority through Twitter communication practices. *Human Relations*, 1–31.

Dobusch, L., & Schoeneborn, D. (2015). Fluidity, identity, and organizationality: The communicative constitution of Anonymous. *Journal of Management Studies, 52*(8), 1005–1035.

Goffman, E. (1974). *Frame analysis: An essay on the organization of experience*. Cambridge, MA: Harvard University Press.

Gioia, D. A., Schultz, M., & Corley, K. G. (2000). Organizational identity, image, and adaptive instability. *Academy of Management Review, 25*(1), 63–81.

Grothe-Hammer, M. (2019). Organization without actorhood: Exploring a neglected phenomenon. *European Management Journal, 37*(3), 325–338.

Güney, S., & Cresswell, A. M. (2012). Technology-as-text in the communicative constitution of organization. *Information and organization, 22*(2), 154–167.

Kavada, A. (2015). Creating the collective: social media, the Occupy Movement and its constitution as a collective actor. *Information, Communication & Society, 18*(8), 872–886.

Koschmann, M. A. (2013). The communicative constitution of collective identity in interorganizational collaboration. *Management Communication Quarterly, 27*(1), 61–89.

Kuhn, T. (2008). A communicative theory of the firm: Developing an alternative perspective on intra-organizational power and stakeholder relationships. *Organization Studies, 29*(8–9), 1227–1254.

Kuhn, T., Ashcraft, K. L., & Cooren, F. (2017). *The work of communication: Relational perspectives on working and organizing in contemporary capitalism.* New York: Routledge.

Kuhn, T., Ashcraft, K. L., & Cooren, F. (2019). Introductory essay: What work can organizational communication do? *Management Communication Quarterly, 33*(1), 101–111.

Laapotti, T., & Mikkola, L. (2019). Problem talk in management group meetings. *Small Group Research, 50*(6), 728–758.

Larson, E. W. (2020a). Where is an organization? How workspaces are appropriated to become (partial and temporary) organizational spaces. *Management Communication Quarterly, 34*(3), 299–327.

Larson, E. W. (2020b). Creating home at work: Humanistic geography and placemaking in organizations. *Culture and Organization,* 1–19.

Larson, G. S., & Gill, R. (2017). *Organizations and identity.* Cambridge, UK: Polity Press.

Leonardi, P. M. (2011). When flexible routines meet flexible technologies: Affordance, constraint, and the imbrication of human and material agencies. *MIS Quarterly,* 147–167.

Leonardi, P. M. (2012). Materiality, sociomateriality, and socio-technical systems: What do these terms mean? How are they different? Do we need them? In P. M. Leonardi, B.A. Nardi, & J. Kallinikos (Eds.), *Materiality and organizing: Social interaction in a technological world* (pp. 25–48). Oxford, UK: Oxford University Press.

Leonardi, P. M. (2013). Theoretical foundations for the study of sociomateriality. *Information and organization, 23*(2), 59–76.

Leonardi, P. M., & Vaast, E. (2017). Social media and their affordances for organizing: A review and agenda for research. *Academy of Management Annals, 11*(1), 150–188.

Martine, T., Cooren, F., Bénel, A., & Zacklad, M. (2016). What does really matter in technology adoption and use? A CCO approach. *Management Communication Quarterly, 30*(2), 164–187.

Novak, D. R. (2016). Democratic work at an organization-society boundary: Sociomateriality and the communicative instantiation. *Management Communication Quarterly, 30*(2), 218–244.

Orlikowski, W. J. (2007). Sociomaterial practices: Exploring technology at work. *Organization Studies, 28*(9), 1435–1448.

Orlikowski, W. J., & Scott, S. V. (2008). Sociomateriality: Challenging the separation of technology, work and organization. *The Academy of Management Annals, 2,* 433–74. doi: 10.1080/19416520802211644.

Orlikowski, W. J. (2010). The sociomateriality of organisational life: considering technology in management research. *Cambridge Journal of Economics, 34*(1), 125–141.

Pälli, P., & Lehtinen, E. (2013). How organizational strategy is realized in situated interaction. A conversation analytical study of a management meeting. *LSP Journal-Language for special purposes, professional communication, knowledge management and cognition, 4*(2).

Porter, A. J., Kuhn, T. R., & Nerlich, B. (2018). Organizing authority in the climate change debate: IPCC controversies and the management of dialectical tensions. *Organization Studies, 39*(7), 873–898.

Putnam, L. L. (2013). Dialectics, contradictions, and the question of agency. In D. Robichaud & F. Cooren (Eds.) *Organization and organizing: Materiality, agency, and discourse* (pp. 23–36). New York: Routledge

Putnam, L. L. (2015). Unpacking the dialectic: Alternative views on the discourse–materiality relationship. *Journal of Management Studies, 52,* 706–716.

Ricoeur, P. (1981). *Hermeneutics and the human sciences: Essays on language, action and interpretation.* Cambridge, UK: Cambridge University Press.

Robichaud, D., Giroux, H., & Taylor, J. R. (2004). The metaconversation: The recursive property of language as a key to organizing. *Academy of Management Review, 29*(4), 617–634.

Schoeneborn, D., Kuhn, T. R., & Kärreman, D. (2019). The communicative constitution of organization, organizing, and organizationality. *Organization Studies, 40*(4), 475–496.

Scott, S. V., & Orlikowski, W. J. (2012). Great expectations: The materiality of commensurability in social media. In P. M. Leonardi, B.A. Nardi, J. Kallinikos (Eds.), *Materiality and organizing: Social interaction in a technological world* (pp. 113–133). Oxford, UK: Oxford University Press.

Scott, S. V., & Orlikowski, W. J. (2014). Entanglements in practice. *MIS Quarterly, 38*(3), 873–894.

Sveningsson, S., & Alvesson, M. (2003). Managing managerial identities: Organizational fragmentation, discourse and identity struggle. *Human Relations, 56*(10), 1163–1193.

Szabo, A. (2016). Organizing the (sociomaterial) economy: Ritual, agency, and economic models. *Critical Discourse Studies, 13*(1), 118–136.

Taylor, J. R. (1999). What is "organizational communication"? Communication as a dialogic of text and conversation. *Communication Review, 3*(1–2), 21–63.

Taylor, J. R. (2006). Coorientation: A conceptual framework. In F. Cooren, J. R. Taylor, & E. J. Van Every (Eds.), *Communication as organizing: Empirical and theoretical explorations in the dynamic of text and conversation* (pp. 141–156). Mahwah, NJ: Lawrence Erlbaum Associates.

Taylor, J. R. (2009). Organizing from the bottom up? Reflections on the constitution of organization in communication. In L. L. Putnam & A. M. Nicotera (Eds.), *Building theories of organization: The constitutive role of communication* (pp. 153–186). New York: Routledge.

Taylor, J. R., & Cooren, F. (1997). What makes communication 'organizational?': How the many voices of a collectivity become the one voice of an organization. *Journal of Pragmatics, 27*(4), 409–438.

Taylor, J. R., Cooren, F., Giroux, N., & Robichaud, D. (1996). The communicational basis of organization: Between the conversation and the text. *Communication Theory, 6*(1), 1–39.

Taylor, J. R., & Robichaud, D. (2004). Finding the organization in the communication: Discourse as action and sensemaking. *Organization, 11*(3), 395–413.

Taylor, J. R., & Van Every, E. J. (2000). *The emergent organization: Communication as its site and surface.* New York: Routledge.

Taylor, J. R. & Van Every, E. J. (2011). *The situated organization: Studies in the pragmatics of communication research.* New York: Routledge.

Treem, J. W., & Leonardi, P. M. (2013). Social media use in organizations: Exploring the affordances of visibility, editability, persistence, and association. *Annals of the International Communication Association, 36*(1), 143–189.

Vásquez, C., & Kuhn, T. (Eds.). (2019). *Dis/organization as communication: Exploring the disordering, disruptive and chaotic properties of communication.* New York: Routledge.

Vásquez, C., Schoeneborn, D., & Sergi, V. (2016). Summoning the spirits: Organizational texts and the (dis) ordering properties of communication. *Human Relations, 69*(3), 629–659.

Wilhoit, E. D., & Kisselburgh, L. G. (2015). Collective action without organization: The material constitution of bike commuters as collective. *Organization Studies, 36*(5), 573–592.

Wilhoit, E. D., & Kisselburgh, L. G. (2019). The relational ontology of resistance: Hybridity, ventriloquism, and materiality in the production of bike commuting as resistance. *Organization, 26*(6), 873–893.

4

THEORIZING COMMUNICATION AND CONSTITUTION OF ORGANIZATIONS FROM A FOUR FLOWS (STRUCTURATIONAL) PERSPECTIVE

Joel O. Iverson, Karen K. Myers and Robert D. McPhee

Theorizing Communication and Constitution from a Four Flows (Structurational) Perspective

"We teach success. That's what it's all about: success. It's going to happen to you." These words spoken by Donald Trump in the video advertisements for Trump University (TrumpU) represent the image sold to people from 2005 to 2010. In 2017 a $25 million settlement of two class action lawsuits and a fraud case resolved the claims of over 6,000 people that they were sold false promises and a scam institution (Domonoske, 2017). Although TrumpU was never a university, it sold seminars and programs purporting to teach real estate investment to potential "students" or attendees (we also refer to them as targets). TrumpU became a series of ballroom seminars designed to sell larger and larger packages of services that ranged up to $34,995 for the Gold Elite Package (Boser et al., 2016). Although TrumpU became "Trump Entrepreneur Initiative" after the New York State Education Department stated it was operating without a license (Tuttle, 2016), TrumpU was an organization. We explore TrumpU as a communicatively constituted organization (CCO) as an exemplar to illuminate the inner workings of the four flows approach to CCO. TrumpU may seem like more of a scam than a legitimate entity, but the simplicity of the organization and the availability of the *Playbook* used to develop the organization and guide its operations make TrumpU a provocative example to illustrate the four flows approach to CCO.

Grounded in structuration theory, the four flows approach to CCO affirms that constitution occurs in embedded practices and identifies four distinct yet overlapping communicative processes that constitute organizations and distinguish them from other social entities (McPhee & Iverson, 2009; McPhee & Zaug, 2000). The four flows approach not only argues

DOI: 10.4324/9781003224914-6

that communication constitutes, it answers the underlying question about *how* communication constitutes organizations. It moves beyond identifying communication that shapes the organization and necessitates probing into constitution as a construct. In this chapter, our purpose is to offer two extensions to CCO theory, delving deeper into the four flows. We draw on *conlocutions* to explain the constitutive power of communication and action working through the four flows. To illustrate, we offer an exemplar of Trump University (TrumpU) to articulate the basis of constitution. Finally, we position our structurational approach within the larger context of CCO issues and make suggestions regarding its future use.

The Four Flows Model

The four flows approach to CCO began with McPhee and Zaug's (2000) paper that outlined the theory of four communicative flows for organizations. That paper was based on Giddens's (1984) structuration theory, which specified that individuals simultaneously draw on structure and agency as they interact in social systems. According to the four flows model, organizations are constituted through four communication flows: membership negotiation, self-structuring, activity coordination and institutional positioning. They describe flows as "circulating systems or fields of messages" (McPhee & Zaug, 2009, p. 29). However, because the communication is more than a message, the term *flow* is a useful metaphor to illustrate its fluid nature and its ability to change that which it contacts. Further, the flow metaphor recognizes the intermingling of the flows and the boundary-spanning nature of communication, and includes the material in complex ways. The four flows serve at least two important ontological functions. First, the four flows articulate distinct yet mutually dependent processes that decades of scholarship have shown to have ontological status in the social constitution of organizations. The basis for the theory has resonated with scholars and influenced organizational scholarship. The four flows have been used as an analytical tool for understanding the multiple aspects of an organization (Browning et al., 2009; Bruscella & Bisel, 2018; Schoeneborn et al., 2014). Second, the four flows are a useful heuristic to analytically divide and group the field of organizational communication into four (again, intermingled) areas. For example, membership negotiation provides a means to collectively examine assimilation, identity, identification, belonging, and other theories of membership. Likewise, institutional positioning is a useful construct to analyze the organization as a social entity that operates in a macro system of organizations as well as to explore the array of communication that influences how individuals—members and non-members—perceive the organization, its identity, mission, collaborations and other conceptions of the organization in its environment. The four flows approach offers a means of understanding each flow as a facet of organizations, but also the interconnected system as communicatively constituted as a product of the intersecting flows. Next, we review the foundation of the four flows model, structuration theory.

Structuration Theory

Briefly, structuration theory explicates the relationship between human agency (capacity to act otherwise) and structure—the production, reproduction, and transformation of systems and structure (Giddens, 1984). As specified by Giddens (1979, 1984), human activity relies on *structure*, which includes rules and resources that guide behavior. Structure is created by human action that both constrains and enables behavior. Structure includes *rules*, both formal and informal, that guide individuals' behaviors. *Resources*, another form of structure, can facilitate and also restrict activity. Agency has a very specific focus: it is a knowledgeable capacity to act otherwise and to reflexively monitor the social system (Iverson, McPhee & Spaulding, 2018). Non-living objects may appear to have agency, but they do not have the ability to change course based on their perceptions of probable outcomes. This position conflicts with others' notions of agency (Cooren, 2018; Kuhn, 2017) that broaden its definition to include the capacity to act by a range non-living objects (ranging from pencils to organizations and social movements) that were created by humans and other aspects of materiality.

In structuration theory, the duality of structure specifies that structure is created and shaped through practices. Reciprocally, structure cannot exist or continue without production. Practice relies on structure because individuals draw on structure (rules and resources) to guide practices and activities. Practices are enabled and constrained by structures but they also reproduce and reinforce those very structures and practices. In creating new practices, individuals borrow from existing practices and, most especially, from structures as resources. When a practice is changed, by conscious decisions or not, structures similarly adjust.

Extending Structuration into Constitution

While Giddens explores the constitution of society, he under-theorizes the phenomenon of constitution itself. Giddens uses *constitute* to point to the duality of structure (McPhee & Zaug, 2000), indicating that constitutive force creates the means and outcome of social systems such as organizations. McPhee and Zaug (2000; 2009) attempt to elucidate patterns and distributions among "types of interaction that constitute organizations insofar as they make organizations what they are, and how basic features of the organization are implicated in the system of interaction" (p. 27). We define constitution as an ongoing accomplishment that creates and recreates the organization through a defined process of communication and action. While Giddens indicates that action-structure constitutes society in general, we extend Giddens's work by suggesting social structures come into being through communication that is transformed in conlocution as an ongoing process of constitution.

In order to be constitutive, the interaction that enacts structures must involve three fundamental elements: its constitution as meaningful; as a moral order (norms); and as power-laden (Giddens, 1976). As affirmed by structurational hermeneutics (see McPhee & Iverson, 2009, for a deeper explanation), these elements emerge from life in a social world in which values and expectations are derived which color daily and ongoing behaviors. As these interactions occur, something notably human, like a supervisor-subordinate relationship and its context (the organization), is constituted. On this basis, constitution represents the process of agents drawing on rules and resources in interaction that develops a recognizable entity we can call an organization.

McPhee and Iverson (2002, 2009) introduce *conlocutions* to describe the transformation from illocution to constitutive force. The notion of conlocutions represents discursive accomplishments (McPhee & Iverson, 2002); it draws on the terminology of Speech Act Theory (Searle, 1969, among others) to illustrate the additional outcomes, the not-necessarily-intended consequences of discourse. Though not offered as a part of Speech Act Theory, conlocutions represent the social system accomplishments of discursive acts. (A full description of conlocutions is offered in McPhee and Iverson [2002], which includes a comparison of conlocutions in two organizations; McPhee and Iverson [2009] provide an applied example of conlocutions.) Briefly, the concept of conlocutions affords us a clear prototype to illustrate how communication is constitutive, representing "categories of discursive accomplishments" (McPhee & Iverson, 2002, p. 7). For example, initiating new members is more than a ceremony with words. The illocutionary act of saying the words of initiation does not merely result in others reacting to people as new members (a perlocutionary act—the response of a listener), but also constitutes the organization as it accomplishes both membership and the organization (McPhee & Iverson, 2009). The accomplishment lies between the illocutionary act (discursive acts) and perlocutionary act (reaction by others), but it is useful to point toward the accomplishment. The organization, as accomplishment, is communicatively constituted in the process of communication. Thus, the organization results as the currents of the four flows are communicatively constituted together, as we illustrate below. For example, a nonprofit engaging in a fundraising event not only communicates with words and images (illocution) leading to donation decisions (perlocution), but is also constituting complex social systems in an interactive way. McPhee and Iverson recognize that accomplishments are interactive, but also naturalizing, meaning the capacity to act otherwise is not clearly seen, only the choice. A constituted organizational context provides the structures for illocution to perlocution, and is implied by that linkage: that pattern *constitutes* the organization. The conlocutions draw upon, produce/ reproduce the organizational context to accomplish things (functionally or dysfunctionally, but relevantly to the organization) in specific recursively constituting ways. Conlocutions are bound to situations and can vary significantly, though they constitute the four flows, and thus accomplish organizations in a variety of ways.

Constitutive Flows in TrumpU

We now demonstrate the constitutive effects of the four flows, and of the conlocutions they involve, in producing and reproducing an organization. In this exemplar, we show membership negotiation, self-structuring, activity coordination and organizational positioning in action in TrumpU.

Flow 1: The Membership Negotiations of TrumpU

Membership negotiation involves individuals developing-maintaining a relationship with, and collaboratively situating themselves as members of the organization. It involves multidirectional and multilayered communication that defines relationships between the individual and others also associated with the confluence of flows; this communication also delineates the relationship with the organization itself, and what it means to be a member. Organizational roles emerge from self-structuring by leadership, but daily interaction and practices are necessary in defining the meaning of membership and putting that membership into play—that's why we say "negotiation".

Individuals initially contribute to the flow by joining the organization. The socialization provided by management has meaning as it orients newcomers to the culture and mission of the organization. Training provides the directives about how members are expected to perform their membership. These illocutionary acts become constitutive when newcomers perform their membership at least in part, as communicated by leaders. Thereafter, ongoing supervision is meant to ensure members' activities contribute to organizational goals, as specified in self-structuring the organization. These illocutionary acts of orienting and training have important meaning and help members understand the expectations, encouraging them to contribute to the communicative flow. To some extent, these actions attempt to channel the flow of performing membership because newcomers typically adapt, at least partially, to fit the mold that's been created for them. Nevertheless, we also recognize the less organizationally desired processes of membership negotiation: managers, colleagues or third parties all exerting surreptitious control over members; members enacting their roles by politically manipulating organizational goals and programs to increase their own power; and members surreptitiously acting or generating roles to pursue dysfunctional programs.

As new members settle into (and resist) their roles, they negotiate with supervisors and coworkers and enact membership in ways that best suit their capabilities and preferences, sometimes without supervisor consent. Their enactment of the role pushes and enhances the membership flow with constitutive effects. Members' support or resistance shapes not only what it means to be a member; it is also constitutive of an essential element of the organization. In many cases, members develop identification when they feel aligned with and unified by the organization's goals and they perceive that their actions support those goals. Some members may choose to push back on leaders' directives and feedback, performing in deviant ways that may create a counter-culture among members.

Membership in TrumpU meant performing two competing roles. While members' outward-facing role may have been "admissions counselors", "real estate experts", and even "university president", their membership titles communicated and constituted an organization that appeared educational. However, most of their engagement with their targets and their actions were as "sales representative", "higher-level sales representative", and "senior-level sales representative", which was constitutive of the organization whose functions were driven by sales. Although the contrast between official titles and their actual purpose in the organization might seem problematic for members who may have desired to participate in an educational organization, it seemed to be a concern only for a handful of TrumpU employees. Most members of TrumpU appeared to recognize the actual meaning of their membership—to sell classes to individuals who dreamed of getting rich through real estate opportunities that only TrumpU could offer. Based on the evidence, TrumpU leadership hired individuals based only on their ability to sell: "those willing to browbeat attendees into purchasing an expensive Trump University course package" (*The Atlantic*, as cited in Tuttle, 2016). In fact, individuals who were labeled by the company as real estate experts had little real estate experience and were instead hired because of their ability to sell. This pushed the membership flow to constitute an organization focused on selling, rather than educating.

The depth and detail of members' sales training was clear and fully described in the TrumpU *Playbook*, as will be described in the self-structuring flow. Forceful directives were evidence that TrumpU did not trust members to customize their sales pitches. Instead, due to the detailed scripts contained in the *Playbook*, members must have recognized that they were mere tools (highly constrained) to act on behalf of TrumpU leaders. Communication from leaders made clear that members were expected to ignore what might be natural compassion for those less fortunate—single mothers struggling to feed their families, elderly or disabled who were persuaded to drain their savings or apply for new credit cards to finance their TrumpU tuition. The *Playbook* reminded members "Attendees are looking for solutions to solve their problem. An attendee's problem represents a golden opportunity … . Attendees want to be a part of Trump University … . Money is never a reason for not enrolling in Trump University", and "You are not doing any favor by letting someone use lack of money as an excuse" (p. 99). These examples demonstrate the thrust of the flow from leaders to members was to impress attendees that TrumpU was the solution to their financial problems and well worth the cost. The guise of a "university" and the recognized Trump brand gave it legitimacy and power. Their words and activities contributed to the flows that constituted it into a sales-driven guise that was not primarily focused on the well-being of the "students". Instead, the members' discourse and activities played a part in making TrumpU what it was—a channel for making money off the backs of trusting, hopeful students.

Flow 2: The Reflexive Self-Structuring of TrumpU

Organizations are created and maintained to fulfill goals or a mission. It can also be said that organizations live in constrained chaos, and one goal of those seeking organizational power is to create as much constraint, in their own favor, as possible while attaining their organizational goals. For both purposes, the primary tool possessed by members high in the hierarchy is self-structuring to simultaneously guide members to fulfill those goals while also constraining them. Among the tools for self-structuring, three crucial ones are formal documents, organizational culture, and organizational technology. One value of the four flows model is that it displays the functionality among these very different phenomena.

Official documents—the organizational legal documents such as the charter, formal descriptions of the organization including hierarchical diagrams, travel vouchers and similar forms, and membership rosters—are good prototypes of self-structuring in an organization such as TrumpU. The conlocutive effect occurs when they officially convey how members should perform their membership by enabling some behaviors and constraining others. For instance, the TrumpU *Playbook* stipulates some of the behaviors required of "members". For instance, related to free "Preview" events intended to sell packages of courses and services to new members, the *Playbook* includes some specific rules like: "All TrumpU Team Members must be professionally dressed at least one-hour prior to the beginning of the Preview" (p. 15), or "ALL TRUMP UNIVERSITY TEAM MEMBERS WILL BE REQUIRED TO HAVE THE BELOW IMAGE AS THEIR DESKTOP BACKGROUND AT ALL TRUMP UNIVERSITY EVENTS" (p. 66). Compared to the rules and regulations formulated in other organizations, these are very microspecific. However, by giving microspecific directives, leaders are clearly attempting to constrain member behavior and to closely control the constituting process of the organization. For example, and as noted in the membership negotiation section, some of the rules allow upper-level members, including speakers, program coordinators, and sales coordinators, to evaluate members by, e.g., taking two distinct forms of attendance, or "audits", to check on up-to-date fee payments prior to each session. Formal structural rules like this allow for several processes to occur that epitomize human organizations. One is that they set up an official shared language with labels for "members" and "program coordinators" so that they can be understood and used for processes including membership negotiation. In most organizations, formal self-structuring tools are subject to informal supplement, explication, and undermining.

TrumpU's training and operations manuals prohibit member adaptation of titles and procedures. That communication exerts extreme control of members via feedback and rewards. Such self-structuring may specify what form communication may take and the "channels" or consecutive contexts it must flow through. As noted in the membership negotiation section, such formal communication requirements contribute to, among other things, determining the distribution of power in the organization. From the *Playbook* it is easy to see the stringent guidelines recruits have about their role. Formal communication also informs members that they are required to follow the rules laid out in the *Playbook*, and the consequences to their membership if rules are not followed. This is one of the most pronounced examples of leaders effectively controlling constitutive practices by members. Through the organization's design, a high-level executive can stipulate features of lower units, e.g., the number of program coordinators and types of computer equipment available. That lets executives choose arrangements that are the best pattern for putative goals. But as with any communication, formal self-structuring can have multiple levels of meaning for different actors, which can facilitate or block movement toward any goal, however noble (McPhee, 1985; McPhee et al., 2014).

A very different phenomenon from formalities is organizational culture. It is typically unwritten and only partly recognized by members. But culture in organizations consists of the enduring tacit values, assumptions, and broad behavior patterns that are conformed to by nearly all members of the organization. Organizational founders and leaders exert considerable power in forging and shaping the organizational culture through self-structuring. For example, leaders impose values by designing reward systems that direct member behaviors and create patterns of behavior reflecting those values. Reward systems can reflect and emphasize values such as innovation, efficiency, customer service, education or profitability. As members respond to those reward systems, they constitute organizations that are largely defined by those values.

Despite their vast difference from formal structure, cultural tenets are considered to be part of the second flow because they too involve organizations structuring themselves reflexively and powerfully. A very good example of this sense of organizational culture is found in Weider's (1974) book about prison tacit culture in organizations (TrumpU-like organizations, actually). Specifically, he describes their cultural practice of not "telling the code" to outsiders as an informal structure to keep other prisoners from cooperating with prison staff. Similarly, reading between the lines of the *Playbook* lets one recognize the emphasis placed on money and sales, regardless of TrumpU claiming to be student-centered. This tacit, but Trump-generated, culture is very narrowly and prescriptively focused and to be followed by all TrumpU workers, as noted in the membership negotiation section.

A final kind of self-structuring has come into prominence in perhaps the last 50 years. Organizational technology has evolved from a set of simple tools for information conveyance to a physical network to a vital, impactful resource, so impactful that it, rather than any formal documents, structures organizational power and member communication. The type and amount of technology used in organizations, nearly always directed by leaders, also exhibits important constitutive qualities. When leaders introduce new technologies, they communicate messages about the identity of the organization (institutional positioning) and also reinforce certain priorities. Those identities and priorities are enacted in member behavior with constitutive effects. The use of technological features in TrumpU is fairly primitive, with paper and pencil still used for most tasks, and computers used purely for boss-member communication of financial data. This, of course, has implications for how TrumpU members coordinate their work.

Flow 3: The Activity Coordination of TrumpU

The third flow, activity coordination, involves members working together to complete tasks that they otherwise could not complete on their own. While self-structuring defines the organizational mission and over-arching areas of responsibility for members, they must still communicate with others to ensure that tasks necessary to attain short- and long-term goals are completed in such a way to communicate their organization's desired identity, as discussed in the section on institutional positioning. Through activity coordination, day-to-day processes are adjusted to facilitate work that relies on interdependencies. The conlocution occurs when members communicate to coordinate, others recognize the meaning and legitimacy of the message toward guiding their collective work to achieve objectives and their efforts contribute to the organization's mission. This need to coordinate is especially relevant in times of change when uncertainties require that members manage their interdependencies to adapt practices.

Policies and interdependencies can mostly be defined as part of self-structuring, but the day-to-day details of how individuals work together often require interaction (Klein et al.,

2005; Myers & McPhee, 2006). Activity coordination flow and the conlocutive effect is seen when one member asks another a question to ensure that their tasks will complement each other. Both recognize the inquiry is linked either distantly or directly to organizational goals. Because the activity is so linked, the second member perceives the legitimacy of the question that may help them to complete their tasks. While members often have personal preferences about working together in a synchronized way, most members recognize the power of coordinating interactions because their activities affect the organization's success. As members throughout the organization engage in similar activity coordination, their collective flows constitute more than the immediate effect of their joint work. Certainly, some members may not contribute as freely to the organization's success, and may actively push back against the activity coordination flow. Regardless, activity coordination that synchronizes with the dominant flow, or that obstructs elements of it, is constitutive. Without these flows, the organization no longer exists.

In most organizations, activity flow emerges somewhat organically between members with the guidance and oversight from management, but in TrumpU leaders sought to control activity coordination at events which were its primary function. TrumpU leaders sought to control the activity coordination flow down to the most minute detail through self-structuring. Communication from leadership makes it clear that they (leaders) are more knowledgeable than members about how members must work together to drive sales. This constituted a tightly controlled organization in which activity coordination was micromanaged from the top. For example, one *Playbook* directive is "All TrumpU Team Members are responsible for learning all parts of the preview set up process and working cohesively to do everything within their power to contribute to a successful event" (*Playbook*, 2009, p. 15). This example demonstrates not only the need to coordinate, but also the interconnectedness of self-structuring and activity coordination.

Although the leaders attempt to position the organization as educational, the *Playbook* makes clear the real objective. Members coordinated activities at the registration desk, presentation and follow-up sales pitches designed "to convince the targets that Trump University is there to help them" (Shireman, 2018, p. 769). Before events, members are told to communicate and work to "Peak [sic] interest and/or 'set the hook'" (*Playbook*, p. 19). During the presentation, members ensured that the room was conducive to keeping the targets focused on the talk (keeping the room cool, reducing the likelihood of disruptions, and ensuring no one left the room). Following the presentation, during the "sales time", each member stationed themselves in locations to slow individuals' exit from the room and to facilitate sales as members recited scripted sales tactics to increase the likelihood of sales success.

Once, when a member felt uncomfortable in closing a sale that would have required a cash-strapped couple to pay $35,000 for classes, his colleague stepped in to complete the transaction—evidence of activity coordination, even against the will of a member (Barbaro & Eder, 2015). The conlocutive effect draws from the flow of self-structuring—a precisely defined way that members should respond when other members are not performing according to the *Playbook*. The colleague adjusted his activities to reflect the (mis)behavior of his colleague by moving in to close the sale. The organization was constituted to take money even from targets who could not afford it. The *Playbook* appears to recognize that it cannot completely structure ongoing practice. It instructs members to coordinate activities with the following message from TrumpU leaders: "Team works together to identify potential buyers with student profile sheets", which include how to rate potential buyers based on their available liquid assets (p. 36). Together, their communication to organize their efforts and enact activities combined with the other flows to establish a larger current that *is* the organization.

Flow 4: The Institutional Positioning of TrumpU

Institutional positioning involves the constitution of organizations within an array of institutional contexts. This flow illuminates the ongoing communicative process of acting organizationally, such as individuals from an organization negotiating a contract on behalf of their organization by spanning the boundaries of the organization to represent *the organization*. By acting for an organization, agents interact with individuals outside and inside their organization as well as other organizations. Institutional positioning both provides definition to the organization as entity and also positions it as an active participant within a broader social system with other organizations (McPhee & Iverson, 2009). Organizations enter into competition, partnerships, service agreements, regulatory contexts, media events and many more conlocutionary acts. As a construct and process, institutional positioning has proved to be a useful means of representing this essential communication and its relation to organizing. For example, Bruscella and Bisel (2018) focus on institutional positioning of the militant group ISIL for recruiting members but also their identity as an institution.

Institutional positioning actions not only constitute the organization, but also participate in the constitution of the broader social systems. Mann (2015) provides the example of La via Campesina, a network of over 160 rural peoples' organizations. While each organization engages in its own actions, the collective nature of broader contexts such as the UN Food and Agriculture Organization, world markets, and broader systems are developed. Institutional positioning provides a heuristic to examine the process of (re)producing the organization as an identifiable social entity as well as the broader social system.

Institutional positioning for TrumpU is illustrated through internal documents, the public events, social media presence, critical news coverage and even legal proceedings. First, TrumpU positions itself with its identity. The use of the Trump name is designed to draw on the image of Donald Trump for the purposes of establishing TrumpU as a credible entity following the success of *The Apprentice*. The meaning of TrumpU is enacted for recruiting clients as well as training its employees. Its identity is further solidified when TrumpU workers congratulated rather than thanked attendees (as required by the *Playbook*) in an attempt to make TrumpU alluring and desirable.

Second, TrumpU was positioned within the context of universities. TrumpU communication clearly focused on establishing itself as elite, focused, and valued. As Shireman (2018) points out:

> In a promotional two-minute video for his eponymous school, Donald Trump said, "We're going to teach you better than the business schools are going to teach you— and I went to the best business school".

TrumpU was positioned as a more practical education than traditional universities. For the promotion, Trump stated it was better, and staff pushed the futility of humanities and other courses. For those who chose to invest in the seminars, they interacted with staff who were pressuring them, acted as their friend, and made TrumpU seem like an investment they must quickly act upon. As a conlocution, selling the prestige of TrumpU not only created a reaction of investing by people, it constituted the image of TrumpU for them as a wise investment in (false) comparison to other higher-educational institutions.

Further, TrumpU critics described it as a scam institution. Shireman (2018) defines TrumpU as a predatory college that is similar to and representative of a set of organizations that draw upon the idea that investing in education is important. However, like many other service products, it is inherently difficult to gauge the quality of the product that consumers receive. Yet this question appeared to be somewhat settled when a court settlement positioned TrumpU as fraudulent (Boser et al., 2017).

Final Considerations

Overall, our example of TrumpU provides a means for analysis, an opportunity to think about each flow, and an illustration of how the process of communicating can be constitutive of multiple flows. Even with this simple, short-lived organization, if one examines communicative moments, the flows are often difficult to separate: during the sessions, for instance, sales staff are engaging in recruiting, upselling, and enacting the *Playbook*. Membership negotiation, self-structuring, activity coordination, and institutional positioning are conlocuted during that communicative process. Rather than merely separate communicative acts into each of the four flows, four flows analysis allows creating analytically separate considerations of each flow while also recognizing the interconnected nature of communication that accomplishes multiple flows and constitutes the organization.

Conlocutions are accomplished in the ongoing practices of organizational communication. When recruiting, persuading people to enroll, and convincing them to upgrade packages, the members of TrumpU are reproducing their membership in TrumpU as they attract "students" and sell them on the prospect of TrumpU. Recognizing those as conlocutions provides us an ability to analytically recognize the social accomplishment of organizations separate from other similar acts. Two individuals trading used books is not equivalent to selling someone a $35,000 package from TrumpU in more ways than location and price point because engaging in neighborhood commerce is different from organizational accomplishments. The four flows and conlocutions acknowledge the constitutive processes as organizational processes. Further, conlocutions provide an opportunity to analyze those accomplishments *as* organizational, perhaps descriptively different than other instances, while also recognizing how they are enacting the four flows of organizations.

As a theory of CCO, the four flows model is grounded in communication and is analytically useful as an approach to examine how structures interact with communication and action to create, sustain and transform the organization. Any one of these elements—communication without action or action without communication—is not sufficient to have constitutive, conlocutionary power. The four flows model identifies essential thrusts of communication that are recognizable, foundational communicative processes that are needed for organizing, giving the model a type of ontological validity. The four flows independently recognize the constitutive processes of each flow while also recognizing that together the flows acknowledge a complex social process of organizing beyond the independent efforts of each flow. When the flows merge and work together they constitute an organizational entity that may claim to be something it is not, but when the flows are examined, as we have done with TrumpU, we can recognize the organization for how it was designed and maintained.

Future Directions

Our structurational approach to constitution offers noteworthy implications for several key issues currently discussed in organizational communication and other views of CCO. As we have described here and elsewhere (McPhee & Iverson, 2009; McPhee & Zaug, 2000), four flows of circulating communication that are distinct, yet intermingle with each other, are constitutive of organizations. In this chapter, we use the four flows model to examine communication that constituted TrumpU into the entity that it became for its members, clients (targets), and society. We conclude with a consideration about how our approach fits into the current streams of conversation around CCO theorizing and respond to critiques of the four flows model.

Since the four flows approach to CCO was introduced, it has received criticism by some, as previously acknowledged, but it has enjoyed recognition by many in the field who find the approach unpretentiously and logically simple, but also comprehensive. The four flows model and/or elements of the model have been cited more than any other CCO approach (Koschmann & Campbell, 2017). Recently, the approach has been adopted by researchers to evaluate when and whether a collective can be designated an organization (Layne, Canary & Beach, 2019) and how the flows influence other organizational phenomena such as the development of organizational identification (Giles & Myers, 2020). Just as studies used the four flows model to examine the constitution of organizations, others have drawn on the model to identify an organization's demise. For example, Bean and Buikema (2015) offered an innovative study of texts to pinpoint how various disruptions of the four flows led to the decline of al-Qa'ida. Their examination of the 17 Abbottabad texts identify emergent disruptions in each of the flows and outcomes that eventually stifled the organization's ability to thrive.

We contend that the four flows approach offers answers that may not completely resolve, but advance the conversation between CCO theories in general. We provide brief answers to some issues in this chapter, but provide a more detailed account in our book (McPhee et al., forthcoming) that articulates the four flows, conlocutions and other advancements of the four flows theorizing.

Although many conversations and mutual critiques exist between CCO approaches, recently Kuhn (2021) offered a clearly articulated provocation of three epistemological "blind spots" for practice-based understandings of social systems, which provide a useful framework for discussion. He contends CCO thinking answers two of these, but suffers from a third, for which we propose a forward-thinking answer. These three issues provide an excellent outline to engage in analysis of the four flows approach overall. First, Kuhn points out that CCO theorizing moves past organizations as mere context. Theorizing the organization as entity, verb and even adjective is certainly possible with the four flows approach as well other CCO approaches. Specifically, we contend that institutional positioning as a flow offers a unique means to consider the higher system level of organization in a system while also considering the production and reproduction of the organization.

Second, Kuhn (2021) contends that the conception of agency as limited to the person is a blind spot and that agency needs reconceptualization and offers the Luhmanian and Montreal school approaches as answers. We see significant common ground with those approaches, but recognize differences that create a healthy dialogue and offer an opportunity for clarification of our position. Given that Kuhn cites Giddens and structuration to exemplify the agency problem, we clearly resemble that remark, but contend that Kuhn and others oversimplify their analysis of a structurational view of agency and minimize the uniquely human communicative process of constituting social systems as meaningful. Rather, we contend (see Iverson et al., 2018, 2019, for more detailed analysis) that agency is a human capacity to "act otherwise" (Giddens, 1984), which fits clearly with practice theories (Cohen, 1989), and the four flows approach, with its attention to conlocutions, centers communication as the process of humans knowledgeably, reflexively making action meaningful. While some analysis may use this definition of agency to be anthropocentric and relegate other material forces as merely tools, that position is not inherent to our view nor do we see anthropomorphizing objects with agency and conflating action with agency or constitutive force as answers. We recognize that "humans and nonhumans are constitutively entangled in action" (Kuhn, p. 5), but differ when it comes to referring to that entangled action as *agency*—or that "action, accordingly is the production of an ensemble, plenum, of agencies" (p. 5). The structurational view of agency allows for entanglement, significant impact, and can recognize the same complexities, but it recognizes, through conlocutions, that the meaning-based processes for communicatively constituting something like TrumpU is a *human* creation that draws upon knowledgeability and reflexive monitoring to act otherwise.

Finally, Kuhn points to the need to re-imagine critical theorizing and offers a promising new materialist approach to the issues of power, domination, control, and resistance. We also are working in this direction with future explication of transtructions in our forthcoming book that we introduced (Iverson et al., 2019) as the intersection of power, norms and meaning (see the modalities in structuration theory) as they intersect in communicative practices. We feel this is an important direction for CCO theories to move and engage in meaningful conversation.

Overall, the four flows approach recognizes the complex ontology of organizations as constituted in communication. Each flow represents a critical facet of organizing and its interconnectedness. Through the conlocution process, organizing that occurs through these distinctive flows has power and meaning beyond the obvious immediate interaction. They constitute organizations that legitimately fulfill their espoused mission, but they are equally constitutive of organizations that lack legitimacy in the eyes of their members, clients, society and, at times, courts of law. TrumpU illustrates not only each flow, but the conlocutionary process of communicatively constituting organizations. For the people who were fleeced by TrumpU, Donald Trump's phrase "That's what it's all about: success. It's going to happen to you" emerged in the form of a $25-million-dollar court settlement as a final act of the organization.

References

Barbaro, M., & Eder, S. (2015, July 28). Under oath, Donald Trump shows his raw side. *The New York Times*. Retrieved from www.nytimes.com/2015/07/29/us/politics/depositions-show-donald-trump-as-quick-to-exaggerate-and-insult.html.

Bean, H., & Buikema, R. J. (2015). Deconstituting al-Qa'ida: CCO theory and the decline and dissolution of hidden organizations. *Management Communication Quarterly, 29*(4), 512–538.

Boser, U., Schwaber, D., & Johnson, S. (2013). Trump University: A look at an enduring education scandal. *American Progress*, March 17. www.americanprogress.org/article/trump-university-look-enduring-education-scandal/.

Boser, U., Schwaber, D., & Johnson, S. (2017, March 30). Trump University: A look at an enduring education scandal. *Center for American Progress*. Retrieved from www.americanprogress.org/issues/education-postsecondary/reports/2017/03/30/429573/trump-university-look-enduring-education-scandal/.

Browning, L. D., Greene, R. W., Sitkin, S. B., Sutcliffe, K. M., & Obstfeld, D. (2009). Constitutive complexity: Military entrepreneurs and the synthetic character of communication flows. In L. L. Putnam & A. M. Nicotera (Eds.), *Building theories of organization: The constitutive role of communication* (pp. 89–116). New York: Routledge.

Bruscella, J. S., & Bisel, R. S. (2018). Four Flows theory and materiality: ISIL's use of material resources in its communicative constitution. *Communication Monographs, 85*(3), 331–356. https://doi.org/10.1080/03637751.2017.1420907.

Cohen, I. J. (1989). *Structuration theory: Anthony Giddens and the constitution of social life*. New York: St. Martin's Press.

Cooren, F. (2018). Acting for, with, and through: A relational perspective on agency in MSF's organizing. In B. H. J. M. Brummans (Ed.), *The agency of organizing: Perspectives and case studies* (pp. 142–169). New York: Routledge.

Domonoske, C. (2017, March 31). Judge approves $25 million settlement of Trump University. *NPR*. Retrieved from www.npr.org/sections/thetwo-way/2017/03/31/522199535/judge-approves-25-million-settlement-of-trump-university-lawsuit.

Giddens, A. (1976). *New rules of sociological method: A positive critique of interpretative sociologies.* New York,: Basic Books.

Giddens, A. (1979). *Central problems in social theory: Action, structure and contradiction in social analysis.* Berkeley, CA: University of California Press.

Giddens, A. (1984). *The constitution of society: Outline of the theory of structuration.* Berkeley, CA: University of California Press.

Giles, M., & Myers, K. K. (2020). *Organizational identification, organizational identity and the four flows of the communicative constitution of organizations.* Paper presented to the Organizational Division of the National Communication Association, Indianapolis, IN.

Iverson, J. O., McPhee, R. D., & Spaulding, C. W. (2018). Being able to act otherwise: The role of agency in the four flows at 2-1-1 and beyond. In B. H. J. M. Brummans (Ed.), *The agency of organizing: Perspectives and case studies* (pp. 43–65). New York: Routledge..

Iverson, J. O., McPhee, R. D., & Myers, K. K. (2019, July 4). Transtructions and modalities: Theorizing communication and constitution from a four flows (structurational) perspective. 35th European Group for Organizational Studies Colloquium, Edinburgh, UK.

Klein, G., Feltovich, P. J., Bradshaw, J. M., & Woods, D. D. (2005). Common ground and coordination in joint activity. *Organizational simulation, 53,* 139–184.

Koschmann, M., & Campbell, T. (2017). Taking stock of taken up: The legacy and relevance of CCO in non-scholarly outlets. Paper presented to the Organizational Division of the National Communication Association, Dallas, TX.

Kuhn, T. (2017). Communicatively constituting organizational unfolding through counter-narrative. In S. Frandsen, T. Kuhn, & M. Wolff Lundholt (Eds.), *Counter-narratives and organization* (pp. 25–50). New York: Routledge.

Kuhn, T. (2021). (Re)moving blinders: Communication-as-constitutive theorizing as provocation to practice-based organization scholarship. *Management Learning, 52*(1), 109–121. https://doi.org/10.1177/1350507620931508.

Layne, R. B., Canary, H., & Beach, E. (2019). Becoming an organization: Ambiguity as a catalyst to communicative constitution flow Patterns. Presented in the Organizational Division at the International Communication Association conference, Washington DC.

Mann, A. (2015) Communication, organisation, and action: Theory-building for social movements. *Communication Research and Practice, 1,* 159–173.

McPhee, R. D. (1985). Formal structure and organizational communication. In R. D. McPhee and P. K. Tompkins (Eds.), *Organizational communication: Traditional themes and new directions* (pp. 149 177). Beverly Hills, CA: Sage.

McPhee, R. D., & Iverson, J. O. (2002, November). Discourse systems structurate organizations and their discursive resources. Paper presented at the National Communication Association Convention, New Orleans, LA.

McPhee, R. D., & Iverson, J. O. (2009). Agents of constitution in Communicad: Constitutive processes of communication in organizations. In L. Putnam & A. Nicotera (Eds.), *Communicative constitution of organization* (pp. 49–88). London: Laurence Erlbaum.

McPhee, R. D., Iverson, J. O., & Myers, K. K. (forthcoming). *The communicative constitution of organizations: The four flows model.* Wiley Blackwell.

McPhee, R. D., Poole, M. S., & Iverson, J. O. (2014). Structuration theory. In L. L. Putnam & D. K. Mumby (Eds.), *The SAGE handbook of organizational communication* (pp. 75–99). Thousand Oaks, CA: Sage.

McPhee, R. D., & Zaug, P. (2000). The communicative constitution of organizations: A framework for explanation. *Electronic Journal of Communication/La Revue Electronique de Communication, 10*(1–2). www.cios.org/getfile/MCPHEE_V10N1200.

Myers, K. K., & McPhee, R. D. (2006). Influences on member assimilation in workgroups in high reliability organizations: A multilevel analysis. *Human Communication Research, 32,* 440–468. https://doi.org10.1111/j.1468-2958.2006.00283.x.

Playbook. (2009). One Company, One Culture, One Goal. Achieving Sustained Profitability in 2010. Trump University. https://static.politico.com/25/88/783a0dca43a0a898f3973da0086f/trump-university-playbook.pdf.

Schoeneborn, D., Blaschke, S., Cooren, F., McPhee, R. D., Seidl, D., & Taylor, J. R. (2014). The three schools of CCO thinking interactive dialogue and systematic comparison. *Management Communication Quarterly, 28*(2), 285–316.

Searle, J. R. (1969). *Speech acts: An essay in the philosophy of language.* Cambridge University Press.

Shireman, R. (2018, Winter). Selling the American dream: What the Trump University scam teaches us about predatory colleges. *Social Research: An International Quarterly, 85*(4), 767–794. Retrieved from: *Project MUSE* muse.jhu.edu/article/716114.

Tuttle, I. (2016, February 26). Yes, Trump University was a massive scam. *National Review.* Retrieved from: /www.nationalreview.com/corner/trump-university-scam/.

Weider, D. L. (1974). *Language and social reality: The case of telling the convict code.* The Hague: Mouton

5

THE COMMUNICATIVE CONSTITUTION OF THE WORLD

A Luhmannian View on Communication, Organizations, and Society

Michael Grothe-Hammer

Introduction

Niklas Luhmann is one of "contemporary sociology's most prominent icons" (Bamyeh, 2014). Although internationally best known for his seminal contributions to sociology (Sohn, 2020), Luhmann in fact started his scientific career as an organization theorist (Seidl & Mormann, 2014). However, in contrast to other prominent sociologists who began similarly organization-focused in the 1960s but then lost their interest in organizational phenomena, Luhmann kept developing his organization theory over the decades and constantly included organizations in all areas of his overarching theory (Ahrne et al., 2016).

As a result, his organization theory comes embedded in a complex grand theory – ranging from his own version of social constructivism over countless social theory contributions to an advanced combination of micro-, meso- and macro-sociological theory. Specifically, this includes theories of communication, face-to-face interaction, organization, social movements, power, risk, trust, love, paradoxes, the welfare state, ecological problems, as well as macro-societal differentiation in general, and societal domains in specific such as politics, economics, science, the legal system, art, religion, and the mass media (Becker, 2005). Hence, Luhmann's theory can spawn fascination as well as intimidation. His theory is probably the most extensive sociological theory there is and therefore offers an unmatched explanatory potential. Any introductory text on his works therefore faces the problem that it must opt for a very specific glimpse highlighting certain aspects while ignoring most areas of Luhmann's oeuvre. In this respect, there have been numerous excellent introductions (e.g., Cooren & Seidl, 2019; Nassehi, 2005; Schoeneborn, 2011; Seidl, 2005; Schirmer & Michailakis, 2019), which have fueled and accompanied a dramatic increase of Anglophone research works drawing on Luhmann's theory in recent years (Sohn, 2020).

A substantive international debate across several disciplines has emerged which is engaged in further developing Luhmann's theory as such. This includes his organization theory. There

DOI: 10.4324/9781003224914-7

have been, for instance, interesting works on the notion of membership (Andersen & Born, 2008), the organizational adoption of new technologies (Højlund & Villadsen, 2020), or the interrelation between organizations, families, networks, and social movements (Kleve et al., 2020). A major recurring theme is the relation between organizations and macro-societal differentiation (e.g., Andersen, 2020; Apelt et al., 2017; Will et al., 2018), which will be a focus of this chapter.

Related to this development, one can also identify several discourses in organization studies, which took considerable inspiration from the Luhmannian framework but depart from it in several ways. In particular, Göran Ahrne and Nils Brunsson were critically inspired by Luhmann's insights. In their famous theories of meta-organization (Ahrne & Brunsson, 2008) as well as partial organization (Ahrne & Brunsson, 2011) they relied crucially on Luhmann's assertion that decisions are key for understanding organizational phenomena. Related and partly inspired by this development, Luhmann's framework is nowadays also considered one of the three main approaches of the CCO perspective (Brummans et al., 2014; see Cooren & Seidl, this volume). Accordingly, several scholars have drawn on Luhmann within this research stream, for instance, in works on "degrees of organizationality" (Dobusch & Schoeneborn, 2015; see Schoeneborn et al., this volume), when defining "organizations as networks of communication episodes" (Blaschke et al., 2012), or when discussing how organizations are constituted through oscillating between order and disorder (Grothe-Hammer & Schoeneborn, 2019; see Vásquez et al., this volume).

Against this backdrop, the main goal of this chapter is twofold. Firstly, I will offer an introduction to Luhmann's organization theory with special attention to communication, which is aimed at giving unfamiliar readers a concise glimpse into the theory and allowing them to connect to the expanding debate of the recent years. Like other theorists, Luhmann conceived of organizations as social systems constituted through communications. In particular, he defined organizations as communicatively constituted systems that are created through decision-making. Decisions are thereby understood as communications as well, and specifically as inherently paradoxical communications that attempt to select a certain option while simultaneously communicating discarded alternatives that could have been selected instead. As a result, decisions are fragile events typically provoking opposition and rejection. Organizations can be understood as social phenomena that are capable of de-paradoxifying decisions by featuring these very decisions as their main mode of operation. However, theorizing way beyond the focus on organizations, Luhmann moreover asserted that not only organizations, but our entire social world is constituted through communication.

Hence, I will secondly highlight the role of macro-societal differentiation. When reading "macro-societal" differentiation, one might at first think of social classes or other forms of stratification. But this is not mainly meant here. While Luhmann acknowledged the importance of stratification, he argued similarly to other sociologists (Abrutyn & Turner, 2011; Bourdieu, 1988; Weber, 1946) that on a macro-level, society is differentiated into thematically distinctive domains such as politics, economics, and science. However, in contrast to other theories, the Luhmannian take on this is the assertion that these societal domains are best understood as systems that are constituted communicatively. In this respect, this chapter will also provide an introduction to this highly abstract theorization of society. As I will point out, the Luhmannian framework offers a communication-based counter program to the contemporary mainstream debate of institutional logics in the field of organization studies. I will thereby add to the existing literature by illustrating how different macro-societal systems are connected through single communication events and how they are structurally coupled via organizations.

The World as Communication

The Emergence of Communication "in-between" Human Beings

Luhmann's systems theory builds on a constructivist understanding of social reality (Luhmann, 1994). Like several other theorists in CCO research and related fields, Luhmann defines organizations as constituted by communication (Brummans et al., 2014). However, Luhmann is far more radical than most of them. According to him, not only organizations but the whole social world as such is constituted by communication and by communication only (Luhmann, 2012, 2013). The theory does not mean to question if there is some kind of "real" reality in a physics sense or that there are consciousnesses of human beings, chemical processes, and biological beings. The crucial point is that these "real" realities have no meaning (Luhmann, 1995b). They simply exist, and as such they can only be observed – and ultimately given meaning – in social processes.

The social reality is understood as a distinct level of reality that emerges out of the relation between human beings. Luhmann adopts a relational approach in this respect (Guy, 2018). The world is therefore not constructed by human beings; it is constructed by what emerges "in-between" human beings, i.e., social processes that, according to Luhmann, take the form of "communication" (Luhmann, 1996b, p. 260). At least one human being has to utter something (speak or gesture or act in some way) while another has to perceive this utterance and establish an understanding that some information has been uttered. However, as I outlined on another occasion:

> "Understanding" thereby does not mean that someone "understood" what another person wanted to say – that would be simply impossible since one cannot think in the head of the other. Understanding simply means that it was understood that an utterance (i.e., something was expressed in a certain way, e.g., in words or gestures) is different from the information (i.e., the actual content) that has been uttered.
>
> *Grothe-Hammer, 2020, p. 484*

Therefore, Luhmann identifies three basic elements that constitute communication – *utterance, understanding, information* – and communication only occurs when all three are present (Luhmann, 1992). An utterance can only be there if there is something that is uttered, i.e., information – and the one can only exist in occurrence with the other. Without understanding, on the other hand, there would not be information or an utterance in the first place, because then no social process would emerge. Perhaps there might be attempts to utter something (e.g., someone screaming towards another one who stands far away), but without an understanding the attempt to communicate would remain a mere attempt. Understanding, however, might also mean instances in which the involved people might think they misunderstood something or did not understand at all what another one was saying. But such descriptions would already be interpretations, which are only possible because on a basic level it was understood that there was an utterance that said something, even if the "something" – the information – appears to remain unclear. Even something uttered being unclear is already information – and as such it can be built on, e.g., by engaging in further communication for clarification, or by avoiding exactly this because one wants to leave it unclear. This is the main difference from events that simply happen – like a tree falling over or the sun going down. In such events there is no difference between utterance and information – these events simply happen and meaning can only be attributed to them through communication.

In a similar manner, a person might act without this action having any social relevance or meaning. Someone might be sitting at home alone talking to the wall. As long as no one else is there to process the talking, it is socially irrelevant. This talking does not become real in a social sense – notwithstanding that this all might exist in some physical reality. Only when the action of talking becomes processed as an utterance and thereby part of a communication process, actual social meaning arises.

Hence, (at least two) human beings are an important pre-condition for the emergence of communication; but the communication emerges in their interrelation and develops a life of its own (Luhmann, 1992). It is not possible to trace back the meaning that is constructed to a single individual. What the communication means is not identical with what someone has uttered, nor is it determined by what another one might understand psychologically.

Social Reality as Process

Human beings provide a necessary (double) *indeterminacy*[1] through which novel meaning is possible (Esposito, 2017). They are non-trivial (psychological and biological) systems that behave neither deterministically nor randomly but contingently. Usually, we can expect certain behaviors of certain people or in certain situations, but behaviors can always happen differently from what we expected. Hence, human beings can neither fully predetermine what meaning emerges socially nor can they directly translate social meaning into psychological meaning and vice versa. Rather, the coupling between human beings and communication can be understood as a bilateral triggering of changes of state:

> One reads, for example, that tobacco, alcohol, butter, and frozen meat are bad for one's health, and one is changed (into someone who should know and observe this) - whether one believes it or not! One cannot ignore it any longer.
>
> *Luhmann 1995a, p. 148*

Triggered by one communication event, a human being then triggers further communication events, and so on – creating a never-ending chain of communication events. Certain communication episodes might "end" – e.g., a conversation, the watching of a movie, a mail exchange – but in the context of society in general, communication constantly goes on, creating a recursive network of communication episodes spanning time and space (Luhmann, 2012, pp. 40–49). Thereby, the one communication event – one event of utterance, understanding, information – is only established in the next communication event. The understanding of the information of one utterance only means something if at least one ensuing utterance builds on it, thereby triggering the emergence of new meaning, and so on (see Figure 5.1). This "connection" can take place directly or indirectly; "connection" merely means that the meaning constructed in one communication event affects the meaning construction of following communication events. While "direct" connections might be obvious – e.g., writing an e-mail in response to an e-mail, or someone saying something in response to another person saying something – indirect connections might be hard to trace. Good examples are the watching of movies or the reading of books. In these cases, direct responses are impossible, and nevertheless most would probably agree that these are instances of communication. To draw on an anecdote here: I can remember that reading "All Quiet on the Western Front" (Remarque 1998/1929) changed how I communicated (and behaved) at work behind a bar – although probably no observer would be able to trace certain things I said back to the book that I had read. I had

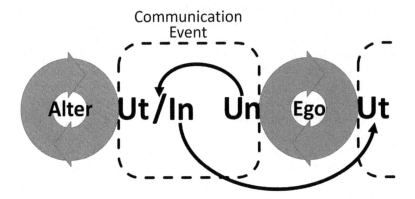

Figure 5.1 The three elements of a single communication event: utterance ("ut"); understanding ("un"); information ("in"). The one event is only established through the ensuing one(s), which can, of course, address the same persons again.

been changed in state psychologically and this has changed the state of further communications I have participated in (as illustrated by these very sentences).

Thus, *social reality only exists in the process*. These processes are thereby shaped by social structures, i.e., more or less stable expectations. But these structures in turn also only exist in the process – reproduced and constantly shifting from one communication event to another.[2] Communication processes, moreover, spawn the emergence of social systems, i.e., processual entities (conceptualized next) that are constituted as soon as "certain communications connect to certain other communications and exclude the rest" (Grothe-Hammer, 2020, p. 484). Then a boundary between an inside and an outside is created, marking a distinguishable system – which can take manifold forms ranging from face-to-face interactions over conflicts, social movements, macro-societal domains, to organizations (Luhmann, 2012, 2013).

Social Systems as Processual Entities

Social systems are *both closed and open systems at the same time* (Luhmann, 1995a, p. 37). On the one hand they are operatively closed since only certain communications connect to certain communications. "Certain communications" mean specific characteristics that these have that make them distinctive from other communications. Any type of social system has its own peculiarities characterized by its own special mode of communication (Kühl, 2020). On the other hand, systems are open in several ways. They can observe their environment through their processes, thereby making their own meaning out of it, and they are triggered by their environment through certain couplings that cannot be evaded. Couplings are certain connecting points between systems and their environments in which certain events on the one side inevitably trigger a change of state on the other – as, e.g., discussed above regarding the relation between human beings and communication (Hagen, 2000). There are countless couplings between social systems and their physical and biological environment, and between social systems themselves – most of which I cannot discuss here in further detail, but I will come back to this when it comes to unfolding how different societal domains as systems are coupled among each other.

Organizations as Systems of Decisions

One specific type of social systems is organizations. These are constituted through a specific kind of communication, i.e., decisions (Luhmann, 2018). To understand how Luhmann could derive such an unusual definition of organizations, it is important to stress that he departs significantly from other established understandings of decisions. Most works treat decisions as psychological events by assuming that it is a person who makes a decision and then communicates it (Grothe-Hammer et al., forthcoming); and, with such a definition in mind, most scholars would probably argue that it makes no sense to define organizations as systems constituted through decision-making. However, Luhmann defines decisions as mere social events, i.e., as communications

> which communicate their own contingency ('contingency' here in the sense of 'also possible otherwise'). In contrast to an ordinary communication, which only communicates a specific content that has been selected (e.g. 'I love you'), a decision communication communicates also – explicitly or implicitly – that there are alternatives that could have been selected instead (e.g. 'I am going to employ candidate A and not candidate B').
>
> *Seidl, 2005, p. 39*

Consequently, decisions are inherently *paradoxical* communications because they attempt to select a certain option while simultaneously communicating discarded alternatives (Luhmann, 2018). Therefore, decisions always fix and open up meaning at the same time (Grothe-Hammer & Schoeneborn, 2019). As a result, decisions are fragile events typically provoking opposition and rejection, because other options are always visible and inevitably bring up the question if another possibility could have been selected instead.

This paradox is unsolvable because a decision is only possible if options are available. In situations in which a certain course of action indeed appears as being "without any alternative", there would be no choice to make and hence no decision. Scholars have accordingly pointed out that, in a sense, decisions are always "undecidable" because they are necessarily fixed and non-fixed at the same time (Andersen, 2003).

This paradox provides the basis for the phenomenon we call "organization". In most social settings, the acceptance of a decision as a premise for ensuing decisions or behavior is improbable. Decisions are fragile "because rejecting a decision implies the possibility of just ignoring it" (Grothe-Hammer & Schoeneborn, 2019). However, organizations can be understood as those social phenomena that are capable of de-paradoxifying decisions by featuring these very decisions as their main mode of operation (Schoeneborn, 2011). Organizations constitute and reproduce themselves through decisions and communications oriented towards decisions (Luhmann, 2018).

Let me clarify this in the following, since this assertion might seem counter-intuitive at a first glance. Many have argued that the importance of decisions in and for organizations should not be overestimated, because decisions are said to often not translate into action (Brunsson & Brunsson, 2017, p. 6). However, Luhmann argues that this is not an adequate description of what is happening empirically in organizations. From a Luhmannian perspective such a clear-cut distinction between decision/action would be an analytical attribution – retrospectively applied, for instance, by a researcher. Luhmann thus points out that in organizations so-called "actions" that might or might not be based on a previous decision, in fact are (or can be) treated as decisions themselves. This is hence one of the main characteristics of organizations, i.e., every event that is treated as part of the organization is or can be treated as a decision.

> Particularly in organizations … practically all behavior – even machine operation, dealing with enquiries, or coming late to work – can, in the event of problematization, be thematized as decisions.
>
> *Luhmann, 2018, p. 45*

This "totalization" of decisions as the basic operational element then produces organizations' unique characteristics in comparison to other types of social systems. While in other social settings – like in an informal face-to-face interaction – a decision might simply be rejected or ignored, in organizations rejecting or ignoring a decision produces the need for new decisions. Rejecting a decision can only be achieved by another decision. As outlined above, even the ignoring of a decision can be treated as a decision in case of problematization – whether the "ignorer" meant it this way or not.

Hence, organizations produce constant "decision necessities" (Nassehi, 2005) through which "one decision calls for ensuing decisions, resulting in a self-reproducing stream of decisions" (Ahrne et al., 2016, p. 95). In doing so, organizations are capable of stabilizing the fragility of decisions to some degree, thereby producing complexities that no other social phenomenon can provide. This is one of their main relevances in modern society. Without more or less stable decisions, modern society would not be possible (Ahrne et al., 2016; Grothe-Hammer et al., forthcoming), so it is dependent on organizations to provide such. Only organizations are capable of producing those complex decisions needed to allow for modern medicine, air travel, the internet, disaster response, building construction, and so on.

One important aspect is their capability to produce certain decisions that become accepted as relatively stable premises for further decisions. Drawing on Herbert A. Simon (1997), Luhmann (2018) calls these (decided) "decision premises", i.e., those decisions that are used as premises in ensuing decisions. Decision premises are the organization's structures. Decided decision premises can take many forms. Luhmann repeatedly distinguished three broad categories: "communication channels", which define who is supposed to communicate with whom, and who can issue orders for whom (vertical and horizontal hierarchies); "programs" in the form of rules, regulations, and goals; and "personnel" selection, deployment, and transfers (see Seidl, 2005). Whereas these three categories offer the possibility to map an organization's structures comprehensively, one can employ less abstract notions when describing certain concrete structural elements. Scholars (including Luhmann) have, for instance, also described structural elements such as membership, hierarchies, rules, goals, organizational statements, monitoring systems, and sanctioning mechanisms as decision premises on which the organization can decide (Apelt et al., 2017; Christensen et al., 2013; Luhmann, 2013). Decision premises shape future decisions by limiting "the possibilities of what is accepted as decisions in organizations" (Grothe-Hammer & Schoeneborn, 2019). For instance, in most organizations, only those who were selected as members can participate in the organization's decision processes, and only those who have a higher position in the vertical hierarchy have the right to issue decisions for other members (Luhmann, 2020).

In the above outlined understanding of communication, decided decision premises are certain decision events that become recurrently re-actualized and therefore "remembered" in ensuing decisions. The premises are remembered through the individuals participating in the decision events and whose psychological states have been influenced by the foregoing premises, therefore influencing the shape of ensuing utterances and understandings in communication, and ultimately the produced meaningful information (Luhmann, 1996a). Every decision premise is therefore re-actualized and hence more or less slightly re-confirmed, adapted, or re-shaped in each event. A certain position in the hierarchy might be seen as in charge for a certain issue by certain people, while others might see another position in the hierarchy as in charge. A certain rule might lead to a particular action in one instance and to another action in another instance. A rule such as "the shower needs to be cleaned after every usage" needs re-interpretation in every actualization. What does "to be cleaned" mean? What qualifies as "usage"? Of course, one can try to overspecify such rules. However, the question is how far one needs to go to get rid of ambiguities. It should be immediately plausible that most rules in an organization cannot be specified in an ISO standard manner. Which researcher has not already experienced some ambiguities in manuscript submission guidelines of a journal when readying a paper for submission – even in cases in which these guidelines already have a length of 13 pages? And as soon as one thinks of structures other than algorithmizable rules – goals, communication channels, recruitment demands, hierarchical responsibilities, etc. – underspecification is unavoidable, and often facilitates ever new specifications.

Moreover, some decision premises might just be ignored – what technically de-premises them for the moment. The cleaning rule for the shower might simply not be followed at all. The authority of an official hierarch might just not be accepted and orders by them ignored. The recruitment demands might just be overthrown by someone giving the job to a friend, and so on. In these cases, we would come back to the abovementioned point: all these instances of rejections of decision premises can be treated as decisions themselves – perhaps even as the setting of alternative decision premises instead. The shower-cleaning rule issued by the head office might be substituted by a local cleaning rule – perhaps an unofficial one, but still a decided decision premise.

Apart from such "decided" decision premises, Luhmann (2018, pp. 193–203) also sees the relevance of "undecided" decision premises, which he describes as the organization's culture. In particular, this concerns all the aspects of an organization that are not decided but that nevertheless shape the decisions the organization makes. In this understanding, organizational culture takes the form of undecided but nevertheless relevant expectations that serve as premises for how organizational decisions are made. This can be implicit norms, ambiguous values, or collegiality. An important aspect is that culture in this sense can be in fact undecidable. Some aspects like implicit norms might be turned into explicated norms through decisions and, hence, into decided premises for decision-making. However, many aspects such as a nice working climate, collegiality or mindfulness cannot be decided. Indeed, an organization might try to decide such issues as well – such as explicitly outlining norms of collegiality – but this will never prevent the emergence of undecided forms of collegiality (or un-collegiality) that escape the decisions. These are rather elementary or self-emergent forms of social structure that can perhaps be influenced by certain decisions but not directly decided.

Society and Macro-societal Domains as Systems of Communication

As outlined above, Luhmann identifies several different kinds of social systems that are all constituted through communication. Apart from organizations, he also defines face-to-face interactions, social movements, families, conflicts, as well as society as such, and several societal domains as social systems (Luhmann, 1995a, 2012, 2013). He describes modern society as the all-encompassing social system that consists of all communications. According to him, modern society can only be comprehended as one world society, because nowadays all communication in the world is somehow directly or indirectly connected (Luhmann, 1982).

In this view, organizations, as well as other social systems, can only be seen as subsystems of this overall world society – meaning that although they are autonomous and distinctive systems, their communications only exist (and gain their meaning) as embedded in the overall network of communications happening in society. One can argue that all the different kinds of social systems represent some kind of internal differentiation of society into organizations, interactions, movements, and so. However, in addition to these kinds of systems, Luhmann (1982) also argued that society as such is differentiated on the macro-level itself.

Specifically, he argued that society is primarily differentiated into thematically or functionally distinctive domains: politics, economics, judiciary, medicine, sciences, education, mass media, art, religion, and love (Luhmann, 2012, 2013; Apelt et al., 2017) – nowadays complemented by sports and social help (Schirmer & Michailakis 2019; Stichweh 2013). Other forms of differentiation, i.e., stratified differentiation into strata, classes, and castes, segmentary differentiation in, e.g., nation states and military alliances, and center-periphery differentiation, e.g., into city and countryside, are, of course, still highly relevant. However, the main argument of Luhmann (2012, 2013) is that modernity distinguishes itself from pre-modern societies by featuring thematic differentiation as its main form of differentiation (for an excellent introduction see Schirmer & Michailakis, 2019). Without being able to go into more specifics here, it is probably worth noting that the idea of society being mainly differentiated into thematically distinctive realms is considered far from "exotic" in sociology. Many other theorists developed similar concepts (Apelt et al., 2017). For example, Max Weber (1946) called these realms "value spheres" (which in neo-institutional theory underlie so-called "institutional logics"; Friedland, 2014), (old) institutional theorists have defined these as "institutional domains" (Abrutyn and Turner, 2011), and Bourdieu (1988) called them "social fields".

Luhmann defined these societal domains as "functional systems" (Luhmann, 2013) – and hence as systems which consist of communication and of communication only. These systems are "functional" in the sense that they provide functions that are elementary for society. Politics, for example, provides collectively binding decisions, science produces scientific knowledge, and the economy distributes scarce resources.

However, while organizations gain their operative distinctiveness by privileging decisions, societal domains orient communications thematically. Societal domains can be understood as social systems because they consist of interconnected communications that are thematically distinctive from communications in other societal domains. They feature their own logic of communication, and hence their own special mode of meaning-making. To grasp these logics of communication, Luhmann proposed to theoretically condense these into binary communication codes. He argued that the economic system only reproduced communication in the code having/not having, the political system only in power/non-power, and so on. However, we must not misunderstand these codes as something that is explicitly applied in practice (at least not all the time). The mere idea behind the binary code is to theoretically capture the empirical situation that each societal domain constructs the world through its own specific lens, i.e., by observing the world and communicatively constructing its own system-specific representation of it. The economic system constructs its view of the world in economic terms, the political system in political terms, and so on. The same event or object will have different meanings in different societal domains.

Let us think of a simple example like a dinner table. The dinner table has different meanings depending on which societal domain currently observes it. One can observe the dinner table through the lens of all societal domains. We can talk about the dinner table economically in terms of its price and potential maintenance costs (economic system), we can admire its aesthetic design (art system), use it as a device to set up the chess board (sports system), we might wonder if the used materials were even legal (juridical system), or perhaps even judge it based on its potential value for romantic activities such as a candlelight dinner (love system), and so on.

In terms of communication, this practically means that we can switch between societal domains within an ongoing face-to-face interaction. Thus, these societal domains are not some abstract substances or spheres with strict boundaries hovering somewhere above the clouds or so. It might be worth reminding us here that social systems are nothing else than networks of interconnected communications that progress through time and space, thereby distinguishing themselves from each other by including only certain kinds of communications. And while organizations create inclusion criteria by narrowing down the spectrum of what counts as internal by employing decision premises, the belonging of a communication to a societal domain is determined by its thematic focus. Thus, societal domains are dynamic communication systems and as such traverse all parts of social life – ranging from face-to-face interactions over organizations or social movements, to the globalized world.

Thus, objects, events, and activities may have a certain economic meaning when thematized in the economic domain, while having quite different meanings in other domains. One might simply think of how our scientific outputs are observed by societal domains other than science (if they are at all). Research results may develop a life of their own when reported on in the news (mass media system), or may trigger very different interpretations than imagined when used in teaching (educational system).

At the same time, the different societal domains trigger and influence each other constantly. They observe each other and, in many cases, even rely on each other's performances. The economic domain usually is quite dependent on scientific research results to develop or adjust new products, and it is dependent on the education system to produce knowledgeable and skilled personnel. The education system in turn is quite dependent on scientific knowledge (science systems) – e.g., in history class one could not teach much without historical research – and, of course, on funding (economic system).

But, if we accept the assertion that these societal domains are systems of distinctive and autonomous communication processes, how is it then possible that communication processes connect to each other? As outlined above, each social system is operatively closed in the sense that only certain communications belong to it while the rest is environment. Economic communication is only economic communication, educational communication is only educational communication, and so on. However, referring to Luhmann (1995a), I have also already argued that all systems are open to each other at the same time. So, how is this simultaneous closedness and openness possible? How can we imagine this seeming contradiction?

After all, these societal domains do not appear as visible entities in our everyday lives. In this respect, Luhmann restricted himself mostly to rather abstract explanations. In the following I will unfold this theoretical abstraction by breaking it down to the smallest elements of communication – something that to my knowledge has not been done so far. To this purpose, let us come back to the basic definition of communication and its three constitutive elements: utterance, understanding, information.

An important point I want to repeat is that a single utterance can be understood multiple times, thereby multiplying into ever new meanings. Think of a university professor giving a lecture. What they say is understood differently through each individual student, thereby each time producing slightly (or maybe even not so slightly) different meanings of what the professor utters. This phenomenon becomes most obvious in cases in which utterances are stabilized in time through material form – as in case of a book or a TV show (both representing utterances or bundles of utterances), a sculpture, etc. The same utterances can be understood countless times – for instance, when millions read the same book or watch the same TV show – thereby producing countless different understandings and slightly different meaningful information. Let us briefly adapt Figure 5.1 accordingly (Figure 5.2).

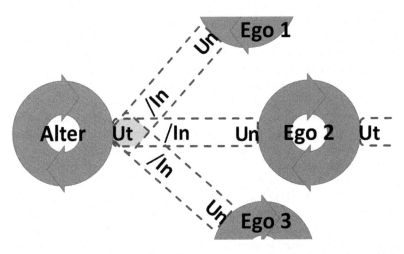

Figure 5.2 One utterance ("ut") can be understood ("un") multiple times by multiple recipients thereby producing differing information ("in").
Derived from Luhmann, 2013, p. 7.

Having this *multiplication of communication* in mind, I would like to apply this insight to the case of different societal domains. Let us think of a hypothetical example from film production and imagine a meeting of the director, the assistant director, the production manager, the director of photography, and the production's lawyer during pre-production. Let us assume the director says the following: "I want to shoot in St. Tropez on a yacht and Taylor Swift comes over." We can now think about the different understandings located in different societal domains that this utterance might lead to. Immediately, the production manager might answer: "This is too expensive", thereby constructing a meaning located in the economic domain. The assistant director might say that this is a good idea and will probably attract many viewers, which would create meaning and connection in the mass media domain. The director of photography might on the other hand react by praising the beauty of the location and what beautiful pictures they can shoot there – and hence constitute meaning in the art domain. And finally, the lawyer might immediately note that this will pose a number of legal challenges that need to be solved – producing a communication in the juridical domain.

Hence, in this simple example we can easily identify four different communications in four different societal domains spawned from one single utterance. Breaking down the communication process into its three basic elements – utterance, understanding, information – makes it therefore possible to understand how one utterance (one single action) can be an element of several different communication systems, and to understand how these systems can be open and closed at the same time. This connection of different systems via single instances is what Luhmann (2012, p. 126) called "*operational coupling*", i.e., the coupling between systems through communicative operations. This aspect of coupling brings us finally back to organizations, and more specifically how organizations couple different societal domains.

Organizations and Societal Domains

We have now introduced the notions of communication, organization, organizational structures (decision premises), societal domains, and couplings between systems. At this point we can bring these notions together to provide an understanding of how organizations combine different societal domains. It is now possible to understand that the same utterances can co-exist as elements of different systems, i.e., face-to-face interactions, organizations, different societal domains. Organizations can, hence, be seen as "multi-referential" – meaning that all societal domains traverse an organization (Apelt et al., 2017). Every organizational decision communication can also simultaneously appear as a communication of a societal domain, or even be multiplied into several societal domains. The organization might decide to spend money on something – which is an example of a communication belonging to the organization and a communication belonging to the societal domain of economics. Perhaps the organization decides to place a commercial on TV – thereby spawning the simultaneous appearance of an organizational, an economic, and a mass media communication in a single instant. These are examples of operative couplings because several systems are coupled in one operation of communication.

As outlined above, these couplings are only possible because communication provides the possibility of multiplying a single utterance into different communications with different meanings that can belong to different systems. Every utterance made in context of the organization system can also connect to societal domains. For example, an autopsy report as an utterance usually spawns a medical meaning and a juridical meaning, while at the same time also an organizational meaning: one utterance with at least three different communicative connections.

However, organizations can also turn operative couplings into *structural couplings*, so that organizations can implement relatively stable couplings between different societal domains. To do so, they make certain decisions that install such couplings between societal domains as organizational structures (Luhmann, 2018). Drawing on the above outlined concept of decision premises, an organization can, in particular, decide on certain communication channels, programs, and personnel issues – and design them in a way that they couple different systems. Let us begin with the structure of communication channels. In this respect, departmentalization is a well-known form of how to decouple societal domains to allow for specific instances of coupling (Besio & Meyer, 2015). The law department is then responsible for juridical communication, the research and development department is concerned with science, and so on. The actual coupling of societal domains then takes place via those arrangements within an organization that bring these departments together at certain points. These can be certain meetings, joint committees and working groups, boundary departments concerned with managing the relations between departments, and so on.

In terms of programs, one can think of goals and rules. Many organizations couple societal domains by prominently installing competing goals that correspond to different societal domains. Examples for such organizations are universities with their shared dedication to science and education, for-profit hospitals with their shared goals of treating sick people (medical domain) and making profits (economic domain), media companies with their shared goals of producing media content for lots of people (mass media domain) and making profits (economic domain), or museums that want to present artistic works (art domain) while being educational as well (education domain). In these cases, societal domains are coupled on a programmatic level leading an organization to constantly address two different societal domains at the same time. However, one can also think of certain rules that organizations implement that couple societal domains in an if-then manner. Hospitals might specify that certain treatments (medical system) are only performed after a payment (economic system). And a specialized news outlet might decide to publish only articles (mass media system) that are related to sports (sports systems).

Last but not least, organizations can also produce structural couplings between societal domains via personnel decisions. On the one hand, organizations might purposely employ people who are professionalized in one societal domain to work mainly in another. One might, for instance, think of political parties that appoint scientists to run for public votes, or of corporations that employ politicians to leverage political connections for economic purposes. On the other hand, one might also think of cases in which organizations design certain positions or roles in a way that they systematically combine different societal domains. At the university, the dual goal of science and education is implemented by having professor positions that combine both orientations in one role. Or to pick up the example of the autopsy report: such reports are produced by forensic pathologists who combine a medical orientation with a juridical one.

Conclusion

This chapter had two main purposes. First, I wanted to offer an introduction to Niklas Luhmann's theories of communication, organization, and macro-societal differentiation in a manner that differs from several (excellent) introductions that already exist. Second, I have demonstrated how the Luhmannian framework can offer an elaborated understanding of how organizations relate to different societal domains, and how organizations interrelate these societal domains among each other through their decisions on the level of single communicative events and on the structural level.

For the future, it might be worth exploring how the potential of the Luhmannian framework can be used better than now. When it comes to researching the relation between organizations and macro-societal differentiation, most organizational research is nowadays taking place within the neo-institutional framework, namely the debate revolving around so-called "institutional logics". However, the consequent works often suffer from a simplified view of organizations as containers of individual actors (cf. Hallett & Hawbaker, 2021) who then do something with these logics. Moreover, these works also suffer from a virtually non-existent macro-societal theory. While institutional logics are explicitly defined as being located in so-called macro-societal value spheres as famously outlined by Max Weber (Friedland, 2014), the theory of value spheres itself remains extremely underspecified. Max Weber (e .g., 1946) only wrote a couple of shorter pieces on these, and there have been in fact only very few works that aimed at further developing the theory. Among these are mainly works by Friedland and colleagues who try to provide a more thorough meta-theorization by taking institutional logics indeed out of sociology as such and instead resort to philosophizing the concept. Institutional logics are then described as grounded in some meta-physical "substance" (Friedland et al., 2014, p. 334) that is explicitly defined as "unobservable" (p. 337) and treated "as if 'it' exists" (p. 336).

The Luhmannian framework makes a counteroffer. It provides extensive works on nearly all macro-societal domains, and an integrated theory of organization – both being built on a framework of the communicative constitution (and construction) of social reality. In this respect I hope that my chapter can help to make the Luhmannian approach a bit more "digestible", so that a communication-based perspective might become a bit more valued in the debates on macro-societal differentiation in organization studies.

Notes

1 Also often called "double contingency".
2 In this respect, Luhmann 1995a, p. 293, explicitly builds on Anthony Giddens, 1979.

References

Abrutyn, S., & Turner, J. H. (2011). The old institutionalism meets the new institutionalism. *Sociological Perspectives*, *54*(3), 283–306. https://doi.org/10.1525/sop.2011.54.3.283.

Ahrne, G., & Brunsson, N. (2008). *Meta-organizations*. Edward Elgar.

Ahrne, G., & Brunsson, N. (2011). Organization outside organizations: The significance of partial organization. *Organization*, *18*(1), 83–104. https://doi.org/10.1177/1350508410376256.

Ahrne, G., Brunsson, N., & Seidl, D. (2016). Resurrecting organization by going beyond organizations. *European Management Journal*, *34*(2), 93–101. https://doi.org/10.1016/j.emj.2016.02.003.

Andersen, N. Å., & Born, A. W. (2008). The employee in the sign of love. *Culture and Organization*, *14*(4), 325–343. https://doi.org/10.1080/14759550802489664.

Andersen, N. Å. (2003). The undecidability of decision. In T. Bakken & T. Hernes (Eds.), *Autopoietic organization theory: Drawing on Niklas Luhmann's social systems perspective* (pp. 235–258). Abstrakt.

Andersen, N. Å. (2020). Potentialization: Loosening up relations between public organizations and societal function systems. *Management & Organizational History*, *15*(1), 65–89. https://doi.org/10.1080/17449359.2020.1815548.

Apelt, M., Besio, C., Corsi, G., von Groddeck, V., Grothe-Hammer, M., & Tacke, V. (2017). Resurrecting organization without renouncing society: A response to Ahrne, Brunsson and Seidl. *European Management Journal*, *35*(1), 8–14. https://doi.org/10.1016/j.emj.2017.01.002.

Bamyeh, M. A. (2014). From the editor. *International Sociology*, *29*(5), 373–373. https://doi.org/10.1177/0268580914544427.

Becker, K. H. (2005). Annotated bibliography of selected works by Niklas Luhmann. In D. Seidl & K.-H. Becker (Eds.), *Niklas Luhmann and organization studies* (pp. 411–422). Liber.

Besio, C., & Meyer, U. (2015). Heterogeneity in world society: How organizations handle contradicting logics. In B. Holzer, F. Kastner, T. Werron, & M. Albert (Eds.), *From globalization to world society: Neo-institutional and systems-theoretical perspectives* (pp. 237–257). New York: Routledge.

Blaschke, S., Schoeneborn, D., & Seidl, D. (2012). Organizations as networks of communication episodes: Turning the network perspective inside out. *Organization Studies*, *33*(7), 879–906. https://doi.org/10.1177/0170840612443459.

Bourdieu, P. (1988). *Homo academicus*. Stanford University Press.

Brummans, B. H., Cooren, F., Robichaud, D., & Taylor, J. (2014). Approaches to research on the communicative constitution of organizations. In D. K. Mumby & L. L. Putnam (Eds.), *The SAGE handbook of organizational communication: Advances in theory, research, and methods* (pp. 173–194). Sage.

Brunsson, K., & Brunsson, N. (2017). *Decisions: The complexities of individual and organizational decision-making*. Edward Elgar.

Christensen, L. T., Morsing, M., & Thyssen, O. (2013). CSR as aspirational talk. *Organization*, *20*(3), 372–393. https://doi.org/10.1177/1350508413478310.

Cooren, F., & Seidl, D. (2019). Niklas Luhmann's radical communication approach and its implications for research on organizational communication. *Academy of Management Review*, *45*(2), 479–497. https://doi.org/10.5465/amr.2018.0176.

Dobusch, L., & Schoeneborn, D. (2015). Fluidity, identity, and organizationality: The communicative constitution of Anonymous. *Journal of Management Studies*, *52*(8), 1005–1035. https://doi.org/10.1111/joms.12139.

Esposito, E. (2017). Artificial communication? The production of contingency by algorithms. *Zeitschrift für Soziologie*, *46*(4), 249–265. https://doi.org/10.1515/zfsoz-2017-1014.

Friedland, R. (2014). Divine institution: Max Weber's value spheres and institutional theory. *Research in the Sociology of Organizations*, *41*, 217–258. https://doi.org/10.1108/S0733-558X20140000041015.

Friedland, R., Mohr, J. W., Roose, H., & Gardinali, P. (2014). The institutional logics of love: Measuring intimate life. *Theory and Society*, *43*(3–4), 333–370. https://doi.org/10.1007/s11186-014-9223-6.

Giddens, A. (1979). *Central problems in social theory: Action, structure and contradiction in social analysis*. Macmillan.

Grothe-Hammer, M. (2020). Membership and contributorship in organizations: An update of modern systems theory. *Systems Research and Behavioral Science*, *37*(3), 482–495. https://doi.org/10.1002/sres.2683.

Grothe-Hammer, M., Berkowitz, H., & Berthod, O. (forthcoming). Decisional organization theory: Towards an integrated framework of organization. In M. Godwyn (Ed.), *Research handbook on the sociology of organizations*. Edward Elgar.

Grothe-Hammer, M., & Schoeneborn, D. (2019). The queen bee outlives her own children: A Luhmannian perspective on project-based organizations (PBOs). In C. Vásquez & T. Kuhn (Eds.), *Dis/Organization as communication: Exploring the disordering, disruptive and chaotic properties of communication* (pp. 60–79). Routledge. https://doi.org/10.4324/9780429492327-4.

Guy, J.-S. (2018). Is Niklas Luhmann a relational sociologist? In F. Dépelteau (Ed.), *The Palgrave handbook of relational sociology* (pp. 289–304). Springer International. https://doi.org/10.1007/978-3-319-66005-9_14.

Hagen, R. (2000). Rational solidarity and functional differentiation. *Acta Sociologica, 43*(1), 27–42. https://doi.org/10.1177/000169930004300104.

Hallett, T., & Hawbaker, A. (2021). The case for an inhabited institutionalism in organizational research: Interaction, coupling, and change reconsidered. *Theory and Society, 50*(1), 1–32. https://doi.org/10.1007/s11186-020-09412-2.

Højlund, H., & Villadsen, K. (2020). Technologies in caregiving: Professionals' strategies for engaging with new technology. *New Technology, Work and Employment, 35*(2), 178–194. https://doi.org/10.1111/ntwe.12161.

Kleve, H., Köllner, T., Schlippe, A. von, & Rüsen, T. A. (2020). The business family 3.0: Dynastic business families as families, organizations and networks—Outline of a theory extension. *Systems Research and Behavioral Science, 37*(3), 516–526. https://doi.org/10.1002/sres.2684.

Kühl, S. (2020). Groups, organizations, families and movements: The sociology of social systems between interaction and society. *Systems Research and Behavioral Science, 37*(3), 496–515. https://doi.org/10.1002/sres.2685.

Luhmann, N. (1982). The world society as a social system. *International Journal of General Systems, 8*(3), 131–138. https://doi.org/10.1080/03081078208547442.

Luhmann, N. (1992). What is communication? *Communication Theory, 2*(3), 251–259. https://doi.org/10.1111/j.1468-2885.1992.tb00042.x.

Luhmann, N. (1994). "What is the case?" and "what lies behind it?" The two sociologies and the theory of society. *Sociological Theory, 12*(2), 126–139. https://doi.org/10.2307/201859.

Luhmann, N. (1995a). *Social systems.* Stanford University Press.

Luhmann, N. (1995b). The paradox of observing systems. *Cultural Critique, 31*, 37–55. https://doi.org/10.2307/1354444.

Luhmann, N. (1996a). Membership and motives in social systems. *Systems Research, 13*(3), 341–348. https://doi.org/10.1002/(SICI)1099-1735(199609)13:3<341::AID-SRES92>3.0.CO;2-5.

Luhmann, N. (1996b). On the scientific context of the concept of communication. *Social Science Information, 35*(2), 257–267. https://doi.org/10.1177/053901896035002005.

Luhmann, N. (2012). *Theory of society: Volume 1.* Stanford University Press.

Luhmann, N. (2013). *Theory of society: Volume 2.* Stanford University Press.

Luhmann, N. (2018). *Organization and decision.* Cambridge University Press.

Luhmann, N. (2020). Organization, membership and the formalization of behavioural expectations. *Systems Research and Behavioral Science, 37*(3), 425–449. https://doi.org/10.1002/sres.2689.

Nassehi, A. (2005). Organizations as decision machines: Niklas Luhmann's theory of organized social systems. *The Sociological Review, 53*(1_suppl), 178–191. https://doi.org/10.1111/j.1467-954X.2005.00549.x.

Remarque, E. M. (1998). *Im Westen nichts Neues* (2nd edn.). Kiepenhauer & Witsch. (Original work published 1929)

Schirmer, W., & Michailakis, D. (2019). *Systems theory for social work and the helping professions.* Routledge.

Schoeneborn, D. (2011). Organization as communication: A Luhmannian perspective. *Management Communication Quarterly, 25*(4), 663–689. https://doi.org/10.1177/0893318911405622.

Seidl, D. (2005). The basic concepts of Luhmann's theory of social systems. In D. Seidl & K.-H. Becker (Eds.), *Niklas Luhmann and organization studies* (pp. 21–53). Liber.

Seidl, D., & Mormann, H. (2014). Niklas Luhmann as organization theorist. In P. Adler, P. du Gay, G. Morgan, & M. Reed (Eds.), *The Oxford handbook of sociology, social theory, and organization studies* (pp. 125–157). Oxford University Press. https://doi.org/10.1093/oxfordhb/9780199671083.013.0007.

Simon, H. A. (1997). *Administrative behavior: A study of decision-making processes in administrative organizations.* The Free Press.

Sohn, Y. J. (2020). 40 years of Luhmann's legacy in the Anglophone academic community: A quantitative content analysis of Luhmannian research. *International Review of Sociology, 30*(3), 469–495. https://doi.org/10.1080/03906701.2020.1853005.

Stichweh, R. (2013). Sport as a function system in world society. *European Journal for Sport and Society,* *10*(2), 87–100. https://doi.org/10.1080/16138171.2013.11687913.

Weber, M. (1946). Science as a vocation. In H. H. Gerth & C. W. Mills (Eds.), *From Max Weber: Essays in sociology* (pp. 129–156). Oxford University Press.

Will, M. G., Roth, S., & Valentinov, V. (2018). From nonprofit diversity to organizational multifunctionality: A systems–theoretical proposal. *Administration & Society, 50*(7), 1015–1036. https://doi.org/10.1177/0095399717728093.

6

THE MULTIPLE ROLES OF MATERIALITY WHEN COMMUNICATION CONSTITUTES ORGANIZATIONS

Elizabeth Wilhoit Larson and Jeanne Mengis

Introduction

Decentering the focus from human communication to recognize the role that materialization (Cooren, 2020), material actants (Latour, 1999), or non-humans play in organizing processes has been an important contribution of the communicative constitution of organization (CCO) approach not only to organizational communication, but to the communication and management disciplines more broadly. In this chapter, we examine four different ways how materiality enters the communicative constitution of organization.

The material turn in organizational communication came in response to the critique that communication-centered approaches to organizing "stressed symbolic over material aspects of organization" (Ashcraft, Kuhn, & Cooren, 2009, p. 2). It followed the broader concern of the new materialist project that the linguistic, semiotic and interpretive turns had "granted [language] too much power" and that what seemed to matter was everything except matter (Barad, 2007, p. 132). Yet, the critique of privileging communication or discourse over matter risked reinforcing a bifurcated worldview with communication and discourse on the one side, and materiality on the other (Ashcraft et al., 2009; Cooren, 2015; Putnam, 2015). For communication scholars, one could avoid such a trap by asking how communication involves materiality, starting to develop different positions of how organizational communication theories could account for materiality (Ashcraft et al., 2009).

As scholars have developed material understandings of communication, they have sought to describe the relationship between the two without separating materiality and discourse or privileging communication over materiality. Scholars of both the materiality camp (Barad, 2007; Latour, 2013; Law & Mol, 1995; Orlikowski, 2007; Orlikowski & Scott, 2008, 2014) and the communication camp (Ashcraft et al., 2009; Cooren, 2020; Putnam, 2015) have attempted to reduce these risks by proposing relational accounts that examine "how these factors work together" (Barad, 2007, p. 25) in organizational endeavors. For example, scholars have analyzed how the material and the discursive become "imbricated" (Leonardi, 2012), "intertwined"

DOI: 10.4324/9781003224914-8

(Hardy & Thomas, 2015), "entangled" (Orlikowski, 2010; Orlikowski & Scott, 2008) or how they are in "tension" (Putnam, 2015) and co-develop in interdependent, dialectic relationships (Putnam, Fairhurst, & Banhart, 2016). Yet, Cooren (2020) has recently argued that much of this work still reinforces a bifurcated view. Given the interest in materiality in organizing and organizations over the last 15 years, particularly within the communicative constitution of organization literature (Ashcraft et al., 2009), understandings of materiality, its roles, and its relationship with communication have evolved. As scholarship in this area has increased, varying perspectives on the relationship between materiality and communication have emerged. In this chapter, we attempt to draw distinctions and lay out four perspectives on materiality and their role in communication (see Table 6.1 for a summary). Our aim is not to create divisions, but to map the fine distinctions between perspectives and how these matter for our explanations of organizational phenomena. These perspectives are helpful to orient and position future research and to further advance a materially sensitive and communication-centered understanding of organizations.

Four Perspectives on Materiality

Materiality as Sensible Matter Mediating Human Interaction

A communication-centered approach to organizations, in particular the CCO perspective, has argued organizing is achieved through communication (Brummans, Cooren, Robichaud, & Taylor, 2014; Schoeneborn, Kuhn, & Kärreman, 2019), and that organizational endeavors such as how we coordinate, innovate, practice leadership, or shape organizational identities are communicative accomplishments. Communication has then been understood primarily as a meaning-centered process, expressed, for example, as Ashcraft et al. (2009) describe (and then trouble) a common definition of communication: "Communication entails the dynamic, interactive negotiation of meaning through symbol use" (p. 6). Communication's constitutive force for organizations is closely related to this meaning-making capacity: "[s]eeing communication as constitutive of meaning (and thus of organizational reality) positions communication as a vital explanation for organizational phenomena" (Schoeneborn et al., 2019, p. 476).

For a long time, this focus on meaning also meant focusing on the symbolic. So although materiality did receive some scholarly attention, for instance as an aspect of organizational culture, it was seen as another symbolic carrier of meanings. Today, there are still some strands of CCO research, such as the four flows framework (see Iverson, Myers, & McPhee, this volume), which, drawing on Giddens (1984), argues that only humans can have agency (McPhee, 2014). Yet, there has been a growing attention to the collective construction of meaning in communication – e.g. sensemaking as a communication-centered (e.g. Cooren, Kuhn, Cornelissen, & Clark, 2011; Taylor & Robichaud, 2004; Taylor & Van Every, 2000; Weick et al., 2005) or a discursive social practice (e.g. Brown et al., 2015; Rouleau & Balogun, 2011) – is "multisemiotic" (Iedema, 2007, p. 933) and involves not only words or text, but also visuals, gestures, architectures or "extra-linguistic auditory signs" (Fairclough et al., 2004, p. 5; Höllerer, Jancsary, & Grafström, 2018).

A first way, then, that scholars have understood the material quality of communication is to consider how communication practice, in particular talk, is a multimodal accomplishment involving documents, pictures, machines, screens, bodies, spaces, smells, among other types of actors. For example, Asmuss and Oshima (2018) showed how strategy-making is a multimodal communicative practice as strategy actors negotiate issues such as entitlement through multiple verbal, embodied, or technological resources. Sergi and Bonneau (2016) analyzed how

Table 6.1 Summary of the four approaches to materiality and communication

	Materiality as sensible matter mediating human interaction	Materiality as hybrid actors mobilized in and animated by human interaction	Materiality as the materialization of (non-human) relations	Materiality as the performative effects of sociomaterial practice
Materiality	The quality of things to be tangible to the senses, for example to be touched, smelled, or seen.	The quality of how things come to be embodied, incarnated, materialized through communication (Cooren, 2010). Things are, at the same time, material and immaterial.	The process of materialization, that is how something comes to materialize itself, to take on certain properties, to become the substance of how something is made and sustains its existence (Cooren, 2018).	That which comes to matter, that is the agential cuts performed over time through material-discursive practices as they come to produce, i.e., materialize phenomena.
Communication	A central process of organizations as it entails the dynamic, interactive negotiation of meaning through symbol use (Ashcraft et al., 2009).	The central constitutive process of organizing and organizations involving multiple agencies and building on a continuous oscillation between being animated by and mobilizing others in and through communication.	The central constitutive force of organizational phenomena by virtue of its relational quality: "communication is the materialization of relations *through* something or someone" (Cooren, 2018, p. 279).	A central practice where meaning and power are performed and the authorship of sociomaterial entanglements is temporarily established.
Relationship between communication and materiality	Communication and materiality are two separate, but always present entities acting upon each other.	Communication and materiality are animated by and productive of hybrid agencies. Communication as the primary, constitutive process with materiality coming in through communication and never independently of it.	The social and the material are properties of everything that exists and are constituted in communication as a key relational process.	The social and the material gain their qualities through intra-action and together become productive of reality. Communication is central to how entanglements are established in material-discursive practices.
Preferred methodology	Focused on multi-modal discourse analysis often involving video-based methods.	Focused on interactions and conversations as the terra firma (e.g. conversation analysis).	Focused on how things, people, practices become related (e.g. ethnographies).	Focused on how embodied, situated practices of sayings and doings become related (e.g. sensory ethnography, visual methods).

conversations that arise from "working out loud" tweets create relationships and professional collaborations as a form of (temporary) organization. In order to account for the multimodal quality of communication, scholars are asked to "retool" their methodological practices, for example, by employing multimodal vignettes during interviews or multimodal mappings for observations (Dille & Plotnikof, 2020). The latter suggests, for instance, scholars to be attentive, when observing, to how actors accomplish specific organizational ends (e.g. position their management status) not only through verbal means, but through affective, bodily, and object-oriented forms of relating (p. 495).

In these multimodal accounts, materiality is generally understood as what is made of physical matter to be touched, tasted, smelled, heard, and seen (Ashcraft et al., 2009) as people interact through multiple material and sensorial means. This perspective then sees communication mainly as a practice between people, and it is people who do the talking, the writing, and the bodily gestures in order to strategize, temporarily organize, and position management. Although this perspective recognizes that bodily gestures, objects, visual artifacts, affective engagements, and movements in space are an important part of communicative practice, the focus remains human-centric. In this perspective then, communication and materiality are always separate, but acting upon each other.

Materiality as the Relational Medium of Human Interaction

The second perspective is one pioneered by CCO scholars, which offers a materially sensitive reading of communication, focusing on a relational understanding of materiality and stressing the hybrid quality of communication. The perspective suggests that "[c]ommunication is im/material because it is both material/incarnated/embodied and immaterial/disincarnated/disembodied" (Cooren, 2010, p.10). Communication's hybrid nature thereby goes further than addressing how the symbolic, immaterial process of communication relates to – or is in a dialectical relationship with (Putnam, 2015) – material actors and practices outside of communication, such as bodies, sites, and artifacts (Ashcraft et al., 2009). Rather, the call is to understand the symbolic-material relation *within* communication. This view recognizes that communication and discourse never work in practice without material support (Hardy & Thomas, 2015); communication necessarily always has a "material dimension" (Cooren, 2020, p. 4) such that we can understand "discourse as materiality" (Philips & Oswick, 2012, p. 470). At the same time, material actors, such as the chair you are sitting on that is giving you a backache, also contain symbolic qualities such as histories of use and representation, which come to co-define how the chair comes to matter in organizational practice (Toraldo & Mengis, 2020).

In light of this perspective, a second, more semiotic and relational understanding of materiality has been proposed, the "symbolic material" (Robichaud & Cooren, 2013, p. xiii). This perspective has been developed primarily through the notion of ventriloquism (Cooren, 2010, 2012). Cooren (2010, 2012) uses the metaphor to further decenter the communicative practice from humans only as the communication of the ventriloquist and her figure (dummy) shows how entities of varying ontological statuses (human and non-human) speak through and with each other. When a ventriloquist makes the figure speak, it appears that the figure is talking on its own. However, it is the ventriloquist who is making the figure speak, or is mobilizing it. At the same time, the ventriloquist is also animated by the figure as it makes the ventriloquist speak in certain ways. Ventriloquism then shows how communication is shared with material actors distributed in time and space (see Nathues & Van Vuuren, this volume).

These material actors can come into communication in two ways. First, other actors can come into a communicative interaction *upstream* by *animating* the communication and "making us say things" (Cooren, 2010; Latour, 2010, p. xiv). For example, someone who is concerned about carbon emissions might choose to ride their bike to work instead of driving; they are *animated* by environmental concerns. By addressing how in interaction we (the dummies!) are always animated by values, emotions, passions, rules, institutions, we can de-center interaction from the humans alone and recognize the variety of non-human figures and agencies participating. Second, ventriloquism can take place *downstream* when people *mobilize* other actants as they communicate, when "we make do things" with our interactions, such as provoking others to respond, to frown, to distance their bodies (Cooren, 2010; Latour, 2010, p. xiv). For example, if a cyclist gets into an argument with a driver and cites traffic laws as allowing them to legally bike in the road, the cyclist has invoked – mobilized – the law as a justification for her behavior, making it communicate.

Both movements – to be animated by or to mobilize another in communication – are not one-way activities, but oscillate. The ventriloquist not only makes the figure speak, but also speaks through the figure that she is animating, being thus both animated by and mobilizing the figure. Returning to the example of the cyclist, when s/he invokes the law about riding a bicycle in the street, this invocation will also act back on her, making her defend certain positions (Cooren, 2012). Following Actor Network Theory (Latour, 2005), this oscillation means that it is difficult to ever find an origin for action and that agency is always distributed. At the same time, we note that materiality here is not understood as sensorial "tangibility and visibility" as the first perspective does (Cooren, 2020, p. 3). Here, materiality becomes part of the conversation quite differently than in a multimodal account where material stuff, i.e. things that are tangible to the senses such as objects or bodies, are part of the interaction. In contrast, in the exchange between the cyclist and the driver, materiality enters the communicative practice as the law, ideologies, emotions, etc. are invoked, that is *materialized* and embodied (Cooren, 2020, p. 11) in conversation. Here then, materiality is understood as how things become embodied, incarnated, materialized through communication (Cooren, 2010).

It is important to note that most of the research in this area has been done by CCO scholars using conversation analysis (CA) as their preferred method (Wilhoit, 2016). CA can be very useful for seeing how mobilization and animation take place in conversation. However, fixing the gaze on conversations might make us overlook how non-humans participate in communication. Indeed, one critique of this understanding of materiality's role in the communicative constitution of organization is that humans remain center stage since they are ultimately the ones who do communicative acts, even if they share this action with non-humans (Wilhoit & Kisselburgh, 2015). In response, research has begun to expand both notions of materiality and communication and methodologically by drawing on interview and ethnographic data looking for a broader accounting of the role of non-humans in communication (e.g., Koschmann & McDonald, 2015; Long, King, & Buzzanell, 2018; Wilhoit & Kisselburgh, 2015, 2019). However, research with this approach to materiality still sees materiality as primarily coming to matter as it is invoked in conversation (see Aggerholm, Asmuß, Ladegaard Johannesen & Feddersen Smith, this volume). The next view of materiality allows materiality to make a difference on its own and in relation to other material actors.

Materiality as the Materialization of (Non-Human) Relations

The third approach that we consider understands communication as the establishment of relationships and therefore considers relationships of any kind, including between non-humans, as communication that can then play a constitutive role for organizing (Cooren, 2015, 2016, 2018; Wilhoit & Kisselburgh, 2019). This understanding of communication is founded in a relational ontology, which takes the relationships between entities as primary for understanding their being rather than the entities in and of themselves (Cooren, 2015). Putnam (2015), for example, suggests:

> Communication is not treated as synonymous with the social, the symbolic, or the discursive; instead, it surfaces in the spaces between them as the processes through which materiality and human agencies become imbricated and as ways that the mangle registers or reveals reality.
>
> *p. 713*

This approach to CCO makes it conversant with other relational theories such as practice theory and Actor Network Theory (ANT), which similarly aim to overcome dualistic debates and to explain social phenomena by tracing the nexuses of multiple, hybrid practices (see Arnaud, Fauré, & Mengis, 2018, for an integration of CCO and practice theory). It particularly draws from ANT and its understanding of agency as relational (Latour, 1992, 2005).[1] ANT sees all action as shared or distributed among entities; one cannot act alone (Latour, 2005). For example, Latour shows the weakness of the NRA slogan, "Guns don't kill people; people *kill* people" (Latour, 1999, p. 176). A gun on its own does not have the same possibilities for action as when a relationship is established between a gun and a person holding it. Similarly, the person cannot act in the same way when she is not holding a gun. The relationship between person and object allows for action (Latour, 2005).

CCO research then builds on this idea to show how communication establishes relationships. Cooren (2016) has suggested that organizational communication scholars define communication as "the establishment, through something or someone, of a link, relation or passage between two or more entities" (p. 81). This understanding of communication shows that communication is much more than two people talking to each other and can include "rooms communicating with each other (through a doorway), machines interacting with each other (through optical fibers), [and] governments exchanging viewpoints (through their representatives)" (Cooren, 2018, p. 284). In all these situations, a third entity holds two entities in common, which is the key to communication.

This understanding of communication is important because it de-centers the role of humans in communication and allows for non-humans to communicate amongst themselves. Human intention is only important to the extent that people position themselves within these relations and take them up in their interactions and attributions of meanings. Another aspect of this understanding is that the definition of materiality changes, overcoming the bifurcation between the material and the social and instead focusing more on processes of materialization. Materiality denotes the *process of materialization*: how something comes to "materialize itself" and take on certain properties (Cooren, 2018). Materiality becomes a process and shifting property, rather than a fixed characteristic of an object. More specifically for organizational communication, materiality is that which matters to encapsulate a range of non-humans who make a difference for organizing (Cooren, 2018; Martine, Cooren, Bénel, & Zacklad, 2015). Examining the etymology of *materiality*, Cooren (2018) concludes that materiality means the substance of something or what sustains something else. He uses the example of a cell phone that is material through not only the substances and materials it is made from (e.g., glass, plastic, electronics), but also the knowledge that supported the design of the phone and the assembly of the physical components. Such an understanding of materiality demonstrates that it is more ephemeral, not permanent, and that materiality does not need to be limited to the sensorial properties and features of given things, rather, it corresponds to a processes of materialization (Cooren, 2020).

This perspective shows that there are many things that *matter* that are not physical. For example, one's work history *matters* when seeking a new job or one's emotions might *matter* when having a difficult conversation. Studying organizations in this way allows scholars to pay attention to more things that make a difference for organizing that might be left out of other analyses. In addition to de-centering the physical as matter, this perspective also demonstrates that materiality is not an intrinsic "property" of the thing it makes up – it is always the result of appropriation or attribution processes (Bencherki & Snack, 2016). The personal leadership qualities of a manager (e.g. his emotional intelligence, her narcissism) or the qualities of a spatial arrangement (e.g. an activity-based office organization with room designs allowing for concentrated individual vs. group work and communication) cannot be seen as exclusive proprieties of the individual or of the space in question. These properties emerge in the complex relational dynamics (e.g. conflicts, co-orientations, integration) between practices, objects, individuals, spaces, etc., including those with the histories of attribution and appropriation processes of identities or with the designers of spaces and objects.

In approaching materiality this way, the bifurcation of the social and material is rejected (Martine et al., 2015). Instead, Cooren (2018) has suggested that materiality and sociality are two ways that all things can be experienced. When one approaches an entity in terms of its sociality, one is made aware of the relationships that allow the entity to exist and that give it identity (Cooren, 2020). When one approaches the same entity in terms of materiality, one is made aware of what something is made of or anything else that is materialized in an entity (Martine et al., 2015). This perspective then views the social and material not as entangled (Orlikowski, 2007), but as properties that all entities always have (Cooren, 2020).

This view on materiality has several implications. First, it centers communication because communication is the materialization of these relations (Cooren, 2018). Second, *human* communication is de-centered, as communication becomes the materialization of relations through various media, including, but not limited to, humans (Cooren, 2015, 2018). Third, many other views of materiality have a priori separated the social and material, which leads to seeing entities as having fixed properties and relations. Taking a relational view both invites a more fluid view of materiality, as well as rejecting the separation between the observer and the observed in which some "objective" view of the world emerges (Martine et al., 2015). This relational approach to communication and materiality has been used by CCO scholars to understand resistance (Wilhoit & Kisselburgh, 2019), online suicide prevention chats (Cooren, Higham, & Huët, 2017), organizational wikis (Martine et al., 2015), and the configuration of art museums (Cooren, 2015). With its relational focus on how artifacts, technologies, processes, and practices become interrelated in communication, this approach enhances the opportunity to address more than locally, spatially and temporally confined "micro" phenomena, a critique often put forward to conversation-centered explanations of organizations (Llewellyn & Spence, 2009). This emphasis is accompanied by ethnography as a preferred research approach as scholars seek to see how communication and relationships are materialized beyond the here-and-now.

To briefly illustrate this approach to materiality, we elaborate on the first author's research on bike commuters. Wilhoit and Kisselburgh (2019) studied bike commuters in the American Midwest, a place where very few people ride their bikes to work. They found that bike commuters in the area they studied rode their bikes to work for personal reasons, whether it was health, environmental concerns, or saving money. Although bike commuters did not understand their act of biking to work as resistance, Wilhoit and Kisselburgh (2019) demonstrate that their activity is resistance through a relational approach to materiality.

Bike commuters necessarily enact alternative practices that are put into relationship with dominant practices, communicating with them. For example, many bike commuters described dressing casually in order to bike to work and caring less about their professional appearance in contrast to colleagues who came to work looking more professional and polished. Additionally, there was very little cycling infrastructure in the studied towns, meaning that bikes were often present in spaces where cars were the dominant form of transportation (like roads). In these situations, dominant and normative practices (driving a car), dress codes (elegant work wear), artifacts and infrastructure (e.g. cars, roads) were put in relationship with alternative ones (biking, casual sportswear, bikes). These normative and alternative practices and objects only acquire their meaning through their relationship with each other. It is through their contrasting relationship that some things are seen as reproducing power and control while others are seen as resistance. Similarly, in organizations, practices, objects, spaces, technologies come to materialize practices of control, iconic innovations, spaces of experimentation, etc. only by becoming related in communication. This process does not necessarily happen through people taking them up in their conversations and interactions, but by being temporally and spatially juxtaposed, over-imposed, contrasted, and combined. It is in this materialization of (non-human) relations where meanings also emerge and something like a practice, an object, a dress comes to *matter* as a practice, object and dress code of resistance. It is in this way that organizational practices, artifacts, technologies, and spaces are both material (through mattering and being materialized) and social (through their relationships). Additionally, for those who are skeptical that when communication is a relationship, everything is communication and it loses its analytical value, as the previous example demonstrates, understanding these communicative relationships can lead to new understandings of organizing. A relational perspective on communication can also be useful for studying organizing that may be outside formal organizations. By tracing relationships (and therefore communication), organizing patterns can become visible. This view of materiality is significant for re-centering communication while challenging the idea that materiality equals physicality.

Materiality as the Performative Effects of Sociomaterial Practice

A fourth way (which has many similarities with the third) that materiality and communication work together in processes of organizing comes from the "sociomaterial turn" (Schultze, Van den Heuvel, & Niemimaa, 2020) or sociomateriality (Orlikowski, 2007; Orlikowski & Scott, 2008), often informed by the work of Karen Barad (2007). This work has found inroads into the organizational literature particularly in information systems (Orlikowski & Scott, 2008; Leonardi, 2012; Cecez-Kecmanovic, Galliers, Henfridsson, Newell, & Vidgen, 2014), to some extent in practice theoretical accounts of organizing (Carlile et al., 2013; Gherardi, 2016; Keevers & Kykes, 2016; Mengis et al., 2018) and more recently in the CCO literature (Cooren, 2020; Dille & Plotnikof, 2020; Kuhn, Ashcraft & Cooren, 2017; Kuhn & Burk, 2014; Martine et al., 2015).

Barad (2007) focuses on the context of quantum physics to propose an agential realist account, which rejects the notion that objects have "determinate properties" (p. 127) and suggests that phenomena – such as quants, universes, but also organizations, strategies, innovations, or identities – come to be through ongoing material-discursive practices. These practices, over time, produce "agential cuts" on phenomena, thereby providing them with certain characteristics (e.g. a wave quality to quants, a rebellious identity to a group of people). In this way, subjects and objects do not exist ex-ante or have intrinsic qualities or features. Rather, through the practice of material and discursive intra-relating (Barad prefers intra-relating and intra-action because they do not imply pre-formed, individual agents), boundaries are gradually drawn around objects and subjects, allowing them to take on certain determinacies or qualities. This view implies that discourse and materiality do not exist "prior to each other – as they only become 'something' when entangled in intra-actions" and in ongoing relational practice (Dille & Plotnikof, 2020, p. 487).

For Barad, it is important to underline that processes and things acquire determinacy not only through discursive or communicative constructions. In fact, materiality should not be "turned into a matter of language or some other form of cultural representation" (Barad, 2007, p. 132). Materialization is not a process where immaterial cultural or communicative dynamics alone inscribe certain marks of meaning (e.g. gendered, discursive constructions of effective leadership become appropriated by female leaders). Rather, matter is "an active agent participating in the very process of materialization" (Barad, 2007, p. 151), such that the material exclusion of women in the upper echelons of an organization, their body sizes and forms, or the lower pay all contribute to performing female (and male) leaders. Matter thereby is "not a fixed essence; rather, matter is substance in its intra-active becoming – not a thing but a doing, a congealing of agency," which over time becomes productive of boundaries, surfaces, or fixities (p. 64/184). The approach is not far from the third perspective of materiality and communication presented above if we recognize that communication is not a dematerialized process. Both approaches share a relational, processual and performative worldview and an integration of their bodies of work could lead to a more materially sensitive understanding of organizations.

CCO scholars have started to integrate sociomateriality in their research, both for strengthening the role of material actants in organizational endeavors (Arnaud & Fauré, 2016; Kuhn & Burk, 2014; Novak, 2016) and for expanding their methodological toolbox favoring sociomaterial explanations (Dille & Plotnikof, 2020). For instance, Kuhn and Burk (2014) studied the design of a laboratory building from a CCO cum sociomaterial vantage point to address the role of space design in how space enters organizations. Rather than attributing to space a specific or fixed agency in organizing (e.g., to physically emplace employees in specific ways), the recognition is that a space's agencies are always the result of assemblages of multiple sociomaterial practices (Orlikowski & Scott, 2008) that are taking place in the everyday designing of a space. These assemblages involved not only people's interests and intentions worked into the physical structure, but also the material affordances of the space, for example, aspects of costs or construction feasibility that often "acted back" in the design process and disrupted its orderliness (p. 161). Kuhn and Burk's (2014) CCO sensitivity makes them ask how such an assemblage takes on the authority to perform space in specific ways, making reference to the importance of "authoritative texts" as abstract, intertextual representations of a collective that provide co-orientation to everyday practice (p. 155). Their intertextuality underlines a processual understanding of organizing, namely that the designing of a space is never authorized once and for all through a single unifying text, but continues to evolve through multiple contradictions and temporal shifts (Kuhn & Burk, 2014), even well into the physical construction and use of a space (cf. Petani & Mengis, 2017). Such integrative work can enrich the CCO literature in further strengthening a material-sensitive account even as one can see that a CCO reading of sociomateriality, such as the one by Kuhn and Burk (2014), continues to focus predominantly on abstract text and dialogic practices such as meetings while only occasionally referring to technologies, bodies, bricks and mortar. For future CCO scholarship further integrating a sociomaterial perspective, we see an opportunity for scholars to focus more on how the physical, sensorial quality of things, bodies, spaces, or technologies are relevant in creating relationships, for example, in how they create physical co-orientations in space, draw people in atmospherically, or create new developments in view of aesthetic clashes or misalignments, without necessarily having to be taken up by humans in their conversations and texts. An integrative effort is also helpful to a sociomaterial approach in revising its view on the quality and role of communication in organizing, in particular in establishing connections and entanglements between diverse, and often conflicting, practices.

Not all CCO scholars, however, have wholeheartedly embraced the sociomaterial turn, and some have advanced critical considerations, primarily because of the dematerialized notion of communication and discourse put forward by sociomateriality scholars (Cooren, 2020; Putnam, 2015). Relatedly, scholars like Cooren (2020) have critiqued the sociomaterial view for remaining analytically anchored within a bifurcated worldview. To Cooren, the solution lies in "acknowledging the irreducible materiality of communication" (p. 6), which to him brings the advantage of not needing to revert to the "entanglement" (Barad, 2007; Orlikowski & Scott, 2008) of matter and meaning as separate entities. Yet, Barad (2007) is explicit that entanglement does not mean to be simply "intertwined with another, as in the joining of separate entities, but to lack an independent, self-contained existence" (p. ix), which is also why she talks of intra-action rather than interaction. Indeed, a sociomaterial perspective does caution us to not view communication as taking place between or through given subjects and objects, which would still assume essences. Rather, it invites us to explore objects' and subjects' wider sociomaterial entanglements that can explain stabilizing and de-stabilizing dynamics, to address the performances of sociomaterial practices and show how they come to matter, thus accounting for their processual becoming. A sociomaterial account would further be critical of addressing only "materiality *in communication*" (Cooren, 2018, p. 281, italics added) as it privileges the one over the other and assumes a conceptual stability in communication.

Yet, rather than identifying shortcomings between the two approaches, a Baradian take on the integrative effort of CCO and sociomateriality would remind us to engage in a "diffractive" reading (Barad, 2010; Barad in Dolphijn & Van der Tuin, 2012). A diffractive approach involves reading one approach through another, thereby engaging not only different theoretical distinctions, but also theory-method packages (Nicolini, 2017), which would allow one to "enact [...] new patterns of engagement" (Barad, 2010, p. 243) and become attentive to new meanings that emerge in intra-action (Mengis & Nicolini, 2021). For example, by experimenting with multiple video-based methods in a single study and reading one through the other, one can learn that video-recordings using an "American shot" (a steady camera with a mid-angle shot) will foreground humans interacting even if involving their bodies and artifacts (first perspective on materiality), while a roving camera that follows the collective practice de-centers humans and foregrounds the interactions and rhythms between artifacts, bodies, etc. (our fourth perspective) (Mengis, Nicolini, & Gorli, 2018).

A diffractive practice between CCO and sociomateriality can thus lead to inventive provocations and theory development on how to strengthen a material cum communicational agenda without necessarily placing the one (communication) over the other (materiality) but allowing them to emerge through intra-actions. In particular, a further integration of sociomateriality and CCO may be particularly useful for understanding organizing processes, particularly for more novel forms of organizing. For example, what are the sociomaterial factors that move an online social justice group into real-world protests and activism? Organizing like this is highly sociomaterial and new insights can likely come through a communicative examination of sociomaterial entanglements that can consider subtle shifts in entanglement that produce organization. Although CCO and sociomaterial work have thus far been rather separated from each other, we see productive potential in integrating these approaches.

Conclusion

In this chapter we have attempted to provide some clarity to the ongoing debate to the relationship between community and materiality in organizing. We have presented four different ways that organizational communication scholars have conceptualized the relationship between materiality and communication: materiality as sensible matter mediating human interaction, materiality as the hybrid actors mobilized in and animated by human interaction, materiality as the materialization of (non-human) relations, and materiality as the entanglement of sociomaterial practice. These varied perspectives represent a maturing of the field in which competing views of the communication/materiality relationship have crystalized and also indicate that there is the potential for more conceptualizations to emerge.

To conclude, we propose some future avenues for researching and theorizing materiality in organizational communication. First, we suggest that although CCO theory is very friendly to non-human and material agency, very little CCO research considers the multi-modal, sensorial, "hard" materiality perspective (Wilhoit & Kisselburgh, 2015). In many ways it seems that CCO scholars skipped over this perspective in their consideration of materiality as they sought to expand what can be conceived of as material, with some conceptualizations of materiality seeing everything as material (Cooren 2018, 2020). As a result, empirical CCO research often focuses on more intangible forms of materiality like attitudes (van Vuuren & Cooren, 2010), authority (Benoit-Barné & Cooren, 2009), or tasks that need to be done (Cooren, Fox, Robichaud, & Talih, 2005). Consequently, research and theorizing on the physical stuff of organizations is lacking and we invite scholars to continue to study this important aspect of organizations. Second, scholarship on communication and materiality needs to take into account how senses and affect act in communication. A turn to affect allows scholars to consider bodies, senses, and felt relations (Ashcraft, 2020). It has the potential to challenge how communication is defined, as well as to contribute to solving social problems and attend to the political aspect of bodily experiences (Kuhn, Ashcraft, & Cooren, 2017; 2019). Affect is an emerging area of research that has the potential to challenge many of the existing ways that communication, materiality, and organizing have traditionally been viewed.

Finally, we also encourage scholars to be aware of the performative quality of their methodological engagements and consider how they can better account for the material in their research (Wilhoit, 2014; 2017; see also Part 3 of this volume). Conversation Analysis, the preferred method of many CCO scholars, is very useful for seeing how various non-humans are materialized in conversations, but it has limits for understanding how the communicative relationships formed between people, buildings, furniture, vehicles, and technologies, among others, play a role in constituting organizations. We suggest that scholars continue to explore more sensory methods (see Wilhoit, 2017) and expand CCO usage of ethnographic methods. Particularly as materiality scholarship extends into affect, new methods will be needed to account for more bodily and sensorial materiality.

In this chapter, we have suggested four different ways that the materiality–communication relationship has been conceptualized. We suggest that this rich diversity of thought demonstrates the maturity of this field and encourage scholars to continue to study materiality in organizational communication from new perspectives to create additional perspectives and add to the richness of existing scholarship.

Note

1 Both this and the second approach draw on ANT, but tend to draw on different facets of the theory. The second approach, which focuses on how human interaction is mediated by materiality emphasizes

the *actor* part of ANT, which argues that we never act alone, but act through and with other actants. This approach, which emphasizes the relational aspect of communication, emphasizes the *network* of ANT, looking at the relationships that allow hybrid agency to emerge.

References

Arnaud, N., & Fauré, B. (2016). A communicative approach to sociomateriality: The agentic role of technology at the operational level. *Communication Research and Practice, 2*(3), 290–310.

Arnaud, N., Fauré, B., Mengis, J., & Cooren, F. (2018). Interconnecting the practice turn and communicative approach to organizing: A new challenge for collective action?. *M@n@gement, 21*(2), 691–704.

Ashcraft, K. L. (2021) Communication as constitutive transmission? An encounter with affect. *Communication Theory.* https://doi.org/10.1093/ct/qtz027.

Ashcraft, K. L. (2021). Communication as constitutive transmission? An encounter with affect. *Communication Theory, 31*(4), 571–592. https://doi.org/10.1093/ct/qtz027.

Asmuß, B., & Oshima, S. (2018). Strategy making as a communicative practice: The multimodal accomplishment of strategy roles. *M@n@gement, 21*(2), 884–912. https://doi.org/10.3917/mana.212.0884.

Bencherki, N., & Snack, J. P. (2016). Contributorship and partial inclusion: A communicative perspective. *Management Communication Quarterly, 30*(3), 279–304. https://doi.org/10.1177/0893318915624163.

Benoit-Barné, C., & Cooren, F. (2009). The accomplishment of authority through presentification: How authority is distributed among and negotiated by organizational members. *Management Communication Quarterly, 23*(1), 5–31. https://doi.org/10.1177/0893318909335414.

Barad, K. (2007). *Meeting the universe halfway: Quantum physics and the entanglement of matter and meaning.* Duke University Press.

Barad, K. (2010). Quantum entanglements and hauntological relations of inheritance: Dis/continuities, SpaceTime enfoldings, and justice-to-come. *Derrida Today, 3*(2), 240–268. https://doi.org/10.3366/drt.2010.0206.

Brown, A. D., Colville, I., & Pye, A. (2015). Making sense of sensemaking in organization studies. *Organization Studies, 36*(2), 265–277. https://doi.org/10.1177/0170840614559259.

Brummans, H. J. M., Cooren, F., Robichaud, D., & Taylor, J. (2014). Approaches to the communicative constitution of organizations. In L. Putnam & D. Mumby (Eds.), *The Sage handbook of organizational communication* (pp. 173–194). Sage.

Carlile, P. R., Nicolini, D., Langley, A., & Tsoukas, H. (Eds.). (2013). *How matter matters: Objects, artifacts, and materiality in organization studies.* Oxford University Press.

Cecez-Kecmanovic, D., Galliers, R. D., Henfridsson, O., Newell, S., & Vidgen, R. (2014). The sociomateriality of information systems. *MIS Quarterly, 38*(3), 809–830. www.jstor.org/stable/26634999.

Cooren, F. (2010). *Action and agency in dialogue: Passion, incarnation and ventriloquism.* John Benjamins.

Cooren, F. (2012). Communication theory at the center: Ventriloquism and the communicative constitution of reality. *Journal of Communication, 62*(1), 1–20. https://doi.org/10.1111/j.1460-2466.2011.01622.x.

Cooren, F. (2015). In medias res: communication, existence, and materiality. *Communication Research and Practice, 1*(4), 307–321. https://doi.org/10.1080/22041451.2015.1110075.

Cooren, F. (2016). Organizational communication: A wish list for the next 15 years. In B. Czarniawska (Ed.), *A research agenda for management and organization studies* (pp. 79–87). Edward Elgar.

Cooren, F. (2018). Materializing communication: Making the case for a relational ontology. *Journal of Communication, 68*(2), 278–288. https://doi.org/10.1093/joc/jqx014.

Cooren, F. (2020). Beyond entanglement: (Socio-)materiality and organization studies. *Organization Theory, 1*(3), 1–24. https://doi.org/10.1177/2631787720954444.

Cooren, F., Fox, S., Robichaud, D., & Talih, N. (2005). Arguments for a plurified view of the social world: Spacing and timing as hybrid achievements. *Time & Society, 14*(2–3), 265–282. https://doi.org/10.1177/0961463X05055138.

Cooren, F., Higham, L., & Huët, R. (2017). Analyzing online suicide prevention chats: A communicative constitutive approach. *Language and Dialogue, 7*(1), 3–25. https://doi.org/10.1075/ld.7.1.02coo.

Cooren, F., Kuhn, T. R., Cornelissen, J. P., & Clark, T. (2011). Communication, organizing and organization: An overview and introduction to the special issue. *Organization Studies, 32*(9), 1149–1170. https://doi.org/10.1177/0170840611410836.

Dille, M. H., & Plotnikof, M. (2020). Retooling methods for approaching discourse – materiality relations: a new materialist framework of multimodal sensitivity. *Qualitative Research in Organizations and Management: An International Journal*, 15(4), 485–501. https://doi.org/10.1108/QROM-09-2019-1821.

Dolphijn, R., & Tuin, I. van der. (2013). New *materialism: Interviews & cartographies.* London: Open Humanites Press. www.openhumanitiespress.org/books/titles/new-materialism/.

Fairclough, N., Graham, P., Lemke, J., & Wodak, R. (2004). Introduction. *Critical Discourse Studies*, 1(1), 1–7. https://doi.org/10.1080/17405900410001674489.

Gherardi, S. (2016). Sociomateriality in posthuman practice theory. In A. Hui, T. Schatzki, & E. Shove (Eds.), *The nexus of practices* (pp. 50–63). Routledge.

Giddens, A. (1984). *The constitution of society: Outline of the theory of structuration.* University of California Press.

Hardy, C., and Thomas, R. (2015). Discourse in a material world. *Journal of Management Studies*, 52(2), 680–695. https://doi.org/10.1111/joms.12113.

Höllerer, M. A., Jancsary, D., & Grafström, M. (2018). 'A picture is worth a thousand words': Multimodal sensemaking of the global financial crisis. *Organization Studies*, 39(5–6), 617–644. https://doi.org/10.1177/0170840618765019.

Iedema, R. (2007). On the multi-modality, materially and contingency of organization discourse. *Organization Studies*, 28(6), 931–946. https://doi.org/10.1177/0170840607075264.

Keevers, L., & Sykes, C. (2016). Food and music matters: Affective relations and practices in social justice organizations. *Human Relations*, 69(8), 1643–1668. https://doi.org/10.1177/0018726715621368.

Koschmann, M. A., & McDonald, J. (2015). Organizational rituals, communication, and the question of agency. *Management Communication Quarterly*, 29(2), 229–256. https://doi.org/10.1177/0893318915572386.

Kuhn, T. R. (2012). Negotiating the micro-macro divide: Thought leadership from organizational communication for theorizing organization. *Management Communication Quarterly*, 26(4), 543–584. https://doi.org/10.1177/0893318912462004.

Kuhn, T., Ashcraft, K. L., & Cooren, F. (2017). *The work of communication: Relational perspectives on working and organizing in contemporary capitalism.* Taylor & Francis.

Kuhn, T., Ashcraft, K. L., & Cooren, F. (2019). Introductory essay: What work can organizational communication do? *Management Communication Quarterly*, 33(1), 101–111. https://doi.org/10.1177/0893318918809421.

Kuhn, T., & Burk, N. (2014). Spatial design as sociomaterial practice: A (dis)organizing perspective on communicative constitution. In F. Cooren, E. Vaara, A. Langley, & H Tsoukas (Eds.), *Language and communication at work: Discourse, narrativity, and organizing* (pp. 149–174). Oxford University Press.

Latour, B. (1992). Where are the missing masses? The sociology of a few mundane artifacts. In W. Beijker & J. Law (Eds.), *Shaping Technology* (pp. 225–258). MIT Press.

Latour, B. (1999). *Pandora's hope: Essays on the reality of science studies.* Harvard University Press.

Latour, B. (2005). *Reassembling the social: An introduction to actor-network theory.* Oxford University Press.

Latour, B. (2010). Foreword: Who is making the dummy speak? In F. Cooren (Ed.), *Action and agency in dialogue: Passion, ventriloquism and incarnation* (p. XIII–XVI). Amsterdam: John Benjamins.

Latour, B. (2013). *An inquiry into modes of existence.* Harvard University Press.

Law, J., & Mol, A. (1995). Notes on materiality and sociality. *The Sociological Review*, 43(2), 274–294.

Leonardi, P. M. (2012). Materiality, sociomateriality, and socio-technical systems: What do these terms mean? How are they different? Do we need them? In P. M. Leonardi, B. A. Nardi, & J. Kallinikos (Eds.), *Materiality and organizing: Social interaction in a technological world* (pp. 25–48). Oxford University Press.

Llewellyn, N., & Spence, L. (2009). Practice as a members' phenomenon. *Organization Studies*, 30(12), 1419–1439.

Long, Z., King, A. S., & Buzzanell, P. M. (2018). Ventriloqual voicings of parenthood in graduate school: An intersectionality analysis of work-life negotiations. *Journal of Applied Communication Research*, 46(2), 223–242. https://doi.org/10.1080/00909882.2018.1435901.

Martine, T., Cooren, F., Bénel, A., & Zacklad, M. (2015). What does really matter in technology adoption and use?: A CCO approach. *Management Communication Quarterly*, 30(2), 1–24. https://doi.org/10.1177/0893318915619012.

McPhee, R. D. (2014). Agency as the Four Flows. *Management Communication Quarterly*, 29(3), 487–492. https://doi.org/10.1177/0893318915584826.

Mengis, J., & Nicolini, D. (2021). Practicing diffraction in video-based research. In S. Grosjean & F. Matte (Eds,), *Organizational video-ethnography revisited. Making visible material, embodied and sensory practices* (pp. 79–94). Palgrave.

Mengis, J., Nicolini, D., & Gorli, M. (2018). The video production of space: How different recording practices matter. *Organizational Research Methods, 21*(2): 288–315.

Nicolini D. (2017). Practice theory as a package of theory, method and vocabulary: Affordances and limitations. In M. Jonas, B. Littig, A. Wroblewski (Eds.), *Methodological reflections on practice oriented theories.* Springer. https://doi.org/10.1007/978-3-319-52897-7_2.

Novak, D. R. (2016). Democratic work at an organization-society boundary: Sociomateriality and the communicative instantiation. *Management Communication Quarterly, 30*(2), 218–244. https://doi.org/10.1177/0893318915622455.

Orlikowski, W. J. (2007). Sociomaterial practices: Exploring technology at work. *Organization Studies, 28*(9), 1435–1448. https://doi.org/10.1177/0170840607081138.

Orlikowski, W. J. (2010). Engaging practice in research: Phenomenon, perspective, and philosophy. In D. Golsorkhi, L. Rouleau, D. Seidl, & E. Vaara (Eds.), *The Cambridge handbook on strategy as practice* (pp. 23–33). Cambridge: Cambridge University Press.

Orlikowski, W. J., & Scott, S. V. (2008). Sociomateriality: Challenging the separation of technology, work and organization. *The Academy of Management Annals, 2*, 433–474. https://doi.org/10.1080/194165 20802211644.

Orlikowski, W. J., & Scott, S. V. (2014). What happens when evaluation goes online? Exploring apparatuses of valuation in the travel sector. *Organization Science, 25*(3), 868–891. https://doi.org/10.1287/orsc.2013.0877.

Petani, F. J., & Mengis, J. (2017). Is space time's blind spot? Towards a processual theorizing of space representation. In *Academy of Management Proceedings* (Vol. 2017). Academy of Management.

Phillips, N., & Oswick, C. (2012). Organizational discourse: Domains, debates, and directions. *Academy of Management Annals, 6*(1), 435–481. https://doi.org/10.5465/19416520.2012.681558.

Poole, M. S. (2014). Systems theory. In L. L. Putnam & D. K. Mumby (Eds.), *The SAGE handbook of organizational communication: Advances in theory, research, and methods* (3rd edn., pp. 49–74). Sage.

Putnam, L. L. (2015). Unpacking the dialectic: Alternative views on the discourse-materiality relationship. *Journal of Management Studies, 52*(5), 706–716. https://doi.org/10.1111/joms.12115.

Putnam, L. L., Fairhurst, G. T., & Banghart, S. (2016). Contradictions, dialectics, and paradoxes in organizations: A constitutive approach. *The Academy of Management Annals, 10*, 65–171. https://doi.org/https://doi.org/10.1080/19416520.2016.1162421.

Rice, A. K. (1953). Productivity and social organization in an Indian weaving shed: An examination of some aspects of the socio-technical system of an experimental automatic loom shed. *Human Relations, 6*(4), 297–329. https://doi.org/10.1177/001872675300600402.

Robichaud, D., & Cooren, F. (2013). Introduction: The need for new materials in the constitution of organization. In D. Robichaud & F. Cooren (Eds.), *Organization and organizing: Materiality, agency, and discourse* (pp. xi–xix). Routledge.

Rouleau, L., & Balogun, J. (2011). Middle managers, strategic sensemaking, and discursive competence. *Journal of Management studies, 48*(5), 953–983. https://doi.org/10.1111/j.1467-6486.2010.00941.x.

Schultze, U., van den Heuvel, G., & Niemimaa, M. (2020). Enacting accountability in is research after the sociomaterial turn(ing). *Journal of the Association for Information Systems, 21*(4), 10. http://doi.org/10.17705/1jais.00620.

Schoeneborn, D., Kuhn, T. R., & Kärreman, D. (2019). The communicative constitution of organization, organizing, and organizationality. *Organization Studies, 40*(4), 475–496. https://doi.org/10.1177/0170840618782284.

Sergi, V., & Bonneau, C. (2016). Making mundane work visible on social media: A CCO investigation of working out loud on Twitter. *Communication Research and Practice, 2*(3), 378–406. https://doi.org/10.1080/22041451.2016.1217384.

Taylor, J. R., & Robichaud, D. (2004). Finding the organization in the communication: Discourse as action and sensemaking. *Organization, 11*(3), 395–413. https://doi.org/10.1177/135050840 4041999.

Taylor, J. R., & Van Every, E. J. (2000). *The emergent organization: Communication as its site and surface.* Lawrence Erlbaum.

Toraldo, M. L., & Mengis, J. (2020). Chair as a mediating technology of organization. In T. Beyes , R. Holt & C. Pias (Eds.), *The Oxford handbook of media, technology, and organization studies*. Oxford University Press.

van Vuuren, M., & Cooren, F. (2010). "My attitude made me do it": Considering the agency of attitudes. *Human Studies, 33*, 85–101. https://doi.org/10.1007/s10746-010-9137-x.

Weick, K. E., Sutcliffe, K. M., & Obstfeld, D. (2005). Organizing and the process of sensemaking. *Organization Science, 16*(4), 409–421. https://doi.org/10.1287/orsc.1050.0133.

Wilhoit, E. D. (2016). Ventriloquism's methodological scope. *Language Under Discussion, 2*(1), 45–49. https://doi.org/10.31885/lud.2.1.243.

Wilhoit, E. D. (2017). Photo and video methods in organizational and managerial communication research. *Management Communication Quarterly, 31*(3), 447–466. https://doi.org/10.1177/089331891 7704511.

Wilhoit, E. D., & Kisselburgh, L. G. (2015). Collective action without organization: The material constitution of bike commuters as collective. *Organization Studies, 36*(5), 573–592. https://doi.org/10.1177/0170840614556916.

Wilhoit, E. D., & Kisselburgh, L. G. (2019). The relational ontology of resistance: Hybridity, ventriloquism, and materiality in the production of bike commuting as resistance. *Organization, 26*(6), 873–893. https://doi.org/10.1177/1350508417723719.

7

DISRUPTING CCO THINKING

A Communicative Ontology of Dis/Organization

Consuelo Vásquez, Timothy Kuhn and Mie Plotnikof

Observers of the social world have long understood the problem of order as a key issue shaping social action. Each major move in social theory presents a novel answer to how order is accomplished—sometimes planned, sometimes spontaneous—against the ever-looming threat of disorder (Hechter & Horne, 2009). Those social theories nominate constructs like norms, discursive formations, institutions, power relations, network ties, and cognitive predispositions to explain the production of order, but tend to exclude the implied complement, disorder. Organization is also invoked in such theories, both as a site for the production of social stability and as the process of activity, coordination, and control. In foregrounding order, such frameworks fail to account for a messier, contingent, and conflicted vision of organizations— one that foregrounds disorder, tensions, and paradoxes. In reaction to this normative and ordering vision of organization, alternatives that focus on disorganization have arisen from processual, complexity science, and postmodern thinking.

A paradigmatic shift in understandings of disorganization, initiated by Cooper (1986), has been embraced in organizational communication scholarship, and more recently among scholars of the Communicative Constitution of Organization approach (e.g., Vásquez & Kuhn, 2019). Questioning the emphasis on order that characterizes the foundational works of CCO theorizing (cf. the ordering properties of communication [Cooren, 2000], co-orientation [Taylor & Van Every, 2000], and the four flows model [McPhee & Zaug, 2000]), contemporary CCO scholars highlight the disorganizing dimensions of communication, which derives from its inherent indeterminacy. These scholars argue that the constitutive value of communication lies in its capacity to create order and disorder *simultaneously*. Hence, to study disorganization entails diving into the disordering, disruptive and chaotic properties of communication.

Before proceeding with our argument, a semantic clarification is needed to distinguish what we mean by dis/organization and dis/ordering. Following Cooper (1986), we define disorganization as the "call to order", i.e., the motivation or trigger for coordination, classification, control, and systemization. What Cooper calls organization/disorganization implies a perpetual movement between the excess and absence of meaning (disorganization), which triggers attempts of ordering by reducing chaos, controlling it and fixing it (organization). Importantly for Cooper, this movement is at the heart of the mutual constitution of the process of organization/disorganization, and can be explained by the indeterminacy of meaning (for a similar argument see Vásquez & Kuhn, 2019). Hence, we define dis/ordering as "communication-based

DOI: 10.4324/9781003224914-9

organizing processes through which meaning is simultaneously opened (i.e. disordering) and closed (i.e. ordering)" (Vásquez et al., 2016, p. 630). A central argument in these definitions is the simultaneity of these processes (marked in the use of the slash: dis/organization and dis/ordering) and the communicative constitution of organization as processes of opening and closing of meaning (for more details see the section "CCO-based Inquiries of Dis/Organization as Communication") below.

This inquiry, as we will see in this chapter, can take various theoretical and methodological paths. However, focusing on communication in its manifold expressions (e.g., events, tensions, paradoxes and contradictions, texts and objects, struggles over meaning and plenum of agencies) remains the common denominator of these studies.

In this chapter we present this emergent trend in CCO thinking by asking: *how is dis/organization communicative?* We present this question as a route to engaging with the organization/disorganization ontology by starting from (and not arriving at) communication (Cooren, Taylor, & Van Every, 2013). This guiding question invites us to interrogate how communication generates and provides a capacity to recognize dis/organization, to study it, and even trigger it. Communication is thus seen as an explanatory framework to understand dis/organization, as well as a strategy to infuse dis/organization into collective practices. Taking into consideration this twofold status of communication, this chapter discusses the implications for both research and practice for embracing this ontological shift. In line with the guiding question, the goals of this chapter are to first present the emergent CCO literature on dis/organization and outline its particularities vis-à-vis other renderings of dis/organization that mainly stem from organization studies. The second goal is to show what CCO scholarship can become if it truly embraces dis/organization as both research and practical agenda.

Renderings of Dis/Organization in Organization and Management Studies

Three and a half decades ago, Robert Cooper (1986) interrogated the conventional vision of organization as a site for the production of social stability and a process of activity coordination and control. Arguing that foregrounding order (and displacing disorder) is an epistemological choice, Cooper explored the consequences of that choice and provided a conceptual apparatus to enable an engagement with the formation of organization/disorganization. Organization studies has typically understood organization to be a bounded system: an entity set apart from, but existing inside, an environment. Cooper was interested in pursuing the ontological questions of what lies beyond organization and what potentials that "beyond" presents (Spoelstra, 2005). Grounding his thinking on the "beyond" in the efforts of Mauss, Lévi-Strauss, and Derrida to show the inherent and irreducible excess and absence of meaning in the symbolic-linguistic domain, Cooper saw the play of difference (or, with Derrida, *différance*) as that which creates meaning continuously. Yet because meaning is always deferred, because it always escapes the grasp of the symbolic, undecidability is an ever-present participant in organization. Recognizing the centrality of *un*decidability led Cooper to posit that processes of dis/organization require the structures of rationality, power, and boundary creation to generate *decidability* and reduce ambiguity; those structures, in turn, generate social systems (Munro, 2003).

Cooper, however, was careful not to engage too deeply with the social systems thinking dominant in organization studies (see Poole, 2014). Systems theorizing frames its units of analysis—be they cells, persons, groups, organizations, or ecologies—as *organisms* with attendant needs, goals, and capacities to differentiate themselves from their environments. In this model, there can be no beyond that is not also a system: all systems are nested in larger systems, *ad infinitum*. We would do better, Cooper insists, to break from systems theorizing and instead consider organizations and organizing processes to be the contingent outcomes of the play of difference that make them possible. From this perspective, "organization is the appropriation of order out of disorder" (Cooper 1986, p. 328) and, as such, organization is always bound up with *dis*organization. Cooper's argument, then, is not as simple as the system theorist's assertion that entropy (disintegration) and negative entropy characterize open systems (Boulding, 1985). Instead of assuming an ordered system as the ground for organizational action (e.g., a capitalist system or an ecosystem), Cooper invites us to consider the productive capacity of difference. The challenge, for scholars of organization, is to think beyond organization without relying on systems metaphors: to imagine how (that which we take to be) organizations and organizational phenomena are the emergent, and invented, products of action (Vásquez & Kuhn, 2019).

Drawing inspiration from Cooper's ontological challenge, a growing number of investigations in the organization studies field probe the implications of thinking with dis/organization. One route is pursued by process perspectives, which (re)frame the world as comprised by continuous flows of interconnected activities to highlight the instability, precariousness, and fluctuations in what are often taken to be stable organizational entities (e.g., Hernes, 2014; Tsoukas & Chia, 2002). Although process perspectives vary widely, they generally show how tensions, contradictions, and paradoxes are fully expected elements of organizing (Putnam, Fairhurst, & Banghart, 2016). Framing these complex processes as normal implies that order and disorder are parasitical upon one another: in routine organizing, the justification for ordering is often to counter disorderliness, and challenges to determinate meanings associated with disorganization tend to respond to ordering moves (Munro, 2003). A second move is to turn to events as the processual happenings of dis/organization, such as in Knox, O'Doherty, Vurdubakis and Westrup's (2015) study of an ambiguous event at an airport and the multiple, intersecting dis/orderings that emerged in response to the practical problems the organizing responses encountered.

A third path for building on Cooper's thinking is to focus on boundaries, framing them not as stable markers of organizational insides and outsides, but as actions that "continuously redefin[e] the actual out of a cloud of potentialities" (Spoelstra, 2005, p. 114). One might then think about *boundarying* practices, instead of what lies inside boundaries, which would lead to a recognition that in creating boundaries, organization creates itself continually anew (Heracleous, 2004). A fourth line connects this *boundarying* to the delineation of bodies in organizing. Thinkers here pay particular attention to the features of bodies, including non-human bodies, that create excesses of meaning with the potential to not merely be disciplined in the organizational interest, but which can exercise an uncontrollability that escapes human intentionality (Dale & Latham, 2015). Across these four themes, Cooper's ontological challenge has borne evident fruit by enabling thinking of excess, indeterminacy, and events as key notions for grasping the practices that engage with the world's inchoate differences in the doing of dis/organization. Stated more simply, engaging with Cooper's thinking helps us understand events as many dis/organizational things at once (Bercherki & Emholdt, 2020).

In slight contrast to these ontological reconceptualizations, other scholars take up the problem of (dis)order in terms of its generative capacity for organizational operations. Indeed, many see disorganization as *functional* for organizations. Some thinking along these lines sees the events that challenge orderliness as a disturbance to a system that reconfigures existing ordering. This can be seen in so-called "new science" theorizing that draws on chaos, non-linear dynamics, and complex adaptive systems approaches. Although these views tend to avoid Cooper's ontological gauntlet by retaining a primary interest in systems' operations, they reject the notion that such systems can ever accomplish a stable equilibrium. Instead, the continual adaptations involved in organizing suggest that issues move through organizations unpredictably

(Dawkins & Barker, 2020), knowledge is continually re-negotiated (Kuhn & Corman, 2003), and meaning-making is unavoidably unstable (Plotnikof & Pedersen, 2019).

Another rendering of the generativity of disorganization is in sensemaking literature on resilience. Drawing largely from Karl Weick's (1979) portrayal of organizing as a sensemaking process responsive to equivocal stimuli, organization scholars examine how disorder can provide instrumental benefits. For instance, some examine how crises, shocks, and strains—framed as events or ongoing processes—catalyze responses that either restore a prior order or develop new capabilities to respond to ongoing disturbances (Williams, Gruber, Sutcliffe, Shepherd & Zhao, 2017). Frequently, studies point to the sensemaking process as generating organizational resilience; for example, in cases of high-reliability organizations maintaining their abilities in the face of threat (see Jahn and Rice, this volume), or of organizations seeking to alter sedimented practices. On the latter theme, Ford and Ivancic (2020) studied victims of workplace sexual harassment, showing how sensemaking theorizing draws attention to the intersections between individuals' resilience and the capacity to alter organizational structures by presenting novel points of practical intervention. Beyond establishing anti-harassment policies and mechanisms for reporting, they argue that sexual harassment can be a disruption that develops a system capable of continually acknowledging that sexual harassment could occur and, thereby, is prepared with routines to address its presence—as productive responses to disorder.

In sum, then, the lines of inquiry in organization and management studies drawing upon the dis/organization theme—both ontological and the operational investigations—show the value of pursuing Cooper's conceptual re-direction. They turn away from a systems orientation, complicating our analytical foci. As this section demonstrated, organization and management studies scholars have found this move fruitful, producing explanations that shed new light on old questions. A similar ambition guides CCO scholars who engage with dis/organization, as addressed in the next section.

CCO-based Inquiries of Dis/Organization as Communication

Rather than reviewing "pillars", or schools of thought, characterizing CCO, we present CCO-based inquiries that problematize dis/organization by focusing on different features of communication, namely (a) events, (b) tensions, paradoxes and contradictions, (c) texts and objects, (d) struggles over meaning and (e) plenum of agencies. All these lines of inquiry have a common ontological positioning that stands along the following premises:

Organization is a process of becoming that stems from the mutual constitution of ordering and disordering. Hence, stability, certainty, and structure are moments in a stream of activity that exhibits order and disorder simultaneously. This first premise is directly in line with Cooper's (1986, p. 316) ontology of organization/disorganization explained earlier. Following a similar argument, Putnam (2019) draws attention to four features, or forces, of organization/disorganization that energize the order-disorder relationship. These are: w*orking on boundaries*, the means by which logics of inclusion-exclusion, inside-outside, and association-dissociation unfold; *struggling over authority*, recognition, and rationality; *negotiating meaning* in the face of the linguistic excess and indeterminacy; and *re-presenting context*, such that meanings are situated in nested practices and, thus, are available for dislocation into new contexts.

Organization/disorganization is situated in communication. As Putnam (2019, p. 22) aptly notes, "the locus of order/disorder centers in the communicative processes that set (dis)organization in motion". This premise entails two interrelated assumptions. The first, shared by CCO scholars, refers to the communicative constitution of organization. Organizations emerge, are maintained, and transformed through communicative actions (Cooren, Kuhn, Cornelissen & Clark, 2011). The second assumption departs from emphasizing the organizing properties of communication (cf. Cooren, 2000), to instead stress its *disorganizing* features (Vásquez, Schoeneborn, & Sergi, 2016). Hence, from this view, communication derives its constitutive value from its inherent indeterminacy (Kuhn & Burk, 2012; Mumby, 2016). Depending on the line of inquiry, as we will see next, the indeterminate character of communication is explained in different ways: struggle over meanings, structural properties of language and text, and multiple agencies and trajectories, to name a few. Exploring the dis/organizational features of communication is a common quest for CCO scholars studying dis/organization.

Organization is made up of relations. This third shared assumption in CCO-based inquiries of dis/organization stems from a relational ontology, which assumes that "everything that is has no existence apart from its relation to other things" (Langley & Tsoukas, 2010, p. 3). Organizations, from this point of view, only exist in relation, which is another way to say that they exist in communication. Cooren, Bencherki, Chaput and Vásquez (2015) defined communication as *"the establishment of a link, connection or relationship through something"* (Cooren, 2000, p. 367, emphasis in the original). To put it differently, communication is considered as a "dynamic practice through which things and being are connected/linked/ related" (Kuhn, Ashcraft & Cooren, 2017, p. 27). This "communicative relationality" puts forth the work of communication in assembling and reconfiguring things and being in a particular way, one that is anchored in neoliberal relations of production/consumption (Kuhn et al., 2017, p. 27). Applying a relational communicative ontology to the study of dis/organization highlights the importance of mattering, nicely summarized by Barad's (2003, p. 801) well-known expression "making matter matter". Focusing on mattering invites us to question how some material reconfigurations become more significant than others, and how by doing so they present themselves as "order", eliminating what they claim to be disorder. For example, the discourse of entrepreneurship is materialized in the context of startups through specific reconfigurations (the narrative of the hero entrepreneur, technologies as saviors, playful settings, performance evaluations, and so forth) (Kuhn et al., 2017). These reconfigurations constitute the ideal type of startups in a particular way (i.e. neoliberal way), excluding other possible arrangements. Yet at the same time, because these material arrangements are always in the process of becoming and are contextually dependent they can engender surprise, flux uncertainty and disrupt normative discourses of entrepreneurship.

Events

A first line of inquiry that explores the communicative constitution of dis/organization focuses on communication events, i.e. "a sequence of instances of communication (i.e. texts and conversations) that are performed in a distinct space-time" (Vásquez et al., 2016, p. 634). As noted by Schoeneborn and Vásquez (2017, p. 3), studying communication events "highlights the eventful nature of communication and invites CCO scholars to study the occurrence of organizational communication events on the microlevel". What a dis/organization approach adds to this focus on practices is that it looks at how order/disorder is generated in and through communication. For example, Vásquez et al. (2016) studied three communication events taken from three distinct project organizing contexts. Mobilizing the Derridean notion of presence/ absence, they examine the role of organizational texts-in-use to show how they simultaneously opened and closed meaning, creating both order and disorder at the same time. In one of the cases, a blank space in a project form created a small but significant disruption in the meeting between the project manager and her assistant. This blank space was seen as a threat as it opened to a multiplicity of meanings (whatever they wanted to fill in), which in the context of an orderly and formatted form did not make any sense. Hence, after discussing the (non)significance of this blank page, they tore it out and followed with the next case. This study shows that the (dis)ordering properties of communication are at play in the use and movement of texts. The locus of dis/ordering "lies in the communication event itself (i.e., as soon as actors make use of language and/or texts) and becomes visible in the (re)negotiation of meaning" (Vásquez et al., 2016, p. 631). Importantly, this dynamic of meaning negotiation—a process that takes place in every communication event—is key for setting the organization in motion and ensuring its continuity (Plotnikof & Pedersen, 2019).

Grothe-Hammer and Schoeneborn's (2019) study further advances this processual conceptualization of organization/disorganization by employing a Luhmannian perspective. For these authors, the paradoxical nature of communication (thus its capacity of creating order and disorder simultaneously) relies on meaning-making: "a process of constantly drawing distinctions – an ongoing ever-changing selection of certain possibilities (i.e., the attempt of fixation of one particular meaning) in distinction to other possibilities that remain unactualized" (Grothe-Hammer & Schoeneborn, 2019, p. 62). This process is realized in every communication event, which draws on previous events and relates to subsequent ones in a recursive manner. A main argument in Grothe-Hammer and Schoeneborn's (2019) study is that this recursivity is key in maintaining a sense of continuity. Disconnection occurs when earlier communication events are not treated as decision premises for follow-up decisions. May we note that these disruptions do not necessarily imply an ontological break. Decisions, as communication events, will always divert an organization from its path onto a new one because they "provoke opposition, alternation, revision and rejection" (Grothe-Hammer & Schoeneborn, 2019, p. 65) by questioning why a particular alternative has been selected over another. Moreover, disruptions can pry open organizing practices to display contingency, surprise, and ambiguity. The latter point is unpacked by Knox and colleagues (2015) in the study of the airport happening presented above, as they elucidate how everyday work events can be rife with ambiguity that creates dis/order.

Studies concerned with organizational (in)stability and change processes also show the potential of studying how these constitutive processes are becoming and connected by dis/organizing communicative events. Drawing on Cooren's (2010) ventriloqual theory, Matte (2019), for example, shows how the contradictory yet complementary figures of extremeness and normalcy are mobilized as a discursive token to push forward a specific medical agenda in the organization of a large-scale vaccine campaign in the Republic of Congo. Those extreme contexts are always opened to negotiation, triggering dis/organizing processes where the meaning of normalcy can be contested. Matte's findings suggest that this rhetoric of dis/organization is key in ensuring inter-organizational collaboration, particularly in settings where instability and chaos are ordinary. Concerned with instability, Mease (2020) introduces a Deleuzian perspective to CCO scholarship. She (2020, p. 2, original italic) argues that: "communicative constitution of organization is *always* a balance of (in)stability or (dis)organization and *always* an act of power." She shows the potential of this approach in a re-examination of Albu's (2019) study of human rights violations, analyzing the connecting and actualizing affordances of force and techniques. More specifically she first focuses on identifying collection of forces and the way they are arranged in patterns (or machines to take the Deleuzian term), for example by identifying the connections to an authoritative text. Second, she addresses how forces come together, i.e., the techniques of articulation. By looking at these techniques, she thirdly analyses instability. Through this analytical framework, Mease unfolds how micro-level communicative events connect (dis)organizational (in)stability, rendering visible large-scale constructions of power. Focusing on change processes, a few other studies (e.g., Plotnikof, 2015; Plotnikof & Pedersen, 2019) also explore communicational events as unstable (dis)organizing in powerful ways—in these cases within governance contexts. In particular, they unpack how changing goals in collaborations are constituted through struggling and disordering meaning negotiations connecting across multimodal agencies and various communication events.

Tensions, Paradoxes, and Contradictions

A second line of CCO-related inquiry asserts that the aforementioned tendency to give preference to order misses the tensions, paradoxes, and contradictions that are irredeemably present in all organizing. There is now a voluminous literature that examines the complexity of organizing via tensions and the like, but much of it is content to describe and catalog the challenges created by these ubiquitous elements of organizational life. Constitutive scholarship has made important strides in examining the complex interrelating of tensions, along with their concomitant consequences for organizing (Putnam et al., 2016). Literature based on CCO has done so in two important ways.

First, communicative theorizing is distinctive in that it provides an explanation for how tensions, paradoxes, and contradictions *constitute* organizations and organizing phenomena. In their encyclopedic review of scholarship in this realm, Putnam et al. (2016) depict how conflicting discourses emerge in concrete socio-historical conditions, interpenetrate tensions associated with multiple levels and sources, and require situated choice-making in response to them. Understood in this way, tensions, paradoxes, and contradictions recursively enable and constrain organizing processes like participation, double binds, or transformation. Those processes, in turn, can constitute the realities that characterize organization because they open up, and also close off, potential meanings circulating in organizing (Plotnikof & Pedersen, 2019). For instance, Porter and Jackson (2019) studied an organization devoted to broadening digital civic participation in a US community they called Mesa, examining one significant incident that implicated both enactments of technology and two other local organizations associated with civic participation. In investigating episodes related to this incident, they noticed that, in the interaction of these interests and forces, meanings *interfered* with one another: the meanings were inherently multiple and in tension. Yet because these meanings occurred at different epistemological levels, they were continually de- and re-contextualized; none of the organizations in the site controlled the trajectory of the practice. In terms of accounting for how tensions, paradoxes, and contradictions constitute organizing phenomena, this work shows how the intersections of conflicting meanings, interests, and conceptions of technology (re)produced difference and, at the same time, constituted digital civic participation.

A second contribution of communicative theorizing on tensions, paradoxes, and contradictions is associated with its commitment to understanding how such are "knotted" together in the production of organizational processes. Acknowledging multiplicity is much easier than examining it, however: "While most analysts concern themselves with multiple tensions conceptually, they rarely do so empirically" (Fairhurst & Sheep, 2019, p. 82). An example of a constitutive communication response to this shortcoming is Sheep, Fairhurst, and Khazanchi's (2017) study of a corporate subsidiary that was spun off and later re-acquired by a parent firm. Employing the metaphors of prisms and knots to consider how tensions can amplify or attenuate one another in organizing, they showed that when analysts consider tensions to exist not in individuals' minds but in the discourses that pervade action, they can better grasp those tensions' multiplicative power. This move enables research on knotted tensions to explain dis/order as resulting from the presence of either an authoritative account of a given organizational reality or the potential for contested meanings (Vásquez et al., 2016). Those contested meanings can, in turn, manifest disorder as disequilibrium, and—to return to the notion that disorder can be functional for organizations, introduced above—as key to a system's capacity for growth (Fairhurst & Sheep, 2019).

Literature on tensions, paradoxes, and contradictions does not necessarily engage with dis/organization as we introduced the notion above. Frequently, work in this vein is content to display the presence of opposing forces in organizational life, or to acknowledge that actors' observations of disarray often prompt efforts at classification and systemization, which in turn can stimulate organizational mess (e.g., Abrahamson, 2002). CCO scholarship, however, frames tensions, paradoxes, and contradictions as the opening and closing of meaning, created from the always-indeterminate communication practices; building on this foundation has led to the valuable insights on organizing described in this section.

Dis/ordering Devices

A third line of CCO-based scholarship focuses on dis/ordering devices, such as texts and other tools (e.g., ICT) that are created to order and structure action, but at the same time have the potential to bring about disorder. Vásquez et al. (2016) propose an analytical framework to study the role of organizational texts as dis/ordering devices based on three dimensions: (1) the genre of the text, which formalizes (i.e., gives form to) meaning that, in turn, allows for its transformation; (2) the language used in the text that excludes (other) signs and (other) meanings, which then "haunt" those included for ordering; and (3) the decontextualization and recontextualization of text, which inscribe the process of meaning negotiation in a broader context, therefore opening it to multiple spaces and times (p. 631). Vásquez et al.'s (2016) study shows that communication, and specifically text-in-use, has (dis)ordering properties, because it opens and closes meaning at the same time. Hence, disordering is an integral part of efforts of ordering. In their words dis/ordering, "is not just a characteristic or 'side effect' of organizational life. It is, on the contrary, woven into the very fabric of organizing" (p. 652).

Extending Vásquez et al.'s (2016) work, Banerjee and Bloomfield (2019) explore the political and organizational effects of the dis/ordering properties of texts by revisiting Rice's (1953) seminal *Human Relations* article, which set the basis for the generalization of the Tavistock Institute's sociotechnical system theory. Drawing on Taylor and Van Every's (2000) text/conversation dialectic, the authors show how Rice's article brought order into the apparent "chaotic" work organization of the mills at Ahmedabad in India, where the experiments took place, mostly by removing the cultural and political dimensions of work relations. To disrupt Rice's reading of the Ahmedabad mills, Banerjee and Bloomfield introduce documented conversations about labor union and worker resistance that were happening during the time of the experiments at the mills, and yet were excluded from Rice's account. Banerjee and Bloomfield's historiographical study can be seen as an invitation to disorder (i.e., open-up meaning) and disrupt normative texts through their recontextualization.

Moving from the disordering properties of textual devices to that of other objects and materials, we find the work of Albu (2019) on ICTs. Albu (2019) explores what she terms the "paradox of (in)visibility" in the use of ICTs by an international civil rights organization based in Morocco that relies on visibility management to work in both overt and covert ways. ICTs, Albu argues, "create order by rendering visible conversations, information, connections, data, etc. At the same time, ICTs create disorder (through ellipsis) by rendering invisible some information, connections, events, etc." (p. 155). This ethnographic study shows that, ICTs, as dis/ordering devices, can both generate and avoid surveillance, aggregate and lose information, and facilitate and disrupt coordination at the same time. Another example is Winkler and Seiffert-Brockmann's (2019) study, who introduce White's concept of styles to argue that disorder is not only a trigger for ordering but can also be seen as a particular form of organizing in itself. Styles represent a form of social organizing that reproduces established meanings, role expectations, and socio-material affordances through irritating and subverting. Drawing on the example of two widely known Internet memes, the Obama Hope meme and the Trump's first order in business meme, the authors reveal recurring patterns of subverting established meaning, manipulating audience expectations, and outwitting affordances and algorithms of the Web as basis modes of reproduction of this digital subverting style.

Agency and Contingent Trajectories of Practice

A fourth line of CCO studies explores how dis/organization is emerging and performed through a multiplicity of (human/nonhuman) agencies. Mainly inspired by ANT and New Materialism, this work approaches entanglements of communicative practices as precariously shaping organization—not in spite of, but intertwined with disorganization (Kuhn & Burk, 2014). Three points are central here: the relationality of non/human agencies, the affectivity of communication, and the performativity shaping contingent trajectories of dis/organization.

Leaving behind the idea that primarily humans respond to the turmoil of everyday dis/organization, CCO scholars propose to view organization/disorganization as a relational matter characterized by the multiplicity and interdependency of human and nonhuman agency. In zooming into the netted and messy communicative practices, they unpack the relational forces that both order and disorder daily work life (Ashcraft & Kuhn, 2018; Dille & Plotnikof, 2020). Cooren and Caïdor (2019) exemplify, in the context of healthcare, how one set of communicative actions introducing new benchmarking indicators and practices to measure healthcare professionals' efficiency may also disorganize other healthcare practices through more paperwork, taking time away from patients (2019, pp. 47–48). Also, Porter (2014) shows the potential of studying relations of non/human agencies with regard to (dis)organization. In her study of a university-based organization supporting blended learning technologies, she shows how this organizational entity and the technology coordinators become entangled through three (dis)organizing performances involving both discursive and material agencies. Likewise, Dille and Plotnikof (2020) explore how multimodal communication both orders and disorders the positioning of a new educational middle-manager role, showing that this precarious accomplishment is (dis)organized through entangled agencies such as bodies, talks, books, aisles, meeting rooms.

Relatedly, some CCO studies accentuate affect as an overseen agentic force, which saturates the communicative dis/organization of everyday work life by intensifying felt practices and embodiments (Ashcraft & Kuhn, 2018). Drawing on affect theory, they indicate the agency of affect that draws together bodies and things, which—by their relation—become real and felt. Ashcraft (2019, p. 100) stresses affective agency as "the ebb and flow of sensory encounter that continually brings bodies into distinction through relation". In various works (2017, 2021) she unpacks dis/organization in communicative acts of differentiation that move and spread affects amongst non/human agencies. For example, she shows how efforts of organizing academic performance in excellence systems (2017), or of understanding issues of hoarding (2019), seek to categorize and control differences by regulating affect, to avoid a disorganization of uncontrollable differences. In refocusing CCO scholarship, such work attunes it to a politics of affect, enabling new senses of dis/organizing control and resistance. This work emphasizes the ordering and disordering capacities of affect in communication of difference that move sensory encounters, stressing how affect (not always obviously or pleasantly) also partakes in dis/organizing everyday life.

Thirdly, efforts to push CCO theorizing beyond micro-macro distinctions (Kuhn, 2012; Putnam, 2019), without leaving the realm of communicative practices, stress the performative shaping of contingent trajectories as dis/organization. Vásquez and colleagues (2018, pp. 7–8) remind us that "all kinds of things – feelings, concerns, principles, collectives, texts, interests, artifacts, etc. – can be said to literally and figuratively participate in communication events", and by unpacking their interrelated performativity, they show the communicative efforts that dis/organize what comes to matter at work. In this piece, they show how "matters of concern" become "matters of authority" in a strategy process, by the communicative agencies that voice and negotiate those matters, transport and materialize them in texts, and legitimize them. However, such communicatively constituted strategy processes may also involve ruptures: e.g., disalignment of actions or opposition to a strategy object. These disorganizing performativities partake in the interweaving of communication—as interstices, intermediaries or in-betweens, that co-constitute the emerging trajectory of, for example, a strategy (Vásquez et al., 2018; Cooren et al., 2015).

Struggles over Meaning in Communicative Capitalism

Lastly, a body of CCO scholarship looks beyond "the" organization to consider how late capitalism itself is a project of dis/organization. In contrast to the conventional image that capitalism is an organized system with stable rules that efficiently govern individual and organizational action, writers in the dis/organization tradition show how the communicative character of contemporary capitalism fosters disruption and precarity as a relatively new logic of capital accumulation (Mumby, 2019).

Work in this vein starts with the recognition that the contemporary economic environment has seen radical shifts over the past few decades. Specifically, the rise of post-Fordism positioned intangible assets like images, knowledge, emotions, and brands as central in the production process. It is not merely that images, knowledge, emotions, and brands are components of tangible products; they are, increasingly, the products themselves. Because those products emerge in communication practices, the shifts to this new economy are often captured under the broad mantle of *communicative capitalism* (Dean, 2005; Hill, 2015), a term recognizing that organizations' value production has gradually become more about making meanings than making things (Mumby, 2016, 2019). Hence, struggles around meaning, along with the management of meaning, are at the heart of communicative processes that constitute our societies and collectivities (Mumby & Plotnikof, 2019).

Scholars of dis/organization are particularly interested in communicative capitalism because it relies on generating insecurity and precarity in the individuals who produce value. If brands were produced only inside firms and transmitted to consumers (as is the case with traditional commodities), precarious forms of employment would make little sense, since exploiting employees—the producers of images, knowledge, emotions, and brands—would reduce the value those individuals would create. The claim of communicative capitalism, however, is that value is no longer produced "inside" the firm (or factory), but in the micropractices of everyday life—and especially in the lives of consumers. Brands have moved well beyond their role as markers of product quality; they exist centrally as signifiers of meaningfulness in the lifeworld.

Branding is thus as much the work of consumers on social media who take the brand to be self-constituting as that of a firm's employees. Taking the argument a step further, in a gig economy marked by ever-present individualized risks, the branding of the self—the whole self—has become the primary mode of navigating our social and organizational worlds. The insecurity and precarity marking individual lives make brands and branding, as devices for securing meaningfulness, instead foment disorder and anxiety. Yet, because brands are rooted in indeterminacies and struggles around meaning, they are always subject to contestation and resistance (Mumby, 2016). Brands embody a contradiction: they try to fix meaning while striving at the same time on a surplus of meaning, which is the essence of the conception of dis/organization offered at the outset of this chapter. As put by Mumby (2019, p. 135), "A brand whose meaning becomes fixed eventually dies". This contradiction is increased by the brand's political ambivalence, in which it mediates the tension between the entrepreneurial neoliberal self and a collective self, formed around political and social issues.

Inspired by Honneth's (1997) work on struggles for recognition, Fassauer (2017) focuses on how communication provides moral evaluations of the relation to self and identity. While she does not directly engage with communicative capitalism, her proposition echoes this line of CCO thinking as the notion of struggles for recognition puts forward instability and disorder as preconditions for organizing and points out the potential for disorder that comes with a moral dimension of communication. As a form of conflict, resistance and demand for change, struggles for recognition describe a communicative situation in which moral standards are scrutinized and disrupted. This instability is one of the main principles of organizing. Recognition is thus both the trigger and the means to settle these struggles: both ordering and disordering at the same time.

Toward a Research and Practical Agenda

The work presented in this chapter moves CCO thinking away from what Bisel (2009, p. 632) called an "organizing bias" in organizational communication, which sees communication as "constituting order and coordinated action rather than disorder and inability to coordinate action". By emphasizing disorder, indeterminacies, tensions, struggles, and varied agencies as co-constitutive of order and organization, this line of work challenges rational and consensual definitions of (organizational) communication. In doing so, it furthers our comprehension of the constitutive role of communication by recognizing that the indeterminate character of communication is not a failure in organizing, but rather a prerequisite and a driver of organization. Said differently, approaches to communication as dis/organization show that if communication organizes, it disorganizes at the same time, and more importantly that this capacity of communication to organize/disorganize is central to understanding the mode of existence of collectives and society. Hence, studying processes and practices of dis/organization is fundamental for pursuing CCO explorations into the constitutive role of communication and advancing CCO thinking in manifold ways.

Moving beyond Meaning Negotiation

A shared standpoint of CCO approaches is that communication is "a process of meaning production and negotiation" (Schoeneborn, Kuhn & Kärreman, 2019, p. 476), which resides in and emerges from practices. As mentioned, a dis/organizational lens understands this process as the opening (i.e., disordering) and closing (i.e., ordering) of meaning (Vásquez et al., 2016). Mease (2020) fairly criticizes the central stage that this indeterminacy of meaning has taken in

CCO accounts of dis/organization, which tends to reduce disorganizing events to meaning-making. As she notes, "[this] risks limiting the explanatory power of communication as the primary constitutive element of organizations" (p. 7). Relational ontologies and alternative frameworks (e.g., Deleuze's techniques and forces; see Mease, 2020) can help to conceptualize communication beyond meaning-making by redirecting attention to the "erratic and material circulation" (Kuhn et al., 2017, p. 91) of affects, bodies, things, values, and goods.

Strengthening Critical CCO Perspectives

The relation with power in CCO approaches has been quite ambiguous (Schoeneborn et al., 2019). While some scholars have directly addressed it (e.g. Kuhn, 2008; Mumby & Plotnikof, 2019), others have avoided the term and preferred that of authority (e.g., Taylor, 2011). A dis/organizational lens puts power at the center as an inherent and constitutive organizational and societal feature. For example, Mumby (2019, p.133) calls for an alternative CCO perspective, one that interrogates the relation between Communication, Capital and Organization, by questioning how communication mediates and constructs the capital-labor relationship in everyday life, transforming life itself into living labor. This shift of focus has two major implications: first, and as mentioned previously, it moves the study of organizing beyond organizations to consider how late capitalism itself becomes a project of dis/organization; second, it questions the *flatness* of the flat ontology that characterizes most of CCO scholarship and favors a more historically contingent explanation of the modes of organizing (see del Fa & Kärreman, this volume). Reconsidering power in the equation of the constitution of organization implies recognizing that even if the world may seem flat, deep-down power infused features—we could call Discourses, logics, mechanisms, relations—affect the course of actions. Attending to these features implies then to anchor the processes of dis/organizing (inside and outside organizations) in the genealogies of power politics.

Problematizing Dualisms

The problematization of dualisms is at the core of CCO theory-building: organization/organizing (Cooren et al., 2011), agency/structure (McPhee & Zaug, 2000), symbolism/materialism (Ashcraft et al., 2009), and text/conversation (Taylor & Van Every, 2000) are some of the dualisms that have been interrogated. Dis/organizational renderings also partake in this endeavor by considering the mutual constitution of order and disorder as an ontological feature of dis/organizing. Whether questioning the organization/disorganization relation in terms of mutual constitution, or labeling it in terms of paradoxes and tensions, these renderings lead, to some extent, to a reinforcement or reification of the dualisms they try to contest. Constructs such as the opening/closing of meaning (Vásquez et al., 2016), the paradox of (in)visibility (Albu, 2019) or organizational (in)stability (Mease, 2020) put the poles in opposite relationship, while keeping them together. A new vocabulary is needed to avoid the trap of dualism. Dialectics and "both-and" approaches, imbricated processes, becoming and the use of verbs and adverbs, and dialogical accounts can offer a "way out" of the trap of dualism that is inscribed in language.

Conclusion

Besides these several theoretical paths, embracing communication as dis/organizational can also contribute in developing a practical agenda, one that infuses disruption, disorder, irrationalities, disobedience into organizational practices and also civic engagement. Our invitation here is to go beyond (or outside) the study of organization/disorganization to extend our concern with and take part in dis/organizational actions by engaging with messy empirical realities. This can be explored with more experimental pedagogies, but also with collaborations with industry, policy and activists. Another way would be to further develop action-research with social movements, civic organization or non-profit organizations. Our hope is that we can develop an ethico-political agenda that recognizes the centrality of dissensus, instability and struggles as constitutive and transformative of collective realities.

References

Abrahamson, E. (2002). Disorganization theory and disorganizational behavior: Towards an etiology of messes. *Research in Organizational Behavior, 24*, 139–180.

Albu, O. B. (2019). Dis/ordering: The use of information and communication technologies by human rights civil society organizations. In C. Vásquez & T. Kuhn (Eds.), *Dis/organization as communication: Exploring the disordering, disruptive and chaotic properties of communication* (pp. 151–171). New York: Routledge.

Ashcraft, K. L. (2017). 'Submission' to the rule of excellence: Ordinary affect and precarious resistance in the labor of organization and management studies. *Organization, 24*(1), 36–58.

Ashcraft, K. L., & Kuhn, T. (2018). Agentic encounters: Performativity and affect meet in the bathroom. In B. H. J. M. Brummans (Ed.), *The agency of organizing: Perspectives and case studies* (pp. 170–193). New York: Routledge.

Ashcraft, K. L. (2019). Feeling things, making waste. In C. Vásquez & T. Kuhn (Eds.), *Dis/organization as communication: Exploring the disordering, disruptive and chaotic properties of communication* (pp. 99–124). New York: Routledge.

Ashcraft, K. L., Kuhn, T. R., & Cooren, F. (2009). 1 Constitutional amendments: "Materializing" organizational communication. *Academy of Management Annals, 3*(1), 1–64.

Barad, K. (2003). Posthumanist performativity: Toward an understanding of how matter comes to matter. *Signs: Journal of Women in Culture and Society, 28*(3), 801–831.

Banerjee, A., & Bloomfield, B. (2019). Disorganizing through texts: The case of A.K. rice's account of sociotechnical systems theory. In C. Vásquez & T. Kuhn (Eds.), *Dis/organization as communication: Exploring the disordering, disruptive and chaotic properties of communication* (pp. 172–176). New York: Routledge.

Bencherki, N., & Elmholdt, K. T. (2020). The organization's synaptic mode of existence: How a hospital merger is many things at once. *Organization.* doi:10.1177/1350508420962025.

Bisel, R. (2009). On a growing dualism in organizational discourse research. *Management Communication Quarterly, 22*(4), 614–638.

Boulding, K. (1985). *The world as a total system.* London: Sage.

Cooper, R. (1986). Organization/disorganization. *Social Science Information, 25*(2), 299–335.

Cooren, F. (2000). *The organizing property of communication.* Amsterdam: J. Benjamins.

Cooren, F. (2010). *Action and agency in dialogue: Passion, incarnation and ventriloquism.* John Benjamins.

Cooren, F. & Caïdor, P. (2019) Communication as dis/organization: How to analyse tensions from a relational perspective. In C. Vásquez & T. Kuhn (Eds.), *Dis/organization as communication: Exploring the disordering, disruptive and chaotic properties of communication* (pp. 36–59). New York: Routledge.

Cooren, F., Bencherki, N., Chaput, M., & Vásquez, C. (2015). A communicational approach to strategy making: Exploring the constitution of matters of concerns in fleeting moments of strategy. In D. Golsorkhi, L. Rouleau, D. Seidl, & E. Vaara (Eds.), *Cambridge handbook of strategy as practice* (2nd edn., pp. 365–388). Cambridge: Cambridge University Press.

Cooren, F., Kuhn, T., Cornelissen, J. P., & Clark, T. (2011). Communication, organizing and organization: An overview and introduction to the special issue. *Organization studies, 32*(9), 1149–1170.

Cooren, F., Taylor, J. R., & Van Every, E. J. (Eds.). (2013). *Communication as organizing: Empirical and theoretical explorations in the dynamic of text and conversation.* Routledge.

Dale, K., & Latham, Y. (2015). Ethics and entangled embodiment: Bodies–materialities–organization. *Organization, 22*, 166–182. doi:10.1177/1350508414558721.

Dawkins, C. E., & Barker, J. R. (2020). A complexity theory framework of issue movement. *Business and Society, 59*(6), 1110–1150. doi:10.1177/0007650318762404.

Dean, J. (2005). Communicative capitalism: Circulation and the foreclosure of politics. *Cultural Politics*, *1*, 51–74.

Dille, M. H., & Plotnikof, M. (2020). Retooling methods for approaching discourse-materiality relations: A new materialist framework of multimodal sensitivity. *Qualitative Research in Organizations and Management*. doi:10.1108/QROM-09-2019-1821.

Fairhurst, G. T., & Sheep, M. L. (2019). Rethinking order and disorder: Accounting for disequilibrium in knotted systems of paradoxical tensions. In C. Vásquez & T. Kuhn (Eds.), *Dis/organization as communication: Exploring the disordering, disruptive, and chaotic properties of communication* (pp. 80–98). New York: Routledge.

Fassauer, G. (2017). Organization as communication and Honneth's notion of struggles for recognition. In S. Blaschke & D. Schoeneborn (Eds.), *Organization as communication. Perspectives in dialogue* (pp. 27–44). New York: Routledge.

Ford, J. L., & Ivancic, S. R. (2020). Surviving organizational tolerance of sexual harassment: An exploration of resilience, vulnerability, and harassment fatigue. *Journal of Applied Communication Research*, *48*(2), 186–206. doi:10.1080/00909882.2020.1739317.

Grothe-Hammer, M., & Schoeneborn, D. (2019). The queen bee outlives her own children: A Luhmannian perspective on project-based organizations (PBOs). In C.Vásquez & T. Kuhn (Eds.), *Dis/organization as communication: Exploring the disordering, disruptive and chaotic properties of communication* (pp. 60–79). New York: Routledge.

Heracleous, L. (2004). Boundaries in the study of organization. *Human Relations*, *57*, 95–103.

Hernes, T. (2014). *A process theory of organization*. New York: Oxford University Press.

Hechter, M., & Horne, C. (Eds.). (2009). *Theories of social order: A reader* (2nd edn.). Palo Alto, CA: Stanford Social Sciences.

Hill, D. W. (2015). *The pathology of communicative capitalism*. Basingstoke, UK: Palgrave Macmillan.

Honneth, A. (1997). Recognition and moral obligations. *Social Research*, *64*(1), 16–35.

Knox, H., O'Doherty, D. P., Vurdubakis, T., & Westrup, C. (2015). Something happened: Spectres of organization/disorganization at the airport. *Human Relations*, *68*(6), 1001–1020. doi:10.1177/0018726714550257.

Kuhn, T. (2008). A communicative theory of the firm: Developing an alternative perspective on intra-organi-zational power and stakeholder relationships. *Organization Studies*, *29*, 1227–1254.

Kuhn, T., Ashcraft, K. L., & Cooren, F. (2017). *The work of communication: Relational perspectives on working and organizing in contemporary capitalism*. Taylor & Francis.

Kuhn, T., & Burk, N. (2012). Spatial design as sociomaterial practice: A (dis)orga-nizing perspective on communicative constitution. In F. Cooren, E. Vaara, A. Langley, & H. Tsoukas (Eds.), *Language and communication at work: Discourse narrativity and organizing* (pp. 149–174). Oxford University Press.

Kuhn, T., & Corman, S. R. (2003). The emergence of homogeneity and heterogeneity in knowledge structures during a planned organizational change. *Communication Monographs*, *70*, 198–229.

Langley, A., & Tsoukas, H. (2010). Introducing perspectives on process organization studies. In T. Hernes & S. Maitlis (Eds.), *Process, sensemaking, & organizing* (pp. 1–26). Oxford: Oxford University Press.

Matte, F. (2019). Extreme context as figures of normalcy and emergency: Reorganizing a large-scale vaccine campaign in the DR Congo. In C. Vásquez & T. Kuhn (Eds.), *Dis/organization as communication: Exploring the disordering, disruptive, and chaotic properties of communication* (pp. 245–267). New York: Routledge.

McPhee, R.D., & Zaug, P. (2000). The communicative constitution of organization: A framework for explanation. *Electronic Journal of Communication/La Revue Electronique de Communication*, *10*(1/2), 1–16.

Mease, J. J. (2020). Techniques and forces and the communicative constitution of organization: A Deleuzian approach to organizational (in) stability and power. *Management Communication Quarterly*, 0893318920969969.

Mumby, D. K. (2016). Organizing beyond organization: Branding, discourse, and communicative capitalism. *Organization*, *23*(6), 884–907.

Mumby, D. K. (2019). Communication constitutes capital: Branding and the politics of neoliberal dis/organization. In C. Vásquez & T. Kuhn (Eds.), *Dis/organization as communication: Exploring the disordering, disruptive, and chaotic properties of communication* (pp. 125–147). New York: Routledge.

Mumby, D., & Plotnikof, M. (2019): Organizing power and resistance: From coercion, to consent, to governmentality. In J. McDonald & R. Mitra (Eds.), *Movements in organizational communication research: Current issues and future directions* (pp. 35–55) New York: Routledge.

Munro, R. (2003). Disorganization. In R. Westwood & S. Clegg (Eds.), *Debating organization: Point-counterpoint in organization studies* (pp. 283–297). Malden, MA: Blackwell.

Porter, A. J. (2014). Performance as (dis) organizing: The case of discursive material practices in academic technologies. *Canadian Journal of Communication, 39*(4).

Porter, A. J., & Jackson, M. H. (2019). The paradox of digital civic participation: A disorganization approach. In C. Vásquez & T. Kuhn (Eds.), *Dis/organization as communication: Exploring the disordering, disruptive, and chaotic properties of communication* (pp. 197–219). New York: Routledge.

Plotnikof, M. (2015). Negotiating collaborative governance designs: A discursive approach. *The Innovation Journal: The Public Sector Innovation Journal, 20* (3), 1–22.

Plotnikof, M., & Pedersen, A. R. (2019). Exploring resistance in collaborative forms of governance: Meaning negotiations and counter-narratives in a case from the Danish education sector. *Scandinavian Journal of Management, 35*(4), 1–11. https://doi.org/10.1016/J.SCAMAN.2019.101061.

Putnam, L. L. (2019). Constituting order and disorder: Embracing tensions and contradictions. In C. Vásquez & T. Kuhn (Eds.), *Dis/organization as communication: Exploring the disordering, disruptive and chaotic properties of communication* (pp. 17–35). New York: Routledge.

Putnam, L. L., Fairhurst, G. T., & Banghart, S. G. (2016). Contradictions, dialectics, and paradoxes in organizations: A constitutive approach. *Annals of the Academy of Management, 10*, 1–107. doi:10.1080/19416520.2016.1162421.

Schoeneborn, D., & Vásquez, C. (2017). The communicative constitution of organization (CCO). *The international encyclopedia of organizational communication.* Chichester: Wiley Blackwell.

Schoeneborn, D., Kuhn, T. R., & Karreman, D. (2019). The communicative constitution of organization, organizing, and organizationality. *Organization Studies, 40*(4), 475–496. https://doi.org/10.1177/0170840618782284.

Sheep, M. L., Fairhurst, G. T., & Khazanchi, S. (2017). Knots in the discourse of innovation: Investigating multiple tensions in a reacquired spin-off. *Organization Studies, 38*(3–4), 463–488. doi:10.1177/0170840616640845.

Spoelstra, S. (2005). Robert Cooper: Beyond organization. *The Sociological Review, 53*, 106–119. doi:10.1111/j.1467-954X.2005.00544.x.

Taylor, J. R. (2011). Organization as an (imbricated) configuring of transactions. *Organization Studies, 32*, 1273–1294.

Taylor, J. R., & Van Every, E. J. (2000). *The emergent organization: Communication as its site and surface.* Routledge.

Tsoukas, H., & Chia, R. (2002). On organizational becoming: Rethinking organizational change. *Organization Science, 13*(5), 567–582.

Vásquez, C., Bencherki, N., Cooren, F., & Sergi, V. (2018). From 'matters of concern' to 'matters of authority': Studying the performativity of strategy from a communicative constitution of organization (CCO) approach. *Long Range Planning, 51*(3), 417–435.

Vásquez, C., & Kuhn, T. (Eds.). (2019). *Dis/organization as communication: Exploring the disordering, disruptive, and chaotic properties of communication.* New York: Routledge.

Vásquez, C., Schoeneborn, D., & Sergi, V. (2016). Summoning the spirits: Organizational texts and the (dis) ordering properties of communication. *Human Relations, 69*(3), 629–659.

Weick, K. E. (1979). *The social psychology of organizing* (2nd edn.). New York: McGraw-Hill.

Williams, T. A., Gruber, D. A., Sutcliffe, K. M., Shepherd, D. A., & Zhao, E. Y. (2017). Organizational response to adversity: Fusing crisis management and resilience research streams. *Academy of Management Annals, 11*(2), 733–769. doi:10.5465/annals.2015.0134.

Winkler, P., & Seiffert-Brockmann, J. (2019). Organizing from disorder: Internet memes as subversive style. In C. Vásquez & T. Kuhn (Eds.), *Dis/organization as communication: Exploring the disordering, disruptive and chaotic properties of communication* (pp. 220–245). New York: Routledge.

8

THE COMMUNICATIVE CONSTITUTION OF ORGANIZATIONALITY

Dennis Schoeneborn, Blagoy Blagoev and Leonhard Dobusch

(1) What is Organizationality?

In the history of organization studies as a field, we can distinguish three basic orientations (see Schoeneborn, Kuhn, & Kärreman, 2019): studying organization as either a noun, verb, or adjective. In the field's historical origins, scholars have traditionally been concerned with studying *the* organization as a (formal) *entity or noun* (as exemplified by metaphorical imaginations of the "organization as machine", "organization as organism", "organization as brain", etc.; see Morgan, 1986). Over the past 30 to 40 years, we can also observe a growing interest in grasping organization and organizing primarily as a *process or verb* (as implied in imaginations of "organization as flux" or "organization as becoming", etc.; see also Morgan, 1986; Weick, 1995; Tsoukas & Chia, 2002). Recently, however, organizational scholars have directed their attention increasingly also to studying organization as an *attribute or adjective* of a broad range of social collectives (e.g., social movements, communities, networks, etc.). In this "adjectivic" orientation of organizational scholarship (Schoeneborn et al., 2019), the core question becomes which degree of such "organizationality" a social collective can accomplish. Importantly, this theoretical move allows organizational scholarship to gain a clearer positioning within the broader spectrum of the social sciences (see Ahrne, Brunsson, & Seidl, 2016).

The notion of organizationality initially goes back to an article by Dobusch and Schoeneborn (2015). Based on a study of the hacktivist collective Anonymous, the authors suggest considering organization as a matter of degree; in other words, a social collective like Anonymous may exhibit higher or lower degrees of organizationality at different points in time. For instance, Anonymous tends to have low degrees of organizationality (e.g., open boundaries that, in principle, allow various individual actors to conduct hacker operations on its behalf; Coleman, 2014). Yet, the social collective can situationally mobilize higher degrees of organizationality (e.g., when it exposes an individual hacker's identity as a means of exclusion and boundary-drawing, thus temporarily exhibiting "classical" elements of organization, such as membership, hierarchies, or sanction mechanisms; see Ahrne & Brunsson, 2011). In this chapter, we argue that the notion of organizationality can serve as an umbrella term that can encompass various streams of recent organizational scholarship that are all united by an adjectivic understanding of organization as a matter of degree.

DOI: 10.4324/9781003224914-10

Another prominent example of adjectivic conceptualizations of organization is Ahrne and Brunsson's notion of "partial organization" (2011). In their article, the authors propose to understand organization as "decided order" (i.e., a particular type of social order that is created as a result of interconnected processes of decision-making), while partial organizations are decided orders that lack one or more of classical elements of organization (i.e., membership, hierarchies, rules, monitoring and sanction mechanisms). One example of partial organization is a customer loyalty club (such as the IKEA Family Club) that is primarily based on membership but that lacks the other typical elements of organization (Ahrne & Brunsson, 2011, p. 87). Also, the notion of partial organization can be used as a theoretical lens to examine various social formations beyond formal organizations (e.g., families, networks, or markets; see Ahrne & Brunsson, 2019) and to assess their organizational character. In that way, the notion of partial organization helps develop a broader "zoology" of organizational forms than the field of organization studies would be traditionally concerned with if it were to restrict itself first and foremost to formal exemplars of organization (see Du Gay & Vikkelsø, 2016).

In a similar spirit, a number of further studies have been conducted to trace and explore phenomena of organization beyond the boundaries of formal organization (e.g., Bennett & Segerberg, 2012; Cnossen, this volume; Mumby, 2016, 2018; Nielsen, 2018; Wilhoit & Kisselburgh, 2015). They focus on a broad set of empirical phenomena such as digitally facilitated social movements (Bennett & Segerberg, 2012), social media hypes (Mumby, 2018), or bike commuter collectives (Wilhoit & Kisselburgh, 2015). Bennett and Segerberg (2012), for instance, study how the organizing activities during the Arab Spring movement, facilitated by mobile digital media and what they refer to as the "logic of connective action", have led to the emergence of new forms of organization out of communicative processes. Similarly, Mumby (2018) describes the case of an emergent and eruptive process of organizing that developed as a social-media hype around a good-looking cash desk employee at the US retail chain Target.

Strikingly, many of these works do not originate from the "core" area of organization studies but from adjacent disciplines such as political or organizational communication studies. In this chapter, we aim to explain why a communication-centered understanding of organizational phenomena goes especially well together with the notion of organizationality (i.e., as a gradual understanding of organization). These considerations build the basis for comparing two empirical cases of organizationality in particular: the case of the hacktivist collective Anonymous (cf. Dobusch & Schoeneborn, 2015) and the case of coworking spaces (cf. Blagoev, Costas, & Kärreman 2019). Our transversal analysis of the two cases demonstrates how communication can serve as an explanatory lens for the emergence of organizationality in distinct forms. We conclude the chapter with reflections on future trajectories of research at the intersection of communication and organizationality.

(2) Value-added of a Communication-Centered View on Organizationality

In this section, we elaborate on three reasons why communication-centered perspectives lend themselves particularly well to studying organizationality. First, communication-centered views in organization studies, especially those that consider communication as constitutive of organization (CCO; e.g., Ashcraft et al., 2009; Cooren et al., 2011), offer a *low-threshold understanding of organization* (see Schoeneborn & Vásquez, 2017; Vásquez, Kuhn, & Plotnikof, this volume). Rather than understanding organization only in the formal sense (i.e., by referring to exemplars of a state bureaucracy or incorporated business firm), a CCO perspective advances a broader understanding of organization as occurring in communication. Thus, it invites us to consider forms of organization that emerge beyond the boundaries of formal organization (e.g., Mumby, 2016). In this view, organization is an inherent by-product of human (and non-human) inter-action (e.g., Cooren, 2000). In other words, organization, if broadly understood as co-orien-tation toward a common reference point through language use (Taylor & Van Every, 2000; Schoeneborn, Vásquez, & Cornelissen, in press), tends to emerge in instances of communica-tion of various kinds. These include not only interactions that we would conventionally con-sider as *organizational* communication, but also conversations on the interpersonal level (e.g., the talk among friends who help each other with a sizable task) or on the societal level (e.g., media reports about recent terrorist attacks that are attributed to the same perpetrators). In that sense, CCO scholarship and work on organizationality share a common interest in organizational phenomena that transcend the boundaries of formal organization.

However, embracing a CCO view that understands organization as ultimately consisting of something as loose and ephemeral as communication raises the "composition problem" (Kuhn, 2012): how do various and dispersed communication episodes get interconnected over time and space so that they constitute a (more or less) coherent organizational phenomenon (see also Cooren & Fairhurst, 2009; Blaschke et al., 2012)? In that regard, CCO scholars and researchers of organizationality share a common interest in how different degrees of "decided order" (Ahrne & Brunsson, 2011), "coordinated action" (Wilhoit & Kisselburgh, 2015), or "connective action" (Bennett & Segerberg, 2012) arise and become stabilized over time. The answers to this question vary though, not least depending on which tradition of CCO scholar-ship researchers draw on (for an overview, see Schoeneborn et al., 2014).

Second, CCO scholarship emphasizes that *the* main constitutive element of organiza-tion is a particular type of process, that is, communication (understood here as a dynamic process of negotiating and transforming meanings; see Ashcraft et al., 2009). It follows that CCO scholarship considers organizational phenomena first and foremost as *processual entities* (Blaschke et al., 2012). In this understanding of what an organization is, organizational phe-nomena only exist from one communicative episode to the next (Taylor & Cooren, 1997) "for another next first time" (Garfinkel, 2002, p. 182), making them necessarily precarious accomplishments.

We argue that this inherently processual focus of CCO scholarship can help capture the dynamics that lead to higher or lower degrees of organizationality. For instance, in their appli-cation of the notion of partial organization to CSR standards, Rasche, de Bakker, and Moon (2013) have called for studying dynamic trajectories of partial organization over time (see also Rasche & Seidl, 2019). Similarly, Schoeneborn and Dobusch (2019) have demonstrated that social collectives such as Anonymous can vary situationally between lower degrees of organizationality (e.g., behaving like a loose and dispersed network that can hardly be inhibited) and higher degrees of organizationality (e.g., by expelling a member and thus mobilizing typical elements of full-fledged exemplars of organization). In the same context, a communication-centered view can help explain why and how degrees of organizationality can vary over time. Accordingly, CCO scholarship can provide research on organizationality with an explanatory lens on the particular communicative mechanisms that lead to less or more organizationality.

These considerations directly point us to a third important argument: CCO scholarship rests on the assumption that communication tends to have *performative* and, in that sense, "world-cre-ating" capabilities. The idea of the performativity of language use (Gond, Cabantous, Harding, & Learmonth, 2016) has its roots in speech act theory, following the tradition of Austin (1962) and Searle (1969) (see also Butler, 1990). Accounting for the performativity and action-like character of language use can also help explain how something as ephemeral as communi-cation can lead over time to something more manifest, consequential, and binding, such as organizational phenomena (Ford & Ford, 1995). Accordingly, acknowledging this two-sided character of communication—in which (a) the open-ended and fluid character of meanings are negotiable through communication and (b) there are possibilities to fix meanings and create bindingness through communication (see also Vásquez, Schoeneborn, & Sergi, 2016)—offers particular promise to explain how phenomena of organizationality are maintained over time in the very interplay of fluidity and stability (see Schreyögg & Sydow, 2010).

In the following, we demonstrate the usefulness of a communication-centered lens by discussing two empirical studies on organizationality: (a) the hacktivist collective Anonymous (Dobusch & Schoeneborn, 2015) and (b) the coworking space betahaus in Berlin (Blagoev, Costas, & Kärreman, 2019). We chose these two cases for two main reasons: first, they stem from very different contexts, allowing us to illuminate the diversity of contexts in which organizationality can emerge. Second, both studies involved members of the author team of this chapter, which allows us to draw on the rich empirical data the two studies were based on. After presenting the main contours of both case studies and the organizationality they reveal, we discuss which insights can be derived from a comparative analysis of similarities and differences across the two cases.

(3) Exemplary cases of Organizationality—and Transversal Insights

a. *The Organizationality of Hacktivist Collectives: The Anonymous Case*

The first case we present is a study on the "hacktivist" (a neologism that combines the terms hacker and activist) collective Anonymous.[1] Anonymous is a network of hackers who are loosely held together by particular ideals (though they may vary across time and geography), such as propagating free software, open access to knowledge, or Internet freedom more generally (Beraldo, forthcoming; Coleman, 2013). One the one hand, Anonymous has a rather fluid character, for instance, by leaving the boundary open, in principle, regarding who can conduct hacker activities on its behalf and thus contribute to the collective endeavor (Coleman, 2014). On the other hand, and despite this fluidity, Anonymous exhibits quasi-organizational features by sparking coordinated action or effectively expelling individual "members" who violate specific rules or norms. The most typical example of such coordinated action is what Anonymous activists call "operations" (or #ops), that is, a project-like collaborative organizing of and often mobilizing for attacks (e.g., DDoS = distributed denial-of-service attacks to shut down a website) against certain religious groups, corporations, or other targets.

Operations attributed to Anonymous are usually launched by postings on public image boards such as 4Chan or forums such as AnonNews, which are open to anonymous postings and highly ephemeral; 4Chan, for example, only hosts a limited number of postings and continuously deletes older posts as new posts are added. Given these circumstances, someone posting calls for a new Anonymous operation on one of these public websites "doesn't mean every single Anon[2] is in agreement", as a press release posted on AnonNews emphasized in an attempt to denounce another posting on the very same platform. Hence, in our earlier research (Dobusch & Schoeneborn, 2015) we asked the question: how are social collectives (like Anonymous) able to accomplish and maintain organizationality despite the fluidity inherent to their ephemeral and anonymous setup?

As shown in our research (Dobusch & Schoeneborn, 2015), Anonymous exhibits all three layers of organizationality (which, in turn, can be seen as a "minimum definition" of organization): first, the hacktivist collective features episodes of *interconnected decision-making*. The project-like hacker operations as such usually comprise a sequence of decision-making episodes through which hackers coordinate who is supposed to be attacked, as well as when and how. This coordination usually occurs both via public digital media channels (e.g., pertinent Twitter and Facebook accounts or collaborative web-authoring tools such as etherpads) and via private media channels (e.g., private and in some cases encrypted chat rooms). But episodes of decision-making do not only get interconnected *within* single hacker operations but also *across* different ones. For example, social media channels such as @YourAnonNews, with 6.8 million followers on Twitter (as of December 2020),[3] historically shared calls for Anonymous operations that turned out to be "real" in the sense of leading to actual hacktivism. This history of contributing to operations perceived as successful, or at least consequential, attracts followers and increases credibility of future calls for operations shared on these channels. This interconnecting takes place at minimum by orienting hacker operations toward the same reference point, that is, Anonymous as a social address.

This leads us directly to a second important layer of organizationality, that is, *collective actorhood* (see also King, Felin, & Whetten, 2010). To some degree, the anonymity of (individual) contributors to Anonymous's operations strengthens the (collective) actorhood of Anonymous. Operations may be conducted by an individual anonymous hacker, e.g., a live website hack during a radio interview, or by a great number of participants running software programs on their computers in distributed denial-of-service (DDoS) attacks on websites. In both these examples, the combination of contributor anonymity and public attribution of these acts to the collective social address of Anonymous constitutes the collective actor (cf. Bencherki & Cooren, 2011; Savage, Cornelissen, & Franck, 2018), which is externally reinforced by third parties corroborating said attributions by reiterating respective claims (e.g., press reports by journalists).

Third, as noted further above, Anonymous is a fluid social phenomenon in the sense that individual hackers can contribute to the organizing activities without having to subscribe to formal rules or attain formal membership status; in other words, fixed membership is replaced here with fluid contributorship (Bencherki & Snack, 2016; Grothe-Hammer, 2020). Importantly, as soon as a social collective relies on a contributorship-based (rather than membership-based) mode of organizing, its boundary is drawn in a different way. The boundary is not drawn by making decisions on which individuals are considered as "inside" or "outside" the organization (as traditional forms of membership negotiation would imply; see Luhmann, 2019, or McPhee & Zaug, 2000). Rather, it is drawn based on distinctions between what types of contributions count as belonging to the social endeavor and which ones do not (see Bencherki & Snack, 2016; Grothe-Hammer, 2020).

This setup makes Anonymous's identity and boundary inherently precarious: "If anyone can speak on behalf of Anonymous, who *cannot?*" (Schoeneborn & Dobusch, 2019, p. 326). Empirically, we can observe that the social collective's boundary is maintained via *identity claims*, that is, communicative practices which attempt to demarcate what an entity is or does. Across different operations we find a particular need to carefully craft, prepare, and "stage" identity claims in such a fluid organizational arrangement—especially in situations where the "open organizing" character of Anonymous leads to communicative contestations of what Anonymous is or should be. In such contexts, Anonymous is able to gain (at least temporarily) the status of a collective actor (i.e., that attacks other actors and maintains a relatively clear boundary around the social phenomenon). In other words, the organizationality lens allows us to study how phenomena like Anonymous are able to oscillate between a rather fluid, social-movement-like character and a tighter, quasi-organizational character. In this regard, the concept of organizationality offers potentials to theorize the very oscillation between movement and organization and consider them as temporary states rather than separate social forms. In so doing, it contributes to research at the intersection of social movement research and organization studies (e.g., Bennett & Segerberg, 2012).

One example of identity claims that allow the temporary accomplishment of organizational actorhood status is the carefully crafted and staged practice of *doxing* (i.e., compiling documents and personal information for exposing of another hacker's identity). For instance, when one hacker announced (in 2011) a collaborative hacker attack against Facebook, it led to public contestations of whether or not such an attack should "count" as being part of Anonymous. In such contestations, the practice of doxing served as an effective means of proving that those hackers who revealed the other hacker's actual identity were more skilled, and thus need to be seen as the "real" contributors to Anonymous. Accordingly, in the case of the operation targeting Facebook (#OpFacebook), the practice of doxing and exposing the initiator's personal identity (including home address, phone number, etc.) successfully settled the debate. By literally "naming" the individual responsible for the operation, a communicative boundary was drawn and made clear that this particular hacker operation should be considered as being outside (rather than part of) the collective: anyone can speak on behalf of Anonymous, as long as he or she remains anonymous. In sum, the Anonymous case allows us to exemplify how organizationality can be constituted through three communicative practices that are closely intertwined: interconnected decision-making, acting on behalf of a collective actor, and performing identity claims. Furthermore, although Anonymous lacks a specific and confined physical location, the label Anonymous as a social address, combined with pertinent digital channels on which one can find Anonymous-related communication, serves as an important substitute in that it provides a reference point toward which hacker operations are oriented (see also Beraldo, forthcoming). Finally, while the fluidity and a rather low degree of organizationality seem to be a "design principle" of Anonymous (Coleman, 2014), in practice the social collective tends to oscillate temporarily between low and high degrees of organizationality (see also Schoeneborn & Dobusch, 2019).

b. *The Organizationality of Coworking Spaces: betahaus in Berlin*

betahaus is one of the most popular and largest coworking spaces in Berlin.[4] Coworking spaces (Blagoev, Costas, & Kärreman, 2019; Garrett, Spreitzer, & Bacevice, 2017; Spinuzzi, 2012) represent a relatively new form of organizing so-called independent work, that is, work which occurs largely outside the boundaries of formal organization and traditional employment (e.g., Petriglieri, Ashford, & Wrzesniewski, 2019). At first sight, betahaus simply provides an open architectural infrastructure of shared, "on demand" workspaces: everyone is welcome to rent a desk flexibly from a single day to a whole year. Doing so also provides access to separate meeting rooms, Wi-Fi Internet, and other basic office facilities, such as a mailbox, printers, and photocopiers. In addition, betahaus usually serves as a platform for various socializing events, such as parties and breakfasts, as well as workshops. Yet, attendance at such events is non-mandatory and everyone is, at least in principle, "free to come and go as they wish". This openness of the betahaus community was also communicatively reinforced by actors at betahaus who often described the coworking space as an "open society", a "culture of openness", or "open space". Such communicative practices suggested a non-binding and fluid character which one interviewee likened to a hotel:

> If you had your own office, then you would indeed have to empty the trash and stuff like this … it's a bit … it has something of a hotel, when I think about it now. You come and use it when you need it or stay a bit, and then you go again.
>
> *Doris*[5]

A closer look at the communicative dynamics within betahaus reveals how the latter can assume an organizational character to varying degrees, depending on its ability to pattern the work activities of its members. On the most fundamental level, betahaus is an open community for independent workers without a traditional organizational affiliation. These independent workers, though engaged in entirely unrelated activities and occupations, end up sharing the same office space. As a result, the coworkers' initially independent decisions could become interdependent. Over time, the community came to exhibit features of *interconnected decision-making*, the most fundamental layer of organizationality (cf. Dobusch & Schoeneborn, 2015). For example, actors at betahaus engaged in episodes of interconnected decision-making when it came to organizing joint activities and events on behalf of the coworking space. Such events entailed, for instance, the weekly betabreakfast but also larger events such as the "People at Beta" festival. On a more subtle level, interconnected decision-making at betahaus also entailed the shared routines and tacit forms of social control through communicative practices that emerged within the coworking space (cf. Barker, 1993). For example, betahaus coworkers developed a particular temporal routine. People arrived at work pretty much the same time in the morning every day (between 9 and 10 a.m.), and at 6.30 p.m. the coworking space was almost always empty (apart from the days when workshops took place followed by parties). This temporal routine was enforced communicatively: When someone came in at an unusual time, people would ask them why they were late (or early). In addition, interviewees reported how the sheer material co-presence at the coworking space had a disciplining effect on their work:

> I just find it hard to motivate myself at home. [...] And here ... there are so many people, this also motivates me and, in the end, in the phases when I sit in front of the computer, I am much more concentrated and efficient.
>
> *Sandra*

The coworking space, thus, served as a platform for inter-connecting a large number of independent workers' everyday decisions to go to work, be productive, and share a daily routine with other fellow coworkers without necessarily working on the same tasks.

In addition, betahaus also acquired some degree of *collective actorhood* by virtue of the internal communicative dynamics within the space and external attribution. For instance, on multiple occasions coworkers decided to appear and act on behalf of betahaus as a collective actor, for instance, in terms of supporting certain social causes (e.g., hosting the "Decolonizing Berlin" conference in September 2020 aimed at, e.g., changing Berlin street names to promote a culture of remembrance about Berlin's colonial past) or when participating in popular city-wide events:

> Three weeks ago, someone had the idea to put on a stage for Fete de la Musique, and they [the space operators] picked it up and asked the startups: "Hey can you support us with a small amount? Or just by doing something?" And then there was a really cool stage with a solid music program.
>
> *Nigel*

It is also important to note that betahaus is portrayed as both a local actor and a participant in a global coworking space network. betahaus coworking spaces have already opened their doors in Hamburg, Barcelona, Sofia, Tirana, and Milan, with each "branch" being openly accessible for users of the other ones.

Appearing and behaving as a collective actor also strengthened the sense of *identity* that betahaus provided its members with. Identity claims were communicated both in a centralized and in a decentralized manner. For example, the betahaus website communicated some central features of identity—the idea of providing a fixed point, a stable place in the fluid and non-binding world of independent work:

> To express our idea of a new workplace, we first came up with terms from the area of software development, such as "beta version" or "beta phase". They best describe the way we'd like to design and develop the betahaus: as an open-ended process. [...] *"Perpetual beta": the betahaus is never really complete but keeps on evolving.* [...]. Finally, the word "betahaus" was created [...]: a real place in the digital world; a fixed point and physical home for creative professionals and other "digital Bohemians".
>
> *betahaus, 2015*

In a more decentralized manner, people working at betahaus also continually engaged in communicating identity claims. To them, the most important point of distinction was demar-cating a boundary between betahaus—which at the end of the day looked a lot like an open-plan office, but more colorful—and traditional employment:

> Coworking is definitely a little bit different than when you rent an office … . Ok, you sit in an open-plan office [...] But actually, what you get here, especially at betahaus, you just get more, you get a *community*.
>
> *Norbert*

Coworkers particularly stressed the absence of hierarchy as well as the egalitarian feel of betahaus as a distinguishing identity feature:

> First and foremost, it is a *non-hierarchical togetherness* because … at almost all companies you have superiors, who always have a special status … even in the open-plan office, [...] it is a hierarchical structure. Here you are equal among equals.
>
> *August*

Coworkers found this distinction important and attractive, as it enabled them to "just be them-selves" at work:

> And unlike the classic corporate office people are not pigeonholing you. [...] *Here you can just be yourself.* You don't have to fulfil any clichés in order not to be frowned at.
>
> *Sandra*

Overall, the betahaus coworking space become a recognizable, physical reference point (a "social address" in the terminology of Dobusch & Schoeneborn, 2015) in Berlin's large scene of independent workers and entrepreneurs. Many of them chose to come and work at betahaus, because doing so provided them with an identifiable affiliation within the scene, something that is important for independent workers who often have to cope with precarious working conditions and feelings of social isolation (e.g., Petriglieri et al., 2019). Above and beyond a sense of affiliation, betahaus also provides independent workers with a flexible degree of organizationality, including elements of interconnected decision-making, collective actorhood, and identity. Indeed, the sheer "co-habitation" in the shared physical space seemed to facilitate the emergence of shared routines, rituals as well as forms of discipline and control. In that sense, betahaus functioned as a sort of "surrogate organization" (Petriglieri et al., 2019), a platform that provided independent workers with varying and customizable degrees of organizationality by mobilizing a material infrastructure of shared office space.

c. Comparative Analysis and Discussion

In the next step, we compare and contrast the two selected cases of organizationality—to identify shared and recurrent patterns across the cases as well as potentially theoretically relevant differences. Table 8.1 provides a summary and overview of these cross-case observations. As we have seen in the description of the two cases, both exhibit the three layers of organizationality: (1) interconnected decision-making, (2) collective actorhood, and (3) identity claims—even if they manifest themselves in different ways.

First, in terms of interconnected decision-making, Anonymous appears to operate primarily in project-based form, with interconnecting decisions both within the project (i.e., to make the hacker operation happen) and across projects (via the label Anonymous as the joint reference point). Somewhat similarly in the betahaus case, organizationality is partly accomplished through project-like activities that emerge among the freelancers sharing the same space. However, on top of this, one can also observe day-to-day routine-like patterns that emerge among users of the coworking space. Such patterns, in turn, intensify the character of a quasi-organization or "surrogate organization" (we will come back to this notion at the end of this section). Second, in terms of collective actorhood, it is noteworthy that in both cases a clearly identifiable label or "social address" serves as the main reference point through which collective actorhood has the chance to arise. In the Anonymous case, hacker operations are enacted "on behalf of" Anonymous, thus charging the social address with actorhood. In the betahaus case, even if more strongly bound to local physical place, the brand name and social address *betahaus* serves as reference point that connects different activities (e.g., given the fact that users of the betahaus Berlin coworking space can check into other coworking spaces in the betahaus network, such as in Hamburg). Third, in terms of identity claims, both cases draw on an interplay of assertive (i.e., low-performativity) speech acts—to define who they are or what they do—and declarative (i.e. high-performativity) speech acts—to perform collective identity, not least by defining what or who they are not (see Dobusch & Schoeneborn, 2015). In the Anonymous case, the collective tends to mobilize highly performative speech acts (e.g., publicly revealing a hacker's personal identity) to distance itself from certain hacker attacks that were perceived as misaligned with the collective identity. At betahaus, coworkers especially distanced themselves from traditional employment and its associated "look and feel" in terms of office space.

Apart from the three layers of organizationality, we identified a number of further striking similarities between the two cases. First, regarding the role of the social address, in both cases the clearly identifiable label or brand name is what holds together the diverse contributions to the organizational endeavor. At the same time, the social address allows for scalability in the sense that new contributions can be added fairly easily to the existing setup, for instance, by endorsing new hacker attacks that contribute to Anonymous as an organizational endeavor, or by adding new, in principle independent, coworking spaces to the betahaus network. Second, regarding the role of contributorship, both cases in principle leave the boundary open in terms of who can add activities to the organizational endeavor—as long as these contributions are largely in line with shared values among contributors. In the betahaus case though, the "open organizing" character (Dobusch, Dobusch, & Müller-Seitz, 2019) is restricted by the fact that only a certain number of people can be simultaneously present at the coworking space (due

Table 8.1 Comparative analysis of the two exemplary cases of organizationality (Anonymous and betahaus)

	Case A: Anonymous	Case B: betahaus
I. Three layers of organizationality		
(1) Interconnected decision-making	Interconnecting of decisions within and across (project-like) hacker operations	Emergence of day-to-day routines as well as project-like activities among otherwise disconnected freelance workers
(2) Collective actorhood	Hacker operations are enacted on behalf of Anonymous, thus contributing to its collective actorhood	Organization of internal events and participation in external, city-wide events on behalf of betahaus as collective actor
(3) Identity claims	Interplay of assertive speech acts that aim to define what Anonymous is or does—and declarative speech acts that "perform" its identity	Interplay of assertive speech acts that aim to define betahaus as part of the larger "openness" movement—and declarative speech acts that distinguish it from traditional, "hierarchical" office spaces/forms of work
II. Further similarities across the cases		
(4) Role of the social address	Clearly identifiable label/social address as necessary condition for organizationality (while also allowing for scalability)	
(5) Role of contributorship	Boundaries are drawn mainly by self-recruited/voluntary contributions compatible with the organizational endeavor (and, in case B, if space permits)	
(6) Role of material configurations	Pertinent channels in digital media/confined physical space serve as "material anchors" for co-orientation	
III. Further differences across the cases		
(7) Global vs local scope	Global/dispersed with regard to location of contributors	Local physical space that hosts contributors
(8) Temporality	Oscillation between high and low degrees of organizationality	Trend toward adding more layers of organizationality (while remaining optional and "customizable")
(9) Strategy vs emergence	Organizationality as strategic/intentional act	Organizationality/"surrogate organization" as emergent and customizable "side-product"

to its limited size) and that users need to pay in advance to make use of the space. At the same time, sheer co-presence is insufficient for organizationality to arise quasi-automatically. Rather, and just like in the Anonymous case, the collective depends on self-recruited and voluntary contributions to the common endeavor to recurrently constitute organizationality. Third, regarding the role of material configurations, in both cases organizationality becomes more tangible through materially visible places where one can "find" betahaus or Anonymous. In the betahaus example, this tangibility is rather straightforward with carefully designed office buildings that are accessible for their users. In the Anonymous example, where such clear physical space is lacking, tangibility is accomplished through pertinent digital media channels where Anonymous hackers would typically make their announcements. Hence, across both cases, we can perceive the importance of such "material anchoring" (Dobusch & Schoeneborn, 2015) that can provide some degree of stability in otherwise rather fluid organizational settings.

Finally, the cross-case comparison also allows for an identification of noteworthy differences between Anonymous and betahaus. A first difference refers to the global vs. local scope of contributors and their activities. While in the betahaus case one needs to be physically present in the coworking space in Berlin (or other subsidiaries) to add to its day-to-day activities and routines (even if these freelancers may engage in dispersed activities for their respective employers for the rest of the day), the Anonymous case is an example of a global and dispersed scope of contributors and their activities to further the common cause. Second, in terms of temporality, the Anonymous case has been described as alternating or oscillating between phases of lower degrees of organizationality (e.g., appearing to serve as a rather loose network in between hacker operations) and higher degrees of organizationality (e.g., when the collective on certain occasions is quasi-organizational, as in the #OpFacebook case mentioned above); accordingly, Schoeneborn and Dobusch (2019) have mobilized the metaphor of an "accordion" to describe such back-and-forth movements between different degrees of organizationality. In contrast, the betahaus case can be seen as part of a process that adds further organizationality and routines over time (and, in that way, might be comparable to the trajectories described by Rasche et al., 2013, or Rasche & Seidl, 2019). At the same time, because working at betahaus as such does not contribute to its organizationality (but only if these activities are oriented toward betahaus as the joint social address), the latter remains customizable for the individual user (i.e., the freelancers who work at betahaus can choose whether they want to engage in activities for their varying other employers and/or in activities for betahaus). This leads us directly to a third and final point. Whereas the rather fluid organizational setting of Anonymous seems to be a deliberate organizational design choice (cf. Coleman, 2014), in the betahaus case the organizationality seems to emerge without being strategically planned for; instead, it appears as a fluid and continuously evolving "surrogate organization", a customizable "by-product" of co-habitating in the shared coworking space.

(4) Concluding Remarks

In this chapter, we have outlined and compared two exemplary cases of organizationality, the hacktivist collective Anonymous (Dobusch & Schoeneborn, 2015) and the coworking space betahaus (Blagoev et al., 2019). We have also used the two cases to make the (somewhat abstract) concept of organizationality more tangible by embedding it into concrete contexts. While the two cases appear to be very different at first glance, they exhibit similarities regarding some of the key elements that need to be in place to enable the emergence of organizationality even in fluid or informal settings, such as a clearly identifiable social address, open but clear boundaries for a steady influx of new contributions, and material anchoring in concrete (digital) channels or (physical) spaces. Also, we have shown that across both cases communication plays a constitutive role in creating organizationality through the performance of communicative practices that are oriented toward a joint social address (e.g., Anonymous or betahaus). However, the specific communicative practices differ, depending on the two case contexts.

Taken together, the concept of organizationality allows us to not only better understand how organization emerges from other forms of sociality but is also able to capture temporarily changing degrees of organizationality over time. To some degree, this is of fundamental importance for research that routinely classifies social actors as either "organizational" or something else entirely. Organizationality as a concept enables—but also requires—acknowledging organization as a continuous communicative accomplishment. The exceptionally fluid and informal contexts of the admittedly extreme illustrative cases of Anonymous and betahaus, in turn, showcase that organizationality happens also in-between and beyond the set of traditional organizational building blocks commonly dealt with in the literature (e.g., Ahrne & Brunsson, 2011). Moreover, as emphasized further above, we believe the concept of organizationality adds to previous research at the intersection of social movement research and organization studies (e.g., Bennett & Segerberg, 2012) a theorization of how social collectives are able to oscillate between both movement and organization as different temporary social states rather than definite and separate social forms.

More generally, for future research, we see the identified similarities and differences between the two cases as a chance for further theoretical and empirical inquiries into the heterogeneity of organizationality (similar to the rich "zoology" of partial organization offered by Ahrne & Brunsson, 2019) and the boundary conditions under which organizationality can be accomplished. For instance, the importance of material anchors seems to be similarly pronounced in other empirical investigations of organizationality, such as the digital platforms that support the organizationality of crowdfunding collectives (Nielsen, 2018), or how mobile technologies facilitated the organizationality of the Arab Spring movement (Bennett & Segerberg, 2012), or the ways in which the materiality of bike riding and equipment helps constitute the organizationality of bike commuter collectives (Wilhoit & Kisselburgh, 2015). In turn, the two exemplary cases, Anonymous and betahaus, differed quite significantly in terms of the temporal trajectories toward higher and/or lower degrees of organizationality, as we have seen. Here, our elaborations call for studying the dynamic developments of organizationality (between partial and complete organization) over time (see also Rasche & Seidl, 2019).

Research on organizationality is still in its infancy. Nevertheless, it can provide the field of organization studies with opportunities for developing new theoretical vocabularies that can help gain a deeper scholarly understanding of the heterogeneous and dynamic landscape of organizational phenomena beyond the boundaries of formal organization (for a similar research impetus, see Ahrne & Brunsson, 2019). As our chapter aimed to show, in this regard communication-centered perspectives can help rethink what organization *is* and to identify (new) forms of organizationality that arise from communication. At the same time, the concept of organizationality helps to further develop CCO scholarship, which has been primarily focused on studying exemplars of formal organization, by elucidating the communicative constitution of a much broader spectrum of organizational phenomena beyond the boundaries of formal organization as such.

Notes

1 We draw here on research that was published in more extensive form in a prior publication of ours (Dobusch & Schoeneborn, 2015).
2 The label used in the community to signify Anonymous activists.
3 Cf. https://twitter.com/YourAnonNews (accessed 20 December 2020).
4 The following draws on an ethnographic study of the Berlin-based coworking space betahaus (Blagoev et al., 2019).
5 All names have been replaced by pseudonyms to protect the identities of those involved in the study.

References

Ahrne, G., & Brunsson, N. (2011). Organization outside organizations: The significance of partial organization. *Organization, 18*, 83–104.

Ahrne, G., & Brunsson, N. (Eds.). (2019). *Organization outside organizations: The abundance of partial organization in social life*. Cambridge, UK: Cambridge University Press.

Ahrne, G., Brunsson, N., & Seidl, D. (2016). Resurrecting organization by going beyond organizations. *European Management Journal, 34*(2), 93–101.

Ashcraft, K. L., Kuhn, T. R., & Cooren, F. (2009). Constitutional amendments: "Materializing" organizational communication. *Academy of Management Annals, 3,* 1–64.

Austin, J. L. (1962). *How to do things with words.* Oxford, UK: Clarendon Press.

Barker, J. R. (1993). Tightening the iron cage: Concertive control in self-managing teams. *Administrative Science Quarterly,* 408–437.

Bencherki, N., & Cooren, F. (2011). Having to be: the possessive constitution of organization. *Human Relations, 64,* 1579–1607.

Bencherki, N., & Snack, J. P. (2016). Contributorship and partial inclusion: A communicative perspective. *Management Communication Quarterly, 30*(3), 279–304.

Bennett, W. L., & Segerberg, A. (2012). The logic of connective action: Digital media and the personalization of contentious politics. *Information, Communication & Society, 15*(5), 739–768.

Beraldo, B. (forthcoming). Movements as multiplicities and contentious branding: Lessons from the digital exploration of #Occupy and #Anonymous. *Information, Communication & Society.*

Blagoev, B., Costas, J., & Kärreman, D. (2019). 'We are all herd animals': Community and organizationality in coworking spaces. *Organization, 26*(6), 894–916.

Blaschke, S., Schoeneborn, D., & Seidl, D. (2012). Organizations as networks of communication episodes: Turning the network perspective inside out. *Organization Studies, 33*(7), 879–906. https://doi.org/10.1177/0170840612443459.

Butler, J. (1990). *Gender trouble: Feminism and the subversion of identity.* London: Routledge.

Coleman, G. (2013). *Coding freedom: The ethics and aesthetics of hacking.* Princeton, NJ: Princeton University Press.

Coleman, G. (2014). *Hacker, hoaxer, whistleblower, spy: The many faces of Anonymous.* New York: Verso.

Cooren, F. (2000). *The organizing property of communication.* Amsterdam: John Benjamins.

Cooren, F., & Fairhurst, G. T. (2009). Dislocation and stabilization: How to scale up from interactions to organization. In L. L. Putnam & A. M. Nicotera (Eds.), *Building theories of organization: The constitutive role of communication* (pp. 117–152). New York: Routledge.

Cooren, F., Kuhn, T., Cornelissen, J. P., & Clark, T. (2011). Communication, organizing and organization: An overview and introduction to the special issue. *Organization Studies, 32*(9), 1149–1170.

Dobusch, L., Dobusch, L., & Müller-Seitz, G. (2019). Closing for the benefit of openness? The case of Wikimedia's open strategy process. *Organization Studies, 40*(3), 343–370.

Dobusch, L., & Schoeneborn, D. (2015). Fluidity, identity, and organizationality: The communicative constitution of Anonymous. *Journal of Management Studies, 52*(8), 1005–1035.

Du Gay, P., & Vikkelsø, S. (2016). *For formal organization: The past in the present and future of organization theory.* Oxford: Oxford University Press.

Ford, J. D., & Ford, L. W. (1995). The role of conversations in producing intentional change in organizations. *Academy of Management Review, 20*(3), 541–570.

Garfinkel, H. (2002). *Ethnomethodology's program: Working out Durkheim's aphorism.* Lanham, MD: Rowman & Littlefield.

Garrett, L. E., Spreitzer, G. M., & Bacevice, P. A. (2017). Co-constructing a sense of community at work: The emergence of community in coworking spaces. *Organization Studies, 38*(6), 821–842.

Gond, J. P., Cabantous, L., Harding, N., & Learmonth, M. (2016). What do we mean by performativity in organizational and management theory? The uses and abuses of performativity. *International Journal of Management Reviews, 18*(4), 440–463.

Grothe-Hammer, M. (2020). Membership and contributorship in organizations: An update of modern systems theory. *Systems Research and Behavioral Science, 37*(3), 482–495.

King, B. G., Felin, T., & Whetten, D. A. (2010). Finding the organization in organizational theory: A meta-theory of the organization as a social actor. *Organization Science, 21*(1), 290–305.

Kuhn, T. (2012). Negotiating the micro-macro divide: Thought leadership from organizational communication for theorizing organization. *Management Communication Quarterly, 26*(4), 543–584.

Luhmann, N. (2019). *Organization and decision.* Cambridge, UK: Cambridge University Press.

McPhee, R. D., & Zaug, P. (2000). The communicative constitution of organizations: A framework for explanation. *Electronic Journal of Communication, 10*(1–2).

Morgan, G. (1986). *Images of organization.* Beverly Hills, CA: Sage.

Mumby, D. K. (2016). Organizing beyond organization: Branding, discourse, and communicative capitalism. *Organization, 23*(6), 884–907.

Mumby, D. K. (2018). Targeting Alex: Brand as agent in communicative capitalism. In B. H. J. M. Brummans (Ed.), *The agency of organizing: Perspectives and case studies* (pp. 98–122). New York: Routledge.

Nielsen, K. R. (2018). Crowdfunding through a partial organization lens: The co-dependent organization. *European Management Journal, 36*(6), 695–707.

Petriglieri, G., Ashford, S. J., & Wrzesniewski, A. (2019). Agony and ecstasy in the gig economy: Cultivating holding environments for precarious and personalized work identities. *Administrative Science Quarterly, 64*(1), 124–170.

Rasche, A., De Bakker, F. G., & Moon, J. (2013). Complete and partial organizing for corporate social responsibility. *Journal of Business Ethics, 115*(4), 651–663.

Rasche, A., & Seidl, D. (2019). Standards between partial and complete organization. In G Ahrne & N. Brunsson (Eds.), *Organization outside organizations: The abundance of partia l organization in social life* (pp. 39–61). Cambridge, UK: Cambridge University Press.

Savage, P., Cornelissen, J. P., & Franck, H. (2018). Fiction and organization studies. *Organization Studies, 39*(7), 975–994.

Schoeneborn, D., Blaschke, S., Cooren, F., McPhee, R. D., Seidl, D., & Taylor, J. R. (2014). The three schools of CCO thinking: Interactive dialogue and systematic comparison. *Management Communication Quarterly, 28*(2), 285–316.

Schoeneborn, D., & Dobusch, L. (2019). Alternating between partial and complete organization: The case of Anonymous. In G. Ahrne & N. Brunsson (Eds.), *Organization outside organizations: The abundance of partial organization in social life* (pp. 318–333). Cambridge, UK: Cambridge University Press.

Schoeneborn, D., Kuhn, T. R., & Kärreman, D. (2019). The communicative constitution of organization, organizing, and organizationality. *Organization Studies, 40*(4), 475–496.

Schoeneborn, D., & Vásquez, C. (2017). Communication as constitutive of organization. In C. R. Scott & L. K. Lewis (Eds.), *International encyclopedia of organizational communication*. Hoboken, NJ: Wiley.

Schoeneborn, D., Vásquez, C., & Cornelissen, J. P. (in press). Theorizing the role of metaphors in co-orienting collective action towards grand societal challenges: The example of the Covid-19 pandemic. *Research in the Sociology of Organizations*.

Schreyögg, G., & Sydow, J. (2010). Organizing for fluidity? Dilemmas of new organizational forms. *Organization Science, 21*(6), 1251–1262.

Searle, J. R. (1969). *Speech acts: An essay in the philosophy of language*. Cambridge, UK: Cambridge University Press.

Spinuzzi, C. (2012). Working alone together: Coworking as emergent collaborative activity. *Journal of Business and Technical Communication, 26*(4), 399–441.

Taylor, J. R., & Cooren, F. (1997). What makes communication "organizational"? How the many voices of a collectivity become the one voice of an organization. *Journal of Pragmatics, 27*, 409–438.

Taylor, J. R., & Van Every, E. (2000). *The emergent organization: Communication as its site and surface*. Mahwah, NJ: Erlbaum.

Tsoukas, H., & Chia, R. (2002). On organizational becoming: Rethinking organizational change. *Organization Science, 13*(5), 567–582.

Vásquez, C., Schoeneborn, D., & Sergi, V. (2016). Summoning the spirits: Organizational texts and the (dis) ordering properties of communication. *Human Relations, 69*(3), 629–659.

Weick, K. E. (1995). *Sensemaking in organizations*. Sage Publications.

Wilhoit, E. D., & Kisselburgh, L. G. (2015). Collective action without organization: The material constitution of bike commuters as collective. *Organization Studies, 36*(5), 573–592.

9

THE COMMUNICATIVE CONSTITUTION OF EPISTEMIC AND DEONTIC AUTHORITY

Epistemological Implications of a Second-Order Construct

Letizia Caronia and Nicola Nasi

1. Introduction[1]

Contemporary debate on the constitution of organizations shows how and to what extent language in interaction – as well as other semiotic artifacts – is constitutive of what an organization is in terms of, for instance, social and professional identities, organizational statuses, roles, and even policies and practices. In this chapter, we focus on two distinct although related constitutive dimensions of any organization: epistemic and deontic authority, i.e. who or what, in a given circumstance, is or should be (recognized as) the one who knows and the one who decides. When dealing with authority (Bencherki, Cooren, & Matte, 2020), one of the main issues is the analyst's positioning as to the typical dilemma between a top-down, structuralistic approach according "causal power to […] structures, divorced from linguistic and communicative constitution" (Kuhn, 2012, p. 546), and a bottom-up approach programmatically focusing on the emergent properties of language and on the constitutive role of communication as to social structures and orders. If the former bears the lingering assumption that human action is produced by a system of forces that "human subjects can neither control nor understand" (Duranti, 2004, p. 452), the latter conceives the subject as a novel Adam, free of constraints in his daily creation of local meanings which do not "survive" until the next day. As pointed out by Bencherki et al. (2020), interactionist approaches to organizations have often been criticized in relation to the latter "fallacy", i.e. "for their alleged incapacity to deal with questions of power, coercion and domination" (p. 8). Their commitment to a radically bottom-up perspective would prevent them from noticing how the macro (i.e. the structures of an organization) affects the micro (i.e. local interaction) as much as the micro-order of interaction locally produces the macro-order of structure.

Assuming the co-constitutiveness of agency and structure (Giddens, 1984), in this chapter we contend that an approach informed by constitutive communication theory does not necessarily imply underestimating structure or neglecting the passive side of human sociality. To

DOI: 10.4324/9781003224914-11

illustrate this claim, we focus specifically on epistemic and deontic authority (hereafter, EDA) and make a case for its being *at the same time presupposed and constituted by participants in and through interaction*. As we will show, by means of the ways they manage their turn-at-talk and mobilize other available semiotic resources, members constantly display their orientation to these dimensions of organizational authority (see the Montreal School notion of co-orientation; Kuhn, 2012, p. 551) and talk them into being by locally (re)creating "who knows best and who decides what to do". From this perspective, agency and structure appear to constantly permeate each other, *at least from the analyst's point of view*. Indeed, while aligning with the CCO perspective on the local interactive crafting of authority and power (see Bartesaghi, 2009; Benoit-Barné & Cooren, 2009; Taylor & Van Every, 2014), in this chapter we go one step further by claiming that the notion at the core of CCO theory, literally, the *communicative constitution* of organization,[2] does not necessarily mirror the members' "natural attitude" (Schütz, 1967/1932) on their own communicative practices. With reference to the long-lasting debate on the emic/etic divide in organizational studies (see Morey & Luthans, 1984; Peterson & Pike, 2002; Kuhn, 2002; Buckley et al., 2014), we advance and empirically illustrate that the communicative constitution of organization is an experience-distant, second-order construct (Kohut, 1971; Fuchs, 2001) which appears significantly detached from members' understandings and accounts of their everyday life-world. If one of the accomplishments of CCO scholars has been to "denaturalize" the organizational world, i.e. to question members' taken-for-granted notions regarding the ontological reality of organizational entities, it came at a price: surreptitiously, this perspective risks depicting members, or at least those who account for their behavior as caused by already given overarching structures, as naive inhabitants of their everyday world. As we illustrate by making the case for EDA, the CCO theoretical attitude risks granting epistemic primacy to the researcher's viewpoint over members' ways of describing and interpreting the reality "out there". In doing so, it renews the relevance of the (perhaps unavoidable) clash between the members' and the analyst's stances, thus making researchers rethink the unresolved etic/emic dilemma in social sciences and compelling them to take a stance in relation to these fairly different modes of explaining organizational behavior. We argue that this possible clash should be explicitly addressed by scholars engaging in exploring the local constitution of (organizational) realities. When first- and second-order interpretations cannot be aligned (as is the case in our illustration), they should at least be juxtaposed, as they both are legitimate ways of making sense of organizations' life.

The chapter is structured as follows. In the first section, we outline one of the main challenges CCO studies have to cope with: the micro-macro link (see Kuhn, 2012). The second section reviews CCO studies on authority and expertise, whereas the third shifts the focus to the contribution of Language and Social Interaction studies (hereafter, LSI) in setting the framework for investigating epistemic and deontic authority in organizations. Finally, an illustration from fieldwork in an Intensive Care Unit exemplifies how the epistemic and deontic authority of the Responsible Clinician are both presupposed and locally constituted by the members in interaction. We conclude by claiming that dealing with the communicative constitution of EDA makes it inescapable for the researcher to take a stance toward the never resolved emic/etic dilemma in social science research.

2. Communication and the Micro-Macro Link

Since the phenomenological turn in social sciences (Caronia & Orletti, 2019), the ensuing groundbreaking notion of the social construction of reality, and the renewed attention to the micro (communicative) details people use to do "being ordinary", a relevant concern has challenged the study of the social world: what relationship, if any, exists "between the way people construct social reality and the obdurate social and cultural reality that they inherit from those who preceded them in the social world" (Ritzer, 2011, p. 219)? How can the link between shared cultural worlds (e.g. norms, rules, folk and professional theories, cultural models) and local (inter)actions be conceived of and analyzed?

Although the issue of the micro-macro link (Alexander et al., 1987) is anything but new, demonstrating how this link works and connects structure and agency, "cultural knowledge" and individuals' everyday praxis, is still a challenging topic for organizational communication studies. To avoid the risks of over-interpretation, intentionalism, and even cultural determinism, scholars in ethnomethodological, conversation analysis and CCO traditions propose a clear analytical perspective: following and analyzing (Cooren & Malbois, 2019) (talk-in-)interaction and the instances where people "talk into being" (Heritage, 1984, p. 290) supra-individual, structural entities such as principles, statuses, norms as well as artifacts, spaces and the material configuration of the world around them. This restricted analytical perspective amounts to a "cautious" approach: the analyst avoids referring to any pre-existing, extra interactional dimension as an explanatory notion of what is going on, unless participants do refer to it in the interaction under scrutiny, in an observable and demonstrable way.

Basically, this perspective has questioned the (in)famous "bucket theory of context" (Drew & Heritage, 1992, p. 19; for a recent uptake of the dispute on context see Antaki, 2012, Bartesaghi, Livio, & Matte, 2020) and is extremely convincing: it is largely shared in social research and still provides the theoretical and methodological framework for a huge amount of empirical research. Less common is illustrating how culture, social structure, and moral horizons, as well as the plethora of entities inhabiting the social world, shape social interaction and the forms of talk. Investigating or taking into account (also) the *passive side* of human sociality is still an underexplored phenomenon in CCO scholarship (but see Caronia & Cooren, 2014; Cooren, 2010; Brummans, Higham, & Cooren 2021). As depicted by Taylor (oral communication, 2015) while delineating the contemporary challenges of CCO-informed studies, the analytical cautiousness as to the role of context opens an analytical problem: narrowing the focus of analysis on the process (e.g., organiz*ing*, author*ing*, position*ing*) risks failing to account for the role played by the "constituted entities" (organization, authority, position) on the practices. This "restricted analytical geography" (Goodwin 2011) would amount to missing the point: showing how (constituted) entities have a life of their own and make a difference in the unfolding of interaction, i.e. have an independent agency (see Cooren, 2010; Brummans, 2018). If local interactions create a not-so-ephemeral array of agentive organizational entities – as the CCO perspective in organizational communication studies has demonstrated in the last 20 years[3] – the reverse is also true: already constituted, maintained, and crystallized entities shape the forms within which agency is deployed and "haunt" everyday social action (Cooren, 2009). In the next sections, we illustrate this point by making the case of epistemic and deontic authority as, at the same time, presupposed and constituted in communication.

3. Knowledge, Status and the Communicative Constitution of Authority

Contemporary CCO approaches to authority try to further develop insights from Follett (1940), Barnard (1938) and Simon (1947) on its situational accomplishment and deeply relational nature (see Bencherki, Cooren, & Matte, 2020). Despite such references to mid-twentieth century scholars, the origin of CCO approaches on authority can be traced back to the seminal work of Taylor and Van Every (2000), which considered authority as an interactive and iterative phenomenon, both presupposed and recursively constituted by members on an everyday basis. Since then, several authors have tried to depict the micro-physics of authority and to reconcile the clash between *entitlement* – i.e. the perceived legitimate right to influence and decide on organizational matters – and *negotiation* (Benoit-Barné & Cooren, 2009, p. 10; see among others Cooren, 2009; Taylor & Van Every, 2014) as well as the entanglement between knowledge and authority subsumed by the notion of expertise (Collins & Evans, 2007).

Within organization studies, the fruitful distinction between *authority of position* and *authority of expertise* (Barley, 1996) has been revived by Taylor and Van Every (2014) to emphasize the tension that a misalignment between these two dimensions can cause. The recognition of expertise as a central tenet of the notion of authority amounts to the investigation of individuals' authoritative claims beyond and despite their structural position and their being (or not) grounded on knowledge (on the [interactional] management of knowledge and its significance for organizational matters, see Kuhn & Jackson, 2008; for an encompassing overview see Barley, Treem, & Kuhn, 2018.) When grounded in knowledge, authority appears to be relative to a specific situation and to the actor's access to and skillful deployment of *relevant* knowledge (Alvesson & Kärreman, 2001). Ultimately, if authority is not something people have but something people do, one of the means to perform it is precisely the skillful management of (types of) knowledge in interaction (Ashcraft, Kuhn, & Cooren, 2009; Caronia, Saglietti, & Chieregato, 2019). This radically situated perspective on knowledge stresses the local nature of expertise, i.e. a heterogeneous accomplishment embedded in everyday workplace practices (Orlikowski, 2002). These practices involve a multiplicity of human and nonhuman actors (Kuhn & Porter, 2011) and represent the *locus* where decisions about expertise location and the deployment of relevant knowledge are continuously made.

In organizational interaction, these struggles over meaning become particularly visible in actors' *classifications* (i.e., naming/defining/framing the situation) and *closures* (i.e. establishing that a sequence is over, for example by selecting knowledge which is deemed sufficient) related to problem-posing/solving sequences (Kuhn & Jackson, 2008, p. 463; on the relevance of closures for the exercise of authority see also Cooren & Fairhurst, 2004). These actions can be considered part of the more general process of *decision-making*, in which "the turn-by-turn accomplishment of influence is made almost tangible" (van de Mieroop, 2020, p. 596). Notwithstanding the growing number of studies on the local constitution of "who knows" (best) and "who decides" (Bencherki et al., 2020), demonstrating how the turn by turn negotiation of expertise and leadership in decision-making concurrently affects and is affected by organization hierarchical structures still represents a challenge for CCO scholars. In the next section, we illustrate the contribution of Language and Social Interaction studies in rethinking this issue in light of what has been called the epistemic and deontic order of interaction (Stevanovic & Svennevig, 2015).

4. Making Epistemics and Deontics Actionable through Communication: The Contribution of LSI Studies

Using at times a different vocabulary, scholars within the LSI tradition have also addressed the issue of authority, trying to avoid any "possessive epistemology" – i.e. the idea that authority is something people *have* (or achieve as the outcome of their having something; Bencherki et al., 2020, p. 3). Rather than speculating on its ontological nature, they define authority as a socially constructed category which participants (might) locally orient to, and focus on authority displays and negotiations in and through talk-in-interaction (Boden, 1994). In the last decade, this focus on the communicative constitution of authority has been narrowed down by distinguishing between *epistemic authority*, i.e. the (relative) authority of knowing best or being entitled to know best about a specific topic (Heritage, 2012b; Stivers, Mondada, & Steensig, 2011), and *deontic authority*, i.e. the (perceived) right to establish what to do next and to determine future courses of action (Stevanovic & Peräkylä, 2012).[4] Although these two entitlements (to know and to decide) are often embodied in and enacted by the same actor, they are not necessarily co-existent and co-extensive: their embodiment depends on situational factors (e.g. "a person may regard another person as an epistemic authority in a certain field or as a deontic authority in a certain domain of action"; Stevanovic & Svennevig, 2015, p. 2) and is often distributed among human and non-human actors (as, for instance, when a physician consults a test as the knowledge source that entitles her to decide what to do [Sterponi et al., 2019]; see the notions of "textual agency" [Cooren, 2004; Brummans, Higham, & Cooren, 2021] and "presentification" [Cooren, 2006]).[5]

Although LSI interest in epistemics can be traced back to several pioneering studies (among others, Labov & Fanshel, 1977, and Pomerantz, 1980), it is only since the seminal work of Heritage and Raymond (2005) that scholars have started to systematically account for the management of knowledge in interaction, i.e. for its central role in action formation and recognition and in everyday negotiations of participants' identities, roles, and statuses (Heritage, 2012a,b; Mikesell et al., 2017). A central tenet of this perspective on knowledge is its *public nature*, i.e. its being both locally claimed by and attributed to interlocutors *and* influenced by social organization, that is, by the "rights and entitlements and obligations and distributions of knowledge according to types or categories of persons" (Drew, 2018). These two (intertwined) dimensions have been usefully addressed with the concepts of epistemic *status* and *stance*: the former refers to participants' relative access, rights and responsibilities to (types of) knowledge, whereas the latter concerns participants' situated displays of their epistemic status relative to one another (Heritage, 2012b). These studies clearly point out the situated, emergent character of (epistemic) authority: claiming and being granted an authoritative role, i.e. being the one who knows (best), depends on participants' communicative competence in managing knowledge in interaction and making it "actionable-through-talk" or other semiotic resources, as when participants point to/evoke/refer to entities or sources of knowledge that make them more knowledgeable than others. However, epistemics does not cover the field of authority-in-action. As mentioned above, the act of deciding can be independent of epistemic status and stance: the notion of *deontic* authority is supposed to account for the possible negotiations around "who decides".

Although the concept of deontic authority emerged as a topic in some early studies in the 1990s (among others, Peräkylä, 1998; Macbeth, 1991), a consistent research interest in a person's "legitimate power to determine action" (Stevanovic, 2018) was sparked by an article by Stevanovic and Peräkylä (2012), which set the agenda for the subsequent stream of studies (see among others Stevanovic, 2015; Svennevig & Djordjilovic, 2015). If epistemic authority concerns *knowing* how the world "is", deontic authority refers to participants' ability to *determine* how the world "ought to be" (Stevanovic, 2018). Recently, the distinction between *status* and *stance* has also been advanced for the deontic order: similar to what has been suggested for epistemics, the concept of deontic *status* refers to the relative position of power that a participant might be considered to have (or not to have) irrespective of what he or she publicly claims, whereas deontic *stances* concern participants' situated, public displays of their "authority to decide" in a specific domain of action. A further, crucial conceptual distinction regards *distal* and *proximal* deontic claims (Stevanovic, 2015); while the former is relative to "people's rights to control and decide about their own and others' future doings" (ibid., pp. 85–86), the latter refers to "people's rights to initiate, maintain or close up local sequences of conversational actions" (ibid.). Therefore, the deontic order concerns the rights and responsibilities to decide about the local interactional agenda (i.e. what is talked about, and when, and how) *as well as* future courses of action.

LSI research has convincingly shown how deontic claims are both ubiquitous in social life and the object of continuous negotiations by participants; together with epistemics, they can account for ongoing authority and power[6] negotiations, underscoring the complex array of local strategies by which authority is enacted, acknowledged, and resisted in (organizational) interaction.

5. Epistemic and Deontic Authority in Organizational Communication: An Illustration

The above-mentioned distinction between epistemic and deontic *status* and *stance* can help disentangle "the tension between the pre-discursive organizational structure [...] on the one hand, and the way the actual interaction unfolds and which identities (e.g. leader or follower) are constructed on a turn-by-turn basis on the other hand" (van de Mieroop, 2020, p. 598). Notwithstanding the relevance of such a conceptual distinction, there are still few accounts of the complex interplay between these dimensions in organizational studies (but see Svennevig & Djordjilovic, 2015; Stevanovic, 2015; Clifton et al., 2018). Furthermore, as EDA is deeply embedded in and enacted through situated interactions, a major aspect that needs to be explicitly addressed is participants' *interactional competence*.

In the next section, we provide an empirical illustration of how epistemic and deontic authority are, at the same time, presupposed by members and locally constituted through communication. Particularly, we illustrate how and to what extent interactional competence plays a role in such processes.

5.1. To Treat or not to Treat? Insights from Antibiotic Stewardship in a Hospital Ward

One of the most pressing contemporary challenges in healthcare organizations consists in rethinking antibiotic use to combat the increase of multi-drug resistant bacteria (MDRB). Deciding when to prescribe antibiotics and under which circumstances is, therefore, a pivotal moment in medical decision-making, especially when the single patient's immediate interest has to be balanced with the ecology of the ward. Drawing on ethnographic fieldwork in an intensive care unit (ICU), we focus on how this decision is collectively taken by the members of the team as aligned to the clinical line established by the *Responsible Clinician* (hereafter RC). We will show how his epistemic and deontic authority are communicatively constituted by means of the ways doctors manage their turn-at-talk and mobilize other available semiotic resources. The case is particularly perspicuous: no member has (or is recognized to have) specialized knowledge concerning the management of infectious diseases. Notwithstanding this flat epistemic hierarchy, one physician emerges as the one "who knows best and who decides what to do". We illustrate how his epistemic and deontic authority results from the entanglement of structure (e.g. pre-existing hierarchically organized roles) and members' constant engagement in communicatively constituting who has the right and responsibility to decide.

CEICU is a trauma-specific intensive care unit. As is the case with most hospital wards, it is a highly hierarchical, structured organization. Andrea is the RC of the ward, i.e. the senior physician in charge of the clinical line of both the ward and any single inpatient. He is a renowned specialist in brain injuries and recovery, but he does not have any specialty in infectious disease management. The issue is far from being irrelevant as Andrea adopted a policy of antibiotic stewardship that *strongly contrasts with the international guidelines for antibiotic treatment (ATBT) in ICUs* (Hranjec et al., 2012). In fact, while the guidelines clearly prescribe the use of empirical therapy *at the first signs of a possible infection* (i.e. they recommend starting treatment on the first suspicion of an infection), CEICU adopts the so-called "watch and wait" approach (Eggimann & Pittet, 2001). This policy consists in avoiding, as far as possible, the empirical therapy (i.e. not treating on suspicion) and prescribing ATBT only when it is clear: (a) that an infection is at stake, (b) what the germ(s) responsible for the disease are, (c) where the infection is located. Until all or – at least – most of these conditions are established: do not treat, "wait", monitor and assess again 24 hours later. Although this approach relies on a broad range of clinical practices (see Caronia & Chieregato, 2016), still this guidelines-non-conforming policy has strong clinical as well as ethical implications: it gives relative priority to the ward ecology over what may be perceived as the single patient's immediate interest (see Hranjec et al., 2012). CEICU's "watch and wait" approach is not a written protocol, yet it is officially stated and acknowledged by CEICU members as the "line of the ward".

How does the responsible clinician manage to (im)pose and pursue this policy despite its being "off label", the team members' explicit and implicit disagreement, and his not having an epistemic vantage point with respect to his colleagues? To investigate the local emergence of the RC's epistemic and deontic authority, we have selected the "morning briefings" as the main locus of analysis as "meetings are the very social action through which institutions produce and reproduce themselves" (Boden, 1994, p. 81).

Focusing on the local management of turns-of-talk, we identified the practices through which the RC managed to lead the ongoing diagnostic talk and make his clinical perspective prevail. The excerpts below illustrate how the RC: (1) manages the opening and closing of the sequences of the night physician's report, (2) behaves as the principal addressee, and (3) pursues the watch-and-wait approach by means of two main strategies, (a) "doing nothing with treatment implicative information" and (b) "making relevant no-treatment implicative information".

Figure 9.1   The morning briefing: orienting to RC's status through body and gaze.

Excerpt 1: "the 30th he had?"
LEGEND: RC = responsible clinician, NP = night physician, CM = case manager

[CEICU_GAR_03]

```
1 RC    the man, this [strange man in bed seven]
2 NP                  [the man, this strange man bed seven,
3       Garetti Gianluca, a fifty-year-old man
4       he is in his fifth day, it is an aneurysm of the
5       anterior communicating artery, treated with embolization,
6       (.)
7       patient issues. temperature thirty-eight point four
8       with an increasing trend in the past two days
9       (.)
10      the white cells are ten thousands but he has
11      foul smelling and dense secretions,
12      the urines from the 30th are negative,
13      there is a bas ongoing, the x-ray from the thirty
14      shows a probable right basal density
15      (.)
16      from a respiratory point of view
17      in the past few days there has been
18      [a progressiv-]
19 RC   [the thirth he was]at? his third day, the patient?
20 NP   yes.
21 RC   hmm. ok.
```

In 1 the RC initiates the macro section concerning the patient in bed number 7, thus indicating the conclusion of the assessment and planning of the previously discussed case. In doing so, he also tacitly selects the next speaker, the night physician (NP), who has primary access to the inpatient status and is the institutionally ratified knowledgeable reporter. The NP takes the turn he has been given and repeats literally what the RC just said. In doing so, he contributes to defining the RC as the authoritative voice that – in this case at least – appears to be a joint communicative construction.

In 4 the NP provides information concerning the day of the patient's stay: he is in his fifth day. This information is relevant to decision-making concerning the beginning of ATBT: this patient is close to the typical day when patients in this ward usually begin an ATBT. This "merely descriptive" information is followed by data concerning the fever: his body temperature is rising (lines 7–8), which is a typical symptom of a possible infection. Right after the NP adds information that does not support an infectious disease diagnosis: his white cells are ten thousands (10), the implied assessment is that they are not as high as they are expected to be when an infection is out there. This no-treatment implicative information is immediately followed by an adversative introducing new information concerning the status of his bronchial secretions: they are foul smelling (note the emphasis on the first syllable) and dense (11). When referred to the bronchial secretions of a patient in his fifth day of stay and with a rising fever, these report-formatted assessments make relevant that the (expected) Ventilator Associated Pneumonia is out there.

In 12 the NP adds the lab results concerning the urine test: it is negative. Referring to this negative result narrows the diagnostic field toward pneumonia as it excludes other possible (and less threatening) loci such as the vesicle and cystitis caused by the catheter. This latter infection is less treatment-implicative than pneumonia, since cystitis often disappears without using ATB by simply removing the device. Note that no diagnosis has been delivered, although the symptoms of pneumonia are there. While the NP continues along this implied trajectory (lines 13–18), the RC takes the turn with a competitive overlapping (19), opens an insertion sequence and comes back to the urine exams. Note that the NP gives up his turn, therefore acknowledging RC's rights to interrupt.

Although the RC uses an interrogative form and, therefore, asks for confirmation, he introduces an element that makes relevant the possibility that the vesicle is the loci of the possible infection: these exams were done the third day of the patient's stay, and the fact that they appear to be negative cannot be meaningful, since in the meantime the patient could have developed cystitis that could cause the fever. With this insert sequence, the RC makes relevant a counter diagnosis with respect to the one silently suggested by the NP: whereas the NP's projective diagnosis is treatment-implicative, the RC's is not. In 20 the NP confirms the information (the urine test was done three days after the patient's recovery) and the RC does not push forward. But still, he introduced the cystitis hypothesis, and therefore non-treatability, to the team's representational field (Heritage & Raymond, 2005, p. 16).

How does the conversation go on?

Excerpt 2: "That's ok go on"

```
22       [...]
23  NP   the white cells yesterday were ten thousand . decreasing
24       today I don't know if::
25  CM   nine thousands.     (.) (here from the) cultures
26       I am miss - I am missing a[bas
27  RC                          [so that's okay. go on?
28       (.)
29  NP   hum  [(tram-)]
30  RC        [cultu]res [((name CM)), you were saying, should
31       they be done?
32  CM                   [but it is miss- no. but-
33       they were repeated this morning but it is missing,
34       I am missing the bas from the [thirty still.
35  NP                                 [it's not here, (    )
36       still ongoing it was written.
37  RC   that's okay.
38  CM   it is still ongoing.
39       (.)
40  NP   so from a neurological point of view
```

The NP has resumed his account of the patient's clinical situation, therefore displaying his first-hand-knowledge-based epistemic status; after a few turns (not shown), he recycles already given information that is not treatment-implicative (the reduction of white cells, 23), thus aligning to the RC's watch-and-wait approach. The case manager (CM) intervenes with information confirming the decreasing trend of the white cells (25). Yet, right afterward, she recalls a piece of information (already provided by the NP in 13): the results of the exam of the last bronco aspirate (BAS) are not on the record yet. This information evokes the possibility that this exam could confirm the unstated yet implicitly projected diagnosis: pneumonia. In 30 and 31 the RC comes back to the status of culture tests and asks the case manager if they should be done: she specifies once again that the tests were done this morning again and that the result of the BAS taken on the 30th is missing.

The NP confirms this information by mobilizing the clinical record as an authoritative source of information: the BAS is still ongoing (lines 35–36). In 37, the RC closes the sequence (he opened in 30) with an agreement token and does not further explore the topic at hand, i.e. the possibility that the ongoing test confirms the suspected pneumonia. The CM further insists on the fact that the results are in progress (38).

By underlining three times that they are waiting for the BAS, the NP and the CM are doing at least three things: first, they highlight the pneumonia diagnostic trajectory (over cystitis); secondly, they project a possible course of action, i.e. calling the lab to have the intermediate results of the BAS which could confirm that a pneumonia is at stake (see Caronia & Chieregato, 2016) and, thirdly, they (therefore) point toward treatability. Note that the RC does not exploit any of the transition-relevant points he could use to intervene regarding this information, making it relevant. In 15 he does not take the turn upon the pause; in 27 and in 37 he provides an acknowledgment token with a conclusive intonation, and in 39 he does not exploit the pause once again. In 37 he signals the possible completion of the report sub-sequence concerning information relevant to an infectious disease diagnosis ("that's ok"). The NP aligns with the suggested closing of this discursive trajectory by changing the topic and reporting on the neurological status of the patient (41). In doing so, he interactionally cooperates once again in constituting/confirming the RC as the authoritative voice of the team.

Although never explicitly formulating any diagnoses nor stating the decision not to treat with antibiotics, the team practically decided, that day, not to treat under what was (de) constructed as suspected but not yet confirmed pneumonia. As in most decision-making occurrences observed during our fieldwork, the RC silently guided decision-making according to the watch-and-wait policy.

5.2. The Communicative Constitution of Epistemic and Deontic Authority: The Role of Interactional Competence

During our fieldwork, we discussed several times the issues of "doing being off-label" and of possible disagreement with different members of the team. As one of them told us, the watch-and-wait approach was "the line of the ward", established by Andrea who – as a senior told us – is "our chief". The overall priority was to follow one single policy, as Dr. Sylvia A. told us: "one ward one clinical line".[7] Clearly enough, Andrea's being the responsible clinician (the "chief") made a difference: when accounting for their behavior, members justified it by invoking his status-based authority as if it were a "real and enduring state of affairs" (Heritage, 2012b, p. 6) and his view weighed more heavily than others by virtue of skill and hierarchical advantage (Ashcraft et al., 2009). The "passive side" of their sociality was evident in the ways they accounted for their workplace life: he had the authority to decide. Despite this "evidence", the typical CCO suspicion concerning any conception of authority as "possessed" by somebody constrained us to search for what possibly went unseen by members.

As our analysis shows, the RC appeared to skillfully manage the interactive competence required to do "being the epistemic and deontic authority" of the ward. First of all, he enacted an authoritative role by opening and closing the macro-sections of the briefing as well as the inner phases of any macro-section: the report, the assessment and the plan (see ex.1, line 1 and ex. 2, line 37; see Cooren & Fairhurst, 2004; Holm & Fairhurst, 2018). The RC's ability in strongly influencing the decision-making process (i.e., in pursuing the watch-and-wait approach) is mostly apparent in his treatment of the NP's first-hand knowledge: on the one hand, he made relevant non-treatment-implicative information, e.g. by interrupting his colleague's account and asking for confirmation of a specific detail (ex.1, 19); on the other hand, he "did nothing" with treatment-implicative information, as he did not exploit transition-relevant places and used minimal acknowledgment tokens in response to his colleague's treatment-implicative contributions, without expanding on the matter (ex. 1, lines 6, 9, 15, and ex. 2, lines 27, 37, 39; see the similar concept of "disqualifications" in Kuhn & Jackson, 2008, and the category "prioritizing" in Holm & Fairhurst, 2018). Further, he managed to delay the diagnosis, e.g. by avoiding undertaking the implicitly suggested action of calling the lab to know the intermediate test results (ex. 2, 37; see "delaying conclusion" in Holm & Fairhurst, 2018). As regards the "followership", the other participants locally ratified the RC's authoritative position by selecting him as the ratified addressee through body orientation and gaze direction (see Figure 9.1), by aligning to his interactional moves (ex. 1 lines 2, 20 and ex. 2 lines 29, 40) as well as, at times, by lining up behind the clinical trajectory. For example, the NP also made relevant information which was compatible with the watch-and-wait approach endorsed by the RC, as when he reported the low level of leukocytes a second time (ex.2, line 23).

In a few words, participants clearly displayed their orientation to RC's authoritative status, and yet the RC provided a significant amount of interactional work in order to maintain this "state of affairs" and skillfully influence the decision-making process without imposing his view (see Pomerantz & Denvir, 2007; Wodak, Kwon, & Clarke, 2011). By cooperatively staging the process as distributed, participants moved toward a collective decision informed by the guidelines-non-conforming clinical line of the ward endorsed by the RC. As the analysis illustrates, (a) hierarchical positions affected the decision-making process, even though they needed to be ratified and maintained in interaction, (b) deontic and epistemic statuses and stances were markedly influenced by the participants' interactive competence, and (c) rather than being an *individual* property, EDA was claimed, attributed, and challenged collectively by several participants. In a few words, and borrowing John Heritage's words, the RC's epistemic and deontic authority appeared to be at the same time "a presupposed or agreed upon, and therefore real and enduring, state of affairs" (Heritage, 2012b, p. 6) *and* "evidenced and made real and enforceable for the participants" through interaction (Heritage, 2004, p. 224).

6. For Whom is Epistemic and Deontic Authority Communicatively Constituted? EDA as a Perspicuous Case of the Emic/Etic Dilemma in CCO Studies

CCO approaches to organizations share a major theoretical problem with emergentialist perspectives on human sociality: while they are very well suited to account for agency and the local production of social order, they are less equipped to deal with the reverse side of the recursive relationship between agency and structure, i.e. to show how structure and social orders impact on agency. In the aim of avoiding Whitehead's fallacy of misplaced concreteness, constitutive approaches risk underestimating how organiz*ing* produces a given (observable, describable, analyzable, labelable) organiz*ation* that – once communicatively constituted – sets constraints and projects possibilities for (communicative) action (Taylor, oral communication, 2015). The problem is far from being only theoretical. It becomes epistemological as it challenges one of the basic assumptions of constructivism-oriented social research: the mandate of taking an "emic perspective", i.e. aligning second-order constructs with first-order constructs and describing the world "from the members' point of view". As we illustrated by exploring the communicative constitution of "epistemic and deontic authority" in a hospital ward, a question arises: for whom are these kinds of authority communicatively constituted?

Clearly enough, a CCO-informed theoretical framework coupled with coherent analytical constructs and techniques (see Cooren & Malbois, 2019) would allow the analyst to see how and to what extent the team members of the hospital ward communicatively and jointly produced who – in a given circumstance – was the one who knows and the one who decides. However, in accounting for their communicative behavior, members focused exclusively on the "passive side" of social action: they invoked structural entities (e.g. pre-existing hierarchically organized roles) as making a difference in the ways they acted. None of the team members naturally (i.e. independently from the researcher's intervention) acknowledged their communicative contribution in crafting the RC's epistemic and deontic status. Rather, when talking with the researcher, junior as well as senior members recognized that they acted as they acted because he was "the chief", "our head", and – as a senior physician told us – "you cannot always say what you think, there are power issues at stake". In a few words, from the members' point of view, structure determined the members' attitudes as well as communicative behaviors, not the other way round: paraphrasing Moermann (1988, p. 102), deontic authority was a noun not a verb, a preformed thing not a social activity (see also Weick, 1995).

Adopting a CCO perspective, it would have been pretty easy to claim that this position was affected by "the fallacy of misplaced concreteness" and to advance that, on the contrary, a jointly accomplished process of communicative constitution of EDA was at stake. In advancing such an experience-distant account, wouldn't we have delegitimized participants as reliable witnesses of the world they lived in? Wouldn't we have delegitimized our informants' ability to account for their workplace life-world? A clash of stances was clearly at stake. To overcome it, we mobilized the (LSI) distinction between *status* (a static category pointing to presupposed and enduring structures of social action) and *stance* (the correlated dynamic notion relative to the contingent interactive bringing into being of any "enduring" state of affairs), which made it possible to account for the co-constitutiveness of organizational structures and members' interaction. As we have shown, by means of the ways physicians and nurses managed their turn-at-talk and mobilized other available semiotic resources, they displayed their orientation toward the RC's status (e.g. by their body posture) as an already existing state of affairs, and at the same time locally (re)created it. Once the analyst's perspective was equipped with these analytical categories, the social world of the organization appeared both a verb *and* a noun; a social activity *and* a pre-formed thing. But even in this case, our interpretation did not mirror nor was coextensive with the members' one.

The Communicative Constitution of Organization and the Denaturalization of Social Order: Concluding Remarks

As we illustrated by making a case of EDA, when assuming a CCO approach to the social life of organizations the analyst is most likely put in front of the never-resolved epistemological and methodological dilemma of social research: finding a way to balance first-order (i.e. members') constructs and second-order (i.e. analyst's) constructs. In this chapter we argued that the analytical distinction between status and stance could partially rebalance the emic/etic divide by focusing on both the pre-discursive entities that affect members' local interactions (status) and their enactment/deployment and, ultimately, constitution in interaction (stance). Despite its limits (e.g. a privileged focus on human over non-human actors), this analytical construct allows to consider both sides of the agency/structure recursive relationship and, thereby, to "take seriously" members' accounts without leaving the *terra firma* of interaction. Having said that, this rebalance of the divide does not lessen the relevance of the epistemological dilemma per se: the *communicative constitution* of EDA (and, we contend, any other ontological trait of organization) is a second-order construct, not always nor necessarily oriented to members' perception or "natural attitude". If – as we suggest – the active role of members in communicatively constituting their organizations is an experience-distant concept, then we have to admit that in advancing it we risk perpetuating the same error post-structural-functionalistic research attributed to structuralist approaches to organizations: considering members' as "cultural dopes" unable to reflexively account for their practices. Even if more subtly than in the past, we still risk situating our perspective in an upper position with regard to the informants' eyes upon the reality they inhabit, and treating their practices as nothing more than naive first-level data. Perhaps they are. But in this case, we have to accept that our analysis is often from "outside" and not necessarily aligned with the members' view. If one of the heuristic advantages of CCO approaches is the denaturalization of the organizational order and the capability to see what goes unseen (but still operating) for the members, then we have to admit and re-legitimize the heuristic advantages of the (in)famous "gaze from afar" (Caronia, 2018). While fascinating and not easily contestable from a CCO point of view, the communicative constitution of EDA as well as other organizational entities is a claim that does not necessarily mirror members' point of view on their life-world, nor an *emic* account of how organizing unfolds. Rather, it is a crucial advance in the scientific (and not always "emic") understanding of organizations' lives.

Notes

1 We would like to thank Dr. Marzia Saglietti for her precious insights on a previous draft of this chapter.
2 As Cooren, Kuhn, Cornellissen, & Clark (2011) contend, "several versions of the CCO approach can be identified". However, they all share "the same general claim […]: if communication is indeed constitutive of organization […] it cannot be merely the vehicle for the expression of pre-existing realities; rather it is the means by which organizations are established, composed, designed, and sustained. Consequently, organizations can no longer be seen as objects, entities, or 'social facts' inside of which communication occurs" (p. 1149). For the purposes of this chapter, when referring to CCO research, we point to this basic theoretical claim which lies at the core of the different CCO approaches and stances (on the three main stances within CCO research see Kuhn, 2012).
3 The local interactive constitution of collectives and organizational entities can be conceived of as the main empirically demonstrated assumption of CCO research; see note 2.
4 Following Searle, Stevanovic and Peräkylä exemplify the distinction between these two orders of interaction by stating that "epistemic authority is about getting the *words to match the world*, and deontic authority is about getting the *world to match the words*" (2012, p. 298).
5 Claiming that authority is distributed between human and non-human actors raises an issue as to who or what embodies or attributes the competence of exercising authority. For reasons of space we cannot enter the long-standing debate on actor vs. agent, the different definitions of agency (see Ahearn, 2001; Duranti, 2004; Caronia & Orletti, 2019) and the related issue of the agency of non-human entities, i.e. their capacity of making the difference in the unfolding of interaction. Following the Montreal School of organizational communication and drawing on the notion of hybrid agency (Caronia & Cooren, 2014), we contend that human and non-human beings do perform authority (and leadership; see Clifton, Fachin, & Cooren, 2021), although in different ways related to their different ontologies. As Latour (1996) had it, once delegated by humans and provided with the competence to act (or "authorize"), things set constraints and possibilities for action and actively participate in

meaning-making and in constituting intangible yet operating realities such as "authority" (e.g. a police badge authorizing a person to act as an authority).

6 As Taylor and Van Every had it, power and authority are "commonly linked", but it is difficult to clarify "the basis of their relationship" (Taylor and Van Every 2014, xviii; on the elusiveness of power, authority and related notions see also Bencherki et al., 2020). For the purposes of this study, we define authority as the attributed, socially ratified, or emerging status that confers (a) the right to know and decide and/or (b) the power to do things and make people do things (on power as the probability of obtaining compliance see Weber 1968/1922). For reasons of space, we cannot elaborate on the issue of "unpacking authority" and on its (not mutually exclusive) constituents and articulations (i.e. epistemic, deontic, moral, and interactional).

7 As we discovered during extensive fieldwork, coherence and consistency in the management of any single patient was perceived and positively evaluated by the patients' relatives, who strongly appreciated the fact that, as the father of a young inpatient told us: "at least, here anyone tells us the same thing". From the ward ecology viewpoint, coherence and consistency in the antibiotic policy was also a benefit in terms of reducing MDRB selection. Moreover, the consistent adoption of an "off-label" clinical policy was a kind of "identity badge" members used to mark their difference with respect to the other hospital wards, and to create internal cohesion in the face of disruptions and conflicts related to its adoption.

References

Ahearn, L. M. (2001). Language and agency. *Annual Review of Anthropology, 30*, 109 137. https://doi.org/10.2307/3069211.

Alexander, J. C., Giesen, B., Münch, R., & Smelser, N. J. (Eds.). (1987). *The Micro-macro link.* Berkeley: University of California Press.

Alvesson, M., & Kärreman, D. (2001). Odd couple: making sense of the curios concept of knowledge management. *Journal of Management Studies, 38*(7), 995–1018.

Antaki, C. (2012). What actions mean, to whom, and when. *Discourse Studies, 14*(4), 493–498.

Ashcraft, K.L., Kuhn, T., & Cooren, F. (2009). 1 Constitutional amendments: "Materializing" organizational communication. *The Academy of Management Annals, 3*(1), 1–64

Barley, S. (1996). Technicians in the workplace: Ethnographic evidence for bringing work into organizational studies. *Administrative Science Quarterly, 41*(3), 404–441.

Barley, W.C., Treem, J.W., & Kuhn, T. (2018). Valuing multiple trajectories of knowledge: A critical review and research agenda for knowledge management research. *Academy of Management Annals, 12*(1), 278–317.

Barnard, C. (1938). *The functions of the executive.* Cambridge: Harvard University Press.

Bartesaghi, M. (2009). How the therapist does authority: Six strategies for substituting client accounts in the session. *Communication & Medicine, 6*(1), 15–25.

Bartesaghi, M., Livio, O., & Matte, F. (2020). The authority of the "broader context": What's not in the interaction? In N. Bencherki, F. Matte, & F. Cooren (Eds.), *Authority and power in social interaction: Methods and analysis* (pp. 18–36). New York: Routledge.

Bencherki, N., Cooren, F., & Matte, F. (2020). Introduction: In Search for the specific unfolding of authority and power. In N. Bencherki, F. Matte, & F. Cooren (Eds.), *Authority and power in social interaction: Methods and analysis* (pp. 18–36). New York: Routledge.

Benoit-Barné, C., & Cooren, F. (2009). The accomplishment of authority through presentification: How authority is distributed among and negotiated by organizational members. *Management Communication Quarterly, 23*(1), 5–31.

Boden, D. (1994). *The business of talk. Organization in action.* Cambridge: Polity Press.

Brummans, B. (2018). *The agency of organizing.* New York: Routledge.

Brummans, B., Higham, L., & Cooren, F. (2021). The work of conflict mediation: Actors, vectors, and communicative relationality. *Human Relations*, 1–28.

Buckley, P., Chapman, M., Clegg, J., & Gajewska-De Mattos, H. (2014). A linguistic and philosophical analysis of emic and etic and their use in international business research. *Management International Review, 54*, 307–324.

Caronia, L. (2018). How 'at home' is an ethnographer at home? Territories of knowledge and the making of ethnographic understanding. *Journal of Organizational Ethnography, 7*, 114 – 134.

Caronia, L., & Chieregato, A. (2016). Polyphony in a ward. Tracking professional theories in members' dialogues. *Language and Dialogue, 6*, 395 – 421.

Caronia, L., & Cooren, F. (2014). Decentering our analytical position: The dialogicity of things. *Discourse & Communication, 8*, 41 – 61.

Caronia, L., & Orletti, F. (2019). The agency of language in institutional talk. An introduction. *Language and Dialogue* [Special Issue, *Dialogue in Institutional Settings*], *9*(1), 1–27.

Caronia, L., Saglietti, M., & Chieregato, A. (2020). Challenging the interprofessional epistemic boundaries: The practices of informing in nurse-physician interaction. *Social Science & Medicine, 246*, 112732. https://doi.org/10.1016/j.socscimed.2019.112732.

Clifton, J., Fachin, F., & Cooren, F. (2021). How artefacts do leadership : A ventriloquial analysis. *Management Communication Quarterly, 35*(2), 256 280. https://doi.org/10.1177/0893318921998078.

Clifton, J., Van De Mieroop, D., Sehgal, P., & Bedi, A. (2018). The multimodal enactment of deontic and epistemic authority in Indian meetings. *Pragmatics, 28*(3), 333–360.

Collins, H., & Evans, R. (2007). *Rethinking expertise*. Chicago: The University of Chicago Press.

Cooren, F. (2004). Textual agency: How texts do things in organizational settings. *Organization, 11*(3), 373–393.

Cooren, F. (2006). The organizational world as a plenum of agencies. In F. Cooren, J. R. Taylor, & E. J. Van Every (Eds.), *Communication as organizing: Practical approaches to research into the dynamic of text and conversation* (pp. 81–100). Lawrence Erlbaum.

Cooren, F. (2009). The haunting question of textual agency: Derrida and Garfinkel on iterability and eventfulness. *Research on Language and Social Interaction, 42*(1), 42–67.

Cooren, F. (2010). *Action and agency in dialogue: Passion, incarnation and ventriloquism*. Amsterdam: John Benjamins.

Cooren, F., & Fairhurst, G. (2004). Speech timing and spacing: The phenomenon of organizational closure. *Organization, 11*(6), 793–824.

Cooren, F., & Malbois, F. (2019). How to follow and analyze a diversity of beings: An introduction. In F. Cooren & F. Malbois (Eds.), *Methodological and ontological principles of observation and analysis: Following and analyzing things and beings in our contemporary world* (pp. 1–12). New York: Routledge.

Drew, P. (2018). Epistemics in social interaction. *Discourse Studies, 20*(1), 163–187.

Drew, P., & Heritage, J. (1992). Analyzing talk at work: an introduction. In P. Drew & J. Heritage (Eds.), *Talk at work: Interaction in institutional settings* (pp. 3–65). Cambridge: Cambridge University Press.

Duranti, A. (2004). Agency in language. In A. Duranti (Ed.), *A companion to linguistic anthropology* (pp. 451–473). Malden, MA: Blackwell.

Eggiman, P., & Pittet, D. (2001). Infections control in the ICU. *CHEST, 120*(6), 2059–2093.

Follett, M. P. (1940). *The dynamic administration: The collected papers of Mary Parker Follett*. New York: Routledge.

Fuchs, S. (2001). *Againts essentialism. A theory of culture and society*. Cambridge, MA: Harvard University Press.

Giddens, A. (1984). *The constitution of society: Outline of the theory of structuration*. Berkeley: University of California Press.

Goodwin, C. (2011). Contextures of action. In J. Streeck, C. Goodwin, & C. D. LeBaron (Eds.), *Embodied interaction: Language and body in the material world* (pp. 182–93). Cambridge: Cambridge University Press.

Heritage, J. (1984). *Garfinkel and ethnomethodology*. Cambridge: Cambridge University Press.

Heritage, J. (2004). Conversation analysis and institutional talk : Analysing data. In D. Silverman (Ed.), *Qualitative research: Theory, method and practice* (2nd edn., pp. 222–245). Sage. www.sscnet.ucla.edu/soc/faculty/heritage/Site/Publications_files/SILVERMAN_2.pdf.

Heritage, J. (2012a). The epistemic engine: Sequence organization and territories of knowledge. *Research on Language and Social Interaction, 45*(1), 30–52.

Heritage, J. (2012b). Epistemics in action: Action formation and territories of knowledge. *Research on Language and Social Interaction, 45*(1), 1–29.

Heritage, J., & Raymond, G. (2005). The terms of agreement: Indexing epistemic authority and subordination in talk-in-interaction. *Social Psychology Quarterly, 68*(1), 15–38.

Holm, F., & Fairhurst, G. (2018). Configuring shared and hierarchical leadership through authoring. *Human Relations, 71*(5), 692–721.

Hranjec, T., Rosenberger, L., Swenson, B., et al. (2012). Aggressive versus conservative initiation of antimicrobial treatment in critically ill surgical patients with suspected intensive-care-unit- acquired infection: A quasi-experimental, before and after observational cohort study. *Lancet Infectious Diseases,* *12*(10), 774–780.

Kohut, H. (1971). *The analysis of the self.* New York: International University Press.

Kuhn, T. (2002). Negotiating boundaries between scholars and practitioners. Knowledge, networks, and communities of practice. *Management Communication Quarterly, 16*(1), 106–112.

Kuhn, T. (2012). Negotiating the micro-macro divide: Thought leadership from organizational communication for theorizing organization. *Management Communication Quarterly, 26*(4), 543–584.

Kuhn, T., & Jackson, M. (2008). Accomplishing knowledge: A framework for investigating knowing in organizations. *Management Communication Quarterly, 21*(4), 454–485.

Kuhn, T., & Porter, A. (2011). Heterogeneity in knowledge and knowing: A social practice perspective. In H. Canary & R. McPhee (Eds.), *Communication and organizational knowledge: Contemporary issues for theory and practice* (pp. 17–34). New York: Routledge.

Labov, W., & Fanshel, D. (1977). *Therapeutic discourse: Psychotherapy as conversation.* New York: Academic Press.

Latour, B. (1996). On interobjectivity. *Mind, Culture, and Activity, 3*(4), 228 245. https://doi.org/10.1207/s15327884mca0304_2.

Macbeth, D. (1991). Teacher authority as practical action. *Linguistics and Education, 3*(4), 281–313.

Mikesell, L., Bolden, G., Mandelbaum, G., et al. (2017). At the intersection of epistemics and action: Responding with *I know. Research on Language and Social Interaction, 50*(3), 268–285.

Moermann, M. (1988). *Talking culture: Ethnography and conversation analysis.* Philadelphia: University of Pennsylvania Press.

Morey, N., & Luthans, F. (1984). An emic perspective and ethnoscience methods for organizational research. *Academy of Management Review, 9*(1), 27–36.

Orlikowski, W. (2002). Knowing in practice: Enacting a collective capability in distributed organizing. *Organization Science, 13*(3), 249–273.

Peräkylä, A. (1998). Authority and accountability: The delivery of diagnosis in primary health care. *Social Psychology Quarterly, 61,* 301–320.

Peterson, M. F., & Pike, K. L. (2002). Emics and etics for organizational studies: A lesson in contrast from linguistics. *International Journal of Cross-Cultural Management, 2*(1), 5–19.

Pomerantz, A. (1980). Telling my side: "Limited access" as a fishing device. *Sociological Inquiry, 50*(3–4), 186–198.

Pomerantz, A., & Denvir, P. (2007). Enacting the institutional role of chairperson in upper management meetings: The interactional realization of provisional authority. In F. Cooren (Ed.), *Interacting and Organizing: Analyses of a management meeting* (pp. 31–52). London: Lawrence Erlbaum.

Ritzer, G. (2011). *Sociological theory.* New York: McGraw–Hill.

Schütz, A. (1967/1932). *The phenomenology of the social world.* Evanston, IL: Northwestern University Press.

Simon, H. (1947). *Administrative behavior: A study of decision-making processes in administrative organizations.* New York: Macmillan.

Sterponi, L., Zucchermaglio, C., Fatigante, M., & Alby, F. (2019). Structuring times and activities in the oncology visit. *Social Science & Medicine (1982), 228,* 211–222.

Stevanovic, M. (2015). Displays of uncertainty and proximal deontic claims: The case of proposal sequences. *Journal of Pragmatics, 78,* 84–97.

Stevanovic, M. (2018). Social deontics: A nano-level approach to human power play. *Journal for the Theory of Social Behavior, 48*(3), 369–389.

Stevanovic, M., & Peräkylä, A. (2012). Deontic authority in interaction: The right to announce, propose, and decide. *Research on Language and Social Interaction, 45*(3), 297–321.

Stevanovic, M., & Svennevig, I. (2015). Introduction: Epistemics and deontics in conversational directives. *Journal of Pragmatics, 78,* 1–6.

Stivers, T., Mondada, L., & Steensig, J. (2011). Knowledge, morality and affiliation in social interaction. In T. Stivers, L. Mondada, & J. Steensig (Eds.), *The morality of knowledge in conversation* (pp. 3–26). Cambridge: Cambridge UP.

Svennevig, I., & Djordjilovic, O. (2015). Accounting for the right to assign a task in meeting interaction. *Journal of Pragmatics, 78,* 98–111.

Taylor, J. R., & Van Every, E. J. (2000). *The emergent organization: Communication as its site and surface.* Mahwah, NJ: Lawrence Erlbaum.

Taylor, J. R., & Van Every, E. J. (2014). *When organization fails: Why authority matters*. New York: Routledge.

Van De Mieroop, D. (2020). A deontic perspective on the collaborative, multimodal accomplishment of leadership. *Leadership, 16*(5), 592–619.

Weber, M. (1968 [1922]). *Economy and society: An outline of interpretive sociology*. New York: Bedminster Press.

Weick, K. E. (1995). *Sensemaking in organizations*. Thousand Oaks, CA: Sage .

Wodak, R., Kwon, W., & Clarke, I. (2011). 'Getting people on board': Discursive leadership for consensus building in team meetings. *Discourse & Society, 22*(5), 592–644.

10

UNCRITICAL CONSTITUTION

CCO, Critique and Neoliberal Capitalism

Sophie Del Fa and Dan Kärreman

Introduction

Since the Frankfurt School, the means of communication are not merely viewed as channels of information's transmission that coordinate interaction or as a means of mass manipulation. Communication has also been established as a social process that produces and reproduces the capitalist logic thereby contributing to the emergence of mass consumption, globalization and industrial production. Through their conception of cultural industries for instance, Adorno and Horkheimer (1972) highlight how the means of communication, such as radio, films, and magazines, generate alienation and passivity and how mass-produced culture is dangerous for individuals and society at large. In their portrait of the North American society of the 1950s and 60s, the means of communication were portrayed as transforming everything into commodities that serve economic purposes. Building on a Marxian perspective, this early version of Critical Theory established communication as the *locus* of capital accumulation (Fuchs, 2020). Since Adorno and Horkheimer's writing, communication scholars took over this critical stance (Aubin & Rueff, 2016) addressing media (e.g. Ott & Mack, 2009), labor (e.g. Fuchs, 2020) or technology (e.g. Wajcman, 2007), among others.

Whereas communication fields ranging from media studies to intercultural communication adopted rather early a critical stance, organizational communication has been slower in taking this turn. Long confined to functionalist or interpretivist approaches, scholars were mainly addressing how communication "in" organization could be optimized to ensure its proper functioning. The communicative constitution of organization perspective (hereafter CCO) can be traced to the 1980s when interpretative and critical scholars started to question the functionalist paradigm (Boivin, Brummans, & Barker, 2017, p. 4). Although the CCO perspective – which we in this paper operationalize to scholarship influenced by the Montreal School, although we think that our argument has longer reach – has made a fundamental theoretical contribution in organizational communication, it lacks a critical dimension. We acknowledge that several CCO scholars are sensitive to the critical potentialities of seeing communication as constitutive of organization, focusing on gender issues (Ashcraft, 2004; Mumby & Ashcraft, 2006), branding (Mumby, 2016, 2019), power and authority (Bencherki, Matte, & Cooren, 2019; Benoit-Barné & Cooren, 2009), resistance in the workplace (Mumby, 2020; Mumby, Thomas, Martí, & Seidl, 2017), or alternative organizations (Del Fa & Vásquez, 2020; Wilhoit

DOI: 10.4324/9781003224914-12

& Kisselburgh, 2019). However, critical CCO scholars can be counted on the fingers of one hand; also, few of them focus on neoliberal capitalism in their conception of both communication and organizations. Even if some propose an alternative route to pursue "critical" theorizing via new materialism (see Kuhn, 2021), it's still a blindspot in the CCO perspective. This chapter makes a modest attempt to rectify this shortfall. Indeed, we do believe that developing a theory of the social (which CCO purports to be in some respects) must consider the hegemonic social order already put in place by neoliberal capitalism.

Thus, drawing on the invitation of Kuhn, Ashcraft and Cooren (2017) to understand neoliberal capitalism as a participant inextricably bound up in socioeconomic practices that "make" communication, we state that capitalism participates in the *organization* of the social. From that premise, we consider it imperative to consider capitalism as such to develop a critical perspective of CCO. Moreover, building on the theoretical premise that communication is a *relational practice* (Cooren, 2020) by which various beings relate to each other through other beings, we will question the character of this relation by stating that, fundamentally, this relation is formed or informed by capitalism. By forming and informing, we understand capitalism as the main way individuals have been socialized to engage with the world and have thus internalized a capitalist way of living (we will come back to that). Considering capitalistic practices this way permits us to address, for example, questions of power and innovation, but also alternative organizing and anti-capitalist resistance. In doing so, this chapter aims to develop CCO's ability to make a critical contribution. Informing a theoretical perspective will bring us to open up empirical questions and propose avenues to empirically explore these issues.

This chapter aims at theorizing a critical approach to CCO in several ways: first by showing that CCO's scholars' interpretation of pragmatism occludes a critical dimension in their analyses; second, by engaging with critical theorizing and its connection points to CCO; and, third, to show how the lack of a critical understanding of neoliberal capitalism is hampering the critical potentialities of CCO.

The Constitutive Approach to Communication: The Linguistic Turn and Pragmatism

At heart, the key contribution of the CCO perspective is an attempt to keep the intellectual promise of the linguistic turn for understanding organizing and organization. The standard interpretation of the linguistic turn is that language is somehow important in the creation and maintenance of organization (see, for example, Alvesson & Karreman, 2000). As pointed out by Deetz (2003), this interpretation occasionally becomes highly problematic: "[t]he problem of language as the 'mirror of nature' that preoccupied the positivist was replaced by simply focusing on the 'mirror' as an object" (Deetz, 2003, p. 425)

What does the linguistic turn mean if pushing further than language is somehow important? It attacks, on philosophical-theoretical grounds, the widely accepted idea that language is a system of reference attributed with the power of denoting objects "out there" (Cooper, 1989). Rather, "language is a structure of material marks or sounds which are in themselves 'undecidable' and *upon which meaning has to be imposed*" (Cooper, 1989, p. 480, emphasis in original). Symbolic systems such as language do not contain meaning. On the contrary, meaning is assigned by users to distinguish certain experiences from one another. Language is external and real. It – and potential meanings generated through it – forego any experience of what is external to it, since experience gains its shape and intelligibility through language.

Deetz (2003) points in particular to how the linguistic turn may be used to problematize taken-for-granted dualisms, such as the subject-object distinction. He also shows how the standard interpretation of the linguistic turn reintroduces this dualism by turning language into an object and the perspectivism implied by accepting that all seeing is seeing-as-something into subjectivist points of reference of equal rank: "the personalization of the idea of 'standpoint' or 'position' has protected personal experience and alternative forms of knowledge from an inter-rogation of their politics and construction" (Deetz, 2003, p. 425).

We don't deny that the CCO perspective is well equipped to deliver on the promise of the linguistic turn. In particular, we accept that it is particularly useful for doing away with the obfuscation that is inherent in dualisms such as subject-object, micro-macro and structure-agency. However, we claim that the CCO perspective has largely failed to tap into the origins of the linguistic turn to offer a deeper and sharper critique and understanding of the role of language and communication for organizing and organization. In particular, the CCO perspective typically fails to problematize the relationship between language and social reality by refusing to explore the possibility that social reality might already be constituted by frozen social relations, held together by ideology and fixed power relations.

The Blind Spots of Pragmatism

The CCO perspective avoids the personalization of position but has instead introduced its own version of avoiding a political and critical understanding, primarily by understanding language as an unprejudiced tool. We trace this turn of affairs to the pragmatic theoretical roots of the CCO perspective. In doing so, we can understand why and how CCO has developed as a non-critical approach. The founders of CCO (James Taylor, Elizabeth Van Every and François Cooren) anchored their thinking in pragmatism coined by Dewey, Mead, Peirce, Garfinkel, Sacks, Schegloff and Wittgenstein, to mention just a few (Brummans, Cooren, Robichaud, & Taylor, 2014). This philosophical influence, and the way CCO scholars have appropriated its premises, is not without consequences and contributes to a sort of "neutralization" of the concept of communication (and, by extension of interactions and of the organization).

It's important, first and foremost, to recall that pragmatism was born in the United States while liberalism was emerging and spreading. It is influenced by empirical social sciences and cognitive fields such as psychotherapy. It breaks with European philosophy which relies upon literature and European linguistics, which was speculative and less data-driven (Taylor & Van Every, 2000). Pragmatism was coined as a method for which the truth is relative: what is true is always useful according to the interests of life. Moreover, for pragmatists (such as James, for instance), truth is always linked with actions, as actions and experience are at the core of this philosophy. Indeed – and of importance for the CCO approach – for pragmatists such as Sacks or Garfinkel, the origin of the social world is to be found in interactions. As Cooren says with great clarity in Schoeneborn et al. (2014):

> A pragmatist epistemology calls into question both subjectivism and idealism, on the one hand, and empiricism and materialism, on the other, *by refusing to determine a starting point in the act of knowing, inquiring, or investigating.*
>
> *p. 288, emphasis added*

The last sentence seems quite problematic as it tends to neutralize the interaction and exclude from it everything that seems to be "not there". Also, it obfuscates what is really going on, as it is more accurate to state that pragmatic inquiry starts haphazardly (and also inevitably informed by structural bias) rather than from nowhere. Indeed, supposing that there is nothing outside the text, no "starting point whatsoever", refuses to acknowledge the existence of a regime of truth à la Foucault (2012), a point we will develop below.

In other words, pragmatism applied this way seems to purge society of norms, values and social order. As Lewis Munford writes, as he talks about "pragmatic liberalism", pragmatism (1940, n.p.):

> minimized the role of instinct, tradition, history; it was unaware of the dark forces of the unconscious, it was suspicious of either the capricious or the incalculable, for the only universe it could rule was a measured one, and the only type of human character it could understand was the utilitarian one (…).

Munford's quote illustrates our point, which consists in underlining how pragmatists "flatten reality" in focusing only on what is seen. As it disregards the complexity of the implicit (or not) rules that dictate behaviours, beliefs, relationships, consumption, decisions-making, etc., pragmatism empties reality from what *organizes* it.

Furthermore, pragmatism is represented by a variety of authors who did not share the same political opinions. For instance, we recall the famous Dewey-Lippmann debate, which opposed two very distinctive view of liberalism: a progressive liberalism for Dewey and a "new liberalism" for Lippmann (which will prevail and pave the way to neoliberalism [Stiegler, 2018]). Even if the two authors did not share the same political views, they share the assumption that social science is a research posture in which the researcher is key in the transformation of the social (see for example, Dewey, 1938). In that sense, pragmatism is not merely theoretical but has in its roots the will to act concretely on society. Pragmatism can be seen as the origin of action research and the definition of social science not solely as analytical theorizing but also as an invitation to act and change society. CCO scholars have avoided this element of their pragmatist stance. Indeed, few are the CCO researchers who are willing to change or act upon a phenomenon. On the contrary, they often stand on their theoretical ground. In that sense, if the CCO approach claims to be pragmatist it has to reconnect with this transformative gesture as a first step towards a critical stance. Moreover, a similar critique has been lobbed at critical theory in organization studies which testify the need to address it bluntly and seriously to find avenues of action for social changes (Spicer et al., 2009; Parker, 2018).

Finally, a core assumption in the CCO approach is "that a variety of forms of agency is always in play in any interaction", a phenomenon that Cooren calls, metaphorically, "ventriloquism" (2012, p. 4). Ventriloquism refers to our capacity to make other beings say or do things while we speak (Cooren, 2012, p. 4). We don't disagree that a variety of forms of agency is in play in any interaction, but it is important to realize that interactions only rarely happen in open play. Ventriloquism stated this way may overestimate the free play of agency. To be fair to Cooren, his argument does not exclude constraints on ventriloquism, but it is clear that the fascination is on the play of agency, not its limits. This obfuscates the rather plain insight that a lot of interactions, if not most, play out in games that are rigged, where actors are framed, and where agency benefits distinct interests.

Critique and Organizational Communication

Being critical: what is the point? After all, critique only exists in relation to something other than itself: it is an instrument, a means for a future or a truth that it will not know nor happen to be, it oversees a domain it would want to police and is unable to regulate. It is a function which is subordinated in relation to what philosophy, science, politics, ethics, law, literature, etc.

positively constitute (Foucault, 2007). At heart, a critical approach advances the idea that we are not stuck with a particular social world at hand. The social world is understood as a construction that is welded together through social processes and thus could have developed differently. "Critical" in this context means to interrogate society at large and in relation to particular cases while acknowledging power relations (inequality, racism, sexism, etc.) and means to overcome them (social justice, peace, resistances, etc.). Here, a critical understanding is understood as an engagement with ideas, ideologies and institutions to encourage liberation and reduce repression. Put bluntly, a critical understanding explores the effects of power, resistance, the division of labor, marginalization, tension, and difference.

Why do we need a critical approach of CCO? In order to answer this, we turn to Foucault, who famously asks the question, "what is critique?" (2007). Even if this question may appear innocuous, it addresses the relation directly between individuals, truth, power, and what Foucault refers to as the "art of being governed". Indeed, for Foucault, being critical (and developing a critical theory) is an attitude that asks two questions: how are humans governed? And how could they not be governed *like that* (2007, p. 44)? He recalls that through history humans have been governed in a certain way and following a specific "regime of truth" that subjugates individuals through mechanisms of power (2007, p. 47). Foucault calls this way of being governed "forms of governmentalization", an expression that stresses that governing humans is an ongoing process that oscillates according to the regime of truth in power.

The critical attitude aims at transgressing this "governmentalization" or way of being governed and gives individuals the right to question the regime of truth (2007, p. 47). In other words, a critical attitude is "the art of voluntary insubordination" (Foucault, 2007, p. 47). Thus, it is definitely an act of resistance that creates a breach in the form of governmentalization. Therefore, it supposes a double thought process: firstly, defining very precisely the regime of truth at play regarding the object of study; and secondly, considering disruptions and resistances. In other words, cultivating the art of insubordination while exploring the politics of truth (Chamayou, 2018). For these reasons, the critical attitude is *relational*, as it is not exterior to the truth it wants to overcome and to the ruptures it aims at.

Considering critique as such for CCO scholars has two main implications. First, we have to acknowledge that capitalism is a dominant regime of truth according to which large tracts of "the social" are organized. More than merely acknowledging it, we indeed have to explore it closely and identify its mechanisms through communication. Secondly, we have to be attentive to, and aware of, the possible breaches created and the moments when this regime of truth vacillates. In other words, the point is to explore the (un)doing of capitalism with a CCO perspective.

Critique and Organizations

Mumby and Ashcraft (2017) have done a substantial job in reviewing critical approaches in organizational communication. They start from critical approaches in communication to explore the question in organization studies and then in organizational communication. They disclose the various influences of the critical stance from Marxism to poststructuralism and post-colonialism, and recall the premises of critical approach in management with the emergence of the Critical Management Studies community in the early 1990s.

As Mumby and Ashcraft (2017) summarize, critical approaches of communication focus on discursive struggle, the relationship between democracy and organization in contemporary capitalism (e.g. corporate colonization: Deetz, 1992), the promise and limitations of alternative organizational forms, and attention to identity. Above all, critical approaches to organizational communication have shown increasing concern for investigating communication as it constitutes the power of organizing. In other words, attention has gradually shifted away from organizational communication as a political phenomenon that occurs within already established organizational containers, and toward communication as a mode of explaining the formations and practices of power that constitute the organizing process (Mumby & Ashcraft, 2017, p. 20) .

Foucault's take on critique has been incorporated in a more general form in management and organization studies by way of critical management studies (CMS). CMS highlight the power relations implied in managerial and organizational arrangements. At the heart of CMS, the idea of "management" is systematically questioned, and treated with suspicion. The purpose is not to question the usefulness of management practices per se, but rather to scrutinize the social costs of these practices (Adler, Forbes, & Willmott, 2008; Alvesson, Bridgman, & Willmott, 2009; Alvesson & Willmott, 1992; Parker, 1995; Parker & Parker, 2017).

Fournier and Grey (2000), in their seminal article on CMS, state that a critical perspective draws primarily on three principles: "non-performativity", "de-naturalization", and "reflexivity" (see also Grey & Willmott, 2005). By non-performativity they draw on Lyotard (1984) and argue that critical perspectives should resist attempts to equate efficiency with progress and that instrumental rationality per se might be destructive, as seen in Habermas's (1987) argument about the colonization of the life world. De-naturalization states that CMS involves a deconstruction of the false claim that social reality is given and not an artifice emerging from social construction processes (Fournier & Grey 2000, p. 8). By reflexivity, they mean that CMS should be explicit about the assumptions and vocabularies it engages with, and reflect upon framing effects, limits, and shortcomings.

We argue that denaturalization has particular weight for understanding the potential of critique inherent in the CCO perspective. Fournier and Grey render denaturalization as primarily an ontological and political move. For them, denaturalization is a matter of realizing that existing knowledge emerges from already established perspectives. It is organized around what is written in, as well as with what is written out: denaturalization questions the privileged position of the established truths established by particular perspectives, vocabularies, and groups of people, and opens up space for what is written out – voices and experiences not covered by established epistemic practices. It also opens up the possibility of generating knowledge about a radically different society, either as giving voice to the muted or the voiceless, or by providing a space in which "whereas-if" and "what-if" realities can be articulated.

Deetz's (1992) concept of discursive closure provides an illustration of how an organizational communication perspective can be mobilized for purposes of critique. Discursive practices, Deetz observes, are not in themselves neutral. They have capacities to lead to the potential suspension of preformed convictions and relatively unconstrained production of understanding. However, they also have the capacity to lead to the suspension of dissent, difference, and discussion. Discursive closure is driven by the latter kind of practices. Since the practices themselves are "tactical", rather than "substantive", they are often hard to notice.

Discursive closure can happen in numerous ways. Deetz enumerates eight important ones: disqualification, naturalization, neutralization, topical avoidance, subjectification of experience, meaning denial and plausible deniability, legitimation, and pacification. For the purposes of this chapter, we will pay attention to naturalization as discursive closure, as it illustrates the importance of denaturalization as critique. Naturalization occurs, per what we discussed above, when something is written in, at the expense of what is written out (Fournier and Grey, 2000). It happens when a way of approaching a subject matter is presented, and accepted, as the way things are by nature and default. Naturalization often appears as an engagement with social relationships and subjective constructions as natural, fixed and external objects. For example, in neoliberal capitalism, freedom is rendered as choice between options, need fulfillment as consumption, and human enterprise as trade, all regulated through the market mechanisms and the superpowers of authoritative finance. Liberty becomes choice, needs become wants, and self-realization becomes the accumulation of wealth.

Processes of naturalization deny alternative formulations of experience. Taken far enough, they deny the possibility of alternative experience itself. The naturalization process becomes materialized and emerges as a social fact. Neoliberal capitalism, for example, can be questioned as a matter of intellectual exercise but it cannot easily be decolonized from our lived experience. Over time, discourse and language have power effects. There is power in the rendering of society in a particular way. Foucault's ideas of truth regimes and power/knowledge show us how this dynamic unfolds: discourse establishes realities that power can operate from, which makes new forms of discourse possible, which makes new manifestations of power possible to operate, and so on.

The Ideological Content of Neoliberalism

Even if the term "neoliberalism" was coined for the first time in the late nineteenth century, it is associated with a specific transformation of capitalism in the 1980s. More specifically, neoliberalism is an ideological reaction from capitalists who felt threatened after the uprisings of the end of 1970s (Brown, 2017; Chamayou, 2018; Gibson-Graham, 2006; Harvey, 2005). Some tend to date its advent to Reagan's election in 1981, since he was inspired by liberal economists such as Milton Friedman and Friedrich Hayek, who were strong advocates of Adam Smith's *laissez-faire* capitalism. Neoliberalism is also associated with economic liberalization including deregulation, privatization, free trade and austerity (e.g. Dardot & Laval, 2009; Harvey, 2005). Decolonial and feminist thinkers add to this list social oppression, such as sexism, patriarchy and systemic racism (Braidotti, 2019; Federici, 2019; Haraway, 1988; Lorde, 1984; Vergès, 2019). Other terminologies can refer to neoliberalism such as advanced capitalism (Pineault, 2008), platform capitalism (Srnicek, 2016), surveillance capitalism (Zuboff, 2019), or communicational or informational capitalism (Dean, 2009; Fuchs, 2020). We chose to stick with the term neoliberal capitalism as we believe that it includes all of these specificities.

There is not any great secret about it: neoliberal capitalism has numerous negative effects for both human and non-human (see among many others: Braidotti, 2019; Deleuze & Guattari, 1980; Stengers, 2008). Neoliberalism, the "new spirit of capitalism" (Boltanski and Chiapello, 2011), is not merely a political economy dominated by free-trade and financial transactions. Indeed, as Dardot and Laval (2009, p. 5) put it, "neoliberal capitalism is about the way we live, feel and think" (our translation). In short, it "is no more and no less the very form of our existence, meaning the way we *have* to behave, to relate to each other and to ourselves" (2009, p. 5, our translation and emphasis). This definition brings the two authors to consider neoliberalism as a form of rationality that structures and organizes the rulers' actions and the behaviors of those who are governed (Dardot and Laval, 2009). The main consequences of neoliberalism rendered this way are global competition, economic struggles and inequalities, ordering of social relations within the model of the market, transformation of the individuals and the state into corporations (corporatization), exploitation of the subalterns (women, people of color, individuals from "undeveloped" countries), and earth destruction (Federici, 2019; Haraway, 2015; Malm, 2017; Vergès, 2019).

Following these broad definitions and claims of effects, we understand neoliberal capitalism as a complex and multifold hegemonic ideology that governs our behaviors, bodies, minds, actions, etc. Ideology is an evergreen in social science. It has many meanings and uses. In early Marxism ideology was used to explain false beliefs covering up a dominant social order. These false beliefs refer to the notion coined by Marx of "false consciousness" which points to the fact that the tenants of the dominant ideology (a.k.a. the capitalists and the *bourgeoisie*) are blinded by the illusion that capitalism is an eternal and fundamental part of history. Their false consciousness prevents them from considering the totality of history and the historical processes that bring an established state of facts. Because of its link with the notion of false consciousness, ideology has a persistent bad connotation. More recently ideology is typically understood as a system of ideas and values (Freeden, 2003). Geertz (1973) summarizes the key differences between these conceptions in distinguishing between an interest and a strain theory of ideology. The interest theory of ideology uses the concept to explain a social group's or class's quest for power. The strain view considers ideology as a concept for understanding how social groups engage in ways to reduce stress and anxiety due to lack of cultural resources (see also Swidler, 1986; Kunda, 1992).

In this chapter we align our argument to the strain theory of ideology. We use ideology to refer to avenues for decontestation (Freeden, 2003) – making essentially contestable concepts less contentious, a move that will help us propose a critical approach to CCO. In this sense, ideology is primarily a device to cope with ambiguity and the indeterminacy of meaning. Understood this way, ideology offers a way to understand how communicative practices become materialized. The neoliberal ideology, in our contemporaneous era, orders and governs patterns and suppresses surplus meaning: it frames liberty as choice (rather than other kinds of freedom), fulfillment as consumption (rather than maturity and autonomy), and self-realization as accumulation of wealth (rather than other ways to grow and develop as human). Indeed, it aligns language and symbols with strategies for action (Swidler, 1986) and suppresses and marginalizes dissent and difference. Nonetheless, as an ideology, neoliberal capitalism is neither solely an economic system nor it is a "background" or a "frame"; rather, following Foucault (2004), we view it as a mode of being organized and governed: as a *regime of truth*. It's an imposed and created way of living that has been integrated into our life and bodies (Brown, 2017; Federici, 2019; Guattari, 1981). Moreover, as Gibson-Graham puts it: "We cannot get outside capitalism" because "it has no outside. It becomes that which has no outside by swallowing up its conditions of existence" (2006, p. 258). However, this is not to say that life can be reduced to neoliberal capitalism only. We think of neoliberal capitalism as we think of family: impossible to escape, which does not mean that it is always in your face, but always in some ways affecting you. Following this, we make the assumption that neoliberalism is *an organizing ideology* that emerges through a patchwork of politico-socio-economic (and communicational) practices (Kuhn, Ashcraft, & Cooren, 2017) which is constitutive of our modern and occidental existence. This is the fundamental assumption of our conceptualization of the communicational constitution of neoliberalism. In some ways it echoes Mumby's (2019) CCC (for Capital Constitutes Communication), but with slight differences that we review further. Furthermore, even-if neoliberal capitalism is all-encompassing it is not at totalitarian system emptied from the potentialities of resistances and decontestation. Following a more Gramscian-inspired conception of ideology, the hegemonic ideology can shift following revolution or classes struggle. So, it is still possible to create and imagine breaches (Holloway, 2010). Recognizing the hegemonic status of neoliberal capitalism does not equal refuting the possibilities of unpacking it, on the contrary, it opens the ways to think how is it possible to transform it from the inside. There are also places in the world where neoliberal capitalism is not hegemonic. For example, the situation in China is better characterized as authoritarian state capitalism (Xing & Shaw, 2013), rather than neoliberal capitalism.

The Communicative Constitution of Neoliberalism

Three Challenges

Kuhn, Ashcraft and Cooren (2017) invite us to think of capitalism in the conceptualization of communication as constitutive of organizations. Thus, capitalism is there defined not as a background figure nor as an external force, but as a set of socioeconomic practices constitutive of organizations. Such an approach echoes Mumby's (2016, 2019) work and his "CCC". Focusing on marketing strategies, Mumby states that a brand is the symptom of communicative capitalism. Drawing on Dean's (2009) idea of communicational capitalism, Mumby shows how capitalism is organized and organized in return through communication (and more specifically through branding practices). On the other hand, Kuhn et al. think that capitalism organizes practices and action. In both cases, "doing capitalism is communication" (2017, p. 28). We want to extend these two avenues to consider capitalism in a constitutive approach by (1) reaffirming that *doing capitalism is communication* (even if we avoid to reduce communication to branding as Mumby tends to do); (2) insisting that *communication is doing capitalism*, in the sense that as an organizing principle, neoliberalism also constitutes communication; and (3) finally stressing that this avenue opens up a breach to *undo* neoliberal capitalism.

Neoliberal capitalism offers three challenges for CCO: the formation of *meaning*, the rendering of *agency*, and the making up of *speaking objects*. First, meaning is challenging to the CCO perspective in the sense that in neoliberal capitalism, ideology is loading the dice of meaning production: some meanings matter more than others. For example, enterprise is a matter of creation of wealth, not about exploring the horizons of what is possible. Liberty is having choices from pre-set menus, not about freedom of expression. Need fulfillment is about consumption of given goods and services, not about self-actualization and self-realization. CCO does have notions that may be helpful here: for example, the idea of authoritative texts, as discussed by Kuhn (2008, 2012). However, there is also a widely shared concern that dealing directly with the concept of meaning would be beside the point and counterproductive; this position is most clearly staked out by the Montreal School. Indeed, from its perspective, what really matters is what communication *does*, not what it *means* nor whether meanings are to be found "within" the communication process (Bencherki, Matte, & Pelletier, 2016).

The problem here is that sometimes meaning – perhaps oftentimes – is the mechanism through which communication *does* things, in the sense that communication is typically done by competent speakers who share a universe of understanding. For example, the negotiation of a salary is impossible to make sense of without a preunderstanding of the selling of labor according to market prices in a neoliberal order. This competency (or the lack of it) frames people's capacity to participate in communication. In this sense, it is the social order that *constitutes communication*, not the other way around.

One way to better incorporate the neoliberal shaping of meaning into the CCO perspective, in a way that is compatible with this perspective's focus on tensions and struggle, is to recognize that tensions and struggle predominantly run up against a pre-existing order. This point is not a bid to recover fundamentalist assumptions about how human groups are colonized and fully regulated by shared meaning. We are arguing that it is important to be able to show how preformed and decontested meanings "do" communication and how they introduce vectors for action.

Second, the expansion of agency beyond human beings to include objects, devices, and "stuff" is helpful and productive. However, it also raises the question of where agency is preformatted by the social order at hand. It might be theoretically true that just about everything can operate as a communication device and "make a difference" (Cooren, 2006) in social situations. However, this is empirically unlikely. The critical question is the co-optation of agency. An object may have an agency, but this might be by design, if the object is human-made. The question here is to what we attribute agency and the (power) effects of its intervention. For example, in the case of a control system for regulating organizational performance, does agency reside in the system itself, among the technicians who designed the system, or among the managers who reap its benefits? Or in all of the above?[1]

Third, there is also the issue of selecting the "speaking" objects. In a world where agency is the exclusive domain of humans, this question is relatively easy to resolve. Basically, the "speaking" objects are the people involved in the context under study, since they are the only objects that are deemed competent to speak. In a world where objects and devices also "speak", or at least partake in communication processes (see Rennstam, 2012), this question becomes more complicated. Cooren's (2010, 2012) notion of ventriloquism offers a way to understand the mechanism of speaking for others, but it does not provide an account for which actors are *given the right to speak*, and what they are entitled to speak of. It is also possible to argue that ventriloquism per se facilitates naturalization as it obfuscates who is actually talking.

Communication as a Relation

These three challenges are intrinsically related to one of the main CCO premises: that communication is a relation. Relationality, as Kuhn and colleagues recall, "can facilitate novel ways of attending to social problems" (2017, p. 4). And they indeed pave the way to a relational and communicational perspective of a crucial trio in our social world: work, capitalism, and organization.

Following a constitutive approach of communication, assume that we organize ourselves *through* communication. Phenomena of all kinds emerge and are organized through the interactions of several and multiple-genre actors (usually referring to "non-humans" or other than humans) who populate "reality". In this view, communication is not a medium, rather it is the fundamental dynamic principle of our existence (Cooren, 2018, 2020). Communication has thus a highly relational function: it puts things in relation on a communicational scene where interactions constitute organizations (seen as arrangements or dispositions). In a specific place, at a specific time, things in interaction are disposing themselves to create a specific arrangement. To be interested in a relational definition of communication shifts the focus from people who speak and write towards the links, the relations that move humans and things in the world. Communication should therefore be conceived of as a set of relational practices – by which various beings relate to each other through other beings that or who act as their intermediaries/voices/media/representatives:

> If someone or something indeed makes a difference (i.e., is the author of an action), it is because it is not only he/she/it who/that is acting, but also what or who he/she/it represents, i.e., make present (again).
>
> *Cooren, 2020, p. 9*

That conception of communication is highly influenced by new materialism (see Cooren, 2020), which stipulates a fundamental relationality of the world (the universe). Relationality is thus defined as an ontological dimension. Seeing communication through this conception invites one to consider communication thus also as ontological.

Moreover, building on those premises, communication refers to the way two (or more) beings "are held in common" together through a third being[2] (Cooren, 2018, 2020). In some ways, this conception of communication echoes how some liberals conceptualized the private firm in the 1970s. Indeed, Chamayou (2018) shows how management scholars back then defined the private firm as a nexus of horizontal relations, emptying it of class struggles and power relations. An organization was not taken to be a real entity anymore: it was merely a "misleading name given to a set of contractual relations" (Chamayou, 2018, p. 148, our translation). Seeing organizations just as relations equals emptying them of everything that makes the organization for instance unequal, sexist and/or authoritative. The CCO approach, in focusing only on relations, tends to do the same as the liberals of the 1970s: it avoids defining the organization and neutralizing the relations. The task at hand is thus to *redefine* this relation approach of both organizations and communication. And we think it passes through the characterization of the *relations* CCO scholars are talking about.

Indeed, a question remains unanswered: *how* are people/things/other-than-human held in common? Or, to put it differently, what is the nature of the relations that hold people/things/other-than-human together? Following our critical stance, we state that these relations are informed by neoliberal capitalism (as defined above from the concept of ideology). Thus, we have to consider it as a fundamental actor in this relational (and communicational) process. Indeed, as we have already highlighted, neoliberal capitalism is an organizing ideology that structures how to behave, live, think, relate to nature, etc. That echoes Dardot and Laval's definition of neoliberal capitalism cited above, as well as Kuhn, Ashcraft and Cooren's (2017) statement in which they agree that:

> what is commonly taken to be actors and factors creating contemporary capitalism – individuals, organizations, markets, public policies, structures, as well as the very figure of the "new economy" – emerge from, and are performed in, communication (when communication is understood as a dynamic practice).
>
> *2017, p. 27*

This definition of relationality supersedes a conception of relations as "connections", only, and acknowledges that these relations are "the effects of [communicational] practices" (Kuhn et al. 2017, p. 27) that are themselves moved and informed by a specific ideology/"regime of truth" (as Foucault would say): neoliberal capitalism. The definition we bring here highlights the three challenges mentioned. Indeed, the formation of *meaning*, the rendering of *agency*, and the making up of *speaking objects*, all three are entangled and moved by the hegemonic organizing ideology that neoliberal capitalism incarnates today.

We can thus add to our definition of communication, seen as a set of relational practices, that this set of relational practices is moved by neoliberal capitalism in the sense that the latter penetrates the way we "hold in common". It is in this conception of relations that we state that neoliberal capitalism *does* communication and that communication *does* neoliberal capitalism. And this is accomplished through a variety of practices which range from interactions, discourses, actions, affects, and so on. Thus, the organization is not merely a set of neutral relations but rather the product of a series of neoliberal practices which define how people (and things) relate, how decisions are made, how texts are written, etc.

Moreover, such a conceptualization of communication and organization is useful to address further questions of resistance within organizations. Indeed, practices of resistance are part of this unmaking of neoliberal capitalism. Practices in-formed by neoliberal capitalism can be substituted and unmade by other ways of organizing (cooperatives, self-governance, participatory democracy, decolonial rules, etc.). And if organizations are the effects and products of neoliberal relations that induce negative power relations, work exploitation, unequal gender divisions, and so forth, we have to undertake a close scrutiny of the practices that can *deconstruct* this factual situation. In that sense, the CCO perspective can become an important theoretical tool for change. In this vein, Wilhoit and Kisselburgh (2019) mobilize a CCO approach of resistance. More specifically, using a study on bike commuters, they show that resistance is the product of multiple human and non-human actants. Their work is a promising avenue to theorize resistance (outside the workplace) with a CCO approach anchored in relationality. However, they still miss the central question: *what* are people resisting through bike commuting? To put it differently, they obfuscate the hegemonic and dominant ideology that makes bike commuting into a "thing". Our critical approach of CCO would question first and foremost the source of the resistance and on what basis it takes place. That – we think – is an avenue to consider the "undoing" of hegemonic ideology and a way thus to deconstruct it through communicational practices.

Implications and Conclusion

As we have shown, the constitutive approach of communication, in its pragmatic roots, presents several drawbacks. However, CCO can be freed from its origins to deepen its critical potentialities. This is possible by focusing on its relational dimension and by engaging with the "material turn". Our proposition has several implications. First, it opens up the reflection and the study of how we (collectively and individually) *do* neoliberal capitalism through our communicative practices. Secondly, it permits us to address further, for example, questions of power but also alternative organizing and resistance as ways of "undoing" capitalism. Indeed, once we agree that we are intrinsically entangled in capitalistic communicative practices, we must ask how we can (un)do these relationships. We have to think breaches, gaps, resistances and alternatives.

In sum, our approach invites one to consider the political potentialities of CCO. When we consider the neoliberal dimension of communicative practices, we invite a study of neoliberalism in terms of interactions (interactionally) but also of transactions (Taylor, 2011). We emancipate ourselves from a merely "macro" vision of neoliberal capitalism, viewed as a transcendent system. Viewing neoliberalism communicationally, as a relation that holds people/things together, allows analysts to dissect society at large. In sum, as such, the constitutive approach gets out of the organization and permits us to think what holds society in common.

Now, the next step is to focus on the empirical stakes. Indeed, some questions still need discussions and reflections: how can we "follow" the neoliberal relations? Which methods are appropriate to render the neoliberal organizations of both organizations and the social world? As CCO scholars we have to engage in empirical work towards such a perspective to disclose the *doing* of neoliberal capitalism in order to transform it from the inside out.

Notes

1 The Montreal School assumes that no single thing has or possesses agency, but that agency is always a hybrid term. Indeed, agency is always the result of a multiplicity of "things" acting together (Bencherki, 2018; Cooren, 2020; Latour, 2006).
2 As Cooren recalls, the proto-Indo-European root of the word "communication" is "ko-moin-i", which means "held in common" (2018, pp. 283–284).

References

Adler, P. S., Forbes, L. C., & Willmott, H. (2008). Critical management studies. In *The Academy of Management annals*, Vol. 1 (pp. 119–179). New YorkY: Taylor & Francis /Lawrence Erlbaum.

Adorno, T., & Horkheimer, M. (1972). *Dialectics of Enlightenment*. New York: Herder and Herder.

Alvesson, M., Bridgman, T., & Willmott, H. (2009). *The Oxford handbook of critical management studies*. Oxford: Oxford University Press.

Alvesson, M., & Karreman, D. (2000). Varities of discourse: On the study of organizations through discourse analysis. *Human Relations, 53*, 1125–1149.

Alvesson, M., & Willmott, H. (1992). On the idea of emancipation in management and organization studies. *The Academy of Management Review, 17*, 432–464.

Ashcraft, K. L. (2004). *Reworking gender: A feminist communicology of organization*. Sage.

Aubin, F., & Rueff, J. (Eds.). (2016). *Perspectives critiques en communication: Contextes, théories et recherches empiriques* (1st edn.). Montréal: Presses de l'Université du Québec.

Bencherki, N. (2018). Écrire les objets/laisser les objets s'écrire. *Revue internationale de psychosociologie et de gestion des comportements organisationnels, XXIV*, 133–152.

Bencherki, N., Matte, F., & Cooren, F. (2019). *Authority and power in social interaction*. New York: Routledge.

Bencherki, N., Matte, F., & Pelletier, E. (2016). Rebuilding Babel: A constitutive approach to tongues-in-use. *Journal of Communication, 66*, 766–788.

Benoit-Barné, C., & Cooren, F. (2009). The accomplishment of authority through presentification: How authority is distributed among and negotiated by organizational members. *Management Communication Quarterly, 23*, 5–31.

Boivin, G., Brummans, B. H. J. M., & Barker, J. R. (2017). The institutionalization of CCO scholarship. *Management Communication Quarterly, 31*, 331–355.

Boltanski, L., & Chiapello, E. (2011). *Le nouvel esprit du capitalisme*. Paris: Gallimard.

Braidotti, R. (2019). *Posthuman knowledge*. Wiley.

Brown, W. (2017). *Undoing the demos: Neoliberalism's stealth revolution*. Princeton University Press.

Brummans, B., Cooren, F., Robichaud, D., & Taylor, J. R. (2014). Approaches to the communicative constitution of organizations. In D. K. Mumby & L. L. Putnam (Eds.), *The SAGE handbook of organizational communication: Advances in Theory, Research, and Methods* (pp. 173–194). Sage.

Chamayou, G. (2018). *La société ingouvernable: Une généalogie du libéralisme autoritaire*. Paris: La Fabrique.

Cooper, R. (1989). Modernism, post modernism and organizational analysis 3: The contribution of Jacques Derrida. *Organization Studies, 10*, 479–502.

Cooren, F. (2006). The organizational world as a plenum of agencies. In J. R. Taylor & E. J. Van Every (Eds.), *Communication as organizing: Empirical and theoretical explorations in the dynamic of text and conversation* (pp. 81–100). Mahwah, NJ: Lawrence Erlbaum.

Cooren, F. (2012). Communication theory at the center: Ventriloquism and the communicative constitution of reality. *Journal of Communication, 62*, 1–20.

Cooren, F. (2018). Materializing communication: Making the case for a relational ontology. *Journal of Communication, 68*, 278–288.

Cooren, F. (2010). *Action and agency in dialogue: Passion, incarnation and ventriloquism* (Vol. 6). John Benjamins Publishing.

Cooren, F. (2020). Beyond entanglement: (Socio-) Materiality and organization studies. *Organization Theory, 1*, 1–24.

Dardot, P., & Laval, C. (2009). *La nouvelle raison du monde: Essai sur la société néolibérale*. Paris: La Découverte.

Dean, J. (2009). Technology. The promises of communicative capitalism. Communicative capitalism and left politics. In *Democracy and Other Neoliberal Fantasies*. (pp. 19–48). Durham: Duke University Press.

Deetz, S. (1992). *Democracy in an age of corporate colonization: Developments in communication and the politics of everyday life*. New York: State University of New York.

Deetz, S. (2003). Reclaiming the legacy of the linguistic turn. *Organization, 10*, 421–429.

Del Fa, S., & Vásquez, C. (2020). Existing through differantiation: A Derridean approach to alternative organizations. *M@n@gement, 22*.

Deleuze, G., & Guattari, F. (1980). *Mille plateaux: Capitalisme et schizophrénie 2*. Paris: Les Éditions de Minuit.

Dewey, J. (1938). *Experience and education*. Kappa Delta Pi.

Federici, S. (2019). *Beyond the periphery of the skin: Rethinking, Remaking, and reclaiming the body in contemporary capitalism*. Oakland: PM Press/Kairos.

Foucault, M. (2004). *Naissance de la biopolitique: Cours au Collège de France (1978–1979)*. Paris: Gallimard: Seuil.

Foucault, M. (2007). What is critique? In *The polics of truth*. Los Angeles: Semiotext(e).

Foucault, M. (2012). *Il faut défendre la société, Cours au Collège de France (1975–1976)*. Paris: Gallimard: Seuil.

Fournier, V., & Grey, C. (2000). At the critical moment: Conditions and prospects for critical management studies. *Human Relations, 53*, 7–32.

Freeden, M. (2003). *Very short introductions available now:* Oxford: Oxford University Press.

Fuchs, C. (2020). *Communication and capitalism: A critical theory*. London: University of Westminster Press.

Geertz, C. (1973). *The interpretation of cultures: Selected essays*. New York: Basic Books.

Gibson-Graham, J. (2006). *The end of capitalism? (As we knew it). A feminist critique of political economy*. Minneapolis: University Of Minnesota Press.

Grey, C., & Willmott, H. (2005). *Critical management studies: A reader*. Oxford: Oxford University Press.

Guattari, F. (1981). Le capitalisme mondial intégré et la révolution moléculaire. *Centre d'Information Sur Les Nouveaux Espaces de Liberté*, 1–9.

Habermas, J. (1987). The idea of the university—Learning processes. *New German Critique*, 3–22.

Haraway, D. (1988). Situated knowledges: The science question in feminism and the privilege of partial perspective. *Feminist Studies, 14*, 575–599.

Haraway, D. (2015). Anthropocene, capitalocene, plantationocene, chthulucene: Making kin. *Environmental Humanities, 6*, 159–165.

Harvey, D. (2005). *A brief history of neoliberalism*. Oxford: Oxford University Press.

Holloway, J. (2010). *Crack Capitalism*. Pluto Press.

Kuhn, T. R. (2008). A communicative theory of the firm : Developing an alternative perspective on intra-organizational power and stakeholder relationships. *Organization Studies, 29*(8 9), 1227 1254. https://doi.org/10.1177/0170840608094778.

Kuhn, T. R. (2012). Negotiating the micro-macro divide : Thought leadership from organizational communication for theorizing organization. *Management Communication Quarterly, 26*(4), 543 584. https://doi.org/10.1177/0893318912462004.

Kuhn, T. (2021). (Re)moving blinders: Communication-as-constitutive theorizing as provocation to practice-based organization scholarship. *Management Learning, 52*, 109–121.

Kuhn, T., Ashcraft, K. L., & Cooren, F. (2017). *The work of communication: Relational perspectives on working and organizing in contemporary capitalism*. New York: Routledge.

Kunda, G. (1992). *Engineering culture: Control and commitment in a high-tech corporation*. Temple University Press.

Latour, B. (2006). *Nous n'avons jamais été modernes: Essai d'anthropologie symétrique*. Paris: La Découverte.

Lorde, A. (1984). *Sister outsider*. Ten Speed Press.

Lyotard, J.-F. (1984). *The postmodern condition*. University Of Minnesota Press.

Malm, A. (2017). *L'anthropocène contre l'histoire: Le réchauffement climatique à l'ère du capital*. Paris: La Fabrique.

Mumby, D. K. (2019). Communication constitutes capital: Branding and the politics of neoliberal dis/organization. In C. Vásquez & T. Kuhn (Eds.), *Dis/organization as communication. Exploring the disordering, disruptive and chaotic properties of communication*. London: Routledge.

Mumby, D. K. (2016). Organizing beyond organization: Branding, discourse, and communicative capitalism. *Organization, 1*.

Mumby, D. K. (2020). Theorizing struggle in the social factory. *Organization Theory, 1*, 1–14.

Mumby, D. K., & Ashcraft, K. L. (2006). Organizational communication studies and gendered organization: A response to Martin and Collinson. *Gender, Work and Organization, 13*, 68–90.

Mumby, D. K., & Ashcraft, K. L. (2017). Critical approaches. In C. R. Scott, J. R. Barker, T. Kuhn, J. Keyton, P. K. Turner, & L. K. Lewis (Eds.), *The international encyclopedia of organizational communication* (pp. 1–23). Hoboken, NJ: John Wiley & Sons.

Mumby, D. K., Thomas, R., Martí, I., & Seidl, D. (2017). Resistance redux. *Organization Studies, 38*, 1157–1183.

Mumford, L. (1940). The corruption of liberalism. *The New Republic*. Retrieved from https://newrepublic.com/article/119690/lewis-mumfords-corruption-liberalism.

Ott, B. L., & Mack, R. L. (2009). *Critical media studies: An introduction*. Chichester: Wiley Blackwell.

Parker, M. (1995). Critique in the name of what: Postmodernism and critical approaches to organization. *Organization Studies, 16*, 553–564.

Parker, M. (2018). *Shut down the business school: What's wrong with management education*. London: Pluto Press.

Parker, S., & Parker, M. (2017). Antagonism, accommodation and agonism in critical management studies: Encouraging alternative organizations. *Human Relations, 70*, 1366–1387.

Pineault, É. (2008). Quelle théorie critique des structures sociales du capitalisme avancé? *Cahiers de recherche sociologique*, 113.

Rennstam, J. (2012). Object-control: A study of technologically dense knowledge work. *Organization Studies*, *33*, 1071–1090.

Schoeneborn, D., Blaschke, S., Cooren, F., McPhee, R. D., Seidl, D., & Taylor, J. R. (2014). The three schools of CCO thinking: Interactive dialogue and systematic comparison. *Management Communication Quarterly*, *28*, 285–316.

Spicer, A., Alvesson, M., & Karreman, D. (2009). Critical performativity: The unfinished business of critical management studies. *Human Relations*, *62*(4), 537–560.

Srnicek, N. (2016). *Platform capitalism*. Polity.

Stengers, I. (2008). *Au temps des catastrophes. Résister à la barbarie qui vient*. Paris: La Découverte.

Stiegler, B. (2018). *Il faut s'adapter: Sur un nouvel impératif politique*. Paris: Gallimard.

Swidler, A. (1986). Culture in action: Symbols and strategies on JSTOR. *American Sociological Review*, *51*, 273–286.

Taylor, J. R. (2011). Organization as an (imbricated) configuring of transactions. *Organization Studies*, *32*(9), 1273 1294. https://doi.org/10.1177/0170840611411396.

Taylor, J. R., & Van Every, E. (2000). *The emergent organization: Communication as its site and surface*. Mahwah, NJ: Routledge.

Vergès, F. (2019). *Féminisme décolonial*. Paris: La Fabrique.

Wajcman, J. (2007). *Technofeminism*. UOC.

Wilhoit, E. D., & Kisselburgh, L. G. (2019). The relational ontology of resistance: Hybridity, ventriloquism, and materiality in the production of bike commuting as resistance. *Organization*, *26*, 873–893.

Xing, L., & Shaw, T. M. (2013). The political economy of Chinese state capitalism. *Journal of China and International Relations*, *1*(1).

Zuboff, S. (2019). *The age of surveillance capitalism: The fight for a human future at the new frontier of power* (1st edn., p. x). New York: PublicAffairs.

11

QUEERING CCO SCHOLARSHIP

Examining Communication as Constitutive of (Hetero)normative Organizations and Organizing

Jamie McDonald

Queering CCO Scholarship: Examining Communication as Constitutive of (Hetero)Normative Organizations and Organizing

Queer theory is a broad, interdisciplinary, and evolving body of thought that has roots in both queer activism and intellectual traditions such as feminism, postmodernism, post-structuralism, and gay and lesbian studies (de Lauretis, 1991). Although queer theorists have varied stances on the scope and aims of queer theory, they share broad commitments to challenging heteronormativity, celebrating difference, and conceptualizing gender and sexuality in a fluid and performative manner (Wiegman & Wilson, 2015). Queer theory has been making inroads to communication studies since the early 2000s when Yep, Lovaas, and Elia (2003) began the conversation of what it might mean to "queer" communication in a special issue of the *Journal of Homosexuality*. However, queer theory only began to find some traction within organizational communication in the mid-2010s (Compton & Dougherty, 2017; Harris & McDonald, 2018; McDonald, 2015), and queer theory continues to occupy a marginal position in management and organization studies more broadly (Rumens, 2013, 2018a).

To date, the literatures on queer theory and the communicative constitution of organization and organizing (CCO) have developed separately, with no prior engagement between the two bodies of research. Although queer theory and CCO scholarship come from different intellectual traditions and have yet to formally engage with each other, they do share several affinities. For one, both queer theory and CCO are broad perspectives with a great deal of internal heterogeneity, rather than unified theories in the traditional sense. Moreover, both queer theory and CCO are process-oriented perspectives that emphasize performativity; that is, how social phenomena are constituted in interaction. Indeed, a central claim of CCO theorizing is that organizations are communicative accomplishments and, as such, do not exist outside of communication. That is, rather than start with the assumption that organizations exist and explaining communication processes within already constituted organizations, CCO holds that analyses of organizational phenomena should *begin* with communication (Schoeneborn et al., 2019). In this sense, communication is the *explanans* that explains organization and

DOI: 10.4324/9781003224914-13

organizing (Ashcraft et al., 2009). This claim resonates with a main tenet of queer theory, which is to question the existence of pre-existing identity categories, particularly as they relate to gender and sexuality (Seidman, 1997). Queer theory suggests that rather than treating identity categories as objectively identifiable and stable, they should be understood as performative accomplishments with no stable essence (Sedgwick, 1990). As such, queer theory examines the processes through which categories such as "man", "woman", "straight", and "gay" are performatively constituted and become recognizable as such (Butler, 1990). Thus, both CCO and queer theory are interested with understanding the ways in which commonly taken-for-granted elements of social life, namely organizations and identity categories, are performatively created, enacted, and constituted.

The goals of this chapter are to put CCO and queer theory into conversation for the first time and, in so doing, to contribute to the development of an emerging critical perspective on CCO (e.g., Del Fa & Kärreman, this volume; Long et al., 2018; Mease, 2020; Mease & Terry, 2012; Mumby, 2019; Wilhoit & Kisselburgh, 2019). To begin, I first summarize some of the key tenets of queer theory, as well as ongoing interdisciplinary conversations among queer theorists. I follow by discussing the ways in which queer theory has been taken up in organizational scholarship to date. Afterwards, I reflect on how queer theory can inform CCO scholarship by posing the provocative question: *what might it mean to queer CCO scholarship?* To this end, I argue that queering CCO entails interrogating how heteronormative assumptions are embedded into the communication processes that constitute both organizations and organizing. Moreover, I suggest that queering CCO scholarship entails reflecting on how we might organize differently to resist heteronormative organizations and organizing.

Queer Theory

Queer theory first became recognizable as a distinct body of thought at a conference organized by Teresa de Lauretis at the University of California, Santa Cruz in 1990. The goal of the conference was to challenge the dominant discourse of gay and lesbian studies at the time, which was premised upon what Seidman (1993) has called an ethnic identity model. This logic presumed stable, universal notions of gay and lesbian identities and sought mainstream acceptance by minimizing claims of difference. Although this minoritizing logic proved effective in mobilizing some lesbians and gay men in the quest for equal rights, it was also critiqued on numerous grounds (Seidman, 1997). In particular, people of color challenged the implicit whiteness of this ethnic identity model, which presumed a universal white and middle-class subject and failed to account for many members of the larger lesbian, gay, bisexual, transsexual, and queer (LGBTQ+) communities (Ford, 2011). As an alternative to the universalizing and assimilationist tendencies of mainstream gay and lesbian activism at the time, queer activism and queer theory promoted an alternative politics that eschewed claims to "normality", celebrated difference, and resisted the notion of a unitary gay and lesbian identity (Warner, 1999; Yep, 2003).

In line with queer theory's rejection of claims to normality and celebration of difference, the concepts of normativity and heteronormativity are at the core of queer thought. To this end, *normativity* refers to the processes that construct certain identities and forms of difference as the desirable standard against which everything else is judged, whereas *heteronormativity* refers specifically to the normalization and privileging of a narrow form of heterosexuality over all other sexual identities and practices (Yep, 2003). Heteronormativity marginalizes not only non-heterosexuals, but also heterosexuals who engage in sexual practices that are considered deviant and fall outside the purview of what is rendered desirable and normal, including but not limited to sex outside of marriage, having children outside of marriage, non-monogamous relationships, promiscuity, and BDSM practices (Elia, 2003). Heteronormativity is maintained through both localized practices, such as casual conversations in which normative heterosexuality is silently assumed and taken-for-granted unless one discloses an alternative sexual identity, and centralized institutions, such as the privileging of the traditional married nuclear family type in policies as varied as health, tax, adoption, and immigration (Cohen, 2005). Drawing from Foucault (1976), who demonstrated that the regulation of sexuality is a primary way through which power has been and continues to be exercised in society, queer theory critiques and resists heteronormativity and heteronormative processes that privilege some expressions of sexuality over others.

Although some queer theorists have argued that the scope of queer theory should be limited to sexuality because of the roots of queer activism in specifically challenging repressive sexual norms (Alexander, 2003; Bersani, 1995), many more have suggested that queer theory can serve as a lens through which to critique how multiple forms of normativity constrain subjectivities (Butler, 2004; Cohen, 2005; Halperin, 2003). In taking a broad stance against normativity, queer theory has a large scope and is much more than a theory of gender and sexuality (Jagose, 2015; Warner, 1999). Rather, queer theory provides a framework to examine how heteronormativity is intertwined with other normalizing regimes. In particular, queer of color scholars have demonstrated the importance of simultaneously critiquing both heteronormativity and whiteness to avoid reifying a universal white queer subject (Eguchi & Asante, 2016; Johnson, 2001; Yep, 2013).

Beyond challenging and critiquing (hetero)normativity, another core feature of queer thought is its challenging of stable identity categories in favor of an anticategorical approach to difference that is informed by postmodernism and poststructuralism (Jagose, 1996). Butler's (1990) theory of gender performativity has been particularly influential in developing queer theory's performative and anticategorical approach to difference. According to Butler (1990), identities do not exist outside of discourse and the performative acts that constitute them. That is, "it is the very performance of identity which produces that identity itself" (Harding et al., 2011, p. 929). As such, gendered and sexual subjects only become recognizable through the repeated and ritualized performance of the performative acts that constitute gendered and sexual identities. Without the accomplishment of these gendered acts, there would be no gender as we know it because, for Butler (1990, 1993), gender only exists through its (re)enactment and performative accomplishment.

Although Butler's (1990) initial articulation of gender performativity can be critiqued for emphasizing discourse over materiality, she later emphasized that the performative acts that constitute gendered and sexual subjects are very much embodied (Butler, 1993). To illustrate her argument about the performativity of gender and sexuality, Butler (1990, 1993) relies heavily upon an analysis of drag performances. For Butler (1990, 1993), drag is a practice through which performers expose and enact the normative gendered practices that performatively accomplish gendered identities such as "woman" and "man". Drag is also a subversive practice because it disrupts the stability of gender and shows how gendered identities can shift and be subverted.

The performative, anticategorical approach to identity described above is favored by queer theorists for two key reasons. First, queer theorists are wary of the differences that are glossed over when making generalized claims about people within a given category. Indeed, queer theory emerged out of a rejection of the ethnic identity model to gay and lesbian identity described earlier, which presumed a stable, universal homosexual subject and failed to account for the important differences that exist among LGBTQ+ subjects (Seidman, 1997). Because there is a great deal of heterogeneity within identity categories, individuals cannot be presumed to share a common experience or political agenda simply by virtue of sharing a particular identity (Sedgwick, 1990). The second reason queer theorists reject a categorical approach to identity is because, following Foucault (1976), queer theory views identity categories as instruments of power, normalizing forces, and disciplinary structures. That is, individuals can be compelled to enact the performative practices that are associated with identity categories to which they are assigned (Seidman, 1997). As a classic example, boys may be disciplined for throwing "like a girl" and thus feel compelled to throw in a way that aligns with the normative, gendered expectations of how boys should throw (Young, 1980). By not identifying with categories that come with normative expectations about how these categories should be enacted, queer theorists suggest that individuals can regain agency and express themselves in freer, more liberating ways (Seidman, 1997). Although individuals may still use categories to make sense of their identities, queer theorists contend that these categories should be understood in a way that is permanently open and devoid of fixed meaning in order to resist their regulatory force (Love, 2011). Queer theory thus advocates a strong anti-essentialist position and rejects generalized and essentialist claims about identity groups (Seidman, 1997).

In this section, I have summarized two key features of queer theory: (1) a commitment to exposing and challenging (hetero)normativity; and (2) the development of an anticategorical, performative approach to understanding and analyzing identity. I now turn to a discussion of the ways in which queer theory has been taken up in organizational scholarship.

Queering Organizational Research and CCO

The first mention of queer theory in organizational scholarship was in a short essay by Gibson-Graham (1996), who reflected on how queer theory might enable organizational scholars to destabilize the hegemony of capitalist organizing and "open up a space for alternative economic representations, one in which non-capitalist economic practices are viable and prolific, and not necessary subsumed to capitalist dominance" (p. 543). However, the first substantial engagement with queer theory by organizational scholars didn't appear until the early 2000s, when Parker (2001, 2002) laid out a framework for queering management and organization. For Parker (2001), queering is an ongoing practice that entails adopting "an attitude of unceasing disruptiveness" (p. 58). As such, the process of queering management and organization subjects commonly accepted assumptions about organizational life to critical interrogation in order to imagine alternative possibilities (Parker, 2016). This follows Seidman (1997), who conceptualizes queering as a practice that seeks "to make strange or 'queer' what is considered known, familiar, and commonplace, what is assumed to be the order of things, the natural way, the normal, the healthy, and so on" (p. xi).

Since Parker (2001) first proposed queering management and organization, organizational scholars have sought to queer our understandings of phenomena such as gender and sexual identities at work (Compton & Dougherty, 2017; McDonald, 2013; O'Shea, 2018; Rumens et al., 2019), leadership (Ashcraft & Muhr, 2018; Chang & Bowring, 2017; Harding et al., 2011; Muhr & Sullivan, 2013), diversity management (Bendl et al., 2008, 2009; Bendl & Hofmann, 2015), organizations that are deemed "gay-friendly" (Burchiellaro, 2020; Rumens, 2015; Williams et al., 2009), closeting processes (Dixon, 2018; Eger, 2018; Harris & McDonald, 2018; McDonald et al., 2020), and research methods (McDonald, 2016, 2017; Riach et al., 2016; Rumens, 2018b).[1] Together, this body of scholarship serves to demonstrate how difference—including but not limited to sexuality—is a constitutive and thus omnipresent feature of organizations and organizing, expose and critique (hetero)normativity in organizations and organizing, and illustrate the fluidity and performativity of identities in organizational contexts (McDonald, 2015).

Despite the modest inroads that queer theory has made into organizational scholarship, queer theory has not yet engaged with CCO. Queering CCO research would draw from an emerging critical perspective on CCO, which recognizes that "the communicative constitution of organization is *always* an act of power connected to a broader social context" (Mease, 2020, p. 2). Specifically, queering CCO research emphasizes how the communicative constitution of organization is connected to power as it relates to (hetero)normativity, as well as always intertwined with relations of difference. That is, a queer perspective on CCO holds the assumption that in addition to communication, (hetero)normativity and difference are constitutive features of organizations and organizing. Queering CCO research thus entails exploring and critiquing the ways in which (hetero)normativity and difference are embedded into the processes that constitute organizations and organizing, as well as imagining alternative ways of organizing that break with (hetero)normativity.

In addition to explaining what queering CCO entails, it is important to emphasize what queering CCO is *not*: examining the communicative constitution of a "queer" organization and/or "queer" organizing practices. To claim that a particular organization or organizing practice is discernably "queer" would go against the philosophical assumptions that underpin queer theory, which resist categorization and stability (Rumens, 2018a). As such, queering CCO is not the same as and does not imply identifying a queer organization or queer organizing practices.

Because CCO is a diverse theoretical perspective, queering CCO can take many forms. Below, I discuss specifically how queer theory can inform our understanding of the communication flows approach, the text and conversation approach, ventriloqual analysis, and constitutive approaches to organizational space.

Queering Communication Flows

The four flows model to CCO, originally developed by McPhee and Zaug (2000), is premised on the idea that while not all communication is organizational, there are four specific types of communication that are inherently organizational and that, when they intersect and become interrelated, lead to the constitution of organizations. McPhee and Zaug (2000) identify these four communication flows as membership negotiation, organizational self-structuring, activity coordination, and institutional positioning. Membership negotiation refers to interactions about the relationship of members to an organization; organizational self-structuring refers to interactions pertaining to an organization's structures and rules; activity coordination pertains to interactions about how work is organized and accomplished; and institutional positioning refers to interactions that position an organization in relation to external stakeholders and society at large (McPhee & Zaug, 2000).

In a later piece, Lutgen-Sandvik and McDermott (2008) added a fifth flow, which they named the syncretic superstructure. The syncretic superstructure refers to messages that "represent deeply rooted beliefs and ideologies that are strongly influenced by culture and history" (Lutgen-Sandvik & McDermott, 2008, p. 311). As such, the syncretic superstructure communication flow refers to discursive formations and ideologies that inform the communicative processes that constitute organizations. Because heteronormativity has long been one of the most pervasive and powerful discursive formations in contemporary society (Foucault, 1976), the syncretic superstructure flow accounts for how heteronormativity is embedded into the communicative constitution of organization.

Queering the communication flows approach to CCO would entail paying particular attention to how (hetero)normativity is embedded into the syncretic superstructure communication flow by focusing on interactions pertaining to the organizational, professional, occupational, and cultural norms that permeate organizational life and lead to the constitution of organizations. However, because queer theory views (hetero)normativity and difference as relevant to all aspects of organizational life, queering the communication flows approach to CCO would also entail looking at how (hetero)normativity and difference are embedded into interactions pertaining to membership negotiation, organizational self-structuring, activity coordination, and institutional positioning. For instance, membership negotiation pertains to the identities of organizational members and who "fits" with the organization. Interactions pertaining to membership negotiation can thus function to exclude those with non-normative identities from either joining the organization or being seen as full-fledged members. Moreover, interactions pertaining to organizational self-structuring can lead to the creation of structures and rules that favor some members, while disadvantaging those with non-normative identities and characteristics. Because work is organized around normative conceptions of difference (Ashcraft, 2011), (hetero)normative assumptions can also be embedded into activity coordination. Lastly, institutional positioning can reproduce (hetero)normativity when organizations ignore external stakeholders who embody difference in non-normative ways, instead only positioning themselves in relation to stakeholders who embody normative conceptions of difference.

Another way to apply queer theory to the communication flows approach to CCO would be to examine a case study of an organization that considers itself "gay-friendly". In this sense, researchers could analyze the communication flows that constitute a "gay-friendly" organization in a similar way to how Lutgen-Sandvik and McDermott (2008) examined the communication flows that constitute an employee-abusive organization. However, in line with queer theory's political impetus, such research would not uncritically celebrate the constitution of a so-called "gay-friendly" organization. Indeed, the very notion of a "gay-friendly" organization has been critiqued in existing queer organizational scholarship on multiple grounds. In particular, this research has shown that (hetero)normativity remains rampant in such organizations and that open expressions of a LGBTQ+ identity can only be accepted in limited ways and to the extent that they produce value for the organization (Burchiellaro, 2020; Rumens, 2015; Williams et al., 2009). Adopting a communication flows approach to the study of such organizations would enable us to better identify how (hetero)normativity can manifest itself in interactions pertaining to membership negotiation, organizational self-structuring, activity coordination, institutional positioning, and syncretic superstructure, even in so-called "gay-friendly" organizations. Using the communication flows approach to investigate the processes that constitute "gay-friendly" organizations also has the potential to identify how these organizations can queer organizing practices related to each of the four flows, thereby challenging conventional and normative organizing processes.

Queering Text and Conversation

As an alternative to the constitutive flows approach, the Montréal School approach to CCO is heavily intertwined with the concepts of text and conversation. Here, conversation refers to situated interactions and "the lively and evolving co-constructive side of communication" (Ashcraft et al., 2009, p. 20), whereas text refers to more stable "forms of communication that may be extended in time and space beyond the bounds of a single time/space setting" (Taylor, 2009, p. 157). For the Montréal School, conversation is the site where organization is accomplished, whereas text is where organization is identified and described (Ashcraft et al., 2009). The textual and conversational modalities of conversation are heavily intertwined, as texts both shape conversation and are products of conversation (Kuhn, 2008; Taylor & Van Every, 2000).

Applying a queer theory lens to the dynamic of text and conversation would seek to identify how (hetero)normativity is a feature of the situated interactions that form the conversational modality of communication, as well as how these conversations "scale up" (Cooren & Fairhurst, 2009) to become incarnated and codified in the more enduring, textual modality of communication. In this sense, analysts would be concerned with illustrating the localized processes through which organizations become constituted in ways that uphold (hetero)normativity. Moreover, a queer lens on text and conversation would also examine how the organization, as a text, can function to shape localized conversations in ways that reproduce (hetero)normativity.

Kuhn's (2008) concept of authoritative text, which refers to a particular and enduring representation of an organization that is understood by most members to be legitimate and official, is also relevant from a queering perspective. According to Kuhn (2008), authoritative texts exercise power and discipline organizational members by portraying certain forms of knowledge and action as either appropriate/inappropriate or desirable/undesirable. As such, authoritative texts represent particular values and ideologies that can bear down upon the actions and conversations of organizational members. For instance, Koschmann and McDonald's (2015) study of an AIDS service organization demonstrated how inclusion functioned as an authoritative text that shaped the work of the organization and that was made present in everyday organizational life through the organization's rituals. Queer theorists can draw from this research to examine how (hetero)normativity is embedded into an organization's authoritative text in a way that disciplines organizational members. As an example of this, Burchiellaro's (2020) research on gay-friendly organizations found that, in the terms of CCO, inclusion was very much a part of the authoritative texts of the organizations that she studied. However, she also found that the organizations' authoritative texts viewed inclusion in a highly circumscribed and (hetero) normative manner. Future research can thus apply a queer lens to the concept of authoritative text to explore how authoritative texts can participate in the constitution of particular types of organizations that suppress difference and uphold (hetero)normativity.

Queering Ventriloqual Analysis

Grounded in the Montréal School of CCO theorizing, ventriloqual analysis was developed by Cooren (2010, 2012) as a way to account for how communication is a relational process that never involves just one individual speaking to another. Rather, humans ventriloquize—that is, mobilize, make present, and give voice to—various figures through communication, including other humans and nonhumans. Examples of nonhuman figures that humans ventriloquize in communication include, but are not limited to, objects, principles, values, interests, norms, and experiences (Cooren et al., 2013). However, in line with ventriloquism's relational conceptualization of agency, it is not just humans who are ventriloquists and have agency. Indeed, humans can also be *ventriloquized*; that is, figures ventriloquize humans by leading them to say certain things rather than others (Bergeron & Cooren, 2012; Schoeneborn et al., 2014). For instance, a bureaucratic rule is a figure that can ventriloquize a human who communicates to enforce that rule. In this sense, the ventriloquist approach problematizes who or what is speaking in a given interaction and accounts for both human and nonhuman agency (Cooren, 2010).

Because the ventriloqual approach addresses how figures such as ideologies, norms, and interests shape communication processes, it is amenable to critical research that views power as a fundamental feature of communication. In this regard, ventriloquism has been mobilized as a framework in feminist organizational research to shed light on topics such as women's meanings of work in China (Long, 2016) and how parents in graduate school negotiate tensions between work and life (Long et al., 2018). For instance, Long et al. (2018) show

how graduate student parents both ventriloquize and are ventriloquized by particular ideologies. In particular, they show that parents can ventriloquize and be ventriloquized by dominant understandings of the ideal worker norm, which leads them to legitimize prioritizing work over family and to experiencing feelings of anxiety and guilt (Long et al., 2018). This research also leads Long et al. (2018) to develop a ventriloqual approach to intersectionality, which examines how certain intersectional identities, such as race, gender, and sexual orientation, act as figures in specific contexts. Intersectional identities can both be ventriloquized by participants who make them present in interactions, as well as ventriloquize individuals by shaping their subjectivities and both enabling and constraining possibilities for action. This is in line with the Foucauldian assumption that identity labels can function as disciplining, normalizing forces.

From the perspective of queering organizational research and CCO, the ventriloqual approach is promising. Because queer theory views (hetero)normativity as a defining and constitutive feature of organizational life, a ventriloqual analysis can help identify how (hetero)normativity is a figure that ventriloquizes organizational members and that organizational members ventriloquize in their daily interactions. Moreover, a ventriloqual analysis can help identify how the ideology of (hetero)normativity is embedded into other figures that may be present in interactions, such as professionalism. Indeed, Rumens and Kerfoot (2009) showed that many gay male professionals that they interviewed drew upon the discourse of professionalism to desexualize their identity performances at work, as well as disparage other gay men whom they found to be excessively camp and flamboyant in professional settings. A ventriloqual analysis could account for how those gay men are both ventriloquizing and being ventriloquized by a (hetero)normative understanding of professionalism. Because ventriloqual analysis emphasizes how individuals ventriloquize and are ventriloquized by multiple figures, such an analysis would also enable researchers to identify additional figures that are being invoked in the *terra firma* of interaction, as well as how they intersect with (hetero)normativity.

As mentioned previously, queer theory views identity categories as disciplinary power structures that contain agency (Seidman, 1997). Applying a queer theory lens to ventriloqual analysis could thus help identify how identity categories are invoked and become prominent figures in organizational interactions. Moreover, ventriloqual analysis could help identify how "queer" itself may appear as a figure in certain organizational interactions. In this sense, queer is a figure that can ventriloquize individuals and be ventriloquized by individuals as they resist the (hetero)normativity) of organizational life.

Queering Organizational Space

In addition to queering approaches to CCO such as the communication flows, text and conversation, and ventriloquism, key CCO concepts can also be queered. One example of such a concept is space, which has become integral to CCO theorizing over the past several years with considerations about how space participates in the communicate constitution of organizations (Vásquez, 2016; Wilhoit, 2016, 2018; Wilhoit Larson, 2020). Wilhoit's (2016) constitutive theory of organizational space recognizes that space is a product of communication and thus an integral feature of organizations and organizing. Wilhoit (2018) also shows that space can be an active agent that communicates. From a critical perspective, this finding is important because it demonstrates that space can communicate power and that "the use and creation of space can be an exercise of power" (Wilhoit, 2018, p. 258). Moreover, Wilhoit and Kisselburgh (2015, 2019) show how resistance can also be accomplished through organizational space as individuals, both actively and passively, create spaces that challenge power relations.

Applying a queer theory lens to the notion of space has the potential to advance the existing CCO scholarship on constitutive approaches to space. Vitry (2020) claims that dominant capitalist organizing practices construct organizational spaces in ways that align with normative bodies; that is, bodies that are white, male, abled, and straight. By adopting a queer perspective to one of the approaches to CCO mentioned earlier, it would thus be possible to examine the ways in which organizational space—and by extension organizations—are constituted in (hetero)normative ways that presume certain bodies and exclude others. In this regard, Vitry (2020) invites us to explore how bodies that do not align with these norms negotiate organizational encounters in (hetero)normative spaces that are communicatively constituted.

Another contribution of queer CCO scholarship could be to examine the organizing processes through which queered space can be constituted. For Vitry (2020), queered space is where "bodies are not presumed to follow specific lines" (p. 6). As such, queering space disrupts dominant capitalist organizational spaces and enables us to imagine how we might organize to create more liberating spaces—and organizations—where bodies can move freely and are not aligned with or constrained by (hetero)normativity.

Importantly, Vitry (2020) notes that the process of queering space is very different from the process of constituting what might be considered a "queer space" or a "gay space". Indeed, the very notion of a queer or gay space presumes normative alignments of particular bodies, where a person in a particular space is expected to identify as queer or gay. Such a space can produce new forms of normativity, which is inconsistent with the spirit of queering as a fundamentally antinormative endeavor (Vitry, 2020). As an example of how a queer or gay space can reproduce (hetero)normativity, Branton and Compton (2021) found (hetero)normativity to be a feature of gay bars, especially as these establishments engage in neoliberal branding practices that are targeted at promoting a narrow version of inclusivity designed to make straight patrons feel more comfortable. Drawing from this work, queer CCO scholarship can examine the processes through which even so-called queer or gay spaces may be constituted in ways that reproduce (hetero)normativity, as well as identify how these spaces could be constituted in ways that align with the spirt of queering; that is, spaces that open up possibilities to act and live in ways that are not constrained by dominant (hetero)normative assumptions.

Conclusion and Future Directions

Because queer theory and CCO have not previously engaged with each other, my goals in this chapter have been to introduce CCO scholars to queer theory and to develop a conceptual framework that can serve to queer CCO research and, by extension, our understandings of the communication processes that constitute organizations and organizing. I have argued that queer theory advances our understanding of CCO by treating not only communication as a constitutive feature of organizations and organizing, but also difference and (hetero)normativity. Concretely, I have outlined how future empirical research can queer CCO by applying a queer theory lens to existing CCO approaches and concepts, most notably the communication flows approach, text and conversation, ventriloqual analysis, and organizational space.

In addition to the theoretical implications of queering CCO research that have been the primary focus of this chapter, queering CCO has methodological implications that can be explored in future research. As Rumens (2018b) states, queering methodologies is a process through which "we can destabilise and disrupt the methodological norms that currently govern how organisational research has been, and ought to be, carried out" (p. 107). Adopting a queer perspective can thus enable CCO researchers to rethink the dominant methodological assumptions that underpin CCO research. For instance, CCO research rarely accounts for fieldwork as an embodied process (Matte & Boivin, 2020). By adopting a queer perspective, researchers could recognize the research process as embodied by engaging in reflexivity about how they constitute the data that they collect and analyze, as well as how (hetero)normativity and difference shape the research process. Moreover, queering CCO research opens up possibilities for bringing non-traditional and innovative methodologies, such as autoethnography, into the purview of CCO research (Matte & Boivin, 2020).

Academics and practitioners who adopt a managerial ideology may question the practical utility of queering CCO research. In this regard, it is true that queering is a process that is decidedly *not* concerned with managerial values such as productivity, efficiency, and profit (Rumens, 2018a). As such, the goal of queering CCO research is not to help organizations become more productive, efficient, or profitable. Rather, the value of queer perspectives on organizational life—and by extension on CCO—lies in their ability to disrupt taken-for-granted views of social life in favor of more complexed and nuanced understandings. As Parker (2016) has claimed, if queering is stopped, "then thinking stops too" (p. 73), as queering is a process that forces thought by refusing commonsensical explanations. In this sense, queering CCO has much practical utility. First, it can help us better understand the ways in which communication constitutes organizations that suppress difference, uphold (hetero)normativity, and function as "normalizing regimes" (McDonald, 2015, p. 322). Moreover, queering CCO can help us imagine how organizations could be constituted *differently* and in ways that resist the (hetero) normativity of organizational life, celebrate difference, and are ultimately more liberatory.

I conclude this chapter by reiterating two basic premises of CCO research: (1) organizations are not stable entities, and (2) organizations do not naturally exist. Because organizations are dynamic entities that are constituted through communication, organizations can be changed—and queering invites us to imagine *how* they could be changed (Rumens, 2018a; Vitry, 2020). In this regard, Harding et al. (2011) have drawn from queer theory to suggest that organizations could become "places of pleasure rather than places of domination" (p. 942). They also suggest that instead of "workplaces being sites of domination, subordination, boredom and alienation, they should become places of pleasure as well as production, of fulfilment alongside employment, of enjoying our lives while earning a living" (Harding et al., 2011, p. 943). Relatedly, Vitry (2020) invites us to imagine how organizations could be changed in a way that removes expectations for punctuality and maximum productivity. From a queer CCO perspective, organizations like the ones described by Harding et al. (2011) and Vitry (2020) do not have to remain fictional, but can be constituted by communication processes. As such, queering CCO offers much hope for us to challenge the status quo, change organizations and organizing practices as we know them, and disrupt the (hetero) normativity of organizational life.

Note

1 For an extensive review of how queer theory has been mobilized in organizational scholarship, see McDonald and Kenney (forthcoming).

References

Alexander, B. K. (2003). Queerying queer theory again (or queer theory as drag performance). *Journal of Homosexuality, 45*(2–4), 349–352. https://doi.org/10.1300/J082v45n02_19.

Ashcraft, K. L. (2011). Knowing work through the communication of difference: A revised agenda for difference studies. In D. K. Mumby (Ed.), *Reframing difference in organizational communication studies: Research, pedagogy, practice* (pp. 3–29). Sage.

Ashcraft, K. L., Kuhn, T., & Cooren, F. (2009). Constitutional amendments: 'Materializing' organizational communication. In A. Brief & J. Walsh (Eds.), *The Academy of Management annals* (Vol. 3, pp. 1–64). Routledge.

Ashcraft, K. L., & Muhr, S. L. (2018). Coding military command as a promiscuous practice?: Unsettling the gender binaries of leadership metaphors. *Human Relations, 71*(2), 206–228. https://doi.org/10.1177/0018726717709080.

Bendl, R., Fleischmann, A., & Hofmann, R. (2009). Queer theory and diversity management: Reading codes of conduct from a queer perspective. *Journal of Management & Organization, 15*(5), 625–638. https://doi.org/10.1017/S1833367200002467.

Bendl, R., Fleischmann, A., & Walenta, C. (2008). Diversity management discourse meets queer theory. *Gender in Management, 23*(6), 382–394. https://doi.org/10.1108/17542410810897517.

Bendl, R., & Hofmann, R. (2015). Queer perspectives fuelling diversity management discourse: Theoretical and empirical-based reflections. In R. Bendl, I. Bleijenbergh, E. Henttonen, & A. J. Mills (Eds.), *The Oxford handbook of diversity in organizations* (pp. 195–217). Oxford University Press.

Bergeron, C. D., & Cooren, F. (2012). The collective framing of crisis management: A ventriloqual analysis of emergency operations centres. *Journal of Contingencies and Crisis Management, 20*(3), 120–137. https://doi.org/10.1111/j.1468-5973.2012.00671.x.

Bersani, L. (1995). *Homos.* Harvard University Press.

Branton, S. E., & Compton, C. A. (2021). There's no such thing as a gay bar: Co-sexuality and the neoliberal branding of queer spaces. *Management Communication Quarterly, 35*(1), 69–95. https://doi.org/10.1177/0893318920972113.

Burchiellaro, O. (2020). Queering control and inclusion in the contemporary organization: On 'LGBT-friendly control' and the reproduction of (queer) value. *Organization Studies.* https://doi.org/10.1177/0170840620944557.

Butler, J. (1990). *Gender trouble: Feminism and the subversion of identity.* Routledge.

Butler, J. (1993). *Bodies that matter: On the discursive limits of "sex".* Routledge.

Butler, J. (2004). *Undoing gender.* Routledge.

Chang, J., & Bowring, M. A. (2017). The perceived impact of sexual orientation on the ability of queer leaders to relate to followers. *Leadership, 13*(3), 285–300. https://doi.org/10.1177/1742715015586215.

Cohen, C. J. (2005). Punks, bulldaggers, and welfare queens: The radical potential of queer politics? In E. P. Johnson & M. G. Henderon (Eds.), *Black queer studies: A critical anthology* (pp. 21–51). Duke University Press.

Compton, C. A., & Dougherty, D. S. (2017). Organizing sexuality: Silencing and the push–pull process of co-sexuality in the workplace. *Journal of Communication, 67*(6), 874–896. https://doi.org/10.1111/jcom.12336.

Cooren, F. (2010). *Action and agency in dialogue: Passion, incarnation and ventriloquism.* John Benjamins.

Cooren, F. (2012). Communication theory at the center: Ventriloquism and the communicative constitution of reality. *Journal of Communication, 62*(1), 1–20. https://doi.org/10.1111/j.1460-2466.2011.01622.x.

Cooren, F., & Fairhurst, G. T. (2009). Dislocation and stabilization: How to scale up from interactions to organizations. In L. L. Putnam & G. T. Fairhurst (Eds.), *Building theories of organization: The constitutive role of communication* (pp. 117–152). Routledge.

Cooren, F., Matte, F., Benoit-Barné, C., & Brummans, B. H. J. M. (2013). Communication as ventriloquism: A grounded-in-action approach to the study of organizational tensions. *Communication Monographs, 80*(3), 255–277. https://doi.org/10.1080/03637751.2013.788255.

de Lauretis, T. (1991). Queer theory: Lesbian and gay sexualities. *differences: A Journal of Feminist Cultural Studies, 1*(2), 3–18.

Dixon, J. (2018). Looking out from the family closet: Discourse dependence and queer family identity in workplace conversation. *Management Communication Quarterly, 32*(2), 271–275. https://doi.org/10.1177/0893318917744067.

Eger, E. K. (2018). Transgender jobseekers navigating closeting communication. *Management Communication Quarterly, 32*(2), 276–281. https://doi.org/10.1177/0893318917740226.

Eguchi, S., & Asante, G. (2016). Disidentifications revisited: Queer(y)ing intercultural communication theory. *Communication Theory, 26*(2), 171–189. https://doi.org/10.1111/comt.12086

Elia, J. P. (2003). Queering relationships. *Journal of Homosexuality, 45*(2–4), 61–86. https://doi.org/10.1300/J082v45n02_03.

Ford, R. T. (2011). What's queer about race? In J. Halley & A. Parker (Eds.), *After sex?: On writing since queer theory* (pp. 121–129). Duke University Press.

Foucault, M. (1976). *Histoire de la sexualité I: La volonté de savoir*. Gallimard.

Gibson-Graham, J. K. (1996). Queer(y)ing capitalist organization. *Organization, 3*(4), 541–545. https://doi.org/10.1177/135050849634011.

Halperin, D. (2003). The normalization of queer theory. *Journal of Homosexuality, 45*(2–4), 339–343. https://doi.org/10.1300/J082v45n02_17.

Harding, N., Lee, H., Ford, J., & Learmonth, M. (2011). Leadership and charisma: A desire that cannot speak its name? *Human Relations, 64*(7), 927–949. https://doi.org/10.1177/0018726710393367.

Harris, K. L., & McDonald, J. (2018). Introduction: Queering the "closet" at work. *Management Communication Quarterly, 32*(2), 265–270. https://doi.org/10.1177/0893318917742517.

Jagose, A. (1996). *Queer theory: An introduction*. New York University Press.

Jagose, A. (2015). The trouble with antinormativity. *differences: A Journal of Feminist Cultural Studies, 26*(1), 26–47. https://doi.org/10.1215/10407391-2880591.

Johnson, E. P. (2001). "Quare" studies, or (almost) everything I know about queer studies I learned from my grandmother. *Text and Performance Quarterly, 21*(1), 1–25. https://doi.org/10.1080/10462930128119.

Koschmann, M. A., & McDonald, J. (2015). Organizational rituals, communication, and the question of agency. *Management Communication Quarterly, 29*(2), 229–256. https://doi.org/10.1177/0893318915572386.

Kuhn, T. R. (2008). A communicative theory of the firm: Developing an alternative perspective on intra-organizational power and stakeholder relationships. *Organization Studies, 29*(8–9), 1227–1254. https://doi.org/10.1177/0170840608094778.

Long, Z. (2016). A feminist ventriloquial analysis of hao gongzuo ("good work"): Politicizing Chinese post-1980s women's meanings of work. *Women's Studies in Communication, 39*(4), 422–441. https://doi.org/10.1080/07491409.2016.1224991.

Long, Z., King, A. S., & Buzzanell, P. M. (2018). Ventriloqual voicings of parenthood in graduate school: An intersectionality analysis of work-life negotiations. *Journal of Applied Communication Research, 46*(2), 223–242. https://doi.org/10.1080/00909882.2018.1435901.

Love, H. (2011). Queers _____ This. In J. Halley & A. Parker (Eds.), *After sex?: On writing since queer theory* (pp. 180–191). Duke University Press.

Lutgen-Sandvik, P., & McDermott, V. (2008). The constitution of employee-abusive organizations: A communication flows theory. *Communication Theory, 18*(2), 304–333. https://doi.org/10.1111/j.1468-2885.2008.00324.x.

Matte, F., & Boivin, G. (2020). A CCO perspective on autoethnography: researching, organizing, and constituting. In A. F. Herrmann (Ed.), *The Routledge international handbook of organizational autoethnography* (pp. 484–497). Routledge.

McDonald, J. (2013). Coming out in the field: A queer reflexive account of shifting researcher identity. *Management Learning, 44*(2), 127–143. https://doi.org/10.1177/1350507612473711.

McDonald, J. (2015). Organizational communication meets queer theory: Theorizing relations of "difference" differently. *Communication Theory, 25*(3), 310–329. https://doi.org/10.1111/comt.12060.

McDonald, J. (2016). Expanding queer reflexivity: The closet as a guiding metaphor for reflexive practice. *Management Learning, 47*(4), 391–406. https://doi.org/10.1177/1350507615610029.

McDonald, J. (2017). Queering methodologies and organizational research: Disrupting, critiquing, and exploring. *Qualitative Research in Organizations and Management, 12*(2), 130–148. https://doi.org/10.1108/QROM-06-2016-1388.

McDonald, J., Harris, K. L., & Ramirez, J. (2020). Revealing and concealing difference: A critical approach to disclosure and an intersectional theory of 'closeting'. *Communication Theory, 30*(1), 84–104. https://doi.org/10.1093/ct/qtz017.

McDonald, J. & Kenney, S. C. (forthcoming). Queer studies and organizational communication. In I. L. West (Ed.), *Oxford encyclopedia of queer studies and communication*. Oxford University Press. https://doi.org/10.1093/acrefore/9780190228613.013.1289.

McPhee, R. D., & Zaug, P. (2000). The communicative constitution of organizations: A framework for explanation. *Electronic Journal of Communication, 10*(1–2).

Mease, J. J. (2020). Techniques and forces and the communicative constitution of organization: A Deleuzian approach to organizational (in)stability and power. *Management Communication Quarterly*. https://doi.org/10.1177/0893318920969969.

Mease, J. J., & Terry, D. P. (2012). [Organizational (performance] of race): The co-constitutive performance of race and school board in Durham, NC. *Text and Performance Quarterly, 32*(2), 121–140. https://doi.org/10.1080/10462937.2011.653390.

Muhr, S. L., & Sullivan, K. R. (2013). "None so queer as folk": Gendered expectations and transgressive bodies in leadership. *Leadership, 9*(3), 416–435. https://doi.org/10.1177/1742715013485857.

Mumby, D. K. (2019). Communication constitutes capital: Branding and the politics of neoliberal dis/organization. In C. Vásquez & T. Kuhn (Eds.), *Dis/organization as communication: Exploring the disordering, disruptive and chaotic properties of communication* (pp. 125–147). Routledge.

O'Shea, S. C. (2018). This girl's life: An autoethnography. *Organization, 25*(1), 3–20. https://doi.org/10.1177/1350508417703471.

Parker, M. (2001). Fucking management: Queer, theory and reflexivity. *Ephemera, 1*(1), 36–53.

Parker, M. (2002). Queering management and organization. *Gender, Work & Organization, 9*(2), 146–166. https://doi.org/10.1111/1468-0432.00153.

Parker, M. (2016). Queering queer. *Gender, Work & Organization, 23*(1), 71–73. https://doi.org/10.1111/gwao.12106.

Riach, K., Rumens, N., & Tyler, M. (2016). Towards a Butlerian methodology: Undoing organizational performativity through anti-narrative research. *Human Relations, 69*(11), 2069–2089. https://doi.org/10.1177/0018726716632050.

Rumens, N. (2013). Organisation studies: Not nearly 'queer enough'. In Y. Taylor & M. Addison (Eds.), *Queer presences and absences* (pp. 241–259). Palgrave Macmillan.

Rumens, N. (2015). Is your workplace 'gay-friendly'?: Current issues and controversies. In F. Colgan & N. Rumens (Eds.), *Sexual orientation at work: Contemporary issues and perspectives* (pp. 181–196). Routledge.

Rumens, N. (2018a). *Queer business: Queering organization sexualities.* Routledge.

Rumens, N. (2018b). Queered methodologies for equality, diversity and inclusion researchers. In L. A. E. Booysen, R. Bendl, & K. Pringle (Eds.), *Handbook of research methods in diversity management, equality and inclusion at work* (pp. 103–121). Edward Elgar.

Rumens, N., de Souza, E., & Brewis, J. (2019). Queering queer theory in management and organization studies: Notes toward queering heterosexuality. *Organization Studies, 40*(4), 593–612. https://doi.org/10.1177/0170840617748904.

Rumens, N., & Kerfoot, D. (2009). Gay men at work: (Re)constructing the self as professional. *Human Relations, 62*(5), 763–786. https://doi.org/10.1177/0018726709103457.

Schoeneborn, D., Blaschke, S., Cooren, F., McPhee, R. D., Seidl, D., & Taylor, J. R. (2014). The three schools of CCO thinking: Interactive dialogue and systematic comparison. *Management Communication Quarterly, 28*(2), 285–316. https://doi.org/10.1177/0893318914527000.

Schoeneborn, D., Kuhn, T. R., & Kärreman, D. (2019). The communicative constitution of organization, organizing, and organizationality. *Organization Studies, 40*(4), 475–496. https://doi.org/10.1177/0170840618782284.

Sedgwick, E. K. (1990). *Epistemology of the closet.* University of California Press.

Seidman, S. (1993). Identity and politics in a "postmodern" gay culture: Some historical and conceptual notes. In M. Warner (Ed.), *Fear of a queer planet: Queer politics and social theory* (pp. 105–142). University of Minnesota Press.

Seidman, S. (1997). *Difference troubles: Queering social theory and sexual politics.* Cambridge University Press.

Taylor, J. R. (2009). Organizing from the bottom up? Reflections on the constitution of organization in communication. In L. L. Putnam & A. M. Nicotera (Eds.), *Building theories of organization: The constitutive role of communication* (pp. 153–186). Routledge.

Taylor, J. R., & Van Every, E. J. (2000). *The emergent organization: Communication as its site and surface.* Lawrence Erlbaum.

Vásquez, C. (2016). A spatial grammar of organising: studying the communicative constitution of organisational spaces. *Communication Research and Practice, 2*(3), 351–377. https://doi.org/10.1080/22041451.2016.1221686.

Vitry, C. (2020). Queering space and organising with Sara Ahmed's queer phenomenology. *Gender, Work & Organization.* https://doi.org/10.1111/gwao.12560.

Warner, M. (1999). *The trouble with normal: Sex, politics, and the ethics of queer life.* The Free Press.

Wiegman, R., & Wilson, E. A. (2015). Introduction: Antinormativity's queer conventions. *differences: A Journal of Feminist Cultural Studies, 26*(1), 1–25. https://doi.org/10.1215/10407391-2880582.

Wilhoit, E. D. (2016). Organizational space and place beyond container or construction: Exploring workspace in the communicative constitution of organizations. *Annals of the International Communication Association, 40*(1), 247–275. https://doi.org/10.1080/23808985.2015.11735262.

Wilhoit, E. D. (2018). Space, place, and the communicative constitution of organizations: A constitutive model of organizational space. *Communication Theory*, *28*(3), 311–331. https://doi.org/10.1093/ct/qty007.

Wilhoit, E. D., & Kisselburgh, L. G. (2015). Collective action without organization: The material constitution of bike commuters as collective. *Organization Studies*, *36*(5), 573–592. https://doi.org/10.1177/0170840614556916.

Wilhoit, E. D., & Kisselburgh, L. G. (2019). The relational ontology of resistance: Hybridity, ventriloquism, and materiality in the production of bike commuting as resistance. *Organization*, *26*(6), 873–893 https://doi.org/10.1177/1350508417723719.

Wilhoit Larson, E. (2020). Where is an organization? How workspaces are appropriated to become (partial and temporary) organizational spaces. *Management Communication Quarterly*, *34*(3), 299–327. https://doi.org/10.1177/0893318920933590.

Williams, C., Giuffre, P., & Dellinger, K. (2009). The gay-friendly closet. *Sexuality Research & Social Policy*, *6*(1), 29–45. https://doi.org/10.1525/srsp.2009.6.1.29.

Yep, G. A. (2003). The violence of heteronormativity in communication studies: Notes on injury, healing, and queer world-making. *Journal of Homosexuality*, *45*(2–4), 11–59. https://doi.org/10.1300/J082v45n02_02.

Yep, G. A. (2013). Queering/quaring/kauering/crippin'/transing 'other bodies' in intercultural communication. *Journal of Intercultural and International Communication*, *6*(2), 118–126. https://doi.org/10.1080/17513057.2013.777087.

Yep, G. A., Lovaas, K. E., & Elia, J. P. (2003). Introduction: Queering communication: Starting the conversation. *Journal of Homosexuality*, *45*(2–4), 1–10. https://doi.org/10.1300/J082v45n02_01.

Young, I. M. (1980). Throwing like a girl: A phenomenology of feminine body comportment motility and spatiality. *Human Studies*, *3*(1), 137–156. https://doi.org/10.1007/BF02331805.

PART II

Opening Up CCO's Methodological Approaches

12

THE UMBRELLA OF DISCOURSE ANALYSIS AND ITS ROLE IN CCO

Theresa Castor

The Umbrella of Discourse Analysis and Its Role in CCO

With the interpretive and linguistic turns, discourse has played an important role in theorizing and researching organizations/organizing as communicatively constituted. As Deetz and Eger (2014) explain, "Language is core to the process of coconstituting the indeterminate and ambiguous internal, social, and external world into specific objects and events" (p. 33). In tracing the development of CCO from the interpretive paradigm, Boivin, Brummans, and Barker (2017) state that discourse "came to be seen as the constitutive force of organizations, and organizations were increasingly seen as 'discursive constructions' (Fairhurst & Putnam, 2004)" (p. 334; also see Cooren, 2015b; Fairhurst & Cooren, 2018; Fairhurst & Putnam, 2004). Jian, Schmisseur, and Fairhurst (2008, p. 300) even argue that "common to discourse studies are the assumptions that discourse is constitutive of organizations (Fairhurst and Putnam, 2004)".

Discourse analysis itself is an umbrella term that:

> represents a broad class of approaches examining the constitutive effects of language; processes of text production, distribution, and consumption; and reflexive, interpretive analysis aimed at deciphering the role of discourse in a socially constructed reality (Grant et al., 2011, p. xvii).
>
> *Fairhurst & Cooren, 2018, p. 82*

This broadness can be daunting, especially to "newcomers to discourse analysis" (Wood & Kroger, 2000, p. 18) given that there is not just one method of discourse analysis, let alone a uniform and agreed upon way to parse discourse analysis as a set of methods. In other words, there is not *a* discourse analytic approach, rather, there are a multiplicity of discourse analytic approaches. An additional, problematizing circumstance is the ambiguity of the term "discourse analysis". In their analysis of CCO scholarship, Boivin, Brummans, and Barker (2017) noted that slightly more than half of the studies that they identified:

> Used a combination of conversation, discourse, and/or interaction analysis. *The distinction between these approaches was not always clear, however, and terms such as "conversation*

DOI: 10.4324/9781003224914-15

analysis," "discourse analysis," and "interaction analysis" were often used interchangeably or synonymously. Moreover, many authors did not specify their type of analysis at all. (p. 340, emphasis added)

Boivin et al. also note that, in CCO research generally, there has been a "lack of methodological explicitness and clarity" (p. 340) in specifying data collection and analysis procedures.

Given the importance of discourse in CCO theorizing, the purpose of this chapter is to explicate the relationship between discourse, discourse analysis, and the Communicative Constitution of Organization. Several works have already provided thorough reviews of discourse analysis in organizational communication and organization studies (e.g., Alvesson & Karreman, 2000; Chia, 2000; Cooren, 2015b; Fairhurst & Putnam, 2014; Grant, Hardy, Oswick, & Putnam, 2004; Hardy, Grant, Keenoy, Oswick, & Phillips, 2004; Philips & Oswick, 2012). In addition, there are journal special issues that feature debates regarding the nature and status of discourse in organizational studies (e.g., Alvesson & Kärreman, 2011; Jian, Schmisseur, & Fairhurst, 2008; Phillips & Oswick, 2012). This chapter's aim is to describe the nuanced relationship between DA and CCO with the goal of explaining how DA can be applied for analyzing constitutive processes. In the following, discourse analysis as a methodology will be explained with attention to differentiating it from other qualitative approaches. This will be followed by a discussion of the relationship between discourse, discourse analysis, and the CCO perspective. The chapter concludes by addressing two, inter-related challenges in applying DA in CCO research—analyzing materiality and multi-modal data.

What is Discourse Analysis?

This section proceeds by, first, defining discourse and discourse analysis; second, delineating some communities of practice associated with DA that are oriented toward analyzing organizational communication; third, describing what DA is and is not; and fourth, identifying similarities and dissimilarities between DA and other qualitative approaches.

Discourse and Discourse Analysis: Definitions and Delineations

Discourse can be described as "language use" in contrast to notions of language that are abstracted from what people actually say (Van Dijk, 1997). Fairhurst and Cooren (2008) state that discourses are "meaning systems anchored in socio-historical time that source and constrain communicating actors simultaneously" (p. 82). Philips and Oswick (2012) add that discourse is "a structured collection of texts (Parker, 1992) along with associated practices of textual production, transmission and reception" (p. 3). Classifications of organizational discourse have tended to focus on "level of analysis" or "type of method" (Phillips & Oswick, 2012, p. 435). For the purpose of presenting basic background, in the following, I first describe "levels of analysis" of discourse and then discuss some methods of discourse analysis, noting that this division is not without its problems (see Phillips & Oswick, 2012).

Commonly, discourse has been delineated as *d*iscourse (with a little 'd') and *D*iscourse (with a big 'D') (see Alvesson & Kärreman, 2000). Little 'd' discourse focuses on the "micro" or situated uses of language in interactions. Big 'D' Discourse is often referred to as a Foucauldian approach and attempts to "cut through the variation at the local levels through summaries and syntheses that identify overarching themes operating in specific situations" (Alvesson & Kärreman, 2000, p. 1134). In their analysis of organizational discourse studies published between 1981 and 2006, Jian, Schmisseur, and Fairhurst (2008) identified varied meanings of "discourse". showing "that the differentiation between little 'd' and big 'D' discourses continues to be a viable marker characterizing two distinct approaches to organizational discourse" (p. 304). They also noted a third usage that "deals with the interplay between little 'd' and big 'D' discourses" (p. 304).

Discourse analysis is *both* a perspective *and* methodology "based on a radical constructivist epistemology" (Hardy, 2001, p. 28). As methodology, discourse analysis encompasses approaches such as conversation analysis, discursive psychology, ethnomethodology, semiotics, speech act analysis, narrative analysis, critical discourse analysis, Foucauldian discourse analysis (Cooren, 2015b; Jian, Schmisseur, & Fairhurst, 2008). This diversity can be attributed to the multiple disciplines from which DA approaches were developed such as sociology, linguistics, anthropology, communication, and literary studies (Phillips & Oswick, 2012; also see Grant et al., 2004).

Discourse analysis as applied to the study of organizations is associated with varied "communities of practice". Cooren (2015b) explains of the development of "organizational discourse" that:

> this academic movement – which was, at the outset, UK based, mainly in British business schools – posited that the detailed and systematic study of discourse could be a very innovative and productive path to better understand, analyze, or denounce how organizations function or fail to do so. (p. 2)

Grant and Iedema (2005) distinguish Organizational Discourse Studies (ODS) from Organizational Discourse Analysis (ODA): ODS emerged from within organization and management studies, whereas ODA approaches are "linguistic-based" (p. 38). Subsequently, ODS consists of management scholars who pay attention to discourse, whereas ODA consists of discourse analysts who study organizational discourse. A key distinction between organizational discourse analysis and discourse analytic studies within organizational contexts lies in the research questions being posed and whether or not a given study that examines discourse does so with the goal of contributing to the understanding of processes of organizing. There are conceptual entailments associated with the very idea of discourse—these include naturally occurring language use, symbols and meanings, interaction, and context. Key to discourse analysis is that it is not just about studying verbal communication or about using qualitative research to study communication.

Similarities and Dissimilarities between DA and Other Approaches

Philips and Oswick (2012) distinguish between discourse analysis and traditional qualitative methods in that discourse analysis:

> does not take the social world as it is and seeks to understand the meaning of this world for participants … . Instead, it tries to explore the ways in which the socially produced ideas and objects that populate the world come to be, or are enacted, through discourse. (p. 12)

Given some of the specific guidelines of doing discourse analysis, in the following I describe some commonly used qualitative methods to identify what it is about these approaches that are similar to, as well as different from, a discourse analytic approach. In their review of CCO studies, Boivin, Brummans, and Barker (2017) noted that 86.8% used "naturalistic or (quasi-)ethnographic approach[es]", 54.4% "used a combination of conversation, discourse, and/or interaction analysis", and 30.9% used "other qualitative methods such as thematic analysis or narrative analysis" (pp. 340–341). For this reason, I focus on distinguishing discourse analysis from ethnography and thematic analysis.

Discourse and Ethnography

Ethnography refers to specific types of methods for gathering data that involve qualitative data and participant-observation research on what people do in their everyday lives (as opposed to in a lab, unless the "lab" itself is the context of interest, e.g., Latour & Woolgar, 1979). This research method can also include data such as interviews or documents (Burgess, 2002; Spradley, 2016). While ethnography and discourse analysis have productive intersections, doing ethnography is not the same as doing discourse analysis. This section begins with a brief explanation of ethnography to lay the groundwork for delineating how it is distinct from DA.

Ethnography has a specific meaning and history within anthropology:

> In etymological terms, "ethnography" means "writing about people," or "writing an account of the way of life of a particular people." In early anthropology, the aim was a descriptive account of distinctive social or cultural features of a particular society. In this, ethnography was sometimes contrasted with ethnology, which was concerned with the comparative analysis of cultures, often in terms of some evolutionary scheme.
>
> *Hammersley, 2015, online*

Ethnography is a process of data gathering (i.e., "doing ethnography") as well as the product of the research (i.e., "writing an ethnography").

How ethnographic data is analyzed depends on the theoretical perspective. Ethnography can be utilized for discourse analytic research *if* language use in social interactions is the subject matter being studied (Atkinson, Okada, & Talmy, 2011). For instance, the ethnography of communication (Hymes, 1964; Philipsen, 1992; Ray, Biswas & Bengal, 2011) and cultural discourse analysis (Carbaugh, 2014) are ethnographic and discourse analytic. While these have been applied mainly in cultural communication, there are applications for analyzing organizational communication (Kalou & Sadler-Smith, 2015). As addressed elsewhere in this volume (see Brummans & Vézy), ethnography itself has been applied productively in CCO projects. For example, Cooren's ethnographic research on Médecins sans Frontières has advanced CCO theorizing on authority (Benoit-Barné & Cooren, 2009) and organizational presence (Cooren, Brummans, & Charrieras, 2008; Fairhurst & Cooren, 2009). Brummans' ethnographic research of a Buddhist monastery has provided insights on mindfulness and organizing (Brummans, 2012, 2014).

While ethnography may include the study of verbal communication, the analysis of verbal or textual data does not in and of itself constitute discourse analysis. Ethnography may use verbal communication as part of the information that is described in a researcher's field notes of observations, but the collection of discursive data does not in and of itself constitute discourse *analysis*. What distinguishes discourse analysis as such is that discourse itself is a prominent aspect of what is being studied. In other words, a discourse analytic perspective would be interested in the nuances of language use which is not necessarily a defining characteristic of ethnography.

Thematic Analysis

Boivin, Brummans, and Barker (2017) note the prominence of CCO studies that "relied on ... qualitative methods such as thematic analysis or narrative analysis" (p. 341; see also Schoeneborn &

Vásquez, 2017). While narrative analysis is a form of discourse analysis (Cooren, 2015b), this is not the case for thematic analysis, which involves the identification of common topics and subjects within the communication being studied. Owen (1984) defined the criteria of force-fulness, recurrence, and repetition for identifying themes. Thematic analysis has also been used in conjunction with qualitative coding (see Lofland & Lofland, 1995; Miles & Huberman, 1994; Strauss & Corbin, 1990). While thematic analysis attends to verbal communication, it differs from DA in the focus of analysis, as the remainder of this section explicates.

Thematic analysis is versatile in that it can be applied to qualitative data generally, whether collected through interviews, field observations, or documents. Thematic analysis has been used for CCO research alone (e.g., Koschmann, 2013; Koschmann & McDonald, 2015; Wilhoit & Kisselburgh, 2015) as well as in conjunction with other forms of qualitative analysis (e.g., Grosjean, Bonneville, & Redpath, 2019).

Thematic analysis can be compared to some strands of DA. In particular, the distinction between thematic analysis and the study of Discourse is blurry. Phillips and Oswick (2012) explain that the study of Discourse focuses "not so much on the specifics of the language used, but more on the coherence of the underlying concepts and ideas contained in a particular set of texts" (p. 10). Cooren (2015b) provides a similar description in associating the study of Discourse with a "focus on the repetition, reproduction, or iteration of specific topics of discussion, styles of communication, and rights to speak" (pp. 6–7).

Fairhurst and Cooren (2018) describe a distinction between grounded theory and discourse analysis that can also be applied to thematic analysis in that these "mainly rely on actors' language to identify content themes in the data in order to translate them into scientific concepts (Charmaz, 2006; Tracy, 2013)" (p. 83). In contrast to DA, the organizing functions of language use and language use as an organized activity are not the subjects of study in thematic analysis.

Doing Discourse Analysis

In this section, I offer general guidelines for doing discourse analysis by describing characteristics of data, analysis, and forms of analytic claim that generally characterize discourse analysis, noting that how one does discourse analysis will depend on the specific discourse analytic approach.

What counts as data? Discourse analysts examine language use, talk, conversations, and/or texts. Other labels can be applied that also point to specific analytic frameworks such as narratives, speech acts, metacommunication, accounts, etc. A starting step in doing discourse analysis involves the identification of a *discursive* unit of analysis. Jian et al. (2008) summarize attention to little 'd' discourse as involving the study of "moment by moment talk-in-interaction and creation of local texts" (p. 304). Big 'D' discourse involves the study of "culturally standardized interpretive frames historically rooted in systems of power/knowledge" and includes "linguistic and extra-linguistic activities" (p. 304). Whether studying discourse or Discourse, common across these is an interest in naturally occurring language—words matter.

What counts as analysis? Discourse analysis stems from the linguistic turn in that language is not viewed as a "reflection" or representation of reality. When discourse analysts study language, it is to understand how social reality is discursively constituted. Coming from a little 'd' orientation, Antaki (2002, online) identified the following "ways of treating talk and textual data … which fall short of discourse analysis": under-analysis through summary; under-analysis through taking sides; under-analysis through over-quotation or through isolated quotation; the circular identification of discourses and mental constructs; false survey; and analysis that consists in simply spotting features.

Analysis of discourse involves attending to the specifics of language use in context. For example, in our study of Louisiana emergency management teleconferences during the Hurricane Katrina disaster, my colleague and I analyzed metacommunication and "reporting" to interrogate how problems were discursively constructed as well as obfuscated through meeting talk (Castor & Bartesaghi, 2016).

What are the forms of analytic claims? Discourse analysis goes beyond describing or summarizing, but involves interpreting and making sense of what was said or written. Antaki (2002) is critical of "over-quotation" and focusing on the "isolated" quotation. These shortcomings overrely on quoting as a substitute for analysis. As a guide, Antaki suggests being aware of "a low ratio of analyst's comments to data extracts" (p. 6). Also, he cautions against taking quotations out of context, which could result from focusing on the isolated quotation. Discourse analysis does not just repeat what is stated in a transcription or written text. Rather, DA takes discourse as a starting point for analyzing the role of specific uses of language in constitutive processes.

The Relationship of Discourse Analysis to CCO

To address the relationship between DA and CCO, I describe background theorizing on "organizations as discursive constructions" before turning to specific applications of DA to understanding CCO processes.

The Discursive Construction of Organizations

Acknowledging the growth of discourse analysis in studying organizations at the time of their groundbreaking article, Fairhurst and Putnam (2004) laid out three framings with respect to the relationship between discourse and organizations: object orientation; becoming orientation; and grounded in action. The "object" orientation views organizations as an "already formed object with discursive features or outcomes" (p. 10). In this orientation, discourse does not play a constitutive role in organizing, rather, discourse is an "outcome" or product of the organization. This perspective is also known as the "container" perspective of organizations. In the "becoming" orientation, discourse plays a fundamental role in organizing: "discourse exists prior to organizations because the properties of language and interaction produce organizing" (p. 13). Discourse constitutes the "micro- and macroaspects of organizations" (p. 13). In the "grounded in action" orientation, the relationship between discourse and organization is more nuanced: "action and structure are mutually constitutive" and "the organization never assumes the form of an identifiable entity because it is anchored at the level of social practices and discursive forms" (p. 16). Because it is "grounded in action", this perspective emphasizes little 'd' discourse analytic approaches such as ethnomethodology and conversation analysis.

Fairhurst and Putnam (2004) highlighted the multi-faceted relationship between discourse and organization, and how these perspectives are consequential for our understanding of organizations. The three perspectives are not mutually exclusive and may complement each other in that they can "play off each other to reveal different aspects of the communication-organization relationship" (Putnam & Fairhurst, 2015, p. 377).

Approximately a decade later, in reflecting on "organizations as discursive constructions", Putnam and Fairhurst (2015) state regarding connections with CCO approaches:

> the three orientations that we set forth in [Fairhurst & Putnam, 2004] served as a precursor to and a parallel development with the work on CCO that was surfacing at this time. It explored how scholars could make the leap from organizing as enacted

through communication to organization as anchored in discursive forms. Thus, it joined with but differed from two schools of thought about CCO. (p. 378)

Putnam and Fairhurst described the Montréal School approach as a "grounded-in action" approach and the Four Flows approach as addressing all three orientations.

Theorizing on the "discursive construction of organizations" establishes a basis for understanding how discourse analysis can be used to understand CCO processes. Schoeneborn and Vásquez (2017) explain:

Yet, one important source of novelty in CCO thinking is that it puts to the fore an ontological inquiry: what is an organization? Whereas other discourse-communication perspectives do not question the ontology of organization, CCO approaches take it as starting point. The constitutive premise can be seen as a preliminary answer to what could be considered as a programmatic agenda: unfolding and detailing the role of communication (in its various forms) to develop an answer as to how communication constitutes organization. (p. 14)

Schoeneborn and Vásquez are careful in identifying that not all discursive perspectives of organizations are CCO. There should be caution exercised in assuming that a given discourse analytic study of organizational communication is by default a CCO study given that discourse analysis itself does not neatly align with a specific paradigm or ontological and epistemological assumptions. As Grant et al. (2004) explain:

Within the broader social sciences, [discourse analysis] has been used in order to promulgate various positivist, social constructivist and postmodern perspectives about a range of social phenomena (Brown & Yule, 1983; Fairclough, 1995; Potter & Wetherell, 1987; Schiffrin, 1987; Silverman, 1993; Van Dijk, 1997a, 1997b). (p. 1)

Further complicating the organization, discourse, and communication relationship, Jian, Schmisseur, and Fairhurst (2008) noted in their analysis of organizational discourse studies that only a little more than half used the term "communication", and these studies had a diversity of perspectives on communication: as information transmission; as meaning construction; and, as inter-action. Organizational discourse studies published within communication journals tended to adopt a constitutive view of communication. Conversely, the articles published in outlets outside of the communication discipline tended to adopt an information transmission or interaction perspective.

While not all organizational discourse studies are CCO projects, conversely, not all CCO studies are discourse-oriented in that there is a difference between a "discourse constitutes" and "communication constitutes" approach (Putnam & Fairhurst, 2015; also see the 2008 special issue of *Discourse and Communication*) in that the notion of discourse tends to either exclude or downplay the role of "non-discursive" artifacts in the communicative constitution of organization. A DA-CCO project is one in which the study of discourse is a prominent (though not exclusive) aspect of understanding the communicative constitution of organization. The claims advanced within a DA-CCO project would shed light specifically on constitutive issues such as the ontological nature of organizations or specific constructs relating to organizational communication such as authority (e.g., Bencherki, Matte, & Cooren, 2019) or organizational failure (e.g., Taylor & Van Every, 2014). Next, I describe some DA approaches that have been used in CCO projects highlighting how those approaches have also provided insight into understanding constitutive processes.

(Some) Discursive Approaches for Understanding CCO Processes

While several discursive approaches can be applied to understanding CCO, there are some that stand out given their close connection to developing theorizing in CCO. Also, I wish to note that while any given CCO approach could utilize discourse analysis, the Montréal School is closely associated with discursive approaches. The DA approaches I highlight are speech act theory, conversation analysis, narrative analysis, and ventriloquism.

Speech Act Theory

Speech act theory was developed by British philosopher John L. Austin (1962) and added to by his student, American philosopher John Searle (1969; Cooren, 2015b). A key contribution of speech act theory is the understanding of the performative nature of language (i.e., words *do* things), in contrast to representational views of language. Cooren (2015b) explains:

> speech acts can be considered the building blocks by which organizing takes place (Cooren, 2000; Taylor, 1993), which, of course, means this approach clearly demonstrates how organization and organizing are *communicatively constituted*. (p. 30)

Bisel (2009) identified speech acts as common across some organizational discourse approaches. Speech acts are also pertinent to understanding a significant way that agency has been conceptualized from within the Montréal School approach. For example, Cooren (2004a) has argued for the agency of texts (i.e., "textual agency") vis-à-vis the analysis of speech acts.

The application of speech acts is not exclusive to the Montréal School, however, as Dobusch and Schoeneborn's (2015) study of the hacker collective *Anonymous* illustrates. They ground their work broadly within CCO, drawing eclectically from the Montréal School, Four Flows, and Luhmann's (1999) organizational systems work. Dobusch and Schoenenborn illustrate a growing refinement of CCO in addressing what is "organizational" about a social collective. Schoeneborn, Kuhn, and Kärreman (2019) describe this as taking an "adjective" approach by asking what is "organizational" about a social collective rather than framing their constitutive research question in terms of "what is an organization" ("noun" approach) or how organizing takes place ("verb" approach) (also see Schoeneborn, Blagoev, & Dobusch, this volume).

Analyses that apply speech act theory start with transcripts and, from there, identify "the organizing effects of different speech acts performed during an episode" (Fairhurst & Cooren, 2004, p. 140). In doing this, researchers make inferences on what is "being accomplished" through the talk.

Conversation Analysis

Conversation analysis (CA) "focuses on the detailed organization of talk-in-interaction" (Fairhurst & Cooren, 2004, p. 134; see Aggerholm, Asmuß, Ladegaard Johannesen & Feddersen Smith, this volume). CA is based on American sociologist Harold Garfinkel's work in developing ethnomethodology, a micro-sociological approach that calls attention to the role of everyday practices in constituting social life and social order: "Ethnomethodology literally means the study of the methods (*methodo-*) people (*ethno-*) mobilize in their daily life to generate social order" (emphasis in original, Cooren, 2015b, p. 31). Developed by Harvey Sacks, Emmanuel Schlegoff, and Gail Jefferson, conversation analysis is an "empirical" approach to analyzing the "ethnomethods" described by Garfinkel. A contribution of CA is attention to the details of interactions such as turn-taking, pauses, intonation, interruptions, and more (Sacks, Schegloff, & Jefferson, 1978).

While Garfinkel's theorizing has close associations with the study of work (e.g., Garfinkel, 2017; Rawls, 2008), Boden's (1994) *The Business of Talk* is a key work in applying CA to the study of organizations. As Taylor and Van Every (2000) explain of Boden's work,

> it integrates not only principles of ethnomethodology informed by a grounding in conversation analysis, but also is sensitive to both sociological theories (the structuration theory of Giddens, in particular) and several well-known management theories of organizations (Weick, Stinchcombe, Pfeffer, and March among others). (p. 13)

Conversation analysis studies organizations as they are "talked into being". This entails a close grounding to what is present in conversation. In terms of methodological process, CA requires a detailed transcription of conversation that represents not just what was said, but also *how* it was said, as well as nonverbal communication (see Antaki, 2002, for a useful online guide). After transcription, Clifton (2019) explains that analysis, then:

> focuses on the sequential organisation of talk, turn design, and the action that these turns and sequences of talk achieve. The underlying question that motivates such analyses is: why this (utterance, turn, sequence, etc.) now? (p. 346)

Clifton (2019) provides an excellent illustration of applying CA to the study of leadership as an *in situ* practice from a CCO perspective. Clifton's analysis shows how, in turn by turn sequences, a leader presented ("downgraded") epistemic claims through modifiers ("a bit like") and hesitations ("er") and established rapport through humor, and, through these, facilitated an organizational decision.

Additional examples of the application of CA for CCO research include Cooren's (2004b) study of the "achievement of collective minding" in a board meeting, Cooren, Brummans, and Charrieras's (2008) study of organizational presence, and Vásquez and Cooren's (2013) study of "spacing practices". Although CA has been useful in showing how organizations are communicatively constituted moment-by-moment within interactions, it has been critiqued for ignoring the role of context and factors not visible from within a conversation (see McPhee, Myers, & Trethewey, 2006, as well as Cooren, 2006, for a rejoinder).

Narrative Analysis

In examining organizational stories, narrative analysis calls attention to relations among organizational actors and how they make sense of the organization and related events (see Czarniawska, 2007). Narrative analysis takes into consideration broader units of talk than speech act analysis or conversation analysis. Narrative analysis does have some divergences from CCO in that the latter focuses more sharply on materiality and disorder (Schoeneborn, Kuhn, & Kärreman, 2019).

Despite the divergences, narrative analysis has been applied in fruitful ways within CCO. For instance, scholars working within the Montréal school have drawn on the narrative work of Algirdas J. Greimas (see Bencherki & Cooren, 2011; Cooren, 1999; Taylor & Van Every, 2000). Narrative analysis illustrates how organizational actors make associations between other actors and entities which in turn has implications for understanding agency (i.e., who or what is doing something) as well as action (i.e., what was done). Drawing from Greimas, Cooren (1999) explains the stages of a narrative as consisting of: (1) a triggering event that disrupts the social order ("manipulation phase"); (2) the protagonist commits to restoring the social order, enlisting helpers and overcoming barriers ("competence phase"); (3) the protagonist takes actions to accomplish the mission ("performance phase"); and, (4) the conclusion where the protagonist is praised for success or blamed for failure ("sanction phase").

In conducting narrative analysis, one can analyze data gathered from a single communication episode, as in Robichaud, Giroux, and Taylor's (2004) study of a city's public meeting, or from across multiple episodes, as in Cooren's (2001) study of an environmental controversy surrounding a proposal for a dam development project of the Great Whale River in Québec. Common across these projects is the gathering of a wide range of data that includes organizational documents and texts as part of understanding the narrative context. Cooren's project also illustrates how narrative analysis can be inclusive of communication events across time and space; in other words, narrative analysis can draw from multiple different communication events in different physical locations.

Ventriloquial Approach

Ventriloquism theory was developed by CCO scholar François Cooren (2010; Cooren, Matte, Benoit-Barné, & Brummans, 2013). Using ventriloquism as a metaphor, this theory advances that when one speaks, it is on behalf of others, whether it be humans, texts, or "nonhumans" such as objects. While ventriloquism has relied upon some specific discourse analytic approaches such as ethnomethodology, conversation analysis, narrative analysis, and others, it has reached a level of development such that it has been described with its own specific methodology (see Nathues, van Vuuren, & Cooren, 2020). For this reason, I group the ventriloquial approach as residing within the constellation of discourse analytic approaches applied for understanding CCO processes. However, whereas the methods described so far in this section originated outside of and preceding CCO, the ventriloquial perspective was developed as a CCO theory (see Nathues & Van Vuuren, this volume).

In terms of data gathering, ventriloquial analysis has similarities to conversation analysis as well as narrative analysis in that it is attentive to the details and nuances of naturally occurring language use and is inclusive of context and multi-site interactions. However, the ventriloquial approach diverges from CA and narrative analysis in its theoretical commitments. It is both theory and method, and as such it is specifically interested in describing how people, documents or technologies are made to speak on behalf of someone or something else (i.e., how "vents" lend their voice to "figures" that speak through them). Vasilyeva, Robles, Saludadez, Schwägerl, and Castor (2020) describe how to conduct ventriloquial analysis using a three-step process: (1) record or collect recordings of interactions; (2) identify markers in which "figures appear to recurrently and iteratively express themselves in the interactions" (p. 48); and (3) develop interpretations related to what the figures appear to be saying. Nathues, van Vuuren, and Cooren (2020) provide, for their part, a four-step framework: (1) identifying; (2) grouping and assigning activities; (3) relating; and (4) showing. Nathues et al.'s steps two and three correspond to Vasilyeva et al.'s steps one and two, respectively. Nathues et al.'s relating step involves "relating clusters and collections to main voices by tracing back chains of authorship, possibly including a visual model" (p. 6), and showing entails choices regarding data display.

Post-Discourse: Departure or Evolution?

Current research and theorizing in CCO has also addressed challenges accompanying discourse analytic approaches. Here, I address some of the ways that this has been done by highlighting re-theorizing of the material and video-ethnography as a methodology. In addressing these,

I recognize that there is a fine line between describing these as "departures" or as evolution in theorizing and research using discourse analysis. I prefer to think of these as evolutionary given that the fundamental insights and methodologies of discourse analysis are still used as a basis for understanding CCO, along with other bases.

Addressing the Material

Phillips and Oswick (2012) described four ways in which discourse and materiality can be related: as competing ("discourse *not* materiality"); as complementary ("discourse *or* materiality"); as connected ("discourse *and* materiality"); and as co-constituted ("discourse *as* materiality") (p. 39, emphasis in original). The first approach minimizes the role of the material. The second and third approaches assume that discursively constructed world(s) *and* material worlds co-exist but while the second approach acknowledges this, the third approach combines the study of both in a "realist" approach (Phillips & Oswick, 2012; Reed, 2004). The fourth relationship is best aligned with a CCO approach. However, Phillips and Oswick (2012) caution that,

> the study of 'discourse *as* materiality' may be a philosophical imperative, but it is extremely difficult to achieve at a practical and pragmatic level. Not least because in order to study the nature of the co-constitution of discourse and the material one has to attempt to disaggregate them for the purposes of understanding the nature of their relationship and co-constitution. (p. 50)

Why should materiality matter for an organizational discourse analyst? Kuhn, Ashcraft, and Cooren (2017) explain regarding a practical consequence of the linguistic turn,

> emphasis on discourse tended to relegate what had previously been considered *objects* to secondary positions … . The linguistic turn's aim of transcending subject/object divisions too often turned the material into the symbolic, refusing to consider the thingness of things, the mattering of the material. (pp. 30–31)

Such a linguistic-focused stance fails to account in meaningful ways for the importance of things such as spaces, places, objects, technologies in communication generally, and in the communicative constitution of organization specifically (see Wilhoit & Mengis, this volume).

One way that CCO scholars have addressed the discourse-materiality challenge is through a relational ontology (Cooren, 2018; also see Brummans, Higham, & Cooren, 2021; Kuhn, Ashcraft, & Cooren, 2017; Robichaud, 2006). In a relational ontology, "things are not pre-bounded entities that exist before they come into contact with humans. Rather, ever-unfolding contact produces 'things' as they are" (Kuhn, Ashcraft, & Cooren, 2017, p. 32). Inclusion of the material highlights the significance of describing a constitutive perspective of organizations as the *communicative* rather than discursive constitution in that things, places, and other entities that are not discourse "matter" in how organizations are constituted.

In methodological practice, one way to address materiality in analyses and theorizing about organizing/organization is to include materiality as one communicative feature, *along with* discourse. As Phillips and Oswick (2012) state:

> By widening the methods used and bringing together methods that focus on the discursive and the material, organizational discourse analysis can make much more of a contribution to our understanding of organizations and organizing. (p. 44)

Video Ethnography

In line with the material and visual turns in organizational theorizing, researchers have taken into consideration the material through the use of video-ethnography and video-shadowing as research methods (Boxenbaum, Jones, Meyer, & Svejenova, 2018; Fairhurst & Cooren, 2018; Vásquez, Brummans, & Groleau, 2012; Wilhoit, 2017). A video-recorder can document discourse *as well as* other materially present aspects of a scene. Wilhoit (2017) explains regarding the benefit of this:

> organizational communication is unique from other areas of communication research because it usually deals with larger-than-human entities (organizations). Although many aspects of organizations cannot be pointed at with a camera lens, a substantial material and discursive reality of organizing always exists as contextual or constitutive for any interaction. (p. 450)

Video-recording enables a researcher to record in detail spoken interactions, addressing the expectations of rigorous attention to language held for discourse analytic studies, in addition to getting at details of silent, yet materially present features in interactions such as nonverbal communication (e.g., eye gaze, gestures, body orientation, etc.) as well as objects (e.g., tables, statues, machines, etc.). Video-recordings enable discourse analysts to take into consideration how nonverbal communication and objects interact with verbal communication in constitutive processes. Video-ethnography and video-shadowing have been utilized within the Montreal School of CCO in ways that also incorporate attention to discourse (e.g., Benoit-Barné & Cooren, 2009; Cooren, 2015a). As an example to illustrate how video can enhance discourse analysis, with the aid of a video-recorder, Benoit-Barné and Cooren (2009) were able to note nonverbal communication such as handshaking, room transitions, speaker orientation to intended recipient, gestures towards objects, the "messiness" of a room, and a "note" that became a significant part of the authors' analysis related to "the role of nonhumans in the achievement of authority" (p. 21). While all of these could have been noted by very thorough field notes, the camera can function as a supplemental data-gathering tool that allows for the review of otherwise fleeting moments of verbal and nonverbal interaction. In turn, "seeing" interactions can aid in understanding and interpreting what may be occurring. For instance, "deference" to the authority of a supervisor may be indicated silently through gaze and body orientation, as Benoit-Barné and Cooren described; conversely, the opposite of deference such as hostility or ill will may also be indicated silently through eye-rolling and folded arms.

In order to do video-ethnography and video-shadowing, one dilemma is the issue of access. To do video-ethnography, one must gain access to organizational places and interactions. However, some interactions may be challenging to gain access to. The issue of access may explain why there has been a healthy amount of research done on organizational meetings that are public or pseudo-public (e.g., Castor, 2016, 2020; Cooren, 2013). While video ethnography can provide informative data, the use of the video-camera should not be applied in a way that engages in "a naive 'epistemology of common sense' (in which the world as it appears before us in its 'natural attitude' actually captures its essence)" (Mumby, 2011, p. 1153). The camera is however, an additional tool that can aid a discourse analyst in interpreting the interplay between discourse and nonverbal communication, visual communication, and other material aspects of interactions.

Concluding Reflections

Phillips and Oswick (2012) argue for an "opening up" of ODA and going beyond "parochialism and isolationism" by becoming "multi-level in orientation and multi-method in approach" and by "paying serious attention to aspects of materiality" (p. 33). Brummans, Cooren, Robichaud, and Taylor (2014) also advocate:

> Thus while it is important to investigate the here-and-now discursive and material accomplishment of everyday organizational practices by zooming in on what people say and do and the active role of tools, materials, and so on, these methods need to be combined with zooming out methods, such as trailing connections between practices through multi sited ethnographies (Marcus, 1995), shadowing (Vásquez, Brummans, & Groleau, 2012), and studying the effects of practice-networks (see Nicolini, 2009). (pp. 188–189)

Given the importance of discourse for constitutive processes, discourse analysis should continue to play a significant role in CCO. In recognizing the range of communicative practices, discourse analysis should be considered as one focusing lens for understanding CCO. In addition, I wish to demarcate what makes a discourse analytic project a study in the communicative constitution of organization/organizing/organizationality. A DA-CCO project examines how discourse *constitutes* organizing in that the so-called organization itself is problematized. In doing so, a DA-CCO project articulates research questions that contribute to understanding discourse as part of the collective of communicative practices that constitute organizations, organizing, and/or organizationality.

References

Alvesson, M., & Kärreman, D. (2000). Varieties of discourse: On the study of organizations through discourse analysis. *Human Relations, 53*(9), 1125–1149.

Alvesson, M., & Kärreman, D. (2011). Decolonializing discourse: Critical reflections on organizational discourse analysis. *Human relations, 64*(9), 1121–1146.

Antaki, C. (2002). An introductory tutorial in Conversation Analysis. Online at http://ca-tutorials.lboro. ac.uk/sitemenu.htm. Accessed on April 21, 2021.

Antaki, C., Billig, M., Edwards, D., & Potter, J. (2003). Discourse analysis means doing analysis: A critique of six analytic shortcomings. *Discourse Analysis Online, 1*. Retrieved from: www.shu.ac.uk/daol/previous/v1/n1/index.htm.

Atkinson, D., Okada, H., & Talmy, S. (2011). Ethnography and discourse analysis. In K. Hyland & B. Paltridge (eds.), *Continuum companion to discourse analysis* (pp. 85–100). London: Contiunuum.

Austin, J.L. (1962). *How to do things with words*. Cambridge, MA: Harvard University Press.

Bencherki, N., & Cooren, F. (2011). Having to be: The possessive constitution of organization. *Human Relations, 64*, 1579–1607. https://doi.org/10.1177/0018726711424227.

Bencherki, N., Matte, F., & Cooren, F. (Eds.). (2019). *Authority and power in social interaction: Methods and analysis*. Routledge.

Benoit-Barné, C., & Cooren, F. (2009). The accomplishment of authority through presentification: How authority is distributed among and negotiated by organizational members. *Management Communication Quarterly, 23*(1), 5–31. https://doi.org/10.1177/0893318909335414.

Bisel, R. S. (2009). On a growing dualism in organizational discourse research. *Management Communication Quarterly, 22*(4), 614–638.

Boden, D. (Ed.). (1994). *The business of talk*. Polity.

Boivin, G., Brummans, B. H. J. M., & Barker, J. R. (2017). The institutionalization of CCO scholarship: Trends from 2000 to 2015. *Management Communication Quarterly, 31*(3), 331–355. https://doi.org/10.1177/0893318916687396.

Boxenbaum, E., Jones, C., Meyer, R. E., & Svejenova, S. (2018). Towards an articulation of the material and visual turn in organization studies. *Organization Studies, 39*, 597–616.

Brummans, B. H. (2012). The road to Rizong: Buddhist mindful organizing amid natural disaster in the Indian Himalayas. *Qualitative Communication Research, 1*(4), 433–460.

Brummans, B. H. (2014). Pathways to mindful qualitative organizational communication research. *Management Communication Quarterly, 28*(3), 440–447.

Brummans, B. H. J. M., Cooren, F., Robichaud, D., & Taylor, J. R. (2014). Approaches to the communicative constitution of organizations. In D. K. Mumby & L. L. Putnam (Eds.), *The SAGE handbook of organizational communication: Advances in theory, research, and methods* (pp. 173–194). Sage.

Brummans, B. H. J. M., Higham, L., & Cooren, F. (2021). The work of conflict mediation: Actors, vectors, and communicative relationality. *Human Relations.* https://doi.org/10.1177_0018726721994180.

Burgess, R. G. (2002). *In the field: An introduction to field research.* Routledge.

Carbaugh, D. (2014). *Cultures in conversation.* Routledge.

Castor, T. (2016). The materiality of discourse: Relational positioning in a fresh water controversy. *Communication Research and Practice, 2*(3), 334–350.

Castor, T. R. (2020). On streams and lakes: Metaventriloquism and the technologies of a water controversy. *Language and Dialogue, 10*(1), 29–48.

Castor, T., & Bartesaghi, M. (2016). Metacommunication during disaster response: "Reporting" and the constitution of problems in Hurricane Katrina teleconferences. *Management Communication Quarterly, 30*(4), 472–502.

Chia, R. (2000). Discourse analysis organizational analysis. *Organization, 7*(3), 513–518.

Clifton, J. (2019). Using conversation analysis for organisational research: A case study of leadership-in-action. *Communication Research and Practice, 5*(4), 342–357.

Cooren, F. (1999). Applying socio-semiotics to organizational communication: A new approach. *Management Communication Quarterly, 13*(2), 294–304.

Cooren, F. (2001). Translation and articulation in the organization of coalitions: the Great Whale River case. *Communication Theory, 11*(2), 178–200. https://doi.org/10.1111/j.1468-2885.2001.tb00238.x.

Cooren, F. A. (2004a). Textual agency: How texts do things in organizational settings. *Organization, 11*(3), 373–393.

Cooren, F. (2004b). The communicative achievement of collective minding: Analysis of board meeting excerpts. *Management Communication Quarterly, 17*(4), 517–551.

Cooren, F. (2006). Arguments for the in-depth study of organizational interactions: A rejoinder to McPhee, Myers, and Trethewey. *Management Communication Quarterly, 19*(3), 327–340.

Cooren, F. (2010). *Action and agency in dialogue: Passion, incarnation and ventriloquism* (Vol. 6). John Benjamins Publishing.

Cooren, F. (Ed.). (2013). *Interacting and organizing: Analyses of a management meeting.* Routledge.

Cooren, F. (2015a). *In medias res*: Communication, existence, and materiality. *Communication Research and Practice, 1*(4), 307–321.

Cooren, F. (2015b). *Organizational discourse analysis.* Cambridge: Polity.

Cooren, F. (2018). Materializing communication: Making the case for a relational ontology. *Journal of Communication, 68*(2), 278–288.

Cooren, F., Brummans, B. H. J. M., & Charrieras, D. (2008). The coproduction of organizational presence: A study of Médecins Sans Frontières in action. *Human Relations, 61*, 1339–1370.

Cooren, F., & Fairhurst, G. T. (2008). Dislocation and stabilization: How to scale up from interactions to organization. In L.L. Putnam & A. Nicotera (Eds.), *Building theories of organization: The constitutive role of communication* (pp. 117–152). New York: Routledge.

Cooren, F., Matte, F., Benoit-Barné, C., & Brummans, B. H. (2013). Communication as ventriloquism: A grounded-in-action approach to the study of organizational tensions. *Communication Monographs, 80*(3), 255–277.

Czarniawska, B. (2007). Narrative inquiry in and about organizations. In J. Clandinin (Ed.), *Handbook of narrative inquiry: Mapping a methodology* (pp. 383–404). Sage.

Deetz, S., & Eger, E. K. (2014). Developing a metatheoretical perspective for organizational communication studies. In L. L. Putnam & D. K. Mumby (Eds.), *The SAGE handbook of organizational communication : Advances in theory, research, and methods* (pp. 27–48). Sage.

Dobusch, L., & Schoeneborn, D. (2015). Fluidity, identity, and organizationality: The communicative constitution of Anonymous. *Journal of Management Studies, 52*(8), 1005–1035.

Fairhurst, G. T., & Cooren, F. (2004). Organizational language in use: Interaction analysis, conversation analysis, and speech act schematics. In D. K. Mumby & L. L. Putnam (Eds.), *The Sage handbook of organizational discourse* (pp. 131–152). Sage.

Fairhurst, G. T., & Cooren, F. (2009). Leadership as the hybrid production of presence(s). *Leadership, 5*(4), 469–490.

Fairhurst, G. T., & Cooren, F. (2018). Organizational discourse analysis. In C. Cassell, A. L. Cunliffe, & G. Grandy (Eds.), *The SAGE handbook of qualitative business and management research methods* (pp. 81–101). Sage.

Fairhurst, G. T., & Putnam, L. L. (2004). Organizations as discursive constructions. *Communication Theory, 14*(1), 5–26.

Fairhurst, G. T., & Putnam, L. L. (2014). Organizational discourse analysis. The SAGE handbook of organizational communication: *Advances in theory, research, and methods* (pp. 271–296). Sage.

Garfinkel, H. (Ed.). (2017). *Routledge revivals: Ethnomethodological studies of work (1986)*. Routledge.

Grant, D., & Iedema, R. (2005). Discourse analysis and the study of organizations. text. *Interdisciplinary Journal for the Study of Discourse, 25*(1), 37–66. https://doi.org/10.1515/text.2005.25.1.37.

Grant, D., Hardy, C., Oswick, C., & Putnam, L. L. (Eds.). (2004). *The Sage handbook of organizational discourse*. Sage.

Grant, D., Putnam, L. L., & Hardy, C. (2011). History, key challenges, and contributions of organizational discourse studies. In D. Grant, C. Hardy, & L. L. Putnam (Eds.), *Organizational discourse studies* (pp. xvii–xlii). Sage.

Grosjean, S., Bonneville, L., & Redpath, C. (2019). The design process of an mHealth technology: the communicative constitution of patient engagement through a participatory design workshop. ESSACHESS–Journal for *Communication Studies, 12*(1(23)), 5–26.

Hammersley, M. (2015). Ethnography. *The Blackwell encyclopedia of sociology*. John Wiley & Sons, Ltd. https://doi.org/10.1002/9781405165518.wbeose070.pub2.

Hardy, C. (2001). Researching organizational discourse. *International Studies of Management & Organization, 31*(3), 25–47.

Hardy, C., Grant, D., Keenoy, T., Oswick, C., & Phillips, N. (2004). Organizational discourse. *Organization Studies, 25*(1).

Hymes, D. (1964). Introduction: Toward ethnographies of communication. *American Anthropologist, 66*, 1–34.

Jian, G., Schmisseur, A. M., & Fairhurst, G. T. (2008). Organizational discourse and communication: The progeny of Proteus. *Discourse and Communication, 2*(3), 299–320. https://doi.org/10.1177/1750481308091912.

Kalou, Z., & Sadler-Smith, E. (2015). Using ethnography of communication in organizational research. *Organizational Research Methods, 18*(4), 629–655.

Koschmann, M. A. (2013). The communicative constitution of collective identity in interorganizational collaboration. *Management Communication Quarterly, 27*(1), 61–89.

Koschmann, M. A., & McDonald, J. (2015). Organizational rituals, communication, and the question of agency. *Management Communication Quarterly, 29*(2), 229–256.

Kuhn, T., Ashcraft, K. L., & Cooren, F. (2017). *The work of communication: Relational perspectives on working and organizing in contemporary capitalism*. Taylor & Francis.

Latour, B., & Woolgar, S. (1979). *Laboratory life: The construction of scientific facts*. Sage.

Lofland, J., & Lofland, L. H. (1995). *Analyzing social settings: A guide to qualitative observation and analysis*. Florence, KY: Wadsworth.

Luhmann, N. (1999). Sign as form. *Cybernetics & Human Knowing, 6*, 21–37.

McPhee, R. D., Myers, K. K., & Trethewey, A. (2006). On collective mind and conversational analysis: Response to Cooren. *Management Communication Quarterly, 19*(3), 311–326.

Miles, M. B., & Huberman, A. M. (1994). *Qualitative data analysis: An expanded sourcebook* (2nd edn.). Thousand Oaks, CA: Sage.

Mumby, D. K. (2011). What's cooking in organizational discourse studies? A response to Alvesson and Kärreman. *Human Relations, 64*(9), 1147–1161.

Nathues, E., van Vuuren, M., & Cooren, F. (2020). Speaking about vision, talking in the name of so much more: A methodological framework for ventriloquial analyses in organization studies. *Organization Studies*. https://doi.org/10.1177/0170840620934063.

Owen, W. F. (1984). Interpretive themes in relational communication. *Quarterly Journal of Speech, 70*, 274–287.

Parker, I. (1992). *Discourse dynamics : Critical analysis for social and individual psychology*. Routledge.

Philipsen, G. (1992). *Speaking culturally: Explorations in social communication*. SUNY Press.

Phillips, N., & Oswick, C. (2012). Organizational discourse: Domains, debates, and directions. *Academy of Management Annals*, *6*(1), 435–481. https://doi.org/10.5465/19416520.2012.681558.

Putnam, L. L., & Fairhurst, G. T. (2015). Revisiting "Organizations as discursive constructions": 10 years later. *Communication Theory*, *25*(4), 375–392. https://doi.org/10.1111/comt.12074.

Rawls, A. W. (2008). Harold Garfinkel, ethnomethodology and workplace studies. *Organization Studies*, *29*(5), 701–732.

Ray, M., Biswas, C., & Bengal, W. (2011). A study on Ethnography of communication: A discourse analysis with Hymes 'speaking model'. *Journal of Education and Practice*, *2*(6), 33–40.

Reed, M. (2004). Getting real about organizational discourse. In D. Grant, C. Hardy, C. Oswick, & L. Putnam (Eds.), *Handbook of organizational discourse* (pp. 413–420). London: Sage.

Robichaud, D. (2006). Steps toward a relational view of agency. In F. Cooren, J. R. Taylor, & E. J. Van Every (Eds.), *Communication as organizing: Practical approaches to research into the dynamic of text and conversation* (pp. 101–114). Lawrence Erlbaum Associates.

Robichaud, D., Giroux, H., & Taylor, J. R. (2004). The metaconversation: The recursive as a key property of language to organizing. *Academy of Management Review*, *29*(4), 617–634.

Sacks, H., Schegloff, E. A., & Jefferson, G. (1978). A simplest systematics for the organization of turn taking for conversation. In J. Schenkein (Ed.), *Studies in the organization of conversational interaction* (pp. 7–55). Academic Press.

Schoeneborn, D., Kuhn, T. R., & Kärreman, D. (2019). The communicative constitution of organization, organizing, and organizationality perspectives: The communicative constitution of organization. *Organization Studies*, *40*(4), 475–496. https://doi.org/10.1177/0170840618782284.

Schoeneborn, D., & Vásquez, C. (2017). Communicative constitution of organizations. In C. R. Scott & L. K. Lewis (Eds.), *The international encyclopedia of organizational communication* (pp. 367–386). Wiley. https://doi.org/10.1002/9781118955567.wbieoc030.

Searle, J. R. (1969). *Speech acts: An essay in the philosophy of language*. London: Cambridge University Press.

Spradley, J. P. (2016). *The ethnographic interview*. Waveland Press.

Strauss, A. L., & Corbin, J. (1990). *Basics of qualitative research*. Newbury Park, CA: Sage.

Taylor, J. R., & Van Every, E. J. (2000). *The emergent organization: Communication as its site and surface*. Routledge.

Taylor, J.R., & Van Every, E.J. (2014). *When organization fails: Why authority matters*. New York: Routledge.

Van Dijk, T. A. (Ed.). (1997). *Discourse as structure and process*. Sage.

Vasilyeva, A., Robles, J.S., Saludadez, J.A., Schwägerl, C., & Castor, T. (2020). The varieties of (more or less) formal authority. In N. Bencherki, F. Matte, & F. Cooren (Eds.), *Authority and power in social interaction: Methods and analysis* (pp. 37–56). Routledge.

Vásquez, C., Brummans, B. H. J. M., & Groleau, C. (2012). Notes from the field on organizational shadowing as framing. *Qualitative Research in Management and Organization*, *7*, 144–165. doi:10.1108/17465641211253075.

Vásquez, C., & Cooren, F. (2013). Spacing practices: The communicative configuration of organizing through space-times. *Communication Theory*, *23*(1), 25–47.

Wilhoit, E. D. (2017). Photo and video methods in organizational and managerial communication research. *Management Communication Quarterly*, *31*(3), 447–466.

Wilhoit, E. D., & Kisselburgh, L. G. (2015). Collective action without organization: The material constitution of bike commuters as collective. *Organization Studies*, *36*(5), 573–592.

Wood, L. A., & Kroger, R. O. (2000). *Doing discourse analysis: Methods for studying action in talk and text*. Sage.

13

ACTING *IN THE NAME OF* OTHERS

How to Unpack Ventriloquations

Ellen Nathues and Mark van Vuuren

Introduction: Who or What is (Really) Talking and Acting?

In recent years, organizational communication scholars have argued for a reconceptualization of organizations as forming *in* communication (Ashcraft et al., 2009; Schoeneborn et al., 2019). There is not communication on the one hand and organization or organizing on the other (Cooren, 2012). Instead, we have learned that what is talked about in an interaction is essentially what constitutes it (Cooren, 2015, 2018). Organization and organizing happen through communication, which is why communication constitutes what becomes organizational.

Ventriloquism (Cooren, 2010) problematizes the question of who or what is communicating. The notion illustrates how we make present additional voices whenever we speak or act. Take the few lines we have so far written as an example: We could argue that the words are not just ours but also François Cooren's. He materializes through his work that we cite (Cooren, 2010, 2012, 2015, 2018) but also through what we say about it. What materializes through our particular descriptions of his work may further be our experiences of collaborating with him (Nathues et al., 2021; van Vuuren & Cooren, 2010). In some respects, the words also belong to ventriloquism as a construct itself and relate to the Montreal School of CCO as the broader research tradition standing behind the ventriloquial idea. Ventriloquism questions the distinctions between who is talking (which is already a bundle of this chapter, its words, and ourselves as its authors) and what is talked about (François, ventriloquism as a concept, CCO, etc.) and helps us reveal how the people, things, and abstractions that we refer to are in fact additional voices or actants that partake in our interactions. Thereby, it decenters our analyses and contributes to more complete understandings of what constitutes organizational situations and phenomena. Let us consider two more (fictitious) examples to further unpack the ventriloquial idea: first, an employee explaining why she did not perform a task and second, a CEO giving a speech to organizational stakeholders.

To justify why she did not complete her assignment, the employee might invoke her supervisor's voice ("I was told by my manager to first solve a customer request"). Alternatively, she might name lack of time ("I had to work on a customer request that consumed all my time") or issues with her equipment ("I really meant to work on it, but I could not with the hardware I had") as reasons for why she could not deliver as promised. We can see how additional actants join the employee in making a good case for her defense. It is not only her doing the talking,

DOI: 10.4324/9781003224914-16

but also the people and things (the supervisor, the lack of time, the malfunctioning equipment) that express themselves in her talk and support her position (Cooren & Sandler, 2014).

When naming her supervisor's order as her excuse, our professional seems to describe herself as a dummy, acting on her manager's behalf. She positions her action—or rather her failure to act—as caused or *animated* by someone else, while also making her supervisor say something, thus essentially *animating* them as giving an order. This is similar to how a ventriloquial artist (called *vent*) presents himself as responding to his puppet while also causing his puppet to speak. When the employee talks about the malfunctioning hardware, she seems to be trying to also make something else responsible for her neglect, so that it is not just her that is to blame but also the flawed equipment. The focus is thus put on how she is now *animating* the presence and presumable liability of the hardware, positioning this hardware as a *figure* that shares responsibility, only to portray herself as passively *animated*—or, more accurately, passivated—and prevented from acting. Ventriloquial effects work in both these ways, as voices can be *made present* by interactants but can also *make themselves present* by leading interactants to (re)act as they do (Cooren, 2010). The ventriloquial act requires both, as a figure can only be a figure in combination with a vent and vice versa: none of them can stand on their own. The oscillation between the two is a key aspect of ventriloquism: when I speak in the name of something, I can only do so because the very same something enables me to speak in its name. The ventriloquial voice is always vent *and* figure, but it can teeter towards one end or the other from one situation to the next. Highlighting either figure or vent as the focal agent in the chain that binds them is then a matter of "selection of agency" (Castor & Cooren, 2006, p. 580).

Now, imagine a CEO giving a talk about her organization's development. This scene might look straightforward at first: a person communicating a statement to an audience. However, it appears more complex once we start unpacking the voices present in the speech. Let us assume that the talk's script has been written by the CEO's assistant. We could then argue that the words the CEO utters when giving her speech are also (at least partially) her assistant's words. Yet, in her writing, the assistant was probably acting on her boss's orders (the CEO told her to do so), trying to make present the statements her boss asked her to incorporate. The assistant might have also been influenced by her experiences as an organization member, for example adding the voice of a satisfied customer that she once talked to. As we see, the apparently simple script is already composed of nested voices so that when the CEO speaks in the script's name, she also implicitly speaks in the name of her assistant and this assistant's experiences, the satisfied customer, the statements the CEO herself authored to be included in the script, etc. Again, we can witness a constant oscillation between these voices: in one moment it might seem as if the CEO is the dummy *animated* by the script and the assistant on whose behalf she speaks, yet in the very next it might appear that the CEO was all the time pulling the strings of her figures and *animating* them.

When giving her talk, the CEO openly acts as a spokesperson for her organization. What she says, questions, or directs attention to is not just understood as *hers* but also as *her organization's*. That does not mean that her own voice disappears, but that what she says gets related to more than just her. For example, the CEO might unconsciously raise her voice when speaking about diversity as this is a value she has a strong personal attachment to. Thereby, the CEO's voice, the organization's voice, and diversity's voice blend together, conjointly constituting the situation of the organizational speech. Voices indeed can become so entangled that it is hard to decipher each one individually, which is why ventriloquial communication or *speaking in the name of others is essentially a matter of interwoven chains and shared relations*, without a singular starting point. If an audience member wanted to disentangle the different voices, she would be impoverishing the communicative event as it is precisely this blending that organizes meaning: audience members cannot tell apart the different voices, which is why the organization that the CEO is representing becomes associated with the CEO's attachment to diversity. Voices present in an interaction link back and forth between one another and together constitute the ins and outs of what happens.

Ventriloquism hence reminds us that agency has no absolute origin (Cooren et al., 2012; Kuhn et al., 2017). Whenever I speak or act, I also ventriloquize, that is, I bring in additional actants through my action of ventriloquation. By speaking or acting *in the name of others* (Cooren, 2012), these others speak or act through me, which means that they also *speak in my name*. We spell out the underlying premises of this oscillating connection by closely studying the meaning of the phrase "*in the name of*" through a vignette borrowed from our Montreal colleagues (Cooren et al., 2021): what functions do ventriloquial connections rest on?

Ventriloquation-in-Action: Four Workings of *in the Name of*

Ventriloquism claims that, when communicating, humans act and speak *in the name of* others, which makes these others partake in the communication. When communication relates, connects, or engages us together (Pomerantz et al., 2018), then ventriloquism allows us to see that it is not just we that get related but also many additional things and beings.

Popular dictionaries define multiple meanings of the phrase *in the name of*, including *for the sake of* or *in appeal or reference to*, *by the authority of*, *as belonging to*, and *as reason or excuse for* something (Cambridge, Collins, & Merriam-Webster, all n.d.). For simplicity, we argue that these can be sorted into four functions (Table 13.1). Each function corresponds to a different ventriloquial feature constituting the ventriloquial connection. First, a ventriloquation can be understood as an *appeal* to a figure: an interactant can ask someone or something else *to speak for* herself or act in her place. For instance, a nurse could point at a box of gloves to remind, *for her*, a doctor of hygiene protocols (Caronia & Cooren, 2014) or a construction site manager could install a warning sign to do the warning *for him* (Nathues et al., 2021). Second, ventriloquation can designate an interactant and a figure's *shared authorship* of an action, suggestion, or the like, thereby bolstering their joint *authority* (Benoit-Barné & Cooren, 2009). For example, an accountant could present a strategic advice to his client *and* make the company's financial spreadsheets argue for the same recommendation; in this sense, the accountant and the spreadsheets both press for the same advice *with* or *next to* one another. Third, ventriloquation can express *possession* of a figure's actions, resources, abilities, etc. by

Table 13.1 Four ventriloquial connections

Appeal	Authority and authorship	Appropriation	Attribution (metaventriloquism)
Asking someone or something else to speak in one's name or act in one's place: *when a ventriloquial figure speaks or acts **for** an interactant*	Multiplying authorship of an utterance or action, thereby strengthening one's authority: *when a ventriloquial figure speaks or acts **with** or **next to** an interactant*	Making or claiming an action, resource, ability, etc. as one's own: *when a ventriloquial figure expresses an interactant's possession **of** something*	Attributing one's or others' sayings and doings to (again) others: *when a ventriloquial figure depicts an interactant's attachments **to** someone or something else*

appropriating this figure (Bencherki & Cooren, 2011). For instance, an organizational member could appropriate his organization's expertise by highlighting his membership—such as by writing his university affiliation on an article—or a graphic designer could express her (partial) possession of a successful idea by pointing out that parts of the idea are built on her initial visualizations. Finally, ventriloquation can also be a matter of *attributing one's own (or others') actions to someone or something else*. For example, a hotel guest could defend her extensive front desk tipping by ascribing it *to* local standards or a speaker could impute certain motives to a city in a public water controversy (Castor, 2020). The latter dynamic has been described as *metaventriloquism* as it invokes another's animations or attachments, thus is essentially about ventriloquizing another's ventriloquation(s) (Castor, 2020).

We borrow a vignette from our Montreal colleagues (Cooren et al., 2021) to further illustrate the four ventriloquial workings. The vignette is taken from a session in which a mediator (M) tries to bring two parties into agreement. Specifically, a citizen (C) required compensation for a traffic accident that he was involved in; he also asked for an official statement that confirms his inability to drive, as well as for paid training for a career change. However, all of his claims were denied. Instead of immediately proceeding to court, C and a government representative (R) agreed to an alternative dispute-resolution process, in which M is acting as a mediator. At the session start, C reads out a document that is supposed to convey his perspective on the situation. Once he has finished summarizing his position, the following happens:

Vignette 1 (taken from Cooren et al., 2021)

```
123   M   Thank you. I will try to summarize↑
124   C   Yeah=
125   M   =My understanding of what you just read to us was that there is a
126       legitimate, in your perspective uh or possible uh, that the accidents that
127       occurred left you with des séquelles, with impeachment of driving
128       accurately and you are afraid that you might be involved in an accident
129       because of the uhm, the the uhm, les acti-
130   C   Residual uh
131   M   Les blessures, how do you say blessures in English
132   R   Injuries
133   M   Thank you, because of the injuries, so you are afraid that the injuries that
134       you incurred, that occurred while you were in your first and second
135       accidents, will make you have a new injury
136   C   No, I'm not afraid. I know the inherent risks that are there, I'm an ex
137       police officer, I have knowledge of what causes accidents and things like
138       that. So being cognizant of this (2.0)
```

In line 127, M actually means 'impediment' when she talks about impeachment.

When we unpack this situation's ventriloquial dynamics and relations, we can observe this: first, to summarize his position, C reads from a document that he himself created. This document materializes C's viewpoints in textual form. When reading it aloud, C hence *essentially appeals to the document to speak for him*. It is the document that brings forward C's experiences, feelings, and claims, with C simply being a medium that gives voice to the document.

Second, we can observe how M is using this document to connect C to his accidents (line 126) and injuries (line 133). Specifically, M brings forward a reading of the document according to which these figures (the accidents and injuries) are reasons for C's fear ("so you are afraid", line 133). That is, M is forming a relation based on *attribution, where C's fear is attributed to his accidents and injuries*. What is important is how M positions C as passive, while both the accident and the injuries are presented as active or as doing something: "the accidents

[…] left you" (lines 126–127) / "the injuries […] will make you" (lines 133–135). Through M's ventriloquations, C is depicted as the dummy acting under his fear. We can observe how M is not simply putting words into C's mouth, but how she *appropriates* the meaning of C's documents by presenting her own reading of it as "summarizing" what C (and his document) said.

However, C counters M's interpretation ("No, I'm not afraid", line 136). Rather than fear, C explicates that he has knowledge that M does not have (lines 136–137), thereby appropriating back this knowledge as his own. C substantiates this possession or appropriation by reminding everyone of the fact that he is an ex-police officer (lines 136–137). That is, he bases his *appropriation of knowledge*—i.e., of what caused his injury—on additional things that he possesses, namely his profession as a police officer and his working experience. It could then also be said that C *attributes his knowledge to the broader professional group that he is part of* and that possesses this sort of knowledge. This linked configuration is crucial here: C essentially positions himself as knowledgeable because his broader professional group also is knowledgeable, which helps C to make an overall better case for his explanation. He is not just bringing forward his personal viewpoint but is also acting on behalf of his profession *that argues for his case with him, thereby enforcing C's authoritative position*. Parts of police officers' jobs are about figuring out what causes accidents ("I know the inherent risks […] I have knowledge of what causes accidents", lines 136–137) and C here presents himself as simply following his profession's standards ("so being cognizant of this", line 138).

C hence rejects M's attempt at describing him as passively acting under his fear (caused by his accidents and injuries). Instead, he depicts himself as actively acting under the guidance of the knowledge he and his professional field possess. Both versions involve the sharing of agency with additional figures through ventriloquations and communicative relations, and we will turn to how we can unpack these hybrid agencies and nested relations next.

Methodological Application: Ventriloquism as an Instrument for CCO

Understanding communication as ventriloquism helps us to understand the communicative constitution of realities, meanings, situations, and organizations by looking at how multiple voices are brought together into specific configurations. We have translated the ventriloquial idea into an analytical method elsewhere (Nathues et al., 2021) and have outlined four phases that analysts can move through (Table 13.2). We believe that ventriloquism is a valuable analytical lens for research endeavors that embrace relational conceptualizations of agency (Caronia & Cooren, 2014) and that understand materiality as a communicative (not physical) resource (Cooren, 2020).

In the following, we will zoom into each of these four phases separately. We unpack how analysts can apply a ventriloquial perspective onto their empirical material and outline some of what we consider important techniques and subtleties. Vignette 1 (the excerpt from Cooren et al., 2021) as well as our fictitious examples from the beginning of the chapter serve as illustrations.

Phase 1: Identifying Ventriloquial Voices

In phase 1, the ventriloquial analyst identifies the ventriloquial effects present in her dataset. For orientation, she can mobilize three analytical questions that can help her spot ventriloquial effects. First, she can address her dataset with the question *what is a person invoking with what*

Table 13.2 Four-step framework for ventriloquial analyses

Phase 1: Identifying	**Identifying ventriloquial effects by addressing the empirical material with three ventriloquial analytical questions**
	(a) What is a person invoking with what she is saying or doing?
	(b) What voice can be recognized in what a person is saying or doing?
	(c) What appears or is presented to lead a person to say what she is saying or do what she is doing?
Phase 2: Grouping	Grouping the identified ventriloquial effects, working through two rounds
	(a) Sorting voices into clusters
	(b) Arranging clusters into overarching collections
Phase 3: Relating	Relating the separate bits of the analysis (voices, clusters, collections) into an integrated model by tracing chains of authorship, relations, and workings of ventriloquations
Phase 4: Showing	Selecting vignettes from the empirical material and showing ventriloquial voices through detailed elaborations

she is saying and doing?, looking for explicit invocations of a ventriloquial figure. These explicit invocations are clearly named in the material and appear through direct references. That is why they are most straightforward to identify, of all ventriloquial effects. In vignette 1, for example, we identified C's "knowledge" (line 137) and his previous job as a "police officer" (line 137) as explicit figures that C invoked to build a better argumentation. In our example of the employee explaining her task non-performance, the manager asking her to prioritize other assignments was overtly mentioned, too. Explicit figures appear in straightforward manners and thereby come to contribute to the ins and outs of a situation.

An important question that then begs attention is: is every subject or object that an interactant names an explicit figure? Or put differently, what is a figure and what is *not* a figure? In our own ventriloquial analyses, we have so far operated from the assumption that every figure that is explicitly ventriloquized in a situation matters for this situation. If a person brings up a regulation, for example, that is because she believes it to be of matter for the situation that she finds herself in. When doing a ventriloquial analysis, we are then less interested in why this person thought that this figure mattered but more in the invocation's unfolding effects: what is the figure's performativity and consequentiality on the situation?

When looking for implicit figures, the analyst can inspect her dataset with the question *what voice can be recognized in what a person is saying and doing?* in mind. Here, we are looking for figures that are not overtly present; they may be implied in utterances and conveyed through actions. In other words, they are enfolded in interactants' sayings and doings and mediate their presence through *other* words and practices. These invocations are not as straightforward to identify as explicit figures. They require analytical unpacking and pondering over what a person might be trying to accomplish with what she says and what voice(s) substantiate her doings and sayings—voices that may be at once absent from the situation and yet very present in their effects.

Think back to the CEO's speech from earlier in the chapter: the assistant's voice is both absent and present in the speech's script, as it is the assistant's experiences and words that make up the speech that the CEO then utters. Identifying these dual effects of absence and presence, in the form of implicit invocations, requires intense familiarization with the empirical material. Repeated readings can help to build a sense of what interactions are about and of what appears to matter. Spending time in the field, shadowing professionals in their work, and talking to people about their experiences and perceptions can help to further sensitize the ventriloquial analyst to the context and content of her study and to what exactly happens in her material. For example, in our own research, we not only observed an organization's strong security concerns in what a professional said and did, but gained similar impressions in interviews with this professional's team members and by visiting the organization ourselves. Specifically, someone from inside the company always had to pre-register our visit, we then had to show our ID when entering the building, after which we proceeded to a gate to meet someone to escort us to our meeting room. The ventriloquial analyst can thus gather evidence that goes beyond interaction transcripts as cues from additional experiences and materials can substantiate what is found in them.

However, gathering information from outside of the communicative situation may lead to overinterpretation on the analyst's part and to *assuming* the presence of implicit voices (Pomerantz et al., 2018). To avoid this analytical trap, reflexivity and the ability to interrogate one's own findings with a critical perspective are important skills. The ventriloquial analyst needs to ask herself what, in the data, tells her that an implicit figure is present and of matter. Collaborative analyses—for instance in the form of "data sessions"—are another helpful strategy, as analysts can compare, question, and challenge one another's interpretations. Finally, an implicit figure could also be checked with the persons studied: do people recognize the figure, and does it make sense to them?

Third, the analyst can explore her dataset with the question w*hat appears or is presented to lead a person to say what she is saying and do what she is doing?* To answer this question, we must keep in mind the oscillation effect we mentioned earlier and identify what *animates* a person's utterances and actions.

When we first developed our framework (Nathues et al., 2021), we intended this third analytical question only for the interactant speaking. We argued that what animates a speaker can be spotted through voice-level increases or repetitions, as both signal the strong attachment needed for animation. However, from studying vignette 1, and in line with Castor's (2020) work on metaventriloquism, we can see that a person cannot just be animated by a ventriloquial voice herself but can also attribute animations to others. For instance, in vignette 1, M described C as being animated or acted upon by his accidents and injuries. While we originally named emotions, attitudes, values, and the like as typical animations, the attribution of vents as we see it here widens the scope of what can be identified as animation. Cues that help identify animations beyond emotions, attitudes, etc., can be gathered from the syntactical construction of what people say: for example, when a person positions something as actively doing or having done something to someone else; just as M did with the accidents ("the accidents that occurred left you with the séquelles", lines 126–127). Prepositions or conjunctions such as *because of, due to,* or *so* can also be animation cues. Indeed, M presents C's injuries as the cause of C's fear by using the prepositions and conjunctions "because of" and "so" (line 133).

At the end of phase 1, the ventriloquial analyst should have identified in the name of what or whom people and things appear to speak and act within her dataset. To work towards better overview and some initial abstraction, she will need to group the ventriloquial voices.

Phase 2: Grouping

We propose working through two rounds of grouping. To start, the ventriloquial voices can be grouped into *clusters*, that is, first arrangements that bring together similar or related voices. If the analyst seeks to work towards further abstraction, she can perform a second grouping round and arrange the various clusters into overarching *collections*. It is important to keep in mind the studied organizational phenomenon or activity as well as the relevant literature as both can help the ordering and sensemaking process. The analyst can ask herself questions such as:

(a) what are the groups and categories that previous studies have found, and do I see them coming back in my data?
(b) if not, what alternative distinctions or groupings can I observe?
(c) are there ventriloquial voices in my empirical material that are always named together and, if so, can I identify what groups them?

As a simple example, we could group the ventriloquial effects of vignette 1 into two clusters: *psychological/emotional causes* and *rational/factual causes* for C's situation (see also Cooren et al., 2021). C's attributed fear would then be part of the psychological/emotional causes, while his knowledge and professional experience would fall under the rational/factual causes (he seems to present himself as possessing accurate knowledge). Grouping is important for creating structure and overview, but it also supports the later writing-up of findings. In most cases, it will be impossible to name and explain every single ventriloquial effect. Working with clusters and collections can make insights more manageable.

Phase 3: Relating

In phase 3, the separate bits of the analysis are related into a more integrated structure. Ventriloquism argues against an absolute origin of action, which instead propagates through agency chains where multiple actants accomplish a situation, activity, or momentary end. Phase 3 aims to account for this interlinkage by bringing actants together. To do so, we recommend tracing chains of authorship and relations. The four workings of the phrase *"in the name of"* that we spelled out before can be of particular practicality for this endeavor as they enable us to specify and hence better understand what connects an interactant and a figure. We suggest that ventriloquations can relationally weave together configurations by *appealing to figures to speak for oneself*, by *sharing authorship with figures*, by *expressing possession of figures*, or by *attributing action to figures*.

For vignette 1, for example, C's accident, his injuries, as well as his fear all appear to be part of a chain that authors C as an emotion-driven victim, presented as such by M through the attributions she makes about C. In contrast, C's previous work as a police officer and his knowledge and experience author him as a rationality-driven character and responsible citizen. These two chains thus tell different stories of one and the same situation or person, which is why they disorganize the common ground that M and C are trying to build. It is important to stay open to these possible disorganizing effects of communication during the analytical process as CCO-research acknowledges and embraces how communication's constitutive powers can be both organizing and disorganizing, which in many ways is a departure from other stances (Vásquez & Kuhn, 2019; Vásquez et al., this volume).

Phase 4: Showing

Ventriloquism will provide analysts with rich insights. Yet, findings will usually have to be communicated in limited spaces. We generally recommend using a vignette approach (Langley

& Abdallah, 2011), which consists of presenting selected data excerpts to readers and elaborating detailed findings along them. By adopting this *showing* strategy, the ventriloquial analyst can provide deep insight into what she has observed while readers get their own chance of assessing findings and interpretations, which increases credibility. Such a strategy also openly exposes the researcher(s) behind the writing, which accentuates that interpretation and selection have come about. A figure essentially says, "I am interpreted" and a vignette says, "I am chosen", which declares subjectivity and encourages the reader to think along.

Good vignettes are "powerfully illustrative" (Langley & Abdallah, 2011, p. 127). Such illustrative power can be indicated by density of ventriloquial effects. Usually, the ventriloquial analyst will deeply immerse herself in her dataset during analysis, but some data parts might stick with her even beyond the actual activity of analyzing—they might have surprised, sparked curiosity, or even overwhelmed her. These parts can be good starting points when selecting vignettes. Whether the analyst should choose one longer or multiple shorter vignettes should be guided by her research questions, aims, and findings. For instance, for longitudinal designs, selecting vignettes that punctuate different moments in time is certainly useful to convey process and progress. To provide a coherent story, it might further help to follow certain aspects, decisions, etc., across the longitudinal process and select vignettes based on these. Another useful strategy is to select and provide vignettes guided by the clusters and collections identified in phase 2.

When writing up the elaborations that accompany the vignette(s), authors should try to stick close to the displayed data. One of their goals should be to unpack their ventriloquial insights in such a way that readers can follow authors' thinking alongside the presented excerpt—findings should be shown, not just told. Ensuring that vignette and text are closely intertwined is hence a good strategy. However, from time to time, authors might need to move away from the singular situation displayed in the vignette and elaborate on their empirical material's broader picture. That is especially the case for accounts of animations that are identified through repetition beyond a single vignette. Here, explanations about how often these animations have been observed within the entire dataset can help to provide the needed bigger picture information.

Overall, one of the framework's main gains is that it allows analysts to approach their analyses with a shared view. It sensitizes us for what to look for in each of the phases and thereby facilitates comparison and concerted efforts across researchers and studies. It also provides us with a bedrock that we can fall back on to corroborate our impressions, and which reminds us to be critical and reflexive of our findings. All this does not mean that the framework is static or rigid, quite the contrary: we construed it to be flexible and adaptable, with room for additions, refinements, etc. For example, in this chapter we added Castor's (2020) metaventriloquial idea and spelled out four functions or connections of ventriloquations that analysts might want to consider. This chapter is then also an invitation for others to work with and on this ventriloquial analytical framework—possibly across schools.

Ventriloquism across CCO Schools

Three major schools of CCO thinking have been identified (Schoeneborn & Vásquez, 2017): the Montreal school, the Four Flows, and the Luhmannian approach. While each of these schools has distinct strengths, dialoguing and thinking *across* them is an important element of CCO's collective strengthening and advancement (Schoeneborn & Blaschke, 2014). We hence seek to end this chapter with the following exercise: tracing the Montreal School's idea of ventriloquism in Four Flows and in work inspired by Luhmann. To perform this exercise, we turn to

221

an Air Force maintenance squadron (as an example of the Four Flows, taken from Browning et al., 2009) and the hacker collective Anonymous (illustrating the Luhmannian school, taken from Dobusch & Schoeneborn, 2015).

Four Flows: Structuration through Ventriloquation

McPhee and Zaug (2000) introduced four communication flows that they deemed essential for organizational constitution: membership negotiation (demarcating boundaries between those who are in or out), reflexive self-structuring (where shared memory is triggered through recognized utterances), activity coordination (integrating everyone's activities to make contributions fit), and institutional positioning (representing the organization in the broader network). These four flows constitute a structure that can afford and constrain organizational action and agency (Iverson et al., this volume). Ventriloquation could then, for instance, be identified in the references made to this structure as a rule or resource for future actions.

Browning and colleagues (2009) illustrated the flows' communicative complexity and overlap in their study of an Air Force maintenance squadron. They explained how training-base technicians learned what made the difference between successful and failed requests: whether they could demonstrate that they had the actual air combat command's support or not. One interviewee put it like this:

Vignette 2 (taken from Browning et al., 2009, pp. 97–98, italics added)

```
"We're a training base. Our major command is Air Education
Training Command. However, the real power broker in the F-15
community is not AETC. It's headquarters ACC [Air Combat Command]
out of Langley. Their F-15's, you know, have real missions as
opposed to training missions. And if you convince them – they
backed us on a lot of our other successes. And if they're not
backing you, you can almost forget about it. You could look at
Langley as a very strong ally. When ACC says it, they're speaking
on behalf of front-line F-15 fighter units".
```

By and large, the interviewed technician describes their training base's activities as contingent on the ACC ("if they are not backing you, you can almost forget about it"). Speaking as a representative of his group ("*We*'re a training base. *Our* major command [...]"), the technician explains how *the training base depends on the ACC to speak for them* and their training missions—more than they depend on their actual command, the Air Education Training (AETC). Thereby, he positions their training base as not just a part of the AETC, but also of the ACC—they are *members* of the broader collective [i.e., *membership negotiation*]. Through the technician's descriptions, the training base's *activities* are hence tied to the ACC's work [i.e., *activity coordination*]. This also means that the training base cannot act without the ACC: ultimately, their activities must be in line with (or more precisely, animated by) the Langley headquarters [i.e., *reflexive self-structuring* and *institutional positioning*].

Compared to the ACC, both the AETC and the training base are in less powerful positions (in consequence of their activity coordination): they possess only the "training missions" while the ACC has the "real missions". As explained by the technician, the ACC appropriates these real missions because of the F-15 fighters that he presents the ACC to speak "on behalf of" and that actually possess these missions ("their F-15s, you know, have real missions"). This *appropriation of the real missions through the F-15 units* strengthens the ACC's power or authority: what this command center decides and communicates reflects not just their own position, but also the positions of the fighter units that need to operate in real missions. In other words, while the training base's activities are animated by the ACC, the ACC's decisions are presented as being driven by the "front-line F-15 fighter units".

The technician hence invokes the broader relations surrounding their training base and emphasizes how their base is connected to the "real power broker[s]". He *attributes the training base's work to that of the Air Combat Command and the fighters* and presents a meticulously constructed chain of voices that the training base is being organized around. As a result, the technician is able to produce an account or *institutional positioning* of their group as much more than just a training facility.

Luhmann: Autopoiesis and Decision Communication through Ventriloquation

One of Luhmann's core assumptions is that autopoietic systems reproduce themselves by actively deciding that previous decisions were indeed decisions: when a previous decision is followed up by a new decision, this ratifies the first one (Grothe-Hammer, this volume). Ongoing decisions then constitute what is or what is not an organization or organizational. Ventriloquism could be identified in the invocation of these decisions and/or the system making or endorsing them: as animations, decisions could request or lead to behaviors that (re)establish the system; when they are the dummy, decisions could, for example, be invoked to justify or typify an organizational action. The determination of what decision to make in crucial moments of undecidability (where there is no obviously better choice; see van Vuuren & Cooren, 2010) is itself influenced by the commitment to previous decisions. Decisions thereby can become each other's vents and dummies and constitute a system through which consistency and organizationality (Schoeneborn et al., this volume) are enforced.

An interesting case of decisions and undecidability is presented by Dobusch and Schoeneborn (2015) in their analysis of Anynomous's Operation Facebook. By definition, an anonymous hacker collective struggles with identification and legitimation of authority: who gets to say what Anonymous should do? In the specific case that Dobusch and Schoeneborn studied, two opposing voices (both declaring to speak as Anonymous) are presented on different social media platforms. On Facebook, a new group acting with the name Anonymous announced a war directed at Facebook, calling upon "the right not to be surveilled" (Dobusch & Schoeneborn, 2015, p. 1025) and claiming that this operation is in accordance with Anonymous's principles. By so doing, *this group appropriated Anonymous's principles*: their operation followed Anonymous's principles, which expressed a possession of these principles. Thereby, the group positioned their war as being operated under the designation of Anonymous: *they attributed their (planned) actions to the collective*.

However, a Twitter account that has already been speaking as Anonymous for a longer period claimed that "[Operation Facebook] is just ANOTHER FAKE!" (Dobusch & Schoeneborn, 2015, p. 1025). These opposing statements, both uttered as coming from Anonymous, constituted a moment of undecidability: what exactly is Anonymous's decision regarding its war on Facebook? Or, in other words, which group is Anonymous's leading ventriloquist, the Facebook or the Twitter one? This paradoxical situation (or ventriloquial conflict) was resolved when the Twitter Anonymous group revealed the Facebook Anonymous group initiator's identity, literally and figuratively proving that he was not anonymous (at least not any more). By revealing his identity, they reduced his communicative acts to just him: *he was speaking in his own name only, and not in the name of Anonymous.* Thereby, the Facebook group's appropriation of and attribution to Anonymous's principles did no longer hold. This in turn strengthened the overall system, where the Twitter Anonymous account gained enforced organizationality: this account was able not only to present Anonymous and speak in its name, but also to name those that were not; appropriating the (momentary) right to decide what and who is or is not Anonymous.

Concluding Thought

Ventriloquism provides us with a rich metaphor to think about communication and offers us an intriguing analytical lens when unpacking the processes of communicative constitution. In this chapter, we explained the ventriloquial idea alongside multiple examples, explicated four workings of ventriloquial connections, described the methodological steps of doing a ventriloquial analysis, and showed how ventriloquial acts can transcend schools' boundaries. We look forward to seeing new ventriloquial analyses, hoping that one day this chapter will have turned into a dummy itself.

References

Bencherki, N., & Cooren, F. (2011). Having to be: The possessive constitution of organization. *Human Relations, 64*(12), 1579–1607.

Benoit-Barné, C., & Cooren, F. (2009). The accomplishment of authority through presentification: How authority is distributed among and negotiated by organizational members. *Management Communication Quarterly, 23,* 5–31.

Browning, L. D., Greene, R. W., Sitkin, S. B., Sutcliffe, K. M., & Obstfeld, D. (2009). Constitutive complexity. Military entrepreneurs and the synthetic character of communication flows. In L.L. Putnam & A.M Nicotera (Eds.), *Building theories of organization: The constitutive role of communication* (pp. 89–116). Routledge.

Caronia, L., & Cooren, F. (2014). Decentering our analytical position: The dialogicity of things. *Discourse & Communication, 8,* 41–61.

Castor, T. (2020). On streams and lakes: Metaventriloquism and the technologies of a water controversy. *Language and Dialogue, 10,* 29–48.

Castor, T., & Cooren, F. (2006). Organizations as hybrid forms of life: The implications of the selection of agency in problem formulation. *Management Communication Quarterly, 19,* 570–600.

Cooren, F. (2010). *Action and agency in dialogue.* John Benjamins.

Cooren, F. (2012). Communication theory at the center: Ventriloquism and the communicative constitution of reality. *Journal of Communication, 62,* 1–20.

Cooren, F. (2015). *In medias res*: Communication, existence, and materiality. *Communication Research and Practice, 1,* 307–321.

Cooren, F. (2018). Materializing communication: Making the case for a relational ontology. *Journal of Communication, 68,* 278–288.

Cooren, F. (2020). Beyond entanglement: (Socio-)materiality and organization studies. *Organization Theory, 1,* 1–24.

Cooren, F., Fairhurst, G., & Huët, R. (2012). Why matter always matters in (organizational) communication. In P. M. Leonardi, B. A. Nardi, & J. Kallinikos (Eds.), *Materiality and organizing* (pp. 296–314). Oxford University Press.

Cooren, F., Higham, L., & Brummans, B. H. J. M. (2021). Epilogue: The ventriloquism of media: Communication as delegation and tele-action. In J. Baron, J. Fleeger, & S. Wong Lerner (Eds.), *Mediaventriloquism: How audiovisual technologies transform the voice-body relationship* (pp. 241–260). Oxford University Press.

Cooren, F., & Sandler, S. (2014). Polyphony, ventriloquism, and constitution: In dialogue with Bakhtin. *Communication Theory, 24,* 225–244.

Dobusch, L., & Schoeneborn, D. (2015). Fluidity, identity, and organizationality: The communicative constitution of *Anonymous. Journal of Management Studies, 52,* 1006–1035.

In the name of [Def. 1]. (n.d.). In *Cambridge Dictionary*, retrieved November 16, 2020, from https://dictionary.cambridge.org/dictionary/english/name?q=in+the+name+of.

In the name of [Def. 2]. (n.d.). In *Collins Dictionary*, retrieved November 16, 2020, from www.collinsdictionary.com/dictionary/english/in-the-name-of.

In the name of [Def. ½]. (n.d.). In *Merriam-Webster Dictionary*, retrieved November 16, 2020, from www.merriam-webster.com/dictionary/in%20the%20name%20of.

Kuhn, T., Ashcraft, K. L., & Cooren, F. (2017). *The work of communication: Relational perspectives on working and organizing in contemporary capitalism.* Routledge.

Langley, A., & Abdallah, C. (2011). Templates and turns in qualitative studies of strategy and management. In D. D. Bergh & D. J. Ketchen (Eds.), *Research methodology in strategy and management* (Vol. 6, pp. 201–235). Emerald Group.

McPhee, R. D., & Zaug, P. (2000). The communicative constitution of organizations: A framework for explanation. *Electronic Journal of Communication, 10*(1/2), 1–16.

Nathues, E., van Vuuren, M., & Cooren, F. (2021). Speaking about vision, talking in the name of so much more: A methodological framework for ventriloquial analyses in organization studies. *Organization Studies, 42*, 1457–1476.

Pomerantz, A., Sanders, R. E., & Bencherki, N. (2018). Communication as the study of social action: On the study of language and social interaction. *Communiquer, 22*, 103–118.

Schoeneborn, D., Blaschke, S., Cooren, F., McPhee, R. D., Seidl, D., & Taylor, J. R. (2014). The three schools of CCO thinking: Interactive dialogue and systematic comparison. *Management Communication Quarterly, 28*, 285–316.

Schoeneborn, D., & Vásquez, C. (2017). Communicative constitution of organizations. In C. R. Scott, L. Lewis, J. R. Barker, J. Keyton, T. Kuhn, & P. K. Turner (Eds.), *The international encyclopedia of organizational communication* (Vol. 1, pp. 367–386). Wiley.

Schoeneborn, D., Kuhn, T. R., & Kärreman, D. (2019). The communicative constitution of organization, organizing, and organizationality. *Organization Studies, 40*, 475–496.

Van Vuuren, M., & Cooren, F. (2010). "My attitude made me do it": Considering the agency of attitudes. *Human Studies, 33*, 85–101.

Vásquez, C., & Kuhn, T. (2019). *Dis/organization as communication: Exploring the disordering, disruptive, and chaotic properties of communication.* Routledge.

14

ETHNOMETHODOLOGICAL CONVERSATION ANALYSIS AND THE CONSTITUTIVE ROLE OF ORGANIZATIONAL TALK

Helle Kryger Aggerholm, Birte Asmuß,
Henrik Ladegaard Johannesen and Leo Feddersen Smith

Ethnomethodology and the Communicative Constitution of Organization (CCO) approach view communication in general, and organizational talk in particular, as residing in social practices (Schoeneborn, Blaschke, Cooren, McPhee, Seidl, & Taylor, 2014; Schoeneborn, Kuhn, & Kärreman, 2019). From an ethnomethodological approach, these social practices are intersubjective in nature, interactively constructed, negotiated and accomplished. Consequently, organizational talk becomes observably evident in participants' coordination of their turns-at-talk and responses to each other's communicative actions. Such organizational "talk" is constituted not only by means of verbal actions, but multimodally by means of verbal, non-verbal, embodied, and material resources, all of which provide the contexts in which the interactions acquire particular meanings. A growing number of researchers attempt to elucidate how communicative organizational practices constitute organizational phenomena. These researchers share the belief that ethnomethodological conversation analysis offers a methodology that is specifically well-fitted to analyse the naturally occurring work life practices that are constitutive of organizational life.

Linking CCO and Ethnomethodology: Material Agency and Social Interaction

Since the evolvement of the field of organizational communication in the 1990s (for an overview see Jablin & Putnam, 2001), communication has been considered important when seeking to understand organizational phenomena. Instead of conceptualizing communication and organization as distinct phenomena that mutually inform each other, the CCO paradigm (McPhee & Zaug, 2009; Putnam & Nicotera, 2009) has moved this field forward in acknowledging that communication and organization are indistinguishable in that communication is constitutive for organizational action (Cooren, Kuhn, Cornelissen, & Clark, 2011). Placed within the broader discursive turn in organization studies (Cooren, 2007; Vaara, 2010), one

DOI: 10.4324/9781003224914-17

of the central contributions of CCO has been the move towards materiality, i.e., the acknowledgement of non-human agents as important for accomplishing organizational goals (Latour, 1987; Ashcraft, Kuhn, & Cooren, 2009). In recent years, it has become clear that the material environment, in the form of objects, bodies and sites (Ashcraft, Kuhn, & Cooren, 2009; Lê & Spee, 2015), shapes the way organizational members act in organizations in general and forms how organizational members specifically interact. This more recent inclusion of materiality in the study of organizations generates a natural linkage between the CCO approach and the use of an ethnomethodological methodology, in specific multimodal conversation analysis.

Starting out with a focus on verbal structure (Sacks, 1992; Sacks, Schegloff, & Jefferson, 1974), ethnomethodological conversation analysis has, over the last decades, developed a strong focus on social actions as being accomplished by means of multimodal resources (Stivers & Sidnell 2005; Mortensen 2013; Asmuß 2015; Mondada 2007; LeBaron 2012), which include verbal, non-verbal, embodied and material resources (Mortensen, 2013; Asmuß, 2015; Nevile, 2015). Studies have shown how various communicative actions consist of multiple modalities (e.g. Asmuß & Oshima, 2012; Glenn & LeBaron, 2011; Heath & vom Lehn, 2008; Mondada, 2011) that participants in interaction can make use of and systematically orient to when communicating. Rather than participants' retrospective accounts of their actions, conversation analysis has proven to have great potential in capturing the dynamics and sequential organization of real-time interaction as it relies on authentic interactions. Studies have for instance highlighted the importance of textual documents (Pälli & Lehtinen, 2014), material artifacts like computers (Asmuß & Oshima, 2012) and PowerPoints (Nissi & Lehtinen, 2016) for the accomplishment of organizational goals. In its recent focus on time (Johannesen, 2018), space (Cnossen & Bencherki, 2019) and emotions (Ruusuvuori, Asmuß, Henttonen, & Ravaja, 2019), an ethnomethodological perspective contributes to acknowledging the socio-material (Cooren, 2020) as well as temporal, spatial and emotional ressources available for organizational members when conducting organizational work.

Similar to CCO, the ethnomethodological perspective places social norms and communicative processes at the core of organizational life. An area within organization studies where this joint interest has proven to be specifically fruitful is the practice perspective in general (Nicolini, 2012), and the strategy-as-practice approach in specific (Golsorkhi, Rouleau, Seidl, & Vaara, 2010). In relation to strategy work, numerous studies have addressed the communicative foundations of strategy work (Aggerholm & Asmuß, 2016a; Asmuß & Oshima, 2018; Samra-Fredericks, 2003, 2005) as well as the need to acknowledge embodied ressources when doing strategy work (Gylfe, Franck, LeBaron, & Mantere, 2016). Within the field of organizational routines (Feldman & Pentland, 2003), an ethnomethodological perspective, with its focus on embodied and communicative actions, has provided fundamental insights into the interactive organization of work routines (LeBaron, Christianson, Garrett, & Ilan, 2016), as well as the performative aspects of organizational routines (Aggerholm & Asmuß, 2016b).

Ethnomethodological Conversation Analysis

Informed by ethnomethodology (Garfinkel, 1967) and Goffman's interaction order (Goffman, 1983), conversation analysis is founded on Harvey Sacks's lectures at the University of California in the late 1960s (Sacks, 1992), and consists in a systematic method to analyze how social beings intersubjectively create meaning and understanding (Sidnell & Stivers, 2012).

Conversation analysis is aligned with ethnomethodology in its interest in uncovering the normative regularities that human beings orient to in social life. More precisely, it attempts to describe the orderliness, structure and sequential patterns of interaction. This orderliness is also referred to as the *conversational machinery* (Sacks, Schegloff, & Jefferson, 1974), and it builds centrally on the sequential structuring of organizational talk, which is "the organization of courses of action enacted through turns-at-talk – coherent, orderly, meaningful successions or 'sequences' of actions or 'moves'" (Schegloff 2007, p. 2).

A *sequential analysis* forms the basis for any conversation analysis and it is fundamentally concerned with the analysis of what a turn is doing and how it is related to its sequential context, i.e., to what comes before and directly after this turn at talk. For that purpose, *next turn proof procedure* is a central analytical tool: it focuses on how a next turn responds to the current one. This response is taken as an indication of what kind of action the prior turn accomplishes (Hutchby & Woofitt, 2008). For instance, the way the audience responds will tell whether a question like "How are you today" actually is an authentic inquiry about a person's state of mind, or whether it is a mere greeting. Sequential analysis is concerned with two central interactional phenomena: *turn taking* and *repair organization*, as first described in the seminal papers by Sacks, Schegloff and Jefferson (1974) and Schegloff, Jefferson and Sacks (1977). Turn taking organization describes the set of regular interactional practices that social beings use to allocate and construct turns at talk. Repair organization is concerned with interactional problems like mishearings or misunderstandings and how they are dealt with locally in the ongoing talk. These phenomena enable the analytical identification of social norms and and moral order as accomplished through interaction, which means that organization and organizing takes place in the interactional here and now.

Doing Conversation Analysis

When doing conversation analysis, the first step is to collect adequate data. Here, it is crucial to rely on *naturally occurring* data, that is data that has not been produced for the sake of the analysis, but data that stem from interactional settings and actions that also would have taken place without the researcher's interest and involvement (Sidnell & Stivers, 2012). In its focus on the micro analytical level, conversation analysis makes use of audio and video recordings in order to make fine-grained transcriptions of the data so that the primary data can be listened to and watched repetitively, thus allowing for a change in focus along the line of the analysis. When deciding whether to use audio or video recordings as the preferred data material, the criterion of *participants' perspective* is relevant. It takes the position that the data for analysis should be as closely identical with the original interactional setting as possible. That means when the interlocutors have visual access to each other, the analyst should too, and in that case video data would be preferred. On the other hand, if interlocutors talk over the phone, video recordings would not make sense as participants are not able to see each other. In this case, audio recordings would do.

The second step for moving into the analysis would be the transcription of the data. In a conversation analytic tradition, it is important to keep in mind that while a close transcript of all interactional details on the one hand forms the basis for any analysis, it on the other hand also stays true to the data in that the transcript is never seen as a form of data, instead it is just a tool. This means that the original data in form of audio or video recordings will always be considered as the main data source that needs to be used continously throughout the data anlaytical process.

As one of the three pioneer academics who originally shaped the field of conversation analysis, Gail Jefferson has developed a transcription system that focuses on the close description of verbal and prosodic features, paying close attention to elements such as speaker emphasis, overlap organization, and pauses (Jefferson, 1984, 2004; Bolden, 2015; Hepburn & Bolden, 2013). Here, Jefferson aimed at creating a balance between the inclusion of as many details as possible, in order to be close to the recording, while also ensuring the readability of the transcripts. As a consequence of the increased focus on video-recorded face-to-face encounters, which also entailed a greater inclusion of embodied and material aspects of interaction, this system has been developed further to also include multimodal features (Goodwin, 1986; Hepburn & Bolden, 2013; Raclaw & Ford, 2015). Here, it is important to note that every transcript, irrespective of its level of detail, will be subjective in the way that each researcher will have to make decisions about which details to include in the transcript and which ones to disregard. Therefore, many conversation analytic transcripts will be revised throughout the analytic process in accordance with the precise research interest. When transcribing other languages than the one in which the research will be published, for instance English, the detailedness of the transcription system makes it relevant not only to include an intelligible translation of the original data into English, but also to include a word-by-word translation. This way, all relevant features of the turn design (overlap, pauses, sequential patterning) can be precisely identified.

The third step is the actual analysis. As a starting point, the data would be approached without having a precise assumption on what to go for or what to find. "Unmotivated looking" (Psathas, 1995), which refers to the basic conversation analytic principle to set the data centre stage, means that the data is browsed for anything that attracts the researcher's attention. These initial observations form the basis of a more in-depth analysis.

A way to move forward from first observations to actually describe an interactional phenomenon would be to do a single case study or to make collections of the phenomenon under investigation (Heritage, 1995; Schegloff, 1993), and most collections are actually based on an initial in-depth single case analysis. When building a collection, and depending on the phenomenon of interest, the researcher would try to identify similar instances across the data that in sum constitute the collection. A basic principle of collections would be to look for deviant cases (Sidnell, 2012), that is cases of the phenomenon under investigation that, at first sight, do not comply with or support the regularities found in the rest of the collection. The inclusion of deviant cases increases the robustness of the findings, in that it helps to identify the social norms that participants talk into being when communicating with each other.

Writing up the analysis, excerpts that best shed light on the phenomenon under investigation would be identified, and an analytic story would be built around those. Many of Gail Jefferson's papers are excellent examples of a conversation analytic procedure for collection building (Jefferson, 1978, 1987), where the robustness of the phenomenon becomes compelling due to the detailedness and transparency of her collection-building procedure and analytical detailedness.

Conversation Analysis and Constitutive Organizing

In the following, two exemplary analyses are shown to explicate how multimodal conversation analysis can help understand the emergence of organizational structure through interaction.

The first exemplary analysis will show how organizational structure in general, and temporal structure in particular, are accomplished in materially embedded turns of talk. We conceptualize temporal structure using McPhee's structurationist approach, which understands organizations as composed of four communicative flows: *membership negotiation, reflexive self-structuring, activity coordination,* and *institutional positioning* (McPhee & Zaug, 2009). Temporal artifacts such as schedules, timetables, and procedures are central to the communicative flow of reflexive self-structuring processes that distinguish formal organization from informal organization (McPhee & Zaug, 2009). However, such processes are neither unidirectional, internally consistent or effective in and of themselves, nor can they provide exhaustively for the emergence of temporal structure. Rather, they must be amended and enacted through activity coordination at the level of ordinary interaction (McPhee & Zaug, 2009). This view contrasts with studies that emphasize either the "subjective" or "objective" side of temporal structuring processes (Orlikowski & Yates, 2002).

Using video recordings of authentic workplace interaction, we track the sequential organization of a possible transition from work into lunch as it is projected, and ultimately rejected, by the members of a work team. We have chosen a case where the participants pursue different trajectories as it reveals the normative horizon on which "expected" conduct is produced and recognized (Garfinkel, 1967). The use of a case where the projected "temporal normalcy" (Zerubavel, 1981) is "breached" (Garfinkel, 1967) enables us to show just how the interplay between different communicative "flows" unfolds in ordinary interaction.

The data was produced as part of a larger ethnographic study of temporal structuring in flexible workplace settings (Johannesen, 2018). The site for the study was a temporary project office with members from a public contractor and a number of private subcontractors. The participants in the interaction are Svend (SVD), who was employed directly by the public contractor, and Pil (PIL) and Jonas (JNS), who were employed by one of the subcontractors. They are editing a document for the tender package for one of the subprojects in the entire project. Karl (KAR), another employee from the subcontractor, has been called in to answer some questions and is leaving at the beginning of the interaction.

```
                @ delimits embodied conduct by SVD¹
                Δ delimits embodied conduct by KAR
                * delimits embodied conduct by PIL
                + delimits embodied conduct by JNS

1     svd:      @>>reads document--->1.25
      kar:      Δ>>closes door--->

2     KAR:      nu går jeg til frokost
                now walk.PRS i.1SG to lunch.SG.INDF
                i'm having lunch now

3     PIL:      >ja det fint<.Δ
                yes that_be.PRS fine
                yes that's fine
      kar:                     --->Δ

4               +(0.5)#(0.5)+
      fig:            #fig 1
      jns:      +-----1-----+
                1: looks at wristwatch

5     JNS:      m det gør vi vel oss+
                that do.FUT we.1PL PRT also
                i guess we'll do so as well
      jns:                         +adjusts the screen--->

6     PIL:      det gør vi oss ja
                that do.FUT we.1PL also yes
                we'll do so as well yes
```

```
7              (0.6)+ +(1.0)
    jns:       -->+ +moves hand to trackpad--->

8   PIL:       skynd dig å gemme+
               hurry_up.IMP you and save.INF
               hurry up and save
    jns:                       -->+

9              (0.8)

10  JNS:       nå for søren+ (alligevel)
               oh dang it
               oh dang it
                             +presses key--->
    pil:                     *looks at JNS--->

11             (0.4)+(0.2)*(0.4)
    jns:       -->+
    pil:             -->*

12  PIL:       at der ikk' lige pludselig går et eller andet koks
               that there not just suddenly walk.PRS one or other wrong
               that something doesn't go wrong all of a sudden

13             (0.2)@(1.2)
                       @rotates pencil and taps document--->

14  JNS:       ja@
               yes
               yes
    svd:       -->@
```

Karl announces in l. 2 that he is having lunch now, and Jonas proposes in l. 5 that they have lunch as well. He delivers the proposal with epistemic primacy (Stivers, Mondada, & Steensig, 2011) by designing the turn with flat intonation and the modal particle "vel" which expresses the expectation to have some opinion or notion confirmed. He prefaces his turn with a short look at his watch (Figure 14.1a), which displays that the time of the clock is relevant for his proposal. One way of understanding his gesture is that it indexes a lunchtime schedule for the members of the project office. As such, the embodied delivery of his turn can be said to *ventriloquize* (Cooren, Matte, Benoit-Barné, & Brummans, 2013) the proposal to have lunch. Pil confirms the proposal in l. 6 by changing it to a declarative format and appending a positive response particle. Lexically, the construction of her turn is almost identical with the construction of Jonas's first turn, and it can be seen as aligning structurally with the suggestion to have lunch.[2] Jonas proceeds in l. 7 by moving one of his hands to the trackpad. The position of his hands displays that he is about to do something in the electronic document, but probably not anything that involves typing. Pil proposes a likely next action by asking him to save the document, which further develops the transition into lunch (l. 8). Saving the document is, of course, not final in any way, and new revisions can be made at any time. However, it projects a sequential position where the closing of the document, and by extension the activity, can happen.

She attends to the saving of the document as somehow volatile by using, in her turn of talk, the verb "at skynde"/"to hurry". This may relate to the risk of losing the work that has been done until now to a software glitch, or it may relate to the risk of discovering new problems that must be solved before lunch. In any case it underscores the need to save the progression that has been made.

```
15          (2.5)
16   SVD:   .hh HHHHH °duh duh ⌜duh⌝ duh duh duh°

17   PIL:                    £⌞hhh⌟£

18   PIL:   *det en ond og uretfærdig vi lever i*
            it_be.PRS a cruel and unjust we.1PL live.PRS in
            it's a cruel and unjust we live in
            *pulls ring binder closer----------*

19   PIL:   °en uretfærdig *verden vi lever i°=
            an.SG.INDF unjust world.SG.INDF we.1PL live.PRS in
            an unjust world we live in
            *looks down----*
                        *sorts documents--->
```

Thus, over a number of turns, Pil and Jonas have collaboratively worked towards a closure of the work activity. However, instead of aligning with the projected transition into lunch, Svend produces continuous displays of working on the document. He does not participate in his co-participants' talk in ll. 2-14, but keeps his gaze on the document in front of him. He proceeds by tapping his pencil on the document (l. 14) and producing a hearable exhalation (l. 16). His embodied actions are ambiguous, but a likely understanding is that he *would like* lunch as well, but that lunch should *not* happen as long as they have unresolved problems. Pil responds to his exhalation by producing a laughter particle (l. 17) and a proverbial phrase (l. 18). She gets the phrase wrong at first and repairs it in an extended turn (l. 19). The phrase is difficult to translate, but it is typically used jokingly to say something like "that's just the way it is". Hence, she attends to his exhalation as designedly hyperbolic, but she also aligns with his display of "duty". Moreover, as she is delivering her turns in ll. 18-19, she pulls the ring binder in front of her closer and sorts through some of the documents, which may indicate that she is returning to the revision of the document.

```
20   JNS:   =MEN DET HER (0.7) *afsnit her
            but this here section.SG.INDF here
            but this section here
     pil:                      -->*

21          *>det kan vi jo sådan set s-<
            that can.PRS we.1PL PRT like see.PST.PTCP
            we might as well
     pil:   *looks at monitor--->>

22          (0.8)
```

```
23        +jo godt slette det #alligevel ikk',
           good delete.INF it anyway not
           delete it anyway right
           +supports head with hand--->>
                            #fig2

24        (0.5)

25  PIL:  oss *svend @ve du @er du enig i det?@@
           also svend want.PRS you.2SG agree in that
           also svend do you want do you agree with that
     pil:      *points at monitor--->>
     svd:       -->@
     svd:                    @looks up---------@
     svd:                                    @looks at
                                             monitor--->>
```

Svend does not respond to Pil's turn in ll. 18–19, but keeps looking at the document. Jonas proceeds in ll. 20–23 by suggesting a paragraph that can be deleted from the document. His turn is aligned with the displayed return to the work task, and it lacks the normal "beat" between turns-at-talk, which may indicate that he did not want to have "ownership" of the transition into lunch. However, even if he is quick to abandon the projected transition into lunch, he displays some reluctance. Specifically, he produces a display of physical exhaustion by sinking into his seat and resting his head in his hand as he is making the suggestion (Figure 14.1b). During the delivery of the last part of the turn, Pil stops organizing her documents and shifts her gaze from the folder in front of her to the monitor with the suggested revisions (l. 21). She proceeds in l. 25 by directing Svend's gaze at the monitor and asking for his confirmation. Both she and Jonas are now actively involved in the continued work on the document instead of the projected closure of the activity.

Figure 14.1a Jonas looks at his watch.

Figure 14.1b Jonas supports his head.

By tracking the sequential organization of a possible transition into lunch, the analysis shows how multimodal conversation analysis can explicate the ways in which organizational structure is accomplished in authentic workplace interaction. Specifically, it shows that the participants invoke different temporal structures to project, and resist, a transition into lunch as the *normatively expected* trajectory of the present work activity, namely a conception of lunch as something that should happen in a particular timeslot (i.e., during lunchtime) and a conception of lunch as something that should happen in a particular sequence (i.e., not before the present problem is resolved). From a CCO perspective, this, in turn, sheds light on the way in which reflexive self-structuring processes provide the horizon for, yet at the same time are amended and enacted through, activity coordination processes at the level of ordinary interaction (McPhee & Zaug, 2009).

The second empirical example serves to illustrate the constitutive role of multimodal interaction for accomplishing the important organizational task of mentoring (Allen, Eby, Chao, & Bauer, 2017). The data is part of a large collection of stories told in pre-hire mentorships (Spitzmüller et al., 2008), which is a specific type of employer branding activity in which a mentor from a specific company volunteers to mentor a young student. The aim of such mentorships is to both help students prepare for life in the labor market, and brand the company as caring about young people, while spotting potential future employees. From a CCO perspective, these mentoring practices are part of the institutional positioning flow, as they involve the communicative constitution of who the company is in the broader labor market (McPhee & Zaug, 2009).

Mentoring involves a great number of interactional micropractices and corresponding roles. According to the practitioner literature, one such mentoring practice is storytelling (Megginson & Clutterbuck, 2005; Poulsen, 2008). Indeed, the role of stories as meaning-making tools in organizations has been widely researched in organizational studies since the so-called narrative turn (Boje, 1991; Czarniawska, 2004; Fenton & Langley, 2011; Gabriel, 2000; Robichaud, Giroux, & Taylor, 2004). Likewise, the broader branding literature has also emphasized the importance of stories in terms of positioning (Lundqvist, Liljander, Gummerus, & van Riel,

2013; Aaker & Aaker, 2016). However, these studies tend to look at the stories in a vacuum, neglecting to consider that stories-in-interaction are told somewhere by someone to someone else. Put differently, much emphasis has been given to the story, and very little to the telling. This is a shortcoming because, like mentoring, storytelling is not something that just is; it is something that members accomplish in interaction. As demonstrated by Sacks's (Sacks, 1992) early explorations of the subject in his lectures, stories emerge as members engage in practices that are distinguishably "storytelling" both for members and for observers. Conversation analytic scholars have investigated various aspects of storytelling, such as how stories may be prefaced (Sacks, 1992, pp. 222–228), how recipients demonstrate recipiency (Stivers, 2008) or even change the trajectory of the story-in-progress (Mandelbaum, 1989) and how the meaning of the story is negotiated (Kjærbeck & Asmuß, 2005). For organizational settings, these findings are of relevance in that they show how storytelling practices can help accomplish various organizational goals.

In the following analysis, the emphasis is on the multimodal means through which mentors and mentees make sense of a story and how these micro-level actions constitute the intersubjective accomplishment of organizational mentoring. The following excerpt is taken from a collection of 71 naturally occurring storytelling sequences in organizational mentorships (Smith, 2018). The excerpt consists of the punchline sequence of a storytelling activity (Kjærbeck & Asmuß, 2005), constituted by the punchline itself and the subsequent meaning negotiation.

The excerpt is from the very beginning of the first mentor conversation between the mentor L (to the left) and the mentee T (to the right).

```
1. L  :  Ø:::hm ±>for<=to  år    siden var man³ ±tyve    mand,
    :  U:::hm >prt<=two year ago   was one twenty man,
    :  Uhm two years ago there were twenty people,
   L:  -----±Raises left hand------±downward gesture--,
   T:  Gaze at L------------------------------------,
       Fig 2a         Fig 2b                Fig 2c
2. L  :  .hh ±i dag er  vi de he:r (.) ±lig- lige knap
          ±halvtreds.
    :  .hh today are we these       jus- just under fifty.
    :  .hh today we are about jus- just under fifty
   L  :  -----±Raises left hand--------±downward
          gesture-±Repeat--,
   T  :  -----------------------------------------------,
       Fig 2d                Fig 2e  Fig 2f
```

In line 1, the mentor presents the number of people employed by the company two years ago. The turn is designed to constitute the first part of a compound turn construction unit (TCU) (Lerner, 1991), meaning that the turn is produced hearably as the first part of a two-part unit. Verbally this is achieved by "ago" combined with rising intonation. The latter projects that the mentor is going to continue talking while the former indicates that the current situation, or "now", is going to be the focus of what is to follow, resulting in a comparison between two years ago and now. The comparison is emphasized by the vocal emphasis on the number twenty and the embodied movements. The mentor raises his hand (Figure 14.2a) after producing the "uhm" and then lowers it sharply when uttering the number twenty (Figure 14.2c). This movement strengthens the verbal emphasis, so two semiotic modes are used to indicate that the number twenty is of particular importance. In the context of the story-in-progress it assists the mentee in foreseeing that a punchline might be forthcoming.

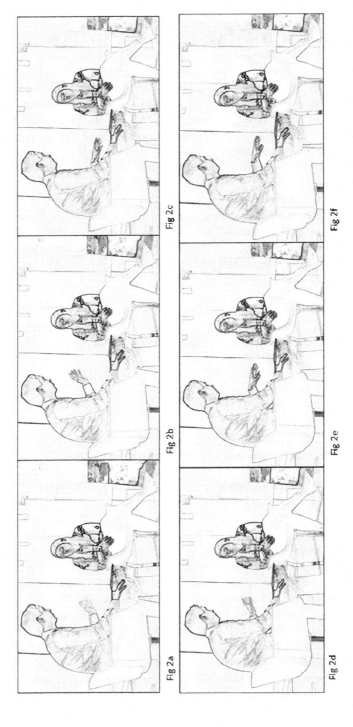

Figure 14.2 A six-panel strip showing mentor L speaking with mentee T. Mentor L's left arm is outstretched and his hand gestures change as he speaks.

In line 2, the mentor continues by presenting the current number of employees – fifty. This is hearable as a punchline because he presents this part as the second part of the compound TCU indicated in line 1. His hand gesture emphasizes this as well, as he repeats the raising and sharp lowering gesture from line 1. The embodied behavior mirrors line 1 quite perfectly. The hand is raised at the time indicator (at "two years ago in" line 1, and "today" in line 2) and it is lowered when producing the number ("twenty" in line 1, and "just under fifty" in line 2).

The emphatic embodied movements work in tandem with the verbal production to allow the mentee to orient to this turn as a potential punchline, which refers to the change from 20 employees two years ago to just under 50 employees today. Therefore, the punchline of the story is hearable as pertaining to the growth and success of the company, and thus has the potential to constitute a micro-instance of institutional positioning. However, much like a joke, the "success" of a storytelling largely depends on the story-receiver responding properly to the punchline. How the mentee responds to the potential punchline is therefore as important for the communicative constitution of the institutional positioning of the company as the story itself.

```
1. L : ≠.hh Så det' gået    ≠rigtig ±[rigtig    stærkt. ]
   : .hh So it's gone       really  [really     fast.  ]
   : So it's gone really            [really     fast   ]
      L :----------------------±Gaze at chart-----------→
      T : ≠Nod raised eyebrows≠ gaze at chart-----------→
            Fig 3
2. T :                              ±[De:t' gået tjept. ]
   :                                 [It's  gone snappy.]
   :                                 [It's gone snappy  ]
```

For the punchline to succeed, Kjærbeck and Asmuß (2005) have shown that the first step is for the story recipient to treat the modality of the story, that is, whether the story was sad, happy, surprising, etc. In line 3, the mentee's initial treatment of the potential punchline is a single downward nod, raising her eyebrows, and pulling the corners of her mouth down (Figure 14.3). Her embodied behavior thus treats the modality of the story as impressive. The mentor does not leave her much room to verbally comment on the modality of the story as he initiates a formulation in line 3 with the turn-initial "So" after a short but hearable in-breath. Before the mentor completes his assessment, the mentee overlaps with her own assessment in line 4. In doing so, she exhibits understanding (Sacks, 1992, p. 252) of the nature of the growth as "snappy". The assessment is produced as an unmarked first assessment in the form of a simple declarative, whereby the mentee claims access to the assessed and exhibits knowledge about what constitutes a fast growth rate (Heritage & Raymond, 2005). By overlapping to make her assessment, the mentee does being knowledgeable and treats this as important since she is willing to compromise the normative rule of talk-in-interaction that only one person should speak at a time (Sacks, Schegloff, & Jefferson, 1974). However, the overlap is less confronting because multimodally it can be seen as a natural continuation of her initial embodied response.

By means of multimodal conversation analysis, we have demonstrated the importance of seemingly trivial actions, such as raising eyebrows, hand gestures, gaze, and overlapping talk by showing how they form the building blocks of meaning-making. It is through various multimodal interactional practices that the mentor and the mentee enact their respective roles,

Figure 14.3   A single-panel figure showing mentor L speaking with mentee T.

and co-negotiate the institutional positioning of the company. Moreover, the analysis provides empirical evidence for the co-construction of organizational phenomena, a fundamental assumption of the CCO approach. The organizational members co-create meaning about the company, and thus they by means of organizational micro-practices like storytelling co-construct and co-interpret the organization. The analysis also shows how participants come to enact their respective roles as mentor and mentee, namely that storytelling is something relevantly done by mentors. In that way it becomes obvious that the co-creation of hierarchy and authority is embedded in the storytelling activity.

The two analyses of organizational talk show how EMCA can ground fundamental CCO concepts in empirical studies of authentic interaction in "real time" (Llewellyn & Hindmarsh, 2010). We have so far referred primarily to the communicative "flows" in the structurationist approach within the larger CCO tradition (Brummans et al. 2014). However, building on concepts from the Montréal School approach, we can extend the analyses further. It is a central notion in CCO that any kind of organizing is necessarily triadic (Taylor & Van Every, 2010). It involves not only a subject acting on an object (a dyadic relationship), but a conceptual scheme for the action (a triadic relationship), a "thirdness" (Taylor & Van Every, 2010, p. 19). Garfinkel (1967, p. 36) describes such schemes as "the socially standardized and standardizing, 'seen but unnoticed,' expected, background features of everyday scenes" that render activities recognizable *as* activities of a certain sort. However, *formal* organization involves particular kinds of thirdness which are typically inscribed in symbolic and material artifacts (e.g., policies, plans, schedules, logos, charts, etc.). Such artifacts can be invoked in interaction in order to authorize, author, or dictate certain actions (Cooren, 2015, p. 82). They enable participants to act (i.e., become subjects) by letting themselves be acted on by the organization (i.e., become objects) through processes of "imbrication" (Taylor & Van Every, 2010, p. 29).

A multimodal conversation analysis in the tradition of EMCA allowed us to show how the participants are "doing being" the objects of organizational action in order to pursue different actions. In the first analysis, Jonas designs his proposal to have lunch as elicited by a schedule that specifies when certain activities should take place. Svend resists the proposal by producing a display of "working because I have to, not because I want to" in order to deal with the task at hand. In the second analysis, the mentee and mentor jointly accomplish the roles of storyteller and story recipient, and in doing so they make the growth rate of the company remarkable, and display an understanding of the expectations of the mentor-mentee relationship, and of a mentorship program.

However, we can also notice the potential pitfall of stretching the analyses too far. The distinction between formal and informal organization is slippery since imbrication frames are not necessarily explicated in interaction (Cooren, 2015; Taylor & Van Every, 2010). The organization is the "absent (but present) third party" (Taylor & Van Every, 2010, p. 52). In the first analysis, Jonas is invoking a schedule by making a public display of checking the time, but it may not be a formal schedule for the organization. It may just as well be informed by larger cultural rhythms that divide the day into central periods (morning, afternoon, evening) and central meals (breakfast, lunch, dinner) (Zerubavel, 1981). Svend is invoking something that compels him to keep working, but it may not necessarily be the formal values of the organization. It may also be, say, a performative display of his personal work ethic. Similarly, the mentee's assessment of the growth of the company in the second example may just as well be a display of competence in the local, sequential context, with no particular regard to the organization as such.

Nevertheless, the question of whether the participants are invoking one thing or another is largely irrelevant for the practical task of accomplishing the timing of lunch or the telling of a story. It is a fundamental principle in EMCA that analysts should not aim for a higher degree of explication than the participants in the interaction (Stokoe, 2012). Thus, EMCA principles can ground, and at times also hinder, the analytical imagination of CCO studies. Moreover, the somewhat myopic, sociological emphasis of EMCA could be a contributing factor as to why EMCA as a methodological approach still represents a small minority of studies in the field of organization studies compared to other disciplines like medicine (Heritage & Maynard, 2006), psychotherapy (Peräkylä, Antaki, Vehviläinen, & Leudar, 2008) and psychology (Potter & Edwards, 2012).

Understanding Organizations through Multimodal Ethnomethodological Conversation Analysis

An ethnomethodological conversation analysis clarifies the intersubjective and locally situated nature of organizations and organizing. By means of rich, observational video-data and subsequent multimodal conversation analysis, it is possible to reveal the collaborative, co-constructive elements of organizing as a sequential row of carefully designed verbal, embodied and material practices that make relevant and account for specific actions, making it possible to fully understand the processual and complex network of actions that form the foundation of organizations.

Acknowledging Materiality, Talk and Bodily Gestures

The micro-ethnographic methodology of conversation analysis adds to our understanding of the material and interactive turn in organizational studies (Vaara, 2010; Cooren, 2007), in that it clearly shows how material actions are used and positioned in line with verbal and embodied actions. This challenges the traditional emphasis on language, which is replaced by a resource view, acknowledging materiality, talk and the body as part of the large array of resources that participants in interaction have at their disposal for the collaborative co-construction of organizations.

While building on important insights concerning the CCO approach (Putnam & Nicotera, 2009) and its focus on material agency (Ashcraft, et al., 2009; Lê & Spee, 2015), and thus considering organizational practices as not only based on human actions, but also on the non-human, material world, a conversation analytic approach advances our understanding of the importance of material agency in organizational performance by empirically showing the importance of acknowledging the interactional and sequential nature of materiality in organizational practices. Material agents do not perform social actions in isolation, but they are part of an array of closely coordinated, sequentially ordered social actions that organizational members can make use of when collaboratively constituting organizations. For the purpose of uncovering how material agents become part of this interaction, multimodal conversation analysis (Nevile, 2015) serves as a relevant methodological tool for uncovering the multimodal and sequentially organized micro-foundations of organizational practices.

The Sequential Organization of Real-Time Interaction

Ethnomethodological conversation analytic studies like the ones briefly presented in this chapter have in many ways been peripheral within organization studies until now. However, when conceiving organizations as constituted by relational processes, the main interest lies in how organizations and organizational processes emerge and unfold through day-to-day experiences and practices. By means of ethnomethodological conversation analysis, it becomes clear how verbal interactions, bodily gestures and material artifacts become center stage in the collaborative accomplishment and constitution of organizations, which we understand as a practice-based, collaborative micro-level display of actions. And, hence, we would argue that in order to theorize organizing as a relational, collective process, it is necessary to understand the fine-grained relational, collective and interactional work in all its practical details, which by use of other – more traditional – methods would remain invisible. Conversation analysis has the potential to advance CCO approaches in that it allows one to capture the dynamics and sequential organization of real-time interaction. The use of video-observations makes it possible to detect how meaning, moment by moment, is negotiated through both verbal and embodied means. Getting such detailed insights into the constitutive micro-moves of organizational dynamics would not have been possible, for instance, through the use of retrospective data obtained with interviews or surveys.

The strengths of the conversation analytic method for a constitutive approach to organizational communication thus lies in its ability to show in depth how recurrent interactional micro-level multimodal actions play a crucial role for the emergence of organizations and organizing. It allows us to apply a resource view on organizational practices, and enables us to acknowledge intersubjectivity as a fundamental condition for accomplishing organizational life.

Notes

1 The transcription of the participants' embodied conduct follows Mondada's (2019) conventions.
2 A number of scholars have described the use of repetition in aligning turns. Tannen (1987), for example, lists displays of participation among the functions of repetition in conversation, and Warren (2006, p. 61) describes lexical repetition of some or all of the lexical items in the first turn as one way of producing an aligning second turn: "By repeating all or part(s) of a preceding utterance, a speaker indicates convergence and co-operative intent which in turn contributes to the management of the discourse."

3 This "man" is different from the "man" in line 1. While the latter can be fairly unproblematically translated with a general you, this "man" is not general at all; it refers to the company. It is, so to speak, a specific reference masquerading as a general one.

References

Aaker, D., & Aaker, J. (2016). What are your signature stories? *California Management Review*, *58*(3), 49–65.

Aggerholm, H. K., & Asmuß, B. (2016a). A practice perspective on strategic communication: The discursive legitimization of managerial decisions. *Journal of Communication Management*, *20*(3), 195–214.

Aggerholm, H. K., & Asmuß, B. (2016b). When "good" is not good enough: Performative aspects of organizational routines. In J. Howard-Grenville, C. Rerup, A. Langley, & H. Tsoukas (Eds.), *Organizational routines: How they are created, maintained and changed* (pp. 140–178). Oxford University Press.

Allen, T. D., Eby, L. T., Chao, G. T., & Bauer, T. N. (2017). Taking stock of two relational aspects of organizational life: Tracking the history and shaping the future of socialization and mentoring research. *Journal of Applied Psychology*, *102*(3), 324–337. doi:10.1037/apl0000086.

Ashcraft, K., Kuhn, T. & Cooren, F. (2009). Constitutional amendments: "Materializing" organizational communication. *The Academy of Management Annals*, *3*(1), 1–64.

Asmuß, B. (2015). Multimodal perspectives on meeting interaction: Recent trends in conversation analysis. In J. A. Allen, N. Lehmann-Willenbrock, & S. G. Rogelberg (Eds.), *The Cambridge Handbook of Workplace Meetings* (pp. 277–304). Cambridge University Press.

Asmuß, B., & Oshima, S. (2012). Negotiation of entitlement in proposal sequences. *Discourse Studies*, *14*(1), 67–86.

Asmuß, B., & Oshima, S. (2018). Strategy making as a communicative practice: The multimodal accomplishment of strategy roles. *M@n@gement*, *21*(2), 884–912.

Boje, D. M. (1991). The storytelling organization: A study of story performance in an office-supply firm. *Administrative Science Quarterly*, *36*, 106–126.

Bolden, G. (2015). Transcribing as research. "Manual" transcription and conversation analysis. *Research on Language and Social Interaction*, *48*(3), 276–280.

Brummans, B. H. J. M., Cooren, F., Robichaud, D., & Taylor, J. R. (2014). Approaches to the communicative constitution of organizations. In L. L. Putnam & D. K. Mumby (Eds.), *The SAGE handbook of organizational communication: Advances in theory, research, and methods* (3rd edn., pp. 173–194). Sage.

Cnossen, B., & Bencherki, N. (2019). The role of space in the emergence and endurance of organizing: How independent workers and material assemblages constitute organizations. *Human Relations*, *72*(6), 1057–1080. https://doi.org/10.1177/0018726718794265.

Cooren, F. (Ed.). (2007): *Interacting and organizing. Analyses of a management meeting*. Lawrence Erlbaum.

Cooren, F. (2015). *Organizational discourse. Communication and constitution*. Polity Press.

Cooren, F. (2020). Beyond entanglement: (Socio-) Materiality and organization studies. *Organization Theory*, *1*(3), 1–24. https://doi.org/10.1177/2631787720954444.

Cooren, F., Kuhn, T., Cornelissen, J., & Clark, T. (2011). Communication, organizing and organization. An overview and introduction to the special issue. *Organization Studies*, *32*(9), 1149–1170.

Cooren, F., Matte, F., Benoit-Barné, C., & Brummans, B. H. J. M. (2013). Communication as ventriloquism: A grounded-in-action approach to the study of organizational tensions. *Communication Monographs*, *80*(3), 255–277. doi:10.1080/03637751.2013.788255.

Czarniawska, B. (2004). *Narratives in social research*. Sage.

Feldman, M. S., & Pentland, D. T. (2003). Reconceptualizing organizational routines as a source of flexibility and change. *Administrative Science Quarterly*, *48*(1), 94–118.

Fenton, C., & Langley, A. (2011). Strategy as practice and the narrative turn. *Organization Studies*, *32*(9), 1171–1196.

Gabriel, Y. A. (2000). *Storytelling in organizations: Facts, fictions, and fantasies*. Oxford University Press.

Garfinkel, H. (1967). *Studies in Ethnomethodology*. Prentice-Hall.

Glenn, P., & LeBaron, C. (2011). Epistemic authority in employment interviews: Glancing, pointing, touching. *Discourse & Communication*, *5*(1), 3–22. https://doi.org/10.1177/1750481310390161.

Goffman, E. (1983). The interaction order: American Sociological Association, 1982 presidential address. *American Sociological Review*, *48*(1), 1–17.

Golsorkhi, D., Rouleau, L., Seidl, D., & Vaara, E. (2010). What is strategy as practice. In D. Golsorkhi, L. Rouleau, D. Seidl, & E. Vaara (Eds.), *Cambridge Handbook of Strategy as Practice* (pp. 1–20). Cambridge University Press.

Goodwin, C. (1986). Gestures as a resource for the organization of mutual orientation. *Semiotica, 62*(1/2), 29–49.

Gylfe, P., Franck, H., LeBaron, C., & Mantere, S. (2016). Video methods in strategy research: Focusing on embodied cognition. *Strategic Management Journal, 37*, 133–148.

Heath, C., & vom Lehn, D. (2008). Configuring "interactivity": Enhancing engagement in science centres and museums. *Social Studies of Science, 38*(1), 63–91. https://doi.org/10.1177/0306312707084152.

Hepburn, A., & Bolden, G. (2013). The conversation analytic approach to transcription. In J. Sidnell & T. Stivers (Eds.), *The handbook of conversation analysis* (pp. 57–76). Wiley-Blackwell.

Heritage, J. (1984). *Garfinkel and ethnomethodology*. Polity Press.

Heritage, J. (1995): Conversation analysis: Methodological aspects. In U. M. Quasthoff (Ed.), *Aspects of oral communication* (pp. 391–417). De Gruyter.

Heritage, J., & Maynard, D. W. (Eds.). (2006). *Communication in medical care: Interaction between primary care physicians and patients*. Cambridge University Press.

Heritage, J., & Raymond, G. (2005). The terms of agreement: Indexing epistemic authority and subordination in talk-in-interaction. *Social Psychology Quarterly, 68*(1), 15–38.

Hutchby, I., & Wooffitt, R. (2008). *Conversation analysis*. Polity Press.

Jablin, F. L., & Putnam, L. L. (Eds.). (2001). *The new handbook of organizational communication: Advances in theory, research, and methods*. Sage.

Jefferson, G. (1978). Sequential aspects of storytelling in conversation. In J. Schenkein (Ed.), *Studies in the organization of conversational interaction* (pp. 219–248). Academic Press.

Jefferson, G. (1984). Notes on a systematic deployment of the acknowledgement tokens 'yeah' and 'mm hm'. *Papers in Linguistics, 17*, 197–216.

Jefferson, G. (1987). On exposed and embedded correction in conversation. In G. Button & J. R. E. Lee (Eds.), *Talk and social organisation* (pp. 86–100). Multilingual Matters.

Jefferson, G. (2004). Glossary of transcript symbols with an introduction. In G. H. Lerner (Ed.), *Conversation analysis: Studies from the first generation* (pp. 13–31). John Benjamins. https://doi.org/10.1075/pbns.125.02jef.

Johannesen, H. L. (2018). The moral ordering of work time. Unpublished doctoral dissertation. Aarhus University.

Kjærbeck, S., & Asmuß, B. (2005). Negotiating meaning in narratives: An investigation of the interactional construction of the punchline and the post punchline sequences. *Narrative Inquiry, 15*(1), 1–24.

Latour, B. (1987). *Science in action. How to follow scientists and engineers through society*. Harvard University Press.

Lê, J., & Spee, P. (2015). The role of materiality in the practice of strategy. In D. Golsorkhi, L. Rouleau, D. Seidl, & E. Vaara (Eds.), *Cambridge handbook of strategy as practice* (pp. 582–597). Cambridge University Press.

LeBaron, C. (2012). Microethnography. In W. Donsbach (Ed.), *The international encyclopedia of communication* (pp. 3120–3124). Wiley-Blackwell. https://doi.org/10.1002/9781405186407.wbiecm082.pub2.

LeBaron, C., Christianson, M. K., Garrett, L., & Ilan, R. (2016). Coordinating flexible performance during everyday work: An ethnomethodological study of handoff routines. *Organization Science, 27*(3), 514–534.

Lerner, G. H. (1991). On the syntax of sentences-in-progress. *Language in Society, 20*(3), 441–458. doi:10.1017/s0047404500016572.

Llewellyn, N., & Hindmarsh, J. (2010). Work and organisation in real time: an introduction. In N. Llewellyn & J. Hindmarsh (Eds.), *Organisation, interaction and practice: Studies in ethnomethodology and conversation analysis* (pp. 3–23). Cambridge University Press.

Lundqvist, A., Liljander, V., Gummerus, J., & van Riel, A. (2013). The impact of storytelling on the consumer brand experience: The case of a firm-originated story. *Journal of Brand Management, 20*(4), 283–297. doi:10.1057/bm.2012.15.

Mandelbaum, J. (1989). Interpersonal activities in conversational storytelling. *Western Journal of Speech Communication, 53*, 114–126.

McPhee, R. D., & Zaug, P. (2009). The communicative constitution of organizations: A framework for explanation. In L. Putnam & A. M. Nicotera (Eds.), *Building theories of organization: The constitutive role of communication* (pp. 39–66). Routledge.

Megginson, D., & Clutterbuck, D. (2005). *Techniques for coaching and mentoring*. Routledge.

Mondada, L. (2007). Multimodal resources for turn-taking : Pointing and the emergence of possible next speakers. *Discourse Studies, 9*(2), 194–225. https://doi.org/10.1177/1461445607075346.

Mondada, L. (2011). Understanding as an embodied, situated and sequential achievement in interaction. *Journal of Pragmatics, 43*(2), 542–552. https://doi.org/10.1016/j.pragma.2010.08.019.

Mondada, L. (2019). Conventions for multimodal transcription. www.lorenzamondada.net/multimodal-transcription.

Mortensen, K. (2013). Conversation analysis and multimodality. In C. A. Chapelle (Ed.), *The encyclopedia of applied linguistics* (pp. 1061–1068). Wiley-Blackwell.

Nevile, M. (2015). The embodied turn in research on language and social interaction. *Research on Language and Social Interaction, 48*(2), 121–151.

Nicolini, D. (2012). *Practice theory, work, and organization. An introduction.* Oxford University Press.

Nissi, R., & Lehtinen, E. (2016). Negotiation of expertise and multifunctionality: PowerPoint presentations as interactional activity types in workplace meetings. *Language & Communication, 48,* 1–17.

Orlikowski, W. J., & Yates, J. (2002). It's about time: Temporal structuring in organizations. *Organization Science, 13*(6), 601–740.

Pälli, P., & Lehtinen, E. (2014). Making objectives common in performance appraisal interviews. *Language & Communication, 39,* 92–108. https://doi.org/10.1016/j.langcom.2014.09.002.

Peräkylä, A., Antaki, C., Vehviläinen, S., & Leudar, I. (Eds.). (2008). *Conversation analysis and psychotherapy.* Cambridge University Press.

Potter, J., & Edwards, D. (2012). Conversation analysis and psychology. In J. Sidnell & T. Stivers (Eds.), *The handbook of conversation analysis* (pp. 701–725). Wiley-Blackwell.

Poulsen, K. M. (2008). *Mentor+ guiden - om mentorskab og en-ti-en relationer.* Virum: KMP+ Forlag.

Psathas, G. (1995). *Conversation analysis. The study of talk-in-interaction.* Sage.

Putnam, L. L., & Nicotera, A. M. (Eds.). (2009). *Building theories of organization: The constitutive role of communication.* Routledge.

Raclaw, J., & Ford, C. (2015). Meetings as interactional achievements: A conversation analytic perspective. In J. Allen, N. Lehmann-Willenbrock, & S. Rogelberg (Eds.), *The Cambridge handbook of meeting science* (pp. 247–276). Cambridge Handbooks in Psychology. Cambridge University Press. doi:10.1017/CBO9781107589735.012.

Robichaud, D., Giroux, H., & Taylor, J. R. (2004). The metaconversation: The recursive property of language as a key to organizing. *Academy of Management Review, 29*(4), 617–634.

Ruusuvuori, J., Asmuß, B., Henttonen, P., & Ravaja, N. (2019). Complaining about others at work. *Research on Language and Social Interaction, 52*(1), 41–62. doi: 10.1080/08351813.2019.1572379.

Sacks, H. (1992). *Lectures in conversation* (E. A. Schegloff & G. Jefferson, Eds. Vol. 2). Blackwell.

Sacks, H., Schegloff, E. A., & Jefferson, G. (1974). A simplest systematics for the organization of turn-taking for conversation. *Language, 50*(4), 696–735. doi:10.1353/lan.1974.0010.

Samra-Fredericks, D. (2003). Strategizing as lived experience and strategists' everyday efforts to shape strategic direction. *Journal of Management Studies, 40*(1), 141–174.

Samra-Fredericks, D. (2005). Strategic practice, "Discourse" and the everyday interactional constitution of "Power Effects". *Organization, 12*(6), 803–841.

Schegloff, E. A. (1993). Reflections on quantification in the study of conversation. *Research on Language and Social Interaction, 26*(1), 99–128.

Schegloff, E. A. (2007). *Sequence organization in interaction: A primer in conversation analysis.* Cambridge University Press.

Schegloff, E. A., Jefferson, G., & Sacks, H. (1977). The preference for self-correction in the organisation of repair in conversation. *Language, 53,* 361–382.

Schoeneborn, D., Blaschke, S., Cooren, F., McPhee, R. D., Seidl, D., & Taylor, J. R. (2014). The three schools of CCO thinking: Interactive dialogue and systematic comparison. *Management Communication Quarterly, 28*(2), 285–316.

Schoeneborn, D., Kuhn, T. R., & Kärreman, D. (2019). The communicative constitution of organization, organizing, and organizationality. *Organization Studies, 40*(4), 475–496.

Sidnell, J. (2012). Basic conversation analytic methods. In J. Sidnell & T. Stivers (Eds.), *The handbook of conversation analysis* (pp. 77–99). Wiley-Blackwell.

Sidnell, J., & Stivers, T. (Eds.). (2012). *The handbook of conversation analysis.* Wiley-Blackwell.

Smith, L. (2018). Storytelling as fleeting moments of employer brand co-creation. Unpublished PhD dissertation. Aarhus University.

Spitzmüller, C., Neumann, E., Spitzmüller, M., Rubino, C., Keeton, K. E., Sutton, M. T., & Manzey, D. (2008). Assessing the influence of psychosocial and career mentoring on organizational attractiveness. *International Journal of Selection and Assessment, 16*(4), 403–415.

Stivers, T. (2008). Stance, alignment, and affiliation during storytelling: When nodding is a token of affiliation. *Research on Language & Social Interaction, 41*(1), 31–57. doi:10.1080/08351810701691123.

Stivers, T., Mondada, L., & Steensig, J. (2011). Knowledge, morality and affiliation in social interaction. In T. Stivers, L. Mondada, & J. Steensig (Eds.), *The morality of knowledge in conversation* (pp. 3–24). Cambridge University Press. doi:10.1017/CBO9780511921674.002.

Stivers, T., & Sidnell, J. (2005). Multi-modal interaction. *Semiotica, 156*(1/4), 1–20.

Stokoe, E. (2012). Moving forward with membership categorization analysis: Methods for systematic analysis. *Discourse Studies, 14*(3), 277–303. https://doi.org/10.1177/1461445612441534.

Streeck, J., Goodwin, C., & LeBaron, C. (2011). Embodied interaction in the material world: An introduction. In J. Streeck, C. Goodwin, & C. LeBaron (Eds.), *Embodied interaction: Language and the body in the material world*. Cambridge University Press.

Tannen, D. (1987). Repetition in conversation: Toward a poetics of talk. *Language, 63*(3), 574–605.

Taylor, J. R., & Van Every, E. J. (2010). *The situated organization. Case studies in the pragmatics of communication research*. Routledge.

Vaara, E. (2010). Taking the linguistic turn seriously: Strategy as a multifaceted and interdiscursive phenomenon. *Globalization of Strategy Research: Advances in Strategic Management, 27*, 29–50.

Warren, M. (2006). *Features of naturalness in conversation*. John Benjamins.

Zerubavel, E. (1981). *Hidden rhythms. Schedules and calendars in social life*. University of Chicago Press.

Conversation analytic transcription conventions

Based on the Jefferson transcription conventions as described in Atkinson and Heritage (1984) and Mondada (2011).

right	speaker emphasis
YES	noticeably louder than surrounding talk
u:	stretched sound
ka-	sharp cut-off of the prior sound
?	rising intonation
,	continuing intonation
;	small falling intonation
.	falling intonation
=	latching between utterances and words
•<	noticeably quicker than surrounding talk
< >	noticeably slower than surrounding talk
↑	rising intonational shift
↓	falling intonational shift
.hh	audible in-breath
hh	audible outbreath
yehhs	laughter in word
(.)	micropause (less than 0.2 seconds)
(0.5)	time gap in tenths of a second
[yes]	overlapping talk
[no]	
()	unintelligible talk
@	delimits embodied conduct
Δ	delimits embodied conduct
•	delimits embodied conduct
•	delimits embodied conduct

15

ARCHIVES IN CCO RESEARCH

A Relational View

Joëlle Basque,[1] Heidi Hirsto and Régine Wagnac

Introduction

CCO research is typically premised on detailed analysis of communication *in situ* to study how organizations and organizational phenomena come into being (Cooren et al., 2011). In contrast to other streams of organizational communication and discourse studies, which often turn to organizational texts to learn about their content and meaning, CCO research draws attention to the interactional *work* or *functions* of texts and other symbolic objects – i.e., how they are used and what they *do* as they participate in interaction and communication networks (Bencherki et al., 2019; Cooren & Matte, 2010). Indeed, documents and other archival objects are interesting for CCO research primarily when they are evoked directly or indirectly by participants in the course of interaction and, in this way, "presentified" and made to speak for something or someone, like a rule, a principle, or a person in authority that is not physically present in the situation (Benoit-Barné & Cooren, 2009). More broadly, texts are seen to act "across space and time from a distance" (Koschmann, 2013, p. 66), as they crystallize past conversations into a representation of what was previously discussed, and make it available as a basis for current decisions. This orientation leads to an interesting stance towards utilizing archival texts and objects, which are typically understood as remnants of communication from a distant past, detached from their original context of use.

In this chapter, our aim is to elaborate on the role and potential of archives in CCO research. Our starting point is that archives may be expected to be of value for CCO research, because they invite us to engage with the material aspects of time and temporality in organizations, such as the various ways in which traces from the past are mobilized to shape organizational present(s) and future(s). At the same time, however, the detached and power-laden nature of archives seems to contradict some of the basic premises of CCO, creating methodological challenges.

We start by defining the notion of archive and discussing some methodological considerations of working with archives in social and history studies. We then proceed to discuss how a "relational view of organization" (Bencherki & Elmholdt, 2020, p. 2) may inform and shape the meaning and use of archives, and finally provide our own definition of archive for CCO research. After that, we propose a typology of five ways of using archives in CCO research, discussing methodological implications and challenges along the way by referring to

DOI: 10.4324/9781003224914-18

studies that use CCO or a compatible theoretical frame. This allows us to reflect on the role of the researcher in studying archives in a CCO perspective, and to provide useful insights for researchers wanting to use this type of material in their work.

Perspectives to Archives

In the Meriam Webster dictionary, an archive is defined as "a place in which public records or historical materials (such as documents) are preserved [...] also: the material preserved". It is further defined as "a repository or collection especially of information". According to Manoff (2004), most writers subscribe to the latter definition, and while some researchers differentiate archives, libraries and museums depending on the repository's content, the distinction remains ambiguous. For those looking past these distinctions or nuances, an archive is a repository of many things such as documents, books, newsletters and other media, or of objects, artifacts, and even bodily remains, which may have been preserved for a variety of reasons (Cifor, 2017; Manoff, 2004).

Within organization studies, Schultz and Hernes (2013) make a distinction between textual, material and oral forms of memory, inspiring us to say that different types of archival objects present themselves to actors through different processes. For example, written texts often present themselves through "symbolic" or interpretational processes, whereas artifacts may present themselves primarily through their sensory and physiological aspects. According to them, "the form in which [a memory] is evoked shapes the meaning of an experience" (Schultz & Hernes, 2013, p. 4). With the digital age, we have come to talk about the digital archive, which, for some scholars, means "everything currently existing in digital format" (i.e. documents, manuscripts, images, sound, multimedia, text, etc.), while for others, it refers to a "discrete collection of related electronic documents" (Manoff, 2004, p. 10).

Regarding the authenticity of archives, historians have traditionally been "seeking to gain some certainty as to the facts of the past" (Bricknell, 2008, p. 2). With skepticism towards historical record at its core, source criticism is one research method that is used to establish "[the] 'original' context or [the] 'original' setting against which to read a text" (Mathewson, 2002, p. 15). According to Alvesson and Sköldberg, "the source critic is, at least to some degree, a knowledge realist, believing in the existence of an underlying reality, which is expressed, albeit in an incomplete, opaque way, in the sources" (2017, p. 172). Thus, historians usually regard archives primarily *as data* that offer evidence about the past and may do so more or less reliably. Archives may be interpreted as "remnants", i.e., as signs that something has happened (for instance, that a statue has been built or a report published), or as "narrative sources" that tell a version of past events (Alvesson & Sköldberg, 2017, p. 174). However, this is not the only way to use archives in research. Kjellstrand and Vince (2020) provide an example of using archival photographs as elicitation material whose purpose is to trigger discussion and reflection about organizational phenomena in an interview, that is, to help *generate data*. In the latter approach, the traditional idea of source criticism, including the evaluation of the authenticity of a document or object, needs to be reconsidered, as the relevance of archives relates not to the past, but to the present or to the future.

The authenticity of archives is also a concern for postmodernist, feminist and postcolonial researchers, who have been "suspicious of the historical record" and denounced "[the] absences and the distortion of the archive" (Manoff, 2004, p. 14). Also, as Manoff writes: "Derrida's work has contributed to scholarly recognition of the contingent nature of the archive – the way it is shaped by social, political, and technological forces" (2004, p. 12). Absences, exclusions, gaps and distortions of the archive can all be seen as the result of different dominant forces.

Some postmodernists like Foucault have entirely redefined the notion of archive. Foucault does not use this word to refer to a collection of texts that reflect parts of history; instead, he defines the archives as: "the law of what can be said, the system that governs the appearance of statements as unique events" (Foucault, 1972, p. 145).

In line with postmodernist theory, as well as with recent works emphasizing the contingent and productive dimensions of archives (Howard-Grenville et al., 2013; Kjellstrand & Vince, 2020), a CCO mindset invites us to see archives as *performative*, while not putting aside the idea of the archive as a repository. Considering heterogeneous traces of the past from this perspective allows us to highlight their relations to other things and beings such as (other) archives, spaces, and people. In line with a CCO approach, our focus is on how archives, within networks of relations, participate in organizations and organizing. We therefore ask: how do archives come to make a difference? How do they "make themselves present throughout space and time" (Cooren, 2020, p. 2) and, in that way, make a difference for organizing processes? A CCO perspective would consider the archive as an agent, as Cifor (2017) aptly puts it:

> Conceptualising the archives as agential in the relations that co-constitute matter and meaning leads to novel understandings of them as vigorous and changeable. This perspective challenges the common conceptualisation of the archives, even by scholars deeply engaged in them, as static, dusty, and the collectors of dead things and past times. Through new materialism, it is possible to understand that archives are actually in a state of constant flux, shifting with each new intra-action of the various and changing actors that constitute it. (p. 18)

Relational Ontology and Methodological Implications

Among the CCO tradition, the Montréal School is unique in presenting a "decentered vision of agency" (Cooren, 2020, p. 7), where agents of different ontologies act in relation with each other. Research in this perspective has shown that communication is performed not only by humans, but also by non-human actors. This is often (but not only) done when people mobilize elements such as principles, previous agreements, contracts, tools and so on, and refer to them in their conversations, allowing them to produce structuring effects (Cooren et al., 2006) and to participate in the performance of authority (Benoit-Barné & Cooren, 2009) or power (Cooren & Matte, 2010). In addition, CCO scholars, inspired by actor-network theory and Latourian philosophy, have shown how tangible agents (such as human bodies, spaces and objects) are imbricated in complex relationships with immaterial agents (such as rules, work habits, laws, and so on) (Wilhoit & Kisselburgh, 2019).

Embracing such a view of distributed agency means relying on a *relational ontology*, that is the idea that "everything or everyone is literally made of relations" (Cooren, 2020, p. 4), and that "agents always act with and through other agents" (Wilhoit & Kisselburgh, 2019, p. 874). Working with archival material implies starting with specific tangible traces from the past, which may be, as we have mentioned above, texts, but also artifacts, photographs, buildings, and sometimes bodily remains (Cifor, 2017). These objects can be said to have *materiality*, an attribute that is often taken for granted by researchers and historians, and distinguished from "immaterial" elements such as discourse, ideas, principles, and emotions. Adopting a CCO perspective, however, means that the dichotomy between materiality and discourse should not be assumed or taken for granted. As Cooren (2020, p. 2) points out, materiality is a necessary property of all phenomena – including communication – and, indeed, of their very existence. Drawing from this, we suggest that researchers should focus on *materialization effects.* In terms of materiality, abstract entities and other things need other actors to exist. They continue their existence through others, so to speak. Therefore, research from a CCO perspective should explain the relations that unite the agents and allow them to act and, thus, to have an agency: that is, "to make a difference" in the course of action (Castor & Cooren, 2006, p. 573).

In other words, we embrace Bencherki and Elmholt's vision according to which, relying on Spinoza's thinking, "to exist, a being must find others that can continue its action through their own, taking it up and continuing it; hence, existence is inherently relational" (2020, p. 6). Following these premises, existing is a matter of degree, meaning that a thing can exist more or less depending on the number of other things that materialize its existence (Cooren, 2020, p. 3).

Adopting such a relational view to understand archives does not deny the inherent material nature of archival data, but stresses that research using archives in CCO should focus on studying the productive relations of the archive with other agents that allow it to act, to make a difference, to make the past speak and change the course of action in an organization, or even constitute the organization itself. The archive also materializes through its (re)mediations: we could imagine the archive as a bunch of papers in a box, which can become a DVD, and then a website. A letter written by Mr. X in the nineteenth century takes on many material forms, and is again re-published in a book, quoted, and so on (Basque & Langley, 2018). Thus, starting with the relational perspective could lead CCO researchers to use a very broad yet simple definition of archives that defies the traditional view of historical studies and instead conceives of archives as an agent. For the purpose of this chapter, we propose the following definition of archives: they are *traces of the past that communicate through materialization effects.*

Drawing on the relational perspective inherent in CCO and especially in the Montréal School theoretical frame, this chapter focuses on situations where pieces of archive come into contact with other beings such as organizational members, spaces, and the researcher. We reflect on how archives gain agency and act through these relations and how they produce materialization effects, for example, by bringing some aspects of organizational identity or culture into (stronger) existence. We suggest a typology based on five different situations where archives can make a difference: archives in relation with organizational members in both naturally occurring and facilitated settings (1 and 2); archives in relation with each other (3); with space (4); and with the researcher (5). These different situations, each presented as a research focus, can be combined (and often are) in the same research project, but we separate them here for heuristic purposes, starting with archives in naturally occuring settings.

1. Archives and Organizational Members in Naturally Occurring Settings

One obvious way that CCO researchers may consider archives, such as documents or artifacts, is through observing references to or uses of such objects in everyday organizational settings. Participants in a meeting, for example, may refer to a painting of the company founder on the wall of the meeting room – or the bronze bust of the school's founder, as Bruno Latour (2011) describes in his piece about organizing as a mode of existence – while discussing organizational practices or values, in a sincere or ironic sense. Organizational histories and memory may be evoked through rituals such as a weekly silent moment in front of a memorial wall (Koschmann & McDonald, 2015), and strategy processes may dig into archives in attempts to (re)define organizational identity or brand heritage (Schultz & Hernes, 2013, 2019).

In observing such cases, archives and archival objects become visible and relevant for study through their agency (Koschmann & McDonald, 2015), i.e., the performative effects they have, here and now, on the flow of discussion, in sensemaking processes, or in organizational identity work. In Hatch and Schultz's (2017) study, for example, researchers observed organizational members in the context of a strategic process of identity reconstruction, showing how organizational members evoked organizational histories and continuities through engaging with archival documents and artifacts, as well as oral narratives unfolding in social interaction. Similarly, Howard-Grenville et al. (2013) used observation and interviews to depict a process of identity resurrection, which was based on community leaders marshaling and orchestrating material and symbolic resources – including historical places and figures – and community members authenticating them through participation and lived experience.

The unfolding relation of archives and (human) organizational actors can work to transcend time and place in many ways. Archives may, for example, be used to presentify other times, other spaces, or other people and their voices (Benoit-Barné & Cooren, 2009). Reminiscences of history in their varied materialities may exert agency on human organizational members (Cooren et al., 2013), who may echo historical voices and discourses in more or less conscious or intentional ways (Ashcraft, 2020). For example, Ashcraft's (2007) study of airline pilots' occupational identity shows how normalized and non-conscious practices of workplace communication in the airline industry carry gendered and class-based meanings that can be connected to decades of cultural narratives and images across multiple cultural sites. From this perspective, everyday expressions such as *junior guys*, *rites of respect*, or *little soldiers* (Ashcraft, 2007, p. 22) enact relations to particular historical discourses, (re-)materializing them and thereby contributing to the production of broader-scale effects such as occupational segregation.

In this type of research, archival materials are not used (primarily) as data or evidence to inform researchers about past realities. Therefore, the main emphasis is not on analyzing the content of archival objects as documents (Prior, 2008, pp. 824–826) or assessing their authenticity as remnants of the past (Alvesson & Sköldberg, 2017). In contrast, archives are analyzed for their agential role in organizational communication.

In this section, we discussed a type of research that focuses on how organizational members themselves orient to and evoke archives in naturally occurring organizational settings. In these kinds of settings, the reseacher's role, ideally, is to observe organizational life as it occurs, in an unobtrusive way. However, the boundaries between naturally occurring and facilitated settings are not clear-cut, which is evident in some of the studies we have referred to (e.g., Schultz & Hernes, 2013), where organizational members themselves organized events to deliberately tap into collective memories and sensemaking processes. Researchers thus change their focus from considering how archives are mobilized and used in naturally occuring settings, to facilitated settings.

2. *Archives and Organizational Members in Facilitated Settings*

Sometimes, it is difficult to observe the use of archives in naturally occurring settings, because not all organizations make frequent references to their past, even when archives are available, or researchers may have limited access to situations where they do. In the absence of such opportunities, researchers can create and facilitate encounters by organizing events such as workshops, focus groups, or interviews, where organizational members are exposed to archives of different forms. Researchers can then observe how participants interact with these archives, what such interactions create in the discussion, what feelings and memories particular artifacts convey, and so on. In this way, the archive's agency may be observed *in situ*, as people are invited to manipulate and discuss the material in a collective (or individual) manner. Hence, archival objects are used primarily as a device to generate data (Kjellstrand & Vince, 2020).

Focus groups and interviews are research methods that are less common in CCO, although interviews have recently been used and recognized as valuable settings for collecting data in a CCO perspective (Jahn, 2016; Koschmann & McDonald, 2015; Wilhoit, 2014; Wilhoit & Kisselburgh, 2019). Interviews, focus groups or other interactive discussions, where archives are deliberately made available as resources for meaning-making, can provide interesting insights into their potential agency in organizational life. For instance, Schultz and Hernes (2013), in their study on identity reconstruction at the LEGO Group, analyzed workshops and meetings that were co-organized by one of the researchers and that used archives to evoke organizational memory. Their study showed that the more organizational members engaged with different forms of memory, including archives, the more complex and elaborate the process of redefining an organization's identity became. As the authors put it:

> Bringing forward past experiences through a wider range of memory forms, such as reports on failures, stories from critical moments, artifacts from the origin of the company, and prototypes from fundamental innovations, enabled the top managers to include more identity claims in the conception of the future organization and to note a broader range of identity claims to be redefined or eliminated.
>
> (Schultz & Hernes, 2013, p.15)

Archive photographs and objects are increasingly recognized in organization studies as valuable tools for eliciting reactions and reflection on organizational phenomena and lived experience. Through photo and video elicitation methods, archives can become tools that "facilitate new forms of communication" (Wilhoit, 2017, p. 452), serving as a common denominator between participants and researchers during focus groups or interviews. For example, in their study on organizational change in Kazakhstan's transition from a Soviet to a post-Soviet economy, Kjellstrand and Vince (2020) used pairs of photos during interviews. They favored this photo elicitation method to generate projections of individual and collective experience and to facilitate engagement "with the possibilities and impossibilities of change" (2020, p. 51). What is crucial here from a CCO point of view is that archival photographs in these settings are considered "as much about the present as they are the past", stimulating "here and now reflection on the current state, and [...] helping the respondent to position him or herself emotionally within the social or organizational issues being investigated" (Kjellstrand & Vince, 2020, p. 42). Photo-elicitation may thus help the researcher ask different questions and the participants share thoughts and experiences that might not have been mentioned otherwise (Wilhoit, 2017, p. 450). In this way, researcher(s), participant(s) and archive(s) are jointly constructing the organizational phenomenon of study.

Shortt and Warren (2019) propose combining such a "dialogical" approach to photographs with an "archeological approach" to image-sets. In their study of work space and identity construction in hair salons, they asked field-study participants to take (or in their words, "make") photographs of meaningful spaces, and used the resulting images both for prompting dialogue in interviews, and for recognizing recurring patterns across image-sets. Of interest to CCO research, the methodological combination grasped the constitution of organization on many levels. The taking/making of photographs rendered selected organizational spaces and practices meaningful for organizational members and materialized them in new ways, thus enhancing their existence, so to speak. At the same time, the photographs also materialized broader cultural and field-specific practices and values that were not necessarily recognized by individual participants but became visible through the analysis of image-sets. Similarly, in their study of a community-based organization fighting for the housing conditions of underprivileged residents, Bencherki and Bourgoin's (2019) analysis of a community-based photography project showed that images do much more than represent and remind viewers of past events: "Images and photographs are semiotic devices that attach us to places, organizations and identities" (p. 500). The image's materiality thus intensifies the relations that substantiate social phenomena and actors (Bencherki & Bourgoin, 2019).

In addition to photographs, other types of (archival) objects may also be used for similar purposes in a way of "object-elicitation" (De Leon & Cohen, 2005). For example, in Everett and Barrett's study on the relationships of visitors to museums, the researchers used "works of art, cultural artifacts, and natural history specimens" (2012, p. 36) as a starting point from which to explore the participants' engagement with the museum and to create more reflective interviews.

These studies, while not necessarily dealing explicitly with archives, illustrate how introducing more agents, such as photographs and objects, to the research context increases the number of meaningful relations and encounters. These, in turn, have the potential to rearticulate and reframe the relationship between the present and the past, and may generate new understandings of organizational phenomena. In studies using facilitated settings, the researchers' role is to create the situation in which they will be able to observe the effect of bringing archives to the conversation. From a relational ontology perspective, archives are here regarded as partners in interaction and relational processes of constitution through which organizations and organizational phenomena gain (more) existence (Bencherki & Elmholdt, 2020; Cooren, 2020). In facilitated settings, the researcher often plays a central role in selecting the archival objects used for elicitation, and needs to reflect and account for the selection based on research goals and questions. Selection is also important when it comes to the interconnections of archives.

3. The Interconnections of Archives through Time

Another set of relations that researchers might consider is the one between archives themselves. We are here considering the interconnection of archives through time, in particular in the case of documents understood as concrete texts. When it comes to the use of documents in the social sciences, it is usually their content that has been the focus of research: "Data analysis strategies concentrate almost entirely on what is in the 'text' (via various forms of content analysis, thematic analysis, or even grounded theory)" (Prior, 2008, p. 825). Some analyses have, however, focused on the "use and function" of documents, seen as a resource that human actors use or have used for "purposeful ends", or as things that function in social interaction organization through driving human action (Prior, 2008, p. 825). From both standpoints, the archive–archive relationship can be seen as a "work of connection and collection" of texts (Latour, 2005, p. 8). In other words, archives as text, together but also individually, can be seen as a textual network (Kuhn, 2008).

(Re)constituting an organization from a network of archives entails "assembling, and mobilizing" (Sergi & Bonneau, 2016, p. 382) texts and other objects that have lasted through space and time such as documents, emails, chats, tweets, images, videos, and so on. Interconnecting archival content within or across archives can then serve to create descriptions of past and present organizations and organizing. In this regard, archival material that is selected and made to speak together is similar to a "collage" providing a textual visualization of organizing processes. Sergi and Bonneau (2016) used archived tweets in that way. By analyzing the interconnections in their content, they were able to illustrate working out loud (WOL) practices on social media (narrating one's own work and relating to others while doing so), and how these "tweets have the potential to actively participate in the constitution of work and professional identity of workers engaging in working out loud" (p. 378). Dobusch and Schoeneborn (2015) have also used digital archives to study the organizationality of a collective. By putting tweets, posts, press reports and material from the academic literature in relation, they were able to describe the communicative constitution of the hackers' collective *Anonymous*.

The interconnections of archives can, furthermore, be seen when texts from one era call upon texts from an older era. When this is visible, intertextuality, which refers to the "sequential (or syntagmatic) relationships between texts" (Hodges, 2015, p. 43), is at play. Direct quotes, paraphrases and implicit allusions, from one text to another, can show for instance how a particular organizational narrative or identity comes to gain credibility, legitimacy, authority and/or durability through time and space. It is the strategic interconnection of archives that can be seen through this intertextuality. For example, drawing on an internal magazine's 80-year archive, Basque and Langley (2018) show the intertextual connections of historical documents' content. Using mainly excerpts from an internal magazine, but also history books, newspaper articles and government documents, their analysis shows how Alphonse Desjardins, the founder of Desjardins Group (a financial cooperative), had been invoked throughout the years to construct organizational identity.

Basque and Langley's (2018) case study allows researchers to see the use and function of archival texts by organizational actors themselves. Looking closely at their writing, more specifically focusing on their published articles and what (or who) they invoked in them, Basque and Langley (2018) highlight the strategic use and interconnection of old texts. Since articles in the magazines were written by managers and other members of the financial cooperative, researchers can observe how these actors were strategically quoting, literally and metaphorically, the deceased founder. Basque and Langley (2018) point out that, as a key source of truth and authority for their actions, these actors were strategically invoking Alphonse's name, his ideas, and his extensive writing, many years after his death. This means that Alphonse's writings were "lifted from [their] originating context (decontextualized) and inserted into a new setting where [they were] recontextualized for that purpose" (Hodges, 2015, p. 43). Exposing such strategic interconnections between archives serves to show managers' agency in the evolution of their organizational identity throughout the years.

Shultz and Hernes' (2019) study on identity construction at the Carlsberg brewing company showed similar uses and re-uses of organizational and cultural archives, such the "Golden words" of the founder. Their study extends beyond textual archives, and includes "matter" from the past, for instance showing how the original yeast recovered from old bottles of beer was reproduced and re-interpreted in organizational texts and products to link future-oriented strategy formulations with the longer time horizon of organizational identity.

In studies that focus on the interconnections of archival texts and objects through time, researchers play a role that only requires them to be lightly involved. Whereas studies of this type use data that exists and has been preserved without their involvement, researchers' involvement consists of selecting which archives to study, choosing texts and objects for detailed analysis, making sense of them, and looking at how they speak together, to account for the constitution of organizations, or organizational processes.

4. *Archives in Relations with Space*

Research driven by a CCO theoretical frame can serve to highlight how traces of the past, taking the form of archival objects, are inserted in, perverted, or erased from dedicated spaces, and describe the practices through which these assemblages contribute to (or harm) the organization's existence and persistence through time. Archival objects are the locus of such practices in all kinds of organizations and public spaces, as shown by de Vaujany and Vaast

(2014), who documented how university staff re-used NATO's office furniture left behind by previous occupants of the building. They show how the furniture functioned as a constant reminder of the particular history and the prestige of their building, impacting how people interacted with it and, later on, how some walls were tagged with graffiti, masking the prestigious history of the building from the new generation.

In CCO, space has been conceptualized as "an ongoing construct of multiple and heterogeneous sociomaterial interrelations, which coexist and affect each other" (Vásquez & Cooren, 2013, p. 27), or as an "organizational assemblage" (Cnossen & Bencherki, 2019, p. 1059) that exists through practices. In both these definitions, space is enacted: it exists through interrelations and practices and is not fixed or separated from the agents that inhabit it, whether humans or non-humans. In a similar way, we argue that a CCO perspective on archives focuses on their various materializations, that is their relations with other agents that allow them to make a difference in the situation. These ways of conceiving of space and archives are consistent with a relational ontology, and invite CCO researchers to observe archives in relations with their surroundings through the practices that mobilize them and infuse them with meanings.

For example, the role of archival objects could be to maintain a sense of coherence with the past, as seen in Basque and Langley (2018). The article includes a photograph of delegates from the *caisses populaires* (the bank branches) posing under a giant picture of the founder, after electing their new president. This photograph illustrates how the past is made present in the situation through this picture, creating a form of blessing from their precious founder (deceased 80 years prior to this picture being taken) upon their actual decisions (see Figure 15.1).

However, coherence with the past through spatiality might sometimes become an obstacle in building an organization's legitimacy over time, as shown in the (previously cited) study by de Vaujany and Vaast (2014) on Dauphine University in Paris, located in a building originally designed to be NATO's headquarters. The study of subsequent appropriation and dis-appropriation practices, documented through ethnography, interviews and extensive study of various archival data (such as photographs, architectural plans, and videos), revealed how the building, its configuration, as well as the artifacts that remained from its past, all played different roles (and thus, displayed agency) in orienting and constraining their uses by students and faculty members through the years. Together, these various agents (the building, objects and organizational members) contributed to construct the organization's legitimacy (or lack thereof), as the inhabited space and "spatial legacies" ended up displaying obsolescence, which contradicted the organization's preferred identity: an elite and innovative institution.

Similar to de Vaujany and Vaast, who used ethnography as one of the main data-gathering methods, Vásquez and colleagues present a shadowing technique as an option for studying archives in relation with space (Vásquez et al., 2012). Delineating the object of study is an important and ongoing part of the shadowing process. Preliminary observations are made in order to identify specific actors that seem to play a key role in materializing archives in relation to space and through it. Such relations must remain the focus of observation, to understand how the past is made present in the organization's physicality and how it serves to (re)produce the organization through time and space (Vásquez & Cooren, 2013). The researcher's aim is to observe and unpack the organizational assemblage that results from encounters between archival objects in and through various spaces (headquarter buildings, employee's offices, parks, public transportation facilities, and so on).

In shadowing, the researcher can be mobile or immobile, and embrace various ways of describing space and everything that inhabits it. As van Vuuren and Westerhof explain, "spatial descriptions can take three forms (i.e., survey, route, and gaze)" (2015, p. 327). The observation

LA REVUE DES
DIRIGEANTS
ET DU
PERSONNEL

DESJARDINS

Municipalités
dévitalisées
La relance passe
par la mobilisation
du milieu

Forum « Feu vert
à la prévention » :
une première !

Alphonse Desjardins
(1859 - 1920)

Volume 74 · Numéro 3 · Juin-juillet-août 2008

Convention nᵒ 41372012

Desjardins
Conjuguer avoirs et êtres

Assemblée
des représentants

En route
vers 2012

Figure 15.1   Cover image, *Revue Desjardins*, 74(3), 2008. Mouvement Desjardins Archives.

of the way archival objects – including mundane objects such as old containers, a shopping cart, and a logo with a nebulous history – relate together can be considered along with field notes, in-depth or on-the-spot interviews with organizational members or passers-by, which can be part of the ethnography, as in Cnossen and Bencherki's (2019) study. Their analysis shows that, in the description of what unfolds, the researcher must account for the intricate ways in which space constrains and orients practices, but also for the ways in which these practices constitute space and infuse it with meanings. Archival objects play a key role in these practices and ways of inhabiting space, as they are moved from places, shared, exchanged, even robbed or vandalized (de Vaujany & Vaast, 2014).

We can also imagine that practices do not need to be the focus of such research, if the researcher takes the stance of a ventriloquist and makes the relations between archival objects and space speak. Wilhoit & Kisselburgh (2019) offer an interesting description of this relation using Cooren's (2015) work:

> Cooren (2015) has shown that through relational ontology and ventriloquism, com-munication can take place between things. He described a woman who told a story relating two pieces of artwork near each other in a museum. This example shows that a person can observe a relationship between things (in this case, pieces of artwork) and make them say something about their relationship. Although this connection could be entirely imaginary on the part of the human, and not intended by the artists or curators, the fact that the juxtaposition between these artworks is there, can be noticed, and made to speak means that the artifacts also contribute to the meaning found in this relationship. (pp. 877–878)

This depiction of a woman making sense of the relationship of an artwork in relation to the space and objects that surrounds it echoes Cifor's description of her own encounter with Harvey Milk's blood-tainted suit in a museum (2017, pp. 11–12). She explains carefully how the relationship of the archive with space (the suit being folded and put behind a glass, accom-panied by a quote from Milk, etc.) created various effects on her, for instance putting her in the position of a distant observer, that would differ from her subsequent encounter with the object several years later when she could touch it and interact with it. While, in this section, we saw that the researcher's role is to delineate the object of study, make observations and analyze the practices that construct archives' agency in relation with space, the relation of the archive with the researcher is the last of our typology, and this last method will demonstrate a particular kind of involvement and engagement with archives.

5. *Archives in Relations with the Researcher*

Ultimately, the archive always comes alive in relation to the researcher as a subject studying the interaction of archives with (other) humans, archives, or spaces. While the reflexive and inter-pretive role of the researcher is always present to some extent in CCO studies, the researcher's position can vary a great deal. In studies drawing, for instance, on ethnomethodological and conversation analytical traditions, the researcher subject often mainly adopts an observing, reporting, and theorizing role. By contrast, in studies drawing from participatory ethnography, autoethnography, or feminist theory, the dynamic relationship between the researcher and the objects and materials of the study becomes more focal. For example, Sergi and Hallin regard performing qualitative research as an "emotional, embodied and deeply personal experience" (2011, p. 19) in which the researcher is fully immersed. Cifor (2017), drawing from fem-inist theory and new materialism, focuses on the "liveliness" of archives that results from the researcher's embodied and affective encounters with the materiality of archives and archived (bodily) matter. Similarly, Winkler's (2013) autoethnographic study of identity work, while not focusing on archives as such, takes the connection between the "inside view" of the researcher (including remembered experiences and feelings, as well as traces thereof in the form of diaries) and the "social outside" of the cultural surroundings as the main object of study.

A reflexive approach to the dynamic relationship and encounters between the researcher and the archive opens up yet another perspective to the performativity of archives. From the perspective of CCO, the relation may be understood as co-constitutive and regarded, for instance, through the conceptual lens of ventriloquism (Cooren, 2012; Cooren et al., 2013). On the one hand, the researcher as ventriloquist brings the archive "to life" and makes it "speak" – not so much as an informant but more as a partner in generative dialogue – which can be done as part of immersive and affective methods of inquiry and reporting (Sergi & Hallin, 2011), whereby the researcher mobilizes emotions, memories, and a personal connection with the archive. At the same time, the researcher also acts as the dummy through which the archive acts by making them feel, remember, and reconstruct events in ways that are partly out of their conscious control. CCO researchers have been documenting how such phenomena unfold in the field, as they are animated, transformed, and moved by the multiple agents that constitute the organization (Matte & Bencherki, 2018). As explained by Matte and Bencherki (2018), the body of the researcher becomes a medium through which materializations occurs; it becomes haunted, so to speak, by the elements of the organization it encounters.

For example, in her research work, the second author of this chapter has written on the way in which she was moved by a particular set of archives, namely children's magazines published by banks. In her research notes (see Hirsto et al., 2020), she writes:

> I bought the first set of The Golden Piggybank Club magazines from the 1980s–1990s online from a private collector who delivered them to me on the parking lot of a gas station. When I received the box of magazines, I was not thinking about my topic, the formation of economic citizens. I felt excited – ridiculously excited on the mere prospect of holding one of those magazines again in my hands: of sensing how the paper feels, how it smells; to be able to turn the pages, see the colors and the layouts. When I picked up the first magazine, I felt deeply moved. It seemed to bring me back to childhood, and let me meet my 10-year-old self again. These magazines, which were at their time so mundane and insignificant, felt precious, and I handled them with great care.

The author's emotions are visible when she describes how she felt while holding the old magazines in her hands. Upon the encounter, these magazines clearly did something to her, she was deeply moved by them, they reminded her of her childhood, and in a way summoned the spirit of her 10-year-old self. Further, the encounter led to her expressing these feelings in different academic contexts, and redirecting the focus of her research. From an analytical viewpoint, then, it is important to account for the sensibilities that animate us in selecting (and eliminating) some traces from the past and that affect us enough so that we make them speak through our research work. In Cifor's (2017) study, for example, the researcher accounts how her strong affective reactions to handling the blood-stained clothes of Harvey Milk connected her to the material history and performative power of the GLBT movement and the role of San Francisco's community-based GLBT Historical Society in preserving its legacy.

In supporting this sort of reflexive process, the method of historical empathy may provide additional guidance. Historical empathy in history studies and pedagogy refers to an effort at gaining "intuitive understanding 'from within' of the object of investigation" (Alvesson & Sköldberg, 2017, p. 179) through a process that involves both cognitive and affective engagement (Endacott & Brooks, 2013, p. 41). It can be simplified as putting yourself in the shoes of a figure in the past, for example as the (imagined) producer or recipient of a text, in order to relate to her lived experience. From this position, it is possible to consider questions such as the following ones, which are raised in the second author's research notes on magazines from a more distant past: *What might a young woman, living in a rural village in the 1920s, have thought or felt when reading this story or seeing this advertisement in a bank magazine? What kinds of hopes, aspirations, or reflections might have arisen?* (Hirsto et al., 2020). From the perspective of relational ontology and CCO, empathy may thus be considered a method for animating and intensifying the relation between archival material and the researcher by means of eliciting an emotional connection with past events and people, as well as identifying with their circumstances and aspirations. This is a way of using historical empathy, or we could also say historical *compassion*, for the purpose of embracing the same passion, and being animated or set in motion by the same figure (Cooren, 2010) that inhabited our predecessors, who created and possessed the objects that have now become archives.

Understanding research as a situated performance and attending to the affective and "subjective" (but always material) dimensions of knowledge production seems generally well suited for the relational and performative premises of CCO (Matte & Bencherki, 2018). According to Sergi and Hallin (2011, p. 192) such dimensions are not only inextricable to research, but in fact may help to produce richer analyses of social and human phenomena. Many types of archival objects, notably artifacts and photographs representing the past, tend to evoke strong affective reactions (Kjellstrand & Vince, 2020; Schultz & Hernes, 2013) and, as Cifor's (2017) study shows, researchers are not immune to such effects. Adopting a relational approach to research helps to regard affective reactions as part of the materialization effects of archives, and to include them in the process of knowledge production.

Conclusion

In this chapter, we have discussed ways of using archives in CCO research. Archives are often primarily associated with historical research, where their role is to provide evidence of past events, and where authenticity and source criticism appear as key concerns. We have demonstrated that a CCO perspective to archives is, and needs to be, very different. CCO research, especially the Montréal School, regards communication as something that occurs in dynamic relations between a variety of human and non-human agencies. Regarded from this relational perspective, it may be argued that archives do not differ in essence from other potential agencies in communication. They, too, should be considered primarily for the different roles they assume and are assigned in communication, the (inter)actions they take part in, and the constitutive or materializing effects that their relations and encounters with other beings produce.

We defined archives, for the purposes of CCO, as "traces from the past that communicate through materialization effects". This means that archives are not studied as windows to the past but as agents that, through their participation in communicative processes and encounters, contribute to the existence of organizations or organizational phenomena. In other words, in order to "count" from a CCO point of view, archives need to be(come) or be made relevant in relation to other agents.

From this starting point, we discussed five broad ways of relating to archives in different types of research designs (summarized in Table 15.1), where the researcher's role varies from external observer of organizational life, to active arranger of research settings, and to a reflexive participant in affective encounters with archives. Archives may be regarded in these designs in a relatively traditional way as objects of (inter)textual analysis, but also, crucially, as agents

Table 15.1 Five ways of using archives for research from a CCO perspective

Focus of analysis	Examples of methods for data collection	Researcher's role in relation to archives	Archive's role
Archives and organizational members in naturally occuring settings	Observation and recording of organizational life Ethnography Video-shadowing	Not involved – exterior Observing meaningful encounters with archives	Agent in naturally occurring relations
Archives and organizational members in facilitated settings	Focus groups Interviews Photo-elicitation Object-elicitation	Involved – creating the encounter with archives	Device to generate data, "added agent" to the discussion
The interconnections of archives through time	Collection and selection of archives to constitute a corpus	Lightly involved Selection of archives Analyzing intertextual relations	Object of analysis, "text"
Archives in relations with space	Ethnography Autoethnography Video-shadowing	Involved – delineating the object of study Making observations Analyzing practices	Agent in naturally occurring relations
Archives in relations with the researcher	Autoethnography Reflexive methods	Deeply involved – Affective encounter with archives Source of data	Device to generate data Participant in reflexive process

participating in processes of communicative constitution through their relations and encounters with organizational members, space, time, and the researcher subject.

Even though archives are, in many ways, similar to other participants in communicative events, their temporal aspect holds special potential for CCO research. In our view, the value of an archive, whether convoked spontaneously by organizational members or introduced by the researcher for elicitation purposes, lies in its ability to mobilize personal and collective histories, always "imaginary" to some extent, for the purpose of shaping the meaning and existence of organizations in the present. Therefore, considering archival material through a CCO lens may help to deepen our understanding of the ways in which traces from the past are interwoven in the communicative constitution of organization.

Note

1 Authors listed in alphabetical order; all contributions were equal.

References

Alvesson, M., & Sköldberg, K. (2017). *Reflexive methodology: New vistas for qualitative research* (3rd edn.). Sage.

Ashcraft, K. L. (2007). Appreciating the 'work' of discourse: Occupational identity and difference as organizing mechanisms in the case of commercial airline pilots. *Discourse & Communication, 1*(1), 9–36. https://doi.org/10.1177/1750481307071982.

Ashcraft, K. L. (2020). Communication as constitutive transmission? An encounter with affect. *Communication Theory.* https://doi.org/10.1093/ct/qtz027.

Basque, J., & Langley, A. (2018). Invoking Alphonse: The founder figure as a historical resource for organizational identity work. *Organization Studies*, 0170840618789211. https://doi.org/10.1177/0170840618789211.

Bencherki, N., & Bourgoin, A. (2019). Property and organization studies. *Organization Studies*, 40(4), 497–513. https://doi.org/10.1177/0170840617745922.

Bencherki, N., & Elmholdt, K. T. (2020). The organization's synaptic mode of existence: How a hospital merger is many things at once. *Organization*. https://doi.org/10.1177/1350508420962025.

Bencherki, N., Sergi, V., Cooren, F., & Vásquez, C. (2019). How strategy comes to matter: Strategizing as the communicative materialization of matters of concern. *Strategic Organization*, 1476127019890380. https://doi.org/10.1177/1476127019890380.

Benoit-Barné, C., & Cooren, F. (2009). The accomplishment of authority through presentification: How authority is distributed among and negotiated by organizational members. *Management Communication Quarterly*, 23(1), 5–31. https://doi.org/10.1177/0893318909335414.

Bricknell, D. (2008). Historical analysis. In R. Thorpe & R. Holt (Eds.), *The SAGE dictionary of qualitative management research*. Sage. https://doi.org/10.4135/9780857020109.n50.

Castor, T., & Cooren, F. (2006). Organizations as hybrid forms of life : The implications of the selection of agency in problem formulation. *Management Communication Quarterly*, 19(4), 570–600. https://doi.org/10.1177/0893318905284764.

Cifor, M. (2017). Stains and remains: Liveliness, Materiality, and the archival lives of queer bodies. *Australian Feminist Studies*, 32(91–92), 5–21. https://doi.org/10.1080/08164649.2017.1357014.

Cnossen, B., & Bencherki, N. (2019). The role of space in the emergence and endurance of organizing: How independent workers and material assemblages constitute organizations. *Human Relations*, 72(6), 1057–1080. https://doi.org/10.1177/0018726718794265.

Cooren, F. (2010). *Action and agency in dialogue*. John Benjamins.

Cooren, F. (2012). Communication theory at the center: Ventriloquism and the communicative constitution of reality. *Journal of Communication*, 62(1), 1–20. https://doi.org/10.1111/j.1460-2466.2011.01622.x.

Cooren, F. (2015). In medias res: Communication, existence, and materiality. *Communication Research and Practice*, 1(4), 307–321. https://doi.org/10.1080/22041451.2015.1110075.

Cooren, F. (2020). Beyond entanglement: (Socio-) Materiality and organization studies. *Organization Theory*, 1(3), 2631787720954444. https://doi.org/10.1177/2631787720954444.

Cooren, F., Kuhn, T., Cornelissen, J. P., & Clark, T. (2011). Communication, organizing and organization: An overview and introduction to the special issue. *Organization Studies*. https://doi.org/10.1177/0170840611410836.

Cooren, F., & Matte, F. (2010). Obama, Médecins Sans Frontières and the measuring stick. *Pragmatics & Society*, 1(1), 9–31.

Cooren, F., Matte, F., Benoit-Barné, C., & Brummans, B. H. J. M. (2013). Communication as ventriloquism: A grounded-in-action approach to the study of organizational tensions. *Communication Monographs*, 80(3), 255–277. https://doi.org/10.1080/03637751.2013.788255.

Cooren, F., Thompson, F., Canestraro, D., & Bodor, T. (2006). From agency to structure: Analysis of an episode in a facilitation process. *Human Relations*, 59(4), 533–565. https://doi.org/10.1177/0018726706065373.

De Leon, J. P., & Cohen, J. H. (2005). Object and walking probes in ethnographic interviewing. *Field Methods*, 17(2), 200–204. https://doi.org/10.1177/1525822X05274733.

de Vaujany, F.-X., & Vaast, E. (2014). If these walls could talk: The mutual construction of organizational space and legitimacy. *Organization Science*, 25(3), 713–731. www.jstor.org/stable/43660905.

Dobusch, L., & Schoeneborn, D. (2015). Fluidity, identity, and organizationality: The communicative constitution of Anonymous. *Journal of Management Studies*. https://doi.org/10.1111/joms.12139.

Endacott, J., & Brooks, S. (2013). An Updated theoretical and practical model for promoting historical empathy. *Social Studies Research and Practice*, 8, 41–58.

Everett, M. C., & Barrett, M. S. (2012). "Guided tour": A method for deepening the relational quality in narrative research. *Qualitative Research Journal*, 12(1), 32–46. https://doi.org/10.1108/14439881211222714.

Foucault, M. (1972). *The archeology of knowledge* (2nd edn.). Routledge.

Hatch, M. J., & Schultz, M. (2017). Toward a theory of using history authentically : Historicizing in the Carlsberg group. *Administrative Science Quarterly*, 62(4), 657–697. https://doi.org/10.1177/0001839217692535.

Hirsto, H., Basque, J., & Wagnac, R. (2020). Making archives speak: Archival material in CCO research. Paper presented at the 36th European Group for Organizational Studies Colloquium (EGOS),

University of Hamburg, Germany. https://egosnet.org/jart/prj3/egos/resources/dbcon_def/uploads/gEYmj_EGOS2020_shortpaper.pdf.

Hodges, A. (2015). Intertextuality in discourse. In D. Schiffrin, D. Tannen, & H. Hamilton (Eds.), *The Handbook of Discourse Analysis* (pp. 42–60). John Wiley & Sons. https://doi.org/10.1002/9781118584194.ch2.

Howard-Grenville, J., Metzger, M. L., & Meyer, A. D. (2013). Rekindling the flame: Processes of identity resurrection. *Academy of Management Journal, 56*(1), 113–136. https://doi.org/10.5465/amj.2010.0778.

Jahn, J. L. S. (2016). Adapting safety rules in a high reliability context: How wildland firefighting workgroups ventriloquize safety rules to understand hazards. *Management Communication Quarterly, 30*(3), 362–389. https://doi.org/10.1177/0893318915623638.

Kjellstrand, I., & Vince, R. (2020). A trip down memory lane: How photograph insertion methods trigger emotional memory and enhance recall during interviews. *Research Methods in Strategy and Management, 12*, 39–53. https://doi.org/10.1108/S1479-838720200000012015.

Koschmann, M. A., & McDonald, J. (2015). Organizational rituals, communication, and the question of agency. *Management Communication Quarterly, 29*(2), 229–256. https://doi.org/10.1177/0893318915572386.

Kuhn, T. R. (2008). A communicative theory of the firm: Developing an alternative perspective on intra-organizational power and stakeholder relationships. *Organization Studies, 29*(8 9), 1227–1254. https://doi.org/10.1177/0170840608094778

Latour, B. (2005). *Reassembling the social: An introduction to actor-network-theory*. Oxford University Press.

Manoff, M. (2004). Theories of the Archive from Across the Disciplines. *Portal: Libraries and the Academy 4*(1), 9–25. doi:10.1353/pla.2004.0015.

Mathewson, D. B. (2002). A critical binarism: Source criticism and deconstructive criticism. *Journal for the Study of the Old Testament, 26*(4), 3–28. https://doi.org/10.1177/030908920202600401.

Matte, F., & Bencherki, N. (2018). Being followed by an organization: A hauntological perspective on organizational ethnography. In F. Malbois & F. Cooren (Eds.), *Methodological and ontological principles of observation and analysis: Following and analyzing things and beings in our everyday world* (pp. 202–232). Routledge. https://doi.org/10.4324/9781315201610-8.

Prior, L. (2008). Repositioning documents in social research. *Sociology, 42*(5), 821–836. https://doi.org/10.1177/0038038508094564.

Schultz, M., & Hernes, T. (2013). A temporal perspective on organizational identity. *Organization Science, 24*(1), 1–21. https://doi.org/doi:10.1287/orsc.1110.0731.

Schultz, M., & Hernes, T. (2019). Temporal interplay between strategy and identity: Punctuated, subsumed, and sustained modes. *Strategic Organization, 1476127019843834.* https://doi.org/10.1177/1476127019843834.

Sergi, V., & Bonneau, C. (2016). Making mundane work visible on social media: A CCO investigation of working out loud on Twitter. *Communication Research and Practice, 2*(3), 378–406. https://doi.org/10.1080/22041451.2016.1217384.

Sergi, V., & Hallin, A. (2011). Thick performances, not just thick descriptions: The processual nature of doing qualitative research. *Qualitative Research in Organizations and Management: An International Journal, 6*(2), 191–208. https://doi.org/10.1108/17465641111159152.

Shortt, H. L., & Warren, S. K. (2019). Grounded visual pattern analysis: Photographs in organizational field studies. *Organizational Research Methods, 22*(2), 539–563. https://doi.org/10.1177/1094428117742495.

van Vuuren, M., & Westerhof, G. J. (2015). Identity as "knowing your place": The narrative construction of space in a healthcare profession. *Journal of Health Psychology, 20*(3), 326–337. https://doi.org/10.1177/1359105314566614.

Vásquez, C., Brummans, B. H. J. M., & Groleau, C. (2012). Notes from the field on organizational shadowing as framing. *Qualitative Research in Organizations and Management: An International Journal, 7*(2), 144–165. https://doi.org/10.1108/17465641211253075.

Vásquez, C., & Cooren, F. (2013). Spacing practices: The communicative configuration of organizing through space-times. *Communication Theory, 23*(1), 25–47.

Wilhoit, E. D. (2014). Ventriloquism's methodological scope. *Language Under Discussion, 2*(1), 45–49. https://doi.org/10.31885/lud.2.1.243.

Wilhoit, E. D. (2017). Photo and video methods in organizational and managerial communication research. *Management Communication Quarterly*, *31*(3), 447–466. https://doi.org/10.1177/089331891 7704511.

Wilhoit, E. D., & Kisselburgh, L. G. (2019). The relational ontology of resistance: Hybridity, ventrilo-quism, and materiality in the production of bike commuting as resistance. *Organization*, *26*(6), 873–893. https://doi.org/10.1177/1350508417723719.

Winkler, I. (2013). Moments of identity formation and reformation: A day in the working life of an academic. *Journal of Organizational Ethnography*, *2*(2), 191–209. http://dx.doi.org/10.1108/JOE-11-2011-0001.

16

ADVENTUROUS IDEAS FOR ETHNOGRAPHIC RESEARCH ON THE COMMUNICATIVE CONSTITUTION OF ORGANIZATIONS

Boris H. J. M. Brummans and Camille Vézy

Imagine it's 1815 and you're a merchant-trader traveling through Ladakh with a pack of mules, transporting goods from Tibet. Ladakh, a northern region of India at the border with Tibet, is a high-altitude plateau in the Himalayas with much of it being over 3,000 m (9,800 ft). The sun has been beating on you and you're tired. The mules are equally fatigued. They move slowly, stubbornly, up a winding road. You push on as dark clouds are gathering and you sense a thunderstorm is about to break. The following thoughts form in your mind: "I should quickly pitch a camp here." And: "I should dig a hole, so that it might fill up with water for my mules to drink." So, you pitch the camp, dig the hole, tie up the mules, and seek shelter, hoping for the best. While the rain pours down, you eventually doze off.

When you wake up the next morning, you find clear skies and a hole full of water.

Several weeks later, you return along the same route after profitable trading. When you arrive at the place where you pitched your encampment, you find to your surprise that the hole is still full of water, though it hasn't rained in the meantime—Ladakh is notoriously dry in the summer. Still in disbelief, your hands touch the water, and when you drink it, you feel its revitalizing force entering your body.

Being a devout Buddhist, discovering the water compels you to perform a puja *(a ceremony of honor, worship, and devotional attention) on the spot. The event's auspiciousness strikes you so profoundly that you vow to build a Buddhist monastery here to honor this auspicious occasion.*

Filled with inspiration, you gather your mules and return to your village, where you start conveying to people what has happened: Each time you tell your story, words pour out of you, and it feels like an external force is driving you to persuade others to help you build the monastery.

Your fire catches on. People even come and volunteer. Slowly, but surely, you collect enough labor forces as well as donations to buy the required materials, and the monastery gets built.

Now imagine traveling to the present, to the same place where you dug that hole in 1815, and look up ... .

DOI: 10.4324/9781003224914-19

Figure 16.1 Rizong Monastery.

This magnificent monastery arises in front of you (see Figure 16.1). It's an integral, natural part of the environment in which it resides, meshing with its surroundings; it feels alive like the bustling monks you see walking throughout the monastery or the fluttering snow partridges moving up and down the mountain sides. This is Rizong Monastery (or Rizong Gonpa in Ladakhi), which you founded two centuries ago. Below are some pictures of its surrounding landscape as well as its beautiful interiors with colorful statues and murals (see Figure 16.2). The last picture shows your name, "Lama Tsultim Nyima, founder of Rizong Gonpa".

Unfortunately, we only have a few pages in an obscure book, published in 1961 and distributed by the monastery itself, that describe without much detail the moment of discovering that the hole was still filled with water after Lama Tsultim Nyima returned from his trading (see Jivaka, 1961, pp. 195–196). How can the eventful nature of communication in the constitution of a social collective like this monastery be studied in both its linguistic and extralinguistic richness? Drawing inspiration from process philosophy, this chapter shows that ethnography can be employed in adventurous ways to investigate this question. Thus, it contributes new theoretical and methodological insights for investigating the communicative constitution of organizations (CCO).

Since its birth, CCO research has been theoretical and grounded in empirical research (Boivin, Brummans, & Barker, 2017). Most CCO is qualitative in nature (for some excellent exceptions, see Blaschke, 2018; Blaschke, Schoeneborn, & Seidl, 2012). Only a handful of qualitative empirical CCO studies, however, are expressly ethnographic and they vary significantly in their conception and implementation of ethnography (Boivin et al., 2017).

Figure 16.2 Quadriptych of Rizong Monastery. Left: view from one of the monastery's rooms. Top right: Buddhist statue and wall painting. Bottom right: base of the *stupa* of Rizong monastery's founder, Lama Tsultim Nyima (a *stupa* is a Buddhist sepulchral monument).

Particularly those associated with or influenced by the Montréal School of CCO research (Brummans, 2006; Brummans, Cooren, Robichaud, & Taylor, 2014) often use long-term immersion in and reflexive engagement with one or multiple (organizational) field sites; they use participatory and non-participatory data collection methods in their fieldwork, including shadowing (Vásquez, Brummans, & Groleau, 2012); and they produce different "tales of the field" through textwork (Van Maanen, 1988/2011a)—these practices are the hallmarks of organizational ethnography (see Neyland, 2008; Van Maanen, 2011b; Ybema, 2009; see also Taylor et al., 2021). Some, for example, have examined how communication makes Médecins Sans Frontières (MSF) present in the Congo and other African countries (Cooren, Brummans, & Charrieras, 2008); how authority is accomplished in MSF's interactional contexts by invoking sources of authority (Benoit-Barné & Cooren, 2009); and how tensions in this humanitarian organization's field operations are produced communicatively by mobilizing contradictory figures (Cooren, Matte, Benoit-Barné, & Brummans, 2013). Others have studied the role of spacing-timing practices in the organizing of a Chilean science and technology diffusion program (Vásquez & Cooren, 2013); material elements in the organizing of a US biking collective (Wilhoit & Kisselburgh, 2015); space as a material assemblage in the endurance of Dutch creative hubs (Cnossen & Bencherki, 2019); absence-presence differentiation practices in the constitution of a Canadian university's alternativeness (Del Fa & Vásquez, 2019); information communication technology as a Moroccan human rights civil society organization's dis/ordering device (Albu, 2019); and invocational practices in the authoring and materialization of a Taiwanese Buddhist NGO (Brummans, Hwang, & Cheong, 2013, 2020). Ethnographic Montréal School CCO research frequently relies on interaction analyses of video/audio recorded materials, at times combined with the analysis of field notes, interviews, websites, and social media posts. Hence, it tends to foreground communication as linguistic and paralinguistic expression. How could ethnography be employed to not only gain insight into the para/linguistic but also the *extra*linguistic richness of micro-moments in organizational constitution—like the auspicious moment when Lama Tsultim Nyima discovers the water in the hole he dug illustrated by the introductory vignette?

Moving with the turn toward *relationality* and *affect* in organizational communication and organization studies (for an overview, see Kuhn, Ashcraft, & Cooren, 2017; see also Ashcraft, 2017, 2021; Cooren, 2015, 2018a, 2018b; Gherardi, 2017; Gherardi et al., 2019; Jahn, 2018; Kuhn, 2021; Ashcraft & Kuhn, 2018; Orlikowski, 2007; Vásquez, 2020), we aim to explore this question here. The mentioned micro-moments may only last a few seconds, yet they make a key difference in the constitution of the *events* (Massumi, 2011; Ramos, 2019, 2020a) that bring forth social collectives (see also Hussenot & Missonier, 2016) with different degrees of *organizationality*—defined by (1) the interconnection of instances of decision-making taking place on behalf of the collective; (2) the collective's ability to act as an actor, which depends on the attribution of actorhood by other actors; and (3) the collective's ongoing demarcation and negotiation of its (organizational) identity (Dobusch & Schoeneborn, 2015). Communication is vital in this process, not so much because it enables the transmission of messages or the co-construction of shared meaning between human beings, but because it enables events to come into being through the expression of language and extralinguistic forces (see Massumi, 2002a, 2019; see also Ritchie, 2018). The adventurous ways of conducting ethnographic CCO research presented here enable research to attune to this dynamic richness, for they provide insight into how an organization takes form and transforms as a "field of relation" (Massumi, 2015, p. 200; see also Cooper, 2005) through communication as extra/linguistic expression.

Thus, in this chapter, we follow in the footsteps of organizational scholars like Robert Chia (1995, 1997), Tor Hernes (2014), Shiv Ganesh and Ying Wang (2015), Anthony Hussenot and Stéphanie Missonier (2016), and Jennifer Mease (2021), who drew inspiration from process philosophy. Our aim is to draw from process philosophy to develop a new theoretical perspective on how an organizational field of relation unfolds as events that become *enacted* (Weick, 1979) or *actualized* in the course of extra/linguistic communication—*in-acted,* as Brian Massumi (2011, p. 16) would say. Subsequently, we propose new ways of ethnographically studying organizational in-act processes by drawing from various disciplines of the humanities and social sciences.

A Process Philosophy Perspective on the Communicative Constitution of Organizations

While Montréal School CCO research has been critiqued for being too microscopic, for staring itself blind on conversation-analytic transcripts of interactions that last a few minutes at the longest, we believe it could be even *more* microscopic in its explorations, because second-by-second moments are, as the Rizong vignette shows, incredibly rich. They therefore deserve to be investigated in even greater depth, not only linguistically or paralinguistically, but also extralinguistically—by taking into account how emerging feelings, ideas, and so forth *move* organizational constitution in conjunction with para/language. The vignette also reveals that it's worthwhile to study organizational in-act processes by including the actual as well as potential (see Massumi, 2011)—or the *manifest* and *latent* in Robert Cooper's (2005) terms. For example, attuning to the moment when Lama Tsultim Nyima discovers the water entails tapping into what *compels* him to perform a *puja* and then to build the monastery. What compels or moves him is affect, which Massumi (2015) defines as "a power to affect and be affected [that] governs a transition, where a body passes from one state of capacitation to a diminished or augmented state of capacitation. This comes with the corollary that the transition is *felt*" (p. 48, emphasis in original; see also Massumi, 2002b; Ramos, 2019; Spinoza, 1985). Hence, affect and relation go hand in hand (see Massumi, 2015, p. 50). The feeling that moves Lama Tsultim Nyima, for example, makes a crucial difference in the string of events leading to the emergence of Rizong as a relational field (performing the *puja*, going to the village and speaking with villagers, starting the building of the monastery, etc.).

What's remarkable about the work of process philosophers like William James and Alfred N. Whitehead, as well as the work of contemporary process philosophers who draw from James and Whitehead, such as Erin Manning, Brian Massumi, and Ana Ramos, is how it invites new ways of experiencing or sensing life's openness. Their writings reveal how life teems with vitality and creativity, yet is also sensitive to how what has come before informs the actualization of its infinite potentialities. As the Rizong vignette illustrates, discovering the water is momentous: seeing the water makes a "qualitative difference" (Massumi, 2011, p. 92) that is "felt" (p. 3). This felt-difference sets in motion other differences—felt or experienced by humans and other-than-humans—that move Rizong's formation and subsequent transformations. The vignette shows how important it is to take into account the events that follow from, and those prior to, this momentous event (Massumi, 2011).

When paying attention to the processual nature of experience, it therefore becomes more insightful to trace constellations or fields of relation in their ongoing formation and transformation, rather than to analyze interactions *between* subjects and objects, as is common in (multimodal) conversation analysis (see Mondada, 2019). The latter focuses attention on interacts, turns of talk, and so on as units of analysis. It centers the senses on the para/linguistic actions between (inter) already formed, already constituted entities, be they human or other-than-human. In contrast, process philosophy accentuates how events are made of felt micro-moments—*actual occasions* in Whitehead's (1978) vocabulary (see also Ramos, 2019). This view doesn't imply that entities cease to exist. It rather implies that entities don't exist outside events (see also Cobb, 2007; Ramos, 2020b); they're *immanent to* them (Massumi, 2011; Ramos, 2019). In turn, communication is no longer viewed as the transmission of content or the co-construction of shared meaning between human beings—a view suggested, for example, by Hussenot and Missonier's (2016) "events-based approach" to organizational process research (see p. 533). It's the expression of language and extralinguistic forces through which events are in-acted in singular ways (Massumi, 2002a, 2019; Ramos, 2019; Ritchie, 2018).

Seen from this process philosophy perspective, language becomes only "one form of communication among many" (Halewood, 2005, p. 72, cited in Murphie, 2019, p. 26). Rizong monastery, for example, is a relational field that unfolds through a series of events that express themselves extra/linguistically. Extra/linguistic expression is the communicative act through which qualitative differences become felt from one micro-moment to another. Such moments enable events to come into being (be in-acted) in the form of a relational field. Communication becomes the extra/linguistic activity through which a relational field is constituted, moment by moment, in the moment: the feeling of fatigue expressing itself in the mules because of their physical exertion in the hot sun hitting the dry and dusty valley of the Indian high-altitude plateau; the decision to halt and dig a hole expressing itself in Lama Tsultim Nyima's mind when sensing that a thunderstorm is about to break; feelings of amazement and auspiciousness expressing themselves when seeing, touching, and consuming the water upon his return several weeks later; the feeling of spiritual devotion expressing itself in his speech when talking with villagers, who then become affected by it; and so on. Note how Lama Tsultim Nyima is immanent to the events that form Rizong monastery as an organizational field of relation. He's but one *vector* (Whitehead, 1978) among many in this dynamic field. The lama's and monastery's becoming are indissociable in the relational manifold that unfolds, eventfully—one moment becoming actualized through grasping, apprehending, or *prehending* (Whitehead, 1933/1967, 1978) the previous one, and tending toward a new moment, again full of potential (see Massumi, 2011).

As Massumi notes, in this view of communication, "nothing makes a difference unless it makes 'ingression' into [takes effect in and for] a situation under way" (B. Massumi, first author's personal communication, April 3, 2020). Transmission still happens, Massumi notes, "but there are multiple channels of transmission into the event". These channels, are irreducible to "point-to-point transmission through a technical medium". They include "bodily disposition, affect, inflections from the surrounding situation of reception, modulation by what came before, activation of tendencies inherent in the way in which the technical medium is embedded in the everyday, sparking of potential and virtualities, etc.". When paying attention to the singular manner in which events are in-acted extra/linguistically, the world becomes "a medium for the transmission of influences" (Whitehead, 1978, p. 286; see also Massumi, 2019; Murphie, 2019). These influences are forces that are transmitted vectorially, "from elsewhere" (Whitehead, 1978, p. 116). In turn, the "content" of communication becomes "everything that factors into the event, whether it is directly signified or not, as enveloped in its taking-effect (as immanent to the event)" (B. Massumi, first author's personal communication, April 3, 2020).

This conception of communication is consequential for research on the communicative constitution of formal, goal-oriented organizations in which coordination and accountability are key, as well as networks of more or less informal relations, such as terrorist groups, or social movements in which organizational and individual actors are united by critical cultural experiences, historical moments, and so on (see Comas, Shrivastava, & Martin, 2015)—different types of social collectives with different degrees of organizationality (Dobusch & Schoeneborn, 2015). It provides a new theoretical perspective for studying how a social collective becomes a field of relation with a certain degree of organizationality through events that express themselves extra/linguistically (see also Ramos, 2020b). For example, it could reveal how the relational field that is now the Rizong's monastic *total institution* (Goffman, 1961) emerged as a series of events expressed through feelings of fatigue, surprise, auspiciousness, and devotion, conjoined with persuasive language and the force of labor. It consequently also provides a novel lens for analyzing how the extra/linguistic expression of a series of events *dis/organizes* (Vásquez & Kuhn, 2019) a relational field with a certain degree of organizationality.

New ways may be developed to conduct empirical CCO research from this process philosophy perspective. What's important, in this regard, is that these ways attune CCO researchers to the dynamic richness of micro-moments and their role in constituting events. Drawing guidance and inspiration from various fields and areas of the humanities and social sciences, including post-qualitative research (St. Pierre Adams, 2018) and research-creation (Chapman & Sawchuk, 2008), we'll now explore how ethnography can be employed to conduct CCO research in adventurous ways from this perspective.

Techniques for Ethnographically Studying the Communicative Constitution of Organizations from a Process Philosophy Perspective

One way of ethnographically investigating a social collective's communicative constitution is by *mapping* or *tracing* how the extra/linguistic expression of events makes felt qualitative differences in trans/forming a relational field with a degree of organizationality. This way of conducting CCO research is inspired by Fernand Deligny's beautiful mappings of the movements of autistic persons living in a social collective in the Cévennes mountains in southern France, which we discovered in Manning's (2013) *Always More Than One*. Deligny's community was captured in Renaud Victor's (1976) film, *Ce Gamin, Là* (see www.youtube.com/watch?v=i20VWKO9Sdk), and is described as follows by Leon Hilton (2015):

> In the 1950s, Deligny conducted a series of collectively run residential programs ... for children and adolescents with autism and other disabilities who would have otherwise spent their lives institutionalized in state-run psychiatric asylums. Militantly opposed to institutions of every kind ... Deligny was critical of the dominant psychiatric, psychoanalytic, and positivist educational doctrines of the time. He rejected the view that autism and cognitive disability were pathological deviations from a preexisting norm. He did not try to force the mostly nonspeaking autistics who came to live with them to conform to standards of speech. [In] the desolate Cévennes region, Deligny and his colleagues [pursued] "the network as a mode of being"—one that would be far less concerned with interpreting behavior and experience according to the hidden intentions and secret desires of individual human subjects, and more focused on "tracing" the trajectories, detours, and wander lines that compose a given social milieu. It was here that Deligny consummated his longstanding preoccupation with mapping the gestures, movements, and trajectories of the autistics living within his networks ... Deligny ... and [his] collaborators began to follow their autistic counterparts as they made their way through the Cévennes's rocky terrain, making rudimentary line drawings to indicate their direction of movement across the rural encampment and into surrounding wilderness. No attempt was made to interfere with the children's movements, or to explain or interpret them. The focus remained on the process of tracing itself.

Some of Deligny's mappings are shown in his book, *The Arachnean and Other Texts* (Deligny, 2015). Figure 16.3 shows two mesmerizing examples.

The first drawing shows a map of "Le Serret":

> [It] designates a more expansive portion of the territory than the living area that is usually designated by this name. The broad lines in black pastel (the main one of which crosses the entire map) transcribe the journeys of an adult, Jean Lin. The wander line of an autistic child, Anne, is traced in India ink. The adult and the child are accompanied by a flock of sheep, whose hoofprints are sprinkled throughout the map. The ringing of sheep bells is represented by tiny clusters of dots. The sounds of a flute and a bell are represented in three places (at the top, in the center, and at the bottom) by three strokes. At the top, Anne strayed from Jean Lin's path; the *black flower* marks a stopping point and a rocking motion. In the center, a chaotic zone of lines and schematically-drawn stones designates the place where they stopped to cut wood (note the sketch of a machete). Farther down, in two places, the child's wander line deviates from the main path for short detours or *swerves*.
>
> *Deligny, 2015, p. 230, emphasis in original*

The second drawing shows a map of the "Y House" in Monoblet:

> The background map is a freehand sketch of the kitchen in "Y House" and its furnishings (table and stools at the top, stove and sink at the bottom). The entrance

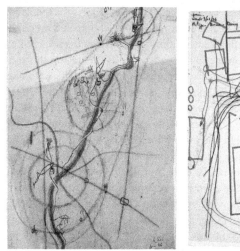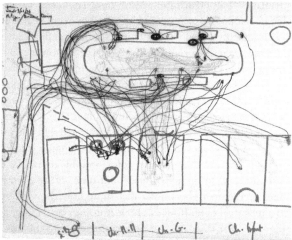

Figure 16.3 Diptych of mappings. Left: "Le Serret, juin 1976". The journeys of Jean Lin and an autistic child, Anne, with a herd of goats in the vicinity of the living area. A map and a tracing drawn by Jean Lin, 45 × 30 cm. Right: "La maison Y à Monoblet." The movements of two adults and three autistic children, Anne, Philippe, and Dany, in the kitchen, while making bread. A map and a tracing drawn by Thierry Bazzana and Marie-Madeleine Godet, 37 × 50 cm. Originals appeared in *Maps and Wander Lines: Traces of Fernand Deligny's Network, 1969–1979,* edited by Sandra Álvarez de Toledo (2013), L'Arachnéen.

to the room is on the left. The wander lines are drawn in India ink on tracings superimposed on the background map. They transcribe the movements of the three autistic children while bread is being made. The "eyes" mark the children's places around the table. The "hands" are recognizable, as well as the strings of saliva (with which one of the children is playing), represented by little wavelets.

Deligny, 2015, p. 232

Manning (2013) calls Deligny's mapping a "cartography of everyday life" (p. 191). Its "explicit mandate [is] to invent modes of relation that do not necessarily rely on words" (p. 191). Following Manning, we don't view this mapping or tracing as a *method*, such as the one typically used in time-and-motion studies that track the movements of hospital care team members (e.g., see Sinsky et al., 2016) or in research that uses sensor technology like socio-metric badges to analyze team interactions (e.g., see Endedijk et al., 2019; Kim et al., 2012). We rather view it as a *technique* that aims to attend to the dynamic richness of micro-moments and their role in constituting events (see Manning, 2016). This technique may be acquired and appropriated in creative ways by CCO researchers, depending on the organizational in-act processes they're investigating. Thus, as a CCO researcher, you may ask yourself: "What kind of tracing technique(s) can I develop to examine how the extra/linguistic expression of events makes felt qualitative differences in trans/forming the organizational field of relation I'm investigating?"

For example, imagine you're conducting an ethnography of a youth detention center in 1950s France. You've become part of this center by living among its juveniles and staff, being, moving, becoming with them every day. Perhaps, one day, you witness the following scene: https://www.youtube.com/watch?v=yYqmZW1n8U0. This is the famous ending of François

Truffaut's 1959 French New Wave film, *Les Quatre Cents Coups*. The film depicts the semiauto-biographical story of Antoine Doinel, a boy who, neglected by family and school, ends up on the streets of Paris and subsequently in a youth detention center, from which he tries to escape.

How incredibly rich the string of events you see in this video clip is for tracing this total institution's communicative constitution: Imagine capturing the unexpectedly unfolding scene on film (for more on organizational video-ethnography, see Grosjean & Matte, 2021). Afterward, you watch the recording and use it to begin drawing lines that trace Antoine's *affective movements* (Harris & Holman Jones, 2021), as well as the guard's and your own, within the unfolding relational field that is co-in-acted by the unwinding path on which Antoine, the guard, and you moved; the sounds of the singing birds; the smell of fresh air, trees, grass; and so forth. You vary their shape, color, and thickness, like Deligny, to signify variations in speed, intensity, and so on across space and time. *In the creative act of drawing*, this technique reveals lines or vectors of becoming that show how the youth detention center unfolds dynamically as a relational field. It reveals how Antoine's becoming, as well as the guard's, yours, the path's, the bird's, the trees', and so on are immanent to the unfolding events, which come into being through the extra/linguistic expression of moment-to-moment felt qualitative differences—for example, feeling your feet as they make contact with the path and the path feeling the impact of your feet in return; or hearing the ebbing and flowing of bird sounds, while the birds hear you approaching through the sound of your footsteps and breathing. You subsequently use this tracing technique as one (retrospective) way *into* the youth detention center's communicative constitution. For example, it provides a starting point for analyzing the dis/organizing effects of this series of events, expressed by extralinguistic forces and the complete absence of (verbal) language—especially *disorganizing* in this case, as it shows a clear *breach*.

This mapping could be complemented by using Clifford Geertz's (1973) *thick description* in your drawing at key moments in the scene shown in the clip, based on the detailed ethno-graphic fieldnotes (Emerson, Fretz, & Shaw, 1995/2011) you wrote after returning to your room and complemented while watching the video recording. The idea of *thick co-composition*, inspired by Manning's (2013) concept of *composing-with*, could be developed as a technique to enrich Geertz's original idea. As Manning notes, "To compose-with is to place language within an ecology of practices. It is to think-with in the time of the utterance's becoming-expression. To compose-with is to collectively write time in the shaping" (p. 16). As a complement to your tracing technique, thick co-composition is a second technique that enables you, *in the creative act of writing*, to *feel with* the surface of the path, the sounds of the birds, the smell of fresh air, trees, grass. While re-watching the video recording, you pause regularly to write. You feel, in writing, how the sound of Antoine's movements expresses a felt sense of freeing from institu-tional constraints (and from his own past). You also feel how this sense of liberty is co-composed with the surrounding sounds, smells, and so on—and with you, the ethnographer who became complicit in his escape attempt by filming him without intervening. Thus, the act of carefully describing—or *in*-scribing—the felt expression of the unfolding events provides multidimen-sional, multisensorial, and multimodal retrospective insight into the total institution's unfolding constitution and dis/organization.

In *Forms of Vitality*, Daniel Stern (2010) provides inspiring examples of how felt quali-tative differences that bring events into being might be expressed through/in writing. For Stern, "[l]ife shows itself in so many different forms of vitality" (p. 5). "The experience of vitality", he states, "is inherent in the act of movement. Movement, and its proprioception, is the primary manifestation of being animate and provides the primary sense of aliveness" (p. 9). Words like "exploding", "swelling", "cresting", "rushing", "relaxing", "pulsing", "powerful", "gentle", "accelerating", "fading", and "weak" are helpful, Stern (2010, p. 7)

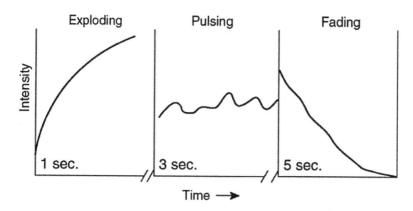

Figure 16.4   Time × intensity (force) graphs for three possible vitality forms. Original appeared in *Forms of Vitality* by Daniel Stern (2010, p. 8), Oxford University Press.

suggests, for expressing the moving lines or vectors of becoming you've traced in the act of writing. Figure 16.4 shows some examples of how different forms of vitality might be expressed by combining lines and words (see Stern, 2010, p. 8)—the x- and y-axes could be left out to create more life-like maps such as the ones drawn by Deligny. As Stern notes (p. 8), words like these are "curious". "[They are not] emotions … . They are not motivational states … . They are not direct cognitions in any usual sense. They are not acts, as they have no goal state and no specific means. They fall in between all the cracks." Hence, words like these "are felt experience of force—in movement—with a temporal contour, and a sense of aliveness, of going somewhere".

In other situations where (verbal) language is used by the human beings involved, these tracing and thick co-composition techniques also enable you to include people's verbatim at specific moments in your mapping in order to understand how language affects and is affected by the youth detention center's trans/formation as a field of relation. Your ethnographic field-work could also include other forms of shadowing in different situations to create a longitu-dinal micro-momentary view of this center's communicative constitution. If the fieldwork was conducted in the present time, for example, you could give GoPro cameras to the center's employees and youth, and ask them to video record their movements throughout the day (see also Wilhoit, 2017). This would provide a different way into key events than if you were to record these persons yourself, as you did with Antoine. Subsequently, you could ask these per-sons to watch their own recordings, draw their own maps, and complement them with their own thick co-composition, turning them into co-composers of your ethnography.

These techniques bring to light how important it is for ethnographers to be reflexive of the ways ethnographic work plays into the constitutive processes they're investigating (see also Vézy & Brummans, 2021). They acknowledge that you (the ethnographer) are an integral (*feeling* and *felt*) constituent of the relational field-in-formation, not a mere (participant) observer *of* it: someone who affects its enactment and is at the same time affected by it (see Ramos, 2020a). In other words, acquiring and appropriating these techniques makes you aware of the fact that you're not the "primary [human] data-gathering instrument" (Lincoln & Guba, 1985, p. 39), but rather a vector that affects and is affected by the unfolding organizational field of relation you're trying to study. These techniques therefore attune you and all those *with* whom you're co-composing this relational field to the complex ethical aspects of ethnographic fieldwork, deskwork, and textwork (Yanow, 2000), well beyond traditional questions of consent, confidentiality, and so on.

Using these techniques, I (the first author) am now eager to return to Rizong monastery, where I conducted ethnographic research on Buddhist *mindful organizing* over several years (see Brummans, 2007, 2008, 2009, 2011, 2012, 2014, 2017), to gain further insight into this total institution's communicative constitution. Figure 16.5 shows the road that connects Rizong with Chulichan nunnery and the village below.

Each day, the Chulichan nuns and Rizong monks walk up and down this road. In walking, the pedestrians, road, surrounding rocky landscape, sky, and so on co-create, moment by moment, second by second, an essential physical communication channel between the relational fields that are the monastery, nunnery, and the world "outside" their community. Unfortunately, the recent creation of this asphalted road also means that heaps of tourists and backpackers now have easy access to this once-remote community, introducing constant disruption of the nuns' and monks' disciplined round of life through the coming and going of vehicles, people causing all sorts of

Figure 16.5 The road to Rizong Monastery and Chulichan Nunnery.

Figure 16.6   Triptych of monks walking back to Rizong Monastery.

pollution, talking loudly, and flashing around the newest technological gadgets. However, in its ongoing becoming, the road also enables transportation of useful goods, resources, and services. It also provides an unfolding trajectory for *en route* informal conversation, individual contemplation, prayer, and meditation. Especially the latter can be seen in the pictures of a small group of monks, taken during my (the first author's) fieldwork in 2006, in Figure 16.6.

Figure 16.7 shows how essential walking for the Chulichan nuns is as well. Like the monks, the nuns frequently go off the beaten path and "lay down a path in walking" (Varela, 1987, p. 63), for example to wash their robes in the nearby creek, as can be seen in the second picture. While washing their robes, the echoing sound of their chatting voices can often be heard while it meshes with that of the babbling water.

How illuminating it would be to appropriate the tracing technique in combination with thick co-composition in ethnographic research on the role of communication as event-expression in trans/forming Rizong, Chulichan, and Ladakhi society as a complex relational field consisting of multiple sub-fields without clear geographical boundaries or limits (for more on this multi-sitedness, see Marcus, 1995). Employing these techniques, it would be enlightening, for example, to study how Rizong and Chulichan are constituted as dynamic, multisensorial relational sub-fields in everyday acts like walking or washing clothes. As I (the first author) experienced during five summers, while peaceful on the surface, the larger field enfolding Rizong and Chulichan is rife with latent and manifest tensions stemming from the monastery's historical domination over the nunnery. Although many Buddhist philosophies foster gender equity rather than male dominance, they're often institutionalized in sexist ways (see Gross, 1993, 1998). For example, the Chulichan nuns used to do arduous manual labor for the Rizong monks. They've slowly become more emancipated, though, in part due to the creation of their own school and the support of the fourteenth Dalai Lama, Tenzin Gyatso. While living with them, it would be intriguing to trace the nuns' and monks' affective movements within their respective communities and along the road shown above, as well as to ask them to trace their own "round of life" (Goffman, 1961, p. xiii). These maps could be complemented by thick co-composition and form the basis for analyzing the dis/organizing effects of specific strings of events, expressed extra/linguistically, to deepen understanding of these power dynamics. It would also provide insight into my (the first author's) *complicity* (Marcus, 1997, 2001) in these and other dynamics.

Figure 16.7 Diptych of nuns walking back to Chulichan Nunnery (left) and washing clothes in a creek (right).

The techniques we've presented could be further enriched and complemented in numerous ways. For example, eventful interview techniques like *walking interviews* (Feinberg, 2016) could be used to understand human beings' ambulatory *sensemaking* (Weick, 1979)—how they make sense with all their senses. Moreover, *soundwalking* could be included in ethnographic CCO research by "listening and sometimes recording while moving through a place at a walking pace" (McCartney, 2014, p. 212). How intriguing it would be to interview members of a social collective while walking through organizational spaces and environments, or to record the sounds that play into processes of organizational constitution. For example, the sonic richness co-composing Chulichan and Rizong could be captured through sound recording while helping the nuns wash their clothes in the creek, or while walking over the road to Rizong and listening to the monks' conversations. These sounds could then be mapped like Deligny's lines and thickly co-composed with the help of Stern's vocabulary of vitality (for an example of *sound-mapping*, see Tejaswinee Kelkar and Alexander Jensenius's [2018] analysis of free-hand sound-tracings of melodic phrases; see also Thulin, 2018).

It would also be intriguing to conduct the kind of retrospective micro-analytic interviews described by Stern (2004) in *The Present Moment* with members of a social collective. Stern initially referred to these interviews as "breakfast interviews" (p. 9). They're used, as Stern explains (p. 9), to "identify present moments and the affective happenings that occur during them [, which last about five seconds]." Individuals are asked: "What did you experience this morning at breakfast?" Together, Stern and the individual then conversationally delve into what was experienced in those five seconds, exploring "what they did, thought, felt, saw, heard, what position their body was in, when it shifted, whether they positioned themselves as an actor or an observer to the action, or somewhere in between" (p. 9).

Interestingly, Stern also relies on a kind of mapping in these interviews:

> The subjects and I try to draw or graph the experience along a timeline, where time stretches out on the horizontal axis and the intensity, effort, and fullness of the event/ feeling/sensation/thought/affect/action is delineated on the vertical axis … .This process may sound tedious, but it actually generates great interest and curiosity in

both the subject and [the psychotherapist], despite the apparent banality of the events. Although the present moments are ordinary, they are triggered by novelty, the unexpected, or a potential problem or trouble … . [W]e become increasingly amazed at all that is recalled as happenings in such short stretches of ordinary life moments and how the[se] micro-dramas are resolved. (pp. 10–11)

This technique would be helpful for analyzing how a social collective's members and you (the ethnographer) co-compose specific series of events in the trans/formation of an organizational field of relation during semi-structured interviews/conversations.

What would also be valuable, especially if you're aiming to transform the social collective you're studying, is that all the mentioned techniques attune organizational members and you to their and your own day-to-day, second-by-second becoming in relation with countless other processes of becoming. This would benefit a member's mindful organizing—members' "awareness of the dynamic, interdependently arising nature of anything that appears to have a permanent, independent existence (including one's own self)" (Brummans, 2014, p. 441), and their cultivation of this awareness to "[bounce] back from unexpected events by using whatever is at hand in a given situation with wisdom and compassion" (Brummans, 2017, p. 4). It would also benefit your mindful researching—your ability to "understand an organization's enactment by folding into, or with, the concrete situations that bring forth this enactment" (Brummans, 2014, p. 444; see also Brummans, in press).

Finally, in the 1960s and 70s, Fluxus members had already noted that an event cannot be *re*communicated (Fluxus was an international avant-garde network or collective of artists, poets, and musicians that aimed to bring attention to the artistic process, rather than its finished product). As Stern also notes, you can only invite others to *re*experience an event. The question becomes therefore: What creative new ways can be developed to express—multisensorially, multimodally—the knowledge gained through ethnographic CCO research from a process philosophy perspective? Here, CCO researchers might turn to poetic language, film, sound, and so on, and the work of Elizabeth Wilhoit Larson (2017, 2020) on photo and video methods as well as books like Johanna Drucker's (2014) *Graphesis* (the study of the visual production of knowledge) provide plenty of promising pathways. In addition, there are plenty of other interesting forms of mapping that could be helpful for analyzing the felt extra/linguistic expression of events, such as those presented in Karen O'Rourke's (2013) book, *Walking and Mapping*. Collaborating with architects, artists, designers, or geographers would be fruitful in this regard—for promising starting points, see the following websites:

- www.lib.sfu.ca/help/publish/dh/dhil/about
- www.sensorystudies.org
- www.walkingartistsnetwork.org

A Conclusion and a Beginning

Over the past 20 years, CCO research has undergone a number of turns. It started out as part of the discursive turn in organizational communication and organization studies, and contributed significantly to it (see Fairhurst & Putnam, 2004; Putnam & Fairhurst, 2015), as it did with the more recent material turn (see Ashcraft, Kuhn, & Cooren, 2009). Now a turn to relationality and affect is under way (see Kuhn et al., 2017). This chapter suggests that the latter would benefit from a strong, deep engagement with process philosophy. By proposing an approach to ethnographic CCO research grounded in this philosophy, our chapter contributes new theoretical and methodological insights for investigating the communicative constitution of organizations. Our hope is that this approach is sufficiently open, so other CCO researchers can develop their own approaches and techniques for ethnographically studying processes of organizational constitution. Rather than regarding the approach we've presented here as a methodological manual, we encourage others to find their own creative ways to immerse themselves into "the situationality of everyday [organizational] life" (Brummans, 2014, p. 442), and to "embrace" (p. 442) this situatedness in order to comprehend how the everyday unfolds moment by moment, in the moment. Like Elizabeth Adams St. Pierre (2018, p. 603), that is, we invite CCO researchers to "follow the provocations that come from everywhere in the inquiry that is living and writing", instead of "rushing to preexisting research methodologies". Thus, we believe, research on the multidimensional, multisensorial, multimodal nature of communication and its role in *organizational becoming* (Chia, 1995, 1997) can continue to advance in adventurous ways.

Authors' Note

This chapter started as an invited presentation at the University of Colorado Boulder, given by the first author on November 6, 2019, and organized by Bryan Taylor. Its title is inspired by Alfred N. Whitehead's (1933/1967) book, *Adventures of Ideas*. We're most grateful to Erin Manning, Brian Massumi, and Ana Ramos for introducing process philosophy to us. Moreover, we kindly thank the editors of this handbook, Joëlle Basque, Nicolas Bencherki, and Timothy Kuhn, as well as Renata Azevedo Moreira, Brenda Berkelaar, François Cooren, Natalie Doonan, Beth Haslett, Brian Massumi, Ana Ramos, and Mark van Vuuren for their valuable comments on earlier versions of this text. This chapter is dedicated to Johan Hubert Brummans, who was born during the writing of this text amid the COVID-19 pandemic.

References

Albu, O. B. (2019). Dis/ordering: The use of information and communication technologies by human rights civil society organizations. In C. Vásquez & T. Kuhn (Eds.), *Dis/organization as communication: Exploring the disordering, disruptive and chaotic properties of communication* (pp. 151–171). Routledge.

Álvarez de Toledo, S. (Ed.). (2013). *Maps and wander lines: Traces of Fernand Deligny's network, 1969–1979*. L'Arachnéen.

Ashcraft, K. L. (2017). "Submission" to the rule of excellence: Ordinary affect and precarious resistance in the labor of organization and management studies. *Organization, 24*(1), 36–58.

Ashcraft, K. L. (2021). Communication as constitutive transmission? An encounter with affect. *Communication Theory, 31*(4), 571–592.

Ashcraft, K. L., & Kuhn, T. R. (2018). Agential encounters: Performativity and affect meet communication in the bathroom. In B. H. J. M. Brummans (Ed.), *The agency of organizing: Perspectives and case studies* (pp. 170–193). Routledge.

Ashcraft, K. L., Kuhn, T. R., & Cooren, F. (2009). Constitutional amendments: "Materializing" organizational communication. *Academy of Management Annals, 3*(1), 1–64.

Blaschke, S. (2018). The distribution of decision rights at ICANN: A Luhmannian perspective on agency. In B. H. J. M. Brummans (Ed.), *The agency of organizing: Perspectives and case studies* (pp. 28–42). Routledge.

Blaschke, S., Schoeneborn, D., & Seidl, D. (2012). Organizations as networks of communication episodes: Turning the network perspective inside out. *Organization Studies, 33*(7), 879–906.

Benoit-Barné, C., & Cooren, F. (2009). The accomplishment of authority through presentification: How authority is distributed among and negotiated by organizational members. *Management Communication Quarterly, 23*(1), 5–31.

Boivin, G., Brummans, B. H. J. M., & Barker, J. R. (2017). The institutionalization of CCO scholarship: Trends from 2000 to 2015. *Management Communication Quarterly, 31*(3), 331–355.

Brummans, B. H. J. M. (2006). The Montréal School and the question of agency. In F. Cooren, J. R. Taylor, & E. J. Van Every (Eds.), *Communication as organizing: Empirical and theoretical explorations in the dynamic of text and conversation* (pp. 197–211). Lawrence Erlbaum.

Brummans, B. H. J. M. (2007). Travels of a Buddhist mind. *Qualitative Inquiry, 13*(8), 1221–1226.

Brummans, B. H. J. M. (2008). Preliminary insights into the constitution of a Tibetan Buddhist monastery through autoethnographic reflections on the dual/nondual mind duality. *Anthropology of Consciousness, 19*(2), 134–154.

Brummans, B. H. J. M. (2009). Travels of a Buddhist mind: Returns and continuations. *Qualitative Inquiry, 15*(6), 1127–1133.

Brummans, B. H. J. M. (2011). What goes down must come up: Communication as incarnation and transcension. *Communication and Critical/Cultural Studies, 8*(2), 194–200.

Brummans, B. H. J. M. (2012). The road to Rizong: Buddhist mindful organizing amid natural disaster in the Indian Himalayas. *Qualitative Communication Research, 1*(4), 433–460.

Brummans, B. H. J. M. (2014). Pathways to mindful qualitative organizational communication research. *Management Communication Quarterly, 28*(3), 441–447.

Brummans, B. H. J. M. (2017). Mindful organizing. In C. R. Scott & L. K. Lewis (Eds.), *The international encyclopedia of organizational communication*. Wiley Blackwell.

Brummans, B. H. J. M. (in press). Eight ways to notice mindfully in process organization studies. In B. Simpson & L. Revsbæk (Eds.), *Noticing differently: The reading, writing and doing of empirical process studies*. Oxford University Press.

Brummans, B. H. J. M., Cooren, F., Robichaud, D., & Taylor, J. R. (2014). Approaches to the communicative constitution of organizations. In L. L. Putnam & D. K. Mumby (Eds.), *The SAGE handbook of organizational communication: Advances in theory, research, and methods* (3rd edn., pp. 173–194). SAGE.

Brummans, B. H. J. M., Hwang, J. M., & Cheong, P. H. (2013). Mindful authoring through invocation: Leaders' constitution of a spiritual organization. *Management Communication Quarterly, 27*(3), 346–372.

Brummans, B. H. J. M., Hwang, J. M., & Cheong, P. H. (2020). Recycling stories: Mantras, communication, and organizational materialization. *Organization Studies, 41*(1), 103–126.

Chapman, O., & Sawchuk, K. (2008). Research-creation: Intervention, analysis and family resemblances. *Canadian Journal of Communication, 37*, 5–26.

Chia, R. (1995). From modern to postmodern organizational analysis. *Organization Studies, 16*(4), 579–604.

Chia, R. (1997). *Essai*: Thirty years on: From organizational structures to the organization of thought. *Organization Studies, 18*(4), 685–707.

Cnossen, B., & Bencherki, N. (2019). The role of space in the emergence and endurance of organizing: How independent workers and material assemblages constitute organizations. *Human Relations, 72*(6), 1057–1080.

Cobb, J. B. (2007). Person-in-community: Whiteheadian insights into community and institution. *Organization Studies, 28*(4), 567–588.

Comas, J., Shrivastava, P., & Martin, E. C. (2015). Terrorism as formal organization, network, and social movement. *Journal of Management Inquiry, 24*(1), 47–60.

Cooper, R. (2005). Peripheral vision: Relationality. *Organization Studies, 26*(11), 1689–1710.

Cooren, F. (2015). In medias res: Communication, existence, and materiality. *Communication Research and Practice, 1*(4), 307–321.

Cooren, F. (2018a). Acting for, with, and through: A relational perspective on agency in MSF's organizing. In B. H. J. M. Brummans (Ed.), *The agency of organizing: Perspectives and case studies* (pp. 142–169). Routledge.

Cooren, F. (2018b). Materializing communication: Making the case for a relational ontology. *Journal of Communication, 68*(2), 278–288.

Cooren, F., Brummans, B. H. J. M., & Charrieras, D. (2008). The coproduction of organizational presence: A study of Médecins sans Frontières in action. *Human Relations, 61*(10), 1339–1370.

Cooren, F., Matte, F., Benoit-Barné, C., & Brummans, B. H. J. M. (2013). Communication as ventriloquism: A grounded-in-action approach to the study of organizational tensions. *Communication Monographs, 80*(3), 255–277.

Del Fa, S., & Vásquez, C. (2019). Existing through differantiation: A Derridean approach to alternative organizations. *M@n@gement*, *22*(4), 559–583.

Deligny, F. (2015). *The arachnean and other texts* (D. S. Burk & C. Potter, Trans.). Univocal Publishing.

Dobusch, L., & Schoeneborn, D. (2015). Fluidity, identity, and organizationality: The communicative constitution of Anonymous. *Journal of Management Studies*, *52*(8), 1005–1035.

Drucker, J. (2014). *Graphesis: Visual forms of knowledge production*. Harvard University Press.

Emerson, R. E., Fretz, R. I, & Shaw, L. L. (2011). *Writing ethnographic fieldnotes* (2nd edn.). The University of Chicago Press. (Original work published 1995.)

Endedijk, M. D., Hoogeboom, A. M. G. M., Groenier, M., de Laat, S., & van Sas, J. (2019). Using sensor technology to capture the structure and content of team interactions in medical emergency teams during stressful moments. *Frontline Learning Research*, *6*(3), 123–147.

Fairhurst, G. T., & Putnam, L. (2004). Organizations as discursive constructions. *Communication Theory*, *14*(1), 5–26.

Feinberg, P. P. (2016). Towards a walking-based pedagogy. *Journal of the Canadian Association for Curriculum Studies*, *14*(1), 147–165.

Ganesh, S., & Wang, Y. (2015). An eventful view of organizations. *Communication Research and Practice*, *1*(4), 375–387.

Geertz, C. (1973). *The interpretation of cultures: Selected essays*. Basic Books.

Gherardi, S. (2017). One turn… and another one: Do the turn to practice and the turn to affect have something in common? *Management Learning*, *48*(3), 345–358.

Gherardi, S., Murgia, A., Bellè, E., Miele, F., & Carreri, A. (2019). Tracking the sociomaterial traces of affect at the crossroads of affect and practice theories. *Qualitative Research in Organizations and Management*, *14*(3), 295–316.

Goffman, E. (1961). *Asylums: Essays on the social situation of mental patients and other inmates*. Aldine.

Grosjean, S., & Matte, F. (Eds.). (2021). *Organizational video-ethnography revisited: Making visible material, embodied and sensory practices*. Palgrave Macmillan.

Gross, R. M. (1993). *Buddhism after patriarchy: A feminist history, analysis, and reconstruction of Buddhism*. State University of New York Press.

Gross, R. M. (1998). *Soaring and settling: Buddhist perspectives on contemporary social and religious issues*. Continuum.

Halewood, M. (2005). On Whitehead and Deleuze: The process of materiality. *Configurations*, *13*(1), 57–76.

Harris, A., & Holman Jones, S. (Eds.). (2021). *Affective movements, methods and pedagogies*. Routledge.

Hernes, T. (2014). *A process theory of organization*. Oxford University Press.

Hilton, L. (2015, July). Mapping the wander lines: The quiet revelations of Fernand Deligny. *Los Angeles Review of Books*. https://lareviewofbooks.org/article/mapping-the-wander-lines-the-quiet-revelations-of-fernand-deligny/

Hussenot, A., & Missonier, S. (2016). Encompassing stability and novelty in organization studies: An events-based approach. *Organization Studies*, *37*(4), 523–546.

Jahn, J. L. (2018). Genre as textual agency: Using communicative relationality to theorize the agential-performative relationship between human and generic text. *Communication Monographs*, *85*(4), 515–538.

Jivaka, L. (1961). *Imji Getsul: An English Buddhist in Rizong monastery*. Rizong Monastery.

Kelkar, T., & Jensenius, A. R. (2018). Analyzing free-hand sound-tracings of melodic phrases. *Applied Sciences*, *8*(135), 1–21.

Kim, T., McFee, E., Olguin, D. O., Waber, B., & Pentland, A. S. (2012). Sociometric badges: Using sensor technology to capture new forms of collaboration. *Journal of Organizational Behavior*, *33*(3), 412–427.

Kuhn, T. (2021). (Re)moving blinders: Communication-as-constitutive theorizing as provocation to practice-based organization scholarship. *Management Learning*, *52*(1), 109–121.

Kuhn, T., Ashcraft, K. L., & Cooren, F. (2017). *The work of communication: Relational perspectives on working and organizing in contemporary capitalism*. Routledge.

Lincoln, Y. S., & Guba, E. G. (1985). *Naturalistic inquiry*. SAGE.

Manning, E. (2013). *Always more than one: Individuation's dance*. Duke University Press.

Manning, E. (2016). *The minor gesture*. Duke University Press.

Marcus, G. E. (1995). Ethnography in/of the world system: The emergence of multi-sited ethnography. *Annual Review of Anthropology*, *24*, 95–117.

Marcus, G. E. (1997). The uses of complicity in the changing mise-en-scene of anthropological fieldwork. *Representations*, *59*(Summer), 85–108.

Marcus, G. E. (2001). From rapport under erasure to theaters of complicit reflexivity. *Qualitative Inquiry*, 7(4), 519–528.

Massumi, B. (2002a). Introduction: Like a thought. In B. Massumi (Ed.), *A shock to thought: Expression after Deleuze and Guattari* (pp. xiii– xxxvix). Routledge.

Massumi, B. (2002b). *Parables for the virtual: Movement, affect, sensation.* Duke University Press.

Massumi, B. (2011). *Semblance and event: Activist philosophy and the occurrent arts.* MIT Press.

Massumi, B. (2015). *Politics of affect.* Polity.

Massumi, B. (2019). Immediation unlimited. In E. Manning, A. Munster, & B. M. S. Thomsen (Eds.), *Immediation II* (pp. 501–543). Open Humanities Press.

McCartney, A. (2014). Soundwalking: Creating moving environmental sound narratives. In S. Gopinath & J. Stanyek (Eds.), *The Oxford handbook of mobile music studies* (Vol. 2, pp. 212–237). Oxford University Press.

Mease, J. J. (2021). Techniques and forces and the communicative constitution of organization: A Deleuzian approach to organizational (in)stability and power. *Management Communication Quarterly*, 35(2) 226–255.

Mondada, L. (2019). Contemporary issues in conversation analysis: Embodiment and materiality, multimodality and multisensoriality in social interaction. *Journal of Pragmatics*, 145, 47–62.

Murphie, A. (2019). The world as medium: Whitehead's media philosophy. In E. Manning, A. Munster, & B. M. S. Thomsen (Eds.), *Immediation I* (pp. 16–46). Open Humanities Press.

Neyland, D. (2008). *Organizational ethnography.* SAGE.

Orlikowski, W. J. (2007). Sociomaterial practices: Exploring technology at work. *Organization Studies*, 28(9), 1435–1448.

O'Rourke, K. (2013). *Walking and mapping: Artists as cartographers.* MIT Press.

Putnam, L. L., & Fairhurst, G. T. (2015). Revisiting "organizations as discursive constructions": 10 years later. *Communication Theory*, 25(4), 375–392.

Ramos, A. (2019). Affective (im)mediations and the communication process. In C. Brienza, L. Robinson, B. Wellman, S. R. Cotton, & W. Chen (Eds.), *The M in CITAMS@30: Studies in media and communications volume 18* (pp. 181–194). Emerald.

Ramos, A. (2020a). Enter the event: How is immanent participation? *AM Journal of Art and Media Studies*, 23(October), 67–75.

Ramos, A. (2020b). Vers une conception de la culture organisationnelle sous l'angle de la philosophie processuelle. *Communication & Organisation*, 58(2), 41–54.

Ritchie, M. (2018). Brian Massumi and communication studies. In *Oxford research encyclopedia of communication* (pp. 1–18). Oxford University Press.

Sinsky, C., Colligan, L., Li, L., Prgomet, M., Reynolds, S., Goeders, L., … & Blike, G. (2016). Allocation of physician time in ambulatory practice: A time and motion study in 4 specialties. *Annals of Internal Medicine*, 165(11), 753–760.

Spinoza, B. de. (1985). *The collected works of Spinoza* (Curley, Edwin, Trad.; Vol. 1). Princeton University Press.

Stern, D. N. (2004). *The present moment in psychotherapy and everyday life.* Norton & Company.

Stern, D. N. (2010). *Forms of vitality: Exploring dynamic experience in psychology, the arts, psychotherapy, and development.* Oxford University Press.

St. Pierre, E. Adams. (2018). Writing post qualitative inquiry. *Qualitative Inquiry*, 24(9), 603–608.

Taylor, B. C., Barley, W. C., Brummans, B. H. J. M., Ellingson, L. L., Ganesh, S., Herrmann, A. F., Rice, R. M., & Tracy, S. J. (2021). Revisiting ethnography in organizational communication studies. *Management Communication Quarterly*, 35(4), 623–652.

Thulin, S. (2018). Sound maps matter: Expanding cartophony. *Social & Cultural Geography*, 19(2), 192–210.

Truffaut, F. (Director). (1959). *Les quatre cents coups* [Motion picture]. Les Films du Carrosse.

Van Maanen, J. (2011a). *Tales of the field: On writing ethnography* (2nd edn.). The University of Chicago Press. (Original work published 1988.)

Van Maanen, J. (2011b). Ethnography as work: Some rules of engagement. *Journal of Management Studies*, 48(1), 218–234.

Varela, F. J. (1987). Laying down a path in walking. In W. I. Thompson (Ed.), *GAIA, a way of knowing: Political implications of the new biology* (pp. 48–64). Lindisfarne Press.

Vásquez, C. (2020). (In)habitée par le cancer: Récits critiques des trajectoires affectives d'un terrain miné d'émotions. *Recherches qualitatives*, 39(2), 193–214.

Vásquez, C., Brummans, B. H. J. M., & Groleau, C. (2012). Notes from the field on organizational shadowing as framing. *Qualitative Research in Organizations and Management, 7*(2), 144–165.

Vásquez, C., & Cooren, F. (2013). Spacing practices: The communicative configuration of organizing through space-times. *Communication Theory, 23*(1), 25–47.

Vásquez, C., & Kuhn, T. (Eds.). (2019). *Dis/organization as communication: Exploring the disordering, disruptive and chaotic properties of communication.* Routledge.

Vézy, C., & Brummans, B. H. J. M. (2021). La recherche CCO comme pratique réflexive: Une approche relationnelle. *Communication & Organisation, 59*, 141–153.

Victor, R. (Director). (1976). *Ce gamin, là* [Motion picture]. Les Films du Carrosse.

Weick, K. E. (1979). *The social psychology of organizing* (2nd edn.). McGraw-Hill.

Whitehead, A. N. (1967). *Adventures of ideas.* The Free Press. (Original work published 1933.)

Whitehead, A. N. (1978). *Process and reality* (D. R. Griffin & D. W. Shelburne, Eds.). The Free Press.

Wilhoit, E. D., & Kisselburgh, L. G. (2015). Collective action without organization: The material constitution of bike commuters as collective. *Organization Studies, 36*(5), 573–592.

Wilhoit, E. D. (2017). Photo and video methods in organizational and managerial communication research. *Management Communication Quarterly, 31*(3), 447–466.

Wilhoit Larson, E. (2020). Where is an organization? How workspaces are appropriated to become (partial and temporary) organizational spaces. *Management Communication Quarterly, 34*(3), 299–327.

Ybema, S., Yanow, D., Wels, H., & Kamsteeg, F. (Eds.). (2009). *Organizational ethnography: Studying the complexities of everyday life.* SAGE.

Yanow, D. (2000). *Conducting interpretive policy analysis.* SAGE.

PART III

How CCO Handles Classic Management Themes

17

AUTHORITY ACCORDING TO CCO

Recursivity, Emergence, and Durability

Chantal Benoit-Barné and Stephanie Fox

Authority According to CCO: Recursivity, Emergence, and Durability

On contemplating how to begin a chapter on authority from a CCO perspective, our initial thoughts turned to the influence of James R. Taylor and Elizabeth J. Van Every in making authority and authoring key concepts in CCO research. As early as 2000, with the publication of *The Emergent Organization: Communication as Its Site and Surface*, and more recently, with the publication in 2014 of *When Organization Fails: Why Authority Matters*, issues of authority have been a constant in Taylor and Van Every's work. Authority is a classical management notion central to understanding how organizations are formed and sustained. It is often defined as a legitimate form of power that supports integration, predictability, and order within organizations (Benoit-Barné & Fox, 2017; Kahn & Kram, 1994; Weber, 1978). According to Taylor (2011), authority is not only central to understanding how organizations are formed and sustained, it is "the primary mechanism responsible for coherence of purpose and identity (…) in that the persons of both organization and members must be continually 'authored' for them to exist" (p. 1273).

For those of us affiliated with the Communication Department at the Université de Montréal, authority became an ongoing subject of discussion from 2007 and on, during our research group's weekly meetings, as Jim and Elizabeth shared their insights about the data they had collected in New Zealand during their fieldwork with a police agency. They were working on a new book, which would become *When Organization Fails: Why Authority Matters*, and, relying on the work of Charles Sanders Peirce, they had in mind that authority should be understood as resting upon thirdness—the agreed-upon interpretation that confers meaning to a relationship and makes it a transaction, an idea to which we will return later. Through their questions, comments, and suggestions, Jim and Elizabeth enabled us to see the place of authority as thirdness in our own data and research projects, inspiring several articles on the topic (e.g., Benoit-Barné & Cooren, 2009; Brummans, Hwang, & Cheong, 2013; Cooren, 2010) and laying the groundwork for the relational view of authority that we wish to emphasize in this chapter.

DOI: 10.4324/9781003224914-21

Over the years, CCO scholarship has contributed to a better understanding of the organizing effects of authority, both in terms of the communicative practices that uphold its local interactional achievement and from the point of view of the organizational structures (in the form of expertise, hierarchy, line of command, rules, etc.) by which authority manifests itself in the workplace. In this chapter, we propose to review the CCO literature on authority to highlight its original take on the notion, in particular the idea that authority is essentially communicational and relational. We begin by explaining this relational view and specifically focus on how the relationships that provide the basis for the accomplishment of authority have been conceived of as transactions that are communicatively sustained through practices of presentification. We then address a fundamental question in CCO research with regard to the notion of authority: How can it be both emergent and enduring, communicatively accomplished in work interactions *yet* lasting beyond the local interactions of organizational members? We propose that one way to answer this question is to consider that authority has its roots in the recursive relationship between text and conversation. Finally, we present some empirical applications of this view of authority as well as methodological considerations.

Authority as Communicational and Relational

One of the key contributions of CCO scholarship has been to advance a conception of authority as essentially communicational and relational (see Benoit-Barné & Cooren, 2009; Benoit-Barné & Fox, 2017; Benoit-Barné, Marsen, Wang, & Yang, 2019; Bourgoin, Bencherki, & Faraj, 2020; Taylor & Van Every, 2011, 2014). This is to say that authority is a property of relationships established through and by a communicative process of coorientation as those involved in interaction relate to one another and to objects of interest to them. Authority is therefore not conceived of as an attribute of the individuals involved in the relationships (e.g., in the form of expertise) or strictly as a product of the existing organizational structures that frame the exchanges (such as hierarchy or chain of command). Rather, authority characterizes the relationships between these elements. As Taylor and Van Every (2014) explain: "Nobody has it. It is not possessed by someone. It governs a relationship ..." (p. 198). In this sense, authority is emergent and dynamic yet enduring, because it is created through communication and continually supported by the relationships that are (re)created through communication. For instance, Bourgoin, Bencherki, and Faraj (2020) adopt a relational conception of authority, linking its emergence to the relational ontology advanced by actor-network theory (ANT), a main source of inspiration for many CCO scholars.

To say that authority is relational and that it characterizes relationships has clear analytical implications. It means that relationships are the starting point of our investigation of authority because they are conceived as (re)producing both the organization and the authority on which it relies for integration, predictability, and order. We find the notion of *action net* proposed by Czarniawska (1997, 2004) useful to clarify the meaning of this proposition and to shed light on the organizing properties of relationships in work environments. For Czarniawska, connecting is "a central activity in all organizing" (2004, p. 782). Lindberg and Czarniawska (2006) explain that the action net concept is based on the assumption that organizing "requires that several different collective actions be connected according to a pattern that is institutionalized at a given time and in a given place" (p. 293). Czarniawska insists on the differences between a network as conceived by ANT and the idea of an action net. Whereas a network emphasizes the existence of *actors* who establish connections with each other, an *action* net emphasizes the existence of relations at various degrees of stabilization that generate the identity of the actors and their organized milieu. In other words, analytical focus is on relations rather than on the actors who enact them, and on those relations' organizing properties.

From this standpoint, an organization, for instance a university, exists and is maintained by the connections or relationships that bring it to life and give it form: professors teaching students, students defending their dissertations, juries evaluating their work, support staff assisting students in their course choices, etc. These activities all implicate and enact relationships. Note that this is different from saying that the university exists as a network of actors (professors, students, support staff, etc.,) who then create relationships by connecting to each other. It means that the university exists as a configuration of more or less enduring, stabilized, and institutionalized *relationships* sustained through communication, such that if the actors change, the organization would not disappear because the relationships it entails would be maintained: professors (albeit new ones) would continue teaching students, students would continue defending their dissertations, support staff would continue guiding students, and so on. In view of these ideas, saying that authority is relational means that CCO researchers can contribute to its investigation by identifying how communication generates and maintains the relationships by which it is established.

In the next three subsections, we present three main conceptual contributions made by the CCO literature regarding authority. First, we explain how this literature has theorized the relationships that sustain authority as transactions, and with what theoretical implications. Then, we present theoretical explanations of how authority is communicatively established and negotiated, notably through different practices of presentification (speaking for, invocation, activation and passivation). Third, we discuss how authority, as the property of relations, can be described as both emergent and enduring, when it is investigated as the outcome of the recursive relationship between text and conversation. In particular, we make explicit how authoritative texts and practices of presentification are recursively imbricated in the establishment of authority.

The Transactive Nature of the Relationships by which Authority is Established

For Taylor and Van Every (2014), authority is built by and through transactions that are communicatively sustained. This proposition is, in our view, their most significant contribution to the study of authority. A transaction entails both *acting on* a situation and *acting for* a third, which, we can recall, refers to an agreed-upon interpretation that confers meaning to a relationship. Organizational actors *act on* a situation as they relate to each other and to objects of interest to them, thus authoring the meaning of their practice and relationship. They *act for* a third as they engage with each other on the basis of a transactional framework entailing mutual obligations, rights, duties, rules of conduct, etc. Take as an example of this dual communicational process a meeting between a graduate student and the professor supervising her master's thesis. At Université de Montréal, where we work, this advisee-supervisor relationship has been formalized by the creation of a form, the *Global Study Plan (GSP)*, to be filled out by both parties as they start working together as supervisor and advisee. The form is composed of two parts: a planned schedule for when the coursework and key mandatory steps of the master's thesis will be fulfilled, and a collaboration agreement allowing both parties to make explicit and discuss their respective expectations and responsibilities regarding the supervising relationship. The GSP is signed by both parties, yet it is clearly not a contract, and professors will generally insist on this fact when meeting with their students to fill out the form, pointing out that it may be revised at any time to account for changes in the student's program of study.

Even so, a lot is going on as professor and student meet to fill out this form: They must answer questions regarding the number and frequency of their meetings, whether or not the student must submit a text prior to a meeting, and the expected delay for feedback from the supervisor. The form, through its many sections and questions, guides the understanding of both parties while setting the transactive framework for their relationship. It allows for the emergence of an authoritative text regarding the graduate advisor–supervisee relationship at the Université de Montréal, in the sense advocated by Kuhn (2008): "an abstract text (...) that represents the [organization] as a whole. This 'authoritative text' emphasizes the relations of legitimacy and power characterizing [organizational] practice. It also depicts the [organization's] structure in a way that specifies activities and outcomes, what knowledge is valued, and roles, duties, and authority" (p. 1236).

Note that, as mediator in the emergence of an authoritative text, the GSP does not, by its mere existence, condition the relation between an advisor and a supervisee. Studying authority as it is based on transactive relationships involves understanding how the terms of a transaction are communicatively negotiated and fixed: how, for instance, a graduate student and a professor completing a GSP form set the parameters for their respective authority by negotiating the terms of their relationship through filling out the form, nudged by the GSP to think about their respective commitments as they answer the questions described above. The authoritative text is key to the communicative accomplishment of authority precisely because it allows for the interaction and mediates it without entirely controlling it. This is an important point as it characterizes a CCO approach toward authority. As emphasized by Taylor and Van Every (2014), authority is built by and through transactive relationships because they involve both acting on a situation through *authoring* (e.g., the mutual definition *in situ* of what this form and each question mean to both parties and how it informs their mutual understandings of what they are to each other) and acting for a third who, although absent, is made communicatively present in the situation in such a way that it frames the exchange, in this case the university through the GSP form. It is this effect of presence that Benoit-Barné and Cooren (2009) describe with the notion of *presentification*, which we will discuss in the following section.

Presentification and the Communicative Practices by which Authority is Accomplished

A focus on the precise functioning of communicative processes and practices in relation to the achievement of authority is a defining characteristic of a CCO approach to investigating authority. CCO studies of authority have documented the specific communication practices by which it is relationally accomplished to have organizing effects. We will focus here on the practices of presentification, such as speaking for, ventriloquism, invocation, and activation and passivation.

Benoit-Barné and Cooren (2009) rely on the notions of *agent* and *principal* to describe the transactive nature of the relations that sustain authority. They argue: "The relation between agent and principal calls attention to the fact that a worker is not only *acting for* his or her organization during work interactions; he or she is *acting with* his or her organization through presentification, in the sense that he or she makes the organization present by acting on its behalf" (p. 13). From their standpoint, establishing authority involves a communicative process of presentification by which effects of presence and absence are interactionally realized. The notion of presence and the idea that communication involves a process of making present, or presentification, is borrowed from rhetorical studies. Based on Perelman and Olbrechts-Tyteca (1969), rhetoric is conceived as a way to engage with and create connections to an audience.

It implies establishing a presence for the things and ideas being discussed. For Perelman and Olbrechts-Tyteca, establishing presence is a rhetorical imperative that guides the entire process of what rhetoricians call "invention," from the formulation of arguments to the selection of figures of speech (Jasinski, 2001). By articulating this idea with Derrida's (1974, 1982) reflections on "presencing" and "hauntology," Benoit-Barné and Cooren conceive of interactions as spectral in the sense that they involve human and non-human entities whose presence and absence are not acquired once and for all but rather must be continually rhetorically established, amplified, or minimized. Cooren (2010) later relied on the metaphor of ventriloquism to more specifically theorize this process (see Nathues & Van Vuuren, this volume).

Benoit-Barné & Cooren (2009) explain that *speaking for* is a common communication practice of presentification when it comes to authority. Relying on video recordings of interactions involving a medical coordinator for *Médecins Sans Frontières* (MSF, or Doctors Without Borders) and the technicians of a hospital supported by the humanitarian organization, their study documents how the medical coordinator achieves authority by *speaking for* MSF in the sense that, during her work interactions with the technicians, she states what the organization is, and they do not question or challenge her on this. More specifically, what is important is the fact that she speaks for MSF such that its presence is established in the "here and now" as she engages with the technicians. Her authority is relationally accomplished as an effect of presence because it is both her ability to speak on behalf of the organization in a way that establishes its presence *and* the compliance of the technicians that sustain her influence.

Brummans, Hwang, and Cheong (2013) advance a concurring argument in their study of a spiritual organization. They describe *invocation* as a practice of presentification by which revered figures are called upon to make sense of a situation and to shape collective action. The authors insist, "Invocation does not merely imply speaking and acting in a revered figure's name but trying to speak in her voice, using her same discourse, intonation, rhythm, and so on, and acting in ways that are similar to hers" (p. 366). Members of spiritual organizations therefore establish their authority by speaking for a revered figure in such a way that they embody or incarnate her, thus making her vividly present for all involved.

This interest in ways of speaking and their relation to the establishment of presence/absence and authority finds an echo in Bourgoin et al. (2020). The authors advance a performative and relational view of authority "by specifying how relations become authoritative, and describing the micro-processes through which a focal actor (…) may orient collective action" (p. 1135). Their aim is to understand how organizational actors can shape a situation in such a way that it orients collective action when they cannot rely on classical bases of authority, such as a fixed place in the hierarchy or the recognition of expertise. This situation is increasingly common for workers in post-bureaucratic environments, such as the management consultants on whom Bourgoin et al.'s study is based, and this makes a CCO approach to authority even more relevant. The authors explain that in a post-bureaucratic context, there is "a gradual erosion of the hierarchical basis of authority; instead of the clear rules laid down by hierarchy, control is increasingly exercised through broadly defined and emergent principles that are negotiated by peers with different occupational affiliations" (p. 1134).

With regard to the communicative accomplishment of authority, Bourgoin et al. (2020) propose two mirroring processes held in tension: "activation and passivation, through which relations are either leveraged or downplayed to shape the situation and steer collective action" (p. 1134). We contend that both processes are forms of presentification. *Activation* involves orienting collective action by speaking or acting in a way that emphasizes one's relation to other actors while minimizing one's own contribution to the unfolding of the situation, for example, teaming up with others to share agency and state that the others are in fact doing most of the work. In contrast, *passivation* implies speaking and acting in a way that disassociates oneself from others, be they human or non-human, and insisting on one's own contributions to the situation, such as claiming that a decision was based on one's unique professional experience, rather than on an established operating procedure, for instance.

As a whole, Bourgoin et al. (2020) extend the general idea that authority involves a dual communicative process of association and dissociation (see Benoit-Barné et al., 2019), or, put otherwise, that it relies on authoritative moves such as bridging and decoupling (see Porter, Nerlich, & Kuhn, 2018). Starting from the premise that organizational actors gain authority as they share their agency with others, they are able to show that it is the oscillation between activation of one's relation to other actors (others are acting, not me) and the passivation of one's relationships (I am the main source of action) that allows an actor to orient collective action in a given situation, thus establishing his or her authority.

Accounting for Authority's Emergence and Durability through the Recursive Relationship between Text and Conversation

In the discussion above, there is a clear focus on the presentification practices and processes by which authority is accomplished in interactions (speaking for, invocation, activation and passivation), that is, in "how authority happens" (Fauré, Brummans, Giroux, & Taylor, 2010, p. 1268) *in situ*. However, there is simultaneously theoretical interest in how authority endures beyond the locally situated interaction. In this regard, theorizing about authority takes up another foundational CCO concept: the conversation-text dialectic.

The basic tenet of the conversation-text dialectic is that organizing occurs through distinct, yet interconnected, communicative episodes in which texts play a crucial structuring role as they are mobilized and spoken for in situated interaction. Communicative practices in situated talk are the basic medium through which organizational members accomplish collective actions while at the same time making sense of the "organization" itself and producing its foundational texts (see Dawson, this volume). Taylor and Robichaud (2004) explain the basic dialectic, tying together communication as conversation and communication as text in the following way (they refer to communication as discourse here):

> As text, discourse is a manifestation of human sensemaking (Weick, 1995). The making of text is how organizational members reflexively (Giddens, 1984) and retrospectively (Weick, 1995) monitor, rationalize, and engender the action of organizing. As conversation, discourse is an instrument of organizational action, and text is a resource that enters into its construction. Linked to the purposes of organizing, conversation is tied to object-oriented and materially based activity. In contrast, discourse as text constructs the organization as an object of reflection and interpretation. (pp. 396–397)

Specifically, Robichaud, Giroux, and Taylor (2004) argue that this dialectic must be understood as a recursive process. Conversations and texts do not merely inform each other in a punctual way; they are woven together in the sense that they take each other as objects of sensemaking, thus defining and presupposing each other.

Robichaud, Benoit-Barné, and Basque (2012) argue that this recursive process is essential for understanding how authority can emerge through talk in interaction while persisting beyond the situation of interaction. They call attention to Spee and Jarzabkowski's (2011) contribution to our understanding of recursivity in relation to authority. Spee and Jarzabkowski describe how a strategic plan was progressively endowed with authority as it "absorbed those contextual nuances that reflected each stage of the plan production cycle" (p. 1236). More specifically, they draw on Ricoeur's (1981) notions of decontextualization and recontextualization to theorize the recursive cycle between conversation and text in the progressive development of the strategic plan. By analyzing the work meetings of those involved in its creation, they show how each meeting allows the previously produced text to be "recontextualized" in the specific context of the current meeting. The text thus takes on a new meaning in light of the readings, interests, and identities of the participants, making modifications that are all "decontextualized" again as they are integrated into a new version of the text. This new version will be recontextualized again at the next meeting, thus sustaining the recursive process that progressively endows the strategic plan with authority. Spee and Jarzabkowski explain:

> [The organization's] strategic plan is constructed through an iterative cycle of recontextualization and decontextualization. However, these iterations are not simply discrete and episodic. Rather, there is a recursive relationship between talk and text, with the meanings expressed in talk and text shaping each other and becoming progressively more interpenetrated throughout the planning text production cycle until they culminate in Unico's final strategic plan. (pp. 1230–1231)

Spee and Jarzabkowski allow us to see that the strategic plan's authority has its roots in the recursive relationship between text and conversation, and we believe that this idea ought to be applied more broadly to the establishment of authority as a whole. Authority can be understood as both emergent and enduring because text and conversation are recursively woven together in such a way that they co-define and presuppose each other.

We are not aware of any study of authority in the CCO literature that takes the recursivity of talk and text as its primary object of study. However, the issue has been accounted for in different ways. For instance, according to Kuhn (2008), an authoritative text is authoritative precisely because it can (more or less easily) be decontextualized and recontextualized through conversations. Indeed, the notion of authoritative text is a key conceptual element in CCO theorizing of authority because it allows researchers to identify and describe both what emerges from the recursive process between conversation and text and what allows it to take place. A similar argument can be developed concerning the notion of presentification. It allows CCO researchers to identify and describe the communicative practices (speaking for, invocation, activation, passivation) by which texts are woven into the daily activities of organizations, thus also enabling the recursive process between talk and text. As such, although the notions of authoritative text and presentification each seem to emphasize one pole of the text-conversation dynamic as it informs the accomplishment of authority, they are complementary and both necessary to conceive of authority as emergent and enduring.

We can best make explicit how authoritative text and practices of presentification are recursively imbricated in the establishment of authority by returning to our example of a graduate student meeting with a professor to complete a GSP form. Let us imagine that, during their initial meeting, the student committed to submit a first draft of her thesis project by a specific date and the professor said that she would give feedback within 10 days. The student sends her draft on time, but the professor is unable to provide feedback as expected. She sends the following e-mail: "Thanks for sending your draft on time. I look forward to reading it. Unfortunately, I won't be able to give feedback as promised. I have agreed to chair a hiring committee that is taking up a lot of my time at the moment. We will have to be flexible and adjust our schedule accordingly. Sorry about this." The student replies, "No problem. I understand."

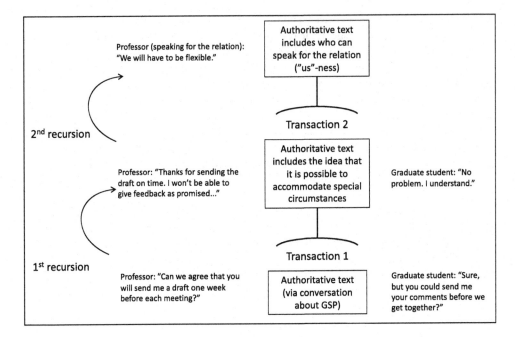

Figure 17.1 Authority through recursivity.

Figure 17.1 is adapted from Robichaud et al. (2004) to schematize how authoritative text and the practices of presentification are recursively imbricated in the establishment of authority taking place in this example. The figure emphasizes the fact that two recursions are taking place, each with its own effects on the achievement of authority.

The first recursion takes place as the professor thanks the student for sending her draft on time and explains why she will not be able to provide feedback within 10 days, as promised. With these opening remarks, the professor embeds their previous transaction (when they filled in the GSP; Transaction 1 in the figure) into the new transaction that she initiates with her email (Transaction 2). She does so by making present the authoritative text that emerged from their first meeting (she recalls their respective commitments to each other and sanctions the fact that the student fulfilled her side of the deal) and recontextualizes the authoritative text for the current situation (the conditions have changed because she is chairing a hiring committee that is taking up a lot of time). As a result, she creates the conditions for a slightly modified version of the authoritative text, one that can account for the idea that it is possible to accommodate for special circumstances. At this stage, we can see that the first recursion sustains the establishment of authority because it both reaffirms the authoritative text and allows for its slight incremental modification.

The second recursion takes this process one step further, as it establishes the existence of an "us-ness," a "we" that can be reflected upon, talked about, and spoken for. As Figure 17.1 makes explicit, the second recursion takes place as the professor speaks for the relation ("we have to be flexible ..."), thus asserting its existence as an object of reflection and acting as its legitimate spokesperson. This constitutive effect is precisely what Robichaud and al. (2004) call attention to as they theorize the recursive property of language and its implication for organizing through the notion of meta-conversation. They explain: "A meta-conversation ... is a conversation that embeds, recursively, another conversation" (p. 621). They later argue: "The meta-conversation literally creates entities that did not exist before by closing the black box of the previous conversations that sustained them" (p. 630). We can see this is happening here, as the professor-student relation become an entity that is talked about and for, thus opening up new possibilities for the establishment of authority. This observation is also in keeping with Benoit-Barné and Cooren's (2009) idea that speaking for a third (here the relation or us-ness) is a key presentification practice involved in establishing authority. By speaking for the relation, the professor presents herself as one who can state what the situation means, to each other, and also eventually, to people outside of the relation.

To summarize, Figure 17.1 shows that authority is both emergent and enduring because it is achieved through the recursive imbrication of one transaction into another. This imbrication is sustained by practices of presentification and allows for the incremental establishment of an authoritative text. The figure also calls attention to the fact that an us-ness emerges through the recursive process and that this opens up new possibilities for the establishment of authority, as the relation now exists as an entity that can be spoken for. Having laid out the main conceptual contributions of the CCO literature to our understanding of authority, we now present ways that the notion of authority has been explored in empirical literature that embraces a CCO approach. We do so to demonstrate how dynamic authority has become as a CCO concept, as well as to explore the variety and empirical richness of the contexts explored and the issues raised.

Empirical Applications of the CCO Notion of Authority

In the literature that we surveyed for this chapter, almost all the empirical studies of authority adopt a processual focus, investigating the communicative practices and processes involved in constituting various organizational phenomena, often emphasizing implicitly or explicitly one side of the conversation-text dialectic over the other. This processual focus is consequential to both the kinds of questions asked and the methodological approaches employed. We present a curated review below.

A commitment to viewing authority as emergent and enduring in communication practices and processes correlates with an empirical focus on questions of organizational change and becoming, as well as on the negotiation of identity and relationships. This has allowed scholars to open up conceptions of organizing and authority that reflect the contemporary organizational landscape in what has been called the post-bureaucratic era, where hierarchy and roles are not necessarily given. For instance, as discussed above, in their study of management consultants during a restructuring assignment, Bourgoin et al. (2020) examine how relations become authoritative in the absence of clear organizational structure such as hierarchy, through the practices of activation and passivation that are linked to presentification in interaction. Likewise, Jahn (2016) demonstrates how authority happens through Cooren's (2010) notion of ventriloquism to explain how members of a non-hierarchical workgroup of wildland firefighters in the United States operate. Team members "leveraged" safety rules to refuse to participate in another, "gung-ho" team member's plan to fight fires (p. 381). Thus, making present the safety rules bolstered their own interactional authority and amounted to tipping the balance of authority in their relationship. Similarly, Koschmann and Burk (2016) use the notion of authoritative text to study how members of the National Science Center managed a change in organizational culture following a physical move that threw together professionals from distinct yet hierarchically equal silos. They found that a previous shared metaphor of "how things work here" (i.e., an authoritative text)—the "wild-wild west"—had to be de-authored, and thus deauthorized, as organizational members moved to a new understanding of their operations from the frame of collaboration. These studies all examined non-hierarchical contexts in which authority is continually negotiated.

Political contexts are another empirical domain where issues of authority are key, in particular regarding the negotiation and relationships. With regard to the relational dimension of authority, in Clifton and de la Broise's (2020) study of the communicative constitution of the "*gilets jaune*" (yellow vests) protest movement in France, the very identity of the movement is constituted by speaking *against* (rather than for or with) the established "authority," namely President Macron and his government. Similarly, Porter et al. (2018) apply the notion of authority as authoring to examine the climate-change debate in the Netherlands, where high-profile errors cast doubt on the legitimacy of an official report by the Intergovernmental Panel on Climate Change, spurring a public dialogue between climate skeptics, climate scientists, policy makers, and authors of the report. Porter et al. identify the relational, authoritative moves by which these actors managed the tensions inherent in this debate. They found that actors with similar but distinct discursive positions who officially authored the report gained authority by bridging their differences to align and *speak with* one another (similar to activation), while also decoupling (i.e., distancing themselves, or passivation) from climate skeptics whose discursive positions jeopardized the legitimacy of these official authors. As with the *gilets jaunes*, the excluded actors managed tension with an authoritative move of their own: resistance, and, ironically, their exclusion thus legitimized their own transactional identities and relative positions in the debate.

Leadership is another terrain where authority is a particularly salient focus of study, in particular regarding its emergence. Some scholars have applied CCO conceptions of authority to leadership studies where authority can be understood as the ability to author legitimate meanings (Fairhurst, 2005; see also Bisel, Fairhurst, & Sheep, this volume). "Leadership and authority are so closely related that the two terms are often equated," write Holm and Fairhurst (2018, p. 695). However, it is the "exercise of leadership that is rooted in authority and, more specifically, in the practices of dominance and deference, where deference, over time, results in authorization, that is, the conferral of authority, even without deliberate decision" (p. 695). They investigated how authority is negotiated and accomplished when traditional lines of hierarchical authority are blurred, analyzing meetings of a high-ranking manager and his team of leaders in a new department of a restructured Danish municipality, where the leaders were considered to be hierarchically equal. Their analysis resulted in a typology of members' authoring moves through which leadership-as-meaning-management (i.e., authoring) is negotiated: authoring claims (i.e., dominance), such as using hierarchical position or expertise to advance a task; grants to authoring (i.e., deference); and resistance through contestations, interruptions, and subversive humor. Interestingly, they found that, initially, there was a preference for shared leadership (i.e., co-authoring), but that, over time, members expressed a preference for hierarchical leadership (e.g., using one's final say to definitively author meaning). In a similar vein, Meier and Carroll's (2020) study of identity formation in a leadership development program in Denmark also saw authority as accomplished through claims and grants. Like Jahn (2016), the authors show the accomplishment of authority through ventriloquism, where epistemic authority (i.e., an interactional claim to authority stemming from one's relative expertise; see Caronia & Nasi, this volume) is fluid and negotiated in interactions, and new leadership identities are co-authored by instructors, students, and non-humans, especially texts.

Other studies more specifically examine how authority becomes enduring. The notion of the authoritative text has been used in studies investigating issues of long-lasting features of organizational reality, such as identity, values, and commitments, for instance longitudinal studies of strategic planning. We discussed in the previous section the conceptual contributions made by Spee and Jarzabkowski (2011), who examined the recursive conversation-text trans-lation in the production of a strategic plan. More specifically, the authors examine talk in meetings and iterations of the strategic plan text at Unico, a British university adapting to the appointment of a new vice-chancellor. They thus delve into the emergence-durability dynamic in their data: The strategic plan organized talk to the extent that it shaped the sequence and topics of talk, thus illustrating its authoritative nature, but meeting participants also shaped the next iteration of the plan by offering their current and sometimes multiple interpretations of the text. Likewise, Vásquez et al. (2018) examine the development of a strategic plan in a non-profit housing organization, explaining how "matters of concern" become "matters of authority": As a given reading of the strategy becomes dominant during the recursive develop-ment of the strategy document, that reading can be considered an authoritative text that comes to legitimize certain courses of action over others.

Continuing with authority as authoritative text, Koschmann and McDonald (2015) offer a new take on organizational rituals, demonstrating how organization members of the AIDS Support and Advocacy Group in the United States adhered to performing several rituals during their meetings because the rituals—as authoritative texts—reminded members of the organization's goals, values, and commitments. Certain rituals' authority even usurped the hier-archical leader's authority in that members insisted on performing the rituals, when the leader would have omitted them from meetings. Finally, Kopaneva and Sias (2015) compare the authoritativeness of official organizational mission and vision statements (as authoritative texts) by measuring their congruence with employees' descriptions of their understanding of their organization's values and commitments in interviews.

Conclusion

We have described authority from a CCO perspective as relational, dynamic, and fluid. It emerges from, is negotiated in, and endures through communicative processes. We first explained how authority inheres in the transactive nature of relationships, entailing both acting on a situation and acting for a third. We then explained how authority is at once emergent, through practices of presentification during *in situ* interactions, and enduring, through the conversation-text dialectic by which authoritative texts are authored and come to govern shared understandings of organizational situations and identities. This allowed us to emphasize the fact that authority has its roots in the recursive relationship between text and conversation. Finally, we explored how this CCO understanding of authority has been deployed in empirical research. This curated review shows that authority is an analytically useful term that has led to a deeper understanding of how organizations are formed and sustained (Taylor, 2011) and to a rich variety of empirical research.

In conclusion, we wish to make explicit two methodological issues that are particular to the study of authority as a phenomenon of communication linked to the recursive properties of language. The first is access to research sites. The second is related to detecting the recursions by which authority emerges and endures, which requires the longitudinal collection of a var-iety of data sources.

Regarding the first, CCO generally holds a methodological commitment to studying the "terra firma" of interactions (Cooren, 2006) to understand organizational phenomena. Regarding authority, Benoît-Barné and Cooren (2009) recommend looking for moments of presentification. Indeed, such studies logically tend to favor the emergent, conversation side of the dialectic, and rely on audio- or video-recorded observations of interactions that are transcribed and analyzed using methods inspired by conversation analysis and ethnomethodology.

However, if observing and recording interactions is often presented as a *sine qua non* for conducting CCO research (whether or not authority is an analytical focus), negotiating such access remains an enduring challenge for researchers. For instance, in Fauré et al.'s (2010) investigation of authority in the accounting processes of a French construction firm, the authors were forced to rely on detailed observation notes of meetings, as they were not permitted to record. Certainly, in some organizational contexts, even conducting observations is simply impossible, sometimes for safety or liability reasons. Jahn (2016) acknowledges this challenge in her study of wildland firefighting teams, which, being high-reliability organizations, are not welcoming of external observers. She worked around it by interviewing team members and focusing on critical incidents related to how they negotiated authority. To interpret the data, she relied on her own extensive personal experience as a wildland firefighter.

Indeed, privileging an autoethnographically inspired approach is one way to "circumvent" constraints to access and be able to observe the communicative establishment of authority. In this regard, autoethnography has been favored by other researchers, such as Bourgoin et al. (2020) in their investigation of management consultants, where the first author used his status as a consultant to gain access, and Vásquez et al. (2018), who analyze their own practices as strategy consultants to the housing organization in their study of the longitudinal process by which this document becomes authoritative. Another example is Meier and Carroll (2020), who relied on the first author's experience in the leadership development program to conduct their focused ethnography.

Overall, an ethnographically inspired methodology allows for the *longitudinal* collection of data from a variety of sources, such as observations, interviews, documents, and, where possible, recordings of interactions. It offers, in our view, the greatest potential to study authority from a CCO standpoint, especially recursivity, because it gives organizational communication scholars the opportunity to describe how the communication practices that enable its interactional emergence are also what allows authority to endure and sustain itself beyond a particular communicative event.

References

Benoit-Barné, C., & Cooren, F. (2009). The accomplishment of authority through presentification: How authority is distributed among and negotiated by organizational members. *Management Communication Quarterly, 23*(1), 5–31.

Benoit-Barné, C., & Fox, S. (2017). Authority. In G. R. Scott (Ed.), *The international encyclopedia of organizational communication*. Wiley Blackwell.

Benoit-Barné, C., Marsen, S., Wang, N., and Yang, Y. (2019). Decentering the analysis: The authority of spectators, journalists and others. In N. Bencherki, F. Cooren, & F. Matte. (Eds.), *Authority and power in social interaction: Methods and analysis*. Routledge.

Bourgoin, A., Bencherki, N., & Faraj, S. (2020). "And who are you?": A performative perspective on authority in organizations. *Academy of Management Journal, 63*(4), 1134–1165. https://doi.org/10.5465/AMJ.2017.1335.

Brummans, B. H. J. M., Hwang, J. M., & Cheong, P. H. (2013). Mindful authoring through invocation: Leaders' constitution of a spiritual organization. *Management Communication Quarterly, 27*(3), 346–372.

Clifton, J., & de la Broise, P. (2020). The yellow vests and the communicative constitution of a protest movement. *Discourse and Communication, 14*(4), 362–382. https://doi.org/10.1177/1750481320910516.

Cooren, F. (2006). The organizational world as a plenum of agencies. In F. Cooren, J. R. Taylor, & E. J. Van Every (Eds.), *Communication as organizing: Empirical and theoretical explorations in the dynamic of text and conversation* (pp. 81–100). Mahwah, NJ: Lawrence Erlbaum Associates.

Cooren, F. (2010). *Action and agency in dialogue: Passion, incarnation and ventriloquism*. Amsterdam: John Benjamins.

Czarniawska, B. (1997). *'Narrating the organization': Dramas of institutional identity*. Chicago: University of Chicago Press.

Czarniawska, B. (2004). On time, space, and action nets. *Organization, 11*(6), 773–791. https://doi.org/10.1177/1350508404047251.

Derrida, J. (1974). *Of grammatology* (G. Chakravorty, Trans.). Baltimore: Johns Hopkins University Press.

Derrida, J. (1982). *Margins of philosophy* (A. Bass, Trans.). Chicago: University of Chicago Press.

Fairhurst, G. T. (2005). Reframing the art of framing: Problems and prospects for leadership. *Leadership, 1*(2), 165–185. https://doi.org/10.1177/1742715005051857.

Fauré, B., Brummans, B. H. J. M., Giroux, H., & Taylor, J. R. (2010). The calculation of business, or the business of calculation? Accounting as organizing through everyday communication. *Human Relations, 63*(8), 1249–1273. https://doi.org/10.1177/0018726709355658.

Holm, F., & Fairhurst, G. T. (2018). Configuring shared and hierarchical leadership through authoring. *Human Relations, 71*(5), 692–721. https://doi.org/10.1177/0018726717720803.

Jahn, J. L. S. (2016). Adapting safety rules in a high reliability context: How wildland firefighting workgroups ventriloquize safety rules to understand hazards. *Management Communication Quarterly, 30*(3), 362–389. https://doi.org/10.1177/0893318915623638.

Jasinski, J. (2001). Presence. In *Sourcebook on rhetoric: Key concepts in contemporary rhetorical studies* (pp. 455–458). Sage. www.doi.org/10.4135/9781452233222.n103.

Kahn, W. A., & Kram, K. E. (1994). Authority at work: Internal models and their organizational consequences. *Academy of Management Review, 19*(1), 17–50.

Kopaneva, I., & Sias, P. M. (2015). Lost in translation? Employee and organizational constructions of mission and vision. *Management Communication Quarterly, 29*(3), 358–384. https://doi.org/10.1177/0893318915581648.

Koschmann, M. A., & Burk, N. R. (2016). Accomplishing authority in collaborative work. *Western Journal of Communication, 80*(4), 393–413. https://doi.org/10.1080/10570314.2016.1159728.

Koschmann, M. A., & McDonald, J. (2015). Organizational rituals, communication, and the question of agency. *Management Communication Quarterly, 29*(2), 229–256. https://doi.org/10.1177/0893318915572386.

Kuhn, T. R. (2008). A communicative theory of the firm: Developing an alternative perspective on intraorganizational power and stakeholder relationships. *Organization Studies, 29*(8–9), 1197–1224.

Lindberg, K., & Czarniawska, B. (2006). Knotting the action net, or organizing between organizations. *Scandinavian Journal of Management, 22*(4), 292–306. https://doi.org/10.1016/j.scaman.2006.09.001.

Meier, F., & Carroll, B. (2020). Making up leaders: Reconfiguring the executive student through profiling, texts and conversations in a leadership development programme. *Human Relations, 73*(9), 1226–1248. https://doi.org/10.1177/0018726719858132.

Perelman, C., & Olbrechts-Tyteca, L. (1969). *The new rhetoric: A treatise on argumentation*. Notre Dame: Notre Dame Press.

Porter, A. J., Kuhn, T. R., & Nerlich, B. (2018). Organizing authority in the climate change debate: IPCC controversies and the management of dialectical tensions. *Organization Studies, 39*(7), 873–898. https://doi.org/10.1177/0170840617707999.

Ricoeur, P. (1981). *Hermeneutics and the human sciences* (Thompson, J. B. , Ed.). New York: Cambridge University Press.

Robichaud, D., Benoit-Barné, C., & Basque, J. (2012, June). Strategic text @ work: How texts frame managerial work and how managers help them to do so. Paper presented at the Fourth International Symposium on Process Organization Studies, Kos, Greece.

Robichaud, D., Giroux, H., & Taylor, J. R. (2004). The meta-conversation: Recursivity of language as a key to organizing. *Academy of Management Review, 29*(4), 617–634.

Spee, A. P., & Jarzabkowski, P. (2011). Strategic planning as communicative process. *Organization Studies, 32*(9), 1217–1245. https://doi.org/10.1177/0170840611411387.

Taylor, J. R. (2011). Organization as an (imbricated) configuring of transactions. *Organization Studies, 32*(9), 1273–1294. https://doi.org/10.1177/0170840611411396.

Taylor, J. R., & Robichaud, D. (2004). Finding the organization in the communication: Discourse as action and sensemaking. *Organization, 11*(3), 395–413.

Taylor, J. R., & Van Every, E. J. (2011). *The situated organization: Case studies in the pragmatics of communication research*. New York: Routledge.

Taylor, J. R., & Van Every, E. J. (2014). *When organization fails: Why authority matters*. New York: Routledge.

Vásquez, C., Bencherki, N., Cooren, F., & Sergi, V. (2018). From "matters of concern" to "matters of authority": Studying the performativity of strategy from a communicative constitution of organization (CCO) approach. *Long Range Planning, 51*(3), 417–435. https://doi.org/10.1016/j.lrp.2017.01.001.

Weber, M. (1978). *Economy and society: An outline of interpretive sociology* (G. Roth & C. Wittich, Eds.). Berkeley: University of California Press.

18

CCO THEORY AND LEADERSHIP

Ryan S. Bisel, Gail T. Fairhurst and Mathew L. Sheep

Leadership studies have a long and complex history. Leadership has been studied as a trait, differentiated into skills, styles, and types, and depicted as set of relationship negotiations. Historically, the emphasis has been individualist, cognitive, and heroic, although an increasing amount of work is collective, communicative, relational, material, and power-laced (Fairhurst, 2007; Fairhurst et al., 2020). The communicative constitution of organization (CCO) fits well within the latter trajectory, although it makes few claims about the role of leaders or leadership as central to organizing. At times, the CCO implications for leadership are easy to draw; at least one CCO school concerns itself with authority, which is often mistaken for leadership (Heifetz, 1994). At other times, the idea of leadership has an ambivalent or uneasy connection with CCO. The goal in this chapter is to draw out the insights of CCO for those interested in studying leadership. We draw from the Four Flows model, Montreal School, and Luhmannian School, separately and in combination, to explore leadership as flow mixing, hybrid acting, and system irritating, respectively. Along the way, we make the case that CCO adds complexity to traditional notions of leadership; meanwhile, leadership is a site for challenging CCO.

Four Flows (FF) and Leadership

McPhee and Zaug (2000) offered a concise and rich explanation of the idea that communication constitutes organization, called the Four Flows (FF) model. The authors later explained their main aim: "The key tenet of the Four Flows model is that no single process, even as broad as a text-conversation dialectic ... decision-making, or ventriloquism ... suffices to explain organizations" (Iverson et al., 2018, p. 47). In other words, the FF model of CCO theory describes the varied ways communication makes organizations what they are. The theory identifies four types (or flows) of constitutive organizational communication processes and adds that an *interplay between and among* those processes is necessary for constitution. McPhee and Zaug (2000) contended not all communication has *organizationally* constitutive force. Twenty years later, their original paper remains highly influential in both general and specific ways (Boivin et al., 2017). Despite the original paper's broad approach, leaders and leadership were not the focus in addressing communicative constitution; however, given our vantage point 20 years later, some connections can be made to leadership and extensions can be offered.

DOI: 10.4324/9781003224914-22

The *Flows.* The model was inspired by Anthony Giddens's (1984) Structuration theory (ST) in that it takes for granted that human agents (re)produce the social structures that enable and constrain their actions. Here, *organizational* structures are endogenous to human *communicative* action (Bisel, 2010). The idea of the FF model is that the communication processes of activity coordination, membership negotiation, reflexive self-structuring, and institutional positioning contribute to organizational constitution whenever these processes mix, overlap, and inter-mingle (McPhee & Zaug, 2000).

Activity coordination refers to the meaning-making of co-action or the mutual adjustments needed to get work done together, such as work-talk, huddles, directive-giving and receiving, meetings, and collaborative conversation. Membership negotiation refers to meaning-making involved with socializing individuals into members (and back again), such as hiring, onboarding, renewal rituals, and terminations. Self-structuring refers to meaning-making involving reflexive control and formulations of authority, responsibilities, and the division of labor, such as organizational chart discussions, strategic organizational planning, and restructuring dialogues and the creation of associated artifacts (Bean & Buikema, 2015). Institutional positioning refers to meaning-making that projects and situates the organizational image to stakeholders so that they treat the collective as having a coherent image with a distinctly organizational meaning, such as advertising, marketing, branding, regulatory adaptation, political activism, and vendor negotiations (Lammers, 2011; Shumate & O'Conner, 2010). Organization, then, is a "confluence" of many flows. In sum, the FF model involves an expansive, holistic, and multilayered view of how communication constitutes organizations—one that is not reducible to a singular mechanism (Iverson et al., 2018).

Materials and the Flows. The complexity of the model was later expanded to account for a growing critique that CCO theories exaggerate social constructionism at the cost of neglecting the role of material realities. Bruscella and Bisel (2018) provided the following three additions to the model: first, the scholars, drawing from Saussure (1916/1959) and McPhee and Zaug (2000), posited that, "all that is communicative is, at least partially, material; but not all that is material is communicative or organizationally constitutive" (p. 334). Second, materials and material resources enable and constrain human agents' ability to enact constitutive flows successfully. The addition might be called the "unequal constitutive capacity argument" in that it suggests materials—such as capital, facilities, and equipment—play into perceptions of (il) legitimacy of flow enactment such that not everyone is equally capable of (or powerful in) achieving constitutive uptake. To be clear, the claim is not prescriptive but merely descriptive in nature. Similarly, Iverson et al. (2018) affirmed that "agents are limited or conditioned by lack of power, decision access, racial prejudice, or structural divergences" (p. 62). Third, Bruscella and Bisel (2018) suggest that imbuing materials with organizational significance through two or more of the flows is an important means through which the communicative constitution of organization occurs. This last addition might be called the "materials-as-symbols argument". Taken together, the additions soften the excessive social constructionism that could be read into the original formulation of the model, while also preserving a central role for human action in the communicative constitution of organization.

Leadership in the Flows. The FF model is limited in terms of its explicit explanation of the role played by leadership and leadership communication in communicative constitution. On one hand, that absence is important because it tends to honor or bolster the constitutive value of *many* members' interactions; that perspective is important as it contrasts with a top-down, heroic management perspective that is a default position of many accounts of organizational ontology. On the other hand, the role played by members in leading or influencing organizational constitution (or "constitutive leadership") is implied in several flows and can be drawn out with little difficulty. For example, reflexive self-structuring conversations often generate authoritative texts (e.g., employment agreements, organizational charts) that serve as potent power-related contexts for other flows, such as activity coordination. Here, leadership is positional and conflated with management. Elsewhere, however, we can easily imagine how individuals' activity coordination communication that functions to produce branding and reputational influence within an industry (i.e., institutional positioning) can be crucial to constitution efforts, whether the individual is invested with formal organizational authority or not. How, then, does leadership emerge through a constitutive FF process? Namely, constitutive leadership activities involve mixing flows. Some constitutive leadership activities are recognized by others as "leadership", some are not. A partially recursive relationship exists in the sense that as flows are enacted and mixed, some enacting members and their activities—but not all—will be labeled as leaders or engaging in leadership retrospectively. Then, those who obtain the label of leader may gain unequal constitutive capacity in the eyes of beholders in achieving constitutive uptake moving forward.

Other observations about leadership and leadership communication can be inferred from the model. Here, we argue that organizational constitution requires distributed constitutive leadership. From one perspective, the model implies that leading the constitution of organizing (verb) is relatively simple in that the mixing of flows can be enacted by many members (not only those with formal organizational authority). Yet, more accurately, and paradoxically, the model implies that leading the constitution of organization (noun) is difficult in the sense that constitution requires the overlapping of multiple flows among members and nonmembers as well as across time and space. That difficulty is only compounded when we include the unequal constitutive capacity and materials-as-symbols arguments within the FF model (Bruscella & Bisel, 2018). Constitutive leadership is much too multifaceted to be situated in any one individual's communication efforts. Thus, the model implies that constitutive leadership is a *distributed* process wherein many members participate.

New Directions. The next frontier for the FF model involves exploring issues related to constitutive quality. To date, the FF model, as with each of the CCO traditions, is concerned with whether organizing/ation is present or absent, but does not attend to matters of better and worse quality communicating and organizing. Constitutive quality matters because it is inevitably related to how leadership and leadership communication practices are evaluated, critiqued, and eventually recommended. Distributed constitutive leadership that yields unethical organizing demands an evaluation and critique of those members and their activities. Bisel (2018) wrote that CCO, "rarely explore[s] whether communication is calling better or worse organization into being. Yet, … . When organizational members communicate in adaptive ways, the net result is calling into being a more durable organization, one that can stave off entropy" (p. 162). Iverson et al. (2018) move toward this point as they suggest that the model "may help leaders or managers diagnose and respond to problems" (p. 63).

A diagnostic use of the Four Flows model implies that it could help us understand and remedy problematic organizational communication patterns. Future studies should continue to expand upon these theories in order to account for the ways influential (and distributed) constitutive leadership activities call a quality of organization into being. Of course, it should be noted here that such studies should continue to avoid a bias for seeing organizing as opposed to disorganizing (Bisel, 2009; Putnam, 2019) and order instead of disorder (Fairhurst & Sheep, 2019)—or, analogously, to avoid an assumption that all constitutive leadership is necessarily healthy in terms of operations and ethics (Conrad, 2011). Researchers could begin by asking, "What does poor constitutive quality entail and what distributed constitutive leadership communication moves encourage, suppress, or avoid it?" For example, (un)ethical leadership communication remains a perennially important topic. Research could explore how distributed constitutive leadership activities invite the (un)ethical.

The Montreal School

The Montreal School (MS) of organizational communication is one of the defining CCO approaches (Putnam & Mumby, 2014). Its roots are in actor-network theory (Latour, 2005), Weick's (1979) theory of organizing; Greimas's (1987) narratology, ethnomethodology (Garfinkel, 1967), and American and European pragmatism (Cooren, 2014). The works of James Taylor and Elizabeth Van Every (2000, 2014) are foundational, although François Cooren (2010; 2012) and colleagues (Brummans et al., 2014; Cooren et al., 2008; Cooren, Matte et al., 2013) are the leading voices of MS today. On the subject of leadership, MS's primary interest is with authority, which some may conflate. As we explain below, we distinguish between these terms.

Text-Conversation. According to Taylor and Van Every (2014), authority and authoring are deeply entwined. In their view, those who are "authentically translating the purposes of the organization" legitimately influence and decide organizational matters (p. 27; see also Barnard, 1938). However, authoring is as much transactional as interactional because actors orient around a common object or purpose that establishes legitimacy as it adds value to the organization. Authoring communication assumes a material form, first, in conversations that negotiate the terms of the transaction and rules of association and, second, in the subsequent texts that inscribe such terms and rules in written documents, scripts for action, tacit understandings, or other forms (Taylor & Van Every, 2000, 2014). It is the conversation/text dynamic that continually (re) produces the organization, providing a basis for shared sensemaking and the power to organize, especially as texts become increasingly authoritative (Giddens, 1984; Taylor & Van Every, 2000).

Agency. Drawing from actor-network theory (Latour, 2005), MS imputes agency to nonhumans, such as texts, objects, spaces, bodies, or any "thing" that makes a difference in social interaction (Cooren, 2004). For MS scholars, it is the heterogeneous engineering of situations (Law, 1987) that creates hybrid acting and relational ontologies—terms signifying how *in situ* humans and nonhumans are each different because of the other. Cooren (2010, 2018) extended relational ontology to suggest that human beings should be seen more generally "as media through which other beings communicate", and this includes ideologies, values, emotions, and policies as much as objects, numbers, architecture, or technologies (p. 279). In short, the social and material coalesce in every aspect of organizational life, and no*thing* should be excluded as an agent if it makes a difference to a situation.

Presentification. This term is often used in concert with materialization, embodiment, and incarnation, all of which represent the ways that actants or "figures" manifest themselves *in situ*, the human in and through the nonhuman and vice versa (Benoit-Barné & Cooren, 2009; Cooren, 2010). Presentification is a performative act that can embody both uniqueness and recurrence, where human-nonhuman configurations emerge and evolve, but must also be acknowledged *for another next first time* as they *re*-present a "first time" again and again (Garfinkel, 2002). This ethnomethodological concept is central to ventriloquism.

Ventriloquism. Also known as a pragmatist approach, human actors are conceived of here as both ventriloquists and dummies (Cooren, 2010). That is, analysts look for the ways human actors position and are positioned by objects, sites, bodies, principles, values, interests, emotions, and so on, which are *"made to speak* to accomplish particular goals or serve particular interests" (Cooren et al., 2013, p. 256, emphasis added). A ventriloquial analysis focuses on what happens when *any* situational dynamic, accompanied by its iterative social and material entailments, takes on a life of its own. The analysis then oscillates between controlled and controlling situational elements, iteratively staging the evolution of what transpires, including paradoxical dynamics (Cooren et al., 2013; Cooren & Caïdor, 2019). In addition to oscillation, a ventriloquial analysis examines authority by adding authors to situations, as well as how they come to matter to situational outcomes through the resistances to be overcome (Fauré et al., 2019). Collectively, ventriloquism, in addition to text-conversation, nonhuman agency, and presentification, infuse this perspective with a level of animation unique among CCO approaches.

MS and Leadership. Although MS has shown relatively little interest in leadership per se, it predisposes analysts to conceptualize leadership in four ways. First, because communication is performative and consequential (Schoeneborn et al., 2020), it avoids casting leadership as a psychologism (individuals with strong inner motors). Instead, leadership is collective accomplishment due to ventriloquism's polyphony (the plurality of human and nonhuman voices; Clifton, 2017). MS thus gives the term "collective" new meaning, as traditional leadership studies would restrict it to human beings who share and exert control. Second, leadership ties closely to authority. Historically, the exercise of leadership is rooted in authority, specifically, in dominance and deference practices, where deference, over time, results in authorization (i.e., the conferral of authority, even without deliberate decision; Heifetz, 1994). Work by Holm and Fairhurst (2018) on authoring in text-conversation dynamics (Taylor & Van Every, 2014) and Clifton (2017) using ventriloquism demonstrates how authority factors into leadership, if leadership is equated with organizational role or position.

Third, in MS research, leadership assumes many forms, thus it retains a plastic quality. In leadership situations, humans and nonhumans are both actors and acted upon, thus making leadership contestable on more grounds (Schoeneborn et al., 2020). Plasticity is also evident in MS studies of leadership in its many forms, for example, charismatic leadership (Fairhurst, 2007), heroic versus failed political leadership during a crisis (Cooren & Fairhurst, 2009), routine building management (Cooren et al., 2012), and shared versus hierarchical leadership (Holm & Fairhurst, 2018), to name a few. Fourth, drawing from its ethnomethodological roots, power is not relevant to leadership within MS unless actants make it relevant (e.g., through a situation's figures that are "made to speak" as in ventriloquism). Here, MS's engagement with power is rather flat, as larger socio-cultural forces are reduced to figurative traces. Yet, prior to MS's theorizing, little work conceptualized the power-laced role of leadership actors speaking for or on behalf of their organizations.

In the leadership literature's historical emphasis on heroic individuals, individualism reigned, cognition was foregrounded, communication was backgrounded, the material was immaterial, and leadership was essentialized (Fairhurst, 2007). MS's answer to this state of affairs is to foreground communication as spatiotemporal, meaning-centered, and materially distributed among human and nonhuman actants. By implication, then, MS resists essentializing leadership by attending to ontology, the likes of which were scarcely conceived of in the surveys and seven-point scales of traditional leadership research.

New Directions. Power is under-studied (and under-taught) in leadership generally; as Collinson and Tourish (2015) state bluntly, "leadership needs to go beyond a 'rotten apple' theory of dysfunctionality and corruption to examine the barrel within which the apples have soured"

(p. 586). MS's work on responsible management can contribute to a post-heroic view of leadership by decentering the agency of individuals to focus on the myriad of forces that enable and constrain leadership agency for good or ill (Schoeneborn et al., 2020). Will this be enough to understand leadership's role in capitalist modes of production driven to excess (e.g., banking crises, income inequality, climate change)? As power dynamics grow more complex, MS's relatively recent turn to study paradoxical tensions may be key to unraveling power's complexities (Cooren & Caïdor, 2019; Cooren et al., 2013).

A second key MS challenge for the future involves taking a stand on the age-old questions of leadership research. What is leadership? What is followership? Who gets to decide? For example, Holm and Fairhurst's (2018) study of authoring using text-conversation dynamics in meeting interactions also collected attributions of leadership (or lack thereof) from the participants. Patterns of authoring supported the presence of shared leadership, as team meetings were highly participative for the nearly six-month period of study. However, team members saw this as a failure of their designated leader because he could not rein in the group to do anything but talk about problems, which grew tiresome. Holm and Fairhurst argued: (a) leadership should not be equated with authority, even though authoring patterns clearly inform leadership dynamics, and (b) multiple definitions of leadership should be held in creative tension to account for both analyst *and* actor perspectives whether leadership (or the lack thereof) is present. It is not at all clear how MS would respond to these specific circumstances, a point we further consider in the Discussion.

Luhmannian Systems Theory

The third tradition of CCO theory is based on the systems theory of Niklas Luhmann (1927–1998), an influential German sociologist whose work has recently gained wider exposure after being translated into English. While it is beyond our scope to summarize Luhmann's theory comprehensively, there are a number of useful reviews—e.g., that of Cooren and Seidl (2020) based on the translation of Luhmann's (2018) magnum opus, *Organization and Decision*. Others have called attention to the analytical potency of Luhmann's theory (e.g., Schoeneborn, 2011; Seidl & Becker, 2005, 2006). Luhmann's theory is deemed a "radical communication perspective" (Cooren & Seidl, 2020, p. 486) because it conceptualizes an organization as a system/network of linked "decision communications" and, at least for analytical purposes, nothing else. That is, "organizations were the only systems that consisted *entirely* of decision communications" (Cooren & Seidl, 2020, p. 481).

Decision Communications. Decision communications are a kind of communication that "contains information about a particular content … but at the same time … contains information about alternatives to that content" (Cooren & Seidl, 2020, p. 481), or else it would not require a decision. Decision communication marks what is and is not part of the organization, its membership, identity, policies, strategies, mission, and so on—as well as "its reasons, its justification, the effort involved" (Luhmann, 2018, p. 148). However, decisions are paradoxical. Their purpose is to create certainty (by eliminating alternatives), but in so doing, they also create uncertainty "by demonstrating that the future is chosen; so it could be different. In this way, decisions pave the way for contestation" (Ahrne & Brunsson, 2011, p. 90). Luhmann (2018) memorably frames this "decision paradox" as follows:

> The decision has to inform about itself, but also about the alternative, thus about the paradox that the alternative is an alternative (for otherwise the decision would not be

a decision) and at the same time not an alternative (for otherwise the decision would not be a decision). (p. 111)

Thus, communication events deparadoxify (reduce uncertainty in) an organization system by resolving (deciding) questions of organizational identity, practices, membership, and so on. Once decided, the decision is *counted as* made—albeit illusory or "covered" (Seidl & Becker, 2006, p. 29)—and as constitutive of the limits of subsequent communication. However, "irritations" (see below) from *structurally coupled* systems in the environment can again cause communication to take on paradoxical/contingent characteristics that require more communication to "decide". Indeed, if this cycle ceases to occur, Luhmann would say that the system ceases to exist because it is no longer self-(re)producing (or *autopoietic*; Schoeneborn, 2011, p. 670).

Events. Moreover, only decision communication *events* are constitutive of the organization, and events are never a single utterance or text. That is because communication is conceived of as a unity of three selections: information (content), utterance (form), and understanding (consequentiality). Only in the understanding of information and utterance does an event occur. That is, "the meaning of a communication … is only determined retrospectively through the later communications" (Seidl & Becker, 2006, p. 20). Communication events are interactionally emergent with meanings based on the *difference* one communication makes in subsequent others, as well as how the communication is taken up or understood subsequently as accepted, modified, or rejected. Therefore, Luhmannian analysis is directed at communication events in series of interactions, but not at the intent or purposes of human actors, which are not accessible to observation. Rather, psychic systems are only observable in the ways they irritate the organization's discourse(s), and only within-system communication is seen as system-constitutive. As Luhmann (2018) put it, "A decision is accordingly a communicative event and not something that happens in the mind of an individual" (p. 110).

Luhmann and Leadership. Human agency is thus replaced by the agency of communication itself, although human psychic systems are available in the form of *irritations* that an organization system constructs as making a difference. In effect, the communication system *decides* how human psychic systems (or environmental irritations) can be treated (Cooren & Seidl, 2020; Luhmann, 2018).

In Luhmannian theory, the notion of a leader and leadership becomes what Luhmann (2018, p. 64) himself asserts is a "fiction", or "control illusions" that allow managers to "feel good":

> The individual manager is a fiction, and for all important decisions a leadership team has to be presupposed … . (p. 64)

Luhmann here agrees with the other two CCO schools that, if there is such a thing as "leadership", then it is at a minimum attributable to a collective (system) and not to individual agency, but that collective is not to be construed as a collection of humans with agency but as a series of interactive communication events that "decide".

Since "heroic leadership" is still a mainstay of scholarly and practitioner literature, Cooren and Seidl (2020) acknowledge that "the organization treats decisions *as if* they were the product of a decision maker, rather than the product of the communication system itself" (p. 491). Nonetheless, a Luhmannian perspective would limit notions of "leadership" to decisions that are internally focused as system communication, and not externally directed to stakeholders, as these are outside the organization system. The organization system may only perturb or irritate other social systems (e.g., the societal system of which it is a part, political and legal systems, financial institutions, markets, and so on), just as it can only be irritated by other systems—including human "psychic" systems.

Luhmannian communication events attempt to: (a) deparadoxify the decision paradox and (b) avert deconstruction of the decision in order to avoid making it once again paradoxical. Thus, for Luhmann, if a "leadership" role of communication is to be entertained, then its primary purpose as decision communication is to reduce (not create) uncertainty (although, due to the decision paradox, uncertainty is made possible, anyway). Traditionally, leadership theories view decision-making—particularly those decisions in which problems are ill-defined—as a (sometimes distributed) leadership function. As noted by Cooren and Seidl (2020), "Luhmann argued that decisions ... are differences that make a difference in the decisions that follow" (p. 484). "Making a difference" begins to sound much like leadership.

However, this difference runs contrary to popular leadership theories, in which leadership is viewed as spearheading change by challenging and upending the status quo—not creating and protecting it (e.g., Kotter, 1996). Yet, for Luhmann, deparadoxification of the decision paradox (that there are alternatives, yet there are none—because the decision has been decided) is the mechanism by which organization systems continue to exist by *reducing* uncertainties in the system. According to Cooren and Seidl (2020), reducing uncertainty implies its own kind of power: "Decisions, to the extent that they are not questioned but are taken as the basis for further decision-making, provide ensuing decisions with stable points of reference ... the uncertainties involved in the original decision do not matter anymore" (p. 483).

New Directions. Once decided, a main concern of further decision communication is to prevent the *deconstruction* of the decision to reveal the paradox once more.

Thus, a primary communicative task of an organization system (requiring a persuasive type of communicative influence, if not a leader) is to manage the *deparadoxification versus deconstruction* paradox, and this is the crux of the Luhmannian perspective. The organization is seen as "a communicative entity that is driven by the continuous need to handle this paradox and thus tends to oscillate between visibilizing and invisibilizing the alternativity of decisions" (Schoeneborn, 2011, p. 674). In sum, from a Luhmannian perspective, if we think of leadership communication as efficacy to influence subsequent system communication by deparadoxification (uncertainty reduction through decisions) and prevention of deconstruction (re-paradoxification by resurrecting alternatives), then there are two arenas of influence that may prove to be fruitful lines of inquiry: (a) within-system decision communication events and (a) between-system irritations.

Within-System Decision Communication Events. How stable/enduring are decisions that are constitutive of organization systems, and why? Similar to leadership identity construction (DeRue & Ashford, 2010), which requires leadership claims to be granted reciprocally by followers, decisional communications cannot simply be asserted as decided. Rather, they must be attended to as decided as revealed in subsequent communication. Of course, decisions may also be rejected or contested, as Luhmann (2013) would account for what he terms a *conflict system* (i.e., conflict conceptualized as a highly integrated system). In such systems, the acceptance of one component in a conflict produces tighter system integration by limiting "degrees of freedom" in other components (p. 250).

More research is needed to investigate how acceptance or rejection is contested in system communications, and how they are subsequently addressed in further communication. Saying "no" to a proposed alternative reduces the "options, states, and qualities that a system can have"

(Luhmann, 2013, p. 250). However, the "possibility of saying no" (p. 252) can be strengthened by reducing integration within the system or by the irritating influence of other structures (e.g., legal) that protect the option of rejecting propositions. In such cases, the question of undecidability is again opened, and paradoxicality and uncertainty are increased. Research programs that more fully theorize Luhmannian conflict systems have the potential of advancing our knowledge regarding how decision communications are made more or less enduring and resistant to deconstruction. The question becomes: which conditions are conducive to system change, system reproduction, or system fragmentation and disintegration?

Between-System Irritations. Luhmann also triggers another question: how and why do organization systems attend to some irritations from psychic systems and not others? How is the communicative construction of human agency, or the operational fiction of a decision-making leader, brought off systemically? As Cooren and Seidl (2020) note, "the Luhmannian approach … invites examinations of how human agency is referred to and thus constructed in the communication process itself" (p. 491). Moreover, what are the effects of the irritation on subsequent within-system communication, and how would the researcher observe this happening in communication? What are the "mechanisms of creating and sustaining the fiction of the decision maker" (Cooren & Seidl, 2020, p. 491)? Thus, we ask: does the systemic decision to attend to the irritations of a certain psychic (human) system(s) and not to others constitute a "leadership" role for that psychic system? Does treatment of a psychic system as having/ deserving more irritational influence within the communication system (organization) equate to granting it leadership? If so, is the leader/leadership entirely a fiction? If not, how is the "influential" psychic system different from our traditional understandings of leadership and influence?

Discussion

Admittedly, few CCO papers have seriously engaged with leadership explicitly; yet, some insights about leadership can be drawn out. The question becomes, "what are the key comparison points among the three approaches for thinking about leadership in tandem with CCO?" For us, issues related to agency and materiality are good starting points: first, in terms of agency, MS acknowledges that humans' capacity for reflexivity and sensemaking distinguishes them from nonhumans (Bencherki et al., 2019), but focuses exclusively on *any* actant's capacity to make a difference *in situ*. The FF model defines agency only in terms of humans' ability to act otherwise, their knowledgeability, and their reflexive monitoring (Iverson et al., 2018). Meanwhile, Luhmannian systems theory discounts *both* texts (nonhuman actors) *as well as* human agency. Within the tradition, there are notions similar to authoring or authority, but it is not because of any direct attributions to human (or nonhuman) actors or actants; instead, these are viewed as mere irritations to the organization system. These divergent agency-related assumptions are important because they direct analytical attention and serve to rule out (or in) explanations. In other words, these assumptions tell us where to look for the (leadership) action.

Consider that, since at least the 1980s, leadership has equated with (human) agency or action in the mainstream leadership literature. Individual leaders are conceived of as forces for change, while managers are framed as maintaining the status quo (Kotter, 1996). Paradoxically, a great deal of psychological leadership research undertheorizes agency or exaggerates it (Fairhurst, 2007). Untheorized agency results from studying leadership without regard to its organizing implications (Hosking, 1988); here, leadership floats ethereally above task accomplishment

(Robinson, 2001). Exaggerated agency stems from a (heroic) leader focus, with Gronn (2000) pejoratively referring to it as "belief in the power of one" (p. 319). The CCO theories on leadership thus take agency in very different directions.

All three CCO schools strike a blow to heroic, essentializing theories of leadership in favor of the study of its relationalities; it is a distributed phenomenon. The FF model comes the closest to a distributed view because agency is embodied in the (human) mixing of communication flows. As such, constitutive leadership *can be* accomplished by management, but it can also occur wherever members' communication mixes flows. MS recasts leadership agency in three ways, including hybrid human-nonhuman acting. But MS also casts leaders (or followers) as macro-actors, speaking for or on behalf of the organization (Taylor & Van Every, 2000, 2014) and, more recently, as a ventriloquized "figure" animated with a life of its own as it comes to "matter" in a situation (Cooren, 2010; Cooren et al., 2013). As such, leadership and management may prove to be different animating figures, although definitional conundrums emerge when CCO analysts are ill-equipped to differentiate among the family resemblance of leadership language games (Kelly, 2014). When everything falls under a leadership banner, leadership loses its meaning.

Luhmann (2018) upends the apple cart completely by treating (traditional notions of) leadership and management as fictional illusions of control. At best, human psychic systems are irritants to organizational systems because only communication can assume the necessary agency to perturb the system's decision-making apparatus. Communication thus makes use of the human being, not the other way around (Cooren & Seidl, 2020). As mentioned above, if there is such a thing as leadership or management, it is a communication-granting "authoring" decision narrowly focused internally as system communication.

Second, all three CCO schools grapple with materiality, but MS leads the way in its recognition of nonhuman agency, recalling Grint's (1997) wry observation that "naked, friendless, money-less, and technology-less leaders are unlikely to prove persuasive" (p. 17). More subtly, the relational ontology of MS decenters all actants (Cooren, 2010, 2018). The social is not privileged as in the FF model, nor is the material secondary to the (collectively human) communicating system as in Luhmann. Recent work in the FF model is redressing the lack of attention to materiality, but much work remains (Bruscella & Bisel, 2018). Meanwhile, Schoeneborn (2011) described Luhmann as "almost 'immaterial' [and] ... instead identifies the inherent need for deparadoxification as the main driving force that triggers the next instance of communication and thus enables the organization to perpetuate" (p. 678).

We suspect that materiality is an avenue through which power can be more adequately theorized and integrated into the CCO traditions' casting of leadership. In all three approaches, the operations of power are more implicit than explicit. They emerge in the ad hoc judgments of analysts who observe asymmetries in (a) flow mixing among those with unequal constitutive capacity created by material resource disparities (FF), (b) human-material pairings and blackboxing in episodic networking (MS), or (c) system misclassifications, deparadoxifications, or deconstructions leading to or away from closure (Luhmann).

Finally, many critical and constructionist theories of leadership take as their starting point that there is no single definition of leadership; as mentioned, there is only a family resemblance among language games (Collinson, 2014; Fairhurst, 2007; Kelly, 2014). Actors, not just analysts, are knowledgeable and must be allowed to define their circumstances (Boden, 1994; Giddens, 1984). However, all three CCO schools favor the "doing" of organizing with a manifest ambivalence to leadership's plasticity, actor knowledgeability, or any distinction that might make leadership and management different discursive disciplinary regimes. If, as Hosking (1988) suggested, leadership really is about organizing, then all three CCO perspectives say

"Yes!" and unabashedly leave leadership's definitional conundrums to others. That's a shame because this stance threatens what we learn about leadership and its other family members as CCO leadership research accumulates.

Conclusion

Can MS work in conjunction with FF and/or a Luhmannian approach to address today's leadership challenges (e.g., climate change, globalization, poverty)? Certainly, it would require a dual analytic ability to zoom in to situational manifestations of the problem and zoom out to understand broader system dynamics (Jarzbkowski et al. 2019). Zooming in is MS's *raison d'être*, while the other two perspectives zoom out to capture system dynamics. Could their alternating or combined use inform each other? The problems of leadership today demand that we ask.

References

Ahrne, G., & Brunsson, N. (2011). Organization outside organizations: The significance of partial organization. *Organization, 18*(1), 83–104.

Barnard, C. I. (1938). *The functions of the executive.* Boston, MA: Harvard University Press.

Bean, H., & Buikema, R. J. (2015). Deconstituting al-Qa'ida: CCO theory and the decline and dis-solution of hidden organizations. *Management Communication Quarterly, 29*, 1–27.

Bencherki, N., Bourgoin, A., Chen, H.-R., Cooren, F., Denault, V., & Plusquellec, P. (2019). Bodies, faces, physical spaces and the materializations of authority. In N. Bencherki, F. Matte, & F. Cooren (Eds.), *Authority and power in social interaction: Methods and analysis* (pp. 77–98). New York: Routledge.

Benoit-Barné, C., & Cooren, F. (2009). The accomplishment of authority through presentification: How authority is distributed among and negotiated by organizational members. *Management Communication Quarterly, 23*(1), 5-31.

Bisel, R. S. (2009). On a growing dualism in organizational discourse research. *Management Communication Quarterly, 22*, 614–638.

Bisel, R. S. (2010). A communicative ontology of organization?: A description, history, and critique of CCO theories for organization science. *Management Communication Quarterly, 24*, 124–131.

Bisel, R. S. (2018). *Organizational moral learning: A communication approach.* New York: Routledge.

Boden, D. (1994). *The business of talk: Organizations in action.* Polity Press.

Boivin, G., Brummans, B. H., & Barker, J. R. (2017). The institutionalization of CCO scholarship: Trends from 2000 to 2015. *Management Communication Quarterly, 31*, 331–355.

Brummans, B. H. J. M., Cooren, F., Robichaud, D., & Taylor, J. R. (2014). Approaches to the communicative constitution of organizations. In L. L. Putnam & D. K. Mumby (Eds.), *The SAGE handbook of organizational communication : Advances in theory, research, and methods* (pp. 173–194). Sage.

Bruscella, J. S., & Bisel, R. S. (2018). FF theory and materiality: ISIL's use of material resources in its communicative constitution. *Communication Monographs, 85*, 331–356.

Clifton, J. (2017). Leaders as ventriloquists: Leader identity and influencing the communicative construction of the organization. *Leadership, 13*(3), 301–319.

Collinson, D. (2014). Dichotomies, dialectics and dilemmas: New directions for critical leadership studies. *Leadership, 10*, 36–55.

Collinson, D., & Tourish, D. (2015). Teaching leadership critically: New directions for leadership pedagogy. *Academy of Management Learning & Education, 14*(4), 576–594.

Conrad, C. (2011). *Organizational rhetoric: Strategies of resistance and domination.* Malden, MA: Polity.

Cooren, F. (2004). Textual agency: How texts do things in organizational settings. *Organization, 11*, 373–393.

Cooren, F. (2010). *Action and agency in dialogue: Passion, incarnation, and ventriloquism.* Amsterdam: John Benjamins.

Cooren, F. (2012). Communication theory at the center: Ventriloquism and the communicative constitution of reality. *Journal of Communication, 62*(1), 1–20.

Cooren, F. (2014). Pragmatism as ventriloquism : A reply to comments. *Language Under Discussion, 2*(1), 65–86. https://doi.org/10.31885/lud.2.1.246.

Cooren, F. (2018). Materializing communication: Making the case for a relational ontology. *Journal of Communication, 68*(2), 278-288.

Cooren, F., Brummans, B. H. J. M., & Charrieras, D. (2008). The coproduction of organizational presence: A study of Mèdecins sans Frontières in action. *Human Relations, 61*(10), 1339–1370.

Cooren, F., & Caïdor, P. (2019). Communication as dis/organization: How to analyze tensions from a relational perspective. In C. Vásquez & T. Kuhn (Eds.), *Dis/organization as communication: Studying tensions, ambiguities and disordering* (pp. 36–59). London: Routledge.

Cooren, F., & Fairhurst, G. T. (2009). Dislocation and stabilization : How to scale up from interactions to organization. In L. L. Putnam & A. M. Nicotera (Eds.), *The communicative constitution of organization : Centering organizational communication* (pp. 117–152). Lawrence Erlbaum Associates.

Cooren, F., Fairhurst, G. T., & Huët, R. (2012). Why matter always matters in (organizational) communication. In P. M. Leonardi, B. A. Nardi, & J. Kallinikos (Eds.), *Materiality and organizing: Social interaction in a technological world* (pp. 296–314). Oxford: Oxford University Press.

Cooren, F., Matte, F., Benoit-Barné, C., & Brummans, B.H.J.M. (2013). Communication as ventriloquism: A grounded-in-action approach to the study of organizational tensions *Communication Monographs, 80*, 255–277.

Cooren, F., & Seidl, D. (2020). Niklas Luhmann's radical communication approach and its implications for research on organizational communication. *Academy of Management Review, 45*(2), 479–497.

DeRue, D. S., & Ashford, S. J. (2010). Who will lead and who will follow? A social process of leadership identity construction in organizations. *Academy of Management Review, 35*(4), 627–647.

de Saussure, F. (1916/1959). *Course in general linguistics.* New York: McGraw Hill.

Fairhurst, G. T. (2007). *Discursive leadership: In conversation with leadership psychology.* Thousand Oaks, CA: Sage.

Fairhurst, G. T., Jackson, B., Foldy, E. G., & Ospina, S. M. (2020). Studying collective leadership: The road ahead. *Human Relations, 73,* 598–614.

Fairhurst, G. T., & Sheep, M. L. (2019). Rethinking order and disorder: Accounting for disequilibrium in knotted systems of paradoxical tensions. In C. Vásquez & T. Kuhn (Eds.), *Dis/organization as communication: Exploring the disordering, disruptive, and chaotic properties of communication* (pp. 80–98). New York: Routledge.

Fauré, B., Cooren, F., & Matte, F. (2019). To speak or not to speak the language of numbers: Accounting as ventriloquism. *Accounting, Auditing & Accountability Journal, 32*, 337–361.

Garfinkel, H. (1967). *Studies in ethnomethodology.* Cambridge, UK: Polity Press.

Garfinkel, H. (2002). *Ethnomethodology's program: Working out Durkheim's aphorism.* Lanham, MD: Rowman & Littlefield.

Giddens, A. (1984). *The constitution of society: Outline of the theory of structuration.* Berkeley: University of California Press.

Greimas, A. J. (1987). *On meaning : Selected writings in semiotic theory.* University of Minnesota Press.

Grint, K. (1997). *Leadership: Classical, contemporary, and critical approaches.* Oxford: Oxford University Press.

Gronn, P. (2000). Distributed properties: A new architecture for leadership. *Educational Management and Administration, 28, 317–338.*

Heifetz, R.A. (1994). *Leadership without easy answers.* Boston, MA: Harvard University Press.

Holm, F., & Fairhurst, G. T. (2018). Configuring shared and hierarchical leadership through authoring. *Human Relations, 71*(5), 692–721.

Hosking, D. M. (1988). Organizing, leadership and skillful process. *Journal of Management Studies, 25,* 147–166.

Iverson, J. O., McPhee, R. D., & Spaulding, C. W. (2018). Being able to act otherwise: The role of agency in the FF at 2-1-1 and beyond. In B. H. J. M. Brummans (Ed.), *The agency of organizing: Perspectives and case studies* (pp. 43–65). New York: Routledge.

Jarzabkowski, P., Lê, J., & Balogun, J. (2019). The social practice of coevolving strategy and structure to realize mandated radical change. *Academy of Management Journal, 62*(3), 850–882. https://doi.org/10.5465/amj.2016.0689.

Kelly, S. (2014). Towards a negative ontology of leadership. *Human Relations, 67*, 905–922.

Kotter, J. P. (1996). *Leading change.* Cambridge, MA: Harvard Business School Press.

Lammers, J. C. (2011). How institutions communicate: Institutional messages, institutional logics, and organizational communication. *Management Communication Quarterly, 25*, 154–182.

Latour, B. (2005). *Reassembling the social: An introduction to actor-network-theory.* Oxford: Oxford University Press.

Law, J. (1987). Technology and heterogeneous engineering: The case of Portuguese expansion. In W. E. Bijker, T. P. Hughes, & T. Pinch (Eds.), *Social construction of technological systems* (pp. 111–34). Cambridge, MA: MIT Press.

Luhmann, N. (2013). *Introduction to systems theory*. Malden, MA: Polity Press.

Luhmann, N. (2018). *Organization and decision*. Cambridge, UK: Cambridge University Press.

McPhee, R. D., & Zaug, P. (2000). The communicative constitution of organization: A framework for explanation. *Electronic Journal of Communication, 10* (1–2).

Putnam, L. L. (2019). Constituting order and disorder: Embracing tensions and contradictions. In C. Vásquez & T. Kuhn (Eds.), *Dis/organization as communication: Exploring the disordering, disruptive, and chaotic properties of communication* (pp. 17–35). New York: Routledge.

Putnam, L. L., & Mumby, D. K. (2014). Introduction: Advancing theory and research in organizational communication. In L. L. Putnam & D. K. Mumby (Eds.), *The SAGE handbook of organizational communication* (3rd edn., pp. 1–18). Los Angeles, CA: Sage.

Robinson, V. M. J. (2001). Embedding leadership in task performance. In K. Wong & C.W. Evers (Eds.), *Leadership for quality schooling* (pp. 90–102). London: Routledge/Falmer.

Schoeneborn, D. (2011). Organization as communication: A Luhmannian perspective. *Management Communication Quarterly, 25*(4), 663–689.

Schoeneborn, D., Trittin-Ulbrich, H., & Cooren, F. (2020). Consensus vs. dissensus: The communicative constitution of responsible management. In O Laasch, R. Suddaby, R. E. Freeman, & D. Jimali (Eds.), *Research handbook of responsible management* (pp. 451–467). Cheltenham: Edward Elgar.

Seidl, D., & Becker, K. H. (Eds.). (2005). *Niklas Luhmann and organization studies*. Copenhagen: Copenhagen Business School Press.

Seidl, D., & Becker, K. H. (2006). Organizations as distinction generating and processing systems: Niklas Luhmann's contribution to organization studies. *Organization, 13*(1), 9–35.

Shumate, M., & O'Conner, A. (2010). The symbiotic sustainability model: Conceptualizing NGO-corporate alliance communication. *Journal of Communication, 60*, 577–609.

Taylor, J. R., & Van Every, E. J. (2000). *The emergent organization: Communication as its site and surface.* Mahwah, NJ: Erlbaum.

Taylor, J. R., & Van Every, E. J. (2014) *When organization fails: Why authority matters.* New York: Routledge.

Weick, K. E. (1979). *The social psychology of organizing* (2nd edn.). New York: McGraw-Hill.

19

EXPLORING IDENTITY MATTERS IN THE COMMUNICATIVE CONSTITUTION OF ORGANIZATION

Mathieu Chaput and Joëlle Basque

Organizational identity has garnered a high level of interest among scholars for the better part of the last four decades. While the concept finds its origins in organizational studies and remains a central focus for research in that field (Brown, 2019; Pratt et al., 2016), our aim in this chapter is to highlight the shift in perspective that can be applied when noting the contributions emerging from the field of organizational communication, where communication's constitutive role – including in identity formation – is increasingly recognized. More specifically, the chapter will focus on studies and reflections on identity that follow the six premises outlined by Cooren and his colleagues (2011, pp. 1151–1154) in their attempt to conceive of a precise, but inclusive, research agenda for the communicative constitution of organization (CCO) scolarship:

1. CCO scholarship studies communicational events.
2. CCO scholarship should be as inclusive as possible about what we mean by (organizational) communication.
3. CCO scholarship acknowledges the co-constructed nature of (organizational) communication.
4. CCO scholarship holds that who or what is acting is an open question.
5. CCO scholarship never leaves the realm of communication events.
6. CCO scholarship favors neither organizing nor organization.

Our suggestion is that existing research that adopts these six premises has shown that identity is (1) constituted in communication (Chreim, 2002; Kuhn & Nelson, 2002), (2) expressed through materializations (Brummans et al., 2009; Chaput et al., 2011), (3) central to major organizational processes (McPhee, 2004; McPhee & Zaug, 2009), (4) contributing to the emergence of organizational actorhood (Dobusch & Schoeneborn, 2015; Koschmann, 2013), and (5) constituted in an autoreferential manner (Cheong et al., 2014). These five features of identity illustrate what can be gained from adopting a CCO perspective to study identity matters,

DOI: 10.4324/9781003224914-23

and what CCO has contributed to the literature on this topic. They are the pillars upon which this chapter is organized. A broader panorama of organizational identity in the field of organizational communication can be found in the reviews by Cheney et al. (2014), Larson & Gill (2017), Wieland (2017) and Scott (2020).

This chapter starts by defining organizational identity in the field of organizational communication and explaining how the main CCO schools of thought have theorized and studied it through the five features identified above. Building on these contributions, we analyze what we conceptualize as "identity matters" in a police organization, as we take a closer look at a group conversation on institutional change. We conclude by suggesting directions for future work on identity. In particular, scholarship could borrow from authors such as Kenneth Burke, Paul Ricoeur, Michel Foucault and Judith Butler, to address identity explicitly. We also highlight potential methodological discussions that could be held regarding identity and classic methods of inquiry versus new methods related to technological advances. Last, we identify related themes that could be explored with regard to the research subject: branding, authority, and the political dimensions of identity.

Organizational Identity and the CCO Perspective in Organizational Communication

Identity is Constituted in Communication

Originally framed as the central, enduring, and distinctive attributes of the organization (Albert & Whetten, 1985), organizational identity has since been recognized as an evolving construct. A lingering effect of this shift in perspective is the important tension in identity research between the concept of identity as a given, and the concept of identity as a process. This tension has long pervaded the literature on organizational identity, with studies that consider identity as a given suggesting that it is a more or less durable and fixed property of the organization, whereas the process view considers it as a *social construction* resulting from stakeholders' interactions and interpretations of shared experiences (Corley et al., 2006; Hatch & Schultz, 2002). This latter view is manifest in studies that conceptualize identity as an ongoing quest for an individual and collective sense of self, and focus on how people answer the question: "Who are we as an organization?" (Whetten, 2006).

This conceptual tension reflects a disciplinary divide between cognitive conceptions of identity, which predominate in organizational studies, and communicative conceptions of identity, found in organizational communication (Scott, 2007; Wieland, 2017). From a CCO perspective, however, the distinction between identity as a given and identity as a process appears as a false dichotomy in the sense that, although identity emerges from interactions and joint interpretations of the (collective) self, it may nonetheless be *constructed as a given* and built into a stable and permanent staple of an organization – even if it may not be so from an ontological standpoint.

A shining illustration of the non-contradiction between identity's stability and its ever-changing nature is the *Farine Five Roses* illuminated sign that brightens the downtown Montréal sky at night (Figure 19.1). The sign, advertising a flour brand, has been a visual urban landmark since 1948. Its ostensible endurance dissimulates its many forms throughout the years, as well as its physical degradation, countless hours of maintenance work, multiple owners, and an uncertain future (Soar, 2009). In the same way, organizational identity can materialize in more durable forms that may give the impression that it is a distanced, delocalized, and almost timeless property. The seeming immutability (Cooren et al., 2007), (con)substantiality (Chaput et al.,

Figure 19.1 Farine Five Roses Sign. By Rachelita — Personal Work, CC BY-SA 3.0.
https://commons.wikimedia.org/w/index.php?curid=29435572.

2011) or singularity (Koschmann, 2013) of an organization would, then, be qualities that, in fact, need to be *continuously performed and materialized in communication*, with more or less stabilizing and long-lasting effects.

In CCO, the study of individual identities has been one of the first sites where this false dichotomy opposing the "given" and "socially constructed" views has been explored. In these works, the emphasis is put on the process of building affiliation and sharing interests with the organization through communicative practices (identification), rather than on the outcome (identities) (Chreim, 2002; Kuhn & Nelson, 2002). Identity is both a temporarily stable entity (when it is used as a resource) and an evolutive entity, since it is the subject of definition and redefinition through the processes of identification and coparticipation in the organization's activities, in a recursive manner (Kuhn & Nelson, 2002). These processes have implications for the construction of professional identities (van Vuuren & Westerhof, 2015), or for the construction of organizational identity, as seen in a recent study by Sörgärde (2020) explaining how members can influence dominant organizational narratives in a dialogical and multi-authored manner.

Identity is Expressed through Materializations

If we accept the idea that organizational (and individual) identity could best be conceived of as a joint communicative accomplishment, we can wonder, next, how an identity can be observed if there is nothing stable to be seen. Is an identity something that can be grasped in its totality? Are there some essential features that must be observed in order to be able to say that we have "seen" someone's or something's identity? Without claiming to solve this puzzle, the premise that "CCO scholarship never leaves the realm of communication events" (Cooren et al., 2011, p. 1153) suggests that studying organizational identity requires a focus on its *materializations* in communication practices (Cooren, 2020). Identity materializes in communication situations verbally, textually, visually, emotionally, viscerally, tactilely, or audibly, and can be observed even when it is not the primary research focus. Indeed, one way identity matters have been explored from a CCO perspective is indirectly, through the study of the ontology of the organization, meaning how its existence in the world is communciatively brought about, and how this is tied to different modes of being (Latour, 2013). In these works, organizational identity is not mentioned explicitly; rather, it is linked to the notion of presence, i.e., how an entity – such as an organization – exists for others and is recognized as such, through the effects of presentification (Brummans et al., 2009; Cooren et al., 2008), consubstantialization (sharing of interests as a basis for collective action; see Chaput et al., 2011), institutional positioning (Bruscella & Bisel, 2018), self-referential practices (Cheong et al., 2014), or by membership and activity attributions of the members themselves and/or of observers (Schoeneborn & Scherer, 2012; Bencherki & Snack, 2016). In most of these studies, identity is a by-product of its presence being intensified by successive incarnations through its spokespersons and through the materialization of its accomplishments in various spaces and times. This presence has to be acknowledged by an audience for the organization to be identified as such, hence the interactive aspect of this process. As Brummans et al. (2009, p. 57) explain:

> "if something or someone is indeed made present, it means that it was somehow embodied or incarnated. The incarnation that enables presentification occurs through the interplay between spoken and written language (conversations, speeches, documents, memos, posters), nonverbal language (gestures, symbols), context (circumstances, previous interactions) and materialities (costumes, buildings, desks, computers). (...) Hence, it is through presentification that an organisation identifies itself, and becomes or is identified.

Studying presentifiaction through the effects of materialization also allows CCO scholars to understand how an organization, or any collective, can come to exist and have an identity, even without assuming intentionality from its (human) members (Wilhoit & Kisselburgh, 2015). Through aggregation effects and repetitive use, objects and spaces become infused with meaning and create a common community goal that can be recognized as such from the outside, even when its members ignore its existence. This was demonstrated in Wilhoit and Kisselburgh's (2015) study of a biker community that brought about attitude and infrastructure changes without explicit coordination or identity. This is quite distinctive from the usual theorizing on identity and identity work, which often puts the emphasis on conscious efforts to define one's identification to an organization, or to produce organizational identity per se.

Identities, then, exist through people, objects and spaces: business signs (as seen above), social media publications (Dawson 2018; Sörgärde, 2020) or gossip (Fan et al., 2020), for instance, are not poor, partial or biased perceptions of what an organization "really" is, but rather are many different materializations of an organization's performed identity. In this sense, a CCO perspective on "identity matters" – taking into account the materiality of identity – blurs boundaries, and bridges internal and external communication (Cheney et al., 2014; Meisenbach & Mcmillan, 2006).

Identity is Central to Major Organizational Processes

Identity matters infuse most, if not all, organizational concerns and processes, as well as their outcomes, in the sense that *organizing and the constitution of organizations both require, produce and reproduce identities*. A CCO perspective on organizational identity thus invites analysts to explore how communication recursively affects identities, which, in turn, further influence the performance of organizational activities. Turning our attention to the structurationist, Montréal School and Luhmannian schools of CCO (Brummans et al., 2014; Schoeneborn et al., 2014), we can note how the Four-Flows Model (McPhee et Zaug, 2009), influenced by Giddens's structuration theory, best exemplifies an emphasis on the prevalence of identity matters in major organizational processes. Identity is featured in each of the major "flows" that make an organization what it is, according to this model. Indeed, *membership negotiation* supposes the attributions of roles and identities, and of membership itself, as a constitutive category (Bencherki & Snack, 2016). This negotiation process is also central to organizational identification, described as a communicative process whereby identities become resources that are drawn upon and reproduced by members (Scott et al., 1998). Identifications are constitutive as they forge, maintain or alter "linkages between persons and groups" (Scott et al., 1998, p. 304), particularly during transition episodes (Chaput et al., 2011; Kuhn & Nelson, 2002; Larson & Pepper, 2003).

Reflexive self-structuring enables groups to represent themselves and perform identity work at the organizational level, notably through the use of texts (McPhee, 2004). Examples include leadership development programmes that actively reconfigure leaders' identities through texts and conversations (Meier & Carroll, 2020), and self-description in the form of strategy documents, which convey the organization's aspirations regarding corporate social responsibility (Penttilä, 2020). The *activity coordination* flow also generates roles, authority relations and responsibilities, building identities that emerge from the work activities themselves, like a surgical team communicating to conduct an operation effectively, or authors collaborating to write, edit and revise a manuscript (McPhee & Iverson, 2013). Finally, *institutional positioning* amounts to a type of identity negotiation (Putnam et al., 2009), where the organization communicates with its surroundings to develop and maintain its place in a larger social system. This type of communication materializes in printed words and pictures, as in the case of the propaganda outlet analyzed by Bruscella and Bisel (2018), but also involves various other material resources imbued with organizational symbolism. Lastly, as the four flows combine to constitute organizations, they lead to identity negotiation and change (Browning et al., 2009).

Identity is Vital to the Emergence of Organizational Actorhood

One of CCO's seminal texts explains how *identity is essential for the constitution of the organization as an actor* (Taylor & Van Every, 2000). People build and reinforce identities through *conversations* that sediment into a *text*, materialized in meeting minutes, mission statements, policies, strategic plans and other supports. This text changes the organization from a network of practices into a *metaconversation*: "the conversation in which a collective identity is constituted that is larger than that of the smaller communities of practice making up the organization" (Robichaud et al., 2004, p. 618). The recursivity of language, the use of documents, but also materializations of nonhuman agents all participate in the emergence of a collective actor. The latter is shaped by a narrative "that expresses the point of view of the organization *itself* as a single unity", hence, "a collective identity begins to take shape" (Taylor et al., 1996, p. 24; italics in original). Identity is thus performed when an authorized agent, including a text, speaks in its name, through what Austin (1962) would call "declarative" statements. Not unlike McPhee and Zaug's (2009) institutional positioning (see also Bruscella & Bisel, 2018), the organization's identity is negotiated internally, in regard to authority, and externally, as a legitimate, recognizable actor. As Taylor and his colleagues (1996) explain: "only by the ability to participate in interaction as a recognized voice is identity achieved" (p. 26).

At the moment, the exploration of organizational actorhood in CCO is mostly restricted to studies concerned with how performing identity is crucial to organizations that are precarious, temporary (Koschmann, 2013), or even contested or threatened in their existence (Dobusch & Schoeneborn, 2015; Dawson, 2018). Collective identity, in this sense, is tied to an organization's existence and its ability to act, and the absence of collective identity can have dire consequences, for example by leading to inaction (Koschmann, 2013). CCO studies show that collective identity is central in producing authority, because it acts as an authoritative text and key in fostering coordination (Koschmann, 2013; Kuhn, 2008), but also in producing *organizationality* (a notion comparable to actorhood; see Dobusch & Schoeneborn, 2015) and substance (a common basis for collective action; see Chaput et al., 2011; Dawson, 2018). When identity claims uttered in conversation are turned into text, they are detached from their initial context and become reified. In this form, they become available for joint scrutiny and enable coorientation, and as such they are reappropriated by organizational members as a common reference for collective action. This double process of abstraction and distanciation of identity can be the product of day-to-day interactions, and can span across many years and generations of organizational members (Chreim, 2005; Basque & Langley, 2018). Identity claims – by stating what an organization is and what it does, and therefore what actions pertain to it or not – participate in the attribution of an action to an organization, thus producing actorhood (Taylor et al., 1996). CCO studies have thus shown that identity is central to the organization's persistence as an entity, but also that it is fundamental in its capacity to act as a collective actor.

Identity is Accomplished in an Autoreferential Manner

A CCO perspective conceives that *organizational identity is recursively accomplished in communication events, through an ongoing, autoreferential process*. More particularly, the Luhmannian school of CCO (Schoeneborn, 2011; Seidl & Becker, 2006) explains that "the organization only exists as long as it manages to produce further communications, which call forth yet more communications" (Schoeneborn, 2011, p. 670; see also Grothe-Hammer, this volume). Communicating an organization's identity is thus an incessant affair, as decisions that distinguish the organization from its environment are communicated and form the basis of further decisions, thus constituting organizational actorhood (Dobusch & Schoeneborn, 2015). However, this process also reveals the organization's contingency, as communicating decisions also reveals the existence of *alternatives*: indeed, other decisions could have been made instead. Thus, identities pre-suppose *selection*, and therefore the exclusion of alternatives. Understood as a self-referential, autopoietic process, identity becomes a driving force to overcome existential instability and turmoil. Acting to maintain *the self as itself*, it precludes inevitable divisions and tensions, and contributes to reducing "the almost infinite number of potential options" to a limited, more manageable set of options (Schoeneborn, 2011, p. 675). It is through consistent decision-making, dependent on previous decisions being communicated and taken-up again in new decision episodes, that organizations become *identifiable over time* (Chreim, 2005). This understanding of identity thus directs attention to the ways in which recognizable organizational features are generated and reproduced in communication (Cooren & Seidl, 2020; Seidl, 2005).

Auto-referentiality is tightly related to materialization and actorhood, as human agents can delegate the task of deciding between alternatives on the basis of prior decisions to non-human agents (texts, symbols, objects and so on). These non-human agents will, in turn, speak on behalf of the organization and contribute to its presence in the world and its constitution as a collective self (Cheong et al., 2014). In CCO, studying how one identifies with an organization, or how people constitute organizational identity, is therefore not only a matter of observing who speaks on behalf of the organization in an autoreferential manner, but also means documenting how networks of various agents contribute to this ongoing process through various spaces and times.

As a summary to this section, a provisional definition of organizational identity, based on CCO research, can be formulated. *Organizational identity is (1) constituted in communication, (2) expressed through materializations, (3) central to major organizational processes, (4) vital to the emergence of organizational actorhood, and (5) accomplished in an autoreferential manner.* These five features do not exhaust the notion of identity, and our exploration of identity matters will be further developed in the next section. Building on our discussion so far, we introduce the concept of *identity matters* as a heuristic tool to analyze how identity materializes; that is, to explore how it is created and performed without leaving the realm of communication events. In the next section, we analyze a discussion with members of a police organization to illustrate its analytical usefulness, and show how this concept connects to our fivefold definition of identity.

Exploring Identity Matters in a Police Organization

So far in this chapter, we have used the expression *identity matters* without properly defining it. In that expression, we capture the multitude of concerns and issues related to identity, without attempting to list or define them prior to their communicative materialization. Firmly anchored in our CCO-inspired definition of organizational identity, identity matters, as a concept, operates as a heuristic device to think, talk and write about identity while remaining firmly anchored in the realm of communication events. Its aim is to embrace all forms of identity, whether personal, collective or otherwise, and focus analytical attention on their sociomaterial incarnations, presentifications and identifications. What matters for any particular identity is not only up to us to express, as researchers: it is a constant concern for members, leaders, experts, rivals, stakeholders, journalists, commentators, advocates, etc. Through negotiation, the people and things that animate an organization provisionally establish what matters *more or less* for themselves and for their collective, as mattering is not dichotomous, but an issue of degree (Cooren, 2015). The concept of identity matters hints at the fact that, in order to matter *more*, elements that compose an indentity must take on additional materializations – for instance, the same value may be expressed by multiple people in their speech, it may be written on a poster, it may be encoded in a piece of software, etc. Hence, identities become materialized through objects, sites and bodies (Ashcraft et al., 2009) in virtually infinite combinations that include physical traits and body features (Gatrell, 2013; Trethewey, 1999), clothing (Guy & Banim, 2000), language use and tongues (Bencherki et al., 2016), in addition to documents, signs, buildings, artefacts, stories (both of the verbal and Instagram types), and numerous other elements. Studying identity in a communicative perspective, then, implies identifying how and to what degree it is made to matter, as all identity expressions materialize in communication (see Cooren, 2020).

To illustrate the relevance of studying identity matters from a CCO perspective, let us turn our attention to an excerpt from a recorded group interview, in which the second author speaks with members of a Canadian Police Organization[1] (CPO) about their work activities. The excerpt is part of fieldwork conducted over a period of 13 months, during which the second author conducted 80 group interviews with employees at all hierarchical levels of the CPO, who participated voluntarily. Group interviews (with 5 to 20 employees) were loosely structured and centered on five themes: work climate, leadership, decision-making processes, organizational structure and organizational belonging. In this particular excerpt, a group of experienced officers discuss their sense of pride and their work at the CPO, in response to a question from the interviewer derived from one of the themes.

1 2	Interviewer:	Hem, yes. What about the other members, your pride, your sense of belonging here at the CPO?
3 4	Gilbert:	For my part, I lost it about three years ago, because when I was fighting crime, I was happy.
5	Interviewer:	Ok.
6	Gilbert:	Now I'm fighting the CPO administration.
7	Jim:	Yeah.
8	Peter:	And there you go.
9 10	Ned:	We're not doing police work any more. We don't help the client, we [inaudible]
11	Jim:	We're bureaucrats!
12 13	Steven:	Because before, before when we went out on the highway, we went out with our marked vehicle …
14	Ned:	And we had a goal, and …
15 16	Steven:	We went out in uniform, we went out. When the CPO went out, it went out. People …
17	Guy:	They saw us.
18	Steven:	We had a sense of belonging, we were proud to go out and do good.
19	Leo:	You'd see the convoy of vehicles.
20	Ned:	Oh yeah, that was pride.
21	Steven:	When we went somewhere, everyone knew it was coming.
22	[. . .]	
23	Gilbert:	We still feel proud though.
24	(Several):	Yeah, we do.
25	Paul:	That, you can't take it away from me.
26	Interviewer:	Ok.
27 28 29 30	Ned:	Well no, that's it, it's when we were here, when we were involved in [a project] and we were working with [another police organization], and we did interventions, we were in the newspaper, everywhere. Jeez it was fun! Yeah, we were proud to work here.

While not overtly framed as a question about identity, the question from the interviewer nonetheless conveys an invitation to respond in terms of identification. It is also an attempt to ponder the importance of professional identity: their pride in accomplishing police work. Thus, we enter the realm of identity matters, of what matters more *for them*.

Spontaneous responses abound and align to express a shared appreciation, or rather, dissatisfaction, toward their employer. Gilbert answers first (lines 3–6), with subsequent turns of talk by colleagues Jim, Peter, and Ned reinforcing his position (lines 7–11). Steven's reply, although it spans several turns of talk, can be understood as a short narrative about how working for the CPO used to be different in previous years, enriched with comments by fellow officers Guy, Leo and Ned (lines 12–21). Following a pause (line 22), Gilbert takes the floor, once more mentioning an enduring pride (line 23), probably to attenuate his previous statement about losing his sense of belonging (and the conclusion that the listener may draw from his narrative: that he is not proud any more), followed by words of approval from his colleagues (lines 24–30). It seems unclear though, here, whether this sense of pride is targeted towards past accomplishments in the field, or is something felt in regard to current work activities, especially by looking at Ned's story and use of past tense (lines 27–30).

In the CPO officers' responses, the identity expressions, while uttered in the "here and now" of the recorded interview, are effectively *dis-located in time and space* (Hall, 1992), as well as incarnated in *matters*, or at least, in images of material agencies. The temporal dislocation is concretely materialized in talk through Gilbert's explicit mention of the identity transition that would be measurable in years (line 3), as well as in participants' use of terms such as "any more" and "before", and their reliance on the past tense to refer to times when they were proud, in contrast with use of the present tense to indicate their new status as "bureaucrats". The past and present are associated with vocabulary referring to different activities (fighting crime vs fighting the administration), spaces (the field vs, presumably, the office) and embodiments (moving in convoys while wearing uniforms). Their identity, thus, materializes in the contrast between two different temporalities associated with different concrete objects, spaces and embodied movements.

Also, the repeated mention by Steven of the expedition missions, of going out and *being out there* (lines 12–13, 15–16), as well as Ned's allusion to newspaper coverage of their activities (line 29), implies that they were visible and audible, *presentified and materialized*, seen and heard, and recognized, by other people. Guy, Leo and Steven (lines 16–21) voice how their pride is enticingly related to these *public materializations* of the CPO. For them, the CPO convoy was a communication performance they collectively enjoyed and felt pride in. Ned's closing intervention (lines 27–30) astutely summarizes this component of a CPO officer's identity matters, in terms of both what matters for them, and the matters that compose their preferred identity, by speaking of involvement in the mission, a common goal, collaboration with other police organizations whose identity they would perform with them, through interventions and their media repercussions. Pride seems interwoven with their institutional positioning as CPO field officers, and heroes deemed as newsworthy. To rephrase Weick's (1995) formula, these police officers may wonder: *how can we know who we are until we see what they say?*

The materialization of identity is not only seen in the content, but also in the performance of the discussion, as officers participate actively in elaborating on Steven's narrative through successive turns of talk, and providing additional dimensions to the story. Through their collective participation in storytelling, they also move from individual identity (Gilbert explicitly limits the scope of his initial intervention by specifying "For my part", seen on line 3) to collective identity, which is noticeable as they switch to the first person plural (Ned, line 9). While categories and types of identity (personal, group, professional, collective, and others) remain relevant tools for analysis, the relative merit of addressing situations in terms of identity matters is to illustrate how such categories are displayed, discussed or challenged by those observed during interactions. We witness the subtle moves by which the officers transition from individual to a collective narrative of self in their talk, by switching from "I" to "we" but also by approving or completing their colleagues' story. This first occurs as Jim, Peter and Ned voice their support of Gilbert's account (lines 7–11). We witness it once more as Steven's story is backed up by Ned, Guy, Leo and Paul (lines 12–21). Therefore, by sticking to interactions, we can observe how matters play an active part in the narrative by which identities, those of the CPO and its officers, are collectively constituted.

In this short analysis, we see that the concept of identity matters encompasses the five features of identity conceptualization in a CCO perspective. Identity is constituted in communication, not only in the content of the discussion, but in the way this discussion unfolds, as the collective self is materialized through a narrative elaborated in close collaboration. Identity is expressed through successive materializations of various elements that make a difference in the conversation. In this case, these are the officers' pride (or absence of), the public eye (through which these police officers exist as such), or objects that embody and illustrate the police identity. Identity is central to major organizational processes, and these discursive materializations allow for institutional positioning, collaboration, and even membership to be concretized and actualized in talk. Actorhood ensues, as collective selves are created and display agency (or contest the fact that they are denied this agency as they are stuck in bureaucrat roles, in contrast to police officers' roles). Finally, autoreferentiality is seen in the way they relate past and current selves, as well as material agents and principles that embody the organization's mission of serving the public.

Continuing the Exploration of Identity Matters from a CCO Perspective

In this chapter, we discussed how a CCO perspective contributes an original answer to enduring questions about the nature of organizational identity. We uncovered how each of the CCO schools of thought – the structurationist (Four Flows), the Montréal School and Luhmannian approaches – contributes to a communicative theory of organizational identity. Accordingly, the CCO perspective answers the call to theorize identity from within the field of organizational communication (Scott, 2007). The main contribution of a CCO perspective on identity matters, consequently, consists of the formulation of a genuinely communicative view of identity. We've seen that, under the CCO umbrella, conversations, stories, documents, artefacts, images, bodies, etc., create, contest, negotiate, reaffirm, i.e., *accomplish identities*, notably through materializations and autoreferentiality, thus producing membership, collaboration and actorhood, among other things. This can be seen in the small, but rapidly growing, CCO-inspired body of work on identities, illustrating how their conceptual and empirical contributions blur the boundaries between the three schools of thought to explore new and fertile ground in the study of organizational communication. Highlighting these contributions allowed us to bring our own stone to the building as we introduced the concept of identity matters to grasp the materializations of identities. We illustrated its relevance as we analyzed an engaged discussion between police officers regarding the recent evolution of their work situation and the ensuing consequences for them.

However, while we have shown that CCO has the conceptual apparatus to offer this form of theorizing, identity remains an understudied phenomenon in CCO scholarship. That is why we invite further contributions, concluding this chapter with suggestions for future work regarding (1) theoretical developments, (2) methodological preferences, and (3) thematic explorations.

At the theoretical level, we highlighted how the CCO schools of thought emphasized five different dimensions of the communicative foundation of identity in organizations, which inspired us with the concept of "identity matters". Thus, this concept implicitly relies on the combination of diverse theories and theoretical groundings that fuel CCO thinking. To continue in this vein, CCO scholars could enrich their theorizing of identity matters by drawing from authors with solid roots in organizational communication, who have been inspirations for CCO research but have not (or rarely) been used to study identity. We have used some in our own work. We can mention here Burke's (1969) rhetoric of identification (Chaput et al., 2011; Chaput, 2012), and Ricoeur's (1984, 1985, 1988) theory of narrative identity (Basque, 2013). Let us not forget Foucault's (1977, 1978) theory of subjectivity or Butler's (1990, 1993) performative theory of gender (see McDonald, this volume), among others. As shown in this chapter, where the concept of identity matters relies on diverse but complementary CCO theories, cross-fertilization between renowned philosophers of identity and CCO theories and concepts would also open up new possibilities to address identity matters more directly, as they often remain peripheral to the main object of inquiry in CCO studies.

Concerns for methods have been sketched rather roughly in this chapter regarding the study of identity from a CCO perspective. Cited works have relied so far on a diverse array of methods and fields: from the close study of interactions (Chaput et al., 2011) to long-range observations (Koschmann, 2013), from interviews (Wilhoit & Kisselburgh, 2015) to archives (Basque & Langley, 2018). However, the relative merits and potential limitations of each method have yet to be discussed in the context of the exploration of identity matters. Emerging domains of inquiry in the field of organizational communication also raise new methodological challenges and propose new opportunities for innovation in the study of identity from a CCO perspective. This has been well illustrated by the investment in digital ethnographies to pursue social media communicative practices (Albu & Etter, 2016; Clifton & de la Broise, 2020; Dawson, 2018; Dobusch & Schoeneborn, 2015), where the notion of matters itself becomes challenged in different directions.

Contributions on connected themes such as branding (McDonald & Kuhn, 2016; Vásquez et al., 2013) and authority (Benoit-Barné & Cooren, 2009; Koschmann & Burk, 2016) could benefit from, and contribute to, further exploration of identity matters. These crucial issues would help reveal the role of identity as a social and political marker, which has yet to be fully explored from a CCO perspective (see McDonald, this volume). Indeed, identities entail cooperation and belonging, but also exclusion and antagonism. As such, the materialization of identity matters through communication allows reifying and therefore comparing, weighing, or even confronting these matters. Voicing identity matters by saying them out loud in specific ways, using certain words, in this or that sentence, by expressing or concealing them through bodily features, clothing choices, behaviors, and so on, enables participants to discover whether their identities are similar, conflicting, complementary, or something else. In this sense, the study of identity matters could also be employed to investigate more sensitive areas of research and concern, where communication might materialize various forms of suffering, inequality and division.

Note

1 All names are pseudonyms.

References

Albert, S., & Whetten, D. A. (1985). Organizational identity. *Research in Organizational Behavior, 7,* 263–295.

Albu, O. B., & Etter, M. (2016). Hypertextuality and social media: A study of the constitutive and paradoxical implications of organizational Twitter use. *Management Communication Quarterly, 30*(1), 5–31.

Ashcraft, K. L., Kuhn, T. R., & Cooren, F. (2009). Constitutional amendments: "Materializing" organizational communication. *Academy of Management Annals, 3*(1), 1–64. https://doi.org/10.5465/194165 20903047186.

Austin, J. L. (1962). *How to do things with words.* Harvard University Press.

Basque, J. (2013). Narrativité et temporalité dans la construction identitaire en contexte organisationnel. Thèse de doctorat, Université de Montréal. https://papyrus.bib.umontreal.ca/xmlui/handle/ 1866/9858.

Basque, J., & Langley, A. (2018). Invoking Alphonse: The founder figure as a historical resource for organizational identity work. *Organization Studies,* 0170840618789211. https://doi.org/10.1177/ 0170840618789211.

Bencherki, N., Matte, F., & Pelletier, É. (2016). Rebuilding Babel: A constitutive approach to tongues-in-use. *Journal of Communication, 66*(5), 766–788. https://doi.org/10.1111/jcom.12250.

Bencherki, N., & Snack, J. P. (2016). Contributorship and partial inclusion: A communicative perspective. *Management Communication Quarterly, 30*(3), 279–304. https://doi.org/10.1177/0893318915624163.

Benoit-Barné, C., & Cooren, F. (2009). The accomplishment of authority through presentification: How authority is distributed among and negotiated by organizational members. *Management Communication Quarterly, 23*(1), 5–31. https://doi.org/10.1177/0893318909335414.

Brown, A. D. (2019). Identities in organization studies. *Organization Studies, 40*(1), 7–22. https://doi.org/ 10.1177/0170840618765014.

Browning, L. D., Greene, R. W., Sitkin, S. B., Sutcliffe, K. M., & Obstfeld, D. (2009). Constitutive complexity: Military entrepreneurs and the synthetic character of communication flows. In L. L. Putnam & A. M. Nicotera (Eds.), *Building theories of organization. The constitutive role of communication* (pp. 89–116). Routledge.

Brummans, B. H. J. M., Cooren, F., & Chaput, M. (2009). Discourse, communication and organizational ontology. In F. Bargiela-Chiappini (Ed.), *The handbook of business discourse* (pp. 53–67). Edinburgh University Press.

Brummans, B. H. J. M., Cooren, F., Robichaud, D., & Taylor, J. R. (2014). Approaches to the communicative constitution of organizations. In L. L. Putnam & D. K. Mumby (Eds.), *The Sage handbook of organizational communication* (3rd edn., pp. 173–194). Sage.

Bruscella, J. S., & Bisel, R. S. (2018). Four Flows theory and materiality: ISIL's use of material resources in its communicative constitution. *Communication Monographs, 85*(3), 331–356. https://doi.org/10.1080/ 03637751.2017.1420907.

Burke, K. (1969). *A rhetoric of motives.* University of California Press.

Butler, J. (1990). *Gender trouble.* Routledge.

Butler, J. (1993). *Bodies that matter. On the discursive limits of sex.* Routledge.

Chaput, M. (2012). Communiquer la genèse de l'organisation: L'invention rhétorique de Québec solidaire. Thèse de doctorat, Université de Montréal. https://papyrus.bib.umontreal.ca/xmlui/ handle/1866/7011.

Chaput, M., Brummans, B. H. J. M., & Cooren, F. (2011). The role of organizational identification in the communicative constitution of an organization: A study of consubstantialization in a young political party. *Management Communication Quarterly, 25*(2), 252–282. https://doi.org/10.1177/089331891 0386719.

Cheney, G., Christensen, L. T., & Dailey, S. (2014). Communicating identity and identification in and around organizations. In L. L. Putnam & D. K. Mumby (Ed.), *The Sage handbook of organizational communication: Advances in theory, research, and methods* (3rd edn., pp. 695–716). Sage.

Cheong, P. H., Hwang, J. M., & Brummans, B. H. J. M. (2014). Transnational immanence: The autopoietic co-constitution of a Chinese spiritual organization through mediated communication. *Information, Communication & Society, 17*(1), 7–25. https://doi.org/10.1080/1369118X.2013.833277.

Chreim, S. (2002). Influencing organizational identification during major change: A communication-based perspective. *Human Relations, 55*(9), 1117–1137. https://doi.org/10.1177/001872670205 5009022.

Chreim, S. (2005). The continuity-change duality in narrative texts of organizational identity. *Journal of Management Studies*, 42(3), 567–593. https://doi.org/10.1111/j.1467-6486.2005.00509.x.

Clifton, J., & de la Broise, P. (2020). The yellow vests and the communicative constitution of a protest movement. *Discourse & Communication*, 14(4), 362–382. https://doi.org/10.1177/1750481320910516.

Cooren, F. (2015). In medias res: Communication, existence, and materiality. *Communication Research and Practice*, 1(4), 1–15. https://doi.org/10.1080/22041451.2015.1110075.

Cooren, F. (2020). Beyond entanglement: (Socio-) Materiality and organization studies. *Organization Theory*, 1(3), 2631787720954444. https://doi.org/10.1177/2631787720954444.

Cooren, F., Brummans, B. H. J. M., & Charrieras, D. (2008). The coproduction of organizational presence: A study of Médecins Sans Frontières in action. *Human Relations*, 61(10), 1339–1370. https://doi.org/10.1177/0018726708095707.

Cooren, F., Kuhn, T., Cornelissen, J. P., & Clark, T. (2011). Communication, organizing and organization: An overview and introduction to the special issue. *Organization Studies*, 32(9), 1149–1170. https://doi.org/10.1177/0170840611410836.

Cooren, F., Matte, F., Taylor, J. R., & Vásquez, C. (2007). A humanitarian organization in action: Organizational discourse as an immutable mobile: Discourse & Communication. https://doi.org/10.1177/1750481307075996.

Cooren, F., & Seidl, D. (2020). Niklas Luhmann's Radical Communication Approach and Its Implications for Research on Organizational Communication. *Academy of Management Review*, 45(2), 479–497. https://doi.org/10.5465/amr.2018.0176.

Corley, K. G., Harquail, C. V., Pratt, M. G., Glynn, M. A., Fiol, C. M., & Hatch, M. J. (2006). Guiding organizational identity through aged adolescence. *Journal of Management Inquiry*, 15(2), 85–99. https://doi.org/10.1177/1056492605285930.

Dawson, V. R. (2018). Fans, Friends, Advocates, Ambassadors, and Haters: Social media communities and the communicative constitution of organizational identity: *Social Media + Society*. https://doi.org/10.1177/2056305117746356.

Dobusch, L., & Schoeneborn, D. (2015). Fluidity, identity, and organizationality: The communicative constitution of Anonymous. *Journal of Management Studies* https://doi.org/10.1111/joms.12139.

Fan, Z., Grey, C., & Kärreman, D. (2020). Confidential gossip and organization studies. *Organization Studies*, 0170840620954016. https://doi.org/10.1177/0170840620954016.

Foucault, M. (1977). *Discipline and punish. The birth of the prison.* Random House.

Foucault, M. (1978). *The history of sexuality, Vol. 1: An introduction.* Random House.

Gatrell, C. J. (2013). Maternal body work: How women managers and professionals negotiate pregnancy and new motherhood at work. *Human Relations*, 66(5), 621–644. https://doi.org/10.1177/0018726713 2467380.

Guy, A., & Banim, M. (2000). Personal collections: Women's clothing use and identity. *Journal of Gender Studies*, 9(3), 313–327. https://doi.org/10.1080/713678000.

Hall, S. (1992). The question of cultural identity. In A. McGrew, S. Hall, & D. Held (Eds.), *Modernity and its futures: Understanding modern societies, Book IV* (pp. 273–316). Polity Press.

Hatch, M. J., & Schultz, M. (2002). The dynamics of organizational identity. *Human Relations*, 55(8), 989–1018.

Koshmann, M. (2013). The communicative constitution of collective identity in interorganizational collaboration. *Management Communication Quarterly*, 27(1), 61–89. https://doi.org/10.1177/089331891 2449314.

Koschmann, M. A., & Burk, N. R. (2016). Accomplishing authority in collaborative work. *Western Journal of Communication*, 80(4), 393–413. https://doi.org/10.1080/10570314.2016.1159728.

Kuhn, T. (2008). A communicative theory of the firm: Developing an alternative perspective on intra-organizational power and stakeholder relationships. *Organization Studies*, 29(8–9), 1227–1254. https://doi.org/10.1177/0170840608094778.

Kuhn, T., & Nelson, N. (2002). Reengineering identity: A case study of multiplicity and duality in organizational identification. *Management Communication Quarterly*, 16(1), 5–38. https://doi.org/10.1177/0893318902161001.

Larson, G. S., & Gill, R. (2017). *Organizations and identity.* Polity Press.

Larson, G. S., & Pepper, G. L. (2003). Strategies for managing multiple organizational identifications: A case of competing identities. *Management Communication Quarterly*, 16(4), 528–557. https://doi.org/10.1177/0893318903251626.

Latour, B. (2013). *An inquiry into modes of existence.* Harvard University Press.

McDonald, J., & Kuhn, T. R. (2016). Occupational branding for diversity: Managing discursive contradictions. *Journal of Applied Communication Research, 44*(2), 101–117. https://doi.org/10.1080/00909882.2016.1155725.

McPhee, R. D. (2004). Text, agency, and organization in the light of structuration theory. *Organization, 11*(3), 355–371. https://doi.org/10.1177/1350508404041997.

McPhee, R. D., & Iverson, J. O. (2013). Activity coordination and the Montreal School. In D. Robichaud & F. Cooren (Eds.), *Organization and organizing. Materiality, agency and discourse* (pp. 109–125). Routledge.

McPhee, R. D., & Zaug, D. (2009). The communicative constitution of organizations. A framework for explanation. In L. L. Putnam & A. M. Nicotera (Eds.), *Building theories of organization: The constitutive role of communication* (pp. 21–47). Routledge.

Meier, F., & Carroll, B. (2020). Making up leaders: Reconfiguring the executive student through profiling, texts and conversations in a leadership development programme. *Human Relations, 73*(9), 1226–1248. https://doi.org/10.1177/0018726719858132.

Meisenbach, R. J., & Mcmillan, J. J. (2006). Blurring the boundaries: Historical developments and future directions in organizational rhetoric. *Annals of the International Communication Association, 30*(1), 99–141. https://doi.org/10.1080/23808985.2006.11679056.

Penttilä, V. (2020). Aspirational talk in strategy texts: A longitudinal case study of strategic episodes in corporate social responsibility communication. *Business & Society, 59*(1), 67–97. https://doi.org/10.1177/0007650319825825.

Pratt, M. G., Schultz, M., Ashforth, B. E., & Ravasi, D. (Eds.). (2016). *The Oxford handbook of organizational identity*. Oxford University Press. https://doi.org/10.1093/oxfordhb/9780199689576.001.0001.

Putnam, L. L., Nicotera, A. M., & McPhee, R. D. (2009). Introduction. Communication constitutes organization. In L. L. Putnam & A. M. Nicotera (Eds.), *Building theories of organization. The constitutive role of communication* (pp. 1–19). Routledge.

Ricoeur, P. (1984). *Time and narrative, Volume 1*. University of Chicago Press.

Ricoeur, P. (1985). *Time and narrative, Volume 2*. University of Chicago Press.

Ricoeur, P. (1988). *Time and narrative, Volume 3*. University of Chicago Press.

Robichaud, D., Giroux, H., & Taylor, J. R. (2004). The metaconversation: The recursive property of language as a key to organizing. *Academy of Management Review, 29*(4), 617–634. https://doi.org/10.5465/amr.2004.14497614.

Schoeneborn, D. (2011). Organization as communication: A Luhmannian perspective. *Management Communication Quarterly, 25*(4), 663–689. https://doi.org/10.1177/0893318911405622.

Schoeneborn, D., Blaschke, S., Cooren, F., McPhee, R. D., Seidl, D., & Taylor, J. R. (2014). The Three schools of CCO thinking: Interactive dialogue and systematic comparison. *Management Communication Quarterly*. https://doi.org/10.1177/0893318914527000.

Schoeneborn, D., & Scherer, A. G. (2012). Clandestine organizations, al Qaeda, and the paradox of (in)visibility: A response to Stohl and Stohl. *Organization Studies, 33*(7), 963–971. https://doi.org/10.1177/0170840612448031.

Scott, C. R. (2007). Communication and social identity theory: Existing and Potential connections in organizational identification research. *Communication Studies, 58*(2), 123–138. https://doi.org/10.1080/10510970701341063.

Scott, C. R. (2020). Identity and identification. In A. M. Nicotera (Ed.), *Origins and traditions of organizational communication: A comprehensive introduction to the field*. Routledge. www.routledge.com/Origins-and-Traditions-of-Organizational-Communication-A-Comprehensive/Nicotera/p/book/9781138570313.

Scott, C. R., Corman, S. R., & Cheney, G. (1998). Development of a structurational model of identification in the organization. *Communication Theory, 8*(3), 298–336. https://doi.org/10.1111/j.1468-2885.1998.tb00223.x.

Seidl, D. (2005). *Organisational identity and self-transformation: An autopoietic perspective*. Routledge.

Seidl, D., & Becker, K. H. (2006). Organizations as distinction generating and processing systems: Niklas Luhmann's contribution to organization studies. *Organization, 13*(1), 9–35. https://doi.org/10.1177/1350508406059635.

Soar, M. (2009, April 11). A brief history. *Farine Five Roses Art Project*. www.farinefiveroses.ca/a-brief-history-of-the-sign.

Sörgärde, N. (2020). Story-dismantling, story-meandering, and story-confirming: Organizational identity work in times of public disgrace. *Scandinavian Journal of Management, 36*(3), 101105. https://doi.org/10.1016/j.scaman.2020.101105.

Taylor, J. R., Cooren, F., Giroux, N., & Robichaud, D. (1996). The communicational basis of organization: Between the conversation and the text. *Communication Theory, 6*(1), 1–39. https://doi.org/10.1111/j.1468-2885.1996.tb00118.x.

Taylor, J. R., & Van Every, E. J. (2000). *The emergent organization: Communication as its site and surface.* Routledge.

Trethewey, A. (1999). Disciplined bodies: Women's embodied identities at work. *Organization Studies, 20*(3), 423–450. https://doi.org/10.1177/0170840699203003.

van Vuuren, M., & Westerhof, G. J. (2015). Identity as "knowing your place": The narrative construction of space in a healthcare profession. *Journal of Health Psychology, 20*(3), 326–337. https://doi.org/10.1177/1359105314566614.

Vásquez, C., Sergi, V., & Cordelier, B. (2013). From being branded to doing branding: Studying representation practices from a communication-centered approach. *Scandinavian Journal of Management, 29*(2), 135–146.

Weick, K. (1995). *Sensemaking in organizations.* Sage.

Whetten, D. A. (2006). Albert and Whetten revisited: Strengthening the concept of organizational identity. *Journal of Management Inquiry, 15*(3), 219–234. https://doi.org/10.1177/1056492606291200.

Wieland, S. M. B. (2017). Organizational identity. In C. R. Scott & L. K. Lewis (Eds.), *The international encyclopedia of organizational communication* (pp. 1–14). Wiley. https://doi.org/10.1002/9781118955567.wbieoc156.

Wilhoit, E. D., & Kisselburgh, L. G. (2015). Collective action without organization: The material constitution of bike commuters as collective. *Organization Studies, 36*(5), 573–592. https://doi.org/10.1177/0170840614556916.

20

WHAT'S IN A PROJECT? EXTENDING INQUIRIES INTO PROJECTS WITH A CCO PERSPECTIVE

Viviane Sergi

Opening

Projects are endeavours with features that should attract the attention of researchers interested in organizational issues. Three such features come to mind. The first characteristic that imposes itself when we think of projects is their temporary nature, which is integral to what projects are. A second feature is that they have, in comparison to other forms of organization, a clear and single aim. While projects may pursue more than one aim, there is in most instances a dominant objective that centrally justifies the project and directs action. The third defining feature is that *conception* and *execution* efforts continually co-exist in a very obvious way as projects are being realized (Boutinet, 2018). Indeed, being involved in a project implies working to set it up and organizing for it to happen, and at the same time progressively materializing what it aims to achieve. When we speak of "a project", we thus refer to two aspects that are inseparable: what Boutinet (2018) identifies as the *poiesis* of the project (the realization of something that will become concrete at some point) and its *praxis* (the organizing of the project itself).

This third feature makes projects, in my opinion, particularly intriguing. In spite of all the energy invested in planning projects before they actually begin, and of all the expectations of control of the course of action that lurk beneath such efforts in planning, working in projects can never be simply about neatly executing what has been planned and decided before taking action. As action directed towards the completion of something (ranging from the small to the big, from physical products to ephemeral events) progresses, reorganizing its planning to take into consideration what has happened becomes necessary—and usually, more than once (Sergi, 2012). It is in this sense that conception (referring to the elaboration, planning and preparation for project work to take place) and execution (engaging in the work needed to move towards the completion of the project) are constantly in a dynamic state, each one influencing the other. This is not to say that planning is a futile exercise, as such efforts invested in planning are, in most organizational settings, a prerequisite for projects gaining approval. Furthermore, as Suchman (2007) has argued, plans are useful resources for action. The dynamic relationship between conception and execution is rather a reminder that unfolding action can never be fully pinned down in a plan written beforehand and will necessarily escape and overflow what

DOI: 10.4324/9781003224914-24

is planned. Such coexistence of anticipation and action/actual doing may in fact characterize much of what we do, and may not be specific to projects. The same applies to the temporary nature of projects: organizations that are not labelled as projects may appear more durable, but they are, in fact, just as transitory. However, given that projects are explicitly conceived as temporary and set up to make something happen or become "real", such features turn them into especially stimulating sites of inquiry: projects may offer researchers a vivid illustration of such constant oscillation between organizing *for* action and organizing *in* action, as irremediably bounded in limited time. The challenge then becomes how to conceptualize this oscillation—a challenge that, as I discuss, a communication-centred perspective is especially well suited to address.

Hence, this chapter aims to explore the potentialities of a communication-centred perspective (or CCO), especially one that is influenced by the Montréal School, for studying projects. I contend that a CCO perspective can allow researchers to think about projects differently from what we commonly find in the specialized field of project management. I pursue this reflection by engaging in an ontological reflection on what projects are. I start by quickly locating the study of projects. Recognizing that CCO has mainly been absent from the field of project studies, I then propose to extend the ontological reflection that it harbours to the concept of project, by mobilizing a few ideas developed by Jean-Pierre Boutinet, a French thinker who has reflected on this concept from an interdisciplinary standpoint, and then by connecting them with CCO. This allows me to show the ways in which CCO is a fruitful framework for the study of projects, as it can reconfigure conceptualizations as well as extend current lines of inquiry.

As a full-fledged field, project management covers a wide variety of sub-topics: project leadership, governance of projects, project team performance, risk management in projects, critical success factors, etc., that could all be interrogated from a CCO perspective. Here, I focus rather on the general concept of project, understood as a temporary organization. I find in CCO a perspective that offers a series of questions and concepts that can help push forward our understanding of these endeavours. But this chapter is more than a simple application of a *perspective* to an empirical *phenomenon*: I contend that there is a close, even intimate, connection between CCO and projects. By discussing just how fitting a communication-centred perspective is for projects, this chapter is also an appeal to recognize, fully embrace and take seriously the features that define phenomena as projects.

From Project Management to Project Studies to Projects as Communicatively Constituted

In management and organization studies, mentioning projects quickly leads to the field of project management. Projects are far from being new in human activities, but they only have been elevated to a legitimate research and practice field in recent decades—that of project management. Developing a full history of the field is beyond the scope of this chapter (readers interested in this history can consider Söderlund and Lenfle, 2013, or Garel, 2013), but the engineering and technical roots of this discipline have to be acknowledged, as they have conditioned much of the research conducted in this field and continue to exert a clear influence. Given these roots, it is not surprising to note that a vast majority of studies in project management are preoccupied with developing prescriptive knowledge of how projects should be managed, what tools, standards or structured approaches should be used by practitioners to increase project success and/or performance, etc. Hence, an overwhelmingly technical, functionalist and normative literature dominates in project management. This literature only pays scant attention to the actual practice of the specific activities that are associated with managing projects, tending to keep the *doing* of project management black-boxed. This more "technical" literature spans many theoretical and methodological traditions and does not constitute a unified body of literature; lumping together all these studies is necessarily reductive. Nonetheless, there are enough commonalities among this diverse research to contrast this first set of project literature to other perspectives that have arisen in the last two decades or so.

Indeed, the kind of research pursued in project management and the underlying conceptions of projects and project management have not gone unnoticed. Since the mid-1990s, several critiques have been levied at project management, including that quantitative models and studies anchored in a neopositivist epistemology dominate this field, that research prioritizes the elaboration of normative knowledge and that it overemphasizes rationality, planning and control (see for example Lundin and Söderholm, 1995, Packendorff, 1995, Cicmil et al., 2009, among many others). These critiques have also led to the identification of other forms of inquiry relevant for the study of projects and have allowed researchers to branch out and develop studies that approach projects as social phenomenon. Over the last two decades, studies privileging a focus on "social"[1] rather than "technical" issues have multiplied to a certain extent, viewing projects as social, relational, symbolic and political endeavours. The field of project management has thus seen the appearance of qualitative, interpretivist and critical inquiries, considering its underlying assumptions, its discourse, its models and tools and its implications for people working in projects. This in qualitatively documenting the experience of working in projects and the practices that are part of doing projects can be linked to the emergence of the Scandinavian school of project management (Sahlin-Andersson and Söderholm, 2002; notable early examples of contributions in this line include Lundin and Söderholm, 1995, Packendorff, 1995 and Engwall, 2003), and of critical studies of projects (e.g., Hodgson, 2002; Hodgson and Cicmil, 2006, 2016). These studies have been instrumental in counterbalancing the more technical approach to projects, by attending to what Cicmil et al. (2006) have aptly termed the *actuality* of projects. Such studies focus resolutely and primarily on the *lived* experience of projects and adopt a qualitative, longitudinal, and detailed view of the actual process of realizing projects. I thus distinguish—possibly a bit too hastily—studies on projects based on their attention, or lack thereof, to the concrete activities, actions and interactions that happen as projects are in progress and unfolding.

If it is not possible, in the few pages of this chapter, to present the wide variety of studies that I group under the "technical" label, neither is it possible to finely cover all of the contributions made by studies that have, each in their manner, aimed at opening this black box of project management and at challenging its engineering roots. Yet, without minimizing any of these contributions, I consider that there is still room to push our understanding of the actual doing of projects further, as seen from the perspective of what people do and experience on a daily basis, over time. Such an extension can rest on changing or multiplying the theoretical frames selected to approach project issues (as suggested by, among others, Söderlund, 2011, and Floricel et al., 2014; this is also reflected in the recent two-part special issue in *Project Management Journal* comprising 23 essays aimed at advancing theory in project studies[2]). But doing so implies an unequivocal move from a concern for project management, to project organizing and, more fundamentally, to the heart of what projects are. Instead of taking for granted what projects are, I concur with Söderlund (2013) that engaging in an ontological inquiry has the potential to create insights that can lead to novel theorizations of projects. In this sense, recognizing that there is more than techniques and prescriptive knowledge to projects, Geraldi and Söderlund (2016, 2018) have suggested the label of *project studies*, rather than project management studies, to better include topics that are still neglected in this field. With this move, Geraldi and Söderlund take a cue from organization studies, and show that the simple removal of one word is a powerful move, enabling a widening of the field. Adding to their fruitful suggestion, I also take to heart Schoeneborn et al.'s (2019) proposal to reinterpret the field of organization studies

> as a field united by a common theoretical impetus, rather than solely by a joint interest in a subject area; that is, by the study of social phenomena *as* organization, rather than by the study *of* organizations as social phenomena. (p. 490; emphasis in original)

Hence, while a simplistic take on the wide variety of studies that populate the field of project management would divide studies between a technical approach and a social approach, a reinvented scholarship along the lines of Schoeneborn et al. would rather move the inquiry right into *what makes projects organizational.*

I suggest that thinking about what makes projects organizational requires a renewed set of ideas and concepts, which is exactly what a communication-centred perspective brings to the table (or to the field). Another reason justifying why Schoeneborn et al.'s reversal is relevant for projects is that projects are in no way a prerogative of organizational settings: while projects are massively present in organizational settings, they are not limited to entities identified as formal/formalized organizations. As a concept, the project is vast, and the variety of activities labelled as "projects" nowadays include architectural projects, educational projects and even life or existential projects (Boutinet, 2010, 2018). In this sense, the questions raised by a communication-centred perspective could be brought to inquiries that are located in different fields than those that organization studies and organizational communication scholars usually visit. This chapter is limited, however, to projects happening in organizations and set to concretize something of worth for this organization, its partners or clients, or projects set up in relation to work, like entrepreneurial projects.

What should be noted at this point is that the developments proposed by CCO have not, for the most part, reached the shores of project studies. Projects may have, on occasion, featured in studies of organizational topics approached with a CCO perspective, like order and disorder (reconceptualized as (dis)ordering; see Vásquez et al., 2016), but they have rarely been the focal point of the inquiry. For its part, communication in the context of projects is regularly studied, but very rarely *problematized* in the manner that a communication-centred perspective proposes. As is the case elsewhere (e.g., in management organization studies in general), communication in the context of projects is usually[3] (1) defined in terms of transmission, (2) understood as taking place between human actors and (3) happening inside or around projects (cf. Axley, 1984, whose argument is similar to the critique Taylor formulated at the onset of CCO; see the interview with Taylor in this volume). As spelled out in the introduction to this Handbook, CCO explicitly challenges these assumptions. The starting point for a meeting of project studies and a communication-centred perspective may thus lie in the recognition of these postulates concerning communication, and of the possibility to move beyond them.

The cornerstone of a CCO perspective is that communication is the explanation (the *explanans*) of organization, organizing or the organizational (Cooren, 2012; Schoeneborn et al., 2019), hence the inclusion of constitution/constituting in its very name. This raises a basic question for inquiry into projects: what do we see and understand about projects themselves, as temporary organizations, when we propose that they could be communicatively constituted? Going back to the three key features of projects outlined in the opening of this chapter, a CCO perspective offers ontological and theoretical bases as well as a specific conceptual vocabulary to reflect on what makes a project a project, a definitional work that is rarely performed in the study of these endeavours. It might seem slightly strange to propose such an ontological inquiry; after all, projects seem almost self-evident, being so overwhelmingly present in our societies—a situation that leads Jean-Pierre Boutinet (2010), who has devoted a large part of his work to exploring projects from anthropological and psychological angles, to speak of a "project culture" when characterizing our world. This is specifically where CCO enters the room, as it is a perspective that deals directly with such ontological inquiries. One of the foundational questions of this perspective has been "What is an organization?", a seemingly simple question that has sparked a flurry of theoretical and empirical developments. This question can give life to new questions in the study of projects because there is a tendency, in a vast majority of studies on projects, to take for granted not only communication, but the project itself. This is not surprising, as a project is a temporary organization, and as such suffers from the same metaphor-assumption that is found in several studies of organizations: that of being the container in which things happen (Smith, 1993; as discussed by Ashcraft et al., 2009). A CCO perspective allows one to engage in an ontological inquiry about the nature of projects, and also to grasp and conceptualize the dual work of conceiving projects while executing them. This coexistence is integral to the endeavours we label "projects"; accordingly, and following Boutinet, when we use this word, we should remain fully aware that it simultaneously designates its aim (what it has been set up to concretize, and that is not yet concretized) and the set of organized/organizing activities that unfold with the objective to realize this aim. We can see reflected in Boutinet's idea the central claim of CCO regarding the coexistence of organization and organizing, an idea whose potential for projects has not as yet been exhausted.

Let's now consider how a few insights from CCO can help us reflect on what makes an endeavour "a project". I explore how CCO, given its original lines of questioning, reveals less-researched areas of inquiry for project studies.

Reconfiguring What is Taken for Granted

Problematizing Communication. What makes it a bit difficult to write about the potential of CCO for projects is that some of CCO's ideas seem to be—without having to proceed to heavy theoretical work—already present in what projects are all about, if only we see projects in a light that is not solely technical and/or instrumental. I see an intimate resonance between some of CCO's main ideas and the very nature of projects. Let's take the central tenet of CCO, summarized in its simplest form, that the organization happens and exists in communication (Taylor and Van Every, 2000). This communicational explanation of the organization (Cooren, 2012) rests on a processual understanding of reality, as it is in ongoing and situated interactions that this constitution of the organization unfolds and happens. Brought into organization studies, this idea requires, if one is to adopt this ontological position, redefining what the organization is. In other words, for many perspectives on organizations, this implies making change, rather than stability, the key feature of organizations. But when a similar translation is done from CCO to projects, less work may be needed, in a sense: projects are *de facto* processual, even when viewed from a traditional perspective. For example, if we turn to the Project Management Institute, the most important professional association in the field of project management, here is how it defines projects in its key manual, the Project Management Body of Knowledge (PMBOK®): "A project is a temporary endeavour undertaken to create a unique product, service, or result" (Project Management Institute, 2017, p. 3). After having stated that projects create something unique and that they are temporary, the PMI adds: "Projects drive change in organizations. From a business perspective, a project *is aimed at moving* an organization from one state to another state in order to achieve a specific objective" (Project Management

Institute, 2017, p. 6; my emphasis). Projects, whatever their aim, are recognized as being about change, as generating change. Add to this the recognition that, as projects progress, they also change, and it becomes quite natural to see that projects exemplify a process ontology. The only supplementary step needed to connect projects and CCO is to embrace the idea that such a process of change happens in communication. When this is accepted, new forms of inquiry and new questions appear for the study of projects.

Following what is, at its heart, a communication-centred inquiry into projects problematizes communication and leads to paying detailed attention to what is said, done, and accomplished collectively in communication events. This implies looking, in a qualitative and situated way, at the conversations taking place, to investigate what is discussed, who is speaking, what is evoked or invoked, what kind of struggles and negotiations take place, how co-orientation and coordination are achieved, and how all of these communicative practices shape decisions, actions and ultimately how the project and its aim progressively emerge. At the same time, it requires expanding the definition of actor to include all the elements that may make a difference (cf. Latour, 2005) in the situation, including what is generally grouped under the "materiality" label. As Cooren has discussed extensively (2006, 2012, 2015, 2018, 2020a and 2020b, to identify a few key references), this requires a more nuanced and blended conceptualization than is usually found when materiality is taken into consideration, in organization studies at large. Indeed, CCO (especially the Montréal School) is not a perspective that simply "adds objects" to its theoretical propositions, making them sit *beside* human actors (cf. Kuhn, 2020). Building on insights from ANT, Cooren (2006) has proposed, first, to view the organization as a plenum of agencies, that is, to recognize that agency is always hybrid, and that action always involves humans and non-humans (or other-than-humans, as Cooren, 2020b, suggests) coming together. One of Cooren's main arguments is that the social and the material do not designate separate categories, and that a communication-centred perspective leads us to see just how both terms are "essential features of everything that exists" (Cooren, 2018, p. 279; see also 2015 and 2020b). His concept of ventriloquism theorizes and makes this idea actionable: recognizing that when someone is speaking, she is making something speak, while at the same time that thing is animating her and speaking through her—what ventriloquism is all about—directs researchers to actual communication events in which one can identify the figures or the matters of concerns (Latour, 2004) that materialize through speech and other action. This concept derives from an empirical focus on communication events and to an unabated commitment to never leaving "the *terra firma* of interaction" (per Cooren's formulation). In this sense, I see in ventriloquism a conceptual-methodological bundle, a concept that comes with strong methodological implications.

Ventriloquism, then, offers a conceptual-methodological tool to decorticate, in a bottom-up fashion (cf. Cooren and Martine, 2016), how what is presented, said, written, discussed and debated contributes to making the project happen (its organizing) and become a concrete product (its aim). For example, megaprojects are a key concern in project studies, given their scope, the resources they require, and the multiple implications they can have. Stakeholder management becomes important in a context where such megaprojects can elicit strong criticisms from different groups. Think, for example, about projects that have an environmental impact and all the controversies that arise around such projects. A ventriloquial analysis would allow for a detailed analysis of who and what is evoked, convoked or invoked, becomes present, orients or, so to speak, "haunts" the projects through communication events. Similar inquiries could be pursued around many specialized topics in projects studies. But the concept of ventriloquism also allows one to go a few steps further, in terms of reconfiguring research on projects. Going back to the idea of project actuality, Cicmil et al. (2006) describe it in the following way:

'project actuality' encompasses the understanding of the lived experience of organisational members with work and life in their local project environments. Their actions, decisions and behaviours are understood as being embedded in and continuously re-shaped by local patterns of power relations and communicative inter-subjective interaction in real time. [...] actuality research, as a stream of thought, demonstrates a deep interest in lived experience of project actors, with the aim to understand what is actually going on in the arrangements labelled 'project' over time, to give an alternative account of what project managers do in concrete project situations and to explore skills and knowledge that constitute the social and political action in managing projects. Researching the actuality of projects means focussing on social process and how practitioners think in action, in the local situation of a living present. (p. 676)

This translates into a program of research that has, as its objects of inquiry, a number of topics that differ from more traditional objects of inquiry in project management, namely

- "—the understanding of the actors' moral and ethical motives (practical reason) and their sense-making processes (enactment) and how their actions unfold over time and in connection with other, multiple events;
- the experience of emotions and feelings that drive action in complex environments;
- closer insight into intentions, political agendas and personal drives of individual actors; and
- the identification of tensions, power asymmetries and patterns of communicative relating among individuals and groups and how they are being negotiated in the context." (p. 676)

Their program of research is anchored in an ontology of becoming and gives precedence to praxis. I quoted this program extensively for two reasons: first, because I strongly believe that this idea of project actuality still represents a program of research open to more relevant contributions, and, second, because I see many possible extensions with a CCO perspective. Communication already features as a key process in project actuality, but it is not defined as a *constitutive force*. Building on this conceptual move, adding the empirical priority given to situated action and interactions and equipping researchers with the conceptual-methodological tool of ventriloquism would lead researchers to expose just how the dimensions listed above exist in communication, and how these communicative practices shape, influence and materialize—in a word, constitute—the project. Problematizing communication (not taking it for granted) problematizes *at the same time* the project understood as temporary organization: this moves studies of project actuality from attention to what happens "inside" projects to how projects are performed as people engage in the variety of activities oriented towards the realization of its aim, and how such localized performance orients what happens next in the course of action. This resonates with and extends Boutinet's ideas that the project "is an intention translated into language" (2010, p. 59), and that it is a site where an "inextricable relation between action and language" (2010, p. 231) takes place, because it implies efforts to make what is said (or written) fit with what is done.

Moving from Materiality to Materialization(s). Communication-centred analyses do not rest on a separation of the social on one side and the material on the other. While the research program focussing on project actuality recognizes that tools and technologies are part of the doing of projects, it does not go as far as adopting a relational ontology that would locate agency in the relations between all elements, human or otherwise, that are involved in collective action.

Generally speaking, if some studies devoted to projects have included a sensitivity to other-than-humans (e.g., texts, Sergi, 2013; or frogs, Tryggestad et al., 2013), this also represents an area for potential contributions, especially when materiality is redefined through the lens of CCO. If, as suggested by Cooren, materiality and sociality alike are properties of all phenomena, then what differs from one phenomenon to another is their relative expression. Hence, materiality and sociality are *relative* properties, and the focus of inquiry becomes the process by which any phenomenon materializes itself more or less. Cooren thus puts the focus on materialization, and on its variable expression, what he calls degrees of materialization. It should be noted here that materialization is not equated with a linear trajectory that would neatly move something from the immaterial (an idea, a plan, etc.) to the material (a bridge, a new information system, etc.); rather, materialization is what can be studied in interactions or in documents, for example, by asking the question of what and who manifests itself and makes itself present through other beings, which in turn attest to the relationality of the focal phenomenon. This is why Cooren (2020b) argues that, from a CCO perspective, choosing between a transmissive or a constitutive definition of communication is not a choice—both aspects are present in his definition:

> While the ideas of transmission, propagation or diffusion (I here use the words interchangeably, as they each refer to different aspects of the same phenomenon) insist on the relational dimension of organizing and organization, the idea of constitution reminds us that these relations are the ways by which an organization *exists* and *materializes* and organizing takes place. (p. 9; emphasis in original)

Cooren also adds two important specifications with respect to materialization: first, there is no definite starting point from which materialization proceeds (there is always a degree of materiality in anything, even in what we conceive as the most immaterial phenomena, such as someone's thoughts), and second, materialization is always incomplete and relative (things or phenomena only materialize partially in interactions; they can materialize more over time, through repetition, action or efforts—or less if they are not sustained; e.g., Bencherki et al., 2021).

These ideas on materialization can appeal to project scholars. As apparent in the PMI's definition (which is, of course, just one definition among others), projects are set up to make something or to accomplish a specific goal. From this definition, projects could easily be summarized as trajectories of materialization, as projects are what is organizationally created and managed to move from an (immaterial) idea to a (concrete, material) product/change/event. If this idea is already in itself a break from the normative perspective that dominates the field of project management, it still perpetuates the separation between immaterial and material. A communication-centred perspective more significantly reconfigures the perspective on projects, by asking the questions of what makes the project more or less material over its course, how it materializes (or not) as it is being pursued (i.e., efforts are invested in trying to make it become something other than only a project, transforming it from idea to product, change or event), how some of its materializations turn out to be more or less robust, and what relations are established that make it exist and that reveal how its organizing happens (cf. the above quote).

Multiplying the Project(s). Opting for a conceptual and analytical focus on materialization could also have another implication: extending the inquiry into projects outside what is seen, organizationally speaking, as its official beginning and end. Indeed, when and where does a project start and end? I can weave in here another insight from Boutinet, who stresses that there is no project without actor/author. CCO can extend this insight by decentring the analysis from the single individual who would be defined as "the" author of the project to focus on the dynamics of authoring and authority (cf. Taylor and Van Every, 2014), especially important when considering organizational projects, where approval has to be gained, the nature of the project has to be negotiated with many actors, and several concerns will be expressed and possibly compete. The beginning of a project cannot be taken for granted, and may even be thought of in the plural, as there might be several beginnings to a project. While the idea for a project may be easier to trace (note that by idea, I do not mean an immaterial moment when a project would not have any materiality: thinking and imagining are highly material), its end becomes fuzzier. Once the point that is identified as "the completion" of project is reached, we tend to say that the project is finished (and, in a sense, dead). However, a focus on degrees of materialization would see this in a different light: by continuing to exist in documents and other formal traces, in people's memories, in the knowledge they acquired and skills they developed during this organized experience, or even by existing in the shadows of what is deemed "concretized" (the aim of the project that is no longer an aim but that has become a result), the project continues to materialize itself—just *less* so than when people were actively investing effort to reach its goals. I would thus propose that projects bear with them a double materialization: both in the common sense of why they are set up and in the communicational sense that is associated with a CCO perspective.

The object of inquiry then becomes to study how materialization (making something move from idea to concrete result, the process over time) happens through successive materializations (in interactions, through documents, etc.). A key word here is *successive*, because the *raison d'être* of the project (what it aims to materialize) requires sustained efforts, persistence and continual work over time. Not only does its materialization have to *persist* over time (if not, the project's becoming is weakened and the project may be abandoned) but it has to *amplify* (the project has to become more and more material to come close to the point where some people will be able to say that it is completed, that it has achieved what it was set up to do). This highlights the possibility of paying attention to what happens between materializations, how these materializations stay (or don't stay) connected and how the project gains more materiality as time and action unfold. A communication-centred perspective not only puts the spotlight on the importance of persistence and amplification, understood as processes, but allows one to empirically see them at play over time. Moreover, in pursuing this empirical-analytical line of inquiry, we may also be able to address the connections between, on one hand, the projects that a larger and more stable organization might set up formally for different aims (change projects, projects to develop new products, interorganizational collaborations, etc.), and, on the other hand, the persistence (or not) of the organization itself. Could projects—as temporary organizations—launched by a more permanent and/or larger organization be a specific *organizational* modality through which an organization continually prolongs and rematerializes itself, thus playing a part in its endurance? And could we go as far as to propose that projects, understood in the sense of Boutinet, may be one aspect that makes social phenomena *organizational*? Exploring this question may add a feature in current discussions on organizationality (e.g., Dobusch and Schoeneborn, 2015; as well as Schoeneborn, Blagoev and Dobusch in this volume), by possibly showing that projects may play a key part in defining something as organizational.

At the same time, highlighting that materialization is never complete leads us to see that deciding that a project is "completed" is not solely a question of having created something (be it a piece of software, a bridge, an organizational change or an artistic event), but of having reached a point where materialization can be considered "enough". Completing a project is, in this sense, just as much a question of degrees as of materiality. Moreover, as the project progresses, elements will be dropped along the way—elements that will matter less or not at all—and may be considered in the end as missing from the finished project (e.g., features planned but not developed). Boutinet (2018) writes that realizing a project is a constant confrontation of inspiration with facts: working towards the completion of a project implies translating intentions into action, and, as the saying goes, translating is betraying. This also makes the project incomplete in an absolute sense, and makes it persist even after no one is actively working on it, as long as there are traces that attest to these unrealized aspects.

Adding to these elements, it should be noted that, from a CCO perspective, the project also acquires the status of an actor. A ventriloquial approach explains that actors, human or other-than-human, like documents, will speak on behalf of the project ("The project needs …"), and that, at the same time, the project will be speaking through humans and other-than-humans. Interestingly, the project as actor is quite explicitly not the same with each passing day, as the project is moving towards its completion (unless it is stalling). A CCO perspective reveals that this may pose specific challenges to human actors who then need to ask themselves which project appears on the communicational scene: is it the project as it was conceived and planned, the project as it is progressively becoming a reality, or the project that should happen next to correct the course of action? What might appear as a purely conceptual question is, as I suggest, a very down-to-earth and pragmatic question: being able to discern which project people speak of, or speaks through them, may in fact be quite useful to make decisions and adjustments, or to alter the course of action.

In this light, I would like to suggest that a project is never just "a" project. As a project gets approved and actually gets accomplished, a multiplication process begins, through the various versions of the project that may be invoked: the idealized version, the approved version, the version presented in various documents, the version as understood by the people involved in its completion, the image its clients have developed and the adapted versions stemming from the gradual completion. And then other versions of the "same" project can also appear once the project is deemed to be completed: the concretized version, the planned version, the version of the project invoked when other projects are set up and in progress, etc. A constitutive view makes this multiplication of projects visible, as it becomes methodologically possible, through a ventriloquial analysis for example, to trace, in what is said and written, which project appears on the scene. This could be further extended by attending to the ontological multiplicity of projects, when defined as assemblages (Kuhn, 2020). This can lead to asking a novel question for the study of projects, namely what does such a multiplication entail, for the becoming of projects, when considered as projects unfold?

These are the kinds of insights that CCO creates for project studies. Many other original contributions made by CCO scholars, around topics like disorganization, authority and affect, could also be explored with projects, among others to pursue Cicmil et al. 's (2006) program (see for example chapters in this volume by Vásquez et al., Benoit-Barné and Fox; see also Kuhn et al., 2019). The relational ontology of CCO could also extend critical studies of project management discourse (e.g., Lindgren et al., 2014; Cicmil et al., 2016), where the discursive may still remain artificially separated from the material. This chapter has thus only been a first foray into such possibilities for project studies.

In Guise of Conclusion, More Possibilities

I opened this chapter by highlighting that projects may represent an exciting site for inquiring into the oscillation between organizing for action and organizing in action. Given this oscillation, projects can be viewed as sites where the relationship between organizing (understood as practices; here project organizing) and organization (understood as entity; here the temporary organization that the project is/becomes) is especially visible. While this oscillation had already been proposed by Jean-Pierre Boutinet, this idea had up to now remained mainly underspecified, theoretically speaking. I have proposed that CCO offers questions and concepts that allow one to turn Boutinet's insight into a productive line of inquiry. The rest of the chapter has explored what a communication-centred perspective can bring to the study of the phenomenon that we call "a project". Given that project studies have not, as yet, fully seized the potential of a communication-centred perspective, this chapter has mainly made the case for such an embrace, especially by focussing on ventriloquism and materialization. If Boutinet sees the project as "a figure destined to always remain hard to define since it destroys itself as it is realized" (2018, pp. 6–7), the relational ontology of CCO offers theoretical bases to conceptualize this processuality and allows questioning the apparent singularity of a project's trajectory between two points in time. Given its twin preoccupation with theoretical development and empirical exploration, I also see CCO, especially the Montréal School perspective, as one that could be quite relevant for project scholars to "stay close to the ground of practice" (Geraldi et al., 2021, p. 3) while extending theorizations in this field.

If CCO should interest project researchers, projects should also attract CCO scholars, as potentialities do not flow in one direction only. I outline here a few possibilities. A first interesting empirical opportunity afforded by projects to CCO researchers is the possibility of inquiring into the birth of an organization (cf. Nicotera, 2013) ... and its death (or its perpetuation beyond death, as I alluded to). Söderlund (2013) has already argued that considering the life and death dynamics in projects could deepen theories in project studies, and I see a similar potential for CCO. They could also provide relevant ground to explore, from a communication-centred perspective, the dynamics between freedom to act and knowledge about the project, the former decreasing as the latter increases as the project progresses and decisions are made (a trajectory described by Midler, 1993). Also, as briefly outlined, projects—and especially those outside formal organizations—could add to the stimulating body of research on organizationality (Dobusch and Schoeneborn, 2015; as well as Schoeneborn, Blagoev and Dobusch in this volume). Finally, projects are often set up "inside" another organization or "between" organizations. How do multiple processes of organizing connect, or not, and mutually constitute each other? Also, if many organizations are nowadays considered as "projectified", does this imply that organizations are constituted by other organizations? These are under-studied questions that CCO scholars may find relevant for further study.

Finally, braiding CCO with projects highlights another area where cross-fertilization between both is visible: that of critical inquiries. CCO is especially well suited to pursuing critical inquiries, both conceptually and methodologically, as it can investigate, empirically, how power effects are performed in communicative practices—in other words, how communicative practices can reiterate power asymmetries or open the door to forms of contestation and resistance. It could also push further the reflection on the projectification of organizations (Midler, 1995), especially when we move from a structural issue to a discursive framing of this transformation. As Packendorff and Lindgren (2014) argue, projectification can be defined as "[p]rocesses of invoking projects as habitual, legitimate and performative responses" (p. 10). A CCO perspective, along the lines presented in this chapter, could interrogate what organizing and which organization are communicatively constituted by mobilizing this discourse. In turn, attending to this performativity of project discourse could open critical inquiries into the implications of what can also be understood as a form of fragmentation of work (Lindgren et al., 2014). Critical studies of project management could thus make good use of CCO's proposals to further studies of power and politics in projects. At the same time, critical inquiries are still needed in CCO studies (Schoeneborn et al., 2019; Kuhn, 2020), in spite of what this perspective affords. In this sense, CCO scholars could see in projects suitable and relevant objects to investigate the (re)production or transformation of asymmetries that appear in organizational settings and, as such, constitute them.

Ultimately, by joining together projects and CCO, this chapter has documented how application of ideas from one area of study to another is not unidirectional but can be generative for both areas. I, for one, will certainly continue to dig into projects with a communication-centred perspective, and I hope that I will not be the only one.

Notes

1 I use quotation marks to indicate that I am aware that qualifications as social vs technical do not reflect the relational ontology of CCO. They nonetheless reflect how studies in project management tend to be commonly distinguished.
2 This two-part special issue was indeed named "Advancing theory and development in project studies". See *Project Management Journal*, volume 51 issue 4 and volume 52, forthcoming.
3 I am not citing any article here because any list here would be incomplete, and my point is not to highlight the shortcomings of specific research contributions. Rather, I make this observation based on my overview of the field, which is of course partial and incomplete.

References

Ashcraft, K. L., Kuhn, T. R., & Cooren, F. (2009). Constitutional amendments: "Materializing" organizational communication. *Academy of Management Annals, 3*(1), 1–64.

Axley, S. R. (1984). Managerial and organizational communication in terms of the conduit metaphor. *Academy of Management Review, 9*(3), 428–437.

Bencherki, N., Sergi, V., Cooren, F., & Vásquez, C. (2021). How strategy comes to matter: Strategizing as the communicative materialization of matters of concern. *Strategic Organization.* https://doi.org/10.1177/1476127019890380.

Boutinet, J. P. (2010). *Grammaires des conduites à projet.* Presses universitaires de France.

Boutinet, J. P. (2018). *Anthropologie du projet.* Presses universitaires de France.

Cicmil, S., Lindgren, M., & Packendorff, J. (2016). The project (management) discourse and its consequences: On vulnerability and unsustainability in project-based work. *New Technology, Work and Employment, 31*(1), 58–76.

Cicmil, S., Hodgson, D., Lindgren, M., & Packendorff, J. (2009). Project management behind the façade. *ephemera, 9*(2), 1–15.

Cicmil, S., Williams, T., Thomas, J., & Hodgson, D. (2006). Rethinking project management: Researching the actuality of projects. *International Journal of Project Management, 24*(8), 675–686.

Cooren, F. (2006). The organizational world as a plenum of agencies. In F. Cooren, J. R. Taylor, & E. J. Van Every (Eds.), *Communication as organizing: Empirical and theoretical explorations in the dynamic of text and conversation* (pp. 81–100). Routledge.

Cooren, F. (2012). Communication theory at the center: Ventriloquism and the communicative constitution of reality. *Journal of Communication, 62*(1), 1–20.

Cooren, F. (2015). In medias res: Communication, existence, and materiality. *Communication Research and Practice, 1*(4), 307–321.

Cooren, F. (2018). Materializing communication: Making the case for a relational ontology. *Journal of Communication, 68*(2), 278–288.

Cooren, F. (2020a). A communicative constitutive perspective on corporate social responsibility: Ventriloquism, undecidability, and surprisability. *Business & Society, 59*(1), 175–197.

Cooren, F. (2020b). Beyond entanglement: (Socio-) Materiality and organization studies. *Organization Theory, 1*(3), 1–24.

Cooren, F., & Martine, T. (2016). Communicative constitution of organizations. In J. K. Bruhn, R. T. Craig, J. Pooley, & E. W. Rothenbuhler (Eds.), *The international encyclopedia of communication theory and philosophy.* Chichester: John Wiley & Sons.

Dobusch, L., & Schoeneborn, D. (2015). Fluidity, identity, and organizationality: The communicative constitution of Anonymous. *Journal of Management Studies, 52*(8), 1005–1035.

Engwall, M. (2003). No project is an island: Linking projects to history and context. *Research Policy, 32*(5): 789–808.

Floricel, S., Bonneau, C., Aubry, M., & Sergi, V. (2014). Extending project management research: Insights from social theories. *International Journal of Project Management, 32*(7), 1091–1107.

Garel, G. (2013). A history of project management models: From pre-models to the standard models. *International Journal of Project Management, 31*(5), 663–669.

Geraldi, J., & Söderlund, J. (2016). Project studies and engaged scholarship: Directions toward contextualized and reflexive research on projects. *International Journal of Managing Projects in Business, 9*(4), 767–797.

Geraldi, J., & Söderlund, J. (2018). Project studies: What it is, where it is going. *International Journal of Project Management, 36*(1), 55–70.

Geraldi, J., Söderlund, J., & van Marrewijk, A. (2021). Bright and dark spots in project studies: Continuing efforts to advance theory development and debate. *Project Management Journal, 52*(3), 227–236.

Hodgson, D. (2002). Disciplining the professional: The case of project management. *Journal of Management Studies, 39*(6), 803–821.

Hodgson, D., & Cicmil, S. (2006). *Making projects critical.* Basingstoke: Palgrave Macmillan.

Hodgson, D., & Cicmil, S. (2016). Making projects critical 15 years on: A retrospective reflection (2001–2016). *International Journal of Managing Projects in Business, 9*(4), 744–751.

Kuhn, T. (2020). (Re)moving blinders: Communication-as-constitutive theorizing as provocation to practice-based organization scholarship. *Management Learning.* https://doi.org/10.1177/135050762 0931508.

Kuhn, T., Ashcraft, K. L., & Cooren, F. (2019). Introductory essay: What work can organizational communication do? *Management Communication Quarterly, 33*(1), 101–111.

Latour, B. (2004). Why has critique run out of steam? From matters of fact to matters of concern. *Critical inquiry, 30*(2), 225–248.

Latour, B. (2005). *Reassembling the social: An introduction to actor-network-theory.* Oxford University Press.

Lindgren, M., Packendorff, J., & Sergi, V. (2014). Thrilled by the discourse, suffering through the experience: Emotions in project-based work. *Human Relations, 67*(11), 1383–1412.

Lundin, R. A., & Söderholm, A. (1995). A theory of the temporary organization. *Scandinavian Journal of Management, 11*(4), 437–455.

Midler, C. (1993). *L'auto qui n'existait pas: management des projets et transformations de l'enterprise.* Paris: InterEditions.

Midler, C. (1995). "Projectification" of the firm: The Renault case. *Scandinavian Journal of Management, 11*(4), 363–375.

Nicotera, A. M. (2013). Organizations as entitative beings: Some ontological implications of communicative constitution. In D. Robichaud & F. Cooren (Eds.), *Organization and organizing: Materiality, agency, discourse* (pp. 66–89). Routledge.

Packendorff, J. (1995). Inquiring in the temporary organization: New directions for project management research. *Scandinavian Journal of Management, 11*(4), 319–333.

Packendorff, J., & Lindgren, M. (2014). Projectification and its consequences: Narrow and broad conceptualisations. *South African Journal of Economics and Management Sciences, 17*, 7–21.

Project Management Institute. (2017). *A guide to the project management body of knowledge: (PMBOK® guide).* Pennsylvania: Project Management Institute.

Sahlin-Andersson, K., & Söderholm, A. (2002). The Scandinavian school of project studies. In K. Sahlin-Andersson & A. Söderholm (Eds.), *Beyond project management: New perspectives on the temporary—permanent dilemma.* Herndon, VA: Copenhagen Business Press.

Schoeneborn, D., Kuhn, T. R., & Kärreman, D. (2019). The communicative constitution of organization, organizing, and organizationality. *Organization Studies, 40*(4), 475–496.

Sergi, V. (2012). Bounded becoming: Insights from understanding projects in situation. *International Journal of Managing Projects in Business, 5*(3), 345–363.

Sergi, V. (2013). Constituting the temporary organization: Documents in the context of projects. In D. Robichaud & F. Cooren (Eds.), *Organization and organizing: Materiality, agency, discourse* (pp. 190–206). New York: Routledge.

Smith, R. C. (1993). Images of organizational communication : Root-metaphors of the organization-communication relation. Annual Conference of the International Communication Association.

Söderlund, J. (2011). Pluralism in project management: Navigating the crossroads of specialization and fragmentation. *International Journal of Management Reviews, 13*(2), 153–176.

Söderlund, J. (2013). Pluralistic and processual understandings of projects and project organizing: Towards theories of project temporality. In N. Drouin, R. Müller, & S. Sankaran (Eds.), *Novel approaches to organizational project management research: Translational and transformational* (pp. 117–135). Copenhagen Business School Press.

Söderlund, J., & Lenfle, S. (2013). Making project history: Revisiting the past, creating the future. *International Journal of Project Management, 31*(5), 653–662.

Suchman, L. A. (2007). *Human-machine reconfigurations: Plans and situated actions.* Cambridge University Press.

Taylor, J. R., & Van Every, E. J. (2000). *The emergent organization: Communication as its site and surface.* Mahwah, NJ: Lawrence Erlbaum.

Taylor, J. R., & Van Every, E. J. (2014). *When organization fails: Why authority matters.* Routledge.

Tryggestad, K., Justesen, L., & Mouritsen, J. (2013). Project temporalities: How frogs can become stakeholders. *International Journal of Managing Projects in Business, 6*(1), 69–87.

Vásquez, C., Schoeneborn, D., & Sergi, V. (2016). Summoning the spirits: Organizational texts and the (dis)ordering properties of communication. *Human Relations, 69*(3), 629–659.

21

STRATEGIC MANAGEMENT AND CCO

A Generative Nexus

A. Paul Spee

Introduction

This chapter draws attention to scholarship at the nexus of Communicative Constitution of Organization (CCO) and strategic management. Strategic management refers to the discipline, or field of study, concerned with "strategy". To advance understanding of strategy, this chapter provides an overview on the origins, novelty and future trajectory of the nexus of CCO scholarship and strategic management. For the purpose of this chapter, CCO is considered a "theoretical endeavour" advocating a distinct position ascribing "organization" as constituted by communication (Cooren, 2010; Schoeneborn, Kuhn & Kärreman, 2019; Taylor & Van Every, 1999). The rise of CCO as a distinct perspective within the field of organizational communication (Ashcraft, Kuhn & Cooren, 2009) was fuelled by several schools of thought (Brummans et al., 2014; Schoeneborn et al., 2014), ascribing to a "relational ontology" (Kuhn et al., 2017). CCO scholarship has opened lines of inquiry on the basis of "seeing communication as constitutive of meaning (and thus of organizational reality) positions communication as a vital *explanation* for organizational phenomena" (Schoeneborn et al., 2019, p. 476 [original emphasis]). Strategy provides one such organizational phenomenon.

Forming in the late 1960s, strategic management is a distinct domain of scholarship, albeit related to concerns within management and organization studies. Its ascent has been shaped by several disciplinary influences, such as sociology, psychology, economics, and finance (Schendel & Hofer, 1979; Nerur, Rasheed & Natarajan, 2008). CCO provided a distinct theoretical lens to advance insights on strategy. To demonstrate the nexus of CCO and strategic management, this chapter is structured in three parts. First, it points to the origins of CCO, as a distinct lens to examine strategy. CCO aligned with a broader movement of practice-based studies (see Gherardi, 2008, 2019; Nicolini, 2012) and the linguistic turn (see Ashcraft et al., 2009; Fairhurst & Putnam, 2004; Putnam & Fairhurst, 2001; Robichaud & Cooren, 2013), taking hold in management and organization studies as well as strategic management. Second, the novelty of CCO comes to bear in distinct concepts which shaped the conceptualization of strategy. Three themes – communication, authority/materiality and strategic planning – exemplify the novelty to strategic management, although are by no means exhaustive of the full scope of contributions of CCO scholarship to strategy. Third, this chapter concludes by positing future trajectories based on emerging research agendas.

DOI: 10.4324/9781003224914-25

Origins of the Nexus of Strategy and CCO

The domain of strategic management originated in scholars' interest in strategy. It occurred alongside the birth of management and organization studies, which had witnessed a surge since the 1970s. Despite a diverse and eclectic beginning (cf. Schendel & Hofer, 1979), strategy scholarship is well entrenched in assumptions ascribing an entitative status to organizations. Based on a substantialist ontology, an entitative status treats "organization" – like any other phenomena – as made up of objective, discrete substances (cf. Tsoukas & Sandberg, 2011). As a result, scholarship ascribed strategy to an organization, e.g., using proxies such as firm performance (profit, revenue, return to shareholders). In contrast, CCO provided an onto-epistemological foundation to generate novel insights, complementing practice-based approaches to strategy, which provided a counter-movement breaking with dominant approaches to strategy scholarship. To recognize the novelty of CCO for scholarship concerned with strategy, let us commence with a brief overview of the socio-historic evolution of strategic management.

Scholarly interest in strategy was grounded in a concern for the "general manager" which had been absent from the curriculum of business schools in the late 1960s, thus warranting a distinct research agenda (Nag, Hambrick & Chen, 2007; Schendel & Hofer, 1979). In a seminal, edited volume, Schendel and Hofer (1979) set an initial research agenda depicting a process of strategic management deemed close to resembling dimensions faced by managers. Whilst it provided foundational pillars of the strategic management discipline, the ascent of economics took hold and determined subsequent research agendas on strategic management (Rumelt, Schendel, & Teece, 1994). It culminated in a rigid division of the domain into research programs classified as strategy content research and strategy process research (Chakravarthy & Doz, 1992). The focus of strategy content research is to determine influences, e.g., varying environmental conditions, on a firm's optimal performance. Strategy process research "focuses on how a general manager can continuously influence the quality of the firm's strategic position through the use of appropriate decision processes and administrative systems". (Chakravarthy & Doz, 1992, p. 5). A turn to economics, finance and psychology tilted the field (almost exclusively) towards strategy content research (Nerur et al., 2008; Leiblein & Reuer, 2020), favouring firm-level or cognition-based research, to the demise of contributions in the tradition of strategy process research (Nag et al., 2007; Hambrick, 2004).

In response and opposition to an economics/finance-based view of strategy, scholars started drawing upon theories and assumptions from other disciplines, such as philosophy, linguistics or social psychology, to develop alternative conceptualizations of "strategy". A prominent movement advocating such alternatives is practice-based studies on strategy, better known as "strategy-as-practice". Strategy as practice pertains to

> social activities, processes and practices that characterize organisational strategy and strategizing. This provides not only an organisational perspective into strategic decision-making but also a strategic angle for examining the process of organizing, and thereby serves as a useful research programme and social movement for connecting contemporary strategic management research with practice-oriented organizational studies.
>
> *Golsorkhi, Rouleau, Seidl, & Vaara 2015a, p. 1*

The movement heeded a call to consider strategy as located in practice (e.g., Whittington, 1996), in contrast to assumptions ascribing strategy as a property of an organization which came to dominate strategic management (Johnson, Melin & Whittington, 2003). Momentum was fuelled by the creation of a community with likeminded scholars who shared an openness and eclecticism to approaches, engaging with each other during regular workshops and conferences. Several venues provided platforms for intellectual debates such as standing working groups at the European Group for Organizational Studies and the inauguration of the Strategizing, Activities & Practices interest group at the Academy of Management, complementing ad hoc workshops held primarily across Europe and Canada. Paying heed to vivid debates, alternative approaches were advocated in dedicated special issues, with contributions characterizing the eclectic approach, for instance in the *Strategic Management Journal* (Burgelman, Floyd, Laamanen, Mantere, Vaara & Whittington, 2018), *Journal of Management Studies* (Johnson, Melin & Whittington, 2003; Balogun, Jacobs, Jarzabkowski, Mantere & Vaara, 2014), *Human Relations* (Jarzabkowski, Balogun & Seidl, 2007; Cabantous, Gond & Wright 2018), the *British Journal of Management* (Dameron, Lê & LeBaron, 2015) or *Long Range Planning* (e.g., Whittington & Cailluet, 2008).

As an alternative to entity-based conceptualizations on strategy (Chia & Holt, 2006; Jarzabkowski, 2004, 2005; Whittington, 2006), research on strategy-as-practice encompasses a range of theoretical and methodological perspectives and approaches, for instance activity theory, actor-network theory, discourse studies, to mention but a few (for reviews, see Golsorkhi, Rouleau, Seidl & Vaara, 2015b; Jarzabkowski & Spee, 2009; Johnson, Langley, Melin & Whittington, 2007; Vaara & Whittington, 2012). Instead of ascribing strategy to a firm (substantialist ontology/entitative status), strategy-as-practice research locates strategy in social activities, exploring strategy as "what people do" (Whittington, 1996). The multifaceted assemblage of theories comprising strategy-as-practice created fertile grounds and an affinity with assumptions advocated by CCO. The nexus of CCO and strategic management built on the momentum of two alternative approaches: a focus on language and a focus on "practice", each gaining momentum since the 1990s.

Language-Based Approaches to Strategy. Similar to organization studies, the linguistic turn influenced strategic management (Vaara, 2010). The performativity of words (cf. Austin, 1962; Searle, 1969) established a basis to explore the communicative dimension to strategy. Two of the early advocates of such approach were Barry and Elmes (1997), who proposed the study of strategy on the basis of narratives. It opened research on the plurivocality of strategic endeavours (e.g., Aggerholm et al., 2012). Another approach built on ethnomethodology, unravelling the dynamics of strategy conversations turn-by-turn (e.g., Samra-Fredericks, 2003). A Foucauldian approach to strategy introduced the notion of discourse and power (Knights & Morgan, 1991) and was taken forward by scholars advocating a critical discourse analysis (e.g., Kwon, Clarke & Wodak, 2014; Vaara, Kleymann & Seristö, 2004) or a stronger recognition of power dynamics (Kornberger & Clegg, 2011). Locating strategy in language and discourse flourished as scholars expanded language-based approaches, for instance investigating strategy with an emphasis on metaphors (e.g., Heracleous & Jacobs, 2011), exploring the multimodality of strategy work (Jarzabkowski, Burke & Spee, 2015), and others developing a theory of strategy grounded in communication (e.g., Mantere, 2013). For instance, a focus on metaphors invited researchers to capture managers' perceptions as they actively and collectively create a representation of their strategic territory (e.g., Heracleous & Jacobs, 2008). Jarzabkowski et al. (2013) unravelled the material, spatial and bodily aspects of strategic work accomplished through multimodal constellations of semiotic resources.

Additional Approaches Locating Strategy in Practice. In addition to language-based approaches, the practice-turn (Schatzki, Knorr-Cetina & Savigny, 2001) offered approaches to investigate strategy as located in practice. Reckwitz's definition of a practice demonstrates the complementarity to language-based approaches. A practice is defined as

> a routinized type of behaviour which consists of several elements, interconnected to one other: forms of bodily activities, forms of mental activities, 'things' and their use, a background knowledge in the form of understanding, know-how, states of emotion and motivational knowledge.
>
> *Reckwitz, 2002, p. 249*

To advance an understanding on strategy, several theories shaped the focus on practice, including activity theory (Jarzabkowski, 2003; Jarzabkowski & Wolf, 2015) and many proponents of practice theory (cf., Nicolini, 2012; Spee, 2021) such as the work of Bourdieu (Gomez, 2015), Giddens (Whittington, 2015) and Foucault (Allard-Poesi, 2015). In contrast to strategy content research, which remained firmly grounded at the firm-level, it shifted attention to the "doing" of strategy, encapsulated in the notion of strategizing. Instead of ascribing strategy to a firm,

> Strategy is not some transcendent property that a priori unifies independently conceived actions and decisions but is something immanent – it unfolds through everyday practical coping actions.
>
> *Chia and Holt, 2006, p. 637*

On the basis of such a shift, and breaking with an entitative focus on strategy, the realm of strategy went beyond formalized efforts of strategy-making, for instance exploring the strategizing of middle managers (e.g., Rouleau, 2005) or linking strategizing to everyday activities (Balogun, Best & Lê, 2015).

The impact of language-based approaches and approaches locating strategy in practice on the trajectory of the strategic management domain is manyfold. For instance, it revived an interest in strategy process research (e.g., Jarzabkowski, 2008), culminating in a special issue (Burgelman et al., 2018). In addition, it created the basis for a distinct research agenda, for example to explore the materiality of strategy (cf. Dameron et al., 2015; Lê & Spee, 2015) and facilitated a growing acceptance of qualitative research methods, which remained under-represented in strategic management (Molina-Azorin, 2012). A focus on materiality pays heed to artifacts such as spreadsheets, flipcharts and computer screens as essential for strategists to accomplish strategy work (e.g., Jarzabkowski et al., 2013). To capture strategizing, a range of qualitative research methods have been employed, such as ethnomethodology, observations or interviews, and video methods (Gylfe, Franck, LeBaron & Mantere, 2016). On the basis of such novel approaches, it also expanded the phenomena of interest, for instance, speeches of CEOs (e.g., Wenzel & Koch, 2018) or strategy workshops (Johnson et al., 2010).

CCO and its Relation to Language-Based and Practice-Based Studies in Strategy. A focus on language and practice provided a source of liberation from assumptions couching strategy in entitative terms, guiding mainstream research in strategic management. Such shift provided an onto-epistemological affinity with CCO. Whilst strategy-as-practice research is characterized as an eclectic approach comprising several theories (cf., Chia & Holt, 2006; Golsorkhi et al., 2015b; Jarzabkowski & Spee, 2009; Vaara & Whittington, 2012), it is united with CCO in terms of broadly ascribing to assumptions advocated by a relational ontology (Kuhn, Ashcraft & Cooren, 2017; Spee, 2021). In contrast to premises of a substantialist ontology, a relational ontology advocates a world as made up of relations. It focuses on the mutual constitution, e.g., of structure and agency (Giddens, 1984), rather than suggesting entities should be studied independently (Sandberg & Tsoukas, 2011). The impact of a relational ontology on CCO and theoretical approaches fostering strategy-as-practice research goes back to mutual roots. For instance, the work of Giddens and the performativity of language (e.g., Searle, Austin) shaped both the foundation of CCO and strategy-as-practice. The alignment along such assumptions created a fertile basis for scholars interested in CCO and strategy to join forces and explore avenues to generate novel insights, as illuminated in the next section.

Similar to strategy-as-practice, CCO is characterized by several schools (Brummans et al., 2014; Schoeneborn et al., 2014): the Montreal School of Communication, the Luhmannian school and the Four-Flows school. Sharing baseline assumptions, e.g., the formative character of language, each school proposes slightly different conceptual frameworks to explain the constitutive nature of communication. For example, the Montreal school combines a focus on the performativity of language with an emphasis on communication's materiality and the contribution of non-humans (e.g., Cooren, 2010; Taylor & Van Every, 1999, 2011; Taylor et al., 1996). The Luhmannian school advocates organizing as a chain of decisions, with communication conceptualized as a synthesis of information, utterances and understanding (e.g., Blaschke, Schoeneborn & Seidl, 2012; Seidl, 2005), whereas the Four Flows school suggests organizing takes place through membership negotiation, self-structuring, activity coordination and institutional positioning (e.g., McPhee & Iverson, 2009; McPhee & Zaug, 2001). Manifestations and the ascent of the three schools of CCO are interwoven with the trajectory of strategy-as-practice scholarship. Whilst CCO and strategic management are characterized by distinct debates, the evolution of scholarship advocating CCO and strategy occurred in parallel. The influence of the Montreal Schools is perhaps the strongest in terms of shaping debates in strategy (e.g., Bencherki et al., 2019; Fenton & Langley, 2011; Spee & Jarzabkowski, 2011; Cooren et al., 2015; Vásquez et al., 2018). A Luhmannian thread has been advocated particularly by Seidl and colleagues (e.g., Seidl, 2007; Hendry & Seidl, 2003; Jarzabkowski & Seidl, 2008). However, the Four-Flows model is least represented in strategy scholarship compared to the two schools. Nevertheless, Giddens's work, which provided core intellectual pillars for McPhee and colleagues, has shaped research in the tradition of strategy-as-practice (e.g., Jarzabkowski, 2008; Jarzabkowski, Lê & Balogun, 2019; Whittington, 2006).

Novelty Generated at the Nexus of CCO and Strategy: What do We Know?

The congruence of CCO and strategy-as-practice provided a fruitful alliance generating novel insights on strategy. It offered complementarity in terms of onto-epistemological considerations, but a unique set of constructs to advance a burgeoning research interest and movement to liberate strategic management from an entitative view on strategy. Three themes were selected to exemplify such novelty, albeit recognizing that what follows is a mere illustration rather than a comprehensive overview.

Communication in Strategy

In mainstream research on strategic management, wedded to economics, the notion of communication received little consideration. The transmission model (Shannon & Weaver, 1949) was well engrained in descriptive and prescriptive theories of strategy (cf. Schendel & Hofer, 1979). Although the linguistic turn placed an emphasis on a communicative dimension to strategy (e.g., Barry & Elmes, 1997; Samra-Fredericks, 2003), CCO contributed to a revised understanding of "communication" in relation to strategy, establishing the basis for several lines of inquiry (e.g., Bencherki et al., 2019; Cooren et al., 2015; Spee & Jarzabkowski, 2011; Vásquez et al., 2018).

An Alternative Conceptualization of "Communication" in Strategy. A revised understanding of "communication" was developed as scholars drew upon the school of thought in the tradition of the Montreal School of communication (e.g., Aggerholm et al., 2012; Bencherki et al., 2019; Cooren et al., 2015; Spee & Jarzabkowski, 2011) and that of Luhmann (e.g., Seidl, 2007). For instance, Cooren et al. (2015, p. 365) articulated three premises to study strategy-making: "1) to always start from (rather than arriving at) commutation as the motto of every inquiry; 2) to take a broad definition of communication that acknowledges that material and social world in which it takes place; and 3) to account for the many kinds of languages, not only spoken and written, that participate in constituting organization and organizing." Drawing from Luhmann, Seidl (2007) developed a novel systemic-discursive perspective on the field of strategy and the respective role of general strategy concepts. He put forward and substantiated claims demonstrating that every single strategy discourse can merely construct its own discourse-specific concepts. Hendry and Seidl (2003) introduced the notion of strategic episode as an appropriate unit of "communication" to study strategy as it unfolded. The notion of strategic episode was taken up by later studies on strategy (e.g., Jarzabkowski, Burke & Spee, 2015; Jarzabkowski & Seidl, 2008). For instance, Jarzabkowski and Seidl (2008) demonstrated how strategic orientations stabilized and de-stabilized over successive strategy meetings.

Strategy as Metaconversation. The notion of metaconversation provided an additional conceptual grounding to revise the conceptualization of "communication" in strategy (Fenton & Langley, 2011; Sorsa & Vaara, 2020; Spee & Jarzabkowski, 2017). Metaconversation first was theorized in communication theory, to explain the emergence of a collective actor such as a city or organization (Robichaud et al., 2004); the concept provided a basis for exploring how collective meaning is created as "simultaneously pluralistic and unitary, multivocal and univocal" (Robichaud et al., 2004, p. 618). The metaconversation is seen as a higher-order discursive construction that is accomplished through recursive interactions amongst diverse actors. For example, a policy formation process (Chaput, Brummans & Cooren 2011), an organizational change process (Taylor & Robichaud, 2007), a strategic planning process (Fenton & Langley, 2011), or indeed an organization itself (Taylor & Van Every, 2000) might all be considered metaconversations that are constructed through the various communicative interactions of participants. Each actor participates in a metaconversation within his or her own particular set of conversations, such as divisional meetings, each experienced from the actor's own perspective and set of interests. But together these actors create some coherence and collectivity from the multiple different conversations that constitute the metaconversation of the organization, policy, or strategy.

Based on the development of a strategic change initiative, Spee and Jarzabkowski (2017) demonstrated how, as part of jointly accomplishing a collective account, participants position themselves as actors who speak for a particular community. For example, participants in a strategic initiative may situate themselves within and speak from their positions as middle managers or top managers (Mantere & Vaara, 2008), from their functions such as sales managers, designers, or engineers (Balogun & Johnson, 2004; Rouleau, 2005), or as actors representing their geographic divisions (Jarzabkowski & Balogun, 2009). It demonstrated that as a collective account was formed, the metaconversation established coherence from the varied meanings of diverse participants, thus fostering an organizational, policy or strategy trajectory that encompasses multiple communities.

Authority, Materiality and Materializing Strategy

The ascent of the strategic management was fuelled by a growing demand of practitioners to devise strategies. Such a demand resulted in a raft of tools, heuristics and frameworks designed to guide decision-making, with Porter's Five Forces serving as a prominent example. Whilst such tools remain a core element of the strategy curriculum (Jarzabkowski, Giulietti, Oliveira & Amoo, 2013), it was the research agenda of strategy-as-practice which opened lines of inquiry into the materials/artifacts involved in strategizing (Spee & Jarzabkowski, 2009; Molloy & Whittington, 2005; Wright, Paroutis & Blettner, 2013). Since, the focus on tools has continued to study one of the main "artifacts" of strategy-making, namely the strategic plan (Ansoff, 1965; Mintzberg, 1994; Giraudeau, 2008; Spee & Jarzabkowski, 2011) but has also started exploring other artifacts/materials involved in strategizing (e.g., Jarzabkowski et al., 2013; Kaplan, 2008).

Whilst the theme of materials/artifacts has been approached from different theoretical lenses (cf. Lê & Spee, 2015), CCO provided concepts to further insights into the authority/authoritativeness and materialization of strategy. For instance, building on Taylor et al.'s (1996) distinction of conversation and text as well as textual agency (Cooren, 2004; Kuhn, 2008), Spee and Jarzabkowski (2011) demonstrated how the recursive relation of talk and its inscription into the plan shaped the trajectory of efforts to devise a new strategic direction for a British university. It opened avenues for research to advance understanding on the materialization of strategy and its relation with any specific concern's "authoritativeness" in guiding collective action (Bencherki et al., 2019; Vásquez et al., 2018). For instance, Bencherki et al.'s (2019, p. 5) work revealed "how, in interaction and through communication, what is or should be strategic emerges and materializes in the form of strategy".

Strategic Planning

CCO scholarship has had a substantial impact advancing understanding on strategic planning. Strategic planning has been a core aspect of strategic management, defining its early research agenda (Schendel & Hofer, 1979). Despite several definitions, strategic planning refers to a process focused on devising a strategy for a firm which ought to shape resource allocation decisions (for a detailed review, see Langley & Lusiani, 2015), which typically culminate in an articulation of a strategic plan. Ansoff (1965) was a main advocate proclaiming that strategic planning enhances firm performance, an ambivalent claim resulting in mixed support (cf. Miller & Cardinal, 1994), placing strategic planning into the spotlight and subject to heavy criticism (Ansoff, 1991; Mintzberg, 1991, 1994). As a result, scholarly focus on strategic planning declined (Wolf & Floyd, 2017).

Despite critique in the realm of strategic management, strategic planning – as a phenomenon – remained prevalent, as reported in regular surveys of executives (Rigby & Bilodeau, 2018). Such evidence suggested strategic planning was more prevalent than assumed (Mintzberg, 1994), sparking a renewed interest in the phenomenon (Whittington & Cailluet, 2008). Several studies employing CCO have heeded calls, investigating strategic planning efforts in a commercial enterprise (e.g., Aggerholm et al., 2012), tenant associations (e.g., Bencherki et al., 2019; Vásquez et al., 2018) or a university (e.g., Spee & Jarzabkowski, 2011). Such studies advanced understanding on strategic planning beyond the initial intent ascribed to strategic planning by its founding fathers (e.g., Ansoff, 1965). For instance, studies pointed to the increasingly rigid aspects of the plan constraining the planning process (e.g., Spee & Jarzabkowski, 2011). CCO offered an additional basis to unravel on "how" things emerge and become strategic (e.g., Bencherki et al., 2019) and its implication for authority (e.g., Spee & Jarzabkowski, 2011; Vásquez et al., 2018), providing grounds for further research.

A Proposed Trajectory to Advance the Nexus of Strategic Management and CCO

The nexus of strategic management and CCO has been fruitful, generating novel insights on strategy. Building on the current extent of engagement, the nexus may evolve along three distinct trajectories. Each trajectory varies along two dimensions: the *positioning* or starting point in the literature and the *depth of engagement* with strategy as phenomena. In terms of positioning, strategic management and CCO are two distinct scholarly domains, pursuing slightly different goals. Depth of engagement pertains to emphasis on the characteristics of the specific phenomenon depicting "strategy", for instance strategic planning or strategic change. Whilst portrayed as distinct, each trajectory offers a way to move the nexus forward.

Strategy as Illustrative Phenomena

A trajectory may arise treating strategy as an illustrative phenomenon, situating the line of inquiry squarely within the debate on CCO. CCO scholarship has been vibrant, advancing several lines of inquiry within and across each school (cf., Ashcraft et al., 2009; Brummans et al., 2014; Schoeneborn et al., 2019). Instead of engaging with debates in strategic management, instances of "strategizing", e.g., everyday strategy work (e.g., Jarzabkowski et al., 2013), strategy meetings (e.g., Liu & Maitlis, 2014) or board meetings (e.g., Veltrop, Bezemer, Nicholson & Pugliese, 2021), may serve as an organizational phenomenon to foster debates in the realm of CCO.

An instance of strategy-making, such as a strategic planning meeting, may provide an empirical basis to illuminate a conceptual point, e.g., to elaborate on current CCO scholarship. Cooren's (2007) edited book provides a case in point. The volume illuminates communicative dynamics based on a series of events, explicating conversations around the succession of Sam Steinberg, a successful entrepreneur. With the succession having a huge implication for the firm's future (and demise), the series of events illuminated strategic discussions. In the instance of contributions in Cooren (2007), implications of the failed succession planning remained largely in the background. Yet, strategy, as a phenomenon, offers distinct characteristics to illuminate aspects suitable to advance CCO scholarship. In particular, strategic planning (Jarzabkowski et al., 2017) or strategy workshops (Johnson, Prashantham, Floyd & Bourque, 2010) offer distinct characteristics, for instance to reveal the temporal dimension of strategy work (e.g., Kaplan & Orlikowski, 2013). Whilst retaining a focus on CCO scholarship, a strategy workshop, strategic planning meeting or scenario planning session may be placed into the foreground as it provides appropriate instances to illuminate notions of authority/authoritativeness (e.g., Kuhn, 2008; Taylor & Van Every, 2014) or temporality. In both instances – placing strategy into the background or foreground, strategic management – as in the domain of scholarship – is side-stepped or may provide further evidence on the characteristics or support for the prevalence of a particular phenomenon.

CCO as a Lens Enriching an Agenda on Strategizing/Strategy-Making

Another trajectory arises with scholarship positioned in strategic management. CCO provided a distinct lens to generate insights on strategy, advancing debates in strategic management or debates wedded to strategy, expanding the lens on the phenomena. The majority of work employed CCO as a distinct lens, leveraging the foundation and/or specific concepts of CCO. In this instance, the novelty that was generated relates to strategic management.

Advancing Debates in Strategic Management. CCO provided a suitable lens to advance research in strategic management, contributing to the burgeoning strategy-as-practice field. Based on the progress to date, several lines of inquiry offer further opportunities. For example, future research may extend insights about the extent of agreement required among participants to roll out a strategy initiative (e.g., Sorsa & Vaara, 2020; Spee & Jarzabkowski, 2017). A prominent line of inquiry on materiality presents further potential to elaborate the materialization of strategy (Bencherki et al., 2019; Spee & Jarzabkowski, 2011) and to extend insights on matters of authority (Vásquez et al., 2018). Several concepts within CCO, such as metaconversation (Robichaud et al., 2004), contributed to a stronger conceptualization of strategy as narrative (Fenton & Langley, 2011), paving the way for further exploration. Advances based on the Luhmannian school (e.g., Jarzabkowski & Seidl, 2008; Seidl, 2007) present another opportunity to investigate constitutive elements of strategy. The Four-Flows school has received limited attention to date, creating an avenue for further research which strengthens the nexus of CCO and strategic management.

Expanding the Lens on the Phenomena: Advancing Insights on Strategy. To date, a majority of empirical studies at the nexus of CCO and strategy have focused on phenomena related to formalized strategy-making. The scripted characteristics of strategic planning provided a suitable context to study the process of strategy-making (Jarzabkowski, Lê & Spee, 2017). Whilst scholarship advanced insights into the "practice" of strategic planning (e.g., Aggerholm et al., 2012; Bencherki et al., 2019; Spee & Jarzabkowski, 2011, 2017), it may portray a rather lopsided view of strategy-making.

The shift from "strategy" to strategizing advocated by strategy-as-practice opened the field to go beyond formalized episodes of strategy-making, for instance to consider informal strategizing (e.g., Hoon, 2007) or implications of and for middle managers (e.g., Mantere & Vaara, 2008; Rouleau, 2005). Such prior examples provide ample scope to extend the adoption of CCO beyond the realm of formalized strategy-making. Thus, future work may explore strategizing along two dimensions. A recent review may serve as a basis to identify pathways to elaborate on the status quo in strategic management, focusing on instances of strategy implementation (Weiser, Jarzabkowski & Laamanen, 2020). Another dimension relates to the evolving characteristics of the "practice" itself. Recent examples point to "new" phenomena worth exploring further, especially through the lens of CCO, such as "open strategy" (Hautz, Seidl & Whittington, 2017; Dobusch & Kapeller, 2018; Tavakoli, Schlagwein & Schoder, 2017).

A Joint Agenda

Building on recent advances and momentum to foster scholarship at the nexus, it may be timely to consider a trajectory based on a joint research agenda. A joint agenda refers to common interests and advances among the scholarly community of CCO and strategy. Instead of positioning the line of inquiry in "either" strategic management (as proposed in trajectory "*CCO as a lens*") "or" CCO (as proposed in trajectory "*Strategy as illustrative phenomena*"), the argument takes the nexus of CCO and strategy as a starting point.

Existing scholarship at the nexus may offer several potential avenues. Since it is now well established that strategy is constituted in communication (cf. Cooren et al., 2015; Jarzabkowski et al., 2013; Spee & Jarzabkowski, 2011), scholars may extend the role of communicative practices that make matters of concern "strategic". Building on a recent momentum (e.g., Bencherki et al., 2019; Vásquez et al., 2018), lines of inquiry may further elaborate how "things" become strategic, which was also approached from the lens of institutional work (Gond, Cabantous & Krikorian, 2018). Opening lines of inquiry into the material/materializing of strategy paves the way for future work to explore and extend a burgeoning research agenda (Dameron et al., 2015; Jarzabkowski et al., 2013; Lê & Spee, 2015), extending insights into the role of authority/authoritativeness (Bencherki et al., 2019; Kuhn,, 2008; Vásquez et al. 2018) since strategy is all but neutral (Knights & Morgan, 1991; Kornberger & Clegg, 2011).

There may be further opportunity to advance conceptualizations of strategy situated within the nexus of CCO/strategic management, thus extending the broader movement advocated within strategy-as-practice. For instance, research in the field of strategy-as-practice has largely shied away from addressing and exploring the constitutive effects of strategizing, such as how communication (talk/text) manifests itself in structural changes (structure for reporting/ organizational structure), or other materializations consequential for "others" such as staff or stakeholders.

Conclusion

With scholarship in strategic management characterized by different disciplinary influences, CCO furnished research agendas building on and accelerating the momentum of practice-based studies and the linguistic turn on strategy. Congruent with assumptions wedded to a relational ontology, CCO complemented theoretical perspectives characterizing strategy-as-practice (e.g., Bencherki et al., 2019; Cooren et al., 2015; Spee & Jarzabkowski, 2011; Vásquez et al., 2018). United in rejecting entitative thinking of organization and strategy respectively, it forms a powerful alliance and force to carve out future scholarship. Future scholarship may blossom beyond the three distinct trajectories outlined in this chapter to shape and shift understanding of strategy and gain an understanding beyond formalized approaches to strategy-making, for instance to explore phenomena such as open strategizing or strategy jams. Whilst the flow of influence is geared towards CCO influencing debates in strategy, there is potential for the flow of influence to become mutual.

References

Allard-Poesi, F. (2015). A Foucauldian perspective on strategic practice: strategy as the art of (un) folding. In D. Golsorkhi, L. Rouleau, D. Seidl, & E. Vaara (Eds.), *Cambridge handbook of strategy as practice* (2nd edn., pp. 234–248). Cambridge University Press.

Ansoff, H. I. (1965). *Corporate strategy: An analytic approach to business policy for growth and expansion.* McGraw-Hill.

Ansoff, H. I. (1991). Critique of Henry Mintzberg's 'The design school : Reconsidering the basic premises of strategic management'. *Strategic Management Journal, 12*(6), 449–461. https://doi.org/10.1002/ smj.4250120605.

Austin, J. L. (1962). *How to do things with words.* Harvard University Press.

Aggerholm, H. K., Asmuß, B., & Thomsen, C. (2012). The role of recontextualization in the multivocal, ambiguous process of strategizing. *Journal of Management Inquiry, 21*(4), 413–428.

Ashcraft, K. L., Kuhn, T. R., & Cooren, F. (2009). Constitutional amendments: "Materializing" organizational communication. *Academy of Management Annals, 3*(1), 1–64.

Balogun, J., & Johnson, G. (2004). Organizational restructuring and middle manager sensemaking. *The Academy of Management Journal, 47*(4), 523–549. https://doi.org/10.2307/20159600.

Balogun, J., Best, K., & Lê, J. (2015). Selling the object of strategy: How frontline workers realize strategy through their daily work. *Organization Studies, 36*(10), 1285–1313.

Balogun, J., Jacobs, C., Jarzabkowski, P., Mantere, S., & Vaara, E. (2014). Placing strategy discourse in context: Sociomateriality, sensemaking, and power. *Journal of Management Studies, 51*(2), 175–201.

Barry, D., & Elmes, M. (1997). Strategy retold: Toward a narrative view of strategic discourse. *Academy of Management Review, 22*(2), 429–452.

Bencherki, N., Sergi, V., Cooren, F., & Vásquez, C. (2019). How strategy comes to matter: Strategizing as the communicative materialization of matters of concern. *Strategic Organization.* https://doi.org/10.1177/1476127019890380.

Blaschke, S., Schoeneborn, D., & Seidl, D. (2012). Organizations as networks of communication episodes: Turning the network perspective inside out. *Organization Studies, 33*, 879–906.

Brummans, B. H. J. M., Cooren, F., Robichaud, D., & Taylor, J. R. (2014). Approaches to the communicative constitution of organizations. In L. Putnam & D. Mumby (Eds.), *The SAGE handbook of organizational communication: Advances in theory, research, and methods* (pp. 173–194). Sage.

Burgelman, R. A. (1983). A process model of internal corporate venturing in the diversified major firm. *Administrative Science Quarterly*, 223–244.

Burgelman, R. A., Floyd, S. W., Laamanen, T., Mantere, S., Vaara, E., & Whittington, R. (2018). Strategy processes and practices: Dialogues and intersections. *Strategic Management Journal, 39*(3), 531–558.

Cabantous, L., Gond, J. P., & Wright, A. (2018). The performativity of strategy: Taking stock and moving ahead. *Long Range Planning, 51*(3), 407–416.

Chakravarthy, B. S., & Doz, Y. (1992). Strategy process research: Focusing on corporate self-renewal. *Strategic Management Journal, 13*(S1), 5–14.

Chaput, M., Brummans, B. H., & Cooren, F. (2011). The role of organizational identification in the communicative constitution of an organization: A study of consubstantialization in a young political party. *Management Communication Quarterly, 25*(2), 252–282.

Chia, R., & Holt, R. (2006). Strategy as practical coping: A Heideggerian perspective. *Organization Studies, 27*(5), 635–655.

Cooren, F. (2004). Textual agency: How texts do things in organizational settings. *Organization, 11*(3), 373–393.

Cooren, F. (Ed.). (2007). *LEA's communication series. Interacting and organizing: Analyses of a management meeting.* Lawrence Erlbaum.

Cooren, F. (2010). *Action and agency in dialogue: Passion, incarnation and ventriloquism.* Philadelphia, PA: John Benjamins.

Cooren, F., Bencherki, N., Chaput, M., & Vásquez, C. (2015). The communicative constitution of strategy-making: Exploring fleeting moments of strategy. In D. Golsorkhi, L. Rouleau, D. Seidl, & E. Vaara (Eds.), *Cambridge handbook of strategy as practice* (pp. 365–388). Cambridge University Press.

Dameron, S., Lê, J. K., & LeBaron, C. (2015). Materializing strategy and strategizing materials: Why matter matters. *British Journal of Management, 26*, S1–S12.

Dobusch, L., & Kapeller, J. (2018). Open strategy-making with crowds and communities: Comparing Wikimedia and Creative Commons. *Long Range Planning, 51*(4), 561–579.

Fairhurst, G. T., & Putnam, L. (2004). Organizations as discursive constructions. *Communication Theory, 14*(1), 5–26.

Fenton, C., & Langley, A. (2011). Strategy as practice and the narrative turn. *Organization Studies, 32*(9), 1171–1196.

Gherardi, S. (2008). Situated knowledge and situated action: What do practice-based studies promise. In D. Barry & H. Hansen (Eds.), *The SAGE handbook of new approaches in management and organization* (pp. 516–525.) Sage.

Gherardi, S. (2019). *How to conduct a practice-based study: Problems and methods.* Edward Elgar.

Giddens, A. (1984). *The constitution of society: Outline of the theory of structuration.* University of California Press.

Giraudeau, M. (2008). The drafts of strategy: Opening up plans and their uses. *Long Range Planning, 41*(3), 291–308.

Golsorkhi, D., Rouleau, L., Seidl, D., & Vaara, E. (2015a). What is strategy-as-practice. In D. Golsorkhi, L. Rouleau, D. Seidl, & E. Vaara (Eds.), *Cambridge handbook of strategy as practice* (pp. 1–29). Cambridge University Press.

Golsorkhi, D., Rouleau, L., Seidl, D., & Vaara, E. (Eds.). (2015b). *Cambridge handbook of strategy as practice.* Cambridge University Press.

Gomez, M. L. (2015). A Bourdieusian perspective on strategizing. In D. Golsorkhi, L. Rouleau, D. Seidl, & E. Vaara (Eds.), *Cambridge handbook of strategy as practice* (2nd edn., pp. 184–198). Cambridge University Press.

Gond, J. P., Cabantous, L., & Krikorian, F. (2018). How do things become strategic? 'Strategifying' corporate social responsibility. *Strategic Organization, 16*(3), 241–272.

Gylfe, P., Franck, H., Lebaron, C., & Mantere, S. (2016). Video methods in strategy research: Focusing on embodied cognition. *Strategic Management Journal, 37*(1), 133–148.

Hambrick, D. C. (2004). The disintegration of strategic management: It's time to consolidate our gains. *Strategic Organization, 2*(1), 91–98. https://doi.org/10.1177/1476127004040915.

Hautz, J., Seidl, D., & Whittington, R. (2017). Open strategy: Dimensions, dilemmas, dynamics. *Long Range Planning, 50*(3), 298–309.

Hendry, J., & Seidl, D. (2003). The structure and significance of strategic episodes: Social systems theory and the routine practices of strategic change. *Journal of Management Studies, 40*(1), 175–196. https://doi.org/10.1111/1467-6486.00008.

Heracleous, L., & Jacobs, C. D. (2008). Crafting strategy: The role of embodied metaphors. *Long Range Planning, 41*(3), 309–325.

Heracleous, L., & Jacobs, C. D. (2011). *Crafting strategy: Embodied metaphors in practice.* Cambridge University Press.

Hoon, C. (2007). Committees as strategic practice: The role of strategic conversation in a public administration. *Human Relations, 60*(6), 921–952.

Jarzabkowski, P. (2003). Strategic practices: An activity theory perspective on continuity and change. *Journal of Management Studies, 40*(1), 23–55.

Jarzabkowski, P. (2004). Strategy as practice: Recursiveness, adaptation, and practices-in-use. *Organization Studies, 25*(4), 529–560. https://doi.org/10.1177/0170840604040675.

Jarzabkowski, P. (2005). *Strategy as practice: An activity-based approach.* Sage.

Jarzabkowski, P. (2008). Strategy-as-practice. In D. Barry & H. Hansen (Eds.), *The SAGE handbook of new approaches in management and organization* (pp. 364–378). Sage.

Jarzabkowski, P., & Balogun, J. (2009). The practice and process of delivering integration through strategic planning. *Journal of Management Studies, 46*(8), 1255–1288. https://doi.org/10.1111/j.1467-6486.2009.00853.x.

Jarzabkowski, P., Balogun, J., & Seidl, D. (2007). Strategizing: The challenges of a practice perspective. *Human Relations, 60*(1), 5–27.

Jarzabkowski, P., Burke, G., & Spee, P. (2015). Constructing spaces for strategic work: A multimodal perspective. *British Journal of Management, 26*(S1), S26–S47. https://doi.org/10.1111/1467-8551.12082.

Jarzabkowski, P., Giulietti, M., Oliveira, B., & Amoo, N. (2013). "We don't need no education"—Or do we? Management education and alumni adoption of strategy tools. *Journal of Management Inquiry, 22*(1), 4–24.

Jarzabkowski, P., Lê, J., & Balogun, J. (2019). The social practice of coevolving strategy and structure to realize mandated radical change. *Academy of Management Journal, 62*(3), 850–882. https://doi.org/10.5465/amj.2016.0689.

Jarzabkowski, P., Lê, J., & Spee, P. (2017). Taking a strong process approach to analyzing qualitative process data. *The SAGE handbook of process organization studies* (pp. 237–253). Sage.

Jarzabkowski, P., & Seidl, D. (2008). The role of meetings in the social practice of strategy. *Organization Studies, 29*(11), 1391–1426.

Jarzabkowski, P., & Spee, A.P. (2009). Strategy-as-practice: A review and future directions for the field. *International Journal of Management Reviews, 11*(1), 69–95.

Jarzabkowski, P., Spee, A. P., & Smets, M. (2013). Material artifacts: Practices for doing strategy with 'stuff'. *European Management Journal, 31*(1), 41–54.

Jarzabkowski, P., & Wolf, C. (2015). An activity-theory approach to strategy as practice. In D. Golsorkhi, L. Rouleau, D. Seidl, & E. Vaara (Eds.), *Cambridge handbook of strategy as practice* (2nd edn., pp. 165–183). Cambridge University Press.

Johnson, G., Langley, A., Melin, L., & Whittington, R. (2007). *Strategy as practice: Research directions and resources.* Cambridge University Press.

Johnson, G., Melin, L., & Whittington, R. (2003). Micro strategy and strategizing: Towards an activity-based view. *Journal of Management Studies, 40*(1), 3–22.

Johnson, G., Prashantham, S., Floyd, S. W., & Bourque, N. (2010). The ritualization of strategy workshops. *Organization Studies, 31*(12), 1589–1618.

Kaplan, S. (2010). Strategy and PowerPoint: An inquiry into the epistemic culture and machinery of strategy making. *Organization Science, 22*(2), 320–346. https://doi.org/10.1287/orsc.1100.0531.

Kaplan, S., & Orlikowski, W. J. (2013). Temporal work in strategy making. *Organization Science*, *24*(4), 965–995.

Knights, D., & Morgan, G. (1991). Corporate strategy, organizations, and subjectivity: A critique. *Organization Studies*, *12*(2), 251–273.

Kornberger, M., & Clegg, S. (2011). Strategy as performative practice: The case of Sydney 2030. *Strategic Organization*, *9*(2), 136–162. https://doi.org/10.1177/1476127011407758.

Kuhn, T. (2008). A communicative theory of the firm: Developing an alternative perspective on intra-organizational power and stakeholder relationships. *Organization Studies*, *29*(8–9), 1227–1254.

Kuhn, T. R., Ashcraft, K. L., & Cooren, F. (2017). *The work of communication: Relational perspectives on working and organizing in contemporary capitalism*. Routledge.

Kwon, W., Clarke, I., & Wodak, R. (2014). Micro-level discursive strategies for constructing shared views around strategic issues in team meetings. *Journal of Management Studies*, *51*(2), 265–290.

Langley, A., & Lusiani, M. (2015). Strategic planning as practice. In D. Golsorkhi, L. Rouleau, D. Seidl, & E. Vaara (Eds.), *Cambridge handbook of strategy as practice* (pp. 547–563). Cambridge University Press.

Lê, J., & Spee, P. (2015). The role of materiality in the practice of strategy. In D. Golsorkhi, L. Rouleau, D. Seidl, & E. Vaara (Eds.), *Cambridge handbook of strategy as practice* (pp. 582–597). Cambridge University Press.

Leiblein, M. J., & Reuer, J. (2020). Foundations and futures of strategic management. *Strategic Management Review*, *1*(1), 1–33. https://doi.org/10.1561/111.00000001.

Liu, F., & Maitlis, S. (2014). Emotional dynamics and strategizing processes: A study of strategic conversations in top team meetings. *Journal of Management Studies*, *51*(2), 202–234. https://doi.org/10.1111/j.1467-6486.2012.01087.x.

Mantere, S. (2013). 'What is organizational strategy? A language-based view', *Journal of Management Studies*, *50*, 1408–1426.

Mantere, S., & Vaara, E. (2008). On the problem of participation in strategy: A critical discursive perspective. *Organization Science*, *19*(2), 341–358.

McPhee, R. D., Iverson, J. (2009). Agents of constitution in the communidad: Constitutive processes of communication in organizations. In L. L. Putnam & A. M. Nicotera (Eds.), *The communicative constitution of organization: Centering organizational communication* (pp. 49–88). Mahwah, NJ: Routledge.

McPhee, R. D., & Zaug, P. (2001). Organizational theory, organizational communication, organizational knowledge, and problematic integration. *Journal of Communication*, *51*, 574–591.

Miller, C. C., & Cardinal, L. B. (1994). Strategic planning and firm performance: A synthesis of more than two decades of research. *Academy of Management Journal*, *37*(6), 1649–1665. https://doi.org/10.5465/256804.

Mintzberg, H. (1991). Learning 1, Planning 0. Reply to Igor Ansoff. *Strategic Management Journal*, *12*(6), 463–466.

Mintzberg, H. (1994). The fall and rise of strategic planning. *Harvard Business Review*, *72*(1), 107–114.

Molina-Azorin, J. F. (2012). Mixed methods research in strategic management: Impact and applications. *Organizational Research Methods*, *15*(1), 33–56.

Molloy, E., & Whittington, R. (2005). Organising organising: The practice inside the process. *Advances in Strategic Management*, *22*, 491–515.

Nag, R., Hambrick, D. C., & Chen, M. J. (2007). What is strategic management, really? Inductive derivation of a consensus definition of the field. *Strategic Management Journal*, *28*(9), 935–955.

Nerur, S. P., Rasheed, A. A., & Natarajan, V. (2008). The intellectual structure of the strategic management field: An author co-citation analysis. *Strategic Management Journal*, *29*(3), 319–336.

Nicolini, D. (2012). *Practice theory, work, and organization: An introduction*. OUP Oxford.

Putnam, L. L., & Fairhurst, G. T. (2001). Discourse analysis in organizations: Issues and concerns. *The new handbook of organizational communication: Advances in Theory, Research, and Methods*, 78–136.

Reckwitz, A. (2002). Toward a theory of social practices: A development in culturalist theorizing. *European Journal of Social Theory*, *5*(2), 243–263. https://doi.org/10.1177/13684310222225432.

Rigby, D., & Bilodeau, B. (2018). Management tools & trends. Bain & Company. ww.bain.com/insights/topics/management-tools-and-trends/.

Robichaud, D., & Cooren, F. (Eds.). (2013). *Organization and organizing: Materiality, agency, and discourse*. Routledge.

Robichaud, D., Giroux, H., & Taylor, J. R. (2004). The metaconversation: The recursive property of language as a key to organizing. *Academy of Management Review*, *29*(4), 617–634.

Rouleau, L. (2005). Micro-practices of strategic sensemaking and sensegiving: How middle managers interpret and sell change every day. *Journal of Management Studies, 42*(7), 1413–1441.

Rumelt, R. P., Schendel, D., & Teece, D. J. (Eds.). (1994). *Fundamental issues in strategy: A research agenda.* Rutgers University Press.

Samra-Fredericks, D. (2003). Strategizing as lived experience and strategists' everyday efforts to shape strategic direction. *Journal of Management Studies, 40*, 141–174.

Sandberg, J., & Tsoukas, H. (2011). Grasping the logic of practice: Theorizing through practical rationality. *Academy of Management Review 36*(2), 338–360.

Schatzki, T. R., Knorr-Cetina, K., & Savigny, E. von (Eds.). (2001). *The practice turn in contemporary theory.* Routledge.

Schendel, D., & Hofer, C. W. (Eds.). (1979). *Strategic management: A new view of business policy and planning.* Little, Brown.

Schoeneborn, D. (2013). The pervasive power of PowerPoint: How a genre of professional communication permeates organizational communication. *Organization Studies, 34*(12), 1777–1801.

Schoeneborn, D., Blaschke, S., Cooren, F., McPhee, R. D., Seidl, D., & Taylor, J. R. (2014). The three schools of CCO thinking : Interactive dialogue and systematic comparison. *Management Communication Quarterly, 28*(2), 285–316. https://doi.org/10.1177/0893318914527000.

Schoeneborn, D., Kuhn, T. R., & Kärreman, D. (2019). The communicative constitution of organization, organizing, and organizationality. *Organization Studies, 40*(4), 475–496.

Searle, J. R. (1969). *Speech acts: An essay in the philosophy of language.* Cambridge University Press.

Seidl, D. (2005). *Organisational identity and self-transformation.* Aldershot: Ashgate.

Seidl, D. (2007). General strategy concepts and the ecology of strategy discourses: A systemic-discursive perspective. *Organization Studies, 28*(2), 197–218.

Shannon, C., & Weaver, W. (1949). *The mathematical theory of communication.* University of Illinois Press.

Sonenshein, S. (2010). We're changing—Or are we? Untangling the role of progressive, regressive, and stability narratives during strategic change implementation. *Academy of Management Journal, 53*(3), 477–512.

Sorsa, V., & Vaara, E. (2020). How can pluralistic organizations proceed with strategic change? A processual account of rhetorical contestation, convergence, and partial agreement in a Nordic city organization. *Organization Science, 31*(4), 797–1051.

Spee, A. P. (2021). *Introducing social practice theory.* Edgar Elgar.

Spee, A. P., & Jarzabkowski, P. (2009). Strategy tools as boundary objects. *Strategic Organization, 7*(2), 223–232.

Spee, A. P., & Jarzabkowski, P. (2011). Strategic planning as communicative process. *Organization Studies, 32*(9), 1217–1245.

Spee, P., & Jarzabkowski, P. (2017). Agreeing on what? Creating joint accounts of strategic change. *Organization Science, 28*(1), 152–176.

Tavakoli, A., Schlagwein, D., & Schoder, D. (2017). Open strategy: Literature review, re-analysis of cases and conceptualisation as a practice. *The Journal of Strategic Information Systems, 26*(3), 163–184.

Taylor, J. R., Cooren, F., Giroux, N., & Robichaud, D. (1996). The communicational basis of organization: Between the conversation and the text. *Communication Theory, 6*(1), 1–39.

Taylor, J. R., & Robichaud, D. (2007). Management as metaconversation: The search for closure. In F. Cooren (Ed.), *Interacting and organizing: Analyses of a management meeting* (pp. 5–30). Lawrence Erlbaum Associates.

Taylor, J. R., & Van Every, E. J. (2000). *The emergent organization: Communication as its site and surface.* Routledge.

Taylor, J. R., & Van Every, E. J. (2011). *The situated organization: Case studies in the pragmatics of communication research.* Routledge.

Taylor, J. R., & Van Every, E. J. (2014). *When organization fails: Why authority matters.* Routledge.

Vaara, E. (2010). Taking the linguistic turn seriously: Strategy as a multifaceted and interdiscursive phenomenon. *Advances in Strategic Management, 27*(1), 29–50.

Vaara, E., Kleymann, B., & Seristö, H. (2004). Strategies as discursive constructions: The case of airline alliances. *Journal of Management Studies, 41*(1), 1–35.

Vaara, E., & Whittington, R. (2012). Strategy-as-practice: Taking social practices seriously. *Academy of Management Annals, 6*(1), 285–336.

Vásquez, C., Bencherki, N., Cooren, F., & Sergi, V. (2018). From 'matters of concern' to 'matters of authority': Studying the performativity of strategy from a communicative constitution of organization (CCO) approach. *Long Range Planning, 51*(3), 417–435.

Veltrop, D. B., Bezemer, P. J., Nicholson, G., & Pugliese, A. (2021). Too unsafe to monitor? How board–CEO cognitive conflict and chair leadership shape outside director monitoring. *Academy of Management Journal, 64*(1), 207–234. https://doi.org/10.5465/amj.2017.1256.

Weiser, A. K., Jarzabkowski, P., & Laamanen, T. (2020). Completing the adaptive turn: An integrative view of strategy implementation. *Academy of Management Annals, 14*(2), 969–1031.

Wenzel, M., & Koch, J. (2018). Strategy as staged performance: A critical discursive perspective on keynote speeches as a genre of strategic communication. *Strategic Management Journal, 39*(3), 639–663.

Whittington, R. (1996). Strategy as practice. *Long Range Planning, 29*(5), 731–735.

Whittington, R. (2006). Completing the practice turn in strategy research. *Organization Studies, 27*(5), 613–634.

Whittington, R. (2015). Giddens, structuration theory and strategy as practice. In D. Golsorkhi, L. Rouleau, D. Seidl, & E. Vaara (Eds.), *Cambridge handbook of strategy as practice* (2nd edn., pp. 145–164). Cambridge University Press.

Whittington, R., & Cailluet, L. (2008). The crafts of strategy. *Long Range Planning, 41*(3), 241–247.

Wolf, C., & Floyd, S. W. (2017). Strategic planning research: Toward a theory-driven agenda. *Journal of Management, 43*(6), 1754–1788. https://doi.org/10.1177/0149206313478185.

Wright, R. P., Paroutis, S. E., & Blettner, D. P. (2013). How useful are the strategic tools we teach in business schools?. *Journal of Management Studies, 50*(1), 92–125.

22

THE COMMUNICATIVE CONSTITUTION OF CORPORATE SOCIAL RESPONSIBILITY

Lars Thøger Christensen, Visa Penttilä and Neva Štumberger

Introduction

Corporate social responsibility (CSR) is a complex social and political ideal that reflects how society expects contemporary organizations to handle the social and environmental consequences of their operations (Lockett, Moon & Visser, 2006). Although there is no universally recognized definition of the concept (Dahlsrud, 2008; Okoye, 2009), most writings within the field depict CSR as a collection of standards, norms, policies and practices that guide how organizations relate to their stakeholders and the wider common good (e.g., Basu & Palazzo, 2008). Specifically, the literature distinguishes between *implicit* and *explicit* CSR, that is, between responsibility as a taken-for-granted practice, embedded, for example in collective rules, norms and expectations, and responsibility as specified in strategies and programs (Matten & Moon, 2008). Implicit and explicit CSR may involve different types of communication, but tend to influence each other in various ways. While many explicit programs, for example, tend to focus on how the organization complies with norms and expectations, implicit CSR practices, for their part, are increasingly claimed and promoted explicitly by contemporary organizations (Matten & Moon, 2020).

While organizational engagement with responsibility is both timely and significant, it is pertinent to ask how such practice is related to CCO and its understanding of communication as constitutive of organization. Specifically, CCO scholarship suggests that communication is "the means by which organizations are established, composed, designed, and sustained" (Cooren et al., 2011, p. 1150). Communication, in this view, is not a passive vehicle through which an already existing reality is presented, but a performative practice with organizing properties (Cooren, 1999). Accordingly, the relevant question is what is particular about CSR communication and its organizing properties. First, CSR depicts organizations as *moral actors* that can, and should be, held responsible for their behaviors (Cooren, 2020). Second, dealing explicitly with issues of right and wrong, CSR communication tends to mobilize many different types of audiences, both inside and outside the organization, to demand *consistency* between the talk and the action (Christensen, Morsing & Thyssen, 2013). Third, as a highly contested arena that

DOI: 10.4324/9781003224914-26

often attracts critical attention, CSR's *constitutive potential* is frequently questioned and, sometimes, fiercely rejected by organizational scholars (e.g., Fleming & Banerjee, 2016). Because of its controversial status, CSR offers an obvious and unique arena in which to discuss and develop notions of communicative constitution. In particular, the CSR context urges CCO scholarship to acknowledge the influence of multiple stakeholders on what communication can possibly accomplish over time. By foregrounding dimensions of temporality, co-constitution, power and broader social dynamics, this chapter illustrates how the CSR context allows for a more nuanced understanding of organizations' communicative constitution.

CSR and Performativity

Many organizations, these days, claim to be socially and environmentally responsible, declaring in more or less solemn terms to serve the long-term interests of society and its members, and perhaps even to care for the natural environment. Given the salience of these issues in today's world, we should expect such claims to play a prominent role in shaping the moral conduct of contemporary organizations. Yet, the relationship between CSR claims and their organizational implications is less than straightforward, something that triggers much critical attention from NGOs and organizational critics (Christensen, Morsing & Thyssen, 2021).

Such stakeholders want to know whether CSR communication is in fact matched by proper corporate action; in other words, they wonder whether the articulated responsibility and sustainability ideals are fully integrated in organizational practices. Such expectation is understandable. In many cases, responsibility, sustainability and other issues of moral nature seem to conflict with other organizational motives and interests, such as profit or efficiency demands. Corporate talk about these matters is therefore often met with suspicion and contempt (e.g., Banerjee, 2008; Fleming & Jones, 2013). CSR communication, for example, is frequently described as "spin" (Jahdi & Acikdilli, 2009) or as a smokescreen designed to make corporations look more responsible than they really are (Roberts, 2003). Given frequent cases of corporate manipulation and misconduct, such descriptions resonate with the common-sense view that much CSR is nothing *but* talk (Grant, Keenoy & Oswick, 1998). The CCO perspective, however, calls upon us to reconsider this widespread assumption.

Recent CCO-inspired studies have shown, for example, that CSR communication channels perceptions and priorities of managers (Pentillä, 2020), stimulates stakeholder attention and critique (Christensen et al., 2013; Winkler, Etter & Castelló, 2020), mobilizes internal activists (Girschik, 2018; Haack, Schoeneborn & Wickert, 2012) and maintains corporate legitimacy (Iivonen & Moisander, 2015; Schultz, Castelló & Morsing, 2013). Even if CSR communication fails to perform as professed by its senders, it is likely to influence how responsibility ideals and expectations are perceived and debated inside and outside organizations and, eventually, how CSR practices unfold over time. As such, it contributes to the constitution of organizational reality (e.g., Cooren, 2020; Schoeneborn & Trittin, 2013). Importantly, this perspective does not imply that communication about responsibility is necessarily responsible *in and of itself*, that communication does *enough* in terms of achieving organizational responsibility, or even that CSR communication pushes the organization in *the right or most responsible direction*. Rather than assuming such a direct and straightforward relationship between communication on the one hand, and further action on the other, it describes communication as an essential "producer and carrier of organizational reality" (Kuhn, 2012, p. 548). Organizations, in other words, are not pregiven objects or facts, but "ongoing and precarious accomplishments" (Cooren et al., 2011, p. 1150) realized, sustained, and transformed in communicative practices (Schoeneborn, Kuhn & Kärreman, 2018; Taylor & van Every, 2000).

While the notion that communication is performative is widely acknowledged in the fields of organization and management (e.g., Gond et al., 2016), the *extent* to which organizational responsibility might be "talked into being" (Schoeneborn, Morsing & Crane, 2020, p. 7) remains a highly contested issue. In the remainder of this chapter, we address this question from various angles. First, we consider the view that CSR communication fails to stimulate responsible organizational practices. Second, we review CCO-inspired work on CSR, presenting central findings and assumptions. Third, we discuss possibilities for extending extant works, emphasizing in particular issues of temporality, co-constitution, power, and broader social influences. Across these studies and ideas, we consider the conditions under which CSR communication is likely to elicit its performative potential.

CSR as Non-Performative

Much of the communication that transpires in social interaction has little behavioral impact beyond the moment in which it is articulated. It is ignored, forgotten, or outright contradicted by subsequent talk, decisions, or other types of action. As Brunsson (2003) points out, this frequently happens in organizations where conflicting interests and demands make it difficult to sustain consistency between what is said and what is done. Under such circumstances, much communication comes across as "mere talk", that is, as detached from other organizational practices. This view is described by Grant et al. (1998):

> Such commonplace notions as 'action speak louder than words', 'talk is cheap' and that things are 'easier said than done' reflect the cultural privileging of action over discourse in Western culture. [...] First, discourse is generally depicted as being of less value than action. Second, discourse is seen as a passive activity while 'doing' something is seen as active and purposive with a tangible outcome. Third, 'talking' and 'doing' are invariably assumed to be consecutive rather than concurrent or mutually implicated activities. (p. 5)

The inclination to depict talk and action as distinct practices is widespread in social interaction, but it is especially pronounced when the topic concerns issues of higher morals. Notions of corporate social responsibility, in particular, tend to mobilize such a distinction. In this domain, communication is often devalued and described as being in opposition to "real action" (e.g., Kolk, 2003; Roberts, 2003; Winkler et al., 2020).

The CSR literature itself is partly contributing to this perception. The predominant communication perspective in this field is "representational": it assumes that CSR communication is subservient to CSR action and ought to present, promote and otherwise convey what has already been accomplished socially and environmentally (e.g., European Commission, 2011; Matten & Moon, 2008; Seele & Lock, 2015; Sen, Bhattacharya & Korschun, 2006). By disregarding communication as a productive force in and of itself, much of this literature reproduces an ontological distinction between what organizations say about CSR and what they do about it (for a comprehensive review of this literature see Crane & Glozer, 2016). Interestingly, this view is even prevalent in writings that explicitly promote a communication approach to CSR (see, for example, several chapters in Ihlen, Bartlett & May, 2011). Such a distinction is reproduced also in the organizational literature. Brunsson's (e.g., 2003) writings on hypocrisy, for example, suggest that while talk certainly *does* something, its performativity tends to counteract or nullify other types of organizational action: "Talk and decisions in one direction *compensate* for actions in the opposite direction and vice versa" (p. 205, italics in original).

Brunsson's reasoning, which has inspired studies of organizational sustainability (Cho et al., 2015), implies that CSR talk diminishes the likelihood that CSR initiatives will actually be implemented. While it is not difficult to find examples of CSR talk that never materializes, the implication of such counter-performativity is that *talk* about responsibility is a direct opponent of responsible *action* (Christensen, Morsing & Thyssen, 2020).

A number of critical writings explicitly reject the possibility of CSR performativity (e.g., Banerjee, 2008; Fleming & Jones, 2013). In these writings, the power of CSR communication to shape further organizational practices is frequently described as naïve or "overly optimistic" (Fleming & Banerjee, 2016, p. 258). Interestingly, much of this literature seems to acknowledge communicative performativity in *other* contexts than CSR (e.g., Sturdy & Fleming, 2003), a fact that illustrates the highly controversial status of CSR as an organizational practice. Drawing on Austin's (1962) and Butler's (2010) discussions of infelicities, Fleming and Banerjee (2016), for example, highlight the conditional limitations for speech acts to perform, and argue that attempts to talk more responsible practices into existence are likely to fail. Specifically, they claim that "the accumulated social forces guiding organizational behavior" (p. 263), in par-ticular shareholder demands for profit-maximization, tend to override any talk about better and more ethical practices. Recognizing that such demands often seem to take priority over issues of responsibility, we encourage CCO research to consider social dimensions and limitations of communicative constitution (a theme we shall return to below).

Yet, we do not need to consult the CSR arena to acknowledge that many speech acts are failed performatives. As McKinlay (2011) points out, "[a]ll performatives are flawed in some way or another, to a greater or lesser extent" (p. 133). In fact, and as McKinlay emphasizes, it makes no sense to describe something as performative *unless* it can fail. Acknowledging that the risk of failure (or misfire) is inscribed in every performative, however, is not the same as rejecting the possibility that new ways of talking about responsibility can affect the accumulated social forces that guide organizational behavior. In some cases, the responsible thing to do is to talk, for example, acknowledging a faux pas and offering an apology or congratulating a hard-working colleague. In other cases, which we focus on in this chapter, morally superior talk might be a temporary stage toward virtuous action (March, 2007). This is likely to be the case, for example, when the talk raises collective expectations and defines a territory upon which different interests and interpretations can be expressed.

To acknowledge such potential, however, requires a refocus from discrete individual speech acts and their *immediate* effects, as Fleming and Banerjee's (2016) critique concentrates on, to the dynamic interplay between organizational speech acts and their sedimented effects over time (Christensen et al., 2021). Such interplay, which we shall address below, can involve for example reactions of stakeholders, competitors and legislators who are variously affected or inspired by the CSR talk to expect and demand better practices. Obviously, such inter-active effects often take considerable time to unfold and are likely to involve more than "just" talk. Still, talk is likely to play a significant role in shaping attention and expectations among stakeholders and thereby instigate new practices. As Austin (1962) points out, the articulation of the words is often "*the* leading incident in the performance of the act" (p. 8, italics original). This is the case not only in conventional speech act situations where the talk instantly triggers further action – for example, when declarations announce that "the meeting is adjourned" or "the race has begun" – but is relevant also when the articulation of goals describes an ideal and uncertain future (Christensen et al., 2021). In such cases, the talk can lead to what Butler (2010) calls "socially binding consequences" (p. 147). The task of CCO-inspired approaches to CSR, accordingly, is to investigate the conditions under which such consequences unfold. In the following, we review works that discuss such conditions.

CSR Aspirations and Stakeholder Mobilization

In recent years, scholars have begun to theorize "what communication *does* to CSR" (Christensen & Cheney, 2011, p. 491), focusing on how talk *is* action and how the two are intertwined in that particular domain (e.g., Christensen, 2007; Schultz et al., 2013).

Livesey and Graham's (2007) study of the Royal Dutch Shell Group was one of the first empirical works to explore the performative role of CSR-related communication. Specifically, they study how eco-talk (re)shaped Shell's understanding of its identity, including the Group's commitment to the sustainability agenda. Analyzing various texts about Shell, including material written by its critics, Livesey and Graham (2007) conclude that Shell talked itself into more responsible practices by espousing environmental concerns and ambitions in public forums across the globe. While rejecting any unidirectional causality between eco-talk and sustainable practices, they emphasize that Shell's talk about sustainability had performative implications across the corporation's formal boundaries: "Whatever the original instrumental intent, language and symbolic action may have constitutive effects beyond what any particular agents—corporate communication departments, CEOs, other corporate rhetors, or their critics—can control" (p. 336). In their observation, Livesey and Graham do not only describe CSR communication as a potential driver of organizational change, but also indicate that communication about responsibility has broader social implications. Acknowledging that public messages might influence *other* organizations than their corporate senders, Livesey and Graham's study thus encourages CCO research to move beyond its largely organization-centric perspective.

Studying the adoption of a corporate responsibility standard in the financial industry, Haack et al. (2012) have similarly illustrated how communicative constitution traverses formal organizational boundaries. While initial subscription to the standard was only ceremonial, the diffusion and use of the responsibility language mobilized critics, both inside and outside financial organizations, to demand better practices. Describing such process as a "moral entrapment", Haack et al. argue: "merely 'talking the talk' can be consequential as it compels organizations and their individual members to address inconsistencies between actual and idealized reality" (p. 834). Interestingly, the study shows how internal critics reproduced the language of critical NGOs, emphasizing the need for their organizations to change and live up to their own ideals and promises. A similar observation is reported in Girschik's (2018) study of organizational members engaged in developing an organizational blueprint for change. Specifically, Girschik shows how these members rose as internal activists who sought to reframe the responsibilities of their organizations in ways that reflected the perceived expectations and demands of external stakeholders. Together, these studies indicate that communicative constitution, while unfolding in specific organizational contexts, might be shaped by discourses and expectations outside organizational boundaries.

Works on aspirational talk have extended these insights in a number of important respects. Defined as self-descriptions to which current practices cannot yet live up, aspirational talk is a pervasive communication genre often utilized by managers to describe goals or hoped-for futures *as if* they are almost accomplished (Christensen et al., 2013). Such talk has been described as performative at several levels, for example when it stimulates further reflections and debate about the ambitions, mobilizes internal and external audiences to specify what the talk should imply, heightens expectations among stakeholders for better practices and triggers follow-up steps toward fulfillment (Christensen et al., 2021). A number of empirical studies have further specified the conditions under which aspirational talk is likely to perform beyond the moment in which it is uttered. In a study of the Irish food industry, for example, Koep (2017) illustrates how a large corporation navigated the tension between CSR talk and CSR walk through phases of denying, embracing, and finally transcending the tension by combining vague and more concrete aspirations. Specifically, Koep shows how aspirational CSR claims can be the cause of uneasiness and fear of failing among participant organizations. Such feelings, she argues, have performative potential because they motivate various players in the industry to work harder to accomplish their CSR goals. Interestingly, this logic implies that although stakeholders are likely to challenge CSR claims, such talk might be performative even *without* actual stakeholder pressure. Penttilä's (2020) longitudinal study of aspirational CSR talk points in the same direction. Specifically, his study shows how aspirations can be established, elaborated and extended in an organization over time through recursive processing of strategy documents. The recurrent reiteration of responsibility aspirations in authoritative strategy texts, intermittent evaluation of the aspirations, and ongoing references to salient stakeholders in these communicative processes can shape the commitment of managers to their own aspirations.

Taken together, these studies suggest that aspirational talk is performative when internal or external audiences are inspired or provoked to play along with the ambitions, to take the goals seriously and demand further specifications and follow-up action (cf. Bromley & Powell, 2012). Without such collective mobilization, aspirational talk is likely to misfire. Winkler et al. (2020) use this observation to claim that organizational engagement with tensions and dissent is necessary to drive what they call "substantial CSR" (p. 105). With their discussion of vicious and virtuous circles of aspirational talk they furthermore suggest that such talk is *either* "self-persuasive", and thus ignorant of tensions and dissent, *or* oriented towards critical audiences. Interestingly, however, self-persuasion is likely to be efficient especially *if* the CSR aspirations are communicated in contexts characterized by contestation (e.g., Girschick, 2020; Haack et al., 2012; Penttilä, 2020). Conversely, contestation and dissent are more likely to influence CSR performativity if they enter processes of organizational self-persuasion. The self-persuasive potential of aspirational talk, in other words, is closely related to its contestability (see also Christensen et al., 2021). The pertinence of this observation is evident especially in situations where organizations, out of fear of attracting negative attention, respond proactively to potential or imagined critiques of their own aspirations (see for example Koep, 2017). Yet, aspirational talk's self-persuasive character is relevant in all contexts where organizations mobilize notions of "what might happen" if they do or say this or that. In such situations, the communicative constitution of organization is driven by larger social forces and expectations, even if concrete engagement with tensions and dissent seems absent.

Temporality and Discrepancies between Talk and Action

Acknowledging that CSR communication often concerns complex and wide-ranging projects that cannot be accomplished instantly by a single and distinct speech act, CCO-inspired scholarship has begun to theorize how *temporality* influences communicative performativity. In an effort to formalize the temporal relationship between CSR talk and CSR action, Schoeneborn et al. (2020) suggest a tripartite framework that distinguishes between walk-to-talk, talk-to-walk, and t(w)alking. Whereas the first category refers to CSR practices that precede CSR communication (e.g., a human rights report describing existing violations), the communication involved might recursively work back on its communicator and shape its future conduct (e.g., by improving work conditions). The second category depicts situations where CSR communication foreshadows, motivates and drives CSR practices, something aspirational talk has potential to do (Christensen et al., 2013). The third category erases the temporal separation between talk and action, arguing that both may occur simultaneously, for instance when the talk (e.g. an apology) is sufficient action or when organizations are invoked or "ventriloquized" by human or material representations (Cooren, 2020).

Conceptualizing the relationship between talk and action in four different modalities of aspirational CSR talk – exploration, formulation, implementation, and evaluation – Christensen et al. (2021) add further detail to the notion that communicative performativity takes time to unfold. Specifically, they discuss how perceived differences between talk and action in these different modalities may influence what communication can accomplish. Whereas intolerance of temporal differences between talk and action can hamper performativity in some modalities, for example in brainstorms where talk is considered valuable in itself, it is likely to facilitate performativity in others, for example in processes of implementation where pressure for talk-action consistency can be a crucial driver. Based on these and other examples, Christensen et al. argue that, although talk *is* action in a number of important respects, CCO research needs to disentangle the two to fully recognize the complexities of communicative constitution.

Haack, Martignoni and Schoeneborn's (2021) study of CSR adoption addresses another dimension of temporality. Specifically, they use an experimental design to simulate how non-adoption, ceremonial adoption, and substantive adoption of CSR practices develop under regimes of, respectively, opacity and transparency. Among other things, their results indicate that a combination of initial opacity – a condition that allows organizations to adopt CSR practices ceremonially – and a subsequent enforcement of a transparency regime is likely to lead to wider substantial adoption of CSR practices than situations characterized by continual transparency. Put differently, organizations, according to this study, are more likely to improve their CSR practices when temporary opacity allows them to first claim their subscription to a CSR ideal and then only gradually adapt their walk to the talk. This insight adds further substance to the notion that inconsistencies between talk and action can drive better practice. If no inconsistencies are noted, internal and external stakeholders may not think of questioning the goals of organizations and may, therefore, not apply pressure for fulfillment. Public attention to inconsistencies, in other words, is not necessarily a fundamental problem for CSR communication, although it may frequently be perceived that way by corporate communicators. Rather, such attention might, as we have argued above, be considered an important felicity condition for CSR performativity (Christensen et al., 2021).

The focus on temporality, thus, illustrates what precarious accomplishments organizations are. Their constitution is always in the making, dependent on the ability to mobilize, empower and sustain commitment and critical attention of multiple audiences over time. Again, this underscores our recurrent observation that CSR performativity involves actors across organizational boundaries (e.g., Kuhn, 2008). In the remaining section, we address additional dimensions of this observation and consider how incipient works might stimulate further insight along these lines.

Voices of Power

Organizations are defined not only by how they deliberately communicate about themselves, but also by how they are invoked or "ventriloquized" by other human or non-human voices (Ashcraft, Kuhn & Cooren, 2009; Cooren, 2020). The nature of CSR communication, with its focus on the wider common good, underscores the importance of considering the voices of a broader range of stakeholders – including the environment and future generations – and their relative power to define what corporate responsibility is.

CSR as Co-Constitution

Such expanded understanding accentuates what Cooren (2020) calls "the challenge of co-constitution" (p. 17). In the context of CSR, co-constitution describes the fact that the meaning of responsibility and its organizational implications is constituted not only by how organizations themselves communicate about such matters, but also by how others interrupt, challenge and contradict such talk. CSR, in other words, is communicated into being through ongoing negotiations and discussions with stakeholders (see also Schultz et al., 2013).

Knight (2007) labels such negotiations and discussions "communicational politics". Communicational politics, he argues, is prevalent especially in situations where communication is defining and shaping new political arenas. Specifically, communicational politics involves practices such as blame management, multilateralism and proceduralism. Blame management, according to Knight, plays a key role in the efforts of social movements to attribute causes and responsibilities for a particular problem. Emphasizing, for example, the environmental risks associated with certain types of production, such movements can draw attention to the lack of responsibility of powerful corporations and governments and force them to rethink and redefine their practices. By focusing on well-known corporate brands, especially, social movements are often able to mobilize the interest of the media and public opinion and this way construct events discursively. Blame management, of course, presupposes that decisions can be convincingly attributed to a specific organization as an actor that can be held responsible for the problems in question and the necessary steps to overcome them (Bencherki et al., 2019). As Grothe-Hammer (2019) shows, however, organizational actorhood is sometimes dispersed by inter-organizational forms of collaboration that obscure responsibility in questionable ways. Some corporations, as Knight (2007) points out, deliberately seek to counter blame management with multilateralism, which serves to spread the blame to more than one corporate actor, and proceduralism, which relegates responsibility to institutional mechanisms such as investigations, assessments, verifications, reporting, etc.

Co-constitution is strikingly salient in the context of CSR where multiple interests and understandings across formal organizational boundaries invoke different notions of what an organization "is" or *ought* to be. The implied complexity and polyphony, however, is at play in many other contexts. No organization is defined by one voice only, but always speaks through several human and non-human representations (Cooren, 2020; Thyssen, 2005). Yet, the CSR context adds to our understanding of co-constitution by foregrounding and elucidating how dissent, opposition and, sometimes, collaboration can play significant roles in shaping communicative performativity. In this respect also, CSR offers important insights for CCO theorizing.

Power and Authority to Define and Constitute CSR

In a contested arena such as CSR, power and authority play significant roles in shaping communicative constitution. The ability to initiate and dominate debates about organizations and their social responsibilities, however, does not necessarily depend on formal power positions. As Kuhn (2008) points out, "[p]ower does not reside exclusively in persons or offices, but is encoded in discursive formations, linguistic distinctions, and material resources" (p. 1229). This observation is particularly relevant in the context of CSR where many different audiences seek to mobilize discourses that can support their understanding of responsibility. Leclercq-Vandelannoitte (2011), thus, uses Foucault's notion of power–knowledge to argue that power is relational and inherent in the discursive practices of different roles and groups (e.g. managers, supervisors, accountants, NGOs), who strive to define organizational reality in order to achieve their particular goals.

As CCO scholarship has emphasized, authority is communicatively accomplished by making prevailing ideals and perspectives present in discussions and debates (e.g. Bencherki, Matte & Cooren, 2019). The notion of "presentification" (Benoit-Barné & Cooren, 2009) accentuates that the chances of having one's ideals about responsibility and proper organizational behavior heard and respected depend on one's ability to mobilize communicative resources such as authoritative documents, tacit understandings or societal values (e.g., Kuhn, 2008). Social actors with such ability may perform authority without formal expertise or recognized power positions (Bourgoin, Bencherki & Faraj, 2020). This is clearly the case in the context of CSR where authorship is radically dispersed and where official corporate understandings of what responsibility entails are frequently challenged and resisted by unofficial voices. Corporate attempts to brand themselves as responsible social actors, for example, are frequently confronted with strong alternative human and non-human voices (Benoit-Barné & Cooren, 2009). This happened to BP's "Beyond Petroleum" campaign, which was aborted after being challenged by an environmental catastrophe, the Deepwater Horizon explosion, as well as by numerous anti-corporate spoofs (Christensen, Morsing & Thyssen, 2015).

When multiple voices seek to speak in the name of the organization, authority to do so becomes a matter of being able to voice concerns and legitimize them. From a CCO perspective, Vásquez et al. (2017) illustrate how strategy-making transforms matters of concern into matters of authority, i.e. certain matters voiced by certain actors become defining of the organization's future actions. Vásquez et al. state that "[i]n order to have an effect in any particular situation, matters of concern must be recognized as such (as matters and concerns) again and again" (p. 10). This observation indicates that performativity hinges on the power to revisit and re-author organizational goals, and to maintain them over time. While such power is often seen to be the prerogative of managers, the CSR context illustrates the important CCO observation that authority is a contested site shaped by tensions and polyphony. Future CCO research, however, should consider in more detail how authority is accomplished and sustained in contexts where multiple external voices strive for attention.

While official responsibility strategies and aspirations may constitute, at least temporarily, what Kuhn (2008) calls "authoritative texts", it is simultaneously such texts that tend to attract critical attention and mobilize resistance of various sorts. The discursively open and polyphonic nature of CSR, especially, is likely to attract such attention and stimulate ongoing power struggles between organizations and their stakeholders (e.g., Schultz et al., 2013). In the context of CSR, authoritative texts, in other words, are not only canonical reference points "encouraging actors to subordinate personal interests to the collective good", as Kuhn (2008, p. 1236) puts it, but also potential battlegrounds upon which responsibility standards are shaped, challenged and (re)constituted. This was clearly illustrated by Livesey and Graham's (2007) study of Royal Dutch Shell, mentioned above, where the company's eco-talk became detached from its origin because it mobilized new actors inside and outside the organization to call for changes. Future CCO research, accordingly, could use this insight from the CSR arena to further elucidate whose interests and concerns are invoked when strategies, ideals, values and aspirations are communicated within and across organizational boundaries.

Importantly, the dimensions of power and authority in CSR communication cannot be fully grasped by focusing exclusively on distinct organizations and their explicit CSR utterances and claims. When organizations communicate in the CSR arena, they simultaneously engage in a social practice with (self-)disciplinary implications. Organizations can discipline themselves, as we have argued, by activating stakeholder scrutiny and transferring power to their critics to expect and demand better practices. Even when CSR talk is ignored by stakeholders, potential critical reactions from such stakeholders have power to shape the extent to which organizations feel committed to their own words. At the same time, explicit organizational submission to CSR norms and values reinforces the significance of these norms and values as disciplinary mechanisms for *other* organizations as well. What is constituted or presentified when organizations talk about CSR, in other words, is not exclusively the organization referred to in CSR messages, but more fundamentally the voices of standards, norms and trends concerning acceptable corporate behavior. While misfire is a constant companion of any speech act, it is through reiterations, contestations, adjustments and variations across many organizations that talk about complex and wide-ranging projects such as CSR has a chance of inspiring and driving organizational behavior (Butler, 2010; Latour, 2013; see also Christensen et al., 2021). CCO research, accordingly, should study the communicative interactions among organizations, their mobilization of social norms, values and standards and their constitutive effects in society more broadly.

By examining how corporations take a political role in society, research on political CSR (PCSR) offers some insight in this regard (e.g., Scherer & Palazzo 2007). Scherer, Rasche, Palazzo and Spicer (2016) have noted that "[w]hile PCSR research has emphasized how legitimacy is communicatively constructed, scholars often neglect how the interactions among various stakeholder groups also change the business models underlying entire industries" (p. 289). The political activities of corporations and NGOs alike can be seen as communicative practices with which they form alliances, lobby for tighter legislation, and constitute new forms of responsibilities. Taking a communicative perspective on such processes, something CCO-based research is well equipped to do, could elucidate the communicative interactions among stakeholders, their mobilization of social figures and their constitutive effects for businesses across different organizations. A CCO perspective could examine, for example, how sustainability standards evolve, change and become institutionalized within and across organizations (cf. Christensen et al., 2017) or how implicit and explicit types of CSR communication interact and vary across organizations, industries and countries (Matten & Moon, 2008, 2020).

Even though the CSR arena calls for CCO research to expand its notion of communicative constitution to include external stakeholders and social and political dynamics, responsibility concerns and responsibility talk may still have distinct performative implications "inside" the organization. In fact, several of the studies cited above indicate that CSR ambitions announced to external audiences are likely to significantly affect employees and organizational practices (e.g., Girschik, 2018; Haack et al., 2012; Koep, 2017). Costas and Kärreman (2013) add that CSR can function as a kind of "aspirational control" that affects how employees see themselves and their role in the organization. Specifically, they suggest that CSR programs define an ideal corporate self that shapes and disciplines how employees understand their role in the organization. Along the same lines, Siltaoja, Malin and Pyykkönen (2015) argue that CSR makes employees both objects and subjects of corporate responsibility. While the organization is considered responsible for its employees, they in turn are expected to perform responsibly on behalf of their workplace. Accordingly, even though some organizational members may be skeptical about CSR communication and its implied values and priorities, it is likely to play an important constitutive role in contemporary organizations. Future research should further explore how social ideals and discourses, such as CSR, shape notions of the ideal employee.

Conclusion

This chapter has argued and illustrated that corporate social responsibility (CSR) provides a unique arena that challenges CCO scholarship on several significant accounts and urges future research to broaden its notion of communicative constitution. By depicting organizations as moral actors responsible for their behaviors, CSR communication tends to mobilize many different types of audiences, both inside and outside the organization, to demand consistency between the talk and the action. Such mobilization, we argue, is a key dimension of CSR performativity. Because of its contentious status in society, this arena can inspire CCO research to "zoom out" of its typical organizational focus. In particular, the CSR context illustrates the immense complexity of communicative constitution that often extends into an uncertain future and therefore has great risk of failing. By foregrounding and explaining how dissent, opposition and collaboration can play significant roles in shaping and, sometimes, obstructing communicative performativity, the CSR arena adds to our understanding of co-constitution. With its emphasis on critical stakeholders, research on CSR communication further illustrates that communicative constitution, while unfolding in specific organizational contexts, is often driven and shaped by important social and political forces. Future CCO research, accordingly, could use insight from the CSR arena to elucidate how many different interests and concerns are invoked when organizations communicate about their strategies, ideals, values and aspirations within and across organizational boundaries.

References

Ashcraft, K. L., Kuhn, T. R., & Cooren, F. (2009). Constitutional amendments: "Materializing" organizational communication. *The Academy of Management Annals, 3*(1), 1–64.

Austin, J. L. (1962). *How to do things with words*. Oxford: Oxford University Press.

Banerjee, S. B. (2008). Corporate social responsibility. The good, the bad and the ugly. *Critical Sociology, 34*(1), 51–79.

Basu, K., & Palazzo, G. (2008). Corporate social responsibility: A process model of sensemaking. *Academy of Management Review, 33*(1), 122–136.

Bencherki, N., Matte, F., & Cooren, F. (Eds.). (2019). *Authority and power in social interaction*. New York: Routledge.

Bencherki, N., Sergi, V., Cooren, F., & Vásquez, C. (2019). How strategy comes to matter: Strategizing as the communicative materialization of matters of concern. *Strategic Organization*. doi.org/10.1177/1476127019890380.

Benoit-Barné, C., & Cooren, F. (2009). The accomplishment of authority through presentification: How authority is distributed among and negotiated by organizational members. *Management Communication Quarterly, 23*(1), 5–31.

Bourgoin, A., Bencherki, N., & Faraj, S. (2020). "And who are you?": A performative perspective on authority in organizations. *Academy of Management Journal, 63*(4), 1134–1165.

Bromley, P. & Powel. W.W. (2012). From smoke and mirrors to walking the talk: Decoupling in the contemporary world. *Academy of Management Annals, 6*(1), 483–533.

Brunsson, N. (2003). Organized hypocrisy. In B. Czarnaiwska & G. Sevón (Eds.), *The Northern lights – organization theory in Scandinavia* (pp. 201–222). Copenhagen: Copenhagen Business School Press.

Butler, J. (2010). Performative agency. *Journal of Cultural Economy, 3*(2), 147–161.

Campbell, J. L. (2007). Why would corporations behave in socially responsible ways? An institutional theory of corporate social responsibility. *Academy of Management Review, 32*(3), 946–967.

Christensen, L. T. (2007). The discourse of corporate social responsibility: Postmodern remarks. In S. May, G. Cheney, & J. Roper (Eds.), *The debate over corporate social responsibility* (pp. 448–458). New York: Oxford University Press.

Christensen, L. T., & Cheney, G. (2011). Interrogating the communicative dimensions of corporate social responsibility. In Ø. Ihlen, J. F. Bartlett, & S. May (Eds.), *The handbook of communication and corporate social responsibility* (pp. 491–504). Chichester: John Wiley & Sons.

Christensen, L.T., Morsing, M., & Thyssen, O. (2013). CSR as aspirational talk. *Organization, 20*(3), 372–393.

Christensen, L.T., Morsing, M. & Thyssen, O. (2015). The polyphony of values and the value of polyphony. *ESSACHESS. Journal for Communication Studies, 8,1*(15), 9–25.

Christensen, L. T., Morsing, M., & Thyssen, O. (2017). License to critique: A communication perspective on sustainability standards. *Business Ethics Quarterly, 27*(2), 239–262.

Christensen, L. T., Morsing, M., & Thyssen, O. (2020). Timely hypocrisy? Hypocrisy temporalities in CSR communication. *Journal of Business Research, 114*, 327–335.

Christensen, L. T., Morsing, M., & Thyssen, O. (2021). Talk-action dynamics: Modalities of aspirational talk. *Organization Studies, 42*(3), 407–427.

Cho, C. H., Laine, M., Roberts, R. W., & Rodrigue, M. (2015). Organized hypocrisy, organizational façades, and sustainability reporting. *Accounting, Organizations and Society, 40*, 78–94.

Cooren, F. (1999). *The organizing property of communication.* Amsterdam: John Benjamins.

Cooren, F. (2020). A communicative constitutive perspective on corporate social responsibility: Ventriloquism, undecidability, and surprisability. *Business & Society, 59*(1), 175–197.

Cooren, F., Kuhn, T., Cornelissen, J. P., & Clark, T. (2011). Communication, organizing and organization: An overview and introduction to the special issue. *Organization Studies, 32*(9), 1149–1170.

Costas, J., & Kärreman, D. (2013). Conscience as control - managing employees through CSR. *Organization, 20*(3), 394–415.

Crane, A., & Glozer, S. (2016). Researching corporate social responsibility communication: Themes, opportunities and challenges. *Journal of Management Studies, 53*(7), 1223–1252.

Dahlsrud, A. (2008). How corporate social responsibility is defined: An analysis of 37 definitions. *Corporate Social Responsibility and Environmental Management, 15*(1), 1–13.

Deetz, S. (2007). Corporate governance, corporate social responsibility, and communication. In S. May, G. Cheney, & J. Roper (Eds.), *The debate over corporate social responsibility* (pp. 267–278). New York: Oxford University Press.

European Commission. (2011). Green paper: Promoting a European framework for corporate social responsibility. Brussels.

Fleming, P., & Banerjee, S. B. (2016). When performativity fails: Implications for critical management studies. *Human Relations, 69*(2), 257–276.

Fleming, P., & Jones, M. T. (2013). *The end of corporate social responsibility.* London: Sage.

Girschik, V. (2020). Shared responsibility for societal problems: The role of internal activists in reframing corporate responsibility, *Business & Society, 59*(1), 34–66.

Gond, J.-P., Cabantous, L., Harding, N., & Learmonth, M. (2016). What do we mean by performativity in organizational and management theory? The uses and abuses of performativity. *International Journal of Management Reviews, 18*(4), 440–463.

Grant, D., Keenoy, T., & Oswick, C. (1998). Introduction: Organizational discourse: Of diversity, dichotomy and multi-disciplinarity. In D. Grant, T. Keenoy, & C. Oswick (Eds.), *Discourse + organization* (pp. 1–13). London: Sage.

Grothe-Hammer, M. (2019). Organization without actorhood: Exploring a neglected phenomenon. *European Management Journal, 37*, 325–338.

Haack, P., Schoeneborn. D., & Wickert, C. (2012). Talking the talk, moral entrapment, creeping commitment? Exploring narrative dynamics in corporate responsibility standardization. *Organization Studies, 33*(5–6), 815–845.

Haack, P., Martignoni, D., & Schoeneborn, D. (2020). A bait-and-switch model of corporate social responsibility. *Academy of Management Review, 46*(3). doi.org/10.5465/amr.2018.0139.

Ihlen, Ø., Bartlett, J. L., & May, S. (2011). *The handbook of communication and corporate social responsibility.* Chichester: Wiley-Blackwell.

Iivonen, K., & Moisander, J. (2015). Rhetorical construction of narcissistic CSR orientation. *Journal of Business Ethics, 131*(3), 649–664.

Jahdi, K., & Acikdilli, G. (2009). Marketing communications and corporate social responsibility (CSR): Marriage of convenience or shotgun wedding? *Journal of Business Ethics, 88*, 103–113.

Knight, G. (2007). Activism, risk and communicational politics. Nike and the sweatshop problem. In S. May, G. Cheney, & J. Roper (Eds.), *The debate over corporate social responsibility* (pp. 305–318). New York: Oxford University Press.

Koep, L. (2017). Tensions in aspirational CSR communication—A longitudinal investigation of CSR reporting. *Sustainability, 9*(12), 2202. https://doi.org/10.3390/su9122202.

Kolk, A. (2003). Trends in sustainability reporting by the Fortune Global 250. *Business Strategy and the Environment, 12,* 279–291.

Kuhn, T. (2008). A communicative theory of the firm: Developing an alternative perspective on intra-organizational power and stakeholder relationships. *Organization Studies, 29*(8–9), 1227–1254.

Kuhn, T. (2012). Negotiating the micro-macro divide thought leadership from organizational communication for theorizing organization. *Management Communication* Quarterly, *26*(4), 543–584.

Latour, B. (2013). "What's the story?" Organizing as a mode of existence. In D. Robichaud & F. Cooren (Eds.), *Organization and organizing: Materiality, agency and discourse* (pp. 37–51). New York: Routledge.

Leclercq-Vandelannoitte, A. (2011). Organizations as discursive constructions: A Foucauldian approach. *Organization Studies, 32*(9), 1247–1271.

Livesey, S. M., & Graham, J. (2007). Greening of corporations? Eco-talk and the emerging social imaginary of sustainable development. In S. May, G. Cheney, & J. Roper (Eds.), *The debate over corporate social responsibility* (pp. 336–350). New York: Oxford University Press.

Lockett, A., Moon, J., & Visser, W. (2006). Corporate social responsibility in management research: Focus, nature, salience and sources of influence. *Journal of Management Studies, 43*(1), 115–136.

March, J. G. (2007). Ibsen, ideals, and the subornation of lies. *Organizations Studies, 28*(8), 1277–1284.

Matten, D., & Moon, J. (2008). "Implicit" and explicit" CSR: A conceptual framework for a comparative understanding of corporate social responsibility. *Academy of Management Review, 33*(2), 404–424.

Matten, D., & Moon, J. (2020). Reflections on the 2018 decade award: The meaning and dynamics of corporate social responsibility. *Academy of Management Review, 45*(1), 7–28.

Mäkinen, J., & Kourula, A. (2012). Pluralism in political corporate social responsibility. *Business Ethics Quarterly, 22*(4), 649–678.

McKinlay, A. (2011). Performativity: From J. L. Austin to Judith Butler. In P. Armstrong & G. Lightfoot (Eds.), *'The leading journal in the field': Destabilizing authority in the social sciences of management* (pp. 119–142). London: Mayfly.

Morsing, M., & Schultz, M. (2006). Corporate social responsibility communication: Stakeholder information, response and involvement strategies. *Business Ethics: A European Review, 15*(4), 323–338.

Okoye, A. (2009). Theorising corporate social responsibility as an essentially contested concept: Is a definition necessary? *Journal of Business Ethics, 89*(4), 613–627.

Penttilä, V. (2020). Aspirational talk in strategy texts: A longitudinal case study of strategic episodes in corporate social responsibility communication. *Business & Society, 59*(1), 67–97.

Roberts, J. (2003). The manufacture of corporate social responsibility: Constructing corporate sensibility. *Organization, 10*(2), 249–265.

Scherer, A. G., & Palazzo, G. (2007). Toward a political conception of corporate responsibility: Business and society seen from a Habermasian perspective. *Academy of Management Review, 32*(4), 1096–1120.

Scherer, A. G., Rasche, A., Palazzo, G., & Spicer, A. (2016). Managing for political corporate social responsibility: New challenges and directions for PCSR 2.0. *Journal of Management Studies, 53*(3), 273–298.

Schoeneborn, D., Kuhn, T. R., & Kärreman, D. (2018). The communicative constitution of organization, organizing, and organizationality. *Organization Studies, 40*(4), 475–496.

Schoeneborn, D., Morsing, M., & Crane, A. (2020). Formative perspectives on the relation between CSR communication and CSR practices: Pathways for walking, talking, and t(w)alking. *Business & Society, 59*(1), 5–33.

Schoeneborn, D., & Trittin, H. (2013). Transcending transmission: Towards a constitutive perspective on CSR communication. *Corporate Communications: An International Journal, 18*(2), 193–211.

Schultz, F., Castelló, I., & Morsing, M. (2013). The construction of corporate social responsibility in network society: A communication view. *Journal of Business Ethics, 115*(4), 681–692.

Seele, P., & Lock, I. (2015). Instrumental and/or deliberative? A typology of CSR communication tools. *Journal of Business Ethics, 131*(2), 401–414.

Sen, S., Bhattacharya, C. B., & Korschun, D. (2006). The role of corporate social responsibility in strengthening multiple stakeholder relationships: A field experiment. *Journal of the Academy of Marketing Sciences, 34*(2), 158–166.

Siltaoja, M., Malin, V., & Pyykkönen, M. (2015). 'We are all responsible now': Governmentality and responsibilized subjects in corporate social responsibility. *Management Learning, 46*(4), 444–460.

Sturdy, A., & Fleming, P. (2003). Talk as technique – A critique of the words and deeds distinction in the diffusion of customer service cultures in call centres. *Journal of Management Studies, 40*(4), 753–773.

Taylor, J. R., & van Every, E. (2000). *The emergent organization: Communication as its side and surface.* Mahwah, NJ: Lawrence Erlbaum.

Thyssen, O. (2005). The invisibility of the organization. *Ephemera, 5*(3), 519–536.

Vásquez, C., Bencherki, N., Cooren, F., & Sergi, V. (2017). From 'matters of concern' to 'matters of authority': Studying the performativity of strategy from a communicative constitution of organization (CCO) approach. *Long Range Planning, 51,* 417–435.

Winkler, P., Etter, M., & Castelló, I. (2020). Vicious and virtuous circles of aspirational talk: From self-persuasive to agonistic CSR rhetoric. *Business & Society, 59*(1), 98–128.

23

THE BLUE MARBLE EFFECT

Globalization, Visibility and Lenticulation

Shiv Ganesh, Cynthia Stohl and Sam James

Globalization has always tacitly, if not overtly, been conceptualized visually. In fact, the ascendance of visibility as a communicative force is deeply enmeshed with a fundamental driver of globalization: the compression of time and space. Scholars across multiple disciplines, including sociology (Robertson, 1992; Giddens, 1990), cultural and postcolonial studies (Minh-Ha, 2014), and communication (Shome and Hegde, 2002; Hegde, 2011), have grappled with many kinds of communicative transformations related to global time-space compression, including aural, textual, and post-representational forms of communication. However, it is visibility that has emerged, more than these other communicative forms and dynamics, as a dominant, problematic, and quintessentially modern phenomenon (Brighenti, 2007).

This is true for scholars of organizational communication as well. Visibility is implicit in how we approach globalization: as the permeability of boundaries (Stohl, 2005), as affordances of emerging communication technologies (Treem, Leonardi & Jackson, 2010), as increasingly dense social, cultural-political, and economic networks (Castells, 1996), and as intelligence infrastructures, algorithms, and platforms that produce and compile extensive amounts of digital traces (Flyverbom, 2016; Stohl, Stohl, & Leonardi, 2016). However, despite the ascendance of visibility and the rise of visibility studies in organizational studies broadly, scholars of organizational communication have only just begun to come to grips with the need to develop an overtly visual vocabulary for understanding visibility vis-à-vis globalization. Accordingly, our goal in this chapter is to ask scholars committed to investigating the constitutive force of communication in organizing to productively engage with the visibility dynamics of globalization in explicitly visual terms.

We address this goal by employing the metaphor of the Blue Marble, one of the earliest and most iconic renditions of globalization. Taken during the Apollo 17 mission in 1972, the first photograph of the Earth as one entity quickly became a symbol of global unity, and a powerful and resonant metonym (Petsko, 2011). The global environmentalist movement endorsed and used it to effectively promote representations of the world as a fragile interconnected ecosystem suspended in space (Cosgrove, 2014). As an iconic image, the Blue Marble has also played a significant role in corporate communication, ranging from the default iPhone background, the name of dozens of accountancy and communication consulting firms, as well as global training initiatives. Conversely, others have critiqued the image, saying that the image promotes a naïve unity in the face of all available counter evidence, and that it popularizes a rigid and reified understanding of the world (Latour, 2018). As a communicative metonymy, then, the image

DOI: 10.4324/9781003224914-27

Figure 23.1 The 1972 Blue Marble image.
Image credit: NASA.

provides a vivid and provocative backdrop against which an explicitly visual vocabulary for apprehending global organizing dynamics can be generated.

We address our goal in two steps. First, we survey the terrain of existing scholarship on globalization and the communicative constitution of organization (CCO), using Stohl and Ganesh's (2014) framework that identifies three generations of scholarship on globalization, reviewing how these generations are evident both explicitly and implicitly in CCO scholarship. We also identify dominant metaphors of communication evident in such scholarship: interactional, textual, structural, and post-representational. Second, we draw attention anew to the need to understand communication as a visual dynamic vis-à-vis globalization. Here, we draw inspiration from the Blue Marble. We offer the term "lenticulation" to think through the Blue Marble Effect in communicative terms, arguing that in visual terms, globalization *is* lenticulation, and that the Blue Marble Effect is evident in the form of three lenticular practices: transformation, animation, and depth. We then work through each lenticular practice using an exemplar of organizational communication scholarship on globalization to illustrate the utility of a lenticular analysis.

Organizational Communication, CCO and Globalization

As we said at the outset, visual conceptualizations of and metaphors for globalization are evident across the social sciences and humanities and have been for a while. Schivelbusch (1986) for instance, showed how the affordances of erstwhile "new" global technologies – in this case, the railway – "translated into a new architectural regime based on heightened visibility, a form of esthetics of transparency" (Styhre, 2017, p. 40). Carey's generative work on Space, Time, and the Telegraph (1992) similarly illustrated how technological systems were bound up with the idea of a new visuality. Lyon (2001) identified global surveillance as the product of a series of technological, political, and economic arrangements put in place since the 1970s. And Minh-ha (2014) is one among several postcolonial anthropologists who have argued that while modernity produces and privileges visual epistemologies, there are multiple modes of knowing, and seeing is not necessarily believing. The emergence of visibility is thus based upon and generated from text, print and typography and must be seen with and against it in dialectical terms (Brighenti, 2007).

Organizational communication scholars have drawn creatively from these disciplines in both conceptualizing and studying globalization. Such work has flourished in critical scholarship (Zoller, 2004), network studies (Stohl, 1993; Monge, 1998), feminist scholarship (Biwa, 2020), structuration (Banks & Riley, 1993) and postcolonial approaches (Broadfoot & Munshi, 2007). However, the attention to visibility as a communicative force in this body of work has been much more latent than manifest, despite visibility becoming an active topic of inquiry in organizational communication studies.

At the same time, organizational communication scholars whose work is attuned to the communicative constitution of organization (CCO) have productively engaged with broad debates in the humanities and social sciences about new ontologies, materiality and relationality (e.g., Kuhn et al., 2017) to fundamentally rethink what counts as organizational communication itself. Consequently, it makes sense to ground attempts to develop visual metaphors for globalization regarding this body of work. To do this, a critical starting point is the question of how CCO scholars have in fact approached questions of globalization. We attend to this issue in this section by examining implicitly global concepts in CCO scholarship before turning our attention to explicitly global concepts, sorting through studies using Stohl and Ganesh's (2014) identification of three generations of scholarship on globalization. We then turn our attention to conceptions and metaphors of communication in CCO scholarship on globalization, arguing why CCO scholarship on globalization needs to take visibility seriously.

Implicit and Explicit Views of Globalization in CCO Scholarship

While several scholars have explicitly addressed the question of globalization in their work (including Del Fa and Kärreman's assessment of CCO vis-à-vis neoliberal capitalism in this volume), several others have developed *implicitly* global concepts that problematize notions of locality and origin, and consequently invoke the idea of spatiotemporal collapse. For instance, the concept of ventriloquism, understood as "actions through which someone or something makes someone or something else say or do things" (Cooren, 2015, p. 475), implies that communicative interactions are never purely local, rather they are dislocal (Cooren & Fairhurst, 2009), and that points of communicative articulation are always manifestations of forces at play elsewhere. Likewise, Dobusch and Schoeneborn's (2015) work on organizational fluidity places into focus open and changing organizational boundaries, as well as ideas of seamlessness, flexibility, and speed, once again conjuring images of a world where actions in one locale reach across and inflect organizing in other parts of the world almost instantly. We also observe that such work on CCO often draws explicitly on the Deleuzian notion of deterritorialization (e.g., Ganesh & Wang, 2015), a process that, as Castells (1996) has pointed out, in a more structural formulation, lies at the very heart of globalization.

Put this way, we would argue that a considerable portion of CCO scholarship could, in fact, be construed as implicitly global, and that CCO provides a useful explanatory ground in general for understanding temporal and spatial dynamics involved in globalization. For instance, the notion of *spacing practices* as outlined by Vásquez and Cooren (2013) specifies the constitutive role of communication in materializing organization and distributing actors in space and time, by focusing upon presentifying, ordering and accounting practices. Interestingly, their work is grounded explicitly on Massey's work on global space as elucidated in her book *World Cities* (2007). Below, we turn our attention to how CCO scholarship has explicitly articulated globalization as a communicative force.

Generating Globalization and the Communicative Constitution of Organizing

Recent work on CCO that explicitly considers globalization encompasses a range of views and includes all three generations of scholarship on globalization as identified by Stohl and Ganesh (2014): uncertainty, connectivity, and ubiquity. Scholarship in the first generation, *Uncertainty*, focuses upon different communicative manifestations of organizational structures, cultures, and logics in the global landscape, comparing differences and seeking out similarities, to ask whether certain organizational forms could be considered global. The second generation, *Connectivity*, seeks to understand the impact of global forms of organizing, focusing upon networks as the quintessential organizational form, examining different network characteristics, as well as positioning networks as a broad metaphor for organizational life itself. The third generation of scholarship, *Ubiquity*, investigates how global dynamics are ever present, unremarkable, and digitally saturated, and are now in the mundane backdrop of most kinds of organizing practices, both formal and informal.

Tritten-Ulbrech and Schoeneborn's (2017) work on reconceptualizing diversity management from a CCO perspective is a good example of how the first generation of scholarship is manifested in CCO work. Their study spotlights communicative attributes of cultural awareness and accommodation as well as engaging intercultural differences using Bahktin's concept of polyphony. Contemporary CCO scholarship has also engaged with communicative and ontological attributes of the second generation of globalization research, which emphasizes global networks, logics, and practices. Kuhn and Marshall (2019), for instance, employed an ecosystem metaphor to understand recently expanding entrepreneurial hubs, outlining a networking logic of globalization that is characterized by interorganizational actors and boundary spanners. Gibbs, Boyraz, Sivunen, and Nordbäck (2020) engaged in a similar approach in their study of global virtual teams that rely on interorganizational linkages based on expertise and stakeholder relationships. Wenzel and Will's (2019) work on the role of communication in the production and reproduction of academic fields once more illustrates the move from an intergroup logic to a more global networking one. Mann's (2015) work on La Vía Campesina, a transnational network of over 160 rural peoples' organizations in more than 70 countries, also exemplifies this logic in its implicit recognition of a global public sphere that underlies how this social movement is communicatively constituted.

Scholarship on globalization from the CCO tradition has also addressed ubiquity, the third generation of scholarship, positioning globalization as evident not only in formal organizational structures, but as ever present, no longer unusual, and in the backdrop of all forms of organizing. Porter, Kuhn, and Nerlich's (2018) study of the manifestation of authority in digital debates about global climate change is a case in point. The very idea of coauthoring as elucidated by these authors illustrates the always-already global hue of concepts such as climate change. As scholarship on this generation in the CCO tradition develops, the distinction between implicitly global and explicitly global scholarship is likely to blur further, and considerably.

Conceptions of Communication in CCO Scholarship on Globalization

As CCO scholarship has engaged with these three generations of globalization, it has done so using diverse definitions of what counts as communication itself. Four interrelated metaphors in particular stand out: interactional, textual, structurational and post-representational, drawing from the full range of theories that are implicated in the CCO moniker (for a discussion, see Cooren and Seidl, this volume). Studies that emphasize interactional metaphors tend to be conversation-analytic in their sensibility. Cooren, Brummans, and Charrieras (2008), for example, draw from Cooren's ethnographic work with Médecins Sans Frontières to explore how differences between this iconic global health organization and local health clinics in the Congo were interactionally negotiated in meetings. In doing so, they explored first-generational issues in globalization, focusing on cultural valuations of the place of paid versus free healthcare.

Other scholars have employed more textual approaches to the study of CCO. While still working with and drawing from the Montreal School's emphasis upon text-conversation dialectics (Taylor & Van Every, 2010), the analytical focus is upon textual semantics. For instance, Eddington's (2018) analysis of the communicative constitution of hate organizations online deployed semantic network analytic techniques to explore connections between Trump supporters in the US and white supremacist groups in other parts of the world, particularly the United Kingdom. In so doing, it drew from and built upon concerns with networked organizational forms characteristic of the second generation of scholarship on globalization.

Still other scholars have used more structurational metaphors of communication (Brummans, Cooren, Robichaud, & Taylor, 2014) to understand CCO in the context of global organizing. For instance, Aten & Thomas (2016) used McPhee and Zaug's (2001) four flows model, grounded in a structurational analysis of communication, to analyze how the US Navy deployed a far-reaching crowdsourcing technology to develop collaborative strategy around war games. Crowdsourcing, which by definition throws open organizational boundaries to a transnational public, is a quintessentially third-generation phenomenon, resting as it does upon the premise that digital technologies are ubiquitous and far-reaching.

CCO scholarship on globalization has also drawn from broadly post-representational and relational views of communication (Kuhn et al., 2017). For instance, Mease (2020) outlined a view of organizing grounded in a relational ontology, inspired by Deleuzian "techniques and forces" view of communication. She re-analyzed Albu's (2019) account of the communicative interchanges between the Moroccan government and a global civil society organization, where each organization "Protected their organization's primary constitutive force, while fostering a disorganizing relation of forces for the other through the production and imposition of disruptive forces and techniques" (p. 22).

Despite the theoretical breadth of CCO scholarship as well as its engagement with multiple generations of globalization, it is increasingly important for such work to explicitly consider addressing globalization in terms of visibility. In this next section, we discuss why and how visibility has emerged as a central problematic in globalization.

Visualizing the Communicative Constitution of Organization and Globalization

The increasing emphasis upon visibility implicated in technological innovation and the compression of time and space has made visibility a central communication phenomenon in organizational communication studies at large. Ganesh, Stohl and James (in press) refer to it as a fourth generation of scholarship on globalization, the generation of *Visibility*. Global time-space compression (Robertson, 1992; Baumann, 2000) has produced conditions of constant visibility in the form of regimes and networks of global coordination and control that rely on such visual modes of communication as observation, transparency, and surveillance. In the process, visibility has become a major organizing force with considerable work done on it in organizational studies (Stohl et al., 2016; Flyverbom, 2016, 2019; Leonardi & Treem, 2020) but, with some exceptions (e.g., Cruz, 2017), not much organizational communication scholarship has explicitly engaged with visibility in the context of global or transnational organizing.

The *Generation of Visibility* is characterized by, first, recognizing how globalization both produces and magnifies systemic problems by making them visible and invisible and, subsequently, directing research to bring those emerging complexities to light. In this generation of research, the locus of globalization is not so much in formal organizations or networks, or even in the backdrop of organizing, as it is in the relationship between what is in focus and out of focus, between visible and invisible, between movable and immovable. Thus, the locus of globalization is most evident in terms of global flows of money, technology, people, artifacts, ideas, and culture (Ganesh & Stohl, 2020). In this way, it implicates logics of disorganizing and instability as much as organizing and order (see Vásquez & Kuhn, this volume).

Stohl & Stohl's (2011) commentary on Al Qaeda and invisibility, and Schoeneborn & Scherer's (2012) response, is an early example of CCO scholars taking issues of global visibility seriously. Stohl and Stohl's study of clandestine organizations challenged what they framed as the Montreal School's implicit but unexamined assumption that visibility is necessary for the communicative constitution of organization. No one would deny Al Qaeda's existence as an organization, they argued, but its status as a clandestine organizing would pose "theoretical challenges for viewing organizations as communicatively constituted" (p. 1199) and result in a need to view anew the range of social and historical forces that create organizations. In response to Stohl and Stohl's (2011) push for a communication-centered approach to organizational constitution, Schoeneborn and Scherer (2012) argued that Stohl and Stohl's perspective on CCO, while valuable, underestimated both the text-conversation dialectic and the processual ontology of the Montreal school. In their view, the formation of Al Qaeda is characterized by diachronic periods of visibility and invisibility, underscoring the processual ontology of the Montreal School.

However, their work did not outline what a post-dualistic view of visibility itself might entail, perhaps because their work continued to position communication as caught in the text-conversation dialectic, rather than one that considers the interplay between typography and visibility. Brighenti's influential (2007) positioning of visibility as a generative category in the social sciences argues that the supremacy of vision as a sense is dialectically linked with the dominance of print. Visibility as a field that emerges from this dialectic, Brighenti argues, has three characteristics: it is relational, strategic, and processual.

Taking visibility seriously and developing a new vocabulary grounded in an overtly visual language oriented towards this dialectic is a project that aligns well with the move beyond the subject-object dichotomy that characterizes post-representational views of CCO. It also helps with the more recent project of developing a vocabulary for organizing that moves beyond the dualist heritage implied in distinctions between conversation and text, interaction and language, or discourse versus Discourse. We turn back to the Blue Marble to help us with an initial think-through of a CCO perspective on visibility, focusing on the notion of lenticulation and three associated practices.

The Blue Marble Effect

As we said at the outset, the original Blue Marble image (and the many others that followed it over the years) has had considerable visual impact. As all powerful images do, the original photograph communicated a lot in acute and simple terms. Over the next several decades the image became an indelible part of the political and organizing landscape of the 1970s and 1980s, becoming shorthand for the emerging US edge in cold war politics, and the visual impetus for the global environmental movement (Wuebbles, 2012). As policies crafted during the Thatcher and Regan regimes began to take hold, the Blue Marble image was even used on occasion to promote the emerging neoliberal world order.

The image of One World that the Blue Marble connotes has now been resonant for nearly half a century and continues to attract critique and assessment. Latour's (2018) *Down to Earth*, for instance, critiqued the Blue Marble for its flattened, externalized, and two-dimensional representation of life on Earth, arguing instead for a more complete notion of Gaia as a living, three-dimensional entity that includes life in all its forms. Regardless of the stance one takes on the Blue Marble, or the specific critique that one might make, it is indisputable that the idea of "global" as a visual field, force, and ethic as promoted by the Blue Marble image has had a profound foundational impact on how we organize; and perhaps that might be why a graphic version of the image was featured on the cover of *Down to Earth* itself.

Lenticulation

What we are calling the Blue Marble Effect thus encompasses not the reductivity of the image per se, but the enlivening, animating and complexifying impact that the idea of "the Global" has had upon organizing problems, processes, and outcomes. To apprehend this impact in overtly visual terms, and to help understand how one might position such visual vocabulary in terms of a dialectic between print and visibility, we employ the term *lenticulation*. Lenticulation is a technique for printing images, created by an array of magnifying lenses designed so that when viewed from slightly different angles different aspects of the image are magnified ("Lenticular, how it works", 2016).

As a technique, lenticulation encompasses all three features of visibility as a field (Brighenti, 2007). First, it is *relational*: seeing, observing, apprehending, and surveilling as acts of visual communication are produced entirely by the relational stance and spatial arrangements between the seeing agent and the seen. Second, visibility is asymmetrical and always imperfectly reciprocal: the act of seeing and lenticulating is an act of power. Thus, because visibility involves inequality, it acts as a resource, and is hence *strategic*. Third, visibility is *processual*: it is unfolding, dynamic and shifting; as Cruz (2017) points out, this processual aspect implies that the relationship between visibility and invisibility itself is interrelated and complementary rather than oppositional.

Lenticulation as an image-printing technique is composed of three sets of printing practices that involve blending images in different ways ("How Exactly does Lenticular Printing Work?", 2020). The first practice is *transformation*. This involves a wide shift in viewing angle, which consequently changes one image into another. Smaller movements do not change the image until the viewer has reached a specific point, whereupon the image transforms completely. A second lenticular practice is *animation*. This involves a relatively small shift in viewing angle. This slight shift in viewing perspective creates the impression of constant movement, motion, and flow. The printer combines very similar prints to create an image that moves or morphs as the viewer moves. A third practice is *depth*, which involves a miniscule and barely perceptible shift in viewing angle, where viewers can see multiple combined images without moving either themselves or the print. This creates a deeper, three-dimensional or stereoscopic effect.

Our analysis of these three lenticular practices initially involved an informal scan of research on globalization and organizational communication published in the last 20 years, to see how these practices were latently embedded in scholarly work. Our corpus of 107 articles and chapters, made up of work on globalization across multiple traditions in organizational communication studies over the past two decades, showed that while several analyses invoked one or two lenticular practices, often, we found one dominant practice at work in each analysis. All three lenticular practices featured surprisingly evenly: we identified 34 pieces that privileged transformation, 41 that featured animation, and 35 others that emphasized depth.

Rather than present readers with a mechanical and arid review of this distribution, we take up each of these lenticular practices in turn, illustrating and analyzing them using insights from prominent scholarly work on globalization and organizational communication. We explicitly examine their relational, strategic, and processual qualities to help bring out the hitherto latently visual nature of their analysis and critique. Below, we first develop transformation as a lenticular practice using Ganesh, Zoller and Cheney's (2005) piece, *Transforming Resistance*, on globalization and social movement organizing. Next, we turn to a recently published provocative study, *Debunking Eurocentrism*, by Cruz and Sodeke (2020), to examine animation. And finally, we review Dempsey, Parker and Krone's (2011) analysis of transnational feminist networks, titled *Navigating Socio-Spatial Difference*, to cast light on depth as a lenticular practice.

Transformation

Ganesh, Zoller and Cheney's (2005) work explicitly took on the issue of transformation, setting an agenda for theoretical and empirical investigation of globalization and resistance in organizational communication studies, drawing from and analyzing the globalization-from-below movement at the turn of the millennium. While there is some recognition of visual dimensions of communication in their work, most notably in their discussion of image politics (Deluca, 1999), visibility per se remains latent in this piece. Their work implies that the sudden visibility of large coalitions of anti-globalization protesters in Seattle and, as Deluca's analysis implies, shocking (to some) visuals of glass on the streets, resulted in a kind of mutual *relational transformation*; a reckoning, and a visible acknowledgment, on the part of globalization from both "above" as well as "below", that there was considerable public dissatisfaction with the "Washington Consensus". This in fact was echoed in both the organizing moves of activists at subsequent WTO protests, as well as the organizers of the summits themselves, resulting in a cat-and-mouse game of alternating visibility and secrecy as activists organized protests and WTO officials prepared surreptitious security measures in places such as Doha and Hong Kong. The seeing agents, composed of not just organizers but also the general public, were thrust in and out of relational connection with the protests and subsequent summits as their visibility mutually transformed.

The highly visible protests also brought into relief the *strategic* transformations enabled by internet-based mobilizations. The authors cite Prokosch (2002) to explain how loosely networked activists were able to accomplish much more because of the digital technologies at their disposal, and in some ways were able to flip their status as objects that were "seen" to agents that were themselves doing their own kind of seeing—the slogan of Indymedia, which was born in Seattle, was, after all "don't hate the media, be the media" (later shortened on the Indymedia masthead to "be the media").

Finally, Ganesh, Zoller and Cheney's piece also draws attention, albeit implicitly, to the open-ended, *processual*, and ongoing nature of transformation. They cite Falk's (1999) work on globalization from below to argue that the newly visible movement in Seattle was an instantiation of an open-ended, unpredictable, and democratic process that sought reconciliatory forms of democratic transformation in manners that could sometimes, surprisingly, mirror the "openness and dynamism associated with globalization from above" (p. 181) even while they countered its pressures to privatize and marketize the commons.

Animation

Our illustration of animation as a lenticular practice draws from Cruz and Sodeke's evocative piece *Debunking Eurocentrism in Organizational Communication* (2020). Drawing inspiration from CCO scholarship, the authors develop the notion of liquidity as an organizing principle that implicitly challenges globalization. Communities in the Global South that are marginalized by the Global Economy are simultaneously placed in a condition of liquidity by virtue of their marginalization even as they can use this liquidity to maneuver their own visibility. The authors tease out three properties of such liquidity, motion, solvency, and permeability, and derive their insights with vignettes from fieldwork with susu groups in Liberia, the Old Matadi community (a neighborhood in Monrovia), as well as street traders in Lagos. In the process, they outline three features of marginal liquidity that align surprisingly well with relational, strategic, and processual aspects of visibility. Throughout their work, visibility is nascent: not emphasized, but an evident part of organizing.

Relational animation is akin to Cruz and Sodeke's description of motion as one of three properties of liquidity. Motion, in their view, is the movement of individual bodies across sites and locations. In a striking vignette, they describe the constant interplay between traffic in Lagos and hawkers who are selling all kinds of goods; as cars move, the hawkers sprint alongside, and as traffic come to a standstill, so do the hawkers congregate differently. This describes an elaborate, dynamic, and generative process whereby hawkers see traffic and vice versa. The traffic jam itself is therefore a "moving, living, unpredictable space of organizing" predicated on the mutual visibility of hawkers and traffic. Motion, it appears, is a relational construct: how fast something can move and whether it appears to be in place depends entirely on where you are.

Strategic animation is evident in Cruz and Sodeke's notion of solvency, which describes how people can fade into and emerge from their organizing backdrops—or in other terms, how they make themselves visible and invisible. They describe how susu groups dissolved for prolonged periods during the Liberian war, but recongregated, often with the very same members, once it was safe to do so. This ability of groups to fade in and out of the background in the face of acute power asymmetries captures not only an important aspect of resistance to globalization, but also the fact that visibility is never reciprocal, and that an important part of resistance in visual terms is the ability to become invisible.

Finally, the authors describe the third property of liquidity, permeability, and in doing so they highlight the notion of processual animation vividly. By permeability, they refer to the constant infiltration of context and case, foreground with background. For instance, one vignette about women at the market who are also part of a mutual payment susu group describes the interweaving of private (hidden) space and public (visible) space, observing how children often stopped by the market if they needed anything; it is worth reproducing a portion of the vignette below:

[The women] were so deeply embedded in the fabric of daily life that they were indistinguishable from it. For instance, susu groups are only visible when market women exchange daily susu money. At 4:00 p.m., susu mothers walk from stall to stall and ask women for their dues. Even in that case, it takes a trained eye to identify such activity as susu practice because money transactions take place in the market all the time.

This vignette vividly illustrates how seeing something slightly differently changes and animates the texture of organizing.

Depth

The final lenticular practice, depth, is well illustrated by Dempsey, Parker and Krone's (2011) piece titled *Navigating Socio-Spatial Difference, Constructing Counter-Space*. This study of transnational feminist networks (TFNs) examined how feminist groups navigated between universal/global notions of feminisms and the exigencies of regional, local, and particularistic place-based politics that complicated global assertions, as they tried to build a collective identity. Relational depth is evident in their analysis of socio-spatial difference. Here, they argue that a stated commitment by some feminist organizers to honoring difference between groups of women resulted in an acknowledgment and visibility of different contexts, religions, and points of view across different women's groups. The emergence of difference as a relational marker between groups of women adds considerable depth to what counts as women's experience and solidarity.

The authors also allude to a kind of strategic depth in their work when they discuss the emergence of regional imaginaries in transnational feminist networks. The establishment of regional networks in such places as the Mediterranean or the Global South ensured that groups were able to come together and spotlight collective identities that stood on their own terms rather than being framed as "being different". This was depth thus referred to as the making visible of the rootedness of identities in local, regional soil even as they developed transnational solidarity. This in turn performed an important resistive function and prevented them from being othered by the global network. Finally, they talk about processual depth by implying that the potential for conflicts between newly visible regional and particularized identities on one hand, and the universalized and somewhat essentialized network on the other, was never ending, would continue to evolve in unpredictable directions, and therefore needed to continue to be held in tension. In the era of visibility, depth as a practice of lenticulation provides relational, strategic, and processual space to gain a more inclusive, detailed understanding of contemporary global organizing.

Conclusion

In this chapter we sought to lay out how scholarship committed to studying the communicative constitution of organization and organizing could come to grips with the ever-evolving dynamics of globalization. We have shown how such scholarship has used a wide range of metaphors for communicating and organizing as it has examined globalizing processes. While globalization is a vital concern of such scholarship, it has also not engaged much with dynamics of visibility which are beginning to take center stage in the research and study of globalization. Yet, this body of work contains considerable potential to examine globalization in terms of visibility precisely because of the rich conceptions of communication that it contains. We have sought to provide a direction for how this might happen, using the Blue Marble as a metaphor. We positioned the Blue Marble Effect as lenticulation and identified a set of three lenticular practices through which we might analyze globalization in visual terms.

Why was this important to do? After all, organizational communication studies in general and CCO scholarship in particular have been subject to a dizzying array of new terms, concepts, and vocabularies. Why add to that list? There are several reasons. For one, the ascendance of visibility in organizational studies in general makes it important that we place it in a more the-oretically central place than has hitherto been done. Second, while several studies of visibility in organizational communication studies have been published in the last decade, their take on visibility tends to be grounded in informational views of communication. Leonardi and Treem's (2020) positioning of behavioral visibility, for example, considers its antecedents to be datafication, digitization and digitalization. While their perspective is vastly more complex than a transmissional or conduit view of communication, we believe there is much to be gained from using an explicitly visual vocabulary to consider issues of visibility. That is precisely what we have set out to do in this chapter.

For example, we placed Cooren et al.'s (2008) piece on Médecins Sans Frontières in the first generation of globalization scholarship, as it prioritizes discursive differences as a practice of rec-ognizing constituting organization through communication. Adopting a lenticulation perspec-tive may give purchase instead to the practices of animation in the experience of a renowned humanitarian organization working in the Democratic Republic of the Congo, Africa. The emerging visibility of relational, strategic, and processual practice that influences organizational constitution both inside and outside of interactional meetings between stakeholders fosters a deeper understanding of the tangibly global elements of their communicative labor.

Positioning globalization and visibility in visual terms, we have argued, involves the idea that globalization *is* lenticulation. Transformation, animation, and depth as three lenticular practices are what constitute globalization using visual terms. Doing so has some implications for how we might study globalization further. Namely, the lenticular practices taken together offer a helpful template to understand how many forms, contexts and practices of organizing are imbued with a global sensibility even when it is not explicitly mentioned. We have, in fact, already listed several CCO concepts that are implicitly global. As such scholarship moves for-ward, we believe that the lines between implicitly and explicitly global concepts will continue to blur.

Finally, using explicitly visual terms to apprehend visibility helps with the broader project of developing post-representational views within the larger CCO project. We have argued that an attention to visibility has the potential to transcend dualistic thinking that has prevailed in how we understand and position communication between subject and object, discourse and materi-ality, and language and action. Visibility as a force involves focusing on the active and ongoing dynamic between seeing and being seen, regardless of whether those processes are techno-logical, automated, or even animate. We hope that the threefold schema we have proposed here will help with that broad, complex, and useful project.

References

Albu, O. B. (2019). Dis/ordering: The use of information and communication technologies by human rights civil society organizations. In C. Vásquez & T. Kuhn (Eds.), *Dis/organization as com-munication: Exploring the disordering, disruptive and chaotic properties of communication* (pp. 151–171). New York: Routledge.

Apollo 17 Crew. (1972) The Blue Marble [Photograph]. *NASA.* www.nasa.gov/content/blue-marble-image-of-the-earth-from-apollo-17.

Aten, K., & Thomas, G. F. (2016). Crowdsourcing strategizing: Communication technology affordances and the communicative constitution of organizational strategy. *International Journal of Business Communication, 53*(2), 148–180.

Banks, S., & Riley, P. (1993). Structuration theory as ontology for communication research. *Annals of the International Communication Association, 16,* 167–198.

Bauman, Z. (2000). *Liquid modernity.* Cambridge, UK: Polity Press.

Biwa, V. (2020). African Feminisms and Co-constructing a Collaborative Future with Men: Namibian Women in Mining's Discourses. *Management Communication Quarterly, 35*(1), 43–68

Brighenti, A. (2007). Visibility: A category for the social sciences. *Current Sociology, 55*(3), 323–342.

Broadfoot, K., & Munshi, D. (2007). Diverse voices and alternative rationalities: Imagining forms of post-colonial organizational communication. *Management Communication Quarterly, 21*(2), 249–267.

Brummans, B., Cooren, F., Robichaud, D., & Taylor, J. (2014). Approaches to the communicative constitution of organizations. *The SAGE handbook of organizational communication: Advances in theory, research, and methods* (pp. 173–194). Sage.

Carey, J. (1992). *Communication as culture: Essays on Media and Society.* New York: Routledge.

Castells, M. (1996) *The Rise of the Network Society.* (2010 reprint) Chichester: Wiley-Blackwell.

Cooren, F. (2015) 'Studying agency from a ventriloqual perspective. *Management Communication Quarterly 29*(3), 475–483.

Cooren, F., Brummans, B., Charrieras, D. (2008), The coproduction of organizational presence: A study of Médecins Sans Frontières in action. *Human Relations, 61*(10), 1339–1370

Cooren, F., & Fairhurst, G. (2009). Dislocation and stabilization: How to scale up from interactions to organization. In L. L. Putnam & A. M. Nicotera (Eds.), *Building theories of organization. The constitutive role of communication* (pp. 117–152). Mahwah, NJ: Lawrence Erlbaum.

Cosgrove, B. (2014, April 11). *Home, sweet home: In praise of Apollo 17's 'Blue Marble'.* TIME. (2015, June 1). https://web.archive.org/web/20150601092710if_/https://time.com/hive.org/web/20150601092710/http://time.com/3879555/blue-marble-apollo-17-photo-of-earth-from-space/.

Cruz, J. (2017). Invisibility and visibility in alternative organizing: A communicative and cultural model. *Management Communication Quarterly, 31*(4), 614–639.

Cruz, J. M., & Sodeke, C. U. (2020). Debunking eurocentrism in organizational communication theory: Marginality and liquidities in postcolonial contexts. *Communication Theory,* 1–21.

DeLuca, K. M. (1999). Unruly arguments: The body rhetoric of Earth First!, Act Up, and Queer Nation. *Argumentation and Advocacy, 36*(1), 9–21.

Dempsey, S., Parker, P., & Krone, K. (2011). Navigating socio-spatial difference, constructing counter-space: Insights from transnational feminist praxis. *Journal of International and Intercultural Communication, 4*(3), 201–220.

Dobusch, L., & Schoeneborn, D. (2015). Fluidity, identity, and organizationality: The communicative constitution of anonymous. *Journal of Management Studies, 52*(8), 1005–1035.

Eddington, S. (2018). The communicative constitution of hate organizations online: A semantic network analysis of "Make America Great Again". *Social Media + Society, 4*(3), 1–12

Falk, R. (1999). *Predatory globalization: A critique.* Cambridge, UK: Polity Press.

Flyverbom, M. (2016). Digital age| transparency: Mediation and the management of visibilities. *International Journal of Communication, 10,* 13.

Flyverbom, M. (2019). *The digital prism.* Cambridge, UK: Cambridge University Press.

Ganesh, S., & Stohl, C. (2020). Fluid hybridity: Organizational form and formlessness in the digital age. In L. Lievrouw & B. Loader (Eds.), *Routledge handbook of digital media and communication* (p. 268). New York: Routledge.

Ganesh, S., & Wang, Y. (2015). An eventful view of organizations. *Communication Research and Practice, 1*(4), 375–287.

Ganesh, S., Stohl, C., and James, S. (in press). Generational shifts: The emergence of visibility in globalization research. In V. Miller & S. Poole (Eds.), *Handbook of organizational communication.* Boston, MA: DeGruyter.

Ganesh, S., Zoller, H., & Cheney, G. (2005). Transforming resistance, broadening our boundaries: Critical organizational communication meets globalization from below. *Communication Monographs, 72*(2), 169–191.

Gibbs, J. L., Boyraz, M., Sivunen, A., & Nordbäck, E. (2020). Exploring the discursive construction of subgroups in global virtual teams. *Journal of Applied Communication Research, 49*(1), 86–108.

Giddens, A. (1990). *The consequences of modernity* (Reprint, 2008). Polity Press.

Hegde, R. S. (Ed.). (2011) *Circuits of visibility: Gender and transnational media cultures.* NYU Press.

"How Exactly Does Lenticular Printing Work?". (2020). World3D.com. Retrieved 31 March 2021 from www.world3d.com/exactly-lenticular-printing-work/.

Kuhn, T., & Marshall, D. (2019). The communicative constitution of entrepreneurship. In J.Reuer, S. Matusik, & J. Jones (Eds.), *The Oxford handbook of entrepreneurship and collaboration* (pp. 83–116). Oxford University Press.

Kuhn, T., Ashcraft, K. L., & Cooren, F. (2017). *The work of communication: Relational perspectives on working and organizing in contemporary capitalism.* Routledge.

Latour, B. (2018). *Down to earth: Politics in the new climatic regime.* Cambridge, UK: Polity Press.

"Lenticular, how it works". Lenstar.org. Archived from the original on 3 May 2016. Retrieved 31 March 2021 from https://web.archive.org/web/20160503192511/www.lenstarlenticular.com/Lenstar/lenticular.htm.

Leonardi, P., & Treem, J. (2020). Behavioral visibility: A new paradigm for organization studies in the age of digitization, digitalization, and datafication. *Organization Studies, 41*(12), 1601–1625.

Lyon, D. (2001). *Surveillance society: Monitoring everyday life.* Philadelphia, PA: Open University.

Mann, A. (2015). Communication, organisation, and action: Theory-building for social movements. *Communication Research and Practice, 1*(2), 159–173.

Massey, D. (2007) *World city.* Cambridge, UK: Polity Press.

McPhee, R. D., & Zaug, P. (2001). Organizational theory, organizational communication, organizational knowledge, and problematic integration. *Journal of Communication, 51*(3), 574–591.

Mease, J. J. (2020). Techniques and forces and the communicative constitution of organization: A Deleuzian approach to organizational (in)stability and power. *Management Communication Quarterly,* 1–30.

Minh-Ha, T. T. (2014). *When the moon waxes red: Representation, gender, and cultural politics.* New York: Routledge.

Monge, P. (1998). Communication structures and processes in globalization. *Journal of Communication 48,* 142–153.

Petsko, G. A. (2011). The Blue Marble. *Genome Biology, 12*(4), 112.

Porter, A., Kuhn, T. & Nerlich, B. (2018). Organizing authority in the climate change debate: IPCC controversies and the management of dialectical Tensions. *Organization Studies, 39,* 873–898.

Prokosch, M. (2002). Three organizing models. In M. Prokosch & L. Raymond (Eds.), *The global activist's manual: Local ways to change the world* (pp. 119–120). New York: Thunder's Mouth Press/Nation's Books.

Robertson, R. (1992). *Globalization: Social theory and global culture.* London: Sage.

Schivelbusch, W. (1986). *The railway journey: The industrialization of time and space in the nineteenth century.* Oakland: University of California Press.

Schoeneborn, D., & Scherer, A. (2012). Clandestine organizations, al Qaeda, and the paradox of (in)visibility: A response to Stohl and Stohl. *Organization Studies, 33*(7), 963–971.

Shome, R., & Hegde, R. (2002). Culture, communication, and the challenge of globalization. *Critical Studies in Media Communication, 19*(2), 172–189.

Stohl, C. (1993). European managers interpretations of participation. *Human Communication Research, 20,* 108–131.

Stohl, C. (2005). Globalization theory. In S. May & D. Mumby (Eds.), *Engaging organizational communication theory and research: Multiple perspectives* (pp. 223–262). Thousand Oaks, CA: Sage

Stohl, C., & Ganesh, S. (2014). Generating globalization. In D. K. Mumby & L. L. Putnam (Eds.), *The Sage handbook of organizational communication* (3rd edn., pp. 717–741). Newbury Park, CA: Sage.

Stohl, C., & Stohl, M. (2011). Secret agencies: The communicative constitution of a clandestine organization. *Organization Studies, 32*(9), 1197–1215.

Stohl, C., Stohl, M., & Leonardi, P. (2016). Managing opacity: Information visibility and the paradox of transparency in the digital age. *International Journal of Communication, 10*(2016), 123–137.

Styhre, J. (2017). Thinking about materiality: The value of a construction management and engineering view. *Construction Management and Economics, 35,* 35–44.

Taylor, J., & Van Every, E. (2010). *The situated organization: Case studies in the pragmatics of communication research.* New York: Routledge.

Treem, J., Leonardi, P., & Jackson, M. (2010). The connectivity paradox: Using technology to both decrease and increase perceptions of distance in distributed work arrangements. *Journal of Applied Communication Research, 38*(1), 85–105.

Trittin-Ulbrich, H., & Schoeneborn, D. (2017). Diversity as polyphony: Reconceptualizing diversity management from a communication-centered perspective. *Journal of Business Ethics, 144,* 305–322.

Vásquez, C., & Cooren, F. (2013). Spacing practices: The communicative configuration of organizing through space-times. *Communication Theory 23*(1), 25–47.

Wenzel, M., & Will, M. (2019). The communicative constitution of academic fields in the digital age: The case of CSR. *Technological Forecasting and Social Change, 146*, 517–533.

Wuebbles, D. (2012). Celebrating the "Blue Marble". *EOS Transactions, 93*, 509–510.

Zoller, H. (2004). Dialogue as global issue management: Legitimizing corporate influence in the Transatlantic Business Dialogue. *Management Communication Quarterly, 18*(2), 204–240.

24

VOICES, BODIES AND ORGANIZATION

Bridging CCO Scholarship and Diversity Research

Hannah Trittin-Ulbrich and Florence Villesèche[1]

1. Introduction

Organization through and in communication is a central concern of the "communicative constitution of organization" (CCO) perspective (Ashcraft, Kuhn, & Cooren, 2009; Kuhn, Ashcraft, & Cooren, 2017; Schoeneborn et al., 2014). Drawing on a formative or performative understanding of communication, CCO scholars study the organizing effects of communication. Of specific interest to this chapter, the CCO perspective offers a lens to study organizations as "polyphonic" entities; that is, sites that emerge from and consist of a multitude of diverse voices (Cooren & Sandler, 2014; Trittin & Schoeneborn, 2017). From this perspective, organizational diversity, or polyphony in CCO terminology, develops from the interplay of multiple voices that find resonance in organizations, including external and (momentarily) absent voices. In this chapter, our central claim is thus to demonstrate that by focusing on the plurality of voices that constitute organizations, CCO scholars share a vital interest with researchers of diversity in organizations.

Social changes, including global migration and the massive entry of women into the workforce, have led to a growing diversification of the global workforce in many countries. In line with these phenomena, organization and management scholars show a growing interest in the implications of diversity for organizations. Diversity (management) research enlightens us about how the notion of diversity has become a cornerstone of contemporary human resource management (e.g., Alcázar, Fernández, & Gardey, 2013; Scott, Heathcote, & Gruman, 2011), and scholars have also given some attention to how organizations communicate about diversity and diversity work (e.g., Singh & Point, 2006). Generally, diversity studies conceptualize workforce diversity in terms of phenotypic categories and social identities such as gender, race, or disability. Diversity scholars consequently pay particular attention to the experiences of individuals who embody such diversity categories and identities and study how these individuals are taken into account in management practices (e.g., Villesèche, Muhr, & Holck, 2018). This includes, for example, "employee voice" (Wilkinson & Fay, 2011), which corresponds to the ability of diverse organizational members to raise their concerns and to have a say in organizational issues and decision-making.

DOI: 10.4324/9781003224914-28

More critically oriented and post-structural strands of diversity research also encompass communication-related research, in particular by documenting how individuals draw on discourse and narratives to construct their identities and strive for emancipation (Janssens & Zanoni, 2014; Swan, 2009; Zanoni & Janssens, 2004). However, so far, scholars make only limited use of the CCO perspective and of a formative understanding of communication in the study of diversity. We contend that further work with a CCO perspective could provide diversity research with a fresh impulse to study the polyphony that "constitutes" diversity, meaning the multitude of voices, including external, absent or silent voices, that shape organizational engagement with diversity. In turn, we also propose that CCO scholars take inspiration from diversity research and its attention to power struggles, affect, and not least the bodies connected to the voices that constitute organizational polyphony. While we acknowledge and take stock of both streams of literature, particularly studies that have begun to build bridges between the two research agendas, we posit that there is a further need to show how this bridging can enrich both lines of scholarship. This chapter is an additional attempt to do so. In the following, we consider how to bridge from the CCO perspective to diversity scholarship and, vice versa, from diversity to CCO scholarship.

In this handbook chapter, we aim to accomplish three things. First, we want to show that by reading the diversity literature through a CCO lens, we can pave the way for novel ways to do research at the intersection of the diversity and CCO research streams. To start with, we argue that the CCO perspective provides scholars with a rich theoretical vocabulary to study the constitutive character of diversity communication; that is to say, how communication in and around organizations about human diversity shapes organizations. Linking CCO theorizing and diversity research, we show how this can help us pay better attention to the *organizational* consequences of communication about diversity. Second, and conversely, we consider how we can take stock of the diversity literature by further engaging with the notions of power, embodiment and affect when doing work aligned with the CCO perspective. In particular, we argue that diversity research provides crucial insights into organizations as sites of power struggles and where the possibility to articulate voices is often restricted for organizational members who embody particular identities. Drawing on these insights, we see an opportunity to enhance CCO theory's normative and emancipatory potential. Third, we aim to encourage further fruitful collaboration between CCO and diversity scholars – a goal we hope this chapter testifies to.

2. Diversity and Communication: State of the Art

We begin with a brief introduction to diversity research and then focus on how this research has addressed communication and its role and function for diversity. We start with Mor Barak's (2017) definition of diversity, which is itself the outcome of a systematic review of definitions of the term in the diversity literature: "Workforce diversity refers to the division of the workforce into distinction categories that (a) have a perceived commonality within a given cultural or national context, and that (b) impact potentially harmful or beneficial employment outcomes such as job opportunities, treatment in the workplace, and promotion prospects – irrespective of job-related skills and qualifications" (p. 203). Such diversity is approached in three main ways: diversity as separation – used to explain diversity-related difficulties and conflicts; diversity as variety – used to explain the value of diversity and its positive outcomes; and diversity as disparity – used to explain inequality among different (sub)groups (Mensi-Klarbach & Risberg, 2019). Diversity research, in turn, entails studies about individual-level diversity in organizations as well as research about the organizational handling or management of such diversity, though the distinction between the two sub-streams is usually not clear-cut. For example, articles focusing on discriminatory practices in organizations may offer insights for modifying diversity management practices, while studies of diversity management tools may comment on the implications of the application of these tools for organizational members, particularly minorities.

What, then, are those diversity categories? They come in three main kinds: narrow, broad, and concept-based categories (Mor Barak, 2017). The narrow, and dominant, view of diversity categories focuses on visible, phenotypical diversity, with prominent categories being sex/gender and race/ethnicity, and emerging categories including age and disability. The broad take on diversity categories extends interest to invisible characteristics such as nationality, sexual orientation, social class, education, and religion. Finally, when diversity categories are defined in relation to concepts, the focus might be on cognitive diversity or value diversity – often used as proxies for or complements to the study of more "embodied" forms of diversity, as some behaviors, norms or values may overlap significantly with specific social identities. Overall, this stream of research focuses on the empirical phenomenon of diversity in organizations. Yet, in the study of diversity, a variety of paradigms is utilized (which we can loosely classify as positivist, critical and post-structural), as well as different disciplinary takes on the subject (e.g., psychology, sociology, economics, anthropology) and a broad array of focus areas (e.g., teamwork, networking, hiring practices, work–life balance, leadership) exist. This variety makes diversity literature already very rich yet still open to new theoretical lenses. However, this also means that some postures and focuses are dominant in the field and that others, including the communication stream, are marginalized or remain underdeveloped.

Moreover, in both research and practice, the focus is increasingly on the germane topic of inclusion, and there is growing interest in the study of intersectionality (Villesèche, Muhr, & Sliwa, 2018) and masculinities (Gottzén, Mellström, & Shefer, 2019). The concept of inclusion is particularly relevant for our argument in this chapter, as it supposes that there is a need for organizations to act inclusively, to bring diverse bodies and identities – and voices – together. This can, however, also imply that some organizational participants are cast as outsiders, ready to be included, while others are "included" insiders. The related dynamics of inclusion/exclusion and in/out-group formation are studied extensively in diversity scholarship on social identity theory (see, for example, van Dick, van Knippenberg, Hägele, Guillaume, & Brodbeck, 2008), and this work points to the importance of organizational openness to diversity (Lauring & Villesèche, 2019) or the benefits of a climate for inclusion (Nishii, 2013). While scholars pay attention to employees' readiness to obtain diverse input and the ability of a diverse workforce to contribute to the organization, empirical data is generally collected via surveys and, thus, focuses on individuals' perceptions of diversity management practices and on managers' behaviors rather than on the observation of these practices and behaviors through and in communication. For example, due to certain identity traits, individual employees, especially from invisible minorities, are challenged (or inhibited) in raising their "employee voice" and making themselves heard. Diversity management attempts to create an "inclusive organization" (for a critical review, see Dobusch, 2014) by providing voice mechanisms to employees to raise their concerns in a valued, open and direct manner, and to make use of these contributions for the organization (Bell, Özbilgin, Beauregard, & Sürgevil, 2011).

In this chapter, we claim that there could be further and richer work at the intersection of the CCO and diversity research agendas. This does not mean that the topic of communication is absent from diversity scholarship. Yet, arguably, many studies tend to follow a somewhat limited model of communication, with quite a few examples adopting a functional perspective on communication. They approach communication in the form of corporate communication *about* diversity. The focus has been on both internal and external aspects of such communication. For example, Singh and Point (2006) investigate how European firms communicate about their workforce diversity and, more specifically, take interest in the categories of diversity that are communicated about. They also consider whether the business case (i.e., diversity positively affects the bottom line) or the fairness argument (i.e., diversity is the right thing to do) dominates in the firms' online communication. Grimes and Richard (2003) consider how ethnocentric, modernistic and cosmopolitan forms of communication affect outcomes in diverse organizations. Jonsen, Point, Kelan and Grieble (2019) focus on external communication and show how diversity and inclusion are used for corporate branding purposes. Aligned to this, Maier and Ravazzani (2019) consider how to integrate better communication about diversity and corporate social responsibility. A larger stream of work looks at the question of bias in corporate recruitment communication (Gaucher, Friesen, & Kay, 2011) and diversity interventions in such communication (Avery, 2003).

Besides corporate communication-centred approaches to diversity communication, there is also a growing body of work – mainly in the critical and post-structural paradigms – that considers the role of narratives, discourses, or institutional logics in relation to diversity and its management. Kirby and Harter (2003), for example, examine how the metaphor of "managing diversity", and its focus on the managerial bottom line, ultimately marginalizes the ethical aspects of diversity. Perriton (2009) shows how the business case discourse frames and depoliticizes the discussion of gender in the workplace. Elsewhere, we learn about how narratives help (re)create the gender order in the organization, thus concluding that gender is something that organizations "do" (Gherardi & Poggio, 2001). Importantly, these studies suggest not only that communication in the context of diversity is something that organizations do, but also that communication "does" something to the way diversity plays out in and for organizations. We conclude from this (selective) review that diversity research has shown interest in communication-related issues, but that studies tend to follow traditional definitions of communication and that their core interest is on either theoretical or individual-level rather than organization-level implications of such communication. In other words, this literature considers mainly communication as something that is done by organizations *about* diversity, and much less on how communication "performs" diversity at the organizational level.

3. Diversity from a CCO Perspective: Organizations as Polyphonic Entities

How, then, can we better connect key concerns in diversity scholarship with more recent constitutive approaches to communication? To answer this question, we now turn toward the CCO perspective and outline how it provides various pathways for diversity scholars to rethink the communication-diversity-organization nexus. We review the tenets of the CCO perspective that are particularly noteworthy for the study of diversity and discuss how CCO scholars have approached the topic of diversity so far.

While approaches to the study of the constitutive or performative properties of communication may vary, the CCO perspective is most notably concerned with how organization and organizing (as both noun and verb) come into existence. It focuses on the "work of communication" (Kuhn et al., 2017); that is, how communication shapes organizing processes. A constitutive or performative understanding of communication underlines the "organising property of communication" (Cooren, 2000). From this perspective, communication is not just something that happens within the organization, such as communication between (diverse) employees, or something that is done by organizations, such as corporate communication (on diversity). Instead, organizational communication is understood as being consequential for organizations in that certain forms of communication enable their emergence, maintenance, and change. Organizations are viewed as precarious accomplishments that emerge from various communication practices, including communication about diversity (Christensen & Cornelissen, 2011; Schoeneborn & Trittin, 2013). For example, when the lack of female managers in a corporation's board of directors becomes a discussion topic in news media and social media, external voices of journalists, experts, and researchers as well as the general public co-construct what "the corporation" is (and what it is not) alongside other communicative practices, such as the corporation's official communication on its strategic pursuits.

In that sense, CCO scholars approach the concept of diversity in communicative terms. Drawing on the Bakhtinian notion of polyphony (Bakhtin, 1984), CCO scholars propose that organizations are precarious entities that are constituted through multiple, often contradicting voices that reside in or outside of the organization (Cooren & Sandler, 2014; Robichaud, Giroux, & Taylor, 2004; Trittin & Schoeneborn, 2017). Dissonant voices thus are seen as inherent features of organizations and as the source of organizational renewal and survival over time (Schoeneborn, Trittin-Ulbrich, & Cooren, 2020). Following Bakhtin (1984), voices are shaped by the individual's social class, cultural or ethnic background, professional background, historical period or political position and can thus be conceptualized as discourses, opinions or viewpoints. This also means that individuals can be the "vessels" for multiple voices. Organizations, then, emerge through the multitude or polyphony of voices that constantly clash and intersect, but never fully merge. Importantly, raising these voices is not the prerogative of individuals who are members of the organization. Instead, external voices can also contribute to the communicative constitution of the organization (e.g., Cooren, 2020; Trittin & Schoeneborn, 2017). For example, if external observers publicly criticize the lack of diversity in the board of a corporation, they actively co-construct "the organization" as the addressee of those critiques, adding to its polyphony.

Additionally, taking the idea of non-human agency seriously, CCO scholars further suggest that various voices may also "speak" through individuals, making them even more "multivocal". Voices are not individually bound as the notion of "employee voice" suggests. Instead, individuals can mobilize and "ventriloquize" (i.e., stage and express) multiple voices through communication (Cooren, 2012). Drawing on the example of corporate social responsibility, Cooren (2020), for example, suggests that in stakeholder dialogues, the voices of facts, principles, future generations, ecosystems or populations can be made to say something by the participants without being physically present in the debate. In this sense, the discursive polyphony is potentially greater than the diversity of the individuals engaged in the stakeholder dialogue, as people can give voice to other beings, including policies, norms, facts, generations, and so on (see also Nathues, van Vuuren, & Cooren, 2020).

Importantly, drawing on the notion of polyphony, some CCO scholars have begun to discuss diversity and the related concept of inclusion. Notably, Trittin and Schoenborn (2017) propose a re-conceptualization of diversity management. In their theoretical piece, they consider the potential of diversity management as an organizational practice to enhance organizational polyphony. For the authors, applying a CCO lens to diversity management entails shifting the analytical viewpoint from the inclusion of human diversity to the creation of organizational resonance for the communicative plurality of voices. To manage organizational polyphony responsibly in terms of instrumental and normative viewpoints, organizations need to go beyond considerations of how to give voice to organizational members. Instead, they need to "foster structural resonance in order to accommodate the polyphony of contextual voices" (p. 312).

Following this perspective, Caïdor and Cooren (2018) empirically study the implementation of a diversity initiative inside a Canadian organization. Drawing on "ventriloquism", a central notion of CCO theorizing, the authors study how organizational members mobilize (or ventriloquize) different internal and external norms and values when debating their participation in or rejection of the organization's diversity initiative. The authors illustrate how, by letting specific "figures" (e.g., norms and values) speak, those organizational members involved in the implementation of the diversity management initiative change the implementation process of the initiative. The study underlines that individuals can mobilize various voices, including external norms, and that these voices change the organizing process. Together with the study by Trittin and Schoeneborn (2017), this work indicates the fruitfulness of studying diversity management as an organizational practice from a CCO perspective. It clarifies how organizational practice comes into being through and in communication between a polyphony of voices.

To conclude this section, we can say that the CCO perspective provides a vocabulary that could be used to generate further insights into how the diversity of voices in and outside of the organization become uttered and what implications emerge from the continuous clash and dissent of these voices for organizations and their diversity practices. Drawing on a performative understanding of communication, the CCO perspective views organizations as emerging from and in a plurality of voices, including non-human ones, that can be ventriloquized by organizational members. In a way, the polyphonic take thereby links to and extends the poststructural understanding that identities are fragmented, fluid and constructed by ideological intervention and make diversity and its management a contested site of discursive struggles (Ahonen, Tienari, Merilainen, & Pullen, 2013). The CCO perspective thus strengthens the argument that diverse, inclusive organizations are not created merely by adding people with various visible "diverse" characteristics. Instead, creating the diverse organization must involve establishing organizational conditions through which a wide range of voices are articulated and heard.

4. Doing Diversity Research with a CCO View

We ended the previous section by concluding that the CCO perspective can equip diversity researchers with a supplementary theoretical lens for the investigation of the role and function of communication for organizational diversity. In order to provide readers with a more tangible research agenda, we now develop propositions for future research, illustrated with examples of scholarly work that, according to our readings, support our vision. Indeed, as remarked upon in the introduction, with this chapter, we aim at making the fruitfulness of this intersection explicit and unpacking its potential for future research by relying on "pioneering" work to develop our argument.

To start with, diversity scholars could take note of the growing body of research by organizational communication scholars addressing the organizing properties of diversity-related categories of difference. While many of these studies do not directly refer to the CCO moniker, they share a (more or less explicit) understanding of the consequentiality of diversity-related communication for organizing. Ashcraft and colleagues (e.g., Ashcraft, 2013; Ashcraft & Allen, 2003; Ashcraft & Mumby, 2004) draw on a critical view of organizational communication to underline that work and organizing are ordered by gender division and racial boundaries (see, for an overview, Ashcraft, 2006). Aligned with extant organizational communication theorizing, these "indirect" CCO studies stress how organizations are inherently organized by diversity categories such as race and gender.

For example, drawing on the metaphor of the "glass slipper", Ashcraft (2013) argues that occupations come to appear as "naturally" having features that fit certain people yet are improbable for others. Just like a glass slipper, occupations are communicatively framed and narrated so that only specific individuals can take them on. Ashcraft's work essentially exposes that organizations are "sites of difference" (Ashcraft, 2006); that is, they are inherently organized by categories of difference that transcend the organization. In particular, she motivates (diversity) scholars to pay attention to the communicative (re)production of occupational identities that transcend individual organizations and to investigate how embodied difference matters to the organization of occupations (e.g., Ashcraft, 2006). Her work is particularly noteworthy for its critical-normative take on the implications of affected individuals that do not embody the communicatively constructed norm. Moreover, it also exposes how industry-wide external communication on occupational diverse identities is constitutive for work within organizations, mainly along demarcations of gender and racial differences.

In the same vein, discourse studies underline how the concept of diversity is discursively constructed and how it shapes the way single organizations respond to this discourse, thus implicitly demonstrating the organizing properties of the discourse (Oswick & Noon, 2014; Thomas & Davies, 2005; Tomlinson & Schwabenland, 2009). These studies indicate that a CCO-informed understanding of communication enables diversity scholars to extend their focus from "cases" centered on a person or single organization towards more structural concerns about how diversity is constituted and organized (e.g., in industries).

We also found several inspiring examples in publications that are geared towards the diversity studies audience yet explicitly distance themselves from a functionalist view of communication. Inspired by the work of Ashcraft and Mumby (2004), Just and Remke (2019) address affective embodiment through the study of communicative practices about maternity leave. Compared to CCO studies, their study's point of departure is the body rather than voices. Yet the authors' aim is explicitly to connect bodies and voices better, to show how they are related affectively: "Bodies matter, but so does how we talk about them" (p. 47). By studying the communicative practices of leaning in/out and opting in/out, they show how such practices organize individuals and collective identities beyond gender. For example, Yahoo! CEO Marissa Meyer is criticized for "leaning in" and bringing her child and maternal body to work in an effort to show her will to lead. Facebook's Mark Zuckerberg is, however, celebrated for "leaning out" and choosing to take an extended parental leave, as this is not perceived as diminishing his leadership aura, but maybe even as increasing it. In the same way, female homemakers are often negatively evaluated as opting out of work, while stay-at-home dads are celebrated for opting into fatherhood.

A number of other studies have overcome functionalist approaches to diversity communication to address the question of voice (and silence). Such research has been done about minority group members in organizations, such as LGBTQIA+ minorities (Bell et al., 2011). We can also here cite the conceptualization of diversity training as a heteroglossic space where narratives and subjectivities can be disrupted (Swan, 2009). Such studies can inspire diversity scholars who want to go beyond functionalist models of communication in their research.

Additionally, diversity researchers active at the intersection between diversity research and CCO theorizing could pay more attention to the organizational consequences of employee voice and silence. Silence, which is not the absence of (employee) voice but rather the purposeful withholding of ideas, information and opinions (Van Dyne, Ang, & Botero, 2003), can be an act of resistance and emancipation that has consequences for organizations and organizing processes. A speaking pause, for example, can be a momentary space to think or to evaluate, but also to resist without talking: to say nothing, but nonetheless do something.

The research we reviewed in this section thus shows how diversity research has seized some of the opportunities of the CCO approach in order to connect the question of the voices and bodies of minority groups in relation to organizational phenomena. However, there is still ample space to develop research by considering the organizing properties of voice and silence beyond firm boundaries and by questioning the strict equation of bodies with their so-called authentic voice. To this end, the notion of ventriloquism (Cooren, 2020), introduced in the preceding pages, could be a central element for diversity scholars.

5. Doing Diversity-Attentive CCO Research

While the previous section shows how we can rethink the communication-diversity-organization nexus by leveraging the existing CCO vocabulary, to go full circle we also want to discuss how CCO theorizing can be enriched through diversity work at this intersection. Indeed, in line with others (e.g., Scherer & Rasche, 2017), we argue that CCO theorizing is somewhat limited in its ability to address normative questions regarding organizations. For example, the CCO perspective demonstrates how norms and values are voiced in organizing processes, as indicated by Caïdor and Cooren (2018), but it does less well in providing clear answers as to which norms and values *should* become organizational. Indeed, due to its descriptive aim of understanding *how* organizations come into being, few scholars have used the CCO perspective to address ethical or normative concerns (see, for a recent exception, Cooren, 2020). The CCO perspective is still timid in raising questions regarding which voices *should* be constitutive for organizing and in pointing out what the critical, political, and ethical implications of communication are for organizational members (and non-members). In the following, we want to particularly discuss power, bodies and affect.

The first dimension that deserves more attention from CCO scholars, and which has been previously discussed in diversity research, is power. Kuhn (2008) suggests that power is a process of capital attraction and the ability to be involved in the creation of authoritative texts. Consequently, from a CCO perspective, power is the ability to *contribute* to the organization and, thus, to *author* it (Bencherki & Snack, 2016; Vásquez, Bencherki, Cooren, & Sergi, 2018). However, arguably, not all voices are equally powerful and able to contribute to the communicative constitution of the organization. This links back to the growing debate on inclusion in diversity research and how such inclusion is created. For example, most diversity scholars would agree that top management support is of critical importance for changes to take place in organizations, which includes being vocal about this support – that is to say communicatively signaling the importance of the topic for the organization (Ng & Sears, 2020).

If we turn to critical management studies, we can say that critical diversity and identity scholars of identity and diversity, in general, have a strong interest in exposing the mechanisms of social injustice and domination in organizations (Villesèche et al., 2018). Van Eck, Dobusch and van den Brink (2021), for example, argue that low-wage employees, with migrants often making up the majority, tend to be excluded from taking part in the "inclusive organization" and therefore remain silenced. Generally, we find that diversity research is particularly powerful in showcasing how the possibility for "diverse" voices to contribute to an organization is often limited by this "othering". These are important insights that require further attention from CCO scholars. Whose voices, then, should be particularly amplified in the co-constitution of organizations, and according to which principles should this amplification take place? In this sense, CCO scholars could further study what opportunities organizations provide for diverse voices to become agentic and develop "contributorship" (Bencherki & Snack, 2016) to the organization.

Relatedly, the constitutive character of silence could also receive more attention: what voices keep silent or are kept silent? What voices are communicated into existence or not? For example, Syed (2020) shows how assumptions about homogeneity in the employee voice literature limit the efforts to give voice to marginalized identity groups in organizations, and he suggests that practices such as self-governed teams and inclusive climates can mitigate the fear of backlash. More generally, work that conceptualizes norm-critique as a way to question the expected correspondence between particular communicative practices and particular bodies is also an avenue of interest (Christensen, 2018). Notably, CCO scholars could consider documenting how norm-critical practices affect organizing. Taking inspiration from such work could thus be of benefit to the CCO literature in understanding how organizational polyphony is hindered, enabled, or reconfigured.

The second opportunity that we observe in the current CCO debate is the role of the body in the communicative constitution of the organization. In line with other critical approaches to organizational communication, a number of the "indirect" CCO studies we refer to in the previous section show how the organization of work is configured around the body. While CCO theorizing tends to give precedence to communication over materiality, these studies underline that the materiality of the body constrains communication. This suggests that some bodies seem to matter, while others seem to hide, disappear or are talked out of being (becoming taken for granted) through communication, particularly those communicatively constructed as "representational" for a particular kind of work. Diversity research extensively engages with the politics of human bodies in organizations as well as with the emancipatory potential of communication for individuals. As Ashcraft and her colleagues (2009) argue, work (and organizing) is configured around the body, as communication on work creates ideational-material hybrids. In a recent article, Christensen, Just and Muhr (2020) show how racialized subjects are put forward by the organization in terms of their communication, but are taught to voice their minority positions in a way that is recognizable by the (white) majority. The bodies are presented as proof of inclusion of diverse voices, but the voices coming out of these bodies are "hyphenated"; that is, organized in public discourses where others decide how they should speak and to whom.

While these studies could somehow be claimed as CCO studies, we note that they are usually authored by scholars who have published about diversity elsewhere, which hints at a mutual inspiration. In order to understand how the body constrains or limits the polyphony *of* or *within* organizations or organizing processes, we suggest CCO scholars take further note of the diversity literature. It takes its starting point in differences grounded – most of the time – in phenotypic heterogeneity that constitutes the ground for categories and social identities and through which others interpret one's communicative acts.

The third aspect that, we believe, could enrich CCO theory concerns the role of affect in the communicative constitution of organization. In line with Bencherki (2017), we suggest that affect enables the "continuation of personal individuation processes into collective ones" (p. 777), which essentially describes how affect is not limited to individual human bodies, but extends to organizational bodies and can contribute to their existence over time by communicative acts that create "affectivo-emotivity". For CCO scholars who would want to venture down this road, the diversity literature is ripe with examples to draw inspiration from. This includes Fotaki and Pullen's (2018) recent book in which they argue for "reading bodies as sites of affects and power relations. Such an approach ... represents a shift from the organisational management of diverse bodies to recognising the diversity of embodied lives and experiences, which challenge organisational norms that violate, oppress, and discriminate against different groups of people within and outside of the organisations" (p. 6). In a piece on affective ethnography, Holck (2018) discusses how affectivity is pivotal, both for organizational participants and for herself as a researcher, to understanding the multi-voiced responses to intervention-based research about diversity. Also, we refer CCO scholars to the work of Just, Muhr and Burø (2017), who theorize three modes of affective organizing, including the link between affect and queering in communication about minority identities. Finally, going across the topics of power, bodies and affect, we draw attention to a fairly recent special issue of the journal *Organization* (Fotaki, Kenny, & Vachhani, 2017) that connects bodies, affect and organization studies and includes a strong interest in diversity. We expect that such work can inspire CCO scholars to further acknowledge the importance in organizing phenomena of the role of non-verbal forms of communication, the bodily experience of being more or less different or alike and the (shared) affect that underpins intersubjective encounters.

Conclusion

In this chapter, we attempt to bridge two streams of research, the CCO perspective and research concerned with diversity (and its management) in organizations. By doing so, we hope to enrich and extend scholarship concerned with the study of individual and communicative diversity in organizations. We argue that the CCO perspective and diversity (management) research share a common interest in the role of communication for organizations as well as the multiple voices that constitute organizations. Initial approaches from CCO scholars posit that organizations are polyphonic entities that consist of multiple and different voices which reside in and outside of organizations. Diversity research, in turn, is interested in the diversity of organizational members, how organizations make use of this diversity and the consequences of diversity (management) practices for organizational members. By reviewing both streams of research and drawing on studies that exemplify our points, we suggest that there is ample potential to combine CCO theorizing and diversity research. Applying CCO theorizing and vocabulary, diversity scholars may explore the performative nature of diversity-focused communication for organizations as well as the performative implications of employee voice and silence for organizations. In turn, CCO scholars could benefit from taking note of diversity research insights on power, bodies and affect to heighten the emancipatory and normative potential of CCO theorizing.

Note

1 The authors have contributed equally to the manuscript. Authors are listed in alphabetical order.

References

Ahonen, P., Tienari, J., Merilainen, S., & Pullen, A. (2013). Hidden contexts and invisible power relations: A Foucauldian reading of diversity research. *Human Relations, 67*(3), 263–286.

Alcázar, F. M., Fernández, P. M. R., & Gardey, G. S. (2013). Workforce diversity in strategic human resource management models: A critical review of the literature and implications for future research. *Cross Cultural Management: An International Journal, 20*(1), 39–49.

Ashcraft, K. L. (2006). Back to work: Sights/sites of difference in gender and organizational communication studies. In B. J. Dow & J. T. Wood (Eds.), *The SAGE handbook of gender and communication* (pp. 97–122). Thousand Oaks, CA: Sage.

Ashcraft, K. L. (2013). The glass slipper: "Incorporating" occupational identity in management studies. *Academy of Management Review, 38*(1), 6–31.

Ashcraft, K. L., & Allen, B. J. (2003). The racial foundation of organizational communication. *Communication Theory, 13*(1), 5–38.

Ashcraft, K. L., Kuhn, T. R., & Cooren, F. (2009). Constitutional amendments: "Materializing" organizational communication. *The Academy of Management Annals, 3*(1), 1–64.

Ashcraft, K. L., & Mumby, D. K. (2004). Organizing a critical communicology of gender and work. *International Journal of the Sociology of Language, 166*, 19–43.

Avery, D. R. (2003). Reactions to diversity in recruitment advertising - Are differences black and white? *Journal of Applied Psychology, 88*(4), 672–679.

Bakhtin, M. (1984). *Problems of Dostoevsky's poetics*. Minneapolis: University of Minnesota Press.

Bell, M. P., Özbilgin, M. F., Beauregard, T. A., & Sürgevil, O. (2011). Voice, silence, and diversity in 21st century organizations: Strategies for inclusion of gay, lesbian, bisexual, and transgender employees. *Human Resource Management, 50*(1), 131–146.

Bencherki, N. (2017). A pre-individual perspective to organizational action. *Ephemera: Theory and Politics in Organization, 17*(4), 777–799.

Bencherki, N., & Snack, J. P. (2016). Contributorship and partial inclusion: A communicative perspective. *Management Communication Quarterly, 30*(3), 279–304.

Caïdor, P., & Cooren, F. (2018). The appropriation of diversity discourses at work: A ventriloquial approach. *Journal of Business Diversity, 18*(4), 22–41.

Christensen, J. F. (2018). Queer organising and performativity: Towards a norm-critical conceptualisation of organisational intersectionality. *Ephemera, 18*(1), 103–130.

Christensen, J. F., Just, S. N., & Muhr, S. L. (2020). Hyphenated voices: The organization of racialized subjects in contemporary Danish public debate. *Organization*, online first, 1–21.

Christensen, L. T., & Cornelissen, J. (2011). Bridging corporate and organizational communication: Review, development and a look to the future. *Management Communication Quarterly, 25*(3), 383–414.

Cooren, F. (2000). *The organizing property of communication*. Amsterdam: John Benjamins.

Cooren, F. (2012). Communication theory at the center: Ventriloquism and the communicative constitution of reality. *Journal of Communication, 62*(1), 1–20.

Cooren, F. (2020). A communicative constitutive perspective on corporate social responsibility: Ventriloquism, undecidability, and surprisability. *Business & Society, 59*(1), 175–197.

Cooren, F., & Sandler, S. (2014). Polyphony, ventriloquism, and constitution: In dialogue with Bakhtin. *Communication Theory, 24*(3), 225–244.

Dobusch, L. (2014). How exclusive are inclusive organisations? Equality, Diversity and Inclusion: An *International Journal, 33*(3), 220–234.

Fotaki, M., & Pullen, A. (2018). Introducing affective embodiment and diversity. In I. M. Fotaki & A. Pullen (Eds.), *Diversity, affect and embodiment in organizing* (pp. 1–19). Cham: Springer.

Fotaki, M., Kenny, K., & Vachhani, S. J. (2017). Thinking critically about affect in organization studies: Why it matters. *Organization, 24*(1), 3–17.

Gaucher, D., Friesen, J., & Kay, A. C. (2011). Evidence that gendered wording in job advertisements exists and sustains gender inequality. *Journal of Personality and Social Psychology, 101*(1), 109–128.

Gherardi, S., & Poggio, B. (2001). Creating and recreating gender order in organizations. *Journal of World Business, 36*(3), 245–259.

Gottzén, L., Mellström, U., & Shefer, T. (Eds.). (2019). *Routledge international handbook of masculinity studies*. New York: Routledge.

Grimes, D. S., & Richard, O. C. (2003). Could communication form impact organization's experience with diversity? *Journal of Business Communication, 40*(1), 7–27.

Holck, L (2018). Affective ethnography: reflections on the application of "useful" research on workplace diversity. *Qualitative Research in Organizations and Management: An International Journal, 13*(3), 218–234.

Janssens, M., & Zanoni, P. (2014). Alternative diversity management: Organizational practices fostering ethnic equality at work. *Scandinavian Journal of Management, 30*(3), 317–331.

Jonsen, K., Point, S., Kelan, E. K., & Grieble, A. (2019). Diversity and inclusion branding: A five-country comparison of corporate websites. *International Journal of Human Resource Management*. doi:10.1080/09585192.2018.1496125.

Just, S. N., & Remke, R. V. (2019). Nurturing bodies: Exploring discourses of parental leave as communicative practices of affective embodiment. In M. Fotaki & A. Pullen (Eds.), *Diversity, affect and embodiment in organizing* (pp. 47–67). Cham: Springer.

Just, S. N., Muhr, S. L., & Burø, T. (2017). Queer matters – Reflections on the critical potential of affective organizing. In *Feminists and queer theorists debate the future of critical management studies* (Dialogues in Critical Management Studies, Vol. 3) (pp. 203–226). Emerald.

Kirby, E. L., & Harter, L. M. (2003). Speaking the language of the bottom-line: The metaphor of "managing diversity". *Journal of Business Communication, 40*(1), 28–49.

Kuhn, T. (2008). A communicative theory of the firm: Developing an alternative perspective on intra-organizational power and stakeholder relationships. *Organization Studies, 29*(8–9), 1227–1254.

Kuhn, T., Ashcraft, K. L., & Cooren, F. (2017). *The work of communication: Relational perspectives on working and organizing in contemporary capitalism.* New York: Routledge.

Lauring, J., & Villesèche, F. (2019). The performance of gender diverse teams: What is the relation between diversity attitudes and degree of diversity? *European Management Review, 16*(2), 243–254.

Maier, C. D., & Ravazzani, S. (2019). Bridging diversity management and CSR in online external communication. *Corporate Communications, 24*(2), 269–286.

Mensi-Klarbach, H., & Risberg, A. (2019). *Diversity in organizations: Concepts and practices* (2nd edn.). Macmillan International Higher Education.

Mor Barak, M. E. (2017). *Managing diversity: Toward a globally inclusive workplace* (4th edn.). Thousand Oaks, CA: Sage.

Nathues, E., van Vuuren, M., & Cooren, F. (2020). Speaking about vision, talking in the name of so much more: A methodological framework for ventriloquial analyses in organization studies. *Organization Studies.* doi:10.1177/0170840620934063.

Ng, E. S., & Sears, G. J. (2020). Walking the talk on diversity: CEO beliefs, moral values, and the implementation of workplace diversity practices. *Journal of Business Ethics, 164*(3), 437–450.

Nishii, L. H. (2013). The benefits of climate for inclusion for gender-diverse groups. *Academy of Management Journal, 56*(6), 1754–1774.

Oswick, C., & Noon, M. (2014). Discourses of diversity, equality and inclusion: Trenchant formulations or transient fashions? *British Journal of Management, 25*(1), 23–39.

Perriton, L. (2009). "We don't want complaining women!" A critical analysis of the business case for diversity. *Management Communication Quarterly, 23*(2), 218–243.

Robichaud, D., Giroux, H., & Taylor, J. (2004). The metaconversation: The recursive property of language as a key to organizing. *Academy of Management Review, 29*(4), 617–634.

Scherer, A. G., & Rasche, A. (2017). Organization as communication and Habermasian philosophy. In S. Blaschke & D. Schoeneborn (Eds.), *Organization as communication: Perspectives in dialogue* (pp. 1–26). New York: Routledge.

Schoeneborn, D., Blaschke, S., Cooren, F., McPhee, R. D., Seidl, D., & Taylor, J. R. (2014). The three schools of CCO thinking: Interactive dialogue and systematic comparison. *Management Communication Quarterly, 28*(2), 285–316.

Schoeneborn, D., Trittin-Ulbrich, H., & Cooren, F. (2020). Consensus vs. dissensus: the communicative constitution of responsible management. In O. Laasch, R. Suddaby, R. Freeman, & D. Jamali (Eds.), *Research handbook of responsible management* (pp. 453–469). Edward Elgar.

Schoeneborn, D., & Trittin, H. (2013). Transcending transmission: Towards a constitutive perspective on CSR communication. *Corporate Communications: An International Journal, 18*(2), 193–211.

Scott, K. A., Heathcote, J. M., & Gruman, J. A. (2011). The diverse organization: Finding gold at the end of the rainbow. *Human Resource Management, 50*(6), 735–755.

Singh, V., & Point, S. (2006). (Re)presentations of gender and ethnicity in diversity statements on European company websites. *Journal of Business Ethics, 68*(4), 363–379.

Swan, E. (2009). Commodity diversity: Smiling faces as a strategy of containment. *Organization, 17*(1), 77–100.

Syed, J. (2020). Diversity management and missing voices. In A. Wilkinson, J. Donaghey, T. Dundon, & R. B. Freeman (Eds.), *Handbook of research on employee voice* (pp. 486–508). Edward Elgar.

Thomas, R., & Davies, A. (2005). What have the feminists done for us? Feminist theory and organizational resistance. *Organization, 12*(5), 711–740.

Tomlinson, F., & Schwabenland, C. (2009). Reconciling competing discourses of diversity? The UK non-profit sector between social justice and the business case. *Organization, 17*(1), 101–121.

Trittin, H., & Schoeneborn, D. (2017). Diversity as polyphony: Reconceptualizing diversity management from a communication-centered perspective. *Journal of Business Ethics, 144*(2), 305–322.

van Dick, R., van Knippenberg, D., Hägele, S., Guillaume, Y. R. F., & Brodbeck, F. C. (2008). Group diversity and group identification: The moderating role of diversity beliefs. *Human Relations, 61*(10), 1463–1492.

Van Dyne, L., Ang, S., & Botero, I. G. (2003). Conceptualizing employee silence and employee voice as multidimensional constructs. *Journal of Management Studies, 40*(6), 1359–1392.

Van Eck, D., Dobusch, L., & van den Brink, M. (2021). The organizational inclusion turn and its exclusion of low-wage labor. *Organization, 28*(2), 289–310.

Vásquez, C., Bencherki, N., Cooren, F., & Sergi, V. (2018). From "matters of concern" to "matters of authority": Studying the performativity of strategy from a communicative constitution of organization (CCO) approach. *Long Range Planning, 51*(3), 417–435.

Villesèche, F., Muhr, S. L., & Holck, L. (2018). *Diversity and identity in the workplace: Connections and perspectives.* Cham: Springer.

Villesèche, F., Muhr, S. L., & Sliwa, M. (2018). From radical black feminism to postfeminist hashtags: Re-claiming intersectionality. *Ephemera, 18*(1), 1–17.

Wilkinson, A., & Fay, C. (2011). Guest editors' note: New times for employee voice? *Human Resource Management, 50*(1), 65–74.

Zanoni, P., & Janssens, M. (2004). Deconstructing difference: The rhetoric of human resource managers' diversity discourses. *Organization Studies, 25*(1), 55–74.

25

CIVIL SOCIETY COLLABORATION AND INTER-ORGANIZATIONAL RELATIONSHIPS

Matthew Koschmann

Introduction

This chapter focuses on the organizational phenomenon of collaborative work, with an emphasis on civil society collaboration and inter-organizational relationships. Collaboration is a hallmark of modern organizing across all sectors and industries, but it is especially relevant for the civil society sector where the scope and complexity of work often necessitate collaborative relationships between nonprofit organizations, NGOs, government agencies, private businesses, and/or community associations. CCO is a promising theoretical framework to advance this knowledge because collaboration emphasizes the communicative existence of organizational forms (i.e., organizational forms exist *as* communication), while also calling into question the ways in which conventional management theory explains key collaboration features and practices. This means going beyond merely looking *at* communication *in* collaboration, but instead understanding collaboration "communicatively" and investigating how and why various communication practices constitute different aspects of collaboration. In addition, collaboration is a valuable context for developing CCO research, because key concerns of CCO scholars (especially agency, authority, and identity) are magnified in collaborative work.

I begin with some clarifying and qualifying remarks about collaboration and the scope of work covered in this chapter. Next, I provide an extensive review of organizational collaboration research that incorporates communicative constitution—broadly and explicitly—as a theoretical foundation or framework, summarizing what we know about CCO and organizational collaboration and identifying the current trajectory of this work. In doing so, I will show how CCO is already making substantive contributions to our knowledge of civil society collaboration and explain how CCO can further enhance our understanding of this important organizational phenomenon.

Defining Civil Society Collaboration

Civil society involves the public at large, representing a social domain apart from the state or the market, though certainly intersecting with sectors of governance and commerce in a variety of

DOI: 10.4324/9781003224914-29

ways. It is composed of individuals but always entails some sort of shared or communal activity. Civil society derives its power and influence from networks of people and their collective action because it lacks the economic and financial power of the market and the regulatory and authoritative power of the state. The civil society sector encompasses a host of related terms and designations that people are familiar with and often use interchangeably, like nonprofit organizations/sector, nongovernmental organizations, the third sector, the independent sector, charitable organizations/sector, or even community-based organizations. I prefer the term *civil society* because some of those previous labels do not fully capture the work of the civil society sector (which may involve collaborating with private businesses or government agencies), and other terms suggest a negative existence derived from the state and market instead of having affirmative value in its own right, while also implying a more narrow understanding in terms of tax codes and legal status instead of the broader nature of the actual work people are doing. Plus, civil society is a more common term across the world, whereas other labels are more tied to the market-state arrangements of specific countries.

The work of the civil society sector is fundamentally different than the work of the market or the state—especially the charitable and voluntary aspects that usually characterize this work—and often involves several collaborative arrangements among different kinds of organizations, associations, and community groups. Many of these arrangements are relatively informal, involving mainly volunteer labor and ad hoc meetings, what Heath and Frey (2004) refer to broadly as "community collaboration". Yet many other collaborations are more formal, such as multi-party alliances (Zeng & Chen, 2003), cross-sector partnerships (Selsky & Parker, 2005), or business-nonprofit ventures (Austin & Seitanidi, 2012) that exist as distinct legal entities with standing committees and paid staff. Whatever the situation, all civil society collaboration and inter-organizational relationships entail relevant stakeholders organizing around key issues to achieve some degree of cooperation and joint outcomes that they could not (and often should not) accomplish on their own—what Vangen and Huxham (2003) simply call "collaborative advantage".

We should also define collaboration a bit further because it has become such a buzzword in both common vernacular and scholarly discourse that it practically means anything and everything, "hopelessly ambiguous" as some have noted (see Donahue, 2010). Collaboration is used to describe anything from huge, multi-city initiatives across large geographic regions to a few colleagues working together on a small project—and everything in between. Here's my best attempt at a coherent working definition: collaboration is a simultaneous process and structure that involves organizational and/or community representatives who come together in a deliberate manner to address issues that affect multiple stakeholders and are beyond the scope or capacity of any single organization, sector, or group (adapted from Koschmann & Sanders, 2020).[1] Of course there is some fuzziness at the boundaries of this definition, but this covers that vast majority of inter-organizational arrangements described as "collaboration". I'm less concerned with definitional precision here, which usually isn't possible for big concepts like civil society and collaboration anyway. Instead, my aim is to provide a working definition that orients us towards a particular organizational phenomenon that has enough distinctiveness to warrant specialized analysis in this chapter, while also acknowledging some overlap and imprecision that will never be resolved.

Furthermore, this definition distinguishes collaboration from other terms like cooperation or coordination, though again these concepts may cover some of the same reality and I accept that people often use them interchangeably. *Cooperation* is the most generic, overarching term involving anyone merely working together, whereas *coordination* is the alignment of tasks towards goal accomplishment. Collaboration obviously involves cooperation and coordination, but these necessary components are not sufficient to rise to the level of collaboration. For that, we need a greater level of interdependency and collective action among the participants, as well as the emergence of a higher-order organizational entity that transcends the relationships among the cooperating and coordinating partners and cannot be reduced to the contributions of any single member or subset of members—a specific organizational arrangement that is more than just the aggregation of partners.

Thinking Communicatively about Civil Society Collaboration

Now that we have a working definition of civil society collaboration to guide us, let's move on to the various theoretical and conceptual frameworks that inform current research and practice, while also noting the shortcomings of this work that invite more communicative approaches to civil society collaboration and the specific work of CCO scholarship. To date, most of the collaboration research is grounded in broad systems and economic perspectives, which empha-size resource dependencies, transaction cost efficiencies, and the macro-level characteristics of individual organizations and interorganizational domains. This is understandable, given that the scholarly study of collaboration originated mainly in schools and departments of public policy, management, business administration, and city planning (e.g., Austin, 2000, 2003; Gray, 1985, 1989; Gray & Wood, 1991; Innes & Booher, 1999; Pasquero, 1991; Sharfman, Gray, & Yan, 1991; Wood & Gray, 1991). This literature has yielded tremendous insights about the nature of civil society collaboration, especially concerning the inputs, outputs, and processes of effective collaboration, as well as the structural characteristics of various inter-organizational arrangements, all of which are consistent with systems and economic thinking (see Shumate, Atouba, Cooper, & Pliny, 2017, for a more extensive review of various theoretical perspectives that inform the interorganizational collaboration literature).

However, this work also exhibits notable shortcomings that limit our understanding of civil society collaboration, especially regarding communication. That is because systems and economic approaches usually privilege the antecedent conditions, subsequent outcomes, and organizational properties of collaboration but tend to overlook the important social processes that compose the actual work of collaboration, essentially "black boxing" interaction in favor of more abstract structural explanations. The problem is that resource dependency and macro-economic theories tend to conflate structure and process, which results in a sterile conception of communication as a linear exchange of information—communication is just another variable to be managed, not something that has constitutive force of its own to investigate. The point is that we severely limit our range of analysis and practice if we take existing arrangements and economic conditions as given and only look at how people send and receive messages within the system. Thus, we need research that does more to incorporate communication into our understanding of collaboration.

Yet, this does not entail that we need more or better systems and economic thinking that merely adds communication as a topic of inquiry to overcome these shortcomings. After all, the limitations explained above are features, not bugs, of these approaches and therefore over-coming them is outside of their logics, as Kuhn (2008) has argued. Additionally, the mere absence of communication from much of the initial collaboration literature does not necessarily warrant a turn to communication scholarship or alone justify the argument for more communi-cative thinking in future research. Instead, the lack of communication scholarship is a significant shortcoming because of the importance of communication to the understanding and practice of civil society collaboration. Simple observations quickly reveal the centrality of communication for collaboration. Not just the obvious fact that people in collaboration are constantly meeting and talking, negotiating and emailing, sharing information and calling each other on the phone, and making decisions, etc., but rather the more insightful observation that collaboration is *inherently communicative*—everything a collaboration "is" is wrapped up in communication practice. Collaborations lack many of the visible features of "normal" organizations—like permanent buildings, articles of incorporation, and formal employment contracts—so their existence is nothing but the accumulation of their ongoing communication practices (albeit materialized in various documents, websites, memorabilia, physical locations, etc.).

Accordingly, communication is the *mode of being* for collaboration; collaborations exist *as* communication and communication constitutes the organizational form of collaboration. Thus, communication scholarship adds a valuable perspective to the collaboration literature, not by simply looking *at* communication *in* collaboration but rather by seeing collaboration "communicationally" and exploring how and why various communication practices constitute different aspects of collaboration. That is exactly what communication scholars have been doing more recently, and in the next section we will look at the scope of this work and how it has expanded our understanding of civil society collaboration.

Communicative Collaboration Scholarship

The previous sections lay the foundation for what we mean by civil society collaboration, how other theoretical perspective have generally approached this subject, and what a communication perspective brings that is distinct and valuable. Now we turn our attention to the specific work that communication scholars have contributed to the literature, dividing this work into two categories: collaboration scholarship that is *broadly communicative* or "CCO friendly", which entails the bulk of this literature, and collaboration scholarship that is *explicitly CCO*, which represents a smaller yet more targeted collection of studies aligned with specific schools of CCO thinking. This type of distinction is already the norm in the extant CCO literature (see Ashcraft et al., 2009; Koschmann & Campbell, 2019), which acknowledged ideas of communicative constitution embedded in earlier research (e.g., culture, power, networks) long before the moniker of CCO was formally adopted. Likewise with collaboration research, as some scholars have been doing work that was distinctly "communicative" before CCO took off as a defined scholarly project. Thus, CCO should always encompass work that is both broadly communicative and more explicitly aligned with particular schools of thought.

Broadly Communicative Collaboration Scholarship

The majority of communication scholarship on collaboration is best understood as *broadly communicative*, working from a general commitment or orientation to the notion of communication as constitutive (Craig, 1999; Deetz, 1994), and where communication provides the basic explanatory framework for understanding collaboration and collaborative work, yet with no clear alignment with specific schools or theories of CCO thinking. Despite the occasional article or book chapter on communication and collaboration (e.g., Eisenberg, 1995; Heath & Sias, 1999; Keyton & Stalworth, 2003; Stohl & Walker, 2002), this work really gets going in the mid- to late-2000s with three notable contributions: Heath and Frey's (2004) *Communication Yearbook* chapter on community collaboration, Lewis's (2006) *Communication Yearbook* chapter on collaborative interaction, and Keyton, Ford, and Smith's (2008) article in *Communication Theory* that articulated a meso-level communicative model of collaboration.

First, Heath and Frey's (2004) chapter was one of the earliest contributions to call for a clear distinction between civil society collaboration and other forms of inter-organizational collaboration that involved private businesses and professional work groups, with the former characterized by a distinct focus on community development and social change versus capitalizing on market opportunities. They were also some of the first scholars in the collaboration literature to challenge the idea that communication was merely a "tool" used by collaborations but rather should be understood as the *sine qua non* or essential condition of collaboration, calling for a communication-oriented theory of collaboration. Next, Lewis (2006) provided an extensive review of the literature on collaborative interaction and made a definitive call for scholarly development and synthesis across multiple domains. Furthermore, she specifically noted the lack of research in the current literature that was "centrally communicative" and thus the need for more work in this area. Soon after, Keyton et al. (2008) offered the first empirical and explicitly communicative model of collaboration in the literature to date. The value of their contribution was that it provided a strong argument for conceptualizing communication as the "essence of collaboration" (not just one of many components in a larger model), and it presented a clear explanation for understanding collaboration as a simultaneous structure and process (note this in the definition I provided above). Furthermore, all these contributions made a compelling case for collaboration as a key site for communication scholarship because collaboration magnifies so many important aspects of interaction, dialogue, and social construction.

This initial work provided an important foundation for subsequent scholars to pursue a variety of projects that can be considered "CCO friendly" because of their broad commitment to the principles of communicative constitution. A notable exemplar of this work comes from Shumate and her colleagues, who have published an extensive body of empirical and theoretical research on *collaboration networks and communicative co-construction*. These scholars have explored, for example, how boards of directors influence cross-sector collaboration (Ihm & Shumate, 2019), how cross-sector collaboration affects nonprofit capacity (Shumate, Fu, & Cooper, 2018), the role of homophily in international nonprofit collaboration (Atouba & Shumate, 2015), interorganizational networking patterns among development organizations (Atouba & Shumate, 2010), and corporate reporting of cross-sector alliances (Shumate & O'Connor, 2010a). Much of this work seeks to understand civil society collaboration (and more specifically, NGO-corporate alliances) as "communicatively co-constructed" arrangements among stakeholder who "mobilize economic, social, cultural, and political capital" to accomplish their goals (Shumate & O'Connor, 2010b, p. 577). This research is also significant for its impact outside the field of communication in a variety of nonprofit and management outlets.

A second noteworthy collection of work comes from Heath and her *dialogic approach* to civil society collaboration and communication, which argues that our understanding of civil society collaboration should be based on dialogic theories of communication that emphasize participatory democracy and creative outcomes (Heath, 2007). A dialogic approach underscores the symmetry and reciprocity of interactions, plus the setting aside of formal authority relations, which opens stakeholder positions and knowledge claims to contestation (Milam & Heath, 2014). The upshot of this perspective involves fostering stakeholder interactions that enable "dialogic moments" that are generative, grounded in diversity, and critical of power (Heath, 2007). The key insight from this research is that these aspects of dialogue are characteristics of each interaction, not of the general structure of a collaboration. Furthermore, the dialogic approach entails that collaboration is grounded in a principled ethic of democratic and egalitarian participation, which has practical implications on how conversations unfold (Heath & Isbell, 2017). Again, this research makes no mention of CCO per se and does not intentionally seek to advance the CCO literature, but it should still be considered within the "big tent" of CCO scholarship because it provides an approach to civil society collaboration that is distinctly communicative and is informed by many of the same principles of social construction, interpretation, meaning, and/or sensemaking that many CCO scholars work from.

The same is true for another important body of research from the related field of *organizational discourse*, which predates much of the communication literature on collaboration and inter-organizational relationships and has been an important resource for CCO research and communication scholars more broadly. Discursive approaches to collaboration focus on interrelated collections of texts, plus the practices of text production and distribution that bring social realities into being. The research team of Hardy, Grant, Lawrence, Maguire, and Phillips has developed a sizable body of literature on the discursive foundations of collaboration, highlighting the negotiation of the issues to be addressed, the interests of relevant stakeholders, and the actors who represent those interests (see Hardy, Lawrence, & Phillips, 2006; Hardy, Lawrence, & Grant, 2005; Lawrence, Hardy, & Philipps, 2002; Lawrence, Phillips, & Hardy, 1999; Maguire, Phillips, & Hardy, 2001; Phillips & Hardy, 1997). A key contribution of this literature is demonstrating how the potential for effective collaboration lies in the participant's ability to negotiate a shared perspective on issues, interests, and identities that provides an adequate context for knowledge and action (Lawrence et al., 1999). The overlap between organizational discourse and organizational communication research is evident in the way these scholars define collaboration and explain their discursive approach, claiming that "collaboration represents a complex set of ongoing *communicative* processes among individuals" and that adopting a discursive approach "directs attention to the *communicative* practices among participants" while also "highlight[ing] the processual and temporal aspects of collaboration, thus allowing us to view collaboration as a *social accomplishment*" (Hardy et al., 2005, p. 59, emphasis added). A key distinction, however, is that most of this work on organizational discourse is grounded in broader commitments to institutional theory, which emphasizes the "multiple levels on which collaboration occurs" (Hardy et al., 2005, p. 59). Yet much of the current CCO literature is critical of the notion of multiple organizational levels and micro-meso-macro distinctions (see Cooren, Kuhn, Cornelissen, & Clark, 2011, especially their sixth premise of CCO scholarship; and Kuhn, Ashcraft, & Cooren, 2017, especially their commitment to a "flat" ontology), a point of contention explored elsewhere in this handbook (see Cooren and Seidl, this volume).

Beyond these three bodies of literature, communication scholars have published several additional studies that should be considered "CCO friendly" and part of our review here. Although they do not (yet) represent coherent scholarly projects with multiple publications like the research I summarized above, they are still informed by key principles of communicative constitution and thus contribute to the overall literature on civil society collaboration that is broadly communicative. These include studies such as Olufowote's (2016) research on identity construction and interorganizational collaboration; Woo's work on communicative entry and exit strategies in interorganizational collaboration (2019a; Woo & Leonardi, 2018), as well as her theoretical model of tensile structures that explains how collaboration conveners manage tensions to enhance collaborative capacity (2019b); Isbell's (2012) writing on boundary spanners as key communication links in nonprofit collaboration; Koschmann and Isbell's (2009) communicative model of inter-organizational collaboration; Lewis, Isbell, and Koschmann's (2010) study of practitioner experiences in nonprofit inter-organizational relationships; Koschmann's (2013a) analysis of human rights collaboration and the communicative practice of religious identity; Kramer et al.'s (2017) use of structuration theory to examine how collaboration members communicatively manage the balance of participation and efficiency; and Rice's (2018) examination of authority and hierarchy in an emergency response collaboration. What these studies have in common is that they all rely on foundational communication and discourse scholarship to inform their empirical investigations or develop their theoretical frameworks, and thus should be included in the CCO literature that is broadly communicative and informs our general understanding of the communicative constitution of civil society collaboration.

If we cast our nets even broader, we'll see there are still further studies that are beyond the boundaries of what we would formally consider civil society collaboration yet nevertheless offer important insights for understanding collaborative work in any context from a communication perspective. Examples include Barbour and James's (2015) study of compliance and regulation of a toxic-waste facility that focuses on identity tensions in inter-organizational collaboration, which demonstrated how identity tensions contribute to the constitution of collaboration; Barley and Weickum's (2017) communicative framework for understanding collaborative work teams from three approaches (black-box studies, interactional research, and work-oriented research); Just and Muhr's (2019) analysis of how collaboration and contestation function as "narrative drivers" for political leadership, revealing how leadership in this collaborative context is a dynamic co-construction yet also a negotiation of difference that does not necessarily lead to harmony and consensus; Arnaud and Mills's (2012) case study of inter-organizational collaboration in the French furniture-manufacturing sector, which revealed how successful collaboration is founded on collective competence that emerges through repeated interactions across a temporal frame; Koschmann and Burk's (2016) analysis of authority and collaborative work at a scientific laboratory, which showed how collaboration authority involves both authoring and de-authoring as people create new systems of influence and accountability while simultaneously erasing prior authoritative forces that undermine collaborative work; and Beck and Plowman's (2014) investigation of emergent inter-organizational collaboration during the Columbia space shuttle response efforts, which explains how specific organizing actions enabled self-organizing and the development of trust and identity, ultimately leading to a successful unplanned collaboration. All these studies engage with key sources from the established CCO literature to support their investigations, plus they offer conclusions and implications that advance a more communicative understanding of collaborative work and inter-organizational relationships—many of which are relevant for the context of civil society collaboration.

Now that we have a good understanding of collaboration, the civil society sector, and previous research on civil society collaboration that is broadly communicative, we are ready to move on to the most targeted aspect of this review chapter: research literature at the clear intersection of CCO scholarship and civil society collaboration. This body of research is relatively small and new, but momentum appears to be building and the trajectory points towards further development and important contributions. What sets this literature apart from everything we have reviewed so far is its positioning within scholarship that is explicitly CCO (i.e., identifies with particular schools of CCO thinking) and its foregrounding of collaboration as a key organizational phenomenon for investigation (not an incidental research site or background context from which to advance knowledge of other phenomena[2]). As such, we'll spend a bit more time examining the finer points of this material, focusing on particular concepts from the CCO literature that are employed and specific aspects of collaboration that are investigated—all of which serve the broader purpose of this handbook and its efforts to establish the state of the art of CCO scholarship.

Explicitly CCO Collaboration Scholarship

I should acknowledge from the outset that most of this literature comes from me and those I have collaborated with, and thus an unavoidable thread of self-promotion runs throughout this section. But if you will forgive this inevitability, there is much to learn about the valuable contributions to the CCO literature these studies offer, as well as how we can advance our understanding of civil society collaboration through an approach that is distinctly communicative. To date, this literature has focused on four interrelated aspects of collaborative work that are intrinsic to the phenomenon of collaboration itself and where CCO thinking has made distinct contributions: authority, agency, identity, and value. That is, collaborative work raises fundamental questions about how power and influence are exercised among stakeholders apart from hierarchical mechanisms of control (authority), how social collectives develop the capacity to act and make a difference (agency), how organizational forms emerge as distinct entities (identity), and how efficacy and success should be assessed (value). CCO is well-positioned to address these questions and several of its concepts have been employed to investigate and explicate these aspects of collaboration, such as authoritative texts, imbrication, text-conversation dialectics, intertextuality, distanciation, and presentification—most of which are grounded in a co-orientational model of communicative constitution that is chiefly associated with the Montréal School of CCO thinking. To my knowledge, there are no studies to date that explicitly address inter-organizational collaboration based on other approaches to CCO. Let's take a closer look at what these studies contribute to our understanding of collaboration and how they utilize CCO thinking.

The explicit CCO literature on collaboration and inter-organizational relationships gets started with Koschmann, Kuhn, and Pfarrer's (2012) communicative model of value in collaborations and inter-organizational relationships (what we refer to as cross-sector partnerships or XSPs in this study). This study argued that organizational collaborations should be evaluated at the partnership level as distinct organizational forms beyond their individual members, and that communication scholars were in a better position to do this compared to more conventional approaches based on resource dependence and transaction cost economic theories. We developed a conceptual model that situates collaboration value (or overall effectiveness) in its capacity to exhibit collective agency, or to take meaningful and substantive action *as a collaboration* in a given problem domain. Our model explains this collective agency as a characteristic of a collaboration's *authoritative text*, an abstract representation that portrays relations of power and discipline practice through its influence as a collective. Authoritative texts emerge from localized text-conversation dialectics (a.k.a. coorientation) as they gain distance from their initial circumstances (a.k.a. distanciation) and demonstrate the ability to marshal consent and attract various forms of capital. Consequently, collective agency—and thus overall collaboration value—is seen in the *trajectory* of an authoritative text, a qualitative component of the authoritative text that indicates its general direction and what it is "on track" to accomplish. Accordingly, we articulated several theoretical propositions regarding specific communication practices that increase collaboration value potential and to assess overall collaboration value, such as examining how collaboration authoritative texts influence the authoritative text of member organizations and other external constituents, or how practices of naming and narrative construction create distinct and stable identities—thus contributing an alternative model of collaboration value assessment rooted in the principles of communicative constitution and that employs several key concepts associated with the Montréal School of CCO.

Subsequently, my colleagues and I expanded this initial theoretical work with empirical studies that utilized CCO thinking for understanding and explaining collaboration identity, authority, and agency. Koschmann (2013b) reconceptualized the notion of collective identity from a communication perspective, noting that collective identity is an important yet misunderstood mechanism for inducing action in civil society collaboration, thus warranting further investigation. Most existing scholarship understands collective identity as a psychological construct, which foregrounds individual cognition at the expense of interaction, practice, and collective constructions. This approach also positions communication as a mere vehicle to express and share those individual cognitions. Contrary to the cognitive view (and building on the seminal work of other communication scholars of identity), I theorized collaboration collective identity as an authoritative text emerging from processes of coorientation, abstraction, and reification. This enabled me to explain the struggles and inaction of a large civil society collaboration of social service providers, as well as trace the advent of a new collective identity (i.e., authoritative text) that brought a renewed sense of purpose and direction to this collaboration. Additionally, I expanded my work in this research site by exploring how sector differences in collaboration (i.e., nonprofit, business, government) were managed communicatively and how these differences are implicated in the processes of collaboration (Koschmann, 2016a). This study demonstrated how sector differences were used as discursive resources that people drew upon to make sense of uncertainty and frame arguments. The findings also revealed how sector differences were managed communicatively through four specific communication practices: *recognition* of the strengths and weaknesses of each sector, *resistance* to the rationality and values of certain sectors, *translation* of one sector's values and norms into another's, and *mediation* between sectors by trusted individuals who could transcend sector boundaries and speak credibly to both.

Next, Koschmann (2016b) investigated the subject of persistent collaboration ineffectiveness, an uncomfortable reality for collaboration despite the best of intentions. Here I studied the collaborative work of an affordable-housing taskforce, in order to develop a conceptual framework to understand the communicative accomplishment of collaboration failure. Drawing on notions of dialogue, discourse, and coorientation, I explained how ineffective collaboration involved communication practices of aggregation (the mere accumulation of ideas and positions), representation (simply stating and advocating individual interests), and expression (non-participatory practices that just convey information), resulting in a state of failure characterized by accumulated information, disparate identities, and the inability to act authoritatively as a group. Basically, many of the right "pieces" of collaboration seemed to be in place here, but the communication practices of the group and their patterns of interaction did not give rise to an entity capable of exercising collective agency in any worthwhile fashion—they never became more than the sum of their component parts, thus leading to overall failure for what this group was trying to accomplish. Conversely, I proposed notions of emergence (generative knowledge), exploration (openness towards discovery and new ideas), and engagement (encounters of back-and-forth interaction) as alternative communication practices that give rise to collaboration effectiveness (i.e., value). Why? Because these practices are more likely to lead to the *generative* knowledge, *shared* identities, and *collective* agency needed for successful collaboration. In the vernacular of CCO thinking, these practices do a better job of facilitating the imbrication of action and scaling up from individual to collective agencies needed to constitute an organizational form capable of acting substantively and legitimately within a given problem domain.

Furthermore, Koschmann, Kopczynski, Opdyke, and Javernick-Will (2017) used the authoritative text concept to explore the social construction of authority in disaster-relief collaboration in the Philippines after a major typhoon. Rather than conceptualizing authority as a formal position in a hierarchy, collaboration pushes us to understand authority as a distributed phenomenon that is worked out in practice as stakeholders negotiate the meaning of their work. Authority is thus a social accomplishment that is achieved and sustained in communication and subject to continual revision depending on how people interact with each other. CCO offers valuable resources to understand and explain collaboration authority by conceptualizing authority as a process of authoring where people struggle to "write" an official version of their work that conveys particular notions of purpose, direction, and identity (see Kuhn, 2008; Taylor & Van Every, 2014). This approach to authority relates to the textual existence or "modality" of organizations, where interrelated networks of meaning are "read" in certain ways to enable coordination (Kärreman, 2001; Westwood & Linstead, 2001). Our empirical case study explored the textual and discursive resources people drew upon to convey authority, how people authorized themselves in relation to other stakeholders, and how people made forms of authority present (presentification) in their interactions.

Lately, recent empirical studies have made significant contributions towards advancing this initial CCO work. Recall our preliminary article on collaboration value assessment described above (i.e., Koschmann et al., 2012). Typhina and Jameson (2019) provide a valuable empirical assessment of this model and developed a research methodology for scholars and practitioners interested in studying and facilitating cross-sector collaboration. Their participatory mapping method guides collaboration members in charting, negotiating, and ritualizing various aspects of their collective identity based on shared goals and mechanisms for enactment. This research contributes valuable insights about collective identity related to narratives, tacit knowledge, and ecosystem management. Rice's (2022) book homes in on the question of collaboration authority through a two-year study of emergency management collaborations involving multiple civil society partners. She employs CCO concepts of authorship, translation, coorientation, imbrication, and authoritative texts to develop a model of *cumulative authority* where authority is a communicative struggle, created in the accumulation of various sources that can be deployed in member interactions and accepted by others in everyday conversations. Collaboration is a uniquely challenging type of organizing that leads to both ambiguity and opportunity for members to position themselves as speakers of authority, and her book shows how CCO scholarship provides valuable resources to understand and explain this important dynamic. These studies are also important because they indicate clear scholarly progression in the CCO collaboration literature: empirical validation of previous theoretical work and methodological guidance to inform future research.

Altogether, this literature shows that a CCO approach explains effective collaboration (value) as the ability to exert influence among members and stakeholders (authority) in such a way that leads to the existence of a social entity (identity) that has the capacity to act and make a difference (agency) in a specific realm of civil society work.[3] Subsequent research should work to refine this communicative understanding of collaboration, as well as expose any shortcomings that arise when applying these ideas in different contexts or when put in conversation with other models and theories. Furthermore, this literature is relatively small in scope compared with the full corpus of CCO thinking and additional concepts that could be employed. Conceivably, we have much to gain by applying the Four Flows/Structuration model of CCO to the context of collaboration and inter-organizational relationships, especially since the contingent and often fleeting nature of collaboration magnifies issues of membership negotiation, reflexive self-structuring, activity coordination, and (to a lesser extent) institutional positioning. Likewise, Luhmann's theory of social systems is particularly relevant for addressing key issues of collaboration, namely how collaborations maintain their existence over time through decisional events and how collaborations act within their environments or domains of practice. And even though the extant literature relies heavily on concepts and theories most associated with the Montréal School of CCO thinking, there are still relevant ideas from this realm that have not been utilized to study collaboration and inter-organizational relationships (e.g., ventriloquism, materiality). Finally, it is worth noting that the pipeline of future CCO collaboration scholarship looks promising. As evidence, Google Scholar lists several conference papers and unpublished dissertations just within the last couple of years that have "CCO" and/ or "collaboration" in the titles and abstracts, some of which are likely to show up in the scholarly literature soon.

To conclude, the intersection of CCO and collaboration is a valuable site for organizational communication scholarship, both for the way that CCO thinking has informed key aspects of collaborative work and for how insights from the practice of collaboration have informed the development of CCO concepts and theories—and can continue to do so. Of course, much of what I explained above likely applies to the broader literature on inter-organizational collaboration in a variety of other sectors and contexts beyond civil society. Yet civil society collaboration foregrounds and magnifies key issues of value, authority, identity, and agency in distinct ways because of the unique financial, labor, and governing arrangements of civil society work. I highlight civil society collaboration in this chapter because that is what makes up the majority of CCO collaboration literature to date. However, collaboration is a vast topic with many unanswered questions and unresolved issues that CCO scholarship is poised to address. Collaboration is inherently communicative and thus our understanding and explanations should be distinctly communicational. CCO is the most recent and developed attempt to apply communicative thinking to the realm of organizational studies. Whether or not CCO continues as a formal project is secondary (though some continuity would be nice); what's more important is a sustained commitment to communicative work. One way to ensure this is to have a common reference point and a set of conceptual resources, and CCO does provide this. Overall, my hope is that communicative work on inter-organizational collaboration—especially in the civil society sector—continues and flourishes, and that CCO anchors this work as long as it is useful.

Notes

1 I make no claim of originality here; this is just my best attempt to synthesize definitions and ideas from many influential sources such as: Gray (1989); Hardy, Lawrence, & Grant (2005); Hardy, Lawrence, & Phillips, (2006); Heath & Isbell (2017); Huxham & Vangen (2013); Keyton, Ford, & Smith (2008); Lewis (2006).
2 This precludes explicit CCO work that happens to come from empirical contexts related to civil society collaboration but does not foreground collaboration in the investigation or seek to contribute to collaboration scholarship, such as the studies by Cooren and his colleagues on agency and presence with Médecins Sans Frontières.
3 I develop this communicative model of collaboration more fully in chapter 4 of Koschmann & Sanders (2020).

References

Arnaud, N., & Mills, C. E. (2012). Understanding interorganizational agency: A communication perspective. *Group & Organization Management*, *37*(4), 452–485.

Ashcraft, K. L., Kuhn, T. R., & Cooren, F. (2009). 1. Constitutional amendments: "Materializing" organizational communication. *Academy of Management Annals*, *3*(1), 1–64.

Atouba, Y., & Shumate, M. (2015). International nonprofit collaboration: Examining the role of homophily. *Nonprofit and Voluntary Sector Quarterly*, *44*, 587–608.

Atouba, Y., & Shumate, M. (2010). Interorganizational networking patterns among development organizations. *Journal of Communication*, *60*, 293–317.

Austin, J. E. (2000). Strategic collaboration between nonprofits and business. *Nonprofit and Voluntary Sector Quarterly*, *29*, 69–97.

Austin, M. J. (2003). The changing relationship between nonprofit organizations and public social service agencies in the era of welfare reform. *Nonprofit and Voluntary Sector Quarterly*, *32*(1), 97–114.

Austin, J. E., & Seitanidi, M. M. (2012). Collaborative value creation: A review of partnering between nonprofits and businesses: Part I. Value creation spectrum and collaboration stages. *Nonprofit and Voluntary Sector Quarterly, 41*, 929–968.

Barbour, J. B., & James, E. P. (2015). Collaboration for compliance: Identity tensions in the interorganizational and interdisciplinary regulation of a toxic waste storage facility. *Journal of Applied Communication Research, 43*(4), 363–384.

Barley, W. C., & Weickum, N. R. (2017). The work gap: A structured review of collaborative teamwork research from 2005 to 2015. *Annals of the International Communication Association, 41*(2), 136–167.

Beck, T. E., & Plowman, D. A. (2014). Temporary, emergent interorganizational collaboration in unexpected circumstances: A study of the Columbia space shuttle response effort. *Organization Science, 25*(4), 1234–1252.

Cooren, F., Kuhn, T., Cornelissen, J. P., & Clark, T. (2011). Communication, organizing and organization: An overview and introduction to the special issue. *Organization Studies, 32*(9), 1149–1170.

Craig, R. T. (1999). Communication theory as a field. *Communication Theory, 9*(2), 119–161.

Deetz, S. A. (1994). Future of the discipline: The challenges, the research, and the social contribution. *Annals of the International Communication Association, 17*(1), 565–600.

Donahue, J. D. (2010). The race: Can collaboration outrun rivalry between American business and government. *Public Administration Review, 70*(5), 151–152.

Eisenberg, E. M. (1995). A communication perspective on inter-organizational cooperation and inner-city education. In M. C. R. L. C. Rigsby & M. C. Wang (Eds.), *School-community connections: Exploring issues for research and practice* (pp. 101–119). San Francisco: Josey-Bass.

Gray, B. (1985). Conditions facilitating interorganizational collaboration. *Human Relations, 38*(10), 911–936.

Gray, B. (1989). *Collaborating: Finding common ground for multiparty problems.* San Francisco: Jossey-Bass.

Gray, B., & Wood, D. J. (1991). Collaborative alliances: Moving from practice to theory. *The Journal of Applied Behavioral Science, 27*(1), 3–22.

Hardy, C., Lawrence, T. B., & Grant, D. (2005). Discourse and collaboration: The role of conversations and collective identity. *Academy of Management Review, 30*(1), 58–77.

Hardy, C., Lawrence, T. B., & Phillips, N. (2006). Swimming with sharks: Creating strategic change through multi-sector collaboration. *International Journal of Strategic Change Management, 1*(1–2), 96–112.

Heath, R. G. (2007). Rethinking community collaboration through a dialogic lens: Creativity, democracy, and diversity in community organizing. *Management Communication Quarterly, 21*(2), 145–171.

Heath, R. G., & Isbell, M. G. (2017). *Interorganizational collaboration: Complexity, ethics, and communication.* Waveland Press.

Heath, R. G., & Frey, L. (2004). Ideal collaboration: A conceptual framework of community collaboration. *Communication Yearbook, 28*, 189–232.

Heath, R., & Sias, P. (1999). Communicating spirit in a collaborative alliance. *Journal of Applied Communication Research, 27*, 356–376.

Huxham, C., & Vangen, S. (2013). *Managing to collaborate: The theory and practice of collaborative advantage.* Routledge.

Ihm, J., & Shumate, M. (2019). How does a board of directors influence within- and cross-sector nonprofit collaboration? *Nonprofit Management and Leadership, 29*, 473–490.

Innes, J. E., & Booher, D. E. (1999). Consensus building and complex adaptive systems: A framework for evaluating collaborative planning. *Journal of the American Planning Association, 65*(4), 412–423.

Isbell, M. G. (2012). The role of boundary spanners as the interorganizational link in nonprofit collaborating. *Management Communication Quarterly, 26*(1), 159–165.

Just, S. N., & Louise Muhr, S. (2019). "Together we rise": Collaboration and contestation as narrative drivers of the Women's March. *Leadership, 15*(2), 245–267.

Kärreman, D. (2001). The scripted organization: Dramaturgy from Burke to Baudrillard. In R. Westwood & S. Linstead (Eds.), *The language of organization* (pp. 89–111). Thousand Oaks, CA: Sage.

Keyton, J., & Stallworth, V. (2003). On the verge of collaboration: Interaction processes versus group outcomes. In L. R. Frey (Ed.), *Group communication in context: Studies of bona fide groups* (pp. 235–260). Routledge.

Keyton, J., Ford, D. J., & Smith, F. L. (2008). A meso-level communicative model of collaboration. *Communication Theory, 18*(3): 376–406.

Koschmann, M. (2013a). Integrating religious faith in human rights collaboration. *Journal of Communication and Religion, 36*(2), 1–27.

Koschmann, M. (2013b). The communicative constitution of collective identity in interorganizational collaboration. *Management Communication Quarterly, 27*(1), 61–89.

Koschmann, M. (2016a). Economic sectors as discursive resources for civil society collaboration. *Communication Quarterly, 64*(4), 410–433.

Koschmann, M. (2016b). The communicative accomplishment of collaboration failure. *Journal of Communication, 66*, 409–432.

Koschmann, M., & Burk, N. (2016). Accomplishing authority in collaborative work. *Western Journal of Communication, 80*(4), 393–413.

Koschmann, M., & Campbell, T. (2019). A critical review of how communication scholarship is represented in textbooks: The case of organizational communication and CCO theory. *Annals of the International Communication Association, 43*(2), 173–191.

Koschmann, M., & Isbell, M. (2009). Toward a communicative model of interorganizational collaboration: The case of the community action network. *Case Research Journal, 29*(1–2), 1–28.

Koschmann, M., Kopczynski, J., Opdyke, A., & Javernick-Will, A. (2017). Constructing authority in disaster relief coordination. *Electronic Journal of Communication, 27* (3 & 4).

Koschmann, M., Kuhn, T., & Pfarrer, M. (2012). A communicative framework of value in cross-sector partnerships. *Academy of Management Review, 37*(3), 332–354.

Koschmann, M., & Sanders, M. (2020). *Understanding nonprofit work: A communication perspective.* Hoboken, NJ: Wiley-Blackwell.

Kramer, M. W., Hoelscher, C. S., Nguyen, C., Day, E. A., & Cooper, O. D. (2017). Structuration processes in an interagency collaboration: Enabling and constraining participation and efficiency. *Journal of Applied Communication Research, 45*(4), 429–444. https://doi.org/10.1080/00909882.2017.1355558.

Kuhn, T. (2008). A communicative theory of the firm: Developing an alternative perspective on intra-organizational power and stakeholder relationships. *Organization Studies, 29*(8–9), 1227–1254.

Kuhn, T., Ashcraft, K. L., & Cooren, F. (2017). *The work of communication: Relational perspectives on working and organizing in contemporary capitalism.* Taylor & Francis.

Lawrence, T. B., Phillips, N., & Hardy, C. (1999). Watching whale watching: Exploring the discursive foundations of collaborative relationships. *The Journal of Applied Behavioral Science, 35*(4), 479–502.

Lawrence, T. B., Hardy, C., & Phillips, N. (2002). Institutional effects of interorganizational collaboration: The emergence of proto-institutions. *Academy of Management Journal, 45*(1), 281–290.

Lewis, L. K. (2006). Collaborative interaction: Review of communication scholarship and a research agenda. In C. Beck (Ed.), *Communication yearbook 30* (pp. 197–247). Thousand Oaks, CA: Sage.

Lewis, L., Isbell, M. G., & Koschmann, M. (2010). Collaborative tensions: Practitioners' experiences of interorganizational relationships. *Communication Monographs, 77*(4), 460–479.

Maguire, S., Phillips, N., & Hardy, C. (2001). When silence=death, keep talking: Trust, control and the discursive construction of identity in the Canadian HIV/AIDS treatment domain. *Organization Studies, 22*(2), 285–310.

Milam, J. M., & Heath, R. G. (2014). Participative democracy and voice: Rethinking community collaboration beyond neutral structures. *Journal of Applied Communication Research, 42*(4), 366–386.

Olufowote, J. O. (2016). Identity constructions and inter-organizational collaboration: Islamic faith-based organizations and the polio vaccination stoppage in northern Nigeria. *Communication Quarterly, 64*(5), 518–535.

Pasquero, J. (1991). Supraorganizational collaboration: The Canadian environmental experiment. *The Journal of Applied Behavioral Science, 27*(1), 38–64.

Phillips, N., & Hardy, C. (1997). Managing multiple identities: Discourse, legitimacy and resources in the UK refugee system. *Organization, 4*(2), 159–185.

Rice, R. M. (2018). When hierarchy becomes collaborative: Collaboration as sensemaking frame in high reliability organizing. *Corporate Communications: An International Journal, 23*(4), 599–613. doi: 10.1108/CCIJ-04-2017-0032.

Rice, R. M. (2022). *Communicating authority in interorganizational collaboration.* Routledge.

Selsky, J.W., & Parker, B. (2005). Cross-sector partnerships to address social issues: Challenges to theory and practice. *Journal of Management, 31*(6), 849–873.

Sharfman, M. P., Gray, B., & Yan, A. (1991). The context of interorganizational collaboration in the garment industry: An institutional perspective. *The Journal of Applied Behavioral Science, 27*(2), 181–208.

Shumate, M., Atouba, Y., Cooper, R., & Pilny, A. (2017). Interorganizational communication. In Craig Scott & Laurie Lewis (Eds.), *The encyclopedia of organizational communication.* Chichester: Wiley Blackwell.

Shumate, M., Fu, J. S., & Cooper, K. R. (2018). Does cross-sector collaboration lead to higher nonprofit capacity? *Journal of Business Ethics, 150,* 385–399.

Shumate, M., & O'Connor, A. (2010a). Corporate reporting of cross-sector alliances: The portfolio of NGO partners communicated on corporate websites. *Communication Monographs, 77,* 238–261.

Shumate, M., & O'Connor, A. (2010b). The symbiotic sustainability model: Conceptualizing NGO-corporate alliance communication. *Journal of Communication, 63,* 577–609.

Stohl, C., & Walker, C. (2002). A bona fide perspective for the future of groups: Understanding collaborating groups. In L. R. Frey (Ed.), *New directions in group communication* (pp. 237–252). Thousand Oaks, CA: Sage.

Taylor, J. R., & Van Every, E. J. (2014). *When organization fails: Why authority matters.* New York: Routledge.

Typhina, E., & Jameson, J. K. (2019). Participatory mapping method: Improving collaboration through attention to collective identity. *Journal of Applied Communication Research, 47*(6), 667–688.

Vangen, S., & Huxham, C. (2003). Enacting leadership for collaborative advantage: Dilemmas of ideology and pragmatism in the activities of partnership managers. *British Journal of Management, 14*(1), 61–76.

Westwood, R., & Linstead, S. (2001). *The language of organization.* Sage.

Woo, D. (2019a). Exit strategies in interorganizational collaboration: Setting the stage for re-entry. *Communication Research,* 0093650219851418.

Woo, D. (2019b). Reconceptualizing interorganizational collaborations as tensile structures: Implications of conveners' proactive tension management. *Communication Monographs, 86,* 158–183. doi:10.1080/03637751.2018.1526389.

Woo, D., & Leonardi, P. M. (2018). Breaking into collaboration: Communicative strategies for gaining entry when you are not invited. *Journal of Communication, 68,* 1127–1154. doi:10.1093/joc/jqy052.

Wood, D. J., & Gray, B. (1991). Toward a comprehensive theory of collaboration. *The Journal of Applied Behavioral Science, 27*(2), 139–162.

Zeng, M., & Chen, X. P. (2003). Achieving cooperation in multiparty alliances: A social dilemma approach to partnership management. *Academy of Management Review, 28*(4), 587–605.

26

DIGITAL MEDIA

From Tools to Agents Making a Difference

Jean A. Saludadez

The communicative constitution of organization (CCO) framework is founded on the premise that the explanation of organization is in communication. In that sense, Taylor et al. (1996) elaborate on the equivalence between communication and society Dewey (1916) initially articulated: "[organization] exists *in* transmission, *in* communication" (Haug & Cooren, 2020, p. 113). This chapter aims to show that digital media contributes to such communicative constitution of organizing. It briefly describes the different perspectives on studying digital media, it critiques those perspectives—in particular, the affordances and the entanglement perspectives that dominate its study—and then it brings into focus CCO's materialization perspective as a framework for studying digital media as agents that make a difference. This perspective, and CCO's key notion of "matters of concern", is illustrated using the case of an open university's online learning environment.

Perspectives on Studying Digital Media

Digital media has been problematized in terms of its power to create, configure and change organizational relations. Perspectives on studying digital media differ in terms of where they locate its organizing power: in its instrumental capacity to influence organizational outcomes; in the intention and construction of organizational members who use it; in its intrinsic properties and interoperability; or in its inextricable or inseparable relationship with human agency. These perspectives can be generally classified into two broad views of digital media: it is either considered as a *tool* or as an *agent* making a difference. Each of these perspectives stands on different ontological and epistemological grounds pertaining to the relationship between the material/technical and the meaning/social dimensions/domains of organizational reality and how they are studied.

Digital Media as a Tool

Two perspectives fall under the "tool" view of the power of digital media, which can be differentiated according to where such technological power is located: (1) in its instrumental capacity to influence organizational outcomes; and (2) in the intention or construction of organizational members who use it.

DOI: 10.4324/9781003224914-30

1. *The Power of DM is in Its Instrumental Capacity to Influence Organizational Outcomes*

Often designated as the Techno-Centric Perspective, this first perspective looks at digital media as a technology that causes / determines / controls organizational outcomes. This perspective stands on a materialist ontology that ascribes to material conditions the power to influence social life. Within this perspective, digital media is problematized in terms of its role in organizational change. Study interests in this perspective include new media technology's role in developing effective organizational internal communication (Kholisoh & Sulastri, 2017), digital technologies and changes in public organizations (Plesner at al., 2018), and the consequences of cyberbullying behaviour in working life (Muhonen et al., 2017).

2. *The Power of DM is in the Intention or Construction of Organizational Members who Use It*

Called the Human-Centered Perspective, this perspective looks at digital media as socially constructed. This perspective stands on a social constructivist epistemology that "holds that both meanings of and outcomes involving technology are shaped or mediated by the social contexts and interactions into which the new technology is implemented" (Rice & Leonardi, 2013, p. 425). Within this perspective, digital media is problematized in terms of "how people appropriate, make sense of, use and speak about [digital] technology" (Cooren, 2020, p. 5). Research in this perspective studies how social media supports an organization's absorptive capacity and performance (Schlagwein & Hu, 2017), the perceived usefulness of web technologies as organizational media (Ohnabayedo, 2017), and what shapes social media's meaning in an organization (Treem et al., 2015).

This view of digital media as a tool has been criticized as deterministic and reductionist as organizing power cannot be attributed only to either a technology's instrumental capacity or to a human being's intentionality. It limits analysts to choose between the effect of [digital] technology on human action or the effect of human action on the [digital] technology (Martine et al., 2016).

Digital Media as an Agent Making a Difference

As an alternative to viewing digital media as a tool, some researchers consider it to be an agent that makes a difference in the situation in which it participates. Two perspectives fall under this view of the power of digital media, which can be differentiated according to where the agentic power is located: (1) in the intrinsic properties of digital media and its interoperability; and (2) in its inextricable or inseparable relationship with human agency. Cooren (2020) classified these perspectives as different versions of sociomateriality. They both stand on relational and performative onto-epistemologies (Hultin, 2019), but they differ in their view of the nature of the relationship between the social/discursive and the material/technological.

1. *The Organizing Power of DM is in its Intrinsic Properties and Interoperability*

Called the Affordance Perspective, this first way of understanding technology's agency looks at digital media as an agent that makes a difference by attributing such power to its intrinsic properties (such as its interoperability), which provide affordances to accomplish organizational life. This perspective assumes that the social and the material have independent existence. However, while there are some aspects of [digital] technology "that are intrinsic to it and not part of the social context in which the [digital] technology is used" (Rice & Leonardi, 2013), they have "synergistic interaction" (Cooren, 2020 p. 6). Beverungen, Beyes and Conrad (2019), quoting Peters (2016), explain how this relationship happens: "Once rendered symbolically interoperable, digits combined computational and referential powers in ways that allow the stewards of digital systems to manipulate elements of … social reality" (p. 94). Within this perspective, digital media is problematized in terms of its affordances, defined as "the mutuality of actor intentions and [digital] technology capabilities that provide the potential for a particular action" (Faraj & Azad, 2012). Research adopting such a perspective includes the study of how social media affordances lead to their governance in workplaces (Vaast and Kaganer, 2013), the relationship between social media and organizational socialization (Leidner et al., 2018), and with information sharing (Khan et al., 2019).

This perspective is criticized for the rigid separation between human/social agency and material/technological agency, which limits our understanding of the organizing power of digital media. Such separation prevents gaining new insights from the phenomenon being studied, since it already assumes a particular relationship between agencies (Martine & Cooren, 2016). As Pentzold and Bischof (2019) argue "to state that a device affords a certain kind of activity might be obvious but also quite uninformative" (p. 1).

2. The Organizing Power of DM is in its "Inextricable" or "Inseparable" Relationship with Human Agency

Called the Entanglement Perspective, this second view of technology's agency looks at digital media as an agent making a difference by attributing such power to its inextricable link with or inseparability from organizational practices. This perspective assumes that "[t]he social and the material are considered to be inextricably related – there is no social that is not material and no material that is not social" (Orlikowski, 2007, p. 1437). The relationship is described as "constitutive entanglement according to which there is no such thing as independently existing entities with inherent properties" (Cooren, 2020, p. 5). Within this perspective, digital media is problematized in terms of its participation in the enactment of organizational practices. Areas of study include how connections to work through the use of smartphones are experienced and managed (Pritchard & Symon, 2014), mutual constitution of social media use and status hierarchies in global organizing (Kim, 2018), and the role of digital technology in the constitution of meaningful work (Symon & Whiting, 2019).

This perspective is criticized for defying the inseparability of the constitutive (or ontological) entanglement of meaning and matter that it espouses (Martine & Cooren, 2016). As Bencherki and Elmholdt (2020) articulated:

> As such, these proposals, on the one hand, reproduce, perhaps unwantedly, an artificial "bifurcation of nature" into a social and a material realm (Cooren, 2015) and, on the other hand, implicitly take for granted that organizations are first and foremost "social" in nature, thus making their connection with materiality a secondary problem rather than a core ontological consideration. (p. 2)

Even studies that were framed within the CCO framework (see for instance Albu & Etter, 2016; Arnaud & Fauré, 2016; Dawson, 2018) slipped into constitutive entanglement as an explanation for the agentive role of digital media. The confusion, as observed by Cooren (2020), is in "automatically associating matter to something that can be touched or seen, that is, something tangible or visible, an association that irremediably leads us to recreate a dissociation between the world of human affairs and the so-called material world" (p. 1).

The Materialization Perspective of the CCO

The materialization perspective of CCO offers a different way of looking at digital media as an agent making a difference, by attributing such power to the irreducible materiality of communication. This perspective also assumes that there is no social that is not material and no material that is not relational (Kuhn et al., 2019), but rather than entangled, materiality and sociality are considered "essential features" of existence (Cooren, 2018, p. 278) or "(relative) properties of what exists" (Cooren, 2020, p. 2; see also Wilhoit-Larson & Mengis, this volume). Its point of departure from other perspectives in understanding digital media is on the nature of materiality, which to most sociomaterial scholarship only refers to the "intrinsic properties" of (digital) technologies "that are relatively stable throughout space and time" (Cooren, 2018, p. 280), while to CCO it is "a property of all (organizational) phenomena" manifested when human and non-human agencies "come to appear and make themselves present throughout space and time" in communication (Cooren, 2020, p. 2).

Materiality as an essential property of organization refers to what an organization is made of, that is, it is made of relations that materialize in communication "through something or someone" (Cooren, 2018, p. 279). Relations that "make [the organization] what it is" (Cooren 2020, p. 14) materialize in communication. It implies, as Cooren (2020) postulates, that "anything or anyone *can* operate as a medium or channel as long as it is seen as an *in-between* through which other beings act or communicate" and "relationally and communicatively speaking, one can *become* a medium or channel whenever something or someone else appears to embody, materialize, incarnate, or present itself/herself/himself through what one says or does" (p. 11).

The materialization of organizational relations, or simply mediation, can explain how organizations act and become (Bencherki & Cooren, 2011). Mediation as the organizing property of communication is built upon two concepts: (1) action and agency as hybrid and historical and (2) authority as stabilizing and surpassing the present interaction.

1. Action and Agency as Hybrid and Historical

Drawing on the work of Bruno Latour, Cooren (2000) suggests that "when someone acts, others always proceed into action" (p. 217). This leads to a conception of organizational action as hybrid or heterogenous (Robichaud, 2006), that is, shared rather than solely performed by an actor, and as historical, meaning that is a product or effect of an action or interaction that was performed in the past but continues "to have very tangible effects today" (Cooren & Fairhurst, 2009, p. 134). Organizing lies "in the chain of actions" (Cooren, 2006, p. 86) and involves "the *association* of many different actors" (Cooren & Fairhurst, 2009, p. 134). Cooren (2006) located the emergence of collective actors in the appropriation of action:

> By appropriating the action of other actors, one can act from a distance and across time … this teleappropriation can be considered the key phenomenon by which collective actors emerge and their identities can be reinforced. (p. 82)

Taylor and Van Every (2000) claimed that "there is a fundamental difference between actor and agency: *Agents* may take the form of individual persons, but they may also be materialized in technology or represent metonymically collective actors or macroactors. The emergence of the latter is an effect of the constitution of actor-networks, or groups of actors mobilized around a common object of concern. In the end, every action supposes the mediation of a material agent" (p. 172). Drawing on relational ontology of Peirce, Robichaud (2006) defined agency "as a relational configuration" or "a situationally embedded connection of connections between heterogeneous entities" (p. 102). He advanced that organizing is "constituted through a plurality of agencies … but this plurality, despite its complexity is nevertheless textualized in an organizing and operative organizational text" (Robichaud, 2006, p. 113). Agents, therefore, can be human, nonhuman, or "other than human" (Cooren, 2020, p. 17), so long as she/he/it can demonstrate that "the author of the text" is "the network" (Taylor & Van Every, 2000, p. 243) and thus make a difference. This leads to the discussion of authority.

2. Authority as Stabilizing and Surpassing the Present Interaction

Taylor and Van Every (2014) characterize authority as "a foundation of organization because in its absence there would be no unifying force. Mostly, however, authority remains invisible, even to the dedicated observer, precisely because it is so fundamental" (p. xx; see also Benoit-Barné & Fox, this volume). Benoit-Barné et al. (2019) suggest that authority is "a communicative accomplishment" because it is made visible through the process of presentification:

> Authority is a legitimate form of power linked to order and stability because its local emergence and negotiation involve a process of "presentification" whereby established and recognizable entities are brought to bear on the interaction … . Presentification refers to ways of speaking and acting by which actors can make present things and beings that influence the unfolding of the situation in which they find themselves. (p. 119)

The notion of presentification implies authority as stabilizing (or giving legitimacy to) and surpassing (or preceding) the present interaction. In the presentification of authority an interaction can be said to be "never purely local" but "always dislocal", offering a way to explain how organizations interact with each other, that is, through the "actors who are authorized and delegated to act and speak on their behalf" (Cooren, 2010, p. 2).

The authoring of the text of the network points to intention as residing not in the individual or the one acting but in the institution or the organization for whom the agent is acting for. According to Robichaud (2006), "intentions are not a property of human mental activities, but a property of institutionalized nets of practices emerging out of conversations in which we constantly redefine our connections to others, to machines, to nature and to texts". He further explained that "the intentional structure is what allows the sharing of action with nonhumans, especially with text and technologies, not what essentially distinguishes us from them" (p. 113).

Matters of Concern as an Analytical Proposal for the Study of Digital Media as Agent Making a Difference

How can the digital media be studied as a non-human agent making a difference in organizational settings, or how can it be empirically shown that the organizing power of the digital media is in the irreducible materiality of communication? Martine et al. (2016) proposed that analyzing conversations is "a key way by which we can explore how the world, in all its embodiments, materialization, and incarnations, comes to express itself in what people say and do" (p. 185). They also argued that "by taking into account all the matters of concern that express themselves in conversations (and not only the people who voice them)", it would be possible to "show how some concerns came to matter more than others by speaking to, for, with, through, or against each other" (p. 185). Matters of concern refer to what is animated in communication by the participants, whether human or non-human.

By focusing on matters of concern, it is possible to analyze "how things can speak through yet other things that translate their 'objective' language into a verbal language that we, human, can make sense of and that suggests a particular course of action for us to take" (Bencherki, 2018, p. 9). Three perspectives were identified by Bencherki (2018) on how things may speak: "the first consists in describing things that are already textual or discursive in nature; the second consists in considering communication as the circulation of action, beyond linguistic action; and the third consists in observing precise ways through which things enter the linguistic realm" (p. 11). This provides a means to study digital media as a *spokesthing* (Bencherki, 2018, p. 9), that is, it can speak and contribute in the materialization of organizational relations.

Further, focusing on matters of concern allows non-human participants in the conversation to be accounted for as agents making a difference, that is, "they have their own weight of mattering (they do what people make them do but they may also resist them)" (Martine et al., 2016, pp. 184–185). Matters of concern, as an analytical procedure, consist of answering a set of questions that Cooren et al. (2015, p. 379) proposed: (1) what to identify in conversations? (the matters of concern that refer to what seems to recurrently, routinely and persistently animate the participants); (2) how to identify matters of concern/interest? (the matters that appear to matter to define what should be done); (3) how to name a matter of concern/interest? (all the elements that are supposed to count, matter or make a difference in a given situation); and (4) what do these matters of concern do? (they bring with them their own weight or value to define or dictate what should or should not be done). These various beings, whether "human or other than human", are the channels and media that serve as "the *in-between* through which other beings act or communicate" (Cooren, 2010, p. 8). These media become agents that have the capacity to make a difference *when* the organization speaks through them or *when* they become "spokespersons" (Cooren, 2015) or "spokesthings" (Bencherki, 2018, p. 9).

This analytical proposal is applied in studying how the unseen organization, an open university, materializes in communication. Open universities are "higher learning institutions that are primarily concerned with education at a distance, namely, education in which the systematic teaching and the communication between student and teacher or institution take place mainly by a variety of media" (Asian Association of Open Universities, www.aaou.org). In open universities students do not see the teacher and the teacher does not see the students, at least not on the same regular basis as is the case at campus-based universities, if at all.

The study analyzed accounts collected from three open universities in Asia – where most of the open universities are located. Access to the archived recording of class interactions in the two universities was made through the author's participation in faculty exchange programs. Two episodes/exchanges/interactions taken from archived recordings of discussion threads in an online forum were analyzed for matters of concern that animated the participants to the exchange and through which an open university materializes itself. In the transcript, TMA refers to tutor-marked assignment. In an open university setup, the tutor assists the teacher in clarifying lessons taught by the teacher. In the exchanges analyzed, the Tutorial Page and the Forum are part of a learning management system or LMS that refers to any software application for the administration and the automation of educational services.

Exchange 1: Tutor and Student B1 interacting

Tutorial 1

by Tutor - - (Date)

> *Dear All,*
>
> *If you have any question for me, please post it on this page. Tutors will not be replying questions in the public forum. Public forum is meant for discussions among students only.*

Re: Tutorial 1

by Student B1 - - (Date)

> *Hi Tutor,*
>
> *Can I have your email address please. Thanks.*

Re: Tutorial 1

by Tutor- - (Date)

> *Dear Student B1,*
>
> *My email is [ ]. If you have questions on TMA1, please post it in the Tutorial 1 forum so that my reply can be shared with your class friends, but I encourage you to email or post it here so that we can discuss any issues together.*

Contact Information

by Tutor - - (Date)

> *Dear All,*
>
> *I can be contacted at [ ] Best time is Mon-Fri 10pm-12midnight. But, please post questions on TMA1 on Tutorial 1 page. We are living in the age of knowledge economy. Knowledge is meant to be shared and leveraged.*

Exchange 2: Course Coordinator (Teacher) and Student B2 interacting

TMA3 results

by Course Coordinator (CC) - - (Date)

> *Dear All,*
>
> *I shall be uploading the answer guide to TMA2 and 3 either later today or tomorrow. I shall also be uploading some additional exercises for you to try. Perhaps also hints on what to expect in the coming exam.*

Re: TMA3 results

by Student B2 - - (Date)

> *Thanks. Looking forward for the model answers and the additional exercises, hope to receive it soonest as possible, so that we have more time for our revision, as we are all working adults, time is always the factor that limits ourselves.*

Re: TMA3 results

by Student B2 - - (Date)

Dear CC,

I have yet seen any answer guide for TMA 2 & 3 and also additional exercise uploading in forum.

Could you please assist to upload it in soonest possible for our revision purpose. There are only 12 days left towards our exam. Please consider time is very precious for open distance learner and working adult like us. Many thanks.

In the first exchange, the posting of the students' questions at the Tutorial Page (a digital platform that allowed asynchronous interaction between the tutor and the students) was identified as a matter of concern. In the initial post (addressed to the class), the tutor reminded the students that the Tutorial Page is the proper venue for the tutorial session. In the second post (addressed to Student B1), the tutor repeated that the Tutorial Page is the venue for collaborative teaching and learning. In the last post (addressed to the class), the tutor reiterated with a plea that the students post their questions at the Tutorial Page, sharing being a norm in such an educational system.

In the second exchange, the posting of the teacher's answer guide in the Forum (another digital platform that allowed asynchronous interaction between the teacher and the students) was identified as a matter of concern. In a follow-up reply to the teacher's post, the student (Student B2) reminded the teacher that the answer guide and exercises had yet to be seen at the Forum and repeated as a plea to make them available there.

The two digital platforms "enter the linguistic realm" (Bencherki, 2018, p. 11) through the tutor and the students becoming the medium through which the open university speaks on what constitutes the official venue for class discussion and by speaking what is the status of the e-classrooms at particular hours – empty when it should be filled with students (referring to absence of questions in the Tutorial Page), or full but the teacher is late in coming (referring to presence of students at the Forum, and B2 in particular inspecting the forum and seeing that no answers had been posted yet by the CC). It thus tells the mutual obligations that come with teaching-learning. Through what the digital platforms say and do, they become the medium or channel for the teacher-student relation to materialize and in so doing the university and the organization of distance education emerged.

Educating online could be seen as a chain of action where many different actors and mediators are mobilized. The digital media is an agent that makes a difference because it (1) shares in the action of teaching and learning by telling the obligations of the parties involved in education and (2) speaks the authoritative text authored by the network of what distance education is, its philosophy and practices by becoming an "immutable mobile" (Cooren et al., 2007, p. 153) stabilizing the association of actions and actors in educating online, making education possible and (3) materializes the relations that made up the university – student-teacher relations, educational philosophy and learning community – and offered substance to an otherwise unseen university. Distance education works because it is organized, an effect of "an array of mediations" (Cooren & Taylor, 1997, pp. 244–245).

According to Cooren, Taylor and Van Every (2006), "[a]gency is not a capacity to act to be defined a priori. On the contrary, it is the capacity to act that is discovered when studying how [organizational] worlds become constructed in a certain way" (p. 11). Martine and Cooren

(2016) argue that "what or who is communicating to whom or what through what or whom is always a matter of selection in a chain of agency (Cooren, 2006), a selection that the analysts can certainly decide to do, but that participants also do in the way they account for what is happening" (p. 152). This is illustrated in the study above.

Summary and Suggested Direction for the Study of Digital Media as an Agent Making a Difference

This chapter presented a vista of digital media when studied as a tool and as an agent making a difference. It brought into focus the materialization perspective of the CCO as a framework that can provide unique insights for understanding the organizing power of digital media: not in its inherent property as a technology that provides organizations with affordances or in its interoperability as apparatus that is inextricably linked or inseparable with organizational practices that constitute assemblages, but in the irreducible materiality of communication – as a media through which "an organization will manage to act and communicate" (Cooren, 2020, p. 8). Digital media is an agent that makes a difference not because it has instrumental capacity or intrinsic property, nor is inextricably linked with discursive practices, but because of its "relational state" as a "channel, in between or medium" (p. 11) in the communicative constitution of organization. It is in the mattering of the digital media by what the spokespersons say and do and in the mediation of the digital media by what the spokesthings say and do that its agency can be studied, as the illustrative case has shown.

The grounding of agency on relational ontology places human and non-human agents on equal status: both have the same ontological status as speaking on behalf of the organization (1) that materialize organizational relations and (2) that make a difference in organizing, thereby answering the criticism of the communication-centered perspective not addressing the ontological differences between human and non-human agents (Jansen, 2016, as cited by Neff and Nagy, 2018). Through this perspective the organizing power of digital media as a non-human agent making a difference can be understood not in its hazy entanglement with organization but in its clear engagement in materializing organizational relations and in mediating organizational actions.

A suggested direction for research in the study of digital media as an agent making a difference on the account of its relational state as a channel or a medium that materializes the organization is in the area of affect. Ashcraft (2020) defined affect as "the fluctuating intensities of encounter, as bodies of all kinds (not only human) come into contact" (p. 3). She argued that "affect confronts a premise at the heart of our discipline today: the claim that communication is constitutive as opposed to mere transmission. By engaging with affect, we can recuperate potential eclipsed by this contrast and cultivate communication theory that: (a) informs transmission as a constitutive activity, (b) expands what counts as communication beyond human language and social interaction, and (c) recovers disappeared ways that power operates communicatively" (p. 1). A particular question in adapting affect to the study of digital media could be: how is affect transmitted through collective bodies? If the e-classroom were not there any more, for instance because of a technical issue, how would the student community's displeasures and disappointments be moved or channeled to the academic community through the agency of digital media? What could be the focus of analysis, if it is beyond human language and social interaction? When there are no spokespersons or spokesthings, can we turn to what the spokespirits say and do?

References

Albu, O. B., & Etter, M. (2016). Hypertextuality and social media: A study of the constitutive and paradoxical implications of organizational Twitter use. *Management Communication Quarterly, 30*(1), 5–31. https://doi.org/10.1177/0893318915601161.

Arnaud, N., & Fauré, B. (2016). A communicative approach to sociomateriality: The agentic role of technology at the operational level. *Communication Research and Practice, 2*(3), 290–310. https://doi.org/10.1080/22041451.2016.1219615.

Ashcraft, K. L. (2020). Communication as constitutive transmission? An encounter with affect. *Communication Theory.* https://doi.org/10.1093/ct/qtz027.

Bencherki, N. (2012). Mediators and the material stabilization of society. *Communication and Critical/Cultural Studies, 9*(1), 101–106. https://doi.org/10.1080/14791420.2011.629419.

Bencherki, N. (2018). How things make things do things with words, or how to pay attention to what things have to say. In C. Mils & F. Cooren (Eds.), *Discursivity, relationality and materiality in the life of the organization: Communication perspectives* (pp. 6–23). Routledge.

Bencherki, N., & Cooren, F. (2011). Having to be: The possessive constitution of organization. *Human Relations, 64*(12), 1579–1607. https://doi.org/10.1177/0018726711424227.

Bencherki, N., & Elmholdt, K. T. (2020). The organization's synaptic mode of existence: How a hospital merger is many things at once. *Organization.* https://doi.org/10.1177/1350508420962025.

Benoit-Barné, C., Marsen, S., Wang, N., & Yang, Y. (2019). Decentering the analysis: The authority of spectators, journalists and others. In N. Bencherki, F. Matte, & F. Cooren (Eds.), *Authority and power in social interaction: Methods and analysis* (pp. 117–137). Routledge. doi: 0.4324/9781351051668-7.

Beverungen, A., Beyes, T., & Conrad, L. (2019). The organizational powers of (digital) media. *Organization, 26*(5), 621–635. https://doi.org/10.1177/1350508419867206.

Chatterjee, S., Sarker, S., & Siponen, M. (2016). How do mobile ICTs enable organizational fluidity: Toward a theoretical framework. *Information & Management, 54*(1), 1–13. https://doi.org/10.1016/j.im.2016.03.007.

Cooren, F. (2000). *The organizing property of communication.* John Benjamins. https://doi.org/10.1075/pbns.65.

Cooren, F. (2004). Textual agency: How texts do things in organizational settings. *Organization, 11*(3), 373–393. https://doi.org/10.1177/1350508404041998.

Cooren, F. (2006). The organizational world as a plenum of agencies. In F. Cooren, J. R. Taylor, & E. J. Van Every (Eds.), *Communication as organizing empirical and theoretical explorations in the dynamic of text and conversation* (pp. 81–100). Lawrence Erlbaum Associates.

Cooren, F. (2009). The haunting question of textual agency: Derrida and Garfinkel on iterability and eventfulness. *Research on Language and Social Interaction, 42,* 42–67

Cooren, F. (2010). *Action and agency in dialogue: Passion, incarnation, and ventriloquism.* John Benjamins. https://doi.org/10.1075/ds.6.

Cooren, F. (2015). In medias res: Communication, existence, and materiality. *Communication Research and Practice, 1*(4), 1–15. https://doi.org/10.1080/22041451.2015.1110075.

Cooren, F. (2018). Materializing communication: Making the case for a relational ontology. *Journal of Communication, 68*(2), 278–288. https://doi.org/10.1093/joc/jqx014.

Cooren, F. (2020). Beyond entanglement: (Socio-) Materiality and organization studies. *Organization Theory, 1*(3), 1–24. https://doi.org/10.1177/2631787720954444.

Cooren, F., Bencherki, N., Chaput M., & Vásquez, C. (2015). The communicative constitution of strategy-making: Exploring fleeting moments of strategy. In D. Golsorkhi, L. Rouleau, D. Seidl, & E. Vaara (Eds.), *The Cambridge handbook of strategy as practice* (2nd edn., pp. 365–388). Cambridge University Press. doi:10.1017/CCO9781139681032.022.

Cooren, F., & Fairhurst, G. T. (2009). Dislocation and stabilization: How to scale up from interactions to organization. In L. L. Putnam & A. M. Nicotera (Eds.), *Building theories of organization: The constitutive role of communication* (pp. 117–152). Routledge.

Cooren, F., Matte, F., Taylor, J. R., & Vásquez, C. (2007). A humanitarian organization in action: Organizational discourse as an immutable mobile. *Discourse & Communication, 1*(2), 153–190. https://doi.org/10.1177/1750481307075996.

Cooren, F. & Taylor, J. R. (1997). Organization as an effect of mediation: Redefining the link between organization and communication. *Communication Theory, 7*(3), 219–260.

Cooren, F., Taylor, J. R., & Van Every, E. J. (Eds.). (2006). *Communication as organizing: Empirical and theoretical explorations in the dynamic of text and conversation.* Lawrence Erlbaum.

Cooren, F., Thompson, F., Canestraro, D., and Bodor, T. (2006). From agency to structure: Analysis of an episode in a facilitation process. *Human Relations, 59*(4), 533–565. https://doi.org/ 10.1177/ 0018726706065373.

Dawson, V. R. (2018). Fans, friends, advocates, ambassadors, and haters: Social media communities and the communicative constitution of organizational identity. *Social Media + Society, 4*(1), 1–11. https:// doi.org/10.1177/2056305117746356.

Dewey, J. (1916). *Democracy and education.* The Macmillan Company.

Faraj, S., & Azad, B. (2012). The materiality of technology: An affordance perspective. In P. M. Leonardi, B. A. Nardi, & J. Kallinikos (Eds.), *Materiality and organizing: Social interaction in a technological world* (pp. 237–258). Oxford University Press. doi:10.1093/acprof:oso/9780199664054.003.0012.

Haug, C., & Cooren, F. (2020). "The magic of the meeting necessitates having multiple voices heard". An interview with François Cooren about ventriloquism, interaction, and the Montreal School [Pre-production]. *Communiquer, 29*, 111–119. https://doi.org/10.4000/communiquer.5891.

Hultin, L. (2019). On becoming a sociomaterial researcher: Exploring epistemological practices grounded in a relational, performative ontology. *Information and Organization, 29*(2), 91–104. https://doi.org/ 10.1016/j.infoandorg.2019.04.004.

Jansen, T. (2016). Who is talking? Some remarks on nonhuman agency in communication. *Communication Theory, 26*(3), 255–272. https://doi.org/10.1111/comt.12095.

Khan, F., Si, X., & Khan, K. U. (2019). Social media affordances and information sharing: An evidence from Chinese public organizations. *Data and Information Management, 3*(3), 135–154. https://doi.org/ 10.2478/dim-2019-0012.

Kholisoh, N., & Sulastri, R. (2017). New media technology in developing effective organizational internal communication. *Humaniora, 8*(1), 21–29. https://doi.org/10.21512/humaniora.v8i1.3693.

Kim, H. (2018). The mutual constitution of social media use and status hierarchies in global organizing. *Management Communication Quarterly, 32*(4), 471–503. https://doi.org/10.1177/089331891 8779135.

Kuhn, T., Ashcraft, K. L., & Cooren, F. (2019). Introductory essay: What work can organizational communication do? *Management Communication Quarterly, 33*(1), 101–111. https://doi.org/10.1177/08933 18918809421.

Leidner, D. E., Gonzales, E., & Koch, H. (2018). An affordance perspective of enterprise social media and organizational socialization. *The Journal of Strategic Information Systems, 27*(2), 117–138. https://doi. org/10.1016/j.jsis.2018.03.003.

Light, B., Bagnall, G., Crawford, G., & Gosling, V. (2018). The material role of digital media in connecting with, within and beyond museums. *Convergence, 24*(4), 407–423. https://doi.org/10.1177/135485651 6678587.

Martine, T., & Cooren, F. (2016). A relational approach to materiality and organizing: The case of a creative idea. In L. Introna, D. Kavanagh, S. Kelly, W. Orlikowski, & S. Scott (Eds.), *Beyond interpretivism? New encounters with technology and organization. IS&O 2016. IFIP advances in information and communication technology, Vol. 489.* Springer. https://doi.org/10.1007/978-3-319-49733-4_9.

Martine, T., Cooren, F., Bénel, A., & Zacklad, M. (2016). What does really matter in technology adoption and use? A CCO approach. *Management Communication Quarterly, 30*(2), 164–187. https://doi.org/ 10.1177/0893318915619012.

Muhonen, T., Jönsson, S., & Bäckström, M. (2017). Consequences of cyberbullying behavior in working life: The mediating roles of social support and social organisational climate. *International Journal of Workplace Health Management, 10*(5), 376–390. https://doi.org/10.1108/IJWHM-10-2016-0075.

Neff, G., & Nagy, P. (2018). Agency in the digital age: Using symbiotic agency to explain human-technology interaction. In Z. Papacharissi (Ed.), *A networked self and human augmentics, artificial intelligence, sentience.* Routledge.

Onobhayedo, P. A. (2017). Implementing web technologies as organizational communication media: A study of employee adoption likelihood. *Journal of Business Theory and Practice, 5*(2). https://doi.org/ 10.22158/jbtp.v5n2p120.

Orlikowski, W. J. (2007). Sociomaterial practices: Exploring technology at work. *Organization Studies, 28*(9), 1435–1448. https://doi.org/10.1177/0170840607081138.

Pentzold, C., & Bischof, A. (2019). Making affordances real: Socio-material prefiguration, performed agency, and coordinated activities in human–robot communication. *Social Media + Society, 5*(3), 1–11. https://doi.org/10.1177/2056305119865472.

Peters, B. (2016). Digital. In B. Peters (Ed.), *Digital keywords: A vocabulary of information society and culture* (pp. 93–108). Princeton University Press.

Plesner, U., Justesen, L., & Glerup, C. (2018). The transformation of work in digitized public sector organizations. *Journal of Organizational Change Management, 31*(5), 1176–1190. https://doi.org/10.1108/JOCM-06-2017-0257.

Pritchard, K., & Symon, G. (2014). Picture perfect? Exploring the use of smartphone photography in a distributed work practice. *Management Learning, 45*(5), 561–576. https://doi.org/10.1177/135050761 3486424.

Rice, R. E., & Leonardi, P. M. (2013). Information and communication technologies in organizations. In L. Putnam & D. K. Mumby (Eds.), *The SAGE handbook of organizational communication* (3rd edn., pp. 425–448). Sage.

Robichaud, D. (2006). Steps toward a relational view of agency. In F. Cooren, J. R. Taylor, & E. J. Van Every (Eds.), *Communication as organizing: Empirical and theoretical explorations in the dynamic of text and conversation* (pp. 101–114). Lawrence Erlbaum.

Schlagwein, D., & Hu, M. (2017). How and why organisations use social media: Five use types and their relation to absorptive capacity. *Journal of Information Technology, 32*, 194–209. https://doi.org/10.1057/jit.2016.7.

Symon, G., & Whiting, R. (2019). The sociomaterial negotiation of social entrepreneurs' meaningful work. *Journal of Management Studies, 56*(3), 655–684. https://doi.org/10.1111/joms.12421.

Taylor, J. R., Cooren, F., Giroux, N. & Robichaud, D. (1996). The communicational basis of organization: Between the conversation and the text. *Communication Theory, 6*(1), 1–39.

Taylor, J. R., & Van Every, E. J. (2000). *The emergent organization: Communication as its site and surface.* Lawrence Erlbaum Associates.

Taylor, J. R., & Van Every, E. J. (2014). *When organization fails: Why authority matters.* Routledge.

Treem, J. W., Dailey, S. L., Pierce, C. S., & Leonardi, P. M. (2015). Bringing technological frames to work: How previous experience with social media shapes the technology's meaning in an organization. *Journal of Communication, 65*(2), 396–422. https://doi.org/10.1111/jcom.12149.

Vaast, E., & Kaganer, E. (2013). Social media affordances and governance in the workplace: An examination of organizational policies. *Journal of Computer-Mediated Communication, 19*(1), 78–101. https://doi.org/10.1111/jcc4.12032.

27

THE COMMUNICATIVE CONSTITUTION OF ORGANIZATIONAL MEMORY

Salla-Maaria Laaksonen and François Lambotte

Memory and memorizing as organizational phenomena have been extensively addressed within the field of organization studies (Foroughi et al., 2020). Although Organization Memory Studies (OMS) highlight the role of communication and discourse in organizational remembering, it is often described mainly through human agency, without explicitly taking a communication-centered view. When confronted with current works in organization studies, especially scholarship on the communicative constitution of organization (CCO), we believe there is room for knowledge-building as regards the constitutive role of *memory as communication* or *the communicative constitution of memory*. In particular, the communication perspective of CCO would allow for an empirical investigation of the social processes considered essential to organizational memory (Rowlinson et al., 2014; Suddaby et al., 2014). From an epistemological point of view, CCO concepts can help to overcome such dualisms as individual versus material or collective versus collected memories, which are frequently highlighted as a limitation of current OMS (Rowlinson et al., 2010; Foroughi et al., 2020). In contrast, CCO studies have been criticized for their focus on single events without taking into account their historical, temporal, and social embeddedness (Bisel, 2010). Hence, CCO scholars could benefit from OMS, where historical reasoning allows researchers to look back on past events and processes within an organization (Wadhwani & Bucheli, 2014).

In this chapter, we will first synthesize the key contributions and problematics, as well as the research agenda, of works known as Organization Memory Studies (OMS). In doing so, we will explore the limits and challenges that this field faces when addressing memory and remembering practices as key organizational phenomena, and, most importantly, we will question the missing role of communication in the theoretical and empirical dimensions of such studies. Then, we discuss how CCO concepts can enrich OMS along three axes: (1) how remembering and forgetting constitute an organization, (2) how communication constitutes memory in practice, and (3) how traces of past communicative events accumulated across communication platforms contribute to the organizationality of collectives.

A Mechanistic Approach to Organizational Memory

From the 1960s to the late 1980s, there was a tendency to favor a reified and fixed approach to individual and organizational memory. It was a shared belief among scholars that memory is

DOI: 10.4324/9781003224914-31

essentially a practice of acquiring, retaining, and exploiting knowledge and experience based on repertoires of retention that influence individual behavior (Walsh & Ungson, 1991). Following this logic, many studies equated memory with such repertoires, which they considered a feature available not only for humans but also for other things as well. In their seminal, much-cited article, Walsh and Ungson (1991) conceptualize organizations as interpretative information-processing systems, where the central processes consist of information acquisition, retention, and retrieval, and they define organizational memory as "stored information from an organization's history that can be brought to bear on present decisions" (p. 61). This highly influential conceptualization likens organizational memory to that of individuals, who sense their environment, select information for processing (Weick, 1995), and then share these meanings through a common language (Burrell & Morgan, 1979).

According to the mechanistic approach, information is stored by the members of an organization (e.g., Argyris & Schön, 1978) as well as by and through organizational processes, protocols, and documents. Walsh and Ungson (1991) highlight the role of individuals in information acquisition, but they also note that an organizational interpretation system must exist that transcends the level of individuals. Interpretations can be stored also in artifacts and objects, which render them more durable and transferable. Thus, organizational memory is not centrally stored, but rather is dispersed throughout a variety of retention facilities (Walsh & Ungson, 1991). The authors propose a model of five retention facilities, or "bins", for organizational memory: individuals, culture and stories, transformation processes, organizational structures, and organizational ecology (for a summary, see Bannon & Kuutti, 1996). Finally, such external archives as financial archives, media content, or ex-employees might also possess information about an organization's past.

According to Walsh and Ungson's (1991) model, organizational memory has three key roles in organizations. First, it has an informational role since it provides the content needed for decision-making. In turn, all organizational decisions become stored in the organizational memory where they form the basis for subsequent decisions (see also Luhmann, 2018; Blaschke & Schoeneborn, 2016). Second, organizational memory has a control function. Storing the rationales behind decisions already made can reduce the transaction costs associated with new decisions and their implementation. Third, organizational memory has a political role because controlling information is power; it creates dependencies between those who possess knowledge and those who do not. To effectively achieve the key functions of organizational memory, the quality of the information being stored is considered important: "communicable, consensual, integrated knowledge" will help to integrate and coordinate organizational activities (Duncan & Weiss, 1979). Computer science literature has also reinforced this mechanistic view of memory by considering information systems as a solution to the incompleteness and approximate nature of human memory. Studies in the field promise that the use of indexing tools and artificial intelligence will facilitate the retrieval of information and afford an organizational memory whose properties would be superior to those of humans (Huber, 1990). Bannon and Kuutti (1996) deemed such a vision unrealistic given that it reduces human memory to a passive storage device; they advocate instead a processual view of memory as a constructive act where humans play an active role in constructing organizational memory.

Mechanistic approaches have been criticized for their passive and static view of organizational memory. While Walsh and Ungson's bin metaphor "concentrate[s] on formulating a typology of the storage bins in which organizational memory is stored", it "neglects the specific human characteristics of memory" (Rowlinson et al., 2010, p. 76). Studies adopting a mechanistic approach thus do not consider the individual and subjective experience of remembering, nor do they consider the social and historical embeddedness of organizational memory (Feldman

& Feldman, 2006; Schultz & Hernes, 2013). They also disregard how humans make associations and the role of emotions in memory (Feldman & Feldman, 2006). Feldman and Feldman (2006) further note that the mechanistic view fails to open the black boxes of the big concepts it introduces, from individuals to ecology and culture. They are not unpacked, and neither are their relations studied.

Remembering and Forgetting: A Processual Approach to Organizational Memory

The abovementioned critiques have invited organization scholars to explore organizational memory as a social process. Several authors suggest that the classical, reified approach should be abandoned in favor of a processual approach centered on the socially constructed nature of *remembering* as defined by Barlett (1932, as cited in Bannon & Kuutti, 1996, p.161):

> *The action of remembering is not the stimulation of innumerable, fixed and fragmentary traces. It is an imaginary reconstruction or construction based on the relationship of our attitudes to an active mass of actions and experiences of the past, but also to that small detail that appears in the form of an image or an element of language.*

The emphasis, thus, is not on the repertoires of the past, but on how to remember in the proper context. Following this proposition, recent research on organizational memory highlights its enacted and reconstructive nature: instead of being passively stored and processed, the organizational past is continuously recreated and socially constructed by organizational members and stakeholders when they engage in the social practice of remembering (Feldman & Feldman, 2006; Rowlinson et al., 2010). Put another way, it is not a question of ignoring the forms that organizational memory takes but of thinking about them within a process of remembrance: "Telling, doing and writing in a work situation are activities that are part of the work activity itself and that allow for the present activation of knowledge and know-how on the basis of 'traces' which, in turn, come from the past" (Havelange et al., 2002, as cited in Grosjean & Bonneville, 2009, p. 6). These approaches are sometimes titled social memory studies (Olick & Robbins, 1998). In contrast to the mechanistic approach, which focuses on the storage and retrieval of (historical) information, social memory studies emphasize the processual and social nature of memory (e.g., Rowlinson et al., 2010; Casey & Olivera, 2011).

While the main line of difference in OMS could be drawn between mechanistic-functional and social-constructivist processual approaches, Foroughi and colleagues (2020) have further divided the social constructivist approaches into interpretative, critical, and performative perspectives. We will explore these next.

Interpretative and Critical Approaches to Organizational Memory

For Foroughi and colleagues (2020, p. 13), interpretative studies of organizational memory aim to understand how "participants attach meaning to different aspects of the past through remembering and forgetting". Consisting of interpretations of mnemonic traces, organizational voices and narratives, organizational memory is made to exist through a hermeneutic process of interpretation.

Several classical OMS studies have followed this approach in studying the way organizations learn from past experience to improve their production processes (Foroughi et al., 2020). In their seminal work, Brown and Duguid (1991) highlight informal storytelling during meal breaks as a key means of enhancing memory that enables knowledge sharing and building. First, narratives help to elucidate experiences that are difficult to express. Second, stories "act as repositories of accumulated wisdom" (Brown & Duguid, 1991, p. 45), enabling its circulation within the organization and offering possibilities for reinterpretation in a new situation (Brown & Duguid, 2000). Third, stories make it possible to construct a shared interpretation "that binds people together" (Brown & Duguid, 2000, p.107). Juliette Malher's (2009) processual study of organizational learning at NASA during the Columbia and Challenger accidents points to the loss of organizational memory as a result of high personnel turnover at NASA, which created a vacuum in the operationalization of information-gathering procedures. Malher's (2009) findings also highlight the importance of individuals (as storage) for organizational memory and the fragmentation and dispersion of information across an organization and its stakeholders. Moreover, obsolete information systems and rigid access rights made information retrieval and follow-up at NASA extremely difficult. For Rowlinson and colleagues (2010), despite their focus on social processes, the above studies still have a functionalist undertone with a focus on how organizational memory practices enhance the efficiency of organizational learning and knowledge building.

Other works adopt a critical perspective on remembering. Ybema (2014) discusses the power struggles inherent in organizational change and the ways in which actors use versions of the past to win the consent of others or to oppose competing viewpoints. Suddaby and colleagues (2016) highlight memory work as a central phenomenon in organizational identity construction, offering a strategic and creative narrative reconstruction of a given community and its history. The same authors also introduce the concept of "rhetorical history" to emphasize the essentially linguistic nature of identity work as well as the highly competitive resource that the organizational past represents for actors engaged in identity work. Foroughi (2020), drawing on Deetz's polyphonic view of organizations (1992), highlights the multiplicity of mnemonic communities and collective memories. In doing so, focusing on stories retold outside the management team can help develop a more complex view on the constitution of organizational memories. In turn, Casey and Oliveira (2011) call attention to the role of forgetting in organizational memory and call for a better theorization of this phenomenon considering the dynamic, temporal, and sometimes contested nature of memory in organizations.

Many of these accounts highlight the role of communication, discourses, and narratives in organizational memory and remembering. Several authors suggest that organizations remember through storytelling and narratives (e.g., Rowlinson et al., 2014; Suddaby et al., 2016). Suddaby, Foster, and Mills (2014) distinguish between remembering the past as the events of the past and history as the collective narrative and interpretation of those events. These conceptualizations conform to the linguistic turn in organization studies (Deetz, 2003). Yet, they do not escape one of the criticisms by Deetz (2003) that such studies tend to defend subjectivism and ignore the invitation offered by the linguistic turn to overcome the subject/object dualism through the adoption of a relational ontology where "experiences and objects initially arise out of a relation of the constituting and that to be constituted" (Deetz, 2003, p. 423). Moreover, although some works rely on ethnographic data on the practices of remembering and forgetting (e.g., Yberna, 2014; Foroughi, 2020), their analytic strategy remains conservative, privileging an interpretative approach that tends to gloss over interactions that could bring an in-depth understanding of remembering as a series of communicative events.

Performative Approach to Organizational Memory

With the linguistic turn, followed by the socio-material turn, recent studies have adopted a broader understanding of *performativity* that sees memory as "the ongoing enactment of the past" (Foroughi et al., 2020, p. 20). A performative approach draws attention to the ways in which organizational history orients present organizational actions and, thus, works to constitute the present (Blagoev et al., 2018; Wadhwani & Bucheli, 2014). Studies following this line of thinking acknowledge that, whether memory exists as something material or only as interpretations and social practices, it is a resource that can be used to enable, constrain, and shape organizations and organizational activities (Foroughi et al., 2020; Blagoev et al., 2018).

Classical works adopting this approach emphasize the role of human agency in the ways in which the past is enacted or reenacted in practices and show the limits of retention bins if they are not recursively enacted in the intricacies of real-life organizational situations. For example, Whiteman and Cooper (2011) highlight the role of remembering and forgetting in sensemaking during crisis situations, showing how enacting previous personal experience, apprenticeship, or training during crisis situations either contributes to or impedes agents' sensemaking of ecological cues. More recent works highlighting the performativity of memory consider both discursive and material agency, and thus they are associated with socio-materiality studies that discuss the entangled role of the material and discursive in organizational life (Orlikowski, 2007). As a prime example, Blagoev and colleagues (2018) emphasize the active role of material objects in organizational remembering by demonstrating how the specific technologies involved in digitizing a museum catalog affected the activities of organizational actors in the process. In so doing, they conclude that it is not tenable to separate material forms of memory, as put forth by authors adopting both a functionalist and an interpretative view of memory (Walsh & Ungdon, 1991; Schultz & Hermes, 2013), precisely because material and social forms of memory are mutually constitutive.

The performative approach also accentuates strategic uses-of-the-past (Foroughi et al., 2020): organizations can choose to narrate, remember, and forget events and stories from their past in ways that are beneficial for them (Wadhwani et al., 2018; Suddaby et al., 2016). Researchers have shown how, for example, certain historical events and stories (Oertel & Thommes, 2018; Hatch & Schultz, 2017), organizational rituals (Dacin et al., 2010), or figures and narratives of the founders (Basque & Langley, 2018; Maclean et al., 2014) are used to construct organizational identities and maintain institutions. This makes organizational memory a critical and strategic resource for organizational management. In their introduction to a special issue of *Organization Studies*, Wadhwani and colleagues (2018) emphasize the performative role of history in making and unmaking organizational orders. Thus, by exploring the connections between memory and power, this approach adds to the critical approach of OMS.

Finally, these works accentuate the varying forms of social remembering and differentiate between textual, material, and oral memory forms as the means by which organizational actors evoke the past (Schultz & Hernes, 2013). Oral memory forms consist of narratives and storytelling, conversations, and interaction in organizational settings. Textual forms refer to corporate communication and an organization's rules, records, and other official texts. Material memory forms thus again refer to the practices of evoking the past through material objects/arrangements (see also Blagoev et al., 2018). This line of study has paved the way for CCO scholars to address current research challenges in OMS. We suggest that from an epistemological standpoint, CCO concepts can help overcome the dualisms frequently criticized by OMS scholars, such as individual versus material or collective versus collected memories (Rowlinson et al., 2010; Foroughi et al., 2020). In the remainder of this chapter, we discuss how CCO, understood as a research perspective, can advance research on organizational memory.

A CCO Research Agenda to Address Organizational Memory, Remembering, and Forgetting

The mainstay of CCO is a communication-centered approach to the ontology of organizations (Ashcraft et al., 2009; Cooren et al., 2011; Putnam et al., 2009). Organizations are seen as negotiated orders that are continually modified through communicative practices, formed and existing in and through language use and its various manifestations from documents to conversations (Taylor & Van Every, 2000; Cooren et al., 2011). By emphasizing the role of communication in organizing, the CCO approach challenges classical theoretical approaches to organizations that view communication as a means of transmitting information within the container of the organization, or from organizations to their environment.

Literature that would directly link the CCO approach with organizational memory studies is quite limited (cf. Blagoev et al., 2019; Basque & Langley, 2018; Blaschke & Schoeneborn, 2016). As an early notable exception, Olick's (1999) call for a constitutive approach to organizational memory resonates particularly well with CCO's assumptions: "It is not just that we remember as members of groups, but that we constitute those groups and their members simultaneously in the act (thus re-member-ing)" (p. 342). Further, Olick defines remembering as a collective process that takes place through language and dialogue (see also Rowlinson et al., 2010). We argue that there are several potential avenues where these two research approaches overlap and could benefit one another. Particularly, the processual, interpretative, and performative orientations of OMS share similar assumptions with the CCO approach: they both highlight the communicative nature of processes that construct organizational memory—or the organization itself.

As mentioned, some OMS work highlights the role of communication and discourse in organizational remembering, but they often describe it in terms of human agency, without explicitly taking a communication-centered view. These studies consider that individuals re-produce their memories through conversations, stories, and texts and that organizational memory is inscribed in texts, traditions, and procedures. Hence, different modalities of communication make memory accessible to an organization's members, thus susceptible to be negotiated (e.g., Wash & Ungson, 1991; Feldman & Feldman, 2006). We suggest that focusing on the constitutive role of communication, as is typical in CCO research, helps to unravel the social processes deemed essential to the processual and interpretative orientations in OMS (e.g., Rowlinson et al., 2014; Suddaby et al., 2014; Schultz & Hernes, 2013). Interestingly, both fields already make use of similar types of empirical data: conversation logs and transcripts, memos, and documents.

To develop the potential contributions of CCO for a study of organizational memory, we draw on the three main dimensions of CCO scholarship proposed by Shoeneborn, Kuhn, and Kärreman (2019, p.3). The authors distinguish between "works that focused on the communicative constitution of organizations (i.e., the 'noun' or 'entity' dimension), of organizing (the 'verb' or 'process' dimension), or of organizationality (the 'adjective' or 'attitude' dimension)". In the remainder of this chapter, we use these orientations to explore the relationship between constitutive communication and organizational memory.

How Does Memory Constitute an Organization?

Proposition 1: The dialectics between historical texts (stories and figures of the past) and conversations (social remembering) shape and constitute an organization.

For CCO scholarship, "process and entity are ultimately understood as two sides of the same coin and thus organizations are understood here as 'processual entities'" constituted through communication (Schoeneborn et al., 2019, p. 482). One prominent theoretical perspective has been the text-conversation dialectic developed within the Montréal School of CCO (Taylor & Van Every, 2000), where conversations are viewed as situational communicative actions, interacting through language. Texts, then, are the output and input of conversations, the substances behind conversations. Organizing is essentially a continuous loop of translation from text to conversation, and vice versa (Taylor et al., 1996). From the perspective of organization memory studies, this calls us to explore the interplay between textual and oral forms of organizational memory and the ways in which they constitute an organization. To some extent, such thinking also bridges the mechanistic-functionalist approach of organizational memory via the processual approach: Walsh and Ungson (1991) discussed the functioning of an organizational interpretation system where interpretations are stored not only in individuals but also in artifacts and objects, which make them more persistent. In this vein, texts are durable, more stable artifactual forms of organizational memory. Dislocated texts (Cooren & Fairhurst, 2008) become "springboards" for organizational conversations, thus perhaps evoking social processes of organizational remembering.

Further, CCO scholars have explored the constitutive power and relative permanence of texts. Taylor (2011) highlights that texts (and conversations dealing with those texts) overlap and imbricate, and thus gradually gain durability and the power to represent the organization. In the same sense, Kuhn (2008) introduces the idea of an "authoritative text" produced as a representation of the official organization (see also Cooren et al., 2011). Kuhn (2008, p. 1236) writes: "[a]s cooriented conversations and texts become imbricated and validated by interactants, an abstract text is produced that represents the firm as a whole" and encourages "actors to subordinate personal interests to the collective good". The resulting authoritative text is a conception of the organization, depicting and specifying its structure, activities and outcomes, and power relations. It functions as a reference point that represents, mediates, directs attention, disciplines, and links people and practices (Kuhn, 2008).

We suggest that organizational history, whether as a concrete written version (referred to as corporate history by Rowlinson et al., 2014) or more likely as a shared, figurative conception, can serve as an authoritative text for an organization. OMS highlights how organizational histories actively build identities and support sensemaking in organizations (e.g., Schultz & Hermes, 2013; Maclean et al., 2018; see also Basque & Langley, 2018), and thus they help generate an organizational actor that speaks with a single voice (Taylor, 2011). In connection to uses-of-the-past studies in performative OMS, organizational memory texts possess an authority that can be mobilized for strategic purposes. As Wadhwani and colleagues (2018, p. 1664) note, the organizational past is "understood as a source of social symbolic resources available for a wide variety of creative uses". For example, Maclean and colleagues (2018) explain how management can theatralize the history of an organization in order to manage organizational transition and ensure ideological consistency over time. At the border of CCO and OMS, Basque and Langley (2018) study how authoritative figures of founders are invoked to reinstate or reinforce a certain view of organizational identity across time. From an OMS perspective, invocation is a form of remembering practices, whereas it can be studied as "ventriloquism" (Cooren, 2012) from a CCO perspective and the historical founder "treated as the ventriloquist's 'dummy' made to speak by managers to make their own message more authoritative, legitimate, and palatable to audiences" (Basque & Langley, 2018, p. 1704).

How is Organizational Memory Constituted through Communication?

Proposition 2: Analysis of the communication processes involved in the constructing of organizational memory reveals the making of memory and the role and power of agents in the process of organizational remembering.

According to the CCO perspective, "the starting point is the process of communication itself, because communication is understood to display inherent ordering or organizing properties" (Schoeneborn et al., 2019 p. 485). Communicating is equivalent to organizing, and organizations do not exist as entities or containers of communication as such, but instead represent the ongoing accomplishments of organizing. Studies adopting this view might look at the practices within a single organization or at the processes spanning multiple organizations. The viewpoints presented by Schoeneborn and colleagues (2019) invite us to also conceptualize remembering as a process of communication manifested in conversations, emails, documents, and books. In our view, such an approach introduces fruitful theoretical and empirical tools for studying organizational memory. OMS has tried to solve the riddle of how individual memories become collective memories within organizations and explain how the process of remembering unfolds over time (Middleton & Edwards, 1990; Rowlinson et al., 2010; Feldman & Feldman, 2006). Yet, rarely does an explicit, named process of remembering exist within an organization. The work of Grosjean and Bonneville (2009) is a rare antecedent that bridges OMS and CCO by focusing on "the process of organizational remembering involving human and non-human actants" (Grosjean & Bonneville, 2009, p.13). Focusing on the local interactions taking place among ambulance dispatchers, they highlight the role of multiple actants (including a management sheet for the fleet of vehicles) in the remembering process. They show how actants *dislocate* the interaction and *connect* it to other sites as well as other times, which, as a result, then participate in the interaction.

Besides official organizational history projects such as museums, remembering is embedded in other organizational processes as well. Even processes with obviously historical underpinnings, such as annual reporting, are usually described in terms of accountability and stakeholder communication, rather than remembering. Writing an annual report is a prime example of a process that involves many types of communication: the report itself, but also conversations, email threads, and meetings that have usually preceded the concrete report text. As Schoeneborn and colleagues (2019, p. 487) point out, the perspective of organizing as communication also highlights "contradictions, tensions, and paradoxes in processes of organizing". Indeed, the process of writing an annual report is a process of remembering, one where competing histories and historical narratives are contested (Suddaby et al., 2016; Ybema, 2014). Some events and stories are chosen to be included, while others are left out. In this sense, Casey and Oliveira (2011) observe, we know little about the dynamic and temporal process of organizational forgetting and the related power struggles.

We suggest that investigating the constitutive, communicative processes connected to remembering is an important way to study these dynamics: what is not communicated decays; alternatively, traces of communication might reveal explicit decisions regarding what to discard (see Anteby & Molnàr, 2012). Among CCO theories, the perspective of forgetting is also present in the Luhmannian approach to CCO, where organizational systems are conceptualized as systems of decision communication (Schoeneborn, 2011; Grothe-Hammer, this volume). Each decision paradoxically communicates both the decision and its alternatives: it communicates that some alternatives existed, but because a particular decision was made, the alternatives were discarded (Schoeneborn, 2011). Thus, in chains of decision communication, organizations *selectively forget* some information (Luhmann, 2018; Blaschke & Schoeneborn, 2016). Blaschke and Schoeneborn (2016) argue that, for Luhmann, forgetting is the primary function of the process of memory; by selectively forgetting, the organizational system remains open for new irritations.

Another central aspect of CCO theorizing relevant from an organizing standpoint is the interplay between materiality and the social (Ashcraft et al., 2009; Cooren, et al. 2011; Wilhoit Larson & Mengis, this volume), that is, studying how bodies, places, technologies, and other objects become entangled with communication and how they invite themselves into people's conversations. From a CCO perspective, communication is the process that works at the intersection of the social and material worlds (Ashcraft et al., 2009). Likewise, some OMS studies discuss the role of materiality in remembering (see Blagoev et al. (2018) discussed earlier). Focusing on materiality opens avenues to explore how forms of communicative memory and memorizing within organizations are affected and reshaped by the adoption of new communication technologies. For example, we might ask: what do these technologies *afford for organizational memorizing and remembering* (Treem & Leonardi, 2013), and how are some practices of remembering delegated to them?

Internal digital platforms build collective memory by enabling both knowledge sharing and distribution, but also by allowing an organization's members to ask questions and submit queries to the archive (Ellison et al., 2015). What is profoundly different when such technologies are introduced is their ability to store conversations, and to give materiality and permanence to previously ephemeral forms of communication (Lambotte, 2019; Laaksonen, 2021; Bachimont, 1996). This leads to a public space where speech acts are automatically archived and can later be accessed—perhaps by new organizational members who were not present when the actual conversation took place (for a CCO interpretation of archival methods, see Basque, Hirsto & Wagnac, this volume). Affected by the technologies of their retention and retrieval, however, the material traces of stored conversations are inevitably decontextualized and scattered. Another avenue worth investigating is how machines learn from our communication and memorizing practices and act as a result (see also Saludadez, this volume). For example, Gmail's "Smart Compose" feature offers suggestions as you type an email, and knowledge management systems propose automatic tagging of content based on other similar entries. Hence, assessing remembering practices as communication processes between humans and technologies (considered as actants) can help researchers overcome the repository metaphor and highlight how non-human agents actively transform and remodel what matters and what is forgotten.

How Do Communicative Events of Remembering Build Organizationality?

Proposition 3: Memory and communicative practices of remembering are essential in generating organizationality for fluid collectives.

The third, more novel, stream of CCO scholarship investigates what makes different social phenomena organizational. The term *organizationality* refers to the degree to which certain social phenomenon can be said to display features associated with organizations (Schoeneborn et al., 2019). Researchers define three criteria for organizationality: the degree to which (a) the social collective displays interconnected instances of decision-making (b) it is attributed actorhood, and (c) it makes identity claims regarding what it is or what it does (Dobusch & Schoeneborn, 2015). Empirically, such studies have explored the organization-like nature of social formations not commonly regarded as formal organizations, such as online social movements (Dobusch & Schoeneborn, 2015) or bike commuters (Wilhoit & Kisselburgh, 2015).

Studies of organizational memory, in stark contrast, have mostly focused on stable and formal organizational entities, often with long histories, such as large corporations (e.g., Schultz & Hernes, 2013; Maclean et al., 2018) or institutions (Blagoev et al., 2018). But what role could memory and remembering play in fluid social collectives that perhaps do not fulfill the criteria of an organization? Existing studies connect organizational identity and the narrating of an organizational past (e.g., Suddaby et al., 2016; Basque & Langley, 2018; Oertel & Thommes, 2018), and they imply that rhetorical history and storytelling are vehicles to enact collective identities. From the CCO perspective, they could be conceptualized as processes of communication, text, and conversations that are co-oriented towards the emergence of an organizational entity (Taylor, 2011). Therefore, it could be argued that a process of organizing emerges whenever a collective engages in practices of remembering and storytelling about its history.

This proposition raises several questions to explore: do memory and remembering indeed make a loose collective more organizational? What is the role of felt or written history in adopting organizational characteristics? How is such information stored and retrieved, and how do members of the collective make sense of it as organizational? One promising area to pursue when answering these questions is research on digital organizing, such as online forms of collective action. Memory technologies such as the archives of online platforms work as retention facilities for these types of collectives. For instance, the Youth for Climate movement has organized across the globe in various physical locations, but as a global collective it becomes constituted through online communication: through sets of Instagram posts and tweets by its central figures—both global and local, from Greta Thunberg to local high-schoolers. We argue that the digital archive born as a global representation of the movement plays a central role in its identity building, as a form of temporal storytelling (see Rowlinson et al., 2014). Further, the movement builds heavily on future-oriented storytelling, further highlighting the historicity and temporality of the movement (Wadhwani & Bucheli, 2014). Another example would be the #metoo movement, which organized with no central leadership as a global movement to oppose sexual harassment. The movement essentially is about remembering past events, telling stories about them in personal ways, and generating a collective of women through digital platforms. Messages marked with the hashtag #metoo call for responsibility over past decisions and historical, forgotten, and silenced events.

Such loose collectives and the importance of communication to them has been explored in social movement studies (e.g., Bennett & Segerberg, 2013), which also acknowledge the constitutive role of communication. However, an explicit focus on movement memory and communicative organizationality remains unexplored. Therefore, we see this combination as a potential new research avenue for CCO-oriented memory studies.

Concluding Remarks

In this chapter, we offered suggestions on how CCO theories and concepts can enrich organizational memory studies by discussing (1) how remembering and forgetting constitute an organization, (2) how communication constitutes memory in practice, and (3) how traces of past communicative events contribute to the organizationality of collectives. Early studies on organizational memory sought to understand how organizations can *remember*, since they do not exist as thinking entities like individuals. We suggest that the answer is that they remember because they are collectives that are constituted through communication, while communication is also what allows for the memory to become social and organizational. More specifically, we propose that CCO theories can help overcome the dualisms present in various streams of OMS research: individual/organizational, discursive/material, and collective/collected memories.

Using a text-conversation framework can help researchers understand how the individual process of remembering is articulated through the constitution of social/organizational memory. The Luhmannian approach to communication systems can shed new light on the dynamics of remembering and forgetting in decision-making. The relational ontology can renew the debate on the materiality of memory bins in a context where just how conversations are stored needs to be questioned. Moreover, CCO concepts can contribute to understanding the central role played by remembering/forgetting artifacts in the organizationality of collectives. Finally, we noted that the ability of digital devices to continuously record organizational life is reshaping organizational memory practices as well as the modes of existence of memory itself. This also opens new opportunities for empirical investigations.

Further, we suggest that OMS could also benefit from the methodological approaches common to CCO studies, such as observing conversations. Although some OMS works rely on ethnographic data on remembering and forgetting practices (Yberna, 2014; Foroughi, 2020), their analytical strategies remain conservative, privileging thematic analysis over conversation analysis, which could offer an in-depth understanding of remembering during communicative events. Conversations as a modality of communication especially, but also as a modality for remembering and forgetting, have been overlooked in OMS.

Finally, there are also contributions to be made in the opposite direction. For example, the Montreal School of CCO has been criticized for its focus on single events without accounting for their historical, temporal, and social embeddedness (Bisel, 2010), as have organization studies more generally (Maclean et al., 2018). To overcome this limitation, organizational memory studies draw on holistic insights from studies on organizational history, where historical reasoning allows researchers to look back on the past events and processes within an organization, while acknowledging the temporality and social embeddedness of those events (Wadhwani & Bucheli, 2014). This approach, complemented by a focus on communication, would support the effort at shedding light on the processes by which the significance and meaning of those past events are constituted.

References

Argyris, C., & Schön, D. (1978). *Organizational learning: A theory of action perspective*. Addison-Wesley.

Anteby, M., & Molnár, V. (2012). Collective memory meets organizational identity: Remembering to forget in a firm's rhetorical history. *The Academy of Management Journal, 55*(3), 515–540.

Ashcraft, K. L., Kuhn, T., & Cooren, F. (2009). Constitutional amendments: "Materializing" organizational communication. *The Academy of Management Annals, 3*(1), 1–64. https://doi.org/10.1080/19416520903047186.

Bachimont, B. (1996). Intelligence artificielle et écriture dynamique: De la raison graphique à la raison computationnelle. *Au nom du sens* (pp. 290–319). Grasset.

Bannon, J., & Kuutti, K. (1996). Shifting perspectives on organizational memory: from storage to active remembering. *Proceedings of the Twenty-Ninth Hawaii International Conference on System Sciences* (pp. 156–167). ACM.

Bartlett, F. (1932). *Remembering: A study in experimental and social psychology*. Cambridge University Press.

Basque, J., & Langley, A. (2018). Invoking Alphonse: The founder figure as a historical resource for organizational identity work. *Organization Studies, 39*(12), 1685–1708. https://doi.org/10.1177/0170840618789211.

Bennett, L. W., & Segerberg, A. (2013). *The logic of connective action: Digital media and the personalization of contentious politics*. Cambridge University Press.

Bisel, R. (2010). A communicative ontology of organization? A description, history, and critique of CCO theories for organization science. *Forum Management Communication Quarterly, 24*(1), 124–131. https://doi.org/10.1177/0893318909351582.

Blagoev, B., Felten, S., & Kahn, R. (2018). The career of a catalogue: Organizational memory, materiality and the dual nature of the past at the British Museum (1970–Today). *Organization Studies, 39*(12), 1757–1783. http://doi.org/10.1177/0170840618789189.

Blagoev, B., Costas, J., & Kärreman, D. (2019). 'We are all herd animals': Community and organizationality in coworking spaces. *Organization, 26*(6), 894–916. https://doi.org/10.1177/1350508418821008.

Blaschke, S., & Schoeneborn, D. (2016). The forgotten function of forgetting: Revisiting exploration and exploitation in organizational learning. *Soziale Systeme, 12*(1), 100–120. https://doi.org/10.1515/sosys-2006-0107.

Burrell, G., & Morgan, G. (1979). *Sociological paradigms and organizational analysis*. Heinemann.

Brown, J., & Duguid, P. (1991). Organizational learning and communities of practice: Toward a unified view of working, learning, and innovation. *Organization Science, 2*, 40–57.

Brown, J., & Duguid, P. (2000). *Social life of information*. Harvard Business Review Press.

Casey, A., & Olivera, F. (2011). Reflections on organizational memory and forgetting. *Journal of Management Inquiry, 20*(3), 305–310. https://doi.org/10.1177/1056492611408264.

Cooren, F. (2012). Communication Theory at the center: Ventriloquism and the communicative constitution of reality. *Journal of Communication, 62*(1), 1–20. http://doi.org/10.1111/j.1460-2466.2011.01622.x.

Cooren, F., & Fairhurst, G. (2008). Dislocation and stabilization. In L. Putnam & A. M. Nicotera (Eds.), *Building theories of organization: The constitutive role of communication* (pp. 117–152). Routledge.

Cooren, F., Fairhurst, G., & Huet, R. (2012). Why matter always matters in (organizational) communication. In P. Leonardi, B. Nardi, & J. Kallinikos (Eds.), *Materiality and organizing: Social interaction in a technological world* (pp. 296–314). Oxford University Press.

Cooren, F., Kuhn, T., Cornelissen, J. P., & Clark, T. (2011). Communication, organizing and organization: An overview and introduction to the special issue. *Organization Studies, 32*(9), 1149–1170. https://doi.org/10.1177/0170840611410836.

Dacin, M., Munir, K., & Tracey, P. (2010). Formal dining at Cambridge colleges: Linking ritual performance and institutional maintenance. *Academy of Management Journal, 53*(6), 1393–1418. https://doi.org/10.5465/amj.2010.57318388.

Deetz, S. (1992). *Democracy in an age of corporate colonization: Developments in communication and the politics of everyday life*. SUNY Press.

Deetz, S. (2003). Reclaiming the legacy of the linguistic turn. *Organization, 10*, 421.

Dobusch, L., & Schoeneborn, D. (2015). Fluidity, identity, and organizationality: The communicative constitution of Anonymous. *Journal of Management Studies, 52*(8), 1005–1035.

Duncan, P. & Weiss, A. (1979). Organizational learning: Implications for organizational design. In B. M. Staw (Ed.), *Research in organisational behavior* (pp. 75–124). JAI Press.

Ellison, N. B., Gibbs, J. L., & Weber, M. S. (2015). The use of enterprise social network sites for knowledge sharing in distributed organizations: The role of organizational affordances. *American Behavioral Scientist, 59*(1), 103–123. https://doi.org/10.1177/0002764214540510.

Feldman, R., & Feldman, S. (2006). What links the chain: An essay on organizational remembering as practice. *Organization, 13*(6) 861–887. https://doi.org/10.1177/1350508406068500.

Foroughi, H. (2020). Collective memories as a vehicle of fantasy and identification: Founding stories retold. *Organization Studies, 41*(10), 1347–1367.

Foroughi, H., Coraiola, D., Rintamäki, J., Mena, S., & Foster, W. (2020). Organization memory studies. *Organization Studies*. Online first. https://doi.org/10.1177/0170840620974338.

Grosjean, S., & Bonneville, L. (2009). Saisir le processus de remémoration organisationnelle des actants humains et non humains au cœur du processus. *Revue d'anthropologie des connaissances, 3, 2*(2), 317–347. https://doi.org/10.3917/rac.007.0317.

Hatch, M., & Schultz, M. (2017). Toward a theory of using history authentically: Historicizing in the Carlsberg Group. *Administrative Science Quarterly, 62*. https://doi.org/10.1177/0001839217692535.

Huber, G. (1990). A theory of the effects of advanced information technologies on organization design, intelligence and decision making. *Academy of Management Review, 15*(1), 47–71.

Kuhn, T. (2008). A communicative theory of the firm: Developing an alternative perspective on intra-organizational power and stakeholder relationships. *Organization Studies, 29*(8–9), 1227–1254. https://doi.org/10.1177/0170840608094778.

Laaksonen, S.-M. (2021). Posting. In F. Cooren & P. Stücheli-Herlach (Eds.), *Handbook of management communication*. de Gruyter Mouton.

Lambotte F. (2019). A communication perspective on the fabric of thinking infrastructure: The case of social media analytics. In M. Kornberger, G. Bowker, J. Elyachar, A. Mennicken, P. Miller, J. Nucho, &

N. Pollock, (Eds.), *Thinking infrastructures* (Research in the Sociology of Organizations Vol. 62) (pp. 307–319). Emerald. https://doi.org/10.1108/S0733-558X20190000062019.

Luhmann, N. (2018). *Organization and decision.* Cambridge University Press.

Maclean, M., Harvey, C., Sillince, J. A. A., & Golant, B. D. (2014). Living up to the past? Ideological sensemaking in organizational transition. *Organization, 21*(4), 543–567. https://doi.org/10.1177/1350508414527247

Maclean, M., Harvey, C., Sillince, J., & Golant, B. (2018). Intertextuality, rhetorical history and the uses of the past in organizational transition. *Organization Studies, 39*(12), 1733–1755. https://doi.org/10.1177/0170840618789206.

Mahler, J. (2009). *Organizational learning at NASA: The Challenger and Columbia accidents.* Georgetown University Press.

Middleton, D., & Edwards, D. (1990). *Inquiries in social construction: Collective remembering.* Sage.

Olick, J. K. (1999). Collective memory: The two cultures. *Sociological Theory, 17*(3), 333–348. https://doi.org/10.1111/0735-2751.00083.

Olick, J. K., & Robbins, J. (1998). Social memory studies: From "collective memory" to the historical sociology of mnemonic practices. *Annual Review of Sociology, 24*(1), 105–140. https://doi.org/10.1146/annurev.soc.24.1.105.

Oertel, S., & Thommes, K. (2018). History as a source of organizational identity creation. *Organization Studies, 39*(12), 1709–1731. https://doi.org/10.1177/0170840618800112.

Orlikowski, W. (2007). Sociomaterial practices: Exploring technology at work. *Organization Studies, 28*(9), 1435–1448. https://doi.org/10.1177/0170840607081138.

Putnam, L., Nicotera, A. M., & McPhee, R. (2009). Introduction: Communication constitutes organization. In L. Putnam & A. M. Nicotera (Eds.), *Building theories of organization: The constitutive role of communication* (pp. 1–20). Routledge.

Rowlinson, M., Booth, C., Clark, P., Delahaye, A., & Procter, S. (2010). Social remembering and organizational memory. *Organization Studies, 31*(1), 69–87. https://doi.org/10.1177/0170840609347056.

Rowlinson, M., Casey, A., Hansen, P., & Mills, A. (2014). Narratives and memory in organizations. *Organization, 21*(4), 441–446. https://doi.org/10.1177/1350508414527256.

Schultz, M., & Hernes, T. (2013). A temporal perspective on organizational identity. *Organization Science, 24*(1), 1–21. https://doi.org/10.1287/orsc.1110.0731.

Schoeneborn, D. (2011). Organization as communication: A Luhmannian perspective. *Management Communication Quarterly, 25*(4), 663–689.

Schoeneborn, D., Kuhn, T., & Kärreman, D. (2019). The communicative constitution of organization, organizing, and organizationality. *Organization Studies, 40*(4), 475–496.

Suddaby, R., Foster, W., & Mills, A. (2014). Historical institutionalism. In M. Bucheli & R. D. Wadhwani (Eds.), *Organizations in time: History, theory, methods* (pp. 100–123). Oxford University Press.

Suddaby, R., Foster, W., & Trank, C. (2016). Organizational re-membering: Rhetorical history as identity work. In M. Pratt, M. Schultz, B. Ashforth, & D. Ravasi (Eds.), *Oxford handbook of organizational identity* (pp. 297–316). Oxford University press. https://doi.org/10.1093/oxfordhb/9780199689576.013.18.

Taylor, J. R. (2011). Organization as an (imbricated) configuring of transactions. *Organization Studies, 32*(9), 1273–1294. https://doi.org/10.1177/0170840611411396.

Taylor, J. R., Cooren, F., Giroux, N., & Robichaud, D. (1996). The communicational basis of organization: Between the conversation and the text. *Communication Theory, 6*(1), 1–39. https://doi.org/10.1111/j.1468-2885.1996.tb00118.x.

Taylor, J. R., & Van Every, E. (2000). *The emergent organization: Communication as its site and surface.* Lawrence Erlbaum.

Treem, J, & Leonardi, P. (2013). Social media use in organizations: Exploring the affordances of visibility, editability, persistence, and association. *Communication Yearbook, 36*, 143–189.

Wadhwani, R., & Bucheli, M. (2014). The future of the past in management and organization studies. In M. Bucheli & R. Wadhwani (Eds.), *Organizations in time* (pp. 2–30). Oxford University Press. https://doi.org/10.1093/acprof:oso/9780199646890.003.0001.

Wadhwani, R., Suddaby, R., Mordhorst, M., & Popp, A. (2018). History as organizing: Uses of the past in organization studies. *Organization Studies, 39*(12), 1663–1683

Walsh, J., & Ungson, G. (1991). Organizational memory. *The Academy of Management Review, 16*(1), 57–91. https://doi.org/10.2307/258607.

Weick, K. (1995). *Sensemaking in organizations.* Sage.

Wilhoit, E., & Kisselburgh, L. (2015). Collective action without organization: The material constitution of bike commuters as collective. *Organization Studies, 36*(5), 573–592.

Whiteman, G., & Cooper, W. H. (2011). Ecological sensemaking. *Academy of Management Journal, 54*(5), 889–911. https://doi.org/10.5465/amj.2008.0843.

Ybema, S. (2014). The invention of transitions: History as a symbolic site for discursive struggles over organizational change. *Organization, 21*(4), 495–513. https://doi.org/10.1177/1350508414527255.

PART IV

What Difference Does CCO Make for Practice?

28

CCO AND THE ACADEMIC-PROFESSIONAL GAP

Combining Rigor and Relevance in Organizational Communication

Mark van Vuuren and Peter Knoers

CCO and the Academic-Professional Gap: On the Rigor and Relevance of Our Work

Oh yes, we held inspiring meetings between CCO scholars and professionals when EGOS conferences were organized. No, these workshops were not EGOS pre-conferences. We called them pre-EGOS conferences. Here is why.

The importance of the annual meetings from the European Group for Organization Studies (EGOS) for the CCO community cannot be overstated. Scholars from around the world have gathered under its hospitable umbrella, from the initial subthemes to the "Organization as Communication" Standing Working Group, and at other meetings organized before, during and after the conference. Two of these sessions were organized on the intersection of academia and society: in 2014 was the first one in Rotterdam's monumental townhall under the title of "CCO in Practice" (Van Vuuren, Porter, Novak & Knoers, 2014). Here, a group of researchers and consultants gathered for a two-day event to encourage the cross-breeding of ideas and practice. Professionals shared some of their most pressing concerns, which the academics tried to clarify and solve using whatever was available in the CCO toolbox. We did this again in 2017, at the Copenhagen Business School during an academia-meets-practice development workshop, "The practical and social relevance of communication-centered organizational research" (Bencherki, Blaschke, Knoers & Van Vuuren, 2017). This was again both a wonderful as well as a frustrating gathering. On the one hand it was wonderful, as we saw the connections between public agencies and autopoiesis and between charitable foundations and the Four Flows. At the same time, it was frustrating as the tensions between rigor and relevance became very obvious. Pearce's pragmatism and pragmatic professionals are not easily compatible.

As said, these sessions were no official pre-conferences, because none of the visiting professionals were EGOS members, a strict requirement for inclusion in the official program. That was the reason these workshops with professionals became pre-EGOS conferences instead of EGOS pre-conferences. A wordplay which reflects the quest central to this chapter: how to build stronger connections between the separated worlds of academia and practice. A strong

DOI: 10.4324/9781003224914-33

connection between those two spheres would benefit both: the scholarly work of CCO can be invaluable for professionals and practice can inspire CCO scholarship. Achieving this connection between rigor and relevance needs a lot of translation activities.

Rigor and/or Relevance in CCO Scholarship

Even though the key question of CCO scholars is "What is an organization?", it remains hard to answer what is key in what organizations can do with CCO scholarship. Its sophisticated theories, nuanced definitions, and meticulous methodologies can be a source of delight and fierce debate for insiders, but can become insurmountable hurdles for outsiders. To untrained ears, speaking fluent CCOese runs the risk of sounding like obscure gibberish. Which, we insist, it is not! On the contrary: there is nothing as practical for professionals in organizations as a strong theory that describes the very processes of how their organizations emerge, perpetuate and transform (Schoeneborn & Vásquez, 2017). However, there is a caveat. The data presented and used in CCO analyses could not be closer to the daily lives of professionals, including open interviews in the military (e.g. Browning et al., 2009), rich cases in hacker collectives (e.g. Dobusch & Schoeneborn, 2015) and vignettes of team interactions in hospital care (e.g. Fox & Brummans, 2019). But the theorizing about these examples from shopfloor to executive board is then oftentimes embedded in abstract ontological-epistemological frameworks, dense philosophical explorations and counterintuitive paradoxes. One cannot blame the interested practitioner becoming confused by Ricoeurian distanciation (e.g. Lohuis & Van Vuuren, 2017) or by what (dis)ordering means (e.g. Vásquez, Schoeneborn & Sergi, 2016). While the academic community learns to speak this language and sharpens its lens for the dynamics, practitioners oftentimes miss the why, the what and the how. In our view, that is a waste.

The tension between academic insight and practical relevance in the field of organizations is, of course, a struggle recognized by many others. At the end of her term as president of the Academy of Management, Pearce (2004) reflected on what had been useful to her while she was leading this academic community: "[A]s I think about what was useful, and which mistakes I was able to avoid, I became aware that very little of this useful knowledge about my most important challenges came from our scholarly world. Rather, the really useful insights, the knowledge that helped with the tough problems, came from what I am calling our world of shared folk wisdom about management and organizations" (p. 176). Pearce came with an interesting suggestion to solve the problem of the small overlap between folk wisdom and scholarly work. Where one may expect a plea for using more theories to replace folk wisdom on management, she suggested to carefully check folk wisdom against reality.

The so-called research-practice gap refers to the failure of research to impact practice and the lacking translation of practical concerns into research projects. Leaning on Luhmann's system theory, Kieser and Leiner provocatively state that research and practice are ultimately irreconcilable systems, deeming fruitful collaborations between the two doomed to fail for at least one but probably both sides (Kieser & Leiner, 2009, 2011, 2012). They are challenged by others (e.g. Sharma & Bansal, 2020) who see this as a rigid definition of science, showing "how the pendulum has swung in business schools over the decades from being not considered scientific enough to make a contribution to practice to being so scientific, such that we cannot contribute to the practice of management" (Shani & Coghlan, 2014, pp. 435). Again, others (Bartunek & Rynes, 2014) have proposed that the paradoxical relationships between academics and professionals are in themselves generative for practice and fruitful for research. Moreover, talking about the tension reifies both the problem of the struggle as well as the importance of respectable and respective conversations between the two fields. A wide range of solutions are provided to bridge the gap (see Kieser, Nicolai & Seidl, 2015, for a review).

For us, the authors of this chapter, the tension is our daily reality in a literal sense. Peter is an experienced communication professional, organization consultant and managing director with a decades-long interest in academia. Mark is a hybrid academic, combining a role as (part-time, tenured) associate professor of organizational communication with a role as strategic consultant in an attempt to become more relevant for practice. We collaborate at the intersection of theory and practice, getting firsthand experience of the gap. We recognize Pearce's surprise at the wisdom and folly of folk wisdom, Bartunek and Rynes's (2014) struggle with different time horizons (insert apology to the editors of this volume about here), and all the others' descriptions of the ways in which rigor and relevance serve as competing values.

These experiences are the data for the current chapter. We aim to do three things. First, we summarize what we think are the main treasures CCO has to offer to practice. This includes the practical lens of its methodology and the discursive resources of its terminology. Second, we identify the more problematic aspects of translating CCO for practice, namely the rigidity of its philosophy, the confusing debates between the schools, and the ironic complexity of its jargon. Third, we explore how practice can inform our theorizing. To do so we provide a case to show how the CCO toolbox informed professionals what they were experiencing. After these explorations, we conclude with some final reflections on the gap between CCO theory and professional life.

How CCO Can Be(come) Beneficial for Practice

For outsiders, CCO has a rather technical, abstract way of speaking about organizations. Professionals have a hard time to understand the questions and the answers brought up by the academic community. This is not because professionals are stupid – both genius and idiocy can be found in equal measure within and outside of academia. The reason is that the language used within CCO is foreign to them. The perspective has no natural resemblance to the ways in which they look at the world. They don't immediately recognize the relevance of agency nor have they time to read good books about "scholars who define and operationalize the agential dynamics of organizing in different ways" (Brummans, 2018, p. 2). What goes for agency also counts for authoritative texts, agencement, assemblage, actants or autopoiesis. And that is only the letter A! The initial missing enthusiasm would not be a problem if CCO was irrelevant for practitioners. However, in our own our daily practice we witness that the CCO lens does provide a detailed and illuminating perspective to professionals' everyday realities. The relational nature of organizing (Schoeneborn, Kuhn & Kärreman, 2019), to name one example here, provides a counternarrative to the depiction of organizations as institutionalized hierarchical structures. Given that I am the team leader now, one professional asked, why are my colleagues not following my orders? Of course, scholars and professionals would agree, leadership is more complex than that. But on explaining why their realities are more complex, we relied heavily on the CCO approach to present an alternative perspective. We could unpack his observed behavior and present the perspective of role constitution where a leadership relationship is composed of reciprocal and mutually reinforcing identities of leaders and followers. One of the strongest assets of CCO thinking *is the reduction of communication naiveté*. Still, reducing naiveté needs something else than mere abstract sophistication. Bridging the abstract conceptualization and the fine-grained analysis of the way we organize ourselves, CCO can contribute to professionals. But CCO scholars need to prove the freshness of these new ways of seeing, preferably through translating CCO concepts in terminology professionals understand, otherwise in helping them to understand the CCO language.

We, the authors, have broad experience with attempts to translate CCO's concepts in our practice. Our attempts have been met with bewilderment and with flashes of insight.

Generally speaking, CCO has strong potential for enriching the views of practitioners. Through a CCO lens, they become aware of new ways of seeing their organizing. In hindsight, we see a pattern of things that are helpful and some elements that are not helpful. We summarize the most helpful insights of CCO for professionals, as well as the most problematic ones.

CCO's Most Helpful Insights for Practitioners

Seeing Organizing as a Process – The Language of Verbs. The crucial step that we see as a key insight from our journey with professionals is to move away from the discourse of "being" towards performative language: "becoming, doing, relating" (cf. Anteby et al., 2015). The social construction – idea rather than fact. This is a liberating thought for many professionals. Since organizations are constituted through communicative acts they end up as mental constructs. These images are shared but will never be completely overlapping with someone else's image of the same organization. While this idea complicates organizational life, it is closer to reality: "My firm always will be slightly different from your firm." Everyone tends to view their own mental construct of the organization as true, hence the emphasis on "corporate identity". A CCO approach problematizes this approach to organization in a way that many professionals can relate to. For example, Christensen and Cornelissen (2011) describe how corporate communication overlooks the process through which organizations are constantly (re)produced through talk. This is easily recognized in organizations, as professionals struggle with the difficulties of different images of what their organization is or should be. It is a liberating idea for them to realize that organizations have no voice of their own (cf. Taylor & Cooren, 1997) and that the depiction of the organization in any specific setting thus partly depends on the person who is speaking on behalf of the organization. This organizing principle of communication provides them with a better explanation for what they see happening around them than their implicit assumption that every sensible person sees the world in the same way as they do, following humans' innate tendency towards naïve realism (Ross & Ward, 2013).

Organizationality. Opening up one's perspective of what an organization actually is has liberating consequences. Exploring why formal organizations remain the norm for many professionals is beyond the scope of this chapter, but it is evident that the awareness of looser social collectives as organization-like forms that are sometimes even superior to the standard organization is emancipating. We explored the consequences of this idea for people's understanding of their organization and teams. The awareness of organizing as a process loosens some of the strict assumptions professionals have. A prominent example of this is the openness for a wider range of organizational forms beyond the institutionalized bureaucracy to looser social collectives. For example, Comas et al. (2015) present a polymorphic framework to show how terrorist organizations operate in different configurations, including networks (e.g. the self-managing bundles of individuals who perform attacks) and movements (e.g. political ideologies that are discussed on online platforms). We use "organizationality" to capture the range of organizational forms, the term Dobusch and Schoeneborn (2015) introduced for the gradual differentiation of social collectives. They proposed the minimum criteria of what constitutes an organization as combining (a) interconnected decision-making, (b) collective actorhood, and (c) identity claims about what the collective is or does. Understanding the possibility of organizationality (beyond a dualistic organization versus non-organization) has consequences on several levels.

First, the boundaries of an organization are no longer seen as an indispensable aspect of achieving goals. For many assignments, an organization turns out to be part of the problem rather than a solution. Bureaucracies are hindering the needed flexibility. Other forms of organizing such as a network and a movement can be much more effective, as Comas et al. (2015) have shown. This does not disqualify a bureaucracy altogether. It all depends on the task at hand. Deep awareness of organizationality includes that in some cases a bureaucracy is the best way to get a job done. This also counters the idea that network organizations are the holy grail, as can be heard in organizations who are fed up with their strictness. It all depends on the question for which organizing starts. Organizationality radically positions the structure as a consequence of the purpose for which organizing takes place.

Second, the boundaries around teams and between professions need to become problematized. Being able to work in multidisciplinary, interdisciplinary and even transdisciplinary teams becomes a professional core competence. This realization is vividly described by Lifshitz-Assaf (2018), who explored open innovation dynamics in teams. A shift from *how* to work to *why* collaboration was necessary led to what she calls identity refocusing. This breaks the boundaries between groups, as the collective goal becomes more important than keeping the initial professional factions intact. As Taylor and Van Every (2011, p. 43) state: "the game is about whose interpretation [a definition of a given situation] will dominate." This awareness that for the goals of the teams the teams themselves may be blockades is crucial for dismantling the boundaries between groups if they want to deliver the best outcome. We have seen this process regularly when working with professionals in teams. The assumption is made implicitly that the organization should be the ultimate beneficiary of one's actions. Letting go of that opens up new ways of seeing and organizing. Particularly, a CCO view of communication helps to see the work of communication professionals differently. The inherent liminal nature of the communication profession (Reed & Thomas, 2021) makes them realize how their profession deals with constitution rather than "just" information.

The analytical payoff. With the CCO lens comes an interest in details. The analytical payoff of closely following how, for example, decisions are communicatively accomplished in meetings gives a new perspective on how collaboration and negotiation emerge. Spee and Jarzabkowski (2011) provide an example of this that resonates with professionals. Tracing how versions of a strategic text scaffold the whole process shows the power (or agency) of such a text. Of course, doing these analyses is more complex than the straightforward survey or interview, but professionals feel that these analyses provide insights that come much closer to the answers on their real questions than standard audits. We use examples from theories to explain the concepts, and three examples are often seen as most illuminating. First, Brummans's (2007) example of the textual agency of a signed document helps professionals to see how a text can create a persona of and for oneself, transcending space and time. It happened several times that someone came back later, proud of having exposed false claims through references to policies that did not say what it was suggested they would say. Second, Benoit-Barné et al.'s (2009) analysis of the accomplishment of authority explains well how a range of words, gestures and things together establish a sense of authority. Finally, Koschmann's (2013) identification of the way in which a metaphor served as an authoritative text for establishing a sense of identity deserves a special mention here. An authoritative text refers to an abstract textual representation with a dominant reading for a group (Kuhn, 2008). The US Declaration of Independence might serve as a good example. This document in a way represents the soul of that country and what it strives for. In a less dramatic – but oftentimes more strict – fashion, in organizations such texts develop as well. These texts can be written mission statements (e.g. Kopaneva & Sias, 2015), but also metaphors can become authoritative texts, as Koschmann (2013) has shown. He describes how a collaboration initiative gained traction when seeing themselves as a dashboard for making sure "everything is working together" (Koschmann, 2013, p. 78). While the intricacies of authoritative texts are hard to explain, organization members are very aware of the crucial role certain metaphors play in their understanding of their collective. The metaphors range from referees and coaches to Huckleberry Finn and Band of Brothers. With these metaphors identified as authoritative text, they become sensemaking devices for what the group is and could be.

Aspirational Talk. Christensen et al. (2013) define aspirational talk as "communication which announces ideals and intentions rather than reflect actual behaviours" (p. 373). Managers know that announcing ideals can be a tricky business. A lack of proof of the actuality of good behavior can damage an organization's image, especially in skeptical contexts. Expressing good intentions to a cynical crowd may pave the road to a reputational hell. Here words have clear consequences, albeit the opposite to the ones that were hoped for. The impact of this *j'accuse* may deter leaders from considering ambitious policies, thereby hampering needed courageous actions to work towards ideals. Every attempt to get out of this deadlock is worth consideration. Aspirational talk is such an attempt. It provides an alternative situation when words are not reflected in actual behavior – these words could be the announcement of an aspiration, as intended behavior. This type of idealization is better known as "inspiration", a word with a much better press than hypocrisy. According to Christensen et al. (2013, p. 380), this is an essential first phase of actual behavioral change: "To stimulate change and improvement, managers are encouraged to invoke fictions, in a sense to practice hypocrisy." That is the key of aspirational talk: there is a positive version of hypocrisy. This is a relief, which refers first of all to CSR communication (Christensen et al., 2013), but also to other settings, like core values (Van Vuuren, 2015) in a vision document. In one higher education institute where they had become rather cynical about the value of strategic plans, we introduced the distinction between the two types of hypocrisy. Strategic plans are always hypocritical as they depict a situation that is different from the current state. There is a gap between what you say and what you do. The question became whether they wanted to pursue the state they described or not. Translating their strategy as hypocrisy turned out to be helpful in reformulating the strategy in a more realistic future state.

Providing a Sophisticated Language for Communication Processes. For practitioners, there seems to be a curse of successful communication. Paradoxically, for people who assumed communication as a given, communication becomes most visible when it is absent. When a project is a failure, it is often due to "the lack of communication". People are angry, dissatisfied, because they were not informed. In post-project assessments, project teams often list communication as one of the most needed areas for improvement. If "the communication" had been better, the project would have run more smoothly. Rather than a constitutive force, communication is treated as an easy, yet the weakest, link in the whole process. And the communication professionals are responsible. At the same time, the same communication is easily overlooked in the evaluation of a successful project. If things go smoothly and a project went well, claims are made about the strength of leadership, charisma and trust. In that sense, transparent communication is a goal and a curse: as soon as you manage the communication processes so well that people really under-stand each other, "the communication" is transparent, hence invisible. The saying goes "success has many fathers, while failure is an orphan". Communication managers have to put effort into making crystal clear which contribution they made to successes. They have to claim their part of the success that is so easily attributed to leadership, vision, focus and teamwork. Otherwise they will remain – in line with the saying – managers of the corporate orphanage. But – and here is the key – they need the discursive resources to identify the constructive, constitutive and complex nature of communication. This is what CCO can provide. Its focus on constitution provides the language that helps professionals to move beyond a caricatural idea of communication, what we previously called the reduction of communication naiveté. An example of this constitution is CCO's approach to organizational identification. While the importance of identification is reflected in the rich stream of research (see Ashforth, 2016; Ashforth et al., 2008, for a review), the emergence and appearance of this organizational identification in the everydayness of organizational life remained an open question. Chaput, Brummans and Cooren (2011) answered this question with their study of members' attachments to a new political party. They showed that organizational identification is not a mindset that merely becomes explicit through utterances in a meeting, but that it was the action of identifying with a common purpose, a document, a name that created the sense of sameness we call identification. Another example shows the exact opposite: Bean and Buikema (2015) apply the Four Flows model of constitutive communication to show how the decline of the terrorist organization al-Qa'ida was communicatively accomplished. The destabilizing communication activities they proposed include production of distorting fake orders in terrorist networks and other forms of information as a weapon of mass distortion. Whether it is about constitution or dissolution, CCO research shows the pervasiveness of communication in organizational processes. In this sense, one communication professional once compared communication for organizations with water on earth: someone who only sees water in seas and ditches will be surprised to learn that over half of the human adult body is water. In organizations, communication is – still – oftentimes reduced to information, and the sending and reception of messages.

The More Problematic Aspects of Translating CCO for Practice

The Rigidity of its Philosophy. While a constitutive perspective is helpful in understanding certain processes, it serves as an add-on to other perspectives. These other perspectives might have contradictory ontological and epistemological underpinnings. People do leave the *terra firma* of interactions. This is not restricted to professionals only, as scholars also differ in their approaches. For example, Ocasio, Loewenstein and Nigam (2015) link CCO to institutional logics without buying into its ontological claim: their perspective follows a critical realist approach, relying "on the assumption that although institutional logics scale up and thereby emerge from situated communicative events distributed throughout organizations and institutional fields, they have an ontological reality distinct from communication" (Ocasio et al., 2015, p. 30). Czarniawska (2001) shared her musings about the possibility of being a constructionist consultant, vividly describing the clash between different logics (e.g. logics of practice, of theory, and of representation). That is part of the problem: speaking from a particular logic makes it really hard to see the rationale of another logic. When you have made sense of something, it becomes challenging to appreciate an alternative explanation. Those are easily rejected as being stupid, evil or naïve. So when professionals do not follow the abstract CCO logic, they are not stupid. They reside in a lived reality in which some of the CCO language does not make sense. It is really hard to consider social constructionism while you are standing next to a coffee machine.

The Debates between the Schools. Professionals with a strong theoretical interest sometimes look for a thorough understanding of the CCO perspective. The difference between the approaches is a puzzling element here. Of course, they know that rigor and specificity is a hallmark of academic debates, but they don't see the relevance for their work. In this sense, interestingly, of the different streams of CCO, the Four Flows approach (Iverson, McPhee & Spaulding, 2017) has the most natural appeal to practitioners. McPhee and Zaug (2000) were the first to propose that organizations are constituted through the intermingling of four kinds of communication processes. These four flows include membership negotiation (demarcating the boundaries between those who are in or out), reflexive self-structuring (recognizing talk creates shared memories), activity coordination (establishing connections between individual activities so they add up to a collective achievement), and institutional positioning (through which individuals can become representatives of the organization). Professionals recognize the four activities as issues they face in their organization. Moreover, the underlying framework of structuration theory with its duality of structure is something that professionals recognize. Governmental officials immediately recognize the web of rules, regulations and resources that guide, afford and constrain their actions – and also that their dealing with these resources reproduces or transforms their routines. Therefore, the Four Flows rationale oftentimes has more direct resonance with their worldviews than Luhmannian or Montreal School sources, at least in the way we present them.

The Complexity of the Language. The irony is not lost on professionals exploring the CCO approach that a group who insists on the power of language speaks such an impenetrable language that only insiders can understand. Insisting on language as crucial for ordering calls for a certain quality of language itself. The quality of rigor and precision is oftentimes achieved for conversations within the academic community, but for outsiders something else is needed. Translation can work both ways: either practitioners learn to speak CCOese, or scholars with a CCO background formulate their perspective in terminology that practitioners use. It is not strange for professionals to learn new terminology when acquiring new concepts. They learned about lean six sigma and black belts, about agile and sprints, so why not initiate them into imbrication and autopoiesis? The problem remains that these words are part of a whole new way of seeing the world. One can only fully understand imbrication after having felt "imbricated" (i.e. that floating feeling when the awareness strikes that everything might be socially constructed). So separate concepts will not do the trick. Moreover, professionals will need to talk to their colleagues as well. Having a real impact requires language that can also be explained to others. Here the scholar will need to face the challenge of ethnographers: learning the language of the other in order to create relational rapport and a shared understanding (Tanu & Dales, 2016). In our case description below, we give a more detailed example of how we used the Montreal School's concepts to help practitioners make sense of their situation. The rather technical language of the model of organization (see Figure 7.1 in Brummans et al., 2014, p. 177) needed an adaptation in order to overcome our participants' confusion. We created a new version we jokily called the 'Montreal School for Dummies' model (see Figure 28.1). Here we replaced distanciation, textualization and presentification with more accessible words.

The boxes 1–4 are thus taken from the CCO chapter in the *Handbook of organizational communication* (Brummans et al., 2014, pp. 176–182), summarizing the core ideas of the Montreal School in accessible language. These boxes and arrows together depict the process of organizational development. While the description in Brummans et al.'s text focuses on the boxes, it is important to note that the actual message of translation and incarnation is in the arrows (see Arrows A–D in Figure 28.1). It represents how many practices and conversations (Box 1) can scale up to a collective experience over time (Box 2). When the participants continue to

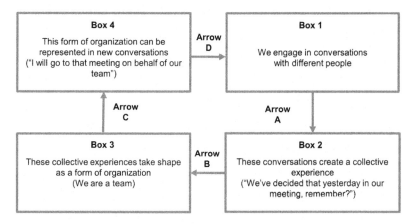

Figure 28.1 The "Montreal School for Dummies" model.

recognize themselves as a coherent unity, they start to refer to this unity as an "it". Through this depersonalization, their collective experiences become authored and turned into text (cf. Taylor & Van Every, 2000). This is the Arrow B translation, where the organization becomes a conversation topic that is extracted from actual practices. "It" becomes a symbolic organizational template, conveying the organization's intentions, code of conduct and identity. Organizations that become texts can be read by (or read to) internal and external publics. This is the Arrow C translation. The traces of yesterday's organizing create predictability for future conversations and provide the template for representation of the collective entity (Box 4). The collectively experienced unity can act when it is represented by people or things that are recognized as typically fitting or incarnating "the organization". Finally, the recognized collective fuels new interactions. The organization in this translation has such a homogeneous substance that it can be recognized (i.e. re-cognize, brought back to mind) and thus be made present again (i.e. re-present-ed) in new interactions (Arrow D).

We will now summarize a case about a collective initiative that became constituted and then dissolved again, to the surprise of many. We analyzed this case and turned it into a learning opportunity for both practitioners and scholars (Van Vuuren, Knoers & Verloop, 2019). We will summarize the case, and then in the conclusion link the learning points to the stronger and weaker elements of CCO mentioned above.

Overheid in Contact: A Tale of Two Narratives

A group of professional experts from different backgrounds, including communication, participation and public services, came up with the idea of creating an online platform to facilitate an ongoing high-quality conversation about improving government-society interaction. Over time, this online conversation was hoped to foster a collective vision, collaboration, and ultimately the increased quality of services and contact with governmental agencies. They called this platform *Overheid in Contact* (OiC, literally: *Government in Contact*). All readers were invited to write articles that would open the discussion. All readers had access to all articles and could comment on each other. On the platform, they shared their views, knowledge and insights into service provision by the government, democracy, participation, working in networks, data, communication and leadership. Ambitions and expectations were high,

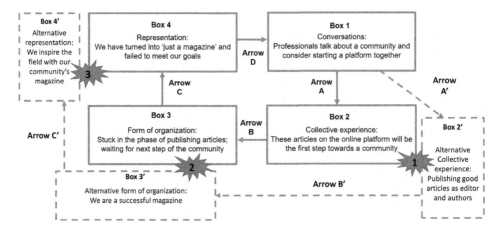

Figure 28.2 The constitution of two different organizations.

yet implicit. Rachel, (a pseudonym for) the initiator of the platform, became the so-called editor-in chief of OiC, and guided the authors in the process to develop their submissions into high-quality articles for the website. The platform published a high-quality article per week on its website between September 2017 and November 2018, widely read by an enthusiastic audience. The amount of and variety in backgrounds of readers grew from the start until the end. Rachel, however, became increasingly frustrated with the way things went. She shut the platform down on November 15, 2018. This left the readers perplexed: how could such a good magazine *not* succeed? Given our connection to both the OiC initiative and the CCO community, we were intrigued by the rise and fall of this new organizational arrangement, by the mix of excitement and frustration, the shock of the readers and Rachel's felt inevitability for making this decision.

The CCO terminology helped us to make sense of the shock, using the Montreal School for Dummies model (Figure 28.1). The constitutive translation dynamics provided the terminology to give a communicative explanation for the rise and fall of the Overheid in Contact initiative, *and the different organizations that were constituted in the process* (see Figure 28.2). Mapping the constitutive translation dynamics, we traced the differences between the participants of what was actually constituted.

We had access to virtually all correspondence, emails, documents, surveys and reports on OiC, ranging from the very initial idea (Spring 2017) to the latest responses after its shutdown (November 2018). Next to these data, we considered that the sequential nature of the four translations might elegantly match a narrative research approach. It is the sequence of translations through which sense emerges. Therefore, we held life-story interviews (Lohuis et al., 2016; McAdams & McLean, 2013) with seven professionals directly involved in OiC. We more or less asked interviewees to "relive their constitution of OiC". This narrative interview helped us to trace the development of the collective, and map it onto the process visualized in the model. Through our analyses, we identified two different narratives of what OiC was and should become. Rachel's conceptualization of OiC differed significantly from the other group members'. Over time, in the minds of the participants, two types of organizations had emerged: a failed community (according to Rachel; Arrows A–D) and a successful magazine (according to almost anybody else; Arrows A'–C').

The leader's Narrative: A Failed Community (Arrows A–D)

A group of professionals came together and talked about the options of starting a platform (Box 1). While there would be many more intensive interactions over the next two years, this was the only time in the entire process that they all met in person. The publication of the first articles was a clear indicator that they were creating something together on this platform (Arrow A). The articles were seen as the first step towards a community, and by all these authors handing in stories, they had something in common (Arrow B). They read each other's texts and were able to share those within their networks. As the hub in the network, the editors took care of the back-office. The editorial team sometimes had to go through many rounds of revisions, sometimes even rewriting the entire text in order to reach the satisfactory quality they set for themselves and all others. The high quality of the articles did not go unnoticed. New readers subscribed to the newsletter every week. As a platform, they took part in activities related to the mission of OiC (Arrow C), including a National Day for "Civil Servants 2.0". Here, they handed out business cards, and had a slide in their presentations explaining the community. "That was a fantastic day." But it was an exception: further, there were no more activities. A scheduled meeting in January 2018 was cancelled because not enough participants showed up. While the high-quality articles were published, read and lauded, it came with a cost: the editorial team spent literally days per week (without payment) to get an article out. During Spring 2018 it became a frustrating endeavor to collect and publish the articles as most authors did not meet their deadlines. The authors took no responsibility as team members as the initiator had hoped for (Arrow D). This was not the type of community she had hoped for. And there was no business case, while the investments were high, particularly for the editors.

The frustration kept growing when the authors continually failed to meet their deadlines. There should be a moment that this initiative would make some money. The investments became severe. A set of masterclasses on topics central to the platform was cancelled as not enough people enrolled for them. The editors felt like being stuck in "just the articles". The community never materialized. It was really frustrating for the editor-in-chief that all their hard work did not move beyond the stage of articles. So, ultimately, she pulled the plug.

The Alternative Narrative: A Successful Magazine (Arrows A'–C')

Other participants had a completely different view on the developments. This is their narrative. A group of professionals came together and talked about the options of starting a platform. The platform took shape, relying on the dominant metaphor of a magazine. With the magazine, a whole set of elements for a collective identity emerged. From the start (Box 1), the interactions were filled with magazine-related terminology: authors, editors, editing, readers, page views, articles, and a format. The activities logically translated the interactions as meetings between editor and authors, and thus it made sense to think of the platform in those terms (Arrow A'). This magazine terminology appeared everywhere in the emails, the website and the narrative. Readers referred to OiC as "the magazine" (Arrow B') and authors used it as explanation for their writing and reading. A key characteristic was that you could learn something from the articles. "They were so good, no one had to react to them. They were done. What could you say? If you wanted response, debate and reactions, you should submit something that is of less quality. Now you read, learned, and remained silent." The timely (weekly) appearance of high-quality articles from different authors was a clear indication that the community was working (Arrow C'). Its success as a magazine became dominant. This muted alternative goals of the platform, like the creation of a community. The magazine metaphor gave the group traction as a collective identity (but it was not helpful for creating a community). Imagine the shock when the successful editor-in-chief pulled the plug … .

How Communication Constituted Two Different Organizations

These two different narratives of the platform led to two different ideas about what OiC was becoming. These ideas clashed in three ways (see collision symbols 1, 2 and 3 in Figure 28.2].

The first tension [Clash 1] was present when different experiences arose. The online-offline incarnations were unbalanced. The platform emerged almost exclusively online. The few moments in which they physically met or collaborated (like organizing workshops on Civil Servant Day) were very energizing. But most often, most authors did not show up at meetings, and the efforts were singularly focused on the online magazine. Looking back, the editor said: "I should not have agreed on cancelling these meetings. You must come together sometimes to form a team." The platform became so tightly dependent on the production of articles, pushing all participants into the roles of author and editor, that an alternative distanciation towards a community would be odd.

The second tension [Clash 2] arose when *a skewed investment of effort and time passed unnoticed* when the platform was shaped. Through the analysis, it became apparent that key conversations were *lacking* in this phase. Given the highly visible output, it was assumed that the "back office" (the editorial work) was smooth and did not need further attention. The depersonalization of this collective experience was a mismatch with the amount of work the editorial duo had to do to realize the publication of the articles. The two days a week editorial work remained invisible, was taken for granted, and was thereby *lost in translation*. This would become frustrating for the editors later on, still out of sight for authors and readers. With such investments, it can become worrisome that OiC did not attract acquisition, contracts, or paid commissions. The single focus on the high-quality magazine left those other voices muted. The editors were hailed for a role they did not want. They wanted to be more than just editors, being highly skilled consultants and experts in digital communication and governmental services.

The third tension [Clash 3] followed logically from the other two tensions: with those different expectations, the failing of the masterclasses (which did not logically flow from the magazine as it would have followed a community) and the disappointment and surprises for the authors and readers when the editor decided to shut down the platform. The success of the magazine and quality of the contributions made them blind to the problematic issues that could only be seen from the hope for a community.

The OiC Case, CCO Theory and Practice

Overheid in Contact looked like a success to everyone except for leader/editor/initiator Rachel. The analysis of the demise of the platform was helpful for the professionals, as they were so surprised about it. It was baffling to them, a group of highly professional collaborators, who made the platform to share their insights on contact, service and collaboration, how could they have overlooked these dynamics? Our analyses showed them the importance of awareness of implicit analogies that people use when they start something new. The alternative reality of the magazine became dominant, leading to people acting like editorial staff. The power of a metaphor in the translation process should therefore not be underestimated (cf. Koschmann, 2013). This dominant translation had a downside: it can mute other translations (e.g. online-offline, or the return on investments from participants) that are also important to achieve successful and sustainable incarnations of organizations. We talked a lot about the becoming of the platform, where things went wrong, and how the platform emerged in a way that the most active person did not want but still actively facilitated. Still, we needed to do a lot of translations. We even created a "Montreal School model for Dummies" in order to show the participants what these boxes and arrows meant.

The impact of the CCO analysis was immediate. After reading the analysis, the editor considered a restart of OiC: "With the insights you gave me that we turned ourselves into a magazine, that messed it all up. So, if we let this go ... then the platform can continue, develop itself organically, like it was meant from the start."

For ourselves, this case was a turning point as well. The impact of such reflections is recognizable for teachers: it enhances their reflexivity too (Kuhn & Schoeneborn, 2015). We were developing an idea to create a community for professionals who work at the intersection of two fields (*Blikopeners*: literally, can opener, but also, a new way of looking). We try to use the learnings from our OiC study in our new community. We focus on "the becoming" of this new community from day 1. We try to make explicit what members feel about the community. We give room to different views, and give all members the freedom to join or leave whenever they want. We are reflective about the ways in which constitution takes place. In this way, we explicitly welcome different views and perspectives, and let everyone explicate the constitution that they see happening.

Concluding Thought: Bridging the Gap or Time for a Map?

For CCO scholars, the setting of collaboration between professionals and scholars can be a fruitful area for research. Experts have to do boundary work, translating their expertise in order to be made useful to nonexperts (Bechky, 2020). This boundary work is now often done by the professionals, and a few scholars in a consulting role. This is really hard. We need help from the CCO community, which has so much to offer to practice. It would be good if insights from CCO were translated in order to become useful to nonexperts. The question is: how?

A creative way to address this question is given by Dipboye (2014), who problematizes the bridging-the-gap metaphor for "its underlying assumption that one can link and make one the worlds of the scholar and the practicing manager" (p. 490). He suggested that scholars and practitioners may have to accept that the realities of the two parties are too different, in both tasks and styles. The very metaphor of gap bridging might be too reductionist. So rather than bridging the gap, he proposes the metaphor of map-making to guide the mutual benefit of each other's efforts and experiences. Scholars are the mapmakers in the world where practitioners travel: "The science of cartography can provide knowledge and a useful tool in the form of a map. However, these are abstractions, and in the journey the traveler will encounter unexpected dangers, uncharted forks in the road, barriers in the path, and other gaps between reality and the map" (Dipboye, 2014, p. 490).

A CCO map of the professional field in which people organize themselves, and are organized by their circumstances, that would be a great idea. In this chapter we sketched some of the elements that could become part of this map. These include of course the strengths of CCO for practice: the language of verbs to unveil the processual nature of organizing; the range of organizational constellations (loosely arranged under the header of organizationality), the eye for detail and its analytical payoff; the freedom provided by the concept of aspirational talk; and the sophisticated language that could capture both the failures and the successes of communication. Also, the more stubborn issues that widen the gap between academia and practice should be considered, including the commitments to specific ontological and epistemological underpinnings and schools that might be relevant within academia, but hinders translation to practitioners, as well as the hard work that needs to be done when translating the concepts to the lived realities of people in organizations.

We are well aware of the fact that not every scholar sees the benefits of investing time to reach out to practitioners to offer collaboration and mutual learning. Oftentimes, institutional incentives to do so are lacking. However, society needs this type of scholar as well, even if both sides are not aware of that. But for most of the academics within this field, we hope to have shown how satisfying and rewarding these interactions with practitioners are. They struggle oftentimes in their work, and the CCO perspective can be beneficial to the core of their activities. Good communication helps, as well as reduced communication naiveté.

A positive sign for crossing bridges, closing gaps and drawing maps is the current Handbook project. In a way this book embodies the coming-out of a group of scholars who have had an inspiring time together in a corner of organization studies, but now they present their ideas to the world. Engagement with other scholars and new questions from professionals will further the discussion.

While the majority of this chapter tries to make scholars move towards professionals in organizations, it is easy to overlook that scholars are organization members too. A collective endeavor to describe university life from a CCO perspective could show how the dynamics scholars see "out there in the field" also explain their own experiences as employees in a system. Notwithstanding the differences between academic and non-academic institutions, there will be shared experiences of populating organizations, just as other professionals do. And, lastly, practitioners went to our schools and universities before entering their organizations. Some who become managers will be our management and communication students first. The notes on a pedagogy of CCO that Kuhn and Schoeneborn (2015) proposed should therefore be taken to heart as well.

But even with all these ideas and intentions, some questions will remain. What would be the best possible map for practitioners? And how can the CCO community guide them through the jungle of elegant theories and thought-provoking concepts? This could be a very exciting topic to organize a meeting, where everyone is invited. Who knows, it may one day even become an official pre-conference.

References

Anteby, M., Chan, C. K., & DiBenigno, J. (2016). Three lenses on cocupations and professions in organizations: Becoming, doing, and relating. *Academy of Management Annals*, *10*(1), 183–244. https://doi.org/10.5465/19416520.2016.1120962.

Ashforth, B. E. (2016). Exploring identity and identification in organizations: Time for some course corrections. *Journal of Leadership & Organizational Studies*, *23*(4), 361–373.

Ashforth, B. E., Harrison, S. H., & Corley, K. G. (2008). Identification in organizations: An examination of four fundamental questions. *Journal of Management*, *34*, 325–374.

Bartunek, J. M., & Rynes, S. L. (2014). Academics and practitioners are alike and unlike: The paradoxes of academic–practitioner relationships. *Journal of Management*, *40*, 1181–1201.

Bean, H., & Buikema, R. J. (2015). Deconstituting al-Qa'ida: CCO theory and the decline and dissolution of hidden organizations. *Management Communication Quarterly*, *29*(4), 512–538.

Bechky, B. A. (2020). Evaluative spillovers from technological change: The effects of "DNA envy" on occupational practices in forensic science. *Administrative Science Quarterly*, *65*(3), 606–643. https://doi.org/10.1177/0001839219855329.

Bencherki, N., Blaschke, S., Knoers, P., & Van Vuuren, M. (2017). Communication constitutes organization: The practical and social relevance of communication-centered organizational research. Pre-EGOS conference, Copenhagen, July 5.

Benoit-Barné, C., & Cooren, F. (2009). The accomplishment of authority through presentification: How authority is distributed among and negotiated by organizational members. *Management Communication Quarterly*, *23*(1), 5–31.

Browning, L. D., Greene, R. W., Sitkin, S. B., Sutcliffe, K. M., & Obstfeld, D. (2009). Constitutive complexity. Military entrepreneurs and the synthetic character of communication flows. In L.L. Putnam & A.M Nicotera (Eds.), *Building theories of organization: The constitutive role of communication* (pp. 89–116). Routledge.

Brummans, B. H. J. M. (2007). Death by document: Tracing the agency of a text. *Qualitative Inquiry*, *13*(5), 711–727.

Brummans, B. H. J. M. (2018). Introduction: Perspectives on the agency of organizing. In B. Brummans (Ed.), *The agency of organizing: Perspectives and case studies* (pp. 1–27). New York: Routledge.

Brummans, B. H. J. M., Cooren, F., Robichaud, D., & Taylor, J. R. (2014). The communicative constitution of organizations: Schools of thought, approaches, and future research. In L., Mumby & D. K. Putnam (Eds.), *The Sage handbook of organizational communication: Advances in theory, research, and methods* (3rd edn., pp. 173–194). Thousand Oaks, CA: Sage.

Chaput, M., Brummans, B. H., & Cooren, F. (2011). The role of organizational identification in the communicative constitution of an organization: A study of consubstantialization in a young political party. *Management Communication Quarterly*, *25*(2), 252–282.

Christensen L.T. & Cornelissen, J. (2011). Bridging corporate and organizational communication: Review, development and a look to the future. *Management Communication Quarterly (25)*, 383–414.

Christensen, L. T., Morsing, M., & Thyssen, O. (2013). CSR as aspirational talk. *Organization*, *20*(3), 372–393.

Comas, J., Shrivastava, P., & Martin, E. C. (2015). Terrorism as formal organization, network, and social movement. *Journal of Management Inquiry*, *24*(1), 47–60.

Czarniawska, B. (2001). Is it possible to be a constructionist consultant? *Management Learning*, *32*(2), 253–266.

Dipboye, R. L. (2014). Bridging the gap in organizational behavior: A review of Jone Pearce's *Organizational Behavior: Real Research for Real Managers*. Academy of Management Learning & Education.

Dobusch, L., & Schoeneborn, D. (2015). Fluidity, identity, and organizationality: The communicative constitution of Anonymous. *Journal of Management Studies*, *52*, 1005–1035.

Fox, S., & Brummans, B. H. J. M. (2019). Where's the plot? Interprofessional collaboration as joint emplotment in acute care. *Journal of Applied Communication Research*, *47*, 260–282.

Iverson, J. O., McPhee, R. D., & Spaulding, C. W. (2017). Being able to act otherwise. In B. H. J. M. Brummans (Ed.), *The agency of organizing: perspectives and case studies* (pp.43–65). Routledge.

Kieser, A., & Leiner, L. (2009). Why the rigour–relevance gap in management research is unbridgeable. *Journal of Management Studies*, *46*, 516–533.

Kieser, A., & Leiner, L. (2011). On the social construction of relevance: A rejoinder. *Journal of Management Studies*, *48*(4), 891–898. https://doi.org/10.1111/j.1467-6486.2009.00886.x

Kieser, A., & Leiner, L. (2012). Collaborate with practitioners: But beware of collaborative research. *Journal of Management Inquiry*, *21*: 14–28.

Kieser, A., Nicolai, A., & Seidl, D. (2015). The practical relevance of management research: Turning the debate on relevance into a rigorous scientific research program. *Academy of Management Annals*, *9*(1), 143–233.

Kopaneva, I., & Sias, P. M. (2015). Lost in translation: Employee and organizational constructions of mission and vision. *Management Communication Quarterly*, *29*, 358–384.

Koschmann, M. A., (2013). The communicative constitution of collective identity in interorganizational collaboration. *Management Communication Quarterly*, *27*(1), 61–89.

Koschmann, M. A., Kuhn, T. R., & Pfarrer, M. D. (2012). A communicative framework of value in crosssector partnerships. *Academy of Management Review*, *37*(3), 332–354.

Kuhn, T. (2008). A communicative theory of the firm: Developing an alternative perspective on intra-organizational power and stakeholder relationships. *Organization Studies*, *29*, 1197–1224.

Kuhn, T., & Schoeneborn, D. (2015). The pedagogy of CCO. *Management Communication Quarterly*, *29*(2), 295–301.

Lifshitz-Assaf, H. (2018). Dismantling knowledge boundaries at NASA: The critical role of professional identity in open innovation. *Administrative Science Quarterly*, *63*(4), 746–782. https://doi.org/10.1177/0001839217747876.

Lohuis, A. M., & van Vuuren, M. (2017). Organization as Communication and strategic change: The dynamics of distanciation. In S. Blaschke & D. Schoeneborn (Eds.), *Organization as communication: Perspectives in dialogue* (pp. 191–212). Routledge.

Lohuis, A. M., Sools, A., Van Vuuren, M., & Bohlmeijer, E. T. (2016). Narrative reflection as a means to explore team effectiveness. *Small Group Research, 47,* 406–437.

McAdams, D. P., & McLean, K. C. (2013). Narrative identity. *Current Directions in Psychological Science, 22*(3), 233–238.

McPhee, R. D., & Zaug., P. (2000). The communicative constitution of organizations: A framework for explanation. *Electronic Journal of Communication, 10*(1/2), 1–16.

Ocasio, W., Loewenstein, J., & Nigam, A. (2015). How streams of communication reproduce and change institutional logics: The role of categories. *Academy of Management Review, 40*(1), 28–48.

Pearce, J. L. (2004). What do we know and how do we really know it?. *Academy of Management Review, 29*(2), 175–179.

Reed, C., & Thomas, R. (2021). Embracing indeterminacy: On being a liminal professional. *British Journal of Management, 32,* 219–234.

Ross, L., & Ward, A. (2013). Naive realism in everyday life: Implications for social conflict and misunderstanding. *Values and knowledge.* New York: Psychology Press.

Schoeneborn, D., Kuhn, T. R., & Kärreman, D. (2019). The communicative constitution of organization, organizing, and organizationality. *Organization Studies, 40*(4), 475–496.

Schoeneborn, S., & Vásquez, C. (2017). Communicative constitution of organizations. In: C. R. Scott et al. (Eds.), *The international encyclopedia of organizational communication* (Vol. 1, pp. 367–386). Hoboken, NJ: Wiley.

Shani, A. B., & Coghlan, D. (2014). Collaborate with practitioners: An alternative perspective: A rejoinder to Kieser and Leiner (2012). *Journal of Management Inquiry, 23*(4), 433–437.

Sharma, G., & Bansal, P. (2020). Cocreating rigorous and relevant knowledge. *Academy of Management Journal, 63*(2), 386–410.

Spee, A. P., & Jarzabkowski, P. (2011). Strategic planning as communicative process. *Organization Studies, 32*(9), 1217–1245.

Tanu, D., & Dales, L. (2016). Language in fieldwork: Making visible the ethnographic impact of the researcher's linguistic fluency. *Australian Journal of Anthropology, 27*(3), 353–369.

Taylor, J. R., & Cooren, F. (1997). What makes communication 'organizational'?: How the many voices of a collectivity become the one voice of an organization. *Journal of Pragmatics, 27*(4), 409–438. https://doi.org/10.1016/S0378-2166(96)00044-6

Taylor, J. R., & Van Every, E. J. (2000). *The emergent organization communication as site and surface.* , Mahwah. NJ: Lawrence Erlbaum .

Taylor, J. R., & Van Every, E. J. (2011). *The situated organization: Studies in the pragmatics of communication research.* Routledge.

Van Vuuren, M. (2015). Reflections on core values as aspirational talk. EGOS Conference, Subtheme 16: Athens, Greece, July 6–8.

Van Vuuren, M., Knoers, P., & Verloop, R. (2019). Translating a community's biography: The surprising incarnation of an online platform. EGOS Conference, Subtheme 5: Edinburgh.

Van Vuuren, M., Porter, A., Novak, D., & Knoers, P. (2014). CCO in practice. Pre-EGOS conference workshop, Rotterdam, July 1–2.

Vásquez, C., Schoeneborn, D., & Sergi, V. (2016). Summoning the spirits: Organizational texts and the (dis)ordering properties of communication. *Human Relations, 69*(3), 629–659. https://doi.org/10.1177/0018726715589422.

29

WHERE ARE THE ORGANIZATIONS?

Accounting for the Fluidity and Ambiguity of Organizing in the Arts

Boukje Cnossen

Introduction: The Absence of the Organization

During fieldwork in a community art organization, I ran into a musician who was running a programme for musical events as part of a local initiative. She tried to explain how this fitted into her other activities. In a matter of seconds, she explained that:

> Everything I do here is part of my artistic practice. Even if I am handing out flyers for music lessons. Working with communities is part of how I define myself as an artist. I am paid for two days a week to coordinate this programme, but I spend much more time on it. For instance, we throw a musical parade every year, and we work on costumes, we create our own instruments with the participants … . That level of community involvement is part of who I am as an artist, but it is not all I do. I am also part of an experimental jazz formation. It is quite avant-garde what we do, so I would never spread the announcement for our concerts here, no one would show up anyway. I also DJ sometimes with the person I run the programme here with. We perform under a different name, so it is clear that it is not part of our work in this programme here.

Based on this small excerpt, this person could be referred to as an artist, a member of a jazz-band, half of a DJ-duo, and a freelancer for a community art programme. These roles do not exist in separate contexts, but rather intersect at times, and this is solved by adopting an alias, or accepting a surplus of organizing work because it can count as part of one's individual art practice.

Looking at this, it is hard to see where being creative and being in a managerial role begin and end. One might say this is specific to the type of art practice this person is active in, working with local communities in temporary projects under precarious circumstances, and that her practice does not exactly fit in the category of "high art". But if we turn to those settings that more easily fit this picture, we encounter a similar difficulty of distinguishing the

DOI: 10.4324/9781003224914-34

"pure" and undiluted art-making from the practical and managerial things surrounding it. Most highly acclaimed painters and sculptors, those who have solo exhibitions in the world's most prestigious museums, have a considerable amount of the creation of their actual artworks done by assistants who graduated from art schools. Artists then become managers and employers, some running studios in several cities at the same time (Thornton, 2008).

Beyond visual art, there is also lots of evidence that artistic practice does not happen in splendid isolation. A lot of artistic practice is organized and contained in larger artistic organizations, such as theatre and ballet companies, opera houses, film production studios, or exhibition halls. Furthermore, the ways in which art is sold to audiences is often the result of strategies of careful curation and the creation of highly aestheticized environments of experience (De Molli, Mengis, & Van Marrewijk, 2019), meaning commercial functions of art organizations, such as branding, heavily rely on aesthetic and artistic techniques, which challenges the presumed separation of art and business as well.

While it has been shown that "creative processes of contemporary art are (...) inseparable from artists' strategies for surviving in the artworld" (Chan, Bruce, & Consalves, 2015, p. 21), CCO scholars have made a more ontological argument about creativity, and its inseparability from organizing or organization. Inspired by actor-network theory, CCO scholarship has argued that "creation is not a solitary endeavour and that the invention (as a thing) is not the product of the inventor, but rather an outcome of the stabilization of the relationships between the interests of many actants, humans, and non-humans" (Bartels & Bencherki, 2013). Other studies from such a relational perspective also challenge the presumed boundary between creating and managing, or between artistic and commercial concerns. Such research reveals that artists and other creators take practical concerns into account all the time, whether this regards the opinions of their funders (Simpson, Irvine, Balta, & Dickson, 2015) and clients (Elias, Chiles, Duncan, & Vultee, 2018), or the practical demands of transportation of artworks (Van den Abeele, 2020). It also shows that cultivating strategic relationships help choreographers create artistically innovative work (Montanari, Scapolan, & Gianecchini, 2016), that Skype conversations provide the feedback necessary for artworks to emerge (Duff & Sumartojo, 2017), and that a well-written project plan helps films materialize not just in terms of their execution, but in terms of the artistic content as well (Strandvad, 2011).

It is to this view of (artistic) creativity as "a socio-materially distributed practice rather than the cognitive privilege of the individual" (Farías & Wilkie, 2018) that CCO research has already made important contributions. For example, in their study of a hackathon event aimed at creating new audience experiences for museum visitors, Martine, Cooren, and Bartels (2017) propose a relational framework for the assessment of creativity. Relying on the same empirical material, Kuhn, Ashcraft, and Cooren (2017) show how artefacts and technological elements participate in the creative process. Taking seriously the socio-material and multiple nature of creativity and creative practice, CCO research has even put forward the idea that thoughts themselves are material, because they have to take shape, and that this taking shape is a form of materialization (Cooren, 2018, 2020).

While this relational view has done a lot to decentre views of creative and artistic endeavours, the question of how these creative practices bring forth organizations, or are supported by them, has remained out of scope. This is surprising, since CCO research puts the ontology of organization and organizing at the centre of its research programme (Bencherki & Elmholdt, 2020; Brummans, Cooren, Robichaud, & Taylor, 2014; Schoeneborn, Kuhn, & Kärreman, 2019). Therefore, in this chapter, I ask: if artefacts and materials contribute to creativity, what does this mean for the idea of the artistic organization? Creativity and creative projects have been studied as relationally constituted, enacted by objects, but what this means for a communicatively constituted view of the organization and the organizing of creative and cultural production remains a puzzle. (Artistic) creativity might have been decentred, its organization has not.

In this chapter, I start with a brief overview of research on artistic organizations and organizing, from which I conclude that art and management are still seen as separate, and that the organization is largely ignored and under-theorized. I then return to CCO literature and related streams of research, to show that this research currently lacks attention for the *organizational* aspects of art production. Finally, I discuss the potential of CCO theory to start investigating the mutually constitutive relationship between the artwork and the organization.

Research on Artistic Organizations and Organizing

A study of the social processes underpinning production and dissemination in the arts has mostly been the domain of cultural sociology and the sociology of the arts. Next to neo-institutional theory (DiMaggio, 1982, 1996; DiMaggio & Useem, 1978), the work of sociologists Howard Becker (1982) and Pierre Bourdieu (1983, 1984, 1993, 1994) has come to shape most of the debates in these subfields of sociology (Bottero & Crossley, 2011; De Glas, 1998; Santoro, 2011). Their views of the arts as social worlds versus fields (the latter being charactized by tension in the strive for dominance), respectively, have been the basis of much empirical research. In empirical applications of Bourdieu's work, the industry or sector is often taken as synonymous to the field (Serino, D'Ambrosio, & Ragozini, 2017). Reviewing these studies, it can be noted that the field can span different countries (e.g., Kuipers, 2011) or be located within one country (e.g., Johansson & Toraldo, 2017; Lindell, Jakobsson, & Stiernstedt, 2020). Within this understanding of fields as the places where artistic and cultural goods are produced, the role of organizations and organizing is often not theorized. Organizations and projects are simply taken as sites for the production of artistic or cultural goods, and although differences between such organizations in terms of, for instance, work culture and hierarchies are sometimes discussed (Kuipers, 2011), the question of how organizations define these fields is mostly left unanswered.

Management and organization scholars have been paying interest to organizing in the arts for at least two decades (Lampel, Lant, & Shamsie, 2000). They too engage with Becker's notion of the art world (e.g., Boutinot, Joly, Mangematin, & Ansari, 2017; Moeran, 2012) or Bourdieu's field theory (e.g., Haunschild, 2003) and his alternative capitals (e.g., Townley, Beech, & McKinlay, 2009; Scott, 2012). Yet, they often do not focus on the organization either. One possible reason for this is that the arts are characterized by project-based work (Lindgren, Packendorff, & Sergi, 2014), which is often informal in nature and relies on networks that span several formal organizations (Moretti & Zirpoli, 2016), or exist completely of contractors (Kauppinen & Daskalaki, 2015). A reliance on informal networks is found in all areas of the arts (Endrissat, Kärreman, & Noppeney, 2017; Hancock & Spicer, 2011; Haunschild, 2003; Hesmondhalgh & Baker, 2011; McRobbie, 2015; Rowlands & Handy, 2012). As a result, there is often no clear focal organization to pay attention to. Another possible explanation lies in the influence of neo-institutional theory in organizational sociology and its application to the study of "the cultural industries" (DiMaggio, 1982, 1996; DiMaggio & Useem, 1978). This perspective continues to influence organizational research (e.g., Jones, Svejenova, Strandgaard Pedersen, & Townley, 2016; Svensson, 2017; Wikberg, 2020) and entails a more macro-level focus on sectors, industries, or nations, rather than on single firms or projects.

Hence, organizational research that takes the arts as its empirical setting often focuses on "manifestations" of organizing, without theorizing how such organizational forms come to be, or how they are maintained over time. For example, organizational research on architectural firms shows an attention to the steep power relations (Bennis, 2003; Brown, Kornberger, Clegg, & Carter, 2010) and the collective nature of the creative work that characterize this profession (Groleau, Demers, Lalancette, & Barros, 2012). Research on design firms has focused on how designers communicate their aesthetic knowledge (Stigliani & Ravasi, 2018) and draw from their cultural toolkit when strategizing (Rindova, Dalpiaz, & Ravasi, 2011), whereas research on managers in the film industry has drawn attention to the different types of leadership found there (Ebbers & Wijnberg, 2012; Sørensen & Villadsen, 2015). Likewise, organizational scholars have focused on the practices of individuals in – to name only a few examples – different types of art markets (Badinella & Chong, 2013; Byerley & Chong, 2015), live music (Hoedemaekers, 2018; Humphreys, Ucbasaran, & Lockett, 2011; Umney, 2016), and national film sectors (Alvarez, Mazza, Pedersen, & Svejenova, 2005; Malik, Chapain, & Comunian, 2017; Mathieu & Stjerne, 2015).

Another focus entails the development of careers of workers in the arts and creative industries over time (e.g., Bennett & Hennekam, 2018; Cinque, Nyberg, & Starkey, 2020), where the focus is longitudinal, yet situated at the individual level as well. Analyses of site-specific dance (Biehl-Missal, 2019) and theatre (Munro & Jordan, 2013) have made contributions to the study of organizational space, while research at a fashion show has contributed to knowledge on embodiment in organizing (Huopalainen, 2015). However, the emergence of the creative firm as a result of such practices, and the ontological nature of such firms, is mostly left unexplored (Clegg & Burdon, 2019, being an exception). CCO, with its inquiry into the constitution of organizations (Brummans, Cooren, Robichaud, & Taylor, 2014; Schoeneborn, Kuhn, & Kärreman, 2019), and its view of organizations as always emergent (Taylor & Van Every, 2000), is a strong candidate to help researchers and practitioners better understand the relationship between art-making and organizing, which are often still thought of as separate realms.

The Absence of the Artwork

Research that does pay attention to the organizational forms that exist within the arts is smaller in size, yet different streams of literature can be distinguished here as well. A first stream regards the clustering of artistic and creative production in space, mostly in the form of creative or cultural hubs, often temporary in nature and part of policies for urban revitalization (e.g., Gill, Pratt & Virani, 2019; Peck, 2012). A second focus concerns the role of loosely structured or informal collectives of individual workers in the arts, often united for political or activist aims (Cnossen, 2018; Jiang & Korczynski, 2019). In most of this research, however, the production of the actual artwork is left out of the analysis of the organizational aspects.

Hence, while these studies often focus on the level of the organization or the team, mostly through a qualitative or even ethnographic approach, this research often disregards the very reason why any form of organizing is there to begin with: the production of art. This is surprising, not only because the artwork is the presumed *raison d'être* for the organizing to begin with, but also because organizational research is increasingly aware of the impact of aesthetic and symbolic elements on the organization (Strati, 1999; Wasserman & Frenkel, 2011). The aesthetics of interior design, for example, have become focal points for understanding hierarchies within the organization (Sivunen & Putnam, 2020; Wasserman & Frenkel, 2015). For some reason, however, when it comes to the analysis of the aesthetics of the artwork that is the product of artistic organizations, this is mostly left unconsidered. Exceptions include Janssens and Steyaert's study (2019) of how a choreography with diverse dancers relates to organizational diversity behind the scenes, Jones and Smith's (2005) research on the recursive relationship between large-scale film production and local identity, and Bazin and Korica (2020) on how Jean-Paul Gautier's take on the bridal gown offers insights into organizational identity.

The lack of attention to how the artwork plays a role in organizations and organizing in the arts may have to do with organizational scholars' reluctance to enter the murky waters of art criticism or aesthetic analysis. One could think, however, that it has to do with a much more fundamental divide than the one between academic disciplines, and is not a matter of division of labour, but rather due to the implicit idea that the making of art is fundamentally different from the doing of organizing. Making art is somehow reserved for a separate realm, one of inspiration and passion, which is removed from the mundane and pedestrian "stuff" that makes up organizing and managing, including any economic, financial and other practical concerns. This idea is a historic one, reflected in the often-found opposition between "creative" and "industrial" (Finkel, Jones, Sang, & Russell, 2017) and going back to the era of Romanticism (Doorman, 2012), in which the realm of art was conceived of as removed from the real world (Den Hartog Jager, 2014). Art and artists went from craftsmen to creators, close to the realm of the divine and the purity of nature (Den Hartog Jager, 2011). In fact, creativity as a notion was long reserved for divine creation only (Hesmondhalgh & Baker, 2011).

The lack of attention to the artwork itself is thus not only a result of the aforementioned theoretical preferences and commitments in the academic literate on art organizations and organizing, but goes back to a historically shaped ontological separation of making art from other practices of making and doing that make up the organizing *around* it. Almost all the organizational literature reflects this historical divide, for instance by talking about a "balancing act" (Lampel et al., 2000) of artistic and economic concerns, clashes between creative and managerial identities (Gotsi, Andriopolous, Lewis, & Ingram, 2010) and ways of working (Laurey, 2019), and artistic versus financial needs (Moeran, 2012). Even research that tries to bridge the divide, for instance by suggesting to talk about a conversation between aesthetic and economic concerns, rather than a conflict (Austin, Hjorth, & Hessel, 2018), often ends up confirming the existence of two opposite sides.

Starting to investigate the role of the artwork in processes of organizing is important for several reasons. First, it would finally help scholars account for what artists often take as a given: that the work demands certain things, that a painting declares itself finished, or that there really is no difference between "the project" and the art itself (Groys, 2002). Given CCO's focus on the performative role of language as well as – in particular within The Montreal School of CCO (Brummans, Cooren, Robichaud, & Taylor, 2014) – non-human actants such as artefacts, documents, tools, and technologies, the potential to theorize the performative effects of artwork for the organization, however small, is present. Although CCO scholars have not focused explicitly on artworks, they have drawn attention to issues of aesthetics and style in other artefacts and practices. They have, for example, shown how genres shape organizational practices (Cooren, 2004; Schoeneborn, 2013), how figurative language helps entrepreneurs bring ventures to life (Clarke, Cornelissen, & Healey, 2019), and how an ad hoc design project brought a community of self-employed creative workers closer together (Cnossen & Bencherki, 2018). In fact, CCO has already been identified as a fruitful perspective from which to study the role of genres in creative labour (Alacovska, 2017, p. 392). There are several ways in which CCO can shed light on the recursive relationship between the artwork on the one hand, and the organizational setting out of which it emerges and by which it is supported, on the other. Several suggestions are provided in the following section.

Constituting Organizations and Organizing in the Arts

When it comes to understanding how organizations and organizing in the arts come into being and persist, CCO theory has several tools to offer. Scholarship adhering to a relational view has already argued for the artistic product and process to be seen as mutually constitutive. What CCO theory can add here is an answer as to how the continuous back-and-forth between creative practices and the creative product can lead to the emergence of a third element, being the organization. Such "thirdness", a notion central to CCO (Taylor & Van Every, 2011), does not need to look like a formal organization, but is identified by looking at communication as it unfolds. For example, Dobusch and Schoeneborn (2015) articulated the concept of organizationality as a way to account for the ways in which loose collectives establish a sense of acting not just on behalf of their group, but in the name of something that is more than the sum of its parts. Relying on Luhmann's theory of decisions being central for the emergence of social systems such as organizations, they argued that social collectives, however dispersed, can acquire a degree of "organizationality" through the repeated presence of some form of coordinated action, as well as through repeated identity claims (Dobusch & Schoeneborn, 2015).

Focusing on the material co-presence of cyclists in the street, Wilhoit and Kisselburgh (2015) also argued collectives are not either organizations or not, but can instead have a degree of what they call "organizationness". Their focus on materiality instead of (human) decision-making differs from the argumentation developed around organizationality (Blagoev, Costas, & Kärreman, 2019; Schoeneborn, Kuhn, & Kärreman, 2019), but the insistence that some form of organization can emerge out of communication without the necessity of any formal organization is shared. This offers opportunities for understanding organizing in the context of the arts, as there is often no formal organization, yet a strong "thirdness". Formally speaking, many artistic and creative projects consist of self-employed workers contracting each other for the duration of a project or production. However, in terms of lived experience, it is often out of a certain thirdness that things are done and decided, exemplified by clichés such as "the show must go on", and statements about "what the work needs".

The CCO literature on attribution and appropriation (Bencherki & Cooren, 2011; Cooren & Bencherki, 2010) offers another piece of the puzzle when it comes to understanding the emergence and persistence of organizations, also (and especially) in contexts where a formal organization is lacking. Attribution and appropriation happen when a certain action or quality is attributed to or appropriated by the organization, thereby contributing to the communicative constitution of this organization (Bencherki & Snack, 2016). It is precisely because of the fact that the arts are largely made up of informal networks that acts of attribution and appropriation proliferate. When reputation and prestige matter, and when working relationships shift fast, it becomes important to emphasize that certain activities belong to a certain prestigious festival, are part of an exhibition, or belong to the oeuvre of a certain artist or designer. This may seem unsurprising, given that authorship and the idea of individual genius still are dominant features of the arts, but the arts are far from exempt from this type of appropriation. The performing arts, while heavily reliant on the work of many talented performers, excel in attributing creative and artistic actions to the opera house, the ballet company, or the orchestra. And in fashion companies, design and architecture firms, and contemporary dance groups, organized creative production is often attributed to an individual author, whose name comes to signify the organization (Brown et al., 2010; Sommerlund & Strandvad, 2012; Strandvad, 2012).

On the other hand, looser collectives in the arts, such as the various forms and activities the artist at the start of the chapter was engaged in, often manage to endure precisely because they make no attempt at *exclusive* appropriation. For example, the artist at the very start of this chapter could attribute some of the (paid) activities for a community art programme to her individual art practice as well. There is some flexibility in this: projects she is particularly proud of could be subsumed under her individual signature, whereas those activities that less clearly fit her aims as an artist can be thought of as simply part of the tasks she is paid to do. Hence, counter to the widely held idea that organizations must have one clear identity, organizing in the arts often relies on selective modes of appropriation. Some actions are attributed to one of the organizational entities while other actions remain appropriated by the artists, volunteers, or creative workers. This seems to allow for a flexible mode of constituting an organization, which can be deviated from if needed, as if the direction towards organizations as entitative beings, or the move "from we to it" (Nicotera, 2013), is reversed from time to time.

Different from other practice-theoretical approaches, CCO has developed unique ways of theorizing the ontology of the organization (Kuhn, 2021), among which are the idea of the inherent fluidity of organization and its existence as a matter of degree rather than kind (Bencherki & Elmholdt, 2020; Dobusch & Schoeneborn, 2015; Wilhoit & Kisselburgh, 2015). A next step would be to investigate practices of attribution and appropriation, and the emergence of organizationality more generally, in order to investigate the role of the artwork in it. This would entail a decentred and processual view of the artwork as well, as current fine art practices often emphasize the open-endedness of art and the role of the viewer in constructing it (Bourriaud, 1998; Gielen, 2013). It would also move beyond a focus on language and material properties, but requires a deeper engagement with its aesthetic and poetic qualities.

If we return once again to the artist who was introduced at the start of the chapter, research could investigate when it is that she benefits from presenting her activities as part of her individual art practice, and when it is that she attributes them to the art organization that employs her on a freelance basis. One might imagine that the alignment of those activities with her individual artistic vision plays a role, but certain field-level dynamics likely play a large role as well. The interplay between opportunities to gain prestige on the one hand, and individual or collective artistic vision on the other, could indicate when certain activities will be attributed to a pre-existing organization, and when they might be appropriated by the artist(s). Finally, one could also ask about the role of audiences and participants in appropriation and attribution. For example, it might be that the participants in her immersive music parades are more willing to attribute the project to her as an artist, or to the art organization, depending on whether and how they feel impacted on an aesthetic or affective level.

To be sure, the question of how the artwork impacts the organization is far from new. In fact, organizational research on artistic interventions has investigated the different ways in which artistic gestures can interrupt or challenge existing organizational contexts (Beyes, 2010; Skoglund & Holt, 2020). While this research has drawn on the work of Jacques Rancière (Beyes, 2010; Mairesse, 2014) and Henri Lefebvre (Skoglund & Holt, 2020), CCO is uniquely equipped to look at the performative effects of words and things, both crucial in art.

There already is a rich tradition of organizational scholars and practitioners taking seriously the potential of the arts for a renewal of the reflection on organizational phenomena by drawing on examples ranging from fine art (Latham, 2014), theatre (Biehl-Missal, 2013; Biehl-Missal & Saner, 2014), street performance (Aslan, 2017; Cnossen, De Vaujany, & Haefliger, 2020), television (Zundel, Holt, & Cornelissen, 2013), music (Bathurst & Williams, 2013), and poetry (Essex & Mainemelis, 2002). However, these analyses often focus on the drawing of parallels or "analogical thinking" (Barry & Meisiek, 2007), whereas words can do so much more than provide analogies. CCO, with its roots in the work of Austin (1962), might be able to look at how art can perform. Again, a deeper understanding of the particulars of words and things in the context of art, a particular type of communication which often aims to confuse and challenge rather than clarify and confirm, would be needed.

In sum, there is a potential for CCO research to theorize the emergence and mainten-ance of the organization in artistic organizations and organizing. A first step is to look more closely at the connection between creativity and the organization, not just because of creativity happening within organizations and being of consequence for organizations, but because cre-ativity *is* organizational. Martine et al. (2017) and Kuhn et al. (2017) show how assessments of creativity do not just happen within the organizational context of a hackathon, but also shape how the event unfolds. At the same time, these studies focus on the communication around the making of the creative product, and do not really engage with the question of how the aesthetic or poetic qualities of the creative product become consequential for the organization.

In Conclusion

In this chapter, I have shown that organizational research on the arts has largely favoured a focus on fields or on micro-level practices, at the expense of a focus on, and theorization of, the organization. I have offered several reasons for this, from the ephemeral character of art-istic organizational forms, to the historically shaped idea of (artistic) creativity and practical and managerial practices as separate "substances", situated in widely removed spheres or realms.

A focus on the emergence and persistence of forms of organizing in the arts is important, because it helps us understand how human and non-human actors can start to act on behalf of something else, and hence leads to a better understanding of agency. It is CCO's focus on the performativity of words and things that can provide the basis for an investigation of the performativity of artwork and their consequences for the organization. This could build on previous research that has seen creative products and creative processes as relational, by showing how the recursive relationship between those two "elements" could lead to the emergence of a third: the organization.

Coming to understand the constitution and agency of forms of organizing in the arts is par-ticularly important given the high precarity of this setting. CCO research has shown that it is humans and things that make organizations act, while organizations help them act too.

Specifically, CCO scholarship has indicated attribution and appropriation as important aspects through which this happens, and this is even more so in precarious settings such as the arts, where people are willing to work in exchange for being associated with a festival, museum, or programme. Often, certain artworks and activities become appropriated by these organizations in communication above all other mechanisms, be they legal or financial. Therefore, dissecting the specificities of these processes in contexts where aesthetic and poetic gestures are involved, and where human actors often have to act under challenging circumstances, is interesting and relevant for researchers and practitioners alike.

References

Alacovska, A. (2017). The gendering power of genres: How female Scandinavian crime fiction writers experience professional authorship. *Organization, 24*(3), 377–396.

Alvarez, J. L., Mazza, C., Pedersen, J. S., & Svejenova, S. (2005). Shielding idiosyncrasy from isomorphic pressures: Towards optimal distinctiveness in European filmmaking. *Organization, 12*(6), 863–888. https://doi.org/10.1177/1350508405057474.

Aslan, A. (2017). Identity work as an event: Dwelling in the street. *Journal of Management Inquiry, 26*(1), 62–75. https://doi.org/10.1177/1056492616656053.

Austin, J. L. (1962). *How to do things with words*. Oxford: Clarendon Press.

Austin, R., Hjorth, D., & Hessel, S. (2018). How aesthetics and economy become conversant in creative firms. *Organization Studies, 39*(11), 1501–1519. https://doi.org/10.1177/0170840617736940.

Badinella, C., & Chong, D. (2013). Contemporary Afro and two-sidedness: Black diaspora aesthetic practices and the art market. *Culture and Organization, 21*(2), 97–125. https://doi.org/10.1080/14759 551.2013.806507.

Bartels G., & Bencherki N. (2013) Actor-network-theory and creativity research. In E.G. Carayannis (Ed.), *Encyclopedia of creativity, invention, innovation and entrepreneurship*. New York: Springer. https://doi.org/10.1007/978-1-4614-3858-8_51.

Bathurst, R. J., & Williams, L. P. (2013). Managing musically: How acoustic space informs management practice. *Journal of Management Inquiry, 22*(1), 38–49. https://doi.org/10.1177/1056492612464543.

Bazin, Y., & Korica, M. (2020). Aesthetic objects, aesthetic judgments and the crafting of organizational style in creative industries. *Journal of Management Inquiry.* https://doi.org/10.1177/105649262 0916519.

Becker, H. S. (1982). *Art worlds*. Berkeley: University of California Press.

Bencherki, N., & Cooren, F. (2011). Having to be: The possessive constitution of organization. *Human Relations, 64*(12), 1579–1607.

Bencherki, N., & Elmholdt, K. T. (2020). The organization's synaptic mode of existence: How a hospital merger is many things at once. *Organization.* https://doi.org/10.1177/1350508420962025.

Bencherki, N., & Snack, J. P. (2016). Contributorship and partial inclusion: A communicative perspective. *Management Communication Quarterly, 30*(3), 279–304. https://doi.org/10.1177/089331891 5624163.

Bennett, D., & Hennekam, S. (2018). Self-authorship and creative industries workers' career decision-making. *Human Relations, 71*(11), 1454–1477. https://doi.org/10.1177/0018726717747369.

Bennis, W. (2003). Frank Gehry: Artist, leader, and "neotenic". *Journal of Management Inquiry, 12*(1), 81–87. https://doi.org/10.1177/1056492602250521.

Beyes, T. (2010). Uncontained: The art and politics of reconfiguring urban space. *Culture and Organization, 16*(3), 229–246. https://doi.org/10.1080/14759551.2010.503499.

Biehl-Missal, B. (2013). And if I don't want to work like an artist...?: How the study of artistic resistance enriches organizational studies. *Ephemera: Theory & Politics in Organization, 13*(1), 75–98.

Biehl-Missal, B. (2019). Filling the 'empty space': Site-specific dance in a techno club. Culture and *Organization, 25*(1), 16–31. https://doi.org/10.1080/14759551.2016.1206547.

Biehl-Missal, B., & Saner, R. (2014). 'I'm as much an anarchist in theory as I am in practice': Fernando Pessoa's anarchist banker in a management education context. *Ephemera: Theory & Politics in Organization, 14*(4), 985–1007.

Blagoev, B., Costas, J., & Kärreman, D. (2019). 'We are all herd animals': Community and organizationality in coworking spaces. *Organization, 26*(6), 894–916. https://doi.org/10.1177/1350508418821008.

Bottero, W., & Crossley, N. (2011). Worlds, fields and networks: Becker, Bourdieu and the structures of social relations. *Cultural Sociology, 5*(1), 99–119. https://doi.org/10.1177/1749975510389726.

Bourdieu, P. (1983). The forms of capital. In J. G. Richardson (Ed.), *Handbook of theory and research for the sociology of education* (pp. 241–258). New York: Greenwood Press.

Bourdieu, P. (1984). *Homo academicus*. Paris: Les Éditions de Minuit.

Bourdieu, P. (1993). *The Field of Cultural Production*. New York: Columbia Press.

Bourdieu, P. (1994). *Raisons pratiques: Sur la théorie de l'action*. Paris: Seuil.

Bourriaud, N. (1998). *L'esthétique relationelle*. Dijon: Les presses du réel.

Boutinot, A., Joly, I., Mangematin, V., & Ansari, S. (2017). Exploring the links between reputation and fame: Evidence from French contemporary architecture. *Organization Studies, 38*(10), 1397–1420. https://doi.org/10.1177/0170840616670433.

Brown, A. D., Kornberger, M., Clegg, S. K., & Carter, C. (2010). 'Invisible walls' and 'silent hierarchies': A case study of power relations in an architecture firm. *Human Relations, 63*(4), 525–549. https://doi.org/10.1177/0018726709339862.

Brummans, B., Cooren, F., Robichaud, D., & Taylor, J. R. (2014). Approaches in Research on the Communicative Constitution of Organizations. In L. L. Putnam & D. K. Mumby (Eds.), *The Sage handbook of organizational communication* (3rd edn., pp. 173–194). London: Sage.

Byerley, A., & Chong, D. (2015). Biotech aesthetics: Exploring the practice of bio art. *Culture and Organization, 21*(3), 197–216.

Chan, J., Bruce, J., & Gonsalves, R. (2015). Seeking and finding: Creative processes of 21st century painters. *Poetics, 48*, 21–41.

Cinque, S., Nyberg, D., & Starkey, K. (2020). 'Living at the border of poverty': How theater actors maintain their calling through narrative identity work. *Human Relations*. https://doi.org/10.1177/00187 26720908663.

Clarke, J. S., Cornelissen, J. P., & Healey, M. P. (2019). Actions speak louder than words: How figurative language and gesturing in entrepreneurial pitches influences investment judgments. *Academy of Management Journal*, 62(2). https://doi.org/10.5465/amj.2016.1008.

Clegg, S. R., & Burdon, S. (2019). Exploring creativity and innovation in broadcasting. *Human Relations*. https://doi.org/10.1177/0018726719888004.

Cnossen, B. (2018). Creative work, self-organizing and autonomist potentiality: Snapshots taken from Amsterdam's art factories. *European Journal of Cultural Studies*. https://doi.org/10.1177/136754941 8786411.

Cnossen, B., & Bencherki, N. (2018). The role of space in the emergence and endurance of organizing: How independent workers and material assemblages constitute organizations. *Human Relations*, 72(6), 1057–1080. https://doi.org/10.1177/0018726718794265.

Cnossen, B., de Vaujany, F.-X., & Haefliger, S. (2020). The street and organization studies. *Organization Studies*. https://doi.org/10.1177/0170840620918380.

Cooren, F. (2004). Textual agency: How texts do things in organizational settings. *Organization*, 11(3), 373–393.

Cooren, F. (2018). Materializing communication: Making the case for a relational ontology. *Journal of Communication*, 68(2), 278–288. https://doi.org/10.1093/joc/jqx014.

Cooren, F. (2020). Beyond entanglement: (Socio-) Materiality and organization studies. *Organization Theory*, 1(3), 1–24. https://doi.org/10.1177/2631787720954444.

Cooren F., & Bencherki N. (2010). How Things do things with words: Ventriloquism, passion and technology. *Encyclopaideia, Journal of Phenomenology and Education*, 14(28), 35–62.

De Glas, F. (1998). Authors' oeuvres as the backbone of publishers' lists: Studying the literary publishing house after Bourdieu. *Poetics*, 25(6), 379–397. https://doi.org/10.1016/S0304-422X(98)90009-2.

De Molli, F., Mengis, J., & Van Marrewijk, A. (2019). The aestheticization of hybrid space: The atmosphere of the Locarno Film Festival. *Organization Studies*, 1–22. https://doi.org/10.1177/017084061 9867348.

Den Hartog Jager, H. (2011). *Het sublieme: het einde van de schoonheid en een nieuw begin*. Amsterdam: Athenaeum-Polak & Van Gennep.

Den Hartog Jager, H. (2014). *Het streven: Kan hedendaagse kunst de wereld verbeteren?*. Amsterdam: Athenaeum-Polak & Van Gennep.

DiMaggio, P. (1982). Cultural entrepreneurship in nineteenth-century Boston: The creation of an organizational base for high culture in America. *Media, Culture & Society*, 4(1), 33–50. https://doi.org/ 10.1177/016344378200400104.

DiMaggio, P. (1996). Are art-museum visitors different from other people? The relationship between attendance and social and political attitudes in the United States. *Poetics*, 24(2–4), 161–180. https:// doi.org/10.1016/S0304-422X(96)00008-3.

DiMaggio, P., & Useem, M. (1978). Social class and arts consumption. *Theory and Society 5*, 141–161. https://doi.org/10.1007/BF01702159.

Dobusch, L., & Schoeneborn, D. (2015). Fluidity, identity, and organizationality: The communicative constitution of Anonymous. *Journal of Management Studies*, 52(8), 1005–1035. https://doi.org/ 10.1111/joms.12139.

Doorman, M. (2012). *De romantische orde*. Amsterdam: Bert Bakker.

Duff, C., & Sumartojo, S. (2017). Assemblages of creativity: Material practices in the creative economy. *Organization*, 24(3), 418–432. https://doi.org/10.1177/1350508416687765.

Ebbers, J. J., & Wijnberg, N. M. (2012). The effects of having more than one good reputation on distributor investments in the film industry. *Journal of Cultural Economics*, 36(3), 227–248. https://doi.org/ 10.1007/s10824-012-9160-z.

Elias, S. R. S. T. A., Chiles, T. H., Duncan, C. M., & Vultee, D. M. (2018). The aesthetics of entrepreneurship: How arts entrepreneurs and their customers co-create aesthetic value. *Organization Studies*, 39(2–3), 345–372. https://doi.org/10.1177/0170840617717548.

Endrissat, N., Kärreman, D., & Noppeney, C. (2017). Incorporating the creative subject: Branding outside–in through identity incentives. *Human Relations*, 70(4), 488–515. https://doi.org/10.1177/00187 26716661617.

Essex, E. M., & Mainemelis, C. (2002). Learning from an artist about organizations: The poetry and prose of David Whyte at work. *Journal of Management Inquiry, 11*(2), 148–159. https://doi.org/10.1177/10592602011002008.

Finkel, R., Jones, D., Sang, K., & Russell, D. S. (2017). Diversifying the creative: Creative work, creative industries, creative identities. *Organization, 24*(3), 281–288. https://doi.org/10.1177/1350508417690167.

Farías, I., & Wilkie, A. (2018). *Studio studies: Operations, topologies & displacements.* London: Routledge.

Gielen, P. (2013). Introduction. In: P. Gielen (Ed.), *Institutional attitudes: Instituting art in a flat world.* Amsterdam: Valiz.

Gill, R., Pratt, A. C., & Virani, T. E. (2019). *Creative hubs in question. Place, space and work in the creative economy.* London: Palgrave Macmillan.

Gotsi, M., Andriopoulos, C., Lewis, M. W., & Ingram, A. E. (2010). Managing creatives: Paradoxical approaches to identity regulation. *Human Relations, 63*(6), 781–805. https://doi.org/10.1177/0018726709342929.

Groleau, C., Demers, C., Lalancette, M., & Barros, M. (2012). From hand drawings to computer visuals: Confronting situated and institutionalized practices in an architecture firm. *Organization Science, 23*(3), 651–671. https://doi.org/10.1287/orsc.1110.0667.

Groys, B. (2002). The loneliness of the project. *New York Magazine of Contemporary Art and Theory, 1*(1).

Hancock, P., & Spicer, A. (2011). Academic architecture and the constitution of the new model worker. *Culture and Organization, 17*(2), 91–105.

Haunschild, A. (2003). Managing employment relationships in flexible labour markets: The case of German repertory theatres. *Human Relations, 56*(8), 899–929. https://doi.org/10.1177/00187267030568001.

Hesmondhalgh, D., & Baker, S. (2011). *Creative labour: Media work in three cultural industries.* London: Routledge.

Hoedemaekers, C. (2018). Creative work and affect: Social, political and fantasmatic dynamics in the labour of musicians. *Human Relations, 71*(10), 1348–1370. https://doi.org/10.1177/0018726717741355.

Humphreys, M., Ucbasaran, D., & Lockett, A. (2011). Sensemaking and sensegiving stories of jazz leadership. *Human Relations, 65*(1), 41–62. https://doi.org/10.1177/0018726711424320.

Huopalainen, A. (2015). Who moves? Analyzing fashion show organizing through micro-interactions of bodily movement. *Ephemera: Theory & Politics in Organization, 15*(4), 825–846.

Janssens, M., & Steyaert, C. (2019). The site of diversalizing: The accomplishment of inclusion in intergenerational dance. *Journal of Mangaement Studies, 57*(6), 1143–1173. https://doi.org/10.1111/joms.12524.

Jiang, Z., & Korczynski, M. (2019). The art of labour organizing: Participatory art and migrant domestic workers' self-organizing in London. *Human Relations.* https://doi.org/10.1177/0018726719890664.

Johansson, M., & Toraldo, M. L. (2017). 'From mosh pit to posh pit': Festival imagery in the context of the boutique festival. *Culture and Organization, 23*(3), 220–237.

Jones, D., & Smith, K. (2005). Middle-earth meets New Zealand: Authenticity and location in the making of The Lord of the Rings. *Journal of Management Studies, 42*(5), 923–945. https://doi.org/10.1111/j.1467-6486.2005.00527.x.

Jones, C., Svejenova, S., Strandgaard Pedersen, J., & Townley, B. (2016). Misfits, mavericks and mainstreams: Drivers of innovation in the creative industries. *Organization Studies, 37*(6), 751–768. https://doi.org/10.1177/0170840616647671.

Kauppinen, A., & Daskalaki, M. (2015). 'Becoming other': Entrepreneuring as subversive organising. *Ephemera: Theory & Politics in Organization, 15*(3), 601–620.

Kuhn, T. (2021). (Re)moving blinders: communication-as-constitutive theorizing as provocation to practice-based organization scholarship. *Management Learning, 52*(1), 109–121.

Kuhn, T., Ashcraft, K. L., & Cooren, F. (2017). *The work of communication: Relational perspectives on working and organizing in contemporary capitalism.* London: Routledge.

Kuipers, G. (2011). Cultural globalization as the emergence of a transnational cultural field: Transnational television and national media landscapes in four European countries. *American Behavioral Scientist, 55*(5), 541–557. https://doi.org/10.1177/0002764211398078.

Lampel, J., Lant, T., & Shamsie, J. (2000). Balancing act: Learning from organizing practices in cultural industries. *Organization Science, 11*, 263–9.

Latham, S. D. (2014). Leadership research: An arts-informed perspective. *Journal of Management Inquiry*, *23*(2), 123–132. https://doi.org/10.1177/1056492613491434.

Laurey, N. (2019). Design meets Business: an ethnographic field study of the changing work and occupations of creatives. Doctoral Dissertation, Amsterdam Business Research Institute.

Lindell, J., Jakobsson, P., & Stiernstedt, F. (2020). The field of television production: Genesis, structure and position-takings. *Poetics, 80*. https://doi.org/10.1016/j.poetic.2019.101432.

Lindgren, M., Packendorff, J., & Sergi, V. (2014). Thrilled by the discourse, suffering through the experience: Emotions in project-based work. *Human Relations, 67*(11), 1383–1412. https://doi.org/10.1177/0018726713520022.

Mairesse, P. (2014). Reversal: le partage de la parole comme expérience sensible, esthétique, et politique. Doctoral Dissertation, Paris 1 & Rijksuniversiteit te Utrecht.

Malik, S., Chapain, C., & Comunian, R. (2017). Rethinking cultural diversity in the UK film sector: Practices in community filmmaking. *Organization, 24*(3), 308–329. https://doi.org/10.1177/1350508416689094.

Martine, T., Cooren, F., & Bartels, G. (2017). Evaluating creativity through the degrees of solidity of its assessment: A relational approach. *Journal of Creative Behavior, 53*(4), 427–442. https://doi.org/10.1002/jocb.219.

Mathieu, C., & Stjerne, I. S. (2015). Artistic practices over the course of careers in film. In T. Zembylas (Ed.), *Artistic practices, social interactions and cultural dynamics*. London: Routledge.

McRobbie, A. (2015). *Be creative: Making a living in the new culture industries*. London: Polity.

Meisiek, S., & Barry, D. (2007). Through the looking glass of organizational theatre: Analogically mediated inquiry in organizations. *Organization Studies, 28*(12), 1805–1827. https://doi.org/10.1177/0170840607078702.

Montanari, F., Scapolan, A., & Gianecchini, M. (2016). 'Absolutely free'? The role of relational work in sustaining artistic innovation. *Organization Studies, 37*(6), 797–821. https://doi.org/10.1177/01708 40616647419.

Munro, I., & Jordan, S. (2013). 'Living space' at the Edinburgh Festival Fringe: Spatial tactics and the politics of smooth space. *Human Relations, 66*(11), 1497–1525. https://doi.org/10.1177/001872671 3480411.

Moeran, B. (2012). A business anthropological approach to the study of values: Evaluative practices in ceramic art. *Culture and Organization, 18*(3), 195–210. https://doi.org/10.1080/14759551.2011.634193.

Moretti, A., & Zirpoli, F. (2016). A dynamic theory of network failure: The case of the Venice Film Festival and the local hospitality system. *Organization Studies, 37*(5), 607–633. https://doi.org/10.1177/01708 40615613369.

Nicotera, A. M. (2013). Organizations as entitative beings. In D. Robichaud & F. Cooren (Eds.), *Organization & organizing: Materiality, agency, and discourse* (pp. 66–89). New York: Routledge.

Peck, J. (2012). Recreative city: Amsterdam, vehicular ideas and the adaptive spaces of creativity policy. *International Journal of Urban and Regional Research, 36*(3), 462 485.

Rindova, V., Dalpiaz, E., & Ravasi, D. (2011). A cultural quest: A study of organizational use of new cultural resources in strategy formation. *Organization Science, 22*(2), 413–431. https://doi.org/10.1287/orsc.1100.0537.

Rowlands, L., & Handy, J. (2012). An addictive environment: New Zealand film production workers' subjective experiences of project-based labour. *Human Relations, 65*(5), 657–680. https://doi.org/10.1177/0018726711431494.

Santoro, M. (2011). From Bourdieu to cultural sociology. *Cultural Sociology, 5*(1), 3–23. https://doi.org/10.1177/1749975510397861.

Schoeneborn, D. (2013). The pervasive power of PowerPoint: How a genre of professional communication permeates organizational communication. *Organization Studies, 34*(12), 1777–1801. https://doi.org/10.1177/0170840613485843.

Schoeneborn, D., Kuhn, T. R., & Kärreman, D. (2019). The communicative constitution of organization, organizing, and organizationality. *Organization Studies, 40*(4), 475–496. https://doi.org/10.1177/0170840618782284.

Scott, M. (2012). Cultural entrepreneurs, cultural entrepreneurship: Music producers mobilising and converting Bourdieu's alternative capitals. *Poetics, 40*(3), 237–255.

Serino, M., D'Ambrosio, D., & Ragozini, G. (2017). Bridging social network analysis and field theory through multidimensional data analysis: The case of the theatrical field. *Poetics, 62*, 66–80. https://doi.org/10.1016/j.poetic.2016.12.002.

Simpson, R., Irvine, K., Balta, M., & Dickson, K. (2015). Emotions, performance and entrepreneurship in the context of fringe theatre. *Organization, 22*(1), 100–118. https://doi.org/10.1177/135050841 3504020.

Sivunen, A., & Putnam, L. L. (2020). The dialectics of spatial performances: The interplay of tensions in activity-based organizing. *Human Relations, 73*(8), 1129–1156. https://doi.org/10.1177/001872671 9857117.

Skoglund, A., & Holt, R. (2020). Spatially organizing future genders: An artistic intervention in the creation of a hir-toilet. *Human Relations.* https://doi.org/10.1177/0018726719899728.

Sommerlund, J., & Strandvad, S. M. (2012). The promises of talent: Performing potentiality. *Theory & Psychology, 22*(2), 179–195. https://doi.org/10.1177/0959354311432561.

Sørensen, B. M., & Villadsen, K. (2015). The naked manager: The ethical practice of an anti-establishment boss. *Organization, 22*(2), 251–268. https://doi.org/10.1177/1350508414558722.

Stigliani, I., & Ravasi, D. (2018). The shaping of form: Exploring designers' use of aesthetic knowledge. *Organization Studies, 39*(5–6), 747–784. https://doi.org/10.1177/0170840618759813.

Strandvad, S. M. (2011). Materializing ideas: A socio-material perspective on the organizing of cultural production. *European Journal of Cultural Studies, 14*(3), 283–297. https://doi.org/10.1177/136754941 0396615.

Strandvad, S. M. (2012). Organizing for the auteur: A dual case study of debut filmmaking. *MedieKultur, 28*(53). 118–135. https://doi.org/10.7146/mediekultur.v28i53.5523.

Strati, A. (1999). *Organization and aesthetics.* London: Sage.

Svensson, J. (2017). Visions and politics in the making of Stockholm's House of Culture: Institutional complexity within extraordinary projects. *Culture and Organization, 23*(3), 197–219. https://doi.org/10.1080/14759551.2015.1029926.

Taylor, J. R., & Van Every, E. J. (2000). *The emergent organization: Communication as its site and surface.* Lawrence Erlbaum Associates.

Taylor, J. R. & Van Every, E. J. (2011). *The situated organization: Case studies in the pragmatics of communication research.* New York: Routledge.

Thornton, S. (2008). *Seven days in the art world.* London: Granta.

Townley, B., Beech, N., & McKinlay, A. (2009). Managing in the creative industries: Managing the motley crew. *Human Relations, 62*(7), 939–962. https://doi.org/10.1177/0018726709335542.

Umney, C. (2016). The labour market for jazz musicians in Paris and London: Formal regulation and informal norms. *Human Relations, 69*(3), 711–729. https://doi.org/10.1177/0018726715596803.

Van den Abeele, H. O. (2020). Materialising careers: The role of artefacts in career making. Doctoral Dissertation, University of Nottingham.

Wasserman, V., & Frenkel, M. (2011). Organizational aesthetics: Caught between identity regulation and culture jamming. *Organization Science, 22*(2), 503–521. https://doi.org/10.1287/orsc.1100.0583.

Wasserman, V., & Frenkel, M. (2015). Spatial work in between glass ceilings and glass walls: Gender-class intersectionality and organizational aesthetics. *Organization Studies, 36*(11), 1485–1505.

Wikberg, E. (2020). Polysemy and plural institutional logics. *Culture and Organization.* https://doi.org/10.1080/14759551.2020.1780596.

Wilhoit, E. D., & Kisselburgh, L. G. (2015). Collective action without organization: The material constitution of bike commuters as collective. *Organization Studies, 36*(5), 573–592. https://doi.org/10.1177/0170840614556916.

Zundel, M., Holt, R., & Cornelissen, J. (2013). Institutional work in *The Wire*: An ethological investigation of flexibility in organizational adaptation. *Journal of Management Inquiry, 22*(1), 102–120. https://doi.org/10.1177/1056492612440045.

30

CCO IN PRACTICE

Spacing and Humanitarian Organizing

Oana Brindusa Albu and Neva Štumberger

The ways in which spacing influences organizing have received increasing attention in organizational research. In recent years, more scholars have turned to the *communication constitutes organization* (CCO) lens to study *spacing assemblages* as the relational weaving of practices, conversations, texts, and other elements that create the practiced, communicative, lived, and even affective qualities of space (Cnossen & Bencherki, 2018; Vásquez & Cooren, 2013; Wilhoit & Kisselburgh, 2015). Such communicative interest is relevant, not the least, for it allows us to explore the manifold consequences of spacing and challenge the assumption that human beings are the only architects of space. In fact, the importance of examining spacing in a humanitarian context is particularly timely because of the unintended social and political implications for those living and working in such contexts. For instance, the so-called refugee[1] crisis following the post-2015 Syrian conflict is an indicative situation of the highly contested ways in which non-governmental organizations (NGOs) engage in spacing: building shelters, predicting movements of refugees, assessing needs, etc., all of which affect both workers and asylum seekers. Research on spatiality and humanitarianism has widely demonstrated that NGOs turn refugee camps into spaces of intensified humanitarian control (Hyndman, 2000). Yet an understanding of the different and unpredictable human and non-human agencies involved in these assemblages in contexts of social and political turmoil is limited (Beyes & Steayert, 2012). The aim of this chapter is therefore to examine the implications of spacing assemblages by drawing on an empirical case of an NGO working in a forced migration hotspot.

While spacing has been widely studied in organizational literature (Taylor & Spicer, 2007), oftentimes there is little interest in the fundamental and formative roles of *spacing assemblages* that act in often unexpected and volatile ways and constitute organizations (see for notable exceptions Cnossen & Bencherki, 2018; Kuhn & Burke, 2014; Wilhoit & Kisselburgh, 2015). As a result, there is a tendency to overlook how agencies are impeded, contested, resisted, or constrained by other relations and agents as a form of transgressing spatial boundaries, and research calls are made for the investigation of such phenomena (Clegg, 1994; Mumby et al., 2017). This is because spacing implies "control through fixing [...] everything and everybody [...] in their rightful places" (Dale & Burrell, 2008, p. 53) and therefore one would always expect resistance to take place. Studies have indeed shown that the spacing activities that are the *raison d'etre* of humanitarian NGOs—placing individuals into shelters that offer emergency aid—are based on forms of humanitarian control that may generate conflicting identities, resistance, and integration problems among both workers and refugees, all of which impede the

DOI: 10.4324/9781003224914-35

ability of these organizations to survive (Thorleifsson, 2016). Yet, there is little knowledge about how spacing assemblages are at the center of such forms of control.

To tackle such a dilemma, this chapter is phenomenon-driven and uses a communication constitutes organization (CCO) lens to understand the implications of spacing and humanitarian organizing in more depth. Accordingly, we bring forward the importance of a communicative approach to spacing, especially in relation to NGOs and forced migration, which sheds lights on the agencies and significant social and political consequences of spacing assemblages. Methodologically, we build on ethnographic methods to describe complex spatial assemblages found in refugee camps. As such, the chapter has a twofold contribution. First, it adds to the literature on space and organizing by mapping how spatial configurations exhibit agencies that are formed through communicative relations between agents, but also how these agencies are impeded, restricted, or constrained by other agents, relations, or assemblages. Secondly, the chapter contributes to CCO research by showing how such a lens is relevant for practice by allowing practitioners to consider political and ethical aspects in humanitarian organizing. Based on these findings, we put forward brief practical considerations potentially relevant for identifying the complexities specific to NGO spacing in a context of forced migration.

The chapter proceeds as follows: the first section explores the relation between organizing, space, and communication. Next, we introduce a framework inspired by the CCO tradition to explore how spatial assemblages situate actors[2] in space while shaping the actions occurring within it in unpredictable and contested ways. After the methodology and case are described, the analysis illustrates the spacing practices of an NGO that operates in a migration hotspot. The last section discusses the limitations of the study and offers few practical considerations and suggestions for future research.

Theoretical Framework

Organizational Space

Research shows that spatiality and organizing are tightly entangled, as space is simultaneously "a social product and a generative force" of organizing practices (Beyes & Steyaert, 2012, p. 48). The production of space is subject to complex processes that amount to not only of "thinking space" (Vásquez et al., 2017), but also of inhabiting and practicing it (Lefebvre, 1991). Space is then both a physical and social landscape which is created by everyday social practices. Space is important as it can trigger identification and meaning-making in organizations, or the loss of it. For instance, when mobile elite workers are situated mostly in "non-places" (Gregory, 2011)—that is, ephemeral, interchangeable, and monotonous spaces of mobility—workers are faced with experiences of ambiguity, disorientation, and loss (Costas, 2013). In this respect, space can be viewed as a specific location, as a wider territory, as consisting of networks, and finally as extending over different scales (Jessop et al., 2008). In other words, space is constituted through communication, actions, and movements, as well as through naming, memories, and living and inhabiting the space. Artifacts and practices are therefore interwoven and dependent on each other (Beyes & Steyaert, 2012).

The attempt to examine space and organizing confronts one with important analytical issues. Research typically draws on Lefebvre's seminal work (1974/1991) to argue that space is not simply a structure but is also practiced in unpredictable ways. Calls are made for rethinking of space as "processual and performative, open-ended and multiple, practiced and of the everyday" (Beyes & Steyaert, 2012, p. 47). For instance, Iedema et al. (2010) showed that the corridor in an outpatient clinic was used in practice not simply to pass between functional rooms. Rather, in the liminal space of the corridor, clinicians temporarily suspended professional distances and engaged in cross-boundary collaborations and "reflection-on/-in action". A liminal space then transcends the presumed conceived or planned qualities of space. Such space is perceived and lived because entities that practice space are "neither here, nor there; but betwixt and between the positions assigned and arrayed by law, custom, convention, and ceremonial" (Turner, 1969, p. 95).

Building on these considerations, this chapter conceptualizes space as not only "produced" by its architects, but also as imagined, represented, and resisted by different objects, bodies, sites, and technologies (Ashcraft et al., 2009). We regard space to be a nexus of not only social structures but also technological and material configurations (such as objects, metrics, ranks, technologies, etc.), where all equally perform the multiple dimensions of space. Space, in this respect, participates in organizing processess. Space is a key ingredient in organizational constitution, existence, and action because space is implicated in both orienting and constraining action and agencies in predictable and unpredictable manners (Cnossen & Bencherki, 2018; see also Wilhoit & Kisselburgh, 2015). We detail such line of thinking about space in the following section.

A Communicative Approach to Spacing

This chapter builds on a communicative view on how spacing as a form of organizing comes to be. Specifically, we use the CCO lens to investigate how space is being produced in the first place (spatial contiguity and alignments, as well as the misalignments, challenges, and negotiations that get constituted through communication), and how the particular human and material composition of a given assemblage results in those effects. In other words, a communicative framework of space enables us to examine the heterogeneous social and material relations that constitute space.

Thinking in terms of *assembling space* allows both considering the individual elements that compose it, and recognizing that its practice cannot be reduced to any single one of them, but rather proceeds from their relational weaving (Cnossen & Bencherki, 2018). The term "assemblage" corresponds to "the processes of arranging, organizing, and fitting together" (Livesay, 2010, p. 18). It suggests the activity of assembling the components rather than the static result of putting different elements together (Thanem, 2011).

Communication is central to such processes. Thus, it is from their ability to communicate—that is, to establish a link, connection, or relationship through something—that the elements of an assemblage can gain their agency, and act in both predictable and unpredictable ways (Vásquez & Cooren, 2013). Applying the CCO lens, communication (as treated in this chapter) then not only concerns (1) how human beings constitute space while speaking with one other about space, but also (2) how material non-human elements communicate to individuals and "space" them in certain locations and (3) how humans communicate through the way they inhabit or resist space by fleeing confined zones, refusing specific identities or dismissing organizational policies.

Following such thinking, we argue that the concept of *assemblage* as a unit of analysis is particularly useful for the understanding of resistance and unintended implications of spacing practices (Cooren et al., 2014). This is because (as we illustrate later in this chapter) elements of spatial assemblages (e.g., a sandbag on the road, a letter or a sign on a wooden pole) can be read, pointed at, or referred to by interlocutors in different ways, with different implications for how the process of organizing comes to be and evolves. Often, such action occurs without intended awareness from human actors who, too, constitute space (Wilhoit & Kisselburgh, 2015). For instance, spatial assemblages act by supplying motives and obligations *to* actors for organizing themselves in certain ways to provide care to refugees (e.g., walk across certain pathways, arrange wooden structures in a specific way, or deliver supplies to specific groups in a refugee camp). But elements of spatial assemblages (natural forces such as drought, inaccurate migration tracking reports, alternative routes, etc.) also act by fostering resistance and disrupting organizing. Resistance, as a product of spacing, then is a process that involves multiple agencies, in which the social and material cannot be separated and in which humans never act alone (Wilhoit & Kisselburgh, 2019). In this respect, it is inevitable that refugee camps are *spacing assemblages* performed by human and non-humans in conflicting ways, and their implications are little understood. There is thus a need to account for how agencies of human and non-human elements form relations and act together to reach a common objective, especially when these communicative relations between humans, non-humans and assemblages can also constrain and disrupt organizing. For example, as described above, a sign on a wooden pole in a refugee camp displaying "Kitchen" acts in conjunction with a volunteer by directing her to what facility she can walk to and what activities (cook, deliver food rations, etc.) and identities she can take on (e.g., cook). At the same time, inaccurate reports about incoming refugee populations act to decide and select which populations receive food supplies and which not, thus restricting the activities of the cook, disrupting aid processes and prompting her to engage in resistance.

Overall, the communicative approach to spacing is especially valuable to studying organizing in the humanitarian context because it allows an examination of "action in all its forms" (Vásquez & Cooren, 2013, p. 29)—including of how both human and non-human elements of spacing assemblages form humanitarian organizing. Due to our organizational focus this chapter zooms in on the spacing practices of one NGO, but we also take into account how other organizations and institutional actors (NGOs, local authorities, political fractions, religious leaders, etc.) can sometimes be involved in spacing assemblages. We also acknowledge the partiality of our observations of the NGO's spacing activities, and thus regard such spacing assemblages to be intimately bound up with a temporality of liminality and enduring temporariness (Ramadan, 2013). That is, the camp exists in a "zone of indistinction" between permanence and transience: "a temporary suspension of the rule of law [...] is now given a permanent spatial arrangement" (Agamben, 1998, p. 169). In these respects, in order to better understand humanitarian spacing and its consequences on organizing, we investigate the following research question:

RQ: How do spacing assemblages shape NGOs' organizing in a migration hotspot?

Methods

Data Contextualization

Empirically, this chapter builds on six months of fieldwork conducted by the first author in 2016 in QPC (a pseudonym), an NGO that aids asylum seekers in Lebanon in the North Bekaa Valley and Beirut. This geographical context was selected because Lebanon is a country that had (at the time of the study) the third highest influx of forced migration worldwide (UNCHR, 2016). The poverty of states such as Lebanon that host refugees is the reason why NGOs such as QPC voluntarily assume the task of raising donations from states and individuals and launch appeals to support the relief programs they mount.

Data Collection

The data collection was based on interviews and observant participation conducted across different in-office and in-field locations with five workers from QPC. The data set incorporates the following: (a) fieldnotes from observations, which amounted to 115 single-spaced pages; and (b) 16 interviews, with an average length of 40 min. Eleven interviews were conducted with QPC managers and five with QPC volunteers. Interviews were transcribed into a document of 127 single-spaced pages. In addition, (c) documentary data containing emails, reports, documentation of different activities and events (providing emergency aid, fund raising, etc.) related to QPC was gathered and compiled in a document of 256 single-spaced pages.

Data Analysis

The first step of the data analysis was open coding. We iteratively clustered the data until we could identify the informants' most relevant practices in relation to space. To classify practices, we relied on situational mapping, which is a relational analytic tool that starts with the observed situation as the unit of analysis. The analysis included questions such as: who, what, and through what practices are involved in spacing? What human (workers, volunteers, etc.) and non-human elements (tents, reports, etc.) are implicated in spacing? The goal of this method is aligned with the CCO tradition and explores an organizational situation by analyzing "all of the analytically pertinent human and nonhuman, material, and symbolic/discursive elements of a particular situation as framed by those in it and by the analyst" (Clarke, 2005, p. 87). Through situational mapping, we thus conducted a relational analysis by comparing situations to show who/what were the actors present in practices, their relations with others, and how they communicated as an assemblage (see Table 30.1). We focused particularly on those assemblages and spacing practices that contributed to the humanitarian organizing of QPC and identified two central themes that structure our findings: *shelters* depicting how these elements control individuals by sorting and situating them in space; and *WASH structures and community centers* illustrating how these elements engender different identities and roles. For each theme, we also show practices of resistance.

It is critical to mention that it is impossible to provide an exhaustive framework of the different spatial assemblages of QPC in this chapter, since such an attempt would fall short of

Table 30.1 Actors, agents, and relations within spacing assemblages

Actors	Agents
Workers, volunteers, refugees, donors, state authorities.	Tents, wooden structures, sandbags, reports, Shelters, WASH structures and community centers, natural territories

Junction of individuals, space, assemblages ↔ identities and organizing

Refugee identities are produced by the junction of individuals with the space and practices happening in these spaces (e.g., an individual living in a shelter or cooking a meal in a center is a refugee; an individual building a WASH center is a worker). These processes in turn create organizing.

Dis-junction of individuals, spaces, assemblages ↔ resistance and dis-organizing

Resistance is produced by the dis-junction of individuals with the space through fleeing or quitting practices (e.g., refugees flee to escape assigned identities and shelter conditions or flooding, drought, etc.; workers move to other functions or quit). These processes in turn create dis-organizing.

an effective analysis of the refugee camp (Ramadan, 2013). Moreover, the focus here is on the organizing of QPC and not on asylum seekers, even though they deserve undivided attention. We selected this focus because of ethical considerations for the vulnerability of asylum seekers. Studies of real-world refugee camps cannot be reduced to a formulaic reading of spaces of exception filled with silenced and disempowered individuals (Agamben, 1998). Such writings risk losing sight of the complex resistance dynamics within refugee camps, and the possibilities of agency on the part of refugees themselves (Thorleifsson, 2016). Therefore, the analysis presented next focuses on the different agencies inhabiting spacing assemblages and their implications for organizing.

Spacing Assemblages of QPC

QPC is part of a network of NGOs that exercise control in different camps, given the lack of a sovereign state. The different mandates of transnational humanitarian institutions (the United Nations, etc.) create a void filled by the activities of smaller NGOs such as QPC. At the time of the fieldwork, QPC had been working in Lebanon for four years to build settlements, and to provide emergency services for vulnerable incoming populations (Syrian and Palestinian Syrian asylum seekers) that experienced forced migration. The two spacing assemblages described in the analysis are contextually dependent on collective interactions that transcend the local communicative situation in which they are enacted. As described next, these spatial assemblages contribute to the humanitarian (dis-)organizing of QPC through their (in)capacity to control movements of QPC workers and constituents, coproduce specific identities such as workers and refugees, and generate resistance to both confined movements and assigned identities.

Shelters

Shelters are white informal tented settlements built by QPC. An official document with directives from local authorities dictates to QPC workers how a shelter should look ("no permanent structures, no concrete, just wood and plastic"). Shelters communicate, on the one hand, a sense of duty and belonging to QPC workers by fostering their identification with QPC: "this is why *we* are here. It's what *we* do", says a volunteer while pointing on a map that showed the distribution of new QPC shelters. On the other hand, these structures communicate where asylum seekers should be placed upon arrival in the camp. In this respect, shelters control the movements of refugees and are spaces of intensified humanitarian control (Hyndman, 2000). For instance, bags filled with sand act as a physical boundary between tents and form pathways that direct where refugees and QPC workers can walk across camps. The movements of QPC members and volunteers working within the shelters are therefore equally controlled by the spatial configuration of these structures. Nevertheless, inclusions and exclusions among refugees are made based on criteria such as gender, family relations, country of origin, or assessed needs. The protection monitoring report of QPC sets such criteria which are key to the organizing of the camp. Specifically, the report has agency because it communicates which forcefully displaced person is to be placed in which shelter and who will benefit from aid services. The agency of the report is, however, highly contested, impeded and hindered by the agencies and relations of other elements of the assemblage such as donors and territories, as indicated in the fieldnote excerpt below:

> We are in a *hilly area* near Beirut. Two workers are standing under a wooden frame that will soon be fixed with a plastic cover and function as a wall for a new shelter. One of

the workers adds in response to my question about who or what decides where individuals are settled: "What *we* do is to implement a 'protection-monitoring program' in refugee communities in North Lebanon and the Bekaa settlements. We monitor refugee communities in order to understand their evolving protection concerns. *Then we create a report that places those refugees in appropriate shelters.* We, of course, don't want to produce metrics that satisfy the needs of the international agencies and donors rather than those of asylum seekers. Others [NGOs] do it. It's all a headache. [laughs] NGO1 never discloses any accurate numbers since they do not want to create panic. NGO2 are less politicized since they have their own donors, so they are more flexible. We, too, work with smaller ones [donors] and we are free to produce our own numbers [of asylum seekers in the reports]. *But these [numbers] change and of course donors' requirements as well.* It is often impossible to track them [asylum seekers] accurately because of the *vast areas at the borders.* So, it's really difficult but the *report decides in the end where everyone goes."*

fieldnote, interview, QPC worker, February 19, 2016, emphasis added

As the QPC worker indicates and as observed on many occasions, the different elements of the shelter assemblage (reports, natural forces, tents, donors, QPC workers and asylum seekers) exhibit unpredictable agencies that collide with each other and affect the ability of QPC to organize. Namely, the spatial assemblage of shelters and the way they are positioned across the camp have agency in that they accommodate incoming vulnerable populations. In so doing, shelters control where people can move, and coproduce specific identities (workers, volunteers, asylum seekers). The protection monitoring report decides where asylum seekers are to be placed and what type of aid they receive, but the report communicates changing numbers about incoming populations because it fails to predict their moves. The agency of the report thus collides with the agencies of asylum seekers, which resist tracking. This fluctuating nature of the report creates unpredictable agencies in terms of designating which asylum seekers need aid. As a result, the report also impacts QPC relations with donors. Donors change their funding requirements based on the reporting they receive, thus exhibiting agencies that often constrain and impede the agencies of QPC workers, volunteers, refugees, and shelters.

The contested and volatile nature of these agencies present in the assemblage of a refugee camp prompted both QPC volunteers and refugees to engage in resistance. Asylum seekers transgressed the spatial rules of the shelters and established hidden routes in search of alternative locations with better access to different facilities. As confirmed by three informants, this happened because asylum seekers did not receive the (expected) protection and placement in shelters from the authorities unless they were financially well-off or had the right connections. Feeling hopeless and apathetic, QPC workers also refrained from doing their job because their agency was restricted by other agents and their relations (for instance, the government). Two workers ultimately quit as an act of definitive resistance due to the conditions of the shelters:

We could not register legally any refugees here in the past two years due to *legislation roadblocks.* The government does not want any permanent structures nor refugees in shelters, as they saw what happened to the Palestinian ones. They are pools of economic drainage, radicalization. Also, there are historical developments with Syria. The [Syrian] army withdrawn in 2006, so then you have all of them coming here in so massive numbers. We have come to think nobody [from the local communities] wants them. So, it's *difficult for us to provide proper assistance in the shelters.* They [asylum seekers] move around despite they risk being arrested because they do not have residence or work permits. So, you start questioning what you do and why. You lose hope often, and you are here to help so it means you cannot do your job properly. We see many staff leaving to other places because of this.

QPC worker, staff meeting, emphasis added

The findings suggest that, in addition to material and human agencies specific to the shelter assemblages, it is also the larger political context of Lebanon and its "legislative roadblocks" that shapes QPC organizing. Assemblages are, then, populated by a *mélange* of agencies, relations and agents that can be at odds with each other and exacerbate resistance and generate feelings of despair, desolation, and apathy. Shelters and their related practices (building tents, reports and metrics, legislative measures, etc.) all make a difference in the organizing of QPC.

WASH and Community Centers

WASH are temporary structures that provide access to water, sanitation, and hygiene. Community centers are mobile structures with several rooms used for gatherings and other joint activities, while "ghatas" are structures that function as portable classrooms. QPC volunteers and refugees assemble these structures together from low-cost locally found materials. QPC workers aim to imbue these spacing assemblages with affective qualities in order to generate feelings of trust, support, safety and hospitality in such alien spaces outside of refugees' home countries. For instance, to assess the perceived safety in these spaces, QPC uses the protection monitoring report based on asking refugees to provide a reading of their community on a scale from one to five. Such assemblage of mobile wooden structures, metrics and reports establishes a space for QPC's humanitarian activities while attempting to assign identities for both workers and the asylum seekers placed within these spaces. Specifically, these assemblages dictate, on the one hand, what it means to be an employee or volunteer of QPC (e.g., providing aid in education, child protection, nutrition, and food safety). On the other hand, assemblages specify what it means to be an asylum seeker. Wooden signs (kitchen, school, etc.) co-constitute identities of asylum seekers by indicating how these groups are different by being physically separated from others and designating them with different roles (cook, pupil, etc.). In this sense, spacing assemblages actively shape identity formation and preservation processes, in which refugees' identities and their central ambitions (e.g., to return to their country of origin; Ramadan, 2009) are being reproduced and sustained.

Resistance occurs because individuals are bound to face a myriad of unexpected and unplanned agencies (e.g., obstacles created by donors in accessing funding, aggressive local authorities, hostile natural forces such as flooding, drought, etc.) that generate contextual shifts in meaningfulness, and in turn dis- or mis-identification (Florian et al., 2018). One of the factors that creates resistance is the failure or inability to prepare for the volatile agencies that inhabit these assemblages:

Honestly, we are not able to provide a straightforward answer to the simple question, 'how many refugees are here [in the region]' and, as a result, our *efforts of providing assistance are increasingly difficult*. Now in Lebanon there are movements of a million refugees or more that take place across large geographical areas, and in some cases, these are remote, weakly administered and environmentally hostile territories. We have many obstacles to effective enumeration: asylum seekers enter at different points along the border. Often, they arrive in such large numbers in the [Bekaa] Valley or

North of Beirut so we can scarcely count them, or we cannot do it because *the authorities do not allow us*. Then we have local residents that want to register as refugees due to poverty. So, the accuracy of any statistics collected is rather distorted.

QPC manager, interview, emphasis added

Practices of gathering data through ranking and forecasting[3] are central to the planning and building of WASH structures and community centers. As explained by a QPC worker, based on their rankings these reports have agency and distribute individuals in space: "we rank exceptional humanitarian cases, and forecast WASH needs for vulnerable incoming populations, and then build them. Same with the community centers" (QPC worker, interview). Importantly, these assemblages are dependent on workers' ability to secure financial resources. The obstacles met in accessing funding and the physical state of the structures also create resistance among workers in the form of distancing (i.e., "going away"). As an informant speaks, we can observe he is moved by his emotions when he talks about the structures and the impossibility of improving them:

> The main problem in accessing humanitarian aid is that funds to construct these structures and centers are not given according to the needs but according to the demographics. Even if we see in our data that Palestinian refugees from Syria are some of the most vulnerable groups, our donors give money only for Syrians so we can only help them. In this case, we try to obtain help from local donations but often it is not enough. So, I feel terrible when we cannot do anything about improving these structures, especially in winter, and I walk away, I try to find something else more meaningful to do.

QPC manager, interview

Workers' emotions become part of the spatial assemblages as well, as they have an effect on agencies and decision. But the subject of contention is created by the very demographics (Palestinian versus Syrian) that the community centers and WASH assemblages host. This is because donors' political and religious affiliations influence the funding made available, which in turn creates obstacles for QPC. This shows how spatial configurations while hosting refugees, controlling their movements, and assigning specific identities also generate resistance and the loss of meaning by fostering dis-identification among workers, as stated by one manager:

> Three years in, we had grown in our scope and ambitions and built additional shelters and centers, and now we need institutional money. But this sort of big money comes with ties that risk contradicting our own principles and ideas—whether it is the decisions and policies of humanitarian donor organizations or—even more complex—money coming directly from governments with their own political agendas. Should we turn a blind eye so that we can help more people—or should we simply stick to what we believe in? A perpetual question that is never easy to answer.

QPC manager, email

In short, the above illustrative examples show how different spatial assemblages (such as shelters, community centers and WASH structures) play an important role in QPC's ability to organize. In the political context of a refugee crisis, spacing is populated not only by predictable but also by contested and conflicting agencies. The spacing practices of QPC provide life-saving solutions, control individuals' movements, and contribute to identity-building processes while generating resistance and creating vulnerability, hopelessness, and disillusionment for both QPC workers and refugees. As a result, such spacing assemblages oftentimes create an environment with widening gaps for civil liberties in zones of chronic conflict (see also Brysk & Stohl, 2019). Refugee camps are therefore spacing assemblages that generate physical relief and welfare and, at the same time, intensified humanitarian control.

Discussion

This chapter investigated refugee camps as spacing assemblages—that is, processes of fitting together relationships, political orientations, bodies, places, settlements, and other artifacts—and how these shape NGOs' ability to organize in migration hotspots. A communicative lens was used to analyze how social, political, material, and technological configurations of spacing assemblages that are established through communication act as important agents that have both organizing and dis-organizing implications for QPC (for a thorough explanation of organizing and dis-organizing, see Vásquez, Kuhn & Plotnikof, this volume). Specifically, we identified the implications of such spacing assemblages to pertain to control, resistance, and identification dynamics that impact individuals' movement and work in such a unique setting (see Figures 30.1 and 30.2). Based on these findings, we discuss our twofold contribution to research and practice.

Firstly, the findings indicate how spacing assemblages steer the conduct of organizations and individuals within the territories these enclose. We thus confirm and extend research on how NGOs exercise humanitarian control, which is intrinsically connected to the production of new spaces (Lauri, 2018; Sahraoui, 2020). Humanitarian assemblages (in our case shelters and WASH structures) actualize a new geography of space in conflict areas, where state borders and gateways to national territories become zones of humanitarian control. In such constrained spatiality of the refugee camps, social practices and materiality interact with one another, and thus enable multiple agents (e.g., humanitarian workers, shelters, centers, forecasting technologies, reports, policy documents, local authorities, international donors, rankings, natural territories, etc.) to exercise different forms of control. This results in generating struggles, contradictions, and resistance among those who operate and reside in such spaces, thus generating disorganizing processes within QPC. As illustrated in the analysis, such forms of humanitarian control

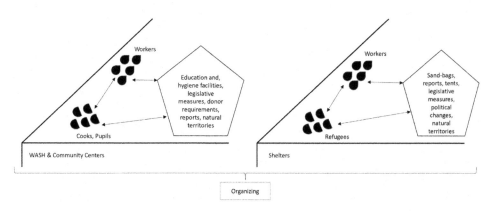

Figure 30.1 Junction of individuals, space, assemblages – identities and organizing.

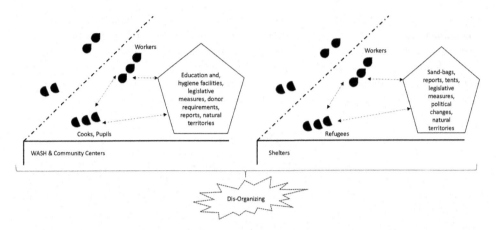

Figure 30.2   Dis-junction of individuals, space, assemblages – resistance and (dis)organizing.

are inherently unstable, dispersed, and not necessarily human-centered—having *de-centralized* and *volatile agency*, that is. We thus extend research that proposes a relational ontology of resistance and control through spacing by showing that the relationship between resistance and control is not a solely human activity but a dynamic contested process between different social and material elements (Wilhoit & Kisselburgh, 2019).

Our findings show that neither religious leaders, groups of refugees, committees of notable people, Lebanese authorities nor QPC members are in full control of the organizing of QPC and its spacing practices. Instead, control is a fluctuating resource that shifted to spacing assemblages under constant reconstruction, shared by many, and not belonging to a single agent. As a result of the *mélange* of discursive, material and political agencies inhabiting spacing assemblages, NGO workers face a significant organizational conundrum: on the one hand, current spacing practices, while providing lifesaving aid, may create bewildering and life-threatening problems for refugees and those working to assist them. On the other hand, the current humanitarian regime suppresses NGO members wanting to improve and change the funding system and silence those who seek innovative spacing due to counter-mobilization from donors (Florian et al., 2018).

The findings also show how spacing assemblages co-produce multiple, divergent, and dissident identities for those who live and work in these spaces while generating potential resistance among them. We thus add to research that shows how tangible configurations of space complicate identification and disidentification processes, especially in spaces of intensified humanitarian control (see Doraï, 2010). Organizational scholars have widely shown that spaces have a constitutive role when it comes to a given territorial identity, with a focus, however, on the social practices taking place within them. For instance, research typically focuses on beliefs and narratives related to bordering classification and categories (us/them, domestic/foreign), legislation defining a border regime, rituals as expressions of solidarity and legitimacy (oaths, religious holidays, celebrations) and symbols (flags and anthems) (see Benezer & Zetter, 2014). However, in this chapter we draw on recent research that considers space as assembling a variety of practices *along* with physical artifacts (e.g., Cnossen & Bencherki, 2018). Our empirical study expands on these notions by showing that the mutually constitutive relationship between material and discursive configurations at play in humanitarian assemblages is, indeed, critical for inciting conflicting identities for those dwelling and working in such spaces (see Martin, Minca & Katz, 2020). Furthermore, next to these configurations, the findings also indicate (albeit only tangentially) that the larger political context that situates spacing assemblages is imperative for understanding how identities of those who partake in such organizing (e.g., members, volunteers) get assigned and shaped. In the case of QPC, the relationship with the host state and the different governmental restrictions imposed on asylum seekers vis-à-vis the existing civil tensions in Lebanon, and the wider region, were significant agencies in organizing. We thus argue that not only humanitarian organizations but also other organizational settings are hybrid and dynamic spaces that are prone to have volatile agencies due to complex and changing spacing assemblages. As such, these processes are worthy of further examination by CCO scholars.

Secondly, this chapter contributes to practice by illustrating how the CCO perspective invites practitioners to think about potential inequalities and differences that spacing creates. It is through assemblages of artifacts, technologies, territories, and social and political practices that space becomes involved in constituting organizations and producing cultural relations (see Shome, 2003). Humanitarian assemblages shape how worker and exile identities, cultures and traditions are performed, sustained, and resisted. In this respect, we make a few practical considerations for those working in the NGO sector to highlight how assemblages may negatively affect their work. Namely:

- Workers and volunteers are at risk of compassion fatigue and burnout because of working with vulnerable populations. There is a dire need for infrastructures that provide emotional support and psychological safety to those who live and operate in the camps. Given the volatility of this space, such services should be available around the clock.
- Clashes and conflicts between the values of donors and the realities and needs of aid recipients frequently happen. A clear risk analysis that accounts for political interests done before launching the funding program might benefit this process.
- Poverty, political instability, and turmoil of local host communities influence the ability of workers to find their job meaningful and be effective in providing aid. A cyclical cultural and environmental analysis that allows job rotation might help workers' stability.

It is important to note that the rare organizational setting of an NGO working with forced migration presented in this chapter provides knowledge most applicable in contexts that share similarities with this one. The limitations of our study amount to the relatively narrow methodological focus and small dataset due to access difficulties, safety concerns and the vulnerability of informants. Nevertheless, these limitations can act as a springboard for future research into the contested nature of space, which transgresses the common-sense understanding of space as a background or a backdrop against which "the real stuff" of history and politics is enacted (Shome, 2003). More research on how aid to asylum seekers can be effectively provided while considering the different agencies at play is needed, especially in a larger political context of a crisis. Research that looks at how effective partnership agreements between assemblages of NGOs, donors, and local host communities can be achieved in order to foster and facilitate inclusion of local actors in actions financed by international funding is necessary. Such multilateral approaches in research, including the adoption of a communicative lens to spacing, are important as they allow analysts to understand how space can challenge and provoke the established order of things.

Notes

1 The term refugee and asylum seeker are used interchangeably in this chapter to denote both situations in which individuals may or may not have yet been granted refugee status under the 1951 Convention relating to the status of refugees.
2 Actors and agents are used interchangeably as elements with agency (Vásquez & Cooren, 2013).
3 Forecasting and ranking technologies, such as agent-based modeling, are used to develop quantitative prediction models to deploy and distribute asylum seekers in community centers (e.g., Groen, 2016).

References

Agamben, G. (1998). *Homo sacer: Sovereign power and bare life.* Stanford University Press.

Ashcraft, K. L., Kuhn, T. R., & Cooren, F. (2009). Constitutional amendments: "Materializing" organizational communication. *The Academy of Management Annals, 3*(1), 1–64. doi:org/10.1080/19416520903047186.

Benezer, G., & Zetter, R. (2014). Searching for directions: Conceptual and methodological challenges in researching refugee journey. *Journal of Refugee Studies, 28*(3), 297–318. doi:10.1093/jrs/feu022.

Beyes, T., & Steyaert, C. (2012). Spacing organization: Non-representational theory and performing organizational space. *Organization, 19*(1), 45–61. doi:10.1177/1350508411401946.

Brysk. A., & Stohl, M. (Eds.). (2019). *Contracting human rights: Crisis, accountability, and opportunity.* Edward Elgar.

Cooren, F., Vaara, E., Langley, A., & Tsoukas, H. (2014). *Language and communication at work: Discourse, narrativity, and organizing.* Oxford University Press. doi:10.1093/acprof:oso/9780198703082.001.0001.

Costas, J. (2013). Problematizing mobility: A metaphor of stickiness, non-places and the kinetic elite. *Organization Studies, 34*(10), 1467–1485. doi:10.1177/0170840613495324.

Cnossen, B., & Bencherki, N. (2018). The role of space in the emergence and endurance of organizing: How independent workers and material assemblages constitute organizations. *Human Relations, 72*(6), 1057–1080. doi:10.1177/0018726718794265

Clarke, A. E. (2005). *Situational analysis – Grounded theory after the postmodern turn.* Sage.

Clegg, S. (1994). Power relations and the constitution of the resistant subject. In J. Jermier, D. Knights, & W. Nord (Eds.), *Resistance and power in organizations* (pp. 274–326). Routledge.

Dale, K., & Burrell, G. (2008). *The spaces of organisation and the organisation of space: Power, identity and materiality at work.* Palgrave Macmillan.

Doraï, M. D. (2010). From camp dwellers to urban refugees? Urbanization and marginalization of refugee camps in Lebanon. In M. A. Khalidi (Ed.), *Manifestations of identity: The lived reality of Palestinian refugees in Lebanon* (pp. 75–92). Institute for Palestine Studies & Institut Francais du Proche-Orient.

Florian, M., Costas, J., & Kärreman, D. (2018). Struggling with meaningfulness when context shifts: Volunteer work in a German refugee shelter. *Journal of Management Studies, 56*(3), 589–616. doi:10.1111/joms.12410.

Groen, D. (2016). Simulating refugee movements: Where would you go? *Procedia Computer Science, 80,* 2251–2255. doi:10.1016/j.procs.2016.05.400.

Gregory, T. (2011). The rise of the productive non-place: The contemporary office as a state of exception. *Space and Culture, 14*(3), 244–258. doi:10.1177/1206331211412264.

Hyndman, J. (2000). *Managing displacement: Refugees and the politics of humanitarianism.* University of Minnesota Press.

Iedema, R., Long, D., & Carroll, K. (2010). Corridor communication, spatial design and patient safety: Enacting and managing complexies. In A. van Marrewijk & D. Yanow (Eds.), *Organizational spaces: Rematerializing the workaday world* (pp. 41–57). Edward Elgar.

Jessop, B., Brenner, N., & Jones, M. (2008). Theorizing sociospatial relations. *Environment and Planning D: Society and Space, 26*(3), 389–401. doi.org/10.1068/d9107.

Kuhn, T., & Burke, N. (2014). Spatial design as socio-materiality practice: A (dis)organizing perspective on communicative constitution. In F. Cooren, E. Vaara, A. Langley, & H. Tsoukas (Eds.), *Language and communication at work: Discourse, narrativity, and organizing* (pp. 147–173). Oxford University Press. doi:10.1093/acprof:oso/9780198703082.001.0001.

Lauri, A. (2018). *Humanitarian borders: The merging of rescue with security and control.* CMI Brief. Retrieved from www.cmi.no/publications/6705-humanitarian-borders.

Lefebvre, H. (1991). *The production of space.* Malden, MA: Blackwell. Original work published in 1974.

Livesay, G. (2010). Assemblage. In A. Parr (Ed.), *The Deleuze dictionary* (Revised, pp. 18–19). Edinburgh University Press.

Martin, D., Minca, C., & Katz, I. (2020). Rethinking the camp: On spatial technologies of power and resistance. *Progress in Human Geography, 44*(4), 743–768. doi:10.1177/0309132519856702.

Mumby, D. K., Thomas, R., Martí, I., & Seidl, D. (2017). Resistance redux. *Organization Studies, 38*(9), 1157–1183. doi:10.1177/0170840617717554.

Ramadan, A. (2009). A refugee landscape: Writing Palestinian nationalisms in Lebanon. *An International Journal for Critical Geographies, 8*(1), 69–99. Retrieved October 16, 2020, from https://acme-journal. org/index.php/acme/article/view/821.

Ramadan, A. (2013). Spatialising the refugee camp. *Transactions of the Institute of British Geographers, 38*(1), 65–77. doi:10.1111/j.1475-5661.2012.00509.x.

Sahraoui, N. (2020). Gendering the care/control nexus of the humanitarian border: Women's bodies and gendered control of mobility in a European borderland. *Environment and Planning D: Society and Space, 38*(5), 905–922. doi:10.1177/0263775820925487.

Shome, R. (2003). Space matters: The power and practice of space. *Communication Theory, 13*(1), 39–56. doi.org/10.1111/j.1468-2885.2003.tb00281.x.

Taylor, S., & Spicer, A. (2007). Time for space: A narrative review of research on organizational spaces. *International Journal of Management Reviews, 9*(4), 325–346. doi:10.1111/j.1468-2370.2007.00214.x.

Thanem, T. (2011). *The monstrous organization.* Edward Elgarg.

Thorleifsson, C. (2016). The limits of hospitality: Coping strategies among displaced Syrians in Lebanon. *Third World Quarterly, 37*(6), 1071–1082. doi.org/10.1080/01436597.2016.1138843.

UNCHR (2016). Global trends in forced displacement in 2016. Retrieved September 10, 2020, from www.unhcr.org/globaltrends2016/.

Vásquez, C., Bencherki, N., Cooren, F., & Sergei, V. (2017). From 'matters of concern' to 'matters of authority': Studying the performativity of strategy from a communicative constitution of organization (CCO) approach. *Long Range Planning, 51*(3), 417–435. doi.org/10.1016/j.lrp.2017.01.001.

Vásquez, C., & Cooren, F. (2013). Spacing practices: The communicative configuration of organizing through space-times. *Communication Theory, 23*(1), 25–47. doi.org/10.1111/comt.12003.

Wilhoit, E. D., & Kisselburgh, L. G. (2015). Collective action without organization: The material constitution of bike commuters as collective. *Organization Studies, 36*(5), 573–592. doi:10.1177/0170840614556916.

Wilhoit, E. D., & Kisselburgh, L. G. (2019). The relational ontology of resistance: Hybridity, ventriloquism, and materiality in the production of bike commuting as resistance. *Organization, 26*(6), 873–893. doi:10.1177/1350508417723719.

Turner, V. W. (1969). *The ritual process. Structure and anti-structure.* Cornell.

31

CONSTITUTING THE BLUE-COLLAR ORGANIZATION

How Social and Material Dimensions Are Discursively Combined to (Re)construct the Factory

Colleen E. Mills

Early organizational and management research was concerned with the efficient management of manufacturing and factories and, as such, it gave the center stage to the material aspects of work. In 1832, Charles Babbage was concerned with "applying machinery to supersede the skill and power of the human arm" (Babbage, 1832, p. 1). Later, Frederick W. Taylor justified his study of scientific management with the need to avoid "Awkward, inefficient, or ill-directed movements of men", which to him were comparable to "the waste of material things" (Taylor, 1911, p. 1). For his part, the French founder of management, Henri Fayol, wrote in 1916 that "To organize means building up the dual structure, material and human, of the undertaking" (Fayol, 1949, p. 7). Then, building on Marxist thought, the middle of the twentieth century witnessed a renewed interest in the material conditions of the working class (Hoggart, 1959; Williams, 1961). However, recent work in organizational and management studies tends to privilege white-collar work and, in doing so, has all but left aside the notion of materiality to emphasize intellectual and discursive practices (with some notable exceptions, such as Kilduff et al., 1997; Korczynski, 2011). Factories and other sites of manufacturing, however, continue to be part of our economic reality, and to be able to account for the work that takes place on these sites, we need theorizing that accounts for the materiality of their organizational reality.

Ashcraft, Kuhn, and Cooren (2009), Barad (2003), Latour (1992), Orlikowski (2010), and Zammuto et al. (2007) all observe that, as a consequence of the linguistic turn (Alvesson & Kärreman, 2000) that spread across the social sciences and humanities, the material world became largely absent from accounts of organizing and organizational life. By enthusiastically embracing the linguistic turn, organizational scholars effectively dematerialized organizational practices. So strong was this effect that Barad (2003) lamented, "Language matters. Discourse matters. Culture matters. There is an important sense in which the only thing that does not seem to matter anymore is matter" (p. 801). She went on to ask why matter was still largely treated as "passive and immutable", only gaining agency through language and culture. Since then a material shift (Robichaud & Cooren, 2013;

DOI: 10.4324/9781003224914-36

Jarzabkowski & Pinch, 2013) has occurred. The literature that once saw the relationship between language and the material world as unequal, with bodies, spaces and matter as represented by language rather than able to act directly, has now been overlaid by studies that reveal how physical bodies and non-human material can exert agency directly on discursive and other types of workplace practice to direct how organizing occurs (e.g., Mills & Cooren, 2018). Inspired by this new literature, this chapter revisits a study (Mills, 2002, 2005) that predates it to look at how this study accounted for the relationship between materiality and communication before the ascendency of the "communicative constitution of organization" (CCO) perspective or "organization *as* communication" as it is known by some (see Schoeneborn & Sandhu, 2013).

Introducing the Communicative Constitution of Organization (CCO) Perspective

The CCO perspective and the three schools that have contributed to it (see Schoeneborn & Blaschke, 2014) assert that communication does not simply happen in and between organizations but actually creates the organization. This perspective turns the view of communication as merely practices occurring in and between organizations on its head by conceptualizing communication as the source of all organizational practices. According to Schoeneborn, Kuhn, and Kärreman (2019), CCO scholarship asserts that "organizations, as well as organizational phenomena, come into existence, persist, and are transformed in and through interconnected communication practices" (p. 476).

The genesis of this influential contemporary perspective is linked to the trailblazing organizational communication scholarship of Gail Fairhurst (Fairhurst, 1993; Fairhurst, Rogers, & Sarr, 1987; Fairhurst, Green, & Courtright, 1995), Marshall Scott Poole (Poole, Folger, & Hewes, 1987), Linda Putnam (Putnam, 2015), and James R. Taylor (1993; Taylor & Van Every, 2000), who proposed in various ways that organizations are continually being constituted through communication – a view that privileged the symbolic over the material. Since then, many of these same scholars (e.g., Ashcraft, Kuhn, & Cooren, 2009; Cooren & Fairhurst, 2004; Putnam & Cooren, 2004) have argued that the symbolic and material dimensions of organizing should be understood as inextricably entangled – a relationship also captured in the concept "sociomateriality" (Orlikowski & Scott, 2008).

Sociomateriality and the CCO Perspective

The sociomateriality concept captures the entanglement of the material and social and recognizes the hybridity of action (Latour, 2005). By capturing the "inherent inseparability" of social and material dimensions of organizing (Bavdaz, 2018; Orlikowski & Scott, 2008; Jarzabkowski & Pinch, 2013), sociomateriality rejects the Kantian subject-object dualism in favor of Latour's focus on relations, and Callon's (1984) and Law's (1992) actor-network theory (ANT), while aligning with feminist views of scholars like Barad (2007) and Suchman (2007).

With origins grounded in research on the technologies of work (see Leonardi, Nardi & Kallinikos, 2012; Kim & Yang, 2020) rather than organizational communication studies, sociomateriality is now a familiar concept across all organizational studies (see Carlile, Nicolini, Langley, & Tsoukas, 2013). Together with the CCO perspective, it is challenging the exclusive preoccupation with humans, and instead draws attention to the non-human agency or the "hybrid agency" that results when human actors "appropriate" (Cooren, 2004, p. 377) what non-human elements do in the organization.

Recent studies (see de Vaujany & Vaast, 2016; Groleau & Demers, 2016; Mills & Cooren, 2018; Arnaud, Mills, Legrand, & Maton, 2016) show how far we have come in this regard. For example, Groleau and Demers (2016) apply an activity theory framework to reveal how design drawings operate as material tools that organize horticulturalists' practice, combining with the social to define the different modes of a specific horticultural project. Similarly, de Vaujany and Vaast (2016) show how the composition, design and distribution of material furnishings in a meeting space at a French university embody values and give legitimacy to communication that occurs in this space. The case described in this chapter suggests that there are still more practices to incorporate into our understanding of how matter and social practices such as communication constitute organizing and some, like sensemaking, have their roots in the interpretive turn championed by Weick (e.g., 1979, 1995) that inspired many of our contemporary views on organizational communication and organizing.

Discovering how the Material and Social Practices Combine to Communicatively Construct Organizing

The remainder of this chapter presents an illustrative case that reveals how the material and social practices combine to communicatively constitute organizing in a factory. The case is the result of an interpretive study of change communication in a food-processing factory that did not start with a pre-emptive conceptual framework such as CCO but rather a simple question: how do workers make sense of change communication? The case is used here to illustrate how blue-collar factory workers' communication and workspace materiality co-constitute organizing and to suggest that a holistic understanding of how communication constitutes such organizations benefits from incorporating consideration of sociomateriality and sensemaking (i.e., the ongoing process of meaning-making).

Method

The Case

The study examined workers sensemaking about workplace communication in a food-processing factory that was replacing its traditional top-down management approach with self-managing work teams designed to empower frontline workers and their line managers. An interpretive ontology was initially chosen because preliminary interviews revealed that the workers held various views about the nature and consequences of the change communication and so the objective was to study their sensemaking about why this inconsistency existed.

The Materiality of the Workspaces

The factory floor was arranged as a series of materially distinct workspaces in which fresh produce was washed, peeled, cut, sorted, packed, frozen, stored and dispatched and containers for transporting the produce were made. Not only were these workspaces physically distinct, the social engagement and collaborative action in and around them was distinctive too.

The tasks performed in each workspace required distinctive forms of coordinated interaction that involved people, machines and space. In some spaces workers collaborated closely to achieve tasks that could not be performed by one person (e.g., in the work center making containers). In others, workers performed alongside each other in a parallel fashion requiring little cooperation (e.g., at the sorting and packaging conveyor belts). In these workspaces communication was constrained by the ambient factory noise and the workers' earmuffs, which not only blocked the factory noise but enabled the worker to listen to the radio as they worked. In a third type of workspace, which included open spaces around the conveyor belts, workers performed their tasks independently and at a distance from each other, moving through these workspaces on forklifts as they transported bins of frozen produce between four pickup points and the freezers.

One work center from each of these three distinctive "geosocial environments" (Mills, 2005, 2002) was chosen. Together, these three work centers comprised a theoretical transect extending from independent through parallel to highly collaborative work. The centers along this transect were distinguished by five dimensions – interactivity, task format, objects in the workspace, noise, and task allocation.

The chosen work centers were given the names Containers (where bins for holding produce were made), Processing (where fresh produce was processed), and Transportation (the department of forklift drivers who moved bins of frozen and packaged produce between pickup points and the freezers).

Data Collection and Analysis

Forty-eight blue-collar workers (i.e., semi-skilled, manual workers) consisting of 13 (N = 16) from Containers, 26 (N = variable) from Processing and nine (N = 10) from Transportation were interviewed and observed as they worked. All had worked in the factory for more than one season and some had worked for the company for more than 15 years. Fourteen were women and 11 were seasonal workers.

In addition to semi-structured interviews and observations, data were gathered using participant observations in Containers and Processing and work breaks in the cafeteria. In the interviews, workers were asked to describe and account for (i.e., make sense of) their workplace experiences, especially in relation to change-related communication, the new ways of working, and the meaning of the concepts they used in their accounts of both.

Data collection and data analysis were coupled in an iterative manner designed to allow the analysis to inform the data collection so that the findings were grounded in data rather than a pre-emptive conceptual framework. This "bottom-up approach" relied on inductive reasoning (Tracy, 2013, p. 36), with the interdependent cycles of coding and analysis mirroring in many respects the constant comparison process integral to the Grounded Theory Approach as it was first described by Glaser and Strauss (1967) and subsequently developed by Glaser (1978, 1992, 1998). However, the approach was not a Grounded Theory approach *per se* as the analysis process also incorporated phenomenographic techniques (Marton, 1981, 1986) and discourse analysis strategies to ensure ideational elements (i.e., concepts, themes, arguments, explanations) and the discursive forms in which these were embedded were incorporated into the analysis. The examination of ideational elements was vital to the analysis as the overarching objective of the study was not merely to understand change communication but to understand how workers made sense of this in relation to the geosocial environments in which it occurred. The research design made it possible to examine the relationships between sense (meaning), communication practice and the corporeal and spatial dimensions that were part of work routines.

Findings

Understanding Workplace Language

The workplace language revealed a bounty of colloquial terms. These referred to (1) types of task-related workplace interaction (e.g., working in with others, getting on with others), (2) specific communication behaviors (e.g., bitching, backstabbing, "having people on"), and (3) states of being (e.g., "pissed off", "knowing what is going on"). A comparative analysis of workers' accounts of the meanings of these terms' revealed that the same term could have different meanings depending on where the workers worked. This finding was significant as it was one of the first empirical clues that there was something constitutive about the materiality of each work center. To pursue this line of thinking, workers' definitions for two terms related to how they worked together were aggregated to create definitional profiles for each one. The final step in the analysis involved comparing the elements in these two profiles with the material and social features of each work center's workspace. The following sections present the findings related to these two widely used terms, which were designated as anchoring concepts because they "attached" the interpretive discourses used to understand change communication to the material and social elements of work practices in particular work centers. How work tasks were done depended on everyone in a work center sharing the same understanding of what the anchoring concept meant. These concepts were the mechanism that coupled the material and the communicative dimensions, so coordinated performances could happen. Importantly, they explained the joint constitutive agency of human and non-human components of each work center. This key point will be returned to in the discussion as it is central to explaining how this case study suggests matter can be incorporated into the CCO perspective.

"Anchoring Concepts" – A Key to Revealing the Coupling of the Material and Language

As already noted, workers' language was richly embellished with informal language including slang. Over time several colloquial terms stood out because of the frequency of their use when referring to work experiences and communication during the roll out of Work Center Management (WCM). The two most commonly heard terms were "working in with others" (WIW) and "getting on with others" (GOW). Workers used them when describing and judging different types of workplace interaction and communication practices. Their definitions suggested these terms provided a means to introduce abstract notions to do with co-operative task-related performance (WIW) and social acceptability (GOW) into conversations using an everyday and widely understood language code. Most significantly, as already noted, they provided a mechanism for anchoring interpretive discourses to the social and material dimensions of specific work centers. Just how they did this is explained in the following section.

The Sociomaterially Situated Nature of Anchoring Concepts

When first encountered, the terms WIW and GOW seemed unremarkable. However, when each work center's definitions were aggregated to create definitional profiles for each concept distinctive differences between the profiles for each work center were revealed. Most significantly, the differences could be linked to the material features (e.g., sorting belts in Processing) and the sort of interaction occurring in the workspace. This finding suggests WIW and GOW were eliminating the symbolic-material duality. In so doing, they demonstrated how human and non-human workspace elements were inextricably entangled in the symbolic tools used to think, talk and go about work. These two examples of the anchoring concepts identified in this study will now be examined in more detail.

(a) 'Working in with' Others (WIW)

Table 31.1 summarizes each work center's geosocial environment (Mills, 2005) and then the central dimensions of its definitional profile for WIW. The correspondence between physical and social elements of the task environment and the definitional profile of WIW construct is evident. Moreover, Table 31.1 allows us to appreciate how the defining dimensions of the anchoring concept WIW changed across the transect from an interdependent task format in Containers to a highly independent one in Transportation and how the work orientation changed correspondingly, from a group orientation to a highly individual one.

Similarly, the way collaboration was viewed changes across Table 31.1 from being considered an inevitable aspect of WIW in Containers to an optional aspect of work in Processing and

Table 31.1 Comparison of the geosocial environments and definitional profile dimensions for WIW for each work center

Dimensions	Containers	Processing	Transportation
Features of task and material environment			
Interactivity	Workers work closely with each other and are interdependent	Workers are adjacent/ alongside each other but work independently	Workers are isolated and work independently
Task format	Collaboratively constructing bins on wooden pallets One person holds the wooden bin sides while another straps these together and then wraps the bin in clear plastic film Job cannot be done alone, without interaction	Standing beside conveyor belt picking out damaged and rotten produce and detritus from the stream of washed and cut produce as it passes on the belt No interaction is necessary	Driving forklifts to pick up and drop off bins containing produce to the freezers and four pickup points across the factory floor No interaction is necessary once jobs are assigned unless a problem occurs
Objects in workspace	Bin sides, pallets, hand-held strapping machine, wrapping machine Forklifts passing through	Conveyor belt and washing and cutting machines Hoses for washing down the equipment	Open spaces and freezers lined with bins of bulk and packaged produce Forklifts
Noise	Loud	Very loud (earmuffs essential)	Variable
Task allocation	Negotiated	Varied by directive	Varied by roster
Dimensions in the WIW definitional profile			
Orientation	Group	Individual	Highly individual
Collaboration	Inevitable	Optional, self- determined	Directed, requested
Factors motivating collaboration	Empathy Reciprocation	Fair share Reciprocation	Self interest Crisis
Task responsibility	Shared (our)	Individual (mine)	Individual (mine)

occurring only when directed in Transportation. The factors that motivated WIW also change from factors that reflect a concern for other workers to factors consistent with workers having a minimal or begrudging concern for others and a strong concern for oneself. This progression across the work center transect is consistent with the different ways task responsibility was conceived: from shared to individual.

In Containers, bin-building was, by necessity, a shared responsibility and people talked in terms of "our task" and would modify their individual actions as they anticipated each other's needs in order to ensure successful task completion. This was in marked contrast to the other two work centers where the actions constituting each worker's tasks were not so tightly dependent on the actions of any other workers in the work center. Instead, the coupling of actions was achieved by workplace materials, the sorting belt in Processing and the delivery points in Transportation. In Processing, each person on the sorting belt was doing the same task. They depended on each other in so far as their additive effect was to remove all detritus and damaged produce from the stream of processed product passing them on the sorting belt. In Transportation, each worker could do their day's work independently. The foreperson's roster dictated which bins of produce were moved and the sequence of pickup points involved in doing this structured worker's activity. If a worker was not rostered to do a particular pickup then they considered that pickup was not their personal concern. This detachment from the collective task is captured in the following excerpt from a Transportation worker (T1). Note that Repack is one of the delivery points that Transportation workers deliver bins of bulk produce to or removed packed product from:

T1: I do Repack every second week. The week you have off in Repack, you don't want anything to do with it. You want to stay away from it.

The following explanation of WIW from another Transportation worker (T2) compares WIW in Transportation to departments like Processing where workers are distributed alongside the inspection belt (i.e., "a line" or "chain"). His account to the researcher (R) makes it clear that WIW is understood as varying according to the material structure of the job.

T2: But on the sorting belt, if you don't sort the product's crap, ... (unclear). So, it's different when you're on a line like that when there's someone following you. But with us, there's no one following us until the end. Changes of shifts, change of shift you put your bins away, and when they come on there's nothing in the loading bay for them.
R: So, is that about the only thing you have to do to work in with other people?
T2: Yeah. Just don't leave extra work. It would be different on a chain or something.

Table 31.2 presents representative data to assist the reader to appreciate how workers' meanings for WIW varied across the workspace transect. The sub-category that applied is in brackets alongside its "parent" dimension.

(b) *"Getting on with" Others (GOW)*

Table 31.3 compares the features of the social environments that prevailed in each work center and then presents the dimensions of the definitional profiles for GOW for each one. Notice how the four dimensions defining the definitional profiles reflect the features of the social environment.

Table 31.2 Illustrating definitional dimensions for WIW

Department	Dimension	Illustrative data
Containers	Orientation (group)	"I've got to rely on you to do your bit so that I can do my bit so he can do his bit and if you don't work in with me I can't work in with him because I'm not getting the supply to give him."
	Collaboration (inevitable)	"Well you have to be part of a team, like you can't do it by yourself so it's all co-ordinated as a team, sort of. One person helps the other and it's just, that's how things get out on time."
	Factors motivating collaboration (empathy, reciprocation)	"It's like you're all together, you know. You just know what the others want and just know exactly how everyone is doing something. [Pause] You know just by second nature of what that person is going to do and if you see them talking in a certain area you know they're going to do that so you don't have to do that … ." "And if you get down and you're not keeping up, as a team member I come and help you out to bring you up to speed to keep him at speed and if I come down you will come and help me. We help each other."
	Task responsibility (shared)	"… They see something and they just go ahead and do it. You know, whether they are doing that particular job before or not. If something needs to be done, they do it."
Processing	Orientation (individual)	"Doing the same thing as you are doing. So like you may be sorting and you're doing you best, head down and just doing it."
	Collaboration (discretionary)	"If someone needs a hand outside your normal range of duties, you give them a hand."
	Factors motivating collaboration (fair share, reciprocity)	"It's very important. Why should you let others work hard, when you are paid the same amount of money as the other one? You should do your share of work." "Well, they should be really good to others. And try to help others. If you help others, people will help you. If you don't help anyone, nobody will help you."
	Task responsibility (individual)	"Getting there and trying to get as much as possible [of the detritus and damaged product] and whoever's working opposite just doing the same thing."
Transportation	Orientation (very individual)	"We don't rely on anyone else. You have got a job to do. You can do it."
	Collaboration (directed, requested)	"…we work in quite well, like X [Stock Controller] sort of makes up a roster, roughly a roster, so you'll be on this one week and then on the other and some days when your quiet you'll be helping X say shift a row." "If they want a hand they'll ask for a hand. You don't go on air and just do it for them, you wait until they're hanging out and then you go and ask them if they want a hand. They'll say if they want a hand or not."

(continued)

Table 31.2 Cont.

Department	Dimension	Illustrative data
	Factors motivating collaboration (self-interest, crisis)	"It's just, don't make any extra effort for anyone else." "If Repack's [Packing room] very busy you sometimes get a bit of a hand from each other and the others will [sic], you just go and help each other when you're looking really stressed sort of thing."
	Task responsibility (individual)	"Working in with means doing your job, letting them do theirs. Don't hinder the job, just do yours, don't try and do theirs and stuff it up."

An earlier version of this table appeared in Mills, 2002, as Table 3, p. 301.

Table 31.3 Comparison of the social elements of the communication environments and definitional profile dimensions for GOW for each work center

Dimensions	Containers	Processing	Transportation
Features of social environment			
Size of work teams/shift	Small 2–5	Large 6–15 (at height of the season)	Small 1–5
Social constraints	Enabling rather than constrained	Communication seen as risky	Oppositional interactional mores
Atmosphere	Relaxed	Tense through to relaxed on night shift	Tense or neutral (especially when only 1 or 2 workers present)
Animation (including humor)	Frequently animated and frequent and regular episodes of humor	Limited animation but regular humorous episodes	Very limited animation and limited irregular episodes of humor and argument
Cohesion			
a. level	High	Variable but high on night shift	Variable, sometimes low
b. primary social maintenance mechanisms in the at work	Collaborative way of working (required) Smoko[2]	Smoko interaction Out of work activities such as meals and bar visits for night shift	Smoko, alliances (son-in-law and father-in-law) Warm-up times (short breaks from freezer)
Competitiveness	Not prominent but some examples	Prominent	Prominent
Interactiveness			
a. task related	Two collaborative task-based groups	Relatively independent	Independent
b. form	Dyads and small groups collaborating on bin-building or chatting in the work center's office	Dyads standing beside each other on the belt	Dyads and triads during warm-up periods
c. frequency in workplace	Group discussions at smoko	Group discussions at smoko	Group discussions at smoko
d. supplementary (out of work)	Frequent interaction in workplace as well as at smoko Very little	Limited to smoko and clean-up phase Some but mainly night shift	Infrequent, limited to warm-ups and smoko Touch rugby after work (not everyone is included)

Table 31.3 Cont.

Dimensions	Containers	Processing	Transportation
Dimensions in GOW definitional profile			
Interactional tone	Light-hearted	Convivial	Discretionary conviviality
Mechanism (process)	Reciprocated assistance	Active association seeking	Satisfactory task performance
Interactional expectations	Active engagement with each other	Inclusion in informal activities	Minimal interaction – civility
Level of intimacy	Disclosure	Reciprocated humor	Acceptance through favor

The comparison between definitional profile dimensions for GOW and the social aspects of the communication environment for each work center suggest the communication environment and GOW were aligned, if not dialectically related. In Containers where the communication environment was characterized by cohesiveness, light-heartedness, supportiveness, and collaboration, the definitional profiles contained elements compatible with this environment. To get on with (i.e., GOW) someone a worker was expected to be light-hearted, reciprocate assistance, actively engage with fellow workers, and be open (i.e., disclose personal information). Similar levels of correspondence between the social environments and the GOW definitional profile elements are evident for the other two work centers.

Table 31.4 shows how GOW was understood to involve more interaction and a higher-level intimacy in Containers, where the geosocial environment required interaction at close quarters so work tasks could be performed. As we progress from this work center's geosocial environment, which supports collaborative action, through to one supporting co-presence but not interaction (i.e., Processing) to Transportation, where collaboration or interaction is not required, it is clear that this progression is mirrored in the definitional profiles created from workers' explanations of how they work in with each other (WIW) in these spaces. Similarly, workers' sense of GOW was as inextricably linked to the materiality of their workspace.

The Interface between Materiality, Ideational Elements and Discourse

The analysis revealed that workers made sense of workplace communication during the change process using a repertoire of five interpretive (i.e., framing) discourses. These framing discourses are described elsewhere (see Mills 2006, 2009) but are summarized here in Table 31.5 and are simply referred to as interpretive discourses in this chapter. They were termed framing discourses because they provided a frame for assembling ideational elements such as themes and anchoring concepts to make sense of workplace sociomaterial practices. In doing so, the discourses provided an interface between materiality, ideational elements and the discursive practices.

Each discourse in this interpretive repertoire provided workers with a framework to combine discursive resources such as WIW and GOW when expressing their sense about some aspect of workplace life such as a change communication event occurring as part of the roll out of Work Center Management.

Workers from all work centers used these discourses but certain discourses were more conspicuous in some and much less so in others. Oppositional and alienated discourses were commonly encountered in conversations among Transportation workers whose physical work environment and way of working limited interaction. The work tools (i.e., forklifts), task

Table 31.4 Illustrating definitional dimensions for GOW

Department	Dimension	Illustrative data
Containers	Interactional tone (light-hearted)	"Well, the people that talk to each other and have a bit of a joke."
	Mechanism (reciprocal assistance)	Me and X, the other forklift driver. We didn't really get on when I first came here but now I helped him out the other day and then he came and helped me out and we start getting on."
	Interactional expectations (active engagement with each other)	"Well, just by the way they talk and the way they act – around each other. … Well the people that talk to each other and have a bit of a joke."
	Level of intimacy (disclosure)	"Yeah, and like we don't just talk about work, we talk about our lives and that."
Processing	Interactional tone (convivial)	"Getting on with I think is getting on with everyone sort of eight hours a day, you know, and it's like friendly as … ."
	Mechanism (active association seeking)	"Oh, just generally associating with them, having your meal with them. Talking to them."
	Interactional expectations (inclusion in informal activities)	"If you get on with being part of the team, they do it to you too [joke] and if you're not part of the team, well they just leave you out."
	Level of intimacy (reciprocated humor)	"You might have a joke or something like that, somebody might fire some beans at you and they go down your neck or something like that, you know, and you turn round and smile or poke your tongue out, you know, things like that."
Transportation	Interactional tone (discretionary conviviality)	"You sort of get on with them but yeah, they're not that important that you have to be nice to them, …"
	Mechanism (satisfactory task performance)	"… how good you are at doing the job and that is how you get on or you don't get on with people."
	Interactional expectations (minimal interaction – civility)	"… you just do your job and be civil, sort of civil, you know. You don't have to lick their ass or anything, eh? If you don't get on you don't get on."
	Level of intimacy (acceptance through favor)	"I'll go out of my way to help them and that's one way of sort of getting people to think, 'Oh he's okay', if I'm stressed out, he'll look at it and see the situation and give me a hand so he's okay. You don't have to go to the pub and drink beer with people to get on with them … ."

An earlier version of this table appeared in Mills, 2002, as Table 4, p. 305.

format (i.e., individually moving assigned product rapidly across large spaces) and time pressure encouraged self-interest and competition rather than collaboration. In contrast, while oppositional discourse was certainly encountered in the data collected from Containers' workers, the aligned discourse, with its defining team metaphor, was more frequently encountered in

Table 31.5 Framing discourses

Discourse	Attitude and position	General features	Language elements
Detached	Neutral or indifferent attitude Commentator or observer	Detached, objective or indifferent view. Low level of personal identification with the workplace or groups in it. Limited emotional engagement.	The pronouns "they", "them", "it" and "one" used often. Rare use of "we". Use of allusive labels language often low. No distinguishing metaphors.
Operational	Positive, neutral or negative attitude Participant in a system or cog in the wheel	Interdependent task or process view. Identification with others as fellow members of a system rather than with any particular group. Low emotional engagement.	Generic "we" but less use of "us" or "our". Technical language and managerial terms used. Mechanistic metaphors.
Aligned	Positive attitude Collaborator	Interdependent, positive group/team view. Identification with a group based upon commonalties within the group. Low emotional engagement.	"Us", personal "we", "us" and "our" used. High use of allusive language. Chain and team metaphors.
Oppositional	Neutral or negative attitude Confederate	Oppositional, group view. Identification with group based upon differences with other groups rather than because of intra-group similarities. High emotional engagement.	Pronouns used included us/them, us/him combinations. Allusive labels and quite graphic phrases used especially when referring to management. Stereotypes used. Ladder metaphor emphasizing hierarchy and combative and war metaphors using language of win/lose.
Alienated	Negative attitude Marginalized individual	Oppositional, negative individual view. Low identification with others. Definition of self in relation to the system (i.e., this place or the company). Concern with personal circumstances. Extremely high emotional engagement.	The pronoun combination me/them common. Allusive labels. Counting or numeric metaphor.

An earlier version of this table appeared in Mills, 2005, as Table 1, p. 26.

workers' sensemaking accounts in Containers. Here, the prevailing social environment was the most convivial of the three work centers and the material and spatial configuration, task profile (i.e., the necessity to work together) and relatively lower time pressure supported team-based collaborative action.

It is not my intention to promote this alignment between workspace materiality, anchoring concepts, and interpretive discourses as a simple relationship. The wider study shows that a worker's level of emotional engagement played a pivotal role (Mills, 2006) when workers selected a framing discourse to make sense of a particular communication practice or event they collaborated in or observed. The combination of choice of discourse and embodied emotion gave a flavor to the language overheard or encountered during the research.

Summary and Conclusion

This chapter has shown how configurations of matter and space can define the ideational resources factory workers use to make sense of communication and physical routines. It shows how "anchoring concepts" provide a mechanism for interpretive discourses to unite communication and materiality in a way that allows them to exert an integrated constitutive agency on thinking and organizing. This integrated constitutive performance can be likened to dancers performing a waltz. Without each partner there is no waltz – no performance to satisfy the norms of the waltz dance genre. Like the waltz, the human and non-human dimensions in a particular workspace become a collection of coordinated sociomaterial practices. These enact recognizable performances that are reflected in the meanings captured in the anchoring concepts in the workers interpretive discourses. Thus, the case in this chapter demonstrates how human (the dancers) and non-human matter are integrated in coordinated ways dictated by the meaning of key concepts that define the "genres" of work practices that prevail in a particular workspace (i.e., work center). At the same time, it recognises that discourse and materiality are empirically distinct but in tensions with each other as they collaborate in a constantly co-emergent interplay (Putnam, 2015).

The correspondence revealed between the interpretive discourses the factory workers' use to make sense of communication, the discursive resources (i.e., anchoring concepts) embedded in these discourses and workplace materiality provides a concrete example of the convergence or interpenetration of symbolic, social and material dimensions of organizing: what Orlikowski (2010, p.127) calls "entanglement in practice" and meaning making. It shows how communication allows the *plenum of agencies* (Ashcraft, Kuhn, & Cooren, 2009, p. 29) across matter, discourse and meaning to constitute the process of organizing and thus the relationships at the heart of the organization itself. Most importantly, the analysis reveals a mechanism by which the material world of work comes to matter as much as the ideational as aspects of work (e.g., language), not just because matter is inextricably active in all organizational practices that constitute organizing (Orlikowski, 2007), but because it dictates what ideas like WIW and GOW mean.

Implications for Research, Theory and Practice

This chapter exemplifies how materiality and discourse can be accounted for jointly rather than as a binary opposition. In doing so, it provides insights into the way organizational communication scholarship can investigate work settings that have largely been left on the curb side: factories and assembly plants and other sites where physical blue-collar work occurs. It suggests that exclusive attention to discourse has its drawbacks as it naturally draws the researcher's attention to contexts where talk is important (e.g., meetings) and where numerous documents are produced. The consequence is that an important proportion of the work contributing to national economies – the semi-skilled manual work – may be overlooked. Additionally, it may give the impression that intellectual work (i.e., white-collar work) is abstracted from its material circumstances.

Theoretically speaking, not only does this chapter illustrate how matter, both human and non-human, comes to matter in conjunction with and as part of communication that constitutes organizing, it also provides a segue between the communication constitutes the organization (CCO) perspective and the concept sociomateriality (Orlikowski, 2007) and sensemaking practices.

The case materializes the *plenum of agencies* (Ashcraft, Kuhn, and Cooren, 2009, p. 29) that come into play when workers interact at work. It also empirically demonstrates how materiality is "an ingredient of social phenomena", and social phenomena are "intercalated constellations of practices, technology, and materiality" (Schatzki, 2010, p. 123), while raising the visibility of meaning-making, which, after all, is at the heart of our most practiced and accepted definitions of communication (Kuhn, Ashcraft, & Cooren, 2017). It sounds complicated, attending concurrently to the social, material and cognitive dimensions of a workplace, but this is necessary in order to gain a dynamic and holistic appreciation of self-sustaining human social systems.

Notes

1 "Pissed off" is a colloquial term meaning angry.
2 "Smoko" is a colloquial term referring to work breaks where workers gather to chat, drink tea or coffee, or eat a meal.

References

Alvesson, M., & Kärreman, D. (2000). Taking the linguistic turn in organizational research: Challenges, responses, consequences. *Journal of Applied Behavioral Science 36*(2), 136–158.

Arnaud, N., Mills, C. E., Legrand, C., & Maton, E. (2016). Materialising strategy in mundane tools: The key to coupling global strategy and local strategy practice? *British Journal of Management, 27*(1), 38–57.

Ashcraft, K. L., Kuhn, T. R., & Cooren, F (2009). Constitutional amendments: Materializing organizational communication. *Academy of Management Annals, 3*(1), 1–64.

Babbage, C. (1832). *On the economy of machinery and manufactures* (4th edn.). London: Charles Knight.

Barad, K. (2003). Posthumanist performativity: Toward an understanding of how matter comes to matter. *Signs, 28*(3), 801–831.

Barad, K. (2007). *Meeting the universe halfway: Quantum physics and the entanglement of matter and meaning.* Durham, NC: Durham University Press.

Bavdaz, A. (2018). Past and recent conceptualisations of sociomateriality and its features: Review. *Athens Journal of Social Sciences, 5*(1), 51–78.

Callon, M. (1984). Some elements of a sociology of translation: Domestication of the scallops and the fishermen of St Brieuc Bay. *The Sociological Review, 32*(1), 196–233. https://doi.org/10.1111/j.1467-954X.1984.tb00113.x.

Carlile, P. R., Nicolini, D., Langley, A., & Tsoukas, H. (Eds.). (2013) *How matter matters: Objects, artifacts, and materiality in organizational studies.* Oxford: Oxford University Press.

Cooren, F (2004) Textual agency: How texts do things in organizational settings. *Organization, 11*(3), 373–393.

Cooren, F., & Fairhurst, G. T. (2004). Speech timing and spacing: The phenomenon of organizational closure. *Organization, 11*, 793–824.

de Vaujany, F.-X., & Vaast, E. (2016). Matters of visuality in legitimation practices: Dual iconographies in a meeting room. *Organization, 23*(5), 763–790.

Fairhurst, G. (1993). The leader–member exchange patterns of women leaders in industry: A discourse analysis. *Communication Monographs, 60*, 321–351.

Fairhurst, G. T., Green, S.G., & Courtright, J. A. (1995). Inertial forces and the implementation of a socio-technical systems approach: A communication study. *Organization Science, 6*, 168–185.

Fairhurst, G.T., Rogers, L.E., & Sarr, R. (1987). Manager–subordinate control patterns and judgments about the relationship. In M. McLaughlin (Ed.), *Communication yearbook* (Vol. 10, pp. 395–415). Beverly Hills, CA: Sage.

Fayol, H. (1949). *General and industrial management* (C. Storrs, Trans.). London: Pitman.

Glaser, B.G. (1978). *Theoretical sensitivity*. San Francisco: University of California Press.

Glaser, B.G. (1992). *Emergence vs forcing: Basics of Grounded Theory analysis*. Mill Valley, CA: Sociology Press.

Glaser, B. G. (1998). *Doing grounded theory: Issues and discussions*. Mill Valley, CA: Sociology Press.

Glaser, B., & Strauss, A. L. (1967). *The discovery of grounded theory: Strategies for qualitative research*. New York: Aldine De Gruyter.

Groleau, C., & Demers, C. (2016). Modes of design tools: sociomateriality dynamics of a horticultural project. *Communication Research and Practice, 2*(3), 211–333.

Hoggart, R. (1959). *The uses of literacy: Aspects of working-class life with special reference to publications and entertainments*. London: Chatto and Windus.

Jarzabkowski, P., & Pinch, T. (2013). Sociomateriality is "The New Black": Accomplishing repurposing, reinscripting and repairing in context. *M@n@gement, 16*(5), 579–592.

Kilduff, M., Funk, J. L., & Mehra, A. (1997). Engineering Identity in a Japanese Factory. *Organization Science, 8*(6), 579–592. https://doi.org/10.1287/orsc.8.6.579.

Kim, Y., & Yang, E. (2020). Theoretical understanding of sociomateriality in workplace studies. *Facilities, 38*(13/14), 927–942.

Korczynski, M. (2011). The dialectical sense of humour: Routine joking in a Taylorized factory. *Organization Studies, 32*(10), 1421–1439. https://doi.org/10.1177/0170840611421256.

Kuhn, T. R., Ashcraft, K. L., & Cooren, F. (2017). *The work of communication: Relational perspectives on working and organizing in contemporary capitalism*. Routledge.

Latour, B. (1992). Where are the missing masses? Sociology of a few mundane artefacts. In W. Bijker & J. Law (Eds.), *Shaping technology, building society: Studies in sociotechnical change* (pp. 225–258). Cambridge, MA: MIT Press.

Latour, B. (2005). *Reassembling the social- an introduction to actor-network-theory*. Oxford: Oxford University Press.

Law, J. (1992). Notes on the theory of the actor-network: Ordering, strategy and heterogeneity. *Systems Practice. 5*, 379–393.

Leonardi, M., Nardi, B. A., & Kallinikos, J. (Eds.). (2012). *Materiality and organizing: Social interaction in a technological world*. Oxford: University Press Oxford.

Marton, F. (1981). Phenomenography - Describing conceptions of the world around us. *Instructional Science, 10*, 177–200.

Marton, F. (1986). Phenomenography - A research approach to investigating different understandings of reality. *Journal of Thought, 21*(3), 28–49.

Mills, C. (2002). The hidden dimension of blue-collar sensemaking about workplace communication. *Journal of Business Communication, 39*(3), 288–313.

Mills, C. E. (2005). Moving forward by looking back: A model for making sense of organisational communication. *Australian Journal of Communication, 32*(3), 19–43.

Mills, C. E. (2006). Modeling sensemaking about communication: How affect and intellect combine. *Southern Review, 38*(2), 9–23.

Mills, C. E. (2009). Making organisational communication meaningful: Reviewing the key features of a model of sensemaking about change communication. *Australian Journal of Communication, 36*(2), 111–126.

Mills, C. E., & Cooren, F. (Eds.). (2018). *Discursivity, relationality and materiality in the life of the organisation: Communication perspectives*. Abingdon: Routledge.

Orlikowski, W. J. (2007). Sociomaterial practices: Exploring technology at work. *Organizational Studies, 28*(9), 1435–1448.

Orlikowski, W. J. (2010). The sociomateriality of organizational life: Considering technology in management research. *Cambridge Journal of Economics, 34*, 125–141.

Orlikowski, W. J., & Scott, S. V. (2008). Sociomateriality: Challenging the separation of technology, work and organization. *The Academy of Management Annals, 2*(1), 433–474.

Poole, M. S., Folger, J. P., & Hewes, D. E. (1987). Analyzing interpersonal interaction. In G. R. Miller & M. Roloff (Eds.), *Explorations in interpersonal communication* (pp. 220–255). Beverley Hills, CA: Sage.

Putnam, L. L. (2015). Unpacking the dialectic: Alternative views on the discourse-materiality relationship. *Journal of Management Studies, 52*(5), 706–716.

Putnam, L. L., & Cooren, F. (2004). Alternative perspectives on the role of text and agency in constituting organizations. *Organization, 11*(3), 323–333.

Putnam, L. L., & Nicotera, A. M. (Eds.). (2008). *Building theories of organization: The constitutive role of communication*. Oxford: Routledge.

Robichaud, D., & Cooren, F. (Eds.). (2013). *Organization and organizing: Materiality, agency and discourse*. New York: Routledge.

Schatzki. T. (2010). Materiality and social life. *Nature and Culture, 5*(2), (123–149).

Schoeneborn, D., & Blaschke, S. (2014). The three schools of CCO thinking: Interactive dialogue and systematic comparison. *Management Communication Quarterly, 28*(2), 285–316.

Schoeneborn, D., Kuhn, T. R., & Kärreman, D. (2019). The communicative constitution of organization, organizing, and organizationality. *Organization Studies, 40*(4), 475–496.

Schoeneborn, D., & Sandhu, S. (2013). When birds of different feather flock together: The emerging debate on "organization as communication" in the German-speaking countries. *Management Communication Quarterly, 27*(2), 301–311.

Suchman, L. (2007). *Human-machine reconfigurations: Plans and situated actions*. Cambridge, UK: Cambridge University Press.

Taylor, F. W. (1911). *The principles of scientific management*. New York: Harper & Brothers.

Taylor, J. R. (1993). *Rethinking the theory of organizational communication: How to read an organization*. Norwood, NJ: Ablex.

Taylor, J. R., & Van Every, E. J. (2000). *The emergent organization. Communication as site and surface*. Mahwah, NJ: Lawrence Erlbaum.

Tracy, S. J. (2013). *Qualitative research methods: Collecting evidence, crafting analysis, communicating impact*. Chichester: John Wiley & Sons.

Weick, K. E. (1979). *The social psychology of organizing*. New York: Random House.

Weick, K. E. (1995). *Sensemaking in organizations*. Thousand Oaks, CA: Sage.

Williams, R. (1961). *The long revolution*. New York: Columbia University Press.

Zammuto, R. F., Griffith, T. L., Majchrzak, A., Dougherty, D. J., & Faraj, S. (2007). Information technology and the changing fabric of organization, *Organization Science, 18*(5), 749–762.

32

CONSTITUTING HAZARDS AND ACTION THROUGH COMMUNICATION

A CCO View of High-Reliability Organizing

Jody Jahn and Rebecca M. Rice

Introduction

The impetus for developing theorizing on high-reliability organizing (HRO) was a broad practical problem: how do organization members manage sources of complexity (e.g., technology, changing conditions, sustained coordinated activities) to plan for contingencies, and avoid accumulating errors and possible catastrophes? Early HRO theorists—Todd LaPorte, Karleen Roberts, Karl Weick, Kathleen Sutcliffe, Gene Rochlin—approached this problem by examining what nuclear submarines, nuclear power plants, and aircraft carriers' crews did "right" to *reliably* notice subtle problems, correct mistakes, and avoid accidents. They coined the name "high reliability organization", which became both a label for the types of organizational contexts that manage such conditions on a regular basis (e.g., an aircraft carrier is *a type of* HRO context), as well as denoting an area of theorizing about organizational process (e.g., emergency management involves *organizing processes* that result in "reliably" accident-free outcomes). In this chapter, we suggest that current theorizing offers partial explanations for how HRO processes occur because it both under-explains the role of communication, and largely overlooks the role of materiality in high-reliability organizing. First, HRO theorizing explains how vigilant coordinated actions constitute an organization's ability to reliably avoid catastrophes, but it mostly focuses on communication's role in coordinating action to the extent that it is involved in exchanging information. Second, HRO theorizing considers *material* actors (e.g., documents, technology, equipment, spaces) as part of the "operating environment" or "context," rather than directly explaining the roles they play as members communicate to organize action. To address these two key deficiencies in high-reliability theory, this chapter proposes ways that possible hazards and tactics are constructed through communication in emerging circumstances. In particular, we apply a communication as constitutive of organization (CCO) perspective to theorize how HRO members construct plans of action as they communicate their knowledge and ideas, and we consider ways various material objects enable and constrain the tactical possibilities they see as being available to them.

This paper proceeds as follows: we briefly review three ways HRO literature talks around communication and materiality without directly addressing their roles in organizing. We then

DOI: 10.4324/9781003224914-37

explain how HRO theorizing would benefit from a communication as constitutive of organization, or CCO, perspective that considers how talk, material objects, and physical spaces actively participate in organizing (Cooren, 2010, 2020; Jahn, 2018; Rice, 2022). In effect, we start with the same practical problems as did early HRO researchers, but we take our theorizing in a different direction—one grounded in a view that sees communication as the primary explanation for how organizing occurs, and which considers human, nonhuman, and material actors to be impactful participants in organizing (Ashcraft, Kuhn, & Cooren, 2009; Cooren, 2010; Kuhn, Ashcraft, & Cooren, 2017; Latour, 2005; Nicolini, 2011). We then revisit the core problems identified in the beginning of the chapter through a CCO lens, using illustrations drawn from emergency management and wildland firefighting.

High-Reliability Organizations and Three Core Organizing Challenges

High-reliability organizations (HROs) are defined by their ability to maintain stable, accident-free outcomes (i.e., reliability) (Weick & Sutcliffe, 2015). Importantly, achieving stable outcomes is a matter of process as organization members maintain constant mindful awareness of their actions and surroundings, and change courses of action as events warrant (Weick & Sutcliffe, 2015). Studies of high-reliability organizations have included a broad range of organizational types, including nuclear power plants (Barbour & Gill, 2014), wildland firefighting teams (Jahn, 2016; Jahn & Black, 2017; Weick, 1993), emergency and crisis collaborations (Rice, 2018, 2021), and military and security organizations (Bean & Rice, 2019; Browning et al., 2000; Weick & Roberts, 1993). High-reliability theorizing grew from an interpretive tradition in which researchers explained how HRO members avoided major accidents through constructing interpretive schemas about three main organizational processes: (1) making sense of operating environments (Rochlin, 1993; Weick, 1995; Weick & Sutcliffe, 2015; Weick, Sutcliffe, & Obstfeld, 1999), (2) coordinating action (Grabowski & Roberts, 1997; Weick & Roberts, 1993), and (3) acquiring organizational lessons (Klein, Bigley, & Roberts, 1995; see Table 32.1). This first section argues that early HRO theorizing implies that communication is important for information exchange but does little to unravel how and why communication might be complex. Early HRO research also acknowledges that materiality (e.g., technology, physical spaces, texts) plays an important role in the real-life operation of HROs, but tends to talk around how material objects, or "figures", participate in constructing an understanding of an emerging situation and what to do about it. This undertheorized area of HRO literature is limiting because both communication processes and material conditions are central (not peripheral) to achieving reliability. That centrality can be more explicitly theorized using a CCO conceptualization of the relationship between human agents and the material world as it unfolds through communication.

Problem 1: Making Sense of the Operating Environment

The *operating environment* consists of the material circumstances to which the organization must be cognizant and flexible, and which can constrain the organization's function. High-reliability organizations are unique because they must operate without major errors and under time pressure, while encountering consequential hazards (Rochlin, 1993). HRO operating environments are complex. There might be ambiguity about lurking hazards or what information might be helpful, and there could be multiple conflicting interpretations about what can or should happen (Weick, 2001). Complexity and ambiguity might arise while managing technology (e.g., nuclear power plant, air traffic control), and elements of nature (e.g., wildland firefighting, disaster response), or while diagnosing bodily maladies (e.g., hospital emergency rooms). In each of these situations, members encounter chaos and consider various explanations and trajectories forward.

Weick and colleagues proposed that HROs avoid catastrophic failures through engaging in *sensemaking* (Weick, 1995) and *mindfulness* (Weick, Sutcliffe, & Obstfeld, 1999). Sensemaking refers to an action-oriented process by which organizational actors develop ongoing explanations of unfolding events through taking actions, and then using their actions as data to build their narrative of what is happening (Weick, 1995). More specific than sensemaking, *mindfulness* refers to organization members maintaining vigilant attention on their surroundings and actions, and adapting as conditions change (Weick & Sutcliffe, 2015; Weick et al., 1999). Three mindfulness "principles" address how members keep track of their operating environment. *Sensitivity to operations* refers to members' focused attention to the circumstances they face, and efforts to share information with others to build a "big picture" awareness of an operation and its risks (Weick & Sutcliffe, 2015). *Reluctance to simplify interpretations* means that members resist jumping to simple conclusions. Rather, they seek out nuanced explanations for what they see and experience so their trajectory of action accounts for as many hazards and back-up plans as possible (Weick & Sutcliffe, 2015). *Commitment to resilience* refers to capabilities to bounce back from setbacks or mistakes; these capabilities form as members develop multiple areas of expertise, and broaden their repertoires of understanding and action (Weick & Sutcliffe, 2015).

These concepts explain how HRO members notice subtle cues in environments, monitor complex technologies, and navigate around known, anticipated, or emergent hazards. However, HRO theorizing grounded in management and social psychology disciplines has only begun to address the complexities with communicating hazards, especially when member's understandings of them are uncertain or provisional (Barton & Sutcliffe, 2009; Jahn, 2019). Further, the materiality associated with technologies and physical spaces is considered to be external or apart from organizing such that they inform organizing efforts but are not theorized as *participating* in organizing. Later in the chapter, we will apply a CCO approach to develop theorizing on both of these matters (Cooren, 2010, 2020; Jahn, 2016, 2018; Rice, 2021, 2022).

Problem 2: Coordinating Action

Another defining characteristic of HROs is that they accomplish complex tasks that require coordination among numerous organizational units and actors (Rochlin, 1993). A coordination focus highlights that reliably avoiding accidents is possible when members can imagine the "big picture" of what their operation aims to accomplish, including understanding how local practices or routines contribute to broader organizational efforts (Grabowski & Roberts, 1997). For example, collective mind refers to individuals who act as though they are a group based on their understanding of how their own actions contribute to a collective goal (Weick & Roberts, 1993). Members may occupy specific roles, but they also have freedom to improvise a wider scope of activities with their group's "big picture" in mind. The mindfulness principle *deference to expertise* also captures the shifting nature of roles and authorities in that it refers to an organization's commitment to empower those who are most knowledgeable about an issue to have authority over it, regardless of their rank (Weick & Sutcliffe, 2015).

Note here that coordinating action for high reliability depends on the assumption that members will build a shared large-scale understanding of an operation so they can fit their individual actions into the broader organizational effort. Such work assumes that a big-picture understanding is both necessary for organizing and possible, yet HRO theorizing generally does not clarify how a widely shared understanding emerges through communication in the first place. To address this gap in HRO theorizing, the second half of this chapter will apply a CCO perspective that attends to the materiality of objects and physical spaces involved in communication that organizes action (Cooren, 2010, 2020; Jahn, 2018; Rice, 2022). Adopting a CCO approach will lead us to suggest that "big picture" understandings of what an organizing effort aims to accomplish might, in fact, not be necessary or possible. Instead, a CCO view helps us see how members constitute hazards and tactics using fragmented, localized meanings, and we will explain the theoretical and practical consequences of such a shift in analytical focus.

Problem 3: Acquiring Organizational Lessons

High-reliability organizations invest substantial resources into understanding accident causes and preventing similar problems in the future. This *preoccupation with failure* results in accident and fatality reports, training, rules, and procedures that codify lessons from mishaps (Weick & Sutcliffe, 2015; Zeigler, 2007). Organizational failures are not simply stored in technical documentation, they also are symbolic stories that evoke member values about safety (Klein et al., 1995). Scholars point to *organizational culture* as the source for reliability, suggesting that the organization's norms for addressing mistakes and failures are at the heart of safe operations (Rochlin, 1993). HROs tend to have safety "cultures" that reward detecting mistakes and learning from them rather than punishing members (Klein et al., 1995).

A focus on acquiring lessons from failures focuses on ways members internalize symbolism from such events to inform their value systems and work. However, while organizational culture might be an important symbolic repository for failure lessons, we will propose that HRO theorizing would benefit from applying a CCO lens to consider additional textual objects (e.g., technical documents) that codify life-or-death lessons, along with ways those objects are invoked, negotiated, and otherwise communicated to both constitute action in the moment (Cooren, 2004, 2010; Jahn, 2016; Rice & Jahn, 2020; Rice, 2021) and help members build expertise (Jahn, 2019).

In summary so far, existing HRO theorizing falls under an interpretive lens, addressing the practical question: *how do organizations interpret chaotic circumstances and complexity to construct an accident-avoidant response?* HRO studies and theorizing generally imply that communication is important and that material actors are present in organizing efforts aimed at *avoiding* hazards and accidents, but they provide limited explanation about how. This chapter embraces the complexity of communication and materiality in HRO contexts. Drawing from communication as constitutive of organizing (CCO) theorizing, we explore the potential for communication processes to construct an actionable understanding of emerging circumstances. We consider how materiality (e.g., texts, physical spaces, technologies) participates in members' efforts to articulate what they see as hazards and formulate trajectories of action in response (see also Wilhoit Larson & Mengis, 2022). Using CCO theorizing, we argue that reliability practices are generated in the relationship among material hazards and communication, or the ways HRO members interact with, interpret, and respond to the material world (Cooren, 2020).

A CCO View of the HRO Phenomenon

If we zoom-out on the broader phenomenon that existing HRO theorizing addresses, we would see that it offers explanations for how to organize for *contingencies*, referring to "a future event or circumstance that is possible but cannot be predicted with certainty" (*Contingency*, n.d.). Bruno Latour (2005) noted that a most universal life experience is stumbling upon puzzling circumstances that force us to reconfigure our knowledge: "A new vaccine is being marketed, a new job description is offered, […] a new catastrophe occurs. In each instance, we have to reshuffle our conceptions of what was associated together because the previous definition has been made somewhat irrelevant" (p. 6). In the spirit of re-shuffling our thinking, we propose shifting HRO thinking away from explaining how organizing processes enable "avoiding" hazards. Instead, this chapter asks how various actors (e.g., humans, texts, physical spaces) configure themselves to materialize hazards (e.g., make them visible and prioritize them) through communication processes. As such, this theory-building effort begins with a question grounded in a CCO perspective: *how do human and non-human actors configure themselves through communication to materialize possible hazards and trajectories for action?*

For this chapter, we adopt a relational view of CCO (Kuhn et al., 2017), which involves decentering human agency to account for the roles of materiality—objects, sites, bodies—in social action. That is, social and material aspects of organizational action are intertwined, or *sociomaterial* (Orlikowski, 2007). A relational view of CCO embraces sociomateriality such that it considers that objects and other material agents can make a difference in how a communicative interaction unfolds, and it does not privilege the influence of human agents over that of material objects (Kuhn et al., 2017). Moreover, relational CCO scholars are concerned

Table 32.1 Re-articulating core HRO problems from interpretive and CCO perspectives

Core problem: interpretive view	Theoretical explanation	Core problem: CCO view	Theoretical explanation
1. Making sense of the operating environment	How HRO members notice subtle cues in environments, monitor complex technologies, and navigate around known, anticipated, or emergent hazards. Concepts: 5 Mindfulness/ HRO principles; Sensemaking	1. Materializing the conditions and possible trajectories	How organizational practices bring together humans, objects and spaces such that their trajectory of action brings attention to particular organizational trajectories. Example: Smartmap
2. Coordinating action	How HRO members work to complement each other's actions, share information, develop a "big picture" of shared goals and concerns. Concepts: Collective mindfulness; Heedful interrelating	2. Mediated coordination	How objects and spaces participate in constructing what needs to be done while also creating blind spots in collective interpretations of the organization. Example: Whiteboard
3. Acquiring organizational lessons	How HRO members learn from historic accidents through organizational stories and texts (e.g., safety rules) because they have limited chances to learn from trial and error. Concepts: Organizational culture; Best practices	3. Cross-modal knowledge performances	How enacting lessons codified in texts transfers the knowledge from a written to a lived modality. How texts enter the action sequence influences the lessons possible to derive from them. Example: Safety rule genre change

with analyzing what occurs in the *flatland* of ongoing interactions (Taylor & Van Every, 2000). Analysts pay attention to the various *figures* (objects, ideas, discourses, texts, symbols, etc.) made present through communication during an episode of interaction (Cooren, 2010), and trace connections among them (Latour, 2005) to understand how hybrid action emerges. A relational view of CCO locates organizing in the *relationship* among social and material elements, thus embracing the CCO commitment to relationality (Cooren, 2020). One way to think about hybrid action is to imagine that "a third actor emerges out of the connection between the human [and the object]" (Robichaud, 2006, p. 106). Some examples of hybrid action include figures (Cooren & Matte, 2010), actor-networks (Latour, 2005; Robichaud, 2006), assemblages (Kuhn et al., 2017), agential-performative linkages (Jahn, 2018), and scripted trajectories (Vásquez, 2013). Considering the latter, Vásquez (2013) flags a multiplicity of possible trajectories as a key challenge for organizing processes that are intended to unfold similarly in different places and times (e.g., following rules or best practices). She proposes that organizations align their geographically and temporally dispersed operations through a *scripted trajectory*, or a main story of what the organizing effort aims to accomplish. With the idea of a scripted trajectory in mind, some scholars propose that organizational *practices* are a useful context to observe hybrid action as it takes place through communication (Kuhn et al., 2017; Nicolini, 2009, 2011).

How hybrid action takes place shapes the meanings of the various sociomaterial actors, or the *plenum of agencies*, involved (Cooren, 2006). An organizational practice, then, provides an analytical site in which to track the co-participation of sociomaterial actors (Nicolini, 2011; Mills, 2022; Wilhoit & Kisselburgh, 2019). Practices combine actor agencies in ways that develop new meanings, change meanings, and instantiate long-standing meanings of objects and sites. Cooren and Matte (2010) demonstrated this in their analysis of a measuring stick used by humanitarian organization Médecins Sans Frontières in Niger, Africa. The measuring stick was used to determine which children qualified for nutritional assistance by measuring their height against scientific growth curves. The authors pointed out that the measuring stick, a material object, together with human agents created courses of intervention, authorized discrimination, and delegated responsibility (or not) for these children. Focusing on organizational practice is compatible with a relational view of CCO, because practices draw attention to sequences of action in which various agents (human or otherwise) participate or make a difference in unfolding communication and activity (Castor & Cooren, 2006). To better understand the role of meaning in hybrid co-action, we need to accept a few assumptions about how existing meanings of various actors do and do not enter our analysis of a practice. First, a relational view of CCO generally assumes that organizational action unfolds *in media res*, or in the middle of things (Kuhn et al., 2017; Latour, 2005). Meanings are neither completely generative, nor entirely deterministic. Rather, some material elements will bring their longer-standing meanings into interactions in ways that influence how action unfolds (Latour, 2005). For instance, Iedema and Wodak (1999) explained that meanings of organizational texts get *recontextualized* when texts travel from one place (or context) to another, and when their meanings are interpreted from one modality to another (e.g., from text to lived experience, such as acting out one's interpretation of a written safety rule). Thus, "recontextualization involves shifts in meaning and materiality away from their previous instantiations" (Iedema & Wodak, 1999, p. 13). The notion of recontextualization captures the idea that organizing processes are constituted in ongoing communication and action, or re-enacted for the next first time, meaning that even familiar routines are subject to change based on current circumstances (Iedema & Wodak, 1999).

Second, a CCO orientation assumes that action occurs in the flatland of ongoing interactions. Attending to the flatland means we see what is operating in each interaction episode, taking care not to take any actions as a given and accepting that some elements act from a distance (Kuhn et al., 2017; Latour, 2005). CCO scholars have proposed numerous perspectives to study this flatland of interaction among agents, including translation (Brummans et al., 2014), presentification (Benoit-Barné & Cooren, 2009), and ventriloquization (Cooren, 2010). We focus on ventriloquization in this illustration. Ventriloquization emphasizes that numerous agents can be voiced in interactions, but that these ventriloquized agents also "speak through" conversants. Ventriloquism makes multiple figures present in the interaction, and these figures then make a difference in the outcome of the interaction. As various actors (human, material or otherwise) combine their agencies, they create unique possible trajectories of action that would not be possible by any actor alone—this relational perspective reminds us that, through communication, actor agencies transform and constitute new potential outcomes (Kuhn et al., 2017). Because it is not given how an actor might participate in organizing, multiple trajectories of hybrid action are possible. The next section returns to the three core problems of HRO theorizing and reconsiders how a relational CCO orientation enables us to see HRO activities differently.

Revisiting the Core Problems of HRO Theorizing

Adopting a relational CCO lens on HRO challenges analysts to attend to both hybrid co-action involving humans, objects, sites, etc., and a preoccupation with the flatland of ongoing interactions. As such, a compatible methodological approach for studying HRO includes exploring organizational practice (Rice & Jahn, 2020). A practice-based approach considers that practices are analytical sites in which human activity, material objects, meaning, and purpose combine in order-producing, knowledge-enacting performances (Nicolini, 2011). For CCO, practices are sites where relationships among human, material and other actors emerge through communication, and act in a hybrid manner to constitute organizations (Cnossen & Bencherki, 2019). Building from Nicolini (2009, 2011), we propose methodological approaches that *zoom in* on, and *zoom out* from, practical communication (see Table 31.1 for overview). Further, empirical illustrations are drawn from emergency management and wildland firefighting research projects.

Problem 1: From Making Sense of the Operating Environment *to* Materializing Conditions and Possible Trajectories

One way to consider how conditions and possible trajectories get materialized in practice is to *zoom in* on practice to examine how communicators ventriloquize materials and tools during everyday work. Nicolini (2009) suggests that tools do not just help human actors to accomplish work, they also *shape* how it is done, by inscribing "norms of cognition, the assumptions of how work should be carried out, and purposes of use" (p. 1406). From a CCO perspective, we can see how, by allowing the tools to be spoken into conversations, these tools also influence activity. Using observation focused on practice can highlight how technologies, the physical environment, and people produce hybrid co-action that both produces and makes sense of hazards.

A central practice for many HROs is *creating situational awareness*—or trying to share information about hazards with everyone involved in the response. In the USA, offices of emergency management (OEMs) exist at the local level to prepare for and respond to hazards impacting populous communities. To create situational awareness, HRO personnel must interrelate with multiple tools to materialize both the hazards and their responses to them.

Situational awareness, then, involves *organizing the space* of the response area. Emergency management staff sit in a shared room so that members can coordinate across jobs and relay information to first responders in the field, which involves a wide variety of technologies. The practice of *mapping hazards* involves hybrid action between staff members and mapping technologies. In the second author's observation of emergency management practitioners, mapping has involved a constellation of technologies, people, and things, including a website where members could enter road closures caused by hazards, and a smartmap that was projected and updated by staff members so that all members could visualize the hazard and related road closures. This smartmap facilitated members' preferred hazard response trajectories by allowing them to visualize and seemingly "contain" the hazard, while also constraining and influencing members by deeming certain information about the hazard as relevant and irrelevant.

For example, OEM members spoke in interviews about challenges to using the map software and the smartmap. The software used to map hazards asked OEM members to enter the intersections of road closures during an emergency, so that first responders could engage the software to know what roads were impassable. However, Paul, a member of the OEM, explained that simply entering the location of a road closure was not helpful, because hazards did not just impact intersections, they could affect several miles of road. In practice, members explained these changes as an important part of the trajectory of their response. They also reinforced the value of changes in the mapping technology by reminding each other to ask first responders in the field for the starting and ending intersections of road closures because the software required multiple data points (fieldnote). In other words, they made the software speak about its needs, in order to build a reliable map to guide them. By doing so, they ventriloquized the map software as guiding their best practices to achieve reliability. However, by allowing the mapping technology to speak, the members also gave the software influence over their practices, agreeing to operate within the constraints of the software.

As this example demonstrates, logics of practice (like mapping) can be shaped by technologies used to accomplish these practices. In mapping practices, emergency management personnel followed norms of cognition about what information about a hazard is relevant to accomplish their work, especially the hazard's impact on space and mobility during the response. However, the web of practices associated with mapping also involved OEM members in ways that guided their priorities, activities, and interactions with other members in the room. By prioritizing the information on the smartmap (over other sources of information), the smartmap influenced what the HRO personnel viewed as the real hazards, and as such marked their trajectory for providing an emergency response.

Problem 2: From Coordinating Action *to* Mediated Coordination

To understand how coordination does not pertain only to shared activities among humans, but is rather mediated with participating objects, Nicolini (2009) suggests following a practice suggests identifying interconnected nodes of different practices that materialize hazards and trajectories in a physical space. This method of zooming out uses ethnographic observation to follow a practice and gain understanding about the multiple sites in which it manifests itself (Nicolini, 2009), and can be used to understand how organizations exist across multiple modes and spaces (Bencherki & Elmholdt, 2020). Bencherki and Elmholdt (2020) suggested tracing "passage" between spaces and entities as a method to study organizing. The focus of this excerpt is how a whiteboard participated in generating an overview, or situational awareness, of an incident. When viewed in relationship to other practices, the sociomaterial practice of situational awareness can reveal how conceptions of work emerge through the passage of information that is materialized across multiple modes of existence.

A central tool to the OEM's mapping practice was the significant events board. One member of the OEM was tasked with creating and updating a whiteboard that contained the key events from the emergency response. The whiteboard was placed in a hallway outside the meeting room, so that people from nearby offices could quickly receive updates as they walked by. OEM members also saw the board frequently, as it was in the hallway near the bathrooms. The situational awareness practices in the OEM were not just about identifying hazards on the whiteboard and smartmap, they were also about managing space to control hazards. The whiteboard and smartmap present in this case created two different representations of the hazard in their co-action with human participants. The whiteboard and the mapping technology involved the transformation of multiple agents, including natural hazards, physical resources, and personnel, into both physical and textual representations that influenced organizational activities. The dropdown menus in the mapping software constrained human understandings of the hazard to road intersections. The technologies themselves, then, shaped the trajectory of the understanding of the hazard and the response to that hazard (Castor & Bartesaghi, 2016).

These practices suggest that emergency management personnel are concerned with sharing information about key locations and with *controlling and managing space* in order to ensure safety. In HROs, the materialization of hazards assigned value to space, which communicated to organizational members about how to respond to and document that space. Moreover, a CCO approach reveals that materializations of space actually create fragmented, highly localized, and narrowly targeted pictures of occurrences. These representations guide interpretation and negotiation of shared actions, and are thus useful to the organization as it attempts to accomplish its goals, but materializations of space can never fully represent those spaces. The consequence of these differing representations is that each suggests different trajectories of action for different audiences. There is no single big-picture understanding of an event, but rather, highly specialized representations generated based on ways the various technologies participate through enabling and constraining how the picture is formed.

Problem 3: From **Acquiring Organizational Lessons** *to* **Cross-Modal Knowledge Performances**

High-reliability organizations depend on accidents to learn as much as possible about elusive hazards in their operations (Rochlin, 1993). To learn, organizations codify failure lessons into technical documents—accident reports, safety rules, and others. Safety rules in particular are a repository for organizational lessons, as they often are the common denominators of recurrent accidents (Jahn, 2018; Zeigler, 2007). HRO literature posits that such lessons are symbolic, and are embedded in culture and best practices. Another way to conceptualize learning from accidents, grounded in a CCO view, is to focus on ways that organization members act out safety lessons (e.g., rules), thereby enacting with their body the conceptual lessons codified in physical texts. Such cross-modal knowledge performances involve bringing safety lessons (from a text modality) to life by acting them out in the lived modality of organizational practice. The sequence by which members act out safety rules (and other texts) is referred to as a *scripted* trajectory, which is the main story that aligns and connects various heterogeneous agents (people, documents, values) toward a particular course of action among many possible trajectories (Vásquez, 2013). The notion of *scripting* is important here because it captures the intention of an organizing process. Drawing from Latour (2013), a script is a *program of action* that hybrid agents perform. Of note, scripted trajectories can change, thereby changing the sequence by which texts participate in action; such changes can impact how hybrid agency unfolds and to what effects (Cooren & Matte; 2010; Jahn, 2018).

In a study on genre change, Jahn (2018) illustrated how a change in safety policy resulted in safety rules entering firefighters' decision process at different times, for new reasons, and with important impacts on how members learned from the lessons rules codify. In particular, the new wildland fire "doctrine" policy removed a requirement that firefighters follow all safety rules; instead, the doctrine policy allowed firefighters to bend or disregard safety rules based on their judgement. Acting in accordance to rules can be considered a *cross-modal* endeavor because it involves translating the lessons in rules from a written modality to a lived modality. To act with knowledge in wildland firefighting involves hybrid action between firefighters and rules in ways that materialize both possible hazards and possible trajectories of activity (Jahn, 2018). This study found that the sequence in which rules entered the decision process shaped whether and how workers materialized hazards. In particular, before doctrine, rules were considered early in the decision process and constrained firefighter's actions if rules could not be followed. After doctrine, firefighter judgement came earlier than rules in the decision process, meaning firefighters described making decisions to act, and then they backed up those decisions by selectively invoking the rules that supported their decisions. The findings suggest how possibilities for a text's participation in a scripted trajectory change when its genre changed. That is, doctrine's privileging of firefighter judgement over the authority of the safety rules seemed to render them less impactful in efforts to voice dissent, which some research identifies as a central mechanism contributing to high reliability (Barton & Sutcliffe, 2009; Jahn, 2019). Given these findings, HRO theorizing would benefit from adopting a CCO view by considering how and when safety rules and hazards (and other figures) participate in practices that define and set trajectories for action (see also Cooren & Matte, 2010).

Conclusions

This chapter identified three core problems that HRO theorizing addresses, and proposed ways a CCO framing of HRO highlights how material objects and sites participate in trajectories of organizing that make hazards visible in different ways. This chapter proposed that future analysts of HROs examine human-material configurations that become apparent in practical communication. We close with three insights about the value of this approach for explaining high reliability.

First, a relational CCO approach to high-reliability organizing reveals how *properties of the objects* participating in defining a situation shape the definition. While early HRO scholars considered how members built a faithful, "accurate" representation of hazards *out there*, CCO analysts attend to human and material configurations that built a representation of events (i.e., "situational awareness") of the disaster area. Taking the properties of objects and technologies into account when theorizing about HROs can highlight the various layers of physical representations (maps, websites, software) by which we become removed from the very circumstances we seek to describe. Instead, coordination efforts are influenced by the representations of these circumstances through material tools and objects. Such an insight can help practitioners identify where certain technologies are helpful and where they could be improved.

Second, a relational CCO approach to HROs demonstrates that there will always be too much information about a hazard and no way to truly generate a shared "big picture". Instead, by examining configurations of humans, objects, and sites, we gain multiple, fragmented, localized representations of events. This insight deflates the triumph associated with traditional

HRO theorists' claim that a "big picture" provides a script that coordinates action in a coherent manner. However, the value of a CCO approach is that it helps to highlight where and why there might be conflicting understandings of events, and blank spots in which certain emergencies or resource needs are not being met. As reliability organizing expands to meet evolving community threats and transcend intraorganizational boundaries (Rice, 2021), a CCO approach encourages scholarship to move beyond the "big picture" to instead consider how various people, objects, and the environment constitute fragmented and partial understandings.

Finally, a CCO approach to explaining high reliability provides a new way to think about organizational knowledge and embodied learning. When organizational knowledge, such as lessons derived from accidents and fatalities, becomes codified in safety rules or other technical documents, the rich lessons lose their nuance. Therefore, organizations like wildland firefighting lament that they keep "learning the same lessons over and over again". A CCO lens on HRO helps us see that lessons are not entirely inscribed in cultural rituals and stories, they also exist as members communicate with each other and engage with safety texts in their decision-making sequences.

Overall, adopting a CCO lens on high-reliability organizing can help theorists and practitioners develop reflexive awareness about ways everyday organizational practices and activities might hinder (or enable) communication and learning about hazards, while also highlighting strategies for invoking various figures to construct meaning, negotiate action, voice dissent, and leverage authority.

References

Ashcraft, K. L., Kuhn, T. R., & Cooren, F. (2009). 1 Constitutional amendments: "Materializing" organizational communication. *Academy of Management Annals*, *3*(1), 1–64.

Barbour, J. B., & Gill, R. (2014). Designing communication for the day-to-day safety oversight of nuclear power plants. *Journal of Applied Communication Research*, *42*(2), 168–189. https://doi.org/10.1080/00909882.2013.859291.

Barton, M. A. & Sutcliffe, K. M. (2009). Overcoming dysfunctional momentum: Organizational safety as a social achievement. *Human Relations*, *62*, 1327–1356.

Bean, H., & Rice, R. M. (2019). Organizational communication and security. In B. C. Taylor & H. Bean (Eds.), *The handbook of communication and security* (pp. 136–152). Routledge.

Bencherki, N., & Elmholdt, K. T. (2020). The organization's synaptic mode of existence: How a hospital merger is many things at once. *Organization*. https://doi.org/10.1177/1350508420962025.

Benoit-Barné, C., & Cooren, F. (2009). The accomplishment of authority through presentification: How authority is distributed among and negotiated by organizational members. *Management Communication Quarterly*, *23*(1), 5–31. https://doi.org/10.1177/0893318909335414.

Browning, L. D., Sitkin, S. B., Sutcliffe, K. M., Obstfeld, D., & Greene, R. W. (2000). Keep 'em flying: The constitutive dynamics of organizational change in the US Air Force. *The Electronic Journal of Communication*, *10*. www.cios.org.colorado.idm.oclc.org/EJCPUBLIC/010/1/01012.html.

Brummans, B. H. J. M., Cooren, F., Robichaud, D., & Taylor, J. R. (2013). Approaches to the communicative constitution of organizations. In L. L. Putnam & D. K. Mumby (Eds.), *The SAGE handbook of organizational communication: Advances in theory, research, and methods* (pp. 173–194). Sage.

Castor, T., & Bartesaghi, M. (2016). Metacommunication during disaster response: "Reporting" and the constitution of problems in Hurricane Katrina teleconferences. *Management Communication Quarterly*, *30*(4), 472–502. https://doi.org/10.1177/0893318916646454.

Castor, T., & Cooren, F. (2006). Organizations as hybrid forms of life: The implications of the selection of agency in problem formulation. *Management Communication Quarterly*, *19*(4), 570–600. https://doi.org/10.1177/0893318905284764.

Cnossen, B., & Bencherki, N. (2019). The role of space in the emergence and endurance of organizing: How independent workers and material assemblages constitute organizations. *Human Relations*, *72*(6), 1057–1080. https://doi.org/10.1177/0018726718794265.

Contingency (n.d.). In *Merriam-Webster Online*, retrieved November 1, 2018, from /www.merriam-webster.com/dictionary/contingency.

Cooren, F. (2004). Textual agency: How texts do things in organizational settings. *Organization*, *11*(3), 373–393. https://doi.org/10.1177%2F1350508404041998.

Cooren, F. (2006). The organizational world as a plenum of agencies. In J. R. Taylor, F. Cooren, & E. J. Van Every (Eds.), *Communication as organizing: Empirical and theoretical explorations in the dynamic of text and conversation* (pp. 81–100). Mahwah, NJ: Lawrence Erlbaum.

Cooren, F. (2010). *Action and agency in dialogue: Passion, incarnation and ventriloquism* (Vol. 6). Philadelphia, PA: John Benjamins.

Cooren, F. (2020). Beyond entanglement: (Socio-) Materiality and organization studies. *Organization Theory*, *1*(3), 2631787720954444. https://doi.org/10.1177/2631787720954444.

Cooren, F., & Matte, F. (2010). For a constitutive pragmatics: Obama, Médecins Sans Frontières and the measuring stick. *Pragmatics and Society*, *1*(1), 9–31. https://doi.org/10.1075/ps.1.1.02coo.

Grabowski, M., & Roberts, K. (1997). Risk mitigation in large-scale systems: Lessons from high reliability organizations. *California Management Review*, *39*, 152–162. http://doi.org/10.2307/41165914.

Iedema, R., & Wodak, R. (1999). Introduction: Organizational discourses and practices. *Discourse & Society*, *10*(1), 5–19. http://doi.org/10.1177/0957926599010001001.

Jahn, J. L. S. (2016). Adapting safety rules in a high reliability context: How wildland firefighting workgroups ventriloquize safety rules to understand hazards. *Management Communication Quarterly*, *30*(3), 362–389. https://doi.org/10.1177/0893318915623638.

Jahn, J. L. (2018). Genre as textual agency: Using communicative relationality to theorize the agential–performative relationship between human and generic text. *Communication Monographs*, *85*(4), 515–538. http://doi.org/10.1080/03637751.2018.1481986.

Jahn, J. L. S. (2019). Voice enactment: Linking voice with experience in high reliability organizing. *Journal of Applied Communication Research*, *47*(3), 283–302.

Jahn, J. L. S., & Black, A. E. (2017). A model of communicative and hierarchical foundations of high reliability organizing in wildland firefighting teams. *Management Communication Quarterly*, *31*(3), 356–379. https://doi.org/10.1177/0893318917691358.

Klein, R., Bigley, G., & Roberts, K. (1995). Organization culture in high reliability organizations: An extension. *Human Relations*, *48*, 771–793. https://doi.org/10.1177/001872679504800703.

Kuhn, T., Ashcraft, K. L., & Cooren, F. (2017). *The work of communication: Relational perspectives on working and organizing in contemporary capitalism*. New York: Taylor & Francis.

Latour, B. (2005). *Reassembling the social: An introduction to actor-network-theory*. Oxford University Press.

Latour, B. (2013). "What's the story?" Organizing as a mode of existence. In D. Robichaud & F. Cooren (Eds.), *Organization and organizing: Materiality, agency and discourse* (pp. 37–51). Routledge.

Mills, C. (2022) Constituting organizations: How social and material dimensions are discursively combined to (re)construct workers' organizational reality and the organization. In T. Kuhn, N. Bencherki, & J. Basque (Eds.), *The Routledge handbook of the communicative constitution of organizations*. Routledge.

Nicolini, D. (2009). Zooming in and out: Studying practices by switching theoretical lenses and trailing connections. *Organization Studies*, *30*(12), 1391–1418. https://doi.org/10.1177/0170840609349875.

Nicolini, D. (2011). Practice as the site of knowing: Insights from the field of telemedicine. *Organization Science*, *22*(3), 602–620. https://doi.org/10.1287/orsc.1100.0556.

Orlikowski, W. J. (2007). Sociomaterial practices: Exploring technology at work. *Organization Studies*, *28*(9), 1435–1448. https://doi.org/10.1177/0170840607081138.

Rice, R. M. (2018). When hierarchy becomes collaborative: Collaboration as sensemaking frame in high reliability organizing. *Corporate Communications: An International Journal*, *23*(4), 599–613. https://doi.org/10.1108/CCIJ-04-2017-0032.

Rice, R. M. (2021). High reliability collaborations: Theorizing interorganizational reliability as constituted through translation. Online first in *Management Communication Quarterly*.

Rice, R. M. (2022). *Communicating authority in interorganizational collaboration*. Routledge.

Rice, R. M., & Jahn, J. L. S. (2020). Disaster resilience as communication practice: Remembering and forgetting lessons from past disasters through practices that prepare for the next one. *Journal of Applied Communication Research*, *48*(1), 136–155. https://doi.org/10.1080/00909882.2019.1704830.

Robichaud, D. (2006). Steps toward a relational view of agency. In J. R. Taylor, F. Cooren, & E. J. Van Every (Eds.), *Communication as organizing: Empirical and theoretical explorations in the dynamic of text and conversation* (pp. 101–114). Mahwah, NJ: Lawrence Erlbaum.

Rochlin, G. I. (1993). Defining high reliability organizations in practice: A taxonomic prologue. In K. Roberts (Ed.), *New challenges to organization research: High reliability organizations* (pp. 11–32). New York: MacMillan.

Taylor, J. R., & Van Every, E. (Eds.). (2000). *The emergent organization. Communication as site and surface.* Mahwah, NJ: Lawrence Erlbaum Associates.

Vásquez, C. (2013). Spacing organization: Or how to be here and there at the same time. In D. Robichaud & F. Cooren (Eds.), *Organization and organizing: Materiality, agency, and discourse* (pp. 127–149). New York: Routledge

Weick, K. E. (1993). The collapse of sensemaking in organizations: The Mann Gulch disaster. *Administrative Science Quarterly, 38*(4), 628–652. https://doi.org/10.2307/2393339.

Weick, K. E. (1995). *Sensemaking in organizations.* Thousand Oaks, CA: Sage.

Weick, K. E. (2001). *Making sense of the organization.* Oxford, UK: Blackwell.

Weick, K. E., & Roberts, K. H. (1993). Collective mind in organizations: Heedful interrelating on flight decks. *Administrative Science Quarterly,* 357–381. http://doi.org/10.2307/2393372.

Weick, K. E., & Sutcliffe, K. M. (2015). *Managing the unexpected: Sustained performance in a complex world* (3rd edn.).Hoboken, NJ: John Wiley & Sons.

Weick, K. E., Sutcliffe, K. M., & Obstfeld, D. (1999). Organizing for high reliability: Processes of collective mindfulness. In R. S. Sutton & B. M. Staw (Eds.), *Research in organizational behavior* (Vol. 1, pp. 81–123). Palo Alto, CA: Stanford: Jai Press.

Wilhoit, E. D., & Kisselburgh, L. G. (2019). The relational ontology of resistance: Hybridity, ventriloquism, and materiality in the production of bike commuting as resistance. *Organization, 26*(6), 873–893. https://doi.org/10.1177%2F1350508417723719.

Wilhoit Larson, E. D., & Mengis, J. (2022) The multiple roles of materiality when communication constitutes organizations. In T. Kuhn, N. Bencherki,& J. Basque (Eds.), *The Routledge handbook of the communicative constitution of organizations.* Routledge.

Zeigler, J. A. (2007). The story behind an organizational list: A genealogy of wildland firefighters' 10 Standard Fire Orders. *Communication Monographs, 74,* 415–442. http://doi.org/10.1080/0363775070 1716594.

33

THE THEORETICAL HITCHHIKER'S GUIDE TO SENSEMAKING, COORIENTATION, AND STATUS ASYMMETRY

Stephanie Fox and Jody Jahn

Introduction

There are various ways of studying how organizational members decide on action around a shared problem or object of concern. In the organizational communication subfield, *sensemaking* (Weick, 1995) theorizing has been particularly influential because it equips scholars with a set of tools for creatively imagining how organization members define problems, set courses of action, and anticipate consequences regarding shared organizational problems. Weick's (1995) notion of sensemaking has appealed to organizational communication scholars largely because it implies that communication is a central process that brings about organization. However, the communicative dynamics—especially pertaining to status differences, or asymmetry, between speakers—tend to be under-specified in this body of work. For example, Weick's theorizing implies that communication is central to the process but it also imposes an assumption that communication is largely egalitarian—or that information carries similar weight regardless of who shares it (which departs from many members' lived organizational experiences). Similarly, sensemaking theorizing pays little attention to ways that hierarchy and status shape how communicators position themselves in relation to each other and their shared object of concern. Status asymmetry between speakers (e.g., due to hierarchy, role, professional expertise) can have adverse impacts on sensemaking because having higher status can give more weight to some voices, while lower status can prevent organization members from raising crucial issues. Both consequences of status asymmetry impact how organization members work together to define problems and decide how to manage them.

There is thus a pressing need to theorize how status asymmetry impacts the ways that organization members collectively decide on actions in uncertain or ambiguous situations. In this chapter, we theoretically "hitch a ride" into the conceptual territory of the communicative constitution of organization (CCO) and propose that its notion of *coorientation* is especially suited to explore how communicators navigate such status asymmetry. This effort responds

DOI: 10.4324/9781003224914-38

to multiple calls to better explain how sensemaking is a communication process steeped in profession-specific politics and vulnerable to ways status differences can elevate some voices and suppress others (Jahn, 2019; Maitlis & Christianson, 2014; Maitlis & Sonenschein, 2010; Weick, Sutcliffe, & Obstfeld, 2005).

This chapter proceeds as follows: first, we summarize how work on sensemaking theorizes how organization members share observations about their circumstances to arrive at shared interpretations. We critique this work for failing to unpack how status asymmetry between communicators (e.g., a doctor versus a nurse) impacts which person's interpretation informs future actions. Second, we propose that sensemaking theorizing would benefit from considering how organization members negotiate interpretations of circumstances in ways that account for communicators' status differences. Toward that end, we draw from the ABX model of coorientation (Newcomb, 1953; Taylor & Van Every, 2000) to theorize how organization members manage their status asymmetry in talk. Therefore, the interpretation communicators ultimately build about a set of circumstances emerges from how they negotiate (e.g., invoke, impose, downplay) situational status asymmetries throughout their interactions. Third, we illustrate our theorizing with an extended excerpt analyzing how an interprofessional healthcare team negotiates decisions about a patient's acute hospital care. This chapter extends sensemaking theorizing because it directs our attention to how cues get highlighted as signal or noise, and how an interpretation of a situation is constructed with the intent to understand and/or act. This chapter also contributes to CCO theorizing by further operationalizing the notion of coorientation; in particular, we highlight how relationships between communicators influence their orientation to their object of mutual interest.

Sensemaking: Interpreting Cues and Planning Action

Sensemaking (Weick, 1995; Weick et al., 2005) involves the "ongoing, retrospective development of plausible images that rationalize what people are doing" (Weick et al., 2005, p. 409). Sensemaking entails scanning the environment to look for the most meaningful information among numerous cues. Individuals *enact* their environment, or take action into it (Weick, 1979, 1995); doing so, they *notice* cues from the environment and begin to draft an explanation of what they are experiencing (Weick, 1979). As organization members consider various pieces of information, they *bracket* plausible explanations for their situation. They *label* the cues according to what they might indicate, then *presume* an explanation of what could be going on. Members *select* from among the various explanations and test them to see if they hold together as an explanation. They then act on presumption and retrospectively assess the extent to which the working explanation of their presumptions and action fits with the circumstances they encountered. If the explanation seems to fit the circumstances, then members will *retain* a particular sensemaking account (Weick, 1995; Weick et al., 2005).

Sensemaking is considered a communicative process to the extent that organization members coordinate their observations and interpretations through interactive talk. However, two sensemaking assumptions hinder our understanding about how communicators negotiate or build sense through communication. First, sensemaking work generally assumes that communicators can see a set of circumstances (e.g., information, cues) similarly in the first place, while it under-explains how interpretations of cues are situated in role-related identities. Second, sensemaking assumes that sense emerges from a shared consensus that labeled and bracketed cues are indeed important, while it under-explains how a particular interpretation ends up winning. Thus, sensemaking theorizing tends to view communication as a means of *transmission* (Putnam & Boys, 2006), or a way to share information to align perspectives;

a limitation of this view is that a narrow focus on the transmission of information overlooks how communicators actively build and negotiate sense based on ways their status asymmetry might inhibit, empower, or shape their contributions and, by extension, influence what communicators collectively determine is "signal" or "noise." With these critiques in mind, the next section reviews how sensemaking literature addresses status asymmetry. We then propose how a communicative constitution of organization (CCO) lens helps to address the above critiques to sensemaking theorizing.

Sensemaking Theorizing and Status Asymmetry

Some sensemaking scholars have drawn from research on employee voice to examine how status asymmetry impacts ways organization members build interpretations about organizational problems and what to do about them. Employee voice refers to expressing opinions and ideas meant to benefit the organization (Botero & Van Dyne, 2009). This work addresses how hierarchy influences members' propensity to exercise voice, whether conceived of as supervisor behaviors or as industry or organizational factors that invite or silence voice (Detert & Burris, 2007; Detert & Trevino, 2010; Milliken, Morrison, & Hewlin, 2003). Some sensemaking studies consider communication episodes as important occasions to pause, re-evaluate circumstances, and revise actions to recover from setbacks (Weick, 2011). Importantly, some studies note that status asymmetry impacts whether members participate in sensemaking in the first place. For instance, Barton and Sutcliffe (2009) found that status asymmetry led less-experienced firefighters to question their own expertise, which prevented them from voicing concerns. Similarly, Blatt et al. (2006) attributed medical residents' silence about concerns to their budding professional identity as physicians. This research tends to focus on whether an organization member engages in voice; however, we still need to know *how* members communicate to manage their status asymmetry because that communication process can potentially shape both the content of sensemaking and resulting actions. The next section proposes the A-B-X model of coorientation, which describes how members orient toward a shared problem and each other.

Coorientation's A-B-X Model: The Building Blocks of Organization

Coorientation refers to a process by which two communicators (A and B) discuss a shared concern (X) from their own perspectives (Newcomb, 1953; Taylor & Van Every, 2000). A and B can be individuals or collectives, and it is possible to analytically include more than two communicators, for instance in studies of teamwork (Fox & Gilbert, 2015). The X has been defined as the topic of conversation (Baxter & Akkoor, 2011), as "the content of what the interactions are about" (Spee & Jarzabkowski, 2011, p. 1219), and as "the practical world of joint activities that actively engage people's attention and care" (Taylor & Robichaud, 2004, p. 401). In conversation, A and B continually make sense of their individual orientations (i.e., thoughts, feelings, attitudes) to X and to their relationship with the other person; they also speculate about the other person's orientation toward X and his or her perception of their communicative relationship (Newcomb, 1953). This A-B-X model of coorientation (see Figure 33.1) is particularly valuable for understanding how members negotiate status asymmetry because it suggests how human actors (A and B) communicate to negotiate their relationship and to constitute their shared organizational situation.

Organizational Predilections. Instances of A-B-X coorientation are the basic units of communication that define situations and develop trajectories of action. As such, coorientation is

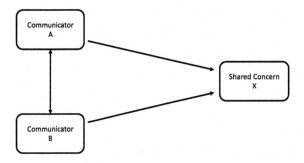

Figure 33.1 Model of A-B-X coorientation.

foundational to the Montreal School's understanding of communication as constitutive of organization (Taylor & Van Every, 2000). Coorientation is considered an ongoing condition of organizational reality, where indeterminateness is the given state of affairs (Cooren, Kuhn, Cornelissen, & Clark, 2011). Indeed, Λ-B-X systems have been referred to as "the building block(s) of all organizational processes and structures" (Arnaud & Fauré, 2016, p. 294; see also Kuhn, 2008) and as "where organizing occurs" (Spee & Jarzabkowski, 2011, p. 1219). Groleau (2006) insisted that coorientation goes beyond simple interaction because it is action- and goal-oriented. Dawson (2018) concurred, claiming coorientation is the "root of organizing because it implies action and collectivity" (p. 3). Kuhn goes even further, specifying that X is "some *objective*" (2008, p. 1233, emphasis added) through which actors relate to one another. Moments of coorientation are *conversations* (e.g., situated interactions unfolding in the moment) that exist and occur in a dialectical relationship with enduring *texts* (e.g., documents, memory traces from past interactions, see Taylor & Van Every, 2000; see also Dawson, this volume). Conversations are thus similar to sensemaking as it happens, whereas texts are similar to records or memories of previous human sensemaking. Texts, whether actual documents or figurative representations of previous sensemaking, are "both the medium and the outcome of conversations" (Koschmann & McDonald, 2015, p. 7), structuring conversations but also providing resources for them by constituting a backdrop of potentiality for coorientation.

Linking explicitly to Weick's (1979) writing about sensemaking, Taylor (2006) explained that coorientation is how events are *enacted*, how "the language-based establishing of compatible beliefs and coordinated responses to events is accomplished" (p. 147). From a CCO vantage point, coorientation unfolds in interaction as follows:

> First, the two agents who are cooriented to what is for them a common object, however different their perspectives on it, need to come to an understanding of the reality that confronts them: the facts of the situation. Second, the two coorienting agents need to agree on what has to be done and who is to do it. Third, how you deal with each other and how you establish your respective roles and privileges in any single encounter will always reflect previous interactions—and set the framework for subsequent interaction.
>
> *Taylor, 2005, p. 207*

As the above excerpt suggests, the first step echoes the sensemaking perspective on the construction of shared meaning about the situation (i.e., "what is going on" or the construction of a cause map or mental model, Weick et al., 2005), while the second step relates meaning making to action planning (i.e., "what to do about 'it'"). However, unlike sensemaking, A and B do not "transmit" information; rather, the meaning of X is negotiated, or jointly established through conversation (Taylor, 2005). What's more, A and B's communication is not analytically isolated to a single episode; instead, their interaction is grounded in ongoing activity, reflexively referring to previous interactions (i.e., texts), and both communicators are interested in proactively making a difference in their environment (Taylor & Robichaud, 2004). Regarding Taylor's third point, we contribute to this theorizing by specifying some mechanisms by which the A-B-X model accounts for the influence of roles and relationships among communicators (i.e., status asymmetry) and their object of communication on sensemaking. We suggest this offers a new way to explore how power and politics are at play in organizational action.

Coorientation's A-B-X Model: Theorizing How Communicators Manage Status Asymmetry Through Talk

The A-B-X model holds potential to explain status asymmetry, but scholarship in this area is only beginning to operationalize the model. Hence, in this section, we flesh out the A-B-X model of coorientation to theorize its potential for explaining how communicators manage status asymmetry through talk, both regarding how they define X and decide what to do about it and relative to one another. Then, we analyze a data excerpt from an interprofessional team in acute hospital care to demonstrate the explanatory power of the A-B-X model with regard to status asymmetry.

Communicators A and B Orienting to X: Asymmetry in Orientations

Symmetry is an important aspect of the A-B-X model. Initially, when social psychologist Theodore Newcomb (1953) introduced the coorientation model to account for the communicative accomplishment of intersubjectivity (or how people come to hold shared meanings), he posited that there exists a psychological preference for symmetry, or similarity, in interlocutors' orientations to their object of communication: the A → X and B → X regions of Figure 33.1. In public relations research, this "strain for symmetry" (Newcomb, 1953, p. 395) has been explored to describe the pull that people feel to share a similar orientation to X when they have favorable orientations to one another (Bentley, 2015). Both Newcomb (1953) and Taylor (2006), who further theorized the model, were concerned with how organizational actors (A and B) come to jointly interpret and act on aspects of their environments (X). However, Taylor extended the concept of coorientation by connecting it with sensemaking theorizing; he proposed that coorientation explains how people organize to address complexity in their environment (Taylor, 2006; Taylor & Van Every, 2000). That is, members organize by negotiating their orientations to the Xs in their environment, reducing complexity and thereby facilitating their efforts to partner on streams of action (Taylor & Van Every, 2000). This chapter continues this theorizing on coorientation (and sensemaking) by attending to the communicative moves by which organizational actors (A and B) negotiate *status* asymmetry between them as they simultaneously make sense of organizational situations (X) and negotiate and implement action.

One central feature of sensemaking is that organization members develop intersubjective meaning about a shared matter of concern, which enables them to move together toward action (Maitlis & Christianson, 2014). The A-B-X coorientation model follows a similar logic, denoting that A is oriented toward X (A → X), and so is B (B → X). However, while Newcomb (1953) suggested communicators strive to achieve symmetry in their orientations, CCO's organizational understanding of the A-B-X model (e.g., Taylor, 2006; Taylor & Robichaud, 2004) does not assume that intersubjective meaning is *required* for coorientation. Rather, coorientation requires that individuals feel concerned by the object of their communication and that their identities both spring from a common source in "the systems of identity that are characteristic of their community. These two parameters leave considerable latitude for negotiating asymmetrical attitudes" (i.e., orientations), because individuals "may be coorienting even while they disagree" (Taylor & Robichaud, 2004, p. 404). These different orientations are often informed by A's and B's *roles* regarding X. Therefore, sensemaking and coorientation are similar because they both pertain to how parties interpret and decide what to do about a shared matter of concern; however, the concepts are different because sensemaking requires a shared mental model between communicators, while coorientation only requires that communicators share a concern for X, even if they disagree on their interpretations and what should be done. For example, a surgeon (A) and a dietician (B), whose professional identities and team roles are inscribed in the same system of professions (Abbott, 1988), might share a concern about a patient's inability to swallow post-surgery (X), while taking different attitudes about what it means and about how to solve their shared problem: for the dietician, the problem might necessitate a change in diet, whereas for the surgeon, it might indicate slow progression in healing. It is important to note that the *expression* and *uptake* of orientations are influenced by the relationship between speakers and their status relative to one another, as we will see next.

Communicators A and B Orienting Toward Each Other: Status Asymmetry

Coorientation assumes that most organizational situations are characterized by *head-complement* relationships that confer differential status to communicators (Labov & Fanshel, 1977; Taylor & Van Every, 2000). In a head-complement relationship, two actors orient toward one another such that their complementary and asymmetrical roles, such as supervisor and subordinate, provide a frame of knowledge about, specifically, the *responsibilities* of the *head*—in this case supervisor—and the *rights* of the *complement*, or subordinate (Labov & Fanshel, 1977; Taylor & Van Every, 2000). Thus, as members interact in relation to some aspect of the organization, they must also establish and/or negotiate their roles and relative status (Taylor & Van Every, 2000). Indeed, while status asymmetry might be partially embedded in their complementary relationship—based on formal rank, for example—that asymmetry is not a given; it can be tied to informal or situated markers of status, and must be communicatively negotiated. It can manifest itself as ability or legitimacy to take the conversational floor. For instance, in their study of family communication patterns, Baxter and Akkoor (2011) studied variance in teens' and parents' orientation to conversation topics, examining various topics (i.e., different Xs) on a continuum from dialogically expansive to contracted. An expansive orientation described teens' and parents' tolerance to diversity in expressed opinions and whether those expressions are equally valued in decision-making, such as in discussions about friends and everyday topics. Conversely, a contracted orientation represented conformity in expressed opinions, for instance regarding sex or drug and alcohol use, and little tolerance for expression of diverging opinions. Importantly, the parent (the higher-status interlocutor) has greater control than the child to set expectations about which topics are expansive versus contracted, shaping which issues the lower-status communicator feels free to discuss, and how.

The A-B-X model, therefore, provides a way to think about status as a situational, ongoing achievement accomplished through imposing, rejecting, or maintaining a head-complement relationship between communicators. The A-B-X model considers how status asymmetry is always up for grabs because communicators can invoke their relationship to each other, and their shared object of concern, in various ways that claim jurisdiction (and thus status) over the emerging interpretation and plan regarding the shared concern. In the healthcare context, there is a status hierarchy in which doctors occupy higher-status positions than nurses and other health professionals in most organizational situations, and nurses, in particular, must often use face-saving communication strategies to advocate courses of action while navigating the status hierarchy (Arber, 2008; Stein, 1967). In subsequent sections, we will refer to the higher-status communicator as A, and the lower-status communicator as B. Due to the status asymmetry entrenched in healthcare's professional hierarchy (Abbott, 1988; Fox & Comeau-Vallée, 2020), we might expect the doctor's (A's) view of the patient (X) to take priority over that of the nurse (B). Thus, the status asymmetry between professions makes a difference in how the patient's care trajectory gets defined, because we can assume that the doctor's view will usually prevail. However, we can easily imagine a scenario in which the nurse (B) knows something important about the patient that the doctor (A) has not considered. In such an instance, the nurse must do more than simply "speak up" (i.e., engage in voice) or share information with the doctor. Rather, the nurse must negotiate the status differential *with* the doctor *while* informing the doctor. The following sections illustrate these ideas using observational data from interprofessional team meetings in acute hospital care.

Empirical Illustration: Coorienting to Make Sense of Mr. Bolshi's Congestive Heart Failure

The A-B-X model helps us map out numerous possibilities for how organization members might navigate status asymmetry with each other, through either maintaining the asymmetry or disrupting it. The following excerpts are from a daily interprofessional team meeting in acute hospital care on a general internal medicine ward. This team's discussions typically followed a sensemaking process whereby they first worked to establish an understanding of the situation and, second, planned actions. The first excerpt illustrates the interactional patterns involved in the former (i.e., determining "what's going on") and a second excerpt illustrates the patterns involved in the latter (i.e., coordinating what to do).

The team members discuss Mr. Bolshi (a pseudonym), a patient in their charge who, as we will learn, is being treated for congestive heart failure. As our coorientation analysis will show, status asymmetry is established and negotiated in this excerpted conversation in two ways: (a) through invoking roles and relationships between A, B, and X, and (b) through defining X, and it manifests itself as team members coordinate planned actions.

In the first excerpt, two members, a hospitalist physician (MD) and the charge nurse (PCC), collectively occupy a higher-status position (A+A) as they ask the bedside nurse (BN), who is the lower-status member (B), for an update on the patient because he is presumed to have the most up-to-date information. BN replies haltingly, trying to mention edema—or swelling, a symptom of congestive heart failure—as concerning. However, when BN is slow to produce an account, the charge nurse interrupts him and asks for a report on the patient's weight. BN's report is deemed less than plausible, and, as we shall see, is subject to sanction. (We followed Jefferson's (1984) conventions for transcription, without attending to pronunciation. The left square bracket symbol "[" indicates the beginning of overlapping talk.)

```
1   MD:    So any comments on him?
2          (…)
3   PCC:   Any comments on him?
4   MD:    From a nursing point of view.
```

```
 5   PCC:   On Mr. Bolshi in 14-2.
 6   BN:    Uh:: not really. (1.0) [Except edema's still ga-
 7   PCC:                          [Did we weigh him this morning?
 8   BN:    Eh, yeah. (2.0) He::'s now:::.
 9          (1.0)
10   PCC:   How much does he weigh today.
11   BN:    (1.0) He'::s no::w.
12   (3.0) ((pages flipping))
13   BN:    73.4 and it's, I think it's (1.0) couple kilos down from the last
            one, so.
14   PCC:   Yeah, he's [still not less than 70, though [and you're trying
            to get less than 70.
15   BN:               [So.                            [No.
16   MD:               [So 73.4?
17   BN:    Yeah.
18   MD:    That's the highest weight I've (.) heard of, so.
19   PCC:   Yeah=
20   BN:    =And, and his legs are (.) still huge.
21   MD:    So do [we know if he's, what was the last measurement?
22   PCC:         [So not going in-
23   BN:    I don't know.
24   MD:    You don't know.
25   BN:    It's not in the, e::r, I can, I can go through [the notes.
26   DIET:                                                 [It's not on
27          theyellow bar? Like a yellow [form in the bar?
28   MD:                                 [Right, so, uh,
29   BN:                                 [It's not in the (inaudible).
30   DIET:  Should be in the yellow, there's a place for weight.
31   MD:    ((chuckles)) Anyway. Yeah. ((clears throat))
32   PCC:   'Kay, so his weight's [obviously still not less.
33   MD:                          [So, so, sounds like it's still high. Um,
34          ((clears throat)), and uh, 'cause it was um sixty:::nine at
            one point there.
35   PCC:   Yeah, 69, and then he went 71, [72 ((Sound of pages rustling,
            PCC is reading))
36   BN:                                   [72.
37   PCC:   72, 73 point [4.
38   MD:                 [73, so, he's getting worse not better.
39   BN:    [Yeah. That's right.
40   PCC:   [And you said today he was what? (0.5) That's you?
41   BN:    Yeah=
42   MD:    =That's his today's, yeah. Alright. ((clears throat)) So, and
            uh is there a standard
43          methodology for weighing them, like, with shoes, without shoes, uh?
44   CCD:   Before breakfast, [after breakfast?
45   BN:                      [((sharply)) Without shoes, the only point,
                              I mean, we can make
46   sure that we weigh him before breakfast, but it's pretty steady so,
     and I [guess
47   e::verybody weighed before breakfast.
48   MD:    [No,
49   no, okay. No, no, fair enough. Good. Fine.
```

The discussion continues in this vein (which we have not included here for space
concerns): higher-status A sets the agenda for coorientation, directing team discussion to
particular cues. Each time MD asks for information or mentions uncertainty, other team

members—except the PCC—respond to his requests for information. Repeatedly, once MD receives the information he is seeking, he speaks over or interrupts the other speakers, most often BN, who is the lowest status member on the professional hierarchy, and moves the discussion on to the next concern.

In the second excerpt, we see that once the MD has interpreted the patient's condition as heart failure, he ignores BN when he tries to raise an additional concern that the patient "cannot do [certain actions] by himself." However, it is the physician's right and responsibility to make the diagnosis, and the bedside nurse's responsibility to follow the MD's instructions, so BN does not press the issue.

```
50  MD:    But, from our point of view, I mean from what you see nursing-
           wise, and
51         otherwise, it sounds like he's, even now, with his less than
           ideally managed what
52         you might say heart failure, he's coping relatively well.
53  PCC:   Uh-hmm.
54  BN:    Uh, he needs [help to-
55  MD:                 [Except for his night time too, his sleep.
56  BN:    His (inaudible) you know, those kind of things. [He cannot do it
           by himself, so.
57  PCC:                                                  [(inaudible)
58  MD:    Okay, and one would think, I mean, don't get me wrong, [I mean it
           sounds like
59  PCC:                                                          [(inaudible)
60  MD:    If he's gained 10 pounds of water in a week? that he should be
           able to lose 5 or 6
61         pounds just the same.
62  PCC:   Yes!
63  MD:    With aggressive therapy. So yes, switch him to IV diuretics
           today.
64  PCC:   'kay.
65  MD:    So you would think, you know, that [today
66  BN:                                       [He was on IV (.) yesterday.
67  MD:    Just one dose.
68  BN:    Yeah, okay.
69  MD:    So, by, you'd think that, you know, you'd be able to, to get four
70         pounds of water off of him in 48 hours.
71  PCC:   Uh-hmm.
72  MD:    Doing that, maybe by Friday morning, he'd be.
73  PCC:   Yes. [Yes.
74  MD:         [You know, at his weight.
75  PCC:   Okay.
76  MD:    Okay. ((clears throat))
77  DIET:  His (electro)'lytes today seemed-
78  MD:    Reasonable. Okay, good. Alright. Anyway that's him.
79  PCC:   (tries to talk)
80  MD:    So it sounds like it's more medical than anything else at the
           moment, right?
81         ((clears throat)) Okay.
82  PCC:   Um, and [then=
83  MD:            [But you (occupational therapist) might want to
                   talk to him
84         about his sort of openness to returning home? [Assuming the medical
           statu-[situation stabilizes.
```

```
85  OT:          [Sure
86  PCC:                                              [Uh-hmm.
87  OT:  Yeah. Okay.
88  MD:  I think that's worthwhile, having that conversation.
89  PCC: Okay, [and=
90  MD:         [And the other guy is Mr. Marsden.
91  PCC: Yes.
```

Because our analytical focus is on status asymmetry, we develop and illustrate this point rather than presenting an analysis of the interaction strictly as it unfolds sequentially, although we recognize that each turn of talk influences subsequent turns. Table 33.1 summarizes our four intertwined analytical steps. In these steps, we identify (a) how communicators negotiate to establish their status relative to one another (i.e., their A-B relationships), and (b) how they consequently negotiate relative status in their sensemaking to define X and to coordinate actions.

The first step in the analysis is to examine the data to note how communicators A and B negotiate a head-complement relationship through their talk. For example, we can see the lower-status bedside nurse (BN) is repeatedly invited to speak by MD and PCC, and has thus been "given" voice to inform the team's sensemaking about the patient's situation. This first analytical step illustrates that, from a coorientation perspective, status asymmetry clearly shapes *how* his contributions are invited and received. As MD and PCC collectively occupy the higher-status A position (A+A → B), these invitations amount to prompts by A for a role performance from lower-status B (the BN) regarding X (the patient): B → X. In terms of the head-complement relationship, A has the relational right (A → B) to request such performances. Moreover, BN accepts the legitimacy of MD's and PCC's relational right as "head"—and by extension, his obligation as "complement"—by performing his role and by accounting for his role performance failure. The negotiated head-complement relationship also grants A the right to *evaluate* B's role performance. In fact, BN's incorrect interpretation of the weight information— as indicating improvement regarding X—triggers a sanction by PCC, and she reminds BN of his goal. Another team member, DIET, aligns with the A position as she "teaches" BN where to find the requested information ("on the yellow bar", lines 26–27, 30).

The second step of analysis is to identify how the negotiated status asymmetry makes a difference in their interaction. This can manifest itself through efforts to maintain the asymmetry, such as the alliance between MD, PCC, and DIET in their collective sanction of BN. As we will see later, such alliances can exclude some voices from participating in sensemaking. Interestingly, however, the invocation of collective roles and relationships is also how status asymmetry is discursively *mitigated*. For instance, we see both MD and PCC use the inclusive pronoun "we" as they prompt BN for a role performance, thereby interactionally underscoring an A+B → X relationship (see Fox & Comeau-Vallée, 2020). In another instance, MD depersonalizes the collective sanction of BN's faulty interpretation by asking about nursing practice on the ward, thereby emphasizing a collective B in the B → X relationship, for which BN is positioned as spokesperson. Again, we see BN accept his attributed role as spokesperson.

The third analytical step is to note where A and B define or redefine X. This is an important step because, as the team coorients to define X, the status asymmetry worked out in steps 1 and 2 manifests itself in the salience accorded to different aspects of X (or cues), and by whom. For instance, water retention, a consequence of congestive heart failure, can be perceived and made relevant (i.e., enacted) both in terms of visual cues—edema or swelling—and as a quantifiable

Table 33.1 Analytical steps for applying the A-B-X coorientation model to conversation data

Analytical step		Examples from excerpt		
Step	Description	ABX relationship	Description	Excerpt lines
1	Note how A and B establish a head-complement relationship in talk	A → B	A's right to prompt role performance	1–5, 21, 24
		B → A	B's obligation to perform	6, 11–13, 20, 23, 25
		A → B	A's right to evaluate role performance	14, 21–41
		A → B	A's right to interrupt B	26, 42
2	Note how status asymmetry makes a difference in A and B's interaction	A+A → B	Alliances toward A maintain asymmetry	1–6, 21–44
		A+B → X	Interlocutors invoke collective team roles to mitigate asymmetry	7, 21
		B+B → X	Interlocutors invoke collective professional practice to mitigate asymmetry	45–47
3	Note moments when A and B define/redefine X	A → X	A provides or interprets information	14, 18, 22, 30, 32, 33–37, 38, 52, 80–84
		B → X	B provides or interprets information	6, 13, 20, 39, 54, 66, 77
		A > B → X	A sets the agenda for coorientation, i.e., decides what cues matter	7, 10, 63–76, 80
4	Interpret how one definition of X becomes accepted	A → X > B → X	One interpretation (A's or B's) prevails over others	32–38, 58–63, 69–70, 80
		A → X	A plans the actions	63, 69–74
		A → B	A assigns action to others (i.e., Bs)	63–68, 83–88

measurement, the patient's weight. As we saw, BN tries to flag the issue of edema on two occasions (lines 6 and 20), thereby giving an account of his previous interaction with the patient (i.e., B → X), wherein he was struck by the size of the patient's legs. However, this voiced concern is not taken up by the others as a defining feature of X. Instead, higher-status PCC sets the conversational agenda as she asks BN about the patient's weight, which BN fails to adequately provide. Ultimately, she and MD work to interpret the information about weight (A+A →X) and conclude (i.e., select an interpretation) that it indicates a deterioration in the patient's situation.

Ironically, BN was pointing to the same concern (worsening congestive heart failure), but through a different cue, and this is ignored by A. Further, the second excerpt shows how MD and PCC converse about the potential to reduce the patient's weight from water retention through a specific course of action without BN's input: They again ignore his attempt to voice a concern, this time about the patient's independent function. The exchange between MD and PCC creates an alliance toward the BN (A + A → B), which consolidates authority over the patient's care with the higher-status professionals, MD and PCC.

The fourth analytical step is to interpret how one interpretation of X becomes accepted, and acted upon, by communicators. This analytical step is attentive to which communicator ultimately makes the interpretation and plans the action. For instance, once MD seems satisfied that his checklist about the patient's condition has been covered (omitted here), he orients the team's discussion toward selecting an interpretation of the discussed information. In particular, he selects that the patient's condition can be treated relatively easily (lines 60–61). The MD guides the group toward action planning, when he assigns tasks to the PCC and BN regarding the patient's care, and later when he directs the PCC and OT to talk with the patient about returning home once the water weight issue is resolved, and they agree to do so. Of note here, PCC and OT take up complement roles to the MD's head role, thus illustrating that these roles are fluid, relative, and constantly negotiated.

In sum, the value of combining coorientation with sensemaking theorizing is that together they make salient two sensitizing questions that can inform data analysis. First, sensemaking directs our attention to how cues get highlighted as signal or noise (i.e., the definition of X), and how an interpretation of a situation is constructed with the intent to understand and/or act. Second, coorientation highlights how relationships between communicators influence their orientation to their object of mutual interest, and also are situational and fluid relative to each other. This approach is particularly useful for understanding how communicators manifest and negotiate status asymmetry while constructing sense.

Theoretical Conclusions and Methodological Suggestions

This chapter makes contributions to both CCO theorizing and sensemaking. First, we explain how organization members coorient from their organizational perspectives to navigate status asymmetry, all while negotiating meaning and action. In the coorientation model, asymmetry can manifest itself in terms of orientations to X (i.e., is there agreement or not?), but it can also manifest itself in terms of hierarchy and status (differences in role obligations and affordances). The latter manifestation of hierarchy is primarily what interested us here, and it is an important issue to address because in most organizations, hierarchy is inescapable, and is often a concrete obstacle to sensemaking. This chapter helps us to think theoretically about hierarchy and status as fluid and subtly negotiated, as enacted as communicators work out "an understanding of the reality that confronts them" (Taylor, 2005, p. 207) and what to do about it. As such, it helps us better understand *how* enacted hierarchy can lead to some cues being taken up as signal, while others are dismissed as noise. While we do not know what ultimately happened to Mr. Bolshi after he left the hospital, it is possible that the second concern that BN voiced— namely, Mr. Bolshi's inability to independently carry out certain tasks—could have negatively impacted his quality of life or his health outcomes if it were not considered during discharge planning. Yet as we saw, this concern was not taken up by MD or PCC as they planned subsequent actions. Relatedly, this chapter showed that interprofessional sensemaking in healthcare is an excellent case to study because of the professional hierarchy that is entrenched in hospital contexts. The interprofessional healthcare team context also is valuable for understanding how communicators negotiate status asymmetry because these teams involve multiple experts who manage multiple, indeed fluid, head-complement relationships in their patient care conversations.

Second, we show how the coorientation model can be operationalized in sensemaking-oriented analyses to articulate interaction nuances that unfold as sense-makers construct meaning. This development extends sensemaking theorizing by considering how it is a socially constructed process (in addition to being interpretive). This allows for communication to be understood as more than information transmission in sensemaking: coorientation (in conversation) is how collective sensemaking happens, how events are enacted by establishing compatible beliefs and coordinating responses through language use (Taylor, 2006). Thus, "signal" and "noise" are no longer understood as neutral determinations that occur during sensemaking but are seen as indicative of and resulting from how roles and head-complement relationships are negotiated in coorientation episodes.

Third, while Taylor's version of the coorientation model offers an abstract explanation of the performative aspects of language use in sensemaking, it is limited in that it does not offer clear indications of how it might be operationalized methodologically, other than pointing to the relationships between the elements in the model (A-B-X). Therefore, we point out in the four proposed analytical steps how the interaction analyst must be attentive to *how* relationships are invoked, keeping in mind that relationships (i.e., identities that are somehow related; Taylor & Robichaud, 2004) imply affordances and obligations. These in turn contribute to coordinating the actions that are accomplished in talk (e.g., organizing the turns of talk). In this way, the coorientation model considers action in two ways: (1) it is an inherent aspect of interaction (Austin, 1962), and this performative aspect of language is what sensemaking ignores; and (2) it also is a way for future actions to become coordinated (this is what sensemaking considers as action).

However, a further limitation of coorientation as a basis for analysis is that it does not distinguish (operationally) between types of activity (in talk), as the sensemaking model does, such as *defining what's going on* (e.g., building a cause map, or enaction/exploration; agreeing on a cause map, or selection), *defining what should be done about it* (planning/coordinating actions), or *making claims about emergent practices* that organization members might carry forward to future interactions. Therefore, we propose that future theorizing about the A-B-X coorientation model (beyond the scope of this chapter) pay attention to how lower-status communicators (B) leverage authority over higher-status ones (A). Here, there is opportunity to "hitchhike" further using CCO thinking about how "figures" become "presentified" or "ventriloquized" (see Nathues and Van Vuuren, this volume) to make a difference in the trajectory of coordinated action members negotiate. This could also include a deeper explanation of the role of texts (see Dawson, this volume) as stabilizers of sensemaking conversations, similar to the notion of assembly rules (Weick, 1979). In conclusion, we argue that, taken together, coorientation and sensemaking are compatible and complementary theoretical frameworks for accounting for ways that status differences can elevate some voices and suppress others as organization members work to understand a set of circumstances and what to do about them.

References

Abbott, A. (1988). *The system of professions: An essay on the division of expert labour.* Chicago: University of Chicago Press.

Arber, A. (2008). Team meetings in specialist palliative care: Asking questions as a strategy within interprofessional interaction. *Qualitative Health Research, 18*(10), 1323–1335. https://doi.org/10.1177/1049732308322588.

Arnaud, N., & Fauré, B. (2016). A communicative approach to sociomateriality: The agentic role of technology at the operational level. *Communication Research and Practice, 2*(3), 290–310. https://doi.org/10.1080/22041451.2016.1219615.

Austin, J. (1962). *How to do things with words.* Oxford, UK: The Clarendon Press.

Barton, M. A., & Sutcliffe, K. M. (2009). Overcoming dysfunctional momentum: Organizational safety as a social achievement. *Human Relations, 62,* 1327–1356. http://doi.org/10.1177/0018726709334491.

Baxter, L. A., & Akkoor, C. (2011). Topic expansiveness and family communication patterns. *Journal of Family Communication, 11*(1), 1–20. https://doi.org/10.1080/15267431003773523.

Bentley, J. M. (2015). Shifting identification: A theory of apologies and pseudo-apologies. *Public Relations Review, 41*(1), 22–29. https://doi.org/10.1016/j.pubrev.2014.10.011.

Blatt, R., Christianson, M. K., Sutcliffe, K. M., & Rosenthal, M. M. (2006). A sensemaking lens on reliability. *Journal of Organizational Behavior*, *27*(9), 897–917. http://doi.org/10.1002/Job.392.

Botero, I. C., & Van Dyne, L. (2009). Employee voice behavior interactive effects of LMX and power distance in the United States and Colombia. *Management Communication Quarterly*, *23*(1), 84–104. http://doi.org/10.1177/0893318909335415.

Cooren, F., Kuhn, T. R., Cornelissen, J. P., & Clark, T. (2011). Communication, organizing and organization: An overview and introduction to the special issue. *Organization Studies*, *32*(9), 1149–1170. https://doi.org/10.1177/0170840611410836.

Dawson, V. R. (2018). Fans, friends, advocates, ambassadors, and haters: Social media communities and the communicative constitution of organizational identity. *Social Media and Society*, *4*(1), 1–11. https://doi.org/10.1177/2056305117746356.

Detert, J. R., & Burris, E. R. (2007). Leadership behavior and employee voice: Is the door really open? *Academy of Management Journal*, *50*(4), 869–884. http://doi.org/10.5465/AMJ.2007.26279183.

Detert, J. R., & Trevino, L. K. (2010). Speaking up to higher-ups: How supervisors and skip-level leaders influence employee voice. *Organization Science*, *21*(1), 249–270. http://doi.org/10.1287/orsc.1080.0405.

Fox, S., & Comeau-Vallée, M. (2020). The negotiation of sharing leadership in the context of professional hierarchy: Interactions on interprofessional teams. *Leadership*, *0*(0), 1–24. https://doi.org/10.1177/1742715020917817.

Fox, S., & Gilbert, J. H. V. (2015). Mapping collective sensemaking in communication: The interprofessional patient case review in acute care rounds. *Health and Interprofessional Practice*, *2*(4), eP1077. https://doi.org/10.7710/2159-1253.1077.

Groleau, C. (2006). One phenomenon, two lenses: Understanding collective action from the perspectives of coorientation and activity theories. In F. Cooren, J. R. Taylor, & E. J. Van Every (Eds.), *Communication as organizing* (pp. 157–180). Mahwah, NJ: Lawrence Erlbaum.

Jahn, J. L. S. (2019). Voice enactment: Linking voice with experience in high reliability organizing. *Journal of Applied Communication Research*, *47*(3), 283–302. https://doi.org/10.1080/00909882.2019.1613555.

Jefferson, G. (1984). On stepwise transition from talk about a trouble to inappropriately next-positioned matters. In J. M. Atkinson & J. Heritage (Eds.), *Structures of social action: Studies of conversation analysis* (pp. 191–12). Cambridge, UK: Cambridge University Press.

Koschmann, M. A., & McDonald, J. (2015). Organizational rituals, communication, and the question of agency. *Management Communication Quarterly*. https://doi.org/10.1177/0893318915572386.

Kuhn, T. R. (2008). A communicative theory of the firm: Developing an alternative perspective on intraorganizational power and stakeholder relationships. *Organization Studies*, *29*(8–9), 1197–1224. https://doi.org/10.1177/0170840608094778.

Labov, W., & Fanshel, D. (1977). *Therapeutic discourse: Psychotherapy as conversation*. New York: Academic Press.

Maitlis, S., & Christianson, M. (2014). Sensemaking in organizations: Taking stock and moving forward. *The Academy of Management Annals*, *8*(1), 57–125. https://doi.org/10.1080/19416520.2014.873177.

Maitlis, S., & Sonenshein, S. (2010). Sensemaking in crisis and change: Inspiration and insights from Weick (1988). *Journal of Management Studies*, *47*(3), 551–580. https://doi.org/10.1111/j.1467-6486.2010.00908.x.

Milliken, F. J., Morrison, E. W., & Hewlin, P. F. (2003). An exploratory study of employee silence: Issues that employees don't communicate upward and why. *Journal of Management Studies*, *40*(6), 1453–1476. http://doi.org/10.1111/1467-6486.00387.

Newcomb, T. (1953). An approach to the study of communicative acts. *Psychological Review*, *50*, 393–404.

Putnam, L. L., & Boys, S. (2006). Revisiting metaphors of organizational communication. In S. R. Clegg, C. Hardy, T. B. Lawrence, & W. R. Nord (Eds.), *The Sage handbook of organization studies* (pp. 541–576). London: Sage.

Spee, A. P., & Jarzabkowski, P. (2011). Strategic planning as communicative process. *Organization Studies*, *32*(9), 1217–1245. https://doi.org/10.1177/0170840611411387.

Stein, L. (1967). The doctor-nurse game. *Archives of General Psychiatry*, *16*(6), 699–703. https://doi.org/10.1001/archpsyc.1967.01730240055009.

Taylor, J. R. (2005). Engaging organization through worldview. In S. May & D. Mumby (Eds.), *Engaging organizational communication theory and research: Multiple perspectives* (pp. 197–221). Thousand Oaks, CA: Sage

Taylor, J. R. (2006). Coorientation: A conceptual framework. In F. Cooren, J. R. Taylor, & E. J. Van Every (Eds.), *Communication as organizing: Empirical and theoretical explorations in the dynamic of text and conversation* (pp. 141–156). Mahwah, NJ: Lawrence Erlbaum.

Taylor, J. R., & Robichaud, D. (2004). Finding the organization in the communication: Discourse as action and sensemaking. *Organization, 11*(3), 395–413. https://doi.org/10.1177/1350508404041999.

Taylor, J. R., & Van Every, E. J. (2000). *The emergent organization: Communication as its site and surface.* Mahwah, NJ: Lawrence Erlbaum.

Weick, K. E. (1979). *The social psychology of sensemaking* (2nd edn.). New York: Random House.

Weick, K. E. (1995). *Sensemaking in organizations.* Thousand Oaks, CA: Sage.

Weick, K. E. (2011). Organizing for transient reliability: The production of dynamic non-events. *Journal of Contingencies and Crisis Managemetn, 1*(19), 21–27. https://doi.org/10.1111/j.1468-5973.2010.00627.x.

Weick, K. E., Sutcliffe, K. M., & Obstfeld, D. (2005). Organizing and the process of sensemaking. *Organization Science, 16*(4), 409–421. https://doi.org/10.1287/orsc.1050.0133.

AFTERWORD

The Emergence of the Communicative Constitution of Organization and the Montréal School: An Interview with James R. Taylor

Mathieu Chaput and Joëlle Basque

Introduction

We conducted this interview with James R. Taylor – known as Jim to his friends and colleagues – in 2009. We were then doctoral candidates and the context was different from what it is now, over ten years later. Yet, upon translating the interview from French to English and reading it, the editors of this Handbook decided to include it as an afterword, to give the last word of this volume to the person who is often recognized as the founder of the communicative constitution of organization, although of course it is difficult to pinpoint a specific starting point for that intellectual project. Taylor gives an overview of CCO's birth and first steps, in particular from the vantage point of the Montréal School, and make its history accessible for its community and future contributors. More than a series of facts, though, Taylor reflects on his journey and on the ideas that he tinkered with and developed throughout his career, and that continue to live on today. Taylor's interview is specially relevant for this Handbook because, as Taylor thinks about the past, he also envisions the future, and expresses the wish to see his provocative ideas continue to evolve through the work of a diverse and prolific community. In a way, this Handbook reflects the fullfillement of that dream.

James R. Taylor's accomplishments are numerous, but for this chapter, it is his innovative theory of organizing and communicating that is of interest. His concepts and sources of inspiration – the product of an inspiring, atypical, iconoclastic journey – distinguish his thought from other theoretical and historical trends in the field of organizational communication. The originality of his thinking led to the birth of the Montréal School, an influential informal group of scholars who are helping – in various places and various ways – to deepen and renew Taylor's radical thought. It is this distinctive journey that forms the substance of our encounter with this passionate scholar, who remained an active and influential thinker of organizational communication long after his retirement from the Université de Montréal in 1999.

The authors naturally wish to thank James R. Taylor for his valuable collaboration in the interview and his subsequent revisions to the manuscript, originally published in French in 2010 in *COMMposite*, a journal for young communication scholars. We are grateful to the

DOI: 10.4324/9781003224914-39

reviewers of the interview for the journal *COMMposite* for their judicious comments and numerous corrections regarding form, and to the editors of the journal for giving us permission to publish this interview in this Handbook. We would also like to thank Stephen Jones for the English translation of the text. Finally, the English version of the interview also greatly benefited from the suggestions and corrections made by Nicolas Bencherki, Timothy Kuhn, François Cooren, but most importantly by Jim himself and Elizabeth Van Every, his wife and long-term collaborator.

Interviewing CCO's founding figure

To view the Communication as Constitutive of Organization movement as a worldwide, multi-generation, quite prolific, and overall unified family, James R. Taylor would easily take the place of its prominent "father" figure: for the lasting impact of his research insights and the deep originality of his communication theorizing – as he nearly single-handedly started what is known today as CCO – but also for the benevolence of his character and his enduring willingness to share his legacy, collaborating for decades with students and young scholars. His personal, professional and academic trajectory proves an invaluable account to better grasp the origins and development of the CCO movement, and in particular the birth and influences of the Montréal School of organizational communication.

James R. Taylor's reputation in academic circles is firmly established: Professor Emeritus at Université de Montréal, founder and former chair of that institution's communication department, former president of the Canadian Communication Association, and promoted in 2006 to the prestigious rank of Fellow by the International Communication Association (one of the most important forms of international recognition for an academic in the field of communication studies). Taylor is the author or co-author of nine published books and has published dozens of scientific papers and book chapters. Rather than the number of his publications, however, the radical originality of his thinking on the organizing effects of language and communication is what has earned him his reputation in the field of organizational communication. His theoretical investigations, backed up by numerous well-substantiated case analyses, led him to radically rethink the concept of "organization", going beyond the bounds of his home field of organizational communication.

It should be borne in mind that, historically, this field developed as it problematized the forms and practices of communication within workplaces, administrations, and associations. Jim Taylor's work, on the other hand, emerges from a converse postulate, taking communication activity itself as a starting point, and then detecting its effects on the makeup of organizational roles, structures, and identities. As one of his collaborators put it neatly: "it is no longer a matter of communication *by* or *in* the organization, but of communication that *is* — *makes* — the organization" (Giroux, 2006, p. 40; our emphasis). To mark out his distancing from traditional organizational communication research, Jim frequently cites the distinction drawn by Ruth Smith (1993) between three different conceptions of the relationship between communication and organization:

(1) In the "container" metaphor – the most widespread orientation that Smith found in empirical research conducted in North America – an organization exists prior to communication, turning the latter into a component of the former, a "conduit", a "flow" or a "transmission" of messages inside the already existing container.

(2) The second metaphor, "production", challenges this anteriority of the container (the organization) over the content (communication), establishing what Derrida would term

the "undecidability" of the communication/organization duo. Either communication produces the organization or, conversely, the organization produces communication. In both cases, they are conceived of as related but separate phenomena.

(3) Lastly, Taylor adheres more readily to the third metaphor evoked by Smith, "equivalence", which incidentally was addressed by only a very small number of publications– and this continues to be the case. From this perspective, communicating "always already" means organizing, in the sense that both concepts are viewed as indiscernible. Thus, organizing can only be effected by the mediation of language in action. Although this conception leads to a reasoning that is disparaged by some as tautological,[1] Taylor cleaves to this radical approach in his work, securing for himself a singular position in the conversation that is organizational communication research (see Fairhurst & Putnam, 1999; Brummans, 2006).

In *The Emergent Organization*, written with his wife, the sociologist Elizabeth J. Van Every, Taylor brings together and lays out the main elements of his theory, which conceives of communication as the *site* and the *surface* of the organization (Taylor & Van Every, 2000). This leads him to distinguish two spaces of communication – conversation and text – each with its organizing properties. In other words, he seeks to index the various ways in which communication makes it possible to act in concert, to constitute roles and identities, to tie widely dispersed and localized actions together by means of a common script and, lastly, to set up spokespersons that act on behalf of the grouping and bestow actorhood on the organization. The conversation thus refers to the multitude of ephemeral local actions, whether formal or informal, by which individuals act collectively and make sense of their actions. Whether verbal or gestural, oral or written, in every case the conversation plays a part in generating a text with structuring effects that is materialized both in the organization's policies and official principles and in more tacit forms, from implicit standards to the discursive formations that govern an era. This text then takes on the role of an agent that constrains action and stabilizes interaction, whether in the form of documents to current procedures, or any of the numerous "non-human" actors that are silently at work in any situation of interaction (a dimension that has been extensively explored by some of Jim's former students: in particular, see Cooren, 2006; Cooren et al., 2005). But text, in its ability to last (both as a material and as a symbolic assemblage), allows communication to transcend the "here and now", breaking free from the local conditions of the conversation to reach other times and other places. Taken together, in a complementary, successive movement, text and conversation play a part in an organization's process of emergence. Text serves as an emergence *surface* since, through its mediation, it renders the organization present: visible and knowable by its members and by the outside world. Conversation, by virtue of the ongoing nature of interactions, serves as the *site* of organizational emergence, that is, those discursive and material spaces where the organization of a collective action takes place.

In the following pages, we reproduce an interview that Jim granted us in September 2009, while he was in the throes of writing his most recent works (e.g. Taylor & Van Every, 2011, 2014). The interview took place in French (and was translated by Stephen Jones for publication in this Handbook). During our conversation, Jim looked back at some of the key moments in an unorthodox academic and professional career which, through meetings with people and works, fashioned the thinking that is today celebrated in the field of organizational communication. His path helps us understand how he came to develop his original thinking about communication, to transform the common conceptions we have of organizations and concerted collective action, revealing that complex configurations of local conversation are at work, transcended by narratives with organizing properties: an autobiographical account of an iconoclastic trajectory, whose ideas today form part of a collective heritage that is materialized, extended and diversified by a group of researchers that some like to call the "Montréal School" (see Brummans, 2006; Mumby, 2007; Taylor, 2006).

Breaking with the tradition of organizational communication studies, employing an occasionally obscure conceptual vocabulary and theoretical references that lay outside the "canon" of communication studies, Jim gained a reputation as a researcher who was not easy to read. The interview format gave him an ideal opportunity to set out in simplified form some of his ideas and concerns regarding communication studies. Here then is a document that we hope will speak to all those who have a long-standing or recent interest in Taylor's work and to those who have yet to discover it. It is a record of thinking that does not stand still, because for many years after his retirement Jim remained no less active – perhaps hyperactive – and no less prolific than before. He continued to devote himself with undiminished zeal to half a century's work as a professor at Université de Montréal. His passion shines through this entire interview, the result of a journey full of twists and turns, with as a backdrop the emergence of an original conception of communication and its institutionalization in the contexts of Canada and Québec. This account is structured around the main themes that have guided not only his work but also his life, as a child from the country who penetrated into the heart of major organizations, as a media professional who ended up in academia, as the nonconformist thinker he remains to this day. Let us now give him the floor, because as well as a brilliant analyst of narrative forms of communication, Jim is above all a captivating, amusing and instructive storyteller.

1. *The Constitutive Authority of Organizations*

James Taylor — Let me begin by telling you a little about my current work. My next book is devoted to the problem of authority and has the following provisional title: *The construction of authority: A communicational perspective* (see Taylor and Van Every, 2014, with the final title: *When organization fails. Why authority matters*). In 2001, my wife Elizabeth and I were invited to New Zealand by Ted Zorn and his colleagues to host a seminar at the Waikato Management School, south of the capital, Auckland. We arrived there with three case studies by my students at Université de Montréal focusing specifically on the Montréal police's implementation of a technology, which turned out to be very messy. It was not exactly what you'd call a resounding success! [laughs] There were all kinds of difficulties because, like any technology, it didn't fit very well into the way people work. I used this case study among others to illustrate what was being taught at Waikato and my teaching assistant said, "Jim, we have a much better case here".

The New Zealand police, a single force for the whole country, had had a lot of communication problems, which had led to a decision to completely replace their infrastructure. They already had a computer system, connected to a mainframe, in which all management data were recorded, but the system dated back to 1975 and had become thoroughly obsolete. They decided to change it, but they also decided to develop an entirely new telephone system, in addition to a completely new integrated system. The police issued a request for proposals and in 1994 signed a contract with IBM to develop and implement a hitherto non-existent system. They invested $100 million in the project, and it was a total catastrophe. The project was finally abandoned in 1999 when IBM pulled out. The New Zealand press labelled the affair a "fiasco". The police were highly embarrassed and wanted to say no more about it. So, we made use of this case, which we found fascinating, and went back to New Zealand on three occasions attempting to find out what had happened, chiefly through interviews. We built up an extensive set of interviews and rounded out the documentation with emails and other elements. Three years ago, we had completed a few chapters, but they didn't really add up to a book, and this material was put to one side while we worked on another book, *The situated organization*.

We discovered that the main problem for the police was maintaining authority. It may seem odd and counterintuitive, but the police were unable to maintain a degree of authority inside their own organization. That is one of the things that really fascinated me: that they didn't know how to do authority. Their headquarters had lost its authority. It no longer had the trust of its own officers. So, by the end we were saying, "Pure irony! The organization that has the most problems with authority is the most authoritarian organization of all: the police!" Precisely because they are authoritarian. The police did not know how to manage and maintain authority because they took their own authority for granted: "I'm the boss because I'm the boss."

Bruno Latour (1986) wrote about power, but in fact he didn't really write about power. Everybody talks about power, but nobody – and this is fascinating – talks about authority. I did some research. I wanted to find out who had written about authority in organizational communication. The answer: nobody! There was a total vacuum. That is, there was absolutely nothing in the way of studies apart from a few that cited Weber (traditional, charismatic and rational-legal authorities), but nothing more. There was nothing on the subject, and it struck me that this is precisely where the problem of conversation and text comes into play, because the word "authority" is directly related to the word "author". If you are unable to establish authority, the text will not be accepted. The problem of authority is a problem of communication.

Any act of communication, whether interpersonal or not, always presupposes "precedence". You cannot ask a question and get an answer unless there is precedence. The police do that: they ask a question and get an answer, because all police officers have to file reports. It's as if head office was asking the questions that they had to answer. But the whole thing was a mess! [laughs] They didn't understand the essence of communication. But for me, the worst thing is that communication researchers had not addressed the subject. You know, everyone loves talking about leadership, power, influence, and all kinds of things, but the word "authority" is one that everyone steers clear of. I don't know exactly why, but people are afraid of the concept of authority. It's probably a way of avoiding the act of communicating, a way of avoiding looking at communication. Those who use the word "power" most often are sociologists: "systems of power, control, etc." Psychologists on the other hand say: "It's a matter of influence and understanding. If we could understand each other, there would be no more problems." Now, any act of communication presupposes the establishment of authority. That is the foundation. And if that foundation is not laid well, things don't work.

2. The Culture of Ideas

J. T. — I'm currently working on another book. Rereading what I have written over the years, I realized that I haven't published the half of it. In a drawer I have a ton of manuscripts of articles that have never been published or disseminated. I thought it might be interesting to explore how these ideas came to me. Where do these ideas that are supposed to be mine come from? I used to be a farmer, and personally, I think that an idea is like a plant and people are like the soil.[2] And, just as plants need soil, ideas need us! [laughs] We imagine that people have ideas, but in fact the opposite is true. People are the place where ideas grow, where they are planted.

To come back to my own path, it has to be said that the field of organizational communication chiefly developed in certain universities of the American Midwest: Purdue, Michigan State, Iowa, Minnesota, Wisconsin, and so on. I studied at the University of Pennsylvania, in the Annenberg School, where at that time teaching and research were strictly focused on the mass media. They accepted me because I had worked for 10 years at the Canadian Broadcasting Corporation (CBC), from 1956 to 1966, and they needed somebody to teach television. We came to an agreement: I could enrol in the doctoral program, provided that I taught television. My interests, however, no longer lay in the mass media. They didn't interest me at all any more.

When I went to Annenberg, Pennsylvania, in 1966, I didn't even know that there was such a field as "organizational communication". I thought I would enrol in a sociology program, or perhaps political science, because I didn't realize that a communication program existed. That was how things stood when I arrived in Philadelphia. At the time, I was working with Michel Chevalier, who was doing a doctorate in urbanism at Pennsylvania. He and I had collaborated earlier, and even published a book (Chevalier & Taylor, 1971), and it was he who invited me to Pennsylvania. Like him, I was working at the time for the Laurendeau-Dunton commission on bilingualism and biculturalism, a Royal Commission on the state of language and culture in Canada. After arriving in Philadelphia to work with him on his report, one night at a gathering at his house I met a political science professor who said to me: "Well, I teach a course on federalism. Could you come tomorrow morning and explain what is happening in Canada?" So I went. The professor was a close friend of the person who ran the Annenberg film and television laboratory, and the next day I got a phone call. "Jim, would you be interested in teaching television with us, given the CBC's reputation?"

They had to come and get me, because at the time I was completely unaware! I didn't even know that there was a doctoral program in communication. Once I was enrolled and settled in, I did my mandatory studies during my first year at Annenberg. After that I went elsewhere. I literally invented a research program, my own program. I did statistics to a very advanced level. I did research on group dynamics from both a sociological and psychological perspective. I worked with people doing urbanism. In particular, I spent two summers working in Baltimore, where a major research program was under way, and so on. So I invented a program. But that had nothing to do with what was happening in parallel at Purdue and elsewhere. That was something completely different. I was totally ignorant of what they were doing and even of their existence, and of course that was mutual! [laughs] So the Montréal School was born out of this difference. The thing that intrigues me is that I came out of this experience with concepts that had very little to do with the prevailing concepts in the field of organizational communication.

Now, I am keen to explore the characteristics that I was able to absorb at the University of Pennsylvania. What really fascinates me, as I reread the texts that I wrote during that whole period, is the following question: how do ideas start to take shape? I left Pennsylvania with ideas that I could barely link up, meaning that there were no precise connections between them. I inherited [ideas] from a number of fields, including cybernetics. My supervisor was Klaus Krippendorf. I was deeply into cybernetics. What interests me at present is to understand the answer to the following question: what was really specific in all that?

3. *The Structuring Effect of Language and Imbrication*

J. T. — When I arrived in Montréal, I had really flunked my dissertation. I had written a dissertation project which was rejected in 1970 and arrived in Montréal in 1971 as an associate professor (without tenure, but I was never an assistant professor) and I became a full professor a year after submitting my dissertation! [laughs] I don't know exactly why, but on my arrival I decided that I absolutely must learn formal logic. I spent several years in Montréal, and all my free time was devoted to learning logic. Gradually, that brought me to the linguistics of Chomsky and all the people around him. My dissertation, submitted in 1977 and accepted in 1978, was on the use of concepts from formal linguistics applied to the study of group dynamics. I also worked with Ken McKenzie, whom I had invited to Montréal because I had plentiful funds: about a million dollars to spend. So there I was, an associate professor before completing my dissertation, with a fortune to spend and a laboratory, hired by the psychology department in spite of the fact that I had never taken courses in psychology!

Today, I am not involved in formal linguistics – the subject no longer interests me. But the effects are still there: what intrigues me about communication is that it is a way of creating structure. Like it or not, that is true. The basic principle of the linguistics invented by Chomsky (1957) is a set of what are called "rewrite rules". So, for me, conversation is a way of establishing a component of a larger unit. When you combine a verb and a noun, for example "wash the dishes", this has to be incorporated into a sentence: "Whose turn is it to wash the dishes? Ah!" There, one component inside another. This is equivalent to the notion of imbrication that I now put forward. One searches for words and "imbrication" is precisely that: a word that is used in French, but is never used in English in that specific sense. This was perfect, and I decided that I would use it because English speakers would be impressed. They don't have that word, so I imported it! [laughs] For me, imbrication has exactly that meaning, that one cannot communicate without providing structure. But structure is not restricted to interpersonal exchanges alone; interpersonal exchanges also feature in compositions, configurations. I really don't want to use the word "structure". It's a way of configuring, and it is done by rewrite rules. But these rewrite rules don't come out of nowhere: they are things that we have inherited.

I was also quite strongly influenced by people from the Palo Alto school, Bateson and Watzlawick. At Annenberg, where I taught television, I had master's students. I was a student myself, and I was directing master's theses! [laughs] One of my students – Alec Campbell – and I worked with a psychotherapist from the Palo Alto tradition. Philadelphia had become a centre for that kind of thing. Alec persuaded a family (father, mother, son, daughter) to come into the studio and reproduce their dysfunctional interactions faithfully in front of the camera. He did his entire master's thesis on the subject, and the thought stuck with me that a family is already a configuring of smaller units: father-daughter relations, father-son, mother-daughter, mother-son, father-mother, son-daughter. When you are looking at a specific interaction, it normally involves two people, maybe three. But all that is encompassed by a system, the family. And the family system doesn't come out of nowhere either. These family configurations tend to perpetuate themselves over time, from one generation to another. As we very well know, children of dysfunctional couples tend to reproduce the configurations that they experienced, although never in quite the same way because people are different. I endeavoured to imagine all this using the linguistics model. It worked up to a point, but beyond that it failed, because linguistics is not communication. Linguistics has its own way of structuring configurations, but that is not what an organization is.

4. Communication and Worldviews

J. T. — Not long after that I dropped the concepts of linguistics. But the problem with ideas is that they leave traces [laughs]. We are captives of our ideas. And out of that, another idea came to me, the idea of "worldview". I had a great many problems with that because unfortunately the word – unlike imbrication – already existed in English. You say the word worldview and everybody goes, "Yeah, yeah, I know" [feigns a yawn]. That is not what I meant by worldview. I learned it in a simulation course. When you try to simulate anything, the simulators attempt to describe a system. For example, my brother-in-law works in information systems. He worked for Shell Oil in Venezuela and his job was to plan the arrivals and departures of ships in a port. They did this by means of simulation, meaning that they invented a system and then ran simulations to identify the best strategies for facilitating the process. What fascinated me is that whenever you simulate any transaction, there are two points of view. If you go to a store to buy something, already there is complementarity. You don't see the world in the same way, because when you go to a store, that's part of the structure of your day, in terms of time, space, and so on. Maybe you had to take a bus, and so you have a journey that is both spatial and temporal. But the person in the store follows a completely different journey. So it is not a meeting of persons, but a meeting of journeys. This is what Consuelo Vásquez (2009) began exploring, and I found it pretty intriguing (see also Taylor & Van Every, 2011, chapter 4). It's a meeting of worldviews, in the sense that it's an organizing of time and space. And this has nothing to do with the ordinary worldview. It is, rather, what every human meeting presupposes … . Elizabeth (Van Every) drove me here this morning because I was running short of time, but she was already on her way somewhere, so when you live with someone, it's already a matter of two journeys. So the worldview concept came to me from there. On this subject, I can assure you that in the established field of organizational communication, nobody can get their head around this idea. It completely escapes my colleagues, they just cannot imagine it, whereas for me it's so obvious.

In information technology people have to choose a worldview. What I found really intriguing is that software must be constructed from one perspective or another. For example, software can be "event-oriented" or "particle-oriented". There are basic applications that are event-oriented and others that are particle-oriented. Let's say that event-oriented is the server perspective and particle-oriented is the client perspective. So, if you are a hospital doctor, for example, you face a sequence of events, "At 10:30, I have a patient, at 11:15, I have another", and so on. So, there's a set of events. And activity is made up like that. Then the patient arrives, and they are particle, a particle that moves through and undergoes a set of events: "I arrived, I had to register, then I had to wait in the waiting room, then the doctor called me into her office, and she told me that I had to have a test." For the particle, this is a set, a sequence of events. However, people who work in the hospital – staff who take X-rays, for example – continually repeat the same movements. They act the same way with every particle, with every patient. So that's an event. In this way, perspectives are fundamentally different. This was a revelation for me.

The act of communicating is not what people generally think. It inevitably presupposes diametrically opposite, different, perspectives. Something irreconcilable. I owe this partly to Buber (1970), to my great surprise. An advantage of being somewhat known is that people will ask you to write an essay. Some people were putting out a book on dialogue and they asked me, "Jim, could you write a chapter on dialogue?" Hmm … I had never read Bakhtin, I had never read Buber, I knew absolutely nothing, but an offer is an offer! [laughs] So I wrote a chapter on dialogue, but from the point of view of Bakhtin (Taylor, 2004). Subsequently, for an article that was rejected, I did read Buber and discovered that he had indeed correctly understood the concept of worldview. During a debate, Carl Rogers said to him, "Yes, I can clearly feel your passion, we are on the same level, I share your experience so much that we can finally understand each other". Buber replied, "No, *you* have just seen passion"[3] (see Anderson & Cissna, 1997). There is an unavoidable fundamental complementarity; every worldview always involves at least two different, complementary ways of seeing the same event, the same situation. The same applies to families, the same applies to teaching. You are obliged to listen to me. I'm not sitting here listening to you, but the reverse! [laughs] That's how life is. We are always experiencing, and we cannot get out of it. The same goes for researchers: they are not objective and they also cannot escape this rule. At the moment, I'm writing about the pragmatism of Peirce and Dewey, and this is what they say. There is no point of view from which I can see everything, where everything I see is objective. We are in the thick of things, we are human beings! [laughs]

Talking about the experience of teaching, about the complementary and irreconcilable viewpoints of the professor and teacher, let's use that as an opportunity to change tack, and talk about the creation of the Department of Communication, a decisive step in the foundation of what some people today call the "Montréal School".

5. *The founding of the Department of Communication*

J. T. — The origins of the department go back to a project conceived by Jean Cloutier, the head of Université de Montréal's audiovisual department. His brother was François Cloutier, then Québec's minister of education. But the two brothers didn't like each other – luckily for me! Jean Cloutier wanted to be the chair of the university's new communication department. But the university decided that he didn't have the necessary academic credentials. He had never studied for a doctorate. I didn't have a PhD, but I had done doctoral studies. They entrusted the setting up of the new program to Father Noël Mailloux. Mailloux was an extraordinary man. He was a Dominican priest who had studied psychoanalysis in Paris in 1920. He serenely combined his religious faith with his faith in research. Freud wasn't exactly religious [laughs], but Father Mailloux didn't see that as a problem.

Mailloux founded four departments at Université de Montréal. First, he founded the psychology department, then the psychoeducation department, followed by the criminology department, and lastly the communication department. The university put him in charge of setting up a communication program and he had decided to put the focus on research. So, there were no undergraduates, only master's and doctoral students. This was exactly the Annenberg model. In February, I got a call from Father Mailloux telling me he was coming to see me in Philadelphia with his dean, David Bélanger (his former student), because they were looking for a chair for the new department of communication. I said: "What?" Because apart from anything else, my fluency in French was really bad. I had all the theoretical elements, because I had studied French for several years. Originally, I even wanted to do my bachelor's degree in French, but I didn't manage to do that. I had all the theory, but little daily practice.

Father Mailloux was a very strongly built man, a very dignified man. He was somebody very special, for whom I developed a great deal of respect during the course of our meetings. David Bélanger and he were looking for somebody to set up a research program, because there was no one in Canada that could do it. There were plenty of communication experts in Canada, especially in Montréal – the city was full of people working in communication – but there was nobody who had done doctoral studies. To set up a master's and doctoral program, they needed somebody with training in research. So, Father Mailloux and David Bélanger arrived, and I introduced them to George Gerbner. We went for a meal at Philadelphia's only French restaurant. The next day, as I was driving them to the airport, they told me they wanted me to be the chair of the new department of communication. I went home and thought, there's no way, because it was 1970, and there were bombs going off in Québec, in Montréal.[4] Appointing an anglophone as the chair of a communication program while francophone culture was being asserted so strongly? I told myself, "That's crazy! Absolute madness! Just impossible!" I phoned Father Mailloux to say no, because I didn't think it was right. But he had such a strong personality that after I hung up I told my wife Elizabeth that I was starting to get positive vibes. About a month later they came back for another try. Since I had to go to Ottawa soon after, I said, "All right, we'll stop by Montréal and come to see you".

It was Sunday, it was a very hot day in June, and we had arranged to meet at the Dominican Office. In the basement, Father Mailloux had a library that was better endowed than the one in the Marie-Victorin Pavilion at Université de Montréal! We arrived, and Father Mailloux brought out the cognac. The vice-rector, Maurice Labbé, joined us a little later. Physically, he was the opposite of Father Mailloux: he was very thin and with his beard he made me think of a Mandarin. At the time, there was a class of people in Québec who had a style that no longer exists; there was a formality, refined manners that you don't come across today. In fact, there was a class of intellectuals in Montréal, a class with a much stronger hierarchy than today, among whom were some exceptional people. For example, Maurice Labbé had done a PhD in mathematics at Princeton University and was now vice-rector of Université de Montréal. They told me, "You *must* come". So, I came and I have officially been a professor at Université de Montréal since June 1970.

I have to say that the early years were very muddled. There were so many contradictory objectives. Professors' meetings during the first eight or nine years were painful affairs. Everybody came from very different horizons and there was no agreement on anything. There were as many Montréal Schools as there were professors.

6. Birth of the Montréal School

J. T. — In 1981, I stepped away from Université de Montréal. I worked as the equivalent of an assistant deputy minister on planning in the federal Department of Communication. I took an entire year, and even when I returned to Université de Montréal, I continued working as an adviser to the federal department. At that time the Canadian government had vast sums to spend, and there was a fund earmarked for Québec. So, projects had to be invented. I had a project: I imagined a research centre devoted not to developing technology, but to understanding how technology was integrated in the country's businesses. I had discovered that this was a major problem for many companies and for government departments. They didn't know what to do with all this new technology. This led to the creation of a research centre in Laval, the Canadian Workplace Automation Research Centre, which existed for a number of years, but is now defunct. But the people in the department were technocrats who refused to look at technology in the context of its use. I therefore found this experience disappointing, but subsequently, in 1988 or 1989, I was a member of the roundtable on the information society, which was a grouping of the most senior public servants in the federal government – that is, at assistant deputy minister level or higher. About 16 or 17 government departments took part in this exercise, which lasted for a number of years. So, for me, the 1980s were mainly devoted to research on the implementation of new technologies. In 1987, the doctoral program began. In 1991 I became department chair for four years. That is when I really returned to the department.

It's interesting to note that, while we are now nearly 20 years later, only the younger professors in the department have a PhD in communication, particularly my former students François Cooren, Daniel Robichaud, Carole Groleau and Lorna Heaton. That is the origin of the "Montréal School". These students continued the research they started as doctoral students at the time and became professors. I was lucky: they were good students. But the person who started to talk of a Montréal School was Boris Brummans. At a Ourepo[5] meeting, he hosted a session entitled "What do you think of the Montréal School?" So, it was Boris Brummans that started it all. He came from outside. Calling it the Montréal School in a sense gave a name to something that already existed in an unexpressed way. Then, in his chapter in the collective book we did (Brummans, 2006), he again referred to the Montréal School. The term was also used by Dennis Mumby (2007).

Personally, I find the term "Montréal School" mildly embarrassing. It's a tad pretentious, don't you think? But it's an interesting question. Why have others adopted the term? I think it's because they have a great deal of difficulty with our ideas. So it's much easier to apply a label such as "Montréal School". It's a way of saying, "It's a little strange, but legitimate …". It's a way of pigeonholing us. It seems that everybody needs to divide things into categories of viewpoints, something that I find very curious. I couldn't care less about categories. In fact, I loathe them! In any case, we are a long way from unanimity inside the so-called "Montréal School"!

6. *Heritage and Future Through Dialogue*

J. T. — I consider my heritage to be dialogue. To have created a dialogue is enough for me. Currently, the really interesting thing is that it's not just my students at Université de Montréal, but people from elsewhere who are keeping my ideas alive. In the United States, everything has become dreadfully conventional! I got discouraged: last year I served on a jury that evaluated 14 doctoral theses for a best-thesis-of-the-year award. I was very disappointed. But elsewhere, there is innovation to be seen! I'm thinking, for example, at what is coming out in France, where they do not seem to be hemmed in by the same constraints. The problem with American universities is that they do three years of intensive courses. This means there is a risk of imprinting models that are … I am tempted to use the word sterile, but let's say conventional instead. So it's one method course after another. I have nothing against method, on the contrary, but I don't like this sort of … rigidity.

To come back to what is being done elsewhere, I am in regular contact with a young researcher in the Netherlands. I met her when teaching a course over there. She was not in my class, but we spoke on several occasions. Subsequently, she contacted me, and we now discuss her research frequently. That's something I find really stimulating. Bertrand Fauré is someone else that I find very interesting: a chapter in my next book comes from his work (see Taylor & Van Every, 2011, chapter 5). Then there is Sandrine Virgili, whom I met in Nice. She had been influenced by some of my ideas, particularly the notion that an organization has a text, but a text that is not often put into words, or even spoken. It's a text because everyone knows how it works. Her research was fascinating (see Taylor & Van Every, 2011, chapter 7). Another student over there worked on a paper with Larry Browning, who is someone I get along with very well. So, the Montréal School is no longer just in Montréal, and I find it exciting to be privileged to know what these people are doing. It's the ultimate reward for me. I will die soon and what I leave behind will be my ideas. It wasn't for nothing that I was a crop grower!

It's flattering that people speak of the Montréal School today. It's a recognition of my work. But perhaps the best thing would be for the Montréal School to disappear, or at least to be no longer located in Montréal, but instead to be a new way of thinking. I feel I have been relieved of the burden that could come with being known for founding this school of thought, because Daniel Robichaud and François Cooren, among others, have carried on.

The thing that is still lacking is a theory of communication. If one had to identify one contribution made by the Montréal School, it would be to have been prepared to tackle this question of communication theory. While I greatly admire Latour's work, I still find that he is not much concerned with communication. Those are my reservations. I am told that he has now set up a section on communication in his program in Paris. François Cooren has been a strong influence on him. Influence is always a two-way process. It's never a one-way street!

Another thing that I would like to say is that Québec had a tendency, particularly back at that time, to withdraw, to stand in the corner, to create barriers. But no society can survive like that. Today I see – and this makes me very happy – people with self-confidence, able to operate in any setting. The future of Québec depends on this. You cannot protect yourself by hiding behind barriers. You have to rise to the challenge. And that, in a way, is what gives me the greatest satisfaction.

Notes

1 If communication equals (=) organization, and organization = communication, logically we can conclude that communication = communication and organization = organization (see Smith, 1993; McPhee & Zaug, 2000).
2 James R. Taylor grew up on a dairy farm in southern New Brunswick in the 1930s.
3 Carl Rogers implies that he and Buber share a common experience, but Buber replies that they don't. "No you have just seen passion" means "you haven't seen a shared experience" because there are none.
4 Between 1963 and 1970, the Front de Libération du Québec (FLQ), a radical political movement, carried out numerous thefts, kidnappings, bombings and other violent actions to promote Québec sovereignty. One of the issues at stake was the emancipation of francophones with respect to anglophones (for more details, see the Radio-Canada archives: http://archives.radio-canada.ca/).
5 Ourepo stands for *l'Ouvroir de recherche potentielle* (which can be translated as the *Research in Development Workshop*), a series of weekly meetings hosted by members of the Language, Organization & Governance research laboratory at Université de Montréal, which included former students of James R. Taylor. Its name and meeting formula are loosely inspired by the *Ouvroir de littérature potentielle*, generally designated under the acronym OuLiPo, an innovative French literature group founded in 1960 featuring authors such as Raymond Queneau, Italo Calvino and Georges Perec.

Bibliography

Anderson, R., & Cissna, K. N. (1997). *The Martin Buber-Carl Rogers dialogue: A new transcript with commentary*. New York: State University of New York Press.
Buber, M. (1970). *I and thou* (W. Kaufman, Trans.). New York: Charles Scribner's Sons.
Brummans, B. H. J. M. (2006). The Montréal school and the question of agency. In F. Cooren, J. R. Taylor & E. J. V. Every (Eds.), *Communication as organizing: Practical approaches to research into the dynamic of text and conversation* (pp. 197–211). Mahwah, NJ: Lawrence Erlbaum.
Chevalier, M., & Taylor, J. R. (1971). Dynamics of adaptation in the federal public service. In *Studies of the Royal Commission on Bilingualism and Biculturalism*, 9. Information Canada.
Chomsky, N. (1957). *Syntactic structures*. The Hague: Mouton.
Cooren, F. (2006). The organizational world as a plenum of agencies. In F. Cooren, J. R. Taylor & E. J. V. Every (Eds.), *Communication as organizing: Empirical and theoretical explorations in the dynamic of text and conversation* (pp. 81–100). Mahwah, NJ: Lawrence Erlbaum.
Cooren, F., Fox, S., Robichaud, D., & Talih, N. (2005). Arguments for a plurified view of the social world: Spacing and timing as hybrid achievements. *Time & Society*, 14(2/3), 265–282.
Fairhurst, G. T., & Putnam, L. L. (1999). Reflections on the organization-communication equivalency question: The contributions of James Taylor and his colleagues. *The Communication Review*, 3(1–2), 1–19.
Giroux, N. (2006). La démarche paradoxale de Karl E. Weick. In D. Autissier & F. Bensebaa (éds.), *Les défis du sensemaking en entreprise: Karl E. Weick et les sciences de gestion* (pp. 25–50). Paris: Economica.
Latour, B. (1986). The powers of association. In J. Law (Ed.), *Power, action and belief: A new sociology of knowledge?* (pp. 264–280). London: Routledge & Kegan Paul.
Les archives de la Société Radio-Canada [online]. http://archives.radio-canada.ca/ (retrieved on February 11, 2010).
McPhee, R. D., & Zaug, P. (2000). The communicative constitution of organizations: A framework for explanation. *The Electronic Journal of Communication/La revue électronique de communication*, 10(1–2), 1–16.
Mumby, D. K. (2007). Organizational communication. In G. Ritzer (Ed.), *The Blackwell encyclopedia of sociology* (pp. 3290–3299). New York: Blackwell.
Smith, R. C. (1993). Images of organization: Root-metaphors of the organization-communication relation. Paper presented at the Annual Conference of the International Communication Association, Washington, May.

Taylor, J. R. (2004). Dialogue as the search for sustainable organizational co-orientation. In R. Anderson, L. A. Baxter & K. N. Cissna (Eds.), *Dialogue: Theorizing difference in communication studies* (pp. 125–140). Thousand Oaks, CA: Sage.

Taylor, J. R. (2006). Communication et la constitution de l'organisation: La perspective de "l'École de Montréal". *Org & Co - Bulletin de liaison bimestrial*, no 16.

Taylor, J. R., & Van Every, E. J. (2000). *The emergent organization: Communication as its site and surface.* Mahwah, NJ: Lawrence Erlbaum.

Taylor, J. R., & Van Every, E. J. (2011). *The situated organization: Case studies in the pragmatics of communication research.* New York: Routledge.

Taylor, J. R., & Van Every, E. J. (2014). *When organization fails: Why authority matters.* New York: Routledge.

Vásquez Donoso, C. (2009). Espacer l'organisation: trajectoires d'un projet de diffusion de la science et de la technologie au Chili. Unpublished doctoral dissertation, Université de Montréal, Montréal.

INDEX

Printed in the United States
by Baker & Taylor Publisher Services